W9-COV-925

▨ Let's Go writers travel on your budget.

"Guides that penetrate the veneer of the holiday brochures and mine the grit of real life."

—*The Economist*

"The writers seem to have experienced every rooster-packed bus and lunar-surfaced mattress about which they write."

—*The New York Times*

"All the dirt, dirt cheap."

—*People*

▨ Great for independent travelers.

"The guides are aimed not only at young budget travelers but at the independent traveler; a sort of streetwise cookbook for traveling alone."

—*The New York Times*

"Flush with candor and irreverence, chock full of budget travel advice."

—*The Des Moines Register*

"An indispensible resource, *Let's Go*'s practical information can be used by every traveler."

—*The Chattanooga Free Press*

▨ Let's Go is completely revised each year.

"Only *Let's Go* has the zeal to annually update every title on its list."

—*The Boston Globe*

"Unbeatable: good sightseeing advice; up-to-date info on restaurants, hotels, and inns; a commitment to money-saving travel; and a wry style that brightens nearly every page."

—*The Washington Post*

▨ All the important information you need.

"*Let's Go* authors provide a comedic element while still providing concise information and thorough coverage of the country. Anything you need to know about budget traveling is detailed in this book."

—*The Chicago Sun-Times*

"Value-packed, unbeatable, accurate, and comprehensive."

—*Los Angeles Times*

Let's Go Publications

Let's Go: Alaska & the Pacific Northwest 2001
Let's Go: Australia 2001
Let's Go: Austria & Switzerland 2001
Let's Go: Boston 2001 **New Title!**
Let's Go: Britain & Ireland 2001
Let's Go: California 2001
Let's Go: Central America 2001
Let's Go: China 2001
Let's Go: Eastern Europe 2001
Let's Go: Europe 2001
Let's Go: France 2001
Let's Go: Germany 2001
Let's Go: Greece 2001
Let's Go: India & Nepal 2001
Let's Go: Ireland 2001
Let's Go: Israel 2001
Let's Go: Italy 2001
Let's Go: London 2001
Let's Go: Mexico 2001
Let's Go: Middle East 2001
Let's Go: New York City 2001
Let's Go: New Zealand 2001
Let's Go: Paris 2001
Let's Go: Peru, Bolivia & Ecuador 2001 **New Title!**
Let's Go: Rome 2001
Let's Go: San Francisco 2001 **New Title!**
Let's Go: South Africa 2001
Let's Go: Southeast Asia 2001
Let's Go: Spain & Portugal 2001
Let's Go: Turkey 2001
Let's Go: USA 2001
Let's Go: Washington, D.C. 2001
Let's Go: Western Europe 2001 **New Title!**

Let's Go *Map Guides*

Amsterdam	New Orleans
Berlin	New York City
Boston	Paris
Chicago	Prague
Florence	Rome
Hong Kong	San Francisco
London	Seattle
Los Angeles	Sydney
Madrid	Washington, D.C.

Coming Soon: *Dublin* and *Venice*

CHINA

2001

Julie Harms editor
Won Park associate editor
Kaitlin Solimine associate editor

researcher-writers

Nancy Chu	Tian Mayimin
Bowen Hsu	Shamiso Mbizvo
Jean Huang	Sue Meng
Josh Levin	Chris Parlato
Elizabeth Little	Julie Wecsler
Charlotte Mangin	

Theadora Sakata map editor

St. Martin's Press ⚹ New York

HELPING LET'S GO If you want to share your discoveries, suggestions, or corrections, please drop us a line. We read every piece of correspondence, whether a postcard, a 10-page email, or a coconut. Please note that mail received after May 2001 may be too late for the 2002 book, but will be kept for future editions. **Address mail to:**

> Let's Go: China
> 67 Mount Auburn Street
> Cambridge, MA 02138
> USA

Visit Let's Go at **http://www.letsgo.com**, or send email to:

> **feedback@letsgo.com**
> **Subject: "Let's Go: China"**

In addition to the invaluable travel advice our readers share with us, many are kind enough to offer their services as researchers or editors. Unfortunately, our charter enables us to employ only currently enrolled Harvard students.

CONTENTS

MAPS

RESEARCHER-WRITERS

Nancy Chu   *Southwest*

All business and no nonsense, Nancy finished her 50-day itinerary in approximately 12 minutes. In the rugged mountains and waterfalls of Zhangjiajie, Nancy found wild beauty, in Guilin and Yangshuo she found rice paddies and karst peaks, and in Sanya she found her true love—porridge. The result? Precise, immaculate copy, done like a true professional. After a summer of R-Wing, Nancy headed back to China for more, and we're sure that Bei Da will be the better for it.

Bowen Hsu   *Chongqing and the Three Gorges*

This model-in-the-making was a model R-W as well. On short notice, Bowen flew up from Thailand to let us in on Chongqing's local secrets and to experience the extent of the Three Gorges tourism culture.

Jean Huang   *Beijing and the North Coast*

Jean hoped to see the Great Wall. And that she did, not one but five times—sometimes a bit too close for comfort (300 splinters in one hand?). In the city, Jean was all business, earning herself the title of Beijinger extraordinaire. She sampled every morsel of international cuisine (from Chinese to French to Israeli to American) in search of the perfect cheesecake. In the process, she touched us with her sparkling prose, sending us packages wrapped in Pooh-bandaged care. Making many friends along the way, she became a dear friend of ours as well.

Josh Levin   *Sichuan, Tibet, Northwest*

What a long, strange trip it's been for Josh, who wrestled with wicked Sichuan accents, bumpy 68-hour bus rides, and a toe-splitting incident or two. Josh was concerned with the people, the environment, and the political situations he encountered along his way. He charmed the lovely ladies of Chengdu, joked with monks in the Jokhang, and enjoyed every drop of yak-butter tea. Josh traveled the Friendship Highway, experienced one of the greatest days of his life as the clouds cleared over Mt. Everest, and ended in Kathmandu on one big, travel-induced high.

Elizabeth Little   *Shanghai and the Yangzi Delta, Yangzi Basin*

Elizabeth took Shanghai by storm, completely revamping the nightlife section. She started what was to be a two-month love affair with dumplings and ice cream on the Bund. Her quest for bargain accommodations led past yellow-hatted tour groups, mildewed carpets, and a bug or two. Rain ruined the famed Beihai sunrise, but Lushan's scenic mountain splendor provided a breath of fresh air before Elizabeth plunged into the furnace of Wuhan. Through it all, Elizabeth's accurate, insightful, and remarkably witty copy kept us entertained all summer long.

Charlotte Mangin   *Northeast, Beijing and the North Coast*

Sent out on the roads less taken, Charlotte traversed the Northeast hinterland with tenacity and a sweetness no cafe mocha could match. Her optimistic attitude kept her copy cool, true, and fresh as she ever so deftly breezed through her challenging itinerary. In the end, Charlotte found her true heaven in the calm beaches and relaxing European atmosphere of Qingdao, a place that matched her personality so well. While the alcohol of choice in Qingdao may be Tsingtao beer, our coffee of choice is Charlotte: mild, sugary sweet, and simply divine.

Tian Mayimin   *Southwest*

A superwoman in her own right, Tian was robbed in Dali, taste-tested snake meat in back alley restaurants, and trekked overnight through the jungle in Banna. Tian proved to be the ultimate survivor; unlike any made for TV approximation of lost-in-paradise living, Tian's experience was the real thing. She explored the backpacker lifestyle while getting to the heart of the minority villages of Yunnan and Guizhou. No matter how her name is translated, Tian remains both sweet and heavenly, a field full of knowledge and insight.

Shamiso Mbizvo
Hong Kong and Macau, South Coast

Enthusiastic, bright, and meticulously organized, Shamiso sent us paper clip-happy copybatches that were a joy to receive. Self-described as "urban-friendly," Shamiso was as colourful, vibrant, and ready for the next challenge as Hong Kong itself. Her love for her adopted city shone through in her highly evocative prose and her keen eye for detail. Despite noisy, insect-ridden hostels, sweltering days, and the challenge of deciphering the language on the mainland, Shamiso never, ever stopped—and in fact insisted that *we* get enough rest.

Sue Meng
Shanghai and the Yangzi Delta, South Coast

After a quick trip to the Hangzhou Hospital ward, Sue set off again with boundless enthusiasm. Even a minor pedicab incident in Quanzhou and repeated offers of *an mo* couldn't dissuade her. The natural delights of Putuoshan and Wuyishan inspired her, Dancing Queen karaoke in Xiamen entertained her, and the heavenly taste of milk ice pops and Sha county-style food nourished her. Come late July, Sue teetered on the edges of rice paddies and slid down dirt hills to the roundhouses of Dadong, where locals welcomed her with open arms. We did, too.

Chris Parlato
Northwest

Some people assume that the Northwest is nothing but a bunch of sand. Not Chris. Chris took a pen to paper to paint a discerning, insightful picture of the vivid landscapes and cultural mysteries of the Northwest. Venturing back from the off-the-beaten Silk Road-path to Yining, Chris marveled as snow-capped peaks slowly receded into desert dunes and bleeding red cliffs over the course of a marathon 36-hour bus ride. After successfully completing his lengthy, tough itinerary, Chris backtracked to Tianchi to sneak in a few days of hiking before heading home.

Julie Wecsler
Central China

Julie explored the imperial splendor of Xian and the culinary delights of Kaifeng's night market. She left behind the monks of Shaolin Monastery to marvel at the fog-shrouded monasteries and mountain passes of Wutaishan. Julie even found the charm in the coal-belching industrial cities of Taiyuan and Datong before heading north to the grasslands of Inner Mongolia. Julie's thoughtful, sticker-decorated copy—full of details, new finds, and her latest adventures—made us feel like we were there, too. And no, she's not from Xinjiang. Best of luck in Shanghai.

John Bachman
Kathmandu

HOW TO USE THIS BOOK

Welcome to *Let's Go: China 2001!* While Mao's little red book it's not, this *is* your big bad red (and yellow) book; use it wisely. We've been working hard to update every fact, add fresh and exciting new places, and give you the best possible information to guide you on your travels. But remember that we are just that—a guide—and not the end all and be all of travel in China. We vow to stand firmly behind you on your adventures, providing motherly insight, fatherly discipline, and sibling humor. It's a big, bad world out there, but with a little help from your comrades, you just may be able to conquer it. Long live *Let's Go: China*.

ORGANIZATION OF THIS BOOK

INTRODUCTORY MATERIAL. First up is **Discover China**, complete with an informative overview of travel in China, including **Suggested Itineraries** to give you an idea of what you shouldn't miss and how long it will take to see it all. **Life & Times** gives overview of the rich art, culture, food, and history of China, from *jingju* (Beijing opera) to *jiaozi* (dumplings). The **Essentials** section covers all those nitty-gritty, practical details you'll need to take care of to prepare for your trip.

COVERAGE. Our coverage of China, like the recent economic progess of China itself, moves westward. We begin in the capital of the Middle Kingdom, Beijing, head down the coast, then go west, ending with coverage of **Tibet** (see the **Table of Contents** for a full chapter breakdown). The **black tabs** in the margins will help you to navigate between chapters quickly and easily.

APPENDIX. The appendix contains a **glossary** of frequently encountered words, useful **conversions** and a climate chart, an extensive ⬛ **phrasebook** (with pinyin transliterations and Chinese characters listed for each phrase), and a handy diagram to help you read those potentially perplexing Chinese train tickets.

A FEW NOTES ABOUT LET'S GO FORMAT

RANKING ESTABLISHMENTS. In each section (Accommodations, Food, etc.), we list establishments in order from best to worst. Our absolute favorites are given Let's Go's highest honor, the *Let's Go* thumbs-up (⬛).

PHONE CODES AND TELEPHONE NUMBERS. The **phone code** for each city or town appears opposite the name of that city or town, and is denoted by the ☎ icon. **Phone numbers** in text are also preceded by the ☎ icon.

THINKING INSIDE THE BOX. Grayboxes at times provide cultural insight, at other times crude humor. In any case, they're amusing, so enjoy. **Whiteboxes** provide important practical information, such as warnings (⚠), helpful hints and further resources (🔖), border crossing information (🛂), and more.

CHINESE, PLEASE. This book provides the pinyin romanization (zhōngguó) and Chinese characters (中国) for every city, train station, establishment, sight, etc. that we mention. The most common phrases (Bank of China, PSB, etc.) are listed in the **appendix** rather than individually in each city. The brave traveler can try pronouncing place names (consult the **Pinyin Pronunciation Guide,** p. 757, for assistance), but the less adventurous can just point at characters.

A NOTE TO OUR READERS The information for this book was gathered by *Let's Go* researchers from May through August of 2000. Each listing is based on one researcher's opinion, formed during his or her visit at a particular time. Those traveling at other times may have different experiences since prices, dates, hours, and conditions are always subject to change. You are urged to check the facts presented in this book beforehand to avoid inconvenience and surprises.

ACKNOWLEDGEMENTS

TEAM CHINA THANKS: Mao—without whom this book would never be red. Tied for first are our R-Ws: without their energy, enthusiasm, and dedicated researching, this book would not have been possible. Ankur (tree cheerleaders on top of each other!), Anne C., Thea, Melissa; typists (Mei Pin, Elizabeth, Emi) and proofers; map-helper Chris; LG China 2000 for forging the way, and to Ting Wang for helping us on the Long March; everyone else who made the China-pod happy.

JULIE THANKS: Team 中国, 饺子, 对面的女孩, Ankur (our 男孩), and LG friends. Skate Asia 1989 and Tsay Laoshi. Chairman Megan, for indoctrinating me into the cult of LG. Four French classes, for keeping me happy in the spring. Jess, Pam, Reggie, Rosie, and others for keeping me happy in the summer. Linda, Jerry, Nathan, Grammy Joy, and Grandma Nita for keeping me happy all the time.

WON THANKS: Zhuli, Hotan, and Wangbadan! Mom, Dad, Marg, and Jason for believing. *Halmoni, halabuhji,* my *gajok* for loving me too much. NB for always thinking of me. FAP 2000 (esp. alan, jim, jason, angelica, sara, angela, greg, eliot, jeff). Dot and LG folks (esp. Angela, Thea, Ann) for putting up with me all summer. Sadie, Becks, Jen, Reagan, Martin, Michelle, Colin, Air, Lynn, Kate, and everyone who gave me a summer life outside of LG. Stev-o, Froggie, Craig, Alex, Seth for good times. Jina for remembering my spirit. Karen, Maya, Michele, Sharon for being true. Caroline, Reera for 20 years. Amen.

KAITLIN THANKS: Zhuli—"Mao." Won—my dumpling. Ankur—cat chow mein? Mom, Dad, and AJ for constant support and sheer silliness-I inherited all my good attributes from you. Gila and Qian—we're the real "Charlie's angels." Erika—the sweetness that kept me sane. Dibs (and fam)—for being as close as family. "Chuck" (Josh)—for finally getting it through my thick skull that loving someone means knowing when to let go. Caitrin and Annie—my heart and soul. Mr. McLaughlin and Ms. Fontaine, Rakhee (and fam), Siggy, Miche, Colleen, Leigh, and all my blockmates. Baba, Chen Xi, and Mama, ni yuan yi zai wo de xin li. For those who think I forgot them, I didn't.

Editor
Julie Harms
Associate Editors
Won Park, Kaitlin Solimine
Managing Editor
Ankur Ghosh
Map Editor
Theadora Sakata

Publishing Director
Kaya "Mao Zedong" Stone
Editor-in-Chief
Kate "Zhou Enlai" McCarthy
Production Manager
Melissa "Deng Xiaoping" Rudolph
Cartography Manager
John "Tiantan" Fiore
Editorial Managers
Alice Farmer, Ankur Ghosh,
Aarup Kubal, Anup Kubal
Financial Manager
Bede "Capitalist Roader" Sheppard
Low-Season Manager
Melissa "Sun Yat-sen" Gibson
Marketing & Publicity Managers
Olivia L. Cowley, Esti Iturralde
New Media Manager
Jonathan "Wangba" Dawid
Personnel Manager
Nicholas "Renmin" Grossman
Photo Editor
Dara Cho
Production Associates
Sanjay Mavinkurve, Nicholas Murphy, Rosalinda Rosalez Matthew Daniels, Rachel Mason, Daniel Visel
Some Design
Mathew Daniels
Office Coordinators
Sarah Jacoby, Chris Russell

Director of Advertising Sales
Cindy Rodriguez
Senior Advertising Associates
Adam Grant, Rebecca Rendell
Advertising Artwork Editor
Palmer Truelson

President
Andrew M. Murphy
General Manager
Robert B. Rombauer
Assistant General Manager
Anne E. Chisholm

RUSSIA

KAZAKHSTAN

Lake Balkhash

MO

Alma-Ata
Yining

★ Bishkek
KYRGYZSTAN

●Kuqa

★ Ürümqi

TAJIKISTAN
●Kashgar

X I N J I A N G

AFGHANISTAN

■■■Dunhuang
Jiayuguan ★

G A N S U

Great Wa

PAKISTAN

Claimed by India,
controlled by China

●Golmud

Xini ★

Q I N G H A I

Yelle

T I B E T

Claimed by China,
controlled by India

Delhi ★

N E P A L

Yarlung Zanbo (Brahmaputra)
Shigatse ●
Kathmandu ★

▲ Mt. Everest
(8848m)

● Lhasa

Nu (Salween)

Claimed by China,
controlled by India

Yangzi

S I

Kangding

Thimphu

BHUTAN

Mekong

Lijiang ●

BANGLA-
DESH

Dali ●

Kunmi

★ Dhaka

Baoshan ●

I N D I A

Y U N

XISHUANGBAN

MYANMAR

LAO

N 👍

Bay of Bengal

0   400 miles
0   400 kilometers

THAILAND

Lake Baikal

RUSSIA

Ulaanbaatar

MONGOLIA

Mohe

HEILONGJIANG

Qiqihar

Harbin

Mudanjiang

Jilin

Changchun

JILIN

LIAONING

Shenyang

NORTH
KOREA

P'yongyang

INNER MONGOLIA

Hohhot

Chengde

Great Wall

Dandong

Baotou

Datong

Beijing

BEIJING

Tianjin

TIANJIN

Dalian

Seoul

SOUTH
KOREA

Yinchuan

Great Wall

Taiyuan

HEBEI

Shijazhuang

Yellow (Huang)

Weihai

Yantai

NINGXIA

Yanan

SHANXI

Anyang

(Huang)

Jinan

Qingdao

Yellow
Sea

JAPAN

anzhou

Tianshui

Xian

Luoyang

Zhengzhou

Yellow

Kaifeng

SHANDONG

SHAANXI

HENAN

ANHUI

JIANGSU

Yangzhou

Zhenjiang

Suzhou

Shanghai

Chengdu

HUBEI

Nanjing

Hefei

Wuxi

SHANGHAI

UAN

Yangzi

Wuhan

Yichang

Hangzhou

Ningbo

East China
Sea

Chongqing

CHONGQING

Leshan

Yueyang

Jiujiang

ZHEJIANG

Zunyi

Changsha

Nanchang

Guiyang

HUNAN

JIANGXI

FUJIAN

GUIZHOU

Anshun

Hengyang

Fuzhou

Guilin

Quanzhou

Taipei

Shaoguan

Xiamen

TAIWAN R.O.C

GUANGXI

GUANGDONG

Nanning

Guangzhou

Shantou

ETNAM

HONG KONG SAR

MACAU SAR

South China
Sea

Hanoi

Haikou

HAINAN

ntiane

Sanya

People's Republic of China

XIII

RUSSIA

N

Ulaanbaatar

ONGOLIA

THE NORTHEAST
180–211

Harbin

Changchun

Hohhot

NORTH
KOREA

Shenyang

Great Wall

P'yŏngyang

CENTRAL CHINA
212–273

Beijing

Tianjin

uan

Taiyuan

BEIJING AND
THE NORTH COAST
92–179

Seoul

SOUTH
KOREA

Yellow
Sea

Qingdao

JAPAN

Xi'an

Nanjing

Hefei

Shanghai

Chengdu

Wuhan

Hangzhou

SHANGHAI AND
THE YANGZI DELTA
274–353

East China
Sea

4–649

ngqing

THE YANGZI BASIN
354–405

Guiyang

THE
SOUTH
COAST
462–523

T'aipei

TAIWAN

HE SOUTHWEST
524–613

Guangzhou

NAM

Hanoi

HONG KONG
AND MACAU
406–461

South China
Sea

Haikou

0   400 miles

0   400 kilometers

China: Chapters

ABOUT LET'S GO

FORTY-ONE YEARS OF WISDOM

As a new millennium arrives, *Let's Go: Europe*, now in its 41st edition and translated into seven languages, reigns as the world's bestselling international travel guide. For over four decades, travelers criss-crossing the Continent have relied on *Let's Go* for inside information on the hippest backstreet cafes, the most pristine secluded beaches, and the best routes from border to border. In the last 20 years, our rugged researchers have stretched the frontiers of backpacking and expanded our coverage into Asia, Africa, Australia, and the Americas. This year, we've introduced a new city guide series with books on San Francisco and our hometown, Boston. Now, our seven city guides feature sharp photos, more maps, and an overall more user-friendly design. We've also returned to our roots with the inaugural edition of *Let's Go: Western Europe*.

It all started in 1960 when a handful of well-traveled students at Harvard University handed out a 20-page mimeographed pamphlet offering a collection of their tips on budget travel to passengers on student charter flights to Europe. The following year, in response to the instant popularity of the first volume, students traveling to Europe researched the first full-fledged edition of *Let's Go: Europe*, a pocket-sized book featuring honest, practical advice, witty writing, and a decidedly youthful slant on the world. Throughout the 60s and 70s, our guides reflected the times. In 1969 we taught travelers how to get from Paris to Prague on "no dollars a day" by singing in the street. In the 80s and 90s, we looked beyond Europe and North America and set off to all corners of the earth. Meanwhile, we focused in on the world's most exciting urban areas to produce in-depth, fold-out map guides. Our new guides bring the total number of titles to 51, each infused with the spirit of adventure and voice of opinion that travelers around the world have come to count on. But some things never change: our guides are still researched, written, and produced entirely by students who know first-hand how to see the world on the cheap.

HOW WE DO IT

Each guide is completely revised and thoroughly updated every year by a well-traveled set of nearly 300 students. Every spring, we recruit over 200 researchers and 90 editors to overhaul every book. After several months of training, researcher-writers hit the road for seven weeks of exploration, from Anchorage to Adelaide, Estonia to El Salvador, Iceland to Indonesia. Hired for their rare combination of budget travel sense, writing ability, stamina, and courage, these adventurous travelers know that train strikes, stolen luggage, food poisoning, and marriage proposals are all part of a day's work. Back at our offices, editors work from spring to fall, massaging copy written on Himalayan bus rides into witty, informative prose. A student staff of typesetters, cartographers, publicists, and managers keeps our lively team together. In September, the collected efforts of the summer are delivered to our printer, who turns them into books in record time, so that you have the most up-to-date information available for your vacation. Even as you read this, work on next year's editions is well underway.

WHY WE DO IT

We don't think of budget travel as the last recourse of the destitute; we believe that it's the only way to travel. Living cheaply and simply brings you closer to the people and places you've been saving up to visit. Our books will ease your anxieties and answer your questions about the basics—so you can get off the beaten track and explore. Once you learn the ropes, we encourage you to put *Let's Go* down now and then to strike out on your own. You know as well as we that the best discoveries are often those you make yourself. When you find something worth sharing, please drop us a line. We're Let's Go Publications, 67 Mount Auburn St., Cambridge, MA 02138, USA (email: feedback@letsgo.com). For more info, visit our website, www.letsgo.com.

DISCOVER CHINA

Five thousand years of history and not anywhere near past its prime, China today is much like the image on the cover of *Let's Go: China*—under construction. The Beijinger going about his daily business, painting the character 建 (jiàn; "to build") on a wall in the nation's capital, was photographed midway through his job. The snapshot has captured something crucial about a changing China: although the skeletal character is only half-finished, it is legible all the same. For travelers to China, this glimpse of a work in progress will be but one of many. Chinese history is a staggeringly long tale of building, destruction, and reconstruction, and this particular moment is no exception. Everywhere, old buildings, roads, traditions, and ideas are being torn down as new frameworks are erected, some making careful use of the past, others branching out in entirely new directions. Although the painter still wears the Mao suit of an era gone by, his message is one for the future: China is wholeheartedly committed to reinventing itself. The question that remains is what this fresh coat of paint, laid over a centuries-old wall, will bring.

CHINA FACTS AND FIGURES

POPULATION: 1.4 billion

LAND AREA: 9.5 million km^2

POP. DENSITY: 127.9 people per km^2

TOTAL NUMBER OF CHICKENS IN CHINA: 3 billion

EGGS LAID PER YEAR: 278.6 trillion

AMOUNT OF TEA CONSUMED PER YEAR: 17.4 billion liters

AMOUNT OF BEER PRODUCED PER YEAR: 20.9 billion tons

NUMBER OF PEOPLE PER YEAR INJURED BY EXPLODING BEER BOTTLES: 470

WHEN TO GO

Even the best-laid travel plans are no match for the monsoons, typhoons, snow-storms, and heavy floods that periodically close China's roads, rails, and airports, sometimes making whole areas seasonally inaccessible. In general, **summer** is hot almost everywhere (except at high altitudes), and rainy and very humid south of the Yangzi River; **winters** range from extremely cold in the far north (especially north of Beijing) to extremely mild in the south. **Late spring** and **early autumn** are usually the best times to travel.

Although most of the country is temperate, southern Yunnan, Guangxi, and Guangdong provinces, as well as Hong Kong, Macau, and Hainan Island, lie in the tropics. Travelers in the summer should watch out for summer **monsoons,** which originate in the South Pacific and can carry rain as far as Mongolia; as a result, rainfall is generally greatest in the southeast, least in the northwest, and heaviest in the summer. **Typhoons** (tropical cyclones) occur year-round in coastal China, but are strongest in late summer and early autumn. Many of China's rivers, particularly the Yellow and the Yangzi, are prone to seasonal **flooding,** especially in June, July, and August. Frequent floods, landslides, and mudslides caused by heavy summer rains can make land travel treacherous, particularly in areas with dirt roads, rickety bridges, and otherwise poor infrastructure. For temperature and rainfall charts, see **Climate,** p. 768.

China's many **festivals** and **national holidays** can both attract and deter travelers. Traveling during the holidays is fraught with hassles—train and bus tickets are usually harder to come by, and hotels are often booked. Visiting during **Chinese New Year** (January 24, 2001) is only for the most determined of festival-goers; travel is extremely difficult all through the week surrounding that date. For a list of the major festivals in China, see p. 44.

THINGS TO DO

From temple-hopping to bar-hopping, there is a great deal of everything in China. Those with specialized interests can indulge to their hearts' content; those without will find no better opportunity to develop them. For more specific regional attractions, see the **Highlights of the Region** section at the beginning of each chapter.

CITY SLICKERS

With more people than any other country in the history of the world, China has produced some spectacular cities: chaotic, teeming, dynamic masses of humanity. More than 100 Chinese cities have over one million inhabitants, and most all of them are experiencing some bumps on the road to modernity. In spite of this, many of the cities of China hold their own against the best cities in the world. **Hong Kong** (p. 406), with its cosmopolitan nightlife and ambrosial shopping, is the obvious pinnacle. **Beijing** (p. 92), grandiose home of a multinational populace and a thriving cultural scene, is also a must-see for travelers interested in living the fast life. And colonial darling **Shanghai** (p. 274) is wasting no time in rediscovering its sordid past. Lesser-known but equally thrilling stops for the avid city-hopper include the fresh-faced harbor city of **Dalian** (p. 207), in Liaoning province; the stately old capital of **Nanjing** (p. 297), in Jiangsu province; the fragrant **Kunming** (p. 545), in Yunnan province; and **Chongqing** (p. 639), a huge, atmospheric (and nearly bike-free) municipality that soaks its feet in the waters of the Yangzi.

IT'S ONLY NATURAL...

The trick to communing with nature in China is to get away from the crowds; after that, the gorgeous sky's the limit. Forests coat the limestone crags in the **Zhangjiajie** nature reserve (p. 392), in Hunan province. Heaven shines in the waters of **Tianchi** (p. 694), in Xinjiang, and elephants and monkeys lurk in the gorgeous rain forest of **Xishuangbanna** (p. 584), in Yunnan. Surfable **sand dunes** (p. 659) beckon the adventurous in **Ningxia** (p. 677) and **Inner Mongolia** (p. 268), which is also home to vast, unforgettable expanses of grasslands. Alpine mountains astound visitors to the remote **Jiuzhaigou** nature reserve (p. 634), in Sichuan province. And of course, **Mt. Everest** (p. 751) towers over it all at the border with Nepal.

DAOIST SIGHTS. Speaking of mountains, China has plenty of them. Daoists, Buddhists, and scenery buffs all have invested them with great significance. The most revered Daoist temple complexes center on a group of five mountains, whose craggy peaks and misty veils are purportedly favored by supernatural forces. The leader of the pack is **Taishan** (Dongyue; p. 160), in Shandong province. The others are **Huashan** (Xiyue; p. 224), in Shaanxi province, **Songshan** (Zhongyue; p. 233), in Henan province, **Hengshan** (Beiyue; p. 258), in Shanxi province, and, for good measure, **Hengshan** (Nanyue; p. 389), in Hunan province.

BUDDHIST MOUNTAINS AND GROTTOES. Chinese Buddhism has also claimed several mountains as sacred sites. Dotted with monasteries and temples, these stately mountains attract scores of pilgrims. They are **Jiuhuashan** (p. 369), in Anhui province, **Emeishan** (p. 631), in Sichuan province, **Putuoshan** (p. 347), in Zhejiang province, and **Wutaishan** (p. 252), in Shanxi province. No list of famed mountains would be complete without **Huangshan** (p. 360), in Anhui province, which, though not sacred, has earned plenty of worshipful praise for its scenic marvels.

In the Northern Wei dynasty, Buddhism solidified its precarious foothold in China with the construction of temples in caves and cliffs. Much of the best-preserved Buddhist art is in grottoes, where big buddhas and carved scenes from religious lore blend seamlessly with the surrounding natural scenery. The mother of all such grottoes is the spectacular **Mogao Grottoes** (p. 687), clustered in the desert around Dunhuang in Gansu province. **Maijishan Grottoes** (p. 675) near Tianshui are a bit hard to reach but no less impressive. **Bingling Temple Grottoes** (p. 668), rapidly losing favor among travelers, and **Xumishan Grottoes** (p. 662) round out the Northwest's grotto contributions. Less far-flung are the **Yungang Grottoes** (p. 257) near Datong, in Shanxi, and the riverside **Longmen Grottoes** (p. 238), outside Luoyang in Henan province. The **Dazu carvings** (p. 644) near Sichuan round out the array.

THE OTHER LITTLE RED BOOK

Ahhh...ideological fervor: crowds of slogan-chanting, armband-wearing Red Guards, top-secret revolutionary cells, peasant uprisings, and...Mao sunglasses?

While this little red (and yellow) book may be all you need for your trip, Chairman Mao's little red book is undoubtedly more important in China as a whole. Tricky though the moral and political issues involved may be, the aesthetic of the Communist revolution has a sort of chicness in certain circles of kitsch connoisseurs. The fierce cult of personality that developed in China around Mao Zedong and other Communist icons has produced plenty of garish and surreal relics, from pocket-sized Little Red Books to musical Mao lighters (and more). Travelers who want to savor these should head first for Mao's home province of Hunan, to the capital **Changsha** (p. 384) and Mao's birthplace in the village of **Shaoshan** (p. 388). Dust off that inner socialist and hum a few bars of "East is Red" and join swarms of Chinese tourists coming to pay romantic or cynical homage to the Great Helmsman. Pilgrims bent on retracing some (or all) of the Long March can stop off at the remote destinations of **Nanchang** (p. 372) and **Jinggangshan** (p. 381), in Jiangxi province, **Zunyi** (p. 611), in Guizhou province, and **Yanan** (p. 227), in Shaanxi province. Finally, what better way to honor thy Chairman than to visit his mausoleum in **Beijing** (p. 118)?

THE BACKPACKER SCENE...

Dirty, hardcore, story-rich, and currency-poor, backpackers turn up in every corner of the globe. Like all cults, that of independent travel has its pilgrimage sites; cheap and scenic, they promise good conversation, plentiful beer, and perhaps the elusive cappuccino. In China, two places fit this bill perfectly: **Yangshuo** (p. 536), in Guilin province, and **Dali** (p. 557), in Yunnan province. Both are small towns blessed with natural splendor, mild climates, friendly residents, and laid-back atmosphere. The desert oasis of **Dunhuang** (p. 683), in Gansu province, is coming to enjoy much the same reputation. Shanghai's **Nanjing Xi Lu** and **French Concession** (p. 274), Beijing's **Sanlitun** (p. 92), Hong Kong's **Lan Kwai Fong** (p. 430), and much of **Guangdong province** (p. 462) welcome more permanent foreign vagabonds.

...AND HOW TO AVOID IT

The backpacker scene does have its drawbacks. The temptation to consort with other Westerners can be overwhelming and can insulate visitors from the very culture that they traveled thousands of miles to experience. Fortunately, a few regions have features (including cheap accommodations, cultural diversity, and striking topography) that *should* attract hordes of backpackers—but don't, at least not yet. The remote **Kaili** (p. 604) region of Guizhou province is filled with tiny Miao, Dong, and other minority villages set amid breathtaking scenery. Much of northwestern China, especially the Silk Road towns of **Kashgar** (p. 707) and **Kuqa**

(p. 704), the Tibetan-style village of **Xiahe** (p. 671), and the **Yili River** region (p. 695) to the far north, presents a vastly different portrait of China, sans tourists. In the southeast, venture to Fujian's **Wuyishan** (p. 502) or the rural areas of **Guangdong** (p. 490) for a glimpse of rice and tea plantations, craggy peaks, and traditional villages left virtually untouched by the region's recent economic success.

▤ LET'S GO PICKS

BEST WAYS TO GET HIGH: Marvel at the pristine alpine forests and snow-capped peaks outside **Yining** (p. 695) or **Ürümqi** (p. 694). Scramble up the stairs in **Shanghai**'s annual race up one of Pudong New Area's tallest skyscrapers (p. 274). Parachute off the enormous Singing Sand Dunes (p. 688) of **Dunhuang.**

BEST PLACE TO GET DEPRESSED: The **Turpan Depression** (p. 698), the second lowest point in the world.

BEST PLACES TO KICK SOME ASS: Go face to face, arm to arm, and leg to leg as you master the art of *wushu* on the practice fields of Henan's **Shaolin Monastery** (p. 233). Wander the Daoist temples and trails of **Wudangshan** to figure out how exactly a magpie's victory over a snake inspired Zhang Sanfeng to found a school of boxing (p. 403). Best way to get *your* ass kicked? Scarf down some red-hot, fiery cuisine in **Sichuan** (p. 614) or **Hunan** (p. 383).

BEST HUGS: Cuddle up to giant pandas in **Wolong Nature Reserve** (p. 626). Meet the locals on **Monkey Island** (p. 522). For some tough love, look up at the stern visage of the **Giant Buddha,** atop Lantau Island (p. 447).

TIGHTEST SQUEEZES: If extricating yourself from the hard seat that you and your newfound friends have occupied for the past 68 hours isn't enough, try one of the following. Squirm through the incredibly kitschy **Dragon Light Cave** near Lake Taihu (p. 319). Hang on to a rusty chain for dear life as you make your way between the ledges of Huashan's narrow **Thousand Foot Cliff** (p. 226). Pile your pack into a closet-sized room at **Hong Kong**'s Chungking Mansions (p. 422).

BEST CUPS OF TEA: Indulge yourself amid the lush hills and sprawling terraced fields of **Longjing tea plantations,** west of Hangzhou (p. 338). Stand back as both the monkeys and "silver needle" tea vie for your attention on Yueyang's **Junshan Island** (p. 392). Sip *ba bao cha* and look out over the steep, rocky landscape of **Lanzhou** (p. 664). Pull up a bamboo chair, take out the *mahjong* tiles, and start sipping in one of **Chengdu**'s many tea gardens (p. 622). Inhale the pungent scent of yak-butter tea wafting through the alleyways in **Lhasa** (p. 730).

BEST DUMPLINGS: Plow into a plateful of heaven at **Kaifeng**'s No. 1 Dumpling Restaurant (p. 242), **Shanghai**'s Changan Dumpling Restaurant (p. 287), **Wuhan**'s Four Seasons Dumpling House (p. 399), **Zhenjiang**'s Yanchun Restaurant (p. 324), or **Harbin**'s Eastern Dumpling King (p. 185), near where the "Northeast dumpling" craze supposedly all began.

GOOD LIBATIONS: Snake brandy, *maotai,* or for tradition's sake, good ole Tsingtao (p. 172). Bottoms up!

BEST REASONS FOR THE SUN TO RISE TOMORROW: Gaze in anticipation at the Beihai sunrise from one of the friendship lock-entwined lookouts in **Huangshan** (p. 367). Emerge from your yurt to watch the sun rise over the gently sloping grasslands of **Inner Mongolia** (p. 264). Join flashlight-wielding pilgrims in the midnight climb up **Taishan** (p. 160). Feel the mist come over Xiamen's **Gulangyu** (p. 515). Stand at attention with crowds of camera-toting tourists and PLA soldiers at the daily flag-raising ceremony in Beijing's **Tiananmen Square** (p. 117).

SUGGESTED ITINERARIES

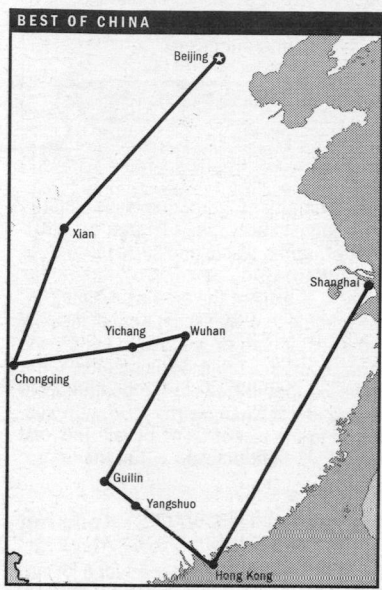

BEST OF CHINA

Beijing
Xian
Shanghai
Yichang   Wuhan
Chongqing
Guilin
Yangshuo
Hong Kong

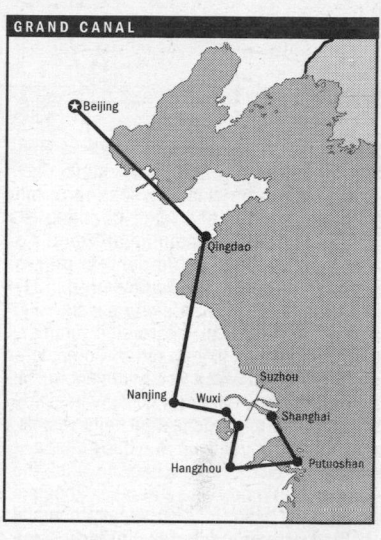

GRAND CANAL

Beijing
Qingdao
Suzhou
Nanjing   Wuxi   Shanghai
Hangzhou   Putuoshan

BEST OF CHINA (2½-3 WEEKS) The capital city of **Beijing** (p. 92) is the perfect starter to a five-course meal of Chinese delights. Beijing's **Forbidden City** (p. 118) is a well-preserved treasure trove of China's long dynastic history, easily combined with a visit to **Tiananmen Square** (p. 117), the largest public gathering space in the world and the site of the 1989 democracy protests (see p. 20). Rounding out Beijing's larger-than-life monuments are the **Summer Palace** (p. 125), a centuries-old royal villa, and the **Great Wall** (p. 127), the only man-made structure visible from space. Xian's **Terracotta Warriors** (p. 222) have also been dubbed the "eighth wonder of the world," and the 7000 clay soldiers arranged in battle formation will have any visitor standing at attention. Leave imperial ostentation behind as you take the train straight from Xian to Guilin, or head to hilly **Chongqing** (p. 639) before jumping on a two-day boat tour through the soon to be submerged **Three Gorges** (p. 646). Disembark at Yichang, catch a minibus to Wuhan, and soon you'll be headed for the storybook scenery of **Guilin** (p. 531). Cruise down the Li River to **Yangshuo** (p. 536) for fruit smoothies and the chance to meet every species of backpacker known to man. Pump up the volume in eye-popping, exhilarating

Hong Kong (p. 406)—dance until the wee hours of the morning in **Lan Kwai Fong** (p. 435), shop the **"Golden Mile"** (Nathan Rd., p. 429), and indulge in **dim sum** (p. 425). Finally, swing north to **Shanghai** (p. 274) for whispers of the colonial past and a fantastic waterfront promenade.

GRAND CANAL (3 WEEKS) Built in the Sui, the Grand Canal links China's two great waterways, the Yellow and Yangzi Rivers. Begin at its northern extreme, in **Beijing** (p. 92), sprawling seat of imperial splendor. Follow the canal south through Shandong, with a quick detour to **Qingdao** (p. 167) to sip beer on the old German concession's beaches. Trundle on to **Nanjing** (p. 297) and stroll down broad boulevards in the historic southern capital. Breeze through **Wuxi** (p. 316) and watch bamboo junks sail by from the shores of **Lake Taihu** (p. 320). Trace the Grand Canal as it meanders past the classical gardens of **Suzhou** (p. 308), dubbed the "Venice of the East." Cruise along like an emperor on a shopping spree to the earthly paradise of **Hangzhou** (p. 330), then head east to the canal-lined streets of **Shaoxing** (p. 338). From **Ningbo** (p. 343), hop a steamer to the fantastic Buddhist island of **Putuoshan** (p. 347). Adjourn in **Shanghai** (p. 274) to admire the Bund's concession-era architecture and to do what everyone goes to Shanghai to do: shop.

DISCOVER

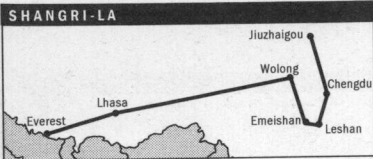

SHANGRI-LA

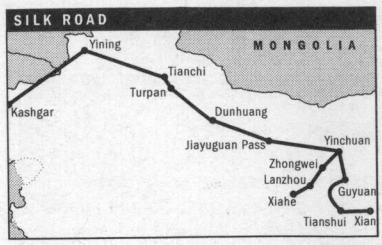

SILK ROAD

SHANGRI-LA (3 WEEKS) Seek ye first enlightenment and peace of mind, then scrub your karma clean by soaring to the heights in Sichuan and Tibet. **Chengdu** (p. 614) is the perfect jumping-off point for nearby heaven-on-earth mountain ranges and nature reserves like **Emeishan** (p. 631) and **Jiuzhaigou** (p. 634), with shimmering, crystal-clear lakes, mist-shrouded temples, and scenic vistas like no other. Combine a trip to Emeishan with a visit to the enormous Big Buddha at **Leshan** (p. 628), where you can climb up on Buddha's toenails or whisper in his ear. Cuddle up to a baby panda at **Wolong** (p. 626). Next, ascend to Tibet, the "Roof of the World," and enter the "Abode of the Gods" (**Lhasa**, p. 730). Meditate in one of the many monasteries, including the **Jokhang Temple** (p. 736) and the **Potala Palace** (p. 735). To finish, careen down the Friendship Highway to gaze at the snow-capped peak that looms over this "Land of Snows," **Mt. Everest** (p. 751).

SILK ROAD (1-2 MONTHS) This journey takes you down the fabled Silk Road, a 2000-year-old trade route that ferried the ancient world's most treasured commodity between Asia and Europe. Leave behind the protection of Xian's mighty **Terracotta Warriors** (p. 222) for China's very own "Wild West." Explore the **Maijishan Grottoes** (p. 675), set in the bleeding red cliffs near Tianshui. Be awed by eerie tombs of forgotten kings near **Yinchuan** (p. 651), and then take a quick detour to **Zhongwei** (p. 659), where you can float down the turbulent Yellow River in an inflated sheepskin raft. Browse through **Lanzhou**'s (p. 664) impressive provincial museum on the way to Xiahe's enchanting **Labrang Monastery** (p. 671), where Tibetan lamas welcome weary travelers with cups of yak-butter tea. Follow the Great Wall westward to the end of its 2000km at **Jiayuguan** (p. 677). Press on to **Dunhuang** (p. 683) for a glimpse of the Buddhist art of the **Mogao Grottoes**, then hitch a camel and go paragliding or tobogganing in the Gobi's **Singing Sand Dunes** (p. 688). As you chug into Xinjiang, the barren Gobi gives way to the rocky Taklimakan, desert of no return. Thirst-quenching sweet hami melons and grapevine-laced trellises await tourist caravans in **Turpan** (p. 690). Tired of barren wastelands? Head north to **Tianchi** (p. 694), a heavenly lake near Ürümqi, or explore the area near **Yining** (p. 695), home to a significant Kazakh minority and spectacular alpine vistas. Loop back down along the Tarim Basin's northern rim to the Sunday Bazaar in the Central Asian crossroads of **Kashgar** (p. 707), now connected to the rest of China by rail. The road leads from here across the **Karakorum** (p. 712) to Pakistan.

SOUTHWEST (3-4 WEEKS) Kunming (p. 545), Yunnan's balmy and laid-back capital, is the perfect starting point for a journey through the Southwest. Go west to **Dali** (p. 557), where the Bai minority and backpacker cultures meld seamlessly and batik turns into tie-dye, amid stunning lakes and mountains. **Lijiang** (p. 565) and its matriarchal Naxi minority await in the north, and tropical **Xishuangbanna** (p. 584) is down south, a place where flora, fauna, and diverse cultures leave unforgettable memories for travelers crossing into Southeast Asia. The journey west has ended. Head east into the rugged **Kaili** region (p. 604), home of the Miao people, then veer north to **Sanjiang** (p. 542), the stronghold of the Dong minority. Return home slowly, stopping in **Guilin** (p. 531) and **Yangshuo** (p. 536) to relax amid mist-shrouded limestone peaks. With peaceful lakes, craggy peaks, and good company, you may never want to leave.

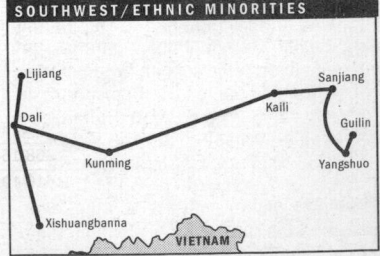

SOUTHWEST/ETHNIC MINORITIES

CHINA

HISTORY

Chinese civilization is the oldest in East Asia, if not in the whole world. In fact, many Chinese advances and inventions predate similar developments in the West. The following is a timeline of major periods in Chinese history.

DYNASTY	PERIOD	YEARS	SITE OF CAPITAL
Xia (recently verified)		ca. 2200-1700 BC	Erlitou, Henan
Shang		ca. 1700-1200 BC	Anyang, Henan
Zhou	Western	1027-771 BC	Xian, Shaanxi
	Eastern	770-256 BC	Luoyang, Henan
Qin		221-206 BC	Xianyang, Shaanxi
Han	Western	206 BC - AD 25	Xian
	Xin	AD 25	Xian
	Eastern	25-220	Luoyang
Three Kingdoms	Wei	220-265	Luoyang
	Shu	221-263	Chengdu, Sichuan
	Wu	229-280	Nanjing, Jiangsu
Jin	Western	265-316	Luoyang
	Eastern	317-420	Nanjing
Sixteen Kingdoms		304-409	
Northern Dynasties	Northern Wei	386-534	Datong, Shaanxi; Luoyang
	Eastern Wei	534-550	Linzhang, Hebei
	Western Wei	535-557	Xian
	Northern Qi	550-557	Linzhang
	Northern Zhou	557-581	Xian
Southern Dynasties	Song	420-479	Nanjing
	Qi	479-502	Nanjing
	Liang	502-557	Nanjing
	Chen	557-589	Nanjing
Sui		581-618	Xian
Tang		618-907	Xian
Five Dynasties-Ten Kingdoms	Later Liang	907-923	Kaifeng, Henan
	Later Tang	923-936	Luoyang
	Later Jin	936-946	Kaifeng
	Later Han	947-950	Kaifeng
	Later Zhou	951-960	Kaifeng
Song	Northern	960-1127	Kaifeng
	Southern	1127-1279	Hangzhou, Zhejiang
Liao		916-1125	Balin Banner, Inner Mongolia
Jin		1115-1234	Acheng, Heilongjiang; Beijing; Kaifeng
Yuan		1206-1368	Beijing
Ming		1368-1644	Beijing
Qing		1616-1912	Shenyang, Liaoning; Beijing
Republic of China		1912-	Nanjing; Taipei, Taiwan
People's Republic of China		1949-	Beijing

CHINA

CLASSICAL CHINA (10,000-221 BC)

PRE-HISTORY & THE GOLDEN AGE OF ANTIQUITY

Prehistoric humanoid presence in China dates back 600,000 years, as documented by the discoveries of the upright walking **Lantian Man** (found near Xian) and the more advanced, fire-using **Peking Man,** who had a cranial capacity two-thirds that of a modern man. The end of the last ice age in 10,000 BC allowed hunter-gatherers to settle in the fertile regions of the Yellow and Yangzi river valleys. The development of agriculture coincided with the growth of pottery and textile production as well as with the evolution of early religion (see **Banpo Neolithic Village,** p. 223).

From 4000 to 2000 BC, contact between emerging Neolithic cultures encouraged rapid technological and artistic progress and the development of complex forms of social hierarchy and government. The use of small-scale weapons and conflict increased as metallurgy improved, and burial finds of bronze offering vessels and sacrificial remains of human attendants indicate the presence of a religious and militaristic upper class by 2000 BC (or around the time of the **Xia** dynasty). The highly organized Longshan culture of central Henan developed into the **Shang** (dated 1766-1122 BC), centered in Erlitou and Anyang (see p. 244). The Shang justified its rule primarily through ancestor worship and oracle bone divination. Eventually, the Shang's special position between the dead and living was not enough, and in 1027 BC, the **Zhou,** a frontier state west of the area under Shang control, overthrew the weakened Shang forces. Because of its hierarchy of territorial rule based on familial ties, the Xian-based Western Zhou period (1027-771 BC) has been loosely compared with the feudal system of medieval Europe.

DIVISION & THE AGE OF PHILOSOPHERS

Attacks by Western tribes forced the Zhou dynasty to move its capital east to a site near present-day Luoyang in 771 BC, marking the beginning of the Eastern Zhou period. In time, the regime lost military, political, and economic power as it splintered into about 170 aristocratic family-states, each with its own walled capital. A strong sense of political discontent and exploration fostered a new generation of philosophers and competing concepts of social governance. During the **Hundred Schools Period,** Confucius, Laozi (Lao Tzu), Mozi, and other scholars decried the decaying morals of their age, traveling from place to place to expound their theories of living to rulers and commoners alike (see **Religion and Philosophy,** p. 31).

SAGE KINGS According to the traditional Chinese view of antiquity, ancient sage kings once ruled the land in perfect peace and harmony. **Yao** was the first of these semidivine paragons of wisdom and justice, and during his 70-year rule the sun, moon, and planets shone more brightly, rice grew more abundantly, and civilization developed more congenially than ever again. Yao was also admired for choosing the virtuous **Shun** as his successor instead of his unspectacular son. The peasant Shun exemplified filial piety through his obedience to a blind father and a wicked stepmother and later demonstrated his supreme sageness by living in harmony with two wives, Yao's two daughters. Shun, in turn, passed the throne to **Yu,** who labored so long and so hard against the devastation of the mythical Great Flood, digging canals to divert entire rivers, that he passed his home several times without pausing to greet his wife and son. Harrowed by Yu's death and reluctant to accept his designated successor, the people elected to follow his less worthy son, and thus established the practice of hereditary succession and founded the first dynasty, the Xia. The golden age of Chinese antiquity is said to have persisted through the Xia, Shang, and Zhou dynasties. In that time one more individual, this one a real historical figure, attained the status of sage king; the **Duke of Zhou,** brother to the founder of the Zhou and regent to the succeeding child emperor, his brother's son, was esteemed as a model statesman for having stabilized the Zhou empire early in the dynasty. Confucius thought so highly of the Duke that he once lamented: "I must have grown really feeble and old, since I have not for a long time dreamed of seeing Duke Zhou."

As diplomacy and contested moral authority failed to mediate conflicts, military might gained the upper hand. Internal social unrest weakened the existing aristocracy and an educated middle class, the *shi*, emerged as a force for cultural and economic advancement. The development of soybean cultivation, new taxation systems, and Sun Tzu's *Art of War* illustrate the rapid growth and bloody division of the **Warring States Period**.

RISE OF EMPIRE (221 BC-AD 589)

QIN & HAN

From Qin (spelled Ch'in in the Wade-Giles romanization) comes China. The highly centralized and martial bureaucracy of the Qin (221-207 BC) transformed an isolated Shaanxi kingdom into a powerful military state that established the rough national boundaries, common currency and written language, and standardized administration system that existed for the next 2000 years. Led by the ruthless **Qin Shihuang**, "First Emperor of the Qin," the Qin swept east and conquered the six other warring states. Supported by Lord Shang and a harsh legal code that allowed for no detractors, Qin Shihuang allegedly destroyed books and buried alive scholars he found seditious. A career militarist famous for his army of terracotta warriors in Xian (see p. 222), the emperor also ordered the expansion of China's northern defense into an elaborate fortification system now known as the **Great Wall** (see p. 130) .

After the death of Qin Shihuang, deep-rooted popular discontent spilled over into open rebellion. The villager Liu Bang, known posthumously as **Han Gaozu**, proclaimed the **Han dynasty** in 202 BC. Han rule drew upon Confucianism (see p. 31) and the model of the Zhou (see p. 8). Historical scholarship came into its own during the Western Han (202 BC-AD 8), with the work of masters such as **Sima Qian**. Likewise, changes in the civil service selection process reflected the importance of Confucian scholarly learning over bureaucratic skills. The influence of the inner court of eunuchs and consort families expanded until the reign of the powerful **Emperor Wu** (141-87 BC). Unpopular taxes and salt and iron monopolies funded the military and economic growth during his reign, yet the arts flourished.

The balance between central control and regional autonomy often proved to separate the men from the boys. The regent of Emperor Ping (1 BC-AD 6), **Wang Mang**, mounted the throne to proclaim his own **Xin** dynasty in AD 9. Natural disaster aggravated the disruptive outcomes of Wang Mang's policy decisions, though, and Xin China collapsed into civil war. In AD 25, a branch of the Han imperial family moved the capital east to **Luoyang** to found the Eastern Han (AD 25-220). The Eastern Han's spectacular first century soon gave way to the same high court intrigue that weakened the Western. The frustrated populace joined anti-dynastic movements inspired by folk beliefs and Daoism, and the crushing of the **Yellow Turbans** in AD 184 gave way to a period of division by AD 220.

PERIOD OF DISUNITY

The Han dissolved into three kingdoms, each led by Western Han military leaders covetous of an imperial mandate. The **Jin** dynasty (265-316) briefly unified China until the death of its first ruler. The resettled non-Chinese "barbarians" in the north sacked the Jin court at Luoyang in 311, forcing the stunned Jin to flee to the southeast. Five successive southern dynasties existed between 316 and 589. The foreign **Xianbei** tribe in 386 forged the **Northern Wei** of 16 overlapping northern kingdoms. The Northern Wei successfully implemented the equal-field system, in which a parcel of farm land was granted to each peasant for the duration of his lifetime. This regime also patronized Buddhist scholarship and art; the cave temples of Longmen Grottoes (see p. 238) stand among its legacies. However, the Xianbei rulers fell victim to their own sinicization as their un-sinicized compatriots at the frontier garrisons turned against them in 589.

FLOWERING OF CHINESE CULTURE (589-1279)

COSMOPOLITAN SUI & TANG

In 589, **Yang Jian,** a prominent northern general of mixed Chinese and Turkish ancestry, ousted the Northern Zhou dynasty and then conquered the Chen dynasty in the south to end 300 years of political division along the Yangzi River. The Sui restored a highly centralized bureaucratic state, established a lasting legal code, boosted agricultural output, restored the Great Wall, and built the **Grand Canal.** Unfortunately, costly campaigns against Korea drained resources, prompting another cycle of repressive taxation, unrest, and rebellion.

When the dust settled in 617, **Li Yuan (Emperor Gaozu)** emerged victorious and founded the Tang dynasty. The Tang first secured an efficient tax base at home and then went on the offensive. Early emperors such as Taizong and Gaozong were skilled tacticians, savvy diplomats, and fearless commanders. Drawing troops from sinicized northern military families and horses from steppe traders, the Tang built a swift strike force that could contend with Central Asia armies. Tang armies and their Uighur allies from Mongolia crushed the Turkish federation in the Tarim Basin in 657, and in the east, Tang armies in 668 handed the Korean peninsula to the **Silla,** a Tang-friendly Korean kingdom. During its heyday in the 7th century, Tang military protectorates extended from western Iran to Vietnam, and forged alliances with the Uighurs and Tibetans.

The empire's radiating influence abroad was reflected in cosmopolitan attitudes at home. Consulates from Byzantium, Zoroastrians from Persia, Nestorian Christians from Syria, scholars from Korea, tributes from Japan, traders from Arabia, and ivory merchants from Vietnam all made their homes in the capital, Chang'an (now known as Xian). Perhaps the most unorthodox event of the era was the emergence of China's only female emperor, **Wu Zetian** in 690. A concubine of two emperors, Empress Wu finally got her chance when she deposed her own son and declared that she was a reincarnation of Maitreya, Buddha of the Future. Though a ruthless politician, she was a generous patron of Buddhism (see **Fengxian Temple,** p. 238, to which she donated her entire cosmetics budget for a year). **Xuanzong** (713-756) reformed the monetary system and extended the Grand Canal before withdrawing to cavort with his favorite concubine, Yang Guifei (see **Huaqing Pool,** p. 223), in later years.

The following years brought about a swift downturn in dynastic greatness. **An Lushan** fomented a palace coup in 755 that dragged on for a decade, leaving much of northern China in ruins. Defeat on foreign battlegrounds near Tashkent effectively ended Chinese dominance in Central Asia, and the Tibetan sacking of Chang'an in 763 drove another nail into the as yet unfinished coffin of the Tang. Once order was restored, a weak Tang court was unable to reign over fractious warlords and starving peasants. In 907, the Tang dynasty dissolved into the fragmented **Five Dynasties-Ten Kingdoms Period,** in which the hereditary aristocracy permanently lost its footing, China gave up its martial vigor, and the acceptance of Buddhism gave way to a yearning for a uniquely Chinese culture.

BUILDING TRADITION: THE SONG

In 960, General **Zhao Kuangyin (Emperor Song Taizu)** reunified much of China and founded the Northern Song dynasty. The reactionary Song rulers concentrated on the preservation of traditional Confucian culture. Scholars such as **Wang Anshi, Ouyang Xiu,** and **Zhu Xi** ushered in **Neo-Confucianism,** a philosophical movement that emphasized selfless behavior and ethical learning for the sake of both service to the state and personal self-cultivation. The Song also promoted progress through a meritocratic civil service examination system, a welfare system, and the introduction of paper money. Song cities, fueled by high agricultural yields, supported booming commerce and iron industries. Vernacular lyrical poetry (see **Literature,** p. 36) and landscape painting (see **Painting,** p. 39) marked the artistic climate, and the growth of Buddhism resulted in the construction of numerous Buddhist temples and pagodas, such as the Iron Pagoda in present-day **Kaifeng** (see p. 240).

Despite the significant reforms and cultural developments at home, the Song dynasty was constantly harassed and threatened by the "barbarians" from the north. Shortly after the founding of the Song, **Khitan** nomads of Mongolia conquered Beijing, secured the Great Wall, and founded the **Liao** dynasty (c. 916-1125). Too weak to drive out the Liao and unwilling to pay tribute, the Song court collaborated with another rising tribe, the Jurchens of Manchuria, who swept south and conquered the Liao, then pressed on to the Song capital of Kaifeng in 1126 and established the **Jin** (Chinese for Golden) dynasty (1115-1234). Liao survivors trekked west and joined the **Western Xia** dynasty (1038-1227) of the Tangut people based in Yinchuan (see p. 651). Although much of northern China was ruled by steppe nomads, these alien rulers quickly adopted the Chinese imperial model of administration and many cultural customs.

Remnants of the Song, led by the emperor **Gaozong**, established the **Southern Song** capital in the present-day city of **Hangzhou** (see p. 330). Cultural achievements continued, but foreign affairs grew increasingly strained and the court became hopelessly corrupt. It was reported that when a concubine informed the emperor that the city of Xiangyang had been surrounded for five years without reinforcements, eunuchs had her executed and the emperor continued with his decade-long orgy. Unable to contend with the expansionist Jin, the Song courtiers eagerly forged an anti-Jin alliance with another powerful nomadic nation to the far north, not knowing that they were about to invite the onslaught of the Mongols.

YUAN & MING DYNASTIES (1279-1644)

MONGOL CAPTURE & RULE: THE YUAN

Prior to the 13th century, the Mongols were a nomadic people composed of dispersed, roving clans. In 1205, **Genghis Khan** unified these clans and stormed across Eurasia, sacking Baghdad, trampling Moscow, and pounding on the gates of Vienna. Genghis died fighting against the Western Xia in 1227, but his sons and grandsons finished the job, conquering the Jin dynasty in 1234, the Nanzhao (Dali) kingdom in 1251, and the Southern Song in 1279. The Mongols even used a converted Song navy to invade Java (1292-93), Vietnam (1282-83 and 1287-88), and Japan (twice unsuccessfully, 1274 and 1281).

Kublai Khan's Yuan dynasty court hosted guests such as Italian explorer **Marco Polo**. Major projects included Beijing's **Beihai Park** (see p. 119), Zhongnanhai Compound (now the residence of top CCP leaders), a stately pleasure dome in Xanadu, and an expanded Grand Canal system. Unlike the Liao and Jin rulers, the Yuan resisted cultural assimilation and maintained a segregated class society where Chinese were of the lowest class and interracial marriages were prohibited. To keep the vast Chinese populace under control, the Mongols employed unusually harsh measures such as confiscating all iron tools and forcing ten families to share one kitchen cleaver. Not surprisingly, many Chinese dreamt of a Song restoration.

Unable to hold government posts, many Chinese intellectuals engaged in private scholarship or took on occupations in medicine, fortune-telling, and theater, all of which brought them in closer proximity to the common people. The vernacular found its way into Chinese literary culture, which had centered around the classical language and more "learned" genres like poetry and philosophy. Theater and fiction (see **Theater**, p. 38, and **Literature: Pre-modern** p. 36) rose to a new prominence in the Yuan. In the visual arts, calligraphy and Buddhist art both flourished.

While the Mongols openly patronized Tibetan Lamaism, the Chinese populace focused on messianic societies such as the **White Lotus Society,** which preached the immediate coming of the Maitreya Buddha, who would put an end to injustice and suffering. In 1352, the **Red Turban Society** (named for the headgear worn by its followers) launched a rebellion that engulfed most of the south for the next three years. Though the Mongols crushed the rebellion, clan member **Zhu Yuanzhang** (posthumously known as Ming Taizu) formed another rebel group that eventually toppled the Yuan in 1368. Ironically, after forming the Ming dynasty, he soon banned all heterodox religious sects, including the Red Turbans.

EXPANSION & EXPLORATION: THE MING

Founding emperor Ming Taizu (r. 1368-1398) established an autocratic and stable government. Taizu initiated extensive reforms in tax, labor, and school systems from his newly built capital in **Nanjing** (see p. 297). His son **Yongle** (r. 1402-24) moved the capital back to **Beijing** and oversaw ambitious public works programs, including the production of a comprehensive literary canon. The Ming dynasty saw **territorial expansion** into Turkestan, Korea, Mongolia, Vietnam, and Myanmar. In the early 15th century, a number of **sea expeditions** brought Chinese ships, people, and goods as far afield as Madagascar. The most famous maritime adventurer of the period was **Zheng He,** a Muslim court eunuch who commanded voyages across the Indian Ocean to India, Arabia, and eastern Africa.

Political and economic stability supported a number of cultural advancements. **Pottery** made great strides as an art form in the Ming; the blue-and-white glazed vases produced in this period were highly valued in Europe (see p. 40). Multiple painting schools flourished in Suzhou, arguably the cultural capital of the Ming (see p. 308). Literature written in the vernacular accompanied a dramatic rise in literacy. Writers like **Feng Menglong** and **Ling Mengqu** transformed the genre of **short fiction,** much of which focused on the lower social classes, into an acceptable venture for intellectuals (see p. 36). The southern form of musical drama known as **kunqu,** an early ancestor to Beijing opera (see **A Night at the Jingju,** p. 112), crystallized in this period. Neo-Confucian thinkers such as **Wang Yangming** formulated new, more individual-oriented interpretations of philosophy.

As time went on, fewer capable leaders came to power. As an autocracy, the Ming government depended on the individual quirks and personalities of the current emperor. **Court eunuchs** held much power, often governing with their own interests in mind (although something seemed to be missing...). The gentry managed to avoid paying their taxes to the imperial center, and the government often was unable to pay salaries. High inflation and constant fighting with Manchu and Mongol armies did not help. Disgruntlement spread among both commoners and officials and in northern Shaanxi, **outlaw gangs** staged small-scale rebellions.

In 1644, a former postal official, **Li Zicheng,** led a brutal but efficient rebel attack on Beijing. The last Ming emperor hanged himself in present-day **Jingshan Park** (see p. 119), and the rebel army entered the city gate's easily. In a last-ditch attempt to save the dynasty, loyalist general **Wu Sangui** allowed Manchu armies into Beijing, hoping that they would assist in putting down Li's rebellion. The Manchus did indeed defeat the rebels, but Wu had literally opened the gates to a foreign power that would rule for more than 200 years.

LATE IMPERIAL CHINA: THE QING (1644-1911)

FOUNDING OF THE QING

The Manchus capitalized on the late Ming's internal disorder to invade China. When Wu Sangui opened the Beijing city gates, the Manchus swept in and declared it the capital of their new dynasty, the **Qing** (Chinese for "pure"). Ming stragglers in the south led by Zheng Chenggong (Koxinga) fled to Taiwan and staved off elimination until Qing Emperor Kangxi conquered the island in 1683. Qing rulers upheld the examination system, patronized Chinese art and literature, and continued to appoint Chinese as well as Manchus to official posts. Most importantly, they used Confucianism as a way to build and maintain political authority. Despite the demand that all Chinese men wear their hair in the distinctive Manchu-style queue (a long braid in the back and shaved head in the front), on the whole Qing emperors adhered very closely to the expectations of Chinese tradition.

Emperor Kangxi (r. 1668-1722), famous for his personal inspection tours and ascetic habits, oversaw distant military campaigns in Russia, Mongolia, and Tibet. Turmoil over Kangxi's successor ended in the reign of Yongzheng (r. 1723-1735), an efficient, tough, and ultimately short-lived ruler. Emperor **Qianlong** (r. 1736-1796), widely regarded as one of the greatest rulers in Chinese history, presided over a period of unprecedented wealth and territorial and population expansion. By the end of Qianlong's reign, however, expensive military campaigns depleted imperial coffers and corruption once again plagued the government. The developing conflict over foreign intrusion exacerbated these problems.

TRADE UNDER THE CANTON SYSTEM

Although maritime trade was essential to the communities of the southeast, Qing emperors remained wary of overseas commerce. Emperor Qianlong restricted all foreign traders to the vicinity of Guangzhou (Canton). The so-called **Canton system** (1760-1843) required all commercial transactions to go through a select group of Chinese merchants *(hongs)* who had been granted a monopoly on foreign trade.

Despite the restrictions of the Canton system, the British had a compelling reason to maintain trade with China: tea (see p. 46). Popularized as a benign alternative to liquor, tea was considered a national necessity by the British. In fact, the East India Company was required by the British Parliament to keep a year's supply in stock at all times, and the British government collected one-tenth of its revenue from a tax on Chinese tea. However, the balance of trade was tilted heavily in China's favor until the introduction of **opium**. By the 1820s, vast quantities of silver were flowing out of China to pay for all this opium, turning a public health issue into a financial crisis. In 1836, the Chinese emperor Daoguang decided to make a vigorous attempt to stamp out opium once and for all. Dealers and users were imprisoned or executed, causing demand for opium to plummet. A few years later, the hardnosed official **Lin Zexu** suspended all trade, blockaded factories, held 250 foreigners hostage, and demanded that the British relinquish their opium. British merchants surrendered over 20,000 chests of opium, which took Lin over 23 days to destroy. The Chinese court was pleased with Lin's apparent success, but Britain decided that the only appropriate response to China's behavior was war.

OPIUM WAR & THE TREATY SYSTEM

The **Opium War** (1840-1842) began when British warships blockaded Guangzhou and moved north toward Xiamen (see p. 510). After several military conflicts and failed negotiations, the Chinese finally consented to the stipulations imposed by Britain's **Treaty of Nanjing,** setting the pattern for tense relations with Western nations during the following century. Five ports were opened to Western trade, the Canton system was abolished, and **Hong Kong** was leased to the British for 99 years (see p. 407). The British also demanded the right to set tariff rates, obtained most-favored-nation status, and used claims of extraterritoriality to restrict the authority of the Chinese legal system over British subjects. Attempts at Sino-Western cooperation centered on suppressing piracy and smuggling but frequently broke down, as in the case of the 1856 **Arrow Affair.** There was no mention of the very controversy that had sparked the war or subsequent events, however, and traders continued to import opium into China until 1917.

TAIPING REBELLION (1850-1864)

After 1850, floods, famine, and overpopulation combined with governmental neglect and corruption to further domestic unrest. Armed uprisings broke out around the country, the most notorious of which was the **Taiping Rebellion.** The leader of the rebellion, **Hong Xiuquan,** a militant evangelist, began preaching his own form of sinicized Christianity after failing the civil service examination for the fourth time. Over 20,000 discontented Chinese responded to Hong's call to arms. This formidable army of "long-haired rebels"—so called because they cut off their queues and refused to shave their foreheads in defiance against the ruling Manchus—captured the capital city of Nanjing in 1853 and eventually numbered over one million. In 1864, loyalist armies led by **Zeng Guofan** finally defeated the rebels.

QING RESTORATION & SELF-STRENGTHENING

The suppression of the Taiping rebellion gave the Qing dynasty one last chance. During the **Tongzhi period** (1862-1874), the government reformed the examination system, tried to eliminate corruption, and established a foreign affairs office to deal with Western powers. Supporters of the **Self-Strengthening Movement** (1874-1894) promoted Western techniques of science and technology while retaining traditional Chinese values and morals. **Empress Dowager Ci Xi**, in a particularly indulgent move, used funds intended for the Chinese navy to build the **Summer Palace** (see p. 125), misconceived marble boat and all. Consequently, when the Sino-Japanese War broke out on the Korean peninsula in 1894, the Japanese sank the underfunded Chinese fleet. This humiliating defeat inspired the short-lived **Hundred Days of Reform**, during which Ci Xi's son, Emperor **Guangxu**, broke free of the iron grip of his mother, that is, until she placed him under house arrest. Advised by a bolder generation of intellectuals led by **Kang Youwei, Liang Qichao**, and **Tan Citong**, Guangxu fought for fundamental political reform. Many intellectuals, including Liang and Tan, sought support abroad from Chinese emigrés such as Sun Yat-sen.

China's military defeat at the hands of the Japanese brought about increased demands for political, economic, and territorial concessions to other imperialist powers. In response to these intrusions, Chinese peasants formed **secret societies** to defend their interests and to express their resentment. During the **Boxer Rebellion**, the Boxers attacked and looted Beijing, killing foreign and Chinese Christians. This inflamed foreign imperial powers, who exacted a hefty settlement and the right to station troops in the capital. Western squabbles led the United States to institute the **Open Door Policy**, allowing all countries equal access and trading privileges at any of the treaty ports in China. This policy was particularly advantageous to the US, which had been a latecomer to trade with China and wanted to secure the same benefits that the European nations already enjoyed.

As China neared the turn of the century, the failure of the Boxers and China's inability to contest the Open Door Policy were indications that the nation had fallen into a serious crisis.

REPUBLICAN ERA (1911-1949)

"Political power grows out of the barrel of a gun."
  —Mao Zedong

At the turn of the 20th century, China was considered the "sick man of East Asia," a backward country ruled by an inept and anachronistic regime that was battered by internal rebellion and foreign domination, and teetered on the brink of collapse. In the ensuing 100 years, China has experienced unprecedented political upheaval, social transformation, and growth, while enduring untold suffering.

FALL OF THE QING & THE 1911 REVOLUTION

As the Qing languished, dissident groups and their leaders debated the future of the country. **Dr. Sun Yat-sen**, a believer that ruling tradition could not be preserved in a traditional monarchy, eventually prevailed. Sun organized the **Tong Meng Hui** (United League), aimed at overthrowing the Qing regime. While Sun was advocating his cause abroad, league members in Wuchang (now part of Wuhan) pulled off a successful armed uprising on October 10, 1911. The **Xinhai Revolution** spread like wildfire, and on January 1, 1912, Sun Yat-sen was inaugurated as the first president of the **Republic of China**. Two months later, the **last emperor**, six-year-old **Pu Yi**, abdicated—so much for the little people. The Tong Meng Hui became known as the **Nationalist Party** or **Guomindang (GMD)**, and October 10 (Double Ten) became the national holiday; it is still celebrated in Taiwan.

Despite the nominal success gained by overthrowing a dysfunctional regime, the revolution barely altered China's power structure. Real political clout remained in the hands of **Yuan Shikai**, a cunning warlord who used the period's confusion to his own advantage. This former Qing general first turned on the boy emperor by proclaiming allegiance to the revolution, then coerced Sun to yield the presidency to him. After the GMD emerged victorious in the election of the national assembly, Yuan had a key GMD leader assassinated and dissolved the legislature, before declaring himself emperor in 1916. This set off a fresh round of rebellions, ending with Yuan's death that same year. Although the Revolution of 1911 failed to establish a republican government, it did break the grip of the dynastic cycle.

WARLORD ERA & THE MAY FOURTH MOVEMENT

On May 4, 1919, 3000 students marched to Tiananmen Square to protest against the terms of the Treaty of Versailles (that ended WWI). The students denounced imperialism and China's internal weakness. The warlord government jailed more than 1000 students, but the **May Fourth Movement** soon spread. In Shanghai, sympathetic workers went on strike and merchants closed their shops. When the entire cabinet resigned, the government finally agreed to reject the treaty.

Many Chinese intellectuals turned their attention to another vehicle for rapid social change, **communism.** In 1921, 11 delegates, including **Mao Zedong,** founder of the Hunan Communist Committee, attended the First Party Congress in Shanghai (see p. 292). Police raids forced the meeting to be moved onto a boat on a lake in Zhejiang, where the Chinese Communist Party (CCP) was officially founded on July 1 of that year. Despite its unceremonious beginnings, the CCP would rule all of China in less than 30 years' time.

Meanwhile, Sun Yat-sen was busy in Guangzhou trying to revitalize the nationalist cause. Despite his presidential title, Sun was dependent on the support of the mercurial warlords. Seeking more solid backing, Sun encountered the all-too-eager Soviets. With the help of Soviet advisors, Sun streamlined the GMD and learned Bolshevik methods of party organization and propaganda dissemination. Moscow brought the GMD and CCP together in an alliance. At the time, the CCP and GMD shared a common platform of anti-imperialism and anti-warlordism. Sun wanted to lead a multi-class revolution and found similarities between his Three People's Principles and Lenin's New Economic Policy. Sun established the **Huangpu Military Academy** in Guangzhou to build the army he would need to wrest power away from the warlords. His brother-in-law, **Chiang Kai-shek,** fresh from training in Moscow, became the first commandant, while **Zhou Enlai,** a capable young communist, served as the political commissar. However, Sun did not live to see the fruits of his labor, dying of cancer in Beijing in 1925. Sun is revered as a national hero by Communists and Nationalists alike; nearly every city in China is stocked with its fill of Zhongshan (Yat-sen) parks and streets, and his mausoleum outside Nanjing (see p. 304) continues to attract visitors.

NORTHERN EXPEDITION & THE LONG MARCH

In 1926, Generalissimo Chiang Kai-shek led the joint forces of the GMD and the CCP on a military campaign against the warlords. In less than a year, the Northern Expeditionary Forces defeated or subjugated all warlords south of the Yangzi River. The GMD capital was moved from Guangzhou to Wuhan. As Chiang's forces approached Shanghai, communist worker vanguard groups organized by Zhou Enlai seized control of the city, at which point Chiang's troops opened fire on them. The Generalissimo, feeling threatened by the increasing Communist presence in the GMD and aided by gangs from the Shanghai underworld, unleashed a bloody campaign that killed and jailed thousands of "reds." Chiang's regime in Nanjing took control, conquering Beijing in 1928.

The jolt of Chiang's sudden purges left the communist movement in disarray. The Comintern (Communist International, led by the Soviet Union) instructed the CCP leaders to foment Bolshevik-style takeovers in GMD cities. But the nationalists' party structure and police force, designed by the Soviets, proved to be much more difficult to dislodge. Worker uprisings in Wuhan, Guangzhou, Changsha, and Nanchang alienated any remaining sympathetic GMD supporters. While the CCP's morale hit an all time low in 1928, the ever-red yet tattered forces of Mao Zedong and Zhu De established a guerrilla base on **Jinggangshan** (see p. 381) in Jiangxi, one of the poorest regions in southern China. Mao believed that the force of the communist revolution lay with China's landless masses, not with the urban proletariat workers as the Comintern had insisted; his **Red Army** thrived in impoverished rural areas where land redistribution campaigns won the support of the peasantry. Mao's Red Army successfully fended off four **Guerrilla Extermination Campaigns** led by Chiang Kai-shek. The Jiangxi Soviet Area expanded and attracted many communists from around the country, including Zhou Enlai, and similar **Red Soviet Areas** were established in other mountainous rural areas.

The Communist resurgence alarmed Chiang Kai-shek, who in 1934 amassed a GMD army of 700,000. Meanwhile, the CCP experienced a change in high command: a group of CCP leaders led by **Wang Ming** and his Communist German strategist Otto Braun (Li De) returned from training in the USSR, promptly took control, and pushed Mao aside. The **Twenty-Eight Bolsheviks** discarded Mao's strategy of indirect enemy engagement and resorted to European-style positional warfare, with disastrous results (go figure). The under-equipped Red Army was overwhelmed by the more powerful GMD and was forced to flee on the infamous Long March. The ragged guerrillas limped into the town of **Zunyi** (see p. 611) in Guizhou, where top CCP leaders convened to decide on the future of the movement. After three days of bitter arguments, Mao Zedong emerged victorious over rival Wang Ming. From this point onward, Mao had the undisputed leadership of the CCP, and the revolution was largely free of Comintern influence. Mao and his army of 90,000 followers continued on the **Long March,** an epic journey across 8000km of China's most rugged terrain, including 18 mountain ranges and 23 major rivers. A year later, Mao and fewer than 8000 of the original marchers finally reached **Yanan** (see p. 227), a Soviet base in northern Shaanxi province. In the course, Mao won the unwavering loyalty of followers.

TWO REGIMES, TWO SOCIETIES

Although both the GMD and the CCP were militaristic dictators, they derived their power bases from different sectors of the highly stratified Chinese society: Chiang from wealthy urbanites, Mao from inhabitants of the backwater countryside.

During the **Nanjing Decade** of 1928 to 1937, China's cities flourished culturally and economically. A pragmatic education system that focused on technical studies and opened its doors to female students developed. Influenced by fascist movements in Europe, Chiang Kai-shek launched the **New Life Movement** in 1934 to shape youths and reinvigorate the Nationalist cause.

In the countryside, however, peasants still scraped together a meager living, much as their ancestors had. Hampered by a lack of capital, primitive farming techniques, taxes, and natural disasters, farmers could not make ends meet. The GMD regime adopted a policy of "local self-rule" that entailed domination by the landlord elite who were backed by local militias. When Mao reached Yanan, he found the northern Chinese countryside just as he wanted: impoverished and opium-stricken. He then applied Marxist theories to Chinese conditions and developed a system known as the **Yanan Way.**

UNITED FRONT & CIVIL WAR

Before the GMD and the CCP could face off to decide China's fate, another player entered the Chinese power game. Japan had long had an interest in the vast resources and market size of its neighbor to the west. In 1895, the "dwarf pirates" (as they were known to Chinese) routed the Qing and annexed Taiwan. Ten years later, Nippon stunned the West by clobbering Czarist Russia in the Russo-Japanese War and by invading Manchuria on September 18, 1931. They set up a puppet state called **Manchukuo** (or Manzhouguo), with former Qing emperor Pu Yi as the figurehead (see **Puppet Emperor's Palace,** p. 195). Despite national outrage at Japanese aggression, Chiang insisted that internal unity must come before resistance to outside powers, and organized the "final red extermination campaign." With a United Front tactic, Mao declared that he was willing to unite with the GMD to fight the Japanese. The message appealed to Manchurian general Zhang Xueliang, who, instead of attacking the Communists as he was ordered, kidnapped Chiang Kai-shek in the **Xian Incident.** The Generalissimo was eventually released in exchange for the promise that he would put aside the civil war and concentrate on fighting Japan. This so-called **Second United Front** came as a great relief to the Communists, who were still recovering from the Long March.

WWII began in China on July 7, 1937, when Japanese troops clashed with Chinese guards at the **Marco Polo Bridge** outside Beijing (see p. 130). The Japanese then started an all-out offensive and took eastern China by storm. Chiang Kai-shek was forced to retreat to Wuhan and then to Chongqing, in Sichuan. In the capital city of Nanjing, the Japanese slaughtered thousands of surrendered soldiers and civilians and raped at least 20,000 women in seven weeks of mayhem, now known as the **Rape of Nanjing** (see p. 305). A few GMD higher-ups, such as Wang Jingwei, surrendered to the Japanese and were made puppet governors.

After the Japanese invasion of Hong Kong and the 1941 Pearl Harbor bombing, Western powers began to help Chiang Kai-shek. Chiang's charismatic wife, the Wellesley College-educated **Song Meiling**, was instrumental in lobbying for American support and supplies. US President Franklin Roosevelt, hoping to build a strong post-war China to counterbalance Japan's presence in East Asia, included the Generalissimo in the **Big Four meetings** with Churchill and Stalin.

Because the Japanese controlled China's major cities, Communist guerrillas moved into the political vacuum left in the rural areas, recruiting volunteers and carrying out small-scale raids against the Japanese and pro-Japanese militias. At the same time, they expanded the size of the Chinese Red Soviet Areas. In 1941, Chiang Kai-shek rescinded his promise of a United Front, and the Nationalists attacked the Communist forces in southern China.

After the Americans bombed Hiroshima and Nagasaki and the Soviet Union invaded Manchuria, Japan surrendered. However, the victory celebration of August 8, 1945 was quickly forgotten in the mad dash to claim former Japanese territories. While Mao's guerrillas raced north in donkey carts, Chiang's troops rode in American battleships to reclaim northern cities. In the midst of this chaos, US President Harry Truman sent George C. Marshall to negotiate a coalition government between the two factions. Mao Zedong personally attended talks in Chongqing, and Chiang Kai-shek even held a formal wedding for Mao and his third wife Jiang Qing (see p. 18). But the thinly disguised veneer of friendship could not bring about peace. Full-scale civil war broke out in 1947 with Chiang's one million soldiers capturing Yanan; Mao's troops had already skipped town.

The Nationalist regime was severely compromised by runaway inflation and corruption. Despite over $2 billion in US aid, soldiers and civilians were starving in the fields. Prices doubled countless times from 1945 to 1948, and Mao's **People's Liberation Army (PLA)** outmaneuvered the better-equipped Nationalists, forcing the GMD to surrender Beijing. The PLA then swept south of the Yangzi River and quickly swallowed up GMD cities from the surrounding countryside. After the fall of Nanjing, Chiang Kai-shek and the Nationalists fled to Taiwan. On October 1, 1949, in typical Mao style, the Chairman stood on the rostrum of Tiananmen (see p. 117), Beijing's "Gate of Heavenly Peace," and declared the founding of the **People's Republic of China**. He proclaimed that the Chinese people had finally risen up after a century of humiliation. Unification was completed with the "liberation" of Xinjiang in 1950 and the liberation of Tibet in 1951.

COMMUNIST ERA (1949-PRESENT)

CAMELOT PERIOD

After winning power in 1949, the Chinese Communists faced the daunting task of transforming a war-torn and bankrupt country into a communist state. In the early years of the PRC, Chairman Mao ruled along with the collective leadership of his comrades-in-arms, including **Zhou Enlai, Liu Shaoqi**, and **Deng Xiaoping**. During this so-called "Camelot Period" (1949-57), the CCP made impressive gains both at home and abroad.

On the foreign policy front, the US and most Western powers continued to recognize the Chiang Kai-shek regime in Taiwan as the legitimate Chinese government. Mao adopted the **Lean to One Side Policy**, choosing to lean sharply toward the Soviet Union. Soviet policy advisors flowed into the country, and Stalinist architecture mushroomed in Chinese cities. During the **Korean War** (1950-53), Chairman Mao backed Communist North Korea and sent over 2.5 million "volunteers" across the Yalu River, where they fought the United States to a draw.

At home, the party leadership initiated a series of campaigns that solidified their hold on Chinese society. In the countryside, the **land reform** already implemented in northern China's Red Areas was extended to the rest of the country. By 1953, land reform had completely transformed the Chinese countryside, as the power of the gentry diminished and peasant political participation increased. The next step in agricultural reform was **collectivization,** the transfer of private land to public ownership. Since Chinese peasants traditionally farmed with extended families, forming farming cooperatives was not difficult.

In urban areas, workers were organized into work units (*danwei*), which provided them with lifetime employment, housing, food ration allotments, schooling for their children, health care, and retirement pensions. These were collectively referred to as the **"iron rice bowl."** For more on the *danwei* system, see p. 29. By 1957, 94% of China's economic output was produced by state-run enterprises.

HUNDRED FLOWERS MOVEMENT & ANTI-RIGHTIST CAMPAIGN

In the early 1950s, while the consolidation of power in agriculture and industry proceeded fairly smoothly, reining in free-thinking intellectuals proved much more difficult. Over the objections of his second-in-command, Liu Shaoqi, Mao Zedong decided to give the intellectuals an opportunity to offer the party leadership suggestions and participate in the party-led socialist transformation. This was known as the **Hundred Flowers Movement,** after Mao's statement: "Let a hundred flowers bloom, and a hundred schools contend." But these hundred schools of intellectuals challenged the legitimacy of party dictatorship, criticized the bureaucracy, and called for genuine elections with opposition parties. Mao was, to say the least, peeved. He clamped down on intellectual dissent, calling the subversive elements "Rightists." (According to the Maoist doctrine, the Left is revolutionary while the Right is counter-revolutionary).

Deng Xiaoping directed the **Anti-Rightist Campaign** of 1957-58, moving swiftly to squash dissent. Hundreds of thousands of writers, artists, ex-GMD officials, and scholars returning from abroad were rounded up, often despite their innocence, and sent to work in camps where they underwent a program of "thought reform." The Anti-Rightist Campaign began a trend that would persist for decades to come in Maoist China—the brutal silencing of Chinese intellectuals.

GREAT LEAP FORWARD

By 1958, agricultural output was unable to keep up with the rapidly growing population, and Mao was growing impatient with the slow pace of industrialization. Instead of adopting technological improvements, as many advisors suggested, Mao turned to his favorite strategy: mass mobilization. In the form of the **Great Leap Forward** (1958-1960), Mao promised that China would surpass Britain in steel production in 15 years, and the US in 20. He ordered massive labor-intensive public works projects. In the countryside, gigantic **People's Communes** (in which up to 1000 peasants farmed and shared harvests) replaced small cooperatives.

At a 1959 party congress in Lushan (see p. 378), defense minister **Peng Dehuai** broke ranks and openly complained that the huge communes were unsustainable. Mao responded by having him "purged." By 1960, the disastrous effects of the Great Leap Forward combined with bad weather in many parts of the country to take their toll. Between 28 and 40 million people in the countryside starved to death in what has become known as the greatest manmade catastrophe in history.

SINO-SOVIET SPLIT

Since the 1950s, Russian leader Nikita Khrushchev had sneered at Mao's fanatical programs, while Mao accused Khrushchev of tampering with Marxist-Leninist doctrine and of cuddling up to the US with his policy of peaceful coexistence. The ideological clash between Mao and Khrushchev led to the **Sino-Soviet Split** of 1960—a complete severing of diplomatic and economic ties between the two countries. In 1962, Mao handed over his position as head of state to second-in-command **Liu Shaoqi.** Liu and Deng Xiaoping set about reviving China's dying economy by reversing the policies of the Great Leap Forward. Unable to gain support for his doctrine-spreading from Liu and Deng (whose popularity soared as the Chairman's plummeted), the Chairman turned to the up-and-comer marshal **Lin Biao**, head of the PLA. Taking a thinker's approach to the military, Lin issued soldiers copies of *The Quotations of Chairman Mao*, or Mao's **Little Red Book** (currently the second most printed book in the world after the New Testament).

In addition to backing from the PLA, Mao had help from an inner council led by his wife **Jiang Qing**, a B-movie actress from Shanghai. The young starlet spearheaded Mao's cultural reforms and tapped into a network of radical intellectuals (from her hometown) that would eventually come to serve as Mao's propaganda organ. All that the Chairman needed was another surge of public enthusiasm to jump-start his next mass mobilization campaign.

CULTURAL REVOLUTION

Mao Zedong initiated a revolution for the simple sake of a having a revolution, ordering the willful destruction of his own government, party, and culture. Although the Great Leap Forward killed far more people, the **Cultural Revolution** (1966-69) inflicted plenty of pain and damage on Chinese society.

Having conquered landlords, capitalists, and intellectuals since his rise to power, Mao finally turned his attention to party rivals. In 1966, Mao ordered Liu Shaoqi to cleanse the party bureaucracy of corruption, but provided no further instructions. When subversive posters appeared on the campus of Beijing University, a confused Liu sent party inspection teams to the campus and suppressed student activities. Jiang Qing and other propagandists spread rumors that corrupt government forces were trying to overthrow the Chairman, and radical students organized **Red Guard** groups to protect him. Within a few short months, millions of youths heeded Mao's call to "bombard the headquarters" of party "capitalists" and "revisionists." He turned against his comrades in arms, accusing Liu of suppressing the voice of the people and diverting China onto a capitalist path. Liu was tried on trumped-up charges and eventually tortured to death; Deng Xiaoping was condemned to manual labor. Thousands of other cadres were purged and sent to hard labor camps. In launching the historically unprecedented **Great Proletariat Cultural Revolution**, Mao hoped to train a new generation of pure visionaries. Red Guards were instructed to purge Chinese culture of the **Four Olds**: old culture, old customs, old habits, and old ideas. Traditional books were burned, and countless historical sites and temples were ransacked and destroyed. Academics and teachers were humiliated in public, and hundreds committed suicide.

By 1967, the violence had veered out of control, as the Red Guards degenerated into fractious infighting. Chinese cities turned into war zones; militant Red Guard factions fought street battles using tanks and missiles looted from arms shipments intended for Vietnam. After shutting down their schools, Mao transported the youth to China's vast countryside, where they were instructed to undergo re-education by the peasantry. In 1968, some 15 million youths left the cities to live on impoverished farms. With the CCP in tatters from repeated "purgings", the PLA moved in to fill the power vacuum. By 1969, the PLA dominated 40% of the Party Congress seats, and Lin Biao's status as Mao's chosen successor was written into the party constitution. The overwhelming presence of the PLA worried Mao however, and Lin's desire to become head of state piqued the Chairman's suspicions. After instigating a failed coup, Lin tried to flee to the Soviet Union, but died in a mysterious plane crash over Mongolia in 1971.

Lin's betrayal dealt a harsh blow to Mao. The Chairman realized his mistake in purging loyal Long March-era comrades and rehabilitated Deng Xiaoping at the recommendation of Zhou Enlai. Zhou had played an active role in promoting moderate policies during Mao's radical campaigns, ordering the protection of many of the country's national relics.

Zhou also played an instrumental role in advancing **Sino-American relations**. In 1969, Chinese and Russian soldiers clashed along the Ussouri River in the Northeast and other points along the border. To offset the Soviet threat, China found a willing partner in the United States, which was also seeking a counterbalance to

USSR power in East Asia. Practical politics overcame ideological differences, and a series of unofficial cultural and athletic contacts known as **Ping Pong Politics** (see **Sports,** p. 43) paved the way for official agreements. After Secretary of State **Henry Kissinger**'s secret visit to China, **Richard Nixon** stunned the world by exchanging toasts with Chairman Mao in Beijing in 1972. The two leaders drafted the Shanghai Communique, which stipulated that the US would recognize the mainland government (and not the Taiwanese regime) as the true government of China.

As Zhou was guiding China toward political moderation, Jiang Qing and her zealous cohorts, known as the **Gang of Four**, sought to keep the flames of the Cultural Revolution alive and positioned themselves to succeed Mao. After Zhou's death from cancer in early 1976, they denounced his policies and banned official mourning. During the Qing Ming Festival in early April, however, thousands of mourners gathered in Tiananmen Square to remember the beloved premier and to vent anger at radical leaders. Militant thugs were called in and violently broke up the demonstration. In the aftermath of the **April Fifth Incident,** Deng Xiaoping was purged and went into hiding under the protection of loyal cadres. Later that year, an enormous earthquake in Tangshan killed 260,000, and a rare lunar eclipse over China served as omens of things to come. The Mao "dynasty" finally came to an end on September 9, 1976, when Mao passed away at the ripe old age of 83. A month later, the Gang of Four was arrested, and Mao's handpicked successor **Hua Guofeng** emerged as China's new leader. The conservative Hua followed the policy of **Two Whatevers,** "whatever Mao said and whatever Mao did." The Chinese population was not quite so "whatever" about the political environment, and political posters sprung up on a Xidan public bulletin board in what came to be known as the **Democracy Wall Movement.** Deng rode a surge of popular support to power and quickly used his old connections to oust Hua.

A DECADE OF REFORMS (1978-1988)

With Deng in control, reform and not revolution would be the path of progress. The "Main Architect," as he was known, pursued the policy of **Four Modernizations:** industry, agriculture, science, and defense. The speed and scope of liberalization quickly became a topic of national debate. While conservative hardliners urged the maintenance of state control, Democracy Wall activists, including Wei Jingsheng (see p. 20), advocated the implementation of a fifth modernization: democracy. Deng jailed Wei, outlawed the Democracy Wall Movement, and started a campaign against "spiritual pollution" from the West. It became clear that China's liberalization would be restricted to the economic sphere, largely bypassing the political.

Deng improved China's economy by undoing Mao's collectivization programs. In the countryside, he de-collectivized communes and introduced an incentive-laden **household responsibility system** that enabled farmers to sell surpluses as well as cash crops on the open markets. Welcome capitalism. The emergence of township and village enterprises reduced the proportion of labor devoted to farm work and brought a measure of prosperity to the countryside. Deng relaxed central control of state industry, encouraged managers to improvise and import Western technology, and advocated the formation of joint-venture enterprises. The opening of China's market to the West brought competition and a measure of efficiency. **Special Economic Zones** (see **Economy,** p. 29) such as Shenzhen attracted foreign capital, which meant increased living standards along with a rise in the almighty power of Lord Cash.

The government also relaxed cultural restrictions. Western fashions replaced Mao suits, and the domestic travel industry revived (luckily for Let's Go). Foreign products invaded the mainland by the thousands, while foreign pop stars such as Michael Jackson and even the basketball star Michael Jordan became familiar names and faces to most Chinese.

POPULAR PROTEST & THE ROAD TO TIANANMEN

From time to time, the government allowed student demonstrations to occur if the theme supported government initiatives. In 1985, there were widespread protests against both the Japanese militarism of 40 years earlier and aggressive commercialism in the country. In the late 1980s, the economy slumped, and soaring inflation eroded consumer savings and undermined public confidence. The economic boom had created great disparities in wealth not seen during the egalitarian Maoist era. Street peddlers became millionaires while underpaid college professors shined shoes on the side. Business opportunities were usually controlled by the authorities and available only to those who had connections *(guanxi)*—codeword for corruption.

As the public simmered, party chief **Hu Yaobang** was fired for being too liberal and permissive. While in power, Hu was dismissed by college students as a ranting liberal buffoon, but after his death on April 15, 1989, Hu was eulogized as a shining progressive cut down by other party members. Thousands of college students marched to Tiananmen Square in memory of Hu Yaobang. They called on the party to grant freedom of the press and freedom of speech, root out corruption, and open elections. As the government debated intensely in the Great Hall of the People, a hunger strike ensued outside. The number of protestors in Beijing ballooned to over one million by May 20th and upstaged the summit meeting between Deng and Mikhail Gorbachev. Attempts at negotiations between student leaders and governement officials failed. As a result, hardliners led by **Li Peng** persuaded Deng to declare martial law. The PLA was called in to disperse the demonstrators, resulting in the **Tiananmen Square massacre** which lasted from June 3rd to the 4th. Western television audiences watched as some 350,000 PLA soldiers poured into Beijing, shooting many, plowing through roadblocks assembled by residents, and even toppling the student-erected Goddess of Democracy statue that stood defiantly facing Mao's portrait. Considered counter-revolutionary, dissenters were quickly captured. Globally, the Tiananmen Square Democracy Movement paved the way for a series of anti-communist demonstrations in Eastern Europe and alerted the West to China's human rights violations (see **Human Rights,** p. 30).

JIANG ZEMIN AND THE 1990S

In the over ten years since Tiananmen, the Chinese government has refused to reverse its verdict on the massacre. After Deng Xiaoping's death in 1997, the transfer of power to current president **Jiang Zemin** proceeded without incident, and Jiang has stayed loyal to Deng's pledge of building "socialism with Chinese characteristics," or, in other words, allowing market reforms controlled by the party dictatorship. Hong Kong passed from British to Chinese hands in 1997 (99 years after the **Treaty of Nanjing**; see p. 13) without major disturbances. The economy continued to expand at a dizzying pace, maintaining a double digit GDP growth rate for much of the 90s before the **Asian financial crisis** of 1997. Compared to the situations of Russia and other nations undergoing more dramatic transitions from socialist to capitalist economies, China's situation has been looking particularly rosy.

RECENT NEWS

The prominent **anniversaries** of 1999—the 80th anniversary of the May Fourth Movement (see p. 15), the 50th anniversary of the People's Republic (see p. 17), the 40th anniversary of the 1959 Tibetan uprising (see p. 727), and the 10th anniversary of the June 4th Tiananmen Square incident (see p. 20)—were alternately welcomed or feared, but nothing too traumatic transpired.

The October 1, 1999 celebration marking the 50th anniversary of the Communist victory was filled with pomp and pageantry. Representatives outfitted in the traditional garb of China's provinces and autonomous regions paraded down Beijing's Changan Dajie in a carefully orchestrated celebration that culminated in Tiananmen Square. Later, fireworks displays lit up the night sky. China again brought out the fireworks for fantastic millennium **New Year's** celebrations in Beijing, Hong Kong, and Shanghai.

The furor over the North Atlantic Treaty Organization (NATO) bombing of the **Chinese embassy** in Belgrade in May 1999 (a mistake that killed three Chinese journalists) gradually died down. The US agreed to pay US$4.5 million in reparations, and US-Chinese relations improved.

GOING, GOING, GONG In July 1999, the Chinese government issued a ban on the meditation and exercise sect known as **Falun Gong** (literally, "exercises of the wheel of law"). Falun Gong was founded in 1992 by Li Hongzhi, who has since claimed the right to be worshiped as a "religious figure." The group's practices, derived from a combination of Buddhist and Daoist principles, center around physical exercises not too different from those of tai chi and qigong. Practitioners assert that the exercises have a positive influence on their health, promoting immunity to disease.

The government ban on the group was issued after members staged a peaceful but alarmingly well-orchestrated demonstration in Beijing: 10,000 practitioners gathered in front of government compounds without the government's prior knowledge. As best observers can tell, this event scared the pants off officials, who felt threatened by Falun Gong's claim to have 100 million followers in China and abroad (in comparison, the ranks of the CCP total only 60 million). Authorities launched an all-out media offensive to discredit the group. Television and newspapers began carrying scathing accusations, describing Falun Gong as fraudulent, exploitative, and disruptive to social order. One oft-cited account was that of a follower who, believing that the wheel of law was lodged in his stomach, cut himself open and died. The government claimed to be attacking the "superstitious" group in the name of "science," and followers were portrayed as doomed and dangerous fanatics.

Supporters of Falun Gong maintain that most practitioners are rational individuals (including middle-aged women, the elderly, and a number of party cadres and military personnel) interested in boosting their physical and spiritual well-being by gathering for harmless morning exercises and meditations in public parks. Outside observers steeped in the principle of freedom of religion reacted with outrage to what they perceived as the government's unjustifiable interference in personal matters. The true extent of the group's influence is still disputed.

Relations with Taiwan continued to be a point of contention, although no major conflicts erupted. In September 2000, the United Nations (UN) General Committee decided not to consider the issue of Taiwan's participation in the UN at the 55th session of the General Assembly, reaffirming the UN's commitment to a "one China" policy (China holds a seat on the Security Council).

US President Clinton made the establishment of **Permanent Normal Trade Relations** (PNTR) with China one of his legislative priorities. In September 2000, the US Senate overwhelmingly approved of this legislation, which Clinton proceeded to sign into law. The passage of PNTR with China will lead to greater foreign business involvement in China. Opponents of the bill point to China's alleged human rights violations. In other economic news, China's Ministry of Foreign Trade and Economic Cooperation expressed hope that China would move from observer to official member status in the World Trade Organization (WTO) by the end of 2000.

PEOPLE

Most Chinese do not cherish the distinction of living in the world's most populous country, with some 1.4 billion inhabitants and counting. Despite the vast land area, three-quarters of the population is crowded into the eastern third of the country, bounded by an imaginary line stretching from the tip of the Dongbei Horn to the Myanmar border. Eastern China is densely packed: more than 100 cities have over 1 million residents each. Although recent economic expansion has led to the rapid growth of urban areas, about 70% of China's people still live in rural areas. The government has tried to curb mass peasant migration to the cities through the use of *hukou*, or residence permits, but recent liberalization has relaxed travel and work restrictions. There is currently a floating population of more than 100 million drifting in and out of China's major cities in search of better jobs. These migrants have been blamed by city dwellers for urban social problems such as rising crime rates and disease outbreaks.

CHINA

FURTHER SURFING: RECENT NEWS.

China Daily (www.chinadaily.com.cn) the national English-language newspaper of China.
People's Daily (www.peopledaily.com.cn) is the official newspaper of the CCP, and is available in Chinese, English, French, Japanese, and Spanish.
South China Morning Post (www.scmp.com), is Hong Kong's major English-language newspaper. Their website has good browsing capabilities and is updated every day.

POPULATION GROWTH

China has a long tradition of meticulous census-taking. Imperial accountants kept careful demographic records for the purpose of tax-collection. At the start of the first millennium (AD 4), there were already 69 million inhabitants living in the Han Empire, and that number reached 100 million during the Song (ca. 1100). More recently, under the Qing, the increase in agricultural productivity led to a huge population boom. Between 1762 and 1834 the population doubled, ballooning to 400 million despite the lack of a similar increase in cultivated land area.

After founding the People's Republic in 1949, the Great Helmsman of mass mobilization movements, Chairman Mao, promoted Stalin's "the more, the merrier" approach. Women who gave birth to five or more children were honored as "Revolutionary Mothers" and awarded government subsidies. Unlike the severely underpopulated Soviet Union, China already had more than half a billion inhabitants. These policies, coupled with improvements in health care and food production, caused the population to swell quickly out of control. Ever since, the immense population has placed enormous strain on resources and hindered the improvement of the standard of living. In the 1980s, the government adopted a series of population control measures, limiting urban couples to one child and rural families to two. Despite stiff penalties, the desire for male heirs and the demands of farming still prompt many couples to ignore government restrictions.

ETHNIC COMPOSITION

Although China is a multicultural nation consisting of 56 officially recognized ethnic groups, over 91% of the population is Han Chinese. The Han trace their ancestry back to the Han dynasty (see **The Rise of Empire**, p. 9) and claim to be the historic guardians of Chinese culture. The remaining 55 groups total 108 million people and live on two-thirds of the nation's land, mainly on China's periphery.

Traditionally, many Han Chinese have distinguished themselves from the other nationalities officially considered to be a part of China. The relationship between Han Chinese and minority peoples has been the source of change and a certain amount of concern. During the Republican Era of 1911-49, Sun Yat-sen envisioned a nationalist state ruled by China's five main ethnic groups: the Han, Manchu, Tibetan, Mongolian, and Uighur. In his early guerrilla days, Mao expressed interest in building a federalist state offering minority groups significant autonomy, similar to Stalin's example of establishing minority republics. After 1949, the CCP, backed by the powerful People's Liberation Army, consolidated its control by organizing minority areas into autonomous regions, counties, and townships that ostensibly enjoyed self-rule. At first, the CCP relied upon compliant local clan and tribal leaders because the party had virtually no support among minorities. Gradually, Beijing-trained minority cadres assumed control and took orders from Han superiors. Radical communist policies in the Maoist period proved disastrously unfit for minority regions. Minority-Han tensions exploded into a number of uprisings, followed by swift government reprisals. Han migration into minority areas, both government-sanctioned and spontaneous, has marginalized minorities in their homelands and contributed to ethnic tension.

In the 1980s, the liberalization policies of Deng Xiaoping (see p. 20) led to nominal recognition of minority cultures and religions. National minorities enjoy special government benefits, such as exemption from the one-child policy, lower academic test scores requirements for secondary school entry, tax breaks, and government subsidies. In general, Han relations tend to be better with groups that have assimilated (Manchu, Zhuang, Korean) and worse with those that have not (Tibetan, Uighur).

MINORITY NATIONALITIES

NORTHEASTERN MINORITIES: MANCHUS AND KOREANS

The **Manchus** (numbering 10 million), and their sub-Siberian relatives, the **Ewenki** and **Oroqen**, once dominated the Northeast. Descendants of the Jurchen tribes that harassed the Song dynasty, the Manchus rose to prominence in the early 17th century and toppled the Ming (see p. 12). The Manchu Qing court demanded that all male subjects wear pony tails (queues) but made few other demands on traditional Han customs. Han migrants were barred north of the Great Wall, and intermarriages were made illegal. Nonetheless, Han influences gradually prevailed. The Han had outnumbered the Manchus in the Northeast even before the fall of the Qing. Even though Manchus are still heavily concentrated in Liaoning and Beijing, today their language is virtually extinct, and, as a people, they are almost indistinguishable from the Han. Farther north in Heilongjiang (see p. 180), Ewenki and Oroqen, formerly hunters and gatherers, have adopted an agricultural way of life. Their cultural traditions have been diluted by Han influences, but many of these peoples still live in traditional clans and worship spiritual deities. In fact, the word "shaman" comes from the Ewenki language.

A large number of **Koreans** live in eastern Jilin, Liaoning, and Heilongjiang provinces (see **The Northeast,** p. 180), along the Yalu River. Most are descended from the masses that fled during the Japanese annexation of the Korean peninsula in 1895. Sharing strong cultural ties with the Chinese and benefiting from decades of friendship between Beijing and Pyongyang, the Koreans have lived peacefully and prospered. Recently, thousands of North Koreans have fled to the Chinese-Korean communities in this region to escape devastating famines in their homeland.

SOUTHWESTERN MINORITIES

Scattered across the mountains of southwestern China are at least three dozen minority nationality groups. For centuries, they have lived in familial clans and practiced primitive slash-and-burn agriculture, planting rice and raising livestock. Most of these peoples were indigenous to the lower Yangzi valley but were gradually pushed southward by Han expansion. The **Dai** in Yunnan (see **Xishuangbanna,** p. 584) share a language and cultural kinship with the Thai of Thailand, Lao of Laos, and Shan of Myanmar. Although several groups such as the **Li** on Hainan Island still worship animist deities and ancestral spirits, the introduction of Theravada Buddhism converted many of the region's ethnic minorities. The **Naxi** (see **Lijiang,** p. 565) follow both Tibetan lamaism and cults of supernatural spirits. A considerable number of the **Miao** and **Yao** in Guizhou are Christians.

The relationship between the Han and these minorities ranges from the Zhuang's embracement of Han culture to the Yi's fierce resistance of it. The largest ethnic minority in China, the 17 million **Zhuang** of Guangxi have all but become Han Chinese, speaking Mandarin dialects and learning Chinese classical literature. The **Wa** people have been influenced by Buddhism. The **Yi** have retained a caste system; their tradition of Han enslavement, though, has been officially outlawed.

FURTHER READING: CHINESE SOCIETY.

China: A Cultural and Historical Dictionary (1998), edited by Michael Dillon.
Contemporary China (1999), by Alan Hunter and John Sexton.
The Living Tree: The Changing Meaning of Being Chinese Today (1994), edited by Tu Wei-ming.
Iron and Silk (1986), by Mark Salzmann.

NORTHERN MINORITIES: HUI AND MONGOLS

The white-cap-donning Hui are most well-known for their refusal to eat pork, the favorite meat of the Han. Although spread throughout China, the **Hui**, or Chinese Muslims, are most heavily concentrated in Ningxia, Beijing, and Shanghai. While most Hui are farmers, urban Hui are often active merchants and craftsmen. Because they speak Mandarin and practice Han social customs, the Hui are often regarded by other minority groups as Chinese, but official Chinese ethnographies trace the ancestry of the Hui to Islamic Persians who immigrated to China in the Tang and Song dynasties. During the days of Mao Zedong's guerrilla war in Yanan (p. 227), many Hui locals joined the communist cause and subsequently rose to power after 1949 and after the establishment of the Ningxia Hui Autonomous Region in 1956. The government assigned many Hui cadres the task of administering other minority groups to achieve their promise of "having minority cadres rule minority people." Despite close ties with the Han majority, tensions stemming from religious differences still exist; during the Cultural Revolution, for instance, the Red Guard destroyed Hui mosques.

Like their 12th century leader Genghis Khan, the **Mongols** are often viewed as hardy, nomadic, yurt-dwelling people who follow their grazing herds across the steppes of Central Asia. They are organized socially into family clans and tribes. In their 12th-century heyday, the Mongols vanquished much of Asia. After encountering the Tibetans, Mongols converted to Tibetan Buddhism (see **Tibetan Buddhism,** p. 729). The short-lived Mongol Yuan dynasty reopened trade routes between China and the West, and the splendor of that empire was documented in Marco Polo's memoirs. The Manchus began the political separation of Mongolia by administering the region as two entities, divided north and south of the Gobi. Han settlers began moving into the southern portion (which became known as Inner Mongolia during the Qing dynasty) to cultivate grazing lands. When "Outer Mongolia" declared its independence in 1921, Inner Mongolia remained part of China.

Today, as a result of past warfare and migration, Mongols in China are spread across the northern rim of the country, stretching from Xinjiang across Inner Mongolia to Heilongjiang. Outnumbered by Hans in their homeland, many Mongols have been sinicized and have become sedentary farmers or city dwellers. Other former nomads have turned to raising sheep for cashmere wool. Closely related to the Mongols are the **Daur** of Heilongjiang and the **Bonan** of Gansu. These two groups have their own spoken languages but use a Mongolian script.

NORTHWESTERN MINORITIES

Xinjiang is a land dominated by **Islam** (see p. 34), the religion of the Uighur, Kazakh, Tatar, Tajik, Uzbek, and Kyrgyz nationalities. All except the Persian-speaking Tajiks use variations of Turkic languages. The **Uighur** (also written Uygur, and pronounced *weiwuer* in Mandarin) are by far the most numerous at 8 million. They are descended from a people that inhabited the Tarim oases a thousand years ago. While the Kazakh and Kyrgyz are pastoral nomads, the Uighur depend on irrigation agriculture, building elaborate underground channels to plant crops in the desert. In Uighur towns, conservative Muslim women still wear veils in public. The northwest is also home to Mongols, Tibetans, **Sibo** (descendants of the Manchu garrisons established during the Qing), and the offspring of **Russians** who escaped to China after the Bolshevik Revolution. Han presence in the region has increased dramatically since 1949, rising from 3.7% to more than half of the population in the last 50 years. The PLA executed thousands of separatists, GMD sympathizers, and nomads in the 1950s. Ethnic tensions during the Great Leap Forward (see p. 18) led to the exodus of 20,000 Uighurs to the Soviet Union.

Riots broke out in Yining, Ningxia in 1995. Uighur separatists, hoping to establish an independent state, bombed a Beijing bus soon afterward, prompting a harsh government crackdown. In March 1996, the Standing Committee of the Chinese Politburo convened a special session to discuss the "Xinjiang question." The Chinese government has since succeeded in securing pledges from Central Asian neighbors to deny support to Uighur separatists.

LANGUAGE

Travelers to China should make an effort to learn a few key phrases and words in Mandarin Chinese. Even minimal knowledge of the language makes visiting China much easier and more rewarding. Most Chinese do not speak any English, especially outside Beijing and Shanghai. This is gradually changing, however, as English is increasingly taught in schools—if you need the assistance of an English speaker, your best bet is to ask teenage or twenty-something students or urban professionals. *Let's Go: China* gives the pinyin and Chinese characters for most Chinese establishment and place names; if you are unable to pronounce something using pinyin, you can always resort to pointing at the Chinese characters and gesturing to convey your meaning. See also the pronunciation guide (see p. 757) and phrasebook (see p. 758) in the **Appendix** for help.

The official language of the People's Republic is **Mandarin Chinese** (pǔtōnghuà; 普通话; "common language"), based on the Beijing dialect. Unofficially, however, there are an astonishing number of different forms of Chinese spoken in China, collectively known by the term **Hanyu** ("Han language") in Mandarin. These varieties of Chinese have more total native speakers than any other language in the world. In northern China, regional linguistic variations are usually referred to as "accents," while in southern China they are called "dialects." In addition to Mandarin, Cantonese (Yue), Shanghainese (Wu), Northern Fujianese (Minbei), Southern Fujianese-Hokkien-Taiwanese (Minnan), Hunanese (Xiang), Jiangxiese (Gan), and Hakka are the main spoken forms. Minority languages like Tibetan, Uighur, Korean, Thai, and Mongolian are also widespread in provinces along China's perimeter (see **Ethnic Composition**, p. 23). Except for the Hui and the Manchu, all of China's non-Han peoples have their own spoken languages (numbering 53), and some 23 have their own written ones. In recognition of China's minority languages, examples of major non-Chinese scripts appear on Chinese paper currency.

PRONOUNCIATION

All forms of spoken Chinese have **tones.** Tones refer to the different inflections placed on syllables that have the same consonant and vowel sounds and that otherwise would be indistinguishable from one another. The number of tones varies; Mandarin only has five, while Cantonese has a mind-boggling, tongue-twisting, ear-wrenching seven or more, depending on whom you ask. Mandarin has a high tone (first tone), a rising tone (second tone), a falling-rising tone (third tone), a falling tone (fourth tone), and a neutral tone; for example, *mā* (妈) means "mother," *má* (麻) "sesame," *mǎ* (马) "horse," mà (骂) the verb "to scold," and ma (吗) a word that can change a declarative sentence into a question. For more information on pronunciation, see the pronunciation guide in the Appendix (p. 757). Another distinctive characteristic of all Chinese languages is the simplicity of their **grammars.** There is a fixed word order (usually subject, time, verb, object), verbs are not conjugated (person is expressed in the pronoun), and tense is expressed by the addition of a time adverb or certain verb complements.

WRITING

Despite the multitude of spoken forms of Chinese, there is a single, non-alphabetic **Chinese writing system** composed of more than 40,000 characters, although only some 6000 to 8000 are used in everyday language. Chinese characters first appeared as logographs (symbols representing entire words) on Shang dynasty oracle bones some 4000 years ago. Although most characters dating to the Shang originally appeared as pictographs (a picture of a mother and child means "love"), the long evolution of the writing system has rendered the pictographic derivations of most characters unidentifiable. Ancient Chinese also adopted the practice of using the same character to represent words with similar pronunciations, which soon led to general confusion, with too many words expressed by the same written symbol. To distinguish between homonyms, an additional element was added

MORE CHINS THAN A CHINESE PHONE

BOOK There is a lot more to a Chinese name than a tongue-twisting jumble of zh, q, x, and w sounds. Since there is no general stock of Chinese Johns and Janes, parents create names out of character combinations that sound pleasant, portend good fortune, express both physical and spiritual beauty, and encourage moral and scholastic achievement.

Former favorites that involved mythological creatures (such as "Dragon Power" or "Phoenix Beauty") are now considered old-fashioned and hokey in the cities but persist in some rural areas. In large farm families, children are sometimes simply enumerated "Big Dog," "Second Monkey," "Third Brat," and so on. Communist ideological fervor brought about a flurry of *Kangmei* (Resist Americans!), *Jianhua* (Build China), and *Maoshengli* (Victory for Maoism) whose bearers are now middle-aged. The post-1949 population explosion (see **Population Growth**, p. 23) led to an unprecedented shortage in the name pool; parents began to scour the dictionary looking for esoteric characters to mirror the uniqueness of their only child. The result: baffled 6-year-olds in penmanship classes learning to ink super-complex 20-plus-stroke character names. The newest fad among the urban *nouveau riche* is to convert Western names into Chinese, but linguistic pitfalls abound: one phonetic translation of Ben means "Dumb."

to similar-sounding characters: pronounced the same in ancient times, "red" (红) and "river" (江) had the radicals for "silk" (纟) and "water" (氵), respectively, appended to the same pre-existing phonetic cypher (工). Thus, compound characters with one component denoting meaning and a second indicating pronunciation came into being. However, spoken Chinese has diverged so far from its ancient roots that today characters sharing a phonetic radical are not necessarily pronounced the same; "red" is said "hóng" and "river" is said "jiāng," for instance.

Although government standardizations of the Chinese writing system date back as far as the Qin (221-206 BC), China's most ambitious language reform project is actually very modern. After 1949, the CCP's Committee for Chinese Language Reform sought to unify and simplify language by reducing the number of strokes in Chinese characters, standardizing Mandarin as the official national language, and introducing a phonetic alphabet. The first of these reforms instituted **simplified characters** (jiǎntǐ; 简体), written with fewer strokes than the **traditional characters** (fántǐ; 繁体). Traditional characters persist in Hong Kong and Taiwan, as well as in calligraphy, but simplified characters now predominate on the mainland.

The last of these reforms established the **pinyin romanization system** (拼音) that standardized Chinese transliteration into the Latin alphabet. Latin letters are used to denote consonant and vowel sounds and accent marks to indicate tones. Today, pinyin is used abroad to teach Mandarin to language students as well as in China to teach Mandarin pronunciation to native speakers of other kinds of Chinese; it is also used in China in dictionaries and indexes, braille for the blind, finger-spelling for the deaf, and telegraphic code. Pinyin has replaced the earlier and more confusing **Wade-Giles romanization** as the international standard for transliterating Chinese personal and place names. *Let's Go* primarily uses pinyin, except when the names of historical figures (such as Chiang Kai-shek and Sun Yat-sen) were romanized according to Wade-Giles or other romanizations and became well known using those spellings.

LAND
GEOGRAPHY

Shaped like a rooster stepping into the Pacific, China's landmass (the fourth largest in the world) dominates East Asia not only in size but in diversity. From snow-capped Himalayan peaks and lush Tarim Basin oases to Hainan Island's white-sand beaches and Yunnan's Stone Forest, China's diverse geographic landscape offers travelers a wealth of unique destinations. Mountains, plateaus, deserts, and foothills render 90% of China's land unsuitable for agriculture, but the remaining 10% supports one-fifth of humankind today.

Flanked by the towering Himalayan, Pamir, Kunlun, and Tianshan ranges in the west, elevation gradually descends from west to east through stair-like mountain chains and basins. **Mount Qomolangma** (Everest), the highest peak in the world, stands 8848m above sea level, while **Lake Aydingkol** in the Turpan Depression is the second lowest point (-154m) on earth. The forbidding **Gobi** and **Taklimakan** deserts separate China from Central and North Asia. With an average elevation of over 5000m, the desolate **Tibetan Plateau,** also called "The Roof of the World," is the largest and highest on earth.

The 6500km long **Yangzi River** (Chang Jiang, literally, "Long River"), at 6500 km, is the longest river in China and the third longest in the world. It winds through the scenic **Three Gorges** and the fertile, rice-producing **Dongting-Poyang Lake** region to the **East China Sea.** As China's most navigable river, it serves the industrial centers of Shanghai, Chongqing, Wuhan, and Nanjing. Central China relies on the 1000km **Grand Canal,** built between Beijing and Hangzhou in the 7th century, for its water transport. The **Yellow River** (Huang He) is China's second longest (5464 km), as well as the world's most heavily sedimented. Roaring through the **Loess Plateau,** the river carries away 1.6 billion tons of yellow, powdery soil into the **Bohai Sea** every year. Known as "China's Sorrow" for its catastrophic floods, the river has changed course at least a half dozen times in the past 3000 years. Nonetheless, the Yellow River Valley, regarded as the cradle of Chinese civilization, is rich with historical sites and ancient capitals such as Anyang, Luoyang, and Xian. 石浦海味饭店

Beyond China's historic northern boundary, the Great Wall, is a region formerly known as Manchuria but now simply referred to as Dongbei (the Northeast). Bordering Siberia, this subarctic region is covered with the forested ridges of Greater and Lesser Xingan to the north and the rolling Dongbei Plains to the south. The warm water harbors of Dalian and Lushun lie at the tip of the Liaodong Peninsula.

Perhaps the single most important climate-determining feature in central China, the **Qinling Mountains** shield the Eastern Plains from the dry air of the arid northwest. To the south, the **Yunnan-Guizhou Plateau** separates the subtropical southwest from the temperate eastern seaboard. Sealed between these two highland areas is the flat and lush **Sichuan Basin,** a historically isolated but prosperous region.

Officially, China's main island is the "Treasure Island" of **Taiwan,** but the largest offshore possession actually controlled by the mainland is **Hainan Island** further south. China's territorial claims in the **South China Sea** also include hundreds of tiny uninhabitable rocks and reefs that extend all the way to the **Zengmu Reefs** off the coast of Malaysia, although these claims are challenged by Vietnam, the Philippines, Taiwan, and Malaysia. The prospect of oil and natural gas deposits around the disputed **Nansha (Spratly) Islands** has added to political tension in the area.

BIODIVERSITY

China is one of the world's most biologically diverse nations, and one of the most environmentally degraded. Thanks to a highly varied topography and climate, the nation is home to many rare and unique plant and animal species. **Xishuangbanna** in southern Yunnan province harbors most of China's tropical flora and fauna, including the white-cheeked gibbon, the Asiatic elephant, and the flying frog, as well as many medicinal plants like the Japanese snowbell and the sandal tree. Farther north, the giant panda (see p. 627) feasts on bamboo in the more temperate forests of Sichuan, Gansu, and Shaanxi provinces, sharing its distinctive habitat with the golden snub-nosed monkey, white-lipped deer, takin, Asiatic black bear, and golden pheasant. The far western reaches of China house snow leopards and wild yaks (see p. 735) in the Tibetan Plateau, while the far north functions as a breeding ground for many of China's distinctive crane species. Chinese alligators, Chinese river dolphins, and South China tigers are thinly scattered throughout the Yangzi River basin.

Nearly all of these animals are on the long list of endangered species in China. Rapid economic and population growth, particularly in the last few decades, threatens much of China's still bountiful natural wealth. In recent years, the Chinese government imposed steep penalties on the **poachers** who have long been a primary cause of decimation of the panda and tiger populations and created a network of **nature reserves.** The percentage of protected land area (8%) now exceeds the global national average. These reserves are typically open to the public and many, like Wolong (see p. 626), Jiuzhaigou (see p. 634), Zhangjiajie (see p. 392), Wudalianchi, Zhalong and Changbaishan (see p. 198), are prime spots to admire scenery and wildlife.

GOVERNMENT & POLITICS

The governmental structure of the People's Republic of China is much the same now as it was when it was created on October 1, 1949. The foundations of the house that Mao built consist of the **Four Cardinal Principles:** the socialist road, the dictatorship of the proletariat, the leadership of the CCP, and Marxism-Leninism-Maoism. China is a communist, one-party republic controlled primarily by the **Chinese Communist Party** or **CCP,** although a few government-approved opposition parties—organized under the Chinese People's Political Consultative Congress (CPPCC)—do exist.

National politics are controlled by both the government and the CCP, and the relationship between the two is vaguely defined and continuously in flux. All government officials are members of the Communist Party, and the leaders of the former tend to be the leaders of the latter, although the two institutions are formally separate. The main legislative body of the government is the **National People's Congress** (governed by the **Politburo** and the **Secretariat**), and the chief executive body is the **State Council.** Local governments follow a similar pattern, with power formally in the hands of government bodies and effectively in the hands of local Communist Party leaders.

Also important to the daily life of individuals is the **danwei** or work unit. Members of a *danwei* live in the same building and attend political meetings and other activities together, and the unit itself oversees everything from marriage permits to changes of residence for its members.

ECONOMY

The saying goes that if you're not a communist before you're 30, you don't have a heart, but if you're not a capitalist after you're 30, you don't have a brain. The CCP seems to have taken this saying to heart (and brain). For nearly 30 years after the creation of the People's Republic of China, the nation had a highly centralized planned economy based on a Soviet model and in line with Marxist-Leninist principles. In his time, Mao aimed to modernize target industries through a series of **Five Year Plans,** which although successful at first eventually led to low levels of production and a sluggish economy as Mao's ideas became more purely socialist.

As the People's Republic neared its 30th birthday, Deng Xiaoping rose to power and immediately began to implement economic reforms that ran contrary to the socialist vision of his predecessor. In 1979, the government established the southeastern coastal cities of Shenzhen, Zhuhai, Xiamen, and Shantou as **Special Economic Zones.** The local governments of SEZs are allowed to foster economic growth and develop governmental infrastructures without the approval of the central government. The phenomenal success of these first four SEZs (their creation led to the quadrupling of the country's GDP and doubling of its agricultural output) has prompted the government to establish others all along the eastern seaboard and down the Yangzi River. Increasing privatization has also led to an improved standard of living for many Chinese: the number of rural poor dropped from 200 million to 80 million in under a decade, and the burgeoning middle class now enjoys such luxuries as DVD players and digital cameras.

China's economic growth has not been entirely painless, however. The government's hybrid system of market socialism means that the country often suffers from the worst problems of both socialism (corruption and a bloated bureaucracy) and capitalism (increased inflation and a growing income gap). In addition to a formidable unemployment problem, the Chinese government must also find a way to deal with the debt-ridden **state-owned enterprises,** industrial dinosaurs that still employ a large number of Chinese workers but operate appallingly inefficiently. The days of the "iron rice bowl" (see p. 20) are coming to an end, as many workers are being paid months late, given extended vacations, or being laid off.

Despite these potential pitfalls, the economy has continued to grow at a solid rate under the guidance of Prime Minister and economic czar **Zhu Rongji.** China managed to keep the *yuan* on the straight and narrow during the **financial crisis** that sent most of Asia into a tailspin in late 1997. And now, China stands ready to receive **Permanent Normal Trade Relations** with the US as well as to possibly gain membership in the **World Trade Organization (WTO),** with negotiations set for late 2000 (see **Recent News,** p. 21).

FURTHER READING: GOVERNMENT & POLITICS.

Evening Chats in Beijing (1992), by Perry Link.
Popular Protest and Political Culture in Modern China (1994), by Elizabeth Perry.
The Coming Conflict with China (1997), by Richard Bernstein and Ross Munro.
Rise of China: The Next Economic Superpower (1993), by William Overholt.
Mandate of Heaven (1994), by Orville Schell.
Intellectuals and the State in Modern China (1983), by Jerome Grieder.
The Origins of the Cultural Revolution (1983), by Roderick MacFarquhar.
China Wakes: The Struggle for the Soul of a Rising Power (1995), by Nicholas Kristof and Cheryl WuDunn.

HUMAN RIGHTS

China's human rights violations have been cause for considerable international concern in the past few decades. The authoritarian government maintains that stability and social order are more important than individual freedoms, and individuals have been detained, arrested, and jailed for peacefully expressing political, religious, and social views that differ from those of the CCP.

Beginning with the crackdown on the **Tiananmen Square Democracy Movement** in 1989 (see p. 20), the past decade has been fraught with worldwide tension over China's suppression of individual rights. In September of 1995, Beijing hosted the **United Nations Fourth World Conference on Women,** inviting thousands of intellectuals, politicians, and activists to discuss the international position of women. Eager to clean up the capital before the start of what was possibly the most high-profile international conference ever held in China, the government executed more than a dozen "criminals" in the weeks leading up to the event. Many urged a boycott of the conference in the name of **Harry Wu,** a naturalized US citizen detained since June 19 of that year after attempting to enter China from Kazakhstan and subsequently sentenced to 15 years in prison on charges of espionage. Several weeks before the conference, Wu was released and expelled from China, returning to the US to once again take up human rights activism. Wu has long been a thorn in the side of the Chinese government. He spent the 19 years from 1960-79 as a political prisoner after criticizing the 1956 USSR invasion of Hungary. Immigrating to the US in 1985, he began his long struggle against **laogai,** the CCP practice of "reform through labor," whereby dissidents as well as common criminals endure forced labor in prison camps.

Initially jailed for criticizing Deng Xiaoping, **Wei Jingsheng** is another one of China's long-term political prisoners who has received international acclaim, including the European Union's Andrey Sakharov Prize for Human Rights. Wei was put in prison in 1979 and, except for a brief stint of freedom in 1995, remained there until November of 1997, when he was released on medical parole and sent to the US for treatment. He was only one of several important dissidents (including the Tiananmen Square student leader, Wang Dan) released in 1997 and 1998, in advance of US President Clinton's 1998 visit to the mainland.

The release of these high-profile political prisoners signaled a loosening of restrictions on personal and political freedoms in 1997 and 1998. In September of 1998, the United Nations High Commissioner for Human Rights visited China for the first time at the behest of the government, and, one month later, the Chinese government signed the **United Nations Covenant on Civil and Political Rights,** although it has not yet been ratified. The signing of the covenant also coincided with the first-ever international human rights conference to be held in Beijing.

Beginning in November and December of 1998, the authorities conducted rounds of arrests, detaining dissidents who were registered with opposition political parties. The government also tightened control over the Internet and print publications, and continued its repression of unauthorized religious organizations including a quasi-religious qigong sect, known as **Falun Gong** (see p. 22).

The much-anticipated 10th anniversary of the **Tiananmen Square massacre** passed without incident in Beijing on June 4, 1999, while the square itself was closed for resurfacing at the time. Amid heavy security presence, only two protesters turned up all day; one opened an umbrella covered with slogans like "Remember the student movement," and the other threw pamphlets with anti-corruption messages. It was a different story entirely in Hong Kong, however, where some 70,000 gathered and were permitted to demonstrate peacefully in Victoria Park with candles to commemorate the dead.

A thorny recurrent issue for the Chinese government has been the human rights abuses in Tibet and Xinjiang. Tibetan dissidents, led by the Dalai Lama and backed by many Western groups like Free Tibet (not to mention Hollywood stars like Richard Gere) have proved remarkably successful at popularizing their cause abroad. At home, however, they have been threatened, arrested, detained, sentenced to hard labor, imprisoned, and even tortured (for more on the conduct of the Chinese government in Tibet, see **Tibet: History,** p. 726). The plight of the Uighurs of Xinjiang is less well received overseas, in no small part because they lack a prominent religious figure like the Dalai Lama to champion the cause. The Uighurs also have not only been known to resort to terrorist activities, but are believed to be responsible for bombings in Beijing and Ürümqi. In regards to the passing of Permanent Normal Trade Relations with China, critics have argued that the US is ignoring China's long history of human rights violations in favor of economic benefits, while US officials argue that the PNTR will indeed bring the Chinese government face to face with such issues.

RELIGION & PHILOSOPHY

Traditional China was dominated by three major faiths: Confucianism, Daoism, and Buddhism. These different faiths coexisted relatively peacefully because none of them required the exclusive professions of faith characteristic of religions in the Judeo-Christian tradition. Acutally, it was not uncommon for a person to feel some affinity with more than one of these faiths; for example, a Chinese believer might practice the filial piety espoused by Confucianism, celebrate Daoist holidays at temples, and pray to Buddhist *bodhisattvas*, all without any conflict of interest. In addition to these major religions, Islam, Zoroastrianism, Judaism, and Christianity also have had minority followings in China.

CONFUCIANISM

Scholars often dispute the characterization of Confucianism as a "religion," arguing that it should be considered a "philosophy." Though "heaven" is a concept frequently seen in Confucian writings, a belief in an otherworldly power is not an explicit tenet of the faith. Confucianism also does not have the hierarchies of monks and nuns that one finds in other world religions, including Buddhism and

Daoism. Nonetheless, Confucianism has inspired the creation of temples and shrines, and has reached a much vaster audience than most purely philosophical systems. Its position between religion and philosophy, is unique in world history.

Confucius is the Latinized version of the name of Confucianism's founder, **Kongzi**. He was born in 551 BC, in the city of **Qufu** (see p. 164) in the state of Lu (the western portion of present-day Shandong province). Like the majority of educated men in his time, he was initially devoted to attaining public office and gaining the confidence of a major ruler, but he never succeeded. After years of wandering from kingdom to kingdom, searching for a ruler who would respect his ideas, he settled down and devoted himself to teaching. His pupils came to honor him as a sage and were the compilers of the **Analects** *(Lunyu)*, a loose and disjointed collection of Confucius's oral teachings that was assembled after his death in 479 BC. Confucius himself is not known to have written a single word.

Confucius did not consider himself to be the originator of a new philosophy but a transmitter of the ideals derived from antiquity. Many consider Confucianism to be fundamentally conservative, and in many ways this is an accurate characterization. According to Confucius, **sacred ritual and ceremony,** or *lu*, should play an important role in the governance of human relations. Society's hierarchies should be strictly adhered to; sons should obey fathers, wives should obey husbands, and subjects should obey their ruler. **Filial piety,** one of the most common Confucian catchphrases, is crucial to guaranteeing social harmony, and social harmony is given priority over the needs of individuals.

In the Analects, it is clear that **self-cultivation** and **right behavior,** rather than noble birth, are the qualities that determine one's status as a gentleman, or *junzi*. The meritocratic examination system that was to develop in later centuries would draw its support from Confucian ideals. The quality of **benevolence,** or *ren*, toward others is listed among the most fundamental of all virtues.

Over the next several centuries after Confucius' death, other thinkers, most notably **Mencius (Mengzi)** and **Xunzi,** made further contributions to Confucian doctrine. Before long, Confucianism evolved into arguably the single most important institution in China. During the Song, **Neo-Confucianism** (see p. 10) adapted Confucian ideals to the behavior of rulers and political leaders. The educational and examination systems focused almost exclusively on the **Confucian classics,** a selection of works on topics ranging from poetry to history that had been compiled and edited by Confucius and his followers. Confucian ideals spread to Japan, Korea, and Vietnam. Although the doctrines provided by Daoism and Buddhism ensured that Confucianism would not be without competition, its significance in the political and philosophical development of the region remained colossal.

By the end of the 19th century, Chinese intellectuals had begun to reject Confucianism in favor of Western ideologies thought to be more modern. Communist leaders also initially condemned Confucianism as a nepotistic political philosophy that legitimized the domination of the "feudal" ruling class at the expense of the the "peasant" or "proletariat." But the effects of Confucian thought on Chinese culture lingered, often unacknowledged, throughout the 20th century. In recent years, scholars have theorized that the ability of certain East Asian societies to adapt well to the demands of modernism is attributable at least in part to the region's Confucian heritage.

DAOISM

In contrast to the overwhelming emphasis on social relations found in Confucianism, Daoism focuses on the individual's relation to nature and to metaphysical reality. The existence of Daoism as a system of thought dates back to the 3rd century BC, when the **Dao De Jing** is presumed to have been written (though Daoist tradition claims that it is the work of a contemporary of Confucius named **Laozi**). The *Dao De Jing* is a subtle and cryptic text that has been subject to a large number of conflicting interpretations. Its clearer assertions concern the inadequacy of language and the power of the *Dao*, an all-encompassing force that guides the workings of the world and that cannot be defined sufficiently in words. In order to rule in harmony with the *Dao*, a sage ruler should stick to a policy of nonaction and passivity except where absolutely necessary. The ultimate relativity of all things and the falsity of binary distinctions are two major themes that run through other works in the Daoist tradition, most notably the humorous, anecdotal **Zhuangzi** (or Chuang-Tzu), attributed to an author by the same name.

Many scholars draw a distinction between the philosophical and religious manifestations of Daoism. As with Confucianism, the distinction between the two is blurry, and the ideas of the former are closely bound to the practices of the latter. Philosophical Daoism is based on the tradition of intellectual exploration started by the texts named above, a tradition that often made forays into mystical and alchemical practices; this is the Daoism of philosophers, monks, and nuns.

Religious Daoism is the Daoism of the common people and other more casual affiliates of the faith. It has little explicit connection with the ideas contained in the philosophical texts. Instead, it is oriented toward the supernatural and draws a number of its elements from age-old Chinese folk beliefs. A belief in various gods and spirits, fortune-telling, magic, and alchemy are all associated with popular Daoism, as are elements of Chinese popular cosmology that predate the Daoist philosophers, such as the idea of man's solidarity with nature and the worship of ancestors. For many, the language and practices of Daoism mixed easily with those of Buddhism to form the base of Chinese popular religion.

Daoism may never have enjoyed the state patronage that Confucianism did, but its influence on Chinese culture was immense nonetheless. The experiments in alchemy prompted by Daoist searches for immortality did much to advance early Chinese science. Daoist conceptions of man's relation to nature influenced generations of landscape painters, and Daoist ideals informed many of the philosophical and personal expressions found in prominent examples of classical poetry.

The Daoist ecclesiastical structure is much smaller in mainland China than that of Buddhism, but scattered clusters of monks and nuns can still be found at prominent temples. The **Five Sacred Daoist Mountains** that are scattered throughout the heart of the country are excellent places to see contemporary Daoism in action; some of the country's largest temples are located there, and the pilgrimage to the summit of each is performed by thousands of Chinese worshipers every year.

BUDDHISM

Unlike Confucianism and Daoism, Buddhism has its origins outside of China. **Siddhartha Gautama,** who would come to be called the Buddha (Enlightened One), was born around 560 BC in Lumbini, just within the modern borders of Nepal. As a prince, Gautama was lavished with comforts in his youth and was prevented from experiencing the life of a normal man. One day, however, Siddhartha convinced his charioteer to take him around the outside world. He went on four outings and saw a very sick man, a very old man, a corpse, and a mendicant. Unsatisfied with the Hinduist explanations of worldly suffering and suddenly taken with the life of the mendicant, Siddhartha fled his posh life as a prince at the age of 29 to wander around the forests of India as an ascetic. He eventually gave up extreme asceticism, realizing it was not the way to the enlightenment, and chose a middle path of meditation. He eventually achieved **nirvana** (enlightenment) and set off to preach his discoveries about escaping the suffering of the world by overcoming desire, in what has become known as the first of the Buddhist *dharma* or teachings.

The Buddha advocated total detachment from the world. Desires for physical and mental things, he said, bring suffering, because they cause one to believe in a self and an individual existence, which are impermanent and fleeting illusions. One's goal should be the end of suffering through the end of desires, which leads to a state of nirvana. The Buddha named right understanding, thought, speech, action, livelihood, effort, mindfulness, and concentration (the **Eightfold Path**) as the way to nirvana. He preserved the doctrine of *karma* and reincarnation drawn from Hinduism, in which an individual's actions in one life determine their position in the next, and became an adamant advocate of universal non-violence.

Chinese Buddhism is part of the **Mahayana** ("Great Vehicle") school, which differs in many ways from the **Hinayana** ("Small Vehicle") school that predominates in most of Southeast Asia. The Mahayana school developed as a popular sect around the first century AD and came to predominate in most of Northeast Asia and Vietnam. Its doctrines argue that the quest for nirvana is a communal affair and not an individual one (as the Hinayana school professes) and stress the importance of compassion for others. Popular worship of Buddha figures is widespread in Chinese Buddhism; among the most prominent are **Amitabha** (*Amitofo* in Chinese), the Buddha of Infinite Light, and **Guanyin** or **Avalokiteshvara,** the Goddess of Mercy.

The first entry of Buddhism into China occurred in the later half of the Han dynasty (see p. 9). Early Chinese Buddhist belief and practice were heavily intermingled with that of Daoism, and the aspects of the faith that were emphasized were those that had the most in common with Daoist ideals. Monastic structures sprang up rapidly, so that by the Sui dynasty Buddhism had become the state religion. A number of competing Buddhist **sects** were founded. The Tiantai and Huayan schools emphasized doctrinal distinctions. The Jingtu, or "Pure Land" sect, was named for the paradise into which enlightened worshipers would be reborn and stressed faith as the route to salvation. **Chan,** better known in Japanese as Zen, taught esoteric meditation techniques.

Toward the end of the Tang, however, the emperor Wuzong undertook a large-scale **persecution** of Buddhism (see p. 33), most likely inspired by fear of the fiscal and political power that the Buddhist clergy had begun to acquire. Chinese Buddhism never quite recovered from this blow. Though it continued to flourish as a religion, its secular power was tightly curbed from this point on, and state-sponsored liquidations of Buddhist assets were undertaken from time to time.

Not surprisingly, the Cultural Revolution also took a heavy toll on Chinese Buddhism as temples were destroyed and monasteries were disbanded. In recent years, Buddhism has rebounded considerably, and monasteries are active centers of worship once again. Though very few Chinese identify themselves as strictly Buddhist, a large number make trips to temples or pilgrimage sites.

A unique form of Buddhism is practiced in Tibet, where Mahayana and **Vajrayana** (Thunderbolt Vehicle) Buddhist traditions are mixed with the indigenous religion, Bön. For more information, see p. 729.

MINORITY RELIGIONS

ISLAM
Islam was founded by the Prophet Muhammad, who lived in Mecca (in what is now Saudi Arabia) during the 7th century AD. The population of ethnic Chinese Muslims, or **Hui,** today numbers about nine million. The Hui are descended from Persian and Central Asian merchants and soldiers who trickled into China between the 7th and 13th centuries and intermarried with the Han Chinese. Today, most Hui are ethnically and linguistically indistinguishable from the Chinese majority, but many of them maintain Muslim beliefs and practices, such as abstaining from eating pork. They are scattered from Beijing to Kunming with high concentrations in Ningxia. See also **Northern Minorities: Hui,** p. 25.

CHRISTIANITY
In the 16th century, the Italian Jesuit priest **Mateo Ricci** entered China on the wave of exploration that had prompted Europeans in this period to seek new economic and evangelical opportunities in East Asia. He mastered the Chinese language and was granted permission by the Qing emperor Kangxi to dwell and proselytize in the capital. His approach to evangelism in China was to adapt the teachings of Christianity to local practice; accordingly, he stressed the integration of Confucian and Christian beliefs. As a consequence, he won a number of Chinese friends and

followers and set the precedent for a long line of Christian missionary activity in China that would continue until the early 20th century.

Today, there are almost 20 million Chinese Christians, concentrated mostly in the southeast. The majority of these are Protestant, but a substantial portion are of Catholic faith. The influence of Christianity on more recent Chinese history has not been negligible; the leader of the bloody Taiping Rebellion of the 19th century drew inspiration from the Bible (see p. 13), and the Boxer Rebellion was a local reaction against Christian missionaries (see p. 14).

JUDAISM

When European missionaries began to flood into China in the 17th century, they found a small community of Chinese Jews in the city of Kaifeng in present-day Henan province (see p. 240). Though scholars are not sure how they arrived in China, most suspect that they arrived via the Silk Road. The Kaifeng Jewish community is no longer active, and only a few relics of their existence remain. During WWII, many Eastern European Jews found temporary refuge in the Hongkou International Settlement in Shanghai (see p. 293).

COMMUNISM AND RELIGION

Following Karl Marx's famous statement that "religion is the opiate of the people," the official religion of Communist China is atheism, and faith in the state and the working people is theoretically supposed to eliminate the need for any deities. Recently, scholars have identified a strong Confucian influence in the Chinese Communist Party's theory and use of authority, but such assertions would not have been looked kindly upon by the CCP for most of its history.

The Cultural Revolution marked the zenith of state-sponsored persecution of religion in China. "To cleanse Chinese culture of its feudal shackles," Red Guards destroyed temples and churches. Monks and nuns of all faiths were forced to renounce their vows and pressed into agricultural or industrial labor, and a number of them were imprisoned. Confucianism was attacked as a remnant of feudal oppression, and Daoism and Buddhism were branded as reactionary superstitions. Christianity was condemned as a vestige of Western exploitation.

In the years following Mao's death, the intense anti-religiosity of the Cultural Revolution began to fade away. Traditional Chinese religion is now officially (and proudly) considered a national relic. In many cases, the government actively promotes the restoration of temples and holy mountains as tourist sites. But the authorities still closely monitor the activities of churches and monasteries, and problems continue to arise when the dictates of religious power structures come into direct conflict with those of the state power structure. Thus, the Catholic Church, which asserts the supremacy of the Pope over all temporal authorities, and Tibetan Buddhism, which claims the Dalai Lama as its spiritual and political leader, have clashed frequently with the government in recent years.

FURTHER READING: RELIGION AND PHILOSOPHY.

The Analects of Confucius, translated by D.C. Lau.
The World of Thought in Ancient China (1985), by Benjamin Schwartz.
Chinese Religion: An Introduction (1988), by Laurence Thompson.
Tao Te Ching: The Classic Book of Integrity and the Way, by Lao Tzu, translated by Victor Mair.
The Buddhist Tradition in India, China, and Japan (1972), edited by William Theodore de Bary.
Buddhism in China: A Historical Survey (1964), by Kenneth Chen.
Christianity in China (1996), by Daniel Bays.
Islam in China (1999), by Dru C. Gladney and S.M. Abedin.

CHINA

ARTS

LITERATURE

ANCIENT & PREMODERN

The **Analects** of Confucius were considered the foundation of any classical literary education, as were the writings of his follower **Mencius.** Other important classics include Laozi's Daoist classic, the **Dao De Jing** (see p. 32), and the Daoist writings of **Zhuangzi** (or Chuang-tzu), which are filled with parables, anecdotes, and jokes.

While drama is considered the prime canonical genre in classical Western tradition, **lyric poetry** is its Chinese counterpart. Basic Chinese literary thought emphasizes the integrity of the individual voice, so poetry was not an "artistic exercise" but the representation of the poet's true feelings at the moment of writing. All of classical poetry, like all classical literature prior to the 20th century, is written in **classical Chinese** (*wenyan* or *guwen*), which was standardized around the time of Han and was markedly different in grammar and vocabulary from the vernacular.

The foundation and standard for all later Chinese poetry is the collection of unauthored song lyrics that is the **Classic of Poetry** (*Shijing*), compiled between the 10th and 7th centuries BC. These poems deal with a wide range of topics, such as love, nature, and politics. Also noteworthy are the **Songs of Chu,** an anthology of works composed in the southern state of Chu (present-day Hubei) during the Warring States Period (see p. 8). The sensual yet deeply spiritual verses bear the influence of Daoism and mysticism.

The Tang dynasty is traditionally considered to be the high point in the history of Chinese poetry; the era's poems are remarkable for their subtlety and range of emotion. Perhaps the most well-known Tang poets are **Li Bai,** who is known for writing bold, individualistic poems, and **Du Fu,** whose works deal with broad historical issues as well as intimate personal concerns. Also written in this era were the intensely visual landscape poems of **Wang Wei,** the socially and politically commentative works of **Bai Juyi,** and the imagistic poetry of **Li He.** In the Song dynasty, a new poetic genre developed. **Ci** (song lyrics) were set to popular musical tunes and written from an explicitly female perspective, even though most *ci* writers were men. Not surprisingly, love and desire were the most common subjects.

Fiction was long regarded as "low art" because of its entertainment value. During the Ming dynasty, however, an increasing number of intellectuals began to write down vernacular narratives handed down by oral storytellers and, eventually, to compose original fiction. Short fiction, written in everyday spoken language, enjoyed tremendous popularity because of their focus on the lives of people of lower social orders. Writers like **Feng Menglong** and **Li Yu** wrote a number of tales set in the urban scene, with prostitutes and poor students as heroines and heroes; many of these stories valued romantic sentiment and individual passion over the obligations of Confucian filial piety.

The great **novels** of the Ming and Qing periods are written in a combination of the classical and vernacular languages. *The Romance of the Three Kingdoms* is a heroic tale set amidst the wars that followed the end of the Han. *The Water Margin*, also translated as *Rebels of the Marsh*, tells the story of a group of virtuous rebels in the Song. *Journey to the West*, or *Monkey*, is based on the life of the Tang dynasty monk Xuan Zang, who journeyed to India to collect Buddhist scriptures. Perhaps best known in the West is *Dream of Red Mansions*, also translated as *The Story of the Stone* or *Dream of the Red Chamber*, by the Qing writer Cao Xueqin. This novel chronicles the romantic and personal intrigues of a large declining family in Beijing at the end of the Ming dynasty.

MODERN

By the late 19th and early 20th centuries, Chinese writers, influenced by the foreign works that were widely available in translation in China, began applying realism and social allegories to their works. In the second decade of the 20th century, a group of

A TRUE ROMANCE NEEDS THREE San Guo Yan Yi (三国演义), known to the Japanese as Sangokushi and to the western world as The Romance of the Three Kingdoms, is one of China's most famed historical novels. Although the epic spans the period from AD 184-286, the plot begins in 220, when the Han dynasty collapsed and the country was divided into the northern Wei, southwestern Shu, and southeastern Wu Kingdoms. Many agree that the hero of The Romance of the Three Kingdoms is Liu Bei, a descendant of the Han and the ruler of the Shu Kingdom, who dedicated his life to destroying Cao Cao, the betrayer of the Han dynasty. What defined Liu Bei were not his twin swords, but his constant weeping; his greatest virtue was neither his brilliance nor his warrior abilities, but his charisma. It was this trait that brought great men such as famous advisor Zhuge Liang to Liu Bei's side. Perhaps the most popular and touching example of Liu Bei's personality is when he and his two greatest generals, Guan Yu and Zhang Fei, make an oath of brotherhood and promise to die as one.

In 264, the Wei Kingdom rose and crushed the Shu. One year later, a usurper stole the Wei throne and founded the Jin dynasty, officially bringing the Three Kingdoms period to a close. As for The Romance of the Three Kingdoms, the Chinese fell in love. Today, three Kingdoms Clubs, personal webpages, TV series, cartoons, comics, video games, and cults of personality around the story's main characters abound.

intellectuals led by Hu Shi began using the spoken vernacular, or **baihua**, in all literary writing in order to create an accessible national literature. This movement proved successful and soon writing in the classical language fell out of fashion.

The May Fourth Movement of 1919 (see p. 15) spawned an intellectual revolution, and writers associated with it began to produce fiction that was explicitly or implicitly critical of contemporary social and political situations. The most famous of the May Fourth writers is **Lu Xun**, whose short stories ("Diary of a Madman," "The Story of Ah Q") portray a China suffering from its inability to modernize. **Lao She** wrote allegorical novels (*Rickshaw Boy*) that document the injustices of Chinese society. **Ba Jin** wrote a trilogy of novels (*Family, Spring*, and *Autumn*) that exposed the conflict between China's premodern traditions and modern aspirations through the story of a family's generational conflicts. The female characters of **Eileen Chang**'s short stories, provide a very different and unique perspective on the historical changes unfolding in China in the first half of the 20th century.

In 1942, Mao Zedong gave two key talks on literature and art in Yanan, declaring that all literature should serve the state and the revolutionary cause. After the Communist victory in 1949, professional writers worked for state-run guilds, and most writing of this period shows the stifling effects of close government control.

From the end of the Cultural Revolution to the present, however, a number of authors have taken advantage of their slowly expanding freedom to experiment and criticize. **Feng Jicai** and **Su Tong** have written satirical tales influenced by "Magical Realism"; Su Tong is the author of "Raise the Red Lantern," which was made popular overseas by Zhang Yimou's film adaptation (see p. 42). The controversial **Zhang Xianliang** has written an account of his experiences in a government labor camp (*Grass Soup*) and a novel that attracted the authorities' suspicion for its explicit sexual content (*Half of Man is Woman*). **Wang Shuo**'s novels portray the vices and disillusionment of young people in present-day China; his works have also been regarded with suspicion by the authorities, but enjoy tremendous popularity. More recently, novels such as **Li Dawei**'s *Dream Collector*, are being written in a post-modern narrative style.

PERFORMING ARTS

MUSIC

Legend assigns the birth of Chinese music to the reign of the semi-mythical Shang emperor Huangdi in 2697 BC. Allegedly, Huangdi sent his advisor Ling Lun to the mountains of the west to find bamboo pipes that could sound the call of the phoenix, and thus, harmonize his reign with the larger workings of the universe. Written and archaeological records indicate that the existence of Chinese music stretches back at least this far. Archaeologists have turned up remains of numerous instruments that were most likely used in burials and ritual ceremonies in the Shang dynasty (1600-1050 BC). Textual evidence of the importance of music in early Chinese society is found in the **Record of Rites** (*Li Ji*, 2nd century BC) and in the **Classic of Poetry** (*Shijing*), which was originally meant to be sung to music.

Traditional Chinese music uses a 12-tone system markedly different from the traditional Western scale. Major **traditional instruments** include the zither (*guqin*), the lute (*pipa*), the horizontal flute (*dizi*), the vertical flute (*dongxiao*), the ceremonial trumpet (*suona*), and the two-stringed viola (*huqin*). Most of the elements of traditional Chinese music are indigenous, but traces of Muslim music (popular during the Tang) can be heard in a number of folk pieces. An excellent resource on traditional Chinese **folk music,** complete with sound clips, is the Internet Chinese Music Archive (http://metalab.unc.edu/chinese-music/).

In the early years of Communism, a number of folk songs were rearranged according to communal principles. Simple tunes sung by a single singer became lavish affairs sung by large choruses. Many lyrics were reconstructed or replaced in order to better represent the "common people." **The East is Red** (*Dongfang hong*) is perhaps the most famous example of a provincial folk tune reworked into a political anthem.

These days, a visitor to China is more likely to encounter pop songs (better known as **Canto-pop**) imported from Taiwan and Hong Kong (see p. 409). But China also has its own popular music industry, which has been steadily developing as authorities relax regulations on music. A great deal of **Sino-pop** tends toward heavily synthesized love songs that emphasize the singer's star qualities, but a full range of styles, including rap and heavy metal derivatives, can be found. Cui Jian, Dou Wei, and Faye Wong (Wang Fei) are popular music stars in China.

THEATER

The important role of instrumental and vocal music in traditional Chinese theater would better characterize it as "opera." All of the various styles of opera tend to share certain common elements, including bare stages, set role types indicated by the type of face paint worn by each actor, complex conventions of symbolism and pantomime, and highly trained performers skilled in operatic movement, singing, and, in many cases, dance, acrobatics, or martial arts.

Chinese theater attained its greatest complexity and widespread popularity during the Song. The **zaju** ("variety plays") of the Northern Song and the **nanxi** ("southern drama") of the Southern Song were written in the vernacular and set to works of popular music. Stories of love and betrayal were the most popular subject matter, and these highly accessible works reached a wide audience.

In the Yuan, operas became more poetic, emphasizing lyrics over plot. Within this highly artistic context, however, the lives and problems of common people were given great attention. During the Ming, a Suzhou scholar, Wei Liangfu, single-handedly incorporated southern folk tunes into a new style of opera called **kunqu,** shifting the center of dramatic innovation from the north of China to the south. For several centuries, *kunqu* enjoyed incredible popularity. Originally an entertainment for the masses, it gradually trickled upward to gain a wide audience among the literati. The love plays of **Tang Xianzu** are among the most well-known works originally written as *kunqu* pieces.

Toward the end of the 18th century, a new operatic form arose. **Jingxi** or **Jingju** ("opera of the capital"), often referred to as "Peking opera," represented a mix of Shanzi and Gansu folk elements, Anhui province singing styles, and Beijing acrobatic styles. *Jingxi* is distinct from *kunqu* in that it uses the flute as its main instrument, instead of cymbals and other percussion instruments. *Jingxi* plots are often military tales that are quicker in pace and involve more elaborate acrobatics; consequently, many think it to be less poetic than *kunqu*. Today, *jingxi* is by far the most popular form of traditional theatre practiced in China (see **A Night at the Jingju**, p. 112).

In the early 20th century, Western-style spoken drama attracted followers from among the intelligentsia. **Cao Yu** was among the first Chinese playwrights to write spoken drama; among his most successful works of the 1930s and 1940s are *Thunderstorm* and *Beijingers*, portraits of the changing social order of urban China. In the face of WWII and the Japanese invasion, nationalist propaganda plays also became quite common. These works provided many ordinary Chinese with their first exposure to spoken drama; many of them also incorporated folk songs and dances to create a uniquely Chinese version of the genre.

After 1949, officials tried to keep theater in accord with the principles laid out in Mao's 1942 **Yanan Talks on Art & Literature** that declared that the foremost function of art was to serve the masses. Most dramas in the 1950s were realistic. In the 1960s, Mao's wife, the former actress Jiang Qing, led a movement to write traditional-style operas that embodied revolutionary principles and made heroes out of the common people. During the Cultural Revolution, many classic operas were banned, and members of notable theater troupes were persecuted. After the Cultural Revolution, however, traditional opera edged back into the public sphere, and contacts with Western dramatic developments were gradually renewed.

"HUNDRED ENTERTAINMENTS"

By the 2nd century BC, a number of vaudevillian entertainments had migrated into China via the nomadic cultures of Central Asia. Sword-swallowing, fire-eating, juggling, acrobatics and tumbling, and other such theatrical tricks were known as the **"hundred entertainments."** These days, **acrobatics and tumbling,** which was one of the rare performing arts approved by the Communist authorities, still remains popular in many parts of China.

Shadow puppet theater is among the more unique ancient art forms to have survived into modern times. Legend says that the form originated around 100 BC, when a priest used a lamp to cast a woman's shadow onto a screen and assured the emperor that his deceased wife had been brought back to life. Chinese shadow puppets are made of leather and brightly colored with a transparent dye that allows the shadows themselves to appear in color. Shadow puppet performances can still be found in parts of China, particularly the South and Northwest.

Traditional Chinese **dance** comes in countless forms—Buddhist ceremonial dance, folk dance, operatic and theatrical dance. Separate dance traditions for each minority community all survive into the present.

VISUAL ARTS

CALLIGRAPHY

An artist only needs the "Four Treasures of the Scholar"—ink, inkstone, brush, and paper or silk—to engage in what is traditionally regarded as the highest form of visual art. Calligraphy, considered an abstract art, values the grace of the calligrapher's strokes more than legibility. To the Chinese, a piece of calligraphy reflects not only the artist's emotions at the moment of composition, but also the refinement and temperament of his person. Since the strokes cannot be altered once on paper, a masterpiece is said to indicate the calligrapher's forethought and confidence. During the Tang, calligraphy was thought to be so demonstrative of character that it was used to appoint high officials in the civil service. Calligraphy is not confined only to manuscripts or paintings; it adorns gates, temples, tombs, mountains, and caves all over China.

PAINTING

Performed with the same basic materials as calligraphy, Chinese painting is typically judged by the same standards. Historically, the Chinese painter has been less concerned with capturing the inner life of the subject through the vigor and expressiveness of his brush strokes. For example, Gu Kaizhi, a brilliant fourth century master, is famed for portraying a scholar's wisdom through the addition of three hairs (just three quick strokes!) to his chin.

China is widely known for its **landscape painting,** which became the culture's most prominent genre from the Song on. Landscape painting allowed for a new perspective on visual art that was not affiliated to political or sacred powers. In this era—widely considered to be the golden age of Chinese painting—bamboo, dragons, cranes, orchids, winter plums, and gnarled pine trees commonly took center stage. **Mi Fei, Ma Yuan,** and **Xia Gui** are some famous figures from this period.

By the middle of the 19th century, Chinese artists were more influenced by Western modernist artistic movements. By the early 20th century, Chinese artists were visiting Europe drawing inspiration from movements like Impressionism. A few artists fused modern Western and traditional Chinese styles, among them **Xu Beihong,** who used the traditional Chinese brush to mimic the realistic effect of pencil and chalk. His figure paintings were a primary influence on post-1949 Socialist Realist artists.

After the Communist victory, sentimental and non-abstract representations of laborers, farmers, and patriotic commoners became the chief subject for painters. Woodblock prints, which were cheaper to produce and purchase than paintings, also grew in popularity. During the Cultural Revolution, many traditional pieces of art that were deemed politically incorrect were destroyed. After Mao's death, Socialist Realist propaganda painting declined as artistic freedom increased. The 1980s were marked by the appearance of abstract Western styles such as Cubism and of non-political subject matter such as the nude figure. Formerly exiled artists returned to the country to foster a new artistic flowering that continues today.

SCULPTURE

Sculptors have traditionally been regarded as craftsmen, not as artists, and most sculpture has served some ceremonial, religious, or practical use. The oldest Chinese sculptures are small, white marble figurines that date to the Shang dynasty. In the Han, sculptures tended to be small, boldly colored carvings of human, animal, and supernatural life. Buddhism became a forceful influence on sculpture when it entered China at the end of the Han, and many elaborate carvings of deities (particularly the many-limbed Avalokiteshvara) were made. By the Tang, Buddhist cave temples became the sites of some of the most innovative sculpture in the world, as life-size and larger-than-life carvings of deities in bronze and limestone were produced.

Pottery, like sculpture, also served practical functions. In the Shang dynasty, lacquer glazes and jade carvings decorated coffins, weapons, and furniture. By the Tang, Chinese ceramics had acquired more of a decorative purpose, and the whiteware and tricolored glazes of this period were slowly turning into prized commodities in international trade. During the Ming, Chinese lacquers and vases were highly sought after in places as far away as Europe, and the pre-eminence of China on the international ceramics scene can still be seen in the use of the English term "china." The famous blue-and-white vases of the Ming were produced in the city of **Jingdezhen** (see p. 375), in present-day Jiangxi province. Production of Yixing ceramics was centered in **Suzhou** (see p. 308).

ARCHITECTURE

Since the Shang (1600-1050 BC), all important buildings in China have faced south. This custom supposedly started with the Emperor's Palace, which faced south because it represented the North Star and allowed the emperor to supervise the earthly world that lay to the South. Another theory suggests that the custom reflects the Chinese indisposition toward their northern neighbors, the barbarian invaders of their past.

A massively ornate and elegantly curved **roof** often dominates many Chinese houses, halls, and temples. Typically, the various chambers of residential buildings are arranged around a central **courtyard.** For eons, the Chinese defended themselves from their attackers by building walls around their homesteads, hometowns, and even their homeland. Walled cities were commonplace in earlier centuries; but today, only portions of a few remain, most notably around the cities of Xian, Nanjing, and Pingyao. The idea of a walled kingdom arose during the Qin dynasty (221-206 BC), when construction of the **Great Wall of China** began (see p.

9). Stretching over 4500 miles, and employing years of conscript labor, the wall was built as a practical tool rather than an aesthetic creation. Nevertheless, the Great Wall stands among the world's most awesome architectural achievements.

Temples have always been a significant part of the Chinese architectural landscape. Temples and palaces often look very similar because Chinese temples were designed with the same principles as secular buildings. There are essentially no architectural distinctions between Buddhist, Daoist, and Confucian temples, except for the **Buddhist cave temple,** the origins of which can be traced to India.

Another functional architectural genre is the **tomb,** which often consists of massive, multi-roomed complexes constructed underground or into the sides of mountains, usually filled with paintings, sculptures, and whatever objects might be important in the afterlife. The thousands of terracotta soldiers buried with the Qin emperor Shi Huangdi (see p. 222) are one example of the concern shown for the afterlives of dead rulers.

Extensive contact with Europe had caused considerable changes in Chinese architecture by the 20th century. Prior to the 1920s, plenty of European-style buildings had been erected in the treaty ports of China, but all of them had been designed and constructed by foreign architects. In 1925, a group of foreign-educated Chinese architects founded the Society for the Study of Chinese Architecture, which sought to find ways of adapting traditional Chinese designs to modern needs. The influence of this movement is more evident in Taiwan than on the mainland. After 1949, utility took priority over aesthetic concerns, and the staggering amounts of construction that have taken place since then reflect this; China has more than its fair share of uninteresting tile high-rises. However, not all examples of Communist architecture are so bland, however: political structures such as the Great Hall of the People (see p. 117) and Mao Zedong's mausoleum in Beijing (see p. 118), exhibit a sense of grandeur all their own.

FILM

China was first exposed to the art of cinematography in 1896. Movies were referred to as "Western Peep Shows" because most early films were foreign-made, and those that were shot in China were often produced by foreign companies and based on Western works of literature. The idea that film was strictly an imported art form began to fade as a domestic film industry flourished in Shanghai from the 1920 to the 1940s under what is now referred to as the "First Generation" of filmmakers. The classic Chinese film noir *Tianya Ernu* was produced in this era.

In the 1950s, the Communist Party realized that cinema could be used for political education, and produced a great number of nationalist-socialist films that had many similarites: zealous heroes, class struggle, and the triumph of progressive protagonists over reactionary forces. In 1966, the Cultural Revolution and the Gang of Four's command over all things cultural (see p. 19) strengthened this cinematic commitment to nationalist-socialist films and solidified the explicitly political function of art.

The end of the Cultural Revolution in 1976 and Deng Xiaoping's rise to power at the same time (see p. 20) brought about a new atmosphere of liberalism, which breathed new life into China's stagnant film industry. A group of gifted directors, commonly referred to as the **"Fifth Generation"** of filmmakers, ushered in the new wave of Chinese cinema. Although Fifth Generation directors like Chen Kaige (*Yellow Earth, Farewell My Concubine*) and Zhang Yimou (*Raise the Red Lantern, Shanghai Triad*) enjoyed the spotlight in film festivals worldwide, at home they had to contend with unreceptive local audiences and hostile government officials who disapproved of their depictions of Chinese society.

A new flock of filmmakers, known informally as the **"Sixth Generation,"** has begun to take on new subjects and styles. In contrast to the historical settings of Fifth Generation films, Sixth Generation works are set in present-day China and often view urban China through a bleak but sympathetic lens. Most of these films have made little impact in China and the West, and getting a hold of them can be very difficult. Directors to look out for include Wang Xiaoshuai (*The Days, Frozen*) and He Jianjun (*The Postman, Red Beads*).

CHINA

RECOMMENDED FILMS

Yellow Earth (dir. Chen Kaige). The first major work of the Chinese New Wave, this exquisite film about a soldier who goes to a rural village to collect folk songs helped to redefine Chinese cinema.

To Live (dir. Zhang Yimou). An epic love story that charts the fortunes (and misfortunes) of several generations of a Chinese family. The film spans several years from the 1940s through the 1960s and is a great way to learn a bit about modern Chinese history.

The Blue Kite (dir. Tian Zhuangzhuang). Told from two perspectives, this is a harrowing but humanistic film about the gradual disintegration of a family targeted by Mao's political reformation movements of the 50s and 60s.

Rouge (dir. Stanley Kwan). A romantic fantasy, Hong Kong style. In the 1930s, a beautiful courtesan and her wealthy lover join in a suicide pact when his class-conscious parents reject their hopes for marriage. She dies, and, 50 years later, her ghost returns to find the delinquent beau.

Raise the Red Lantern (dir. Zhang Yimou). A sumptuous drama about an educated young woman who has been married off against her will to be the fourth wife of a wealthy landlord. The movie recounts the intrigues and injustices associated with polygamous households.

Chungking Express (dir. Wong Kar-wai). Two loosely connected stories about police officers in love linked by a Hong Kong fast food joint. Stylish cinematography, fractured narration, and sexy, quirky characters give the film the hip urban feel that makes it one of Quentin Tarantino's favorite flicks.

Fallen Angels (dir. Wong Kar-wai). A frenetic and exhilarating portrait of honkytonk Hong Kong. A professional hitman, his glamorous agent, and a mute ex-con charge headlong through this neon city of endless night searching for love.

Farewell My Concubine (dir. Chen Kaige). Visually stunning but made, some suggest, with an eye to commercial acceptability rather than artistic innovation, this film recounts the complex relationship between two Beijing Opera stars.

Gate of Heavenly Peace (dir. Carma Hinton and Richard Gordon). A lengthy but nuanced attempt to explore the violent confrontation between student demonstrators and the Chinese government at Tiananmen Square. Hinton and Gordon make excellent use of archival footage, narration, and personal interviews.

The Last Emperor (dir. Bernardo Bertolucci). The true story of the last ruler of the Qing dynasty, this movie was filmed on location in Changchun (see p. 195). The winner of nine Academy Awards, including Best Picture and Best Director.

SPORTS & LEISURE

GAMES

What is known to Western children as "Chinese checkers" is actually a version of a popular Chinese game known as **tiaoqi**, played by up to six players using marbles on a star-shaped board. **Weiqi,** the ancient "game of encirclement," is a military conquest game on a grid using white and black pebbles as opposing "armies." Each side tries to secure board territory by surrounding and gobbling up opponent stones. Though it originated in China, w*eiqi* is currently more popular in Korea and Japan and is known in the West by its Japanese name, *Go.* **Chinese chess,** known as *xiangqi,* is different from Western chess in that it involves a set of character-inscribed wooden pieces with few pawns, no queen, and two artillery pieces. *Xiangqi* is by far the most popular board game in China, and is commonly played in parks by young and old alike. **Mahjong** is a four-person game using a table of green and white ceramic blocks. The objective of the game is to assemble sets of blocks from any of several categories. A *mahjong* match is not considered a *mah-*

jong match unless some form of gambling is involved. During the Cultural Revolution, when gambling was condemned as a form of "spiritual pollution," *mahjong*'s popularity took a hit, but in recent years the game has regained its old popularity at an alarming speed. **Card games** with large followings in China include bridge (Deng Xiaoping's favorite game), poker, and a six-player Chinese version of poker popular on long train rides.

SPORTS

Dismissed during the Maoist era as the lowest of the Chinese sports, the millennia-old practice of **wushu**, or martial arts, is back on the upswing in China—and around the world. There are at least a hundred different forms of *wushu* (also called *gongfu* or kung fu) in China alone. Traditionally, the most important thing *wushu* taught was not self-defense and physical strength, but spiritual development. It made its impact on other branches of Chinese culture as well; *wushu* moves were often incorporated into performing arts such as opera and acrobatics. Famous centers of *wushu* study include the Buddhist **Shaolin Monastery** (see p. 233) in Henan and the Daoist **Wudangshan** temples (see p. 405) in Hubei. For more information on kung fu, see **Boxer Rebellion, p. 233**. Tai chi (or *tai qi*), a toned-down version of *wushu* featuring slow, fluid body movements, is extremely popular with the elderly, who pack into parks at the crack of dawn for morning exercise.

After 1949, sports mingled with politics when the Communist government treated athletics as a means of building and displaying national prestige. The government encouraged participation in sports and built public sports facilities. During the height of the Maoist era, the Chairman, an avid swimmer since childhood, urged the nation's young people to "learn to thrive in the turbulent waves" (both figuratively *and* literally). Millions heeded his call and dove into the nation's rivers and lakes, even as they plunged into the violent tides of politics.

Due to overcrowding in Chinese urban areas, the most popular sports today tend to be the most space-efficient. **Ping pong** and **badminton** took the country by storm mid-century. In the early 1970s, when China was at the height of its international isolation, ping pong matches were the first instances of the unofficial cultural contacts between the US and China that led to the normalization of relations between the two (hence, the phrase **Ping Pong Politics**; see p. 19).

In the last few decades, sports have flourished as leisure activities rather than political promotions. Bowling, billiards, tennis, and racquetball, though increasingly popular, are still considered sports of the well-to-do. Bans on "bourgeois sports" like golf, bowling, and horse-racing have been lifted, though gambling remains officially illegal. Michael Jordan (known as Qiaodan) mania hit China hard, and **basketball** is now popular among young people. In **Olympic competition,** China is traditionally strong in diving, gymnastics, women's volleyball, and table tennis, but overnight successes in swimming and track and field have raised suspicions about the use of performance enhancement drugs. Despite several previous failed bids, Beijing is currently vying for the 2008 Summer Olympic Games. For more information on Beijing's Olympic bid, see www.beijing-olympic.org.cn.

The most popular spectator sport is **soccer,** and the failure of the Chinese men's team to qualify for the World Cup has been the cause of deep national disappointment. Fortunately for fans, Chinese women's teams have continuously succeeded where their male counterparts have not. Winners of six straight Asian championships, the Chinese women are considered one of the premier teams in the world.

KARAOKE

Like spitting, staring, and suffocating crowds, karaoke is something visitors to urban China are guaranteed to encounter. Even smaller towns now have karaoke bars, denoted either by the Chinese transliteration of the word (kǎlā OK; 卡拉 OK) or by the acronym KTV, which indicates the presence of private rooms for individual parties. Originally a Japanese invention, karaoke was introduced to China in the mid-1980s. These days, Canto-pop (see p. 409) and Taiwanese love ballads have largely replaced folk and patriotic tunes as the songs of choice. Even Western tunes have made their way into the repertoire. From simple mikes set up in hole-in-the-wall neighborhood restaurants to glitzy high-tech ventures filled with yodeling businessmen, karaoke is enjoyed by Chinese in all walks of life.

Frankly, some Westerners enter and leave China hating karaoke. Foreign visitors have spent many a long night in hotel rooms just above the in-house karaoke lounge, begging for a hurricane to drown out the never-ending off-key warbling from below. Exercise an open mind (and your vocal cords!), and karaoke can be tolerable and even enjoyable. And, a drink or two couldn't hurt.

FESTIVALS & HOLIDAYS

DATE	FESTIVAL	DETAILS
Jan. 1	Western New Year's Day	Though the Chinese do not celebrate the Western New Year, the day is a state holiday.
Jan. 24-28, 2001	Lunar New Year	The most important holiday in all of East Asia. Families gather to prepare special meals and light fireworks. Red paper decorations and New Year's calendars, thought to bring good luck for the coming year, are hung and given as gifts.
Mar. 8	Working Women's Day	A state holiday.
Apr. 4-5	Qingming (Tomb-Sweeping) Festival	A traditional holiday on which the Chinese visit and beautify their ancestors' graves.
May 1	Labor Day (May Day)	This state holiday honors the nation's workers. Parades are often held.
May 4	International Youth Day	A state holiday honoring the student demonstrators who catalyzed the May 4 Movement (see p. 15) in 1919.
June 1	Children's Day	A holiday for China's youngest citizens.
June 25, 2001	Dragon Boat Festival	Memorializes poet and patriot Qu Yuan, who drowned himself in an act of political protest. Celebrants throw bamboo-wrapped rice dumplings into rivers and race canoe-like dragon boats. See **Dragon Boats Galore**, p. 535
July 1	Anniversary of the CCP's Founding	A patriotic state holiday.
Aug. 1	Anniversary of the PLA's Founding	A state holiday honoring the armed forces.
Oct. 1	National Day	A state holiday commemorating the Communist victory of October 1, 1949.
Oct 1, 2001	Moon (Mid-Autumn) Festival	Celebrated as the night on which the moon is fullest and brightest. A time for eating sweet mooncakes and gazing at the moon.

FOOD & DRINK

China is blessed with a rich variety of raw materials which fuel one of the most distinctive and varied cuisines in the world. Historically, food has commanded interest and respect among Chinese intellectual, political, and artistic leaders. Authors and poets wrote eulogies celebrating food and drink (the Song poet Su Dongpo (or Su Shi) wrote a lyrical poem "In Praise of Pork"). The first act of many newly crowned emperors was to appoint a personal chef for the imperial palace. This obsession with food was not restricted to the wealthy classes—a common greeting which is heard to this day is "have you eaten yet?" ("nǐ chī wán le ma?").

Chinese cuisine strongly emphasizes the division and balance between *fan* (rice and grains) and *cai* (vegetables and meat). Dishes must also satisfy the complex requirements of the **yin-yang equilibrium,** which is based on a Daoist conception of cosmic balance; foods that are dampening should be combined with foods that are drying, heating flavors should be balanced by cooling flavors, and so on. Despite these seemingly complex requirements, Chinese food is also notable for its flexi-

CHOPSTICKS ARE LOTS OF FUN

These are not toys, not curios, and definitely not percussion instruments. Without mastery of chopsticks in China, you will get no peace, no respect, and most critically, no dinner. To begin, it is common habit to rub disposable chopsticks perpendicularly against each other to scratch off unwanted splinters. This must not be done when one is a house guest lest you unwittingly suggest that the host is unable to provide unsplintered utensils. To use the chopsticks, one stick is grasped in the webbed space between the thumb and index finger and kept stable by being pressed against the next to last finger. The second chopstick is held lightly between the tips of the thumb and the first two fingers. Two-thirds of the way from the bottom of the chopsticks is the best place to gain leverage over the food. Beginners should forget altogether about peanuts, while old hands can go ahead and snatch flies out of the air.

The polite chopstick-user will bear the following in mind. If no serving spoon is provided, it is fine to pick items of communal plates with your own chopsticks, but picked items should first make a cursory landing on your bowl or plate, and not go directly into your mouth. Chinese rice is sticky enough to be picked up in small amounts, but placing the bowl against your lower lip and shoveling the rice into your mouth with the chopsticks is completely acceptable between friends. What is not acceptable in any company is sticking the chopsticks straight up in a bowl of rice, which looks like incense in a censer and is reminiscent of a funeral; it is more correct to lay the chopsticks against the side of the bowl or on a special rest.

bility and adaptability. Once the basic principles of food preparation are mastered, a chef has plenty of room for improvisation. Because each dish tends to involve many ingredients, scarce or out-of-season ingredients can be replaced or omitted without destroying the overall distinctiveness of the dish. This ability to adapt to environmental constraints is also evident in rural Chinese people's comprehensive knowledge of "famine plants"—edible flora and fauna that are not a part of everyday cuisine but can be eaten in times of food shortage.

Resource availability was perhaps the most important factor to shape Chinese cuisine. The characteristic Chinese preparation method, in which food is sliced, diced, or otherwise cut into small pieces before cooking, was developed primarily in response to the need to cook food quickly to conserve fast-burning firewood and scarce charcoal. And **chopsticks**, the great multi-use Chinese utensils, were perfectly suited to the task of scooping up these bite-sized morsels.

REGIONAL CUISINE

Rice is the staple crop in much of China, but geographical and climactic differences have given rise to vast variation from region to region. In the North, for example, wheat, rather than rice, is the principal crop, and noodles are the bedrock of every meal. Traditionally, the country is divided into four distinct regional cuisines: Beijing/Shandong, Sichuan, Guangdong, and Jiangsu.

One of Beijing's most famous namesakes, at least in the culinary world, is **Beijing duck,** a delectable delicacy requiring elaborate preparation. (See also **Beijing Duck,** p. 107) In Beijing, Shandong, and other northern regions, noodles, steamed breads, and multiple forms of the sacred **dumpling** are prevalent (see **Small Package, Big Happiness,** p. 195). Beijing cuising makes liberal use of stronger flavored roots and vegetables such as peppers, garlic, ginger, coriander, and leek.

Sichuanese/Hunan cuisine is known for its hell-fire spicy flavors. Chili peppers, indigenous to the region, are used in liberal quantities to give chicken, pork, and river fish a killer kick.

Guangdong cuisine is not for the faint of heart: snail, snake, eel, frog, and turtle all turn up on Cantonese menus. Guangzhou is best known for its **dim sum**, appetizer-sized snacks that add up to a meal. Eaten for breakfast and lunch, dim sum features more small dumplings and buns than you ever thought possible, as well as steamed spareribs, spring rolls, and chicken feet (see p. 425).

Specialties of **Jiangsu** and other east coast provinces feature lots of seafood; shad, mullet, perch, and shrimp are all hauled from the ocean for consumption.

Among favorites in China's Northwest are noodle soups and lamb or beef kebabs and roasted meat.

DRINK

Tea is the single most ubiquitous beverage in China; tea, not water, is the default drink in restaurants. Chinese teas come in an unfathomable variety of specimens and brands; the three major categories, from least to most caffeinated, are **white teas** (báichá; 白茶), **green teas** (lǜchá; 绿茶), and **black teas** (hóngchá; 红茶). Hot water for tea is free and available everywhere, including on trains and in hotel rooms. Particularly during northern winters, Chinese often drink the boiled water without the tea as an excellent way to keep warm and to hydrate without fear of water-borne disease.

Coca-Cola and other Western soft drinks (particularly Sprite and Fanta) can be found almost anywhere. Chinese companies have caught on, and domestic sugary carbonated drinks (some in exotic flavors like lichee and coconut), crowd store shelves. (See also **What's in a Name?,** p. 667.) The Chinese do drink and produce juice drinks, but many are heavily sweetened; a glass of pure OJ will be hard to find. **Bottled water** is sold everywhere.

By no means is China a nation of tea-totallers. The joys of alcoholic imbibement are celebrated in ancient poetry and prose; the brews that inspired many a Tang dynasty poet were not wines, but grain-based spirits every bit as thick and hearty as what is known today as **beer.** Beer is still among the most consumed liquids in the country. Most towns have their own local brews; the famed Tsingtao brand is the product of Qingdao (see p. 168), and Beijing's Yanjing is also well known.

There is no shortage of hard liquor in China. Cheap bottles of the potent, transparent, grain-based substance known as **baijiu** (白酒) are sold everywhere; those who plan to drink it should get used to the unique bouquet of flavors, since chasers and mixers are unheard of at Chinese banquets. While men down large quantities of the stuff on special occasions and karaoke nights, women rarely consume it in public. Higher quality Western liquors are available at upscale bars and stores, and cost about what they would in the West.

ESSENTIALS

FACTS FOR THE TRAVELER

DOCUMENTS AND FORMALITIES

ENTRANCE REQUIREMENTS.
Passport (p. 49). Required for all travelers to China, Hong Kong, or Macau.
Visa (p. 50). Required for all travelers to China. Required for some travelers to Hong Kong or Macau.
Letter of Invitation (p. 89). Typically required to work or study in China.
Immunizations (p. 60). No vaccinations are required to enter China, unless entering from an area infected with yellow fever.
Work Permit (p. 90). Required of all foreigners planning to work in China.
Driving Permit (p. 84). Required for all those planning to drive.

CHINA'S CONSULAR SERVICES ABROAD

Australia: Embassy: 15 Coronation Dr., Yarralumla ACT 2600, Canberra (☎(02) 6273 4780; visa section 6273 4783; fax 6273 4987; www.chinaembassy.org.au). **Consulates:** 75-79 Irving Rd. 3142, **Melbourne** (☎(03) 9822 0604; fax 9822 0320); 15-17 William St., 3rd Fl., Australia Place 6000, **Perth** (☎(08) 9321 8193; visa section 9481 3278; fax 9321 8457); 539 Elizabeth St., Surry Hills 2010, **Sydney** (☎(02) 9319 0678; fax 9319 2430).

Canada: Embassy: 515 St. Patrick St., Ottawa, ON K1N 5H3 (☎(613) 789-3434; fax 789-1911; www.chinaembassy-canada.org). **Consulates:** 1011 6th Ave. SW, Ste. 100, **Calgary,** AB T2P OW1 (☎(403) 264-3322; fax 264-6656); 240 St. George St., **Toronto,** ON M5R 2P4 (☎(416) 964-7260; fax 324-6468); 3380 Granville St., **Vancouver,** BC V6H 3K3 (☎(604) 734-7492; fax 737-0154).

New Zealand: Embassy: 2-6 Glenmore St., Wellington (☎(04) 4721 3823; fax 499 0419). **Consulate:** 588 Great South Rd., Greenlane, **Auckland** (☎(09) 525 1586 or 525 1589; fax 525 0733).

South Africa: Embassy: 972 Pretorius St., Arcadia 0083, Pretoria (☎(012) 342 4194; visa section 342 9366; fax 342 4244; www.chinese-embassy.co.za). **Consulates:** 18 De Villers St., Cape Suites Hotel, #54, **Cape Town** (☎(021) 465 9515; fax 465 9512); 18 Dava en Ave., La Lucia, **Durban** (☎(031) 527 385 or 527 517; fax 562 9890); 25 Cleveland Rd., Fandhursp Sanddton, **Johannesburg** (☎(011) 784 7241; fax 883 5274).

United Kingdom: Embassy: 31 Portland Place, London W1N 3AG (☎(0171) 7631 1430; fax 436 9756; www.china-embassy.org.uk; email webmaster@www.china-embassy.unet). **Consulates:** Denison House, 49 Denison Rd., Rusholme, **Manchester** M14 5RX (☎(0161) 224 8672 or 224 7478; fax 257 2672); 43 Station Rd., **Edinburgh** EH12 7AF (☎(0131) 316 4789; fax 334 6954).

United States: Embassy: 2300 Connecticut Ave. NW, Washington, D.C. 20008 (☎(202) 328-2500; fax 588-0032; visa section 338-6688; visa fax 588-9760; www.chinaembassy.org; email webmaster@china-embassy.org). **Consulates:** 100 W Erie St., **Chicago,** IL 60610 (☎(312) 803-0098; visa section 573-3070; fax 803-0122); 3417 Montrose Blvd., **Houston,** TX 77006 (☎(713) 524-0780; visa section 524-0778; fax 524-7656; email visa@chinahouston.org; www.chinahouston.org); 443 Shatto Pl., **Los Angeles,** CA 90020 (☎(213) 807-8088; fax 380-1961; visa section 807-8018; fax 265-9809; email visachina@aol.com; www.chinaconsulatela.org); 520 12th Ave., **New**

York, NY 10036 (☎(212) 868-7752; fax 502-0245; www.nyconsulate.prchina.org); 1450 Laguna St., **San Francisco,** CA 94115 (☎(415) 674-2900, fax 563-0494; visa office 928 6931, fax 563 4861; www.consulatesf.webchina.org).

> **EMBASSIES AND CONSULATES.**
> The website for **Embassy World** (www.embassyworld.com) has a comprehensive directory of embassies and consulates with information on foreign embassies in China as well as Chinese embassies abroad.

CONSULAR SERVICES IN CHINA

Australia: 21 Dongzhimenwai Dajie, Sanlitun, **Beijing** (☎6532 2331; fax 6532 4349). GITIC Plaza, 339 Huanshi Dong Lu, Rm. 1509, **Guangzhou** (☎8335 0909; fax 8335 0718). Harbour Centre, 25 Harbour Rd., 23rd-24th Fl., Wan Chai, **Hong Kong** (☎2827 8881). 17 Fuxing Lu, **Shanghai** (☎6433 4604; fax 6437 6669).

Canada: 19 Dongzhimenwai Dajie, Sanlitun, **Beijing** (☎6532 3536; fax 6532 4072). China Hotel Office Tower, Liuhua Lu, Rm. 801, **Guangzhou** (☎8666 0569; fax 8666 2401). Exchange Square, Tower 1, 12th Fl., Central, **Hong Kong** (☎2810 4321). Shanghai Centre, Ste. 604, 1376 Nanjing Xi Lu, **Shanghai** (☎6279 8400; fax 6279 8401).

India: 1 Ritan Dong Lu, Jianguomenwai, **Beijing** (☎6532 1908 or 6532 1856; fax 6532 4684). 2200 Yanan Xi Lu, International Trade Center, 10th Fl., **Shanghai** (☎6275 8885; fax 6275 8881).

Indonesia: Office Bldg. B, Sanlitun, **Beijing** (☎6532 5489; fax 6532 5368). 127 Leighton Rd., Causeway Bay, **Hong Kong** (☎2890 4421).

Ireland: 3 Ritan Dong Lu, Jianguomenwai, **Beijing** (☎6532 2914; fax 6532 6857). Chungnam Bldg., 1 Lockhart Rd., Wan Chai, **Hong Kong** (☎2527 4897).

Japan: 7 Ritan Lu, Jianguomenwai, **Beijing** (☎6532 2361). 6 Bao He Lu, Zhongshan Qu, **Dalian** (☎251 2005 or 251 2007). Garden Hotel Tower, 368 Huanshi Dong Lu, 1st Fl., **Guangzhou** (☎8334 3090, ext. 7365; fax 8333 8972). Exchange Square, 8 Connaught Place, Tower I, 46th Fl., Central, **Hong Kong** (☎2522 1184). 1517 Huaihai Zhong Lu, **Shanghai** (☎6433 6639; fax 6433 1008). 50 Shisi Wei Lu, Heping, **Shenyang** (☎2322 7530).

Kazakhstan: 9 Dongliu Jie, Sanlitun, **Beijing** (☎6532 6182; fax 6532 6183).

Kyrgyzstan: Tayuan Diplomatic Bldg., 14 Liangmahe Nan Lu, Sanlitun, **Beijing** (☎6532 6458; fax 6532 6459).

Laos: 11 Dongsi Jie, Sanlitun, **Beijing** (☎6532 1224; fax 6532 6748).

Malaysia: 13 Dongzhimenwai Dajie, Sanlitun, **Beijing** (☎6532 2531-3; fax 6532 6544). CITIC Plaza, Tianhe Bei Lu, Rm. 1915-1918, **Guangzhou** (☎3877 0766; fax 8739 5669). Malaysia Bldg., 50 Gloucester Rd., 24th Fl., Wan Chai, **Hong Kong** (☎2527 0921).

Mongolia: 2 Xiushui Bei Jie, Jianguomenwai, **Beijing** (☎6532 1203; fax 6532 5045).

Myanmar (Burma): 6 Dongzhimenwai Dajie, Sanlitun, **Beijing** (☎6532 1425; fax 6532 1344). Sung Hung Kai Centre, 30 Harbour Rd., Rm. 2421-2425, Wan Chai, **Hong Kong** (☎2827 7929).

Nepal: 1 Xiliu Jie, Sanlitun, **Beijing** (☎6532 1795; fax 6532 3251). 13 Luobulinka (Norbulinka) Lu, **Lhasa** (☎682 2881; fax 683 6890).

New Zealand: 1 Donger Jie, Ritan Lu, **Beijing** (☎6532 2731; fax 6532 3424). Central Plaza, 18 Harbour Rd., Rm. 6503, Wan Chai, **Hong Kong** (☎2877 4488). 1375 Huaihai Zhong Lu, Qihua Tower, #15A, **Shanghai** (☎6471 1127; fax 6431 0226).

North Korea: Ritan Bei Lu, Jianguomenwai, **Beijing** (☎6532 1189; fax 6532 0656). International Trade Center, 2200 Yanan Xi Lu, 4th Fl., **Shanghai** (☎6219 6420; fax 6219 6918).

Pakistan: 1 Dongzhimenwai Da Jie, **Beijing** (☎6532 2504 or 6532 2581).

Philippines: 23 Xiushui Bei Jie, Jianguomenwai, **Beijing** (☎6532 2794). United Centre, 95 Queensway, Rm. 603, Admiralty, **Hong Kong** (☎2823 8500).

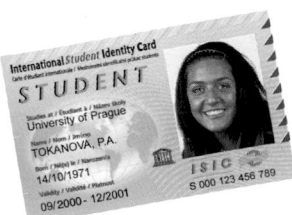

Call the USA

"feel free to call"

1-800-COLLECT

1 8 0 0
COLLECT

When in Ireland
Dial: 1-800-COLLECT (265 5328)

When in N. Ireland, UK & Europe
Dial: 00-800-COLLECT USA (265 5328 872)

Member of
Dublin Tourism

Australia	0011	800 265 5328 872
Finland	990	800 265 5328 872
Hong Kong	001	800 265 5328 872
Israel	014	800 265 5328 872
Japan	0061	800 265 5328 872
New Zealand	0011	800 265 5328 872

Russia: 4 Dongzhimennei, Beizhong Jie, **Beijing** (☎6532 2051; visa section 6532 1267; fax 6532 4853). 20 Huangpu Lu, **Shanghai** (☎6324 2682; fax 6306 9982).

Singapore: 1 Xiushui Bei Jie, Jianguomenwai, **Beijing** (☎6532 2926; fax 6532 2213). Admiralty Centre, 18 Harcourt Rd., Tower I, Rm. 901, Admiralty, **Hong Kong** (☎2527 2212). 400 Wulumuqi Lu, **Shanghai** (☎6437 0776; fax 6433 4150).

South Africa: 50 Liangmaqiao Lu, Lufthansa Center, C801, **Beijing** (☎6465 1941). Great Eagle Centre, 23 Harbour Rd., 27th Fl., Wan Chai, **Hong Kong** (☎2577 3279).

South Korea: China World Tower, 1 Jianguomenwai Dajie, 4th Fl., **Beijing** (☎6505 2609 or 6505 3171). Huiguan Dynasty Hotel, 9 Nanhan Rd., 3rd Fl., **Qingdao** (☎288 8900).

Thailand: 40 Guanghua Lu, Jianguomenwai, **Beijing** (☎6532 2151; fax 6532 1748). White Swan Hotel, 1 Shamian Nan Jie, Rm. 313, Shamian Island, **Guangzhou** (☎8188 6968, ext. 3313; fax 8187 9451). Fairmont House, 8 Cotton Tree Dr., 8th Fl., Central, **Hong Kong** (☎2521 6481). 7 Zhongshan Dong Yi Lu, 3rd Fl., **Shanghai** (☎6321 9371; fax 6323 4140).

United Kingdom: 11 Guanghua Lu, Jianguomenwai, **Beijing** (☎6532 1961; fax 6532 1939). GITIC Plaza, 339 Huanshi Dong Lu, 2nd Fl., **Guangzhou** (☎8331 2799 or 8333 6520; fax 8333 6485). Bank of America Tower, 12 Harcourt Rd., 9th Fl., Admiralty, **Hong Kong** (☎2901 3000). Shanghai Centre, 1376 Nanjing Xi Lu, Rm. 301, **Shanghai** (☎6279 7650; fax 6279 7651).

United States: 2 Xiushui Dong Jie, Jianguomenwai, **Beijing** (☎6532 3831; fax 6532 6057). 4 Lingshiguan Lu, **Chengdu** (☎558 3992). 1 Shamian Nan Jie, Shamian Island, **Guangzhou** (☎8188 8911; fax 8186 2341). 26 Garden Rd., Central, **Hong Kong** (☎2523 9011). 1469 Huaihai Zhong Lu, **Shanghai** (☎6433 6880; fax 6474 6867). 52 Shisi Wei Lu, **Shenyang** (☎282 0057; visa office 2322 2147; fax 282 0074).

Vietnam: 32 Guanghua Lu, Jianguomenwai, **Beijing** (☎6532 1155; fax 6532 5720). Great Smart Tower, 230 Wan Chai Rd., 15th Fl., Wan Chai, **Hong Kong** (☎2591 4510).

CHINA NATIONAL TOURIST OFFICE

Australia: 44 Market St., 19th Fl., Sydney, NSW 2000 (☎(61) 2 9299 4057; fax 9290 1958; email chinainfo@cnto.org.au; www.cnto.org.au)

Canada: 480 University Ave., Ste. 806, Toronto, ON M5G1V2 (☎(416) 599-6636; fax 599-6382).

Japan: Air China Building, 2-5-2 Toranomon, Minato-Ku, Tokyo (☎3591 8686; fax 3591 6886).

Singapore: 1 Shenton Way, #17-05 Robina House, 068803 (☎221 8681 or 221 8682; fax 221 9267).

United Kingdom: 4 Glentworth St., London NW1 5PG (☎(171) 935 9787; fax 487 4842).

United States: 350 5th Ave., Ste. 6413, **New York, NY** 10118 (☎(212) 760 8218; fax 760 8809; email cntony@aol.com; www.cnto.org); 333 West Broadway, Ste. 201, Glen dale, **CA** 91204 (☎(818) 545 7507; fax 545 7506).

PASSPORTS

REQUIREMENTS. Citizens of Australia, Canada, Ireland, New Zealand, South Africa, the UK, and the US need valid passports to enter China and to re-enter their own countries. China does not allow entrance if the holder's passport expires in under six months; returning home with an expired passport is illegal, and may result in a fine.

PHOTOCOPIES. Be sure to photocopy the page of your passport with your photo, passport number, and other identifying information, as well as any visas, travel insurance policies, plane tickets, or traveler's check serial numbers. Carry one set of copies in a safe place, apart from the originals, and leave another set at home. Consulates also recommend that you carry an expired passport or an official copy of your birth certificate in a part of your baggage separate from other documents. If you are staying in China for a significant length of time, it is a good idea to **regis-**

ESSENTIALS

ter your passport with your embassy. US citizens can register their passports online at the US embassy in Beijing (http://www.usembassy-china.org.cn/english/us-citizen/index.html).

LOST PASSPORTS. If you do lose your passport, immediately notify the local Public Security Bureau (PSB; gōng ān jú; 公安局) and the nearest embassy or consulate of your home government (see p. 48). To expedite its replacement, you will need to know all information previously recorded and show ID and proof of citizenship. In some cases, a replacement may take weeks to process, and it may be valid only for a limited time. Any visas stamped in your old passport will be irretrievably lost. In an emergency, ask for immediate temporary traveling papers that will permit you to re-enter your home country. Your passport is a public document belonging to your nation's government. You may have to surrender it to a foreign government official, but if you don't get it back in a reasonable amount of time, inform the nearest mission of your home country.

NEW PASSPORTS. File any new passport or renewal applications well in advance of your departure date. Most passport offices offer rush services for a steep fee. Contact the nearest passport office in your home country for information on where and how to acquire a new passport. Citizens living abroad who need a passport or renewal should contact the nearest consular service of their home country.

VISAS AND PERMITS

VISAS. As of August 2000, citizens of every country need a visa—a stamp, sticker, or insert in your passport specifying the purpose of your travel and the permitted duration of your stay—in addition to a valid passport for entrance to China. Visas are issued at Chinese consulates and embassies worldwide, and in Hong Kong through numerous travel agencies and even some hotels and guesthouses. Getting a Chinese tourist visa in Hong Kong is both easier and cheaper than getting one abroad (see **Hong Kong: Consulates, Visas, and Immigration,** p. 420).

Tourist visas (type "L") are usually issued for 30 days and are typically valid for a single entry only, although tourist visas for longer stays or for multiple entries are not impossible to obtain. Business ("F"), work ("Z"), and student ("X") visas are also available and generally require a **letter of invitation** from the appropriate Chinese corporation, government office, or educational institution. When applying for a visa, make sure your passport is valid six months beyond the date of your intended return and has several blank pages. For more information on working or studying in China, see **Alternatives to Tourism,** p. 89. Students, teachers, and visiting scholars staying in China for more than nine months and business persons staying for more than a year must submit proof of a negative test result for HIV once they have arrived in China.

In general, you can apply in person or by mail for a visa at a Chinese embassy or consulate; you will need a completed application form, a recent passport-sized photo, a valid passport, and the appropriate visa fee. US citizens can take advantage of the **Center for International Business and Travel** (CIBT; ☎ (800) 925-2428), which secures visas for travel to almost all countries for a variable service charge. Be sure to double-check on entrance requirements at the nearest embassy or Chinese consulate for up-to-date info before departure. US citizens can also consult www.pueblo.gsa.gov/cic_text/travel/foreign/foreignentryreqs.html.

> **Australia:** AUS$30 for a single-entry tourist visa, AUS$45 for a double-entry tourist visa, AUS$60 for a 6-month multiple entry, and AUS$90 for a one-year multiple entry. Mail processing is an additional AUS$10; self-addressed stamped envelope required. Cash, money order, and certified check are the accepted forms of payment. Processing takes 1 week. Rush fees are AUS$30 for 2-3 day service and AUS$50 for next-day service.
>
> **Canada:** CDN$50 for a single-entry tourist visa, CDN$75 for a double-entry tourist visa, CDN$100 for a 6-month multiple-entry business visa, and CDN$150 for a one-year multiple-entry business visa. Mail processing is an additional CDN$21.40; self-addressed

stamped envelope required. Mail applications must be sent directly to: Golden Mile Travel Consultant, 203-1390 Prince of Wales Dr., Ottawa, ON K2C 3K6 (☎(613) 224-6863; fax 224-7863). Cash, money order, and certified check are the accepted forms of payment. Processing takes 5 business days. Rush fees are CDN$35 for 2-day service and CDN$50 for next-day service.

New Zealand: NZ$60 for a single-entry tourist visa, NZ$90 for a double-entry tourist visa. Cash and check are the accepted forms of payment. No additional fee for mail processing if envelope is included. Processing takes 7-10 business days. Rush fees are NZ$40 for 2- to 3-day service and NZ$60 for same-day service.

South Africa: SAR180 for a single-entry/transit tourist visa, SAR360 for a double-entry/transit tourist visa, and SAR540 for a 6-month multiple-entry business visa. Cash or postal order are the accepted forms of payment. A refund will not be available if the application is cancelled or refused. Processing takes 5 business days. Rush fees are SAR60 for 3-day service, SAR120 for 2-day service, and SAR180 for next-day service.

United Kingdom: UK£30 for a 3-month single entry visa, UK£45 for a 3-month double entry visa, UK£60 for a 6-month multiple entry visa, and UK£90 for a one-year multiple entry visa. Mail processing costs an additional UK£20. Cash is the only accepted form of payment. Processing takes 3 business days. Rush fees are UK£15 for next-day service and UK£20 for same-day service.

United States: US$30 for a single-entry visa, US$45 for a double-entry visa, and US$60 for a 6-month multiple-entry business visa. Personal checks are not an accepted form of payment. Mail processing costs an additional US$5 and takes 1 month. Processing takes 5 business days. Rush fees are US$10 for 3-day service, US$20 for 2-day service, and US$30 for same-day service. You can obtain a visa application through a fax-back service. Fax-back machine: New York (212) 868-7761; Washington (202) 265-9809. See also www.nyconsulate.prchina.org/Visa Extensions.

Visa extensions are the domain of the Foreign Affairs section of the Public Security Bureau (PSB) in China (listed in the **Practical Information** section of every city). Depending on where you are, it is usually not a problem to get one visa extension for an additional two weeks to a month. Getting a second extension, however, is more difficult. You might be better off heading to Hong Kong for a few days and getting a new tourist visa there. Whatever you decide, **do not overstay the duration of your visa**—you risk being heavily fined and detained when you depart China.

SPECIAL PERMITS. A scant 20 years ago, much of China was off limits to foreign travelers. These days, almost everywhere is open to tourists, but vestiges of the PRC's policy of travel restrictions still linger. Foreigners will need special **travel permits** to visit certain "sensitive" regions in China, while some areas remain entirely closed. In general, only certain border regions, especially those populated by ethnic minorities, require special permits to visit. The list of areas closed to foreign travelers is in a constant state of flux, and official Beijing policy can often take considerable time to reach the hinterlands of Xinjiang. As a result, if you want to know if you need a travel permit to visit a particular region of the country, the answer is: it depends on who you talk to. Those areas most frequently needing special travel permits are Tibet, Northern Xinjiang, certain wilderness areas and other border regions. Travel permits are issued at the discretion of the Public Security Bureau (PSB), which decides how much they cost and how long they take to process. You may be asked to produce your permit when you check in at a hotel or guesthouse, when you buy air, bus, or train tickets, and during police spot checks in these sensitive areas. The local PSB reserves the right to cancel or modify your permit at any time, so it is best to get to your destination as fast as possible once you've obtained a permit for it.

WORK PERMITS. Admission as a visitor does not include the right to work, which is authorized only by a work permit. For more information on documents needed to work in China, see **Working Abroad**, p. 90. For more information, see Alternatives to Tourism, p. 89.

IDENTIFICATION

When you travel, always carry two or more forms of identification on your person, including at least one photo ID; a passport combined with a driver's license or birth certificate is usually adequate. Never carry all your forms of ID together; split them up in case of theft or loss. It is useful to bring extra passport-size photos to affix to the various IDs or passes you may acquire along the way. Don't ever hand over your passport to people whose authority you question (ask to accompany them to a police station if they insist), and **don't ever let your passport out of your sight.**

STUDENT AND TEACHER IDENTIFICATION. The **International Student Identity Card (ISIC),** the most widely accepted form of student ID, provides discounts on sights, accommodations, food, and transport. However, it is not widely recognized in China. If you can get your hands on a **Chinese student card,** you may be able to avoid the "foreigner's surcharge" (see p. 57) that is sometimes tacked onto museum entrance fees and other travel services in China. Some places in backpacker hangouts such as Yangshuo will offer "classes" to foreigners who will then be given a Chinese student card. Anyone studying legitimately on the mainland, for no matter how short a time, can get one of these red plastic-covered wallet-sized booklets. Forged Chinese student IDs are not unheard of in popular tourist destinations, but the government is clued in to the proliferation of fake student cards among foreign travelers; charlatans are almost always exposed. *Let's Go* does not recommend using fake IDs.

Although the ISIC card is not widely recognized in China, it is not entirely useless for travelers; all cardholders have access to a 24hr. emergency helpline for medical, legal, and financial emergencies (in North America call (877) 370-ISIC, elsewhere call US collect +1 (715) 345-0505), and US cardholders are also eligible for insurance benefits (see **Insurance,** p. 66). Many student travel agencies issue ISICs (see p. 73), including STA Travel in Australia and New Zealand; Travel CUTS in Canada; usit in the Republic of Ireland and Northern Ireland; SASTS in South Africa; Campus Travel and STA Travel in the UK; Council Travel (www.counciltravel.com/idcards/default.asp) and STA Travel in the US. The card is valid from September of one year to December of the following year and costs AUS$15, CDN$15, or US$20. Applicants must be degree-seeking students of a secondary or post-secondary school and must be of at least 12 years of age. Because of the proliferation of fake ISICs, some services (particularly airlines) require additional proof of student identity, such as a school ID or a letter attesting to your student status, signed by your registrar and stamped with your school seal. The **International Teacher Identity Card (ITIC)** offers the same insurance coverage but more limited discounts. The fee is AUS$13, UK£5, or US$20. For more information, contact the **International Student Travel Confederation (ISTC),** Herengracht 479, 1017 BS Amsterdam, Netherlands (☎+31 (20) 421 28 00; fax 421 28 10; email istcinfo@istc.org; www.istc.org).

YOUTH IDENTIFICATION. The International Student Travel Confederation issues a discount card to travelers who are 26 years old or under, but are not students. This one-year **International Youth Travel Card (IYTC;** formerly the **GO 25** Card) offers many of the same benefits as the ISIC. Most organizations that sell the ISIC also sell the IYTC (US$20).

CUSTOMS

Upon entering China, you must declare certain items from abroad and pay a duty on the value of those articles that exceeds the allowance established by China's customs service. Note that goods and gifts purchased at **duty-free** shops abroad are not exempt from duty or sales tax at your point of return and thus must be declared as well; "duty-free" merely means that you need not pay a tax in the country of purchase. Tourists are allowed to bring four bottles of wine or spirits and 600 cigarettes with them into China in addition to their personal belongings. Electronic goods (radios, cameras, etc.) cannot be sold in the PRC if they were imported duty-free for personal use. All gifts and items imported on the behalf of others must be declared and may be charged duty. Movie cameras and videotaping equipment must be declared at customs. Chinese customs has a long list of items prohibited from import and export: fire arms and explosives, Chinese currency, pornographic or political literature, narcotics, infected plants, animals, or food-stuffs, and radio transmitters, to name a few. Furthermore, the Chinese government prohibits the export of valuable cultural relics, rare animals and plants, and precious metals and gems. Antiques (real and imitation) need to be marked with a red wax seal if you wish to bring them out of the country. It is wise to make a list, including serial numbers, of any valuables that you carry with you from home; if you register this list with customs before your departure and have an official stamp it, you will avoid import duty charges and ensure an easy passage upon your return. Be especially careful to document items manufactured abroad.

Upon returning home, you must declare all articles acquired abroad and pay a duty on the value of articles in excess of your home country's allowance. In order to expedite your return, make a list of any valuables brought from home and register them with customs before traveling abroad. Also be sure to keep receipts for all goods acquired abroad. For more information, contact your local customs office.

MONEY

CURRENCY

The standard unit of Chinese currency is the **renminbi** (RMB; "people's currency"), commonly referred to as the **yuan**. The *yuan* is divided into 10 units of *jiao* and 100 units of *fen;* 10 *fen* equals 1 *jiao*. Coins are issued in denominations of 1, 2, and 5 *fen*, 5 *jiao* and 1 *yuan*, with size and weight increasing with value. All coins except the bronze-colored 5 *jiao* are silvery. The smaller *fen* dominations are now rarely used. Paper currency comes in denominations of 1, 2, and 5 *jiao*, along with 1, 2, 5, 10, 50, and 100 *yuan*. Paper bills differ in size based on value. Some vendors try to trick foreign tourists by giving change in the smaller *jiao* rather than the bigger *yuan;* be sure to receive bills of the correct size. Almost all prices in China, as well as those in this book, are posted in *yuan* decimal form (which is equal to RMB). When referring to prices orally, the Chinese usually substitute the colloquial *kuai* for *yuan* and *mao* for jiao. For example, Y5 is pronounced *wu kuai;* Y0.60, *liu mao;* and Y5.61, *wu kuai liu mao yi*.

The currency chart below is based on August 2000 exchange rates between Chinese **renminbi** (RMB) and various countries, including those that share borders with the Middle Kingdom (see **Border Crossings**, p. 78). Check a large newspaper or the web (e.g. finance.yahoo.com or www.bloomberg.com/markets/currency/curr-calc.html) for the latest exchange rates.

EXCHANGE

As a general rule, it's cheaper to convert money in China than abroad. Bring enough foreign currency to last for the first 24 to 72 hours of a trip to avoid being penniless after banking hours or on a holiday. Travelers living in the US can get foreign currency from the comfort of their homes; **International Currency Express** (☎888 842 0880) delivers foreign currency or traveler's checks overnight (US$17) or in two days (US$12) at competitive exchange rates.

In China, Hong Kong, and Macau, you can **change money** at any international airport, many upscale hotels (although the service is sometimes restricted to guests), and most banks, all for pretty competitive rates. Watch out for commission rates and check newspapers for the standard rate of exchange. Banks generally have the best rates. Also, money changers who offer good rates and stay open longer than the banks can be found on the streets of most major cities. However, while there is always a possibility that you will end up with a counterfeit bill or two wherever you exchange money in China, the chances are probably slightly greater on the street than in a bank. A good rule of thumb is only to go to banks or money

US$1 = 8.27 RMB	1 RMB = US$0.12
EUR€1 = 7.92 RMB	1 RMB = EUR€0.13
CDN$1 = 5.61 RMB	1 RMB = CDN$0.18
UK£1 = 12.45 RMB	1 RMB = UK£0.08
IR£1 = 9.99 RMB	1 RMB = IR£0.10
AUS$1 = 4.85 RMB	1 RMB = AUS$0.2
NZ$1 = 3.88 RMB	1 RMB = NZ$0.26
SAR1= 1.18 RMB	1 RMB = SAR0.85
KRW1 (SOUTH KOREAN WON) = 0.70 RMB	1 RMB = KRW 134.81
LAK100 (LAOS NEW KIP) = 0.1 RMB	1 RMB = LAK 913.6
MMK1 (MYANMAR KYAT) = 1.32 RMB	1 RMB = MMK .76
100Đ (VIETNAMESE DONG) = 0.06 RMB	1 RMB = 1701.68Đ
PKR1 (PAKISTANI RUPEE) = 0.159 RMB	1 RMB = PKR 6.28
JPY1 (JAPANESE YEN) = 0.078 RMB	1 RMB = JPY 12.88
RUR1 (RUSSIAN RUBLE) = 0.29 RMB	1 RMB = RUR 3.43
MNT100 (MONGOLIAN TUGRIK) = 0.8 RMB	1 RMB = MNT 126.53

THE CHINESE YUAN (Y)

ESSENTIALS

changers that have at most a 5% margin between their buy and sell prices. Keep the receipt of the transaction; you will need it to convert any leftover Chinese currency you end up with back into your home currency at the end of your trip. Also, using an ATM card or a credit card (see p. 56) often gets you the best rates, although this does not tend to be possible outside major urban centers. In **Hong Kong and Macau,** it should be possible to exchange most major currencies, but in China, bank tellers are more likely to exchange US dollars than other currencies.

In many cases, exchanging foreign currency for Chinese RMB abroad yields a lower return. The best alternative is to change some (but not large amounts of) money prior to leaving and then change remaining amounts at any Bank of China. The Bank of China has a standard transaction fee for all currency and traveler's check exchanges.

Store your money in a variety of forms; ideally, you will at any given time be carrying some cash, some traveler's checks, and an ATM and/or credit card. Travelers should also consider carrying some US dollars, which are often preferred by local tellers. However, avoid using US dollars when possible; throwing dollars around for preferential treatment may be offensive, and it can attract thieves.

TRAVELER'S CHECKS

Exchange rates for traveler's checks are actually more favorable than those for cash in China, making traveler's checks the preferred way to carry money on the mainland. There is only one drawback: although traveler's checks are easily exchanged at most banks and upscale hotels, they are not generally accepted at budget hotels and guesthouses, restaurants, or sights.

American Express and **Visa** are the most recognized types of traveler's checks. Several agencies and banks sell them for a small commission. Each agency provides refunds if your checks are lost or stolen, and many provide additional services, such as toll-free refund hotlines abroad, emergency message services, and stolen credit card assistance.

Never countersign checks until you're ready to cash them, and always bring your passport with you to cash them. If your checks are lost or stolen, immediately contact a refund center (of the company that issued your checks) to be reimbursed; they may require a police report verifying the loss or theft. Ask about toll-free refund hotlines and the location of refund centers when purchasing checks, and always carry emergency cash.

ESSENTIALS

American Express: Call (800) 251 902 in Australia; in New Zealand (0800) 441 068; in the UK (0800) 521 313; in the US and Canada (800) 221-7282. Elsewhere, call US collect +1 (801) 964-6665; www.aexp.com. Checks can be purchased for a small fee (1-4%) at American Express Travel Service offices, banks, and American Automobile Association (AAA) offices. American Express offices cash their checks commission-free (except where prohibited by national governments), but often at slightly worse rates than banks. *Cheques for Two* can be signed by either of 2 people traveling together. American Express has offices in Beijing (☎8610 6505 2228 or 6505 2639), Chengdu, Guangzhou (☎8620 8331 1771), Guilin, Hangzhou, Hong Kong, Macau, Nanjing, Ningbo, Shanghai (☎8621 6279 8082), Tianjin, Xiamen, and Xian.

Citicorp: In the US and Canada call (800) 645-6556; in Europe, the Middle East, or Africa call the UK +44 (020) 7508 7007; elsewhere call US collect +1 (813) 623-1709. Traveler's checks available in 7 currencies at 1-2% commission. Call 24hr.

Thomas Cook MasterCard: From the US or Canada call (800) 223-7373; from the UK call (0800) 622 101; from elsewhere, call collect 44 (01733) 318 950. Checks available in 13 currencies. Commission 2%. Thomas Cook offices cash checks commission-free and have locations in Beijing, Hong Kong, and Shanghai, as well as in Banks of China all over the mainland.

Visa: In the US call (800) 227-6811; in the UK call (0800) 89 50 78; elsewhere call UK collect +44 (01733) 31 89 49. Call for the location of their nearest office.. As with Thomas Cook MasterCard, their traveler's checks can be exchanged at any Bank of China.

CREDIT CARDS

Credit cards are accepted almost everywhere in Hong Kong and Macau, but only in fancy hotels and restaurants in China. Major credit cards—**MasterCard** and **Visa** are the most often welcomed—can be used in most of China to obtain cash advances (in local currency) from certain banks and teller machines. Credit card companies get the wholesale exchange rate, which is generally 5% better than the retail rate used by banks and other currency exchange establishments. **American Express** cards also work in some ATMs, as well as at AmEx offices and major airports.

Credit cards may also offer services such as insurance or emergency help, and are sometimes required to reserve hotel rooms or rental cars. However, budget travelers will probably find that few of the establishments they frequent will accept credit cards; aside from the occasional splurge, you will probably reserve use of your credit card for financial emergencies.

Credit cards are also useful for **cash advances,** which allow you to withdraw *yuan* from associated banks and ATMs throughout China. However, transaction fees for all credit card advances (up to US$10 per advance, plus 2-3% extra on foreign transactions after conversion) tend to make credit cards a more costly way of withdrawing cash than ATMs or traveler's checks. In an emergency, however, the transaction fee may prove worth the cost. To be eligible for an advance, you'll need to get a **Personal Identification Number (PIN)** from your credit card company (see **Cash (ATM) Cards,** p. 56). Be sure to check with your credit card company before you leave home, though; some companies have started to charge a foreign transaction fee.

CREDIT CARD COMPANIES. Visa (US ☎(800) 336-8472) and **MasterCard** (US ☎(800) 307-7309) are issued in cooperation with banks and other organizations. **American Express** (US ☎(800) 843-2273) has an annual fee of up to US$55. AmEx cardholders may cash personal checks at AmEx offices abroad, access an emergency medical and legal assistance hotline (24hr.; in North America call (800) 554-2639, elsewhere call US collect +1 (202) 554-2639), and enjoy American Express Travel Service benefits (including plane, hotel, and car rental reservation changes; baggage loss and flight insurance; mailgram and international cable services; and held mail). The **Discover Card** (in US call (800) 347-2683, elsewhere call US +1 (801) 902-3100) is not readily accepted in China.

ESSENTIALS

CASH CARDS (ATM CARDS)

While it should be no problem finding **ATMs** (Automated Teller Machines) that accept foreign ATM cards in Hong Kong and Macau, most ATMs on the mainland take only cards issued by Chinese banks. In Hong Kong (and Macau to a lesser extent) nearly every ATM is linked to an international money network, like Cirrus, PLUS, NYCE, Maestro, Global Access, and many others. Travelers who are going to be in China for an extended time period and wish to carry less local currency with them should consider opening a local account at the Bank of China or another Chinese bank and getting a domestic ATM card that can be used in many mid- to large-sized Chinese cities. All you need is a passport and valid tourist visa. ATMs get the same wholesale exchange rate as credit cards, but there is often a limit on the amount of money you can withdraw per day (around US$500), and unfortunately computer networks sometimes fail. There is typically also a surcharge of US$1-5 per withdrawal. Be sure to memorize your PIN code in numeric form since machines elsewhere often don't have letters on their keys. Also, if your PIN is longer than four digits, ask your bank whether you need a new number.

The two major international money networks are **Cirrus** (US ☎(800) 424-7787) and **PLUS** (US ☎(800) 843-7587). To locate ATMs around the world, call the above numbers, or consult either www.visa.com/pd/atm or www.mastercard.com/atm.

Visa TravelMoney (for customer assistance in China, dial the AT&T access code (10811) and then call toll-free (800) 847-2399) is a system allowing you to access money from any Visa ATM. You deposit an amount before you travel (plus a small administration fee), and you can withdraw up to that sum. The cards, which give you the same favorable exchange rate for withdrawals as a regular Visa, are especially useful if you plan to travel through many countries. Check with your local bank to see if it issues TravelMoney cards. **Road Cash** (US ☎(877) 762-3227; www.roadcash.com) issues cards in the US with a minimum US$300 deposit.

To report lost ATM cards, call collect to Singapore (English ☎(108 650) 345 1345, Chinese ☎(108 650) 336 9586) or Hong Kong (☎(108 852) 2810 8033).

GETTING MONEY FROM HOME

AMERICAN EXPRESS. Cardholders can withdraw cash from their checking accounts at any of AmEx's major offices and many representative offices (up to US$1000 every 21 days; no service charge, no interest). AmEx "Express Cash" withdrawals from any AmEx ATM in China are automatically debited from the cardholder's checking account or line of credit. Green card holders may withdraw up to US$1000 in any seven-day period (2% transaction fee; minimum US$2.50, maximum US$20). To enroll in Express Cash, cardmembers may call (800) 227-4669 in the US; elsewhere call the US collect +1 (336) 668-5041. The AmEx national number in China is toll-free (61) 29 271 8691.

WESTERN UNION. Travelers from the US, Canada, and the UK can wire money abroad through Western Union's international money transfer services. In the US, call (800) 325-6000; in Canada, (800) 235-0000; in the UK, (0800) 833 833; in China, toll-free (10) 6318 4313. Although the service is rather expensive, money can be transferred instantly to Beihai, Beijing, Changzhou, Changle, Changsha, Chengdu, Chongqing, Dalian, Dandong, Fushun, Fuqing, Fuzhou, Guangzhou, Guilin, Haikou, Hangzhou, Harbin, He Yuan, Hohhot, Hong Kong, Jingmen, Jingzhou, Jiujiang, Kunming, Lhasa, Liuzhou, Nantong, Nanjing, Nanning, Ping Xiang, Putian, Qingdao, Shanghai, Shenzhen, Suzhou, Taiyuan, Ürümqi, Wenzhou, Wuhan, Wuxi, Wuzhou, Xiamen, Xian, Yangzhou, Yichang, Yingkou, Yulin, and Zhenjiang. Except in Hong Kong where a variety of money changers and travel services receive the wire, the service is usually handled by the local post office or EMS (Express Mail Service) office. Look for foreign remittance windows in the main post offices of these cities. The rates for sending cash are generally US$10-11 cheaper than with a credit card, and the money is usually available at the place you're sending it to within an hour. To locate the nearest Western Union location to you, consult www.westernunion.com.

US STATE DEPARTMENT (US CITIZENS ONLY). In dire emergencies only, the US State Department will forward money within hours to the nearest consular office, which will then disburse it for a US$15 fee. Contact the Overseas Citizens Service, American Citizens Services, Consular Affairs, Room 4811, US Department of State, Washington, D.C. 20520 (☎(202) 647-5225; nights, Sundays, and holidays 647-4000; http://travel.state.gov).

FEDERAL EXPRESS. Some people choose to send money abroad in cash via FedEx to avoid transmission fees and taxes. While FedEx is reasonably reliable, note that this method is illegal. In the US and Canada, FedEx can be reached by calling (800) 463-3339; in the UK, (0800) 123 800; in Ireland, (800) 535 800; in Australia, 13 26 10; in New Zealand, (0800) 733 339; and in South Africa, (021) 551 7610. In China, FedEx dropoff locations are available in Beijing (☎8610 6434 8448), Shanghai, and Hong Kong.

COSTS

TIERED PRICING SYSTEM. China is gradually getting rid of the government-sanctioned tiered pricing system that has for so long charged foreigners (i.e. non-Chinese) more than overseas Chinese, and overseas Chinese more than mainlanders, for transportation, accommodations, and admission to sights. The remnants of this system are the admission prices levied at many of the most popular sights in the country, which still charge foreigners one-and-a half or two times more than Chinese.

The cost of your trip to China will vary considerably, depending on where you go, how you travel, and where you stay. The single biggest cost of your trip will probably be your round-trip (return) **airfare** to China (see p. 72). The average income and cost of living in China are much lower than in the West, but this doesn't always translate into cheap accommodations and transportation for travelers. A dorm bed in Yangshuo runs a mere US$2 a night, but the cheapest accommodations in Tianjin (and the other booming coastal cities) start at US$15 to US$20. Some hotels or hostels also may not accept foreigners. A bare-bones day in China (camping or sleeping in hostels/guesthouses, buying food at supermarkets) would cost about US$15 to US $20 per day in regions such as Yunnan, Guangxi, Tibet, Sichuan, Gansu, and Xinjiang and around US$30 on the Eastern coast; a slightly more comfortable day (sleeping in hostels/guesthouses and the occasional budget hotel, eating one meal a day at a restaurant, going out at night) would run US$30-40 in the above mentioned regions and US$40-50 for the East coast; and for a luxurious day, the sky's the limit. Don't forget to factor in emergency reserve funds (at least US$200) when planning how much money you'll need.

TIPS FOR STAYING ON A BUDGET. Considering that saving just a few dollars a day over the course of your trip might pay for days or weeks of additional travel, the art of penny-pinching is well worth learning. Learn to take advantage of freebies: for example, cities often host free open-air **concerts**, **movies** and/or **cultural events** (especially in the summer). When at all possible, do your **laundry** in the sink (unless you're explicitly prohibited from doing so), and split **accommodations** costs (in hotels and some hostels) with trustworthy fellow travelers; multi-bed rooms almost always work out cheaper per person than singles. The same principle will also work for cutting down on the cost of **restaurant** meals. Though supermarkets are an up and coming thing in China, your best bet for cheap eats is the endless array of food stalls on many Chinese streets.

TIPPING AND BARGAINING. Tipping is still very uncommon in China, Hong Kong, and Macau. In China, don't feel obligated to tip anyone—they shouldn't expect you to. The same thing goes in Hong Kong and Macau, except in the fanciest of hotels.

While tipping is rare in Asia, **bargaining** for goods and services is commonplace. Except in large department and grocery stores, expensive boutiques, and foreign shops and restaurants, you can expect to bargain for what you buy in China, Hong Kong, and Macau, where street merchants immediately raise prices at the mere scent of a *laowai* (foreigner). Travelers to China should make an attempt to learn the basics of bargaining etiquette, both in order to conduct themselves courteously in a foreign culture and to prevent unwittingly paying too much. As a rule of thumb, if there is no set price given, it is almost certainly negotiable, and even if there is a set price, it may well be negotiable too. This is true whether you're buying souvenirs, ordering dumplings at a food stall, checking into a guesthouse, or hiring a guide to take you sightseeing.

Above all, **be polite.** Bargaining should be more like a fencing match than a barroom brawl, with less brute force and more decorous finesse. Levity, a smile, and good intentions may prove to be your best weapons. Never let your emotions show, no matter how much you may want something. The trick to bargaining, as with many civilized sports, is the ability to bluff convincingly. Many travelers to China bank on the "50% rule," meaning that a bargainer should cut the original price of the item in half and then begin bargaining from there. To see just how low a hawker will go, bargain a little bit (enough to get their attention) and then act as though you really don't want the trinket in question and start to walk away. More often than not, the vendor will give in and offer you a reasonable price (and if not, they probably weren't willing to go lower!). A word of warning: bargaining when you don't intend to buy is an absolute no-no, especially with minority cultures such as those in Tibet. Losing sight of the value of money—and the traveler's place in the world economy—can ruin the bargaining experience and appear downright disgraceful. Cut-throat bargaining to a rock bottom price may result in a temporary sense of satisfaction, but often at the expense of the seller's losing face. When settling on a final price, try to keep some perspective; consider the hours of work and/or the talent that goes into making what you're buying and think about how much an item or service would cost in your own country.

SAFETY AND SECURITY

EMERGENCY!	**110** for police (PSB) **119** in case of fire **120** to call an ambulance

PERSONAL SECURITY

EXPLORING. Familiarize yourself with your surroundings before setting out, and carry yourself with confidence. Be sure someone at home knows your itinerary, and **never admit that you're traveling alone.** At night, stick to busy, well-lit streets and avoid dark alleyways. Do not cross through parks or other large, deserted areas. If you feel uncomfortable, leave as quickly and directly as you can, but don't allow fear of the unknown to turn you into a hermit.

TRANSPORTATION. Although the national **train** system is safe mechanically, one should be wary of long-distance **buses.** Old or low-quality equipment, dangerous road conditions, and reckless drivers can make for risky journeys. Look at your bus before you buy your ticket—if a vehicle looks unsafe, it very likely is. Public city buses, which tend to be overcrowded and (sometimes) recklessly driven, also may be more dangerous than those you are accustomed to at home.

Let's Go does not recommend **hitchhiking** under any circumstances, particularly for women—see **Women Travelers** (<u>p. 84</u>) for more information.

Avoid **driving** altogether in China. If you can get past the expensive bureaucracy of obtaining a driving permit (see p. 84), you will find yourself coping with poor road conditions in rural areas or clogged, chaotic streets in cities.

CRIME AND TERRORISM. Terrorist activity is not a significant problem in China. There have been a small number of bombings in recent years, all of them presumably the work of ethnic (largely Uighur) separatist groups and disgruntled unemployed workers, but foreigners have not been deliberately targeted. The violent crime rate is also low by international standards, and it is rare for foreigners to be targets of such crimes. Property crimes are another issue altogether: rising unemployment and economic transitions have hit certain sectors of the population hard, and presumably affluent foreign tourists are obvious targets for theft.

SELF DEFENSE. There is no sure-fire way to avoid all the threatening situations you might encounter, but a good self-defense course will give you concrete ways to react to unwanted advances. **Impact, Prepare,** and **Model Mugging** can refer you to local self-defense courses in the US (☎(800) 345-5425) and Vancouver (☎(604) 878-3838). Workshops (2-3hr.) start at US$50; full courses run US$350-500.

> **TRAVEL ADVISORIES.** The following government offices provide travel information and advisories by telephone, by fax, or via the web:
>
> **Australian Department of Foreign Affairs and Trade:** ☎(2) 6261 1111; www.dfat.gov.au.
>
> **Canadian Department of Foreign Affairs and International Trade (DFAIT):** In Canada call (800) 267-6788; elsewhere call +1 (613) 944-6788; www.dfait-maeci.gc.ca. Ask for their free booklet, *Bon Voyage...But*.
>
> **New Zealand Ministry of Foreign Affairs:** ☎(04) 494 8500; fax 494 8511; www.mft.govt.nz/trav.html.
>
> **United Kingdom Foreign and Commonwealth Office:** ☎(020) 7238 4503; fax 7238 4545; www.fco.gov.uk.
>
> **US Department of State:** ☎(202) 647-5225, auto faxback (202) 647-3000; http://travel.state.gov. For *A Safe Trip Abroad*, call (202) 512-1800.

FINANCIAL SECURITY

PROTECTING YOUR VALUABLES. Bring as little with you as possible. Buy a few combination **padlocks** to secure your belongings either in your pack—which you should **never leave unattended**—or in a hostel. Carry as little cash as possible; carry traveler's checks and ATM/credit cards, keeping them in a **money belt**—not a "fanny pack"—along with your passport and ID cards. Fourth, keep a small cash reserve separate from your primary stash. This should entail about US$50 (US dollars are best) sewn into or stored in the depths of your pack, along with your traveler's check numbers and important photocopies.

Keep your valuables secure at all times. Economic transitions in China and growing inequalities in wealth mean that the rate of property crimes has risen dramatically in recent years. Property crimes tend to be most prevalent in areas where travelers congregate; be particularly careful in train and bus stations and at major tourist sites. Never count your money in public. If you carry a hand bag, buy a sturdy one with a secure clasp, and carry it crosswise on the side, away from the street with the clasp against you. Secure packs with combination padlocks that slip through the two zippers. Even these precautions do not always suffice; motorcycle riders have been known to cut the straps off passing travelers' handbags.

CON ARTISTS AND PICKPOCKETS. Among the more prevalent aspects of many Chinese cities are **con artists.** They often work in groups, and children are among the most effective. They possess an innumerable range of ruses: sob stories that require money, rolls of bills "found" on the street, drinks spilled (or saliva spit) onto your shoulder to distract you while they snatch your bag. Don't let your bag out of sight; never trust a "station porter" who insists on carrying your bag or stowing it in the baggage compartment or a "new friend" who offers to guard your bag while you buy a train ticket or use the restroom. Beware of **pickpockets** in city crowds, especially on public transportation. If someone stands uncomfortably close, move to another car and hold your bags tightly; some pickpockets slash bags with knives and then remove their contents.

ESSENTIALS

ACCOMMODATIONS AND TRANSPORTATION. Be particularly careful on **buses** and **trains;** theft is common on long journeys (thieves often wait for travelers to fall asleep). Carry your daypack in front of you where you can see it. When traveling with others, sleep in alternate shifts. When alone, use a lock to secure your pack to the luggage rack. Try to sleep on top bunks with your luggage stored above you (if not in bed with you), and keep important documents and other valuables on your person at all times (even when using the bathroom).

In general, hotels in China are safe and secure. Many have an attendant on every floor, and almost all have safes where you can store valuables for free or for a minimal charge. Dormitory rooms are the least secure in most hotels; avoid leaving your belongings unattended, and always store your valuables in a secure place.

DRUGS AND ALCOHOL

Penalties concerning the possession, use, or trafficking of **illegal drugs** are steep— drug dealers and smugglers are regularly sentenced to death—and strictly enforced. Remember that you are subject to the laws (and the penalties) of the country in which you travel, not to those of your home country, and it is your responsibility to familiarize yourself with these laws before leaving. If you carry **prescription drugs** while you travel, it is vital to have a copy of the prescriptions themselves and a note from a doctor; keep these readily accessible whenever you cross national borders. **Avoid public drunkenness;** it can get you in trouble with the authorities very quickly and jeopardize your safety and earn the disdain of locals.

HEALTH

Common sense is the simplest prescription for good health while you travel. Travelers complain most often about their feet and their gut, so take precautionary measures: drink lots of fluids to prevent dehydration and constipation, wear sturdy, broken-in shoes and clean socks, and use talcum powder to keep your feet dry. To minimize the effects of jet lag, "reset" your body's clock by adopting the time of your destination as soon as you board the plane.

BEFORE YOU GO

In your **passport,** write the names of any people you wish to have contacted in case of a medical emergency, and also list any **allergies** or medical conditions of which you would want doctors to be aware. Allergy sufferers might want to obtain a full supply of any necessary medication before the trip. Matching a prescription to a Chinese equivalent is not always easy, safe, or possible. Carry up-to-date, legible prescriptions or a statement from your doctor stating the medication's trade name, manufacturer, chemical name, and dosage. While traveling, be sure to keep all medication with you in your carry-on luggage.

IMMUNIZATIONS. Take a look at your immunization records before you go. Travelers over two years old should be sure that the following vaccines are up to date: MMR (for measles, mumps, and rubella); DTaP or Td (for diptheria, tetanus, and pertussis); OPV (for polio); HbCV (for haemophilus influenza B); and HBV (for hepatitus B). Adults should consider an additional dose of Polio vaccine if they have not already had one during their adult years. **Hepatitis A vaccine** and/or immune globulin (IG), as well as the **Hepatitis B vaccine** is recommended for travelers to China. An inoculation against **Japanese Encephalitis** is recommended for summer travelers or visitors planning to stay longer than two weeks in rural areas. If you will be spending more than four weeks in the country, you also should consider being vaccinated for **typhoid.** For recommendations on immunizations and prophylaxis, consult the CDC (see below) in the US or the equivalent in your home country, and be sure to check with a doctor for guidance.

USEFUL ORGANIZATIONS AND PUBLICATIONS. The US **Centers for Disease Control and Prevention** (**CDC;** ☎ (877) FYI-TRIP; www.cdc.gov/travel) is an excellent source of information for travelers and maintains an international fax information

INOCULATION REQUIREMENTS AND RECOMMENDATIONS
No vaccinations are required to travel to China, except yellow fever if arriving from infected areas (parts of tropical South America and sub-Saharan Africa). Vaccines against measles, diptheria, tetanus, polio, Hepatitis A, and Hepatitis B are all recommended.

service. The CDC's comprehensive booklet *Health Information for International Travelers*, an annual rundown of disease, immunization, and general health advice, is free on the website or US$22 via the Government Printing Office (☎ (202) 512-1800). The **US State Department** (http://travel.state.gov) compiles Consular Information Sheets on health, entry requirements, and other issues for China (and other countries). For quick information on health and other travel warnings, call the **Overseas Citizens' Services** (☎ (202) 647-5225; after-hours 647-4000), contact a US passport agency or a US embassy or consulate abroad, or send a self-addressed, stamped envelope to the Overseas Citizens' Services, Bureau of Consular Affairs, #4811, US Department of State, Washington, D.C. 20520. For information on medical evacuation services and travel insurance firms, see http://travel.state.gov/medical.html. The **British Foreign and Commonwealth Office** also gives health warnings for individual countries (www.fco.gov.uk).

For detailed information on travel health, including a country-by-country overview of diseases, try the **International Travel Health Guide,** Stuart Rose, MD (Travel Medicine, US$20; www.travmed.com). For general health info, contact the **American Red Cross** (☎ (800) 564-1234).

MEDICAL ASSISTANCE ON THE ROAD. Pharmacies, indicated by green crosses, abound in the larger cities. Few are open 24hr. and few pharmacists speak English. The selection of both local and imported brands of pharmaceuticals has increased in recent years, but you may still want to bring your own supplies. In an emergency, head to the nearest major hospital, which is almost certainly open all night and has an in-house pharmacy. Outside the big cities, the going is a bit rougher, although every major town should have at least one pharmacy.

The quality of China's **hospitals** and other medical services varies by region. Major metropolitan centers typically have better facilities than rural areas, but even so, hospital accommodations tend to be basic, and medical technology is not up-to-date. While most doctors and nurses are trained and competent professionals, they often do not speak English. You may have to struggle with charades and use the handy **Phrasebook** (see p. 758). **Expect to pay cash on the spot for treatment.** Foreigners are often charged more than Chinese for medical services, but the

IS THERE A DOCTOR IN THE HOUSE? If a bug hits you in Hohhot or bites you in Baoshan, you will want tender loving care, and you will want it quickly. Unfortunately, Chinese hospitals are not always the nicest to visit. Finding your way to a hospital in any decent-sized city should not be difficult; there are usually several scattered around the city center and its periphery. Once there, the first step is to *guà hào* (挂号; "to take a number"). By paying a fee of Y3.5-5, you will be given a hospital-specific record book, a prescription form to be filled out by the doctor, and a number for the department to which you must report. You and countless other patients will all be seen in rapid succession by a physician, who will *usually* take the time to listen to a thorough explanation of your symptoms before scribbling out your prescriptions. While tenderness and love may be in short supply, the care you receive is likely to be competent. You must pay for your medicine at the cashier's desk before collecting it at the pharmacy. Pills and lotions manufactured by the hospital are often quite inexpensive (only Y2-4); externally manufactured drugs can run into the Y30 range. Make sure you know how and when to take each medicine; when in doubt, return to the doctor who saw you to ask for an explanation.

costs are still considerably cheaper than in most developed nations. For non-emergency care, you can contact your embassy and ask for a suggested list of doctors.

If you are concerned about accessing medical support while traveling, there are special support services you can employ. The *MedPass* from **Global Emergency Medical Services (GEMS)**, 2001 Westside Dr., #120, Alpharetta, GA 30004, USA (☎(800) 860-1111; fax (770) 475-0058; www.globalems.com), provides 24hr. international medical assistance, support, and medical evacuation resources. The **International Association for Medical Assistance to Travelers** (**IAMAT;** US ☎(716) 754-4883, Canada ☎(416) 652-0137, New Zealand ☎(03) 352 2053; www.sentex.net/~iamat) has free membership, lists English-speaking doctors worldwide, and offers detailed info on immunization requirements and sanitation. If your regular **insurance** policy does not cover travel abroad, consider purchasing additional coverage (see p. 66).

Those with medical conditions (diabetes, allergies to antibiotics, epilepsy, heart conditions) may want to obtain a stainless steel **Medic Alert** ID tag (first-year US$35, $15 annually thereafter), which identifies the condition and gives a 24hr. collect-call number. Contact the Medic Alert Foundation, 2323 Colorado Ave., Turlock, CA 95382, USA (☎(800) 825-3785; www.medicalert.org).

ONCE THERE

ENVIRONMENTAL HAZARDS

Air quality: A disproportionate number of the world's most polluted cities are in China. Most of the country burns coal for heat in the winter, and industrial emissions tend to be alarmingly high. This situation will aggravate existing respiratory problems such as allergies and asthma and will often create new problems in healthy travelers. If you suffer from respiratory difficulties, be certain to take inhalers and/or any prescription medication with you, and consult with your doctor for advice before departure.

Heat exhaustion and dehydration: All areas of China, particularly the deserts of the northwest and the subtropical areas of the south and southwest, can be brutally hot in the summer. Heat exhaustion, characterized by dehydration and salt deficiency, can lead to fatigue, headaches, and wooziness. Avoid heat exhaustion by drinking plenty of clear fluids, eating salty foods (e.g. crackers), and avoiding dehydrating beverages (e.g. alcohol, coffee, tea, and caffeinated soda). Wear a hat, sunglasses, and a lightweight long-sleeved shirt in hot sun, and take time to acclimate to the heat before seriously exerting yourself. Continuous heat stress can eventually lead to **heatstroke,** characterized by rising body temperature, severe headache, and cessation of sweating. Victims should be cooled off with wet towels and taken to a doctor.

Sunburn: If you're prone to sunburn, bring sunscreen with you (it's hard to find in many parts of China) and apply it liberally and often to avoid burns and risk of skin cancer. If you are planning on spending time near water, in the desert, or in the snow, you are at risk of getting burned, even through clouds. If you get sunburned, drink more fluids than usual and apply Calamine or an aloe-based lotion. The dangers of sunburn are especially acute in high elevation areas.

Hypothermia and frostbite: A rapid drop in body temperature is the clearest sign of overexposure to cold. Victims may also shiver, feel exhausted, have poor coordination or slurred speech, hallucinate, or suffer amnesia. Seek medical help, and *do not let hypothermia victims fall asleep*—if their body temperature gets too low they may die. To avoid hypothermia, keep dry, wear layers, and stay out of the wind. When the temperature is below freezing, watch for **frostbite.** If a region of skin turns white, waxy, and cold, do not rub the area. Drink warm beverages, get dry, and slowly warm the area with dry fabric or steady body contact until a doctor can be found. **In China, you will need to be particularly careful on long-distance bus rides;** faulty heaters and mechanical breakdowns can be deadly in cold weather or at high elevations at all times of the year.

High altitude: Travelers to high altitudes, particularly Tibet, must allow their bodies a couple of days to adjust to lower oxygen levels before exerting themselves. Alcohol is more potent at high elevations. High altitudes mean that ultraviolet rays are stronger, as well, and the risk of sunburn is therefore greater, even in cold weather. For more information on **Acute Mountain Sickness** (AMS, also called altitude sickness), see p. 725.

INSECT-BORNE DISEASES

Many diseases are transmitted by insects—mainly mosquitoes, fleas, ticks, and lice. Be aware of insects in wet or forested areas, especially while hiking and camping. **Mosquitoes** are most active from dusk to dawn. To stop the itch after being bitten, try Calamine lotion or topical cortisones (like Cortaid), or take a bath with a half-cup of baking soda or oatmeal. **Ticks**—responsible for Lyme and other diseases—can be particularly dangerous in rural and forested regions. Pause periodically while walking to brush off ticks (use a fine-toothed comb on your neck and scalp). Do not try to remove ticks by burning them or coating them with nail polish remover or petroleum jelly.

Malaria: Transmitted by *Anopheles* mosquitoes that bite at night. The incubation period varies from 6-8 days to as long as months. Early symptoms include fever, chills, aches, and fatigue, followed by high fever and sweating, sometimes with vomiting and diarrhea. See a doctor for any flu-like sickness that occurs after travel in a risk area. Left untreated, malaria can cause anemia, kidney failure, coma, and death. It is an especially serious threat to pregnant women. To reduce the risk of contracting malaria, use mosquito repellent, particularly in the evenings and when visiting forested areas, and take oral prophylactics, like **mefloquine** (sold under the name Lariam) or **doxycycline** (ask your doctor for a prescription). Be aware that these drugs can have very serious side effects, including slowed heart rate and nightmares. Risk is greatest in rural areas, so if hiking or staying overnight in certain areas, take weekly anti-malarial drugs. The type of drug you should take depends upon the strain of malaria present in the region you are travelling to; chloroquine is generally recommended for travelers to areas that do not have chloroquine-resistant malaria, while mefloquine is recommended for travelers to areas that do (most of southern China, especially Hainan Island, Guangxi, and Yunnan). See also **Malaria Risk** below.

MALARIA RISK Malaria is a risk in most rural areas in China, with the notable exceptions of Heilongjiang, Qinghai, Tibet, and the northern provinces bordering Mongolia. For travelers visiting cities and popular tourist destinations, the risk is generally very small, and anti-malarial medication is usually not needed. In Guangdong, Guangxi, Yunnan, and Hainan Island, malaria infection is a year-round risk; most of the Yangzi River region and Sichuan is at risk from May to December; north of this area, risk of infection is only from July to November.

Dengue fever: An "urban viral infection" transmitted by *Aedes* mosquitoes, which bite during the day rather than at night. Dengue has flu-like symptoms and is often indicated by a rash 3-4 days after the onset of fever. Symptoms for the first 2-4 days include chills, high fever, headaches, swollen lymph nodes, muscle aches, and in some instances, a pink rash on the face. If you experience these symptoms, see a doctor, drink plenty of liquids, and take fever-reducing medication such as acetaminophen (Tylenol). *Never take aspirin to treat dengue fever.* Risk is greatest in Southern China, although it is rarely prevalent at elevations greater than 1200m (4000ft.).

Japanese encephalitis: Another mosquito-borne disease, most prevalent during the rainy season in rural areas near rice fields and livestock pens. Although Japanese Encephalitis does occur throughout rural areas in both temperate and tropical regions of China, the risk of becoming infected while traveling is generally small. Aside from delirium, most symptoms are flu-like: chills, headache, fever, vomiting, muscle fatigue. Since the disease carries a high mortality rate, it's vital to go to a hospital as soon as any symptoms appear. While the JE-VAX vaccine, usually given in 3 shots over a 30-day period, is effective for a year, it has been associated with serious side effects. According to the CDC, there is little chance of being infected if proper precautions are taken, such as using mosquito repellents containing DEET and sleeping under mosquito nets. In China, transmission season generally lasts through the summer and the fall.

Other insect-borne diseases: Filariasis is a roundworm infestation transmitted by mosquitoes. Infection causes enlargement of extremities and has no vaccine. In scattered, localized areas of China, **the plague** and **relapsing fever,** which are transmitted through fleas and ticks, still occur. The risk to travelers, however, is generally quite low. Treatment is available for both, and a vaccine can prevent the plague.

ESSENTIALS

FOOD- AND WATER-BORNE DISEASES

Prevention is the best cure: be sure that everything you eat is cooked properly and that the water you drink is clean. **In all parts of China, you should never drink unbottled water which you have not treated yourself.** Buy bottled water, or purify your own water by bringing it to a rolling boil or treating it with **iodine tablets.** In risk areas, don't brush your teeth with tap water or rinse your toothbrush under the faucet, and keep your mouth closed in the shower. Ice cubes are just as dangerous as impure water in liquid form.

The food in China is generally safe to eat. Beware, however, of salads and uncooked vegetables (including lettuce and coleslaw), which are full of untreated water. Other culprits are raw shellfish, unpasteurized milk, and sauces containing raw eggs. Peel all fruits and vegetables yourself, and beware of watermelon, which is sometimes injected with impure water. Watch out for food from markets or street vendors that may have been washed in dirty water or fried in rancid cooking oil. Always wash your hands before eating, or bring a quick-drying purifying liquid hand cleaner like Purrell. Your bowels will say *xie xie*.

■ **Traveler's diarrhea:** Results from drinking untreated water or eating uncooked foods; a temporary (and fairly common) reaction to the bacteria in new food ingredients. By far the most common illness among travelers in China. Symptoms include nausea, bloating, urgency, and malaise. Try quick-energy, non-sugary foods with protein and carbohydrates to keep your strength up. Over-the-counter anti-diarrheals (e.g. Imodium) may counteract the problems, but can complicate serious infections. The most dangerous side effect is dehydration; drink 8oz. of water with ½ tsp. of sugar or honey and a pinch of salt, try uncaffeinated soft drinks, or munch on salted crackers. If you develop a fever or your symptoms don't go away after 4-5 days, consult a doctor. Consult a doctor for treatment of diarrhea in children, as the treatment is different.

Cholera: An intestinal disease caused by a bacteria found in contaminated food. Symptoms include diarrhea, dehydration, vomiting, and muscle cramps. See a doctor immediately; if left untreated, it may be deadly. Antibiotics are available, but the most important treatment is rehydration. Consider getting a (50% effective) vaccine if you have stomach problems (e.g. ulcers) or will be living where the water is not reliable. The risk is low for travelers to China, especially if food and water precautions are observed.

Hepatitis A: (distinct from B and C, see below) A viral infection of the liver acquired primarily through contaminated water, ice, shellfish, or unpeeled fruits, and vegetables, as well as from sexual contact. Symptoms include fatigue, fever, loss of appetite, nausea, dark urine, jaundice, vomiting, aches and pains, and light stools. Ask your doctor about the vaccine called Havrix, or ask to get an injection of immune globulin (IG; formerly called gamma globulin). Risk is high in China, especially in rural areas and the countryside; it is also present in urban areas.

Parasites: Microbes, tapeworms, etc. that hide in unsafe water and food. **Giardiasis,** for example, is acquired by drinking untreated water from streams or lakes (see p. 725). Symptoms of parasitic infections include swollen glands or lymph nodes, fever, rashes or itchiness, digestive problems, eye problems, and anemia. Boil water, wear shoes, avoid bugs, and eat only cooked food.

Shistosomiasis: Also known as bilharzia; a parasitic disease caused when the larvae of flatworm penetrate unbroken skin. Risk is present in Southern China. Symptoms include an itchy localized rash, followed in 4-6 weeks by fever, fatigue, painful urination, diarrhea, loss of appetite, night sweats, and a hive-like rash on the body. If exposed to untreated water, rub the area vigorously with a towel and apply rubbing alcohol. Schistosomiasis can be treated with prescription drugs. In general, swimming in fresh water should be avoided.

Typhoid fever: Caused by the salmonella bacterium; common in villages and rural areas in China. While mostly transmitted through contaminated food and water, direct contact with another person can infect you. Early symptoms include fever, headaches, fatigue, loss of appetite, constipation, and sometimes a rash on the abdomen or chest. Antibiotics can treat typhoid, but a vaccination (70-90% effective) is recommended.

OTHER INFECTIOUS DISEASES

Rabies: Transmitted through the saliva of infected animals; fatal if untreated. By the time symptoms appear (thirst and muscle spasms), the disease is in its terminal stage. If you are bitten, wash the wound thoroughly, seek immediate medical care, and try to have the animal located. A rabies vaccine, which consists of 3 shots given over a 21-day period, is available but is only semi-effective.

Hepatitis B: A viral infection of the liver transmitted via bodily fluids or needle sharing. Symptoms may not surface until years after infection. Vaccinations are recommended for health-care workers, sexually-active travelers, and anyone planning to seek medical treatment abroad. The 3-shot vaccination series must begin 6mo. before traveling.

Hepatitis C: Like Hep B, but the mode of transmission differs. IV drug users, those with occupational exposure to blood, hemodialysis patients, and recipients of blood transfusions are at the highest risk, but the disease can also be spread through sexual contact or sharing items like razors and toothbrushes that may have traces of blood on them.

AIDS, HIV, STDS

For detailed information on **Acquired Immune Deficiency Syndrome (AIDS)** in China, call the **US Centers for Disease Control**'s 24hr. hotline at (800) 342-2437, or contact the **Joint United Nations Programme on HIV/AIDS (UNAIDS),** 20 av. Appia 20, CH-1211 Geneva 27, Switzerland (☎ +41 (22) 791 36 66, fax 791 41 87). Council's brochure, *Travel Safe: AIDS and International Travel,* is available at all Council Travel offices and on their website (www.ciee.org/Isp/safety/travelsafe.htm). The Chinese government screens incoming travelers planning to stay in the country for six months or longer and regularly denies entrance to HIV-postive people; students, teachers, visiting scholars, and businessmen staying for 9 months or more are required to submit test results showing they are HIV negative. Contact the nearest Chinese consulate for up-to-date information.

Sexually transmitted diseases (STDs) such as gonorrhea, chlamydia, genital warts, syphilis, and herpes are easier to catch than HIV and can be just as deadly. **Hepatitis B** and **C** are also serious STDs (see **Other Infectious Diseases,** above). Though condoms may protect you from some STDs, oral or even tactile contact can lead to transmission. Warning signs include swelling, sores, bumps, or blisters on sex organs, the rectum, or the mouth; burning and pain during urination and bowel movements; itching around sex organs; swelling or redness of the throat; and flu-like symptoms. If these symptoms develop, see a doctor immediately.

WOMEN'S HEALTH

Women traveling in unsanitary conditions are vulnerable to **urinary tract** and **bladder infections,** common and severely uncomfortable bacterial diseases that cause a burning sensation and painful and sometimes frequent urination. To avoid these infections, drink plenty of vitamin-C-rich juice and clean water, and urinate frequently, especially right after intercourse. Untreated, these infections can lead to kidney infections, sterility, and even death. If symptoms persist, see a doctor.

Vaginal yeast infections may flare up in hot and humid climates. Wearing loosely fitting trousers or a skirt and cotton underwear will help, as will over-the-counter remedies like Monistat or Gynelotrimin. Bring supplies from home if you are prone to infection, as they are hard to find in China. In a pinch, some travelers use a natural alternative such as a plain yogurt (suānnǎi; 酸奶) and lemon juice douche.

Tampons and **pads** can be found in most, but not all, areas of China. Preferred brands are very likely not to be available, so take supplies along. Reliable **contraceptive devices** may also be difficult to find outside of large cities. Women on the pill should bring enough to allow for possible loss or extended stays. Bring a prescription, since forms of the pill vary a good deal. Women who use a diaphragm should bring enough contraceptive jelly. Though condoms are increasingly available, consider bringing your favorite brand, as availability and quality vary.

Women who need an **abortion** while abroad should contact the **International Planned Parenthood Federation,** European Regional Office, Regent's College Inner

Circle, Regent's Park, London NW1 4NS (☎44 (020) 7487 7900; fax 487 7950), for more information. Another useful resource might be the **China Family Planning Association (CFPA)**, No.1 Shenggu Beili Yinghuayuan Xiju, Beijing (☎+ 86 (10) 644 3375; email cfpa@public.fhnet.cn.net).

INSURANCE

Travel insurance generally covers four basic areas: medical/health problems, property loss, trip cancellation/interruption, and emergency evacuation. Although your regular insurance policies may well extend to travel-related accidents, you may consider purchasing travel insurance if the cost of potential trip cancellation/interruption or emergency medical evacuation is greater than you can absorb. Prices for travel insurance purchased separately generally run about US$50 per week for full coverage, while trip cancellation/interruption may be purchased separately at a rate of about US$5.50 per US$100 of coverage.

Medical insurance (especially university policies) often covers costs incurred abroad; check with your provider. **US Medicare** does not cover travel in China. **Canadians** are protected by their home province's health insurance plan for up to 90 days after leaving the country; check with the provincial Ministry of Health or Health Plan Headquarters for details. **Homeowners' insurance** (or your family's coverage) often covers theft during travel and loss of travel documents (passport, plane ticket, railpass, etc.) up to US$500.

ISIC and **ITIC** (see p. 52) provide basic insurance benefits, including US$100 per day of in-hospital sickness for up to 60 days, US$3000 of accident-related medical reimbursement, and US$25,000 for emergency medical transport. Cardholders have access to a toll-free 24hr. helpline for medical, legal, and financial emergencies overseas (US and Canada ☎ (800) 626-2427, elsewhere call US collect +1 (713) 267-2525). **American Express** (US ☎ (800) 528-4800) grants most cardholders automatic car rental insurance (collision and theft, but not liability) and ground travel accident coverage of US$100,000 on flight purchases made with the card.

INSURANCE PROVIDERS. Council and **STA** (see p. 73) offer a range of plans that can supplement your basic coverage. Other private insurance providers in the **US and Canada** include: **Access America** (☎(800) 284-8300); **Berkely Group/Carefree Travel Insurance** (☎(800) 323-3149; www.berkely.com); **Globalcare Travel Insurance** (☎(800) 821-2488; www.globalcare-cocco.com); and **Travel Assistance International** (☎(800) 821-2828; www.worldwide-assistance.com). Providers in the **UK** include **Campus Travel** (☎(01865) 258 000) and **Columbus Travel Insurance** (☎(020) 7375 0011). In **Australia**, try **CIC Insurance** (☎9202 8000).

PACKING

Pack light: lay out only what you absolutely need, then take half the clothes and twice the money. The less you have, the less you have to lose (or store, or carry on your back). A ny extra space left will be useful for any souvenirs or items you might pick up along the way.

Backpack: Internal-frame packs mold better to your back, keep a lower center of gravity, and flex adequately to allow you to hike difficult trails. **External-frame packs** are more comfortable for long hikes over even terrain, as they keep weight higher and distribute it more evenly. Make sure your pack has a strong, padded hip-belt to transfer weight to your legs. Any serious backpacking requires a pack of at least 4000in^3 (16,000cc), plus 500in^3 for sleeping bags in internal-frame packs. Sturdy backpacks cost anywhere from US$125-420—this is one area in which it doesn't pay to economize. Fill up any pack with something heavy and walk around the store with it to get a sense of how it distributes weight before buying it. Either buy a **waterproof backpack cover,** or store all of your belongings in plastic bags inside your pack.

WASHING CLOTHES. Almost every Chinese hotel has laundry service, especially in big cities and on the east coast. A load of laundry usually costs US$1-5 and hotel staff can return it in a day or two. A cheaper and easier alternative is to use a sink: bring a small bar or tube of detergent soap, a small rubber ball to stop up the sink, and a travel clothes line.

ELECTRIC CURRENT. In China, electricity is 220 volts AC, enough to fry any 110V North American appliance. Visit a hardware store for an adapter (which changes the shape of the plug—keep in mind that Chinese sockets come in several different configurations) and a converter (which changes the voltage). Don't make the mistake of using only an adapter (unless appliance instructions state otherwise).

FILM. Chinese brands of film are widely available and inexpensive (about Y10 per roll). Most imported brands, including Japanese (Kodak Y20-22, Fuji Y22-28), are easy to find in cities, but they are not as cheap as Chinese brands. Slide or black-and-white film can be impossible to purchase outside of major cities. Despite disclaimers, some airport security X-rays can fog film, so either buy a lead-lined pouch (sold at camera stores), or ask security to hand inspect it. Always pack it in your carry-on luggage, since higher-intensity X-rays are used on checked luggage.

OTHER USEFUL ITEMS. For minor health problems, bring a compact first-aid kit, including bandages, aspirin or other pain killer, antibiotic cream, a thermometer, a Swiss army knife with tweezers, moleskin, decongestant for colds, motion sickness remedy, medicine for diarrhea or stomach problems (Pepto Bismol tablets or liquid and Immodium), sunscreen, insect repellent, burn ointment, and a syringe for emergency medical purposes (get a letter of explanation from your doctor). Contact lens wearers should bring an extra pair, a copy of the prescription, a pair of glasses, extra solution, and eyedrops. Those who use heat disinfection might consider switching to chemical cleansers for the duration of the trip.

Other useful items include: an umbrella; sealable plastic bags (for damp clothes, soap, food, shampoo, and other spillables); alarm clock; waterproof matches; sun hat; needle and thread; safety pins; sunglasses; plastic water bottle; compass; string (makeshift clothesline and lashing material); towel; padlock; whistle; rubber bands; flashlight; cold-water soap; earplugs; electrical tape (for patching tears); garbage bags; a small calculator for currency conversion; a pair of flip-flops for the shower; a money-belt for carrying valuables; deodorant; razors; tampons; and condoms (see **AIDS, HIV, and STDs,** p. 65).

ACCOMMODATIONS

The country's budget accommodations may be the low point of a trip through China. Travelers can face a host of accommodation-related annoyances, including exorbitant rates, poor sanitation, noise, insects, and bureaucratic red tape. Since quality often varies more than price, choose carefully.

RESTRICTIONS. In most cities, foreigners are barred from staying at the cheapest lodgings and may be relegated to mid-range hotels. China has a five star (wǔ xīngjí) rating system for hotels, and most hotels authorized to accept foreigners (shèwài bīnguǎn; 涉外宾馆) are one star or higher. If you have some Chinese-language skills or are overseas Chinese, you might try your luck at talking the management into letting you stay in a place that officially does not accept foreign guests—in general, the better your Chinese, the more likely they are to relent. In dire circumstances, hotel staff can sometimes be persuaded to call the local PSB to ask for permission to lodge you for one night, but this is by no means guaranteed. Some establishments accepting foreigners insist that they occupy standard rooms even if dorm rooms exist. Most establishments also refuse to allow Chinese and foreigners **to share a room**, especially if of the opposite sex. Less frequently, **unmarried foreign couples** are also barred from staying together; a wedding band or marriage certificate, authentic or not, goes a long way in overcoming this regulation. Remember that an English sign outside does not always indicate a foreigner-friendly establishment.

ESSENTIALS

If you plan on staying in a private residence while in China, you must register with the local branch of the PSB (Public Security Bureau) upon arrival (usually within the first day or two of your stay in the area).

PRICES. A wave of renovations is converting many old budget standbys into upmarket hotels, and prices. While dorm beds in popular backpacker destinations like Yunnan, Guangxi, and Tibet continue to cost around US$2 per night, in many cities along the eastern seaboard it's now hard to find a room for under US$20 a day. The only respite in sight is the low-occupancy rate that plagues most Chinese hotels; this gives travelers bargaining power. At any type of establishment, **always ask for a discount;** discounts of at least 10-20% are common, and as much as 50% is not unheard of. Many low-end hotels use their price charts only as paperweights, giving discounts or padding room rates based on a guest's appearance. Although the two-tiered (foreigner and Chinese) pricing system is disappearing in most places (see p. 57), foreigners are still easy targets for price hikes. Telling the staff that you're a student may help.

CHECKING IN. When checking in to your hotel, you will invariably be required to fill out a **registration form** with vital statistics like your nationality, passport number, and visa type (see p. 50 for an explanation of visa types—most travelers have an "L"-type tourist visa). In the past, hotels commonly kept your passport as a **deposit** on the room, but most establishments have converted to cash; nonetheless, should you be asked by hotel staff to leave your passport, refuse and offer an expired one, some other form of identification, or cash instead. For any deposit you do leave, remember to keep the receipt in order to get a refund upon check-out. Check-out is typically noon, while check-in is generally anytime. Reservations for standard rooms are often accepted, but often not necessary.

HOTELS

Mandarin has several words to distinguish between different types of establishments that are generally all translated as "hotel" in English. In general, the most upmarket hotels are called *dàjiǔdiàn* (大酒店) or *fàndiàn* (饭店) and mid-range hotels are called *bīnguǎn* (宾馆). However, many run-of-the-mill establishments masquerade as *fàndiàn* without any of the expected perks in an attempt to justify exorbitant room rates. More often than not, you will stay at one of these three kinds of hotels, as they are usually the only places in town that accept foreigners. Low-end hotels are called *lǚguǎn* (旅馆), while guesthouses are *zhāodàisuǒ* (招待所), but both of these rarely accept foreigners.

UPMARKET HOTELS. These establishments generally offer several restaurants, business and travel services, IDD/DDD phones and TVs in every room, laundry, 24hr. hot water, A/C, private baths with Western-style toilets, massage parlor, salon, and just about every other amenity under the sun. The luxury doesn't come cheap, however—doubles typically go for US$40 and up.

MID-RANGE HOTELS. Even more common than upmarket deluxe mega-hotels are the somewhat cheaper mid-range hotels. A dime a dozen, these places usually come with a more limited selection of similar amenities (restaurant, TV, A/C, phones, laundry, and karaoke parlor), and a smaller price tag, usually US$15-40 for doubles. Many of these hotels are large, multi-storied buildings with worn linens and upholstery, paper-thin walls, and aging bathrooms. They often have several buildings, wings, or floors with different levels of quality, often called "economy," "standard," and "deluxe" rooms; receptionists will sometimes try to make you stay in the most expensive rooms, so always ask about cheaper options.

LOW-END HOTELS. Often near the train and/or long-distance bus stations, these establishments may not even have a star. Amenities may still include TV, laundry, a restaurant, sometimes phones, and perhaps Western-style toilets. These hotels, sometimes called hostels, often rent rooms by the bed, with most thrifty Chinese happy to bed down next to strangers at a fraction of the price of a room of their own; sadly, this option is rarely open to foreigners. Nonetheless, some budget hotels do let foreigners stay in these "dorm" rooms, especially when they're not full—the best of both worlds, since you pay for only the bed but almost always get the room to yourself. In these dorm accommodations, bathrooms are usually communal, hot water only available limited hours, and cleanliness questionable at times. But the price is right, usually US$3-8 per person per night.

OTHER ACCOMMODATIONS

HOSTELLING INTERNATIONAL (HI). Hostels are located in Hong Kong and five cities in Guangdong province. As of June 2000, only Hong Kong's Ma Wui Hall Hostel accepts reservations via the **International Booking Network** (Australia ☎ (02) 9261 1111; Canada ☎ (800) 663-5777; England and Wales ☎ (1629) 58 14 18; Northern Ireland ☎ (1232) 32 47 33; Republic of Ireland ☎ (01) 830 1766; NZ ☎ (09) 379 4224; Scotland ☎ (541) 55 32 55; US ☎ (800) 909-4776; www.iyhf.org). Most student travel agencies (see p. 73) sell HI cards, as do all national hosteling organizations listed.

UNIVERSITIES. Some university residences in China open their arms to foreign travelers. Beijing, Xian, Nanjing, Hangzhou, Changsha, Hefei, and Suzhou are among the cities that offer such accommodations. These dorms are often close to student areas—good sources for information on things to do—but can be far from major sights or downtown areas. Many universities have had moderate success renting rooms to travelers and have decided to go upscale, charging as much as regular mid-range hotels. Prices for dorms may be as low as US$7.

MONASTERIES AND TEMPLES. Especially in remote areas, monasteries and temples often provide accommodations for just a few *kuai* a night. Frequently lacking electricity and running water, these tend to be the most basic of accommodations (essentially, a bed or a piece of the floor), but those who don't mind roughing it a little are often lured by the thought of trading in the noisy concrete high-rises of the cities for a little serene rusticity. Keep in mind, though, that on popular pilgrimage routes like Emeishan, every other traveler probably has the same idea, so spaces may be scarce.

CAMPING. Camping in one of China's beautiful scenic areas and nature reserves might be an attractive option, but it is unfortunately a largely unfeasible one. Nowhere are there designated camping facilities, and the PSB frowns upon on setting up your own site. A few organized tour groups are permitted to organize camping expeditions, but these are few and far between. *Let's Go* does not recommend camping in China.

KEEPING IN TOUCH

MAIL

SENDING MAIL TO CHINA

Mark envelopes "air mail," "par avion," or 航空 to avoid having letters sent by sea.

Australia: Allow 4-6 days for regular **airmail** to China. Postcards and letters up to 20g cost AUS$1; packages up to 0.5kg AUS$6, up to 2kg AUS$32. **EMS** can get a letter to China in 3-4 days for AUS$28. www.auspost.com.au/pac.

Canada: Allow 4-7 days for regular **airmail** to China. Postcards and letters up to 20g cost CDN$.95; packages up to 0.5kg CDN$10.45, up to 2kg CDN$39.20. www.canada-post.ca/CPC2/common/rates/ratesgen.html#international.

Ireland: Allow 5-7 days for regular airmail to China. Postcards and letters up to 25g cost IR£.45. Add IR£2.30 for Swiftpost International. www.anpost.ie.

New Zealand: Allow 5-7 days for regular airmail to China. Postcards NZ$.80. Letters up to 20g cost NZ$1.60; small parcels up to 0.5kg NZ$9.44, up to 2kg NZ$28.64. www.nzpost.co.nz/nzpost/inrates.

UK: Allow 5-7 days for airmail to China. Letters up to 20g cost UK£0.65; packages up to 0.5kg UK£4.95, up to 2kg UK£19.20. UK Swiftair delivers letters a day faster for UK£3.5 more. www.royalmail.co.uk/calculator.

US: Allow 4-7 days for regular **airmail** to China. Postcards/aerogrammes cost US$0.55/0.60; letters under 1 oz. US$1. Packages under 1 lb. cost US$7.20; larger packages cost a variable amount (around US$15). **US Express Mail** takes 2-3 days and costs US$15. **US Global Priority Mail** reaches select Chinese cities (Beijing, Chongqing, Dalian, Guangzhou, Nanjing, Qingdao, Shanghai, Shenyang, Shenzhen, Suzhou, Tianjin, Wuhan, Wuxi, Xiamen, and Zhuhai) delivers small/large flat-rate envelopes to China in3-5 days for US$9. http://ircalc.usps.gov.

RECEIVING MAIL IN CHINA

There are several ways to arrange pick-up of letters sent to you by friends and relatives while you are abroad. Mail can be sent via Poste Restante (General Delivery; cúnjú hòu; 存局候) to almost any city or town in China with a post office (yóujú; 邮局). Address Poste Restante letters as in the following example:

Jane Ankur
Poste Restante 存局候领
Xian, Shaanxi Province
CHINA 中国 710000

The mail will go to a special desk in the central post office, unless you specify a post office by street address or postal code. It's best to use the largest post office, since mail may be sent there regardless. It is usually safer and quicker, though more expensive, to send mail express or registered. Bring your passport (or other photo ID) for pick-up; there may be a small fee. If the clerks insist that there is nothing for you, have them check under your first name as well. *Let's Go* lists post offices in the Practical Information section for each city and most towns.

American Express travel offices throughout China offer a free **Client Letter Service** (mail held up to 30 days and forwarding upon request) for cardholders who contact them in advance. Address the letter as shown above. Some offices will offer these services to non-cardholders (especially AmEx Travelers Cheque holders), but call ahead to make sure. *Let's Go* lists AmEx office locations for most large cities in **Practical Information** sections; for a complete, free list, call (800) 528-4800.

SENDING MAIL ABROAD FROM CHINA

Sending a post card out of China costs Y4.20. Sending a letter out of China costs Y5.40 (1-10g), Y6.40 (10-20g), and Y8.20 (20-50g). Airmail charges an additional Y10 per gram. Sending letters within China costs Y0.80. **Airmail** from major cities in China to North America averages 4-7 days; to Australia or New Zealand, 4-6 days; to the UK or Ireland, 5-7 days; to South Africa, 5-7 days. Be aware that mail traveling from smaller towns or outer regions may take longer than normal. **Aerogrammes,** printed sheets that fold into envelopes and travel via airmail, are available at post offices. It helps to mark 航空 (hángkōng; "air mail") if possible, though "par avion" is universally understood. Most post offices will charge exorbitant fees or simply refuse to send aerogrammes with enclosures.

Surface mail is by far the cheapest and slowest way to send mail. It takes two to four months to cross the Pacific—good for items you won't need for a while, such as souvenirs or other articles you've acquired that are weighing down your pack.

TELEPHONES

CALLING ABROAD FROM CHINA

A **calling card** is probably your cheapest bet. Calls are billed collect or to your account. You can frequently call collect without even possessing a company's calling card just by calling their access number and following the instructions. **To obtain a calling card** from your national telecommunications service before leaving home, contact the appropriate company listed below (using the numbers in the first column). To **call home with a calling card,** contact the operator for your service provider in China by dialing the appropriate toll-free access number (listed below in the second column).

COMPANY	TO OBTAIN A CARD, DIAL:	TO CALL ABROAD, DIAL:
AT&T	(888) 288-4685	108 11
British Telecom Direct	(800) 34 51 44	108 440
Canada Direct	(800) 564-4708	108 186
Ireland Direct	(800) 25 02 50	not available
MCI	(800) 444-4141	108 12
New Zealand Direct	(0800) 00 00 00	108 640
Sprint	(800) 877-4646	108 13
Telkom South Africa	09 03	108 270
Telestra Australia	13 12 00	108 610

PLACING INTERNATIONAL CALLS. To call China from home or to place an international call from China, dial:

1. The **international dialing prefix.** To dial out of **Australia,** dial 0011; **Canada** or the **US,** 011; the **Republic of Ireland, New Zealand,** or the **UK,** 00; **South Africa,** 09; **China,** 00.
2. The **country code** of the country you want to call. To call **Australia,** dial 61; **Canada** or the **US,** 1; the **Republic of Ireland,** 353; **New Zealand,** 64; **South Africa,** 27; the **UK,** 44; **China,** 86.
3. The **city** or **area code.** Let's Go lists the phone codes for cities and towns in China opposite the city or town name, alongside the following icon: ☎. If the first digit is a zero (e.g., 010 for Beijing), omit it when calling from abroad (e.g., dial 011 86 10 from Canada to reach Beijing).
4. The **local number.**

CALLING WITHIN CHINA

The simplest way to call within the country is to use a coin-operated or public phone. Be aware that sometimes the public phones have extra fees for long distance calls that would not be applied otherwise. **Prepaid phone cards** (diànhuà kǎ; 电话卡; available at China Telecoms everywhere) carry a certain amount of phone time depending on the card's denomination and usually save time and money in the long run. Also be aware that prepaid phone cards are sometimes only available for use within the home province (supposedly Y200 phone cards can be used anywhere in China). Be sure to ask about such restrictions before purchasing a card.

DIGITS. Telephone numbers in China can have anywhere from 4 digits (in Zhangmu, near the Tibet-Nepal border) to 8 digits (in Beijing, Hong Kong, and other major cities). The telephone system is expanding at a rapid rate, and cities are increasing the number of digits in their phone numbers all the time. It is not uncommon for one city to have telephone numbers with different numbers of digits; Macau has 6-, 7-, and 8-digit numbers. When a new digit is added to a phone number, it usually precedes the first digit of the old phone number. If you're having trouble getting through and you suspect you have an old phone number, try to find out what new first digit the numbers in the city you're calling all share and add it to the beginning of the number you're trying. Popular new digits are "2" and "6."

EMAIL AND INTERNET

For the most convenient public Internet access venues, try China Telecom (zhōng-guó diánxìn; 中国电信) offices, cybercafes, university campus computer rooms, libraries, and the business centers of upmarket hotels. Though nationwide coverage is still patchy, *Let's Go* lists at least one establishment where travelers can surf the net in practically every city's **Practical Information** section.

Though in some places it's possible to forge a remote link with your home server, in most cases this is a much slower (and thus more expensive) option than taking advantage of free **web-based email accounts** (e.g., www.hotmail.com and www.yahoo.com). Travelers with laptops can call an internet service provider via a **modem.** Long-distance phone cards specifically intended for such calls can defray normally high phone charges; check with your long-distance phone provider to see if it offers this option.

Web surfers will find that the web pages of many major Western news sources and human rights organizations are not accessible from Chinese computers; this is because of government censorship attempts to curb any Internet information that goes dramatically against Party doctrine.

TIME DIFFERENCES

These times are Standard time. China does not follow Daylight Savings Time; thus, at some times of the year, China may be one hour ahead of the times listed below.

4AM	7AM	NOON	7PM	8PM	10PM
Vancouver	Toronto	London	Hanoi	China	Sydney
Seattle	Ottawa	(GMT)	Bangkok	Hong Kong/	Canberra
San Francisco	New York		Jakarta	Macau	Melbourne
Los Angeles	Washington,		Phnom Penh	Manila	
	D.C.			Singapore & KL	
				Denpasar	

GETTING THERE

BY PLANE

The vast majority of foreign tourists arrive in China by air. Airfare will probably be the largest single expenditure of your trip to China, but a little effort can save you a bundle. If your plans are flexible enough to deal with the restrictions, courier fares (see p. 75) are the cheapest. Tickets bought from consolidators (see p. 75) and standby seating (see p. 75) are also good deals, but last-minute specials, airfare wars, and charter flights often beat these fares. The key is to hunt around, to be flexible, and to ask persistently about discounts. Students, seniors, and those under 26 should never pay full price for a ticket.

Airfares to China peak between June and Sept. Holidays are also expensive times to travel, although most foreign airlines have not caught on to Chinese carriers' policy of jacking up rates for Chinese New Year. Round-trip flights are by far the cheapest; "open-jaw" (arriving in and departing from different cities) and round-the-world, or RTW, flights are pricier but reasonable alternatives. Patching one-way flights together is the least economical way to travel. Flights to the major international cities—Beijing, Shanghai, and Hong Kong—will tend to be cheaper. Round-trip flights to Beijing, Shanghai, or Hong Kong from the US or Canadian East Coast cost US$800-1400 in summer, US$550-1000 in winter; tickets from the US or Canadian West Coast run US$600-1600; from the UK UK$450-800; from Australia or New Zealand AUS$1000-1500.

BUDGET AND STUDENT TRAVEL AGENCIES

Unlike many international destinations, the cheapest tickets to China are usually not offered by conventional student or budget travel agencies (i.e. Council Travel or STA), but by smaller Chinatown agencies that cater mainly to overseas Chinese. These agencies are often able to find prices as much as 20-30% lower than other budget travel agencies. We highly recommend scouring the phone book for travel agencies in your local Chinatown, or picking up a copy of a local Chinese newspaper and flipping to the travel advertisements page to find an agency near you.

While Chinatown agencies sell tickets at unbeatable prices, they typically do not offer services such as travel insurance or student ID cards. Students and non students 26 years or under holding **ISIC** and **IYTC cards** (see **Identification, p. 52**), respectively, qualify for big discounts from student travel agencies.

usit world (www.usitworld.com). Over 50 **usit campus** branches in the UK (www.usitcampus.co.uk), including 52 Grosvenor Gardens, **London** SW1W 0AG (☎(0870) 240 1010); **Manchester** (☎(0161) 273 1721); and **Edinburgh** (☎(0131) 668 3303). Nearly 20 **usit now** offices in Ireland, including 19-21 Aston Quay, O'Connell Bridge, **Dublin** 2 (☎(01) 602 1600; www.usitnow.ie), and **Belfast** (☎(02890) 327 111; www.usitnow.com). Offices also in Athens, Auckland, Brussels, Frankfurt, Johannesburg, Lisbon, Luxembourg, Madrid, Paris, Sofia, and Warsaw.

Council Travel (www.counciltravel.com). Countless US offices, including Atlanta, Boston, Chicago, L.A., New York City, San Francisco, Seattle, and Washington, D.C. Call (800) 2-COUNCIL (226-8624) to find the office nearest you. Office in the UK at 28A Poland St. (Oxford Circus), **London**, W1V 3DB (☎(020) 7437 7767).

CTS Travel, 44 Goodge St., **London** W1 (☎(020) 7636 0031; fax 7637 5328; email ctsinfo@ctstravel.com.uk).

STA Travel, 6560 Scottsdale Rd. #F100, Scottsdale, AZ 85253 (☎(800) 777-0112; fax (602) 922-0793; www.sta-travel.com). A student and youth travel organization with over 150 offices worldwide. Ticket booking, travel insurance, railpasses, and more. In New Zealand, 10 High St., **Auckland** (☎(09) 309 0458). In Australia, 366 Lygon St., **Melbourne** Vic 3053 (☎(03) 9349 4344).

Travel CUTS (Canadian Universities Travel Services Limited), 187 College St., **Toronto,** ON M5T 1P7 (☎(416) 979-2406; fax 979-8167; www.travelcuts.com). 40 offices across Canada. Also in the UK, 295-A Regent St., **London** W1R 7YA (☎(020) 7255 1944).

 FLIGHT PLANNING ON THE INTERNET. The Web is a great place to look for travel bargains—it's fast, it's convenient, and you can spend as long as you like exploring options without driving your travel agent insane. Many airline sites offer special last-minute deals on the Web. Try Air China: www.airchina.com.cn; China Eastern: www.chinaeasternair.com; Cathay Pacific: www.cathaypacific.com; Korean Air: www.koreanair.com; All Nippon Airways: www.ana.co.jp; Asiana Airlines: www.asiana.co.kr. Other sites do the legwork and compile the deals for you—try www.bestfares.com, www.onetravel.com, www.lowestfare.com, and www.travelzoo.com.

STA (www.sta-travel.com) and **Council** (www.counciltravel.com) provide quotes on student tickets, while **Expedia** (msn.expedia.com) and **Travelocity** (www.travelocity.com) offer full travel services. **Priceline** (www.priceline.com) allows you to specify a price, and obligates you to buy any ticket that meets or beats it; expect antisocial hours and odd routes. **Skyauction** (www.skyauction.com) lets you to bid on last-minute and advance-purchase tickets. Just one last note—to protect yourself, make sure that the site uses a secure server before handing over credit card details. Happy hunting!

ESSENTIALS

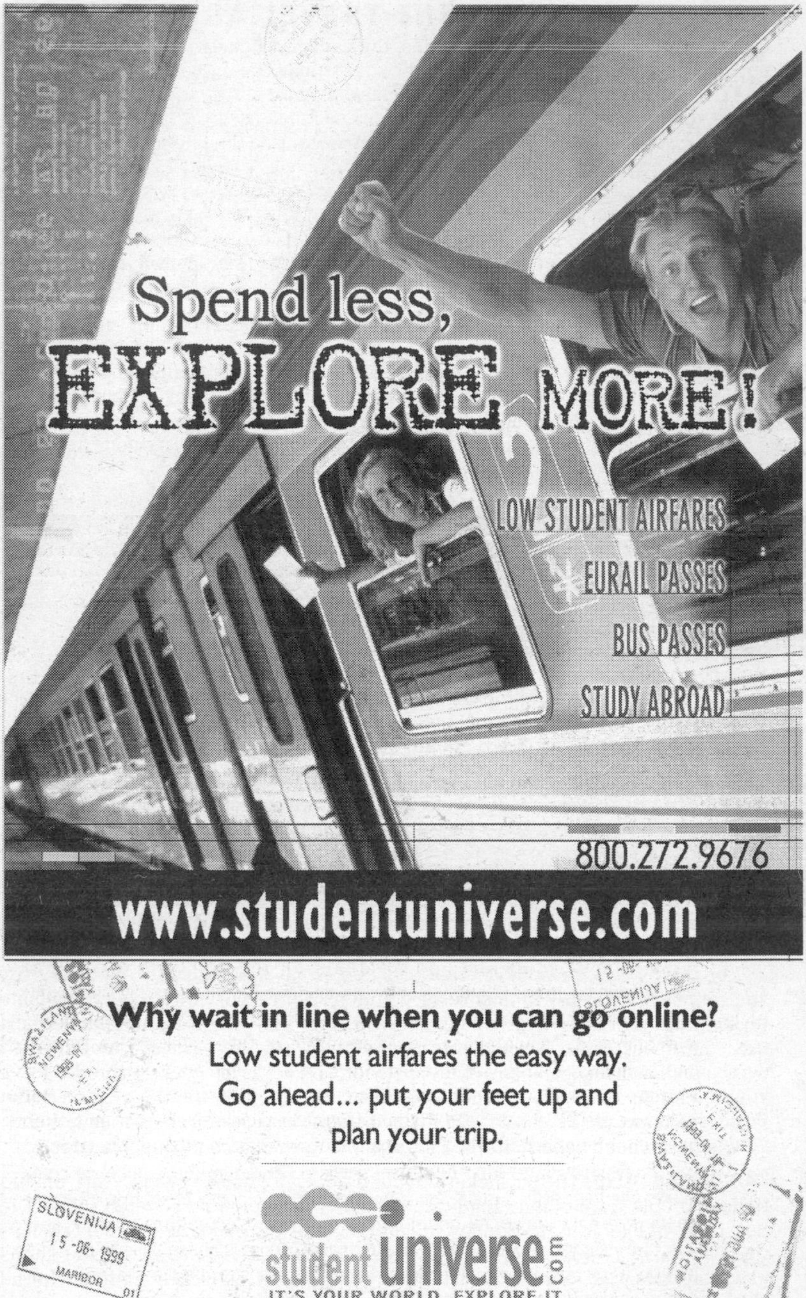
Spend less,
EXPLORE MORE!
LOW STUDENT AIRFARES
EURAIL PASSES
BUS PASSES
STUDY ABROAD
800.272.9676
www.studentuniverse.com
Why wait in line when you can go online?
Low student airfares the easy way.
Go ahead... put your feet up and
plan your trip.
student universe.com
IT'S YOUR WORLD. EXPLORE IT
SLOVENIJA
15-06-1999
MARIBOR

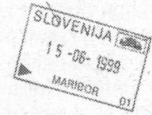

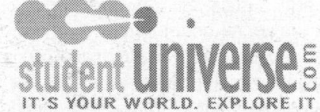

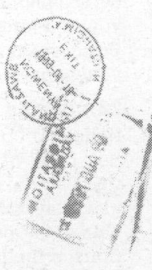

COMMERCIAL AIRLINES

As more and more airlines fly to China, travelers have an increasingly large number of carriers to choose from. The cheapest are often Korean Air, Air China, and China Eastern Airlines. Canadian Airlines, Cathay Pacific, All Nippon Airways, and Asiana Airlines also offer ultra-competitive fares with good service, although some flights may involve overnight stays or lengthy layovers in Tokyo or Seoul.

The commercial airlines' lowest regular offer is the **APEX** (Advance Purchase Excursion) fare, which provides confirmed reservations and allows "open-jaw" tickets. Generally, reservations must be made seven to 21 days ahead of departure, with seven- to 14-day minimum-stay and up to 90-day maximum-stay restrictions. These fares carry hefty cancellation and change penalties (fees rise in summer). Book peak-season APEX fares early; by May you will have a hard time getting your desired departure date.

OTHER OPTIONS

AIR COURIER FLIGHTS. Couriers help transport cargo on international flights by using their checked luggage space for freight. Generally, couriers must travel with carry-ons only and must deal with complex flight restrictions. Most flights are round-trip only, with short fixed-length stays (usually one week) and a limit of a one ticket per issue. Most of these flights operate only out of major gateway cities, usually Hong Kong, and occasionally Beijing or Shanghai. Generally, you must be over 21 (in some cases 18). In summer, the most popular destinations usually require an advance reservation of about two weeks (you can usually book up to two months ahead). Super-discounted fares are common for "last-minute" flights (three to 14 days ahead).

Groups such as the **Air Courier Association** (☎ 800 282 1202; www.aircourier.org) and the **International Association of Air Travel Couriers**, 220 South Dixie Hwy., P.O. Box 1349, Lake Worth, FL 33460 (☎ (561) 582 8320; email iaatc@courier.org; www.courier.org) provide their members with lists of opportunities and courier brokers worldwide for an annual fee. For more information, consult *Air Courier Bargains* by Kelly Monaghan (The Intrepid Traveler, US$15) or the *Courier Air Travel Handbook* by Mark Field (Perpetual Press, US$10).

STANDBY FLIGHTS. Traveling standby requires considerable flexibility in arrival and departure dates and cities. Companies dealing in standby flights sell vouchers rather than tickets, along with the promise to get you to your destination (or near your destination) within a certain window of time (typically 1-5 days). You call in before your specific window of time to hear your flight options and the probability that you will be able to board each flight. You then decide which flights you want to try to make, show up at the airport at the appropriate time, present your voucher, and board if space is available. Vouchers can usually be bought for both one-way and round-trip travel. You may receive a monetary refund only if every available flight within your date range is full; if you opt not to take an available (but perhaps less convenient) flight, you can only get credit toward future travel. Carefully read agreements with any company offering standby flights as tricky fine print can leave you in a lurch. To check on a company's service record in the US, call the **Better Business Bureau** (☎ (212) 533-6200). It is difficult to receive refunds, and clients' vouchers will not be honored when an airline fails to receive payment in time.

TICKET CONSOLIDATORS. Ticket consolidators, or **"bucket shops,"** buy unsold tickets in bulk from commercial airlines and sell them at discounted rates. The best place to look is in the Sunday travel section of any major newspaper (such as the *New York Times* or *Sydney Morning Herald*), where many bucket shops place tiny ads. Call quickly, as availability is typically extremely limited. Not all bucket shops are reliable, so insist on a receipt that gives full details of restrictions, refunds, and tickets, and pay by credit card (in spite of the 2-5% fee) so you can stop payment if you never receive your tickets. For more info, see www.travel-library.com/air-travel/consolidators.html or pick up Kelly Monaghan's *Air Travel's Bargain Basement* (Intrepid Traveler, US$8).

Travel Avenue (☎(800) 333-3335; www.travelavenue.com) searches for cheap flights from anywhere for a fee. Other consolidators worth trying are **Interworld** (☎(305) 443-4929; fax 443-0351); **Pennsylvania Travel** (☎(800) 331-0947); **Rebel** (☎(800) 227-3235; email travel@rebeltours.com; www.rebeltours.com); **Cheap Tickets** (☎(800) 377-1000; www.cheaptickets.com); and **Travac** (☎(800) 872-8800; fax (212) 714-9063; www.travac.com). Yet more consolidators on the web include the **Internet Travel Network** (www.itn.com); **SurplusTravel.com** (www.surplustravel.com); **Travel Information Services** (www.tiss.com); **TravelHUB** (www.travelhub.com); and **The Travel Site** (www.thetravelsite.com). Keep in mind that these are just suggestions to get you started in your research; *Let's Go* does not endorse any of these agencies. As always, be cautious, and research companies before you hand over your credit card number.

In London, the **Air Travel Advisory Bureau** (☎(020) 7636 5000; www.atab.co.uk) can provide names of reliable consolidators and discount flight specialists.

CHARTER FLIGHTS. Charters are flights a tour operator contracts with an airline to fly extra loads of passengers during peak season. Charter flights fly less frequently than major airlines, make refunds difficult, and are almost always fully booked. Schedules and itineraries may also change or be cancelled at the last moment (as late as 48 hours before the trip, and without a full refund), and check-in, boarding, and baggage claim are often slower. However, they can be cheaper.

Discount clubs and **fare brokers** offer members savings on last-minute charter and tour deals. Study contracts closely; you don't want to end up with an unwanted overnight layover.

TO RUSSIA, WITH LOVE

TRANS-SIBERIAN RAILROAD

For years, the Trans-Siberian Railroad was a mysterious voyage past closed cities and missile silos attempted by only the most intrepid of travelers. Today, agencies in both China and Russia have cracked this tough nut, providing help with tickets and visas. Actually, the term Trans-Siberian Railroad is generally misused to refer to three different rail lines. The real Trans-Siberian line runs from Moscow to Vladivostok, connecting the gilded domes and tinted windshields of Moscow with the rest of her proud but crumbling empire. The two lines that are of interest to the traveler in China are the Trans-Mongolian and the Trans-Manchurian. The **Trans-Mongolian** runs from Beijing through Mongolia to Moscow while the **Trans-Manchurian** runs north from Beijing, cutting above Mongolia and crossing the Chinese-Russian border at Manzhouli in Inner Mongolia before going straight to Moscow. The trip takes five or six days depending on the route (the Trans-Mongolian is the shorter of the two). Regardless of which route you take, the train rolls through two continents, seven time zones, and miles of flat land. Although backpackers and tours have discovered this rail line, it still remains a unique, unpolished journey that cannot be matched elsewhere in the world.

TRANS-MONGOLIAN RAILROAD

TICKETS. Tickets for the Trans-Mongolian can be obtained from the **CITS** in Beijing (see p. 102), although you cannot reserve tickets in advance, and tickets are particularly difficult to obtain during the summer. To make advance ticket reservations, try private tourist agencies—you'll have to pay an extra premium, but they will arrange tickets, visas, and sometimes even package tours with stopovers in Mongolia and Russia. Tianhua International Travel Service (see p. 102) in the back of the Jinghua Hotel in Beijing helps arrange tickets and visas. In Hong Kong, a very helpful agency called Moonsky Star (see p. 387) offers an assortment of special packages. Time Travel Services Ltd. (see p. 390), also in Hong Kong, will help arrange tickets and visas.

VISAS. Because the Trans-Mongolian cuts through Ulaanbataar, both a Mongolian visa and a Russian visa are necessary to travel this route. You can obtain a Mongolian visa at the border (entry-exit visa US$24, urgent US$50). Both Mongolian and Russian visas are available from the Mongolian consulate (see p. 48) in Beijing or can be obtained with the help of travel agencies mentioned above. Visitors can either get transit visas (good for 2 days) or tourist visas (90 days).

SCHEDULES. Trains on this route (#3) leave Beijing at 7:40am on Wednesday, pass through Ulaanbataar, and arrive in Moscow on Monday at 4:32pm.

TRANS-MANCHURIAN RAILROAD

TICKETS. Tickets for the Trans-Manchurian are obtained in the same places and in the same manner as tickets for the Trans-Mongolian (see above). Only the head **CITS** office in the Beijing International Hotel (see p. 102) books tickets.

VISAS. A trip on the Trans-Manchurian line only requires passengers to obtain either a transit visa or a tourist visa, but getting your hand on either of these documents requires quite a bit of organization. The transit visa is only valid for 10 days. Since the train ride takes about six, there is very little time to get off the train, especially since you will have to leave time to go from Moscow to your next destination. It is wise to arrange transportation out of Moscow in advance. To obtain a transit visa, you must already have a train ticket and a visa for your next destination in hand. The tourist visa lasts much longer but is a major hassle to obtain. You must present tourist confirmations from hotels you will be staying in during your journey, which means that you will have to have planned your itinerary in advance. Furthermore, you must stay in hotels that are registered with the Russian Ministry of Foreign Affairs which tend to be expensive. Russian visas can be obtained with the help of the same travel agencies that book tickets, though its cheaper to obtain visas yourself from the Russian embassy in Beijing (see p. 49).

SCHEDULES. Trains running the Trans-Manchurian route (#19) leave at 11:10pm on Saturday and travel directly into Russia via Manzhouli (see p. 271), arriving in Moscow the next Friday at 7:50pm.

LIFE ABOARD THE TRAINS. Food in dining cars (as well as those sold by locals) is priced according to local currency, so bringing Russian rubles as well as Chinese *yuan* will prove useful. Bringing US dollars is more convenient, since dollars are more easily exchanged at border crossings. Many travelers also opt to bring their own snacks. Instant noodles are a good idea, since hot water is available.

Try to avoid the first or last compartment in the car because these are next to the toilets, and on trains which don't have attendants, the stench can become unbearable. And remember to bring your own toilet paper.

INTO SIBERIA. Rail routes connect cities in Heilongjiang province with Russian cities across the border. Visas cannot be obtained at the border, and since getting a Russian visa is even more unwieldy than getting a Chinese visa (see Visas, p. 62), it is best to deal with visas in Beijing. Chinese train #Y217 runs from Harbin East and Main Stations to Khabarovsk via Mudanjiang and Vladivostok every Wednesday, Friday, and Saturday. Train #Y218 chugs its way down the reverse route, leaving from Khabarovsk on Monday, Wednesday, and Thursday.

ON A SLOW BOAT FROM CHINA

While travel by ship may hold romantic appeal for those who like to imagine themselves pulling in to ports-of-call with boatloads of silk or spices, the reality today is that international boat travel is too expensive and time-consuming to be worthwhile, except between China and its near neighbors across the East China Sea.

SOUTH KOREA. Many coastal cities have international ferry terminals with a few boats a week heading to Inchon, particularly Dalian (see p. 207), Tianjin's port of

ESSENTIALS

Tanggu (see p. 141), and Qingdao (see p. 168). Citizens of most Western European countries, Canada, and New Zealand can stay in South Korea visa-free for 90 days, citizens of the US, Australia, and South Africa can stay visa-free for 30 days.

JAPAN. Tanggu (see p. 141)) has ferries headed for Kobe, Qingdao for Shimonoseki (see p. 168), and Shanghai for Osaka (see p. 281). Citizens of most Western European, North American, and Oceanic countries can stay visa-free for 90 days, some for as long as six months.

BORDER CROSSINGS

In general, odd-numbered international trains depart from China, and even-numbered trains arrive in China. International train tickets are usually sold at **China International Travel Service (CITS)** or other travel agencies, not at train stations.

SOUTHEAST ASIA

LAOS. The border crossing between China and Laos is located at the town of **Mohan** in the Xishuangbanna region of Yunnan province (see p. 596), which is accessible only by buses or minibuses. Laos visas are not issued at the border; they must be obtained in Beijing or at the Lao consulate in Kunming (see p. 547).

MYANMAR (BURMA). Generally, border crossing into Myanmar from China is for Chinese businessmen, not foreigners. Officially, foreigners can only get to Myanmar by air. However, the Burmese Consulate in Kunming (see p. 547) can make special arrangements for travelers to take a car from **Ruili** (see p. 581) to **Mu-se** in Myanmar, provided that travelers have already obtained a visa from the Burmese Embassy in Beijing (see p. 49).

VIETNAM. Most travelers cross between Vietnam and China via one of two border posts; at Pingxiang in Guangxi province and Hekou in Yunnan province (see p. 596). The crossing at Pingxiang can be reached via train or bus from Nanning (see p. 525). The crossing at Hekou can be reached via train from Kunming (see p. 545). The train leaves Kunming on Friday and Sunday, crosses through Hekou, and arrives in Hanoi two days later. There is also a direct train connection between Beijing and Hanoi; the train leaves on Mondays and Fridays, making the two-day trip to Hanoi via Pingxiang.

Visas cannot be obtained at either crossing. Although Vietnamese visas are available at CITS in Nanning (see p. 528) or possibly from Kunming travel agencies, the cheapest and safest plan is to take care of Vietnamese visas in Beijing or Hong Kong (see p. 49). Chinese visas can be obtained at the Chinese embassies in Hanoi and Bangkok.

THE 'STANS

KAZAKHSTAN. Train #13 leaves Ürümqi on Monday and Saturday for the 26-hour journey to **Almaty** through Alashan Pass; train #14 plies the reverse route, also on Monday and Saturday. Kazakh visas can be obtained at the embassy in Beijing or from the consulate in Ürümqi (see p. 692).

PAKISTAN. Buses leave from the the the Kashgar International Bus Station in Xinjiang (see p. 708) for **Sost, Pakistan,** via **Tashkurgan** and the **Khunjerab Pass** (40hr., noon, hard seat Y270). **Visas** are required and are not issued at the border; the Pakistani embassy in Beijing (see p. 48) is the nearest source of Pakistani visas.

KYRGYZSTAN. From Kashgar in Xinjiang, buses run to **Bishkek, Kyrgyzstan** via the **Torugut Pass** (16hr., M, US$50). You can take a public bus from the Kashgar International Bus Station (see p. 708), but you will need a transit permit (pīzhào; 批照) to make the border crossing, which you can only obtain at a travel agency. However, agencies will require you to take their tour, but ask anyway, since agencies might itemize their tour packages. Permit prices are often listed at around Y300-350 (for groups of 2-5). **John's Information Cafe** (see p. 709) in Kashgar can also arrange permits and tours to Bish kek. Make sure you have a valid entry visa to Kyrgyzstan, available only in Beijing or Hong Kong (see p. 48); reportedly, transit visas are good only for three days.

MONGOLIA. Travelers who want to visit Mongolia must have either a transit visa or a tourist visa (see p. 76). Several **trains** go from China to Mongolia each week: In addition to the Trans-Mongolian train to Russia (see p. 76), train #23 leaves from Beijing on Wednesday and arrives in **Ulaanbataar** (Y560) on Monday or Tuesday. Tickets can be purchased at the Beijing CITS (see p. 102) or at the Tianhua Travel Agency in the Jinghua Hotel (see p. 102). From Hohhot in Inner Mongolia, trains #602/603 and #332/216 leave on Wednesday and Sunday for Ulaanbataar. Both routes cross the border at **Erinhot.** You can also take a **plane** to Ulaanbataar from **Beijing** (2hr.; M,W, Sa-Su) or **Hohhot** (1½hr.; M and Th).

NEPAL

The trip along the **Friendship Highway** from Lhasa to Kathmandu, crossing the border at **Zhangmu/Kodari,** is quite popular; visitors travel in both directions, but going from Tibet to Nepal is far easier, in terms of visas and logistics, than going the other way. For more information, see p. 724 and p. 752. Nepali visas are required and can be obtained at the border crossing for US$30, although it is far more convenient to get one at the Nepali consulate in Lhasa (see p. 732).

NORTH KOREA

Views of North Korea from Dandong (see p. 205) may be the closest you'll come to this isolated country. Generally, only organized tourist groups authorized by the North Korean Government are permitted into the country. One such tourist group is **Koryo Tours** (☎(010) 6464 9276; fax (010) 6418 1722; email NorthKorea8@hotmail.com; www.koryogroup.com), which has been run by Nicholas Bonner (email NicholasBonner@cs.com) since 1993. Independent tourism is extremely limited, and US or South Korean citizens absolutely cannot obtain visas. Contact the North Korean embassy in Beijing (see p. 48) for more information.

GETTING AROUND

BY PLANE

An enormous country, China has enough geographical barriers and unbearably long bus and train rides for even the stingiest of travelers to consider domestic air travel. While the cost of flying is two to five times the price of a hard sleeper, air travel saves precious time and energy for you actually to enjoy your destination. The Chinese government has embarked on a vigorous expansion program, especially in the Northwest. The new terminal at Beijing Capital Airport, Shanghai's new Pudong Airport, and Hong Kong's Chep Lap Kok all have made air travel easier as well. Nearly all domestic flights are less than three hours; *Let's Go* provides only frequencies and approximate prices in Practical Information or Transportation sections. Domestic airline schedules are revised in April and October.

DOMESTIC AIRLINES. The domestic airline industry is overseen by the state-run monopoly of the **Civil Aviation Administration of China** or **CAAC** (zhōngguó rénmín hángkōng; 中国人民航空). Long infamous for its suspect safety record, unsatisfactory service, and mismanagement, the CAAC has begun a massive reform program, buying new aircrafts and safety equipment, training air traffic controllers abroad, and improving its organization. Perhaps its boldest move yet has been to decentralize the industry by forming semi-independent regional airlines that will eventually assume complete autonomy. The six biggest airlines are:

Air China (CA), US and Canada ☎(800) 986-1985, New York ☎(212) 371-9898, San Francisco ☎(415) 392-2162, London ☎(020) 7630 0919, Sydney ☎(02) 9232 7277, Beijing ☎010 6601 7755; www.airchina.com.cn). The flagship of the CAAC, services mainly international routes, as well as a few domestic destinations.

China Eastern Airlines (MU), US and Canada (800) 200-5118, Los Angeles ☎(626) 583-1500, San Francisco ☎(415) 982-5115, Sydney ☎(02) 9290 1148, Shanghai ☎(021) 6247 2255; www.cea.online.sh.cn). Centered in Shanghai, with some flights to Japan and daily flights to Los Angeles from Beijing and Shanghai.

China Southern Airlines (CZ), US and Canada (888) 338-8988, Los Angeles ☎(323) 653-8088, Hong Kong ☎(852) 2861 0288, Guangzhou ☎(020) 8666 1803; www.cs-air.com). Based in Guangzhou, with flights to Europe, Japan, and Southeast Asia.

China Northwest Airlines (WH) (Xian ☎029 831 4452; http://china-window.com/Shaanxi_w/brief/cnwair/main.htm). Dominates Xian and Lanzhou.

China Southwest Airlines (SZ) (Beijing ☎010 6602 4010, Chengdu ☎(028) 667 1841, Chongqing ☎023 6787 8538; www.cswa.com). Centered in Chengdu and Chongqing. Administers most domestic flights to Tibet.

China Northern Airlines (CJ) http://www.cna.ln.cninfo.net Hubs in Shenyang, Changchun, and Harbin.

Major regional airlines include: Changan (2Z), Fujian (IV), Great Wall (G8), Guizhou (G4), Hainan (H4), Nanjing (NJ), Shandong (SC), Shanghai (FM), Shanxi (8C), Shenzhen (4G), Sichuan (3U), Wuhan (WU), Xinhua (X2), Xinjiang (XO), Yunnan (3Q), and Zhongyuan (Z2). **Dragon Air,** a non-CAAC domestic carrier, operates out of Hong Kong.

BUYING DOMESTIC AIR TICKETS. Standard rates are fixed between cities (so Beijing to Shanghai costs the same as Shanghai to Beijing). The round-trip price is always simply twice the one-way price. Prices for foreigners and Chinese are the same. Children over the age of 12 must buy adult fare tickets, those between the ages of 2 and 12 pay half-price, and those under the age of 2 pay 10% of adult fare. Air travel insurance can be purchased with the ticket for Y20. The policy pays indemnities of up to Y200,000 (US$24,000) for death, total paralysis, loss of any limb, and cerebral damages. Policies with higher indemnities are also available.

When booking a domestic flight, be sure to inquire what type of aircraft is flying your route, as the CAAC fleet is a grab bag of some of the world's most advanced and most ancient planes. While flights in and out of more traveled regions utilize modern aircraft, flights in border regions (especially the Southwest and North-west) often employ older, Russian-built aircraft, such as the accident-prone Tupolev 154s (Tu5) or Ilyusin 86 (YLW).

While it is possible to purchase a limited selection of domestic airline tickets from travel agencies abroad, most travelers find it simpler to buy them in China. Most airports have airline ticket offices that sell tickets for domestic flights on any carrier. Although availability varies, many travelers report no problems walking in and buying a ticket for the next departure. Note that it may be more difficult to obtain tickets during Chinese New Year and for some flights in the Northwest, Southwest, and to major tourist destinations like Chengdu. In the past, CAAC ticket offices in most Chinese cities also sold tickets for all of its subordinate carriers, but with the recent wave of decentralization, some local CAAC offices have been turned over to local airlines (for example, the CAAC offices in Xian and Lanzhou are now under the auspices of China Northwest Airlines). The CAAC office in Beijing remains, but dozens of individual airline offices have also popped up.

AIRPORT PROCEDURES. Passenger are instructed by airlines to arrive at the airport at least 30 minutes before departure time. A few extra minutes rarely hurt, as a massive influx of passengers all waiting to have their travel documents and baggage examined can cause long backups at the security counter. Passengers arriving too early, however, often will find themselves waiting for the specified flight check-in counter to open. Upon landing, watch out for the frenzy of passengers racing to get off the plane only to end up in the same slow shuttle bus going from the runway to the arrivals gate. Be prepared for a possible headache at the baggage claim, as most older and under equipped Chinese airports have several arriving flights sharing one baggage claim. The wait can be ridiculously long, and by the time you get all your pieces together, there may not be any baggage carts left. Hopefully the same fate will not have befallen your bags. Lost baggage is compensated at Y40 per kg, and the maximum compensation for checked baggage is Y8000 (US$900).

CHANGES AND REFUNDS. Travelers wishing to modify the departure time, date, or class of a ticket may do so only once. If the new flight is also offered by the same carrier, than the transaction is straightforward. But if the new flight is aboard a different airline under the CAAC umbrella, then the passenger must buy a new ticket and cancel the old ticket at the airline office of the old ticket. Refunds requested over 24hr. before departure are subjected to a 10% cancellation fee; when requested within 24hr. lose 20%, and when requested two hours before take-off lose 30%. No-shows are entitled to only 50% of the original ticket value.

BY TRAIN

Unless you are planning to stay in one city for the duration of your trip to China, you'll certainly have an opportunity to tango with China's extensive train system. The sprawling network of tracks goes to every part of the country except Tibet, but if engineers have their way, that too will change soon. The convenience, speed, and relative comfort of train travel have made it so popular that tickets can occasionally be hard to come by. Some savvy travelers buy a ticket for their next destination as soon as they arrive in a town. While this technique can save time and sanity, often travelers can only purchase tickets two or three days in advance, and smaller stations will only sell tickets on the day of travel. If you are having real trouble acquiring a ticket, most every upscale hotel and travel agent can help with travel arrangements for a fee (generally Y10-50). Paper **train schedules** (in Chinese only) are available at most major stations for about Y1 and up. The Chinese Ministry of Railways offers comprehensive information on schedules and regulations, albeit only in Chinese (www.chinamor.cn.net).

Depending on how much you are willing to pay, you can roll across the country in any position—from squatting to sitting to supine to spitting. Most trains do not have all four classes available. A "K" in front of the number means that train is an express (*kuai*) and will make fewer stops, while a "Y" indicates that the train is a double-decker tourist (*luyou*) or travel class train. For a helpful guide to deciphering train tickets, see the **Appendix,** p. 756.

Once you have a ticket, hold onto it for dear life. First you'll need to show it to access the track area; keep in mind that at the larger stations, there will be many tracks and multiple trains boarding at once and that gates are generally closed about 3 minutes before the train is due to leave. Attendants at many stations again scrutinize your ticket before allowing you to exit the station.

HARD SEAT. (yìng zuò; 硬座). Hard seat is the cheapest class available and, thus, the majority of train travelers buy hard seat tickets. Generally, a hard seat ticket entitles the bearer to a space on train—the seat part is often optional, as more tickets are sold than seats available. Travelers getting on the train at its point of origin may have slightly less trouble securing a seat, but those who embark at a later stop may find all the seats already taken and be forced to spend the journey standing, sitting, or squatting in the aisles until a seated passenger gets off. Even with a seat, the crowded cars, clouds of cigarette smoke (this despite the no smoking signs often posted conspicuously in the carriage), and blaring loudspeakers can make the trip a less than soothing experience. That said, on the more popular routes, new trains with cushier hard seat sections have sprung up; perks include A/C, cleaner bathrooms, seat assignments, and, ironically, well-cushioned seats.

SOFT SEAT (ruǎn zuò; 软座). Soft seat cars exist only on certain routes, usually short trips between major cities. The soft seat section is considerably more comfortable than the hard seat; passengers are given assigned seats so no one is forced to wander up and down the aisles, and smoking is allegedly prohibited.

HARD SLEEPER (yìng wò; 硬卧). Hard sleeper cars consist of several doorless sleeping compartments off a main aisle. Each compartment has room for six people with three bunks on each side; sheets, blankets, and pillows are provided. Not

all bunks are created equal. In the summer, the claustrophia-inducing top bunk is too hot, or, when the train has A/C, too cold, and leaves the passenger sleeping inches from the ceiling next to the loudspeakers. The middle bunk is slightly removed from the hubbub below. The bottom bunk inevitably becomes the communal bench during the day, although bottom dwellers enjoy the benefit of not having to climb to get in and out of bed. Bunk assignments are printed on the ticket, and it is possible make requests at the ticket window (ticket prices rise with bunk elevation). Top is *shàng* (上), middle *zhōng* (中), and bottom *xìa* (下). Once on board, the attendant exchanges your paper ticket with a metal or plastic piece that must be exchanged for your ticket before you reach your final destination.

SOFT SLEEPER (ruǎn wò; 软卧). Soft sleeper passengers ride as close to the lap of luxury as is possible on a train. Compartments are less cramped and more comfortable, with only four well-padded bunks, wall-to-wall carpeting, and a lovely window curtain. The compartment also has a door for added peace and quiet. For travelers faced with the quandary of a night (or two or three) in hard seat because of sold-out hard sleeper cars, soft sleeper may provide a possible, albeit pricy, solution. Soft sleepers may cost nearly as much as airplane tickets.

FOOD AND DRINK. Food is readily available, and most trains have dining cars that serve mediocre Chinese food and beverages. Attendants also push carts through the aisles selling styrofoam boxes of rice with meat or vegetables, cups of instant noodles, and other goodies. Platform sellers at most stops do the same thing. Virtually every car has a hot water tap, so passengers who bring their own cups and beverages can drink tea or coffee.

BY BUS

China's long-distance bus system has several advantages. First and foremost, it goes virtually everywhere—eventually. Second, bus tickets and actual seats or sleepers are almost always easier to purchase than train tickets. And, third, bus trips are often (but not always) cheaper than train trips of comparable distance. On the downside, unpredictable road conditions, poorly maintained vehicles, and unreliable drivers can conspire to make bus trips long and uncomfortable, or even dangerous. It is not uncommon for roads, particularly in the Northwest and Southwest, to be washed out or otherwise impassable for weeks or months at a time.

Virtually every city or town has a **long-distance bus station** (chángtú qìchē zhàn; 长途汽车站) or designated location at which buses can drop off and pick up passengers. **Tickets** are sold at the station itself and need not be booked in advance. A number of routes are traversed by both rickety, older, Chinese-made buses and newer, relatively luxurious, foreign-made buses (for which tickets are more expensive). It is generally a good idea to look at the bus in which you will be riding before you buy your ticket; a few travelers report having been charged the price for a trip on a higher-quality bus only to find themselves on a rattling, run-down vehicle. On overnight trips, more expensive **sleeper buses** with a semi-reclining bunk for each traveler now ply many routes.

Be sure to prepare yourself well for any long trip by bus, and always anticipate the possibility that a trip will take longer than it is meant to. For travel in cold or high-altitude areas, even in summer, bring plenty of **warm clothing;** buses are all too frequently unequipped with working heaters, and mechanical breakdowns in remote areas can prove deadly for those not properly prepared. (See **Environmental Hazards,** p. 62, for more tips on protecting yourself on bus trips.) It is also a good idea to bring enough **food and water** for the trip, since stops may be few and far between. Shorter routes, particularly those between neighboring cities, often are plied by **minibuses** (including the much-touted A/C Iveco minibuses) that pick up passengers in front of train or bus stations or along major thoroughfares. Typically, you pay for your ticket on board the minibus, which leaves when full and stops when the driver feels like it.

BY CAR

What are you, nuts? Most travelers to China wisely never get behind the wheel of an automobile. Foreign tourists are expressly forbidden to drive in and between most Chinese cities, although most wouldn't want to anyway—roads in China are often completely clogged with vehicles, and drivers drive on whichever side of the road is least congested, ignoring traffic laws and blaring their horn all the while. For local use, cars can be rented in Hong Kong, Macau, Beijing, and Shanghai with a credit card and an **International Driving Permit (IDP)**, or sometimes just a current driver's license from your home country.

To get an IDP, valid for one year to those over 18, apply at a national automobile association or club in your home country. An application for an IDP usually requires one or two photos, a current local license, an additional form of identification, and a fee. Info on the IDP is printed in 10 languages, including Chinese.

SPECIFIC CONCERNS

Bear in mind that traveling in China implies a conception of personal space and privacy that may contrast sharply with what many Westerns are accustomed to. A person's threshhold for reacting to perceived threats or intrusions also may need to be adjusted accordingly. Private space is at a premium in most places. Travelers should expect to be jostled about in crowded buses, trains, and buildings, just like any Chinese would be. This behavior, while making some uncomfortable, does not necessarily indicate more serious concerns. Likewise, curiosity about lighter or darker skinned visitors may be represented by hands spontaneously reaching out to stroke the hair or skin that inspired such curiosity in the first place. That said, do not disregard behavior that makes you feel threatened or in danger.

TRAVELING ALONE

There are many benefits to traveling alone, including independence and greater opportunities to interact with the residents of the region you're visiting. Lone travelers need to be well-organized and look confident at all times. If questioned, never admit that you are traveling alone. Maintain regular contact with someone at home who knows your itinerary. Many of the popular backpacker hotels in China have messages boards listing requests from solo travelers for companions.

For more tips, pick up *Traveling Solo* by Eleanor Berman (Globe Pequot, US$17) or subscribe to **Connecting: Solo Travel Network**, P.O. Box 29088, Delamont RPO, Vancouver, BC V6J 5C2 (☎/fax (604) 737-7791; www.cstn.org; membership US$25-35), or the **Travel Companion Exchange**, P.O. Box 833, Amityville, NY 11701, USA (☎ (631) 454-0880 or 800-392-1256; www.whytravelalone.com; publishes the pamphlet *Foiling Pickpockets & Bag Snatchers* (US$4.70) and Travel Companions, a bi-monthly newsletter for single travelers seeking a travel partner (US$48).

WOMEN TRAVELERS

Take heart. China is one of the safest parts of Asia for women travelers. While it is always wise to take precautions to ensure your own safety wherever you are traveling, in China it is fairly easy to be adventurous without taking undue risks. Rape or assault of foreign women in China, although not unheard of, is uncommon.

As always, use your common sense when traveling. Carry extra money for a phone call, bus, or taxi. **Hitching** is never safe for lone women, or even for two women traveling together. Trust your instincts when choosing a place to stay. You might consider staying in hotels or guesthouses which offer single rooms that lock from the inside. Communal showers in some hotels are safer than others; check them out before settling in. Stick to centrally located accommodations and avoid solitary late-night treks or bus rides. At any time of day, look as if you know where you're going (even when you don't) and consider approaching women or couples for directions if you're lost or feel uncomfortable.

Foreign travelers, especially women, often attract a lot of attention in China. Dress conservatively, especially in less-touristed rural areas and in the Muslim areas of China's northwestern provinces. Some Chinese men assume that foreign women traveling alone are in fact seeking out sexual gratification. The chance to practice English and become "good friends" with a foreign woman can be too much too resist. (Strange bedfellows, indeed.) In general, anyone who offers for you to come visit in a hotel that doesn't cast a second glance as you head upstairs without proper documentation should be viewed with a certain skepticism. Unwanted late night phone calls are best avoided by unplugging the phone. Also, never open your hotel door to strangers. That said, wearing a conspicuous **wedding band** may help prevent unwanted overtures. Even the mention of a husband or group of male friends waiting back at the hotel can be enough to deter unwanted male attention and discount your unattached appearance. Some travelers report that pictures of a "husband" or "children" are extremely useful to help document marriage status.

Your best answer to verbal harassment is no answer at all; feigning deafness, sitting motionless, and staring straight ahead at nothing in particular will do a world of good that reactions don't usually achieve. If need be, turn to an older woman for help; her stern rebukes will usually be enough to embarrass the most determined jerks. The extremely persistent can sometimes be dissuaded by a firm, loud, and very public "Go away!," "gǔn," or "zǒukāi."

Memorize the emergency numbers in the **Practical Information** listings of the places you visit, and consider carrying a whistle or airhorn on your keychain. Don't hesitate to seek out a PSB officer or passerby if you are being harassed. Note that overseas Chinese may blend in more and could perhaps encounter a slower response from passersby or even police. A self-defense course will not only prepare you for a potential attack, but will also raise your level of awareness of your surroundings as well as your confidence (see **Self Defense,** p. 60). Also be sure you are aware of the specific health concerns that women face when traveling (see **Women's Health,** p. 65).

OLDER TRAVELERS

Unfortunately, the senior citizen discounts that are so common in North America and Europe are virtually nonexistent in the PRC, and the lack of creature comforts in much of China may make independent travel particularly taxing for senior citizens. However, agencies specializing in senior citizen group travel are growing in enrollment and popularity, and can ease the stress of traveling in China. For travel programs for seniors, investigate the organizations listed below.

ElderTreks, 597 Markham St., Toronto, ON M6G 2L7 (☎(800) 741-7956 or (416) 588-5000; fax 588-9839; email eldertreks@eldertreks.com; www.eldertreks.com). Adventure travel programs for the 50+ traveler in Tibet, parts of Xinjiang, and Yunnan.

Elderhostel, 75 Federal St., Boston, MA 02110, USA (☎(617) 426-7788 or (877) 426-2166; email registration@elderhostel.org; www.elderhostel.org). Organizes 2- to 4-week "educational adventures" in China for those 55+.

The Mature Traveler, P.O. Box 50400, Reno, NV 89513, USA (☎(775) 786-7419, credit card orders (800) 460-6676). Deals, discounts, and travel packages for the 50+ traveler. Subscription US$30.

BISEXUAL, GAY, AND LESBIAN TRAVELERS

Attitudes regarding sexual orientation vary considerably in China, Hong Kong, and Macau. Some Chinese (both male and female) hold hands with members of the same sex as an expression of friendship, at times making it difficult to distinguish between heterosexual friends and homosexual couples. While heterosexual kissing and other romantic acts are becoming more acceptable in public, similar expressions of homosexuality are not. Nevertheless, many Chinese are tolerant of homosexual behavior as long as it does not interfere with one's responsibility to produce children and raise a family.

ESSENTIALS

Not everyone in China today is fully tolerant of homosexuality, however. In 1994, the Chinese Psychiatric Association (CPA) passed the latest Chinese Classification of Mental Disorders (CCMD), in which homosexuality is still listed as a type of mental disorder. The government officially regards homosexuality as a perversion brought to China only recently by the decadent West, despite historical and literary evidence of its ancient prevalence in Chinese culture. While the legal status of homosexuality remains ambiguous, police persecution of homosexuals and bisexuals is quite common. Foreigners need not worry too much, but police raids of gay clubs and meeting places are becoming more frequent, especially in Beijing, Shanghai, Guangzhou, and Hong Kong. Both heterosexual and homosexual prostitution is frowned upon by authorities.

Resources for bisexuals, gays, and lesbians are easier to access from abroad and from select websites than from within China itself. For online information about gay and lesbian resources in Asia, try www.utopia-asia.com. **Out and About** (www.planetout.com) offers a bi-weekly newsletter addressing travel concerns. Listed below are contact organizations, mail-order bookstores, and publishers that offer relevant materials.

Gay's the Word, 66 Marchmont St., London WC1N 1AB (☎(020) 7278 7654; email sales@gaystheword.co.uk; www.gaystheword.co.uk). The largest gay and lesbian bookshop in the UK, with both fiction and non-fiction titles. Mail-order service available.

Giovanni's Room, 345 S. 12th St., Philadelphia, PA 19107, USA (☎(215) 923-2960; fax 923-0813; email giophilp@netaxs.com; www.queerbooks.com). An international lesbian/feminist and gay bookstore with mail-order service (carries many of the publications listed below).

International Gay and Lesbian Travel Association, 4331 N. Federal Hwy., #304, Fort Lauderdale, FL 33308, USA (☎(954) 776-2626; fax 776-3303; www.iglta.com). An organization of over 1350 companies serving gay and lesbian travelers worldwide.

International Lesbian and Gay Association (ILGA), 81 rue Marché-au-Charbon, B-1000 Brussels, Belgium (☎/fax +32 (2) 502 24 71; www.ilga.org). Not a travel service; provides political information, such as homosexuality laws of individual countries.

TRAVELERS WITH DISABILITIES

China, including Hong Kong, is ill-equipped to deal with disabled travelers. Despite the efforts of Deng Pufang (one of the sons of the late Chinese leader Deng Xiaoping) and the China Disabled Persons Federation, physical improvements in disabled access are still slow to be implemented. Attitudes toward disabled Chinese have gradually improved, particularly in larger cities like Beijing, Shanghai, Nanjing, Guangzhou, and Hong Kong, and the May 2000 Asian Special Olympics Games in Beijing represented another means of increasing public awareness.

That said, hospitals cannot be relied upon to replace broken braces or prostheses; orthopedic materials, even in large cities, are undependable. Public transportation in mainland China is almost entirely inaccessible. Some buses in Hong Kong now have special wheelchair lifts, although there may be no room to get on and off. Train and long-distance bus stations may have escalators in the main waiting areas, but platform access is almost always via steps. All but the newest airports lack elevators, offering only stairway access to airplanes. Successfully making special arrangements for the physically disabled may require much prodding and crossed fingers. While classier hotels often have elevators (which may or may not be wheelchair accessible), most budget accommodations don't. Rural areas have potholed roads and no sidewalks, and larger cities are packed with curbs and steps. Even in areas that are accessible, crowded streets and informal pushing and shoving matches present another a potential challenge.

USEFUL ORGANIZATIONS

Mobility International USA (MIUSA), P.O. Box 10767, Eugene, OR 97440, USA (☎(541) 343-1284 voice and TDD; fax 343-6812; email info@miusa.org; www.miusa.org). Sells *A World of Options: A Guide to International Educational Exchange, Community Service, and Travel for Persons with Disabilities* (US$35).

Moss Rehab Hospital Travel Information Service (☎(215) 456-9600 or (800) CALL-MOSS; email netstaff@mossresourcenet.org; www.mossresourcenet.org). An information resource center on travel-related concerns for those with disabilities.

Society for the Advancement of Travel for the Handicapped (SATH), 347 Fifth Ave., #610, New York, NY 10016 (☎(212) 447-7284; www.sath.org). An advocacy group that publishes the quarterly travel magazine *OPEN WORLD* (free for members, US$13 for nonmembers). Also publishes a wide range of info sheets on disability travel facilitation and destinations. Annual membership US$45, students and seniors US$30.

MINORITY TRAVELERS

Every non-Asian traveler to China will find herself or himself in the minority. People will inevitably point and stare, crowds will gather around you, and you will be trailed by a constant murmur of *"laowai!"* (Mandarin for foreigner) wherever you go. People will want to practice their English with you or have their photo taken with you. Your best strategy is to simply take it all in stride and to go about your business politely but firmly. The Chinese reaction to you is more likely to be curiosity than malice.

For any foreign tourist, traveling in China means dealing with often incorrect assumptions about who you are based on your skin color; this problem is exacerbated if you are not white or not overseas Chinese. Non-white and non-Chinese tourists in China face a unique set of challenges and prejudices.. Unfortunately, the darker your skin, the worse your treatment in the PRC. While incidents of racial violence or serious harassment are few and far between, discrimination on the basis of skin color is alive and well, be it from hotel owners, shopkeepers, travel agents, or government officials. Overseas Chinese may face a different set of challenges, in which people assume that they can understand spoken and written Chinese like a native and are surprised and sometimes offended if they cannot.

TRAVELERS WITH CHILDREN

Family vacations often require that you slow your pace, and always require that you plan ahead. When deciding where to stay, remember the special needs of young children and realize that few hotels offer specialized children's services or programs. Cribs or cots for babies are usually not available. Private places for **breast feeding** and changing tables are generally nonexistent, although some train stations may have special waiting rooms for pregnant mothers and mothers with small children. Be sure that your child carries some sort of ID (including instructions and contact information in Chinese) in case of an emergency, and arrange a reunion spot in case of separation when sightseeing.

Many museums and tourist attractions have a children's rate, although exact age and height restrictions (often under 1.3m) vary. Children under two generally fly for 10% of the adult airfare on flights (this does not necessarily include a seat), and children ages 2-11 fly for half price.

DIETARY CONCERNS

Although Chinese food often contains meat, especially pork, or uses meat bases, **vegetarian** dishes abound. Buddhists are the biggest group of Chinese vegetarians, and one of the best places for a good vegetarian meal is often the nearest Buddhist monastery. Very few non-Buddhist Chinese are vegetarians, but non-meat-based dishes, many of which use tofu, are popular nonetheless. Vegetarian restaurants can be found in many cities, and sùcài, or vegetarian dishes, are available at virtually every Chinese restaurant (see **Phrasebook**, p. 758). However, even meatless dishes are usually prepared using animal-based cooking oils and other products; it may be hard, if not impossible, to find food cooked otherwise. Strict vegetarians and vegans may want to consider preparing their own food while traveling.

While **kosher** meals are practically nonexistent in China, a strong Muslim presence makes **halal** (qīngzhēn; 清真) food a large part of the cuisine, especially in the north and west and in Xinjiang. Restaurants and stores certified *halal* are recognizable by their trademark green awnings and Arabic characters and are considered by some to offer more sanitary food than their Chinese non-halal counterparts. **The Jewish Travel Guide,** which lists synagogues, kosher restaurants, and Jewish institutions in over 100 countries, is available in Europe from Vallentine Mitchell Publishers, Newbury House 890-900, Eastern Ave., Newbury Park, Ilford, Essex IG2 7HH, UK (☎ (020) 8599 8866; fax 8599 0984) and in the US ($16.95 + $4 S&H) from ISBS, 5804 NE Hassallo St., Portland, OR 97213 (☎ (800) 944-6190).

CULTURE SHOCK

BATHROOMS. Culture shock can't be measured in volts, but the jolt sent through most Westerners the first time they see and smell a Chinese toilet is roughly equivalent to sticking a fork in a socket. China may show you a lot more of the entire relief process than you ever wanted to see. Unless you're in a mid-range or deluxe hotel, a new department store, or a Western restaurant—and sometimes not even then—you'll find that most public toilets are of the squatting kind. Most smell like a sewer. Stall partitions are often surprisingly low, and stall doors are sometimes entirely absent. Let it be known, however, that within this subspecies of toilet there is quite a bit of variation. Some are flushable basins recessed into the floor (a sort of horizontal urinal at ground level). Some are basic pits without any running water. A small percentage is maintained by a brigade of custodians who often charge you Y0.2-0.5 for the privilege of relieving yourself. Train toilets are a breed of their own. In all cases, toilet paper will most certainly not be provided—and definitely not for free. For more info, see **Taking the "Oooo" Out of Loo,** p. 89.

SPITTING. Polluted cities and poor sanitation mean that respiratory flus are par for the course for everyone living through a Chinese winter, and the Chinese tend to be fairly up front about how they take care of their phlegm. Neither men nor women are shy about hawking back and letting it fly in public. Free and unfettered expectoration is commonplace on Chinese streets, and, though most Chinese will refrain when inside a building, the interiors of trains and buses are fair game. This makes sitting on the floor in public places—a risky option anywhere in the world—particularly unsavory. There is no way to avoid the spitting, so when you hear the trademark clearing of the throat, turn around and get out of the way.

STARING. If you went to China wearing an extra head, you couldn't attract any more attention than you will merely by virtue of being a foreigner. Even in moderately sized East Coast cities, a non-Chinese face still attracts troops of curious onlookers. Staring is not quite the social faux pas in China that it is in the West, and you will almost certainly be stared at by everyone, from small children to store clerks to business people. There is little that you can do to ward off the spectators; take solace in the fact that you have indeed achieved a special place in the pantheon of Chinese tourist sights. Wearing unobtrusive clothing is recommended, and body piercing and brightly colored hair dye are certain to make you stand out even more. Yelling to stop staring (in any language) or showing obvious annoyance will most likely just make the problem worse. If you speak Chinese, striking up a conversation with onlookers is often the best way to deal with unwanted attention. Most Chinese will assume that foreigners speak English and may be extremely eager to practice with you. As always, beware of the occasional moneymaking scam that begins as a simple request to speak English or take a personal guided tour of the city. Most of all, travelers should remember that staring usually represents friendly curiosity, nothing more. See also **Minority Travelers,** p. 87.

BEGGARS. Begging is a fact of life in China. While beggars are relatively scarce in the large, wealthy cities on the eastern seaboard, at some point or another, you are likely to be approached by panhandlers, whether in Beijing or in poverty-stricken Guizhou and Tibet. Rising unemployment means more and more people throughout the country are asking for spare change. In crowded areas like train and bus stations, elderly men and women, handicapped people, mothers with babies, or young children frequently beg for money. The kids, generally around four or five years old, are quite tenacious, often grabbing hold of the legs and arms of pass-

ESSENTIALS

TAKING THE "OOOO" OUT OF LOO

TAKING THE "OOOO" OUT OF LOO Moved by the demands of an increasing number of tourists and international conventions, the Chinese government has decided to clean up its act. Over 4000 toilets in Beijing have undergone renovation, the Chinese Revolutionary Museum has seen three "model toilet exhibitions," and the Great Hall of the People, meeting-ground of the National People's Congress, was the site of a bathroom-designing competition. But China is still a big place and the effects of all this work may not be visible for years to come. Until then, these handy hints may help put relief back in the process of relieving yourself.

1. Public toilets are generally located every few blocks or so and are free unless there is an attendant (about Y0.5). Signs often have "WC" or pictures in addition to Chinese characters. But just in case...men (男) and women (女).

2. Carry your own stash of toilet paper. Never before have those little travel packs of tissue been so ideally suited to a purpose.

3. Keep an eye out for a five-star hotel, McDonald's, or KFC, and inconspicuously mosey into bathrooms with sit-down toilets and toilet paper. Many of the new department stores springing up throughout the country also have excellent bathrooms, manned by staunch cleaners who mop up after each go.

ersby and hanging on. It is ultimately up to you, but if you do give money, you run the risk of being thronged by more beggars hoping to receive the same treatment. Keeping a handful of spare change in your pockets can prevent the spectacle of pulling out wads of bills when you don't intend to.

ALTERNATIVES TO TOURISM

Opportunities for work, study, or other activities conducive to meeting more than (fun as they are) hotel owners, cab drivers, and other tourists abound in China. Many foreigners go to teach English, to study Mandarin, martial arts, or Chinese medicine, or to volunteer. Here are some helpful resources:

STUDYING ABROAD

Foreign students constitute one of the largest parts of China's expatriate population. Summer-, semester-, and year-long programs, especially for Chinese language study, are increasing in number all the time; many are in Beijing, but Harbin, Nanjing, Shanghai, and many smaller cities also run programs.

To study in China for up to 6 months, you will need an "F" visa; an "X" visa is required for students planning to stay for 6-12 months (see **Visas**, p. 50). To obtain either visa, you will need a **letter of Invitation** and a **JW202 form** (further confirmation that you are indeed welcome at the school you will attend) from a school or university in China. Study abroad programs operating in China usually assist participants with getting visas and residence permits. Students enrolling directly in a Chinese university will need to get both of the relevant forms from that university and include those in their visa applications.

Many foreign language programs are run by foreign universities or independent international organizations, in cooperation with Chinese universities. If your Chinese is already proficient, applying directly to Chinese universities can be much cheaper than a US university program, though it can be hard to transfer academic credit. Schools that offer study abroad programs to foreigners are listed below.

China Scholarship Council, 160 Fuxingmennei Dajie, Beijing 100031 (☎(010) 6641 3249; fax 6641 3198; email webmaster@csc.edu.cn; www.csc.edu.cn), a division of the Ministry of Education. Provides financial support and resources for Chinese citizens wishing to study abroad and for foreign students wishing to study in China. Maintains a comprehensive directory of Chinese universities admitting foreign students.

Hopkins-Nanjing Center for Chinese and American Studies, 1619 Massachusetts Ave. NW, Washington, DC 20036 (☎(202) 663-5800; fax 663-7729; email nanjing@jhu.edu;

www.sais-jhu.edu/nanjing), is a joint Johns Hopkins University and Nanjing University program that provides one year of graduate study for Chinese, American, and international students in Chinese and American social sciences. Also offers summer language programs.

Council on International Educational Exchange (CIEE), Beijing Office, Olympic Hotel, 52 Baishiqiao Lu, Rm. 319, Beijing 100081 (☎(010) 6217 5830; fax 6217 5808; email josseyln@public2.est.cn.net). Also at 205 East 42nd St., New York, NY 10017 (☎(888) 268-6245 or (800) 407-8839; www.ciee.org/study), CIEE hosts study abroad programs in Beijing, Hong Kong, Nanjing, and Shanghai. The organization also arranges teaching positions in China.

CET Academic Programs, 1000 16th St. NW, Ste. 350, Washington, DC 20036 (☎(800) 225-4262; fax (202) 342-0317; email cet@academic-travel.com; www.cetacademicprograms.com). Runs academic year and summer language programs in Beijing and Harbin and a summer language program in Nanjing.

Princeton in Beijing, 211 Jones Hall, Princeton University, Princeton, NJ 08544 (☎(609) 258-4269; fax 258-6984; email pib@princeton.edu; www.princeton.edu/~pib). Summer-long intensive Mandarin programs in conjunction with Beijing Normal University.

School for International Training, College Semester Abroad, Admissions, Kipling Rd., P.O. Box 676, Brattleboro, VT 05302 (☎(800) 336-1616 or (802) 258-3267; www.sit.edu). Semester-long program in Yunnan costs about US$10,500. Also runs the **Experiment in International Living** (☎(800) 345-2929; fax (802) 258-3428; email eil@worldlearning.org), which arranges 4-week summer travel programs for high-school students (US$4,900).

WORKING ABROAD

To work in China, you must have an employment visa ("Z"), which requires an invitation letter from the Chinese government or your employer. Most people find work and make the necessary visa arrangements before they go to China, as it is much easier than going to China on a tourist visa, finding a job, and then obtaining a work visa. Working with a tourist visa is, of course, illegal.

There are many opportunities to teach English in China. It is possible to apply directly to a Chinese school or university, and occasionally job openings are posted on the web. Many US organizations help arrange teaching positions. Compensation is minimal by Western standards, but housing is usually provided and the salary should be enough to cover all living expenses. **CIEE** (see **Studying Abroad,** p. 89) also arranges teaching positions in China.

Office of Overseas Schools, US Department of State, Room H328, SA-1, Washington, D.C. 20522 (☎(202) 261-8200; fax 261-8224; www.state.gov/www/about_state/schools). Keeps a comprehensive list of schools abroad and agencies that arrange placement for Americans to teach abroad.

International Schools Services, Educational Staffing Program, P.O. Box 5910, Princeton, NJ 08543 (☎(609) 452-0990; fax 452-2690; email edustaffing@iss.edu; www.iss.edu). Recruits teachers and administrators for American and English schools in China. All instruction in English. Applicants must have a bachelor's degree and two years of relevant experience. Non-refundable US$100 application fee. Publishes *The ISS Directory of Overseas Schools* (US$35).

VOLUNTEERING

Volunteer jobs are available in China, almost always through foreign-sponsored organizations. You may receive room and board in exchange for your labor. You can sometimes avoid the high application fees charged by the organizations that arrange placement by contacting the individual workcamps directly; check with the organizations.

Global Volunteers, 375 E. Little Canada Rd., St. Paul, MN 55117-1628 (☎(800) 487-1074 or (651) 407-6100; fax 482-0915; email email@globalvolunteers.org; www.globalvolunteers.org). Sponsors 2- to 3-week volunteer English and business skills teaching programs in China. No teaching experience is required.

Peace Corps, Office of Volunteer Recruitment and Selection, 1111 20th St. NW, Washington, D.C. 20526 (☎(800) 424-8580; www.peacecorps.gov). Opportunities in 78 developing nations, including China. Volunteers must be US citizens ages 18+ willing to make a 2-year commitment. A bachelor's degree is usually required.

Volunteers for Peace, 1034 Tiffany Rd., Belmont, VT 05730 (☎(802) 259-2759; www.vfp.org). Arranges placement in workcamps in China. Annual *International Workcamp Directory* US$20. Registration fee US$200. Free newsletter.

World Teach, Harvard Institute for International Development, 14 Story St., Cambridge, MA 02138 (☎(617) 495-5527; fax 495-1599; email info@worldteach.org; worldteach.org). Volunteers primarily teach classes in spoken English to students of all ages in China. BA or BS required for 6-month-long (extendable to one year) program; summer program open to anyone over 18. Program fee includes airfare, health insurance and training, and room and board.

WORLD WIDE WEB

Almost every aspect of budget travel (with the most notable exception, of course, being experience) is accessible via the web. Within 10 minutes at the keyboard, you can get advice on travel hotspots or experiences from other travelers who have just returned from China. Listed here are some budget travel sites to start off your surfing; other relevant web sites are listed throughout the book. Because website turnover is high, use search engines (such as www.google.com or www.altavista.com) to strike out on your own.

LEARNING THE ART OF BUDGET TRAVEL

How to See the World: www.artoftravel.com. A compendium of great travel tips, from cheap flights to self defense to interacting with local culture.

Rec. Travel Library: www.travel-library.com. A fantastic set of links for general information and personal travelogues.

Shoestring Travel: www.stratpub.com. An e-zine focusing on budget travel.

CHINA ON THE WEB

CIA World Factbook: www.odci.gov/cia/publications/factbook/index.html. Tons of vital statistics on China's geography, government, economy, and people.

Foreign Language for Travelers: www.travlang.com. Provides free online translating dictionaries and lists of phrases in Chinese.

MyTravelGuide: www.mytravelguide.com. Country overviews, with everything from history to transportation to live web cam coverage of China.

Geographia: www.geographia.com. The highlights, culture, and people of China.

Atevo Travel: www.atevo.com/guides/destinations. Detailed introductions, travel tips, and suggested itineraries.

Columbus Travel Guides: http://www.travel-guides.com/navigate/world.asp. Helpful practical information.

LeisurePlanet: www.leisureplanet.com/TravelGuides. Good general background.

TravelPage: www.travelpage.com. Links to official tourist office sites throughout China.

PlanetRider: www.planetrider.com/Travel_Destinations.cfm. A subjective list of links to the "best" websites covering the culture and tourist attractions of China.

AND OUR PERSONAL FAVORITE...

🏠 **Let's Go:** www.letsgo.com. Our recently revamped website features photos and streaming video, info about our books, stories from our researchers on the road (in China and everywhere else), a travel forum buzzing with stories and tips, and links that will help you find everything you ever wanted to know about China.

BEIJING
AND THE NORTH COAST

China's north coast is something of a jigsaw puzzle, each piece with its own distinct fate, but all fitting together to form an impressive picture of a country proud of its history and culture. At the center stands Beijing, an independent municipality and the nation's capital, trend-setter, and rule-maker. Accustomed to living in the capital's shadow, Hebei province is the traditional getaway of Beijing bigshots, be they emperors lounging in the shade at the Summer Villa in Chengde or cadres sunbathing at Beidaihe. The tiny seaside village of Shanhaiguan anchors one end of the **Great Wall,** which slices through northern Hebei, cresting over Beijing on its 6400km journey west to Gansu province. The **Grand Canal,** the world's longest manmade waterway, also originates here, linking Beijing with Shandong province and snaking south all the way to Hangzhou. Water traffic is not the only thing that keeps trade thriving between Beijing and southern cities. Beijing's proximity to the coast, and to port cities like Tianjin and Qingdao, has ensured that foreign goods and ideas have always made their way toward Beijing.

The area may not have been the birthplace of Chinese civilization (that title undoubtedly belongs to the central provinces of Shanxi, Shaanxi, and Henan), but it was the literal birthplace of the fathers of its longest-lasting and most influential intellectual tradition: **Confucianism.** The man himself was born in Qufu, and Mencius, his most famous disciple, was born in nearby Zouxian. Daoism's most important pilgrimage site, **Taishan,** is but a scant few hours away.

In fact, everywhere a tourist turns, the legacy of dynastic history rears its mighty head—in remnants of the Qin-era Great Wall, the Ming dynasty's Forbidden City, and the Summer Palace's ill-conceived marble boat (see p. 13). The European-style architecture of Qingdao and Tianjin serves as a reminder of the foreign concessions of the late 19th century. On the eve of the bamboo curtain's descent over newly Communist China, Mao proclaimed the founding of the PRC from atop Tiananmen Gate, and his embalmed corpse rests nearby. But, dynastic cycles are exactly that—cycles. And now, from the rough-and-tumble provincial capitals of Shijiazhuang and Jinan to the most refined sector of Beijing, the region is re-outfitting itself in the style of China's latest craze: prosperity and modernity.

HIGHLIGHTS OF BEIJING AND THE NORTH COAST

THE IMPERIAL SCALE of Beijing, home to some of the finest remnants of the country's imperial past, including the **Forbidden City** (p. 118), **Tiantan Park** (p. 122), **Lama Temple** (p. 121), and the **Summer Palace** (p. 125).

LEGENDARY LINE OF DEFENSE at the **Great Wall** (p. 127 and p. 151), just a few hours from Beijing.

REGAL RESPITE at the Imperial Summer Villa (p. 148) in **Chengde.**

HOLIEST OF THE HOLY at **Taishan** (p. 160), one of Daoism's sacred mountains.

THE BREWS ON TAP at the beachside town of **Qingdao** (p. 167).

BEIJING 北京 ☎010

Beijing is a city built for giants. From the gargantuan boulevards to the enormous Forbidden City, the cityscape is conceptualized on a grand scale. As China's political, economic, and cultural nucleus for the better part of 700 years, Beijing is figuratively and literally imposing. Palaces, temples, and parks where generations of emperors lived, worked, prayed, and played are scattered all over the city. In the

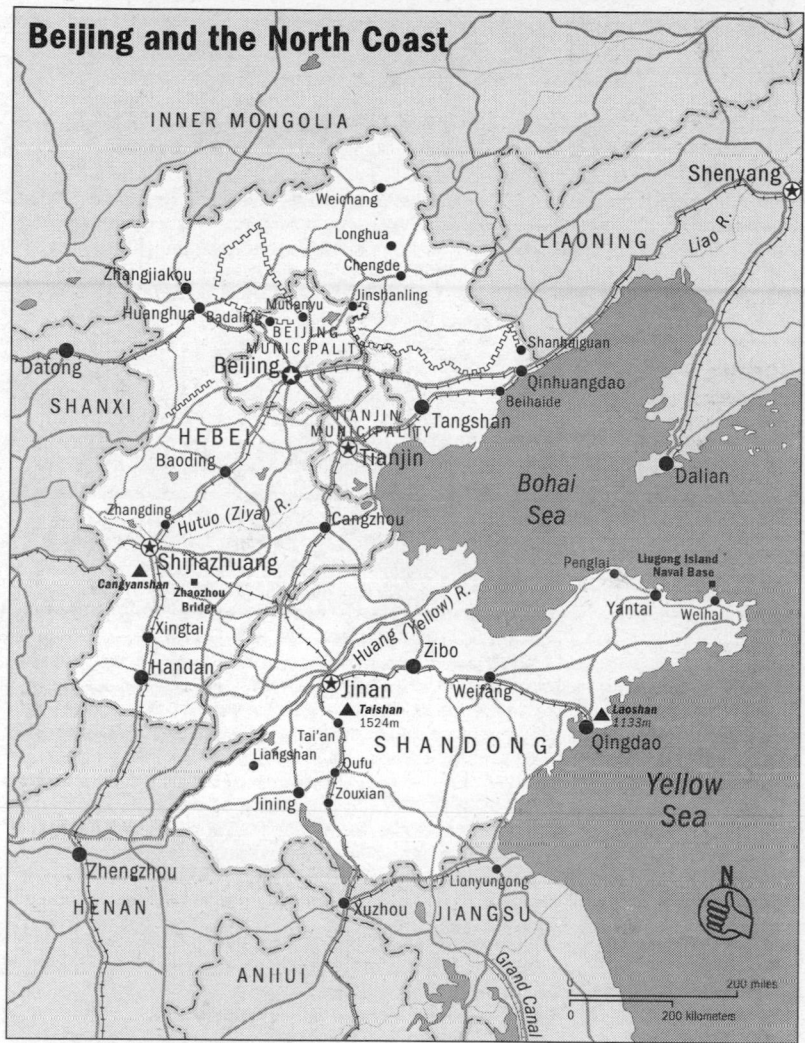

BEIJING & NORTH COAST

city center, the vast concrete swath that is Tiananmen Square edges up against the white marble bridges and bright red palace walls of the Forbidden City; hanging above the crimson archway, Chairman Mao directs his gaze at McDonald's and KFC across the square. The green of capitalism constantly wrestles with communist grays and imperial reds for a place to call home; meanwhile, streams of businessmen toting cellphones, PLA officers in overstuffed army parkas, and uniformed school children hurry down the streets in pursuit of something grand.

Beijing certainly has its hold on China. The whole country runs on Beijing time and learns Beijing Mandarin; the first lesson in elementary school primers nationwide is "I love Beijing." The amusing thing about all this Beijing fever is that visitors to the densely populated and pollution-laden city will often find themselves slave to the sickness, too. Beijing has a way of clearing its thick gray skies and pausing in its rush against time just long enough for a passing visitor to be able to see through the haze. Its imposing atmosphere and Communist rhetoric lighten, and for a moment, if just a moment, it just could feel like home.

Beijing

🏠 ACCOMMODATIONS

Beijing University Shaoyuan Hotel, 1	B1
Big Bell Temple Hotel, 4	C2
Evergreen Hotel, 5	B3
Feng Long Hotel, 7	D6
Furong Hotel, 15	F4
Jing Hua Youth Hostel, 10	D6
Leyou Hotel, 14	F5
Lihua Hotel, 9	D6
Qiaoyuan Hotel, 8	D5
Qinghua Yuan Hotel, 3	C1
Sea Star Hotel, 11	D6
Shangyuan Hotel, 6	C3
Tiantan Haoyuan Hotel, 12	E5
Tiantan Sports Hotel, 13	E5
Zhongguancun Hotel, 2	B1

TO MING TOMBS (50 km),
BADALING GREAT WALL (65 km),
AND HUANGHUA GREAT WALL (100 km)

Datun Lu

TO CAPITAL AIRPORT (25 km),
MUTIANYU GREAT WALL (70 km)
AND SIMATAI GREAT WALL (120 km)

Nanhugu Lu
Jixianqiao Lu

Beiyuan Lu

Beijing College
of Tourism

Chinese Ethnic Culture Park

International Olympics Center

Beisihuan Dong Lu

Huayuan Bei Lu

Badaling Expwy

Beitucheng Lu

Tiyanggong Lu

Ba River

Beisanhuan Zhong Lu

Anding Lu

Sino-Japanese Friendship Hospital

Xinjiekouwai Dajie

Deshengmenwai Dajie

Beisanhuan Dong Lu

Shoudujichang Lu

Shuangyi Lu

Andingmenwai Dajie

Hepingli Station

Liangmaqiao Lu

Liuyin Park

Ditan Park (Temple of the Earth)

地坛公园

SEE CENTRAL BEIJING MAP

Dongzhimen Waixie Jie

Dongzhimen Wai Dajie

Moat

Xihai Lake

Gulou Xi Dajie

GULOU DAJIE

AIDINGMEN

YONGHEGONG

Lama Temple

CHAOYANG

JISHUITAN

Bei Dajie

Xinjiekou Nan Dajie

Xinjiekou

D'anmen Dajie

Gulou Dong Dajie

Dongzhimennei Dajie

DONGZHIMEN

Houhai Lake

Di'anmen Xi Dajie

Di'anmen Dong Dajie

DONGSI SHITIAO

Museum of Agriculture

Chaoyang Park

Nongzhanguan Nan Lu

Beihai Park

北海公园

Gongrentiyuchang Bei Lu

Workers' Stadium

Beihai Lake

Jingshan Park

景山公园

Dongsi Xi Dajie

Chaoyangmennei Dajie

CHAOYANGMEN

Tuanjie Lake Park

Honglingjin Park

Zhonghai Lake

FORBIDDEN CITY

故宫博物院

Chaoyangmenwei Dajie

DONGCHENG

Ritan Park

日坛公园

Chaoyang Lu

Jintai Lu

15

Xidan Bei Lu

Nanhai Lake

AIDAN

TIANANMEN WEST

TIANANMEN

WANGFUJING

DONGDAN

JIAGUOMEN

WORLD TRADE CTR. (GUOMAO)

DAYANG

SIHUI

SIHUI EAST

TO EASTERN QING TUMBS (150 km)

Xi Chang'an Jie

Dong Chang'an Jie

Jianguomen Nei Dajie

Jianguomenwai Dajie

TIAN'ANMEN SQUARE

天安门广场

Dongsanhuan Zhong Lu

Tonghui River

Jingtong Expwy

XUANWUMEN

HEPINGMEN

CHONGWENMEN

BEIJING ZHAN

Beijing Station

Qianmen

Chongwenmen

Dong Dajie

Chongwenmen Xi Dajie

Beijing East Station

Xuanwumen Dong Dajie

Xuanwumen Wai Dajie

Xibianmen

Qianmen Xi Dajie

Qianmen Dong Dajie

Guangqu Lu

Xinhua Jie

Zhushikou Dong Dajie

Guangqumennei Dajie

Guanggumen Wai Dajie

Xidamen

XUANWU

Luomashi Dajie

Hufang Lu

Zhushikou Xi Dajie

CHONGWEN

Majuan Bus Station

Nanmofang Lu

International Post Office

Yongdingmennei Dajie

Tiantan Lu

Tiantan Park (Temple of Heaven)

天坛公园

13

12

Taijing Lu

Taoranting Park

Tianqiao Bus Station

Yaowa Park

Longtan Park

龙潭公园

Panjiayuan Flea Market

14

Yongdingmen Bus Station

8

Malianbao Lu

Shazikou Lu

Tiantan Dong Lu

Beijing South Station

Yongdingmenwai Dajie

Wanfangting Park

10

9

11

Muxiyuan Bus Station

Nanshanhuan Dong Lu

Zhoujiazhuang

Beijing-Tianjin-Tanggu Expwy

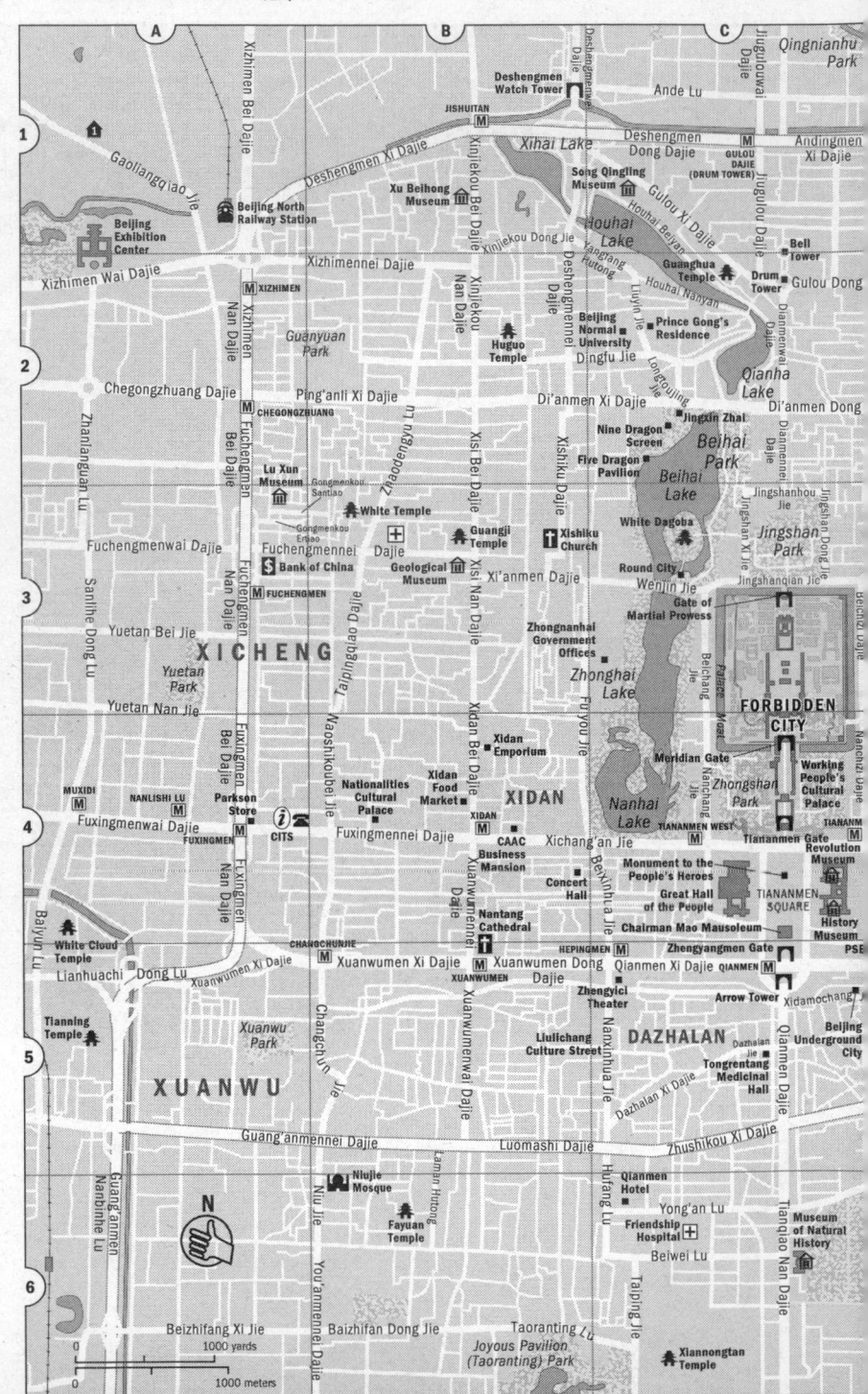

Qingnianhu Park
Deshengmen Watch Tower
Ande Lu
JISHUITAN
Xihai Lake
Deshengmen Dong Lu
Xizhimen Bei Dajie
Gaoliangqiao Jie
Deshengmen Xi Dajie
Kinjiekou Bei Dajie
Song Qingling Museum
Gulou Xi Dajie
GULOU DAJIE (DRUM TOWER)
Andingmen Xi Dajie
Beijing North Railway Station
Xu Beihong Museum
Xinjiekou Dong Jie
Houhai Lake
Houhai Beiyan
Guanghua Temple
Bell Tower
Drum Tower
Gulou Dong
Beijing Exhibition Center
Xizhimennei Dajie
Xinjiekou Nan Dajie
Yangfang Hutong
Luyin Lu
Houhai Nanyan
Xizhimen Wai Dajie
XIZHIMEN
Deshengmennei Dajie
Beijing Normal University
Prince Gong's Residence
Qianhai Lake
Guanyuan Park
Huguo Temple
Dingfu Jie
Diannenmei Dajie
Ping'anli Xi Dajie
Zhaodengyu Lu
Di'anmen Xi Dajie
Di'anmen Dong
Chegongzhuang Dajie
CHEGONGZHUANG
Xis Bei Dajie
Nine Dragon Screen
Jingxin Zhai
Beihai Park
Jingshanhou Jie
Jingshan Dong Jie
Fuchengmen Bei Dajie
Lu Xun Museum
Gongmenkou Santiao
Five Dragon Pavilion
Beihai Lake
Jingshan Park
Fuchengmennai Dajie
Gongmenkou Ertiao
White Temple
Fuchengmennei Dajie
Xishiku Dajie
White Dagoba
Jingshan Xi Jie
Bank of China
Guangji Temple
Geological Museum
Xishiku Church
Round City
Wenjin Jie
Jingshanqian Jie
FUCHENGMEN
Xi'anmen Dajie
Gate of Martial Prowess
Beichizi Dajie
Santihe Dong Lu
XICHENG
Taipingqiao Dajie
Xisi Nan Dajie
Zhongnanhai Government Offices
Yuetan Bei Jie
Zhanlanguan Lu
Zhonghai Lake
Beichang Jie
FORBIDDEN CITY
Nanchizi Dajie
Yuetan Park
Naoshikoubei Jie
Fuchengmen Nan Dajie
Yuetan Nan Jie
Fuxingmen Bei Dajie
Xidan Emporium
Meridian Gate
Zhongshan Park
Working People's Cultural Palace
Fuxingmennai Dajie
Nationalities Cultural Palace
Xidan Food Market
Xidan Bei Dajie
Nanchang Jie
Nanheyan Dajie
MUXIDI
NANLISHI LU
Parkson Store
XIDAN
Nanhai Lake
TIANANMEN WEST
Zhongshan Park
TIANANMEN
Revolution Museum
Fuxingmenwai Dajie
CITS
Fuxingmennei Dajie
CAAC
Xichang'an Jie
Tiananmen Gate
FUXINGMEN
Business Mansion
Beixinhua Jie
Monument to the People's Heroes
History Museum
Fuxingmen Nan Dajie
Nantang Cathedral
Concert Hall
Great Hall of the People
TIANANMEN SQUARE
PSE
Baiyun Lu
Xuanwumen Xi Dajie
CHANGCHUNJIE
HEPINGMEN
Chairman Mao Mausoleum
Zhengyangmen Gate
White Cloud Temple
Xuanwumen Dong
Qianmen Xi Dajie
QIANMEN
Lianhuachi
Changchun Jie
Xuanwumen Dajie
XUANWUMEN
Zhengyici Theater
Arrow Tower
Xidamochang
Tianning Temple
Xuanwu Park
Xuanwumenwai Dajie
Liulichang Culture Street
Nanxinhua Jie
DAZHALAN
Dazhalan Jie
Beijing Underground City
XUANWU
Tongrentang Medicinal Hall
Qianmen Dajie
Dazhalan Xi Jie
Guang'anmennei Dajie
Luomashi Dajie
Zhushikou Xi Dajie
Qianmen Hotel
Guang'anmen Nanbinhe Lu
Niu Jie
Niujie Mosque
Jiaman Hutong
Hufang Lu
Yong'an Lu
Friendship Hospital
Beiwei Lu
Museum of Natural History
Tianqiao Nan Dajie
Fayuan Temple
You'anmennei Dajie
N
Beizhifang Xi Jie
Baizhifan Dong Jie
Taoranting Lu
Taiping Jie
Joyous Pavilion (Taoranting) Park
Xiannongtan Temple
0 1000 yards
0 1000 meters

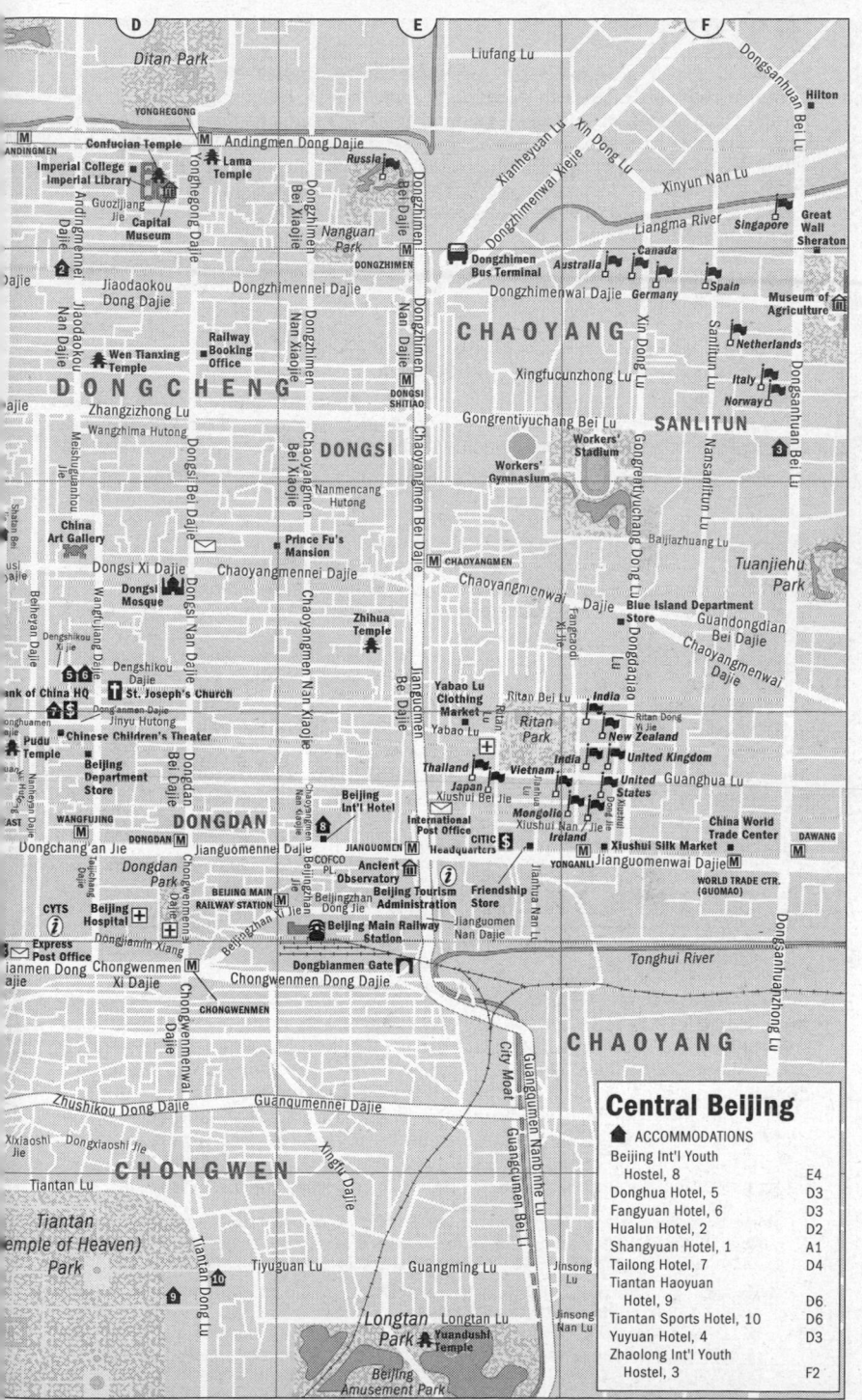

Central Beijing

ACCOMMODATIONS

Beijing Int'l Youth Hostel, 8	E4
Donghua Hotel, 5	D3
Fangyuan Hotel, 6	D3
Hualun Hotel, 2	D2
Shangyuan Hotel, 1	A1
Tailong Hotel, 7	D4
Tiantan Haoyuan Hotel, 9	D6
Tiantan Sports Hotel, 10	D6
Yuyuan Hotel, 4	D3
Zhaolong Int'l Youth Hostel, 3	F2

HISTORY

From Peking Man's stone tools to construction workers' jackhammers, Beijingers have witnessed an unending cycle of building, wrecking, and rebuilding. Over 3000 years ago, Beijing became Yanjing, capital of Yan, one of the six kingdoms later conquered by Qin Shihuang. Early emperors shunned this backwater, Great Wall town, preferring the fertile plains around Xian and Luoyang for their capitals. Not even the construction of the Grand Canal from Beijing to Hangzhou in AD 607 could awaken the city from its provincial doldrums. It was a series of nomadic invasions that caused Beijing's real estate value to rise. Kublai Khan and his Mongol army thundered into China from the grasslands up north, subjugating the Han people and establishing the Yuan dynasty. The Mongols proceeded to dig gigantic lakes in downtown Beijing in an attempt to recreate their idyllic Lake Baikal homeland. The Yuan rulers not only made Beijing pretty; they made her pretty authoritarian as well. For the first time, Beijing had become the political and administrative center of China.

In 1368, the Ming dynasty briefly moved the capital to Nanjing before a nasty succession feud ended with Emperor Yongle moving the court back to Beijing. Dissatisfied with what the Mongols had left behind, the Ming emperor began a fresh round of construction that included the Forbidden City and Tiantan (Temple of Heaven). After the Manchus swept down and relieved the Ming of their heavenly mandate, they settled right in to the Forbidden City. Their dynasty, the Qing, witnessed an explosion of palaces, temples, and parks, including the Old and New Summer Palaces in the northwest of the city. During the last hundred years of the Qing, British and French troops burned the Summer Palace, and Christian missions, consulates, and hotels mushroomed beside Beijing courtyard homes.

When the revolution of 1911 installed the republican capital down south, Beijing was demoted to Beiping, the "city of northern peace." This turned out to be a blessing in disguise; as a newly unimportant city, Beijing was spared the wartime destruction inflicted on its southern counterparts. After a peaceful handover in 1948, the Communists outfitted their new capital with nondescript factories and apartment blocks, the grand hallmarks of socialist architecture. Population growth combined with industrial development and investment to result in a rapid increase in standard of living and infrastructure, setting a pace of development that continues, in fits and starts, to this day.

◪ GETTING THERE AND AWAY

BY PLANE

Beijing's **Capital Airport** (shǒudū jīchǎng; 首都机场; ☎6456 2580) is about an hour from the city center. A taxi to the city costs at least Y80. From the airport, go outside the terminal to the taxi stand; taxi drivers that hover around the arrivals area inside the airport invariably charge far more. A cheaper but slower (and less direct) alternative to or from the airport is the **CAAC shuttle bus** (1-1½hr., Y16). The bus runs to and from various points in the city, but the most reliable place to be picked up is in front of the Aviation Building at 15 Xi Changan Dajie (5:30am-8:30pm) or at the International Hotel, near the Beijing Train Station. For more information on international flights to Beijing, see **Getting There: By Plane** (p. 72).

Domestic Airlines: Dragon Air, Henderson Center, 18 Jianguomennei Dajie, Tower 1, Ste. 1710 (☎6518 2533). **CAAC** headquarters in the Aviation Bldg., 15 Xi Changan Jie (☎6601 7755; 24hr. domestic inquiry ☎6256 7811; international inquiry daily 8am-5pm ☎6256 6783).

Asian Airlines: Air Macau, SCITECH Tower Place, 22 Jianguomenwai Dajie, Ste. 807 (☎6515 8988 or 6515 9398). **All Nippon Airways,** Fortune Bldg., 5 Dongsanhuan Bei Lu, Ste. N200 (☎6590 9191). **Asiana Airlines,** Lufthansa Center, Kempinski Hotel, 50 Liangmaqiao Lu, Ste. W102 (☎6468 4000). **Japan Airlines,** Changfugong Office Bldg., Hotel New Otari, 26 Jianguomenwai Dajie, 1st Fl. (☎6513 0888). **Korean Air,** China World Trade Center, 1 Jianguomenwai Dajie, Ste.

W401 (☎6505 0588). **Malaysian Airlines,** China World Trade Center, Tower 2, Ste. 1005 (☎6505 2681 or 6505 2683). **MIAT Mongolian Airlines,** China Golden Bridge Bldg., A1 Jianguomenwai Dajie, East Gate (☎6507 9297). **Pakistan International Airlines,** China World Trade Center, Ste. 617 (☎6505 1681 or 6505 1682). **Singapore Airlines,** China World Trade Center, Tower 2, 8th Fl. (☎6505 2233). **Thai Airways International,** Lufthansa Center, Ste. S102B (☎6460 8899).

Other Airlines: Aeroflot, Hotel Jinglun, 3 Jianguomenwai Dajie (☎6500 2412). **Air France,** Fenglian Plaza, Chaoyangmenwai Dajie, Ste. 515 (☎6588 1388). **Alitalia,** China World Trade Center, Ste. W501 (☎6505 3505). **Austrian Airlines,** Lufthansa Center, Ste. S103 (☎6462 2161 or 6462 2164). **British Airways,** SCITECH Tower Place, Ste. 210 (☎6512 4070 or 6512 4085). **Finnair,** SCITECH Tower Place, Ste. 204 (☎6512 7180 or 6512 7181). **KLM Royal Dutch Airlines,** China World Trade Center, Ste. W501 (☎6505 3505). **Lufthansa,** Lufthansa Center, Ste. S101 (☎6465 4488). **Northwest Airlines,** China World Trade Center, Ste. W501 (☎6505 3505). **Qantas,** Lufthansa Center, Ste. S120 (☎6467 3337). **Swissair,** SCITECH Tower Place, Ste. 201 (☎6512 3555). **United Airlines,** Lufthansa Center, 1st Fl. (☎6463 1111).

TO	PER DAY	PRICE	TO	PER DAY	PRICE
Changsha	2-4	Y970	Chengdu	11-13	Y1150
Chongqing	3-6	Y1250	Dalian	10-11	Y570
Fuzhou	4-5	Y1240	Guangzhou	10-12	Y1360
Guilin	3-4	Y1430	Haikou	6-8	Y1800
Harbin	8-11	Y770	Hefei	2	Y790
Hohhot	4-6	Y400	Hong Kong	5	XXX
Kunming	5-8	Y1450	Lanzhou	3	Y1070
Lhasa	1	Y1940	Nanjing	8-9	Y810
Qingdao	6-7	Y570	Sanya	3-4	Y1850
Shanghai	21-26	Y900	Shenyang	8-10	Y560
Ürümqi	3-4	Y1930	Wuhan	6-8	Y860
Xlamen	4-7	Y1370	Xlan	10-12	Y840

BY TRAIN

Several train stations serve Beijing. The chandeliers and marble tiles at **Beijing Train Station** (běijīng huǒchē zhàn; 北京火车站; ☎6512 9525 or 6563 3242) hardly lessen the chaos. Sandwiched between Jianguomennei Dajie and Chongwenmendong Dajie, it sits just southeast of the city center, accessible by the subway (Beijing Zhan stop) and a host of buses. The **Trans-Mongolian** train to Moscow departs from here (6 days, W and Sa; see p. 76); tickets can only be bought at the CITS head office in the Beijing International Hotel (see p. 102). This is also the place to catch trains to **Ulaanbataar, Mongolia** (30hr., Sa-Su, Y559-949) and **Pyongyang, North Korea** (22½hr.; M, W-Th, and Sa; Y467-652). The station's **booking office** for international passengers is in the left back corner on the first floor, through the soft seat waiting room. All international train tickets leaving China must be bought through CITS. The table at the end of this section gives details about trains to domestic destinations; Beijing Train Station departures are indicated by "BJ."

Beijing West Train Station (běijīng xī zhàn; 北京西站; ☎6321 6253) is on Lianhuachi Dong Lu near Lianhuachi Park, accessible by bus #52. Trains leaving from Beijing West are denoted "W" in the table below. Destinations of note are **Kowloon, Hong Kong** (28hr., every other day, Y650-777) and **Hanoi, Vietnam** (3 days, M and F). There is a "Booking Office for Compatriots of Hong Kong, Macau, Taiwan, and Foreign Visitors" on the second floor. International train tickets must be bought through a travel agency.

Beijing South Station (běijīng nán zhàn; 北京南站; ☎6303 0031), off Yonganmen Dongbinhe Lu, is accessible by buses #20 and 54. Trains to **Shidu** leave from here. **Beijing North Station** (běijīng běi zhàn; 北京北站; ☎6563 6223) is on the northwest corner of Erhuan Lu, accessible by the subway to Dongzhimen.

The following table provides the departure station, number of trains per day, duration of travel (in hours), and the price (in *yuan*) for all major Chinese cities serviced by trains from Beijing. The prices given range from the cheapest hard seat fare to the most expensive hard sleeper, although short routes have only hard seats available. Travel times vary depending on the speed of the train; faster trains are generally more expensive. For help reading your train ticket, see the ticket reader in the **Appendix** to this book, **p. 756.**

TO	站	PER DAY	HR.	PRICE	TO	站	PER DAY	HR.	PRICE
Baotou	BJ, W	4	14½	55-169	**Beidaihe**	BJ	2	2½	70-90
Changchun	BJ	7	13	137-319	**Changsha**	W	10	16	191-345
Chengde	BJ	4	4-7½	17-59	**Chengdu**	W	1	32	231-418
Chongqing	W	2	32-33	181-430	**Dalian**	BJ	2	10-16	126-269
Dandong	BJ	2	12-22	73-263	**Datong**	BJ, W	4	5-8	31-108
Fuzhou	BJ	1	35	253-458	**Guangzhou**	W	3	24	253-458
Guilin	W	2	30	400	**Guiyang**	W	1	34½	271-490
Hangzhou	BJ	1	14	200-363	**Harbin**	BJ	7	12-30	131-327
Hefei	BJ, W	2	12-15	68-263	**Hohhot**	BJ, W	4	11-12	92-170
Jinan	BJ	14	5-7	64-128	**Kunming**	W	1	46½	320-578
Lanzhou	W	4	29	208-390	**Luoyang**	W	8	11	53-117
Nanchang	W	3	17-24	86-277	**Nanjing**	BJ	2	12-18	73-274
Qingdao	BJ	2	12-14	102-201	**Qinhuangdao**	BJ	5	3	75
Shanghai	BJ	3	14-21	88-327	**Shenyang**	BJ, W	9	10	116
Shenzhen	W	1	33	257-467	**Shijiazhuang**	BJ	29	2½-6	33-40
Suzhou	BJ	1	14½	170-309	**Taiyuan**	BJ	2	10-14	79-224
Tianjin	BJ	14	1½	11-30	**Ürümqi**	W	1	60	363-652
Wuhan	W	16	12-19	102-281	**Xiamen**	BJ	1	44	256-465
Xian	W	2	13	150-274	**Xining**	W	1	32½	238-430
Yantai	BJ	1	15	67-145	**Yinchuan**	W	2	22	94-188
Zhengzhou	BJ, W	27	7-18	57-173	**Zhangjiakou**	BJ	1	5½	17

BY BUS

Only two of Beijing's bus stations are major long-distance hubs. The **Xizhimen Long-distance Bus Station** (xīzhìmén chángtú qìchē zhàn; 西直门长途汽车站; ☎6217 8742), a long walk or one stop on bus #16 from the Xizhimen subway stop, has buses going to: **Chengde** (4hr., every 20min. 6am-5pm, Y41); **Dalian** (16-22hr., 1 per day, Y140); **Qinhuangdao** (9-10hr., 1 per day, Y50); and **Shenyang** (16hr., 1 per day, Y100 and up). More important to budget travelers may be the **Zhaogongkou Long-distance Bus Station** (zhàogōngkǒu chángtú qìchē zhàn; 赵公口长途汽车站; ☎6722 9491), off Nansanhuan Lu in Fengtai district. Buses go to **Qingdao** (16hr., 1 per day, Y123) and **Tianjin** (1½hr., every 10 min., Y31).

◆ ORIENTATION

Beijing is huge. Sprawling. Immense. Really, really big. Everything in Beijing is far away from everything else, and many interesting sights are on the city outskirts.

The metropolis radiates from a definite center; ring roads sprinkled with tourist sights are arrayed around Tiananmen Square and the Forbidden City. In theory, there are four ring roads, but the first doesn't really exist, and the fourth is so far off the radar screen that it may as well not exist for tourists. The second ring road, **Erhuan Lu** (二环路), is generally called by its various component names, which change many times as you go around the loop. The third ring road does actually go by **Sanhuan Lu** (三环路). Most other roads are named in relation to landmarks and former city gates; *bei* (north), *nan* (south), *xi* (west), *dong* (east), *nei* (inner), *wai* (outer), *qian* (front), and *hou* (back) are added

BEIJING & NORTH COAST

to these names to indicate their relative locations. In general, address numbers increase from east to west and from north to south; even numbers are on east and north sides, and odd on west and south. **Changan Jie** (长安街) runs from east to west through downtown, changing names from Jianguomenwai Dajie, Jianguomennei Dajie, Changan Dong Dajie, Changan Xi Dajie, Fuxingmennei Dajie, and finally Fuxingmenwai Dajie.

The **Forbidden City** and **Tiananmen Square,** on either side of Changan Jie, form the city center. From the south side of the square, **Qianmen Dajie** (前门大街) runs through a crowded business district to **Tiantan** before heading to budget hotels in the deep south. **Dazhalan** and **Wangfujing,** southwest and northeast of the Square, respectively, are full of shopping options. To the northeast is **Gongren Tiyuchang Bei Lu** (工人体育场北路), commonly known as Gongti Bei Lu, which leads to **Sanlitun,** one of the city's embassy compounds. Many older neighborhoods and *hutongs* (Beijing alleyways) are preserved in the **Drum Tower** and **Lama Temple** sectors to the north. To the far northwest is the zoo, the silicon district, Beijing and Qinghua Universities, and, farther out, the **Summer Palace** and **Old Summer Palace**.

⌐ GETTING AROUND BEIJING

BY BUS

Take a deep breath and plunge in. The Beijing bus system can be mystifying, but the jam-packed buses, in combination with the subway, are a great way to get around this city on the cheap. Most buses run from 5am to 11pm or midnight. Buses generally cost Y1 regardless of destination; A/C buses are Y2. Bus stops are spaced very far apart, and sometimes the driver skips entire stops if no one appears ready to get on or off. Knowing the characters of your destination often helps in finding the right bus and getting off at the right stop. Get close to the door before you reach your stop to make sure you can scramble off in time.

There is method to the madness of Beijing's 200-odd bus routes. As a general rule, buses #1-125 navigate the city center, while #300 and above ply Beijing's periphery; #200s indicate late night buses; #800s and #900s are air-conditioned. The **minibuses** that trail the regular buses follow the same routes and cost Y2. The table below lists some main bus routes and the areas they serve.

BUS #	ROUTE DESCRIPTION	BUS #	ROUTE DESCRIPTION
1, 4, 58	Changan Jie	5	North-South: Deshengmen-Qianmen Dajie
14	Jiaomen Nan Zhan-Yangqiao-Beihai	20	Beijing Main—Beijing South
21	Beijing West-Fuchengmen	44	Circle Line subway
54	Beijing Main-Yongdingmen	66	Beijing West-Yangqiao-Qianmen
103	Beijing Main-Wangfujing-Beihai-Zoo	106	Dongzhimen Bei Dajie-Yongdingmen
116	Tiantan-Dongsi Dajie-Ditan	300	Sanhuan Lu-Liangmaqiao-Sanlitun
322	Zoo-Summer Palace	808	Beijing Main-Qianmen

BY SUBWAY

Despite its somewhat limited reach, the subway is an escape from the snarl of Beijing traffic. Trains run frequently from 5am to 10:30pm and cost Y3 regardless of destination. Beijing's subway system has two intersecting lines, the Circle Line and Line #1. The **Circle Line** cruises beneath the old city wall in a loop around the center of Beijing, while **Line #1** runs directly under Changan Dajie/Jianguomen Dajie. To transfer between lines, just follow the English signs and the rushing hordes at **Fuxingmen.** Subway platform signs are marked in both characters and pinyin, and stops are announced in Chinese and English.

BY TAXI

You can't swing a cat in Beijing (if you're into that kind of thing) without hitting a cab. Base fare is Y10, and each additional km is Y1.2-2, according to the stickers on the back windows. Always insist that drivers use the meter. Almost no cabbies speak English, few read pinyin, and Beijing is so large that many locations are first time trips for taxi drivers. Call **Beijing Taxi** (☎6837 3399), **Capital Taxi** (☎6515 9604), or **Beijing Tourism Taxi** (☎6832 2561) for taxi pickup. Call **Taxi Complaints** (☎6835 1150) to register a complaint against a taxi company or driver.

BEIJING BY BIKE

As millions of locals have figured out, a bike is a pretty handy way to see Beijing and avoid public transportation. Be warned, however, that there are no road rules in the capital—motorists, cyclists, and pedestrians cross, weave, dash, cut (and crash) at their own peril. Many hotels and hostels rent bikes. Hotels will often lend out only the dregs; ensure that the bicycle is rideable before renting. Also be aware that bike theft is common in Beijing. A hotel will occasionally lend a guest a bicycle and a lock, and then send out a friend or relative with another set of keys to trail the hapless biker and make off with the bike. When parking the bike, cast your eyes around for suspicious characters and use a different lock, if you have one. Bike parking generally costs Y0.2.

☷ PRACTICAL INFORMATION

TOURIST AND FINANCIAL SERVICES

Tourist Offices: Virtually every high-end hotel and the vast majority of mid- to low-end accommodations in Beijing have travel agencies or arrange tours to popular sights. Most establishments also assist guests in booking air and train tickets. There is a **tourist information service** in Beijing (☎6513 0828), but no actual tourism bureau. The **Beijing Tourism Administration,** Tourism Bldg., 28 Jianguomenwai Dajie (☎6515 8252), handles tourist complaints and large groups.

CITS: Beijing International Hotel, 9 Jianguomennei Dajie, west lobby (☎6512 0507; fax 6512 0503). Open M-F 8:30am-noon and 1:30-5pm. Another branch in the World Trade Tower, 1 Jianguomenwai Dajie, Ste. L100A (☎6505 3775 or 6505 2288, ext. 8110; fax 6505 3105). Open M-F 9am-noon and 1-5pm, Sa 9am-noon.

Hualong International Travel Service (huálóng guójì lǚxíng shè; 华龙国际旅行社), Beijing International Hotel, 9 Jianguomennei Dajie, 4th Fl. (☎6522 9299; fax 6512 4448). Open daily 8am-8pm.

Beijing Hotel Travel Service (běijīng fàndiàn lǚyóu bù; 北京饭店旅游部), Beijing Hotel, 33 Dong Changan Dajie (☎6523 2370; fax 6523 2372). Open daily 8am-10pm.

Jinghua Hotel (jīnghuá fàndiàn; 京华饭店), Xiluoyuan Nanli, Yongdingmen Wai (☎6722 2211, ext. 3359; fax 6721 6383), off Nansanhuan Lu. Open daily 8am-midnight. **Tianhua International Travel Service** (tiānhuá guójì lǚxíng shè; 天华国际旅行社; ☎8727 5387; fax 8727 5389), to the left of the business center and lobby of Jinghua. Open daily 8:30am-5pm.

Embassies: Sanlitun and Jianguomenwai are the two main embassy compounds. See **Essentials: Consular Services in China** (p. 48) for complete listings.

Banks: Bank of China, 410 Fuchengmennei Dajie, 2nd Fl., Counter #1 or 2 (☎6601 6688). Other branches: Asia-Pacific Bldg., 8 Yabao Lu, Chaoyang; Capital Airport; Lufthansa Center, 50 Liangmaqiao Lu, Ground Fl.; China World Trade Tower, 1 Jianguomenwai Dajie, Ste. L204. **CITIC Industrial Bank** (zhōngxìn shíyè yínháng; 中信实业银行), CITIC Bldg., 19 Jianguomenwai Dajie (☎6501 9446), Chaoyang, next to the Friendship Store. Most branches open M-F 9am-4pm, with a lunch break.

ATM: There are over 70 ATMs in Beijing, with more sprouting up all the time. Nearly all accept **AmEx, Cirrus, MC, Plus,** and **Visa** cards. Locations include: **Bank of China,** 8 Yabao Lu, Chaoyang; **Palace Hotel,** 8 Jinyu Hutong, Dongdan Bei Dajie; **Landmark Towers,** 8 Dongsanhuan Bei Lu, Chaoyang; **Central Garden Hotel,** 18 Gaoliangqiao Lu,

Haidian; **Capital Airport; Friendship Store,** 17 Jianguomenwai Dajie; **Everbright China,** Changan Bldg., 7 Jianguomennei Dajie; **SCITECH Shopping Center,** 22 Jianguomenwai Dajie; **China World Hotel,** 1 Jianguomenwai Dajie, basement entrance.

American Express: China World Trade Center, 1 Jianguomenwai Dajie, Ste. 2102 (☎6505 2888). For lost checks or problems with American Express credit cards.

LOCAL SERVICES

Bookstores: Beijing Foreign Language Bookstore (běijīng wàiwén shūdiàn; 北京外文书店), 235 Wangfujing Dajie (☎6512 6922), a savior for novel-starved travelers. **The Commercial Press** (shāngwù yìnshùguǎn; 商务印书馆), 36 Wangfujing Dajie, sells bilingual dictionaries and other books. **China Publications Import and Export Company** (zhōngguó túshū jìngchūkǒu gōngsī; 中国图书进出口公司), 16 Gongti Dong Lu, 2nd Fl., Chaoyang, next to Schlotzky's Deli. **Friendship Store** (yǒuyì shāngdiàn; 友谊商店), 17 Jianguomenwai Dajie, 1st Fl., has a great bookstore.

Library: National Library (běijīng túshūguǎn; 北京图书馆), 39 Baishiqiao Lu (☎6841 5566), Haidian, near the zoo. Large foreign language section. Open daily 9am-5pm.

Supermarkets: Park N Shop, COFCO Plaza, 8 Jianguomennei Dajie, Tower B, basement. **Hualian Shopping Center,** across from the Vantone New World Plaza. **Friendship Store Supermarket** (yǒuyì chāojí shāngchǎng; 友谊超级商场), 17 Jianguomenwai Dajie

Health Clubs: Beijing Trend Station Beauty and Fitness Center (běijīng shíshàng kōngjiān měiróng jiànshēn zhōngxīn; 北京时尚空间美容健身中心), 8 Jianguomennei Dajie, COFCO Plaza, Tower C, B3, Dengcheng (☎6526 0795 or 6526 0796). Features aerobics, tae kwon do, weight training, a salon, a massage parlor, a sauna, and a health juice bar (Y50 per visit; Y400 per month). Open daily 10am-10pm. **Capital Gymnasium** (shǒudū tǐyùguǎn; 首都体宇馆), near the intersection of Baishiqiao Lu and Xizhimenwai Dajie, west of the entrance to the zoo. Features fitness center, archery room, and ice skating rink (Y20-30 per hr.). Open daily 9am-10pm.

Weather Conditions: ☎121.

EMERGENCY AND COMMUNICATIONS

PSB: 85 Beichizi Dajie (☎6524 2063; foreigners section ☎6404 7799, ext 2061; visa administrative dept. ☎6512 8871 2860), east of the Forbidden City.

Medical Services: Asia Emergency Assistance International (AEA), BITIC Leasing Center, 1 Bei Lu, Xing Fu San Cun, Bldg. C, Sanlitun (24hr. ☎6462 9100; clinic ☎6462 9112). Handles emergencies, vaccinations, pharmacy needs, pre- and postnatal care, dental work, and more. Renowned for treating foreign dignitaries, the state of the art **Sino-Japanese Friendship Hospital** (zhōngrì yǒuhǎo yiyuàn; 中日友好医院; ☎6422 1122, foreigners ext. 5121), Hepingjie Beikou, Chaoyang, just north of Sanhuan Lu. Take bus #119 from Andingmen. **Beijing United Family Hospital** (běijīng hémù fùér yīyùan; 北京和睦妇儿医院), 2 Jiangtai Lu (24hr. ☎6433 3960), Chaoyang, 5min. east of the Holiday Inn Lido. Specializes in family medicine. Other hospitals: **Beijing Union Hospital** (emergency ☎6512 7733, ext. 251), Dongdan, Dongcheng; **Beijing Hospital,** 15 Dahua Lu (☎6513 2266, foreigners ext. 3130), Dongcheng; **Friendship Hospital,** Yongan Lu (☎6301 4411), Xuanwu; **International Medical Center (IMC),** Lufthansa Center, 50 Liangmaqiao Lu, Ste. S106 (☎6465 1561); **Hong Kong International Center,** Swissôtel Hong Kong Macau Center, Ste. 93 (☎6501 2288, ext. 2346).

Internet Access: Qianyi Internet Cafe (qiányì wǎngluò kāfēi wū; 前艺网络咖啡屋), The Station Shopping Mall, 3rd Fl., opposite the southeast corner of Tiananmen Square. Y10 per 30min. Drinks and snacks (Y5-25) and a TV/VCD. Open daily 9am-around midnight. **Spark Ice Internet Cafe,** China World Trade Center, 1 Jianguomenwai Dajie, 2nd Fl. Y15 per hr. Open daily 9am-2am. **Feiyu Internet Cafe** (fēiyǔ wǎng bā; 飞宇网吧), 36 Haidian Lu, just east of the south gate of Beijing University. Y5-9 per hr., 7-9am free. Open 24hr. **Jinghua Youth Hostel** (p. 105). Y10 per 30min. Open daily 8am-midnight.

Post and Telecommunications: The **International Post Office** (guójì yóujú; 国际邮局; ☎6512 8114 or 6512 8120) is on Jianguomen Bei Dajie. Open daily 8am-6:30pm. EMS, IDD service, Poste Restante (at the glass counter opposite the main service counters), and **Western Union Station.** 9 Qianmen Dong Dajie. Open daily 8am-6:30pm. **Beijing Central Post and Telecommunications Office,** Jianguomennei Dajie, west of the Henderson Center. Open daily 8am-7pm.

Private Couriers: DHL Worldwide Express, China World Trade Center, 1 Jianguomenwai Dajie, Ste. 211, Sinotrans Express Center (☎6505 2173 or 6505 2288, ext. 8103). Open M-F 8am-8pm, Sa 9am-noon. **UPS,** Sinotrans Pekair Parcel International Express Co., Ltd. (liánhé bāoguǒ yùnshù; 联和包裹运输), Beijing Kelun Plaza, 12 Guanghua Lu, Tower B, 1st Fl., Chaoyang (☎6581 2088). **Federal Express** (liánbāng kuàidì; 联邦快递), Gaolan Plaza, 32 Liangmaqiao, 3rd Fl., Chaoyang (☎6468 5566).

▙ ACCOMMODATIONS

In Beijing, budget typically means poor location, so most of the low-end accommodations cluster around the city's southern periphery. The hostels and hotels along the mid-stretch of **Nansanhuan Lu,** between **Yangqiao** and **Muxiyuan** exits, teem with backpackers. These outposts provide dirt-cheap dorms, bike rental, ticket and tour booking, and Internet access. As with the rest of Beijing, the state of budget travel is in constant flux, so budget and location are beginning to merge, even for foreigners—**Beijing International Youth Hostel** and **Zhaolong International Youth Hostel** are two shining examples.

Most hotels have currency exchange capabilities and restaurants on-site, and most do not accept foreign credit cards.

CITY CENTER (WITHIN THE SECOND RING ROAD)

Beijing International Youth Hostel (běijīng guójì qīngnián lǚshè; 北京国际青年旅舍), Beijing International Hotel, 9 Jianguomennei Dajie, Bldg. 2, 10th Fl. (☎6512 6688, ext. 6145 or 6146; fax 6522 9494), at the end of the road leading north from the main train station. Accessible by any bus to Beijing Zhankou or Beijing Zhan, as well as by the subway; the airport bus stops outside, too. Brand spankin' new. Internet access, reading corner, and kitchen. Reservations recommended. 6- to 8-bed dorms with A/C Y50, for non-HI/IYHF members Y60.

Fangyuan Hotel (fāngyuán bīnguǎn; 芳园宾馆), 36 Dengshikou Xi Jie (☎6525 6331), near Wangfujing Dajie and a 20min. walk from Tiananmen Square. Accessible by buses #103, 104, 108, and 111. Large, clean, slightly musty rooms in a terrific area. Breakfast included. Deposit based on room rate. Reservations morning of arrival only. Singles Y126; doubles Y177-267; triples Y342.

Tailong Hotel (tàilóng bīnguǎn; 泰龙宾馆), 51 Donganmen Dajie (☎6525 3498), across from the China Children's Theater. At night, step outside of your comfortable room and land smack in the middle of a market. Doubles Y200 and up; triples Y260.

Yuyuan Hotel (yùyuán bīnguǎn; 御园宾馆), 31 Shatan Bei Jie (☎6405 9955, ext. 104), east of Jingshan Park along Jingshan Houjie. Take bus #2, 60, 103, or others to Shatan or Wusi Dajie. So close to the Forbidden City, it's like being the emperor's next-door neighbor; too bad the rooms aren't imperial sized. Bike rental Y30. Hot water 7am-midnight. Breakfast included. Doubles Y180-200; triples Y210.

Donghua Hotel (dōnghuá fàndiàn; 东华饭店), 32 Dengshikou Xi Jie (☎6525 7531), near the Fangyuan Hotel. The Donghua's location can't be beat, but its small rooms sure can be. Breakfast included. Check-out 2pm. Doubles Y200-288.

Hualun Hotel (huálún fàndiàn; 华伦饭店), 291 Andingmennei Dajie (☎6403 3337), at Gulou Dong Dajie, a 20min. walk south from the Andingmen subway stop, near the Lama Temple. Buses #104, 106, 108, and others stop at Jiaodaokou; walk a block north to the hotel, which is set back from the street and marked by a huge white and blue archway. Decent bedrooms, could-be-better bathrooms. Small discounts for stays of 3 days or more. Singles Y146; doubles Y226.

NORTHEAST OF CITY CENTER (SANLITUN AREA)

■ **Zhaolong International Youth Hostel** (zhàolóng qīngnián lǚshè; 兆龙青年旅舍), 2 Gongren Tiyuguan Bei Lu (☎6597 2299; fax 6597 2288), at Sanhuan Lu, just behind the Zhaolong Hotel. Take bus #3, 43, or 300 to Baijiazhuang; it's a 5min. walk north. The Zhaolong is pure heaven. A perfect day: take a dip in the pool, work out at the fitness center, kick your heels back in the sauna, stuff dumplings in the kitchen, pick up the daily paper in the reading room, and then head out onto the streets of Sanlitun. Sparkling rooms have A/C, and common showers positively glisten. For HI members: 3- to 6-bed dorms Y50, 2-bed dorms Y60. Non-members: Y60, Y70.

EAST OF CITY CENTER

Furong Hotel (fúróng bīnguǎn; 芙蓉宾馆; ☎6557 2921), on Shilipu, next to Hua Tang Shopping Center. Take bus #9 to Xiaozhuang and then #112 or 115 to Balizhuang. Sort of near the Silk Market and far from everything else. Soft beds in otherwise unremarkable rooms lull tired travelers to sleep after silk splurges. Deposit equal to 1 night's stay. Doubles with bath Y240-280.

Leyou Hotel (lèyóu fàndiàn; 乐游饭店), 13 Dongsanhuan Nan Lu (☎6771 2266), in the Panjiayuan area east of Longtan Park. Take bus #28, 35, 52, 58, or 368 to Jinsong Dongkou. Ordinary rooms full of foreigners ready to tackle the flea market. Watch out for the karaoke bar next door. Deposit Y50. Doubles Y320-430; triples Y398.

SOUTHEAST OF CITY CENTER (NEAR TIANTAN)

Tiantan Haoyuan Hotel (tiāntán hǎoyuán bīnguǎn; 天坛吴园宾馆), 9A Tiantan Dong Lu (☎6701 4499, front bldg. ext. 3288, back bldg. ext. 2511 or 2512). Accessible by buses #34 and 36, or just walk south from Tiantan's east gate; the hotel is deep inside the first *hutong* on the right. Splendid rooms envelop an idyllic traditional courtyard. The back (north) building is less expensive. Deposit equal to 1 night's stay. Doubles Y338 and up. Credit cards accepted.

Tiantan Sports Hotel (tiāntán tǐyù bīnguǎn; 天坛体育宾馆), 10 Tiyuguan Lu (☎6711 3388). From the northeast corner of Tiantan Park, take a step east on Tiyuguan Lu, look right, and you're there; it's set back from the street. Buses #6, 35, 39, 41, 43, and 60 stop nearby. For the comfort level, you'll deal with the slightly smallish rooms. Bike rental Y20 per day, deposit Y200. Deposit Y300. Doubles Y298; triples Y400.

SOUTH OF CITY CENTER

■ **Jinghua Youth Hostel** (jīnghuá fàndiàn; 京华饭店), Xiluoyuan Nanli, Yongdingmenwai Dajie, Fengtai (☎6722 2211 ext. 3359; fax 6721 1455), east of the smelly canal from McDonald's. Take bus #66 from Qianmen to Yangqiao. With a pool, 24hr. bar, co-ed dorms, and an unending flow of travelers, the Jinghua is a cauldron of carousal, arousal, and extra-spousal scandal. Waley's Green Bay Bar and Restaurant serves french toast, french fries, but no french kisses. Bike rental Y10 per day, deposit Y100. Internet Y10 per 30min. Deposit Y50. 30-bed dorm Y25; 4-bed dorms Y30-35; 3-bed dorms with bath Y50; doubles with bath Y140 and up.

Qiaoyuan Hotel (qiáoyuán fàndiàn; 侨园饭店), 135 Youanmen Dong Binhe Lu, Fengtai (☎6301 2244, ext. 3161; fax 6303 0119), 500m walk west from the South Train Station. Look for the kooky silver archway and tall tan buildings on your left. After giving up its title as backpacker central to undergo renovations, the Qiaoyuan is eager to reclaim its past glory, with the help of Mr. John, budget travel coordinator extraordinaire. And how better to do that than with A/C and some of the cleanest common baths around? Internet access, travel services, and bike rental (Y5 per day). 10-bed dorms Y15; 4-bed dorms Y25; 2-bed dorms with mini-fridge Y25; doubles with bath Y120-180.

Lihua Hotel (lìhuá fàndiàn; 丽华饭店), 71 Majiapu Dong Lu, Fengtai (☎6721 1144; fax 6721 1367), near Yangqiao. Take bus #14, 66, or 343 from downtown to Lihua, or bus #300, 324, or 368 to Yangqiao, and then head south for 200m. Bright red carpets, 2 restaurants, and nicely furnished A/C rooms. Internet access. Deposit Y50. Doubles Y132, with bath Y198; triples Y168.

Sea Star Hotel (hǎixīng dàjiǔdiàn; 海兴大酒店), 166 Haihutun (☎6721 8855, ext. 3358; fax 6722 7915), Yongwai Mu Xu Yuan, Fengtai. A 20min. walk from bus #66's Yangqiao stop; the terminus of buses #2 (to Tiananmen), 40, 54 (to Beijing Main Train Station), 324, and 366 is also nearby. Dorms are very basic; doubles are nicer than the prices suggest. Deposit Y100 and up. 6-bed dorms Y25, 5-bed dorms Y30; 4-bed dorms Y35; doubles with bath Y170 and up.

Feng Long Hotel (fènglóng bīnguǎn; 凤龙宾馆), 5 Youanmen Dong Jie, Xuanwu (☎6354 5836 or 6353 6413; fax 6353 6452), at the southeastern corner of Taoranting Park, at Taoran Bridge on Erhuan Lu. Take bus #3, 14, 20, 66, or others to Youyongchi and head south to the bridge; the hotel is on the right. The new kid on the budget block, but facilities and standard rooms are rather aged. Deposit equal to 1 night's stay. Singles Y120-180; doubles Y180-280; triples Y270-330. Traveler's checks accepted.

WEST OF CITY CENTER (NEAR THE ZOO)

Evergreen Hotel (wànnián qīng bīnguǎn; 万年青宾馆), 25 Xisanhuan Bei Lu (☎6842 5154). Take bus #300, 323, 374, or others to Wanshousi, or take bus #360 from the zoo to Beiwa Lu, walk east to Sanhuan Lu, and then north for 10min. Unremarkable standard rooms away from everything except possibly the zoo set around a courtyard with the loudest cicadas known to man. Deposit Y300. Doubles Y262; triples Y282.

Shangyuan Hotel (shàngyuán fàndiàn; 上园饭店), 40 Xie Jie, Gaoliangqiao, Xizhimenwai (☎6225 1166, ext. 135 or 136). Take bus #16, 103, 105, 601, or 933 to Zhanlanguan or Shangyuancun. Closed until at least Jan. 2001. The mosque-like exterior and astroturf carpets are an odd mix, but renovations may give a second lease on life. Breakfast included. Deposit equal to 3-night stay. Doubles with bath Y298.

NORTHWEST OF CITY CENTER

Beijing University Shaoyuan Hotel (běijīng dàxué sháoyuán bīnguǎn; 北京大学勺园宾馆), Bldg. 7 (☎6275 2218 or 6275 2200). Buses #320, 355, 375, 710, 718, and 808 stop at Beijing Daxue or Beida Ximen. Enter the west gate of the university on Yiheyuan Lu, pass between two lakes, and bear right past the basketball courts until you see Bldg. 7. Guests need a letter of introduction in order to be received, so you might have to wait at a nearby coffee house for a foreign student or faculty member who might pose as your "guarantee-or." This plan is of course far from fail-safe. Rooms have attached bath. 2-bed dorms Y180; singles Y200; doubles Y230 and up.

Zhongguancun Hotel (zhōngguāncūn jiǔdiàn; 中关村酒店), 19 Haidian Lu (☎6256 5577, ext. 2001 or 2002), about 2 blocks east of the smaller Beijing University south gate. Buses #332 and 808 stop nearby. Ordinary standard rooms are spiced up by the vibrant surroundings you'd expect near a university loaded with discerning youth. Deposit Y400. Doubles Y256. Credit cards and traveler's checks accepted.

Big Bell Temple Hotel (dà zhōng sì fàndiàn; 大钟寺饭店), 18 Beisanhuan Xi Lu (☎6225 3388, ext. 2138). Under the expressway and about a block east from Big Bell Temple, this hotel is heralded by a sprightly fountain and a tall bowling pin. Deposit Y50. Doubles with bath Y232 and up.

Qinghua Yuan Hotel (qīnghuá yuán bīnguǎn; 清华园宾馆), 45-1 Chengfu Jie (☎6257 3355). Take bus #331, 335, or 375 to Wudaokou. Rooms are comfortable but bathrooms are less than dazzling. Deposit Y50. Breakfast included. Singles Y172; doubles Y240 and up. Traveler's checks accepted.

▣ FOOD

The streets of Beijing burst with food options. The *hutongs* overflow with stalls that vary in quality but are consistently low in price; special attention should be paid to the areas around **Qianmen** and **Wangfujing,** and **Tiantan, Ritan,** and **Beihai Parks.** Some great, not-too-expensive restaurants can be found around Liangmaqiao, as well as in a gray building with hanging eaves called **Hualong Jie** on Nan-heyan Dajie, about a 5min. walk west from Wangfujing Dajie. An absolute must-see, the night food market at **Donganmen,** off Wangfujing Dajie, serves treats like fried ice cream and more exotic fare like whole-sparrows-on-a-stick nightly from dusk to 9:30pm. For an easy sit-down meal, just head into any restaurant that advertises *jiachangcai* (everyday family food; 家常菜). Tasty, filling meals are typically about Y10-20 per person, but ask to see the prices first, as foreigners are sometimes knocked over the head with ridiculous prices.

BY REGION

CITY CENTER	PAGE	CUISINE
Fangshan Restaurant	110	Regional
Kentucky Fried Chicken	108	Fast Food
The Sichuan	110	Sichuanese

DONGCHENG (EAST)	PAGE	CUISINE
Donglaishun Restaurant	108	Hotpot
Green Tianshi Vegetarian	111	Vegetarian
Hard Rock Cafe	111	Western
Hong Kong Food City	108	Cantonese
Old Chongqing Hotpot	110	Sichuanese
Shaoshan Mao	109	Special
Wonton Pavilion	108	Dumplings

E. OF CITY CENTER	PAGE	CUISINE
A Funti Hometown	109	Muslim
Almuhan Xinjiang	109	Muslim
Golden Elephant	109	Indian
Mockba Restaurant	110	Special
Mother Earth Cafe	111	Western
Omar Khayyam Indian	109	Indian

E. OF CITY CENTER (*CONT.*)		CUISINE
Sichuan King Hotpot	111	Sichuanese
TGI Friday's	111	Western
Yuntai	110	Sichuanese

S. OF CITY CENTER	PAGE	CUISINE
Dai Family Village	110	Special
Diyilou Sausage	108	Dumplings
Gongdelin Vegetarian	111	Vegeterian
Old Beijing Zhajiang	110	Regional
Qianmen Quanjude	107	Duck

W. OF CITY CENTER	PAGE	CUISINE
Hongda Roast Duck	107	Duck
Laochuan Cai	111	Sichuanese
Sanwa	110	Special

N. OF CITY CENTER	PAGE	CUISINE
Long March	107	Duck
Nengren Ju	108	Hotpot
Pearl River Restaurant	108	Cantonese
Tian Gong Dietetic	110	Regional

BY TYPE

BEIJING DUCK

Food fit for kings, at prices budget travelers can stomach, Beijing duck (kǎoyā; 烤鸭) is as important to Beijing's history as Beijing Opera and the Forbidden City.

Qianmen Quanjude Roast Duck Restaurant (qiánmén quánjùdé kǎoyā diàn; 前门全聚德烤鸭店), 32 Qianmen Dajie (☎6511 2418 or 6701 1379). Founded in 1864 during the 3rd year of Emperor Tongzhi's reign, the Qianmen location is the oldest of the 15 branches. Whatever the surroundings, the duck is the same, and Quanjude's duck is the genuine article. A pictorial menu helps walk tourists through a first-time Beijing duck experience. Meals Y75-100, carving extra. "Fancier" part open daily 11am-1:30pm and 4:30-8:30pm; "less fancy" part 10am-9pm.

Hongda Roast Duck Restaurant (hóngdà kǎoyā diàn; 宏大烤鸭店; ☎6721 5726), Muxiyuan, Fengtai, 500m south of Lijiao Bridge, amid the cluster of backpacker hostels. By hook, crook, or wily nose, most backpackers find their way to Hongda—many times over. The roast duck is cheap, but world-class: Y38 for a good-sized quacker that feeds 4 easily, carving display included. Open daily 10:30am-10:30pm.

Long March Restaurant (cháng zhēng fànzhuàng; 长征饭庄), 17 Haidian Lu, Haidian (☎6253 1550), diagonally opposite Beijing University's south gate. It's a long march to get here, but no real historical significance is waiting at the end: just a big yellow duck at the door and a mind-bending array of every duck part conceivable. Average meal Y35-50. Open daily 11am-1:30pm and 5-8pm.

BEIJING HOTPOT

With vats of bubbling potion, vials of unnerving sauces, and heaps of raw meat, hotpot is much more than just fondue. Vegetarians need not be disheartened—but remember to order an all veggie broth as well as meatless ingredients (see **Appendix**, p. 758). Cooking meat and vegetables in a simmering communal hotpot is an experience that Beijingers relish during the chilly winters, although true devotees are willing to sweat it out over their *shuan yang rou* all year long.

Nengren Ju (néng rén jū; 能仁居), 5 Taipingqiao Dajie (☎6601 2560 or 6606 6993), near White Pagoda Temple. Take bus #102 or 103 to Baima Si; walk east and then south at the first crossing. Nengren Ju is the hotspot for hotpot right now; most patrons eat until they can't move. Beijing style hotpot broth Y18, Y18-25 for the animal parts to dunk in it. Open daily 11am-2am. **Panjiayuan branch** is open daily 10:30am-midnight.

Donglaishun Restaurant (dōngláishùn fànzhuāng; 东来顺饭庄), Sun Dongan Plaza, 138 Wangfujing Dajie, 5th Fl. (☎6528 0931), just to the right of the escalators. Donglaishun used to be the only place to go for old Beijing hotpot. A man scuttles around with a watering can with a meter-long spout filled with soup. Hotpot broth Y15, most meat and vegetables Y4-20. Open daily 11am-2pm and 5-9pm.

CANTONESE

Hong Kong Food City (xiānggǎng měishí chéng; 香港美食城), 18 Dong'anmen Dajie (☎6525 7349), near Wangfujing Dajie. This huge, posh restaurant also serves Beijing duck, hotpot, BBQ, and specialties like shark's fin and pigeon. Most dishes Y20-100. 10% service charge. Open daily 11am-3am.

Pearl River Restaurant (zhūjiāng lóu cāntīng; 珠江楼餐厅), New Century Hotel, 6 Shoudu Tiyuguan Nan Lu, 3rd Fl. (☎6849 1155). Take the bus to Baishi Qiao. Behind its glitzy facade, Pearl River offers a can't-be-beat dim sum deal for lunch Sa-Su, with over 30 dishes at half-price (Y6-12). Entrees and entrails Y30-80. 15% service charge. Open daily 11:30am-2:30pm and 5:30-10pm.

DUMPLINGS

Beijing's dumpling joints offer both quality and quantity, something any visitor with a large stomach and a not so large budget will quickly come to appreciate.

🏮 **Diyilou Sausage Little Steamed Buns** (dìyīlóu guàntāng xiǎo lóngbāozi; 第一楼灌汤小笼包子), 83 Qianmen Dajie (☎6303 0268). Head straight south from Qianmen, and a comforting tiled awning will welcome you into a *baozi* shop renowned among locals for its traditional soup-soaked, oil-drained dough buns. A dozen buns (Y9) in a variety of fillings, including vegetarian, do a filling meal make. The waitresses are scandalized by requests for more. Open daily 8:30am-10:30pm.

Wonton Pavilion (húndùn hóu; 馄饨候), 11 Donganmen Dajie (☎6525 1892), at Wangfujing Dajie. This old guard Beijing eatery serves wonderful wontons. A chef sits behind a glass case making the little delectables all day long. Sesame cakes and pickles are popular accompaniments. Y15 per person is plenty. Open daily 7am-1am.

FAST FOOD

International fast food chains have exploded onto the Beijing scene in the past few years. **McDonald's** (màidāngláo; 麦当劳) now has close to 60 restaurants in the capital; travelers are hard-pressed to find a place where the insidious golden arches don't rear their heads. **Kentucky Fried Chicken** (kěndéjī jiāxiāng jī; 肯德基家乡鸡) has been around since its opening at Tiananmen Square in 1987. **Domino's Pizza** has moved in, and **Pizza Hut** (bìshèngkè; 必胜客) is closing in on the competition, with nine restaurants, including branches next to the Jianguomen silk market and by the zoo. **Marrybrown Family Restaurant, Yongke Da Wang, Uncle Sam's,** and **Viva Curry** all do fast food with a slightly more original twist. **Sammie's Cafe** delivers sandwiches. (☎6234 4487. Open daily 7am-midnight.) For a cup of American coffee, check out one of the many **Starbucks** (xīngbākè; 星巴克), including ones at the China World Trade Center and the Friendship Store. See **Western** for more Western food options.

INDIAN

Omar Khayyam Indian Restaurant (wèiměijiā yìndù cānguǎn; 味美佳印度餐馆), Asia-Pacific Bldg., 8 Yabao Lu, M-01, Chaoyang (☎6513 9988, ext. 20188). The staff greets patrons in English, then takes orders for dishes with Hindi names from Francophones speaking Mandarin. Mesmerizing linguistic Babel aside, the food is deliciously authentic, courtesy of the Indian proprietor, set in an atmosphere that is charmingly romantic. With a motto like "love all, serve all," how could they go wrong? Entrees Y25-100. Open daily 11:30am-2:30pm and 6-10:30pm. Credit cards accepted.

Golden Elephant Spicy Restaurant (jīn xiàng yuàn dōngfāng cāntīng; 金象苑东方餐厅; ☎6417 1650 or 6417 1651), to the right of Sanlitun Lu. Master chefs from Thailand and India cook tempting South Asian cuisine, including mandarin fish, shish kebabs (minced lamb barbecue), and tandoori (grilled in clay ovens). Entrees Y20-70. Weekday lunch buffet Y48. Open daily 11am-midnight.

MUSLIM

Beijing is blessed with a large number of Uighur neighborhoods. Through the smoke pouring from kebab-cookers set up on the street, proprietors approach potential patrons, boasting that their dive is better than the one next door. Truth be told, they're all basically the same: simply sumptuous. Typical Muslim fare includes noodles (*mian*), *nang* flatbread, and kebabs (*rouchuan*, generally beef, or *yangrouchuan*, lamb), topped off by Uighur tea (*sanpao tai* or *ba bao cha*).

A Funti Hometown Restaurant (ā fántí jiāxiāng yīnyuè cāntīng; 阿凡提家乡音乐餐厅), 2A Houguaibang Hutong (☎6525 1071 or 6527 2288), in an alley immediately south of the Chaonei Xiaojie stop (buses #101, 110, and 112). Truly a funti(me). It takes only one glance to fall in love with A Funti, the ultimate Uighur funhouse. Delectable Xinjiang fare (including melt-in-your-mouth "fried mutton with toothpick"/kebabs for Y32) plus the wild ground-stomping and drum-thumping of an exuberant song and dance troupe. On weekends, eat fast before they clear the tabletops for dancing—join them if you'd like. The flier puts it well: a "very impressive performance, which eventually includes at least one drunk *laowai* (foreigner), making a complete idiot of himself, great stuff." Entrees Y30-90. Performances Su-W 8pm, 2hr. band Th-Sa. Open daily 11am-midnight.

Almuhan Xinjiang Restaurant, 26 Dongzhimenwai Dajie, Chaoyang (☎6417 4888 or 6417 3568), opposite the Australian embassy. Almuhan serves up Xinjiang food in countless delicious ways (crisp fried lamb breast, mutton kebabs, mutton pies, and more), in a setting so exotic you can hardly pay attention to your meat. An excellent music and dance troupe enlivens the crowd; at other times, the racy Arab music videos almost do the trick. Most meals Y80. Open daily 11:30am-2pm and 5:30pm-11pm.

REGIONAL/SPECIAL CUISINE

These unusual specialist restaurants add dash to their dishes by combining food with fetish. Spread out over the city, the effort to find them is often repaid with ever-changing forms of mental and sensory stimulation.

Shaoshan Mao Family Cuisine (sháoshān máo jiā cài; 韶山毛家菜), 111 Hualong Jie, 1st Fl. (☎6512 9110), on the east side of Nanheyan Dajie, a 5min. walk west of Wangfujing Dajie. Photos of photos of Mao, paintings of paintings of Mao, and so on, in a restaurant run (surprise!) by his family. Enjoy the same fare the late Chairman did every time he went home to Hunan, including chili bean paste, *xiaolong bao*, bamboo-cooked meals, and his favorite, red-braised pork. Full meals Y50. Open daily 10am-10pm.

BEIJING & NORTH COAST

Dai Family Village Restaurant (dǎi jiā cūn; 傣家村), Guandongdian Nan Jie, Chaoyang (☎6585 8709), near Sanhuan Lu about a block north of the Kerry Center Hotel. Also at 13 Tiyuguan Lu, Chongwen (☎6711 1616), east of Tiantan Park. Dai meals of mushroom, turtle, and snake, complemented by bamboo booze, an outdoor bonfire, and an eager-to-please staff. Most dishes Y20-50, meter-long snakes (slayed and brained before your eyes) Y150, camel paws Y320. Open daily 9:30am-2:30pm and 4:30-9:30pm; performances at 12:30, 6:30, and 7:30pm.

Sanwa Japanese Korean Restaurant (sānhé rìhán shāokǎo huǒguō chéng; 三和日韩烧烤火锅城), Millenium Hotel, 338 Guanganmennei Dajie, 3rd Fl. (☎6375 8888, ext 8382). Take the bus to Guanganmen. An impeccably chic spot to see and be seen. Satiate your hunger with artfully flavored Japanese and Korean dishes (Y15-80) and traditional hotpot (Y68-188). A great buffet includes sashimi, sushi, and various Korean dishes (Y48). Open daily 11am-3pm and 5-10:30pm.

Mockba Restaurant (rìtán mòsīkē fēngwèi fànzhuāng; 日坛莫斯科风味饭庄; ☎6586 3217), at the corner of Ritan Lu and Guanghua Lu, west of the south gate of Ritan Park, near the Russian district on Yabao Lu. Serves up Russian food (Y15-40) to a largely Russian clientele in a classy setting, complete with wood paneling, a balcony, chandeliers, and risqué paintings. Open daily 11am-3am.

Old Beijing Zhajiang Noodle King (lǎo běijīng zhájiàng miàn dàwáng; 老北京炸酱面大王), 29 Chongwenmenwai Dajie (☎6705 6705), straight north from the east gate of Tiantan Park, past the main road. Take the bus to Hongqiao. The menu features pastes, pickles, and mustards that though none too spectacular in aroma, recall the Beijing canteens of a few decades back. Ironically, it is the lively atmosphere and noodle-free specialites that deserve praise—the noodles are coarse and not all that tasty. Average meal Y20-25. Open daily 11am-2pm and 5-8:30pm.

Fangshan Restaurant (fǎngshàn fànzhuāng; 仿膳饭庄; ☎6401 1879 or 6401 1889), inside Beihai Park, midway along the corridor that runs around Qiong Island. The Man-Han style banquet was invented in the royal kitchen that used to present the Empress Dowager Ci Xi with 108 courses at every meal. Apparently she was more than just power-hungry. Try the *wowotou*, dry little corncakes that were Ci Xi's favorite. 14- to 16-course set banquets Y100-200 per person. Open daily 11am-1:30pm and 5-7:30pm.

Tian Gong Dietetic Palace (tiān gōng shí fǔ; 天公食府), 26 Guozijian Jie (☎6401 8155), across from the Imperial College and Confucius Temple. This stone pagoda-style building with an intriguing name serves up Shandong province and Northeast Chinese specialties. Find everything from Kungpao chicken (Y18) to sea slugs (Y200). And no, there's nothing "diet" about it. Open daily 11am-2pm and 5-9pm.

SICHUANESE

Sichuanese food is spicy, pickled, spicy, hot, and spicy—did we mention spicy? It packs enough punch to stun one of Qin Shihuang's terracotta horses, and really isn't authentic unless it leaves your eyes teary and your tongue numb.

The Sichuan (sìchuān fàndiàn; 四川饭店), A14 Liuyin Lu, Xicheng (☎6615 6924), to the left of Prince Gong's Former Residence, behind Beihai Park. If Premier Zhou Enlai had not called for The Sichuan's establishment in 1959, the facial tissue market would never be where it is today. Average meal Y80-100. Open daily 11am-2pm and 5-9pm.

Yuntai Restaurant (yúntái cāntīng; 云台餐厅), Great Wall Sheraton Hotel, 10 Dongsanhuan Bei Lu (☎6500 5566, ext. 2295). Be prepared: 3-pepper dishes are hot enough to melt glass. No-pepper dishes are for those who shouldn't be eating Sichuanese food in the first place. The hanging lanterns, live music, stellar food, and a classy 21st floor location make the prices (Y35-90) palatable. Open daily 11:30am-2pm and 6-10pm.

Old Chongqing Hotpot City (lǎo chóngqìng huǒguō chéng; 老重庆火锅城), Fuhao Hotel, 45 Wangfujing Dajie, Dongcheng (☎6522 2168), across from Capital Theater and the Two Thousand Years Club. Ponderous decor and spicy Sichuan-style hotpot distract your senses while destroying your taste buds. Hotpot Y30-60, plus Y15-88 for each item you throw in the pot. Open daily 10am-2pm and 5-9:30pm.

Laochuan Cai (lǎochuān cài dàjiǔdiàn; 老川菜大酒店), 8 Xizhimenwai Dajie (☎6836 6803), marked by the lit-up sea creatures sign opposite the south gate of Capital Gymnasium. Tickle your taste buds with fiery fare, amid ornate gold dragons, pillars, and lanterns. Dishes Y15-40. Sichuanese hotpot is also available. Open daily 11am-3am.

Sichuan King Hotpot (shǔ wáng huǒguō; 蜀王火锅), 6 Chezhan Lu, Chongwen (☎6303 6791), 100m west of Beijing South Train Station, with high steps in front. Not just another hotpot spot, this restaurant is also worth a try for its turtles, serpents, and home-brewed wines. Hotpot Y20, lamb Y15. Open daily 11am-10:30pm.

VEGETARIAN

Green Tianshi Vegetarian Restaurant (lǜ tiānshǐ cāntīng; 绿天使餐厅), 57 Dengshikou Dajie, 2nd Fl. (☎6524 2349), Dongcheng, east of Wangfujing Dajie. This lovely little restaurant's specialty is "the imitation of real meat, not only in appearance, but also in taste," achieved with ingredients like soybean protein, taro powder, mushrooms, and tofu. Well, it worked: you'll be asking if the "prawn" is *really* vegetarian. Dishes Y50-60 each. Open daily 10:30am-9pm.

Gongdelin Vegetarian Restaurant (gōngdélín sùcài fànzhuāng; 功德林素菜饭庄), 158 Qianmen Nan Dajie (☎6702 0867). Take the bus to Zhushikou. First opened in 1922 on Sakyamuni's birthday (true to its Buddhist bent), Gongdelin is an old pro at culinary deceit. Meals Y25-34. Open daily 10:30am-1:30pm and 5-8:30pm.

WESTERN

In addition to the average Western food joints (see **Fast Food**, p. 108), Western-style bakeries are spreading like hotcakes. **Déli France** sells authentic croissants and other pastries; some Sanlitun bakeries sell convincing French loaves. **Mrs. Shanen's Bagels** (shuānglóng wùzī gōngsī; 双龙物资公司内), 3 Zhaojiu Lu, Jiuxianqiao, Chaoyang, turns out bagels by the dozen—they're not Manhattan bagels, but they're close. (Delivery ☎6435 9561. Open M-Sa 8am-6pm, Su 8am-4pm.)

Hard Rock Cafe, Landmark Towers, 8 Dongsanhuan Bei Lu (☎6590 6688, ext. 2571). HRC Beijing features typical Hard Rock decor and fare, steak, french fries, sky-high prices for mediocre food and American memorabilia...You get the idea. It also holds the unofficial title for biggest and best slice of cheesecake in town (Y38). Entrees Y65-100. Becomes a disco at 10:30pm; live bands nightly. 15% service charge. Open Su-Th 11:30am-2am, F-Sa 11:30am-3am.

TGI Friday's (xīngqīwǔ cāntīng; 星期五餐厅), Huafeng Mansions, 19 Dongsanhuan Bei Lu, Chaoyang (☎6597 5314), beside Baijiazhuang bus stop (#3, 43, 300). Faux Tiffany lighting and trademark red-and-white striped tablecloths. Check out the vintage chandelier from New York's Vanderbilt Hotel and the wooden crew shell lining the upper wall. Entrees Y50-100, soup and half sandwich Y48. Open daily 11am-midnight.

Mother Earth Cafe (dìqiú zhījiā; 地球之家), 1 Baijiazhuang Lu (☎6503 1099), the neon castle just south of TGI Friday's. Pasta, pizza, burgers, and steaks served in a rainforest environment. "Rain" patters down onto the jungle, thanks to an indoor water system, amid claps of thunder and the squawking of parrots. Animal-patterned chairs and waterfalls add to the insanity. Most entrees Y30-70. Open daily 11am-1am.

■ ENTERTAINMENT

ACROBATICS

With gardens full of flower-like plates spinning on poles, beatifically grinning contortionists folded double, trapeze artists, tumblers, and dozens of girls perched precariously on one bicycle, Chinese acrobatics represent a dizzying pinnacle of artistic achievement.

BEIJING & NORTH COAST

A NIGHT AT THE JINGJU There are as many branches of Chinese opera as there are dialects, but Beijing opera (jīng jù; 京剧) has by far the highest reputation. Established in 1790 during the Qing dynasty, Jingju has entertained audiences with dramatic (though perhaps not entirely accurate) accounts of Chinese history and classical tales. Among Jingju's biggest fans were Emperor Guang Xu and Empress Dowager Ci Xi. Guang Xu was not only an amateur Jingju singer but also a capable drummer and orchestra director. Empress Ci Xi, for her part, constructed a three-story theater in the Summer Palace (p. 125) to prove how much she loved opera.

In Beijing opera, there are four main types of roles: *sheng* (positive male role); *dan* (positive female role); *jing* (supporting male role); and *chou* (clown). Each type has unique costuming and facial makeup; the different colors of painted faces represent different personalities. Yellow or white signifies cunning; red, uprightness and loyalty; black, valor and wisdom; blue or green, vigorous and enterprising (often rebellious); and gold or silver, mystic or supernatural. Performances are accompanied by an orchestra of wind, string, and percussion instruments, and often by scrolling translations on an electronic screen (a concession to the modern era) as well. So sit back and ponder the fate of "The Drunken Concubine" or "The Unicorn-Trapping Purse."

Chaoyang Theater (cháoyáng jùchǎng; 朝阳剧场), 36 Dongsanhuan Bei Lu, Hujialou, Chaoyang (☎6507 2421). Tickets Y80-120. Performances nightly 7:15-8:40pm.

Tiandi Theatre (tiāndì jùchǎng; 天地剧场), north of Dongsishitiao Lijiaoqiao and Poly Plaza (☎6502 3984 or 6502 2649). Features the **Children's Team of the China Acrobatics Troupe**. Tickets Y120. Performances nightly 7:15pm.

Wansheng Theater (wànshèng jùchǎng; 万胜剧场), 95 Tianqiao Shichang, Xuanwu (☎6303 7449 or 6702 2324). Features the **Beijing Acrobatics Troupe**. Tickets Y100-150. Performances nightly 7:15pm.

BEIJING OPERA

The sounds of Chinese opera (jīngjù; 京剧) may be an acquired taste, but its worth sampling the genre (see **A Night at the Jingju,** p. 112). Beijing provides training operas for foreigners, which make things a little easier for the hapless musical wanderer. The all-night, top-volume presentations of acting, singing, dancing, and acrobatics are replaced by toned-down, two-hour versions, with translations flashed on electronic screens.

Liyuan Theatre (líyuán jùchǎng; 梨园剧场), 175 Yongan Lu (☎6301 6688, ext. 8860), inside the Qianmen Hotel. Foreign-friendliness expressed through bit-sized segments of opera and well-meaning but senseless English subtitles. Tickets Y30-120; Y30 buys an unbeatable balcony seat. Performances nightly 7:30-8:45pm.

Huguang Guild Hall (húguǎng huìguǎn; 湖广会馆), 3 Hufanqiao, Xuanwu (☎6351 8284 or 6352 9134). Scenes from famous operas presented in an old-style theater. Tickets Y60-180. Performances nightly 7:15-8:45pm.

Zhengyici Theatre (zhēngyǐcí xìlóu; 正乙祠戏楼), 220 Xiheyan Jie (☎6318 9454), south of Hepingmen. Turn left by Quanjude Roast Duck Restaurant and follow the signs. China's first opera house. Tickets Y50-150. Performances nightly 7:30-9:30pm.

Changan Grand Theatre (chángān dà xiyuàn; 长安大戏院), Changan Bldg., 7 Jianguomennei Dajie, Dongcheng (☎6510 1309 or 6510 1308). Acrobatics and special effects in a Western-style theater. Classical stories at weekend matinees, full operas on weekend evenings. Tickets Y20-120. Performances daily 1:30 and 7:30pm.

GALLERIES

Not too long ago, almost all state-run museums in China were woefully lacking any concept of curatorship. Beijing had its share of daring, bold young artists, but they were often deprived of public exhibition space and forced to retreat to warehouses in the countryside. In recent years, though, several galleries have begun to open Chinese and foreign eyes to the tremendous talent in China, and exhibits change regularly in keeping up with the times. Useful websites include: www.chinese-art.com, www.artscenechina. com, and www.china-avantgarde.com.

Wan Fung Art Gallery (yúnfēng huàláng; 云峰画廊), 136 Nanchizi Dajie (☎6512 7338 or 6523 3320), near the southern end of the 1st street east of the Forbidden City. Take bus #3 from Chongwenmen. Some of Beijing's more interesting contemporary exhibits in what could be considered the most beautiful gallery space in Beijing (originally part of the Forbidden City itself). Exhibits change weekly. Free. Open daily 9am-5pm.

Red Gate Gallery (hóng mén huàláng; 红门画廊), China World Trade Center, China World Hotel, 1 Jianguomenwai Dajie, 3rd Fl. (☎6505 2266, ext. 6821). One of the first private galleries in Beijing to challenge the boundaries of acceptable art; contemporary mixed media art displays wind around the halls. Free. Open daily 11am-6pm.

China Art Gallery (zhōngguó měishù guǎn; 中国美术馆; ☎6401 2252), on Chaoyangmennei Dajie, several blocks east of Jingshan Park and west of the Dengsi intersection. Take bus #202 from Fuchengmen or #211 from Chongwenmen to Meishuguan. This multi-winged museum fuses traditional golden eaves and covered walkways with a modern, spacious interior. The galleries are bright and airy, and in warm weather the doors are thrown open. Exhibits change regularly; *China Daily* runs up-to-date listings. No translations. The gift shop stocks an impressive selection of art books, note cards, and calligraphy brushes. Y4. Open daily 9am-5pm; last admission 4pm.

Courtyard Gallery (sìhéyuàn huàláng; 四合苑画廊), 95 Donghuamen Dajie, basement (☎6526 8882). Courtyard has an incredible location, perched by the moat just east of the Forbidden City. This small gallery relentlessly pushes ahead with new art. Exhibits change monthly. Free. Open M-Sa 11am-7pm, Su noon-7pm.

Poly Art Museum (☎6500 1188), on Dongzhimenwai Dajie, at Poly Plaza. An extensive collection of Chinese bronzes from the Shang and Zhou dynasties to the present. Open Tu and Th 10am-3pm. Y20.

▐ TEA HOUSES

Going to a Beijing tea house is sort of like getting a cheat sheet for the Chinese cultural scene. Typical tea houses, besides serving up tea and snacks in traditional Chinese fashion, feature Beijing opera, acrobatics, contortionism, magic tricks, traditional Chinese instruments, and more, often all on one night.

Tea ceremonies take place at several venues, including: **Purple Vine Tea House,** 2 Nanchang Jie (☎6606 6614; open daily noon-2am), at the corner with Xihuamen near the Forbidden City; **Wufu Tea House** (wǔfú cháguǎn; 五福茶馆), 104 Dianmen Bei Dajie (☎6405 9648; open daily noon-1am); **Green Tea House** (zǐyún xuān cháguǎn; 紫云轩茶馆), 53 Tayuancun, Chaoyang (☎6468 5903; open daily 11am-11pm); and **Xichan Tea House** (xīchán chálín; 西禅茶林), 7 Meishuguan Dong Jie, Dongcheng (☎6404 3486; open daily 9am-midnight). Others include:

Lao She Tea House (laǒshè cháguǎn; 老舍茶馆), Dawancha Bldg., 3 Qianmen Dajie, 3rd Fl. (☎6304 6334 or 6303 6830), about a block west of KFC, just across from the Qianmen bus stop. Intended to evoke bygone days with its lacquered wood and covered lanterns. Some of the performances, like opera, instrumental music, and acrobatic swordplay, deserve accolades; slightly cheesy magic tricks add some comic relief. Different seats have different admission prices, but the show is good even from afar, and snacks are free for all. Tickets Y40-130. Shows daily 7:40-9:20pm.

Sanwei Bookstore (sānwèi shūwù; 三味书屋), 60 Fuxingmennei Dajie (☎6601 3204), across from the Minzu Hotel. Sanwei caters to a more mature crowd, with its candles, birdcages, and higher ticket prices. On Saturday nights, ceiling fans whirl while brilliantly executed Chinese folk music pleases an already easily pleased audience. A translator stands ready to explain the history of the pieces and of the traditional instruments on which they are played. A cup of tea here can cost as much as a beer (Y20). Cover Y30. Open Sa 8:30-10:30pm.

SHOPPING

Wangfujing Dajie, an upscale street with lots of stores and lots of action, runs from north to south a bit east of Tiananmen Square. It will make for some good people-watching once the construction that currently tears up the center of the street is done. **Xidan,** a shopping area off Changan Jie in the west, is where Beijing's teenage trendsetters pay their respects to the latest in European and American fashion. The vast **Friendship Store** (yǒuyì shāngdiàn; 友谊商店), 17 Jianguomenwai Jie, is a self-contained commercial cosmos with outlandish prices.

For more upscale and elusive products, try **Watson's** (wòtèsēn; 沃特森) at the Holiday Inn Lido; the **Lufthansa Center** (yànshā shāngchéng; 燕沙商城), also known as the **Kempinski Hotel** (kǎibīnsījī fàndiàn; 凯宾斯基饭店); the **China World Trade Center** on Jianguomenwai; or the **Beijing Department Store** (běijīng bǎihuò dàlóu; 北京百货大楼), on Wangfujing. The glitzy **Hualian Shopping Center** (huāliǎn shāngshà; 花脸商厦), across from Vartone New World Plaza at Fuchengmenwai Dajie, has designer goods and a sprawling basement supermarket.

XIUSHUI SILK MARKET (xiùshuǐ shìchǎng; 秀水市场). Veritable oceans of silk spill into the street here. True to its name, the silk market sells silk of all ilks, including shirts, lingerie, pajamas, and traditional Chinese dresses. The market also peddles brand-name (sometimes authentic) merchandise like Levis jeans and North Face jackets; the nefarious purchase of pirated CD music and "seed-eerongs" (around Y30) is also possible. Accustomed to the smell of rich tourists, vendors scrutinize their potential prey with a practiced eye, on the prowl for easily swindled shoppers. Although the clientele is largely foreign, a good number of repeat customers, savvy and spendthrift to a fault, keep hard haggling possible. Beware, counterfeits abound. *(On Xiushui Dong Jie, a tiny street stretching from the north side of Jianguomenwai Dajie between the Friendship Store and the Jianguo Hotel to the US Embassy. Take bus #1 or 4.)*

LIULICHANG (liúlìchǎng; 琉璃厂). An amazingly modern-looking antique market, Liulichang combines the brilliant reds, blues, and golds of sleek antique restoration with the timeless feeling of getting conned. Stores overflow with vases, scrolls, calligraphy, chops, and carpets, both genuine antiques and convincing imitations. The market sells the pride of China at high-to-exorbitant prices; as price varies more than quality, comparison shopping is usually very fruitful. *(Off Xinhua Nan Dajie, perpendicular to Qianmen Dajie, southwest of Qianmen. Take bus #14 or 66, or take the subway to Hepingmen and walk south on Nanxinhua Dajie. Most stores open daily 9am-5pm.)*

◨ PANJIAYUAN FLEA MARKET (pānjiāyuán jiǔhuò shìcháng; 潘家园旧货市场). Wake up at the crack of dawn to take a peek at one of Beijing's best shopping spots. Antiques and not-so-antiques stretch for what seems like miles. Although the Flea Market has its crooks, overall it is a stellar place to acquire good-quality scrolls and other wares not sold elsewhere, such as traditional Chinese shadow puppets. Nearly everyone leaves itching for more. *(At Panjiayuan, in the southeast part of the city. Accessible by buses #34, 51, 63, 64, and 368. Open Sa-Su around 5am-6pm; most of the action is over by noon.)*

YABAO LU CLOTHING MARKET (yábǎolù shìchǎng; 雅宝路市场). If fur coats are your style, look no further than this bizarre bazaar. A sort of Little Russia, store signs are written in Cyrillic, Russian salutations fill the air, and cheap clothing and fur stalls line the street. Since the early 90s, tons of Russians have been running import businesses in Beijing, mostly on Yabao Lu. After a hard day of bargaining, many a Russian adjourns to the nearby Mockba Restaurant (see p. 110) for a taste of home. *(Off Jianguomennei Dajie. Perpendicular to the entrance to Ritan Park. Accessible from Jianguomen subway or bus #44 from Qianmen.)*

QIANMEN DAJIE AND DAZHALAN. These two streets are lined with stalls selling virtually every article of clothing and clothing-related product known to mankind. The fabric stalls at times give way to stalls selling leather jackets, luggage, purses, shoes, toys, and more. Two more exotic shops in the Dazhalan Pedestrian Zone are **Zhangyiyuan Tea Hall** (zhāngyìyuán cházhuāng; 张一元茶庄) and **Tongren Medicinal Hall** (tóngrén táng; 同仁堂), the place for antlers, cicada shells, and other traditional Chinese herbal remedies. Haggling is the norm. *(Just south of Tiananmen Square. Take bus #2, 54, 59, or 66, or take the subway to the Qianmen stop.)*

ⓜ NIGHTLIFE

Welcome to China, Beijing Journal (www.beijingtour.net.cn) offers an expat insider's look at fun stuff to do in Beijing, from bungee-jumping to bar-hopping. **City Weekend** and **Metro** also list some great night spots and restaurants. Free copies of these magazines can be found in in shopping districts, universities, and large hotels. If partial assimilation or seeing "the real China" are your goals, look elsewhere. If not, go forth and party.

The decadent embassy district of **Sanlitun** (sānlǐtún; 三里屯) in northeast Beijing could just as easily be called *"laowai* central"—bars bursting with foreigners crowd its foreigner-laden streets. A stroll through Sanlitun will unearth dozens of aptly named spots: Comma Bar, Green, Day Off, and Orgasm, just to name a few. There are two main bar streets in Sanlitun—**Sanlitun Lu,** frequented mainly by local night owls, and **Sanlitun Nan Lu,** packed with expat bars and expats. The favorite new place is a mini-Las Vegas at the south gate of **Chaoyang Park,** chock full of cool bars. **Wudaokou** near the Foreign Language Institute has a number of music clubs and bars frequented by students and younger expats.

Gay and Lesbian nightlife is available, though not prevalent. One popular spot is **Half and Half** (hǎitōng jiǔjiā; 海通酒家), on 15 Sanlitun Nan Lu, about half a block northeast of the Kylin Plaza. Fashionable hipsters come here to meet and mingle amid an active pick-up scene. (☎ 6416 6919. Open daily 8pm-5am.)

- ⓜ **Havana Cafe** (hāwǎnnà kāfēi; 哈瓦那咖啡; ☎ 6586 6166), at the north gate of the Workers' Stadium, Chaoyang. This beautiful groove-getting hovel, once the Workers' Stadium ticket booth, is now Beijing's first Cuban bar and restaurant. The *comida* is Latin American, the *bebidas* are international, and the *sangria* works best when sipped on the outdoor terrace. Drinks Y15-35. Around 10pm, a DJ spins hot and sweaty samba beats to jump-start nights of summer passion, while lusty lovers of all ages kick up their heels on the dance floor. Open daily 11am-3am.

- ⓜ **Solutions** (hélǜshén; 和路神; ☎ 6255 8877), down the little lane across from the west gate of Beijing University. With everything from Japanese rap to French hip-hop to dirty old American booty-shakin' tunes, Solutions is the solution if you're dying for music that won't arrive in China for another year. DJs are mostly foreign students itching to spin the latest vinyl for a packed weekend house glowing with black lights. Drinks Y10-25. Sa-Th no cover, F-Sa Y10-30. Open Su-Th 7pm-2am, F-Sa 7pm-6am.

- ⓜ **The Den** (dūnhuáng xī cāntīng; 敦煌西餐厅), 12 Chaoyangmenwai Dajie, Chaoyang (☎ 6592 6290), beside the City Hotel in Sanlitun. A smoky chamber of exotic vices, the Den is an expat favorite for weeknight unwinding and weekend frenzy. A DJ spins vinyl every night starting at 10pm, and the weekend brunch (Sa-Su 11am-3pm) serves a mean eggs benedict. Drinks around Y30, Su-W 10pm-midnight all drinks Y15. Cover Y30 only for those bringing food from the booth next door. 18+. Open Su-Th 10:30am-3am, F-Sa 10:30am-7am.

- ⓜ **The Big Easy** (kuàilè zhàn; 快乐站), 8 Chaoyang Gongyuan Lu (☎ 6508 6776), at the south gate of Chaoyang Park. Looks and feels like a hurricane picked up a piece of New Orleans and dropped it in China. Deliciously authentic cajun and creole food (Y35-100) dished up to the feel-good sounds of the Big Easy band, fronted by the fabulous Jacqui Staton, one of the original Ikettes with Ike and Tina Turner. Motown, R&B, and blues stir expats to sing along. New Orleansese Made Easy: "mo bettah" means the best there is, as in "The Big Easy is one of the mo bettah bars around." Happy Hour daily 5-8pm. Open Tu-Sa 10am-2pm and 5pm-2am.

CD Cafe (CD kāfēi wū; CD 咖啡屋; ☎6501 8877, ext. 3032), on Dongsanhuan Lu, Chaoyang, east of Xiaobawang overpass and 200m south of the Great Wall Sheraton. Known as the best jazz club in town. Every night (except M and W) features an excellent trio or quartet that brings the house down. Regular special concerts. Drinks Y25-45. Su-Th no cover, F-Sa Y20, special performances Y30. Open M-Su 6pm-2am.

Durty Nellie's (dūbōlín xī cāntīng; 都伯临西餐厅), 11A Sanlitun Nan Lu (☎6502 2808), on Dongdaqiao Xi Jie off Gongren Tiyuguan Bei Lu. One of 2 places in Beijing to get Guinness on tap. Everything here has an old Irish pub flavor, from the live bands to the relaxed pool hall around back. In the winter, people come here to warm up—and end up staying. In the summer, they come to get liquored up—and then go hit the dance clubs. Drinks Y30-40. Open Su-Th noon-1:30am, F-Sa noon-2am.

The Loft (cáng kù; 藏酷), 4 Gongren Tiyuguan Bei Lu (☎6501 7501). Follow the signs beside Pacific Century Place around to the bar. Brand new, the Loft has quickly established itself as one of the coolest hangouts around. Bamboo chairs and leafy plants grace the floors and walls, while mini-TVs line the back wall. The live DJ turns the Loft into a jam-packed disco (F-Sa from 10:45pm). Drinks Y22-40. Lunch and dinner (about Y35-100) until 8pm. Cover Y30-50. Open Su-Th 11am-2am, F-Sa 11am-4 or 5am.

Nasa Disco (NASA dísīkè; NASA 迪斯科), 2 Xitucheng Lu, Jimenqiao Beice, Haidian (☎6203 2906). Walk up the gangplank to a vast, weird world of multiple levels and an underutilized but highly sophisticated lighting system. Fake rockets and old jeeps round out the decor. Drinks Y20-30. Cover Y20-30. Open Su-Th 8pm-2am, F-Sa 8pm-2:30am.

Shooters Bar and Grill (shùdéshì xīcān bā; 树德士西餐吧), 4 Gongti Dong Lu (☎6593 2360). Follow the sign to the end of an alley to the right of Sanlitun Nan Lu. The telltale owl, tiny t-shirts, and "More than a bowlful" slogan might seem suspiciously familiar to Americans. Hooters it's not, but it's close. With cheap drinks (Y12-30) and live music (weekends 10pm-1am), Shooters packs in an alcohol-happy younger crowd of mostly foreign students. "Lush Card" Y100 (20 drinks). "All you can drink" Th-Su 6pm-midnight Y88. Tex-Mex fare Y15-70. Open daily 4:30pm-2am.

Porgy's Place, 11 Dongdaqiao Xi Jie (☎6515 9566), near the southern end of Sanlitun Nan Lu, heralded by a bright yellow sign. The only place in town that carries Rolling Rock beer, straight from Latrobe, Pennsylvania. Serving up great soul food and great soul music, as well as some blues, jazz, and R&B, Porgy's features live bands W-Su 10pm-1:30am. Drinks Y20-40, entrees Y20-80. Open daily 6pm-2am.

Nightman (càitè màn; 菜特曼), 2 Xibahe Nanli, Chaoyang (☎6466 2562). Nightman fizzes with pure sensory overload, with lights, strobes, smoke, TV screens, 2 levels of lounges, and a DJ stage featuring unremittingly erotic Chinese dancers. English pop and techno music complete the experience. Drinks Y20-30. No cover for foreigners. Open Th and Su 8pm-3am, F-Sa 8pm-5am.

Nashville (xiāngyáo jùlèbù; 乡谣俱乐部), 14 East Bldg., Chaoyang Dongdaqiao Xi Jie (☎6502 4201), across from Sanlitun Market. Off the beaten track and a nice change of pace. Live rock and country music nightly accompany excellent BBQ and foot-stomping blues on the weekends. Drinks Y25-40, entrees Y20-50. Open daily 6pm-2am.

Jam House (jièmò fáng; 芥茉房), 1 Sanlitun Nanlixi, Chaoyang (☎6506 3845). Down a narrow little alley and through an even narrower door, Jam House is a smoky cavern packed with foreigners. W blues jam sessions, Th-F flamenco, Sa rock. Drinks Y20-40. Open daily from 8pm, usually until 2am Su-Th and 4am F-Sa.

Minder Cafe (míngdà xīcānguǎn; 明大西餐馆), Xinyi Bldg., Gongren Tiyuguan Bei Lu, 1 Houpingfang, Nanjiubajie Lukou, Sanlitun (☎6500 6066). Classic American rock? Check. Faux Tiffany lamps? Check. Darts? Check. If it looks like an expat bar, and sounds like an expat bar, chances are it *is* an expat bar. A mediocre Filipino rock band attracts an older audience. Drinks Y35. Open Tu-Su 11am-at least 2am.

⊛ SIGHTS

CITY CENTER

TIANANMEN SQUARE

Between Chang'an Dajie and Qianmen Dajie. Take the subway to Qianmen. By bus, buses #1, 4, 10, and 20 stop along Changan Jie to the north, while #5, 9, 17, 22, 47, 53, 54, 59, and 307 reach Qianmen to the south. Bus #116 runs along the side of the square.

As one of the largest and most notorious public meeting spaces in the world, Tiananmen Square (tiānānmén guǎngchǎng; 天安门广场), has created enough historical and political cannon fodder to last a lifetime. As the political epicenter of popular protest in modern China, the square has witnessed May Fourth anti-imperialist demonstrations, anti-Japanese protests, Mao Zedong's proclamation of the People's Republic of China, Red Guard rallies of the Cultural Revolution, politically charged outpourings of grief for Zhou Enlai, and pro-democracy protests. For most Chinese, Tiananmen Square remains an ideological mecca, a field of cement where they pay tribute to the heroes and victims of China's tumultuous history. Vivid images of the bloody events of 1989 (see p. 20) may at times surface, but for now, the square seems rooted in an eternally celebratory atmosphere, a prime kite-flying and picture taking site. On the north side of the square, the **Monument to the People's Heroes,** an angular slab of granite erected in 1958, depicts heroic, revolutionary events from recent Chinese history.

TIANANMEN GATE (tiānānmén; 天安门). The huge banner on this "Gate of Heavenly Peace" proclaims "Long Live the People's Republic of China" and "Long Live the Unity of the World's Peoples." It was on the rostrum of this gate that Chairman Mao declared the founding of the PRC in 1949, and his portrait (touched up yearly) gazes out still. Two stone lions stand guard at the five bridges across the Jinshui (Gold Water) River, actually a very small stream. The wound on the lioness's chest comes from a halberd stab made by rebel leader Li Zicheng during his assault on the Forbidden City. Li toppled the Ming and lived in the palace for 100 days before the Qing swooped down and ended his imperial dreams. Two winged totems topped with tortoises are symbols of loyalty, awaiting the emperor's return from distant expeditions. The climb to the top of the gate itself is not very interesting—all that awaits you there is an off-limits collection of dining tables. For a better view of the square, visit Zhengyangmen Gate. *(At the northern end of Tiananmen Square. Open daily 8am-5:30pm. Y15, students Y5.)*

ZHENGYANGMEN GATE (zhèngyángmén; 正阳门). Of the nine original imperial gates *(men)* guarding Beijing, only Zhengyangmen's character for *men* (门) lacked the little hook at the lower corner. The emperor often traveled through Zhengyangmen; as a descendant of a dragon (an aquatic creature), it was believed that the emperor would be snagged by a hook. When the Beijing walls were torn down in 1964 to make room for the subway and second ring road, only Zhengyangmen was left standing. There is a small exhibit on Old Beijing at the top. *(At the southern end of Tiananmen Square. Open daily 9am-4pm. Y5.)*

GREAT HALL OF THE PEOPLE (rénmín dàhuìguǎn; 人民大会馆). This venue of the National People's Congress is a virtual toystore of caucusing cliques. Visitors are brought around a selection of province-themed reception rooms amid impressive chandeliers and marble pillars. The intimate banquet hall seats a hefty 5000. *(On the western edge of the square. Open daily 8:30am-3pm (sometimes until 1pm), except when the Congress is in session. Y15.)*

CHINESE REVOLUTION AND HISTORY MUSEUMS (zhōngguó gémìng lìshǐ bówùguǎn; 中国革命历史博物馆). On the right is the **Museum of History,** a comprehensive chronicle of Chinese civilization. Artifacts and pseudo-artifacts dating from 3000 BC to 1919 are arranged in a timeline defined by Marx's four stages of human development: primitive communal groups, slavery, feudalism, and capitalism/imperialism. On the left, the **Museum of the Revolution** picks up where the Museum of History leaves off, beginning with the founding of the CCP (1919-21). The museum sees frequent re-fittings to accommodate the latest re-inventions of history. For those in Beijing during times of flux or on significant anniversaries, the museums can be gripping. Otherwise, the content is dry, and the significance, given the lack of English translation, is left largely to the imagination. *(On the east side of the square. Open Tu-Su 8:30am-4:30pm; last admission 3:30pm. Museum of History Y5, students Y2; Museum of the Revolution Y5, students Y3.)*

CHAIRMAN MAO MAUSOLEUM (máo zhǔxí jìniàn táng; 毛主席纪念堂). Before the Monument to the People's Heroes lies the resting place of China's widely lauded Chairman, who has lain flag-draped in waxy splendor since 1976. The cult-like adoration that Mao enjoyed during his lifetime seems little diminished by his demise, if the number of offering-bearing mainlanders who flock to the Mausoleum for the allotted quick peek is any reflection of national sentiment; factory lines of reverent visitors are shepherded with strict authority and white gloves through the Lenin-esque tomb. Inside the dimly lit, plush red-carpeted anteroom, signs enjoin viewers to take off their hats and remain silent so as not to disturb the Great Embalmed One. *(In the middle of Tiananmen Square; enter from the north door. Prepare for long lines. Open M-Sa 8:30-11:30am. Free. No bags or cameras allowed; bag check Y8.)*

BEIJING UNDERGROUND CITY (dìxià chéng; 地下城). Any ancient civilization worth its salt should have a subterranean labyrinth. This underground city was constructed in the 1960s when an ultra-idealist China faced nuclear threats from "hegemonic imperialist and revisionist powers" (namely the US and USSR). Most of these bomb shelters have since been converted to storage houses and shopping centers. Not extraordinarily fascinating in its own right (just a bunch of damp tunnels), the free English guide service and silk factory help you get your money's worth. See the process of making silk quilts from start (cocoon) to finish (feather-light blankie), and maybe try your hand at giving the silk a "pull." *(62 Xidamochang Jie. Walk south on Qianmen Dajie and take the 1st alley on the left (just past the underground crosswalk stairs); continue for 15min., bearing right at the fork. Open daily 8:30am-6pm. Y20.)*

FORBIDDEN CITY

*Take any **bus** to Tiananmen Square. Go under the Tiananmen Gate and don't stop until you reach the ticket booths for the Palace Museum. For the North Gate, take bus #101, 103, or 109. **Open** daily 8:30am-5pm; last admission 3:30pm. English translations of most signs. Audio tours (narrated by Roger Moore) Y30, Y200 deposit. **Admission** Palace Museum Y30, all-inclusive admission to Palace Museum, Jewelry Hall, and Clocks Hall Y50. Students half-price, groups of more than 10 Y45, children under 1.2m free.*

During the palace's 500-year history, only 24 emperors and their most intimate attendants could have known every part of its 800 buildings and 9000 chambers. The Forbidden City (zǐjìn chéng; 紫禁城), so named because commonfolk were barred from entry, was opened to the public in 1949. Now referred to as the **Imperial Palace** (gù gōng; 故宫), the complex is the largest and most impressive example of ancient architecture in China. The signs in the Forbidden City usually give at least three dates—of construction, destruction, and reconstruction. The palaces have seen so many face-lifts that it is hard to tell what is original anymore, but no amount of fresh paint can diminish the epic weight they carry.

Construction of the Forbidden City was completed in 1406, the 4th year of Ming Emperor Yongle's reign. It was based on a principle of work before play; the administrative offices and temples are in the front, while the markets are in the back. The Son of Heaven conducted his stately affairs in the **ceremonial halls** of

Taihedian, Zhonghedian, and Baohedian. The first hall is also the hall of the imperial throne. Past the **imperial living quarters,** Qianqinggong, Jiaotaidian, and Kunninggong (now voyeur-friendly peering halls), is the **Imperial Garden** and an impressive artificial **Mountain of Piled Excellence** topped with a pagoda.

The bulk of the palace collections were removed by the Nationalists during the Sino-Japanese War and eventually put on display at the National Palace Museum in Taipei, Taiwan. The **Hall of Paintings** to the west, just before Qianqinggong, is a dimly lit cavern of famous scriptures and paintings graced by imperial ownership. The **Hall of Clocks** is more interesting than it sounds, with room after room of unabashedly ostentatious timepieces, some so overgrown with goldleaf that it's impossible to actually tell the time. *(Open daily 8:30am-5pm; last ticket sold 4pm. Y5.)* North of this is the **Hall of Jewelry,** which is really an assemblage of several halls housing imperial relics so splendid they don't need lighting. Visitors must shuffle about in ridiculous-looking neon orange overshoes (Y2) to preserve the brick floors. *(Open daily 8:30am-5pm; last ticket sold 4pm. Y5.)*

Outside the Forbidden City, two parks offer unexpected respite. To the southwest is **Zhongshan Park** (zhōngshān gōngyuán; 中山公园), where Sun Yat-sen's hearse was temporarily housed in 1925. *(Open daily 6am-10pm; last admission 9pm. Y3, students Y1.5, children under 1.2m free.)* To the southeast is **Working People's Cultural Palace** (láodòng rénmín wénhuà gōng; 劳动人民文化宫) and **Imperial Ancestral Temple.** The inner court, a tiny Forbidden City with its own marble terraces and stairways, is worth a visit if there is a good temporary exhibit or performance. *(Open daily 6am-9pm. Park Y2, students Y1, children under 1.2m free; park and temple Y15.)*

OTHER SIGHTS IN THE CITY CENTER

BEIHAI PARK (běihǎi gōngyuán; 北海公园). Beihai Park, home to the Liao dynasty palace some 800 years ago, is one of the world's earliest imperial gardens. Built in 1651, the **White Dagoba** (a Tibetan-style Lama temple) is the symbol of the park, surging up into the sky and visible from many vantage points. The **Nine-Dragon Screen,** a 5m-long depiction of nine dragons batting pearls about in the water, and the **Jade Buddha,** carved out of a single piece of white jade, are both worth a look. The central island area, **Qiong Island,** is connected to the surrounding land via bridge and ferry (and Y20 per hr. rental boats). It was made from the piled mud that collected as the lake was dug out by hand. The eastern and western shores are home to gardens, religious buildings, and the small temple where Empress Dowager Ci Xi raised silkworms. *(Northwest of the Forbidden City. Buses #6, 101, 103, 109, 111, 202, and 802 stop just outside its main gate in the south. Buses #42, 107, and 113 stop at the North Gate, a less crowded entrance. Open daily 6am-10pm. Park Y5; park and White Dagoba Y10; Round City Y5.)*

JINGSHAN PARK (jǐngshān gōngyuán; 景山公园). This 14th-century park's claim to fame is a locust tree. It was here that Emperor Chongzhen, wracked with despair after insurgents broke into the Forbidden City, hung himself on March 19, 1644, thus ending the Ming dynasty. Jingshan (Vista Mountain), made of an huge mound of the dirt dug up to create the Forbidden City's moat, has nine pavilions; the pavilion perched on top used to be the highest point in the city. The rest of the park is almost criminally tacky, with colored lights, garish life-sized *papier mâché* and polyester dioramas, and a dress-up station where visitors can get bounced around in a faux emperor's palanquin. *(Jingshan Qianjie, directly opposite the north (rear) gate of the Forbidden City. Accessible by buses #101, 103, 109, 111, 114, 202, 211, 802, 810, and 812. ☎6404 4071. Open daily 6am-10pm. Y2.)*

DONGSI MOSQUE (dōngsì qīngzhēnsì; 东四清真寺). Much quieter and smaller than Niujie Mosque across the city, the simple Dongsi Mosque is tucked among busy shops. Its pretty courtyard and trees are functionally attractive, but do not really measure up to the rather hefty admission price. *(13 Dongsi Nan Dajie, a short walk south from the intersection of Chaoyangmennei Dajie and Dong Dajie. Take bus #101 or 106 to Dongsi. No skirts, shorts, or tank tops allowed. Open daily 9am-5pm. Y10.)*

AROUND THE SECOND RING ROAD

The second ring road roughly traces Beijing's old city wall. Subway stops are marked by the old locations of the city gates; although the gates are no longer standing, Beijingers still use the gate names as landmarks. Most sights around the second ring road are easily accessible by subway. Beginning with Deshengmen north of city center, the following gates are arranged clockwise.

DESHENGMEN 德胜门

PRINCE GONG'S RESIDENCE (gōng wáng fǔ; 恭王府). One of the few royal Qing residences remaining in Old Beijing, this crown jewel is an undiscovered paradise. Little commercial blitz mars the environment, and visitors can walk at leisure through the nine small courtyards of Prince Gong's hideaway. The residence, reputedly the model for the setting of the 18th-century literary classic *Dream of Red Mansions*, is arranged so that the viewer can take in the whole scene at once. Craggy rock formations, gardens, *bonsai* trees, and a pond grace the grounds; chirping cicadas run amok, and bamboo-lined paths open onto gardens of fuchsia flowers adorned with a haze of white moths. Thanks to the double meaning of the Chinese word *fu*, the little cave is a place of happiness (福) and of bats (蝠). *(14 Liuyin Jie, north of Beihai Park. Hard to get to by any means other than taxi or pedicab. The closest bus stop is the Beihai Park North Gate. Open daily 8:30am-4:30pm. Guided tours Y60. Y5.)*

DRUM TOWER (gǔ lóu; 鼓楼). Across the lake from Prince Gong's Residence stands the Drum Tower, a vast structure also known by the unfortunate epithet "Drum Tower Curio City." Those who manage to avoid the huge "art museum" can climb steep, 1420-era stairs for a peek at the surrounding sights, including the golden 1990-era arches of McDonald's. About 100m north, up a nearby alley choked with fresh and pickled fruits and vegetables, is the **Bell Tower** (zhōng lóu; 钟楼) and its 63-ton bell. The two towers used to be the origins of "Beijing time." *(Northernmost tip of Gulou Dajie. Take bus #5, 58, or 107, or take the subway to Gulou Dajie and then walk south on Jiugulou Dajie. Open daily 9am-4:30pm. Each tower Y6, both towers Y10.)*

SONG QINGLING MUSEUM (sòng qìnglíng gùjū; 宋庆龄故居). Once belonging to Prince Chun, father of the last emperor Pu Yi, these stately grounds became the estate of Song Qingling, the wife of Dr. Sun Yat-sen. A politically active woman in her own right, Song campaigned for civil rights, democracy, and freedom from aggression and was named Honorary President of the PRC. Following her death in 1981, her home was turned into a museum. There is no English translation of the history exhibit, but the museum's spacious grounds make for a lovely stroll among ponds, pavilions, and willows. *(46 Hanhai Beiyan, between 2 dormant smokestacks, on the northern edge of Houhai Lake. Take bus #5, 210, or 819 to Guozishi, or take the subway to Jishuitan and walk south on Gulou Xi Dajie. Open Tu-Su 9am-4:30pm. Y8, students Y4.)*

XU BEIHONG MUSEUM (xú bēihóng jìniàn guǎn; 徐悲鸿纪念馆). Hailed as the father of modern painting and realist art in China, Xu Beihong enjoyed a long and distinguished career of "making ancient things serve the present" and "making foreign things serve China." At this large and tastefully displayed museum, visitors can view Xu's artwork (including his trademark galloping horses, defiant lions, and crowing roosters) and exhibits tracing his life history and travels. *(53 Xinjiekou Bei Dajie, near the Jishuitan subway stop; also accessible by bus #22 from Qianmen. Open Tu-Su 9am-noon and 1-5pm. Y5.)*

BEIJING HUTONG TOUR. As wrecking balls hired by Hong Kong tycoons turn vast swaths of Beijing's old neighborhoods into office buildings and hotels, tourism may be the last savior of Beijing's urban cultural heritage. For those not confident enough to navigate Beijing's narrow *hutongs* (alleyways) alone, this tour by rickshaw traverses one of the nicest gray brick neighborhoods in Beijing, with stops at Prince Gong's Residence and the Drum and Bell Towers. (☎6615 9097 or 6612 3236. *Tours depart at 8:50am and 1:50pm from: 26 Dianmen Xi Dajie, at Qianhai Xi Jie, 200m west of Beihai Park's North Gate; Beihai Park's South Gate; and the intersection of Ping'an Dajie and Shihai Qian Jie, near Prince Gong's Residence. English tours available; call ahead to reserve. Y180 per person, admission to sights included.)*

ANDINGMEN 安定门

■ **LAMA TEMPLE** (yōnghé gōng; 雍和宫). If you have time to see only one temple in the city, this colorful Tibetan Lamasery (a.k.a. **Yonghe Lamasery**) should be it. Wafting clouds of incense do little to obscure the brilliance of the blue, green, and gold detail of the red pagodas; the intricacy of the decoration both inside and out is arresting. Constructed in 1691 and converted into a lamasery in 1744, Yonghe's architecture successfully combines Han, Mongol, Manchu, and Tibetan elements both in its dominant buildings (three huge archways and five large halls) and its minor ones (two auxiliary halls and four "halls for learning"). The temple boasts three "matchless treasures": an 18m high sandalwood Buddha statue, with a plaque from the Guinness Book of World Records certifying that the Buddha was indeed carved from just one really big tree; the Mountain of 500 Arhats, made of precious stones and less precious metals; and the "niche of Buddha" carved out of wood. An exhibition displays portraits of various Dalai Lamas, beginning with the Great Fifth. *(28 Yonghegong Dajie. Take bus #13, 116, or 807 to Yonghegong or Guozijian, or walk south from the Yonghegong subway stop; enter at the tail end of the temple. Open daily 9am-4:30pm. Y15; temple and exhibition hall Y20.)*

CONFUCIUS TEMPLE AND IMPERIAL COLLEGE (kǒng miào; 孔庙; and guózǐ jiān; 国子监). The 198 stone steles housed here tell the names of 50,000 successful candidates for the *jinshi* degree, the highest level of academic achievement in the imperial civil service examination system. Spanning 600 years and three dynasties, this list conveys the legacy of the oldest meritocracy in the world. The complex also houses the **Capital Museum** (shǒudū bówùguǎn; 首都博物馆). The museum traces the history of Beijing, beginning 400,000 years ago with *Sinanthropus Pekinensis* (Peking Man; see p. 130), and ending with "liberation" in 1949. Shaded courtyards offers a soothing refuge after prayers in front of incense censers. *(13 Guozijian Jie, around the corner from the Lama Temple. Enter through a decorated archway on the west side of the street. Open daily 9am-5pm; last admission 4:30pm. Y10, students Y3.)*

DITAN PARK (dìtán gōngyuán; 地坛公园). Built in 1530, Ditan is Tiantan's (see p. 122) smaller cousin. This park comes alive during the Chinese New Year, when the enormous Miaohui Festivals are held here to welcome the spring planting season and to appease the earth gods. Most halls, such as the **Royal Stables** and the **Storehouse of Sacrificial Utensils,** are free. The broad, elevated stone platforms and crazy echo potential give the **Fangze Altar and Hall of Cultural Relics** a distinctly Tiantan feel. *(Open daily 8:30am-5:30pm. Y5.)* This is also the place to go for croquet or to see lots and lots of *bonsai* trees for sale. *(The South Gate is just north of the Yonghegong subway stop; buses #104, 119, and 407 stop at West Gate. Open daily 6am-9pm. Y3.)*

JIANGUOMEN 建国门

BEIJING ANCIENT OBSERVATORY (běijīng gǔguān xiàngtái; 北京古观象台). Built in 1442, this observatory is in terrific condition. The eight rooftop instruments bear such exotic names as the "Azimuth Theobolite," "Equatorial Armilla," and "Celestial Globe." The downstairs exhibit is a goldmine for astronomy buffs, while the garden is for the mariners among you. *(West of the Friendship Store, southwest of the intersection of the Erhuan Lu and Jianguomennei Dajie. Take the subway to the Jianguomen stop; cross diagonally through the underpass. Open daily 9am-5:30pm. Y10.)*

RITAN PARK (rìtán gōngyuán; 日坛公园). Shielded from the bustle of Jianguomen, Ritan is one of Beijing's oldest and most pleasant parks. Ritan ("Temple of the Sun") has a lofty heritage as a place of sacrifice to the glowing orb. *(At the end of Yabao Lu, in the heart of the embassy district behind the Friendship Store. Accessible by bus #29. Open daily 6am-9pm. Y1.)*

CHONGWENMEN 崇文门

TIANTAN (TEMPLE OF HEAVEN) PARK

South of the city center between Erhuan Lu and Sanhuan Lu, bordered by Tiantan Lu, Yongdingmennei Dajie, Tiantan Dong Lu, and Yongdingmen Dongbinhe Lu. Buses #2, 15, 17, 34, 35, 36, 110, 105, 610, 812, and 943 stop at 1 of the 4 gates. Open daily 6am-8pm; sights open 8am-5:30pm. Park Y4; Y10 to all 3 sights.

A total of four *tan* (imperial shrines) were constructed in Beijing as the sacrificial altarplace for *tian* (heaven), *di* (earth), *ri* (sun), and *yue* (moon). The largest of these, Tiantan Park (tiāntán gōngyuán; 天坛公园) was designed as a venue for the annual imperial ceremony to appease the heavens, secure good harvests, atone for sins, and receive divine direction. The 273-hectare temple complex is rounded at its northern end and square along its southern edge, reflecting the traditional Chinese belief that the earth is square and the heavens are round. Within the park compound, a serene stone boulevard carried the imperial procession from "earth to heaven." Constructed in 1420 and opened to the public in 1949, Tiantan draws crowds of tai chi practitioners, bird cage bearers, and opera singers at dawn.

HALL OF PRAYER FOR GOOD HARVEST (qínián diàn; 祈年殿). The highlight of Tiantan, this 38m high, 30m wide round hall features a triple-eaved roof covered with blue, yellow, and green glazed tile representing the heavens, earth, and the mortal world. The hallmark of Ming engineering, the hall was built entirely without the use of nails, cement, or beams, and is held together by an elaborate network of interlocking pillars. Four gigantic "dragon" pillars represent the seasons and two dozen smaller ones symbolize the 12 months of the year.

ECHO WALL (jiǔ lóng bǎi; 九龙柏). One of Tiantan's many architectural acoustic sites, the wall stretches 65m in diameter. Supposedly, a mere murmur at one side of the wall will be conveyed with perfect clarity all the way to the other. But with visitors hooting and howling, it's a bit hard to put that theory to the test. Inside the courtyard, you can actually test the **Triple Echo Stones** (sān yīn shí; 三音石). Stand on the first stone and clap, and the echo comes back once; on the second stone, the sound returns twice; and on the third, three times. Aside from all the clamor, the courtyard was designed to enclose the **Imperial Vault of Heaven** (huáng qióng yǔ; 皇穹宇), which housed tablets used in sacrificial rites. The vault has a double-eaved roof, tiled in blue, upon which a blue-green gilded dragon plays with a pearl. *(South of the Hall of Prayers for Good Harvests.)*

ROUND ALTAR (yuán qiū; 圜丘). A sight to tickle the numerologist's fancy, the shape of the altar and the surrounding stairs and railings is based on the lucky imperial number "9." The three tiers of the altar represent the heavens, earth, and humankind. Join the other stamping, yelling, and occasionally mooing visitors eager to test out the timeless qualities of physics from the central stone on the top tier; the sound will bounce off the stones. *(Farther south along the main park axis.)*

FASTING PALACE. Emperors would sequester themselves here, away from the wily reaches of meat, drink, and women. The buildings, as one would expect of a fasting palace, are not terribly exciting, but do contain the original furniture from Qianlong's reign. There is also a Ming Dynasty **Big Bell** that anyone can strike (Y1) to accompany fervent prayers. *(Near the West Gate.)*

STAYIN' ALIVE With a 5000-year history lurking around every corner and a traditional preoccupation with brute longevity, it is not surprising that the Chinese feel the pressure to live not just well, but long. To that end, the Chinese have fine-tuned intricate workout routines to keep themselves fit. After **tai chi** and **qigong** at the crack of dawn, possibly the most popular activity is **ballroom dancing**. Have a boombox and 10m^2? Waltz the night away. An evening stroll through any populated area will lead to at least three ballroom dancing schools, set up *ad hoc* in parks and parking lots. Dancers frown with concentration, executing admirably elegant two-steps. Another popular workout is **fan dancing**, where women wave fans while keeping their four-step in time to traditional instrumental music. Other exercises are more minor, but no less well-founded. A good exercise regime includes several of the following:

Tree Slapping: A sort of basic man-to-nature catharsis, this activity allows the slapper (we don't know about the trees) to breathe in fresh air while expelling bad energy.

Head Standing: Meditating with your head and feet in swapped positions allows for increased blood circulation to the brain and clearer thinking, not to mention a new perspective on the world.

Walking Backward: Should not be done on busy highways. Ancient records of an immortal who walked backwards at the speed of light have inspired many to lightfoot it butt-first through the parks. Karmic reversal is also hoped to be an associated benefit.

Walking Barefoot: Because all the body's major acupuncture channels connect to the soles of the feet, walking barefoot is a cheap and easy way of revitalizing the body's main meridians.

Primal Scream: The logic behind the idea that a good, loud yell drives out built-up bad energy in your system is easy enough to understand. It also helps the screamer to remember to breathe. Usually practiced in the workplace by competing hawkers.

Finally, at the end of all the exercise, there's nothing better for keeping the spirit alive than squatting by the side of the road and smoking a pack of Chinese cigarettes while staring at the *laowai*.

OTHER SIGHTS IN CHONGMENWEN

NATURAL HISTORY MUSEUM (zìrán bówùguǎn; 自然博物馆). The largest such museum in China, this place takes satiric delight in its own existence, quoting Gorky ("Man, oh what an arrogant creation!") and musing about the origins of the glorious Chinese civilization. The main halls focus on flora, fauna, and human evolution. Artful taxidermy aside, there is a graphic excess of pickled vaginas and deformed fetuses preserved in formaldehyde, but you can easily avoid those and spend your time with enormous dinosaur fossils and prehistoric beasts. English translations are patchy, unless you can decipher Latin genus names. *(126 Tianqiao Nan Dajie, a few minutes north of Tiantan Park's West Gate. Take bus #2, 6, 17, 20, or others to Tianqiao or Tiantan. Open daily 8:30am-5pm; last admission 4pm. Y15, students Y10.)*

XUANWUMEN 宣武门

GRAND VIEW GARDEN (dàguān yuán; 大观园). Unlike Beijing's countless other parks, Grand View Garden has the selling point of a certain surrealism. Grand View Garden was planned and built according to depictions of the garden in Cao Xueqin's *Dream of Red Mansions;* in fact, the TV movie was filmed here. The landscape is pristine to the point of being unreal, and every chamber houses an incredible exhibit of restrained literary obsession. Peeling paint aside, the colors are bright, the willows lush, and the lakeside paths make for a gorgeous walk in an imagined world. **Hengwu Garden,** residence of the "Frosty Beauty" Xue Baochai, conveys a tidy, cool elegance. *(Nancaiyuan Jie, west of Taoranting along Yongdingmen Dongbinhe Lu. Buses #59 and 351 terminate at the park, and #19, 53, 122, and others stop nearby. Open daily 8:30am-5:30pm; last admission 4:30pm. Carriage rides Y10. Y10.)*

TAORANTING PARK (táorántíng gōngyuán; 陶然亭公园). The Tang poet Bai Juyi once wrote, "Wait until the chrysanthemums are golden and our home-brewed wine matured / Then drink until we are intoxicated with joy *(tao ran)* and contentment." Taoranting offers an amusement park and swimming pool with slides, an "adventure labyrinth," a "floating world," the Yuan dynasty **Temple of Mercy** (used by May 4th revolutionaries as a base), and more. Beyond the temples and the amusement park, Taoranting is one of the most serene parks in the city. *(19 Taiping Jie, between Taoranting Lu and Yongdingmen Dongbinhe Lu. Buses #20, 54, 102, and 106 stop at Taoran Qiao, in front of the park. Open daily 6am-10pm; in spring and autumn 6am-9pm; in winter 6:30am-8:30pm. Y2.)*

NIUJIE MOSQUE (niújiē lǐbài sì; 牛街礼拜寺). Built in 996 by the Arab scholar Nasuratan, the mosque combines Arab and traditional Chinese palace architecture. The brilliant, intricately decorated entrance hall opens up onto panel after panel of gold Arabic script on a red background. This hall, which faces Mecca and spills into a courtyard of green plants and pink flowers, is nothing short of breathtaking. A stele sporting Arabic script, a 300-year-old copy of the Qur'an, and Ming dynasty porcelains are also on display. The mosque is fully operational, and visitors must respect all rules regarding personal 1.5 appearance. Don't despair if you show up in a skirt; the mosque lends out garish checkered pants to anyone not appropriately dressed. Supplies are limited. *(On Niu Jie, south of Guanganmennei Dajie. Accessible by bus #40. Open daily 8am-4pm. No skirts or shorts. Y10, students Y5.)*

WHITE CLOUD TEMPLE (báiyún guàn; 白云观). Beijing's most active Daoist temple complex, White Cloud is a sleeper of a tourist attraction. The **Shrine Hall for the Jade Emperor** contains two large, oddly out of place revolving cones that light up, and the **Shrine for Patriarch Qiu** marks the resting place of the founding father of the Longmen sect of Quanzhen Daoism. Beyond that, White Cloud's biggest attraction is the "wind-containing" bridge. Visitors can hurl tokens (Y0.2) at a large coin with a bell in its center; a hit brings good luck, granted to you by a tiny voice that booms metallically out from under the bridge. *(On Baiyun Lu, Xibianmenwai. Take bus #40 to Tianning Si; head north. Open daily 8:30am-4:30pm; Oct.-Apr. 8:30am-4pm. Y10.)*

FUXINGMEN 复兴门

NATIONAL MILITARY MUSEUM (jūnshì bówùguǎn; 军事博物馆). This enormous Socialist-era building houses a collection of outdated toys for military aficionados. East Wind Missiles, tanks, and fighter planes dominate the main floor; torpedoes, AK-47 assault rifles, and flame throwers are upstairs; and bombers and U2 wreckage rust in the outside arena. Another room is filled with various bronze busts of generals and field marshals. Upstairs there is an interesting exhibit on the history of war in China, complete with weapons, chemicals, and clay soldiers. Pick up your guerrilla-era military gear and Soviet army binoculars in the museum store. *(9 Fuxing Jie. Accessible by bus #1, 4, or 57 from Tiananmen. From the northwest exit of the Junshi Bowuguan subway stop, turn right. Open daily 8am-5pm; last admission 4pm. Y5, students Y2.)*

YUYUANTAN PARK (yùyuāntán gōngyuán; 玉渊潭公园). "Jade Springs Pool" is big, wild, and very much in its natural condition. There are some pleasant gardens, an exercise area, and a good fishing hole. *(Just inside Sanhuan Lu, north of the Military Museum. From the museum, take the first right and cross a dirt field to the park's south gate. Accessible by bus #33. Open daily 6am-9:30pm; in winter 6am-7:30pm. Y2, senior citizens Y1.)*

FUCHENGMEN 阜成门

GUANGJI TEMPLE (guǎngjì sì; 广济寺). Built by a villager during the Jin dynasty (AD 280-316), this temple was excavated during the Ming—images of Buddha, stone turtles, and pillar fragments confirmed the ruined temple's location. Rebuilt in 1460 and again in 1931, the temple became the headquarters of the Chinese Buddhist Association in 1953. Along with towering trees and imposing *steles*, the beautiful temple houses a wall of 18 *arhats*, a Ming dynasty Chinese Tripitaka, and a library of 100,000 volumes of scriptures in over 20 languages. *(25 Fuchengmennei Dajie, at Xisi Dajie. Take bus #13 or 103 to Xisi. Open daily 6am-6pm. Free.)*

WHITE PAGODA TEMPLE (bái tǎ sì; 白塔寺). The White Pagoda's huge, chalky form was designed to look like an upside-down alms bowl. A small collection of Qing-era Buddhist relics and a room full of more Tibetan-style Buddha statues than you can imagine are on display. It is believed that going around the pagoda clockwise, from west to east, brings "merits and happiness, and dispels evils and disease." *(171 Fuchengmennei Dajie. Take bus #13, 103, or 814 from Fuchengmen to Baitasi. Open daily 9am-5pm; last admission 4:30pm. Y10, students Y5.)*

LU XUN MUSEUM (lǔ xùn bówùguǎn; 鲁迅博物馆). This lovingly curated museum offers an in-depth perspective on the author of *The Madman's Diary* and *The Story of Ah Q*. The museum is divided into two areas: the well-protected former residence of the author from 1924 to 1926, and an exhibition that includes over 10,000 manuscripts, letters, journals, and other items. With this collection and a computerized database of Lu Xun's complete works, the spacious and cool museum has become a worldwide center for Lu Xun studies. Not a jot of English explanation is in sight. *(19 Gongmenkou Ertiao. Take the 1st left as you walk east on Fuchengmennei Bei Dajie from the Fuchengmen subway stop. Open daily 9am-4pm; last admission 3:30pm. Y5, students Y3.)*

XIZHIMEN 西直门

BEIJING ZOO (běijīng dòngwùyuán;北京动物园). Weeping willow-shaded paths and placid lakes make the zoo a beautiful spot for a stroll. The zoo's permanent residents, however, don't have it nearly so nice: most of them live in dusty, dirty enclosures and appear bored or on the verge of serious depression. Zoo authorities have apparently woken up to the fact that the zoo is no place for animals, and some grand-scale renovations are underway. The pandas, a major tourist attraction, are kept in more comfortable surroundings. *(West of the Xizhimen subway stop. Accessible by bus #7 from Hepingmen, #15 from Fuxingmen, #27 from Deshengmen, #102 and 105 from Xuanwumen, #103 from Wangfujing, #107 from Dongzhimen, and #111 from Chongwenmen: the terminus for several buses. Virtual tour at www.beijingzoo.com. Open daily 9am-5:30pm; ticket office open 8:50am-4:30pm. Y100, students with ID Y50, "old men" Y80.)*

PURPLE BAMBOO PARK (zǐ zhúyuàn gōngyuán;紫竹院公园). This is where Beijing's lovers go to grow drowsy in one another's arms. Napping consorts aside, the park is a gorgeous emerald maze of waterways and footbridges, with sprawling lawns, pavilions, and lots of bamboo. *(On Zizhuyuan Lu, west of Xizhimenwai Dajie. Take bus #114, 332, or 360 to Zizhuyuan. Open daily 6am-10pm; last admission 9pm. Y2.)*

BEYOND THE THIRD RING ROAD

SUMMER PALACE

The quickest way to the Summer Palace is to take minibus #375 from Xizhimen station. Bus #332 from the zoo stops there. From Qianmen, the Palace is 1½-2hr. away by bicycle. Open daily 8:30am-5pm. Y25-33 for access to all 3 main park areas; Suzhou Jie area only Y10.

Constructed in 1750, the **Summer Palace** (yìhé yuán; 颐和园) is the largest imperial palace and garden complex in China. Scattered across the emperors' enormous summertime playground are over 3000 halls, pavilions, towers, courtyards, and even a re-creation of the southern Chinese city of Suzhou (see p. 308) where empresses could go "shopping" for fine silk. **Suzhou Jie** (苏州街) is the one area far enough off the beaten path not to make it onto the mapped walking tour (Y8); it is a must-see all the same. Cool green water laps the sidewalks, stylized gondolas idle beside dumpling restaurants, and stone walkways wind between water on one side, and shops, snack stands, and street artists on the other.

In the complex's scarcely visited northern half, just south of Suzhou Jie, is **The Tower of the Fragrance of Buddha** (fó xiāng gé; 佛香阁), perfectly situated for emperors seeking divine guidance without leaving their vacation resort. Nearby, the **Buddhist Tenants' Hall** houses bronze images of the Buddhas of the Three Ages, and statues of the 18 *arhats*. *(Y8, students Y4.)* The **Garden of Harmonious Virtue** (dé hé yuán; 德和园), in the cluster of buildings within the east palace gate, was used to entertain royals with Beijing Opera. The ornate stage dominates the center of the courtyard; a privileged few were allowed to watch from hallways. *(Y5.)*

Other sights include Empress Dowager Ci Xi's infamous **Marble Boat** (built in 1888 courtesy of embezzled funds; see p. 13), the **Seventeen Arch Bridge** topped with 544 stone lions, the **Pavilion for Listening to Orioles,** and the **Porcelain Pagoda.** A stroll along the stunning 728m **Long Corridor** (cháng láng; 长廊) winds past 8000 paintings and around most of the sights. Pedal and rowboat rental stations also pepper the shore of the lake. *(Stations open daily 8am-4pm. Y20-30 per hr., deposit Y100.)*

OTHER SIGHTS BEYOND THE THIRD RING ROAD

OLD SUMMER PALACE (yuán míng yuán; 圆明园). Unlike its splendid younger counterpart, the desolate Old Summer Palace remains in ruins from its plunder and pillage by French and British troops during the Second Opium War. For palace- and pavilion-goers, it is a huge disappointment, but the **Labyrinth,** an imitation European-style maze, is an interesting diversion. During the Mid-Autumn Festival, the emperor's palace maids often raced to the center pavilion carrying yellow silk lanterns in the shape of lotus flowers. The names of the two pavilions, Wanchunyuan (Beautiful Spring Garden) in the southeast and Changchunyuan (Eternal Spring Garden) in the east, evoke the palace's former grandeur, and quirky histories surround the ruins of such rooms as "The Birds House" aviary. In fact, a visit to the park is something like visiting a grandfather with great stories from the past. *(Northeast of the Summer Palace. From the Summer Palace, take a minibus (Y5) or taxi (Y10). Bus #375 from Xizhimen also stops outside. Open daily 9am-6pm. Tour guide Y60. Y10.)*

GREAT BELL TEMPLE (dà zhōng sì; 大钟寺). This endearingly enthusiastic temple believes that "every bell is a nutshell of a part of history and culture." The "bell forest" contains several hundred bells, from primitive pottery bells to Maoist bells. One of the world's oldest bells and China's largest, the **Great Bell** has over 230,000 characters from the Buddhist scriptures and prayers carved onto it. For Y2, visitors can climb a set of stairs and toss a coin in the hole of the bell for happiness. You can even make your own small bell (Y5-10). The temple is graced by signs hoping "that this exhibition will arouse your interest in ancient bell culture" and wishing you well—"may the pealing of bells remain fresh in your memory!" *(31A Beisanhua Xi Lu. Buses #300 and 367 stop outside. Open daily 8:30am-5pm; last admission 4:30pm. Y10, students Y4.)*

CHINESE ETHNIC CULTURE PARK (zhōng huá mínzú yuán; 中华民族园). This relatively new addition introduces "the life of the minorities in the metropolitan capital," Disney-style. The package deal includes: an Ewenki yurt, a Wa bamboo house, an Oroqen birch-bark tent, and 13 other villages, including China's largest "Taiwanese village." The Magic Tree of Ali Mountain, iron totem poles, waterfalls, and other "natural" environments are included. *(1 Beichen Lu. Take bus #380, 406, or 407 to Beichen Lu. Open daily 7:50am-7pm; last admission 6pm. Y60, students Y45.)*

🄵 DAYTRIPS FROM BEIJING

FRAGRANT HILLS AND ENVIRONS

FRAGRANT HILLS PARK

*Several buses go to Fragrant Hills Park and the adjoining Azure Clouds Temple. **Bus #318** departs from Pingguoyuan, just under 1km north from the subway station (30min., Y1-2). Bus **#333** runs from the Summer Palace and **#360** from the zoo. The bus terminus is at the foot of the hills, and rickshaws swarm like flies to take you to the park's north entrance. Save Y10 and take a 15min. walk instead. Open daily 6am-7pm. Cable car runs daily 9am-4pm (Y30 one-way, Y50 round-trip, children under 1.2m Y10). Y5, students Y2.5.*

There are several ways to earn a name like Fragrant Hills: be perpetually shrouded in cloudy mists that resemble an incense cumulus; be topped off by an impressive peak in the shape of an incense burner; or be ripe with blossom trees that erupt in a burst of floral aroma. **Fragrant Hills Park** (xiāng shān gōngyuán; 香山公园) pulls off all of these, with a dash of history, a smattering of architecture, and a lot of retired old folks. Built in 1745 under Emperor Qianlong and ravaged by foreign imperial forces in 1860 and 1900, the park underwent some cosmetic surgery after 1949 and is now one of Beijing's most idyllic spots. The park's greenery opens up to reveal an architectural gem or two—namely the faux-Tibetan **Temple of Brilliance** and a glazed-tile pagoda—that managed to escape the razings of the last century, and its natural harmony is sullied only slightly by the vendors hawking the plastic-encased red maple leaves that lend the Fragrant Hills their fiery autumnal glow.

If the hike to the summit doesn't tickle your fancy, fear not: a **cable car** can whisk you up, up, and away in 18 exertion-and-perspiration-free minutes. Other amenities include a lake, a restaurant that serves dead insects and springwater-boiled rice, and the **Xiangshan Hotel** (xiāngshān měngyǎngyuán bīnguǎn; 香山蒙养园宾馆; ☎6259 1155), which has single rooms for Y80 and up.

Through the north gate of the Fragrant Hills Park lies the **Azure Clouds Temple** (bì yún sì; 碧云寺). Built in 1331, the temple complex is comprised of several halls, including the hall to worship two protective deities (Heng and Ha), and the 1748 **Hall of the Five Hundred Arhats.** The red walls and tiled roofs of the other buildings give way to the cool white stone and Indian-style stupas of the Vajra **(Diamond Throne Pagoda).** Elaborate carvings of women and mythical beasts adorn the pagoda walls. *(Open daily 8am-5:30pm; last admission 5pm. Y10.)*

OTHER SIGHTS IN FRAGRANT HILLS

FRAGRANT HILLS BOTANICAL GARDENS (xiāngshān zhíwù yuán; 香山植物园). A huge scientific and ornamental complex, the Gardens are home to 30 varieties of bamboo, 2000 Chinese herbaceous peony trees, and a newly opened glass conservatory with over 3000 kinds of plants. Visitors to the **Sleeping Buddha Temple** (wò fó sì; 卧佛寺) are met by a 250,000kg, 5.3m long representation of a reclining Sakyamuni—and several pairs of his enormous shoes. Over 7000 people were enslaved to build it in 1321. *(A 15min. walk or a Y2 minibus ride from the foot of Fragrant Hills Park. Accessible by bus #318 from the terminus or from Pingguoyuan subway stop. Open daily 6am-8pm. Conservatory and gardens Y50, students Y40; gardens only Y5; Sleeping Buddha Temple Y5.)*

BADACHU (bā dà chù; 八大处). Another short ride from the Fragrant Hills are these "eight great sites" that comprise a rather schizophrenic wooded area featuring eight ancient temples and a slew of modern amusements. Along the path to the left, seven of the eight temples, including a recently refurbished site built to display the Buddha's tooth, are open for viewing; to the right is the **Landsled.** Visitors can pay to ride at breakneck speeds down aluminum tubes carved into the sides of the mountain (up Y20, down Y40, round-trip Y55). A **zipline** is also available. *(From Pingguoyuan terminus, take bus #318 to Pingguoyuan Dong, and change to #389 to Badachu. Otherwise, take #347 from the zoo. Open daily 5:30am-9pm. Y5, students Y3.)*

MING TOMBS

*About 50km northwest of Beijing proper, not far from the Badaling Great Wall. Take bus #5 or 44 to Deshengmen, cross the overpass to the bus terminal, and then take bus or minibus **#345** to **Changping** (昌平). Taxis run to the tombs from Changping (Y20). Trains also cover the distance between Beijing and Changping Main Station and, less frequently, the Changping North Station. Tour buses often take in both the tombs and Badaling (see p. 131). Changling, Dingling, and Zhaoling tombs are open to the public. **Open** daily 8:30am-5pm. **Admission** to each tomb Y20, students Y10, insurance Y1.*

At the foot of the Tianshou Mountains lie the famed Ming Tombs (míng shísān líng; 明十三陵). Zhu Di (Emperor Yongle) moved China's capital to Beijing and in 1409, the 7th year of his reign, commissioned his tomb to be built on the outskirts of the new capital. A final tally of 13 emperors, 23 empresses, eight concubines, and one prince were all entombed here. The 4km **Divine Road to the Changling Tomb,** a path lined with 24 white stone beasts, crosses the **Seven-Arch Bridge** before reaching its final destination. The other tombs are arrayed on either side of Changling.

Although most people knew the area housed lots of dead emperors, authorities worked hard to keep the precise location a secret. Every laborer who had even the slightest knowledge of the location was systematically executed. During World War Two, the Japanese sent a brigade of minesweepers to search for the tomb. The mystery remained unsolved until construction workers working on a nearby reservoir found a stone tablet giving directions to a tomb entrance. Even then, it took archeologists several years to disarm the booby traps inside.

The Ming Tombs ought to be an impressive reflection of Ming achievements in artistry and engineering. They're not. The descriptions convey little more than the rooms' dimensions, and the only decoration in the chambers is the coins and bills that visitors have thrown in as somewhat belated offerings to the emperors. Whether the planned amusement park, swimming pool, aquarium, museums, fishing pier, and camping grounds will bring the place back to life remains to be seen.

EASTERN QING TOMBS

*150km east of Beijing. They're near Zunhua, Hebei, but the tombs are best reached from Beijing. On weekends and holidays, a **tour bus** (7am, Y70) leaves when full from Xuanwumen Church. Otherwise, charter a taxi or minibus. ☎6605 4851. Pedicabs shuttle about the grounds; Y10 round-trip should cover several tombs, including the Cian and Ci Xi Tombs. **Open** daily 8am-5:30pm. **Admission** Y55, students Y35, children under 1.3m free.*

China's largest and most complete set of imperial tombs, the Eastern Qing Tombs (qīng dōng líng; 清东陵) are home to two princesses, three princes, five emperors, 15 empresses, 136 concubines, and an impressive amount of dust bunnies. The imperial superstars Empress Dowager Ci Xi, the dragon lady who ruled China from behind two puppet emperors (see p. 13), and Emperor Qianlong, China's longest reigning emperor (see p. 12), are interred here.

Although the Qing Tombs are more of a hassle to reach than their Ming counterparts, there is a lot more to see. The sprawling 15-tomb estate has been turned into an impromptu, somewhat run-down, collection of bejeweled knicks, knacks, clocks, and corpses. Perhaps most impressive is **Emperor Qianlong's tomb,** comprised of three magnificently carved chambers with Tibetan and Sanskrit engravings. Imperial performances, or spectacles of some sort, take place at **Xiaoling Tomb** (the tomb farthest to the north) daily at 10am and 2pm; a gaggle of ruffians don faded costumes and pretend to be royalty.

SHIDU

Southwest of Beijing. **Trains** *run to Shidu from Beijing South Train Station (1¾hr.; 6:38, 7:30am, and 5:40pm, returning 9:36am, 3:50, and 7:40pm; Y12), near the Qiaoyuan Hotel.* **Bus #917** *(3hr., 7 per day 6am-6:40pm, returning 4:30am-5:30pm) runs from Tianqiao. A tour bus (2hr., 6:30-8am, Y40) leaves from Xuanwumen Church on weekends; it may take a while to attract enough passengers for the driver to leave. From Shidu Train Station to Solitary Hill Camp costs about Y10 one-way; taxis abound for the return trip.*

Shidu (十渡) is absolutely gorgeous. The river connecting Shidu to the next village has so many bends that you cross it 10 times. The train stops at Shidu (10th crossing); most of the tourist trap action is at **Jiudu** and **Badu** (8th and 9th); and if you can get out beyond that, **Qidu** (7th) and below, your soul will thank you for it. Throngs of cab and horse carriage drivers greet new arrivals at the station. Choose a reputable-looking one for the trip to **Solitary Hill Camp** (gūshān zhài; 孤山寨), the best spot for crags, cliffs, paths, streams, and dreams. *(Open daily 7am-9pm. Y20.)* Look out for the **Thread of Sky,** a fissure in the rocks just wide enough for a person to pass through. Drivers may offer to take you to the temple with the pretty steps leading up to it. Avoid it: as of July 2000, that temple is being repaired, and there is nothing to see but an admission booth. If fending off the hordes of taxis isn't sport enough, go **bungee jumping** (Y200) on the way to Jiudu or ride a **zipline** (Y50).

TANZHE AND JIETAI

Tour bus #7 (6-8am, Y42) leaves from the northeast corner of Qianmen on weekends; tours include the two temples and the beautiful Stone Flower limestone cave. Otherwise, take the subway to Pingguoyuan and hop on bus #36 to Hetan. From Hetan, bus #931 (45min.-1hr., every 10min. 7am-5:30pm, Y2-2.5) stops at both temples; a taxi should cost about Y60 round-trip.

TANZHE TEMPLE (tánzhè sì; 潭柘寺). This temple lies at the end of a scenic drive through mountains and lush valleys. Over this serenity, the Liao dynasty emperor's gingko tree presides, 30m tall and 4m wide, with as many trunks growing from the same root as there have been Qing rulers. The monastery dates back over 1700 years to the Jin dynasty. It takes its name from the Dragon Pool (*tan*) behind the complex, and the mulberry trees (*zhe*) on the surrounding hills. The central section houses the largest and most ornate of the buildings, including the main hall of worship and a gorgeous rendering of the four heavenly protectors. The western section is said to feature a brick impression of the footprint of Kublai Khan's daughter, while the eastern section contains the **Floating Cup Pavilion.** The etching on the pavilion floor is said to look like a dragon from one direction, and like a tiger from another. Qing-dynasty poets came to the pavilion to write and play drinking games, floating their cups on the water in the etched grooves of the dragon/tiger. *(Open daily 8am-6pm. Y20, children under 1.2m free.)*

JIETAI TEMPLE (jiètái sì; 戒台寺). Also known as **Temple of the Ordination Altar,** Jietai was built in AD 622, although it didn't acquire its altar until several hundred years later. Like Tanzhe Temple, there are pavilions, stone tablets, and steles, including one with inscriptions in both Chinese and Manchu. Visitors may find themselves pining after the temple's ancient conifers for at least a little while. The **Chinese Scholar Tree,** the protector of Buddhism, is said to be over 1000 years old. The **Embracing Pagoda Pine** redefines the term "tree-hugger," as it wraps its branches around a small pagoda. Originality may not have been the tree namers' biggest attribute; but in the case of **Nine Dragon Pine,** imagination well may have been. *(11km southeast of Tanzhe, on Ma An Hill. Open daily 8am-6pm; in winter 8am-5pm. Y30, children under 1.2m free.)*

MUSEUM OF THE ANTI-JAPANESE WAR

101 Luguoqiaochengnei Jie, 15km southwest of Beijing. Accessible by taxi from Tanzhe and Jietai Temples, or by bus #6 or 50 to Guanganmen and bus #339 or #309 to Luguoqiao. Open daily 8:30am-4:30pm; last admission 4pm. Y15, students Y8.

The Museum of the Anti-Japanese War (zhōngguó rénmín kàngrì zhànzhēng jìniànguǎn; 中国人民抗日战争纪念馆), in the old Ming-dynasty garrison town of Wanping, is of minimally more interest than the Marco Polo Bridge nearby. Explanations are in Chinese, with the occasional Japanese translation. Blood and gore rule the day, from the introductory sign placed on a big red paint splatter to a model scene of a heart-exposing surgery room to video footage of shootings. A screening of the Japanese invasion shows Japanese armies swarming over some of Beijing's more renowned tourist sights.

MARCO POLO BRIDGE

88 Luguoqiaochengnei Xi Jie. Open daily 5am-7pm. Y6, students Y2.

Marco Polo Bridge (lú gòu qiáo; 卢沟桥), topped by anywhere from 485 to 501 stone lions (legend has it that they are uncountable because the lions frolic about at night), is the oldest bridge in Beijing. Begun in 1192, the bridge is noted for its role in stories Marco Polo brought back to Europe and for the original calligraphy by the Qing Emperor Qianlong. It is best remembered, however, for the Marco Polo Bridge Incident of July 7, 1937, when Japan attacked Beijing, catapulting China into the fray of WWII (see p. 16). History buffs excepted, many visitors find that the bridge is not quite worth the hike.

PEKING MAN SITE AT ZHOUKOUDIAN

50km southwest of Beijing, on the boundary between Taihang Range and the North China Plain. Take bus #917 (1¾hr., Y4.5) from the Tianqiao bus station to Fangshan, and then grab a taxi (Y10). Open daily 8:30am-4:30pm. Y20, students Y10.

It seems like all the action happened here half a million years ago, when *homo erectus pekinensis* liked it so much he decided to leave his bones and artifacts to be discovered in 1921. The Peking Man Site at Zhoukoudian (zhōukǒudiàn běijīng yuánrén yízhǐ; 周口店北京猿人遗址) is an exciting site in theory, but the original findings that set archeological hearts aflutter have since been "lost" at sea; all that remains are excavated caves and a dismal museum housing some bone chips and stone tools. Outside the site, there are fossilized plastic and fiberglass mummy and dinosaur exhibits to disappoint would-be enthusiasts.

GREAT WALL 长城

The seven wonders of the world put together are not comparable to this work; and all Fame hath published concerning it among Europeans, comes far short of what I have seen.
    —Ferdinand Verbiest, 7th-century traveler to the Great Wall

An ancient Chinese proverb says that one is not a good Chinese if one hasn't set foot on the Great Wall. From Shanhaiguan (see p. 150) on the Bohai Sea to Jiayuguan (see p. 677) in Gansu province, this mammoth wall extends 6400km across the northern periphery of China, a distance longer than the width of the continental United States. And, as all school-children know, it is the only manmade structure visible from the moon.

In 221 BC, the first emperor of the Qin joined various defensive walls together to create the Great Wall to protect the newly unified nation and to permit communication between the capital Xianyang (near modern-day Xian) and the most far-flung outposts of the country. In an ironic twist of fate, the construction project was eventually held up as one of the emperor's crimes against the people because of its enormous cost. Although the skeleton of the Great Wall is more than 2000 years old, it owes most of its length to the Ming dynasty, when the threat of Mongol invasion spurred emperors to reconstruct the Great Wall and extend it for a thousand kilometers to protect Shaanxi.

At the Mutianyu portion of the Great Wall, a plaque erected in 1989 to thank a German company for their help in restoring the wall reads "Once intended to ward off enemy attacks, today it brings together peoples of the world." To facilitate this exchange, and inevitably to capitalize on the wall's huge economic potential, the government has opened three sections in Beijing to tourists: Badaling, Mutianyu, and Simatai. Anyone looking to avoid all the hoopla and hype surrounding these sections of the Great Wall should visit the more remote section at Huanghua.

BADALING GREAT WALL 八达岭长城

Take bus #5 or 44 from Qianmen to Deshengmen, then walk over the nearby overpass, and hop on **bus #919** *(Y5) from in front of a monstrous circular building. Badaling is the next stop (1½hr., Y5.5). The next best way to Badaling is a local train from Xizhimen Train Station to* **Qinglongqiao** *(before 10am, Y7). Official* **tour buses #1, 2, and 4** *(Y36) leave for Badaling Great Wall and the Ming Tombs from the northeast corner of Qianmen (6-10am), Beijing Train Station (6-10am), and the zoo (6-11am). Hotel services and tour guides are the most expensive means of getting there.* **Open** *daily 8am-8pm.* **Admission** *Y30, students Y17.5; includes the museum and film.*

Badaling is the part of the wall to visit if you want to take pictures and have admirers back home recognize them as the Great Wall. The government has taken great pains to restore this part of the wall to its "original" condition. Every tower and turret stands just as it did when the Mongols overran the country 700 years ago, give or take a few souvenir shops. Guard rails and a cable car (one-way Y40, round-trip Y50) make Badaling the safe, almost easy, way to see the Great Wall. You'll get to rub elbows (literally) with tourists from all around the world. Badaling also features a museum of Chinese history, with photos of dozens of world leaders huffing and puffing up the wall, and the 360° Great Wall Circle Vision Theatre, which shows a 15-minute film on the history and legends of the wall. Chinese narration is scant and English subtitles scanter still, but stampeding hooves, a towering inferno, and more than one stomach-wrenching bird's eye sweep across the mountains and valleys leaves visitors satisfied.

MUTIANYU GREAT WALL 慕田峪长城

70km northeast of Beijing. **Special bus #6** *from the Xuanwumen Church (weekends 6:30-8am, Y43) is probably the best way to get to Mutianyu. On weekdays, take the subway to the Dongzhimen stop. From there, cross the thoroughfare; walk down the street that runs past KFC, turn right, and take bus #916 (Y5) from the long-distance bus station (Y5) to the Langshan Hotel in Huairou County.* **Minibuses** *(Y20-30) take passengers to Mutianyu. For the return, minibuses are harder to find; the better option is to take a taxi (Y40; bargain).* **Admission** *Y20, plus Y1 insurance.*

The Great Wall at Mutianyu was constructed during the Northern Qi Dynasty, over 1400 years ago. Its splendor has held up well, with a little help from its friends in the government tourism bureau. Mutianyu was opened up to take the pressure off Badaling: it's less overrun with tourists and peddlers, although plenty of both do exist. Higher up in the mountains than Badaling, the view at Mutianyu is much more dramatic. The cable car that runs to the top is quicker and sleeker, and this section of the wall features unusual double-serrated ramparts. *(Cable car runs daily 8:10am-4:30pm. One-way Y35, round-trip Y50; students half-price.)* All in all, Mutianyu is less accessible and more expensive than Badaling, but worth it. Even the twisting route going up into the mountains to get there is gorgeous.

SIMATAI GREAT WALL 司马台长城

Jinghua Youth Hostel (see p. 105) runs tours every other day (departs 8:30am, returns 2:30pm; Y60, excluding admission). **Buses** *(7am, Y20) leave from Dongzhimen Bus Station; special bus #12 (Y50) leaves Xuanwumen Church on weekends between 7-8:30am. Chartering a miandi taxi costs around Y360.* **Open** *daily 8am-5pm. Cable car Y30 one-way, Y50 round-trip.* **Admission** *Y20.*

Reputedly the most dangerous part of the Great Wall, Simatai is also hands down the most impressive. As the sole unrestored section of the wall open to tourists, Simatai provides a glimpse of what the old wall once looked like. There are no guardrails or handholds along the wall, and parts of the wall sport 70° inclines, 20cm wide paths, and 500m drops, bringing many hikers down on all fours. Simatai's high elevation grants an absolutely glorious view of the surrounding mountains; stairways lead to cloud-enshrouded turrets, and the unrestored wall curls away 19km into the distance. Although this section of the wall is rough and undeveloped, hawkers move quickly and are starting to capitalize on tourists. Go now to Simatai, before the rest of the tourism bureau kicks in.

HUANGHUA GREAT WALL 黄花长城

About 90km north of Beijing, 22km from Mutianyu. Take the subway to Dongzhimen and paraglide over the thoroughfare; walk down the street that runs past KFC, turn right, and take **bus #961** *(7:40, 9:40am, 3:40, and 5:30pm; Y7-8) from the long-distance bus station. The bus returns to Beijing (5:20, 7am, 1, and 2:50pm). Alternatively, bus* **#916** *leaves Dongzhimen frequently for* **Huairou** *(Y7); take connecting bus #916 (approx. every hr. 5:50am-6:30pm, Y2.5) to Huanghua. This section of the wall has no tourist infrastructure; there are no hours of operation and no admission.*

Built by General Cai Kai, Huanghua took so long to construct that the unfortunate general was deemed inefficient and beheaded. As testament to his tenacity, his headless body stood vigilant without toppling for three days and three nights before the locals had him interred. When the Mongols attacked, Cai Kai's efforts paid off; Huanghua was the only fortress that successfully warded off the enemy. Cai's body was exhumed and reburied with honor near the wall.

Even today, something about Huanghua continues to fend off the negative elements that plague other sections of the wall, making it the Great Wall experience of choice for hardy backpackers who scorn rampant commercialism. There are few postcard and water vendors (locals are more interested in their sheep than in you) and no short films, cable cars, or guardrails. Part of the wall is underwater and becomes submerged at high tide, and many parapets are overgrown with trees—overall, not your typical Great Wall experience. While this section of the wall is beautiful and rugged, it is also quite treacherous in some areas. Be careful, wear good shoes, and don't walk the wall alone. Many hikers choose to spend the night on the wall clinging to gravel. The simple **Jintang Mountain Lodge** (jīntáng shān zhuāng; 金汤山庄), across from the reservoir, offers comfortable rooms well worth the money. (Singles Y100; doubles Y200; triples Y250.)

TIANJIN 天津　　　　　　☎ 022

Tianjin means "passage to heaven"—heaven being the emperor's home in nearby Beijing. This modern city acquired its status as a trading hub during the Ming dynasty, when it served as a handling center for the tribute rice bound for the emperor in Beijing. Today, Tianjin is China's fourth largest city, a huge manufacturing center, and the largest port in northern China. Downtown, there are megastores and trendy shops on nearly every corner, and cell phone-toting locals loudly proclaim the advance of change upon Tianjin. However, visitors strolling down the city's smaller streets and alleys will undoubtedly discover that Tianjin is still infused with the traditions, culture, and history of old China.

After the second Opium War (1856-60), the Treaties of Tianjin granted Britain and France concessions along the banks of Tianjin's Hai River, soon followed by further concessions to other imperial powers. Every other street corner bears the architectural stamp of a different European tradition, be it French, Italian, Austrian, or otherwise. Because of its strategic location, Tianjin has suffered considerably in international power plays. The ancient city wall was destroyed in 1900 while the city was under Western occupation. In 1937, Japanese invasion of the city marked the beginning of the Sino-Japanese War. Twelve years later, the Communists wrested control of Tianjin from the Nationalists. In 1976, a major earthquake wrecked the city, after which Tianjin was rebuilt into what it is today.

Tianjin is a hub for commercial activity of all sorts, from the vendor-filled alleys, where tiny stalls and carts peddle everything from cotton balls to cotton candy, to the mammoth department stores that dot Heping Lu, where fashion shows and makeup counters herald the latest trends. These days, businessmen and bargain-hunting Beijingers comprise the bulk of Tianjin's visitors, resulting in a dearth of

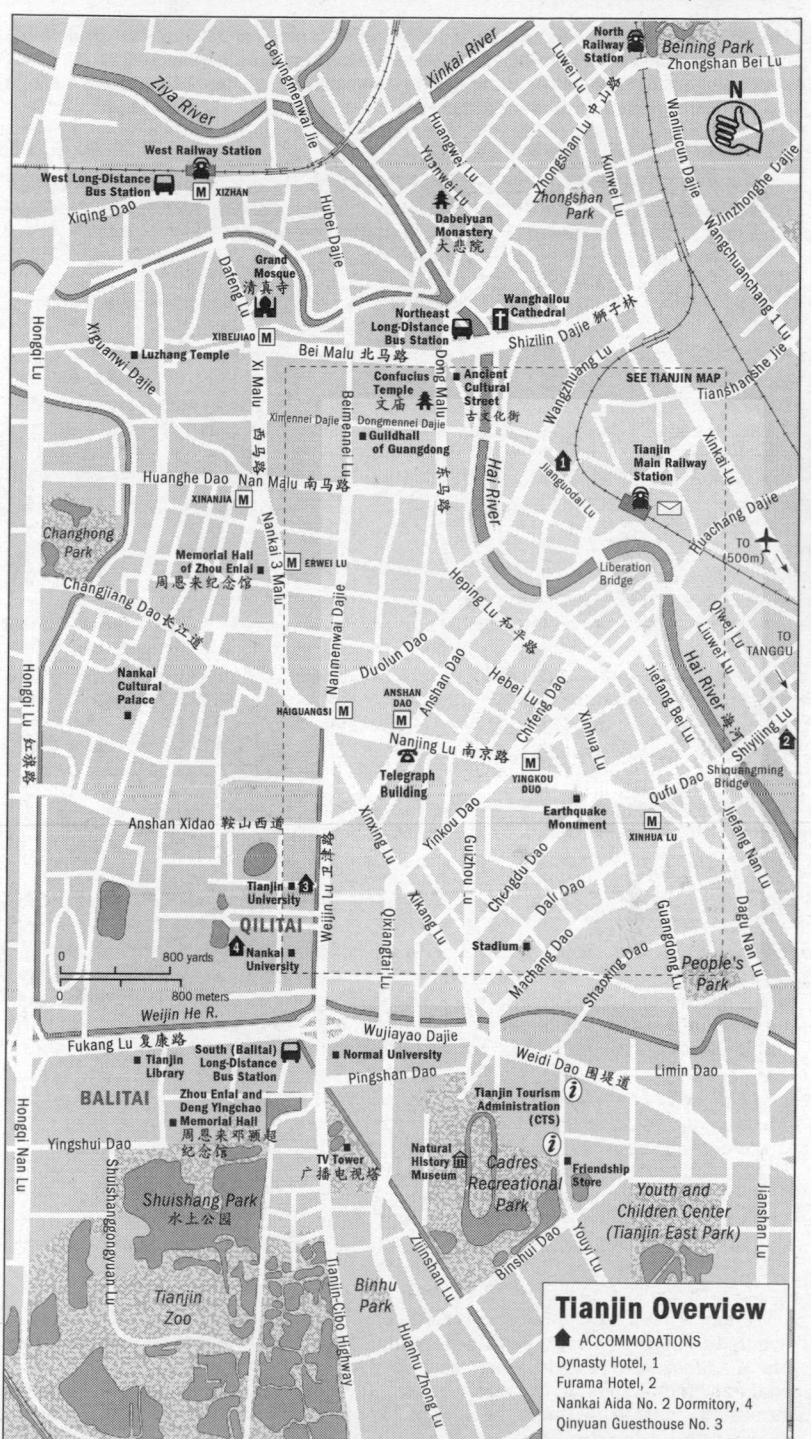

Tianjin Overview

🛏 **ACCOMMODATIONS**

Dynasty Hotel, 1
Furama Hotel, 2
Nankai Aida No. 2 Dormitory, 4
Qinyuan Guesthouse No. 3

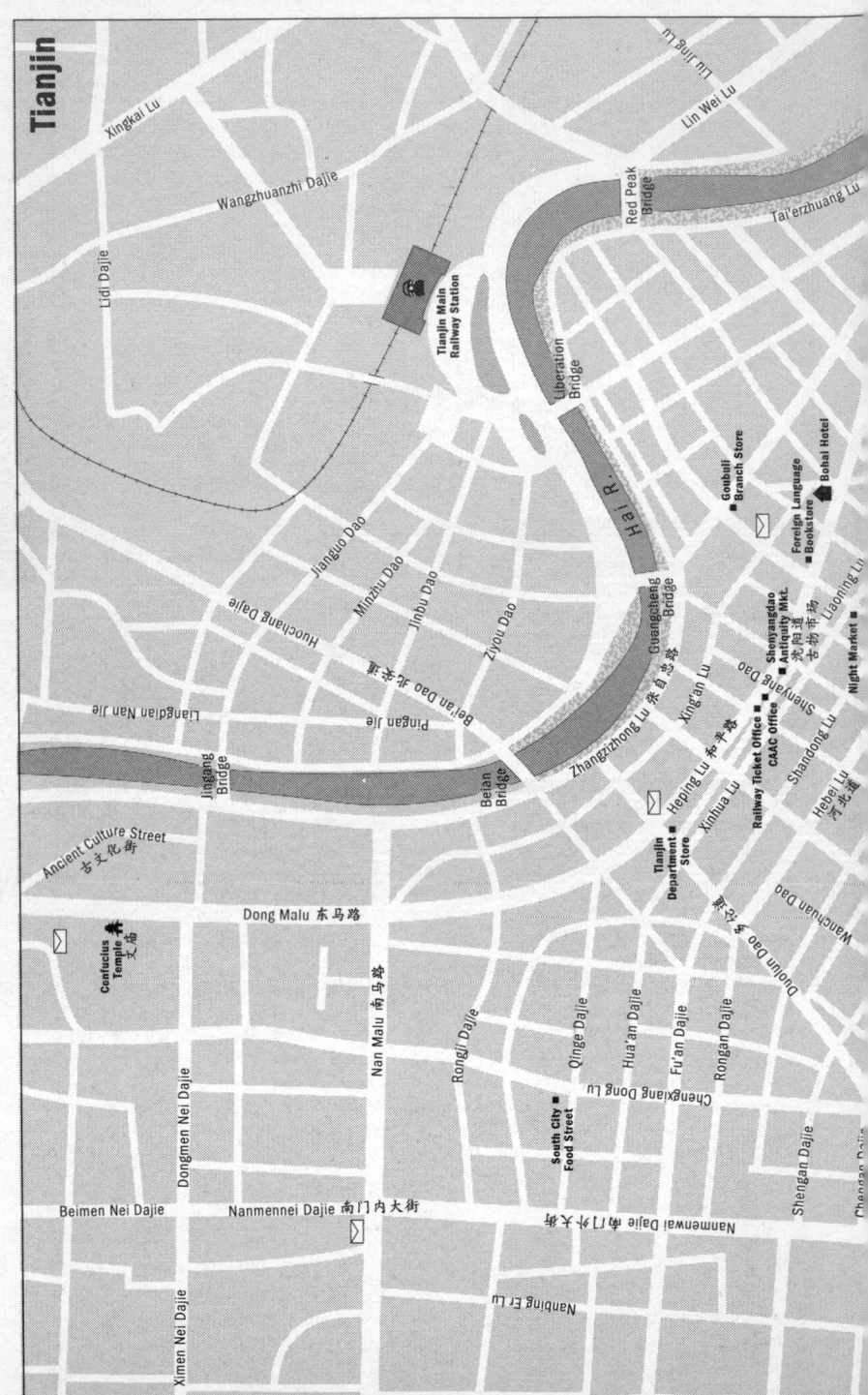

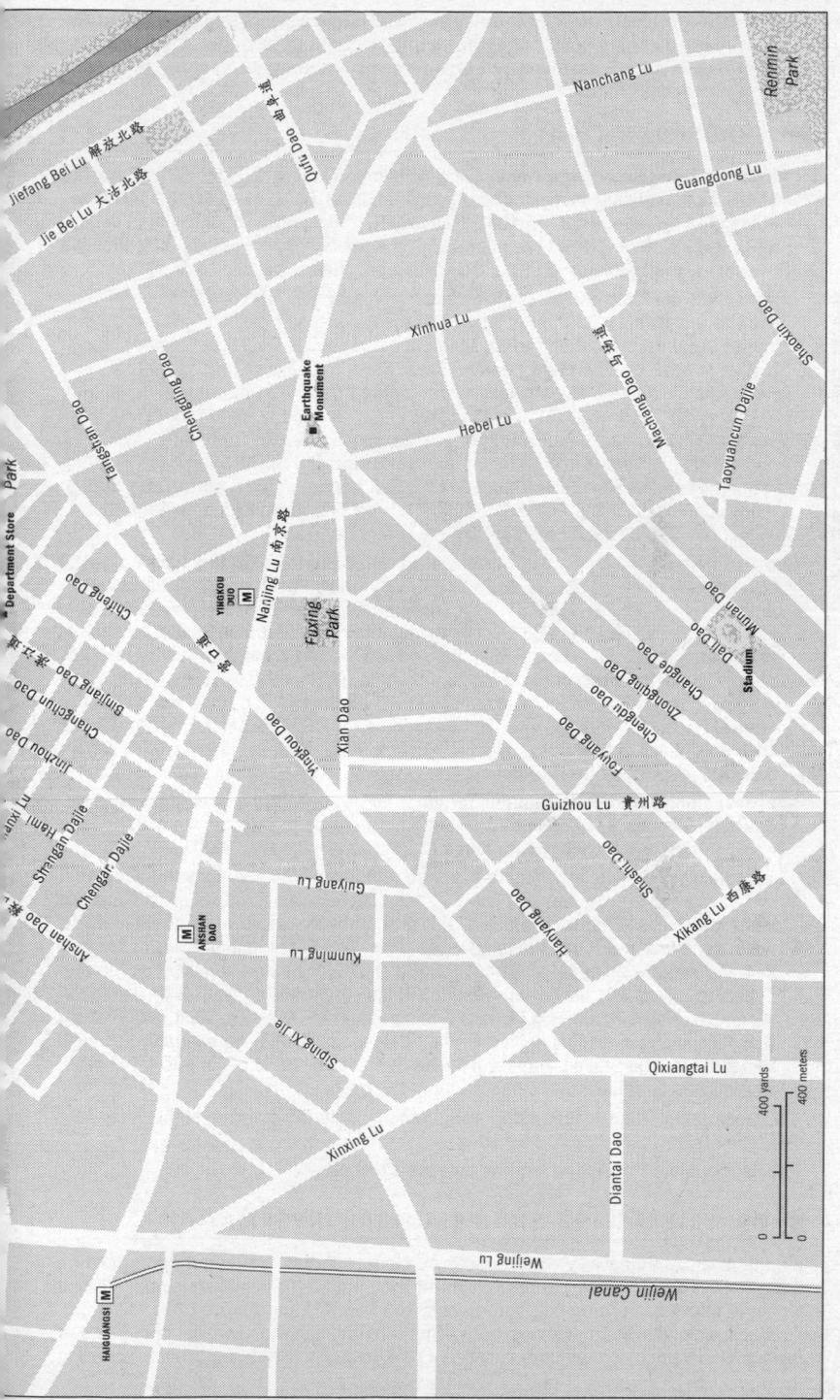

Nanchang Lu

Renmin Park

Jiefang Bei Lu 解放北路

Jie Bei Lu 大沽北路

Guangdong Lu

Qufu Dao

Shaoxin Dao

Xinhua Lu

Changdu Dao

■ Earthquake Monument

Hebei Lu

Machang Dao 马场道

Taoyuancun Dajie

Tangshan Dao

Park

■ Department Store

Chifeng Dao

YINGKOU DAO M

Nanjing Lu 南京路

Fuxing Park

Dali Dao

Minan Dao

Binjiang Dao 滨江道

Changchun Dao

Yingkou Dao

Xian Dao

Zhongqing Dao

Changde Dao

Jinzhou Dao

Fuyang Dao

Stadium

Harbin Dao

Chengdu Dao

Shangan Dajie

Guizhou Lu 贵州路

Chengar Dajie

Guiyang Lu

Shashi Dao

Xikang Lu 西康路

Anshan Dao

M ANSHAN DAO

Kunming Lu

Hanyang Dao

Siping Xi Jie

Qixiangtai Lu

400 yards

400 meters

Xinxing Lu

Diantai Dao

0   0

M

Weijing Lu

HANGUANGSI

Weijin Canal

facilities for foreign travelers. On the plus side, Tianjin's sights remain unassaulted by tour buses, and its fascinating temples and pagodas offer refreshingly peaceful destinations. Unusually affluent but uniquely unspoiled by its wealth, Tianjin has retained a charm all its own.

▐ TRANSPORTATION

Airplanes: Zhangguizhuang Airport (zhāngguìzhuāng fēijīchǎng; 张贵庄飞机场; ☎2490 1114) connects Tianjin to major cities throughout China. Book tickets at the **CAAC ticket office**, 242 Heping Lu (☎2730 4045). Open daily 8:30am-6pm. To: **Chengdu** (1 per day Sa-Th, Y1230); **Guangzhou** (2 per day, Y1360); **Kunming** (4 per week, Y1360); **Qingdao** (1 per day, Y530); **Shanghai** (3 per day, Y820); and **Xian** (1 per day Sa-Th, Y770).

Trains: Both the Main and West Stations are served by the 24hr. bus #24, which shuttles passengers between the Heping Lu and the two stations (Baihuo Dalou stop). During the day, buses #624 and #824 service the same route. Train tickets can be bought 5 days in advance. The **Main (Tianjin) Train Station** (tiānjīn zhàn; 天津站; ☎2430 6444), is on Haihe Dong Lu, just across Jiefang Qiao from downtown. To **Beijing** (1½hr., 12 per day, Y11-30) and **Shanghai** (17hr., 4 per day, Y301). The **West Train Station** (xī zhàn; 西站; ☎2618 2662), is on Xizhan Qian Jie. To: **Beijing** (1½hr., 17 per day, Y24); **Guangzhou** (33hr., 1 per day); **Harbin** (18hr., 1 per day); **Nanjing** (16hr., 2 per day, Y64); and **Shanghai** (17hr., 3 per day, Y301). **North Train Station** (tianjin běi zhàn; 天津北站; ☎2635 2214), is off Zhongshan Bei Lu. To **Beijing** (2hr., 13 per day, Y20-30) and **Shanghai** (16hr., 10 per day, Y301).

Buses: There are three main bus stations in Tianjin. **Balitai Bus Station** (bālítāi chángtú qìchē zhàn; 八里台长途汽车站; ☎2334 4749), near Shuishang Park, runs buses to **Jinan** (11hr., 2 per day, Y31-50). **West Station** (tiānjīn chángtú xī zhàn; 天津长途西 站), 2 Xiqing Dao (☎2732 0688), down the road from the West Train Station, runs buses to **Shijiazhuang** (3½hr., every 30min. 8am-4pm, Y75) and **Zhengzhou** (9hr., 1 per day, Y140). **Northeast Station** (běidōng jiāo chángtú qìchē zhàn; 北东角长途汽车站; ☎2635 2214), near Ancient Culture Street. To: **Beijing** (1½hr., 6-12 per day, Y30); **Chengde** (6½hr., 2 per day, Y40); and **Guangzhou** (17-18 hr., 1 per day, Y100). **Beijing Zhao Gong Kou Bus Station** (北京赵公口站; ☎2732 3477 or 2771 9945), on Rongye Dajie in front of Food Street. To **Beijing** (2hr., every 30min.-1hr. 7am-7:30pm, Y30).

Ferries: Tianjin Harbor Passenger Terminal (☎2570 6728) is open daily 8:30am-6:50pm. Take **bus #102** from the bus station. Ferries go to **Kobe, Japan** (48hr., 1 per week, Y1875) and **Inchon, South Korea** (28hr., 1 every 4 days, Y988).

Local Buses: Tianjin's labyrinthine bus system is intimidating, but worth figuring out since buses run everywhere, cost only Y1-2, and operate 5am-11pm. Signs at bus stops are written only in Chinese characters. Hours of operation are listed on bus stop signs; buses numbered 1-100 tend to run later than the other buses. The following buses stop near the end of Heping Lu at Baihuo Dalou (百货大楼) before trundling on to other major locations: **#8:** Main Train Station, Balitai (right beside Nankai University on Weijin Lu), Waterside Park; **#24** (runs 24hr.): Tianjin Train Station, West Train Station; **#658:** Food Street, Nankai University, Tianjin University; **#693:** Anshan Dao, Hebei Lu; **#818:** North Train Station, Hubei Lu; **#860:** Food Street, Fu An Dajie; **#904:** Hubei Lu, Yingkou Dao, Northeast Bus Station.

Subway: Runs with a limited route along Nanjing Lu in the direction of the West Train Station (Y1).

Taxis: Base fare Y10. Yellow minivan taxis are cheapest.

◤🛈 ORIENTATION AND PRACTICAL INFORMATION

Tianjin is a satisfying city—big enough to be interesting, yet small enough to be easily navigable. The city center is formed by a jumble of commercial streets and old-style alleys branching off from **Heping Lu** (和平路) and **Binjiang Dao** (宾江道), Tianjin's main shopping arteries, both of which only allow pedestrian traffic. As of June 2000, Heping Lu was under massive construction. From the downtown area, the crosses of the Catholic Church point southeast, in the direction of Binjiang Dao. The old city northwest of downtown, dubbed **"Chinatown"** by Europeans, is marked by **Bei** (北), **Nan** (南), **Dong** (东), and **Xi Malu** (西吗路). It is even possible to catch a glimpse of people stringing carpets on the street, practicing one of Tianjin's major cottage industries. Often forgotten is the more tranquil southwestern corner of Tianjin, where three universities converge on **Balitai**.

The **Hai River** cuts through the city diagonally. Cruises run from several points on the north bank of the river, and some of Tianjin's large temples are sprinkled along its northwest corner. The famed architectural legacy of the European concessions is visible throughout the city, but various national styles are concentrated together along **Jiefang Bei Lu,** which runs parallel to the Hai. The **main train station** is just north of the Hai, across Jiefang Qiao from downtown.

TOURIST AND FINANCIAL SERVICES

Travel Agency: China International Travel Service (CITS), 22 Youyi Lu (☎2835 8499 or 2835 8309), opposite the Friendship Store. Open M-F 8:30am-5pm. In the same building and with the same hours is the **Tianjin Overseas Tourist Corporation** (tiānjīn shì hǎiwài lǚyóu zōng gōngsī; 天津市海外旅游总公司; ☎2313 9424).

Bank of China: 80-82 Jiefang Bei Lu (☎2710 2207). Traveler's check exchange and **ATM** (Cirrus and MC). Open M-F 9am-noon and 1:30-5pm. Around the corner, the bank's **Credit Card Department** (xìnyòng kǎ bù; 信用卡部), 22 Datong Dao (☎2326 1234), has an **ATM** (Cirrus, MC, Plus, and V). Open M-F 9am-noon and 1:30-5pm, Sa 9am-noon.

LOCAL SERVICES

Bookstores: Heping Lu is dotted with bookstores. **Xinhua Bookstore** (☎2712 2797), on the corner of Binjiang Dao and Xinhua Lu, sells everything from physics books to picture books in Chinese characters, as well as a small selection of fiction in English and some imports from Hong Kong, Taiwan, and America. Open M-F 9:30am-6pm, Sa-Su 9:30am-7pm. The **Foreign Languages Bookstore** (wàiwén shūdiàn; 外文书店), 182 Machang Dao near Xikang Lu, offers a sizeable English section. Open daily 9am-6pm.

Shopping: Heping Lu and Binjiang Dao are main shopping streets. **Tianjin Department Store** (bǎihuò dàlóu; 天津百货大楼), 172 Heping Lu (☎2730 0723, ext. 3106). Open M-F 9am-7pm, Sa-Su 9am-8pm. **Tianjin Quan Yechang (Group) Co., Ltd.** (quàn yecháng; 劝业场), 290 Heping Lu (☎2721 1111), also has an ATM for Cirrus and MC cardholders. The **Friendship Store** (yǒuyì gōngsī; 友谊公司; ☎2835 3159 or 2835 2160) on Youyi Lu, just beyond Weidi Dao. Open daily 9:30am-8:30pm. **China Photography Store** (zhōngguó zhàoxiàng guǎn; 中国照相馆), 251 Heping Lu (☎2712 6139) offers Kodak film and express processing (1 hr., Y22). Open daily 9am-7pm.

Laundry: Xin'an Laundry (xīn' ān xǐyīdiàn; 新安洗衣店; ☎2731 0529), at the junction of Fu An Jie and Dong Malu. Y15 average for 2-3 day service. Open daily 7:30am-9pm.

EMERGENCY AND COMMUNICATIONS

PSB: 26 Tangshan Dao (☎2731 9000). The **Foreigners Office** (wài guǎn chù; 外管处), 19 Minzhu Dao, near the No. 1 Hospital, grants visa extensions.

Hospital: No. 1 Hospital (yī zhōngxīn yīyuàn; 一中心医院; ☎2336 6914), on Fukang Lu, has English-speaking staff.

Internet Access: Liu Yuan Internet Bar (liú yuán wǎngbā; 留缘网吧), 128 Weijin Lu (☎2353 1143), down the road and under a bridge from Nankai University. Y4 per hr. Open daily 9am-midnight. More centrally located is the newly opened **E-space** (E kóngjiān; E空间), 80 Anshan Dao (☎2722 9358). An oasis of 60 computers in the chaos of downtown, with prices as low as Y4-5 per hr. Open 24 hr.

Post Office: China Post Dongzhan Post Office (☎2430 3459), immediately right of the Main Train Station. Poste Restante and EMS available. Open daily 8:30am-8pm. The **China Post** across from the Nankai University entrance also offers EMS service. Open daily 8:30am-6:30pm. **DHL** (zhōngguó wàiyùn dùnhào gúojì hángkōng kuàijiàn gōngsī; 中国外运顿号国际航空快件公司), 195 Machang Dao (☎2430 3388), is a private courier service. Open daily 8am-5:30pm. **Postal Code:** 300000.

■ ACCOMMODATIONS

Tianjin is a great place to go for a day. Unfortunately, it's not a very cheap place to spend the night. Budget options for foreigners are limited. To stay in the city center, your best bet is to head for one of Tianjin's consistently high-quality hotels, all with private baths, TVs, and room phones. Outside the city center, the dormitories at Nankai and Tianjin Universities offer a comfortable and affordable deal.

Nankai Aida No. 2 Dormitory (nánkāi àidà yīyuán èr hào lóu; 南开爱大一园二号楼; ☎2350 1832), the cheapest of three dormitories on the Nankai University campus. Follow Dazhong Lu from the main university entrance and take a second left onto Yiyuan Lu. Nankai Aida is the brown brick building on the right at the end of the road. Aida makes you feel like you're definitely taken care of: every room comes with TV, phone, A/C, a thermos full of hot water, and, best of all, the daily service of a beaming ayi (chamber auntie) who wants only the best for you. Laundry token Y6. Key deposit depends on length of stay, one night usually between Y100-200. Curfew midnight. Doubles Y150, with 2 rooms Y400; triples Y400.

Qinyuan Guesthouse No. 2 (qìnyuán lìyù; 沁园隶属; ☎2740 7711 or 2740 7508; fax 2335 8714), on the Tianjin University campus. Take Beiyang Dao from the Qilitai entrance and bear left at the roundabout. Qinyuan is the dark brown brick building on the left just after the roundabout, behind two fenced-in ball courts. Qinyuan offers high-quality rooms among what are arguably the prettiest lakes in Tianjin. Reception 6am-11pm. Curfew 11pm (inform the receptionist if you must return later). Doubles with bath, TV, phone, A/C, and mini-fridge Y144.

Dynasty Hotel (wángcháo dà jiǔdiàn; 王朝大酒店), 42 Jianguo Dao (☎2446 4671), a 5 min. walk from the main train station. The Dynasty offers relatively luxurious rooms for relatively affordable prices. Doubles Y188; triples Y218.

Furama Hotel (fùlìhuǎ dà jiǔdiàn; 富利华大酒店), 104 Qiwei Lu (☎2431 0961 or 2431 0795), just south of Shiyijing Lu/Qufu Dao. Although the pagoda-shaped exterior is attractive and the rooms are clean with all standard amenities, this hotel is such a hike from anywhere except the river that guests might be better off heading to central Tianjin. Breakfast included. Doubles Y200-240. Visa accepted.

■ FOOD

Tianjin is a great place for epicures. Snacking is perhaps the best way to discover all that the city has to offer, and **Food Street** (shípǐn jiē; 食品街; open daily 9am-5pm), a pagoda-shaped mall of food stores off Rongye Dajie and Qingge Dajie, is a snacker's Shangri-La. Here an extravagant wealth of cholesterol and color awaits, with rainbow-hued flyers dangling from the ceiling and nuts, candies, and dried fruit blanketing the ground. Hundreds of stores, restaurants, and stalls stacked one on top of the other sell everything from pastries and cured meats (dog meat Y8) to candy. Chances are you'll come away nibbling on something.

Xi Malu in the old city is peppered with several blocks of Muslim restaurants, while **Balitai** has many good Korean restaurants. Be sure to pick up baked goods from the Austrian-founded **Kiesseling's Bakery** for a sample of century-old gastronomic history. Vendors throughout the city sell **Guifaxiang Deep-fried Dough Twists** (guìfāxiáng máhuā; 桂发详祥麻花) and **Fried Eardrum Cake** (ěrduōyǎn zhágāo; 耳朵眼炸糕), two Tianjin specialties.

Goubuli Stuffed Buns (gǒubùlǐ bāozi diàn; 狗不理包子店), 77 Shandong Lu (☎2730 0810), between Binjiang Dao and Changchun Dao. Goubuli is famous for its pork-filled baozi (steamed buns), served either at the downstairs counter or the pricier dining room upstairs (entrees around Y30). The restaurant boasts 98 varieties of buns, but only three kinds are available at the fast-food counter. Red-dotted baozi are filled with chicken or shrimp instead of pork. Meals Y13-16. Piping hot baozi every hour 1-7pm—devotees can make off with a dozen for only Y6. Open daily 7:30am-10:30pm.

WILL THE REAL BUN PLEASE RISE?

Of Tianjin's three specialty pastries (18th Street Fried Dough, Eardrum Fried Cake, and Goubuli Stuffed Buns), the most famous by far is the Goubuli Stuffed Bun. When a 14-year-old Wuqing County native nicknamed Gou (Dog) apprenticed himself to a Tianjin dough-bun master during the Qing dynasty, little did he expect that his buns would one day be praised by the emperor (much less that they would one day be the favorite of former US President George H.W. Bush). The buns eventually were known as Goubuli (literally, "dog doesn't bother") because the master bun-maker was always so engrossed with his buns that he never bothered to talk to his customers. Another version of the legend says that the unfortunate Gou was so ugly that even dogs wouldn't look at him.

Thank goodness that he had his pork-filled claim to fame. Goubuli buns have become so internationally renowned (there are franchises in Singapore, Japan, Korea, and the US) that imitation Goubuli bun restaurants have sprung up throughout Tianjin. The most bizarre bandwagon rider must be Maobuwen (māobùwén; 猫不闻), or "cat doesn't smell" dumplings, produced since 1995. These dumplings aspire to be the fourth Tianjin pastry specialty but lack the extra flavor of a century-old legend.

Ali Baba's (ālǐ bābā; 阿里巴巴), 7 Tiannan Jie (☎2350 5613), on the Nankai University campus. Turn right off Dazhong Lu just before the Student Activities Center and walk nearly to the end of the alley; an Arabic-looking sign heralds Ali Baba's on the right. The menu promises everything from Indian curry rice to American cheeseburgers, but everything comes out tasting distinctly Chinese. Ali Baba's loyal expat clientele is happy to shell out Y15-30 for entrees that are Tianjin's closest approximation to a taste of home. The interior decor, as eclectic as the menu, includes a stuffed Santa and African trinkets. Many stay late to down beers and watch Chinese MTV. Open daily 10am-2am.

JJ's Food and Restaurant (Tianjin) Inc. (jiājiā xiāngdòujiāng zhījiā; 家家香豆浆之家), 1 Dagu Bei Lu (☎2721 6289), immediately south of Guangchang Bridge. This clean, friendly, plastic-and-Formica palace serves a mean bowl of soybean milk (hot or cold, sweet or salty, raw egg optional) for Y2-3. The fried dough fritters or sesame cakes (Y2-6) are popular at breakfast. Noodle and curry rice dishes average Y10. Open 24hr.

California Beef Noodle King (měiguó jiāzhōu niúròu miàn wáng; 美国加州牛肉面大王), 102-104 Xinhua Lu (☎2711 2276 or 2711 5163). This fast-and-filling restaurant serves up tasty noodle dishes for Y6 a bowl. Open daily 10:30am-10pm.

⚑ NIGHTLIFE

Not too many years ago, there were no bars in Tianjin, save those of the five-star hotel, stuffed-suit genre. Now, the reckless carousing scene is growing rapidly. Epicenters for foreigners to meet and greet are **Sgt. Pepper's** (see p. 139) and **Ali Baba's** (see p. 139). Travelers feeling poor after forking over their life savings for a room at one of Tianjin's upscale hotels might enjoy the fountains and night markets (daily 6-9:30pm) that stretch along the north side of the river.

Kanghao (kānghǎo; 康好), 47 Minzhu Dao (☎2446 2686). Where are all the young people in Tianjin? All smashed up against one another on Kanghao's massive disco dance floor, that's where. Kanghao wakes up at 9pm, when the strobes turn on, the lights come up, and a disco full of locals starts grooving to the tunes—American remixes, Chinese pop songs, and more. The 2nd floor sports a lounge and a stage where scantily-clad hires show off choreographed dance moves. Cover Y20 for women, Y30 for men. Open daily 8pm-5am.

Sgt. Pepper's Music Hall Grill & Bar (shājīn yīnyuè xīcāntīng; 沙金音乐西餐厅), 62 Jiefang Bei Lu (☎2312 8138). Featuring the sounds of Hot Stuff (nightly 9:15pm), a Filipino group called "the best band in Tianjin," as well as English, Chinese, Spanish, and Beatles songs (of course!), Sgt. Pepper's is one of the hottest places for foreigners to mix and mingle. Though the food is pricey (entrees around Y40, drinks Y8 and up), the atmosphere is fun and friendly. Y60 spending minimum F-Sa. Open daily 6pm-2am.

Club NUTS (nàsī jǐubā; 纳斯酒吧), on Tiannan Jie in Nankai University, around the corner from Ali Baba's. To the right of the central Nankai lake, Club NUTS is tucked away near the end of an alley and heralded by some risqué oil paint artwork. Black lights, good music, nearly 100 hard-to-find cocktails (Y15-20), and a laid-back atmosphere make Club NUTS a favorite watering hole for international students and young expats. An essential part of the experience is meeting Yan Wen Zhu, the super-friendly one-woman owner, waitress, and DJ between 4pm-midnight. Open daily 11am-midnight.

NYC Music Kitchen (niúyuē yīnyuè chúfáng; 纽约音乐厨房), 212 Weidi Dao (☎ 2353 9600), near Machang Dao, on the 2nd floor above Big Bowl Restaurant. Proclaiming the "Style of New York, Taste of China," NYC touts a classy restaurant and bar with live entertainment Tu-Su. All kinds of people waltz upstairs for Chinese fare (most entrees about Y30), good music, and dancing. Open daily 10am-1am.

◉ SIGHTS

Colorful streets and museums make up Tianjin's tourist sights; most of them are close to the city center but are hard to get to by any means other than taxi. The city has been called a living museum of international architecture, and the energetic walker can scour either bank of the **Hai River** for the 19th-century British, French, German, Russian, and Italian buildings remaining from the concession days.

DABEIYUAN MONASTERY (dàbēiyuàn; 大悲院). Built in the early 17th century and subsequently battered by the ravages of time and revolutions, the Dabeiyuan Monastery was finally restored in 1982. The monastery is large and well cared for, with many prayer rooms, including one honoring the glamorous 24-armed Goddess of Mercy. If you arrive around 2pm on Wednesdays and Sundays, you can catch a glimpse of the fascinating and hypnotic evening prayers. Outside, alms-seekers gather at the door, and street vendors sell charms, incense, prayer mats, and other religious paraphernalia. (*40 Tianwei Lu. To the north of Jingang Bridge, Tianwei Lu is the first left off Zhongshan Lu. The monastery is on the right just past Shiwei Lu. ☎ 2626 1768. Open Tu-Su 9am-4pm. Y4.*)

ANCIENT CULTURE STREET (gǔ wénhùa jīe; 古文化街). Built to mimic the look and feel of ancient China, this is less a street and more a sizable neighborhood, encompassing the area north of central Tianjin. Pagoda-topped buildings and delicately engraved eaves offer an almost-convincing haven from the surrounding socialist architecture. Shops serve up the pride of traditional China—scrolls, swords, ceramics, and jades—with the zeal of unabashed capitalism. (*West of the Hai River, between Jingang Bridge and Jintang Bridge, with an entrance at the corner of Dongma Lu and Beima Lu. Open daily 9am-5pm.*)

At the heart of Ancient Culture Street is **Tianhou Temple** (tiānhòu gōng; 天后宫), which was built during the Yuan dynasty (1279-1368) and restored in 1985. The temple honors Empress Tianhou (born in 960) with incense altars, offerings of money, food, and flowers, and statues of "celestial beings" (among them Qian Li Yan, famed for his farsightedness, and Shun Feng Er, famed for his ability to hear voices a long way off). Her death at the age of 27 came as no surprise; she had led an exhausting life "curing disease, helping the poor, and vanquishing demons and monsters." (*80 Ancient Culture Street. ☎ 2735 5517. Open daily 9am-5:30pm. Y3.*)

ZHOU ENLAI AND DENG YINGCHAO MEMORIAL HALL (zhōu ēnlái dèng yǐngchāo jìniàn guǎn; 周恩来邓颖超纪念馆). Zhou Enlai and his wife Deng Yingchao were revolutionary heroes who are still revered today. While the latter worked for women's liberation in China, former Premier Zhou, a 48-year veteran of the Politburo, is especially respected for resisting Jiang Qing's Gang of Four (see p. 19) and for trying to temper the damages of the Cultural Revolution. This memorial to Zhou and Deng and their lifelong partnership (there is an entire hall devoted to their love) is a massive, near-fetishistic complex more interesting for the everyday trinkets and trivia preserved than for the revolutionary scripts. (*Shuishang Gongyuan*

Lu. Southeast of Nankai University, just across from Waterside Park. ☎ 2352 9257. Open Tu-Su 8:30am-5pm, last ticket sold at 4pm. Y10, students Y5.)

SHENYANG DAO ANTIQUE MARKET (shènyángdào gǔwù shìchǎng; 沈阳道古物市场). Jostling vendors hawk all sorts of goods in a market that sprawls over a staggeringly large area, beginning at Shenyang Dao. Not just for antique collectors, the market proffers a vast array of vases, ceramics, and jades, a respectable offering of scrolls, and a huge variety of Mao memorabilia. Merchants rest on mats and under umbrellas, sleepily guarding their metal flocks against expat wolves. Buyer beware—bargain or else walk away with a tiny bronze turtle for a startling Y500! *(Shenyang Dao, south of Heping Lu. A nondescript alley directly opposite the Shijie Shangsha leads to the market. Open daily 9am-4pm. Th and F mornings are the best times to go.)*

OTHER SIGHTS. Close to Ancient Culture Street, Tianjin's **Confucian Temple** (wénmiào; 文庙), a cultural relic, sits on the northern side of Dongmennei Dajie, offering a quiet escape under the shadow of the huge Carrefour megastore. Goldfish and waterlilies thrive in a small "pan pool" under the bridge leading to some beautifully ornate (but rather dusty) pagodas dedicated to the life of Confucius. Among the exhibits: stringed instruments, regal-looking carriage roofs, and a wall-sized model of a pagoda and offering ceremony. *(☎ 2727 2812. Open Tu-Su 9am-4:15pm. Y4, students Y2.)*

At 415.2m, **Tianjin Radio & TV Tower** (tiānjīn guǎngbō diànshì tǎ; 天津广播电视塔) on Weijin Nan Lu is the fourth highest radio tower in the world and an impressive sight from afar (especially when lit up at night). However, the fee for the top-floor view of Tianjin's flat, building-filled landscape is even steeper than the climb. Still, the lake and rose gardens surrounding the tower are beautiful (and free). *(☎ 2335 5775 or 2334 3557. Open daily 8:30am-10pm. Ground level Y2; tower Y50, children under 1.3m. Y25).* Across Weijin Nan Lu from the TV Tower sits the **Waterside Park** (shǔishàng gōngyuán; 水上公园), where a spectacle of animal shows awaits and water lilies overtake ponds to the point at which even Monet might have objected. *(☎ 2353 3437. Open daily 5am-8pm. Y10.)*

🄳 DAYTRIP FROM TIANJIN

TANGGU 塘沽

Although it is an Economic and Technology Development Zone and one of China's largest international ports, there is little for visitors to see or do in Tanggu, unless one has a thing for smokestacks, cranes, and soda plants (hint: not a botanic curiosity). Tanggu's value lies in its seaside location, though this little district by the water is not cheap to visit.

The **Seaside Amusement Park** (hǎibīn yùchǎng; 海滨浴场) on Haifang Lu (☎ 2531 9020), accessible only by taxi (30min., Y40-50), is the home of the largest waterslides and manmade beaches in China. Look out over the brown waters of the Bohai Gulf as happy music blares from speakers. Get your wallet out again—the waterslides are a separate fee (Y15-30) to ride. (Open 24hr. Summer Y30, before June 16 Y10.) **Bohai Children's World** (bóhǎi értóng shìjie; 渤海儿童世界) is a pretty little park with lots of greenery, a small castle-shaped history museum, several peacocks, and some kiddie rides. (Open daily 8:30am-4pm. Y1.) **Dagu Fort** (dàgū pàotái; 大沽泡台) features an old war plane and a rusted cannon on a barren hillside. The fort has been around since the mid-16th century, but 450 years haven't helped to clarify (or translate) the signs in its small museum of history. (☎ 2588 8544. Open daily 8:30am-4:30pm. Y5, students Y2.)

Buses leave Tianjin for Tanggu from many locations, including the Main Train Station and the South Bus Station (1½hr., buses leave when full, Y4). Trains (Y3.5) cover the distance in 30 min. and leave frequently. Tanggu is surprisingly vast and quite difficult to get around.

Travelers consigned to Tanggu's shores overnight should try one of the two hotels across from the passenger terminal. The **International Seamen's Club** (tiānjīn xīngǎng gúojì hǎiyuán jùlèbù; 天津新港国际海员俱乐部) offers clean rooms with bath, TV, A/C, and phone. (☎6577 0333. Doubles and triples Y160-360.) The **Kangda Hotel** (kāngdá zhùsè; 康达住宿) is another affordable option. (☎2579 5941. Doubles Y60, with bath and A/C Y104-144.) Along the same strip as both hotels are several little restaurants that serve up local fare. The **Xingang Friendship Store** (xīngǎng yǒuyì shāngdiàn; 新港友谊商店) is open daily from 9am to 9:30pm.

HEBEI 河北

"Second fiddle." "Unglamorous." "Lackluster." "Struggles in Beijing's shadow." The number of derogatory statements that have been directed at Hebei is enough to reduce a province to tears. With the powerful municipalities of Beijing and Tianjin geographically (but not administratively) within its borders, Hebei struggles to prove its own worth. But while Hebei may not be sexy—the mountainous tableau in the north is bleak and barren and the monotonous plains in the south are broken only by industrial mining towns—something about it has attracted generations of Beijing's elite away from their beloved city. Chengde, home to the Imperial Summer Villa (literally "Flee-the-Heat Villa"), was a favorite destination for Qing emperors in the 18th century. These days, as sweaty summer hits, the seaside resorts of Beidaihe and Shanhaiguan (where the Great Wall runs into the sea) lure city-weary CCP hotshots and throngs of other not-quite-as-hot-shots to the beach to frolic in the surf. Any criticism of Hebei begs the obvious question: if it weren't for Hebei, where would Beijingers summer?

SHIJIAZHUANG 石家庄 ☎0311

The informal slogan of Shijiazhuang is: "Give us five years." "And we'll be like Beijing" is the implied conclusion of that unrealistic declaration. About 250km southwest of Beijing, the capital of Hebei province houses the largest pharmaceutical plant and PLA military academy in China and thus sees itself as one of the arrowheads of progress in the region. The construction of the railway line has brought Shijiazhuang a booming population and prosperity, but there are not many interesting destinations for the traveler within the city itself. However, Shijiazhuang does serve as a good home base for visitors who want to take in some of the impressive sights in the area.

▐ TRANSPORTATION

Airplanes: Shijiazhuang Airport (shíjiāzhuāng jīchǎng; 石家庄机场) is 45km northeast of the city. Shuttle buses leave from the CITS office (about 6 per day, Y25). **China Eastern Airlines** (zhōngguó dōngfāng hángkōng gōngsī; 中国东方航空公司), Aviation Building, 128 Zhongshan Dong Lu (☎698 1824 or 698 1124). To: **Guangzhou** (1 per day Tu-Su, Y1250); **Haikou** (M, Y1640); **Shanghai** (1 per day W-M, Y790); and **Shenzhen** (1 per day Tu and F, Y1210).

Trains: Shijiazhuang Train Station (shíjiāzhuāng huǒchē zhàn; 石家庄火车站) is accessible by almost every bus in the city. Open 24hr. Ticket reservations permitted 10 days in advance (☎792 2171). Luggage storage Y3 per day. Trains to: **Beijing** (2½hr., 33 per day, 26 express trains; Y30-50); **Chengde** (5½hr., 1 per day, Y32); **Datong** (13hr., 2 per day, Y38); **Harbin** (20½hr., 2 per day, Y114); **Qinhuangdao** (9 hr., 1 per day, Y97); **Shanghai** (16½hr., 1 per day, Y154); and **Xian** (11¾ hr., Y120).

Buses: The **Long-distance Bus Station** (chángtú qìchēzhàn; 长途汽车站; ☎702 5775) is south of the train station. Head as far south as you can on the pedestrian street immediately in front of the station, past the jungle of minibuses, until you see a huge faux gold entrance. To: **Beijing** (3½hr., every 20min. 6am-7:30pm, Y69); **Jinan** (5hr., every 30min. 6am-8:30am and 1:30-5pm); **Qinhuangdao** (11hr., 2 per day, Y104); and **Taiyuan** (3hr., every 20min. 6am-8pm, Y45).

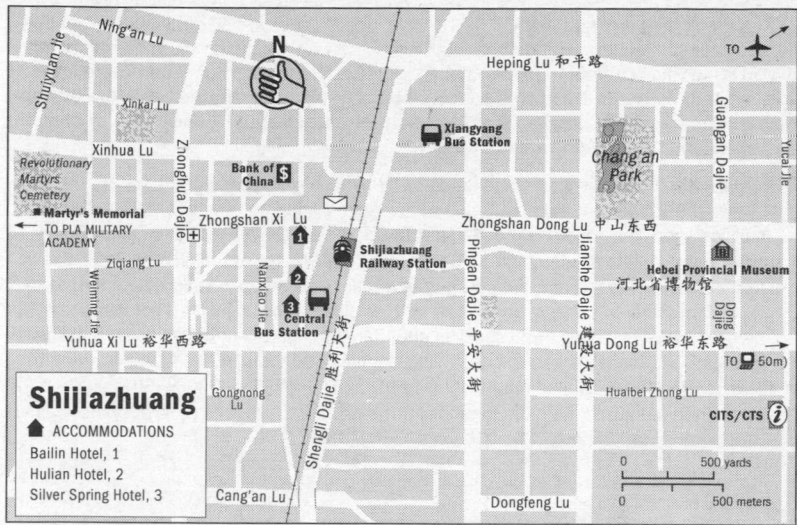

Shijiazhuang

▲ ACCOMMODATIONS
Bailin Hotel, 1
Hulian Hotel, 2
Silver Spring Hotel, 3

Public Transportation: Many **buses** ply the streets of downtown Shijiazhuang, most of them starting from, stopping at, or running past the train station. Buses **#1, 5,** and **6** run east-west along Zhongshan Lu, and bus **#9** runs east along Xinhua Lu.

Taxis: Base fare Y5. Y10-15 should suffice for most places around town.

Bike Rental: South of the train station, across from the Hualian Commercial Building.

ORIENTATION AND PRACTICAL INFORMATION

Downtown Shijiazhuang is laid out in a grid with smaller alleys running off the cardinal lanes. Activity is centered around the plaza outside the train station. **Zhongshan Xi Lu** (中山西路) and **Zhongshan Dong Lu** branch out from there. **Yucai Jie** branches off Zhongshan Dong Lu just past the Provincial Museum. The only in-town tourist attractions are along this road.

Travel Agencies: CITS and **CTS** main offices are in the Tourism Building, 175 Yucai Jie, 4th and 5th Fl., opposite the Hebei Grand Hotel, but they cannot help book tickets or tours. **CITS** branches are in the Railway Building, 97 Zhongshan Dong Lu (☎ 607 6666; open daily 8am-2pm) and 15 Ziqiang Lu (☎ 701 1342), next to the Hualian Hotel (open daily 8am-6pm). **CTS** branches at 140 Yucai Jie (☎ 667 4225; open daily 8am-noon and 3-6pm) and 85 Yucai Jie (☎ 605 6417).

Bank of China: 83 Zhongshan Xi Lu, Congfang Plaza, 1st Fl. (☎ 861 1257 or 861 1258), northeast and within walking distance of the train station. Office through the west entrance changes traveler's checks. MC and V credit card advances but no ATMs. Open M-F 8:30-11:30am and 3-6pm.

Shopping: Shijiazhuang has a small shopping strip along Zhongshan Dong Lu, including the **Beiguo Commercial Building,** at the intersection with Jianshe Dajie. A bit closer to the center of town is the **Dongfang City Plaza Shopping Center,** 83 Zhongshan Xi Lu (☎ 861 1061), about a block west of the train station. Open daily 9am-7:30pm.

Internet Access: Red Leaf Internet Bar (hóng yè wǎngbā; 红叶网巴), 296 Yuhua Dong Lu, just beyond Yucai Jie. There are 10 rather slow computers available for Y4 per hr. Open daily 9am-1am.

Post Office: China Post, 1 Gongli Jie (☎ 702 5736), at the corner of Gongli Jie and Zhongshan Dong Lu, just across a walking bridge from the train station. EMS and IDD phone service daily 7am-9pm. **Postal Code:** 050000.

ACCOMMODATIONS

If you're in Shijiazhuang, you're probably a reluctant itinerant. The hotels know you're stuck here, and your options for budget stays are limited. As most of the hotels are near the train station and in fierce competition, it won't hurt to check out several before making a choice.

Hualian Hotel (huālián héběi fàndiàn; 花联河北饭店), 10 Zhanqian Jie (☎702 5991), across the street from the area between the train station and the bus station. Friendly staff and spacious rooms. Deposit Y100. Check-out 2pm. Doubles Y110-360.

Bailin Hotel (báilín dàshà; 白林大厦), 24 Zhanqian Jie (☎702 1398; fax 702 1887), opposite the train station. Within spitting distance of the next train out of town and unofficial winner of the best bathrooms in town award. Rooms have all standard conveniences. Half-price rates if you check in after 2am and check out before noon. Breakfast included. Singles (with a huge bed) Y158; doubles and triples Y220-420.

Silver Spring Hotel (yínquán jiǔjiā; 银泉酒家; ☎702 6981 or 702 6360), across the street from the bus station. Clean rooms with bath, TV, phone, and A/C. Hot water 6am-8am, noon-2pm. Deposit Y100. Doubles Y110-288.

FOOD

In keeping with Shijiazhuang's stopover identity, the biggest food fads in town are fill-me-up-quick box lunches and stuff-me-to-the-brim buffets. On **Zhongshan Dong Lu,** about 50m east of Beiguo Department Store, **Changan Yuan** (长安园) alley is filled with inexpensive restaurants—the Y6-12 buffets are unbeatable. A similar concept is the **Yong'an Pedestrian Street Market,** with all sorts of cheap snacks and meals sold out of shops, wagons, and baskets. The food court in the basement of **Dongfang City Plaza Shopping Center,** at 83 Dongshan Xi Lu, northwest of the train station, offers a stunning array of delicious, attractive, and super-hygienic local food (Y6-10). For sit-down meals, there is a strip of seafood restaurants running along **Yucai Jie** south of the Hebei Teachers' University.

SIGHTS

Shijiazhuang's sights are rather sparse; if you have some time to kill in Shijiazhuang, it might be more interesting to wander through the massive markets south of **Xinhua Dong Lu** (新华东路) and along **Shengli Bei Jie** (胜利北街), even if their goods are more sundry than souvenir. There are some interesting but hard-to-find sights outside Shijiazhuang proper, but they are not cheap.

HEBEI PROVINCIAL MUSEUM (héběi shěng bówùguǎn; 河北省博物馆). Though currently closed for renovations, the museum plans to open soon. Previously, the main gallery space was given over to a collection called "The Course of Reform and Open-Door in Hebei," an exhibit-cum-trade show, with canned goods and factory-line machinery in the spotlight. A suit of jade armor, a full terracotta army, and a complete mammoth tusk were found upstairs. *(Zhongshan Dong Lu, 2 blocks east of Beiguo Commercial Building. Take bus #1 from the train station. ☎604 5642. Open daily 8:30am-noon and 3-6pm, holidays 9am-4pm. Y5.)*

MARTYR'S MEMORIAL (lièshì língyuán; 烈士陵园). In this expansive park, superhuman busts and statues mingle with refreshing greenery (some of the trees even have camouflage-looking trunks). Several stately buildings house extensive photo collections and relics from the heroes' every aspect of life—from darned socks and old shoes to war helmets and rusted shells. Two foreign names stand out in a sea of Chinese characters: doctors Norman Bethune (1890-1939) and Dwarkanath Shantaram Kotnis (1910-42) are among the honorees. *(343 Zhongshan Xi Lu. Take bus #1, 28, or 24. ☎702 2904. Open daily 7:30am-6pm. Y3.)*

WORLDWIDE CALLING MADE EASY

The MCI WorldCom Card, designed specifically to keep you in touch with the people that matter the most to you.

MCI WORLDCOM   **WORLDPHONE.**

1·800·888·8000

J. L. SMITH

www.wcom.com/worldphone

Please tear off this card and keep it in your wallet as a reference guide for convenient U.S. and worldwide calling with the MCI WorldCom Card.

HOW TO MAKE CALLS USING YOUR MCI WORLDCOM CARD

> **When calling from the U.S., Puerto Rico, the U.S. Virgin Islands or Canada** to virtually anywhere in the world:
1. Dial 1-800-888-8000
2. Enter your card number + PIN, listen for the dial tone
3. Dial the number you are calling :
   Domestic Calls: Area Code + Phone number
   International Calls:
   011+ Country Code + City Code + Phone Number

> **When calling from outside the U.S.**, use WorldPhone from over 125 countries and places worldwide:
1. Dial the WorldPhone toll-free access number of the country you are calling from. ·
2. Follow the voice instructions or hold for a WorldPhone operator to complete the call.

> **For calls from your hotel:**
1. Obtain an outside line.
2. Follow the instructions above on how to place a call.
   Note: If your hotel blocks the use of your MCI WorldCom Card, you may have to use an alternative location to place your call.

RECEIVING INTERNATIONAL COLLECT CALLS*

Have family and friends call you collect at home using WorldPhone Service and pay the same low rate as if you called them.
1. Provide them with the WorldPhone access number for the country they are calling from (In the U.S., 1-800-888-8000; for international access numbers see reverse side).
2. Have them dial that access number, wait for an operator, and ask to call you collect at your home number.

* For U.S. based customers only.

START USING YOUR MCI WORLDCOM CARD TODAY. MCI WORLDCOM STEPSAVERS℠

Get the same low rate per country as on calls from home, when you:

1. **Receive international collect calls to your home** using WorldPhone access numbers

2. **Make international calls with your MCI WorldCom Card** from the U.S.*

3. **Call back to anywhere in the U.S. from Abroad** using your MCI WorldCom Card and WorldPhone access numbers.

* An additional charge applies to calls from U.S. pay phones.

WorldPhone Overseas Laptop Connection Tips —
Visit our website, www.wcom.com/worldphone, to learn how to access the Internet and email via your laptop when traveling abroad using the MCI WorldCom Card and WorldPhone access numbers.

Travelers Assist® — When you are overseas, get emergency interpretation assistance and local medical, legal, and entertainment referrals. Simply dial the country's toll-free access number.

Planning a Trip?—Call the WorldPhone customer service hotline at 1-800-736-1828 for new and updated country access availability or visit our website:

www.wcom.com/worldphone

MCI WorldCom Worldphone Access Numbers

Easy Worldwide Calling

MCI WORLDCOM.

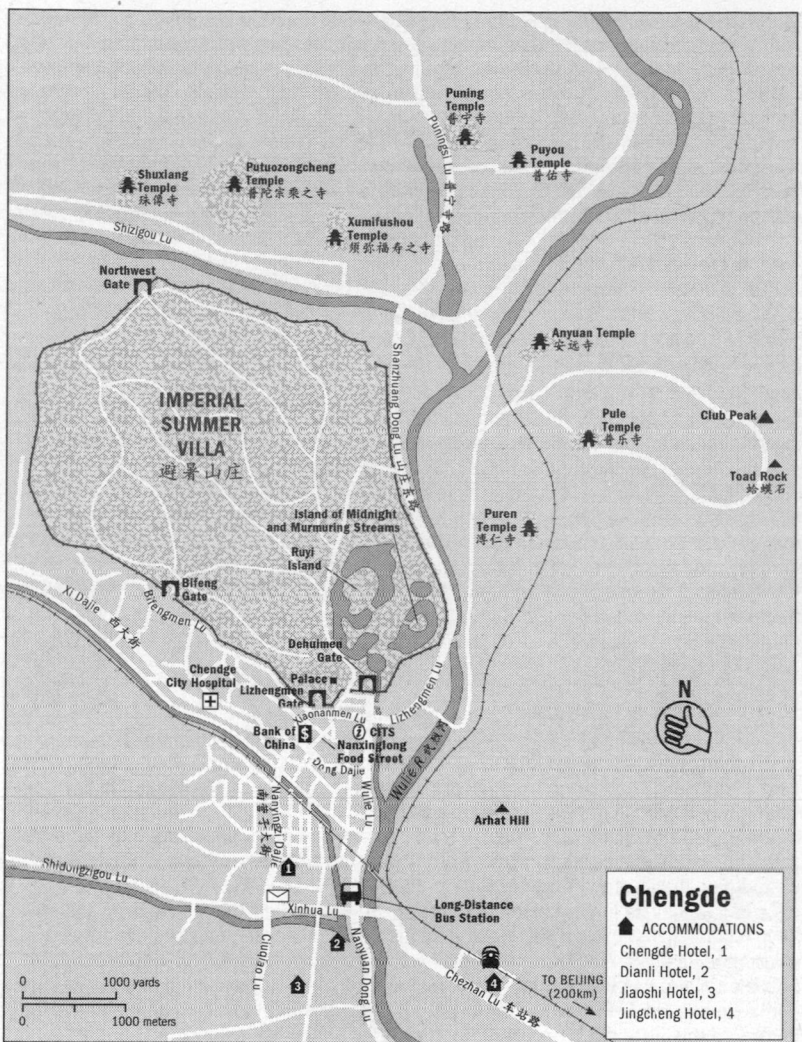

Chengde

📍 ACCOMMODATIONS

Chengde Hotel, 1
Dianli Hotel, 2
Jiaoshi Hotel, 3
Jingcheng Hotel, 4

🏔 DAYTRIPS FROM SHIJIAZHUANG

ZHENGDING正定

15km northeast of Shijiazhuang. Take bus #201 from the train station in Shijiazhuang to Dafo Si, the last stop, about 1hr. away. Open daily 8am-6pm. Y30, children under 1.3m Y15.

Zhengding used to be an important regional center, but has since been eclipsed by the burgeoning economic clout of the capital. Now, Zhengding tries to tout itself as a weekend getaway with ghastly theme parks like The Wild Kingdom (yě chéng; 野城) and The Hall of the Journey to the West (xīyóujì gōng; 西游纪宫). Visitors really only go to Zhengding to visit the Longxing Si (lóngxīng sì; 隆兴寺), popularly known as the **Great Buddha Temple** (dà fó sì; 大佛寺), home to the giant, multi-armed copper Buddha that dominates the main hall. According to the locals, climbing into the upper rafters to shake one of the Buddha's many burnished hands, touch Buddha's nose, or commit some other life-threatening act, demonstrates one's piety. Supposedly the oldest monastery in China, Longxing Si is really an amalgam of structures put together over several dynasties, containing unique and impressive Buddha sculptures such as the "nun with a bag" Matreiya, the two-faced Buddha, the hanging Guanyin, and the 7m wide moving bookshelf that monks used to rotate to get exercise and read the canon simultaneously. At 21.3m, the **Goddess of Mercy** bronze statue with "one thousand hands and eyes" (a gross exaggeration—more like forty and two), was the highest statue in ancient China, and is one of the four wonders of Hebei province.

CANGYANSHAN 苍岩山

90km southwest of Shijiazhuang. Two buses leave for Cangyanshan daily at 8am (2hr., Y10) from the Dongfang Bus Station, at the corner of Xinhua Lu and Youyi Bei Lu. They leave Cangyanshan for Shijiazhuang at 3:30pm. Another option is to charter a taxi for Y180-200. ☎230 0104. Open 24hr. Y25.

Against a dramatic landscape of dropaway peaks and marvelously twisted cypresses, a whole complex of pagodas and monasteries has been stitched into the mountainside, often at the most perilous points possible. The **Hanging Palace** is a spectacular suspended temple straddling a cleft between two cliffs. It is reached by several hundred steps, and is only the first sight on a long, engrossing trail, that takes in 16 scenic spots, up, around, and down the mountain. Some of these are guarded by gatekeepers who'll ask for further admission fees (Y1-3). Save yourself some money and skip these, as there's enough to see on the hike without paying. As Cangyanshan's connections to the outside world are not entirely reliable, you might find yourself stranded for the night. If so, the Cangyan Shan Hotel (cāngyán shān bīnguǎn; 苍岩山宾馆; ☎230 0101), across from the parking lot, has doubles for Y120.

CHENGDE 承德   ☎0334

About 200km northeast of Beijing, Chengde, once called Rehe (Hot River), is a small town that enters Beijing's consciousness every summer when the big city heat and traffic grow too hard to bear. Early in the 18th century, Emperor Kangxi built himself a small mountain lodge that eventually became the immense Imperial Summer Villa of Qianlong's reign. To add to the splendor, Qianlong had the surroundings dotted with temples replicating distinctive minority architecture, including a miniature version of the Potala Palace in Lhasa.

Chengde lost its appeal after the emperors Jiaqing and Xiangfeng both passed away there in 1820 and 1860. Like a swarm of locusts fleeing rain, the imperial court made a quick exit from its apparently unlucky premises. The empty summer complex then was left to suffer the ravages of time. Today, plenty of money is being poured into restoration, and a smattering of mountains and blue skies only complete this little city's pretty picture.

■✦? ORIENTATION AND PRACTICAL INFORMATION

Chengde's roads are perpetually rowdy. Most drama takes place on **Nanyingzi Dajie** (南营子大街). To the north, virtually eclipsing the city, is the **Imperial Summer Villa,** with the **Eight Outer Temples** orbiting farther beyond.

Trains: Chengde Train Station (chéngdé huǒchē zhàn; 承德火车站; ☎202 3690, ext. 2602), east of the river. Ticket office open daily 5-7:30am, 8:20am-6:40pm, and 7:10-11pm. To: **Beijing** (4-7hr., 5 per day, Y17-41); **Shenyang** (12hr., 2 per day, Y45); **Shijiazhuang** (12hr., 1 per day, Y38); and **Tianjin** (9hr., 1 per day, Y30).

Buses: Chengde Long-distance Bus Station (chéngdé chángtú qìchē zhàn; 承德长途汽车站; ☎202 3476), at the junction of Xinhua Lu and Wulie Lu. Open daily 4:30am-9:30pm. To: **Beijing** (4hr., every 20min. 6am-5:40pm, Y40); **Qinhuangdao** (8hr., 5 per day, Y60.5); and **Tianjin** (7½hr., 3 per day, Y38.5).

Local Transportation: Most **buses** run from 6am-6:30pm. Fare Y1. Bus **#5** goes from the train station to the Imperial Summer Villa; **#6** from Nanyingzi Dajie to Puning Temple via the Villa; **#7** between the train station and Nanyingzi Dajie. More frequent but unnumbered **minibuses** also ply the streets.

Taxis: To almost anywhere in the city Y10.

Bike Rental: Check with the guy on a stool at the southwest corner of the train station square, left of the post office. Y5 per day, deposit Y200. Open daily 6am-6:30pm.

Travel Agencies: CITS, 11 Zhonghua Lu, 2nd Fl. (☎203 0448), in a gray building up the street from the villa's Dehuimen Gate. Open daily 8:30am-noon and 2-5:30pm.

Chengde Railway Travel (chéngdé tiĕdào lǚxíngshè; 承德旅行社; ☎208 7124), operates 1- and 2-day tours of Chengde's major sights; tours depart from the Jingcheng Hotel (daily 7am-4pm; Y50, excluding admission).

Bank of China: 3 Dong Dajie. Exchanges traveler's checks and issues credit card advances. Open M-F 8am-noon and 2:30-6:30pm; in winter 8am-noon and 2-5:30pm.

Hospital: Chengde City Central Hospital (chéngdé shì zhōngxīn yīyuàn; 承德市中心医院; ☎202 8468), on Xi Dajie, about 1½ blocks west of Nanyingzi Dajie. English-speaking staff. Open 24hr.

Post Office: About half a block north of the southern tip of Nanyingzi Dajie. EMS. Open daily 8am-6:30pm; in winter 8am-6pm. **Postal Code:** 067000.

ACCOMMODATIONS

If you travel to Chengde by train from Beijing, agents will start accosting you before the trip is half done. They often have discount deals with the better hotels and guarantee a free ride from the train station.

Jingcheng Hotel (jīng chéng fàndiàn; 京承饭店; ☎208 2027), on the east side of the train station square. So big, so nice, so clean, you keep wondering if *you* are good enough. 4-bed dorms Y30, with A/C and bath Y60; doubles Y200-220.

Jiaoshi Hotel (jiàoshī bīnguǎn; 教师宾馆), 16 Tiaoli Jie (☎215 3268), about a 7min. walk south of Xinhua Lu. These pleasant rooms are hard to beat. Hot water 8:30-10:30pm. 4-bed dorms Y25; 2-bed dorms with bath Y60; doubles Y120-180.

Dianli Hotel (diànlì bīnguǎn; 电力宾馆, ☎217 3735), at Daqiao Tou, south of the bus station, just west of the bridge. Breakfast included. 5-bed dorms with bath Y100; 4-bed dorms Y50; 3-bed dorms Y60; 2-bed dorms Y80; doubles with bath Y280 and up.

Chengde Hotel (chéngdé bīnguǎn; 承德宾馆), 33 Nanyingzi Dajie (☎202 3157 or 202 2551). Take bus #7 from the train station. Noisy outside, but the rooms are quiet and all the essential bathroom surfaces are scrubbed down. Enter through the north hall (北楼) just to the left of the entrance, not the one down the ramp. Hot water 6:30-8:30am and 7:30-10:30pm. Deposit Y20. Doubles with bath Y100-120; triples Y90.

FOOD

Where there were emperors, there were attendant armies of the country's best chefs doing everything humanly possible to tickle the imperial taste buds. Although little of that culinary sophistication remains, the wild deer, hare, and pheasant that once fed the son of heaven are still local specialties. **Imperial City Restaurant** (huáng chéng dàjiŭdiàn; 皇城大酒店), 98 Xiaonanmen, outside Dehuimen Gate at the Imperial Villa, offers a taste of the best—for those with at least Y60 to spare. (☎202 5757. Open daily 9am-9pm.) Similar fare is available in rustic, cabin-style rooms decorated with plastic pumpkins at **Drink Two Liang** (hē èr liǎng; 喝二两) in Xiaonanmen, west of the Lizhengmen and Wulie Lu junction. Happy Halloween. (☎203 3362. Open daily 6:30am-10pm.)

Qianlong Dumpling Restaurant (qiánlóng jiǎozi guǎn; 乾隆饺子馆), 10-11 Qingfeng Dong Jie, tucked away in a small alley to the east of a ramp, about a block south of Dong Dajie, serves delicious dumplings. Order in *liang* (7 dumplings); Y10 should suffice. (☎202 8559. Open daily 11:30am-2:30pm and 5:30-9pm.) **Nanxinglong Food**

Street (nánxīnglóng xiǎochī jiē; 南兴隆小吃街) will also please your palate. The bustling, bubbling, brewing street opposite the Lizhengmen entrance of the Imperial Villa dishes up great *sha guo* stews (Y8-18). In the evening, open-air stalls on **Yihua Lu,** about a block west of the bus station, serve up plenty of fresh fruit and vegetables; try Chengde's specialty, **Lulu Almond Juice,** said to beautify all.

🕶 SIGHTS

Temples, palaces, and curious rocks are the order of the day in Chengde. The easiest way to see them all quickly is to attach yourself to one of the minibus tours that race around the city (see **Travel Agencies,** p. 147).

IMPERIAL SUMMER VILLA
At the end of Nanyingzi Dajie, north of the city center. The best entrance is at Lizhengmen Gate, on Lizhengmen Dajie. Take bus #5 from the train station or #6 from Nanyingzi Dajie. Tour buses (40min., 8am-5pm, Y40) leave from between the courtyards and the lake. Open daily 5:30am-9pm; last admission 6:30pm. Y50, children under 1.2m free.

The Imperial Summer Villa (bìshǔ shān zhuāng; 避暑山庄) is the place where the elite meet to beat the heat, where the grounds are impressive, the dealings important, and the former residents imperial. Dubbed the "Mountain Villa for Escaping the Heat," this massive 18th-century estate is twice the size of Beijing's Summer Palace and featured nearly as many Qing intrigues. Since the Summer Villa fell from imperial favor over 100 years ago, the once-resplendent retreat has slipped slowly into a state of disrepair and is now in need of a team of imperial caretakers. Even those who claim the park is a bit over-hyped have to admit that it is still one of Chengde's must-see sights.

There are 120 groups of ancient buildings; the main palace, including the elegant **Hall of Frugality and Sincerity,** has been converted into a museum of weaponry and furniture. In the side halls, the walls are lined with shelves to hold the *Gujintoshujicheng,* a gargantuan encyclopedia of books and illustrations. Behind the courtyard is the lavish **Hall of Refreshing Mists and Ripples,** where Emperor Xiangfeng signed the 1860 Treaty of Beijing. Xiangfeng also took his last breath here, and Empress Dowager Ci Xi contemplated usurping the court—and then did.

The majority of the space has since been surrendered to Empress Nature, taken over by lakes and hills. Although emperors used to flex their hunting arrows on these grounds, it would be foolhardy to cover this land unaided; the hills are the perfect place to get lost. The lake is a patchwork of islands, the prettiest of which are **Ruyi Island** and the **Island of Midnight and Murmuring Streams.** You can walk to all the islands, but renting a boat (Y10-20 per hr., deposit Y50-100) is more fun.

EIGHT OUTER TEMPLES
There were once 12 great temples in the Chengde vicinity, but four have fallen gracefully into disrepair. Of the Eight Outer Temples (wài bā miào; 外八庙) remaining, only six are presentable, and they are being continuously improved at great expense. Built after the fashion of various ethnic styles, these temples were commissioned by Emperors Kangxi and Qianlong less for religious reasons and piety than for intimidating ethnic envoys. The **Eastern Temples** (Anyuan, Pule, and Puren), on the east bank of the Wulie River, are older and smaller, but possess a charm of their own. The biggest money-makers are the **Northern Temples** (Putuozongcheng, Xumifushou, Puning, Puyou, and Shuxiang). The smaller Puren Temple (pǔrén sì; 溥仁寺) and Shuxiang Temple (shūxiàng sì; 殊像寺) are not open to the public. While it may be tempting to strike out independently to cover all the temples, it is easy to overdose on temples; most organized tours only take in two or three of the temples.

PUNING TEMPLE
PUNING TEMPLE (pǔníng sì; 普宁寺). Of the Northern Temples, this is the only one where the chanting you hear doesn't come from tape recorders. Called the "Temple of Universal Peace," this active temple commemorates Qianlong's defeat of the Mongolian rebels in 1755. Two "living Buddhas" bless visitors, but the inanimate star of the temple is the 22m Thousand-Armed-and-Eyed Avalokiteshvara

(Guanyin), the largest wooden statue in the world. *(At the end of Puningsi Lu, east of the villa. Take bus #6 to Dafosi. Open daily 7:30am-6pm; last admission 5:30pm. Y25.)*

PUYOU TEMPLE (pǔyòu sì; 普佑寺). This small, quiet compound was originally the center for the study of Buddhist scripture. In 1937, Japanese occupation forces moved 500 statues here from Arhat Temple. Many were destroyed in a lightning fire in 1964, but 178 remain. See such disciples as "Crazy Ji," who "acted like a lunatic and gave no damn to rules," Liu Hai Chan, who teased toads, and "The Crazy Monk," who swept up treacherous officials with his trusty broom. *(A 2min. walk east from Puning Temple, to the left of the gate. Open daily 8am-6pm; last admission 5:30pm. Y10.)*

XUMIFUSHOU TEMPLE (xūmífúshòu zhī miào; 须弥福寿之庙). Think dragon on a hot tin roof—eight of them, in fact, and made of sparkling gold. Writhing atop the roof, each over 1000kg, the dragons are the outstanding feature of the temple. This "Temple of Happiness and Longevity" was built in 1780 for the 6th Panchen Lama when he came to celebrate the emperor's birthday. The poor lama enjoyed neither happiness nor longevity when he contracted smallpox (some say poison) and was sent home in a coffin. *(On Shizigou Lu, the 1st of the Northern Temples, north of the Imperial Villa and about a 10min. walk west from Puning Temple. Open daily 8am-6pm; last admission 5:30pm. Y20.)*

PUTUOZONGCHENG TEMPLE (pǔtuózōng chéngzhī miào; 普陀宗乘之庙). The granddaddy of the Chengde temples. Generally considered the place to go if you can't make it to Tibet, the Putuozongcheng, also known as the Temple of Potaraka Doctrine, is a one-third scale model of the Dalai Lama's Potala Palace in Lhasa (see p. 735). Even though the great red wall surging up from the mountainous landscape is indeed reminiscent of the Potala, so many Chinese pagodas have been added that it is at best only a faded impression of the original. *(A few hundred meters west of Xumifushou. Open daily 8am-6pm; last admission 5pm. Y20.)*

OTHER TEMPLES. Pule Temple (pǔlè sì; 普乐寺), on the east side and accessible only by taxi (Y10), is a quieter spot that most, with a circular pavilion in the back like that on Beijing's Temple of Heaven (see p. 122). Built by visiting Mongols as a site of worship, the architecture represents a mixture of Mongolian, Tibetan, Chinese, and Islamic influences. *(Open daily 8am-6pm; last admission 5:30pm. Y20.)* **Anyuan Temple** (ānyuǎn miào; 安远庙), about a 10-minute walk north of Pule, is a Xinjiang imitation temple once used as barracks by the Mongolian troops. Nobody lives here now but spiders and weeds. *(Open daily 8am-5:30pm. Y10.)*

OTHER SIGHTS

CLUB PEAK (qìngchuí fēng; 磬锤峰). Looking like a large sore thumb sticking out of the eastern horizon, Club Peak is Chengde's most loved rock formation. Legend has it that this geological marvel came to be when a dragon used his needle to plug a hole in the mountain that was letting the sea through. A 2km walk south lies **Toad Rock** (háma shí; 蛤蟆石). Visitors scramble until they find the perfect angle and then exclaim with delight, "It's a toad, it's a toad!" The climb is especially enjoyable in the early morning, when the paths lack mounds of tourists and early risers can watch the sun rise over the Chinese countryside. *(At the end of Hedong Lu, between Anyuan and Pule Temples. Accessible only by taxi (Y10), but within walking distance of the 2 temples. Open daily 6:30am-6pm. Y15. Cable car round-trip Y15.)*

TWIN PAGODA HILL (shuāng tǎ shān; 双塔山). Since Club Peak is visible from all over the city, and Twin Pagoda Hill has not one but two protuberances, this seems like the better deal to most people. In place of the toad, there is a smaller squat rock that looks like a tortoise bowing before the two pagodas. Some say you can see the profile of one of China's Chairmen—three guesses as to which one. *(About 15km west of Chengde. Accessible by bus #5. Open daily 6am-7pm. Park Y20; temple Y20; cable car round-trip Y25.)*

BEIJING & NORTH COAST

SHANHAIGUAN 山海关 ☎ 0335

Famous for being the spot where the Great Wall meets the sea, Shanhaiguan is a petite and charming place to go to escape the patent lack of foreigner-friendly accommodations in Beidaihe. While Shanhaiguan is often overrun by tourists, the walled town is nonetheless very attractive; it is possible to fall in love with the place while taking a stroll down its streets. Most of the surrounding sights are a bit dull, but the beaches are pleasing and the prices (or lack thereof) even more so. Shanhaiguan is also famous for being the site where Ming general Wu Sangui opened the gates to allow in the Qing armies to quash Li Zicheng's rebels in Beijing, effectively sealing the demise of the Ming dynasty (see **The Ming**, p. 12). Apparently, Li had robbed Wu of his favorite concubine; hers, it could be said, was the face that comprised the impressive line of defense that was the Great Wall.

✴ ⁊ ORIENTATION AND PRACTICAL INFORMATION

The center of town is divided into a grid pattern, anchored by **Bei Dajie** (北大街), **Nan Dajie** (南大街), **Dong Dajie** (东大街), and **Xi Dajie** (西大街). Two main roads run perpendicular to one another through the center of town; everything is within easy walking distance. **Trains** run from Beijing to Shanhaiguan (3½-6hr., 15 per day, Y60-90). The **bus station** is at the junction of Changcheng Dong Lu (长城东路) and Xinkai Dong Lu (新开东路), but the best spot to catch a bus is outside the South Gate of the old walls. **City buses** (Y1) are not allowed within the old city walls, but skirt along their eastern and southern edges; buses **#13, 23, 24,** and **25,** though they run irregularly, cover the route between the First Pass Under Heaven, South Gate, and the Old Dragon's Head. Bus **#34** (Y4) runs from Shanhaiguan to Beidaihe via Qinhuangdao. **Taxis** (base fare Y5) shouldn't be necessary except to more distant sights; make sure the drivers use meters. Rent **bikes** at the bike repair shop in front of the Jingshan Hotel (see **Accommodations and Food**).

CITS is atop a restaurant next to the ticket booth of the First Pass Under Heaven. (☎ 505 2952. Open 24hr.) **Bank of China,** 60 Diyiguan Lu, exchanges traveler's checks. (Open M-F 8-11:30am and 3-6pm; in winter M-F 8-11:30am and 3-5:30pm.) **People's Hospital** (rénmín yīyuàn; 人民医院) is at 46 Nan Dajie. The **post office,** 31 Nan Dajie, offers EMS. (Open daily 8am-5:30pm.) The **postal code** is 066200.

⌂ ⌕ ACCOMMODATIONS AND FOOD

Shanhaiguan blows Beidaihe out of the water when it comes to inexpensive places to stay. **North Street Hotel** (běi jiē zhāodàisuǒ; 北街招待所), 2 Mujia Hutong, off to the left of Bei Dajie just past the Jingshan Hotel, is famous for its age. Peeling and mossy, with stone floors and round doorways, this place feels like it's half-hostel, half-abandoned monastery. (☎ 505 1680. 6- to 8-bed dorms Y20-30; doubles with bath Y120-160.) About 50m west of the First Pass Under Heaven, **Jingshan Hotel** (jīngshān bīnguǎn; 京山宾馆) has plain, comfortable standard rooms under winning, imitation Qing-style roofs. (☎ 505 1130. Doubles Y140, with A/C Y180-280.) If neither of these places can house you, take your money to the **Shanhaiguan Hotel** (shānhǎiguān dàjiǔdiàn; 山海关大酒店), on Xinkai Dong Lu just outside and east of the South Gate. (☎ 506 4488 or 506 4988. Doubles Y288 and up.)

Family restaurants serving fresh seafood line **Xi Dajie** and **Dong Dajie**. After sundown, vendors set up outdoor barbecue stands on **Nan Dajie,** and flatbread and fried vegetables are easy to find.

◉ SIGHTS

There are a fair number of sights in Shanhaiguan. Most of them are wildly overpriced and not terribly interesting; at worst, they are commercialized displays of bad taste. **Beaches** are why all the married Beijingers flock to the coast; from the city center to the coast is a Y10 taxi ride. To go swimming, the eastern gates are free, but the western gates normally charge Y5.

GREAT WALL MUSEUM (cháng chéng bówùguǎn; 长城博物馆). This museum is possibly the most interesting place to visit in Shanhaiguan. A well-curated and well-displayed history of the Great Wall is a good thing: if you can read Chinese, there's enough information here to answer all those questions backpackers are always slinging at one another about the wall. Even if you can't read Chinese, the excellent pictures should make you itch to adjust your travel itinerary. There is also a hall set aside for freakish-shaped rocks. *(On Diyiguan Lu, 3min. south of the First Pass Under Heaven, following the Old City Wall. Open daily 7:45am-6:30pm. Y5; bag check Y1.)*

YANSAI LAKE (yànsāi hú; 燕塞湖). Just about any rock-enclosed patch of water in China is nicknamed a "Little Guilin"—Yansai Lake is no exception, aggressive crowds jostling for photos and all. A pleasant lake cruise (only when there is no drought, Y20) gets you to some of the 14 crags and cliffs imagined by locals to resemble all manner of bestial and divine beings. The park's huge **bird sanctuary** is marked by a pen inhabited by a half-dozen ostriches, looking ridiculous, indignant, and vaguely surprised. A two-way **landslide car** (Y30) takes willing visitors around the park. As a special bonus, the lake's introductory sign features some of the most creative stream of consciousness Chinglish in all of China: "the squrrel is lovely activie and people arehappy it is more skillful than natural things visiting yansai lake returning to nature enjoying your life will mould your personality and enjoy beauty of nature." *(9km northwest of Shanhaiguan. Bus #24 stops at the lake; taxis (Y25) are more reliable. Open daily 6am-7pm; landslide open daily 8:30am-4:30pm. Y30.)*

JIAOSHAN GREAT WALL (jiǎoshān cháng chéng; 角山长城). As you approach it along the broad, smooth avenue, Jiaoshan looks like it is going to be the best Great Wall experience yet. Stately and breathtaking, it surges up along the precipitous peaks of the first real mountain ridge facing the Bohai Sea, earning itself the name "Horn Mountain" for looking like the ridges on the back of a writhing dragon. Up close, Jiaoshan is disappointingly well made. Legend holds that this section of the Great Wall spontaneously dissolved to reveal the bones that had been used to fill in its base; that might explain the extensive restoration since. If you can make it past the first two towers, though, the wall all but disappears, and hikers must scramble hard to make it up to **Qixian Monastery.** *(3km north of Shanhaiguan. Accessible by taxi (Y10). Open daily 6am-7pm. Y15. Cable car round-trip Y20.)*

FIRST PASS UNDER HEAVEN (tiān xià dì yī guān; 天下第一关). This gate was the outermost gate to the world as we know it, at least until the Manchu armies stormed in (followed soon after by souvenir vendors). The essence of the First Pass Under Heaven is an overpowering tower of the Great Wall that now stands tall and lonesome amid squalid touristy splendor. *(At the end of Dong Dajie, on the eastern edge of town. Open daily 6am-7pm. Y35.)*

MENGJIANGNU TEMPLE (mèngjiāngnǚ miào; 孟姜女庙). An entire complex dedicated to a woman who knew how to be a good wife, Mengjiangnu was built in the Song dynasty and restored during the Ming. The temple bears witness to the folklore surrounding Mengjiangnu, who is said to have traveled thousands of miles in search of her husband who died during a term of service at the Great Wall." So many times did she pace back and forth that she left "footprints in the stones," and so moving was her virtuous nature that the wall crumbled to reveal her husband's bones. *(6km east of Shanhaiguan, on Fenghuangshan. Accessible by bus #23. Open daily 7am-5:30pm. Y30, students Y15, children 1.1-1.4m Y15.)*

OLD DRAGON HEAD (lǎo lóng tóu; 老龙头). Named after a carving that once faced the sea, this rock juts out 124m into the Bohai Sea. Restored in 1987 at a cost of three million *yuan*, the easternmost edge of the Great Wall is said to be a perfect juxtaposition of manmade miracle and gorgeous natural scenery. The masses of tourists who flock here apparently agree. *(3km from Shanhaiguan. Mini-buses (Y2) leave from South Gate; buses #13, 23, 24, and 25 take forever to come by the same place. Open daily 4am-7:30pm. Y35.)*

If you ask to be taken to the Old Dragon Head, most taxis will drop you off at the **Great Wall Cultural Center** (cháng chéng wénhùa yóudōngyuán; 长城文化游东园) instead. The exhibitions include a vast amount of papier maché Great Wall, a model of a gruesome attack scene, and what appears to be a Buddhist temple, Elvis style—slightly cheesy and covered with sparkles. *(At the head of the 500m strip leading to the Old Dragon Head. Open daily 8am-5:30pm. Y20.)*

LONGEVITY MOUNTAIN (chángshòu shān; 长寿山). This hefty hiking ground is made of massive granite rocks stacked Lego-style to form impressive mountains, deriving their names from the frequent rock face etchings. Rock rarities such as "Fish-eye stone," which looks like a giant fish with its mouth open, and the "Stone Grotto of Highly Skilled Doctors" are there for your viewing enjoyment. *(9km northeast of Shanhaiguan. Accessible by taxi (30min., Y30). Open daily 8am-7pm. Y15.)*

BEIDAIHE 北戴河 ☎ 0335

Until Beidaihe was "discovered" in the 19th century by Europeans living in the Tianjin concession, it was just a little fishing village. The foreigners' proclivity for sun and surf, however, quickly turned Beidaihe into a miniature Chinese Riviera. Westerners checked out not long after, and the coastal city is now a watering hole for Communist cadres and *yuan*-laden Chinese vacationers. If the promise of Party bigwigs shedding their comrade garb is too rich to resist, then join the scantily clad mainlanders and head to this sparkling oceanic oasis. But be sure to pack lots of money with your swimsuit; seaside fun has its price.

■ ⁊ **ORIENTATION AND PRACTICAL INFORMATION.** The two main streets in Beidaihe are **Haining Lu** (海宁路), running from north to south, and **Dongjing Lu** (东经路), running from east to west about a block inland from the shore. A group of streets branching north from Dongjing Lu are named **An-number Lu** (Anyi Lu, Aner Lu, etc.; 安"X"路); numbers increase from west to east. The streets branching to the south from Dongjing Lu follow suit, going by **Bao-number Lu** (保"X"路). There are three stretches of beach in Beidaihe, of which the closest is **Middle Beach. West** and **East Beaches** are more tranquil, but chunks of the latter are cordoned off by the men in green, specially set aside for party leaders. If you follow **Qiqiao Nan Lu** (七侨南路) down to the beach, you'll find an admission-free entrance.

Trains run from Beijing to Beidaihe Train Station (2½-5hr., 13 per day, Y60-90). **Local buses** run frequently (6am-6:30pm; Y1) between all three towns in this area. Useful routes include: **#5** from the Beidaihe Train Station to Beidaihe Haibin Bus Station via West Beach; **#21** and **22** along Beidaihe's main drag; and **#34** from Beidaihe to Qinhuangdao and Shanhaiguan (1½hr., round-trip Y4). **Taxi** base fare is Y5; from the train station to most hotels costs Y10 (take bus #1 or 21 instead). **Bike rentals** are necessary only if you intend to venture to the quieter beaches toward the east, where taxis and buses are not allowed.

Bank of China, 17 Dongjing Lu, between Anwu Lu and Liuchi Lu, exchanges traveler's checks and issues credit card advances. (Open M-F 8:30-11:45am and 3-5:30pm; in winter 8:30-11:45am and 2-5pm.) **China Telecom,** 76 Dongjing Lu, has IDD service and Internet access. (Open daily 8am-noon and 3-6:30pm. Internet Y0.3 per min.) The **EMS post office,** on Haining Lu about half a block north of Dongjing Lu, also books tickets. (☎ 404 1119. Open daily 8am-6:30pm.) The **postal code** is 066100.

⁊ **ACCOMMODATIONS.** The accommodations situation in Beidaihe is grim. Those not willing to shell out Y600-700 per night have only two places to go. The **Guesthouse for Diplomatic Missions** (wàijiāo rényuán bīnguǎn; 外交人员宾馆), 1 Baosan Lu, set back from Dongjing Lu, is a different definition of "budget," selling decadent living in oceanfront bungalows with access to a pool, tennis courts, and weekend barbecues. (☎404 1287. Open Apr. 20-Oct. Doubles Y650, off-season Y450; triples Y300/200.) The **Yuehua Hotel** (yuèhuá bīnguǎn; 悦华宾馆), 90 Dongjing Lu, is in a big white building just west of Baowu Lu. Plush is as plush does. (☎404 1575, ext. 1111. Doubles Y390-480. Credit cards accepted.)

🍴 **FOOD.** The quality of the **seafood** in Beidaihe is nothing short of spectacular. Pick out your creature of choice from the red and green tubs on the sidewalk; greet it again on your plate. The **Juan Restaurant** (jūān cāntīng; 居安餐厅), a favorite among travelers, is on the southern end of Haining Lu, across from Xinhua Bookstore. (Dishes Y3-10. Open 24hr.) From Haining Lu all the way down **Baoer Lu** toward Tiger Rock is a row of clean, lively, and airy seafood restaurants. **Kiesslings** (qìshìlín cāntīng; 起士林餐厅; ☎404 1043), a branch of the famous Tianjin chain, is near the Guesthouse for Diplomatic Missions, where Baosan Lu and Dongjing Lu meet. Feast on the German *borscht*, sausage, caviar, and sinfully good pastries that the Austrians brought to Tianjin during the concession days.

SHANDONG 山东

The parent of such colorful progeny as Confucius, the Boxer Rebellion (see p. 13), and Jiang Qing (see p. 18), scrappy little Shandong has seen more than its share of action over the past three millennia. The province has traditionally been one of the poorest in China, in no small part because of the caprices of the Yellow River, which meets the sea at Shandong's coast and has spilled cruelly over its banks more times than historians can count. But Shandong is also responsible for a disproportionate amount of China's proudest cultural achievements. Confucius and Mencius were both born and based here, in the ancient state of Lu, which occupied the western portion of the province. Some of Daoism's most revered spirits and sprites are said to make their home here, on the mountain of Taishan, and ancient storytellers located the dwelling of the immortals on Shandong's far eastern coast, in the mythic seaside haven of Penglai. Even China's most highly regarded beer, Tsingtao, is brewed here.

Shandong's staggering cultural wonders, combined with its green hills and many kilometers of craggy coastline, make it a must-see for visitors. Highlights include the sacred mountain of Taishan in the magical little village of Taian; Qufu, the birthplace of Confucius and national center of Confucian thought and worship; and Qingdao, a lovely and decadent former German concession on the sea, with beer and beaches galore.

JINAN 济南   ☎0531

For most travelers, Jinan is just a convenient stopping point on the routes to Qingdao or to Taishan and Qufu. But the capital of Shandong province offers some surprising treasures beneath a thick layer of concrete. Jinan is an industrial megalith and still a staunch adherent to Communism; its "hard-working people" are, by its own assertion, its most valued asset, and the flow of activity here is mostly directed toward making a good living. But colorful towers of fruits and vegetables at street markets and the splendor of Thousand Buddha Mountain and Four Gate Pagoda shimmer through the dust. The people of Jinan and the multitudes of schoolchildren wearing bright yellow caps walk a little slower than most Chinese, reminding visitors that life should be a stroll, not a frantic-paced rush.

▣ **TRANSPORTATION**

Airplanes: Yaoqiang International Airport (yáoqiáng guójì jīchǎng; 遥墙国际机场; ☎694 9400). Tickets can be booked by calling the **Shandong Ticket Center** (☎295 1351), at 8 Kuiyuan Lu, near the intersection with Jingshi Lu. **Shuttle buses** run from the **Silver Plaza Shopping Center** (yínzuò shāngchéng; 银座商城), at the intersection of Luoyuan Dajie and Qianfoshan Lu. To: **Beijing** (2-3 per day, Y500); **Chengdu** (1-3 per day, Y1090); **Chongqing** (1 per day, Y880); **Dalian** (1-2 per day, Y730); **Guangzhou** (at least 2 per day, Y1270); **Guilin** (M-W and F-Sa, Y1350); **Haikou** (1 per day, Y1620); **Harbin** (Tu-Th and Su, Y900); **Nanjing** (M-Tu and Th-Sa, Y640); **Shanghai** (3 per day, Y610); **Shenyang** (at least 1 per day, Y690); and **Xian** (M, W, F-Su, Y700).

Trains: Jinan Train Station (jínán huǒchē zhàn; 济南火车站), on Jingyi Lu, in the city center. To: **Beijing** (4-7hr., several per day, Y64-70); **Fuzhou** (18hr., 1 per day, Y208); **Harbin** (24hr., 1 per day, Y95); **Nanjing** (8½hr., 2 per day, Y81); **Qingdao** (4½hr., 5 per day, Y68); **Shanghai** (12hr., 2 per day, Y125); **Shenyang** (15¼hr., 3 per day, Y68); and **Tianjin** (3½hr., 4 per day, Y50).

Buses: Only one of Jinan's bus stations is of use to travelers. The bus station right in front of the train station (☎691 0927) is the most centrally located and most convenient. To: **Beijing** (8hr., 1 per day, Y71); **Qingdao** (4hr., every hr. 6:30am-5:30pm, Y91); **Qufu** (1½hr., every 30min. 5:30am-5:30pm, Y20); **Shanghai** (20hr., 1 per day, Y160); **Taian** (1hr., every 20min. 5:30am-5:30pm, Y12); **Yantai** (5hr., 5 per day, Y99); and **Weihai** (6hr., 2 per day, Y139).

Local Transportation: Buses #2, 48, and **51** run along Jingshi Lu to the Thousand Buddha Mountain. Many buses, including **#3, 11, 18,** and **34,** also run to and from the train and bus stations. Bus fare Y0.5-4, depending on distance.

Taxis: Base fare Y5-6.

✦ ▐ ORIENTATION AND PRACTICAL INFORMATION

Jinan's **train station** is in the western part of town, on **Jingyi Lu** (经一路), a major east-west street. Immediately to the east, **Tiancheng Lu** (天城路) runs north-south. **Daming Lake** (大明湖), surrounded by Daming Lake Park, is the major landmark in the eastern half of the city, surrounded by **Daming Hu Bei Lu** (大明湖北路) to the north and **Daming Hu Lu** to the south; the major north-south thoroughfare of **Lishan Lu** (历山路) is to the east. **Qianfoshan Lu** (千佛山路) runs through the southern half of the city, toward Thousand Buddha Park; it intersects with **Jingshi Lu** (经十路), which runs from east to west past the Shandong Provincial Museum.

In the southwestern part of the city, the east-west streets are designated as **Jing (number) Lu,** so that, going from north to south, the traveler encounters Jingyi Lu, Jinger Lu, Jingsan Lu, and so on. The north-south streets are designated **Wei (number) Lu,** and the numbers increase from east to west.

Travel Agency: CITS, 88 Jingshi Lu, 4th Fl. (☎296 5858, ext. 6401 or 6402; fax 296 5651; email sdcitsaa@public.jn.sd.cn), near Lishan Lu. Open M-F 8:30am-noon and 2:30-6:30pm.

Bank of China: 22 Luoyuan Dajie (☎699 5026 or 699 5029), exchanges foreign currency and traveler's checks and allows Visa card advances. Open M-F 8am-noon and 2:30-6:30pm; in winter 8am-noon and 1:30-5:30pm.

Bookstore: Xinhua Bookstore (☎691 2729), on the 2nd floor of the overpass at the corner of Jingsi Lu and Weier Lu. Offers a sizable selection of English books. Open Tu-Su 9am-8pm, M 9am-7pm.

PSB: 145 Jingsan Lu (☎691 5454), near Weiwu Lu.

Hospital: Shengli Hospital (shēnglì yīyuàn; 省立医院), 324 Jingwu Lu (☎793 8911), near the corner with Weiqi Lu. 24hr. emergency. Pharmacy.

Internet Access: China Telecom (☎606 5449), Silver Plaza Shopping Center, 5th Fl., at the corner of Luoyuan Dajie and Qianfoshan Lu. Y5 per hr., 1hr. minimum. Open daily 9am-9pm. Closer to the station, **The Fossick Network Bar,** 19 Jinger-Weisan Lu, 2nd Fl. (☎605 0385), is set back from the street beside a room with pool and ping-pong tables. Y3 per hr., 1hr. minimum. Open 24hr.

BEIJING & NORTH COAST

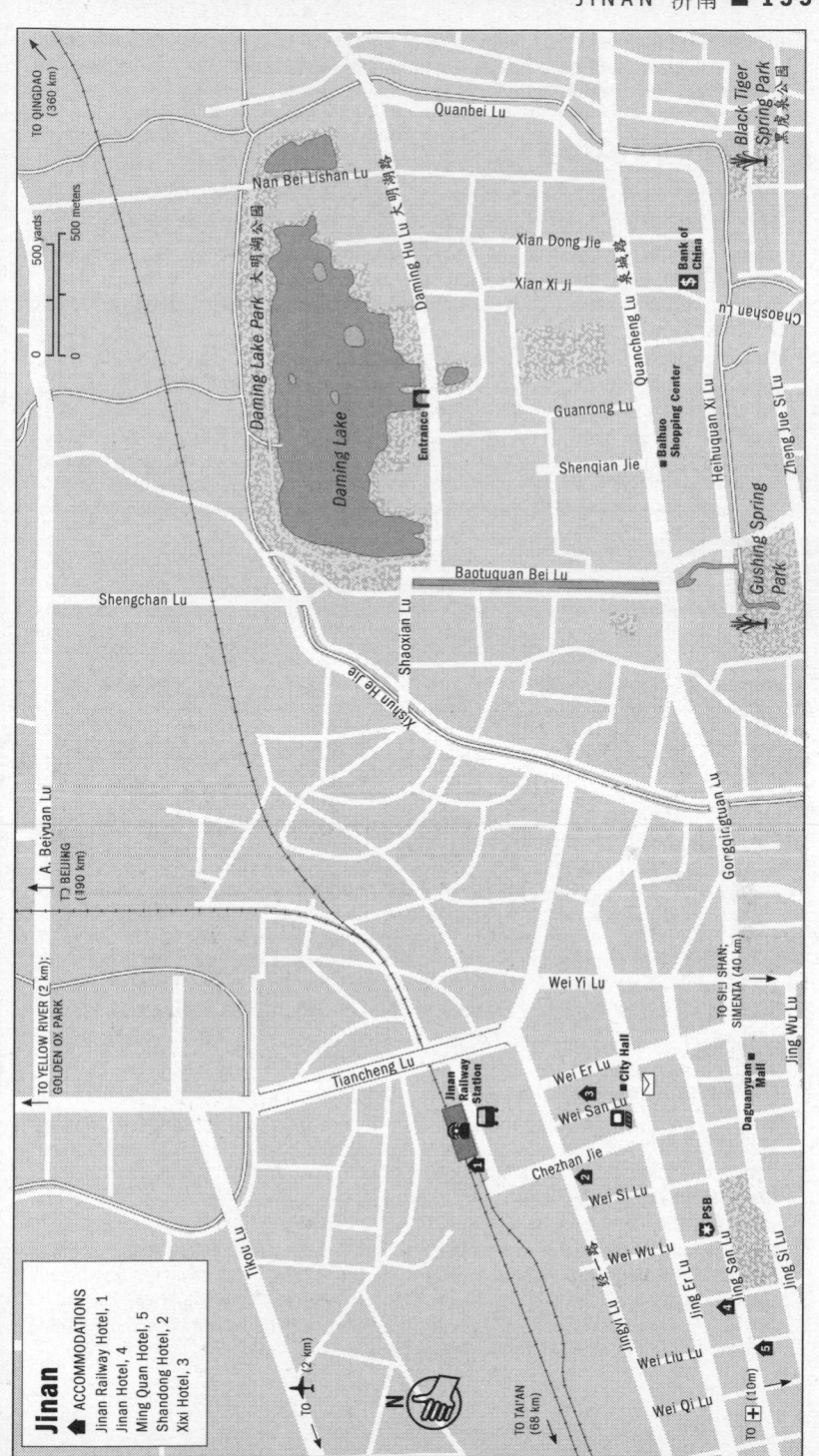

Jinan

♦ ACCOMMODATIONS
Jinan Railway Hotel, 1
Jinan Hotel, 4
Ming Quan Hotel, 5
Shandong Hotel, 2
Xixi Hotel, 3

TO QINGDAO (360 km)

Quanbei Lu

Nan Bei Lishan Lu

Daming Lake Park 大明湖公园

Daming Hu Lu 大明湖路

Xian Dong Jie

Xian Xi Ji

Quancheng Lu

东城路

$ Bank of China

Black Tiger Spring Park 黑虎泉公园

Chaoshan Lu

Daming Lake

Entrance

Guanrong Lu

Shenqian Jie

Bahuo Shopping Center

Heihuquan Xi Lu

Zheng Jie Lu Lu

Gushing Spring Park

Shengchan Lu

Baotuquan Bei Lu

Shaoxian Lu

Xisnun Jie Jie

A. Beiyuan Lu

TO BEIJING (390 km)

TO YELLOW RIVER (2 km); GOLDEN OX PARK

Gonglingtuan Lu

Wei Yi Lu

TO SHI SHAN; SIMENLA (40 km)

Daguanyuan Mall

Jing Wu Lu

Tiancheng Lu

Jinan Railway Station

Wei Er Lu

City Hall

Wei San Lu

Chezhan Jie

Wei Si Lu

Wei Wu Lu

PSB

Jing San Lu

Jing Er Lu

Jing Si Lu

Tikou Lu

Jingyi Lu 经一路

Wei Liu Lu

Wei Qi Lu

TO ✈ (2 km)

N

TO TAI'AN (68 km)

TO ✚ (10m)

500 yards
500 meters

Post Office: China Post, 162 Jinger Lu (☎605 7274), at Weier Lu. EMS and Poste Restante available. Open daily summer 8am-7:30pm, winter 8am-7pm. For EMS pick-up service, dial 185. **Postal Code:** 250001.

ACCOMMODATIONS

Accommodations in Jinan are severely lacking, in number and value. More than a night here will burn a hole not just in your wallet but in your whole backpack.

Shandong Hotel (shāndōng bīnguǎn; 山东宾馆), 92 Jingyi Lu (☎605 7881, ext. 3100; fax 605 7881, ext. 3188), about a block south of the train station, on the corner of Weisan Lu. All rooms have A/C, TV, phone, and bath. Breakfast included. Singles Y130; doubles Y160; triples Y210.

Ming Quan Hotel (míng quán dà jiǔdiàn; 名泉大酒店), 181 Jingsan Lu (☎792 0748, ext. 8118), just past Weiwu Lu. Spacious, clean rooms with decent bathrooms, A/C, TV, and telephone. Breakfast included. Doubles Y178-258.

Jinan Hotel (jǐnán fàndiàn; 济南饭店), 240 Jingsan Lu (☎793 8981; fax 793 2906), just past Weiliu Lu, set back off the road behind a row of tall trees. A little hard to find behind all the foliage, but far enough from the street for a little peace and quiet. Reception desk is in Building 4. Clean and spacious, with a pretty courtyard. Rooms have all standard amenities. Breakfast included. Singles and doubles Y220.

Xixi Hotel (xíxí jū bīnguǎn; 习习居滨馆), 24 Weisan Lu (☎605 7886), down an alley near the Shandong Hotel. The Xixi is not very chichi, with gaudy green vinyl couches in the lobby. "Natural" singles and doubles Y168; "better" singles and doubles Y188-200.

Jinan Railway Hotel (jǐnán tiědào dàshà jiǔdiàn; 济南大厦酒店; ☎601 2118; fax 601 2188), right next to the train station. Guests will have to fend off the stream of beggars and peddlers outside just to reach the comforts of inside. Discounts available to returning customers. Singles and doubles Y230-360.

FOOD

Jinan offers some surprisingly luscious produce in summer. Fruit and vegetable vendors line the alleys, dishing up delights like mangos, kiwis, eggplants, tomatoes, and some gargantuan watermelons. A strip of up-and-coming hipper-than-thou bars and eateries is on **Qianfoshan Lu,** right down the street from the Thousand Buddha Mountain entrance, and **Chezhan Jie** is lined with numerous little restaurants. The basement of the **Silver Plaza Shopping Center,** at the intersection of Luoyuan Dajie and Qianfoshan Lu, offers a wide selection of clean, palate-pleasing foods for ultra-cheap prices (Y1-10). Jingshi Lu is the place to go to get your poultry while it's still clucking. McDonald's and KFC are at 222 Chongqing Lu.

Yuedu Restaurant (yuèdū jiǔlóu; 粤都酒楼), 588 Jingqi Lu (☎793 4825). The one-night stand of meals: patrons choose their dishes (Y8-20) from a window display, and may well leave never knowing their chosen concoction's name. Open daily 6am-9pm.

Tianlong Fast Food (tiānlóng kuàicān; 天龙快餐; ☎602 3742), opposite the train station. The rumble of trains rocks the house, literally, and music blaring from loudspeakers heralds fast, cheap eats and the usual plastic seats and supersonic pace. Dishes Y1-10. Open daily 6am-10pm.

Lao Cheng Dou (láo chéng dōu; 老成都), 213-1 Jinger Lu, just before Weisi Lu. A simple, clean place where patrons select dishes from a long counter full of tasty selections (Y6-12). Open daily 6am-9pm.

Fulinmen Bakery (fúlínmén; 富临门), 31-1 Weier Lu (☎605 5999), just past Jingsi Lu. This gleaming, scrumptious-smelling bakery serves up mouth-watering rolls, cakes, and cookies for Y1-4 each. Open daily 9:30am-10:30pm.

👁 SIGHTS

A few oases of cultural and historical interest stand their ground against the endless crunch of concrete. Most of Jinan's sights are not far from the city center and train station. The Four Gate Pagoda is an exception, but it is definitely more than worth the hike out.

THOUSAND BUDDHA MOUNTAIN (qiān fó shān; 千佛山). The mountain is Jinan's pride and joy. There are a *lot* of Buddhas carved into the face of the mountain (the first was carved around AD 587), and the number of ancient gingkos and cypresses, waterfalls, and temples is still greater than the number of souvenirs produced in honor of the mountain. A hike to the summit takes about one hour; a ride on the rickety cable cars (Y15) takes 10 min. The summit is dotted with temples (admission Y3 to each). The real sleeper attraction is the alpine slide ("Magical Function Skidway") that sends visitors careening down the mountain (Y20), laughing all the way. *(18 Jingshi Lu, on the southern edge of town. Accessible via buses #2 and #48, which run along Jingshi Lu and Lishan Lu, and #51, which runs along Jingshi Lu. Open 24hr., ticket office open daily 6am-7pm. Y15.)*

FOUR GATE PAGODA (sì mén tǎ; 四门塔). Officially, the pagoda is a mere 33km south of town, but locals swear that it is much farther, and the amount of time and ingenuity it takes to get there might make you believe them. The pagoda is a small square stone hut built in AD 611, impressive for its unassuming dignity and gracious sense of past. Spread throughout the surrounding hills is the old burial ground for monks of the Shentong Temple, interred between the Song and Qing dynasties; the "Thousand Year Old Tree," allegedly planted in the Eastern Han; and the Tang dynasty Thousand Buddha Cliff, with one thousand buddhas of varying size and splendor carved laboriously into a rocky mountain face. *(Accessible via bus #22 from Jinan, the pagoda is at least a 1½hr. ride (Y4) on dusty, poorly paved roads. The bus stop is 20-30min. by foot from the pagoda; a motorbike or van-taxi will take you there for Y5. ☎ 284 3051. Open daily 8am-6pm. Y10.)*

SHANDONG PROVINCIAL MUSEUM (shāndōng shěng bówùguǎn; 山东省博物馆). This imposing concrete block houses one of China's more intriguing provincial museums. View a Ming dynasty ship, huge dinosaur fossils (including some from the homegrown *Shandongosaurus Gigantous*— no joke!), and truckloads of thousand year-old pottery shards. An interesting animal exhibit includes exotic birds, huge sea turtles, and a freakish stuffed six-legged calf. *(14 Jingshi Lu. A 5min. walk from Thousand Buddha Mountain; accessible via buses #2, 31, and 48. Open Tu-F 8:30am-noon and 2:30-6:30pm, Sa-Su 9am-6pm. Y20.)*

DAMING LAKE (dàmíng hú; 大明湖). Picturesque Daming Lake sits in the center of the park's amusement grounds, refreshing greenery, and, in the mornings, focused locals practicing tai chi. The paths that meander through the park have a soothing effect—visitors likely will find themselves falling into step just a little bit more slowly than usual. *(271 Daminghu Nan Lu. Take bus #11 or 41. ☎ 608 8928. Open daily 6am-6:30pm. Y15.)*

TAIAN 泰安   ☎0538

Tucked humbly at the foot of the illustrious Taishan, compact little Taian could easily be mistaken for a mere gateway to its towering companion. But every emperor who made the trek up Taishan stopped first at the town's glorious and infinitely complex Dai Temple. The town is home to outstanding calligraphy and medicine shops, and its friendly inhabitants are steeped in a long tradition of healthy pride in their home and the art of sharing it with awestruck visitors. What's more, accommodations and food are significantly cheaper here than on Taishan's summit, making Taian an ideal base.

✦ ⁊ ORIENTATION AND PRACTICAL INFORMATION

With fewer than 500,000 residents and a dense center, Taian feels very manageable. The mountain, positioned directly north of town, is a useful landmark when not hidden by haze. The **train station** is just south of the major thoroughfare, **Dongyue Dajie** (东岳大街), in the western half of town, but everything else of interest to visitors is in the northeastern portion, just south of the base of Taishan. **Hongmen Lu** (红门路) runs south from the mountain, past the Taishan Guesthouse, to the Dai Temple. **Qingnian Lu** (青年路) skirts the western edge of the temple.

Trains: A number of trains pass through Taian, though virtually none originate here. The **Taian Station** (tài'ān zhàn; 泰安站) is in the western half of the city, just south of Dongyue Dajie. Open 24hr. To: **Beijing** (7hr., several per day, Y79); **Jinan** (1hr., Y5.5-30); **Qingdao** (5½hr., several per day, Y34-60); and **Yantai** (9½hr., 2 per day, Y41).

Buses: Taian Long-distance Bus Station (tài'ān chángtú qìchē zhàn; 泰安长途汽车站), on Dongyue Dajie, about 3 blocks east of the train station. To: **Beijing** (12hr., 1 per day, Y60); **Jinan** (1½hr., every 30min. 6am-6:40pm, Y21); and **Qufu** (1hr., every 20min. 6am-6pm, Y13).

Public Transportation: Several **buses** ply through downtown Taian, though their routes are rather limited. Bus **#3** runs along Hongmen Lu from the station area to the foot of Taishan, bus **#4** along Dongyue Dajie, and bus **#7** along Hushan Lu.

Taxis: Base fare Y5 in a *miandi* taxi and Y6-7 in a red cab.

Travel Agency: CITS, 22 Hongmen Lu, 2nd Fl. (☎822 3259; fax 833 2240), a 2min. walk from the Taishan Guesthouse and set back from the street. Open M-F 8:30am-noon and 2:30-6:30pm.

Bank of China: 49 Hongmen Lu (☎822 6057). Changes currency and traveler's checks. Open M-F 8am-noon and 2:30-6pm. A branch at 23 Dongyue Dajie (☎825 5274), across from the Lao Dong Hotel, provides credit card advances but no currency exchange. Open M-F 8am-noon and 2:30-6:30pm.

PSB: 71 Qingnian Lu (☎822 4004), with a main gate around the corner on Dongyue Dajie.

Pharmacy: No. 6 Pharmacy (dìliù yàodiàn; 第六药店), 157 Hushan Lu (☎825 7356). Open daily 8:30am-8pm.

Hospital: Central Hospital (zhōngxīn yīyuàn; 中心医院), 29 Longtan Lu (☎822 4161), near the intersection with Kangfu Lu. Some English-speaking doctors. Pharmacy.

Internet Access: Internet Bar (wǎng xìng bā; 网兴巴), 133 Hushan Lu (☎820 8989). Y3 per hr. Open daily 8:30am-11pm.

Post Office: China Post, in the train station square just west of the station (☎822 3567 or 833 7946). EMS and Poste Restante. Open daily 8am-7pm; in winter 8am-6pm. **Postal Code:** 271000.

▛ ACCOMMODATIONS

The traffic of pilgrims and tourists through Taian keeps accommodation pricing competitive, and Dongyue Dajie is crawling with hotels. Rumors fly that Chinese-only hotels in the train station area will sometimes accept foreigners who are willing to do a little persuading in Chinese.

Mian Ma Hotel (mián má bīnguǎn; 棉麻宾馆), 129 Dongyue Dajie (☎826 5800), about a 5min. walk west of the long-distance bus station. Although renovations in the cheapest rooms clutter the hall somewhat, the Mian Ma, the best budget place in town, is all that and more. Breakfast included. Prices are per person, not room. Rooms contain up to 5 beds. Y12-50; with A/C, TV, and bath Y50-120.

Longtan Hotel (lóngtán bīnguǎn; 龙潭宾馆), 14 Longtan Lu (☎822 6511), at Dongyue Dajie. Rooms are dimly lit but comfortable. All rooms have attached bath and 24hr. hot water. Doubles Y158-218; triples Y150-180; deluxe single Y480. Prices negotiable.

Friendship Grand Hotel (yǒuyí dàjiǔdiàn; 友谊大酒店), 49 Dongyue Dajie (☎822 2288; fax 822 4100), 1 block from the train station. The newer rooms are cushy but not quite cheap, and the older ones are livable but show their age a bit. 24hr. hot water. Older singles and doubles Y160, newer Y260-360.

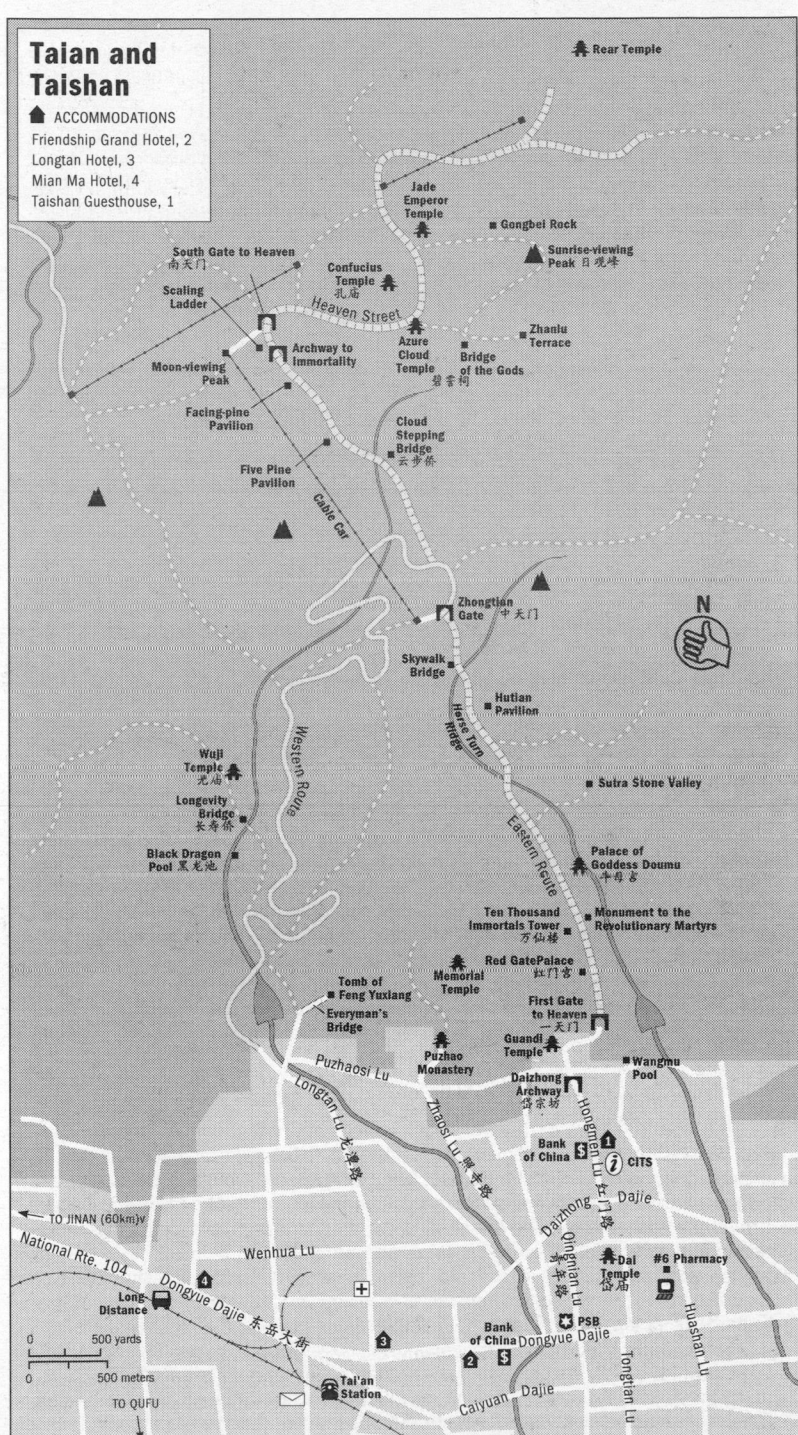

Taian and Taishan

🏠 ACCOMMODATIONS
Friendship Grand Hotel, 2
Longtan Hotel, 3
Mian Ma Hotel, 4
Taishan Guesthouse, 1

Rear Temple

Jade Emperor Temple

Gongbei Rock

Sunrise-viewing Peak 日观峰

South Gate to Heaven 南天门

Confucius Temple 孔庙

Scaling Ladder

Zhanlu Terrace

Moon-viewing Peak

Archway to Immortality

Azure Cloud Temple 碧霞祠

Bridge of the Gods

Facing-pine Pavilion

Cloud Stepping Bridge 云步桥

Five Pine Pavilion

Heaven Street

Cable Car

Zhongtian Gate 中天门

Skywalk Bridge

Hutian Pavilion

Wuji Temple 无极庙

Western Route

Horse Turn Bridge

Sutra Stone Valley

Longevity Bridge 长寿桥

Black Dragon Pool 黑龙池

Eastern Route

Palace of Goddess Doumu 斗母宫

Ten Thousand Immortals Tower 万仙楼

Monument to the Revolutionary Martyrs

Tomb of Feng Yuxiang

Memorial Temple

Red Gate Palace 红门宫

Everyman's Bridge

First Gate to Heaven 一天门

Puzhao Monastery

Guandi Temple

Wangmu Pool

Daizhong Archway 岱宗坊

Puzhaosi Lu

Longtan Lu 龙潭路

Zhaosi Lu 岱宗路

Hongmen Lu 红门路

Bank of China

CITS

Wenhua Lu

TO JINAN (60km)

National Rte. 104

Daizhong Lu 岱宗路

Qingnian Lu 青年路

Dai Temple 岱庙

#6 Pharmacy

Long-Distance

Dongyue Dajie 东岳大街

Bank of China

Dongyue Dajie

PSB

Huashan Lu

Tai'an Station

Caiyuan Dajie

Tongtian Lu

TO QUFU

0   500 yards
0   500 meters

BEIJING & NORTH COAST

Taishan Guesthouse (tàishān bīnguǎn; 泰山宾馆), 26 Hongmen Lu (☎822 4678), within spitting distance of Taishan. Not the budget traveler's haven this place used to be, the Taishan has undergone a facelift to become a typically plush tourist hotel with typically high tourist prices. Doubles Y300-420; triples Y380.

◖ FOOD

Taian is brimming with good food, and the strenuous climb up the mountain is an excellent excuse to stuff your face. **Dai Bei Jie,** a covered street connecting Hongmen Lu and Hushan Lu, is set aside entirely for fresh fruits, vegetables, fish, meat, and food stalls. Hearty Shandong cuisine (basically dumplings galore) is supplemented by a few specialties unique to Taian, most notably **red-scaled fish** (hóng lǐ yú; 红鲤鱼), a species said to be found only in the waters around Taishan.

Zhuanghu City (zhuānghù chéng; 庄户城), 54 Dongyue Dajie (☎833 3373). With 8 locations around Shandong, this place is on its way to chaindom. Polynesian-style decor and impressive fresh fish displays, where you can pick out your dinner while it's still swimming. Dinners average Y20. Open daily 8:45am-10:30pm.

Daguanyuan Duck Restaurant (dàguānyuán kǎoyādiàn; 大观园烤鸭店), 8 Tongtian Jie (☎826 0664), just south of the Dai Temple, at the intersection with Dongyue Dajie. The big white plastic duck at the front door leaves no doubt as to what's inside: a good rendition of Beijing roast duck. Most entrees Y15-30, Beijing roast duck Y28. Open daily 8:30am-2:30pm and 4:30-9:30pm.

Global Bakery Center, 7 Hongmen Lu (☎833 7720), toward the southern end of Hongmen Lu. For those in need of a good old-fashioned European sugar fix before the big climb, this place offers all the breads, cakes, sweet rolls, and even muffins (Y1-6) a sugarholic could ask for. Open daily 7:30am-7:30pm.

California Beef Noodle King USA (měiguó jiāzhōu niúròumiàn; 美国加州牛肉面), 68 Caiyuan Jie (☎825 2751), in the center of town near Qingnian Lu. Heaping bowls of well-seasoned noodles (Y5.5) come with the uniformity you expect from a chain. Also at 243 Caiyuan Jie, about 1½ blocks east of the train station. Both open daily 7am-10pm.

◉ SIGHTS

Yes, there *is* more to Taian than the mountain. There's also the **Dai Temple** (dàimiào; 岱庙). The North Gate is at the bottom end of Hongmen Lu. Optional gates precede the North Gate (Y1 each to pass through). Over 2200 years ago, Emperor Qin Shihuang held sacrifices on the site of what is now the Dai Temple before he set out to climb Taishan. Around that time, emperors began coming here regularly to pay homage to the gods and powers of Taishan, who, as guardians of the eastern edge of the empire, were thought to exercise a crucial influence over a ruler's or a dynasty's fate. Since then, the temple has been fundamentally linked to the experience of Taishan; the full holiness of the latter has been considered unattainable without some exposure to the former.

The main hall, known as the **Hall of Heavenly Blessing,** was built in the Song and is surrounded by murals. Those on the eastern side depict the god of Taishan (often associated with the sun) setting out on a journey, while those on the western side show him returning home. This hall also includes the **Dongyue Throneroom,** home of an engraved stone from the Qin dynasty and the emperors' resting place between sacrifices, and the **Han Cypress Courtyard** (hànbǎi yuàn; 韩柏院), home of five ancient cypresses said to have been planted by a Han dynasty emperor. Well-preserved calligraphic *steles*, some of which are allegedly the handiwork of emperors, dot courtyards at every turn. (☎822 3491. Open daily 7:30am-6:20pm. Y20.)

NEAR TAIAN: TAISHAN 泰山

This is it, the fabled Taishan, the easternmost and holiest of China's five sacred Daoist mountains, a site of both spiritual and political importance for literally longer than anyone knows. Confucius climbed it. The founder of the Qin dynasty climbed it. Emperors and their retinues stood in line to climb it. Mao lumbered on up in his day. Countless Chinese have traveled for miles to offer prayers to the various deities associated with the mountain and to watch the first rays of morning light; watching the sunrise from the summit is considered an indispensable part of the Taishan experience. Trust us: this is one bandwagon you want to jump on.

Western visitors may be a little overwhelmed; well-climbed Chinese mountains are like nothing you are likely to have experienced before. Millennia of tourist traffic means that the natural wonders of Taishan have not been virgin territory for centuries. Stone stairs, built into the side of the mountain over many, many years, line all trails to the summit. A succession of temples and shrines mark visitors' upward progress. Souvenir and food vendors have also staked out every trailside spot from base to summit, and there are enough of them to constitute a small city.

A large part of Taishan's charm and fascination stems from the fact that it is still an active place of worship. For every tour group of Chinese businessmen climbing up the mountain in suits, there are at least five packs of elderly women with walking sticks, making their way up armed with paper money and incense, pausing at every temple to offer prayers for their grandchildren. The mountain's spiritual significance has undergone a startling transformation over the course of its history. Once the ultimate symbol of the stability of imperial power and the stomping ground of emperors and other high and mighty types, Taishan has evolved into a worship center for a mostly elderly and overwhelmingly female subset of the Chinese peasantry. Visitors will see very few men bowing and scraping before the shrines; no one has quite managed to explain the staggering predominance of women among the mountain's pilgrims. But the Princess of the Azure Clouds, a Daoist deity with a large following among women, has definitely replaced the sun god worshiped by emperors as Taishan's dominant deity.

▟ CLIMBING TAISHAN

The climb can take anywhere from three to eight hours. Going up and coming down in one day is recommended only for those who think their legs deserve some severe punishment; the 6600 stairs can reduce the legs of even the fit to two quivering trunks of rubber. Spending the night at the summit and watching the sunrise in the morning is the best of all possible plans. Food and drink are exorbitantly priced but readily available along the trail or at the summit. Naturally, the temperature at the summit is quite a bit cooler than that at the base, and the skies can be temperamental; bring warm and waterproof clothing. Big, cozy PLA coats can be rented at the summit for Y2. It is also wise to bring a good flashlight; the lampposts along the path are often out of order, and climbing at night can be difficult in the dark. Those who find the climb more exhausting than expected can either hire a man-powered carriage for Y150 or hop on a cable car to the summit halfway up, near the Zhongtian Gate. (Open daily 5am-9pm. Y45 one-way, children Y20.) Most hotels in Taian will store luggage for a nominal fee while guests climb the mountain. The ticket gates are open 24hr., since frugal pilgrims often make the climb at night to arrive in time for the sunrise. Admission from March to October is Y50, and from November to Febuary is Y35, payable at the first arch along the trail.

EASTERN ROUTE

This is the more traveled and more interesting of the two routes to the summit. To get to the trailhead, follow Hongmen Lu north from the Dai Temple to the **Daizong Archway** (dàizōng fáng; 岱宗坊), the first Taishan landmark. Built during the Ming, the arch is covered with calligraphic carvings that extol the traditional virtues of generosity and beneficence. Hongmen Lu officially ends at the **First Gate to Heaven** (yì tiān mén; 一天门), which marks the beginning of the imperial ascent.

The next major landmark is the **Red Gate Palace** (hóng mén gōng; 红门宫), named for the two door-like scarlet stones on the southern face of the nearby peak. Temples, littered with money and other offerings to their affiliated deities, surround the gate; this is a good place to stop and store up those blessings before the real strain begins. Next is the **Ten Thousand Immortals Tower** (wànxiān lóu; 万仙楼), built in 1620 and dedicated to Wangmu, the popular "mother goddess." Entrance fees are dealt with here. One kilometer farther up is the **Palace of Goddess Doumu** (斗母宫), a temple that houses a rather creepy statue of Doumu herself, who is also known as "the Goddess of one thousand hands and one thousand eyes" (a shameless exaggeration).

More minor sights (the Sutra Stone Valley, Feng'an Stele, and Cypress Cave) line the rest of the trail to **Zhongtian Gate** (zhōngtiān mén; 中天门), the midpoint of the ascent, perched about 850m above sea level. This is the point where the Eastern route intersects with the Western route, and a veritable village of restaurants, hotels, and trinket vendors awaits. From here, the truly spent can hop on a cable car to the summit or collapse at the busy **Zhongtianmen Guesthouse** (zhōngtiānmén bīnguǎn; 中天门宾馆. ☎822 6740. Dorm beds Y15-50; doubles Y200.)

The first major sight along the second half of the climb is the **Cloud-stepping Bridge** (yúnbù qiáo; 云步桥), about one km past Zhongtian Gate. The bridge offers striking views of a waterfall and glistening streams. Crossing it is supposed to be an experience akin to "stepping among the clouds," though these clouds look an awful lot like vertigo-stricken Chinese tourists snapping photos like there's no tomorrow. Luckily, their enthusiasm is contagious.

A row of prickly sights along the final stretch includes Five Pine Pavilion, Yingke Pine, and Facing-pine Pavilion. The very last landmark before the summit, and the bane of very tired climbers, is the **Scaling Ladder to the Gate of Heaven** (tiānmén yúntī; 天门云梯), comprised of 18 bends and 1600 very steep steps that must be conquered before the weary pilgrim can reach "heaven." By this stage of the game, calling the summit "heaven" seems like no exaggeration at all.

WESTERN ROUTE

Temples, calligraphy, and fellow climbers are much scarcer along the western route, but it makes for a slightly less strenuous climb than the eastern route. The western route begins at the northern tip of Longtan Lu, through **Tianwai Cun**, and follows its own winding path up to Zhongtian Gate; the western and eastern routes converge for the stretch between the summit and Zhongtian Gate (see p. 162).

After entering through Tianwai Cun, the first major sight is the **Black Dragon Pool** (hēilóng tán; 黑龙潭), the source of Taian's famed red-scaled fish. Farther along the trail is **Longevity Bridge** (chángshòu qiáo; 长寿桥), stretching between craggy cliffs. The brook flowing beneath it gives way to a tall waterfall, and the bridge is known by some as "the boundary between life and death." The last major sight before Zhongtian Gate is **Wuji Temple** (wújí miào; 无极庙). Built in 1925 by the warlord Zhang Zongchang in memory of his late wife (whom he hoped would become a Daoist immortal), the temple is a testament to the endurance of the mystique of Taishan.

SUMMIT

Pat yourself on the back, stretch your aching muscles, and then make a point of exploring the maze of buildings and temples at the summit. Perhaps it's just the altitude, but the air here is redolent with magic and mystery. The **South Gate to Heaven,** or **Nantianmen Gate** (nántiān mén; 南天门), built during the Yuan dynasty, marks the very end of the climb. Highlights of the summit include **Heaven Street** (tiān jiē; 天街), lined with shops and restaurants; the **Confucius Temple** (kǒng miào; 孔庙), which Confucius himself is said to have frequented; and, the virtual raison d'etre of modern Taishan, the **Azure Clouds Temple** (bì xiá cí; 碧霞祠). The Princess of the Azure Clouds, a Daoist deity with a fanatical following among the elderly peasant women who make the difficult climb, is the premier cult figure of Taishan. Certain myths claim that the princess was the daughter of the male Taishan god, while others list her as one of seven special women sacrificed by the mythical Emperor Huangdi to the gods of Taishan. By all accounts, she assumed her special status among the deities of Taishan over 900 years ago. As for the temple itself, over 40 monks, identifiable by their distinctive topknots, live and study here.

In the pre-dawn stillness, crowds of tourists appear seemingly out of nowhere, tumbling out of bed and stumbling over to the **Sunrise-Viewing Peak** (rìguān fēng; 日观峰). Unfortunately, clear days are a rarity in this part of Shandong (concentrated mostly in spring and autumn); only the very lucky will see an unobscured sunrise from Taishan. Still, even shrouded in haze, that great surge levitating out of the east, greeted by gleefully pointing and shouting tourists, makes for an impressive sight.

Around the South Gate to Heaven, touts from nearby hotels may accost climbers with alluring offers. Take all of these with a grain of salt; lack of competition, and the difficulty involved in getting supplies to the summit, keep prices high and quality low almost across the board. Try to get a bed quickly, and count yourself lucky if you get a reasonable night's sleep without going broke. The **Daiding Hotel** (dàidǐng bīnguǎn; 岱顶宾馆), at the end of the alley to the left of Nantianmen Gate, is something of an adventure—when demand exceeds supply, they set up beds in the hallways. (☎823 6519. 24hr. hot water. Breakfast included. Dorm beds Y10; doubles with bath Y100.) The most expensive of the contenders, the **Shenqi Hotel** (shénqì bīnguǎn; 神憩宾馆), right next to the Blue King Palace and about a 15-min. walk past the South Gate, comes the closest to Heaven, both literally and figuratively. (☎822 3866 or 833 7025; fax 820 7619. Doubles with bath Y580; quads without bath Y160.) The **Meteorological Observation Hotel** (rìguān fēng qìxiàngtái bīnguǎn; 日观峰气象台宾馆) is to the east, on Sunrise-Viewing Peak. (☎822 6995. 8-bed dorms Y20; 4-bed dorms Y50; doubles Y160; no rooms have bath.) If those options fail, head for the less than stunning **Nantianmen Guesthouse** (nántiānmén bīnguǎn; 南天门宾馆), just past Nantianmen Gate. (☎823 5204 or 833 0988. Dorm beds Y20; doubles with bath Y120-180 per person.)

QUFU 曲阜   ☎0537

Qufu's own local-boy-made-good said in the *Analects*: "Is it not a joy to have friends come from afar?" The tranquil little town likely had no idea how prophetic that seemingly harmless rhetorical question would prove to be. Since Confucius' day (see p. 31), Qufu has seen truly staggering numbers of visitors, reverent scholars, and curious sightseers alike. Present-day Qufu is a miracle of architectural preservation, a rare skyscraper-free zone full to the brim with traditional wooden buildings. In a town where one of every five residents proudly shares Confucius' surname, Kong, reflections of a life lived 2500 years ago still very much appear, the greatest concrete evidence of immortality one could find in the modern age.

◆ ⑦ ORIENTATION AND PRACTICAL INFORMATION

Qufu is compact and easily navigable. Pedicabs or your own two feet should get you anywhere, and the trip is likely to be pleasant. The Confucian Temple and Confucian Mansions, two of the main sights, are right in the center of town, bordered to the east by **Gulou Jie** (鼓楼街) and **Banbi Jie** (半壁街), respectively. One major sight, the Confucian Forest, is sequestered up in the far north. **Lindao Lu** (林道路), the northern continuation of Gulou Jie, connects it to the center of town. The **bus station** is directly south of this area; **Shendao Lu** (神道路) runs between it and the south end of the Confucian Temple.

Trains: Qufu does not have its own train station; the nearest one is a 15min. drive away in **Yanzhou** (兖州). Since mostly slower trains pass through the station, travelers are probably better off making connections in Jinan (see p. 153).

Buses: Qufu Long-distance Bus Station (qūfù chángtú qìchēzhàn; 曲阜长途汽车站), 1 Jingxuan Lu (☎441 1241), a large brown building near Shendao Lu in the southern part of town. To: **Beijing** (14hr., 1 per day, Y61); **Jinan** (1½hr., every 30min. 6:30am-5:30pm, Y21); **Qingdao** (7hr., 4 per day, Y61); **Shanghai** (12hr., 1 per day, Y156);

BEIJING & NORTH COAST

Taian (1hr., every 30min. 7am-5:30pm, Y13); and **Zouxian** (30min., every 15min. 6:30am-5:30pm, Y3.5).

Local Transportation: Pedicabs rule the streets. Rides anywhere in town should be Y2-10; be sure to bargain with the driver and set the price before embarking. **Tours** of all of Qufu's sights average Y30-40. Metered red minivan **taxis** are also available, starting at Y5, and most places in town can be reached for less than Y10.

Travel Agency: CITS, 1 Kuiquan Lu (☎441 2491), about 5min. by pedicab from the Confucian Temple, just east of Dacheng Lu. Follow the red path through the courtyard to the office. Open M-F 8-noon and 2:30-5:30pm.

Bank of China: 96 Dongmen Dajie (☎441 5862), just east of Gulou Bei Jie. Exchanges traveler's checks and does credit card advances. Open daily 8am-noon and 2:30-6pm.

PSB: 1 Wuyuan Tan Lu (☎441 1403).

Hospital: People's Hospital (rénmín yīyuàn; 人民医院), Tianguan Di Jie (☎440 2440).

Internet Access: Zhi Zhuan Internet Bar (zhī zhuān wǎng bā; 职专网吧; ☎445 3559), on Jingxuan Xi Lu across the street from Qufu Normal University, about a 5min. cab ride from the Confucian Temple. Y2.5 per hour. Open 24hr.

Post Office: China Post, 8 Gulou Bei Jie (☎441 2214), two doors down from the Qufu Post Hotel. EMS available. Open daily 7:30am-6pm. **Postal Code:** 273100.

ACCOMMODATIONS AND FOOD

Qufu has a decent range of accommodation options, most of which are convenient to sights. None of its hotels, reaches the soaring heights of value found at a few establishments in Taian; thus, travelers often do Qufu as a daytrip from Taian.

In keeping with its intimate and traditional feel, Qufu offers some wonderful street markets, especially near the Confucian Temple and Mansions.

Qufu Post Hotel (qūfúshì yóuzhèng bīnguǎn; 曲阜市邮政宾馆), 8 Gulou Bei Jie (☎448 3888), just opposite the Confucian Mansions (the real ones, not the hotel listed below). Those in need of a little pampering should go postal. The spacious rooms feel much, much more expensive than they actually are. Economy singles and doubles Y80, with bath Y120; standard singles and doubles Y120, with bath Y260; deluxe singles and doubles Y360, with bath Y388-588. Bargaining possible.

Luyou Hotel (lǚyóu bīnguǎn; 旅遊宾馆), 108 Datong Lu (☎441 1625; fax 441 6207), opposite and to the right of the bus station. Sputtering waterfalls and intriguing aluminum sculptures outside. Rooms with bath are quite a step up from those without. Prices are per person, not per room. Singles Y22, with bath Y120; doubles Y44, Y240; triples Y54, Y195; quads Y60, Y240.

Confucian Mansions Hotel (kǒngfǔ fàndiàn; 孔府饭店), 9 Datong Lu (☎441 2686 or 441 1783; fax 441 3786), opposite the bus station and set back from the street a bit. Hardly as resplendent as the real Confucian Mansions: halls are rather dimly lit but the rooms (all with attached bath) are decent. Doubles Y160; triples Y180; quads Y280.

Queli Hotel (quèlǐ bīnshè; 阙里宾舍), 1 Queli Jie (☎441 1300; fax 441 2022), just south of the Confucian Mansions and east of the Confucian Temple. The architecture is traditional Chinese, but the decor is pure Polynesian. Packed with Western tour groups apparently wishing they were in Hawaii. Singles Y298; doubles Y398.

SIGHTS

Confucius himself, and 2000 years of his staggering influence, are *the* hot topics in this town, and that seems unlikely to change anytime soon. While the tourist brigades drawn by Qufu's sage appeal have injected a minor note of kitsch into the landscape (try day-glo t-shirts reading, in Chinese, "I paid homage to Confucius"), there is much less of a circus feel here than you might expect. The people of Qufu are undoubtedly proud of their link to the sage (one store awning proclaims, "The Seventy-Fifth Generation of Confucius"), but it is a tastefully executed pride.

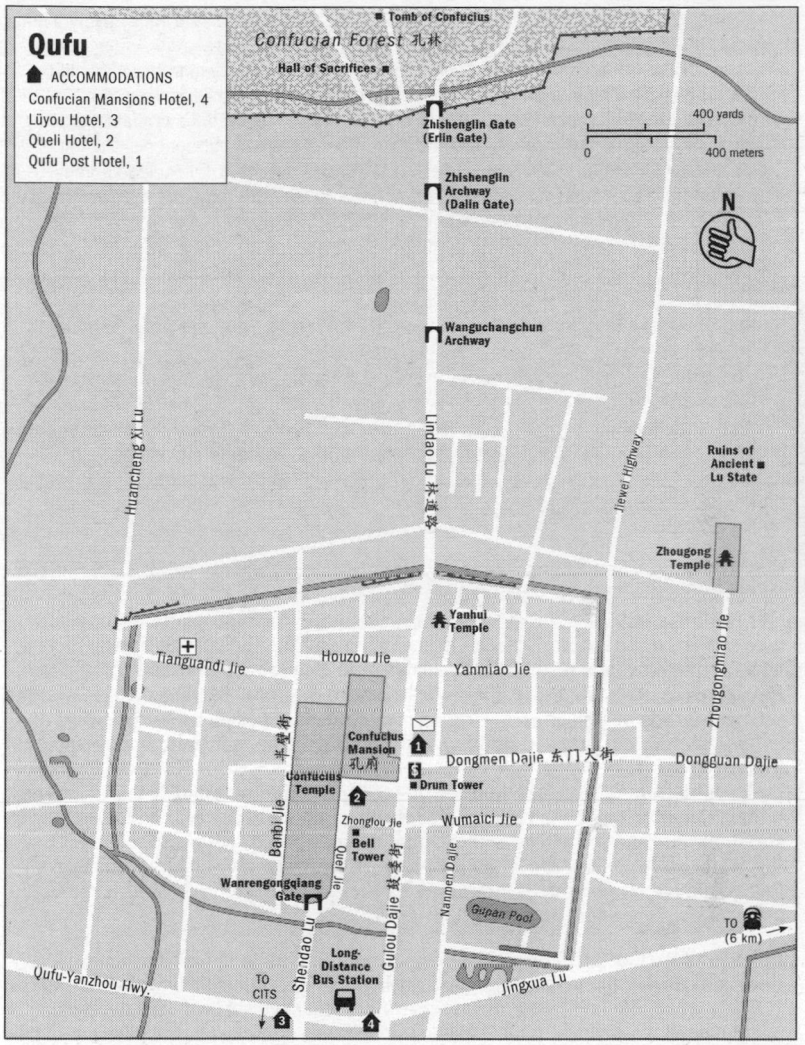

Qufu

🏠 ACCOMMODATIONS
Confucian Mansions Hotel, 4
Lüyou Hotel, 3
Queli Hotel, 2
Qufu Post Hotel, 1

CONFUCIAN FOREST (kǒnglín; 孔林). Daytrippers who overdose on Confucius at the mansions and temple may be tempted to skip this sight, but the Great Sage always recommended resisting temptation, and we have to agree with him on this one. North of the town, the forest contains the tomb of Confucius and the graves of a mere 100,000 of his ancestors and descendants; it is the largest, oldest, and best preserved cemetery for a single family. The surroundings, insulated by a tall brick wall, exude an almost medieval feel; the vegetation is lush, and the grave-sites are mind-bogglingly old. Heading along paths bearing to the right from the entrance will bring you to the tomb of Kong Lingyi, a Confucian descendant (76th generation) who rests peacefully with several wives amid stone statue sentries and towering gnarled trees. Farther along is the grave of Confucius' father. The route eventually circles around to the grave of the man himself, buried next to his son and grandson. *(Hiring a pedi-cab or taxi to the forest is the nice thing to do for your feet. Alternatively, walk north along Gulou Jie until it turns into Lindao Lu; continue north on this road, which runs directly to the forest.*

CONFUCIUS SAY WHAT? The Great Sage, the Superior Man, Master Kong...to most Westerners, he's known simply as Confucius (see **Confucianism, p. 31**). While his role in modern times might be reduced to fortune cookies and tongue-in-cheek jokes ("Man who stands on toilet—high on pot"), his influence on ethics remains strong, although 2000 years have passed since he uttered his wisdoms.

Confucian ethics stresses two virtues: *li* (礼), the rules of proper conduct and etiquette, and *jen* (任), benevolent love or human-heartedness. Confucian morals consist of five fundamental principles in human relations: love between parents and children, justice between king and retainer, difference between husband and wife, order between old and young, and trust between friends. Here are some of Confucius's famous sayings as recorded in the *Analects*:

The obvious: "Shall I teach you about knowledge? What you know, you know, what you don't know, you don't know. This is knowledge."

The inspiring: "If you are virtuous, you will not be lonely. You will always have friends."

The intellectual: "To study and not think is a waste. To think and not study is dangerous."

The outright profound: "It is quite rare to see someone who applies himself to the study of something for three years with having a noticeable result."

The one that never made it into a fortune cookie: "I have never seen one who loves virtue as much as he loves sex."

Optional (but persistent) Chinese-speaking guides Y10. Bike rental within the forest Y5. Free minibuses. Open daily 7:30am-6:30pm. Y20.)

If the trip out to the forest puts you in the mood for more and farther wanderings, a further half-hour pedicab ride (Y6) to the northeast will bring you over wheat-covered roads to the **Mausoleum of Shao Hao** (shǎohào líng; 少昊陵). Shao Hao, the son of the mythical Emperor Huangdi, ruled for 84 years. After living to the ripe old age of 100, he chose a good place to rest in peace; the surrounding area is uncluttered and utterly soothing. The tomb itself is centered among ancient-looking trees; it is built to look like a pyramid with the top sliced off. Tradition calls for visitors to clamber up the corner of the 8.73m pyramid barefoot and pay homage to a statue of Shao Hao at the top. Beware of sneaky tour guides who may spout out information at you without first asking if you're willing to pay the Y15-20 fee. At the other end of the street is a small, picturesque lake surrounded by rocks and two huge stone tablets. Admission is included in the price of a ticket to the mausoleum. *(Open daily 8am-5pm. Y5.)*

CONFUCIAN TEMPLE (kǒngmiào; 孔庙). It didn't take long for Confucius, largely neglected during his lifetime, to start getting his due; this temple was first built in 478 BC, when the soil had barely settled over the sage's grave. Arranged along a perfect north-south axis, the temple is a stately introduction to the practice of the Confucian faith. Stone columns, calligraphy samples, twisted ancient trees, and bas-relief dragons surround the main hall, **Dacheng Hall** (dáchéng táng; 达成堂). The **Apricot Altar Pavilion** (xìngtán gé; 杏坛阁) is said to be the site where Confucius would lecture his disciples, spitting out those maxims that would eventually be compiled in the *Analects*. If you arrive around 3pm, you can catch a glimpse of the daily procession of devotees parading in full regalia through the temple grounds, drums and horns in tow. *(In the center of Qufu, off Gulou Jie, an unmissable sea of red roofs. Open M-Th 8am-5pm, last admission at 4:30pm. Y30.)*

CONFUCIAN MANSIONS (kǒngfǔ; 孔府). Confucius extolled the value of filial piety and respect for one's ancestors. Certainly, his own descendants must have had an easy time conjuring up a little reverence for their own illustrious ancestor, thanks to whom they lived a rather cushy life in the Confucian Mansions. Generations of them resided in the splendid mansions, said to have been the second most luxurious residence in all of ancient China, after that of the imperial family (see p.

118). Many members of the Kong family milked their glorious genetic heritage to the fullest, at various times ruling western Shandong as their own private fiefdom; the halls of the mansions are lined with tributes to some of the more accomplished members of the clan, including the Qing playwright Kong Shangren (see p. 38). The last of the Kongs did not leave the mansions until 1949, when they fled to Taiwan in fear of Communist persecution. Features of the mansions include the **Front Chamber,** where patriarchs lived with their wives; the **Upper Front Chamber,** where celebrations and ceremonies were held; the **Third Hall,** where important family and personal affairs were handled; and the **Great Hall,** where visitors were received. *(Off Gulou Jie in the town center. Open daily 8am-5pm, last admission at 4:30pm. Y20.)*

◪ DAYTRIP FROM QUFU: ZOUXIAN

Zouxian (zōuxiàn; 邹县) is a tiny, struggling town less than one hour from Qufu. Its claim to fame is that it was the hometown of the philosopher Mencius (see p. 31), one of Confucianism's most important adherents. The whole place is something of a poor man's Qufu, less grand and far calmer than its counterpart. The experience of wandering through the quiet, largely deserted sights of Zouxian can actually be quite worthwhile, with the chattering of birds to make up for the absence of tour groups.

The **Mencius Temple** (mèng miào; 孟庙), is on Yashengfu Jie, just a pedicab ride from the bus station (Y3). Knotted trees and a massive bell have their home amidst the pagodas, and the temple echoes with the sound of its own emptiness. *(Open daily 8am-6pm. Y20.)* Just around the corner, the **Mencius Mansions** (mèng fǔ; 孟府) are a green, peaceful reminder of the glory once bestowed upon the descendants of the "other" semi-divine ancient philosopher. Ghosts and remnants are all that remain in the deserted estate. (Open daily 8am-6pm. Admission included in price of temple ticket.)

From the Zouxian **long-distance bus station** on Pingyan Lu, buses run to: **Beijing** (14hr., 2 per day, Y54-75); **Jinan** (2½hr., every 30min. 6am-5pm, Y25); **Qufu** (40min., every 10min. 7am-5pm, Y3.5); and **Taian** (1½hr., every 30min. 6am-5pm, Y16). Pedicabs and minivan taxis abound. For those spending the night in Zouxian, hotel options are rather limited. Spacious and plush rooms are available at the fancy **Zoucheng International Hotel** (zòuchéng guójì fàndiàn; 邹城国际饭店), 62 Taiping Lu, a Y2 pedicab ride from the bus station. (☎525 6666; fax 525 6260. Breakfast included. Laundry. Singles Y300; doubles Y260; triples Y320.) Just down the street is the slightly more affordable **Yishan Hotel** (yìshān bīnguǎn; 译山滨馆), 64 Yishan Lu. (☎526 6688. Breakfast included. Laundry. Singles with bath Y190; doubles without bath Y45; triples with bath Y180.)

QINGDAO 青岛 ☎0532

Qingdao enjoys an unusual degree of name recognition in the West, thanks to its most famous export: Tsingtao beer. Many people enjoy the beer, and even more people enjoy Qingdao, whose charms are as complex and richly satisfying as those of a good brew. This coastal city's green hillsides, numerous beaches, and striking collection of red-roofed Bavarian buildings leave few visitors unmoved. Before the Qing imperial court began garrisoning troops in the area in 1891, Qingdao was just a small scenic fishing village: unrefined, undistilled, and unassuming. In 1897, a German concession was established, and the imperialists began a full-scale makeover of this modest beauty. By the time the Japanese invaded in 1937, Qingdao had already blossomed into the stunning temptress that it is today, with a healthy economy, unique and potent architectural contrasts, and breezy nautical attitude. Chinese tourists flock here on holiday, and foreign travelers are pouring in at increasing rates, but coy Qingdao has gracefully fended off these advances, resisting the obvious temptation to become "touristy." And, yes, the beer is fabulous, especially on tap.

⌐ TRANSPORTATION

Airplanes: Liuting International Airport (liútíng guójì jīchǎng; 流亭国际机场), on Kaiyang Lu (☎484 3331 or 484 2139), 32km northeast of the city. Shuttle buses (departure times vary) leave from the **CAAC ticket office,** 29 Zhongshan Lu (☎287 4275). Open daily 8am-5pm. To: **Beijing** (2-3 per day, Y570); **Dalian** (1-2 per day, Y430); **Guangzhou** (1-2 per day, Y1420); **Hong Kong** (M and F, Y2400); and **Shanghai** (1-2 per day, Y590). International flights to: **Seoul, South Korea** (2hr., 2-3 per day, Y1170); **Singapore** (6hr., Th and Su, Y4980); and **Tokyo, Japan** (Tu and Sa).

Trains: Qingdao Train Station (qīngdǎo huǒchē zhàn; 青岛火车站), 2 Taian Lu (☎286 5741 or 286 4571), north of Taiping Lu. Ticket offices also at 9 Guantao Lu (☎284 3014) and 2 Fuqing Lu (☎587 1814). To: **Beijing** (11hr., 10am and 8:30pm, Y102-213); **Dandong** (27hr., 1:55pm, Y100-212); **Guangzhou** (19½hr., 4pm, Y153-302); **Jinan** (4-7hr., 5 per day, Y48-53); **Shanghai** (20hr., 11am, Y150-287); **Shenyang** (21hr., 10:05am and 1:55pm, Y88-217); **Taian** (5½hr., 7:55am, Y60); **Weihai** (5¾hr., 8:45am, Y27); **Wuhan** (24hr., 4:40pm, Y168-320); and **Yantai** (4hr., 8am and 2:40pm, Y22-36).

Buses: Sifang Bus Station (sìfāng qìchē zhàn; 四放汽车站), 2 Wenzhou Lu (☎371 8061), at the terminus of bus #8. To: **Beijing** (18hr., 9:50 and 11:10am, Y127); **Jinan** (4hr., every 30min. 6am-7pm, Y92); **Nanjing** (9hr., 4 per day 8am-4pm, Y153); **Penglai** (5hr., every 30min. 6:10am-2:40pm, Y31); **Shanghai** (20hr.; 9, 11am, and 12:30pm; Y187); **Taian** (5½hr., 7:30am and 1pm, Y51); **Tianjin** (10hr., 8am, Y126); **Weihai** (6hr., every 30min. 6am-5pm, Y41); and **Yantai** (3½hr., every 30min. 5:50am-5:20pm, Y31-32). **West Station** (qìchē xī zhàn; 汽车西站), 36 Guantao Lu (☎267 6842), just south of the train station. To: **Beijing** (18hr., 10am, Y120); **Jinan** (4hr., every 20-35min. 6am-6:30pm, Y50); **Shanghai** (20hr., 4 per day 10:30am-6pm, Y160); and **Yantai** (3½hr., every 20min. 6am-5:30pm, Y30).

Ferries: Qingdao Ferry Terminal (qīngdǎo gǎng kèyùn zhàn; 青岛港客运站), 6 Xinjiang Lu (☎282 5001). To **Shanghai** (26hr., every 3 days 4pm, Y98-345). International boats to **Inchon, South Korea** (20hr., M and Th, Y1180) and **Shimonoseki, Japan** (36hr., Th 2pm, Y1160). **Lundu Dock** (lúndù mǎtóu; 轮渡码头; ☎287 4275), 21 Sichuan Lu, and **Small Harbor Ferry Terminal** (xiǎo gǎng kèyùn zhàn; 小港客运站; ☎284 4247), 16 Xiaogang Yilu, both have departures for **Huangdao,** Qingdao's Development Zone (30min., every 30min. 6:30am-5pm, round-trip Y6-8).

Local Transportation: Fare Y0.5-4. Useful **bus** routes include: **#1,** from Hubei Lu to Sifang District via Yanan Lu; **#2** and **5,** which run down Zhongshan Lu; **#8,** running from Lundu Dock to the Sifang Bus Station via the train station and Qingdao Ferry Terminal; **#31** from Zhongshan Park to Qingdao University; **#26** from the train station to eastern Qingdao along the coastal Yang Lu, Wendeng Lu, and Xianggang Lu.

Taxis: Base fare Y7.

✴ ⁊ ORIENTATION AND PRACTICAL INFORMATION

Qingdao isn't the easiest city to navigate, mostly because its seven urban districts and five counties are spread far and wide along the coast. The western side of the city, the tip of the peninsula on which Qingdao sits, contains the train station, the ferry terminal, No. 6 Beach, and a number of main drags. **Zhongshan Lu** (中山路) runs from north to south to **Zhanqiao Pier** and is intersected by **Hubei Lu** (湖北路), which leads to the train station. **Taiping Lu** (太平路) runs from east to west along the coast. **Jiangsu Lu** (江苏路), **Daxue Lu** (大学路), and **Yanan Yilu** (延安一路) run from north to south along the coast, eventually crossing Taiping Lu. East of here lie No. 1 and 2 Beaches and the Qingdao World Trade Center. **Nanhai Lu** (南海路) and **Shanhaiguan Lu** (山海关路) run roughly parallel to the coast from **Huiquan Bay** (汇泉角) to **Taiping Bay** (太平角).

Travel Agency: CITS, 9 Nanhai Lu (☎287 0876), in the eastern part of town, on the 4th floor of the building behind the Huiquan Dynasty Hotel, just south of Huiquan Square. Open daily 8:30am-noon and 1:30-5pm.

Bank of China: 68 Zhongshan Lu, next to Parkson Plaza. Exchanges traveler's checks and issues credit card advances. Open M-F 8am-5pm.

Bookstore: Foreign Language Bookstore (wài wén shūdiàn; 外文书店), 165 Zhongshan Lu. Open daily 9am-6pm.

PSB: 29 Hubei Lu (☎286 2787), between Taian Lu and Zhongshan Lu. **Foreign affairs office,** 272 Ningxia Lu (☎579 2555), in the eastern part of town. Take bus #301 from the train station to Xiaoyao Lu. Open M-F 8:30-11:30am and 1:30-5pm.

Hospital: Qingdao Southern District People's Hospital (qīngdǎo shì shìnán qū rénmín yīyuàn; 青岛市市南区人民医院), 29 Guangzhou Lu (☎261 9783), west of the train station. Open 24hr.

Pharmacy: Qingdao Medicine Store (qīngdǎo yīyào qìxiè shāngdiàn; 青岛医药器械商店), 1 Beijing Lu (☎285 9086), at Zhongshan Lu. Open 24hr.

Internet Access: Xinyue Parkson Internet Cafe (xīnyuè báishèng wǎngbā; 新月百盛网吧), Parkson Plaza, 6th Fl., on Zhongshan Lu at Hubei Lu. 25 computers. Y5-6 per hr. Open daily 9am-9pm.

Post Office: China Post, 51 Zhongshan Lu, across from Parkson Plaza. EMS and Poste Restante available. Open daily 8am-6pm. **Postal Code:** 266001.

ACCOMMODATIONS

Cheaper places crowd the train station and ferry terminal areas. More upscale resort hotels line the southern coast.

Fotao Hotel (fótáo bīnguǎn; 佛桃宾馆), 13 Taian Lu (☎287 1581 or 591 1406), a 2min. walk north on Taian Lu from the train station. No need to look—they'll come to you. Hired touts accost foreigners at the station and regale them with tales of cheap rooms and clean tiled bathrooms. True to their word, the rooms are relatively clean and bright, the staff eager to help. Hot water 8-10pm. Singles Y30, with A/C and bath Y160; doubles Y100, with bath Y190, with A/C and bath Y210; triples Y120-270.

Chayuan Hotel (cháyuàn bīnguǎn; 茶苑宾馆), 15 Taian Lu (☎286 3101), next to the Fotao. Almost a carbon copy of its neighbor. Singles with A/C and bath Y180; doubles Y100, with A/C and bath Y240; triples Y120-280; quads Y140.

Railway Hotel (tiělù dàshà; 铁道大厦), 2 Taian Lu (☎286 9927), just north of the train station exit. Not quite as dreamy as the Fotao or Chayuan. 3- to 4-bed dorms Y45; singles and doubles with A/C and bath Y240.

Golden Dragon Hotel (jīnlóng bīnguǎn; 金龙宾馆), 1 Mengyin Lu (☎296 3741), directly across from the train station square and next to the Bank of Communications. Among the more well-kept options near the train station. All rooms have A/C and bath. Singles Y180; doubles Y220; triples Y270.

Peace Hotel (hépíng bīnguǎn; 和平宾馆), 10 Xinjiang Lu (☎282 7851), near the ferry terminal, down an alley behind the International Seamen's Club. Good amenities, but far from the city center. The surrounding area is thick with nautical atmosphere, drunken sailors and all. Doubles Y80, with bath Y170-185; triples Y100; quads Y120.

Friendship Hotel (yǒuyì bīnguǎn; 友谊宾馆), 12 Xinjiang Lu (☎282 8165), next door to a popular Korean restaurant and the Friendship Store. With tacky decor, poor lighting, and a vertigo-inducing elevator, this is a place for the budgeteer with a sick sense of adventure. Public showers 7:30-8:30pm for women, 8:30-9:30pm for men. 2- to 4-bed dorms Y50; doubles with A/C and bath Y180; triples with A/C and bath Y270.

FOOD

While it is tempting to stick to a liquid diet while in Qingdao, you'd be missing out; the food is outstanding. Seafood restaurants are scattered all over, especially along **No. 1 Beach** and **Taian Lu** and **Hubei Lu,** near the train station. For outdoor shish kebab eateries, try the neighborhood east of Zhongshan Lu and north of the Catholic Church (especially **Boshan Lu**). Hearty Shandong cooking (lots of dump-

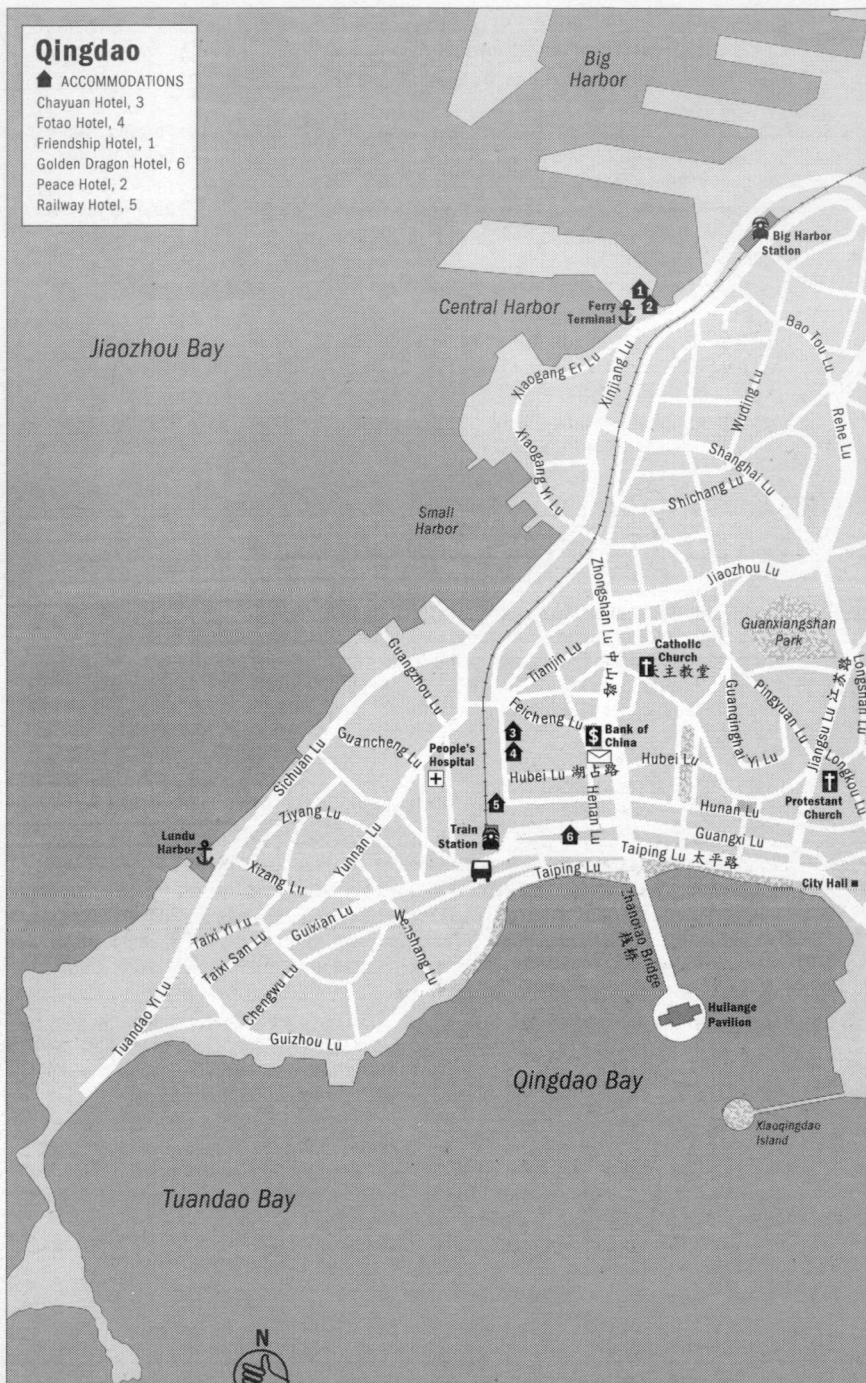

Qingdao

♦ ACCOMMODATIONS
Chayuan Hotel, 3
Fotao Hotel, 4
Friendship Hotel, 1
Golden Dragon Hotel, 6
Peace Hotel, 2
Railway Hotel, 5

Big Harbor

Central Harbor

Ferry Terminal

Jiaozhou Bay

Big Harbor Station

Xiaogang Er Lu

Xinjiang Lu

Xiaogang Yi Lu

Wuding Lu

Bao Tou Lu

Rehe Lu

Shanghai Lu

Shichang Lu

Small Harbor

Jiaozhou Lu

Zhongshan Lu 中山路

Guanxiangshan Park

Tianjin Lu

Catholic Church 主教堂

Guangzhou Lu

Feicheng Lu

Guangdong Yi Lu

Pingyuan Lu

Longshan Lu

Jining Lu 立太路 Longkou Lu

Sichuan Lu

Guancheng Lu

People's Hospital

Bank of China

Hubei Lu 湖占路

Hubei Lu

Protestant Church

Ziyang Lu

Yunnan Lu

Henan Lu

Hunan Lu

Guangxi Lu

Lundu Harbor

Train Station

Xizang Lu

Guixian Lu

Wenshang Lu

Taiping Lu

Taiping Lu 太平路

City Hall ■

Taixi Yi Lu

Taixi San Lu

Chengwu Lu

Shandao Bridge 栈桥

Tuandao Yi Lu

Guizhou Lu

Qingdao Bay

Huilange Pavilion

Xiaoqingdao Island

Tuandao Bay

N

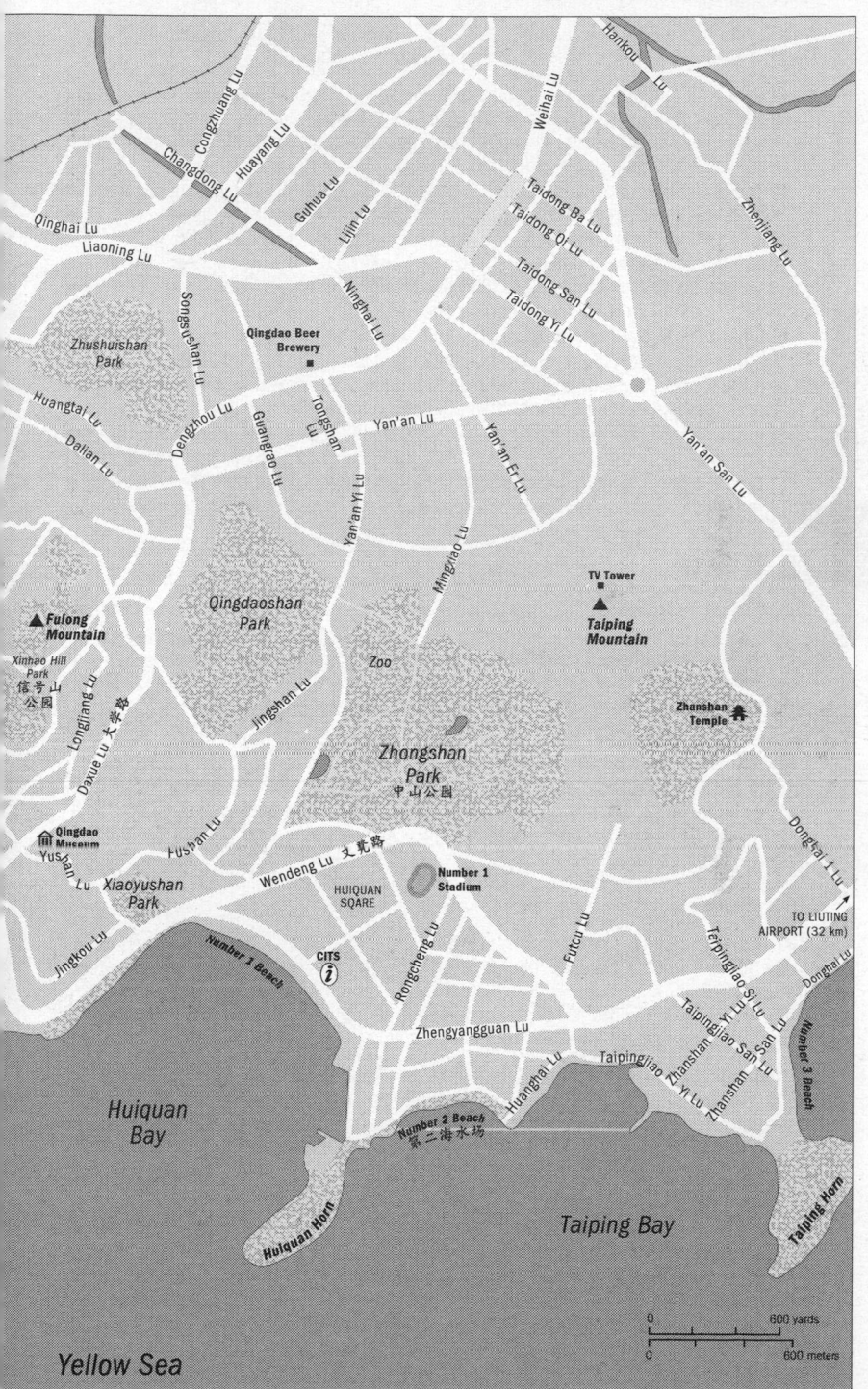

Congzhuang Lu
Hankou Lu
Changdong Lu
Huayang Lu
Weihai Lu
Qinghai Lu
Guhua Lu
Lijin Lu
Taidong Ba Lu
Zhenjiang Lu
Liaoning Lu
Taidong Qi Lu
Taidong San Lu
Ninghai Lu
Taidong Yi Lu
Zhushuishan Park
Songshan Lu
Qingdao Beer Brewery ■
Huangtai Lu
Dengzhou Lu
Tongshan Lu
Yan'an Lu
Dalian Lu
Guangrao Lu
Yan'an Yi Lu
Yan'an Er Lu
Yan'an San Lu
Mingxiao Lu
TV Tower ■
Fulong Mountain ▲
Qingdaoshan Park
Taiping Mountain ▲
Xinhao Hill Park
信号山
公园
Zoo
Longjiang Lu
Jingshan Lu
Zhanshan Temple
Daxue Lu 大字路
Zhongshan Park
中山公园
Qingdao Museum
Yushan Lu
Fushan Lu
Wendeng Lu 文乾路
Number 1 Stadium
Dongei 1 Lu
Xiaoyushan Park
HUIQUAN SQARE
TO LIUTING AIRPORT (32 km)
Jingkou Lu
Number 1 Beach
Rongcheng Lu
Futou Lu
Teipingjiao Si Lu
CITS ⓘ
Teipingjiao Yi Lu San Lu
Dongha Lu
Zhengyangguan Lu
Taipingjiao Zhanshan
Taipingjiao Zhi Yi Lu
Number 3 Beach
Huiquan Bay
Number 2 Beach
第二海水场
Huangshai Lu
Zhanshan
Taiping Horn
Huiquan Horn
Taiping Bay

0   600 yards
0   600 meters

Yellow Sea

lings) can be sampled anywhere. International cuisines, including Muslim, Japanese, and the ever exotic Kentucky, have also left their mark.

Chunhe Lou (chūnhé lóu; 春和楼), 146 Zhongshan Lu, a 5-10min. walk north from the waterfront. The fast-food section (Y5-12) on the 1st floor combines lightning speed with the cleanliness and tastiness you'd expect of a real restaurant; the restaurant on the 2nd floor offers great local specialties (Y10-50). Open daily 6am-10pm.

TV Tower Restaurant (diànshì tǎ fàndiàn; 电视塔饭店), 37 Shangqing Lu, just north of Zhongshan Park. Free buses leave from in front of the Sanbaihui Department Store (三百惠) on Yanan Erlu every 30min. 9:30am-7:30pm. You can either walk up the tower from an entrance on Mingxia Zhi Lu off Yanan Lu or take the elevator. Dine as you spin around at a dizzying height. Elevator service and buffet Y39. Tower open M-Sa 8:30am-9:30pm; meals served daily noon-2:30pm and 6-8:30pm.

Qinghai Muslim Restaurant (qīnghǎi mùsīlín fànzhuāng; 青海穆斯林饭庄), 31 Dexian Lu, between Zhongshan Lu and the back of the Catholic Church. This lively place offers beef tail, beef stomach, and grilled mutton tongue to the brave, with mutton, eggplant, and dumplings for the rest. Dishes Y8-20. English menu. Open daily 6:30am-9pm.

Sun Bar (yángguāng fàndiàn; 阳光饭店), 14 Nanhai Lu (☎288 8855), opposite the Huiquan Dynasty Hotel, near the No. 1 Beach. The sign touting this as a "Western restaurant" is misleading, but the upbeat name heralds good food (Y8-20) and a relaxing atmosphere all the same. Outdoor seating and a bar area. Open daily 10am-2am.

◉ SIGHTS

Qingdao deserves to be seen and savored at a meandering pace. Visitors should not miss **No. 2 Beach, Xinhao Hill Park,** the commercial action of **Zhongshan Lu,** and the intimate **German-style neighborhood** east of Zhongshan Lu and north of the Catholic Church. Every year, beer-guzzling fanatics stumble to the Qingdao Beer Festival (held in late summer), to do what beer-fans do best—drink beer.

▧ QINGDAO BEER BREWERY (qīngdǎo píjiǔ chǎng; 青岛啤酒厂). Qingdao's brewery provides a chug of history amid the odor of hops and barley. Qingdao's most famous export has been fermenting since 1903, when German expats established the country's best-known brewery here. Mineral water from nearby Laoshan is said to be the secret behind the beer's great taste and healthful qualities. Drink Tsingtao—live forever. *(56 Dengzhou Lu. Take bus #1 or 25 from the train station to Shiwuzhong (十五中) on Yanan Lu. ☎383 3437. Open daily 8-11am and 1:30-5pm. Call ahead. 15min. tour of the bottling workshop and unlimited tasting Y10.)*

SIGNAL HILL PARK (xìnhào shān gōngyuán; 信号山公园). This park derives its name from a former beacon that once sat atop the steep hill. The narrow, vegetation-clogged paths that wind their way up to the top are not really for strolling; the top is a 20-minute uphill jaunt, rewarded by majestic views of the city. *(18 Longshan Lu, just east of Jiangsu Lu. Open daily 5:30am-9:30pm. Y12.)*

QINGDAO YINGBIN HOTEL (qīngdǎo yíngbīn bīnguǎn; 青岛迎宾宾馆). Built in 1905 to house the German governor and later used to host Chinese leaders (including Mao himself in the summer of 1957), this imposing, castle-like villa no longer welcomes overnight guests. Sniff the fragrance of faded opulence that infuses every room. *(26 Longshan Lu, up from the Protestant Church and east of Signal Hill. Open daily 8:30am-4:30pm. Y10.)*

CATHOLIC CHURCH (tiānzhǔ jiàotáng; 天主教堂). This grand neo-Gothic cathedral was built in 1934 by German architects. The church suffered serious damage during the Cultural Revolution, but was reopened in 1981. Today it is an active place of worship, with a number of priests and nuns in residence. *(At Zhejiang Lu and Feicheng Lu, east of Zhongshan Lu. ☎286 5960. Open M-Sa 8am-5pm, Su 9am-5pm. Y5. Service Su 7-8:30am.)*

ITSY BITSY TEENIE WEENIE When commentators talk about the hyper-politicization of every aspect of life in China, they aren't joking; even the micro-sized configuration of lycra known as the bikini was once the subject of serious national debate. The bikini debuted in China in 1986, in a Shenzhen body-building contest. At that time, the sight of the nation's precious feminine resources strutting their stuff so shamelessly caused massive contention among officials. The vice-manager of the Shanghai Advertising Corporation, for example, declared that bikinis were "not acceptable to oriental sensibility." In contrast, one of the judges hailed the positive political implications, claiming that women "taking part in such a contest, clad in bikinis, in front of a crowd of onlookers, shows that the women of China, after thousands of years of imbibing traditional feudalistic thinking, are opening their minds." (Presumably, the sight opened the minds of more than a few male onlookers as well.) Since calendars showing women in bikinis were legalized in 1992, advertisements (not just for the cars and cigarettes one would expect, but also for magazines about law and democracy) have featured scantily clad women displaying their (ahem) products. Watch out, chains of feudalism; a firmly tied string bikini is a tough act to follow.

PROTESTANT CHURCH (jīdū jiàotáng; 基督教堂). Like its Catholic counterpart, this stone and stucco-roofed church is a prominent reminder of Qingdao's colonial past. Completed in 1908 by Germans, it houses an intriguing bell and clock tower, which visitors can climb up to see. (*15 Jiangsu Lu, at Zheshui Lu. ☎ 286 5790. Open daily 8-11:30am and 1:30-4:30pm. Y3. Service Sa 9-10:30am.*)

ZHONGSHAN PARK (zhōngshān gōngyuán; 中山公园). This park has a few outdoor cafes and tea houses that exude a relaxed charm, but the rest of what goes on here is a travesty of tackiness. A cable car (Y10) runs to the TV Tower on top of Taiping Hill for a stunning view of the city. (*On Wendeng Lu, just north of Huiquan Square. Accessible by buses #6, 26, 214, and 304, and others. Open daily 6am-10pm. Y12.*)

🏖 BEACHES

NO. 2 BEACH (dì èr hǎishuǐ yùchǎng; 第二海水浴场). Finding a beach in Qingdao is only marginally harder than finding a disgruntled bureaucrat in Beijing. The No. 2 runs circles around its competition. Lush hills hem it in on three sides, and clean sands and sapphire water take care of the fourth. Only the crash and hiss of waves disturbs the quiet. (*Open 24hr. Y2; free after 5pm.*)

At the eastern end of the beach is **Huashi Villa** (huāshí lóu; 花石楼), or "Granite Castle." This old-world stone villa was built in 1930 for a Russian aristocrat and later sold to a British businessman. A succession of Chinese cadres then laid claim to the mansion. Other than the lookout tower, the villa is only mildly interesting. (*18 Huanghai Lu, at Shanhaiguan Lu. Open daily 7:30am-6pm. Y5.*)

Badaguan Scenic Area (bādàguān fēngjǐng qū; 八大关风景区) occupies the surrounding hills, but the scenic attractions are as much manmade as natural. More than 200 European-style villas, left over from the concession era, line the broad avenues that charge through the thick greenery. The area is named and modeled after the eight great passes of the Great Wall, and each "pass" is planted with groves of its own favored tree: pine, gingko, peach, crab-apple, and more. (*South of Zhongshan Park, in the eastern part of town. Accessible by buses #6, 26, 214, 219, and 304.*)

NO. 6 BEACH (dì liù hǎishuǐ yùchǎng; 第六海水浴场). Far too close to the downtown area, the No. 6 Beach is No. 1 in terms of population density, litter, and noise level. It is, however, the gateway to **Huilan Pavilion** (huílán gé; 回澜阁) at the end of Zhanqiao Pier. The pier, built in 1891, is regarded as the symbol of Qingdao, and the octagonal pavilion at the far end echoes with tourists' exclamations and the pounding rhythms of the ocean. (*At the southern end of the city center, south of the train station. The pier is on Taiping Lu at Zhongshan Lu. Open 24hr. 8:30am-6pm. Y2; free after 6pm.*)

NO. 1 BEACH (dì yī hǎishuǐ yùchǎng; 第一海水浴场). Qingdao's longest beach is swamped with tourists, hotels, restaurants, and shark-proof nets. Those who believe that swimming and sunbathing should not be such high-drama affairs had best head for the more deserted No. 2. *(In the eastern part of town, just south of Nanhai Lu. Accessible by buses #6, 15, 26, 312, and others. Free; swimming Y3.)*

⓰ DAYTRIP FROM QINGDAO: LAOSHAN

Take bus #304 from the train station (Y6.5) to Yakou (垭口) or Liuqinghe (流清河), two separate entrances to the park itself. Bus #312 from the bus station (Y6.5) or Zhongshan Park (Y6) stops at Yangkou (仰口) and Liuqinghe. Liuqinghe stops at Weizhu Nunnery, Liuqing River, and Jufeng Peak; Yakou stops at Taiping Palace, Shangqing Palace, Mingxia Caves, and Longtan Waterfall; Yangkou stops at a swimming beach, Taiping Palace, Youlong Cave, Mitian Cave, and several small temples. Minibuses (30min., every 30min. 7am-4pm, Y3) run between Yakou and Yangkou. The last bus to Qingdao departs Yangkou at 4:40pm, Yakou at 5pm. Admission Y40; individual sights Y10-15. Cable car to Taiqing Palace Y20.

The fabled Daoist fairyland of Laoshan (崂山) makes for a magical daytrip from Qingdao. Rising 1133m above sea level, the source of the omnipresent Laoshan Mineral Spring Water is dotted with temples, monasteries, waterfalls, and limestone cliffs hanging over the Yellow Sea. The mountain's Daoist monastic tradition dates back to the Song dynasty, and its significance to the Chinese imperial court dates back even longer. Sights along the scenic paths are staggeringly numerous, and the arduous hikes an incomparable experience. Among the most prominent are the **Shangqing Palace,** the oldest monastery in the area, fronted by a tree said to be more than 1000 years old; the roaring **Longtan Waterfall,** the sight of frequent aquatic rainbows; the bamboo-shrouded **Weizhu Nunnery;** and the **Jufeng Peak** viewing platform. The many monasteries and temples in Laoshan are active worship sites, home to Daoist monks and nuns and host to pilgrims and ordinary tourists.

YANTAI 烟台 ☎0535

Despite its fine specimens of Communist concrete architecture coated with grime, Yantai should not be dismissed as simply a transport link to the marvelous Penglai castle, one hour to the north, or as a ferry connection point to Dalian and Tianjin. A few outdoor markets, beaches, and a neighborhood of well-preserved Western-style buildings give the city a surprising dose of charm.

⓯ TRANSPORTATION

Airplanes: Yantai Airport (yāntái jīchǎng; 烟台机场; ☎624 1330), on Shihuiyao Lu 17km south of the city. **CAAC ticket office,** 6 Dahaiyang Lu (☎624 5596), just south of the train station. Open daily 8am-6pm. To: **Beijing** (5-6 per day, Y550); **Changchun** (Tu and F, Y640); **Guangzhou** (Tu-Th and Sa, Y1540); **Harbin** (1 per day, Y760); **Hong Kong** (W and Sa-Su, Y2610); **Jinan** (Tu-Su, Y470); **Shanghai** (2-3 per day, Y630); and **Shenyang** (1 per day, Y570).

Trains: Yantai Train Station (yāntái huǒchē zhàn; 烟台火车站), 135 Beima Lu (☎624 3917), at Haigang Lu. To: **Beijing** (15hr., 6am and 9pm, Y65-143); **Jinan** (8hr., 5 per day 6:20am-10:20pm, Y36-141); **Qingdao** (4hr., 4 per day 8:25am-6:20pm, Y21-36); **Shanghai** (24½hr., 2:40 and 5:35pm, Y86-188); and **Xian** (16hr., 8:55am and 9:50pm, Y96-208).

Buses: Yantai Bus Station (yāntái qìchē zhàn; 烟台汽车站), 86 Xi Dajie (☎624 2716), at Qingnian Lu, 2 blocks west and 1 block south of the train station. To: **Beijing** (17hr., 10:30am, Y125.5); **Jinan** (6½hr., every 45min.-1hr. 6:45am-5:30pm, Y86.5-99.5); **Penglai** (1½hr., every 20min. 3:30am-5:30pm, Y8); **Qingdao** (4hr., every 30min. 6am-4pm, Y30); **Taian** (10hr., 6:30am, Y73.5); **Tianjin** (17hr., 1pm, Y110.5); and **Weihai** (1hr., every 15min. 6am-6:30pm, Y15). The **Train Station Bus Station** (huǒchē zhàn qìchē zhàn; 火车站汽车站; ☎626 2604) is in front of the train station.

To: Beijing (17hr., 7 and 8:30pm, Y130); **Jinan** (6½hr., every 40min. 5am-6:30pm, Y65); and **Weihai** (1hr., every 15min. 5:30am-6:30pm, Y16).

Ferries: Yantai Passenger Ferry Terminal (yāntái kèyùn zhàn; 烟台客运站), 155 Beima Lu (☎674 1774), just east of the train station on Beima Lu. To **Dalian** (express: 3hr., 4 per day 8:30am-2pm, Y192; regular: 8hr., 6 per day 8am-9:30pm, Y72-560) and **Tianjin** (16hr., July-Aug. 4pm, Y76-214).

Local Transportation: Minibuses (Y1), **public buses** (Y0.5), and **double-decker buses** (Y1) can get you almost anywhere. Buses **#2, 48,** and **52** run the length of Nan Dajie; **#10** and **17** run from the train station to Yantai University via the beaches; **#21** and **22** run to the Development Zone.

Taxis: Base fare Y5.

ORIENTATION AND PRACTICAL INFORMATION

Yantai spreads along the southern shore of the Yellow Sea. **Beima Lu** (北马路) and **Nan Dajie** (南大街) run from east to west. **Dahaiyang Lu** (大海阳路), **Xinanhe Lu** (西南路), **Shengli Lu** (胜利路), and **Jiefang Lu** (解放路) all run from north to south. The area around the train station and the ferry terminal, at the start of Beima Lu, is the city center.

Travel Agency: CITS, 181B Jiefang Lu (☎661 0661), at Sima Lu, south of the Bank of China. Some English-, Japanese-, and Korean-speaking staff. Open M-F 8am-6pm.

Bank of China: 166 Jiefang Lu (☎623 8888), next to the International Hotel just south of Nan Dajie. Exchanges traveler's checks and issues credit card advances. Open M-F 8am-noon and 2-5:30pm.

Bookstore: Xinhua Bookstore, 184 Bei Dajie, at the corner of Beima Lu and Chaoyang Jie. Open daily 8:30am-6:30pm.

PSB: 78 Shifu Jie (☎653 5621), at Chaoyang Jie. **Foreign affairs office** (6th floor) has some English speakers. Open M-Sa 8am-5:30pm.

Hospital: Yantaishan Hospital (yāntáishān yīyuàn; 烟台山医院), 1 Jiefang Lu (☎660 2108), at Binghai Bei Lu. Some English-speaking staff.

Pharmacy: Bei Dajie Pharmacy (běi dàjiē yàodiàn; 北大街药店), 30 Bei Dajie (☎622 2988), in an ornate Chinese-style building on Beima Lu. Open daily 7:30am-9pm.

Internet Access: Meigui Internet Cafe (méiguī wǎngbā; 玫瑰网吧), 164 Bei Dajie, on Beima Lu east of the Golden Gilder Hotel. Y3 per hr. Open 24hr.

Post Office: China Post, 172 Nan Dajie, at Dahaiyang Lu. EMS, IDD service, and Poste Restante. Open daily 7:30am-6pm. **Postal Code:** 264000.

ACCOMMODATIONS

Hotels officially open to foreigners in Yantai are chronically overpriced, but don't expect much pampering—drab is the order of the day.

Golden Gilder Hotel (jīnxiáng dàjiǔdiàn; 金翔大酒店), 172 Beima Lu (☎621 6495), about a 5min. walk east of the train or ferry station. All that gilders is not gold, as shown by this rather sheenless place. Doubles Y128-198; triples Y228; quints Y200.

Dayang Hotel (dàyáng bīnguǎn; 大洋宾馆), 185 Nan Dajie (☎624 3441), 1km from the train and ferry stations. Doubles Y198; triples Y150.

Yantaishan Hotel (yāntái shān bīnguǎn; 烟台山宾馆), 38 Haian Lu (☎622 4491), at Chaoyang Jie. In the heart of what is arguably the most interesting neighborhood in town and within walking distance of the pier and beaches. Clean rooms have A/C and 24hr. hot water. Singles Y160; doubles Y228; triples Y278.

Haiyuan Hotel (hǎiyuán bīnguǎn; 海员宾馆), 68 Beima Lu (☎624 3425), across from the train and ferry stations. Labeled as the "International Seamen's Club," the Haiyuan may not have an especially nautical feel, but it does have surprisingly well-kept rooms for a Yantai old-timer. Hot water at night only. 4-bed dorms Y26; doubles Y160-200.

🍴🎵 FOOD AND ENTERTAINMENT

Thoroughfares like **Beima Lu** and **Nan Dajie** and Yantai's oceanfront street, **Haian Lu**, are strewn with eateries serving local seafood. Bars, including a spin-off of the Beijing's **Keep In Touch** (open 2:30pm-late), line Chaoyang Jie north of Beima Lu.

Jingjing Fast Food (jīngjīng kuàicān; 晶晶快餐), 180 Xinanhe Lu, south of Bei Dajie. Cafeteria-style Chinese fast food with no dish over Y2. Open daily 10:30am-11pm.

Yantai Beer City (yāntái píjiǔ chéng; 烟台啤酒城), 174 Xianhe Lu, south of Bei Dajie and half a block north of Jingjing Fast Food. The beer on tap is understandably the most popular item, but the meat, seafood, and vegetable dishes galore can add to the revelry. Entrees Y15-35, with smaller portions available. Open daily 10am-10:30pm.

Tudali (tǔdàlì; 土大力), 32 Beima Lu, near Chaoyang Jie. This Korean restaurant specializes in skewered meats and vegetables. Lacquered wooden tables and red ceiling lanterns create atmosphere. Entrees Y10-40. Open daily 10:30am-10:30pm.

👁 SIGHTS

While Yantai does not have much to offer tourists, a day here should prove a day well-spent. **Yantai Museum** (yāntái shì bówùguǎn; 烟台市博物馆), 257 Nan Dajie at Shengli Jie, was originally a guild hall built in 1884 by merchants from Fujian. It's worth a visit less for the exhibits than for the intricacies of the buildings, decorated with colorful carvings of dragons and phoenixes, and flowers and figurines inspired from *Romance of the Three Kingdoms*, Eight Immortals, and other Chinese folk stories. *(Open daily 8-11:30am and 1-4:30pm. Y5.)* North of Beima Lu, the intimate streets lined with Western-style architecture lead to **Yantai Hill Park** (yāntái shān gōngyuán; 烟台山公园). The remains of a lookout fort (Y2) and a 1905 lighthouse (Y5) are among the attractions. *(Open 24hr. 6am-8pm Y5; after 8pm free.)* Yantai also has two large **outdoor markets: Sanzhan Wholesale Market** (sānzhàn pīfā shìchǎng; 三站批发市场), off Qingnian Jie north of the bus station, and **Qicai City** (qīcǎi chéng; 七彩城), on Xi Dajie across from the bus station.

🏖 BEACHES

We'd like to think that the local officials who were assigned to name **No. 1 Beach** (dì yī hǎishuǐ yùchǎng; 第 海水浴场) and **No. 2 Beach** (dì èr hǎishuǐ yùchǎng; 第二海水浴场) struggled over the decision for hours. In any case, they did well: the former deserves first place over the latter. No. 1 features an attractive, clean path winding along the waterfront. Be sure to check out the man-in-the-moon statue, in the next cove, a popular spot for marriages and parties. The No. 2 is a bit down the road. Tourists, trash, and fishing boats litter the horizon of this unfortunate runner-up. The beach locals tend to be most proud of is **Yellow Sea Beach** (huáng hǎi hǎishuǐ yùchǎng; 黄海海水浴场), farther down the coast. All three beaches are accessible by bus #17.

🗺 DAYTRIP FROM YANTAI: PENGLAI

Buses run from Yantai to Penglai (1½hr., every 20min. 3:30am-5:30pm, Y8). Buses for the return trip (1½hr., every 30min. 6am-6pm, Y8) leave from the Penglai Long-distance Bus Station, 166 Zhonglou Bei Lu (☎564 2018), at Beiguan Lu. Pavilion open daily 7:30am-6:30pm; in winter 8am-5pm. Y55. Cable car Y18.

The name Penglai (péng lái; 蓬莱) rings with magical associations for those familiar with Chinese mythology. Qin and Han dynasty emperors, including Qin Shihuang and Han Wudi, are said to have come here to find the secrets of immortality and to appease the gods of the sea. In a popular folktale, "Eight Immortals Crossing the Seas," Penglai is portrayed as a fanciful fairyland. Visitors today won't find any hoary immortals or fountains of youth, but the famed **Penglai Pavilion** (pénglái gé; 蓬莱阁), which sits atop oceanside cliffs in all its regal majesty. Built by a

Northern Song general in 1061 AD, this public pavilion has inspired both poets and political leaders. Gardens and temples liven up the long walk over bridges and hills, and the views from the pavilion are a fine reward. The main hall of the pavilion has a golden statue of the Sea Goddess, surrounded by a mural of oceans, magnificent sea dragons, and clouds. The grounds are also the site of a fort and a Chinese maritime history exhibition, as well as the demarcation line between the Bohai Sea and the Yellow Sea. Standing atop the seaside palisades, even the most worn-out travelers will feel positively grand—and perhaps more. Penglai is also famous as the site of the "Penglai mirage," said to occur every few decades. While some see just a hazy mist around them, others claim to glimpse entire cities through the clouds, complete with busy villagers, intricate temples, and mule-drawn carts. Squint hard.

If you're spending the night in Penglai and there's no room at the small inn on the main street of the invisible village, try the **Phoenix Grand Hotel** (fēnghuáng dàjiǔdiàn; 凤凰大酒店), 45 Zhonglou Bei Lu, south of Beiguan Lu and half a block from the bus station in the real city of Penglai. There's nothing grand about it other than the name and the decent prices. (☎564 2074. Doubles Y120; triples Y150.) **Penglai Guesthouse** (pénglái bīnguǎn; 蓬莱宾馆), 11 Zhonglou Nan Lu, is south of the Phoenix. (☎564 2411. Doubles Y60, with bath Y260; triples Y90; quads Y120.) Penglai also offers every kind of **seafood** imaginable, including some beasts that look well-nigh mythical. Small family restaurants line the streets next to the pavilion entrance on **Beiguan Lu** and along **Zhonglou Bei Lou** south of the bus station.

WEIHAI 威海 ☎0631

Originally a home port from which the Chinese fleet fought off Japanese pirates, Weihai became China's Pearl Harbor in 1895, when the entire Qing dynasty's North Sea Fleet, the most advanced armada in Asia, was destroyed by a smaller Japanese flotilla. Now eclipsed by the larger ports of Qingdao and Yantai, Weihai holds tenaciously onto its small niche as a hub for ferry connections to South Korea, which makes for a sizable Korean population and lots of Korean businessmen.

✴ 🛈 ORIENTATION AND PRACTICAL INFORMATION

The city occupies a rugged outcropping that juts into the Yellow Sea, forming a natural harbor with Weihai Gulf to the east. **Haibin Lu** (海滨路) runs along the gulf shore and meets **Kunming Lu** (昆明路) at a perpendicular angle, in front of the ferry terminal. **Qingdao Lu** (青岛路), **Xinwei Lu** (新威路), and **Tongyi Lu** (充一路) run roughly parallel to Haibin Lu. **Wenhua Lu** (文化路) runs from east to west from **City Government Square** (shì fǔ guǎngchǎng; 市府广场) to the International Beach.

Airplanes: Weihai Airport (wēihǎi jīchǎng; 威海机场), 80km away in neighboring Wendeng County, is accessible by taxi (1hr., Y70-80). **CAAC ticket office**, 24-1 Qingdao Bei Lu (☎531 7915), just south of the Bank of China. Open daily 8am-8pm. To: **Beijing** (10:30am and 4:10pm, Y530); **Changchun** (W and Sa 12:25pm, Y630); **Guangzhou** (W and Sa 4:25pm, Y1460); and **Shanghai** (W and Sa 10:30am, Y610).

Trains: Weihai Train Station (wēihǎi huǒchē zhàn; 威海火车站), off Qingdao Zhong Lu in the south of the city. Take bus #1 or 12 from downtown. To: **Beijing** (15hr., 5pm, Y69-258); **Jinan** (13hr., 3-4 per day, Y51-167); and **Xian** (27hr., 8:55am, Y327).

Buses: Weihai Long-distance Bus Station (wēihǎi chángtú qìchē zhàn; 威海长途汽车站; ☎522 2867), at the intersection of Jiefang Lu and Dongcheng Lu, at the terminus of buses #3, 4, 6, 7, and 9. To: **Beijing** (15hr., 10am and 2:45pm, Y142.5); **Dalian** (9hr., 10am); **Jinan** (8hr., every 30min. 8am-5pm, Y79.5-139.5); **Qingdao** (3½hr., every 15min. 6am-6pm, Y42.5); and **Yantai** (1¼hr., every 15min. 6am-6:30pm, Y17.5).

Ferries: Weihai Passenger Ferry Terminal (wēihǎi kèyùn zhàn; 威海客运站), 53 Haibin Bei Lu (☎523 3220). To **Dalian** (7-8hr.; 8:30, 10am, and 8pm; Y60-250) and **Inchon, South Korea** (17hr.; W, F, and Su 5pm; Y75-810).

Local Transportation: Buses cost Y0.5-1. Bus **#1** runs from the Ferry Terminal to the south of the city, along Qingdao Lu; **#2** runs along Huangshan Lu; **#7** runs from the International Beach to the long-distance bus station; **#12** runs to the train station.

Taxis: Base fare Y5.

Travel Agency: CITS, 96 Guzhai Dong Lu (☎521 6175 or 581 8616), across from the broadcasting station. Helpful staff. Open M-F 8am-6pm.

Bank of China: 9 Qingdao Bei Lu, attached to the International Financial Hotel. Open M-F 8am-noon and 2:30-6pm.

PSB: 111 Chongqing Jie (☎521 3620).

Bookstore: Xinhua Bookstore, 1 Heping Lu, at Xinwei Lu. Open daily 8:30am-6pm.

Hospital: Central Hospital (zhōng yīyuàn; 中医院), 29 Qingdao Bei Lu (☎532 1811), south of the Bank of China and north of the train station.

Internet Access: Lingdian Internet Club (língdiǎn wǎngbā; 零点网吧), down an alley to the north of Weihaiwei Mansion, across from the post office. Y5 per hr. Open 24hr.

Post Office: Weihai City Post Office, 40 Xinwei Lu. EMS available. Open daily 8am-5:30pm. **Postal Code:** 264200.

ACCOMMODATIONS AND FOOD

On the whole, Weihai's accommodations are quite expensive, but a few bargains exist. **Shandong University Foreign Students Dormitory** (shāndōng dàxué liúxuéshēng sùshè; 山东大学留学生宿舍), off Wenhua Xi Lu, is within walking distance of the International Beach. The dormitory has a cafeteria, laundry, and Internet access. (☎568 1414. Doubles with bath Y120, with A/C Y160.) The **Blue Star Hotel** (lán xīng bīnguǎn; 蓝星宾馆), halfway down the street perpendicular to Jiefang Lu, south of the long-distance bus station, has tolerable rooms and a restaurant. (Public showers 5-6:30pm for women, 6:30-8pm for men. 4-bed dorms Y25; 3-bed dorms Y30, with A/C Y40; doubles with bath Y140.) **Weihai Grand Hotel** (wēihǎi dàfàndiàn; 威海大饭店), 9 Dongping Lu, in an alley east of Tongyi Lu, is one of Weihai's cheapest two-star hotels. (☎523 3888. Singles Y298; doubles Y348.)

Restaurants are dispersed throughout the downtown area, especially on side streets off **Xinwei Lu.** Small seafood eateries are clustered near the International Beach. Among the numerous Korean food options is **Tudali** (tǔdàlì; 土大力), on 73 Guangming Lu, east of Xinwei Lu. A popular local spot is **Fengshengyuan Restaurant** (fēngshēngyuán càiguǎn; 丰盛园菜馆), 61 Tongyi Lu, on the 2nd floor. Do not be deceived by the not-so-inviting exterior; the restaurant serves delicious seafood (Y10-25) and other local specialties. (Open daily 11am-midnight.)

SIGHTS

Weihai itself has few sights of note, although walking through the Weihai coastal streets provides ample respite from the usual rushed pace of city life. In Weihai center, **City Government Square,** south of the grandiose city government building, is a popular meeting place, especially at night, when ballroom dancers take to the floor. The **International Beach** (guójì hǎishuǐ yùchǎng; 国际海水浴场), on Beihai Lu in the western part of Weihai, accessible by buses #7 and 12, is a wonderful sand beach for strolling, swimming, or sunbathing. Jet skis can be rented at the insane price of Y60 per 4 minutes. *(Open 24hr. Y2.)*

LIUGONG ISLAND

Summer tourist ferries (20min., every 10min. 7am-6pm, round-trip Y20) shuttle visitors to the island from Weihai Tourist Dock (wēihǎi lǚyóu mǎtóu; 威海旅游码头; ☎523 1985), 100m south of the main ferry terminal. There is no accommodation on the island; unless you are prepared to camp, don't miss the last boat back to Weihai at 6pm.

Weihai's biggest attraction, Liugong Island (liúgōng dǎo; 刘公岛) lies in the Weihai Gulf 5km off the coast. After suffering humiliating defeats at the hands of Western powers in the First and Second Opium Wars (see p. 12), the Qing court purchased a new Western-built fleet, giving China the strongest armada in Asia. This North Sea Fleet was installed on Liugong Island to guard against the Japanese threat. However, in 1894, the fleet was attacked by a band of Japanese gunships disguised under American flags. Although the clash ended in a draw, the Qing court, fearing more damage, refused to let the ships see any more action. A few months later, Japanese troops landed in Shandong. Facing enemy fire from both land and sea, the Chinese fleet surrendered, and its admiral committed suicide by swallowing opium. The war ended in the infamous Maguan Treaty, in which China ceded control of Dalian, Lushun, and Taiwan to Japan.

The island gets most of its attention for the **Museum of the 1894-95 Sino-Japanese War** (jiǎwǔ zhànzhēng bówùguǎn; 甲午战争博物馆) housed in the old offices of the North Sea Fleet commanders. Exhibits include photos of warships and relics salvaged from ships sunk in Weihai Gulf. *(Open daily 7am-5:30pm. Some English translations. Y20.)* Visitors had best bypass the **Sino-Japanese Sea War Hall** (jiǎwǔ hǎi zhànguǎn; 甲午海战馆; Y25) and head instead for the six 20-ton Krupp cannons atop the forested hills of **Liugong Island Park** (liúgōng dǎo gōngyuán; 刘公岛公园), on the rugged north coast. The hiking paths are rewarding and the cannons and bunkers truly impressive. *(Open 24hr. Y10.)*

BEIJING & NORTH COAST

THE NORTHEAST

China's Northeast, known as Manchuria to Westerners and as Dongbei to the Chinese, always has dwelt on the cultural and geographic fringes of the empire. The hinterland north of the Great Wall, with its monotonous stretches of plains and wheat fields, bitter winters, forests of smokestacks, and gorgeous but relatively inaccessible scenic wonders, never has been particularly inviting.

Han Chinese have attempted to maintain a foothold in the Northeast since the 3rd century BC, but the region's diverse and volatile inhabitants would not give in easily. Over the centuries, Khitans, Manchus, Mongols, Jurchen, and a host of other peoples fought over various corners of this massive region. In the 17th century, the Manchus burst through the Great Wall to found the Qing dynasty, uniting Manchuria and the rest of China for the first time in history (see **Founding of the Qing**, p. 12). Foreign invasions and Civil War conflicts made the 20th century a particularly tumultuous time. Today, the challenges are of a different sort: massive layoffs at state-owned factories have reduced workers and officials to frustration.

The Northeast can be tough going for travelers. Accommodations tend to be expensive, the landscape dreary, and the established tourist sights not the most thrilling. But those with the time and energy to explore this region on its own terms will discover the Northeast's real virtues: its historical background, its friendly residents, known for their down-to-earth, rough-hewn character, and its short list of dazzling sights.

HIGHLIGHTS OF THE NORTHEAST

LUMINOUS ICE LANTERNS in Russian-styled **Harbin** (p. 180).

SEEING GREEN in **Dalian** (p. 207), one of China's greenest, wealthiest, and most cosmopolitan cities.

TIME WARP in **Shenyang** (p. 201), the former Manchu capital, now a booming modern cityscape.

HEILONGJIANG 黑龙江

Heilongjiang, China's northernmost province, is an industrial stronghold, a place of harsh climactic extremes, and a cultural crossroads—from a tourist's perspective, a thoroughly mixed bag. In the 1950s, the province's rich natural resources drew prospectors in search of coal, petroleum, and thermal power; a thick layer of industry quickly spread over a landscape that had formerly been shaped by Russians, Manchus, and sub-Arctic minorities, as well as Han Chinese. The landscape of Heilongjiang is both bleak, with its unforgiving Siberian winters and city smokestack clusters, and inspiring, with its majestic mountain peaks and sprawling plains. For hardy and thick-skinned visitors willing to scrape beneath the surface, however, Heilongjiang has some unique treats to offer, most prominently the unexpected architecture of the former Russian outpost of Harbin and the forested scenery around Jingbo Lake.

HARBIN 哈尔滨   ☎ 0451

Were it not for the construction of the China Eastern Railway to Heilongjiang province, Harbin might still be the sleepy riverside fishing village that it was before the turn of the 20th century. Instead, due in large part to the Russian-built railway line that once passed through Harbin to link the Trans-Siberian Railroad to

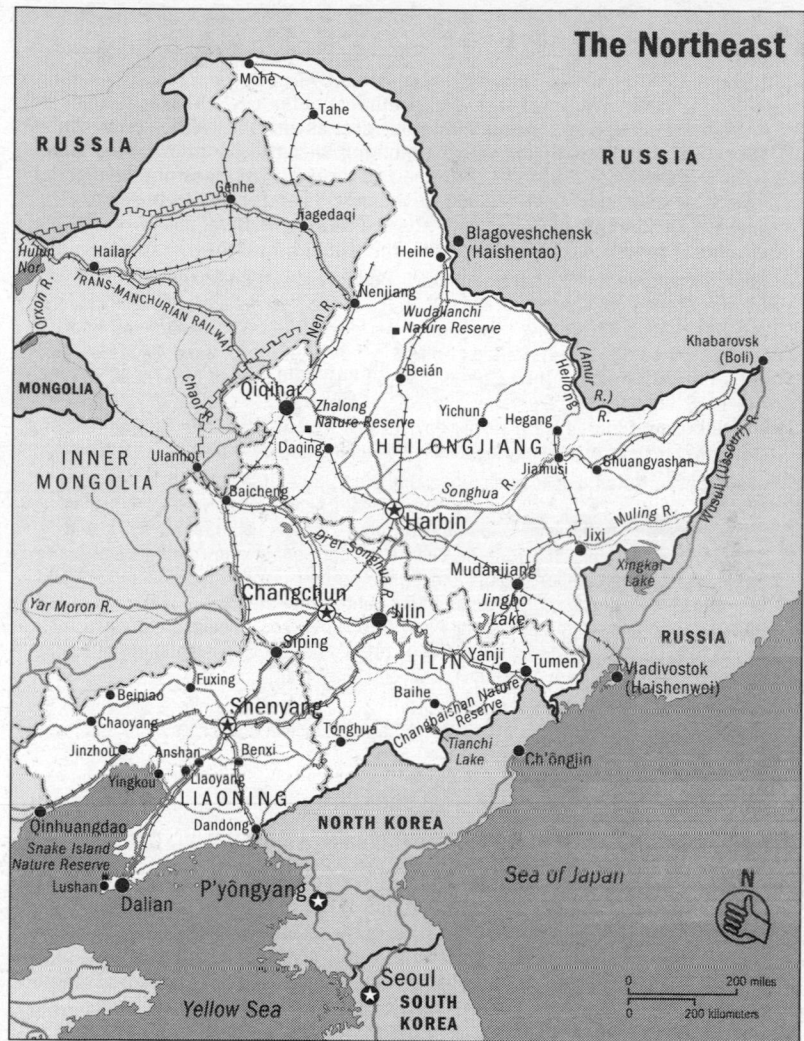

The Northeast

RUSSIA

RUSSIA

Mohe

Tahe

Genhe

Jagedaqi

Blagoveshchensk
(Haishentao)

Hulun
Nor.

Hailar

Heihe

Nenjiang

Khabarovsk
(Boli)

TRANS-MANCHURIAN RAILWAY

Orxon R.

Nen R.

Wudalianchi
Nature Reserve

Chaor R.

Beián

Helong R. (Amur) R.

MONGOLIA

Qiqihar

Zhalong
Nature Reserve

Yichun

Hegang

Wusuli (Ussuri) R.

INNER
MONGOLIA

Ulanhot

Daqing

HEILONGJIANG

Jiamusi

Shuangyashan

Baicheng

Songhua R.

Muling R.

Jixi

Xingkai
Lake

Yar Moron R.

Drer Songhua R.

Harbin

Mudanjiang

Jingbo
Lake

RUSSIA

Changchun

Jilin

Vladivostok
(Haishenwei)

Siping

Yanji

Tumen

NORTHEAST

Fuxing

JILIN

Beipiao

Shenyang

Baihe

Changbaishan Nature
Reserve

Chaoyang

Tonghua

Tianchi
Lake

Ch'ŏngjin

Jinzhou

Anshan

Benxi

Yingkou

Liaoyang

LIAONING

Qinhuangdao

Dandong

NORTH KOREA

Snake Island
Nature Reserve

Lushan

Dalian

P'yŏngyang

Sea of Japan

N

Seoul

Yellow Sea

SOUTH
KOREA

0   200 miles

0   200 kilometers

the port of Vladivostok, Harbin is now the second largest city in northeastern China, with a population of nearly four million. The bone-chilling winters provide the proper climate for the annual ice-sculpting display and competition that is the city's most prominent claim to fame. In the summer, guests can enjoy the cool respite from warmer southern climes. Much of the city was built by Czarist Russia in the early 20th century, when a large population of Russian and other European expatriates lived here. In more recent decades, Harbin has established itself as an industrial center. As a result, the downtown area hosts an eclectic mix of Russian domes, traditional Chinese architecture, and the more typical array of concrete eyesores. Harbin is aesthetically confusing and often startling, presenting the drab and mundane jumbled up with the elegant and exotic. Travelers can encounter the best of what this unique city has to offer in the Daoli District, a well-restored area with a relaxed European feel.

▐▔ TRANSPORTATION

Airplanes: Harbin's new **Taiping International Airport** (tàipíng guójì jīchǎng; 太平国际机场; ☎289 4114), is 1hr. southwest of the city. **Airbuses** go from the CAAC ticket office (Y10); alternatively, cabs cost about Y100. Plane tickets can be booked at the **CAAC ticket office** (mínháng shěng jú hā'ěrbīn shòupiàochù; 民航省局哈尔滨售票处), 99 Zhongshan Lu (☎265 1188), near the Swan Hotel. Open daily 8:30am-5:30pm. To: **Beijing** (at least 6 per day, Y770); **Dalian** (3-5 per day, Y670); **Guangzhou** (2 per day, Y2030); **Nanjing** (several per week, Y1320); **Qingdao** (2 per day, Y760); and **Shanghai** (5-6 per day, Y1410).

Trains: Virtually every train passing through Harbin stops at both stations. The **Harbin Central Station** (hā'ěrbīn zhàn; 哈尔滨站) is at the intersection of Songhuajiang Jie and Hongjun Jie. To: **Beijing** (13-24hr., 7 per day, Y86-308); **Changchun** (4½hr., at least 12 per day, Y20-136); **Dalian** (14hr., 1 per day, Y62-352); **Dandong** (13hr., 1 per day, Y55-140); **Heihe** (11hr., 1 per day, Y56-544); **Mudanjiang** (4½-7hr., 7 per day, Y49-116); **Qiqihar** (3hr., 5 per day, Y39-111); **Shanghai** (32hr., 1 per day, Y276-770); and **Shenyang** (8hr., at least 12 per day, Y159). **Harbin East Train Station** (bīnjiāng zhàn; 滨江站), inconveniently located in the Taiping district, is of little use to travelers.

Local Transportation: Public **bus** routes numbered 28 or less cost Y0.5-1 depending on distance. All run past the train station. Bus **#7** goes between Daowai and Xiangfeng districts, and **#8** runs between Daoli and Nangang districts. **Minibuses,** numbered 50-100, cost Y2. Minibus **#64** runs between Museum Square and Daoli district. **Trolley buses** (Y0.5) are numbered 100 and up. Important trolley routes include: **#101,** between Dongli and Daoli districts; **#103,** between Xiangfeng and Daoli districts; **#104,** Daowai district to the Cultural Park; **#105,** between Taiping and Daoli districts; and **#109,** Daowai district to the Children's Park via the train station. All buses run approximately 5am-10pm in summer; 5am-9pm in winter.

Ferries: Private- and government-run boats (Y2-10) cross the Songhua River from the Flood Control Monument and from the riverbank in Daowai district, going to Sun Island or the Siberian Tiger Park. Boats run 6am-8pm.

Taxis: Taxis between districts cost Y9-20.

✴? ORIENTATION AND PRACTICAL INFORMATION

The railway is both the economic and geographic heart of Harbin; the city is divided into districts demarcated by the railroad tracks. The **main train station** is in the approximate center of the city. To its northwest along the river lies the architectural treasure trove that is **Daoli district** (道理区), with **Zhongyang Dajie** (中央大街) running down its middle. Immediately to the east is **Daowai district** (道外区), filled with street markets and Russian and Chinese architecture. The **Songhua River** (sōnghuá jiāng; 松花江) forms the city's northern boundary. The commercial **Nangang district,** south of the train station, contains **Xi Dazhi Jie** and **Dong Dazhi Jie,** which join at **Museum Square** to create one of the city's major thoroughfares. Outlying districts include **Taiping district** (太平区) in the northeast (home to the Cultural Park and the Harbin East Train Station), **Xiangfang district** in the southeast, and **Dongli district** in the far south (home to Harbin's forest park).

Travel Agency: Heilongjiang CITS, Hushi Building, 2 Tielu Jie, 11th Fl. (☎366 1159; fax 366 1190; email cits@mail.hrb.hl.cninfo.net), to the right of the train station (when standing with your back to the station). Enter the lobby via the Hushi store. English-, German-, Japanese-, Korean-, and Russian-speaking staff. Open daily 8:30am-5:30pm. **Heilongjiang Overseas Tourist Corporation** (hēilóngjiāng lǚyóu zǒnggōngsī; 黑龙江海外旅游总公司), 40 Hongjun Jie (☎360 6607 or 360 6687; www.hljotc.com.cn), east of Museum Square. English-, German-, Japanese-, Korean-, and Russian-speaking staff. Other branches in many hotels in Nangang district. **Harbin Railway International Tourist Agency** (hā'ěrbīn tiědào guójì lǚxíngshè; 哈尔滨

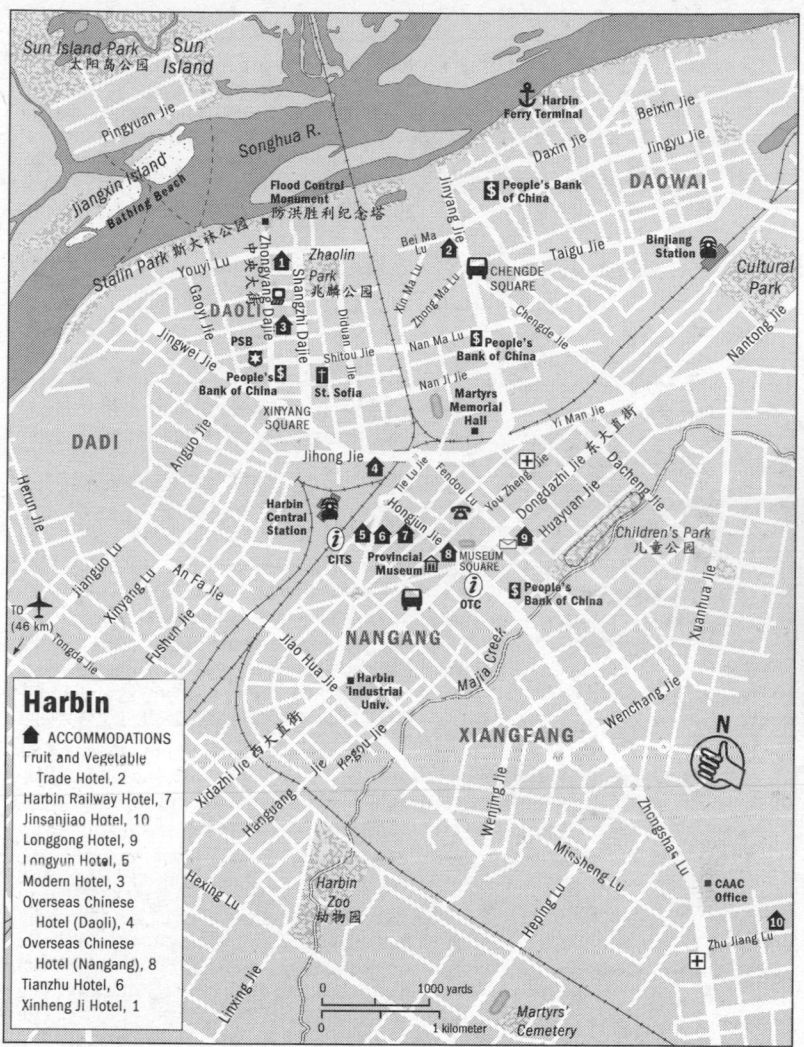

Harbin

🏠 ACCOMMODATIONS
Fruit and Vegetable
  Trade Hotel, 2
Harbin Railway Hotel, 7
Jinsanjiao Hotel, 10
Longgong Hotel, 9
Longyun Hotel, 5
Modern Hotel, 3
Overseas Chinese
  Hotel (Daoli), 4
Overseas Chinese
  Hotel (Nangang), 8
Tianzhu Hotel, 6
Xinheng Ji Hotel, 1

铁道国际旅行社), 8 Tielu Jie, 7th Fl. (☎ 362 1362), sells international train tickets to **Khabarovsk** (Y669) and **Vladivostok** (Y471). Open M-F 8am-5pm.

Bank of China: 20 Hongjun Jie (☎ 363 3518). From Museum Square with your back to Xi Dazhi Jie, take a right onto Hongjun Jie; the bank is a short walk down on the left. Exchanges traveler's checks (2nd floor, window #5) and offers credit card advances. Open M-F 8:30am-noon and 1-4pm, Sa-Su 9am-3pm.

Bookstore: Foreign Language Bookstore, 26 Jingwei Jie (☎ 461 5922). More a bookstore for Chinese learning foreign languages than foreigners seeking in the native tongue. Some foreign language reference books. Open daily 9am-6:30pm.

PSB: 9 Hongxing Jie, between Zhongyang Dajie and Jingwei Jie. The entrance for foreign affairs is around the back of the building at 26 Duan Jie. Open daily 8:30-11:30am and 1:30-4:30pm.

Hospital: No. 1 Hospital (hāyī dà yīyuàn; 哈医大一院), 23 Youzheng Jie (☎362 3180), in Nangang district 1 block from the Children's Department Store on Fendou Lu. Some English-speaking staff. Open daily 8am-5pm.

Pharmacy: Xinyao Pharmacy (xīnyào tèyào shāngdiàn; 新药特药商店), 125 Diduan Jie (☎461 6097), is one of the city's largest. **Zhongyang Pharmacy** (zhōngyāng dà yàofáng; 中央大药房), 77 Zhongyang Dajie (☎461 9156).

Post Office: Nangang Post and Telecommunications Office (nàngáng yóudiàn jú; 南岗邮电局), 104 Dongda Zhi Jie (☎363 8717), just east of Museum Square at Fendou Lu. Film processing and currency exchange. Open daily 8am-7pm; winter 8am-6:30pm. Another large post office is to the right of Harbin Central Station. Open daily 8am-10pm. **Postal Code:** 150001 for Poste Restante, 150000 for the city.

Internet Access: In the **China Telecom** building on the corner of Zhongyang Dajie and Xiwudao Jie; use the stairs to the right of the building. Y5 per hr. Open daily 9am-8pm. **www.hl.cninfo.net** has 4 internet cafes (wǎng bā; 网吧). Y5 per hr., Y3 for subsequent hours. In **Daoli district:** 129 Zhongyang Dajie, 2nd Fl. (over 60 computers) and 55 Xi Shi Sidao Jie, 3rd Fl. In **Nangang district:** 49 Xuefu Lu and 80 Yiman Jie, Rm. 1005.

▟ ACCOMMODATIONS

Many of Harbin's accommodations are expensive, but a few relative bargains can be found. The most conveniently located hotels are clustered around the main train station and Zhongyang Dajie.

DAOLI DISTRICT

Overseas Chinese Hotel (huáqiáo dàshà; 华侨大厦), 18 Jihong Jie (☎469 6584), in a beautiful but dilapidated Russian building. One block from the bridge to the central train station, the hotel is within walking distance to Nangang and Daoli districts. Doubles Y160; triples Y180.

Xinheng Ji Hotel (xīnhēng jī bīnguǎn; 新恒基宾馆), 38 Xitou Dao Jie (☎463 2384; fax 463 2494), 1 block east of Zhongyang Dajie. Refreshingly clean and elegant rooms and friendly staff. Summer travelers can even control the room A/C themselves. Ahhh, love that cold air. Breakfast included. Doubles Y188; triples Y338; quads Y388.

Modern Hotel (mǎdiē'ěr bīnguǎn; 马迭儿宾馆), 89 Zhongyang Dajie (☎461 5846; fax 461 4997), a 10min. walk from the Songhua River and 1 block from KFC and McDonald's. The hotel's location and European ambience attract many foreigners. With a supermarket, business center, sauna, and health center, the Modern is a gem with less-than-dazzling prices. 15% service fee. Singles Y220; doubles Y308; triples Y418.

NANGANG DISTRICT

Tianzhu Hotel (tiānzhú bīnguǎn; 天竹宾馆), 14 Songhuajiang Jie (☎363 4266; fax 364 3720), opposite and to the right of the main train station. Unassuming on the outside, this hotel offers the typical amenities, including a beauty salon, bar, deluxe ballroom, and meeting room. Doubles Y50-188; triples Y35-240.

Harbin Railway and Police Station Hostel (hā tiě gōngānjú zhāodaìsuǒ; 哈铁公安局招待所), 8 Jianzhu Jie (☎642 8540), 1 block east of the central station and around the corner from the Hongjun Jie PSB office. One of the most affordable options in its neighborhood. 6-bed dorms Y30; doubles Y98-140; triples Y228.

Overseas Chinese Hotel (huáqiáo fàndiàn; 华侨饭店), 72 Hongjun Jie (☎364 1479; fax 362 3429), a 5min. walk up Hongjun Jie from the front of the train station. The hotel is on your right, opposite the two glass towers of the North Sinoway Hotel. Staff is accommodating, but the rooms are beginning to show their age, and some travelers find the hall-wandering clientele a bit sketchy. An energy-conscious establishment—with sporadic hot water and A/C. Deposit Y100. Doubles Y100, with A/C Y150.

Longyun Hotel (lóngyùn bīnguǎn; 龙运宾馆; ☎363 4528), opposite the train station. This standard issue hotel provides the expected entertainment room, restaurant, and laundry services, along with affordable rooms. Doubles Y90, with A/C Y104-190; triples Y47 per bed, with A/C Y270; quads Y42 per bed.

Longgong Hotel (lónggōng dàshà; 龙工大厦), 345 Fendou Lu (☎362 1553; fax 362 1553), at Dong Dazhi Jie almost directly across from the post office. The prices tell the story quite accurately: this hotel is quiet, posh, and new. Doubles Y470; suites Y620.

DAOWAI AND XIANGFANG DISTRICTS

Fruit and Vegetable Trade Hotel (guōcài mǎoyī dàshà; 果菜贸易大厦), 42 Beima Lu (☎830 7976 or 830 7977), in Daowai district. About a 10min. cab ride from Daoliqu and a 1min. walk from Jingyu Jie, the Guocai costs less than what it is worth. Foreigners are infrequent clientele, although the spacious rooms all have TV, phone, and Western bathroom. Doubles Y128; triples Y188.

Jinsanjiao Hotel (jīnsānjiāo bīnguǎn; 金三角宾馆), 16 Zhujiang Lu (☎232 7101), a few blocks from the Swan Hotel. Recognizable by its impressive glass pyramid side. Although this hotel leaves much to be desired in terms of upkeep, a dwindling travel budget might tolerate it. The Mongolian hotpot restaurant next door is a plus. Dorms Y20; singles Y60; doubles Y110-160; triples Y120.

◖◗ ♫ FOOD AND ENTERTAINMENT

Local specialties in Harbin tend toward the rich and hearty. **Mongolian hotpot** (shuànyángròu; 涮羊肉) is a do-it-yourself mutton dish; restaurants advertise its availability with drawings of hotpots on windows or signs. Local *jiaozi* are first-rate and available everywhere. The price range of a restaurant is easily determined through a code unique to Harbin: the more **lanterns**, the more expensive the meal. Nearly all establishments hang red lanterns in front. Blue lanterns indicate Muslim restaurants, which serve a range of mutton dishes and no pork. White lanterns with the Korean flag indicate Korean restaurants, notable for a healthy *bibimbap* (bànfàn; 拌饭). The best places to trawl for Western or fast food are **Museum Square** and **Zhongyang Dajie.**

A big hit with locals is the **Bei Bei Dig World Club** (běi běi hànbīng dītǔ gāo; 北北旱冰迪士高), in an underground passageway at the corner of Hongjun Jie and Tielu Jie across from the train station. Listen for the techno music; watch for the glow-in-the-dark wall paintings. This combination bar/danceclub/roller-skating rink should not be missed, if only to gawk at the phenomenon from the entrance. (Open daily 9am-midnight. Y20 admission includes a pair of rental skates.)

▓ **Eastern Dumpling King** (dōngfāng jiǎozi wáng; 东方饺子王), 39 Zhongyang Dajie (☎469 0888). Food fit for a king. Even at off-peak hours, this chain franchise (only 1 branch of the broader kingdom) draws a crowd for truly regal fare. A sure bet (not to mention a well-rounded meal) is the cabbage and pork dumplings. A second location at 213 Jinyang Jie, in Daowai district. Entrees Y12-60. Open daily 10am-10pm.

Portman Western Food Hall (bōtèmàn xī cāntīng; 波特曼西餐厅), 53 Xi Qi Dao Jie (☎468 6888), overlooking an open-air seating area off Zhongyang Dajie. An elegant setting, complete with wooden paneling, skirted waitresses, and European tablecloths. The menu choices (available in English) range from salads and pasta to burgers, pizza, and babyback ribs. Live piano and singing 9-11pm. Open daily 11am-2am.

Huamei Western Restaurant (huáméi xī cāntīng; 华梅西餐厅), 112 Zhongyang Dajie (☎467 5574 or 467 5573), directly across from the Modern Hotel. Almost universally billed as the best Western restaurant in town, the Huamei offers Russian specialties and other fine continental dishes like french fries. Recognizable by the colored lights flashing in the windows. English menus available. Entrees Y16-30. Open daily 11am-8pm.

Paris Bakery (bālī miànbāo fáng; 巴黎面包坊), 4 Xi Dazhi Jie (☎362 6838), and 174 Zhongyang Dajie (☎464 9109). Escape the bustling Chinese streets by entering this "Parisian" café (simulated by jazz music and photos of Parisian sights). Coffee drinks (Y15-20) and turnover puff pastries with such flavors as kiwi and red bean (Y3-6) are favorites of the Chinese and foreign clientele. Open daily 7:30am-10pm.

NORTHEAST

Harharle (hāhālè fàndiàn; 哈哈乐饭店), 52 Hongjun Jie (☎364 1341). With your back to Xi Dazhi Jie at Museum Square, take a left onto Hongjun Jie. Under construction in September 2000, Harharle was said to be reopening "soon"—and good thing too. Local fast food, cafeteria-style; entree, rice, and soda for about Y13. Open daily 11am-4pm and 5-8pm.

Sweet Chocolate Shop, 45 Zhongyang Jie (☎469 3350). For anyone craving that love-inducing, life-giving substance known to the masses as "chocolate." Just keep repeating the mantra: "Chocolate is good for me...Chocolate is good for me..."

👁 SIGHTS

Harbin gets most of its tourist traffic from its winter **Ice Lantern Festival** (bīng dēng jié; 冰灯节), based in **Zhaolin Park** (zhàolín gōngyuán; 兆林公园) in Daoli district. Other winter activities include (surprise!) skiing at local ski resorts. Three popular skiing spots are within a 2 to 3hr. bus ride from Harbin: **Two Dragon Mountain** (èrlóng shān; 二龙山), **Jade Fountain Ski Resort** (yùquán huáxuě chǎng; 玉泉滑雪场), and **Yabuli Ski Resort** (yàbùlì huáxuě chǎng; 亚布力滑雪场). All three are open from early December to mid-February, and trips to each can be organized through Harbin travel agencies. Summer travelers obviously miss out on the ice sculptures and winter sports, but do get to enjoy the rest of the city's attractions in more livable temperatures.

DAOLI DISTRICT (dàolìqū; 道里区). A walking tour of this area is the best way to get a feel for Harbin and its architectural legacy. From the south end of Zhongyang Dajie (around the Holiday Inn), walk north toward the river. Much of the street is closed to vehicular traffic, laid with cobblestones, and lined with posh stores, restaurants, and striking examples of Russian architecture. About five or 10 minutes up the street on the right, live models grace the storefront window of the **Northeast Tiger Fur World** during daylight hours—it's amazing how long these women can stand still. Farther north, the open seating area at **Xi Qi Daolu** (西七道路) lends ample opportunity to people-watch, feast on milky popsicles, and take in the fresh air. At night, neon lights mingle with the stately architecture and the crowds to create a surreal effect. On summer evenings, outdoor movies are shown on a large screen at the corner of Zhongyang Dajie and Xi Shiyi Dao Jie.

At the northern end of Zhongyang Dajie is the **Songhua River.** The imposing **Flood Control Monument** (fánghóng shènglì jìniàn tǎ; 防洪胜利纪念塔) memorializes the civic victory over the devastating floods of 1958; a gold bar on its lower section marks the height that the river reached that year. Along the banks of the river is **Stalin Park** (sīdàlín gōngyuán; 斯大林公园), an excellent place for promenades.

One of Harbin's most impressive architectural landmarks is the **Church of St. Sofia** (shèng suǒfēiyà jiàotáng; 圣索菲亚教堂), at the corner of Zhaolin Jie and Toulong Jie, east of Zhongyang Dajie and across from the Harbin Oolong Manhattan Commercial Building. This massive Russian church sticks out like a sore yet beautiful Let's Go thumb in this commercial area. At present, the gorgeous but decaying church houses no active worship but is home to a fascinating photographic exhibition on Harbin and the Russian influence. The square in front of the St. Sofia has been transformed into a showcase for Heilongjiang cultural artwork. *(Church open daily 9am-5pm. Y10.)*

SUN ISLAND PARK (tàiyáng dǎo gōngyuán; 太阳岛公园). Locals enjoy many a weekend here, but frankly, Sun Island has only modest entertainment options (though a water park of wet and wild rides is open in July and August). Still, the green spaces make for a nice retreat. In the summer, dragons (5 people per boat, Y20) or ducks (2 people per boat, Y10) can be rented for a paddle around Sun Lake. In the winter, an annual snow sculpture show (not to be confused with the ice sculpture show in Zhaolin Park) takes place here. *(In the middle of the Songhua River. Buses labeled Youyi Lu-Taiyang Dao (友谊路-太阳岛) depart for Sun Island from Youyi Lu at the corner of Zhongyang Dajie every 15min.; fare is Y1.5. Boats from the Flood Control Monument Y2-10; cable cars from Stalin Park Y60. ☎819 0365. Open daily 7am-6pm. Y10.)*

SIBERIAN TIGER PARK (dōngběi hǔ línyuán; 东北虎林园). If Sun Island Park is clean, innocent civilization, then the Tiger Park is the raw terror of nature unleashed (well, almost). Occupying over 100 km^2, the park is home to many members of this endangered subspecies. Visitors ride in buses without reinforced doors, as tigers parade by a little too closely, feasting occasionally on live cows or chickens. Bloodthirsty guests can buy livestock to "sacrifice" to the tigers. Binoculars are helpful, and cameras are a must; most likely, you will never again want to be this close to the world's largest felines. *(Minivans (Y10) depart from in front of Sun Island Park. ☎ 409 0098. Tours last approximately 20min. Open daily 9am-5pm; last tour at 4:30pm. Y28.)*

CHILDREN'S PARK (értóng gōngyuán; 儿童公园). This park is a child's fantasy playland come to life, and a great spot for kids of all ages. Inside the castle-like entrance is a 2km kiddie-sized railroad that transports visitors from "Beijing station" to "Harbin station" for Y5. CITS can even arrange a welcoming ceremony for large groups visiting the park. *(295 Fendou Lu. From Museum Square, walk up Dong Dazhi Jie and take a right onto Fendou Lu; the park is a few blocks down on the left. ☎ 367 8325. Open daily 9am-6pm. Y4.)*

HARBIN ZOO (dòngwùyuán; 动物园). As long as the small concrete bunkers that house the various species of monkeys, Siberian tigers, bears, peacocks, birds, deer, and goats do not offend, this zoo can provide some diversion. After the exhibits have closed, a visitor can still stroll around the grounds in the dark and try to guess which fearsome beast is housed in the outdoor cages just feet away. *(95 Hexing Lu, in the southern part of Nangang district. Take bus #10 or 55 from Museum Square. ☎ 634 4230. Animal show daily at 10am. Gates open daily 5am-8pm; animal exhibits open 9am-5pm. Y10, children Y5.)*

QIQIHAR 齐齐哈尔   ☎ 0452

Like many cities in Heilongjiang, Qiqihar was a Russian outpost during the first years of the Trans-Siberian Railroad. Today, it possesses none of Harbin's graceful Russian architecture; instead, it is a confusing mass of concrete, unpaved roads, and construction projects. In fact, if it weren't for Qiqihar's convenient access to the Zhalong Nature Reserve, this jumble of a city most likely would not show up on many tourist itineraries.

⌐ TRANSPORTATION

Airplanes: Qiqihar Airport (qíqíhāěr fēijīchǎng; 齐齐哈尔飞机场) is 15km from downtown. Taxis to the airport take 20min. and cost about Y20. Minibuses (Y5) leave from the **CAAC ticket office,** 2 Minhang Dajie, 2nd Fl. (☎ 242 4445), at Bukui Dajie. Open daily 8am-4:30pm. To: **Beijing** (Tu and F, Y890); **Guangzhou** via **Shanghai**; and **Shanghai** (Tu and F, Y960).

Trains: Qiqihar Train Station (qíqíhāěr huǒchē zhàn; 齐齐哈尔火车站), at the corner of Zhanqian Dajie and Longhua Lu. To: **Beijing** (21hr., 4 per day, hard seat Y98); **Changchun** (7hr., 1 per day, Y34); **Dalian** (19hr., 2 per day, hard seat Y78); **Harbin** (3½-5hr., 7 per day, Y40); **Hohhot** (1 per day); and **Manzhouli** (11hr., 2 per day, soft sleeper Y193).

Buses: Qiqihar Long-distance Bus Station (qíqíhāěr chángtú kèyùn xīzhàn; 齐齐哈尔长途客运西站), on Longhua Lu, 1 block east of Bukui Dajie.

Local Transportation: Buses #14, 101, and **102** run along Longhua Lu between the train station and Bukui Dajie. Daily 6am-7pm. Fare Y0.5.

Taxis: Base fare Y6-10 (☎ 234 9464).

◀※🛈 ORIENTATION AND PRACTICAL INFORMATION

With train tracks to the east and the **Nen River** (嫩江) to the west, Qiqihar's central area is along **Bukui Dajie** (卜奎大街). The area between Bukui Dajie and **Longsha Park** (lóngshā gōngyuán; 龙沙公园) is crisscrossed by smaller streets full of open-air markets. **Longsha Lu** (龙沙路) and **Longhua Lu** (龙华路) both run between the train station and the park.

Travel Agency: Qiqihar Guangda Travel Company (qíqíhāěr guāngdà lǚyóu gōngsī; 齐齐哈尔光大旅游公司), Jinrong Hotel, Rm. 201 (☎241 4553; fax 241 4553), across from the Xinsheng Lu entrance to Longsha Park. English- and Russian-speaking staff organizes tours to Zhalong Nature Reserve.

Bank of China: 3 Bukui Dajie (☎240 9933), near Longhua Lu. Exchanges traveler's checks (window #33) and all major currencies (window #18). Credit card advances. Open M-F 8am-6pm, Sa-Su 8:30am-6pm.

PSB: At the corner of Bukui Dajie and Longsha Lu. The **Foreign Affairs Office** (wàishì; 外 事) is on the 2nd floor. Open daily 8-11:30am and 1:30-5pm.

Hospital: No. 1 Hospital (dìyī yīyuǎn; 第一医院; ☎242 5981), on Gongyuanhou Hutong, north of Longsha Park. English-, Japanese-, and Russian-speaking staff.

Pharmacy: On Longsha Lu, 1 block west of the train station.

Post and Telecommunications: Qiqihar Central Post (☎242 8601), on the corner of Bukui Dajie and Xinsheng Lu, to the right of the **China Telecom** building (☎240 3222). Both open daily 8am-5pm. **Postal Code:** 161000.

ACCOMMODATIONS AND FOOD

Accommodations are centered near the train station and along Bukui Dajie. Restaurants specializing in hotpot (huǒguō; 火锅) and roasted meats line **Longsha Lu** between Bukui Dajie and Longbei Jie. There is also a **Korean restaurant** (marked by the Korean flag) along the same strip. A lively night market on **Xinsheng Lu** is the place to go for fresh, crawling crustacean specialties.

Railway Hotel (tiědào fàndiàn; 铁道饭店), 7 Longhua Lu (☎292 6888), a block west of the train station, past the pink gymnasium building. As one might expect from its name, this hotel caters primarily to train travelers in town for the night. Doubles Y44, with bath Y110; quads Y76.

White Crane Hotel (bái hè bīnguǎn; 白鹤宾馆), 25 Zhanqian Dajie (☎292 1112; fax 212 7639), across the street and just south from the train station. This two-star hotel is better than a two-star value; check out the sauna, bar, and rotating dining hall on-site. A/C and 24 hr. hot water. Singles Y150; doubles Y198; triples Y298.

Military District Hostel (jūn fēnqū zhāodàisuǒ; 军分区招待所), 2 Longbei Jie (☎241 1027), at Longhua Lu. Run and frequented mainly by PLA members. Rooms are spartan but well kept, with attached bath. If the hostel is full, try the **Batehan Hotel** just across the street; it has similar prices but no private baths. Singles Y78; doubles Y116- 236; quads Y304.

Huawei Hotel (huáwēi dàshà; 华威大厦), 50 Junjiao Jie (☎241 4778), on the corner of Longsha Lu and Longbei Jie, just up the street from the Military Hostel. With fluorescent lights outside and karaoke and pool halls within, this hotel certainly stands out from its surroundings. The bathrooms are fancy, but the hard beds leave more to be desired. Doubles Y160-200.

SIGHTS AND ACTIVITIES

The tree-lined lanes of **Longsha Park** (lóngshā gōngyuán; 龙沙公园) offer a pleasant retreat from the bustle of Qiqihar streets. Ducks (the plastic kind) may be rented to paddle around the lake (Y15 per hr.). The park's idle children's rides and run-down zoo verge on the depressing, however. (*Open daily 6am-9pm. Y2.*) The streets east and northeast of the park are filled with markets from morning until night. For a change of pace, wander through the wares up to the **Qiqihar Mosque** (qíqíhāěr qíngzhēn sì; 齐齐哈尔清真寺), on the corner of Rongdong Lu and Xi Daojie.

ZHALONG NATURE RESERVE (zhālóng zìrán bǎohùqū; 扎龙自然保护区). Established in 1979, this reserve is home to over 200 different species of birds. Most famous are its cranes, including the endangered red-crowned and white-naped cranes. During the spring and summer, tens of thousands of birds stop through en route to southern migration areas. Unfortunately, for all but the most seasoned birdwatchers, flying object sightings will likely be limited to the dozen or so caged species, the occasional dragonfly, and perhaps a UFO or two. On weekends, at least a few more visitors flock to the area; renting a boat (Y10 per person for 5min.) to whiz around the lake is a popular activity. A **hotel** on the reserve grounds also has a restaurant. (☎452 0024. Doubles Y320; triples Y180-270; quads Y360.) Casual visitors generally beat a fairly hasty retreat. *(26km southeast of Qiqihar. Buses leave for the 30min. ride from the Qiqihar Long-distance Bus Station at 9am, 11:30am, and 3:30pm, with fewer departures on weekdays; round-trip fare Y10. Taxis can be hired for Y35-40 one-way. Y10.)*

WUDALIANCHI 五大连池 ☎0456

Wudalianchi—literally "the five great linked lakes"—is home to 38 sanitoria, 14 volcanoes, and five lakes that formed when a volcanic eruption close to three centuries ago stopped up the nearby Bai River. Unless you are a geological enthusiast, though, you might consider spending your time elsewhere. The scenery is less exceptional than the "Nature Reserve" designation suggests, although those who do make the trek will find extensive vistas of the entire area from the summit of one of the accessible volcanoes.

Of the 14 volcanoes in the Wudalianchi area, **Black Dragon Mountain** (hēi lóng shān; 黑龙山) and **Fire Burnt Mountain** (huǒ shāo shān; 火烧山) offer the best views of the five lakes in the valley below. The volcanoes last erupted from 1719 to 1721. Today, kilometers of black jagged lava fields skirt each volcano. **White Dragon Cave** (bái lóng dòng; 白龙洞), an underground ice cave, houses fluorescent ice sculptures reminiscent of those in the famous Harbin Ice Festival. Don't be fooled; the cave is a real tourist trap. *(Minivans and motorcycle taxis give tour prices of Y150 and up; Y80 is reasonable. Admission to each site Y10-15.)*

Don't expect to know it when you have arrived in Wudalianchi—the village consists of one intersection with a traffic circle in the middle. **Long-distance buses** arrive and depart from the traffic circle or from the adjacent parking lot of the general store. Buses make the trip to Wudalianchi from: Beian (1½-2hr., 4 per day, Y10.5); Heihe (7hr., 5:40am, Y38.5); and Zhanhe (45min., 2 per day, Y10). There is a **first aid center** and **post office** in the village. Two hostels at the main intersection accept foreigners. The **Rice Paddy Hotel** (shuǐ hétián jiǔdiàn; 水禾田酒店), next to the general store, has dorms with public bathrooms. (☎722 2837. 4-bed dorms Y15.) Around the corner, the **Yingbin Hotel** (yíngbīn lǚdiàn; 迎宾旅店), provides similar facilities (Y10). Both have restaurants attached, and small restaurants abound on the main street, at the other side of the traffic circle.

MUDANJIANG 牡丹江 ☎0453

Mudanjiang is a moderately sized city five hours southeast of Harbin. Foreigners rarely visit here, and those that do are usually passing through en route to Jingbo Lake. Nevertheless, there are a few reasonably priced hotels from which to choose and some lively street markets to peruse.

▐ TRANSPORTATION. Transportation in the region is sparse, and trains are generally the most reliable means of travel. **Mudanjiang Airport** (mǔdānjiāng jīchǎng; 牡丹江机场), 10km south of the city, has flights to: Beijing (1-2 per day, Y950); Guangzhou (2 per week, Y2080); and Shanghai (2 per week, Y1460). CAAC airport buses (depart 1½hr. before flight, Y10) leave from the **CAAC Ticket Office,** at the corner of Dong Ertiao Lu and Aimin Jie. (☎693 9627. Open daily 7:30am-5pm.) Trains from the **Mudanjiang Train Station** (mǔdānjiāng huǒchē zhàn; 牡丹江火车站), at the intersection of Guanghua Lu and Taiping Lu, go to: Beijing (26hr., 1 per day, Y79-550); Dalian (10¾hr., 1 per day, Y65-217); Harbin (4½-7hr., 7 per day, Y21-50); Shenyang (12¼hr., 1 per day); and Tumen (6hr., 1 per day, Y33). **Mudanjiang Bus Station** (mǔdānjiāng qìchē zhàn; 牡丹江汽车站) is in the parking lot outside the train station. **Minibuses** to Jingbo Lake (2-4hr.) leave from the left parking lot (facing away from the train station) daily at 7am (same day return by 4pm, Y20 round-trip). To stay overnight at Jingbo Lake, hire a taxi (Y400).

■ ✦ ORIENTATION AND PRACTICAL INFORMATION. Mudanjiang is cut roughly in half by the train tracks. **Taiping Lu** (太平路) runs from north to south, and **Guanghua Lu** (光华路) runs from east to west, forming the commercial district.

CITS, 34 Jingfu Lu, between Dong Yitiao Lu and Dong Ertiao Lu, is the best place to organize a trip to Jingbo Lake or Changbaishan in Jilin province. (☎695 0062; fax 695 0064. Open daily 8am-5pm.) **Bank of China,** on Taiping Lu 200m from the train station, exchanges traveler's checks (window #3) and offers credit card advances (window #9). (Open daily 9am-4:30pm; window #3 open until 3:30pm.) The **PSB** is at 96 Guanghua Lu. **No. 2 People's Hospital** is at the corner of Taiping Lu and Pingan Jie, 50m from the China Telecom office. **China Telecom,** on Taiping Lu, at Aimin Jie, has no 24hr. phone booths. (Open daily 8am-5:30pm; in winter 8am-5pm.) The **postal code** is 157000.

■ ✦ ACCOMMODATIONS AND FOOD. Most cheap, foreigner-friendly hotels are within a 10 minutes walk from the train station. **Fengyanglou Hostel** (fēngyánglóu lǚdiàn; 凤阳楼旅店), 86 Rizhao Jie, one block from the train station, provides homey accommodations at unbeatable prices, and can also organize minibuses to Jingbo Lake (Y30 round-trip). (☎622 5553. Doubles with bath Y60; triples Y45; quads Y48.) **Dongfang Hotel** (dōngfāng fàndiàn; 东方饭店), 123 Guanghua Lu, east of the train station and across the street from the PSB, has relatively clean and comfortable rooms. (☎692 6341. Breakfast included. Doubles Y98, with bath and A/C Y228; triples Y218.) **Mudanjiang Hotel** (mǔdānjiāng fàndiàn; 牡丹江饭店), 85 Guanghua Lu, about 800m to the left and across the street from the train station, offers typical Chinese two-star accommodations. (☎692 5631. Doubles Y136.)

Many small restaurants dot the side streets off Taiping Lu and Guanghua Lu; most of the department stores along Taiping Lu also have food halls. Night markets in this area offer the possibility of open-air meals in the summer. The *xiangla tudoutiao* ("Delicious Spicy Potato" dish) and dumplings at the **Golden Chopsticks Big Filling Dumpling Restaurant** (jīn kuàizi dà xiàn jiǎozi cūn; 金筷子大馅饺子村), 5 Shizheng Lu (☎628 9561), are special treats.

JINGBO LAKE 镜泊河   ☎0453

Jingbo, or "Mirror" Lake, south of Mudanjiang, was formed on a bend of the Mudan River by volcanic explosions over 5000 years ago. While the lake and the surrounding scenery has its beauty, a visit today is likely to be highly commercialized, with swarms of motorboats and tourists dampening the natural splendor. Winter weather makes Jingbo inaccessible (not to mention inhospitable) for much of the year. Although tourists are fewer and prices are cheaper in the off season (May and June), many of the lake's attractions are open only during July and August.

■ ✦ ORIENTATION AND PRACTICAL INFORMATION. The historic entrance to Jingbo Lake has been replaced recently by a more modern front gate. From there, roads encircle the lake, and well-placed signs in Chinese direct traffic. **Jingbo Village,** the main tourist access point, with parking lots, a beach, and a dock, is on the northern shore.

The nearest **train station** is in Dongjing. Trains travel between Dongjing and Mudanjiang (1¾-2hr., 2 per day, Y4). **Minibuses** travel from the lake to Mudanjiang Train Station and Dongjing. The public minibuses are often teeming with Chinese tour groups; those who don't care to jump on the tourist bandwagon can hire a taxi or leave the group upon arrival. There is a **first aid center** and **post office** in Jingbo Village, near the Shanzhuang Hotel.

■ ✦ ACCOMMODATIONS AND FOOD. Many hotels do not open until June 1; verify in advance. That said, rates are significantly cheaper in May and June than they are later in the summer. Many hotels have decent restaurants on-site. The **Shanzhuang Hotel** (shānzhuāng bīnguǎn; 山庄宾馆) is in Jingbo Village, near the lake, past the post office. (☎627 0012. Open June-Sept. 3-bed dorms Y50; doubles Y100, weekends Y150.) The **Jingbo Lake Hotel** (jìngbó hú bīnguǎn; 镜泊胡宾馆), beyond the Shanzhuang Hotel and up a hill to the right, is quick to announce that

President Jiang Zemin and Premier Li Peng have hung their hats in the luxurious Presidential Suite (Y5800). Frequent the sauna, the karaoke bar, and the bowling alley, and enjoy what must be presidential treatment. (☎627 0091. 50% discount May-June. Doubles Y380.)

🔲🔳 SIGHTS AND ENTERTAINMENT. Although **Jingbo Lake** (jìngbó hú; 镜泊湖) is about 50km long, most tourist facilities are in Jingbo Village on the northeastern shore. From behind the souvenir shops, a path passes several attractive villas, including the decades-old villa of former President Liu Shaoqi, ending at the small **Shaoqi Fishing Pavilion.** Jet skis are available on the beach to the left of the pavilion when you are facing the lake (Y10 per min.). Hour-long boat trips also run out of Jingbo Village (Y30, Y50 for 2 people), and sunbathers and swimmers crowd the beach on warm afternoons. *(Off-season vehicle fee Y20 for cars, Y30 for buses and mini-buses. During peak season, admission Y2-8 more.)*

The **Diaoshui Lou Waterfall** (diàoshuǐ lóu pùbù; 掉水楼瀑布) was formed from a volcanic eruption about 10,000 years ago. The eruption left a crater 60m deep, and in mid-summer, water from the river cascades over lava rock and into the crater. Souvenir vendors hawk live turtles (Y65)—no fossilized remains here. From the top of a hill facing the waterfall, visitors can take a cable car to a **Korean minority village** (20min., Y30).

HEIHE 黑河

Heihe sits on the border with Russia, across the Black River from Blagoveshchensk. Other than the fact that foreigners are often assumed to be Russian and the presence of the occasional street market selling Russian wares, there are few reminders of Heihe's strategic location. Head to Black River Island, however, and the huge trading market, the immigration and customs buildings, and the views of Russian architecture across the river recall where you are.

🔳🔳 ORIENTATION AND PRACTICAL INFORMATION. Streets are arranged in a grid pattern. The train station is quite far from the city center, but most other places are within walking distance. Many of the shops and services cluster around the banks of the Black River (hēi hé; 黑河), the town's namesake. **Heihe Train Station** (hēihé huǒchē zhàn; 黑河火车站) is on the end of Tongjiang Lu, accessible by taxi (Y5) from the town center. Trains go to Beian (7hr., 2 per day), Harbin (11hr., 1 per day), and Qiqihar (11hr., 1 per day). The **Heihe Long-distance Bus Station** (hēihé kèyùn zhàn; 黑河客运站; ☎226 6422), on Xixing Lu, near Huancheng Lu, has buses to Wudalianchi (7hr., 5:40am, Y38.5). **Taxis** to most areas cost Y5-10.

CITS, 148 Wenhua Jie, 2nd floor (☎822 4921), can arrange tours of the area but not Russian visas. **Russian visas** should be arranged at the Russian consulate in Shenyang (see **Consulates,** p. 202), although some travelers report being able to buy day visas at the border for a hefty Y700. The **Bank of China,** 169 Wenhua Jie, at Xundu Lu, exchanges traveler's checks. (Open daily M-Sa 8am-5pm; in winter 8am-4pm; Su year-round 9am-2:30pm.) The **PSB** is at 2 Xundu Lu. (☎826 6648. Open M-F 8am-5pm.) The **District People's Hospital** (dìqū rénmín yīyuàn; 地区人民医院) is on Xingan Jie, at Dongxing Lu, and the **Heihe Pharmacy** (hēihé shì yīyuàn shāngdiàn; 黑河市医院商店) is on Zhongyang Jie, between Youzheng Lu and Xundu Lu. **Internet access** for Y2 per hour is available in the building behind the post office, on Zhongyang Jie. The **post office** is at 168 Wenhua Jie. (Open daily 7:30am-5pm; in winter 8am-4:30pm.) The **postal code** is 164300.

🔳🔳 ACCOMMODATIONS AND FOOD. The **Tianlong Hotel** (tiānlóng bīnguǎn; 天龙宾馆) is to the left of the train station as you exit. (☎822 7795. Doubles Y35, with bath Y55.) In town, the **Caizheng Hotel** (cáizhèng bīnguǎn; 财政宾馆), on Wenhua Jie at Dongxing Lu, has fairly clean rooms, although the water supply may be somewhat erratic. (Doubles with bath Y132.) Some food stands are scattered around the train station and along Wenhua Jie in town.

🎦 **SIGHTS.** The **Black River waterfront promenade** affords views of Russia. In the summer, many locals swim or bathe in the river. One-hour river cruises are also available (Y10 per person). During the day, the **Russian Wares Street** (éluósí shāngpǐn jiē; 俄罗斯商品街), on Hailan Jie between Dongxing Lu and Gongyuan Lu, is lined by vendors selling Russian dolls, hats, and furs (of more questionable Russian origins). **Big Black River Island** (dà hēi hé dǎo; 大黑河岛) contains the immigration and customs facilities and is the departure point for daily boats to the Russian towns on the other side of the river. The **Heihe Black River International Market** (hēihé shì cháng hēi hé dǎo guójì màochéng; 黑河市长黑河岛国际贸城), a huge indoor market, sells more of those Russian trinkets. *(Open M-Sa 8:10am-5pm, Su 8:30am-4pm.)*

JILIN 吉林

Much like its northern neighbor Heilongjiang, Jilin province is an ambiguous blend of industrial banality and cultural and scenic surprises. Formerly known as Kirin, the area was once the home of the Hurka tribe, steppe- and forest-dwellers who offered furs and ginseng as tribute at the Ming court. By the late 16th century, the Manchus had conquered the region, and Han Chinese began settling here by the 18th century. These days, the sooty cities of Jilin and Changchun can be haunting or dreary, depending on how you look at it. The stunning mountain scenery of Changbaishan, however, justifiably attracts scores of tourists, and ethnic Korean villages along the North Korean border help to break up Jilin's cultural monotony.

CHANGCHUN 长春   ☎ 0431

Changchun's name means "eternal spring." While this designation seems to ignore the reality of the region's frigid winters, the capital of Jilin province is indeed an unexpected mixture of greenery and urbanity. Dubbed both the "Detroit of China" and the "Hollywood of China," Changchun is an awkward but lovable mess of contradictions, known for both its industrial utility and its role in the development of Chinese film. During the Japanese occupation from 1931 to 1945, Changchun was the capital of the Japanese-ruled state of Manchukuo; the palace from which the puppet emperor Puyi ruled the region remains. Changchun's broad avenues and vibrant commercial centers indicate that the city is taking care not to dwell too heavily on its past as it surges toward its own unique brand of hyper-modernity.

▗ TRANSPORTATION

Airplanes: Changchun Airport (chángchūn jīchǎng, 长春机场), 28 Luyuan Chuyingbin Lu (☎ 798 7855), west of the city. **CAAC ticket office,** 23-1 Changbai Lu, 2nd Fl. (☎ 298 8888), between the train station and the Post Hotel. Open daily 8am-4:30pm. To: **Beijing** (5 per day, Y770); **Chengdu** (1 per day, Y1630); **Dalian** (2 per day, Y460); **Fuzhou** (1 per day, Y1450); **Guangzhou** (2 per day, Y1950); **Nanjing** (2 per day, Y1170); **Qingdao** (1 per day, Y640); **Shanghai** (3 per day, Y1280); and **Yantai** (1 per day, Y640).

Trains: Changchun Train Station (chángchūn huǒchē zhàn; 长春火车站), 1 Changbai Lu (☎ 282 4022), at the north end of Renmin Dajie. To: **Beijing** (14hr., 9 per day, Y83-249); **Dalian** (11hr., 7 per day, Y61-183); **Dandong** (10hr., 1 per day, Y71); **Harbin** (3½-4hr., 11 per day, Y61-183); **Jilin** (2hr., 6 per day, Y17-26); **Shanghai** (28hr., 2 per day, Y158-437); **Shenyang** (4-5hr., 4 per day, Y20-28); **Tonghua** (8hr., 2 per day, Y21-48); **Tumen** (10hr., 4 per day, Y32-43); and **Yanji** (8hr., 3 per day, Y29-39).

Buses: Changchun Central Bus Station (chángchūn gōnglù kèyùn zhōngxīn zhàn; 长春公路客运中心站), 6 Renmin Dajie (☎ 279 2547), just south of the train station. To: **Beijing** (1 per day, Y180); **Dalian** (8hr., 3 per day, Y157); **Dunhua** (6hr., 4 per day, Y38.3); **Erduobaihe** (6am, Y52); **Harbin** (4½hr., every 15min. 5:30am-5pm, Y40); **Jilin** (1½hr., every 30min. 5:30am-6pm, Y14.5); **Shenyang** (3½hr., every hr. noon-5pm, Y70); and **Yanji** (1 per day, Y103-109). Express buses from Jilin often arrive at the **Changchun Express Bus Station** (chángchūn gāosù gōnglù kèyùn zhàn; 长春高速公路客运站), 219 Renmin Dajie, a Y18 taxi ride from the train station.

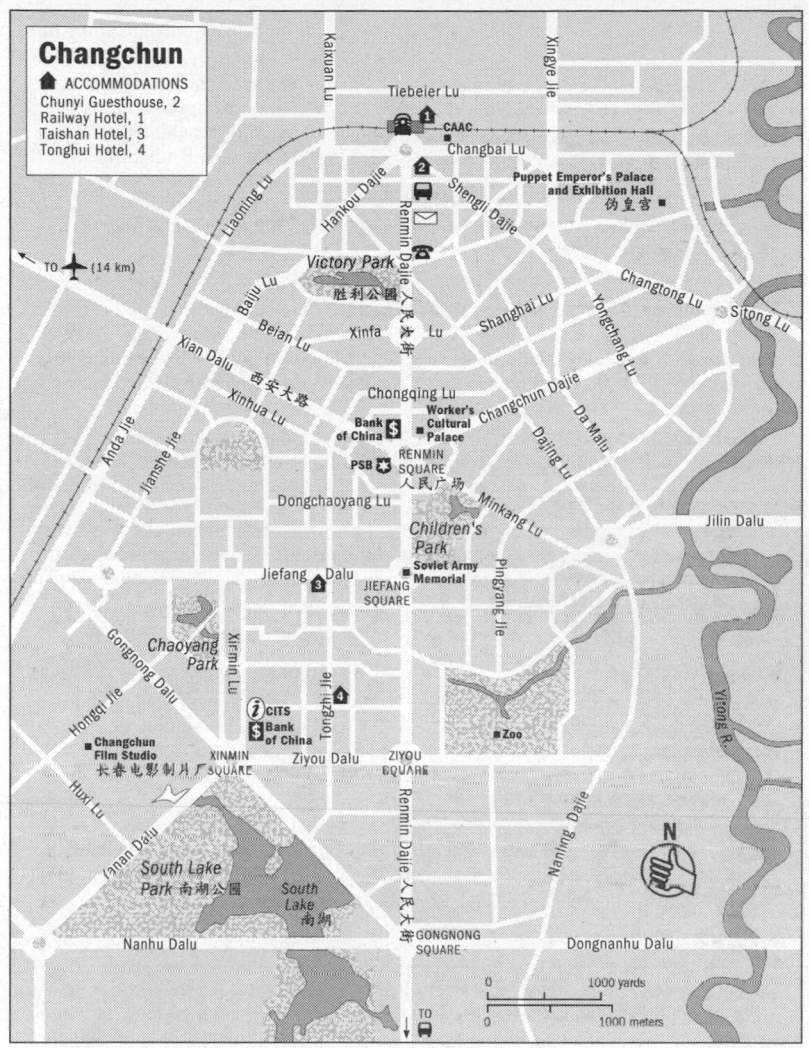

Changchun

⌂ ACCOMMODATIONS
Chunyi Guesthouse, 2
Railway Hotel, 1
Taishan Hotel, 3
Tonghui Hotel, 4

Local Transportation: Most **buses** run 6am-10pm. Fare Y0.5-1. Bus stops are labeled in pinyin. From Renmin Square, bus **#364** goes to the airport, and **#6** runs north to the train station and south to Freedom Square. Buses **#25** and **62** (via Tongzhi Jie) go from the train station to South Lake Park.

Taxis: Base fare Y5. Most destinations Y7-16, to the airport Y20-25.

✵ ? ORIENTATION AND PRACTICAL INFORMATION

Changchun is a vast, sprawling city blessed with wide streets. Several major roads meet at **People's Square** (rénmín guǎngchǎng; 人民广场). **Renmin Dajie** (人民大街) runs from the train station south to and beyond **Freedom Square** (zìyóu guǎngchǎng; 自由广场); **Tongzhi Jie** (同志街) runs south to South Lake Park; and **Xian Dalu** (西安大路) slopes south as it runs from west to east. The **Yitong River** (伊通河) runs from north to south down the length of the city.

Travel Agency: CITS, Yinmao Bldg., 14 Xinmin Lu, 7th Fl. (☎560 9500), behind the Changbaishan Hotel. Open M-F 8:30-11:30am and 1:30-5pm.

Bank of China: Yinmao Bldg., 14 Xinmin Lu, 1st Fl. Exchanges major foreign currencies and traveler's checks (window #6). Open M-F 8:30-11:30am and 1:30-4:30pm.

Bookstore: Foreign Language Bookstore, 44 Tongzhi Jie (☎567 5854), at Huimin Jie. Open daily 9am-8:30pm; in winter 9am-5pm.

PSB: 94 Renmin Dajie (☎898 2107), at People's Square.

Hospital: Changchun Central Hospital (chángchūn shì zhōngxīn yīyuàn; 长春市中心医院), 64 Renmin Dajie.

Telephones: China Telecom, 42 Renmin Dajie, at Beijing Dajie.

Internet Access: Worker's Cultural Palace Internet Cafe (wǎngbā; 网吧), 74 Renmin Dajie, 3rd Fl. (☎891 3369). Over 30 computers; Y3-10 per hr. Open 24hr. **Earth Village Internet Bar** (dìqiú cūn wǎngbā; 地球村网吧), 47-1 Tongzhi Jie (☎565 3704), at Huimin Jie, across from the Foreign Language Bookstore. Y5 per hr. Open daily 8:30am-11pm.

Post Office: 18 Renmin Dajie (☎297 5053), south of the train station. EMS and Poste Restante. Open daily 8:30am-5pm; in winter 8am-4:30pm. **Postal Code:** 130000.

ACCOMMODATIONS

Business travelers on expense accounts make up most of the traffic through the city. Most budget places are clustered near the train station and on Tongzhi Jie.

Railway Hotel (tiělían bīnguǎn; 铁联宾馆), between the station exit and ticket office. Rooms aren't overly shabby, given the price. Doubles Y40-80, with bath Y120-140.

Chunyi Guesthouse (chūnyì bīnguǎn; 春谊宾馆), 2 Renmin Dajie (☎297 9966; fax 896 0171), across the square from the train station. The lobby of the older building is worth viewing; the buffet breakfast is worth tasting. Doubles Y180; triples Y240.

Tonghui Hotel (tōnghuì bīnguǎn; 通汇宾馆), 60 Tongzhi Jie (☎567 1939). It lacks charm, but the price is right. 6-bed dorms Y20; 4-bed dorms Y30; 3-bed dorms Y30; singles and doubles with bath Y120.

Taishan Hotel (tàishān dàjiǔdiàn; 泰山大酒店), 35 Tongzhi Jie (☎563 4991; fax 563 6025), at Jiefang Dalu. So what if this hotel may be named after a mountain that isn't even in the province? With the friendly staff, clean rooms (all with attached bath), and superb location, you won't care one bit. Singles Y150; doubles Y150-200; suites Y230.

FOOD

The side streets and alleyways east of the train station and along **Tongzhi Jie, Guilin Lu,** and **Chongqing Lu** are filled with small, homestyle eateries serving standard fare. The kingdom of the dumpling king extends throughout Dongbei. **Changchun Dumpling King** (chángchūn jiǎozi wáng; 长春饺子王) and **Eastern Dumpling King** (dōngfāng jiǎozi wáng; 东方饺子王) are centrally located on Xinfa Lu, east of Renmin Dajie. For fowler fare, try the Peking duck at **Jinan Food Hall** (jìnǎn shífǔ; 济南食府). Meals average Y20-35. Three locations dot Changchun's streets: 61 Renmin Dajie, north of People's Square; 1 Chengyang Lu, one block south of People's Square; and 131 Renmin Dajie, halfway between People's and Freedom Squares. (Open daily 10am-10pm.) To finish off that hearty meal of feathered friends with a good cup of joe, head to the Western-style cafe in the lobby of the elegant **Changbaishan Hotel** (chángbáishān bīnguǎn; 长白山宾馆), 16 Xinmin Lu.

SIGHTS

One of Changchun's most attractive sites is actually its main street, **Renmin Dajie.** The thoroughfare begins at the train station and runs to People's Square. An impressive Mao statue (juxtaposed with one of Big Bird!) greets comrades at the

THE JOY OF JIAOZI You haven't gotten a taste of China until you've had a good plate of *jiaozi*, one of China's most widely loved foods. Close cousin to *hundun* (wontons) and *guotie* (potstickers), *jiaozi* are morsels of meat or veggie filling, wrapped in thin dough skins and boiled to perfection. *Jiaozi* are served on all occasions, whether it be a friend's farewell party or a huge family gathering. Many families spend New Year's Eve together busily creating piles and piles of dumplings for the celebratory dinner. Pinched tightly into bundles of delight, *jiaozi* are supposed to look like gold or silver ingots to symbolize wealth. Sometimes during the New Year, a coin is placed inside a dumpling, and the recipient is blessed with good fortune (unless a broken tooth results). *Jiaozi* are usually served with soy sauce (*jiangyou*) and malt vinegar (*cu*); more daring *jiaozi* connoisseurs can add a dash of sesame oil or chili pepper to the mix. But whatever the sauce and whatever the occasion, *jiaozi* never fail to delight. Eat and be merry, one small happiness at a time.

small but attractive **Victory Park** (shènglì gōngyuán; 胜利公园), at the corner of Beijing Dajie and Renmin Dajie. In the morning or late afternoon, the park often plays host to impromptu "dance performances" by groups of local women, who gather to dance with fans to the cadence of drums and the clash of cymbals. *(Open daily sunrise-sunset. Y3.)*

PUPPET EMPEROR'S PALACE (wěi huánggōng; 伪皇宫). After the Japanese invaded Manchuria in 1931, they installed the last emperor of the Qing dynasty, Puyi, as puppet emperor of the new state of Manchukuo (see p. 16). Bertolucci's film *The Last Emperor* was filmed here, and, yes, this is where it all happened. The palace covers some $43,000m^2$ and is comprised of the inner court (the private residence of the emperor and his family) and the outer court, where public affairs and ceremonies were handled. The ironically named **Mansion of Serving the Populace,** where Puyi signed treaties cementing Japanese control, and the **Pavilion of Joint Virtue,** where the "last concubine," Li Yuqing, lived, both have been restored. Visitors expecting the opulence of the film may be disappointed, but it's enjoyable all the same. *(In the northeastern part of the city. Take bus #12 from People's Square, or walk from the train station via Shengli Dajie and the street markets of Zhujiang Lu. Open daily 8:30am-5pm; in winter 8:40am-4:30pm. Last admission 40min. before closing. Inner court Y20; outer court Y20.)*

SOUTH LAKE PARK (nán hú gōngyuán; 南湖公园). The park is green, lean, mean, and fairly clean, although miniature red umbrellas hanging from wires strung across the paths can appear terribly tacky. Wrapped around **South Lake** (nán hú; 南湖), the park also offers boat rides (Y20). Along the right bank of the lake are a cluster of rickety kiddie-rides. *(Across Xinmin Square from Changbaishan Hotel and the Bank of China. Take bus #13 from People's Square or #25 or 62 from the train station. Open daily 7am-11pm. 7am-5pm Y5, 5-11pm Y10.)*

CHANGCHUN FILM STUDIO (chángchūn diànyǐng zhìpiān chǎng; 长春电影制片厂). China's Hollywood? It would be unfair to say so. The crumbling remains of what is known as the cradle of the Chinese film industry are the source of much local pride, but the glamor seems to be long gone. Fans of *The Last Emperor* may shiver with excitement to think that it all began right here. The tour and all captions are in Chinese only. *(28 Huxi Lu, west of South Lake Park. Take bus #13 from People's Square. ☎ 596 9175. Y20.)*

JILIN CITY 吉林市   ☎ 0432

Jilin's name means "lucky forest," and the irony of that misnomer is hard to miss in this industrial megalith, where green seems to be an endangered hue. Even Jilin's trees are considered to be most impressive during the winter, when they are bedecked by dignified "ice-rims," the product of evaporation from hydroelectric plants nearby. Still, surrounding mountains liven up the horizon, and a few sights provide more intimate havens from the expansive avenues of the city.

⌐ TRANSPORTATION

Airplanes: Gudianzi Airport (gūdiànzi jīchǎng; 孤甸子机场; ☎306 7450) is in the city's western outskirts, off the northern road to Changchun. **CAAC ticket office,** 121 Chongqing Lu (☎253 1668). Open daily 8am-6pm. To: **Beijing** (2 per day, Y760); **Guangzhou** (1 per day, Y1940); and **Shanghai** (1 per day, Y1170).

Trains: Jilin Train Station (jílín zhàn; 吉林站; ☎292 1222), on Zhongxin Jie, at Zhong-kang Lu. To: **Beijing** (17hr., 2 per day, Y262); **Changchun** (2hr., 7 per day, Y26); **Dalian** (15½hr., 2 per day, Y174); **Harbin** (5½hr., 2 per day, Y170); and **Shenyang** (9¾hr., 1 per day, Y73).

Buses: Linjiang Long-distance Bus Station (línjiáng chángtú qìchē zhàn; 临江长途汽车站), on Xian Lu, between Jiefang Dalu and Songjiang Lu (☎484 0121). To: **Changchun** (1½hr., every 30min. 5:30am-6:30pm, Y30); **Dalian** (9hr., 2 per day, Y183); and **Shenyang** (4½hr., every hr. 8am-10pm, Y88).

Local Transportation: Most buses run from early morning until around 10pm, and many terminate at the Jilin Train Station. Fare Y0.5-1. Bus **#10** runs to the airport; **#7** and **107** go to Beishan Park; **#8** runs between the train and long-distance bus stations; **#103** runs up and down Jilin Dajie; **#13** runs along Tianjin Jie between the train station and the riverfront.

Taxis: Base fare Y5. Train station to Songjiang Lu Y5-10.

⚡☑ ORIENTATION AND PRACTICAL INFORMATION

Jilin's major streets run along the **Songhua River** (松花江), while the rest of the city fans outward from there. **Songjiang Lu** (松江路) winds around the western side of the southern river bend. **Jilin Dajie** (吉林大街) runs from north to south about half-way between the river and the train station. **Cultural Square** (wénhuà guǎngchǎng; 文化广场) is near the center of the city.

Travel Agency: CITS, 3 Wenmiao Lu (☎244 3451; fax 245 3773), around the corner from the Jiangcheng Hotel and near the Confucian Temple. Organizes 3-day trips to Changbaishan (via Yanji) for Y450 per person. Open M-F 8:30am-4:30pm.

Bank of China: 1 Shenchun Jie (☎467 0277), across the Linjiang Bridge. Exchanges traveler's checks and issues credit card advances (windows #3 and 4). Open M-F 8:30am-4pm, Sa-Sun 9am-3pm.

PSB: On Beijing Lu (☎240 9315), at Nanjing Lu.

Hospitals: Jilin's largest hospital is at 4 Nanjing Jie (☎245 6487; fax 244 0643).

Bookstore: Xinhua Bookstore, 110 Henan Jie (☎202 3685). A good selection of traditional Chinese music. Open daily 8:30am-8:30pm.

Internet Access: China Telecom Internet Bar, 31 Nan Malu (☎249 2757), at the corner of Chongqing Jie and Jiefang Dajie. Take bus #3. Y5 per hr. Open daily 9am-10pm.

Post Office: China Post (☎202 6253), on Junchun Jie at Henan Jie. EMS and IDD service available. Open daily 8:30am-5pm. **Postal Code:** 132000.

▮◌ ACCOMMODATIONS AND FOOD

Jilin suffers from the chronic Northeastern lack of budget accommodations, and hostels around the train station offer little respite.

Jiefang Dajie becomes one big surreal neon dream at night, and is a good place for food and fun. The pedestrian street, **Henan Jie,** offers ample food selections, from bakeries to dumpling houses to Sichuanese restaurants. At night, **Chongqing Jie** is also closed off to automobile traffic and the local hotpot restaurants come to life north of Baodeng Lu. Tea houses abound along **Tianjin Jie. Qingnian Lu,** off Nanma Lu, is the place to go for fresh fruit. **Mingmen Restaurant** (míngmén fàndiàn; 名门饭店), 19 Jiefang Dajie, has Y10-20 entrees and an impressive view. (☎203 8888. Open 5:30-10pm.) At **Xincheng Restaurant** (xínchéng fàndiàn; 鑫诚饭店), on

Jiefang Dajie, each party gets its own room, and customers sit on the floor, Japanese-style. Entrees cost Y15-20; guests are allegedly welcome to spend the night in the hostel upstairs for the price of a meal.

Jilin Changlin Hotel (jílín chǎnglín bīnguǎn; 吉林常林宾馆), 216 Tianjin Jie (☎255 7780), near the train station. Not only do you get a clean room, but you also get to take part in the spectacle at the hotel's public showers. Leave your modesty at the door. Doubles Y100, with bath Y180.

Tourism Hotel (lǚyóu bīnguǎn; 旅游宾馆), 88 Chaoyang Jie (☎248 2087), overlooking Cultural Square. An excellent location and surprisingly pleasant rooms one of Jilin's best bargains do make. Doubles Y140, with bath Y160; triples Y200.

Angel Hotel (tiānshǐ bīnguǎn; 天使宾馆), 2 Nanjing Lu (☎248 1848; fax 248 0323), just north of the Catholic Church. With sparkling carpets and bathrooms like these, you might prefer sleeping on the floor or in the tub to sleeping on the beds. Tea house in the lobby. Doubles Y228; triples Y248.

👁 SIGHTS

Jilin gets its chance to shine in the winter, sub-zero temperatures notwithstanding. Thanks to the manipulations of hydroelectric power companies, the Songhua River does not freeze; instead, it perspires ice-rimmed drops of sweat.

BEISHAN PARK (beǐshān gōngyuán; 北山公园). Beishan embodies the best and worst of Chinese leisure spots. The worst is represented by the endless rows of souvenir stands and the shoddy children's park, and the very best is represented by the active Buddhist temples at the top of the hill, with monks and nuns in residence and a permeating air of spiritual devotion. *(Take bus #7 from the train station. Open daily 6am-6pm. Y5 adults, Y3 children; temple Y1.)*

METEORITE SHOWER MUSEUM (yǔnshíyǔ bówùguǎn; 陨石雨博物馆). In 1976, Jilin got lucky when a 1.77 ton meteorite (supposedly the largest meteorite ever to hit the earth) fell nearby. Special "intergalactic decorations" are not nearly as impressive. The museum is not necessarily worth the detour across the river. *(On Jilin Dajie, across the river from Songjiang Jie and in front of the Mao statue. Open daily 9am-4:30pm. Y10.)*

OTHER SIGHTS. On Jiangwan Lu near Tianjin Jie and the north bank of the river, the **Confucian Temple** (wénmiào; 文庙) offers some respite from ferro-concrete urbanity. *(Open M-F 8:30am-4pm, Sa-Su 9am-4pm. Y10.)* Exit this sanctuary and follow the Songhua River east along Songhua Lu for about five minutes. The beautiful **Catholic Church** (tiānzhǔ jiàotáng; 天主教堂) was built between 1906 and 1912 by a French mission. Doors are only open during service hours, but those who walk around to the nunnery on the right may find a kind nun willing to provide a private tour. *(Services M-F 5-6:30am, Sa-Su 8-9:30am; also open for confession before each service.)*

YANJI 延吉 ☎0433

Yanji is the best access point for Changbaishan Nature Reserve (see p. 199), 300km away. As the largest (and fastest growing) city in Jilin province's Korean minority region, it is an interesting cultural crossroads, teeming with bilingual residents and signs. Unfortunately, it has little to offer tourists besides its appealing mix of cultures.

✦✦ ❷ ORIENTATION AND PRACTICAL INFORMATION

Yanji sprawls on both sides of the **Yanji** (延吉) and **Buerhatong Rivers** (布尔哈通河). The commercial center of the city is at the intersection of **Renmin Dajie** (人民大街) and **Guangming Jie** (光明街), northeast of the rivers. The train station and long-distance bus station are across the **Yanji Bridge** (延吉桥) from the city center.

Airplanes: Yanji Airport (yánjí fēijīchǎng; 延吉飞机场), west of the city. The **CAAC ticket office,** 62 Gongyuan Lu (☎272 7666), in the lobby of the Civil Aviation Mansion.

Trains: Yanji Train Station (yánjí huǒchē zhàn; 延吉火车站), at the southern end of Zhanqian Jie.

Buses: Northeast Asia Long-distance Bus Station (dōngběi yā kěyùn zǒng zhàn; 东北亚客运总站) is the central bus station in Yanji. Buses go to **Changbaishan** (4hr.; 5:30am departure, 4pm return; round-trip Y101). Taxi drivers offering similar packages (Y105) swarm about unsuspecting tourists outside. Buses to **Dunhua, Tumen** (1¼hr.; 10 per day, Y8-10), and other cities depart from the square in front of the train station.

Local Transportation: Buses cost Y0.5-1. Buses **#2, 3, 4,** and **5** run between the train station and the long-distance bus station. Bus **#3** to Guangming Jie. Bus **#35** runs along Zhanqian Jie between the train station and the CAAC and CITS offices. Most **taxis** do not use meters, but have a base fare of Y5.

Travel Agency: CITS, 4 Yanxi Jie, 6th Fl. (☎271 5018; fax 271 7906), almost directly across the street from the CAAC. Organizes guided 1- to 3-day tours (3-day Y1300-2400) to Changbaishan. Open 8am-5pm.

Bank of China: On Renmin Lu at Yongle Jie, next to the PSB. Exchanges traveler's checks and issues credit card advances. Open daily 8am-5pm; in winter 8am-4:30pm.

PSB: On Renmin Lu, 1 block east of Juzi Jie (☎256 5021).

Pharmacy: Xinyao Pharmacy (xīnyào dàyàofáng; 新药大药房), at the corner of Renmin Lu and Guangming Jie.

Post Office: Yanji Post, on Renmin Lu, at the corner of Guangming Jie (☎251 1426). **Postal Code:** 133002.

BEANS, BEANS, GOOD FOR YOUR HEART

Wander through any market in China, and you're bound to come across vendors selling strangely-shaped fungi, each one supposedly having special healing powers. The vendors do good business because many Chinese view the body as an organic whole connected by various "channels" and energies. Herbs and drugs are used to improve the body; in some cases, a specific substance has been pinpointed for its helpful effects, but more often than not, it is enough to know simply that a certain herb works, and not necessarily to know exactly why.

Each food is unique in its character, being classified under several categories. There are the four properties of cold, cool, warm, and hot; each "temperature" group has differing effects, though cool and warm differ from cold and hot only by degree. **Cold** and **cool** foods (e.g. barley, celery, crab, green tea, and soy sauce) are said to "clear heat" or "purge fire," relieving feverish symptoms and removing toxic substances. **Hot** and **warm** foods (such as ginger, onion, garlic, peach, pineapple, and coffee) supposedly "disperse cold" and "warm up" the interior body. Some say a **neutral** group (e.g. wheat, corn, potatoes, and grapes) can treat both hot or cold conditions.

Foods are also classified according to five "flavors." **Pungent** foods (e.g. ginger and scallions) promote energy and blood circulation. **Sweet** foods (e.g. potatoes and milk) nourish, tone, and enrich various organs in the body. **Sour** foods (e.g. tomatoes and lemons) stop bodily discharges, such as sweating. **Bitter** foods (e.g. almonds and coffee) clear heat, purge fire, and stop coughing and vomiting. **Salty** foods (e.g. beef and table salt) relieve constipation and resolve hard masses, like tumors. Certain foods also specialize in "channel tropisms," or particular areas of the body. The liver prospers from tomatoes, papaya, and eel. Millet, snap peas, and watermelon are a spleen's best friends, and ginger, onions, pears, and water chestnuts are of use to the lungs. Kidneys take a liking to such specialties as prawn, mutton, duck, and dog. Wheat, lotus seeds, lily bulbs, and yes, red beans, are good for the heart.

ACCOMMODATIONS AND FOOD

Hotels in central Yanji are outrageously overpriced. Accommodations on the southwest side of the river are more reasonable, and hostels line the square in front of the train station.

Given Yanji's location, Korean restaurants are ubiquitous. **Jiefang Lu**, east of Juzi Jie, is lined with Korean joints specializing in dog dishes. **Pama's** (pāimǎsī; 啪玛嘶), on Xinxing Jie, is a tastefully decorated Western-style restaurant that serves good American and European cuisine.

Jiangshan Hotel (jiāngshān fàndiàn; 江山饭店; ☎281 5931), directly across from the train station. With each train station hotel seeming to be more Hitchcockian than the last, the Jiangshan stands out as one of the more pleasant accommodations options around. 3-bed dorms Y15-20; 2-bed dorms Y17.5-40.

Northeast Asia Hotel (dōngběi yà dàjiǔdiàn; 东北亚大酒店), 109 Changbai Lu (☎280 8111; fax 282 0970). A cylindrical building next to the long-distance bus station, the Northeast offers luxury (Yanji-style) with a revolving top-floor restaurant, sauna, coffee shop, and spacious rooms. The travel agency organizes 1- and 2-day trips (Y180-420) to Changbaishan. Doubles Y260.

Civil Aviation Mansion (mínháng dàshà; 民航大厦), 62 Gongyuan Lu (☎275 4001). A standard, 3-star Chinese hotel with simple and fairly elegant rooms to match. Free airport transfers. Singles Y160; doubles Y320.

CHANGBAISHAN 长白山

Deng Xiaoping is reported to have said "Not climbing atop Changbaishan will be a regret harbored for life." The trek to **Changbaishan Nature Reserve**, isolated in the southeast corner of Jilin province along the North Korean border, is a long and arduous one, despite the scenic rewards. Dramatically shaped, multicolored peaks culminate in the two-million-year-old **Tianchi.** Tianchi, filling a crater atop a now-dormant volcano, is the deepest lake in China and the source of the Songhua and Yalu Rivers. Tall waterfalls and springs capable of boiling eggs round out its freakish natural blessings. A resort atmosphere detracts somewhat from the wonder of the place and vacationing Koreans and Japanese have driven up prices. Fortunately, the crisp mountain air and spectacular scenery are ample compensation.

▶ PRACTICAL INFORMATION. The resort and the nearby town of **Erdaobaihe** (二道白河) are accessible via **Dunhua** and **Yanji** (if coming from Changchun or other points north of the resort) or via **Tonghua** and **Baihe** (if coming from Shenyang or other points south of the resort). The CITS offices in both Yanji (see p. 198) and Jilin (see p. 195) organize one- to three-day tours. Prices rise during the summer peak season.

▌ ACCOMMODATIONS. Affordable lodging is rather hard to find. **Hot Springs Villa** (wēnquán shānzhuāng; 温泉山庄) is a two-minute walk down the mountain from Cuckoo Village. Korean-style rooms (no beds, but heated floors) are officially not open to foreigners, but those who insist they are "accustomed" (xíguàn) to such living conditions may get in. (☎ 574 6033. Doubles Y180, off-season Y120.) **Changbai Athletes Village** (chángbáishān yùndòngyuán cūn; 长白山运动员村), in Erdaobaihe, is about a 20-minute ride from the main park entrance. The staff is quick to show prospective guests the room where Jiang Zemin once stayed. (☎ 574 6055. 8-bed dorms Y50; doubles Y360. Off-season: dorms Y30; doubles Y280.) South Korean and Japanese tourists spend fortunes at **Mount Changbai Cuckoo Village** (chángbáishān dùjuān shānzhuāng; 长白山杜鹃山庄), in Erdaobaihe, but less expensive rooms are also available. Relax in the outdoor heated pool. (☎ 574 6088. Doubles Y260, off-season Y180.)

▣ SIGHTS. A tourist brochure praises the forests of the area for their ability to "relate their own stories," and in any season the natural splendor of the area is quite likely to speak for itself. A dirt road leads to the reserve's gate (Y40, students Y20), and from there the climb to the base of the mountain takes about 20 minutes. At the base is a cluster of hot springs (Y50). As it slopes up the mountain, the road (now paved) leads to another ticket gate (Y29) and Tianchi's thundering waterfall (Y10). An hour's walk past here is the lake itself, the shimmering crown of the mountain. As of summer 2000, the metal staircase lining the road to the lake was out of service, and the only way to reach Tianchi was via rented jeep (Y80); inquire around to see if the staircase has been fixed before planning on making the climb on foot. The icy Alpine lake invites gazing but no swimming; frostbite-inducing temperatures aside, the deep waters are rumored to contain massive marine monsters. Many of the hot spring villas in the park offer dorm-style accommodation.

The **Changbaishan Museum** (chángbáishān bówùguǎn; 长白山博物馆), not far outside the main gate, has exhibits on everything from stuffed Siberian tigers and black bears to speculative representations of Tianchi's underwater monsters. *(Open daily 8am-5:30pm. Y15.)*

LIAONING 辽宁

Liaoning is the golden child of China's Northeast. A long coastline, a relatively mild climate, and proximity to South Korea and Japan have contributed to the booming economy. The warm-water seaports of Dalian and Lushun are considered Liaoning's crown jewels; in the countryside, however, unemployment is growing and development is lagging behind. Historically more closely tied to Han China than the rest of Manchuria is, Liaoning was chosen by the Manchu founders of the Qing dynasty as the site of their first capital. Like the rest of the Northeast, the province suffered heavily during the Japanese occupation in the 1930s and 40s, but many parts of the province seem blissfully unfettered by recollections of darker eras. Blessed with lush greenery and even the occasional beach, Liaoning is energizing and occasionally harrowing, with its gaze focused as firmly on the pleasures of the present as on the challenges of the future.

SHENYANG 沈阳   ☎024

Shenyang is a promising metropolis, a swan amid the endless ugly-duckling wheat
fields of Liaoning province. History singled the city out at the beginning of the
Qing dynasty, when the Manchu generals who unified the northeast and conquered the Ming set their capital at Shenyang from 1625 to 1644. In 1931, Shenyang, along with the rest of Manchuria, was once again brought to the forefront of
history when the Japanese army used the region as a base from which to launch
their invasion of China.

In the decades since, Shenyang has been creeping forward with the times. With
a population of 6.8 million, it is the largest and arguably the most important city in
the Northeast. Modernization is more than just a buzzword here: main streets are
being gutted and repaved, high-rises are going up and coming down, and the populace appears to be taking it all in stride. After all, the historical sites that constitute
the cultural heart of the city still stand undisturbed against the ravages of time.
Shenyang gladly invites visitors (donning hard hats) to come to terms with a bit of
a mess, and relish in the contrasts of old and new.

▐ TRANSPORTATION

Airplanes: Taoxian International Airport (táoxiān jīchǎng; 桃仙机场; ☎8939 2900),
on the southern fringe of the city, off the main highway to Dalian. **IATA ticket office**
(guójì hángxié hángkōng shòupiào chù; 国际航协航空售票处), 41 Xiaoxi Lu
(☎2290 2888) and 229 Zhongshan Lu (☎2284 2925). To: **Beijing** (7-10 per day,
Y560); **Dalian** (1 per day, Y150); **Guangzhou** (2-3 per day, Y1850); **Harbin** (1-2 per
day, Y410); **Hong Kong** (2 per week, Y2900); **Qingdao** (1-3 per day, Y540); **Shanghai**
(4-5 per day, Y1040); and **Xian** (2 per day, Y1200). International flights to **Osaka,
Japan** (5hr., 4 per week, Y2350) and **Seoul, South Korea** (2¾hr., 2 per day, Y1850).

Trains: Shenyang Main Train Station (shěnyáng huǒchē zhàn; 沈阳火车站; ☎2206
2222), at the corner of Shengli Dajie and Zhonghua Lu, Heping. To: **Beijing** (10-12hr.,
6 per day, Y150-250); **Changchun** (5hr., 4 per day, Y75); **Dalian** (6-9hr., 15 per day,
Y119); **Dandong** (5hr., 9 per day, Y37); **Harbin** (8hr., 2 per day, Y151); and **Tumen**
(16hr., 1 per day, Y162). **Shenyang North Station** (shěnyáng běi zhàn; 沈阳北站;
☎2252 2085), on Beizhan Lu, Shenhe. To: **Beijing** (9½-12hr., 13 per day, Y114);
Dalian (4-6hr., 15 per day, Y53); **Dandong** (4½hr., 6 per day, Y40); **Guangzhou** (35hr.,
1 per day, Y567); **Jilin** (7hr., 2 per day, Y88); and **Tianjin** (14hr., 2 per day, Y115).

Buses: Shenyang Long-distance Bus Station (shěnyáng chángtú qìchē zhàn; 沈阳
长途汽车站; ☎2351 3112), on Minzhu Lu. To: **Beijing** (13hr., 2 per day, Y110);
Changchun (4½hr., 2 per day, Y50); **Dalian** (4½hr., 5 per day, Y50); **Harbin** (12hr., 2
per day, Y80); and **Tianjin** (13hr., 2 per day, Y100). **Express Bus Station** (kuàisù
kèyùn zhàn; 快速客运站; ☎2251 1222) across from Shenyang North Station. To:
Changchun (3½hr., 18 per day, Y70); **Dalian** (4½hr., 8 per day, Y95); **Harbin** (6½hr.,
6 per day, Y129); and **Jilin** (4½hr., 8 per day, Y95).

Local Transportation: Buses and minibuses cost Y1, larger A/C buses Y2. The **first ring
bus** (yī huán; 一环) loops from the Main Train Station to North Station via Xishuncheng
Jie; **#202** runs between the Main Train Station and North Tomb Park, via City Government Square; **#225** loops from the Main Train Station to South Lake Park and up
Qingnian Dajie to City Government Square.

Taxis: Base fare Y6-7.

◢✦⚡ ORIENTATION AND PRACTICAL INFORMATION

Shenyang sprawls. The city is divided into five districts: the west-central **Heping**
(和平), the east-central **Shenhe** (沈河), the eastern **Dadong** (大东), the northern
Huanggu (皇姑), and the western **Tiexi** (铁西). **City Government Square** (shì fǔ
guǎngchǎng; 市府广场) is the hub of the city, and Heping and Shenhe districts are
the city's commercial and tourist centers. **Taiyuan Jie** (太原街) and **Zhongjie Lu**
(中街路), and the areas nearby, are likely to be of most interest to visitors. The
Hun River (hún hé; 浑河) forms the southern border of the city.

Travel Agency: CITS, 113 Huanghe Nan Dajie, Huanggu (☎8612 2445), near North Tomb. Open M-F 8-11:30am and 1-5pm.

Consulates: Japan, 50 Shisi Wei Lu (☎2322 7530). Open M-F 9am-noon and 1:30-5pm. **Russia,** 109 Huanghe Nan Dajie (☎8611 4963), in the Phoenix Hotel. Organize day visas here if you are planning to visit Russia from border towns in Heilongjiang. **US,** 52 Shisi Wei Lu (☎2322 1198; visas ☎2322 2147). Open M-F 8:30am-4:30pm.

Bank of China: 253 Shifu Dalu, west of City Government Square. Exchanges traveler's checks (2nd fl.) and offers credit card advances. Open M-F 8am-noon and 1-4pm.

Bookstores: Foreign Language Bookstore (wài wén shūdiàn; 外文书店), 43 Taiyuan Bei Jie. Open daily 9am-6pm. **Dongyu Bookstore** (dōngyǔ shūdiàn; 东宇书店), 2 Heping Nan Dajie, at Zhonghua Lu. Open daily 9am-8pm.

PSB: 106 Zhongshan Lu, on Zhongshan Square. Visa questions addressed at 66-1 Beisanjing Jie (☎2285 8987).

Hospital: No. 1 Hospital (dì yī yīyuàn; 第一医院), 140 Minzhu Lu (☎2386 3543).

Internet Access: Linxi Internet Cafe (línxī wǎngbā; 林夕网吧), 357 Zhongshan Lu, near Qingnian Dajie. Y4 per hr. Open 10am-midnight. **Dongyu Bookstore** (see **Bookstores**) has access for Y5 per hr.

Post Office: China Post, 44 Zhongshan Lu, at Taiyuan Jie. EMS and IDD service. Open daily 8am-6pm; in winter 8am-5:30pm. **Postal Code:** 110000.

ACCOMMODATIONS

Accommodations in Shenyang tend to be upscale, but there are some relatively cheap places in good locations. Construction is the sport of choice; call ahead.

SHENHE

Meisan Hotel (méisǎn bīnguǎn; 梅糁宾馆), 48 Xiaoxi Lu (☎2273 5538). Within walking distance of City Government Square, Zhongjie Lu, and the Imperial Palace, this hotel is a real treat. Hardwood floors, bright standard rooms, and friendly staff. Singles Y140; doubles Y180; triples Y240; and quads Y280.

Postal Tower Hotel (yóuzhèng dàshà bīnguǎn; 邮政大厦宾馆), 78 Beizhan Lu (☎2252 8717), just west of the North Train Station. Dwarfed by the almighty Gloria Inn, the much humbler Postal Tower is still a deal. 3-bed dorms Y33; doubles Y90.

Wangfu Hotel (wángfǔ bīnguǎn; 王府宾馆), 5 Youhao Jie (☎2273 5867), south of the North Train Station. Undergoing piecemeal renovations during summer 2000, this hotel offers standard services and relatively clean rooms. Doubles Y120; triples Y180.

HEPING

Peace Hotel (hépíng bīnguǎn; 和平宾馆), 104 Shengli Bei Jie (☎2383 3033), just north of the Main Train Station. Convenient location and a range of room options. Doubles Y90-240; triples Y120-260; quads Y120.

South Pacific Mansion (nán yáng dàshà; 南洋大厦), 96 Zhonghua Lu (☎2341 0688), at Tongze Bei Jie. Brand new and fairly luxurious, but without a coconut grove in sight. Singles Y208; doubles Y268; triples Y348.

Liaobao Hotel (liáobào dàjiǔdiàn; 辽报大酒店), 15 Beisanjing Jie (☎2284 4826), next door to the Liaoning newspaper building on Zhongshan Lu, but a bit removed from the action of Taiyuan Jie. Rooms are immaculate. Doubles Y150-198.

FOOD AND ENTERTAINMENT

Western restaurants and bars are clustered in the Heping district and near Dongbei University. **Zhongshan Market** (zhōngshān shìchǎng; 中山市场), on Beiliu Malu off Zhongshan Lu, is an ideal place for street food. The **Civic Moon Shop** (xìnméng biànlì diàn; 信盟便利店) has 24hr. convenience stores scattered throughout the city, including one on Xiaoxi Lu across from the Meisan Hotel. For more low-key entertainment, check out the Chinese-subtitled American and Hong Kong movies at the **Dream Cinema** across from Star Hollywood (2 films Y20).

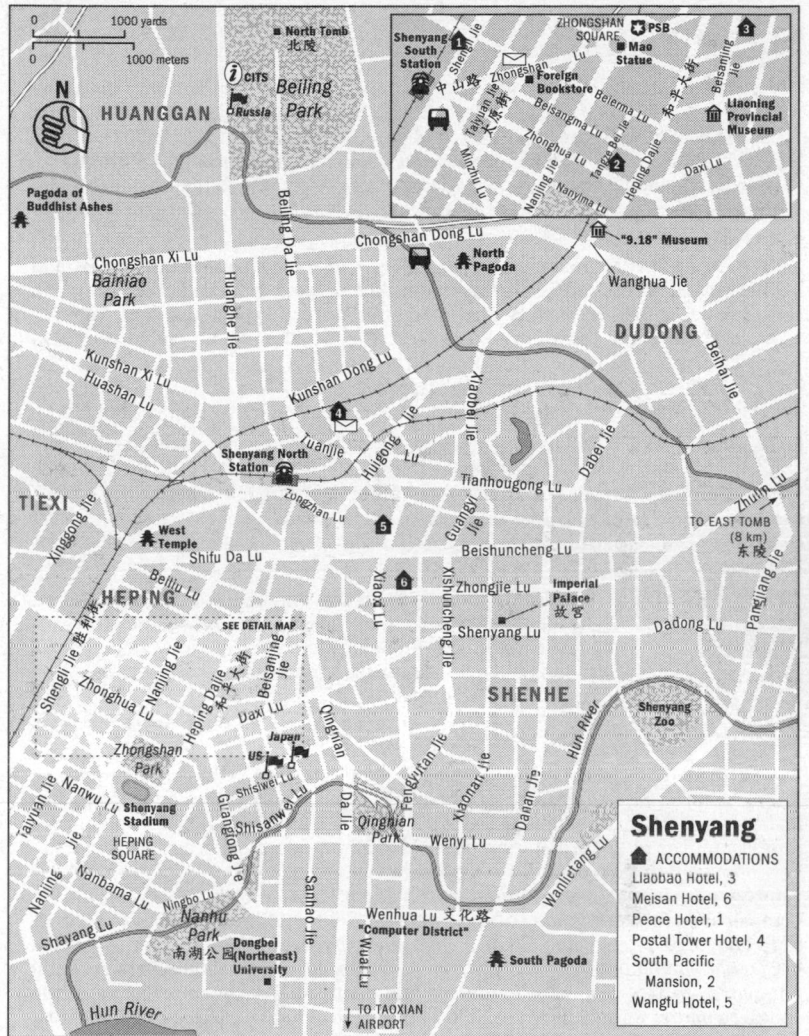

SEE DETAIL MAP

NORTHEAST

Shenyang

ACCOMMODATIONS
Liaobao Hotel, 3
Meisan Hotel, 6
Peace Hotel, 1
Postal Tower Hotel, 4
South Pacific
  Mansion, 2
Wangfu Hotel, 5

Huaxia Folk Village (huáxià mínzú cūn dàjiǔlóu; 华夏民族村大酒楼), 11 Beifang Malu, Heping, a short walk from Zhongshan Square. A great big place, where you can play with children's blow-up toys and hang with the resident parakeets. Entrees Y18-25.

Small Potato (xiǎo tǔdòu; 小土豆), on Xiaoxi Lu. Potato dishes are the specialty, but Small Potato also offers a tummy-pleasing array of other dishes. So popular with locals that it's often hard to find empty tables. Entrees Y10-25. Open daily 10am-11pm.

Fairyland (xiānzōnglín; 仙踪林), 57 Zhonghua Lu, at Tongze Bei Jie. A tea house chain originating in Shanghai, Fairyland serves over 30 different teas (Y6-8). The decor—vines, bamboo, and tree swings—is truly magical. Open daily 10am-9pm.

Star Hollywood Cafe (xīngchén hǎoláiwū měishì cāntīng; 星辰好莱坞美式餐厅), 9 Tongze Bei Lu, Heping, off Zhongshan Lu. A live band (F-Sa 9pm-1:30am) playing Western music brings out foreign patrons to flirt with their Chinese comrades and drink until visions of Hollywood dance in their heads. Drinks Y28-48, entrees Y48-60. Open Su-Th 10am-midnight, F-Sa 10am-2am.

SIGHTS

QING IMPERIAL PALACE (gù gōng; 故宫). This splendid complex was the home of the Manchu founders of the Qing dynasty, Nurhaci and Huangtaiji, in the early 1600s. The 300 rooms are constructed largely on the basis of Han Chinese architectural principles; the palace looks like a smaller version of Beijing's Forbidden City. While Manchu assimilation in Han culture was not complete, Manchu and Mongol architectural elements blend seamlessly into the palace grounds. *(171 Shenyang Lu, Shenhe. Open daily 8am-4:30pm. Y35.)*

NORTH TOMB PARK (běi líng gōngyuán; 北陵公园). This park is the biggest and best Shenyang has to offer. The vaunted tomb contains the remains of Huangtaiji (also known as Abhai). Slightly run-down buildings with grass sprouting from the roofs only add to the character of the place. The same cannot be said for the lackluster lake and monstrous, duck-shaped paddle boats. *(On Beiling Dajie, in Huanggu. Take bus #220 or 242 from the North Train Station or bus #227 from Xishuncheng Jie just west of the Imperial Palace. Park open daily 7:30am-6pm. Y3. Tomb open daily 6am-6:30pm. Y10.)*

EAST TOMB PARK (dōng líng gōngyuán; 东陵公园). The other founder of the Qing dynasty, the "Dragon Tiger General" Nurhaci (1559-1626), lies in these woods with his empress. Perhaps because of the tomb's more remote location or perhaps because he was genuinely less popular, Nurhaci sees fewer post-mortem visitors than does his late partner Huangtaiji. *(210 Dongling Jie. Take bus #218 (45min.) from Xishuncheng Jie just east of the Imperial Palace. Open daily 6am-6:30pm. Park Y2, tomb Y10.)*

"9.18" HISTORICAL MUSEUM (jiǔ yī bā lìshǐ bówùguǎn; 九一八历史博物馆). Named after the "9.18 Incident"—the seizing of Shenyang by the Japanese on September 18, 1931—this museum explores the Japanese occupation of Manchuria (see p. 16). The background explanations are undeniably biased against the invaders, rendering photographs of Emperor Pu Yi's puppet regime and of rows of decapitated heads even more haunting. *(46 Wanghua Nan Jie. Accessible by bus #212 from Xishuncheng Jie west of the Imperial Palace. Open daily 8:30am-4pm. Y20.)*

OTHER SIGHTS. A walk through Heping district's pedestrian **Taiyuan Jie** provides a telling glimpse into the future of Shenyang, from KFC to Giordano. **Zhongshan Square** houses an elaborate **Mao Statue.** Tall, proud, and surrounded by numerous representatives of the proletarian class, Mao stands alert, his heavy arms extending southward toward the Adidas-trodden base of Taiyuan Jie.

In Shenhe district, the commercialized **Zhongjie Lu** contrasts starkly with the Manchu-style reconstructions of Shenyang Lu. South of Zhongjie Lu, at the corner of Renao Lu and Fengyutan Jie, lies Shenyang's largest outdoor market, **Wuai Market** (wǔài shìchǎng; 五爱市场). *(Open daily 5am-2pm.)* **South Lake Park** (nán hú gōngyuán; 南湖公园), off Wenhua Lu and north of Dongbei University in the southern part of the city, is accessible by bus #225 or 609 from the North Train Station. *(Open daily 6:30am-7:30pm. Y1.)*

FETTUCINE ALFIDO Some visitors to China may find themselves cringing at the thought of one so-called Chinese custom: the consumption of dog meat. And, yes, it's true: fluffy pooches are bred and slaughtered for their meat in China. Han Chinese in the Northeast are actually less charmed by Fido's succulent flavors than their counterparts elsewhere in the country, but the presence of ethnic Koreans in the area and the central role that dog meat plays in some regional Korean cuisines mean that restaurants advertising dog meat (góu ròu; 狗肉) are common. Dog hotpot also has attracted quite a following down in Guangxi province.

Dog meat is lean and recommended for those with heart problems. Known for its warming qualities, dog hotpot or broth becomes all the rage when temperatures drop below freezing. This delicacy comes at a price, though. Restaurant owners report that a full dog goes for Y300 or more. Still unfazed? Chefs are often eager to impress tourists by showcasing the uneaten tail, paws, and head of man's best friend. Doggone it.

DANDONG 丹东   ☎0415

A small, unassuming city, Dandong would make its way onto few tourist itineraries were it not for its choice location on the Sino-Korean border. Japanese, South Korean, and Chinese tourists crowd onto the shore, into boats, and along the Yalu River Bridge to peek at the forbidden kingdom beyond. The transformation of the world's most isolated nation into a tourist attraction presents a spectacle every bit as bizarre as the view of North Korea itself.

■*⁊ ORIENTATION AND PRACTICAL INFORMATION

Dandong is easily navigated on foot. Most hotels and local services are clustered around the square in front of the train station, **Zhanqian Square** (zhànqián guǎngchǎng; 站前广场), north of Yalu River Park and the riverbank.

Airplanes: Dandong Airport (dāndōng jīchǎng; 丹东机场; ☎617 6569), 13km from Dandong. **CAAC ticket office,** 50 Jingshan Dajie (☎212 3427). Open daily 8am-6pm. To **Beijing** (Th and Sa, Y500) and **Shanghai** (Tu, Th, and Sa; Y870).

Trains: Dandong Train Station (dāndōng huǒchē zhàn; 丹东火车站; ☎202 1132). To: **Beijing** (14hr., 21 per day, Y73-261); **Changchun** (11hr., 1 per day, Y41-71); **Dalian** (11hr., 1 per day, Y47-99); **Qingdao** (25½hr., 1 per day, Y49-212); and **Shenyang** (4hr., 6 per day, Y21-42).

Buses: Dandong Long-distance Passenger Station (dāndōng chángtú kèyùn zhàn; 丹东长途客运站), 98 Shiwei Lu (☎213 4571), a short walk northeast of the train station. To: **Beijing** (18hr., 10am, Y165); **Dalian** (6hr., 11 per day 5:30am-4pm, Y57.5-59.5); and **Harbin** (20hr., 10am, Y153.5).

Taxis: Base fare Y5. **Pedicabs** generally cost Y2.

Travel Agency: CITS, 1 Zhanqian Dalu (☎213 5854; fax 213 1853), the large building south of the train station on Zhanqian Square. Handles visa applications for North Korea (see **North Korea,** p. 79). Open M-F 8:30-11:30am and 1:30-5pm.

Bank of China: 60 Jingshan Dajie, at Erwei Lu. Exchanges traveler's checks on the 2nd floor. Open M-F 8-11:30am and 1:30-5pm; in winter 8:30-11:30am and 1-4:30pm.

PSB: 15 Jiangcheng Dajie (☎212 7086; visas ☎210 3138), at Shiwei Lu, across from Hualian Store (华联商店). Open daily 8:30-11:30am and 2:30-5:30pm.

Hospital: No. 1 Hospital (dì yī yīyuàn; 第一医院; ☎281 4132), at Qijing Jie where it turns into Gongan Jie.

Internet Access: China Telecom, 76 Liuwei Lu (☎212 1640), around the corner from the main China Post on Qiwei Lu. Fast connections. Y13 per hr. Open daily 8am-5pm.

Post Office: China Post, 78 Qiwei Lu, at Qijing Jie. Open M-F 8am-5:30pm; in winter 8am-5pm. **International Post Office** (guójì yóujú; 国际邮局), 6 Shangmao Luyou Qu, in Yanjiang Development District. EMS. Open daily 8am-5pm. **Postal Code:** 118000.

▟ ACCOMMODATIONS

Most of Dandong's hotels are standard and stodgy. Choicest locations are around the train station and near the Yalu River, but the city is small enough as it is.

Dandong Railway Hotel (dān tiě dàshà; 丹铁大厦), 3 Shiyiwei Lu (☎213 1031), the tower attached to the train station. Favors convenience over chic. Beware: area taxis are horn-happy, especially when trains arrive. Dorms Y18-60; doubles Y120 and up.

CITS Hotel (guó lǚ bīnguǎn; 国旅宾馆), 1 Zhanqian Guangchang, 2nd Fl. (☎212 2166). Standard rooms, especially those facing away from the square, are actually quite nice. Singles Y80; doubles Y120; triples Y180.

Dandong Hotel (dāndōng fàndiàn; 丹东饭店), 31 Qijing Jie (☎212 3529), 1 block east of the post office. This no-frills accommodation offers unbeatable prices. 4-bed dorms Y18; singles Y40-100; doubles Y60-120; triples Y75-150.

FOOD

Dandong's wealth of culinary options is a testament to the power of borders. **Yalu River seafood** is a local favorite. Small Korean restaurants line **Shiwei Lu** between Zhanqian Square and the river, serving cold noodles (lěng miàn; 冷面; Y3-5) and *bi bim bap* (bànfàn; 拌饭; Y5-8).

Andong Pavilion Restaurant (āndōng gé; 安东阁), west of the Yalu River Bridge, along the riverbank in the Yanjiang Development District. An elegant new restaurant with a sought-after (and disturbingly attractive) view of North Korea. Most dishes (including hotpot) Y20-30. Open daily 11am-9:30pm.

Hong Kong Coffee House (xiāng gǎng kāfēi guǎn; 香港咖啡馆), across the street from the Andong Pavilion Restaurant. A cosmopolitan meeting place for Chinese, Koreans, and other foreigners. Drinks Y10-20. Open daily 8:30am-11pm.

Deheng Fat Cow City (déhēng féi niú chéng; 德亨肥牛城), 40 Kaifa Qu'e Qu, between Hong Kong Coffee House and Kaifa Qu Square. Run by a Hui family, this restaurant serves Muslim dishes and hotpot. Dishes Y10-30. Open daily 10am-11pm.

SIGHTS

Dandong's most interesting sights revolve around the Yalu River and the Democratic People's Republic of Korea. Along the Yalu River near Shiwei Lu, **Yalu River Park** (yālù jiāng gōngyuán; 鸭绿江公园) lacks the drama of Dandong's other sights, but is a fine spot for a walk. *(Open daily 6:30am-midnight. Y1; free after 5:30pm.)*

YALU RIVER CRUISES. All along the Yalu River, boat operators aggressively offer their services to tourists. Newlyweds on honeymoon and Japanese tour groups eagerly don their lifejackets for these unconventional cruises. Their enthusiasm, bizarre though it may seem, is quite justified—the ride takes passengers within 10m of one of the most isolated places on earth. Photos are allowed, but the area does not derive its fame from its scenery (and yields little intelligence data). Old boats, children playing in the water, and a few soldiers patrolling the shores constitute the entire visible slice of North Korean life. *(Big boats: 20min., Y6. Speed boats closer to the North Korean shore: 10min., Y13.)*

YALU RIVER BRIDGE (yālù jiāng qiáo; 鸭绿江桥). This old wooden bridge was the site of "US aggression" against North Korea in the 1950s, and the evidence (US shrapnel and damage done to the broken endpoint) has been preserved. Visitors can wear a Chinese Volunteer Anti-Imperialist Force uniform and pose with a gun in front of the North Korean border—for a fee, of course. *(West of Yalu River Park and extending halfway over the Yalu River. Open daily 6:30am-7pm. Y12.)*

DAYTRIPS FROM DANDONG

TIGER MOUNTAIN GREAT WALL

15km northeast of Dandong, beyond the town of Jiuliancheng (九连城). Minibuses depart from the Long-distance Bus Station (30min.; 8 and 10am, returning 1 and 3pm; round-trip Y6). Round-trip taxis cost Y80. Open daily 7:30am-5:30pm. Y15.

A small section built by the Ming dynasty in 1469, Tiger Mountain Great Wall (hǔ shān cháng chéng; 虎山长城) constitutes the easternmost edge of the piecemeal Great Wall. Renovated for tourism in the 1980s, Tiger Mountain Great Wall boasts a half dozen towers snaking along the North Korean border—a proximity more thrilling than the Yalu River vantage from Dandong.

PHOENIX MOUNTAIN

50km northwest of Dandong, near the city of Fengcheng (凤城). Buses (1½hr., approx. every 30min. 5:30am-5:30pm, Y6.1) go from Dandong Long-distance Bus Station to Fengcheng; ask to be dropped off at Fenghuangshan Gate, a few kilometers before Fengcheng city. Buses shuttle visitors between the gate and the park ticket office (Y10). Open May 1-Oct. 1. Y2.

An expansive mountainous area dotted with Daoist temples dating to the Ming and Qing dynasties, Phoenix Mountain (fēnghuáng shān; 凤凰山) makes for some worthwhile hiking. Often treacherous paths chiseled into the rock lead to shrines tended by over 20 Daoist monks and nuns, joined during the day by self-fashioned guides and snack vendors. The hike to the farthest peak takes up to four hours.

DALIAN 大连   ☎ 0411

In much of China, economic prosperity has been won at the price of clean air and charm. Not so in Dalian, whose natural blessings are its biggest economic asset. Dalian made its money the tidy way, through the vast shipping traffic that passes through its harbor, the third largest in China. European commercial intervention in the 19th and early 20th centuries left its architectural mark; rounding out the mix are skyscrapers, covered markets, boutiques, grassy squares, hilly terrain, and all the fresh sea air anyone could want. Today the city is vivid, rich, cosmopolitan, and, all things considered, quite fabulous.

From time to time, people refer to Dalian as the "Hong Kong of the North." Like its southern counterpart, a strategic location has made Dalian a site of contention for some time. Japan first took control after the Sino-Japanese War. The Russians then made a bid for the city, hoping to find a serviceable Pacific port to replace Vladivostok during the months when it was iced over, but they were soundly beaten in the Russo-Japanese War of 1905. Japan held on to Dalian until 1945, when it became an international territory for a few months under the Yalta Agreement. The squabbling was justified; Dalian is very much a prize worth fighting for.

NORTHEAST

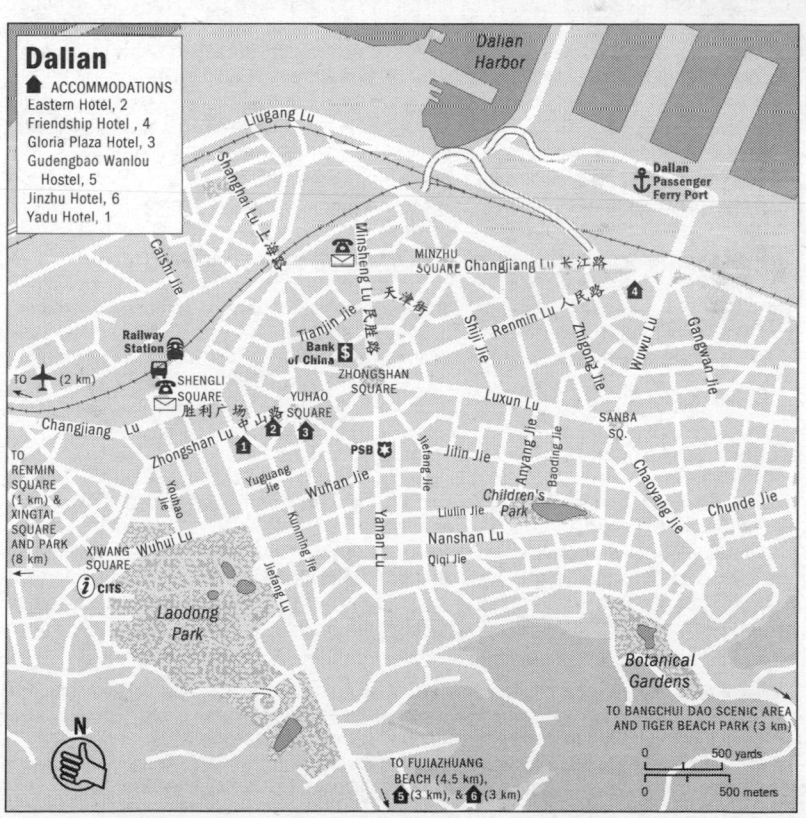

Dalian

⌂ ACCOMMODATIONS
Eastern Hotel, 2
Friendship Hotel , 4
Gloria Plaza Hotel, 3
Gudengbao Wanlou
    Hostel, 5
Jinzhu Hotel, 6
Yadu Hotel, 1

⌐ TRANSPORTATION

Airplanes: The **Dalian Zhoushuizi International Airport** (dàlián zhōushuĭzi guójì jīchăng; 大连周水子国际机场; ☎666 2334) is about 2km northwest of the city. **CAAC ticket office,** Civil Aviation Hotel, 143 Zhongshan Lu (☎363 7480), in Xiwang Square. Open M-F 7:30am-6pm, Sa 8am-5pm. To: **Beijing** (14 per day, Y570); **Changchun** (5 per day, Y460); **Chengdu** (6 per day, Y1450); **Guangzhou** (3 per day, Y1640); **Harbin** (8 per day, Y670); **Hong Kong** (4 per day, Y2870); **Qingdao** (3 per day, Y330); **Shanghai** (14 per day, Y850); **Shenyang** (2 per day, Y150); and **Xian** (4 per day, Y910). International flights to **Tokyo, Japan** (2¾hr., 3 per day, Y3800).

Trains: Dalian Train Station (dàlián huŏchē zhàn; 大连火车站; ☎282 3242), at the head of Shengli Square. To: **Beijing** (18½hr., 4:15 and 8:55pm, Y138); **Changchun** (11hr., 8:40pm, Y49-99); **Dandong** (9hr., 8:10pm, Y47-77); **Harbin** (14hr., 7:40pm, Y125); **Jilin** (14½hr., 6:25pm, Y57); and **Shenyang** (4-6hr., 6 per day, Y38-124).

Buses: Dalian Long-distance Bus Station (dàlián chángtú qìchē zhàn; 大连长途汽车站), 20 Anshan Lu (☎363 0119), at Xinkai Lu, west of the train station. To **Dandong** (6hr., 10 per day, Y46-58). Buses to other cities leave from the road just west of the train station and from in front of the Bohai Pearl Dalian Hotel east of the station. Arrive a few hours early for sleepers. To: **Beijing** (14hr., 4 per day 12:30-6:30pm, Y100-160); **Changchun** (8hr., 4 per day, Y128); **Harbin** (13hr., 5am and 4:40pm, Y180); **Shenyang** (4½hr., 12 per day 7am-6pm, Y98); and **Tianjin** (13½hr., 4:30pm, Y80-150).

Ferries: Dalian Passenger Ferry Port (dàlián kèyùn găng; 大连客运港; ☎263 6061), on Gangwai Jie, at the north end of Renmin Lu. To: **Qingdao** (12hr., 5pm, Y120-550); **Shanghai** (37-39hr., 3-4 per week 4pm, Y118-539); **Tianjin** (13-15hr.; 3, 4, or 6pm; Y125-560); **Weihai** (7hr.; 9am, 7, and 9pm; Y75-340); and **Yantai** (express: 3hr., every 2hr. 8am-2pm, Y190; regular: 6-8hr., 6 per day 8am-8:35pm, Y70-300). A ferry also goes to **Inchon, South Korea** (18hr., Tu and F noon, Y960-1840).

Local Transportation: Fare Y0.5-1. **Buses #2** and **#401** run the length of Jiefang Lu; **#13** runs between the train station and the ferry port; **#19** runs from Shandong Lu to Zhongshan Square; **#23** runs along Zhongshan Lu between Zhongshan Square and Xinghai Park; **#701** shuttles from Zhongshan Square to the airport.

Taxis: Base fare Y8, Y10.5 at night. From city center to the beach Y15-30.

■✻? ORIENTATION AND PRACTICAL INFORMATION

Dalian's public squares, complete with greenery and flocks of pigeons, date back to the time of Japanese rule. **Victory Square** (shēnglì guăngchăng; 胜利广城) is opposite the train station and close to a number of hotels. To the east is **Friendship Square** (yóuhăo guăngchăng; 友好广城), home to hotels, cinemas, and bars. From here, **Zhongshan Lu** (中山路) runs farther east to the city's main square, **Zhongshan Square** (中山广城). A number of major thoroughfares radiate out from here, including: **Yanan Lu** (延安路), running south from the square; **Minsheng Jie** (民生路), which runs north to **Changjiang Lu** (长江路); **Shanghai Lu** (上海路), which runs northwest and intersects with **Tianjin Jie** (天津街); and **Renmin Lu** (人民路), which goes northeast to the ferry port. West of the main train station is the stately **People's Square** (rénmín guăngchăng; 人民广城). Dalian's beaches and scenic drives are in the south of the city along **Jiefang Lu** (解放路).

Travel Agency: CITS, 1 Changtong Jie, Xigang (☎360 2914), in an architecturally unique building off Xiwang Square, opposite the Civil Aviation Hotel on Zhongshan Lu. Open M-F 8:30-11:30am and 1-5pm.

Bank of China: 9 Zhongshan Square (☎280 5711), in a European-style green-domed building. China's largest Bank of China exchanges traveler's checks M-F 8:30-11:30am and 1-4:30pm. On the weekend, try the Dalian Hotel across the street.

Bookstore: Foreign Language Bookstore (wài wén shūdiàn; 外文书店), 178 Tianjin Jie, northwest of Friendship Square. Open daily 9am-6:30pm; in winter 9am-5:30pm.

PSB: 16 Yanan Lu (☎265 8265), 2 blocks south of Zhongshan Square. Visa questions addressed on 2nd floor, windows #2 and 3. Open M-F 8-11:30am and 1-5pm.

Hospital: No. 1 Hospital of Dalian Medical University (dàlián yī xuéyuàn dì yī fùshǔ yīyuàn; 大连医学院第一附属医院), 222 Zhongshan Lu (☎363 5963), just west of People's Square.

Pharmacy: Dalian Medicine Market (dàlián yào fáng; 大连药房), 207 Tianjin Jie (☎263 3304). Open daily 8:30am-7pm.

Internet Access: ▨**21st Century Internet Club** (èrshíyī shìjì wǎngluò kāfēi diàn; 二十一世纪网络咖啡店; ☎263 6701), on Qiqi Jie at Jincheng Jie, a 5-10min. walk south of Zhongshan Square. Over 30 computers and cool decor. Y10 per hr. Open 24hr.

Post Office: China Post, 261 Changjiang Lu, in the Youzheng Hotel. EMS and Poste Restante. Open daily 7:30am-7pm; in winter 7:30am-6pm. **Postal Code:** 116000.

▌ ACCOMMODATIONS

Dalian is bursting at the seams with hotels that cater to the rich and playful. Unfortunately, budget travelers may find themselves outdone by the expensive accommodations that dominate the scene.

CENTRAL DALIAN

Yadu Hotel (yādū bīnguǎn; 雅都宾馆), 11 Kunming Jie (☎264 9822), at Zhongshan Lu. Spanking new, affordable, and 1 block from Victory Square, the Yadu is a rare treasure. Public shower 1-3pm and 6-10pm. 3-bed dorms Y54; singles and doubles Y128.

Eastern Hotel (dōngfāng fàndiàn; 东方饭店), 28 Zhongshan Lu (☎263 4161), near Friendship Square. Old-school hotel with decent rooms. Singles Y180; doubles Y248.

Gloria Plaza Hotel (kǎilái dàjiǔdiàn; 凯莱大酒店), 5 Yide Jie (☎280 8855), off Friendship Square and a 5min. walk from Victory and Zhongshan Squares. Gloria offers her usual high-class service. Off-season discounts available. Singles and doubles Y368.

OUTSIDE THE CITY CENTER

▨ **Gudengbao Wanlou Hostel** (gǔdēngbǎo wánlóu zhāodàisuǒ; 古登堡沴楼招待所), 58 Linmao Jie (☎249 6223), perched like a little castle on a hill near Changchun Lu in the south of the city. Take bus #401 from Jiefang Lu near Victory Square or #706 from Zhongshan Square to Bayi Lu and Changchun Lu; Linmao Jie is a 5-10min. walk up Changchun Lu, on the right. The rooms are neat, but the hairstyles on the friendly staff are wacky and wild—decor kitsch to perfection. Dorms Y35; doubles Y60; triples Y50.

Friendship Hotel (yǒuyì bīnguǎn; 友谊宾馆), 91 Renmin Lu (☎263 4121), a 5-10min. walk north of Zhongshan Square toward the ferry port. Fairly bland, like most of Dalian's mid-range places. Singles Y230; doubles Y280.

Jinzhu Hotel (jīnzhù dàjiǔdiàn; 金铸大酒店), 87 Bayi Lu (☎268 8866), between Changchun Lu and Jiefang Lu. Halfway between downtown and the coast, this standard hotel lacks the fanciful atmosphere of the neighboring Gudengbao. Doubles Y260.

◖ FOOD

Dalian is a port city, and it shows in the food. Seafood restaurants litter the streets close to the shore and **Xiangqian Jie** between Kunming Jie and Friendship Square in the city center. In business and tourist areas like Zhongshan Lu and Tianjin Jie, visitors will find those other creatures that wash up on beaches: **McDonald's, KFC,** and **Dairy Queen** (in the Dalian Grand Plaza Hotel and in Friendship Square). **Captain Nemo's,** on the ground floor of the Grand Hotel, just south of Zhongshan Square, serves up a Y58 Western breakfast buffet. Lots of Chinese restaurants line **Renmin Lu, Zhongshan Lu,** and nearby side streets. The underground mall at Victory Square has an extensive **food court;** enter across from the start of Tianjin Jie.

NORTHEAST

Yixin Roast Meat Restaurant (yīxīn kǎo ròu diàn; 一心烤肉店), 56 Yanan Lu, at Nanshan Lu, south of Zhongshan Square. Also at 216 Youhao Lu and 24-6 Tangshan Jie. Roast meat aficionados mob the place during peak hours, so prepare to wait. Another version of hotpot: waiters place metal "stoves" full of burning coal under a rack in the center of the table for guests to cook pre-seasoned meats themselves (Y15-18). The occasional third-degree burn aside, it's great fun. Open daily 10:30am-10:30pm.

Japan Roast Meat Restaurant (rìběn kǎo ròu diàn; 日本烤肉店), 9 Liulin Jie, between Yanan Lu and Jiefang Jie, south of Zhongshan Square. Do not come here expecting sushi; roast your own fish (and meat) on table stoves. The menu also includes *teriyaki*, *tempura*, and other favorites. Join the crowds of Japanese tourists. English menu. Entrees Y10-70. Open daily 9:30am-1:30pm and 4:30-10pm.

Hollywood Studio Cafe and Pub (hǎoláiwū yǐngchéng; 好莱坞影城), 28 Shengli Guangchang, on Zhongshan Lu. If you came all the way to China to pay Western prices for Western food and atmosphere, then Hollywood is the place for you. Hopping on the weekends (live band F-Sa 8-10pm), but rather listless at other times. Happy Hour M-Th 6-7pm. Entrees Y28-50, drinks Y30-48. Open daily 10:30am-3am.

🎵 ENTERTAINMENT

Dalian's harbor brings both foreign businesspeople and sailors to town, and most nightlife is bound to involve one or the other. The **Holiday Inn** is proud of its "English Pub" (open until midnight), and the **Swissôtel** has a gorgeous outdoor deck (performances Tu-Su 10pm-midnight). **JJ's Disco** (jiéjié dísīkē; 杰杰迪斯科), on Gangwan Jie, south of Gangwan Square near the ferry port, is a popular place for students and foreigners (no cover). **Hollywood Studio Cafe and Pub** (see p. 210), features a band from 8-10pm; after that the dance music gets cranked up and the flashing lights pulse until 3am. A half-dozen intimate cafes and bars line **Yanan Lu** just south of the PSB, across the street from the **Night Cat** music club. A few blocks away, across from the Grand Hotel, is the extravagantly decorated **Xanadu,** where patrons can listen to live performances or try it out for themselves in one of the private karaoke rooms. For low-key (and less off-key) spectator sports, check out the daily **soccer** matches in **Victory Square,** or head to **Zhongshan Square** at night to play **hackey-sack** and **badminton** with the student population.

👁 SIGHTS

Dalian ain't about musty museums or ossified temples. Tourists are usually satisfied with the sea air, the great shopping, the glamorous atmosphere, and, oh, the beaches. After all, markets, malls, and skylines don't require admission fees. In the west, **People's Square** was home until 1999 to one of China's best **Stalin monuments,** now relocated to neighboring Lushun (see p. 211). Farther east on Zhongshan Lu is **Victory Square,** a large elevated plaza with an underground shopping center, soccer field, and outdoor cafe. To the right of the Holiday Inn is **Tianjin Jie,** a jam-packed pedestrian street. A left turn on Shanghai Lu points you toward **Zhongshan Square,** lined with grandiose Western-style buildings.

BANGCHUI ISLAND SCENIC AREA (bàngchuí dǎo fēngjǐng qū; 棒棰岛风景区). This area wears its sparkling blue waters and emerald green hills with no trace of shame. Gardens and waterfalls surround the road, and the clifftops afford spectacular views of the Dalian Port and Bohai Sea. The northern drive features some excellent scenic moments. Dalian's best swimming beach is here, inside the rather exclusive guesthouse and golf course complex. *(About 1hr. outside Dalian. Take the bus to Hutan Gongyuan; from there, a taxi to Bangchui and back to Dalian costs Y40-50. Round-trip taxis from the city center cost Y60-100. Beach complex Y20; northern drive Y5 per person.)* **Tiger Beach Park** (hǔtān gōngyuán; 虎滩公园), about five minutes away, is infinitely tackier than Bangchui. *(Take bus #2 from Victory Square or #4 from Changchun Lu to Hutan Gongyuan. Open daily 5:30am-6pm.)*

FUJIAZHUANG BEACH (fùjiāzhuāng hǎishuǐ yúlè chǎng; 傅家庄海水娱乐场).
Those expecting the Riviera or even the Jersey shore should be forewarned—the
Chinese beach experience is like none other. Barking loudspeakers, bawling children, crowded tents, and the sharp pebbled ground temper the fun just a bit. To
avoid the crowds, walk past a string of trinket vendors and seafood restaurants to
a path that leads to a clifftop. At best, it's a good spot for a picnic and for those
desperate for some ocean exposure. *(Accessible via bus #401 from Victory Square, or a
Y15-20 taxi. Open 24hr. Ticket office open Apr.-Oct. 7:30am-6:30pm. Y1.)*

SOUTHWESTERN DALIAN. Xinghai Square (xīnghǎi guǎngchǎng; 星海广场), once a
garbage dump, is now an oceanfront square reputedly larger than Beijing's Tiananmen. A kilometer away is **Xinghai Park** (xīnghǎi gōngyuán; 星海公园), where the typical array of rickety rides and trinket vendors is supplemented by bungee jumping
(Y160) and **Sun Asia Ocean World** (Y70), with Asia's longest watertank tunnel. *(Both
Xinghai Square and Xinghai Park are accessible via buses #22 from Victory Square and bus #23
from Zhongshan Square. Park open daily 8am-5:30pm. Y15. Aquarium open daily 8am-5pm.)*

■ DAYTRIPS FROM DALIAN

LUSHUN

*35km southwest of Dalian. Accessible by **train** (2hr.; 3 per day 7:10am-5:45pm, returning
9:35am, 3:50, and 5:10pm; Y4.5), **taxi** (approx. Y200 round-trip), and bus. **Blue buses**
(every 5min. 5am-6:30pm, round-trip Y13) go from Dalian's South Road Bus Station (nán lù
kèyùn zhàn; 旅顺南路客运站), west of Xinghai Park at the end of Zhongshan Lu; to get
there, take bus #23 from Victory Square. Buses return from Lushun Bus Station (lǚshùn qìchē
zhàn; 旅顺汽车站) with similar frequency 5am-6:30pm. Hiring a taxi (Y70-100) once in
Lushun is the only way to tour the sites. **Admission** to Lushun sights Y10-30 per sight.*

Truly a must-see for fans of naval war history, the port of Lushun (旅顺) was occupied by the Japanese during the Sino-Japanese War of 1894-95 and then later
leased to the Russians, who held the town until 1954 under the name of Port
Arthur. Lushun's continued role as a naval base means access is highly restricted
for Westerners (seemingly less so for Japanese and Korean tour groups). You can
try your luck and inquire about official permission at the Dalian PSB. Some travelers foolishly choose to go "unofficially"; stepping out of the taxi even once in
Lushun risks a fine of up to Y5000.

Many of the Russian buildings in the downtown area, the train station being
among the most original, have been preserved, and remains of forts and batteries
dot the surrounding hills and cliffs. The **Stalin Monument** formerly residing in
Dalian's People's Square is now next to the Russian cemetery, known as the
"Tombs of the Victims of the Japanese Massacre." The tower atop **Mount Baiyu** offers
a view of Lushun's horseshoe-shaped harbor and strategic lay of the land.

SNAKE ISLAND

*10km off the northern tip of the Liaodong Peninsula. Accessible via the Twin-Island Holiday
Villa (双岛湾度假村), a Y40 taxi ride northeast of Lushun. Boats depart from the Villa dock
at 9am, 1, and 3pm, returning 2hr. later. Round-trip boat ride and island fee Y120.*

Snake Island (shé dǎo; 蛇岛)...paradise lost? Maybe not. This devilish Garden of
Eden is home to numerous species of snakes. Visitors are confined to a "safety
zone" as they observe Eve's slithering temptors; indeed, even herpetologists may
be grateful for this. The **Snake Exhibition Hall** (shé zhǎn guǎn; 蛇展馆) on Youyi Lu
in Lushun has live displays of each of the island's species.

CENTRAL CHINA

Winding through the provinces of Shaanxi, Shanxi, and Henan, the Yellow River both sustains and betrays the people who live along its banks. The splendid history of the area around the river valley, known as the "cradle of Chinese civilization," is testament to the life-giving force of the river, which provides fertile loess soil and is the vital source of irrigation for the otherwise parched land. But the Yellow River's various nicknames ("China's Sorrow" or "The Ungovernable") hint at the other side of the story. The tempestuous river periodically rises above its banks, flooding farmland and leaving devastation in its wake. Despite the perpetual risk of inundation, central China was a hotbed of cultural and political activity from 3000 BC to AD 1000. Numerous ancient kingdoms and every early dynasty established capitals in this region, and the Qin dynasty, the first to conquer and consolidate all of China, maintained its administrative center in the great city of Chang'an (present-day Xian).

Aside from coping with the vicissitudes of the river, it also fell to residents of this region to buffer the rest of the county from repeated northern invasions. This task was made somewhat easier by the construction of the Great Wall, part of which ran along the northern fringes of Shaanxi and Shanxi provinces. Eventually, however, the combined threat of floods and invasion proved debilitating. After the fall of the Tang, the central China region fell on hard times.

Only in the last 50 years has the area's economy picked up, as coal- and iron-rich cities like Zhengzhou, Taiyuan, and Datong have been transformed into important industrial centers. Around the same time, Inner Mongolia was incorporated as China's first autonomous region. Ironically, the land on which China's fiercest enemies were born and raised is now connected by direct rail line with the same provinces that served as China's first line of defense.

All this development has resulted in little that should appeal to tourists; quilts of smog blanket many major central cities. But it has succeeded in opening up one of the world's richest historical stashes to outsiders. Most visitors to China at some time or another make their way to Xian in Shaanxi province, home of the awesome Terracotta Warriors that were buried with Emperor Qin Shihuang. Yet those who make Xian their only stop in Central China will be missing out. Even the most polluted cities offer sights worth seeing, and travelers can get a breath of fresh air as they travel to the lush valleys and green mountains of Wutaishan or the sprawling grasslands of Inner Mongolia.

HIGHLIGHTS OF CENTRAL CHINA

TERRACOTTA THRILLS of Emperor Qin Shihuang's immense underground army near **Xian** (p. 222).

MESMERIZING BEAUTY AND MONASTIC LIFE in **Wutaishan** (p. 252).

BUDDHAS EVERYWHERE in the cliffs and caves of **Yungang** (p. 257) and **Longmen** (p. 238) **Grottoes.**

DESERT DUNES, NOT KARAOKE at the **Singing Sands Gorge** (p. 268) near Baotou.

GRASSLAND GROUPIES near **Hohhot** (p. 264) and, less so, in **Manzhouli** (p. 271).

IMPERIAL SPLENDOR AND FABULOUS FOOD in **Kaifeng** (p. 240).

Central China

N

RUSSIA

MONGOLIA

INNER MONGOLIA

SHANXI

CHINA

SHAANXI

HENAN

Yellow Sea

MONGOLIA

Xilinhot

Linxi

Erenhot

INNER MONGOLIA

Bayan Obo

Wudangzhao Monastery

Jining

Zhangjiakou

Wuyuan

Baotou

Hohhot

BEIJING MUNICIPALITY

Beijing

Dongsheng

Datong

Yellow R.

Wutaishan 3018m

Hengshan 2017m

HEBEI

Tianjin

Tengger Desert

Wuhai

Ghengis Khan Mausoleum

Shenmu

Xinzhou

Yinchuan

Muus Desert

Yulin

Qingxu

Taiyuan

Shijiazhuang

NINGXIA

Suide

Fenyang

Pingyao

Handan

SHANDONG

Luo R.

Yan'an

SHAANXI

Fen R.

SHANXI

Changzhi

Anyang

Hebi

Xiankou

Guokou Falls

Houma

Xinxiang

Hancheng

Yellow R.

Kaifeng

Tongchuan

Sanmenxia

Luoyang

Zhengzhou

Tianshui

Baoji

Xianyang

Wei R.

Shaolin Monastery

Songshan 1440m

GANSU

Huxian

Xi'an

Huashan 2160m

Tonggun Falls

Xuchang

Shangxian

HENAN

ANHUI

Yangxian

Nanyang

Guangyuan

Xiangfun

Xinyang

Huangchuan

SICHUAN

HUBEI

Ankang

CHONGQING

0   200 miles

0   200 kilometers

Wuhan

SHAANXI 陕西

Referring to Shaanxi as the "center of China" elicits more than a few scoffs. Sure, Shaanxi may be the geographical center of China, but Beijing is the center in the meaningful sense of the word. However, for a thousand years, Shaanxi was the center of China politically, economically, and culturally, as well as geographically. The soft, fertile silt of the Yellow River valley in the northern portion of the province was ideal for cultivation, and settlements of farmers sprang up along the banks of the river. Despite the region's drawbacks—bad weather, the danger of floods, and the threat of attack from the north—the Zhou, the Qin, the Han, the Sui, and the Tang dynasties all maintained their capitals in Shaanxi. The ancient capital city of Chang'an, situated along the Silk Route which connected eastern China to Central Asia, grew into a magnificent cosmopolitan center during the Tang dynasty, with a population of over one million. By the end of the 9th century, however, the province's glory days were coming to an end, and when the capital city was sacked in 884, Shaanxi's fall from grace was swift and severe. The next millenium left Shaanxi, plagued by droughts, rebellions, and famines, in a state of dreadful impoverishment, with whole counties virtually wiped out by starvation and disease. It wasn't until the Communists ended their Long March in Yanan and used the city as a base from which to fight the Japanese and the Guomindang that Shaanxi attained any significance.

Nowadays, Shaanxi seems to be pulling out of its thousand-year slump. The dry, dusty northern region of the province is still quite poor, but an influx of investment—both foreign and domestic—has breathed new life into the southern region, turning the city of Xian into an important center of light industry and resulting in burgeoning construction in the entire province. Shaanxi has also become one of China's most popular tourist destinations, due in large part to the famous Terracotta Warriors. Things are looking up for old Shaanxi, but don't call it a comeback—Shaanxi's been here for years.

XIAN 西安 ☎ 029

When tourists hear the name Xian, they immediately think of the armies of terracotta warriors nearby. But Xian is no one-hit wonder; the city itself has a lot to brag about and can back up any boasts with a mighty impressive resumé. The city began to flourish during the golden Han age, but it wasn't until the Tang dynasty that Chang'an really came into its own. Situated on the crossroads between China and Central Asia, Chang'an grew into one of the wealthiest and most sophisticated cities in the world, a metropolis on equal footing with Rome or Constantinople. After the fall of the Tang dynasty, the city's tenure as capital of China came to an end, and for a thousand years, not much happened in Xian, though the city continued to act as the trade broker with Central Asia.

Ironically, it was this millennium of inactivity that left Xian so attractive to tourists today. A latecomer on the industrialization bandwagon, Xian is now undergoing rapid development, and the combination of development and the architecture of the past make the city appear prosperous yet weathered. Xian also contains a vibrant Muslim quarter, which adds an element of architectural and culinary diversity to the mix. This mellow, pungent giant deserves to make it onto many a traveler's list of greatest hits.

✴ ORIENTATION

Although the modern metropolis has long since outgrown the confines of its ancient walls, Xian remains remarkably compact for a city of three million. Typical

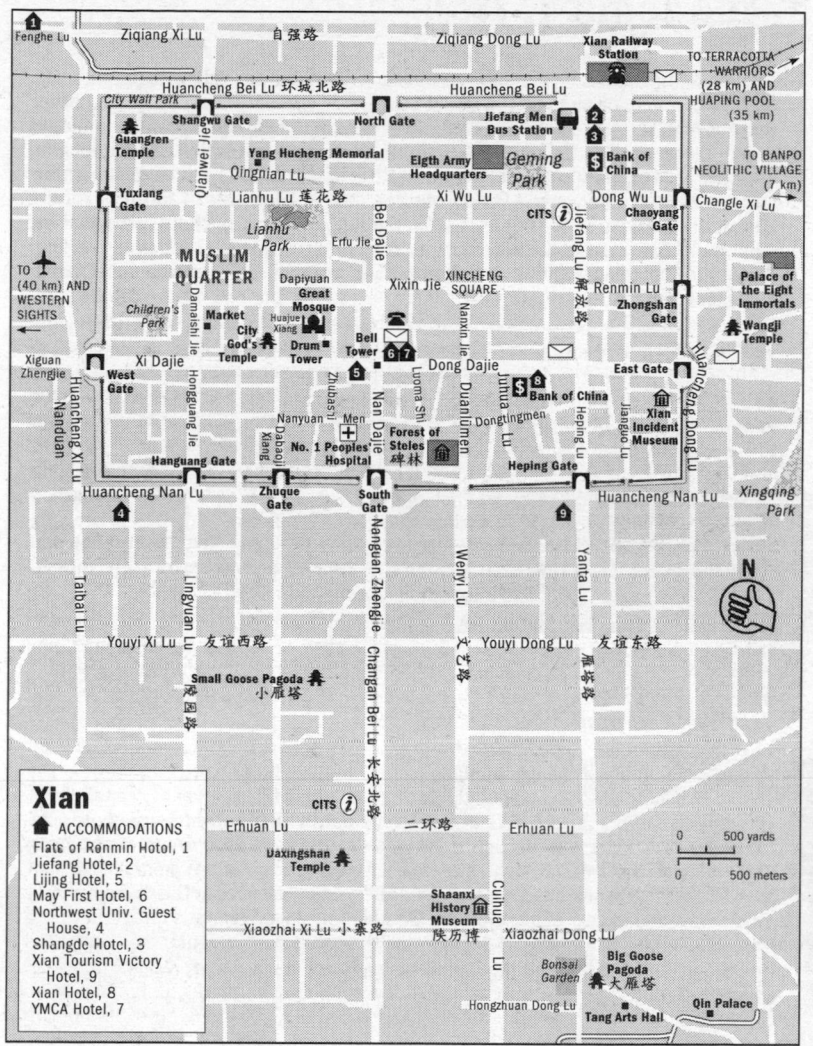

Xian

ACCOMMODATIONS
Flats of Renmin Hotel, 1
Jiefang Hotel, 2
Lijing Hotel, 5
May First Hotel, 6
Northwest Univ. Guest
House, 4
Shangde Hotel, 3
Xian Tourism Victory
Hotel, 9
Xian Hotel, 8
YMCA Hotel, 7

of historic Chinese cities, streets inside the walls are arranged in a grid pattern that ends abruptly in the narrow alleys of the **Muslim Quarter**. The **Bell Tower** (zhōng lóu; 钟楼) marks the city center; from this point, **Bei Dajie** (北大街), **Nan Dajie** (南大街), **Dong Dajie** (东大街), and **Xi Dajie** (西大街) extend to the city gates. **Jiefang Lu** (解放路) runs south from the main train and bus stations to **Heping Gate** (和平门), becoming **Heping Lu** (和平路) south of Dong Dajie. Dong Dajie, Jiefang Lu, and the surrounding quarters are lined with hotels and shops, but many of the major tourist attractions are outside the city walls. Big Goose Pagoda, Small Goose Pagoda, and the Shaanxi History Museum are accessible by bus directly from the train station, as is the Eastern Tour (which includes the Terracotta Warriors). The main train and bus stations are just northeast of the city walls.

◲ TRANSPORTATION

Airplanes: Xian Xianyang Airport (xīān xiányáng guójì jīchǎng; 西安咸阳国际机场; ☎ 870 8450), about 50km northwest of Xian, is accessible by shuttle bus (1hr., every hr. 5am-6pm, Y20) from the **CAAC ticket office,** 296 Laodong Lu (☎ 870 2299). Ticket office open daily 8am-9am. To: **Beijing** (8-9 per day, Y840); **Chengdu** (5-7 per day, Y500); **Chongqing** (Sa-Tu and Th, Y460; **Dunhuang** (1 per day, Y1340); **Guangzhou** (3 per day, Y1190); **Harbin** (M, W, and F; Y1220); **Hong Kong** (1 per day); **Jiayuguan** (seasonal, Y890); **Kunming** (up to 4 per day, Y840); **Lanzhou** (2-4 per day, Y430); **Lhasa** (1 per day Su-M, W, and F; Y1320); **Nanjing** (1-3 per day, Y860); **Shanghai** (at least 4 per day, Y1010); **Ürümqi** (3-7 per day, Y1330); **Wuhan** (3-5 per day, Y550); **Xiamen** (1-2 per day, Y1310); and **Xining** (M-Tu and F-Sa, Y520). International flights to **Nagoya, Japan** (1-2 per day).

Trains: Most travelers arrive in and depart from Xian by train. At certain times of the year, particularly in July, tickets can be difficult to acquire. Hotels and hostels sometimes buy up tickets, jack up prices, and leave travelers to pay the difference. Persistence seems to pay off, though. **Xian Train Station** (xīān huǒchē zhàn; 西安火车站; ☎ 727 6076) is at the north end of Jiefang Lu. Foreigners can buy tickets at any window, but the foreigners' ticketing office is on the south side of the station on the 2nd floor. Open daily 8:30-11:30am and 2:30-5:30pm. To: **Beijing** (14½-17hr., 6 per day, Y263); **Chengdu** (16-19hr., 5 per day, Y124-199); **Chongqing** (28½hr., 1 per day, Y170); **Guangzhou** (28-29hr., 2 per day, Y414); **Lanzhou** (12-14hr., 6 per day, Y104-167); **Luoyang** (9½hr., 1 per day, Y104); **Nanjing West** (18-22hr., 2 per day, Y163-253); **Shanghai** (20-24hr., 5 per day, Y199-301); **Taiyuan** (9½-12hr., 2 per day, Y102-163); **Ürümqi** (48hr., 1-2 per day, Y230); and **Zhengzhou** (7-10hr., 4 per day, Y77-131).

Buses: Jiefang Men Bus Station (jiěfàng mén qìchē zhàn; 解放门汽车站), opposite the Xian Train Station. Open 5:30am-6:30pm. Storage Y2 per bag. To: **Huashan** (2hr., every hr. 6am-4pm, Y12); **Lanzhou** (20hr., 1 sleeper per day, Y105); **Luoyang** (14-15hr., 2 per day, Y58); **Yanan** (8hr., 3 per day, Y50); **Yinchuan** (20hr., 6 per day, Y115); and **Zhengzhou** (12hr., 1 per day, Y75).

Local Transportation: Local buses usually cost Y0.5, with A/C Y2; some routes have no fare collector to make change. **Minibus** prices vary with distance (Y0.5-5). Several key routes, including **#5** (train station to Yike Daxue) and **#18** (Xiaozhai to Zhangjiabao), run 6am-11pm, but most run 7am-7pm (some have shorter winter hours). Buses **#5** and **41** serve Jiefang and Heping Lu, while **#43, 201,** and **205** ply the Xi and Dong Dajie corridor. Bus **#610** is Xian's closest equivalent to a tourist bus; from Jiefang Men Bus Station, this minibus stops at the Bell Tower, Drum Tower, Little Goose Pagoda, Big Goose Pagoda, and the Shaanxi History Museum (runs daily 7am-8pm).

Taxis: Base fare Y5, each additional km Y1.2-1.7. Y0.3 per km surcharge 10pm-6am. Airport to city center Y100-120; train or Jiefang Men Bus Station to city center Y10-15.

Bike Rental: The **Flats of Renmin Hotel** (p. 217) offers bike rentals.

ⓘ PRACTICAL INFORMATION

Travel Agencies: CITS, 48 Changan Bei Lu (☎ 524 1864). Open daily 8am-5:30pm. Other branches at numerous hotels and the airport. CITS arranges tours and books tickets (commission Y60). **China Golden Bridge Travel Service** (zhōngguó jīn qiáo lǚyóu gōngsī; 中国金桥旅游公司), Bell Tower Hotel, Rm. 227 and 231 (☎ 725 8863 or 725 7975) provides similar services (commission Y60) and can arrange discounts at many hotels. Open daily 8am-8pm.

Bank of China: 38 Juhua Lu, 2nd Fl. (☎ 726 1726). Open M-F 9am-noon and 1-5pm.

Bookstores: Shaanxi Foreign Languages Bookstore (shǎnxī shěng wài wén shūdiàn; 陕西省外文书店), 349 Dong Dajie (☎ 726 9844). Decent selection of literature classics, mysteries, Shakespeare, as well as the obligatory dictionaries. Open daily 9am-6pm. **Xinhua Bookstore,** 372 Dong Dajie. Not quite as impressive as the Foreign Languages Bookstore. Open daily 9am-8pm.

Market: Parkson (báishēng gòuwù zhōngxīn; 百盛购物中心), 119 Dong Dajie, near the Hyatt Regency, has a supermarket with a large selection of Western brands. Open daily 9:30am-10pm; in winter 9:30am-9pm.

PSB: 138 Xi Dajie (☎727 5934). Open M-F 8:30am-noon and 3-6pm.

Hospital: No. 1 People's Hospital (dì yī rénmín yīyuàn; 第一人民医院; ☎721 7170), on Nan Dajie Zhong Duan.

Internet Access: China Telecom Internet Club, 169 Dong Dajie, 2nd Fl. (☎723 2017 or 723 2037), near the Bell Tower. Clean and quiet, with fast connections and private booths. Y12 per hr. Open daily 8am-8pm. **Tian Yan Network of Club Old Gun Bar,** 217 Dong Dajie (☎728 1449), in the basement. Y20 per hr. Open 24hr. The **Flats of Renmin Hotel** also offers access.

Post and Telecommunications: China Post, at the Bell Tower, offers EMS (counter #1) and Poste Restante (counter #14; Y2.3 per item). Open daily 8:30am-8pm. **Postal Code:** 710003.

◤ ACCOMMODATIONS

Hotels that accept foreigners cater primarily to business travelers and tour groups. Despite the abundance of four- and five-star hotels, backpackers and other budget travelers can still find several relatively inexpensive options. Such establishments are clustered around the train station, while more upmarket places line Dong Dajie and Xi Dajie in the center of the city. As always, bargain hard.

Flats of Renmin Hotel (rénmín dàshà gōngyù; 人民大厦公寓), 11 Fenghe Lu (☎624 0349), about 5min. from Xinghuo Lu. Bus #9 makes the 30min. trip from the parking lot on the right side of the train station exit to Xinghuo Lu (9th stop); a taxi from the train station should cost about Y10. From the airport, the CAAC bus offers a cheaper alternative to taxis (Y100 or more); the CAAC bus stops at Yuxiang Men, and a Y5 cab ride covers the remaining distance. All rooms in this backpacker enclave have A/C and TV, although the paint is peeling in places, the hot water can be unreliable, and the carpet looks a bit scruffy. Restaurants just outside the door. Internet access Y20 per hr. Arranges tours to the Terracotta Warriors and helps guests obtain train tickets in Xian's competitive market. Western breakfast in Kane's Kafe included. Deposit Y50. 4-bed dorms in the old building Y35, new building Y45; singles and doubles with bath Y160.

Jiefang Hotel (jiěfàng fàndiàn; 解放饭店), 321 Jiefang Lu (☎742 8946), on the left hand side of the train station's main exit. Rooms have A/C, TV, and bath; the more expensive doubles are brighter, with newer appliances and more luxurious furnishings. Rooms facing the train station are generally noisier than those in back. Reservations recommended. Doubles in back building Y180, front building Y220-240; triples Y360.

YMCA Hotel (qīngnián huì bīnguǎn; 青年会宾馆), 339 Dong Dajie (☎726 2288). The Y offers a central location and fantastic deals on their five small, windowless, spotless basement rooms with A/C, TV, phone, common bath, and sauna. Basement: singles Y80; one double Y120; one triple Y150. Upstairs: doubles Y268; triples Y488.

Shangde Hotel (shàngdé bīnguǎn; 尚德宾馆), 198 Shangde Lu (☎742 6164), opposite the Jiefang Men Bus Station and a block south (toward the city center) of the city wall. Convenience is the Shangde's biggest asset. Standard rooms have somewhat worn amenities. Shared triples (Y30 per bed) with showerless bathrooms in the basement. Reservations recommended. Singles Y158; doubles Y158-178; triples Y188.

May First Hotel (wǔ yī fàndiàn;五一饭店), 351 Dong Dajie (☎721 2212), just minutes by foot from the Bell Tower. This establishment's fame is derived mainly from its Chinese restaurant at street level. Walk through the restaurant to the stairs indicated by the pink sign marked "Housekeeping" (客房部). Rooms have all standard amenities; the cheapest ones are windowless. Singles Y178-238; doubles Y280-300; triples Y360.

Liging Hotel (lìjìng jiǔdiàn; 丽晶酒店), 6 Xi Dajie (☎728 8731, ext. 100), at the southwest corner of the Bell Tower Square between Zhubashi and Nan Dajie. Well-maintained

CENTRAL CHINA

rooms with A/C, TV, IDD, and bath. Courteous staff and a central location are a plus. Room discounts available for large groups or longer stays. Singles Y380; doubles Y480.

Xian Hotel (xīān fànzhuāng; 西安饭庄), 298 Dong Dajie (☎ 721 6120), between Juhua Lu and Nanxin Lu. Bus #201 from the train station stops on Dong Dajie not far from the entrance. Large standard rooms make this centrally located hotel appealing, if not quite worth the price. Breakfast included. The only single Y250; doubles Y306; triples Y440.

Northwest University Guesthouse (xīběi dàxué bīnguǎn; 西北大学宾馆; ☎ 830 2975 or 721 1554, ext. 2100), on the Northwest University campus. Bus #205 from behind the train station at the north end of Shangde Lu stops opposite the campus gate at Xibei Daxue (8th stop, 20min.). Cross the overpass and enter the campus, continuing straight for about 5min. Turn right at the sidewalk just past the playing field on the right. The two buildings are inside the gate, and the reception is in the building with a number of official-looking plaques on the front wall. All rooms have private bath and appear clean. With the exception of the cheaper single rooms, A/C, TV, and phone are standard amenities. Student discounts available. Singles Y100; doubles Y160; suites Y280.

Xian Tourism Victory Hotel (shènglì fàndiàn; 胜利饭店; ☎ 785 3042), at the intersection of Huancheng Nan Lu and Yanta Lu just south of the city wall. Take bus #5 or 41 from the train station to Heping Men. From the bus stop, the hotel is a 3min. walk toward the city wall, on the left side of the road at the first intersection. The boxy rooms all have A/C, TV, phone, and bath. Deposit Y10. Singles Y140; doubles Y168.

☑ FOOD

The quality of Xian's cuisine impresses the average cheap food connoisseur, with backpacker cafes and Western-style restaurants constituting just a small portion of the city's dining options. The Muslim food is excellent and very cheap. **Damaishi Jie** (大麦市街), **Zhubashi** (竹笆市), and the other streets around the Great Mosque in the Muslim Quarter are lined with small food stalls designated as *qingzhen*, the Chinese term for "Muslim" (which literally means "pure and true"). *Yangrou paomo*, a mutton soup peppered with torn pieces of dry bread cake, is especially popular (usually Y4-7). Other Xian specialties include rice cakes with sweet filling (*migao*; Y1-2), a mutton and wheat mixture (*fengzhenrou*; Y2-3), and dark noodles (*helaomian*; Y2-3). **Tanshi Jie,** a passage teeming with vendors selling everything edible from dried spices to live fish, runs north of Dong Dajie.

▨ **Jia San Soup Parcel Restaurant** (jiǎ sān bāozi guǎn; 贾三包子馆), 121 Xiyangshi Jie (☎ 725 7507), in the Muslim Quarter. Customers are attracted again and again to this establishment's famed dumplings (10 dumplings for Y5). The uniquely flavored *zhou* (粥; Y2), a sweet rice porridge, is also a favorite. Open daily 7:30am-2 or 3am.

▨ **Kane's Kafe,** 11 Fenghe Lu, conveniently across from the lobby of the Flats of Renmin Hotel. Friendly proprietor Kane dishes up Chinese and Western specialties as well as free travel advice—in English. The extensive English menu includes Kane's special pita bread with pork, beef, or chicken filling (Y5), and beer for Y4-6 per bottle. English music and movies upon request. Kane also works with the Flats Hotel to arrange tours to the Eastern and Western sights. Open daily 7:30am-2am.

Dad's Home Cooking, 2 Fenghe Lu, up the street from its previous choice location across from the Flats. This establishment was left alone after Mum's recently closed its doors, yet it continues to dish up Chinese and Western food (including their famous crepe-like pancakes, Y5-7) to its backpacker clientele. Bike rental, free maps and information, next-day laundry service, tours, and help in finding train tickets out of Xian (average commission Y50) available. Check out the travelers' logbooks for advice and juicy stories. Open daily from 7 or 8am-11pm or midnight.

May First Hotel Restaurant (wǔyī fàndiàn; 五一饭店), 351 Dong Dajie, a short walk east of the Bell Tower. Lots of seats, lots of delectable choices, and lots of hustle and bustle. Walk up to the counters and choose from endless varieties of dumplings, noodles, and soup (generally Y1-10). A good place for a cheap meal, but not a leisurely chat. Open daily 7:30am-9:30pm.

King Palace (wángfǔ dàjiǔdiàn; 王府大酒店), 333 Dong Dajie (☎ 725 1224), on the north side of the street. This enormous restaurant boasts seven floors; go with gravity and stay downstairs for all the fun. Pick out dumplings (Y3-5), noodles (Y3-6), and more. The 2nd and 3rd floors offer Cantonese and Sichuanese cuisine; from the 5th floor up, karaoke and dancing rule the house. Open daily 10:30am-10:30pm.

Laosunjia Restaurant (laǒsūnjiā fànzhuāng; 老孙家饭庄), 364 Dong Dajie (☎ 721 0936). Laosunjia is more than a restaurant—it's a philosophical enterprise. Current owner Ma Mingyan was carefully schooled in Marxism, Leninism, Maoism, and Deng Xiaoping Theory. The famous establishment has five "feature foods," including Muslim *jiaozi* (Y0.7), Xinzheng salt-cured beef and mutton (Y13), beef and mutton buns, and *yangrou paomo*. Upstairs banquet rooms serve delicacies such as peacock (Y98) and fawn (Y58). Ask for a brochure to check out Laosunjia's methods of indoctrinating employees, 10 decades of favorable calligraphic commentary, and mugshots of world leaders and public figures eating mutton. Open daily 7am-10pm.

Anellia, 261 Dong Dajie. Sweeten your palate with an enormous and elaborate selection of cakes, ice cream (Y3 per scoop), breads (Y2-7), and pastries (Y3-7). Open daily 8:30am-10:30pm.

Sushi Restaurant, 223 Dong Dajie (☎ 721 5855 or 724 1148). Small sushi (Y6), soup (Y12-20), and cooked fish (Y20-48). Picture menu available. Open daily 11am-1pm.

Pizzeria Italiana (yìdàlì bǐsàbǐng shǐ; 意大利比萨饼室), 297 Dong Dajie (☎ 723 3693), on the ground floor of the Friendship Supermarket. Pizzas (including dessert and fruit pizzas) Y12.5 (slice) to Y70 (large pizza). Open daily 9am-11pm.

Shaanxi Special Local Fast Food Restaurant (xīan fànzhuāng; 西安饭庄), 298 Dong Dajie, just east of Juhua Lu. Wander around the 12 display stations and then point at assorted plates of *jiaozi, baozi,* veggies, and other unidentifiable but intriguing options (Y0.5-16). More expensive restaurant upstairs. Open daily 7:30am-8pm.

◪ NIGHTLIFE

Most bars, discos, and clubs are concentrated along Dong Dajie between Bei and Nan Dajie and Jiefang Lu/Heping Lu. There is also a smattering of theaters and performance halls in the city. In general, more action can be found on the streets than in the bars. The **Bell Tower Square** is especially lively on warm summer nights, when it is filled with children, couples in love, and peddlers pushing roses to passers-by. Weary travelers might consider forgoing the bar scene and swapping stories over a bottle of Tsingtao at Kane's Kafe or Dad's Home Cooking.

Apollo Music Bar, 348 Dong Dajie (☎ 721 3661). You're on a mission. You ascend the huge marble staircase for a night at the Apollo. A huge stage gracing the front room catches your eye. The low lighting and intimate tables provide the perfect spot for a romantic (if other-worldly) encounter. You touch down and order a space-age drink from the extensive Chinese and English drink menu. Will it be beer (Y20-30), wine (Y78-128), or both? Just as you are about to discover alien life forms, the owner kicks you out. Open daily 2pm-2am.

Hong Fang Pottery Bar (hóngfáng tǎo bā; 红坊陶吧), 207 Dong Dajie, 2nd Fl. (☎ 741 1307), on the north side of the street. This mellow establishment, like its cousins or imitations elsewhere in China, is the ideal place to get down and dirty. There is an instructor on the premises to assist artistically challenged customers. Even on most weeknights, the place is comfortably busy. Liberate your artistic spirit with a few bottles of Budweiser, Tsingtao (Y18), or Corona (Y25). Open daily noon-2am.

1+1 Disco Bar (1+1 dísīkē jiǔbā; 1+1 迪斯科酒吧), 285 Dong Dajie (☎ 721 6265), on the left before Tanshi Jie as you come from the Bell Tower area. Upstairs, the decor is space-age, with stars hanging from the ceiling and futuristic metal architecture. Among the waiters, you just may find your knight in shining armor—or in a metallic silver bow-tie. "Romantic music" until 9pm, followed by a 45min. live act and disco dancing until the wee hours of the morning. Imported beers Y25-28. Open daily 8pm-2am.

Darts Bar (fēibiāo jiǔbā; 飞镖酒吧), 270 Dong Dajie (☎ 727 3560). Try your luck at one of the six dart boards while downing a Heineken (Y20) or Budweiser (Y18-20). Most other drinks Y25 and up. Open daily 2pm-around 2am.

Single One Piano Bar (xīngé màn gāngqín jiǔbā; 辛格曼钢琴酒吧), 216 Dong Dajie, 2nd Fl. (☎ 721 6949), on the south side of the street and just west of Jiefang Lu. The rickety staircase could prove quite treacherous after a night of carousing. The piano music provides a relaxing alternative to the current releases played at top volume in some of Xian's clubs. Tsingtao Y15, Budweiser Y18. Open daily until around 2am.

Peace House (hépíng jiǔbā; 和平酒吧), 191 Dong Dajie (☎ 743 7932), on the north side of the street, east of Shangde Lu and west of Jiefang Lu. Climb the stairs marked by a hot pink sign and "Give Peace a Chance." Tinsel, high rafters, and some live music give a certain charm, but those seeking sweaty dancing crowds had best arrive fashionably late. Tsingtao Y18, Heineken Y21, cocktails Y28. Open daily 7:30pm-1am or later.

◉ SIGHTS

One-day tours organized by tourist agencies and hotels allow tourists to see most of Xian's famous landmarks before catching the next train out of town. The more popular **Eastern Tour** (see p. 222) generally includes the Terracotta Warriors, Banpo Village, Qin Shihuang's tomb, and sometimes Huaqing Pool. The less popular **Western Tour** (see p. 223) typically covers the Xianyang City Museum, several imperial tombs, the Qian Tomb, and Famen Temple.

Within Xian's city walls, the streets near the Great Mosque constitute the **Muslim Quarter,** part of the **Old City,** where most of Xian's Muslim Hui community resides. Good walking streets include Nanyuan Men, Huajue Xiang, and Damaishi Jie, which runs off Xi Dajie. Not only is the food terrific and terrifically cheap here, but it comes in an area that is full of surprises: hidden mosques, winding alleys, and scads of tourist paraphernalia.

XIAN CITY SIGHTS

GREAT MOSQUE (dà qīngzhēn sì; 大清真寺). Established in AD 742, the Great Mosque is gorgeous, featuring charmingly peeling and cracking wood and unusual and arresting bright teal roof tiles. Each of the mosque's four courtyards holds historically fascinating religious records, including a stele called the "Moon Tablet" that bears Arabic inscriptions on the Muslim calendar, made by an *imam*. Other treasures include a handwritten copy of the Qur'an, as well as Chinese and Arabic inscriptions from the Qur'an carved into the ceiling of the hall of worship. In the second courtyard stand tablets inscribed by famous Chinese calligraphers; they are considered some of the best works of art in the country. Non-Muslims are not allowed inside the hall of worship, but the parts of the mosque accessible to the general public are well worth a visit. *(Buses #201, 205, and 610 from the train station stop at the Bell Tower. From Xi Dajie, follow Zhubashi Jie north 1 block until just past the covered tunnel; red signs point the rest of the way. The entrance is down an alley called Huajue Xiang, on the left. Open daily 8am-8pm. Y12, including an English guidebook.)*

SHAANXI HISTORY MUSEUM (shǎnxī lìshǐ bówùguǎn; 陕西历史博物馆). The history museum is a success both inside and out. Opened in 1991, the complex itself is designed on a grand scale. Large Tang-style stone buildings with white tile eaves look out onto wide courtyards of trim grass and more white stone. The exterior feels contemporary and classical at the same time, and the interior is equally well designed. The huge space stores over 3.7 million historical relics, preserved and pampered by all sorts of environmental control systems. The central hall features a permanent exhibit on the history and culture of Shaanxi, focusing on the Zhou, Qin, Han, and Tang dynasties. Other exhibits include a survey of China's Bronze Age and a gallery of ancient pottery and sculptures. The exhibits have English captions. *(91 Xiaozhai Dong Lu. Take bus #610 from the train station. ☎ 525 4727. Open daily 8:30am-6pm; in winter 9am-5:30pm. Y25, students Y12.)*

BELL TOWER (zhōng lóu; 钟楼). First erected in 1384, this 36m pavilion was moved to its present central location at the intersection of Bei, Nan, Dong, and Xi Dajie in 1582 and then repaired and rebuilt in 1740. The second floor houses an exhibit of ancient musical instruments, and the third floor displays calligraphy and Chinese scroll painting. From the top, visitors get a bird's-eye view of the former capital's straight boulevards, and a close-up of the bright colors on the underside of the tower eaves. Elaborate musical performances (every 30min., 9-11:30am and 2:30-5:30pm) even drown out the car horns below. *(Take bus #201, 205, or 610 from the train station to Zhonglou; enter through the pedestrian tunnel. Open daily 8am-7pm. Y15.)*

BIG GOOSE PAGODA. (dà yàn tǎ; 大雁塔). This pagoda, built in AD 652, houses over 600 sets of Buddhist scriptures brought to China from India by Xuan Zang, the most famous monk of the Tang dynasty. Xuan spent 17 years studying Buddhism in India, translating many works from Sanskrit into Chinese. He also taught several Japanese students the ways of Buddhism at the Big Goose Pagoda, catalyzing a religious revolution across East Asia. The pagoda itself, which has been restored many times in the last 1200 years, is a square pyramid of blue brick, 64m tall. On the first story, two steles offer a Tang-era treatise on Xuan Zang's translations of the Buddhist scriptures that were the pride of his time in India. The pagoda was also known in the Tang dynasty for its walls, on which imperial exam degree recipients inscribed autobiographical poems. *(Bus #610 from the train station stops outside the main entrance. ☎ 521 5014. Open daily 8am-6:45pm; in winter 8am-5:30pm. Park admission Y10; pagoda admission Y15, students Y8.)*

LITTLE GOOSE PAGODA (xiǎo yàn tǎ; 小雁塔). Completed in AD 709, the Little Goose Pagoda originally shot up 15 tiers high, but an earthquake later reduced its height to 13 or 14 perspiration-inducing flights ascending 43m. Earthquakes have been something of a theme in the pagoda's history: it has survived over 70 of them. A particularly violent quake in 1487 reputedly left a foot-wide fissure that ran from the top to the bottom of the temple. The crack is rumored to have been mended by an equally violent quake that closed the gap in 1521. Twelve hundred years after its original construction, the Little Goose seems virtually untoppleable. *(Bus #610 stops on Youyi Xi Lu, at Xiao Yan Ta stop; coming from the train station, walk forward about 1 block. Open daily 8:30am-6pm. Park admission Y5; park and pagoda admission Y10.)*

CITY WALL (chéng qiáng; 城墙). Constructed in 1370, long after Xian had fallen as imperial capital to become a mere outpost under the Ming, the 14km long city wall standing today is much less imposing than the grandiose bulwarks of Xian's earlier Sui and Tang heyday. After 1949, Beijing and other cities used hefty state subsidies to tear down city walls to build highways and subways, while central planners thought Xian was too poor to "modernize." When the city finally got funding, it chose to restore the walls and turn them into a tourist draw, complete with Chinese and English explanatory signs. On summer evenings, the sections of the wall at the South Gate (southern end of Nan Dajie) and the North Gate (northern end of Bei Dajie) are popular gathering places for locals. *(From the train station, bus #9 goes to the North Gate, bus #3 goes to the South Gate, and buses #5 and 41 go to Heping Gate. Open daily 8am-10pm. Y8, students Y4.)*

PALACE OF THE EIGHT IMMORTALS (bā xiān ān; 八仙庵). The palace offers a lovely counterpoint to the overabundance of Buddhist temples in China. Its English signs share the story of the goddess who represents the mother responsible for all the stars, among other bits of Daoist lore. Under Yu Xian Bridge hangs the "lucky and peaceful bell." According to legend, if you hit the bell with a coin, you have a predestined relationship with Daoism and will be lucky and peaceful always. An active place of worship, the temple features two huge steles with gorgeous, intricate etchings on their upper sections. *(East of Zhongshan Gate. Open daily 7:30am-5pm. Y5, students Y1.)*

CENTRAL CHINA

DRUM TOWER (gǔ lóu; 鼓楼). Constructed in 1380, the Drum Tower housed a drum beaten to announce the arrival of dusk. The tower's carved beams and painted columns have held up well, with a little help from the friendly restorations bureau. A colorful exhibit of beautifully restored frescoes from the Dunhuang Grottoes, as well as Ming- and Qing-era furniture and vases, make the climb to the top floor well worth the effort. *(On Zhubashi, across a broad square from the Bell Tower. Open daily 8am-7pm. Y12.)*

XIAN FOREST OF STELES (xīān bēi lín; 西安碑林). A gold mine for calligraphers, historians, and philosophers, the Forest of Steles contains over 1000 inscription-etched stone slabs displayed in seven small exhibition halls. The collection includes tablets from copies of Confucius' *Analects*, works by Mencius, and the Dictionary of Terms, all inscribed in AD 183. There is a plan showing the layout of the former capital at Chang'an dating from the year 1000. A message inscribed by peasant rebel Li Zicheng in 1644 lamenting the oppression of the population by the feudal ruling class reads, in part: "Men eating men, and dogs also eating men." While the content of the ancient steles may be intriguing, deciphering the archaic inscriptions is reserved for those with esoteric expertise. *(18 Wenyi Bei Lu, off Shuyuan Men Cultural Street. ☎ 721 3868. Open daily 8am-6pm. Y20.)*

EASTERN TOUR

The Flats of Renmin Hotel (see p. 217) organizes the transportation for an Eastern Tour that excludes Huaqing Pool (departs 8:30am, returns 3:30pm; Y35). Individual admission fees are not included, and a minimum of four people is necessary. Almost every travel agency in Xian also offers the same tour with "more" included for a much higher price. Many visitors opt for public transportation instead.

TERRACOTTA WARRIORS

Buses #306 and 307 from the train station stop outside. Alternatively, minibuses make the trip for about Y5, sometimes dropping people off at the small amusement park about a 15min. walk from the entrance. ☎ 391 1961. A movie explains the history of the warriors, and computer screens in each vault provide English and Chinese explanations. Open daily 8:30am-5:30pm, no admission after 5pm. Y65, students Y35.

When current French President Jacques Chirac came to Xian in 1978, he declared that "with the excavation of the Qin terracotta figures and horses, the world now has its eighth wonder." Chirac's words ring true to anyone who visits the home of Xian's ◧ Terracotta Warriors (bīngmǎyǒng; 兵马俑). Founder of the dynasty that unified China in 221 BC, Emperor **Qin Shihuang** (see p. 9) strove to construct an empire underground that would reflect the glory and dignity of his empire long after his death. Thus, he immortalized his soldiers by directing artisans to carve out a terracotta army for his tomb.

In 1974, a group of peasants digging for water discovered the army, which consisted of over 7000 slightly larger-than-life clay warriors and war horses waiting in battle formation and posed according to Qin dynasty directives on the art of warfare. Each face differs from those around it, and the clay men's hands try to hold the still-sharp and still-poisoned Qin-era weapons that excited archaeologists quickly whisked away. The vaults are all partially excavated. The first vault, measuring 210m by 60m, houses 6000 soldiers; the second contains 1000; and the third holds only 68, accompanied by a war chariot. Despite the sea of soldiers on display, some suggest that the excavated army is just the start, constituting only one part of an even more magnificent system still buried in Qin Shihuang's tomb.

OTHER EASTERN TOUR SIGHTS

TOMB OF QIN SHIHUANG (qín shǐhuáng líng; 秦始皇陵). The Terracotta Warriors are only one section of the tomb of Emperor Qin Shihuang (or Yong Zheng). The famous emperor ascended the throne of the Qin kingdom at age 13, and began his tomb at Mount Lishan immediately after the death of his predecessor. Seven hundred thousand conscripts built the ruler's tomb, which contained model palaces and offices, vessels, and jewels. Because of the high mercury content in the soil, the actual tomb remains unexcavated, awaiting the arrival of better technology. All that visitors can see today is a large mound approximately 1.5km from the vaults of the terracotta warriors. The steps to the top lead to a spectacular view of the surrounding mountains, but after about five minutes, you've seen what there is to see, and your imagination is left to do the rest. *(Buses #306 and 307, from both the train station and the terracotta warriors, stop a short distance away; walk in the direction of the souvenir stands. If coming from the warriors, continue in the same direction taken by the bus back to Xian. Walking from the warriors is not recommended; a minibus should cost Y0.5-1. Open daily 7:15am-6:30pm. Y26)*

HUAQING HOT SPRING (huáqīng chí; 华清池). Dating back more than 2000 years to the Zhou dynasty, the hot springs have been enjoyed by a succession of emperors and other important figures. Qin Shihuang dubbed the area the "Hot Spring of Mount Lishan," and in AD 747 Emperor Xuanzong of the Tang expanded it, naming it Huaqing Palace. In 1936, Chiang Kai-shek came here to set up his field headquarters against the CCP, and was captured in a coup known as the Xian incident (see p. 16). The Lake of Nine Dragons is supposedly 43°C all year long. Visited mainly by Chinese tourists, Huaqing Pool makes for an expensive diversion after a day of sightseeing. *(Bus #306 stops outside the cable car entrance. A minibus back to the train station costs Y3-4. Open daily 7am-7pm. Y30; hot pool and sauna Y20-120 extra.)*

BANPO NEOLITHIC VILLAGE (bànpō bówùguǎn; 半坡博物馆). Part dry archeological exhibit and part kitschy theme park, Banpo is an on-site museum of a 6000-year-old matriarchal clan community in the Yellow River valley, discovered in 1953 and opened to the public five years later. Covering 3000m^2, the **Great Hall** is the excavated dwelling area of the Banpo people. Four houses have been reconstructed at the site, and individual graves, group graves, and children's graves have been unearthed. Near the back of the site, enter the "authentic" reproduction of the matriarchal village through an enormous statue of a reclining woman. Banpo also houses a slightly voyeuristic exhibition of photographs of the "primitive man." *(Bus #105 from the train station stops at Banpo. Take a right onto Banpo Lu at the first intersection; the museum is about 5min. ahead on the left. Open daily 8am-6pm. Y20.)*

WESTERN TOUR

The Xianyang Museum is the only Western Tour sight that is reasonably accessible by public transportation. Minibuses (with Chinese speaking guides) leave from the parking lot behind the train station around 8 or 9am and return by around 7pm. Average cost is Y45 for transportation; as always, if asked to pay a flat fee in advance, be sure to clarify what sights and admission fees this covers unless padding the tour operator's pockets sounds appealing. Many tourists report being overcharged or under-tombed on this tour.

XIANYANG MUSEUM (xiányáng bówùguǎn; 咸阳博物馆). Xianyang witnessed the founding of the Qin dynasty in 221 BC, and was home to 11 ensuing dynasties; that distinction gave rise to both impressive cultural and economic achievements and the nickname "Oriental Pearl." This museum pays tribute to this long and impressive history. Originally a Confucian temple, Xianyang Museum was reconstructed in 1371 during the Ming dynasty and today houses over 5000 objects, primarily relics from the Qin and Han dynasties. The first three rooms contain relics from the Qin dynasty; the fourth contains relics from excavations of Western Han mausoleums. The fifth and sixth rooms house rare colored pottery discovered 30 years ago in Western Han tombs, including a staggering 3000 miniature terracotta soldiers only a foot and a half in height. *(Bus #3 goes from the train station to the terminal, at which point bus #59 takes you to Xianyang. At the clock tower on the left, turn right; when you reach Xining Jie, turn right again. ☎ (096) 321 3015. Open daily 8am-6pm. Y20.)*

MAOLING MAUSOLEUM (màolíng bówùguǎn; 茂陵博物馆). Referred to as the "crown jewel" of Western Han dynasty mausoleums, the Maoling houses the tomb of Emperor Wudi (157-87 BC), as well as those of his relatives and assistants. Displays feature some well-preserved ancient stone sculptures, including a bronze rhinoceros-shaped vessel used for drinking wine. The museum's lush gardens are ornamented with a large fountain; Emperor Wudi's tomb perches dramatically on a 47m high hill. *(40km northwest of Xian. Open daily 7:30am-6:30pm. Y21.)*

QIAN TOMB (qián líng; 乾陵). The largest of the surrounding tombs, this is the burial ground of the third Tang emperor and his wife Empress Wu Zetian. Sculptures of lions and other figures line the long walkway. It's a pleasant 15- to 20-minute walk from one end to the other. Other nearby sites include the 17 smaller tombs of princes, princesses, and ministers. *(Open daily 8am-6pm. Y25.)*

PRINCE YI DE'S TOMB (shǎnxī gānlíng yìdé tàizimù bówùguǎn; 陕西干陵懿德太子墓博物馆). In AD 701, Li Zhongren, eldest son of Emperor Zhong Zong, did the unthinkable: he challenged the system. At the age of 19, the young man demanded to know why certain nobles were favored in the courts and offered official positions. Under the Empress's orders, the lad was flogged to death for his insubordination. When Zhong Zong assumed the throne four years later, he honored his son with the title Yi De (the virtuous) and reburied him alongside an eligible (if deceased) young lady, in what is now Prince Yi De's Tomb. Excavated in 1971, the tomb was refurbished in 1996 with Y12 million from the Taiwanese government, just enough to restore the gorgeous Tang-style buildings, restaurants, exhibition halls, and, the burial vault itself. Corridors, tunnels, and chambers display the pride of the tomb: 450m^2 of frescoes on the walls. *(Open daily 8am-6:30pm. Y21.)*

▧ FAMEN TEMPLE (fǎmén sì; 法门寺). This 1700-year-old Eastern Han dynasty temple was one of the four ancient sacred places in Buddhist history, housing four of the Buddha's finger bones *(sarira)*. The Northern Wei emperor made the place famous in AD 555 when he opened the four-door, single-eaved gold *stupa* in order to worship the *sarira*. During the Tang dynasty, the temple was expanded to 24 courtyards, housing many monks and nuns. In 1981, the *sarira* crypt was restored, yielding more than 1000 sacrificial objects preserved for over a thousand years. They are now kept in an on-site museum; the downstairs vault, in white stone and with elaborate gold decoration, is absolutely gorgeous. Famen Temple is an extraordinary sight, made all the more impressive by its almost two-millennia-long history. *(In Fufeng County, a bumpy 115km northwest of Xian. Open daily 8am-6pm. Temple admission Y15; museum Y20.)*

PRINCE ZHANGHUAI'S TOMB (zhānghuài tàizi mù; 章怀太子墓). Yet another tomb, Prince Zhanghuai's final resting place probably looks like any other to the casual observer. The sloping walls are covered with horses and other frescoes of varying authenticity. *(Open daily 8am-6pm; in winter 8am-5pm. Y12.)*

HUASHAN 华山 ☎0913

Proclaimed one of the five sacred Daoist mountains by Emperor Han Wudi over 2000 years ago, Mount Huashan (also known as Xiyue, or "Western Yue") guards the eastern gateway to Shaanxi. With near-vertical cliffs and plunging ravines, the impenetrable mountain repelled countless invaders of Xian over the centuries. The climb to the 2158m summit—alternately exhilarating and terrifying—makes clear why would-be attackers gave up and went home.

✦🄯 ORIENTATION AND PRACTICAL INFORMATION

Situated approximately 120km east of Xian not far from the main Xian-Zhengzhou rail line, Huashan village lies at the base of the mountain. **Yuquan Lu** (玉泉路) runs from **Jianshe Lu** (建设路) to Yuquan Temple and the entrance to the mountain. A

number of hotels, restaurants, and souvenir stands line the road. The cableway
terminus is about 15 minutes by minibus southeast of Huashan village. Huashan's
administrative center is north of the rail line and mountain.

Trains: Huashan Train Station (huáshān huǒchē zhàn; 华山火车站) is actually about
15km away in Mengyuan, but is linked with Huashan village by frequent minibuses (Y3).
During the evening or for the return trip, a taxi may be necessary. To: **Luoyang** (4-5hr.,
17 per day, Y26); **Taiyuan** (9hr.; 5 per day; Y38, express Y76); and **Xian** (1¾-3hr., 21
per day, Y10). From **Huashan West Train Station** (huáshān xī huǒchē zhàn; 华山
西火车站), a small station in Huashan village, trains depart for **Luoyang** (4hr., 1 per
day, Y21) and **Xian** (3hr., 2 per day, Y9).

Buses: Numerous minibuses to **Xian** (2hr., Y15-20) leave throughout the day from
Yuquan Lu near the Huashan Banking Hotel. **Huashan Bus Station** (huáshān qìchē
zhàn; 华山汽车站) is on Jianshe Lu west of Yuquan Lu, but most travelers find it more
convenient to take the minibus or the train.

Local Transportation: There is **minibus** service around town. Buses #2 and 8 stop at the
train station. Most **taxis** do not use meters; from Yuquan Lu to the train station costs
about Y15.

Bank of China: On the southwest corner of Yuquan Lu and Jianshe Lu. Exchanges foreign
currency but not traveler's checks. Open M-F 9am-5pm, holidays 10am-4pm.

Post Office: Post and Telecommunications Building, at the corner of Dongyue Lu and
Dahua Bei Lu. **Postal code:** 714200.

ACCOMMODATIONS AND FOOD

Most of the cheapest accommodations are clustered along Yuquan Lu near the
trailhead, and fortunately for the budget traveler, rates under Y50 per person are
not uncommon. Quality, however, varies considerably. Many of the upmarket
hotels charge much higher rates to foreigners, although if the hotel is not full, a
discount or the Chinese price may be possible. Up on the mountain, hotels and
hostels generally provide more rugged accommodations.

Restaurants abound along Yuquan Lu in Huashan village. Food (mainly noodles
and fried dishes) is quite expensive here; plain rice is usually Y2 per bowl. On the
other side of Jianshe Lu, however, noodles and soups are dished up for Y3 per
bowl. Refreshment stands are also plentiful along the trail, though the offerings at
the summit are much more limited.

HUASHAN VILLAGE

Huayue Hotel (huáyuè bīnguǎn;华岳宾馆; ☎436 2906, ext. 3808), right of the intersection of Yuquan Lu and Jianshe Lu when facing the mountain. Rooms are relatively
clean, and all have A/C. 3-bed dorms Y30 (Y80 for the room); doubles Y128 (foreigners
Y198), with bath Y218 (foreigners Y298); triples with bath Y258 (foreigners Y328).

Tielu Hostel (tiělù zhāodàisuǒ; 铁路招待所; ☎436 4723), on the left side of Yuquan
Lu just beyond the Huashan Banking Hotel, in a building more readily identified by the
characters for Huashan Dajiudian (华山大酒店) displayed on the front. Rooms are
functional and facilities rather basic. Water supply (especially hot water) can be unpredictable. Room rates tend to be negotiable. Deposit Y100. Single with A/C and bath
Y80-100; doubles Y70.

Xiyue Hotel (xīyuè fàndiàn; 西岳饭店; ☎436 3145; fax 436 4559), on the right side of
Yuquan Lu about 2min. from the Yuquan Temple entrance. The reception is down the
driveway and to the right. For travelers who value their material comforts: all rooms have
A/C, TV, phone, and bath. Discounts. Doubles Y198; quads Y320. MC, Visa accepted.

Wangyue Hotel (wàngyuè jiǔlóu; 望岳酒楼; ☎436 5802), on the right side of Yuquan
Lu about 4min. from the Yuquan Temple entrance. This small, family-run hotel has clean
rooms and decent prices. Hot water after 8pm. Some rooms have A/C and bath. Singles Y50-128; doubles Y60-150.

LOOK ON THE BRIGHT SIDE According to an ancient Shaanxi legend, an old man once owned a beautiful stallion that was the envy of all his neighbors. When the stallion ran away one day, the man's neighbors came to offer their condolences. The old man ever-so-calmly replied: "Nothing is completely good or bad. Let's wait and see." A few days later, the stallion galloped back, bringing with him an even more beautiful wild mare. When his neighbors came to offer their congratulations, the old man repeated his previous words. Weeks later, the old man's only son tumbled off the wild mare, breaking his leg and becoming crippled for life. Yet again the old man repeated his original words. Soon after, a terrible war broke out, and all able-bodied men were called to the front. Few lived to return home, but because the man's crippled son could no longer walk, he was spared.

Yuhua Hotel (yùhuá dàjiǔdiàn; 浴华大酒店; ☎436 5055), on the corner of Yuquan Lu and Jianshe Lu. 24hr. hot water. Doubles Y80-100; triples Y90; quads Y100.

MOUNT HUASHAN

Maonu Dong Shan Branch Hotel (máonǚ dòng fàndiàn; 毛女洞饭店), past the 4km point of the trail up to North Peak. A place to take shelter only if stranded by inclement weather or weak from exhaustion. Small, dimly lit rooms with basic common bathroom facilities on the 1st floor. 10-bed dorms Y20; 5-bed dorms Y30; singles Y90; doubles Y90; triples Y105.

North Peak Hotel (běi fēng fàndiàn; 北峰饭店; ☎430 0062), about a 3min. walk from the North Peak cable car station. Clean rooms with basic bathing facilities (no showers) and common toilets. Restaurant on premises. Beds (during the day only) Y10 per hr.; 30-bed dorms Y30; 14-bed dorms Y40; 8-bed dorms Y50; doubles Y240; quads Y280.

🔼 CLIMBING HUASHAN

Visitors come to Huashan to conquer the mountain, and Huashan does not disappoint. The challenges of the climb make it feel like a real victory. Certain stretches are steep enough that the handrail is transformed from a simple metal chain to a lifeline. Wearing dark clothing is advisable, as it is hard to keep clean when you're hanging on to a rusty guardrail for dear life. At the peak, there are basic accommodations that would be bad value at sea level—maybe currency devalues as altitude increases. If you want to catch the sunrise from East Peak, spring for a room or join the crowds of thrifty tourists who opt for a night climb, setting off around 11pm and ending up on East Peak as the sun comes up. Be careful when hiking in the dark, or dawn won't be the only thing breaking. (Flashlights for rental or purchase are readily available on Yuquan Lu in Huashan village.) A **cable car** ride to North Peak shortens the time commitment and thrill factor considerably. *(Minibuses between the cable car base and Huashan village Y10. ☎436 2683. Cable car runs daily 7am-7pm. Y55, Y100 round-trip.)* Ticket gates are open 24hr. Park **admission** is Y50, plus a mandatory registration fee (Y5) for foreigners, who must fill out a form that asks for passport and visa numbers.

Yuquan Temple (yùquán yuàn; 玉泉院), at the trailhead, is an obligatory first stop. *(Open 24hr. Y8, foreigners Y20. Try to get someone to buy you a Chinese-priced ticket.)* From there, it is a three- to five-hour climb, punctuated by numerous (and overpriced) refreshment stands, to **North Peak** (běi fēng; 北峰). On the way up, be sure to stop and take a look at the scenery once in a while. When not shrouded by fog or mist, the sheer, white granite cliffs are quite imposing. Check out the **Thousand-Foot Cliff** (qiānchǐ chuáng; 千尺幢); it's steep, narrow, and just keeps on going.

The climb to North Peak represents the lion's share of the hike. From North Peak, turn around, or keep going along the **Green Dragon Ridge** trail, which connects North Peak to West, South, and East Peaks. Getting to the other peaks involves first climbing down a bit and then ascending again, which can be confusing since trail markers are exclusively in Chinese. **West Peak** (xī fēng; 西峰) is about one-and-a-half to two hours away. **South Peak** (nán fēng; 南峰) is about 45 minutes from West Peak, while **East Peak** (dōng fēng; 东峰) is about one-an-a-half hours from North Peak.

YANAN 延安   ☎ 0911

Yanan, along with Shaoshan and Jinggangshan, is one of the most important Communist Party pilgrimage sites in the country. Its stark landscape of wind-swept sandstone cliffs and scrub vegetation provided the backdrop for the "birthplace of the revolution" in the late 1930s. From 1937 to 1948, Yanan was the headquarters of the Chinese Communist Party, and the city is now symbolic of a heroic and idealistic phase of the revolution (see p. 16). Much of the revolutionary fervor has diminished since then, but more than 20 sites bear witness to that era.

■✦⏸ ORIENTATION AND PRACTICAL INFORMATION

Yanan's main commercial areas and streets run parallel to the Y-shape formed by the Yan and Nanchuan rivers. **Zhongxin Jie** (中心街), **Daqiao Jie** (大桥街), and **Nanguan Jie** (南关街)/**Qilipu Dajie** (七里铺大街) are the most important thoroughfares. Daqiao Jie becomes **Dongguan Jie** (东关街) on the other side of the river. While the bus station, several parks, and a few revolutionary sites are located near the city center, the train station and many of the revolutionary-era attractions are several kilometers away, although still accessible by public transportation.

Airplanes: Yanan Airport (yánān jīchǎng; 延安机场) is about 5km northeast of city center. Service is very limited; flights run only on Thursdays to **Beijing** (2hr., Y680) and **Xian** (1hr., Y150). Bus service to the airport is available from the booking office next door to the Aviation Hotel or taxis make the trip for around Y10. The **CAAC ticket office** (☎ 211 3854) is open daily 7:30-11am and 2:30-5:30pm.

Trains: Yanan Train Station (yánan huǒchē zhàn; 延安火车站; ☎ 249 6976) is located at the far southern end of town on Qilipu Dajie. Buses #1, 3, and 12 stop right outside, as do numerous minibuses. The ticket office (open daily 8:30-10am, 3:30-5pm, and 8:30-10:30pm) is to the right of the waiting room when facing the station. Window #2 sells hard sleeper tickets starting at 3:30pm for the evening train to Xian; tickets sell out fast, so buy early. Same day sales only. To **Xian** (8-9hr., 2 per day, Y68-74).

Buses: Yanan Bus Station (yánān qìchē zhàn; 延安汽车站; ☎ 211 2531 or 211 3350) is on the right side of Dongguan Jie, as you head away from the city center. Buses #4, 6, and 8 serve the station. To: **Beijing** (27hr., 11am, Y166); **Lanzhou** (25hr., 6:30am, sleeper Y127); and **Xian** (9hr., frequent departures, Y54).

Local Transportation: Eleven **bus** routes 6am-8pm; frequent minibuses to and from the train station and other key areas extends until at least 10pm. Bus fare is Y0.5; minibuses generally charge Y1-3.

Taxis: *Miandi* taxis base fare Y5, each additional km Y1.

Travel Offices: CITS, 106 Dajie (☎ 212 3320). Ticket commission Y10. Several staff members are proficient in English. Open daily 8am-noon and 2:30-6pm.

Bank of China: On the right side of Beiguan Jie, a couple of minutes beyond Xigou Lu (☎ 211 2423). Open M-F 8:20am-noon and 2-6pm.

Hospital: Yanan People's Hospital (yánān dìqū rénmín yīyuàn; 延安地区人民医院; ☎ 211 2038), on Zhongxin Jie across the street from the Yanan Hotel.

Post Office: Post and Telecommunications Building, on the left side of Zhongxin Jie heading away from Daqiao Jie in the direction of the Yanan Hotel. Open daily 8am-midnight. **Postal Code:** 716000.

🖼️ ACCOMMODATIONS AND FOOD

There is only one hotel officially open to foreigners in Yanan. The **Yanan Hotel** (yánān bīnguǎn; 延安宾馆; ☎211 3122), is on Beiguan Jie. Bus #3 from the train station stops outside (Diqu Yiyuan stop); alternatively, a *miandi* costs about Y7-8. The hotel was being renovated in September 2000 and new room rates had not been determined. In the past, foreigners had to pay twice as much as Chinese; in most cases, a 10-20% discount was the only concession the staff will make.

Street stands and small hole-in-the-wall restaurants serve a number of northern Shaanxi specialties. *Heluo* noodles are about Y2-3 per bowl. Food stalls line Dongguan Jie between Daqiao bridge and the bus station. Several Mongolian hotpot restaurants, mostly along Daqiao Jie and Zhongxin Jie, supplement the local cuisine.

👁️ SIGHTS

A number of Yanan's key attractions are located slightly outside the city center. However, the city's compactness makes it possible to see all major sights in one day. Most important sights are indicated by red and white signs.

YANAN REVOLUTION MUSEUM yánān gémìng jìniànguǎn; 延安革命纪念馆). A good first stop, the museum houses an impressive collection of maps, relics, and old photographs. There are no English captions, but, if in doubt, at least one of the people pictured is probably Chairman Mao. Mao's faithful horse (stuffed, of course) also holds a place of honor here. Legend has it that, when its death was near, it turned toward Zhongnanhai, the residential complex of top CCP government officials, and gave three cries as a final farewell to its rider and companion. *(At the northern end of Wangjiaping Bridge. Take bus #1 or 3 from the train station stop outside. Tel. 211 2610. Open daily summer 7:30am-6pm; winter 8am-5pm. Y10.)*

YANGJIALING REVOLUTION HEADQUARTERS SITE (yángjiālíng gémìng jiùzhǐ; 杨家岭革命旧址). Set among the dry loess hillsides outside of Yanan are the Central Committee's meeting hall, offices, propaganda and policy research divisions, and other key administrative departments. From 1938 to 1943, Mao Zedong lived in a dugout nearby; Zhu De and other high-ranking officials also called Yangjialing home. *(Buses #1 and 3 from the train station stop at Yangjialing; the entrance is down the lane on the right side of the road. Open daily 7:30am-6pm. Y10.)*

WANGJIAPING REVOLUTION HEADQUARTERS SITE (wángjiāpíng gémìng jiùzhǐ; 王家坪革命旧址). As one of the CCP strongholds in Yanan, this area includes a meeting hall and the houses of Zhu De, Peng Dehuai, Mao, and others in the Eighth Route Army. *(On Zaoyuan Lu, about a 10min. walk from the Revolution Museum. Take bus #1 or 3 to Wangjiaping, then walk back in the direction of town until the turn-off on the left side of the road. Open daily 7:30am-6pm; in winter 8am-5pm. Y8.)*

BAO PAGODA (bǎo tǎ; 宝塔). Built in AD 766-78, the 44m high pagoda is such a fixture in the Yanan skyline that its silhouette often appears on Mao buttons. The climb up the claustrophobia-inducing staircase has its rewards; on clear days, the city and the hills far into the distance are visible. *(On the east side of Nanchuan River. Take bus #1 to Xiao Dong Men. After buying a ticket, continue along the road walking away from the train station, and take the first right. The walk up to the pagoda takes 15-20min.; taxis also make the trip. Open daily 7am-7pm. Y10; pagoda Y5.)*

QINGLIANGSHAN PARK (qīngliángshān; 清凉山). With more caves and temples than flowers or trees, Qingliangshan may not exactly fit the typical definition of a park. **Ten Thousand Buddha Cave** (wàn fó dòng; 万佛洞) is probably the best-known attraction. Due to the park's position on the side of a hill, any of the paths will provide a good view of the city layout. *(Near the Yanan Bridge on the northern bank of the Yan River. Bus #1 from the train station stops at Daqiao; continue along the same street for 3min. until the entrance to the hillside park appears on the right. Open daily 7am-7pm. Y10.)*

FENGHUANGSHAN REVOLUTION HEADQUARTERS SITE (fēnghuángshān gémìng jiùzhǐ; 奉凰山革命旧址). Not as large or spread-out as subsequent headquarters sites, Fenghuangshan was the CCP base for about two years after the party's 1937 arrival in Yanan. The simple houses of Red Army bigshots Mao, Zhu De, and Zhou Enlai remind visitors of the idealism and equanimity of the fledgling CCP back in the day. There is also a collection of photographs, including some of the Canadian comrade Norman Bethune, a doctor elevated to hero status for his care of wounded CCP soldiers. *(On the left side of Zhongxin Jie, about 5min. before the Yanan Hotel, if walking from the city center. Bus #3 from the train station stops nearby at Diqu Yiyuan. Open daily 7:30am-6pm. Y6.)*

HENAN 河南

In a country known for its lengthy history and illustrious past, Henan province claims a great share of the bragging rights. The area around the Yellow River in the north of the province is the cradle of Chinese civilization, the place where the story started over 3500 years ago. Evidence of the region's early beginnings abound: Henan is home to three ancient national capitals (Luoyang, Kaifeng, and Anyang), and relics and ruins are spread throughout the province. Whatever enchanting charms attracted people here so many years ago are apparently still active today; over 90 million call Henan home, making it the second most populous province in China. Recently, the region has also attracted a number of large foreign investment projects, such as the Xiaolangdi Dam, fueling the growth of Luoyang and Zhengzhou. Like much of the province, these projects seem destined to be perpetually under construction. However, despite centuries of turmoil and decades of development, many remnants of the province's past, most notably in the captivating cities of Kaifeng and Luoyang, are still going strong.

ZHENGZHOU 郑州 ☎0371

Droves of both Chinese and foreign travelers pass through Zhengzhou en route to Shaolin Monastery, Luoyang, or Kaifeng; few, however, actually stick around for more than a night or two. As capital of Henan province, the city has its share of high-rises, specialty stores, and other ventures, but there are few notable tourist attractions within the city itself, save the Henan Provincial Museum and the shiny new exterior of the train station.

▛ TRANSPORTATION

Airplanes: Zhengzhou Airport (zhèngzhōu jīchǎng; 郑州机场) is 5km east of the city center. The CAAC bus (40min., every hr., Y15) goes to the airport from the Aviation Hotel (mínháng dàjiǔdiàn;民航大酒店), 3 Jinshui Lu (☎599 1111). To: **Beijing** (2-3 per day 9:30am-7:10pm, Y550); **Guangzhou** (4-5 per day 8:15am-3:20pm, Y1080); **Hong Kong** (W and Su 9:15am, Y1690); **Kunming** (3-4 per day 8:05am-3:35pm, Y1010); **Shanghai** (3-4 per day 8:20am-4:10pm, Y640); and **Xian** (1 per day, Y400).

Trains: Zhengzhou Train Station (zhèngzhōu huǒchē zhàn; 郑州火车站; ☎835 1111 or 696 3013; ticket info ☎698 8988), near Yima Lu and Erma Lu, southwest of the main commercial center. Open 24hr. Sleeper tickets (or even seats) may be difficult to obtain on trains not originating in Zhengzhou. To: **Beijing** (8hr., 33 per day, Y46-173); **Guangzhou** (23hr., 7 per day, Y189-351); **Luoyang** (2½hr., at least a dozen per day, Y10-15); **Nanjing** (12 hr., 2 per day, Y87-173); **Shanghai** (15hr., 4 per day, Y118-237); **Shijiazhuang** (5½hr., 2 per day, Y24-61); **Taiyuan** (12hr., 2 per day, Y129-237); **Wuhan** (5½hr., 12 per day, Y28-71); and **Xian** (8-9hr., at least 10 per day, Y28-135).

Buses: Zhengzhou Bus Station (zhèngzhōu qìchē zhàn; 郑州汽车站; ☎696 3361), on Xinlong Jie, across the square from the train station. Counter #1 sells Yutong bus tickets to Beijing, Shijiazhuang, and Taiyuan. Buses to: **Anyang** (3hr., Iveco minibuses depart every 30min., Y30); **Beijing** (7-8hr., 1 and 3pm, Y138); and **Shanghai** (18hr., 2:25pm, Y109-169); and **Taiyuan** (8hr., 2 Yutong buses per day, Y120).

Local Transportation: The train station is a hub for local **buses;** stops are spread across Yima Lu, Erma Lu, Xinlong Jie, Datong Lu, and Fushou Lu. Fare on buses with no collector Y1; on buses with someone to make change, fare Y0.5 and up. Bus **#2** leaves from Erma Lu to traverse a circular route extending as far east as Dongming Lu and north to Nongye Lu; **#4** and **201** head west to the Zhengzhou University area; **#29** stops both at the South Bus Station and near the intersection of Chengdong Lu and Jinshui Lu in the north of town. **Minibuses,** including **#16** to the Yellow River, ply many routes 6am-8 or 9pm. Fare Y4 and under.

Taxis: Base fare Y5-6, each additional km Y1.

⚡🗿 ORIENTATION AND PRACTICAL INFORMATION

About 30km south of the Yellow River, Zhengzhou is a major rail transportation hub for the region. The commercial areas around **Jinshui Lu** (金水路) and **Erqi Pagoda,** with streets radiating in five directions, are crowded with department stores, boutiques, restaurants, and hotels. **Erqi Lu** (二七路) and **Renmin Lu** (人民路) are two of the major thoroughfares. Most tourist attractions are away from the city center, with only the Henan Provincial Museum being relatively accessible.

Travel Agency: CITS, Haitong Bldg., 50 Jinqi Lu, 8th Fl. (☎392 7758 or 392 7768), at Weiwu Lu. Li Shengjiang, the European-US manager, speaks English well. Runs tours to Shaolin Temple (Y80-100, not including admission). Train ticket commission Y40. Open M-F 8:30am-noon and 2-6:30pm.

Bank of China: At the intersection of Chengdong Lu and Jinshui Lu. Open M-F 8am-6:30pm; in winter 8am-5:30pm. **Guangdong Development Bank** (guǎngdōng fāzhǎn yínháng; 广东发展银行), 8-3 Jinshui Lu, just west of the Bank of China, has an **ATM** (Cirrus, Visa, Plus). Large hotels in the station area rarely change money for non-guests.

Markets: Zhengzhou Department Store (zhèngzhōu bǎihuò dàlóu; 郑州百货大楼), 49 Erqi Lu, north of Erqi Pagoda. Open daily 9am-8pm.

PSB: 110 Erqi Lu (☎622 2023), near People's Park. Open M-F 8:30am-noon and 3-6:30pm.

Hospital: First Affiliated Henan Medical University Hospital (zhèngzhōu shì yīxué yīyuàn; 郑州市医学医院; ☎691 3114), at the corner of Zhengzhou Lu and Daxue Lu.

Internet Access: China Telecom Internet Bar (zhèngzhōu diànxìn shāngchéng wǎngyuàn; 郑州电信商城网院), on the 1st floor of Tianran Commercial Center just northeast of Erqi Pagoda. Y3-5 per hr.; weekday mornings are cheapest. Must register passport. Open 24hr. A branch on the southwest corner of the intersection of Jinqi Lu and Nongye Lu, across from the Henan Provincial Museum, has the same rates and rules as its Erqi Lu counterpart. Open daily 8:30am-10:30pm.

Post Office: Zhengzhou Post Office, on the south side of the train station square near Yima Lu, to the right when exiting the station. EMS and Poste Restante available. Open daily 8am-7pm. **Postal Code:** 450000.

🏠 ACCOMMODATIONS

The cheaper places are primarily around the noisy train station square. For quieter sleeping quarters, there are several budget options along Jiefang Lu or on the outskirts of the city. Most of Zhengzhou's upscale establishments are near Jinshui Lu, although several three-star hotels are near the station.

Golden Sunshine Hotel (jīn yángguāng dàjiǔdiàn; 金阳光大酒店), 86 Erma Lu (☎696 9999; fax 699 9534), left of the train station's north exit. All rooms have A/C and TV; try the "honeymoon room" (Y388) for a change of surroundings. Standard rooms are large and even have mini-bars. Even the cheapest rooms (without attached bath or ele-

CENTRAL CHINA

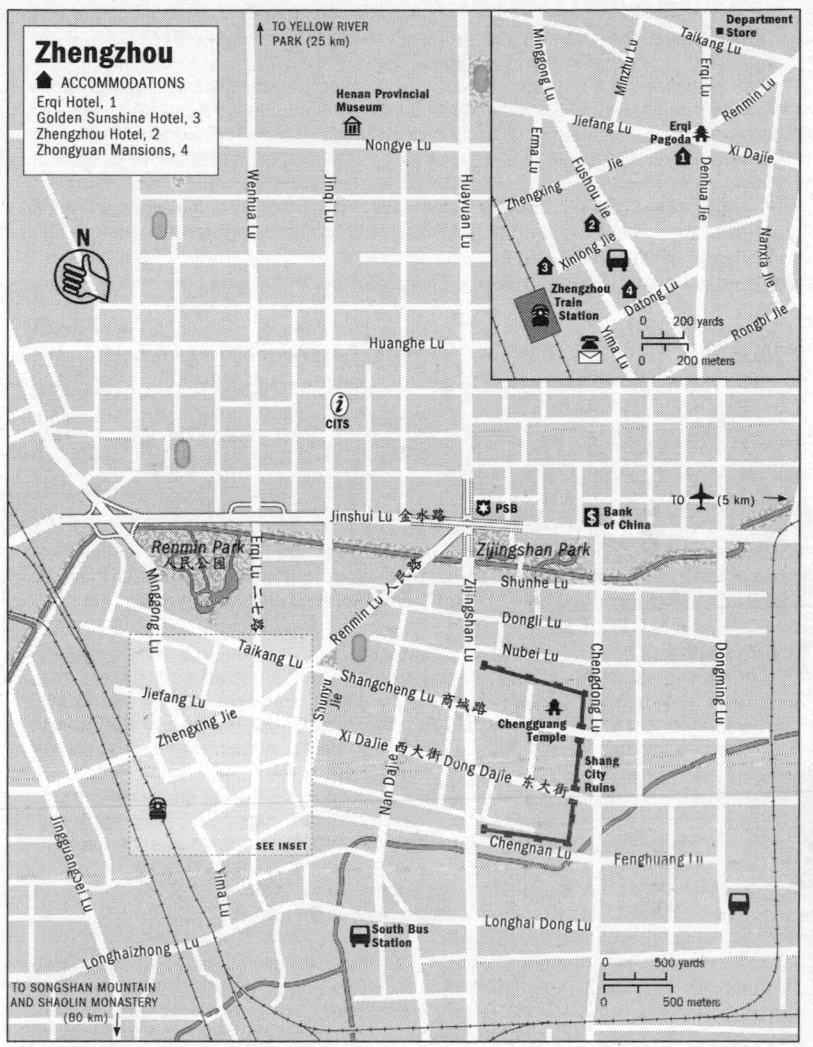

Zhengzhou

♦ ACCOMMODATIONS
Erqi Hotel, 1
Golden Sunshine Hotel, 3
Zhengzhou Hotel, 2
Zhongyuan Mansions, 4

CENTRAL CHINA

vator access) aren't bad. There is a fair amount of noise from the train station, though. Health club and other amenities. Breakfast included with standard rooms. Singles Y40, with bath Y180-328; doubles Y60/160-328; triples with bath Y388.

Zhongyuan Mansions (zhōngyuán dàshà; 中原大厦; ☎696 6172, ext. 481), in front of the train station. This cavernous high-rise features wood- or linoleum-floored rooms with huge windows, A/C, TV, and phone. Deposit Y10. Singles Y60, with bath Y100; doubles Y90, with bath Y120; triples Y105; quads Y100, with bath Y180; quints Y100.

Zhengzhou (Fandian) Hotel (zhèngzhōu fàndiàn; 郑州饭店; ☎696 9941). From the north exit of the train station, walk straight ahead for about 1min.; the entrance is on the left. Not to be confused with the Zhengzhou (Dajiudian) Hotel nearby, this hotel has small rooms with a musty smell. All rooms except the triples without bath have A/C, TV, and phone. Singles with bath Y130; doubles Y80, with bath Y130-160; triples Y90/135; quads with bath Y160.

Erqi Hotel (èrqī bīnguǎn; 二七宾馆), 168 Jiefang Lu (☎696 1169, ext. 183573), at Dehua Jie and Zhengxing Jie near Erqi Pagoda. A 10min. walk from the train station; buses #2, 6, 9, and 32 stop at Erqi Guangchang. Rooms are more functional than elegant. Foreigners must pay for an entire room; bargain. 10-bed dorms Y20; doubles Y80, with bath and A/C Y130; triples Y108/177.

◪ FOOD

Aside from its famous **No. 3 hybrid watermelon,** Zhengzhou is not particularly well known for any local food products. Fortunately, good, cheap food abounds. The Erqi Pagoda neighborhood offers several possibilities for outdoor dining. A night market sets up along Dehua Jie near Zhengxing Jie; restaurants are mainly of the point-and-choose variety. Stalls specializing in *huimian* or *shaguo* noodle soups (Y3-5) line a small alleyway just off Renmin Lu, near the base of the pedestrian overpass and Shangcheng Hotel. A number of restaurants and street stands, often preparing Muslim or Sichuanese cuisine, dot Ziyou Lu and Minzhu Lu off Jiefang Lu, across from the Asia Hotel.

For Western and Chinese fusion, the ▨ **Haoxianglai Restaurant** (háoxiǎnglái; 毫享来), 21 Minggong Lu, a 10-minute walk south of the Minggong Lu entrance to People's Park, is a winner. Take bus #2 from the station to Minggong Lu and walk north for a few minutes; the restaurant is on the left. This clean, cheery place serves everything from curried chicken and dim sum to margaritas and sushi. Set meals cost Y25-50. (☎622 6038. Open 24hr.) There is a **KFC** on the west side of Erqi Lu, just north of Erqi Pagoda, but trying to order during meal hours might be more difficult than buying a hard sleeper to Beijing. (Open daily 9am-10pm.)

◉ SIGHTS

Zhengzhou is best known as a jumping-off point for tours of Shaolin Monastery. The city proper has few points of interest. **People's Park** (rénmín gōngyuán; 人民公园), near Erqi Lu and Xili Lu, is accessible via buses #6 and 24 from the train station. *(Open daily 6:30am-10pm. Y2.)* **Zijingshan Park** (zǐjīngshān gōngyuán; 紫荆山公园), on Jinshui Lu just west of Chengdong Lu, offers similar pleasures but on a smaller scale. Visitors can fish for Y10 (an extra Y8-16 for each fish caught) or stroll through the landscaped gardens. *(Open daily sunrise-sunset. Free.)*

▨ **HENAN PROVINCIAL MUSEUM** (hénán shěng bówùguǎn; 河南省博物馆). This large pyramidal building houses an impressive collection that fills four floors of exhibition space. In addition to displays of Buddhist statues, ceramics, and jade carvings, there is even the occasional vegetable (ivory cabbage and radishes from the Qing dynasty) or dinosaur thrown in for good measure. Full English captions enhance the experience. There is a 30-minute musical performance on ancient instruments daily at 10:30am and 3:30pm. *(8 Nongye Lu, at Jinqi Lu. Bus #32 from the train station stops about 1 block to the east. ☎351 1250. Open daily 8:30am-6:30pm; in winter 8:30am-5:30pm; last admission 30min. before closing. Y20.)*

YELLOW RIVER PARK (huánghé yóulǎn qū; 黄河游览区). For those who have already seen the Yellow River, this trip might not be very worthwhile. The cable car and Five Dragon Park provide the best views; visitors can also hike or ride a horse (for as little as Y2) down to the mud flats. In 1938, the scene was markedly different, as GMD general Chiang Kai-shek's last-ditch attempt at stopping the Japanese advance here resulted in the destruction of the river dikes and the drowning of over one million Chinese. *(About 25km north of Zhengzhou. Minibus #16 leaves from Xinglong Jie or Erma Lu near the station (1hr., Y4). Open daily 6:30am-sunset. Y20.)*

SHANG CITY RUINS (shāngdài yízhǐ; 商代遗址). Mounds of dirt are all that is left of this 3000-year-old settlement; artifacts have long since been carted off for safekeeping. Even residents are hard-pressed to explain where exactly the Shang City

BOXER REBELLION China has two main schools of boxing. One, the "internal" (soft) school, originated in Shaolin; the other, the "external" (hard) school, originated in Hubei province's Wudangshan (see p. 403). As the name suggests, one versed in the external style would answer a kung fu block with another block, while those using the internal style would merely deflect the blow. The external style is said to favor physical force and strength over the breathing and timing.

Shaolin kung fu has a huge variety of systems and sub-systems that incorporate moves imitating everything from a praying mantis to a tiger. In the "drunken system," a boxer stumbles around in an attempt to exhaust his opponent while simultaneously dealing carefully timed blows to the opponent's more sensitive areas. The "crab system" focuses on pinching off the opponent's nerve endings and blood vessels, and the "eagle system" directs vicious attacks to the eye and throat. One of the most important aspects of Shaolin kung fu is breath control, which allows disciples to hang onto a tree using their necks, hang a 50 lb. weight from their testicles, or other feats.

Shaolin kung fu has been criticized both as being overly external and overly internal. So which is it? The famous *wushu* saying "in defense like a virgin; in attack like a tiger" answers this question to a T. As any accomplished Shaolin martial artist will tell you, behind each seemingly hard move is a soft one, and vice versa. A hard blow must be guided by proper breathing and timing, whereas a deflection requires the elements of quick movement and contact with the opponent.

As a Shaolin disciple faced his final test in the quest to become a kung fu master—a rank that very few lived to achieve—deciding how to classify his techniques was probably the last thing on his mind. The disciple would be shown the entrance to a long tunnel filled with fatal traps and pitfalls with an exit blocked by an enormous urn weighing hundreds of pounds and filled with burning hot irons. Only those who survived the tunnel and moved the urn with their bare hands were awarded the well-deserved rank of master. For more on kung fu, *wushu*, and all that jazz, see **Sports**, p. 43.

ruins can be found. The surrounding neighborhood, especially along Dong Dajie, offers an interesting glimpse into daily life away from the hubbub of the train station or Erqi Square; check out the bird markets. *(West of Chengdong Lu in the southern portion of the city. Bus #2 from Erma Lu in front of the train station stops at Shangcheng Dong Lu. The mounds stretch in both directions, perpendicular to Shangcheng Lu.)*

◪ DAYTRIP FROM ZHENGZHOU: SONGSHAN AND SHAOLIN

Stretching 500km across central Henan is Songshan (1492m), a hotbed for Daoist hermits ever since the mountain was designated Zhongyue (Central Peak; one of the 5 sacred Daoist mountains) during the Zhou dynasty. If this sounds like just another one of the *799 Famous Mountains of China*, get a load of Shaolin kung fu. The biggest attraction on this mountain is a Buddhist monastery famous for practicing martial arts.

SHAOLIN MONASTERY

Minibuses make the trip from Zhengzhou, generally departing from the long-distance bus station or the parking lot at the intersection of Fushou Lu and Xinlong Jie. Standard asking price for round-trip tickets is Y40; tour operators generally don't go lower than Y30. A direct trip to Shaolin takes about 2-2½hr., although extra stops (including the Han Tombs, Zhongyue Temple, a tourist souvenir store, the gas station, or a restaurant) can mean a 5hr. ride to Shaolin. For more information on kung fu, contact the **Shifang Martial Arts School** (shífāng wǔshù xuéyuàn; 十方武术学院; ☎(0371) 274 9499 or 274 9968), or any of the other schools upon arrival. **Accommodations** are available at several of the guesthouses and hostels in the area. **Admission** to the 8 sights Y40.

The cult of kung fu lives on in Shaolin Monastery (shàolín sì; 少林寺). Thousands of young trainees, brightly outfitted in the colors of their respective schools, practice the kicks and jabs that made the tradition famous. According to a 30-minute film, almost every technique imaginable has been used to instill discipline in Shaolin *wushu* (martial arts) students. Training methods include ramming logs into a volunteer's stomach, meditating while suspended from a tree, and other strength-testing and character-building exercises. Some schools offer short-term classes for about Y300 per month; living expenses cost an additional Y120-350.

SHAOLIN TEMPLE (shàolín sì; 少林寺). Opened in AD 495, the monastery turned to Chan (Zen) Buddhism after a visit by Bodhidharma in 527 and began to adapt local martial arts to Buddhist teachings. Far from hermits, these monks showcased their fighting prowess by helping Tang Emperor Taizong to vanquish bandit rebels and were rewarded with a major expansion. The main temple area consists of many buildings of varying age and authenticity, most with both Chinese and English explanations. **Li Xue Pavilion** (Standing-in-the-Snow Pavilion) marks the place where the second generation Master Monk Huike stood deep in the snow and cut off his own left arm to fully understand the essence of Chan Buddhism. Above the shrine hangs a commemorative tablet entitled "Snow Imprinting Piety into Heart," handwritten by Qing Emperor Qianlong. One of the most recent additions is **Chuipu Hall,** built in 1984, with 14 displays of figures depicting Shaolin martial arts and the history of the temple. *(Open daily 7am-6pm.)*

SHIFANG MONASTERY (shífāng chányuàn; 十方禅院). Indicated by the English sign "the meditation yard for all directions," this monastery features a collection of about 500 buddhas. Legend has it that visitors must pick one that they find particularly appealing, count down the same number as their age (plus one year), and then read the explanatory note (in Chinese) on the buddha that results. *(Across the street from Shaolin Temple. Open daily 7am-6 or 7pm.)*

OTHER SIGHTS AT SHAOLIN. Shaolin Stupas Forest (tǎ lín; 塔林), on the same side of the road as Shaolin Temple, contains many small dagobas in honor of some respectable monks. At the end of the main road, the **Forest of Birds** (bǎiniáo lín; 百鸟林) is true to its name: a screened-off forest of squawking birds. Watch out for the ostriches—they spit. **Quanzhou Cinema** (quánzhōu yǐngyuàn; 全周影院), **Wushu Hall** (wǔshù guǎn; 武术馆), **Bodhidharma Cave** (dámā dòng; 达摩洞), and **Science Fiction Hall** (kē huàn guǎn; 科幻馆) are included in the admission fee. Most visitors find that observing the martial arts classes (check out the fields on the left side of the road as you come from the main entrance) is a more stimulating activity.

OTHER SONGSHAN SIGHTS

Also on Songshan Mountain, **Zhongyue Temple** (zhōngyuè miào; 中岳庙) is an important Daoist place of worship. Inside the compound, a bit off to the side, stand four figures known as the "Iron Men of the Song." Supposedly, rubbing the figure and then touching a sore spot on your own body will magically eliminate the pain. *(Open daily 7am-7pm; in winter 8am-6pm. Y10.)* The nearby **observatory** (guānxīngtái; 观星台), one of 27 in China, reaches a height of 12.6m. It's too bad the open hours preclude prime star-gazing times. *(Open daily 7am-6:30 or 7pm; in winter 7am-5:30pm. Y10.)* Closer to Zhengzhou, the **Dahuting Han Tombs** (dǎhǔtíng hànmù; 打虎亭汉墓) near Xinmi have been pillaged twice but still feature impressive frescoes in burnt-earth tones. *(Open daily 6am-8pm; in winter 6:30am-7:30pm. Y10.)*

LUOYANG 洛阳 ☎0379

"Paper is expensive in Luoyang," or at least it used to be. This Chinese expression refers to the actual paper shortage caused by the extreme popularity of "The Three Capitals," a series of poems written by Zuo Si after the fall of the Han dynasty. As one of China's seven ancient capitals (see **The Qin & Han,** p. 9), Luoyang witnessed the founding of China's first university, the Guozi Jian, in 29 BC, as well as the invention of the seismograph and paper. Its role as a seat of power,

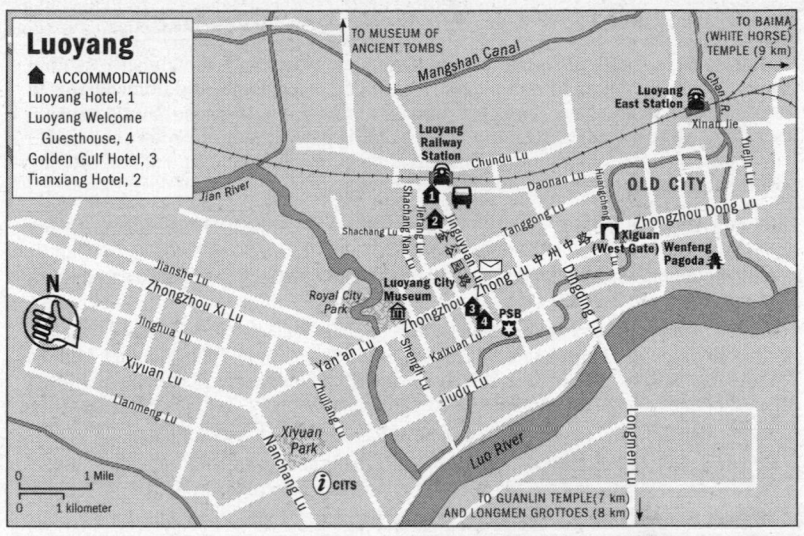

however, made Luoyang particularly vulnerable to political upheaval and power struggles throughout time. In the past 50 years, Luoyang has regained much of its lost prestige. Fortunately, the push for industrial development has not cost the city its tree-lined boulevards or shaded parks, and the high-tech, fancy boutique area of Zhongzhou Lu fades by the time visitors reach the Longmen Grottoes, the White Horse Temple, or other sights. The annual Peony Festival (April 15-25), first celebrated in 1982, showcases over 500 varieties of Empress Wu Zetian's favorite flower.

⌐ TRANSPORTATION

Airplanes: Luoyang Airport (luòyáng jīchǎng; 洛阳机场; ☎393 5301, ext. 510), over 10km north of the city. Bus #83 leaves from Daonan Lu in front of the long-distance bus station. A shuttle bus leaves about 2hr. before departure from the **CAAC ticket office,** 196 Chundu Lu (☎231 0121 or 394 1863), near Shachang Bei Lu west of the train station. To **Beijing** (Tu, Th, and Sa; Y550) via **Zhengzhou.**

Trains: Luoyang Train Station (luòyáng huǒchē zhàn; 洛阳火车站; ☎323 4321), at the intersection of Jinguyuan Lu and Daonan Lu in the northern part of the city. To: **Beijing** (13hr., several per day, Y107-183); **Guangzhou** (28hr., 1 per day, Y319-367); **Shanghai** (19hr., 3 per day, Y140-244); **Taiyuan** (12hr., 1 per day, Y84); **Wuhan** (10hr., 6 per day, Y94-162); and **Xian** (7hr., 4 per day, Y26-53).

Buses: Luoyang Bus Station (luòyáng chángtú qìchē zhàn; 洛阳长途汽车站; ☎323 2945), at the corner of Jinguyuan Lu and Daonan Lu diagonally opposite the train station. To: **Anyang** (4-5hr., 5 per day 8-11am, Y30); **Guangzhou** (27hr., 1 sleeper per day, Y260); **Kaifeng** (3hr., Y30); **Taiyuan** (10hr., 1 sleeper per day, Y80); **Xian** (7-8hr., 2-5 sleepers per day, Y61); and **Zhengzhou** (2½hr., Iveco minibuses every 20min. 7am-7pm, Y23). The ticket office for deluxe buses to **Beijing** (10hr., 2 per day, Y180) is to the right of the main entrance to the waiting hall.

Local Transportation: Most **buses** stop running at 8-9pm, but bus #5 runs until midnight. Fare Y1. Buses **#5** and 48 run along Zhongzhou Zhong Lu and up Jinguyuan Lu to the train station; **#59** runs along Zhongzhou Lu; **#83** goes north from the main train station to the Ancient Tombs Museum and the airport; **#102** and 103 run along Zhongzhou Xi Lu and up Jinguyuan Lu to the train station.

⟦⟧ ORIENTATION AND PRACTICAL INFORMATION

On the northern bank of the Luo River, Luoyang covers an area of nearly 500km. Many of Luoyang's hotels, shops, and restaurants are clustered near **Zhongzhou Lu** (中州路), particularly around **Jinguyuan Lu** (金谷园路). Because Zhongzhou Lu runs from east to west across the entire city, it is an important reference point. The main train and long-distance bus stations are on the northern edge of the city proper, and Luoyang's airport is to the northwest.

Travel Agency: CITS (☎432 3212 or 431 3701), in the Tourist Mansion on Jiudu Xi Lu. Helpful staff and a standard commission of Y30. Open daily 8am-6pm.

Bank of China: 439 Zhongzhou Zhong Lu, in the International Finance Building. Open M-F 8am-noon and 3-6:30pm.

Market: Luoyang Department Store (luòyáng shì bǎihuò dàlóu; 洛阳市百货大楼), 287 Zhongzhou Zhong Lu (☎325 2453). Open daily 9am-7pm. **Xicheng Market** (xīchéng liàngfàn; 西城量贩), inside the Shanghai Cinema on Zhongzhou Lu a block west of Jinguyuan Lu, sells a wide selection of foods. Open daily 8:30am-9:30pm.

PSB: 1 Kaixuan Xi Lu (☎394 8257). Open M-F 8:30am-noon and 2:30-5pm.

Hospital: The **150th Military Hospital** (150 zhōngxīn yīyuàn; 150中心医院; ☎486 1784) has a reputable Foreigner's Building. Accessible by buses #55, 101, or 103.

Internet Access: China Telecom is just north of the post office, but for the past 2 years has been planning a move to the new high-rise on Zhongzhou Zhong Lu just east of the post office. Y5 per hr., deposit Y50. Open daily 8am-noon and 2:30-6pm. **Kaituo Computer City** (kāituò diànnǎo chéng; 开拓电脑城), 1 block from the corner of Zhongzhou Xi Lu and Yanan Lu, on the 4th floor of the China Mobile building. Take bus #101 or 103 to Motuo Dalou; China Mobile is 1 block away on the left. Y3 per hr., deposit Y10.

Post Office: On Zhongzhou Zhong Lu, just east of Jinguyuan Lu. EMS and Poste Restante available. Open daily 8am-7pm. **Postal Code:** 471000.

⟦⟧ ACCOMMODATIONS

Accommodations open to foreigners generally fall into one of two extremes: cheap, noisy hotels near the main train station, or the relatively posh establishments along Zhongzhou Lu in the city center.

Luoyang Hotel (luòyáng lǚshè; 洛阳旅社; ☎393 5181), in the high-rise at the corner of Daonan Lu and Jinguyuan Lu, opposite the main train station. The entrance is at the far left when you arrive from the station. Most rooms share slightly dank common showers and toilets and require a Y10 fee for A/C. 6- to 10-bed dorms Y10; 4-bed dorms Y12; 3-bed dorms Y15; singles Y35; doubles Y20, with bath Y45.

Tianxiang Hotel (tiānxiāng fàndiàn; 天香饭店), 56 Jinguyuan Lu (☎394 0602), about 2min. from the main train station. Slightly quieter than the hotels facing the station, but of similar quality. Most rooms have common showers and toilets and no A/C. There are TVs, but you probably don't want to spend more time than you have to in this somewhat dingy hotel. Luckily, the standard doubles and triples have been renovated recently. Singles Y50; doubles Y33, with bath and A/C Y100; triples Y25-40/100; quads Y56.

Luoyang Welcome Guesthouse (luòyáng yíng bīnguǎn; 洛阳迎宾馆), 6 Renmin Xi Lu (☎393 5156), about 3min. south of Zhongzhou Lu. Take bus #2 from the train station to Youleyuan; the hotel entrance is on the right side of the street. Worn rooms have all standard amenities. Doubles Y232.

Golden Gulf Hotel (jīn shuǐwān dàjiǔdiàn; 金水湾大酒店), 319 Zhongzhou Zhong Lu (☎339 5588; fax 339 5678), between Renmin Xi Lu and Bayi Lu. Take almost any of the buses from Jinguyuan Lu in front of the train station to Xigong. Buses #5 and 81 stop in front of the Luoyang Department Store; from there, walk about 5min. in the other direction along Zhongzhou Zhong Lou. Stay at this 3-star beauty and get Star TV, a fridge, your own personal pair of terry-cloth slippers, and a ton of on-site entertainment options. Discounts often available. Doubles Y460-510.

WATER, WATER EVERYWHERE The famed Luoyang Water Banquet (shuǐxí; 水席) is so named because the main dishes contain soup and are served up almost as quickly as "flowing water." Of the 24 dishes, the first eight (evenly divided between meat and vegetables) are served cold, as are the four saved for the end of the meal. The remaining 12 dishes, divided into sets of three, are the most important part of the banquet. Each of the four groups include one main dish and two side dishes, all of which are similar in taste; this method of serving is known as "a father taking his two sons to court." The famous "Luoyang Swallow Dish" is actually prepared by boiling shredded radishes, chicken, minced pork, and various vegetables into a thin soup; the finished product represents the spring swallow, a symbol of hope. Legend has it that Empress Wu Zetian found this dish so delicious that she consumed no other meat dish for three months. The highlight of the second group, "Happiness for the Whole Family," consists of a variety of braised meats and vegetables. "Eight-Treasure Rice Pudding" (a sweet porridge made from eight grains and beans), the main dish of the third group, expresses the wish for bountiful harvests. The last main dish, "Sour and Spicy Egg Drop Soup," also known as the "Farewell Soup," signifies that the meal is nearly over. Some of the side dishes served include the deceptively named "Field Snail Meat," "Turtle and Chicken," "Steamed Quails," and other delicacies.

FOOD

Luoyang is famous for its 24-course **Water Banquet** (see Water, Water Everywhere, p 237), but for those with neither the time nor the appetite, there are plenty of other options. Street stalls are set up at night all over the city: Renmin Dong Lu just south of Zhongzhou Zhong Lu; Jinguyuan Lu and Jiefang Lu just north of Zhongzhou Lu; Wangcheng Lu opposite Wangcheng Park from Zhongzhou Lu to Kaixuan Xi Lu; and **Xinghua Night Market** (xìnghuá yè shì; 兴华夜市) in the Old City (Yuxi Binguan stop on bus #5) are all particularly crowded with vendors and customers. The fast-food place just off Renmin Dong Lu, across from the back entrance of the Luoyang Department Store, has an English menu.

Popular snacks include lamb kebabs, *doushagao* (sweet cakes made of dates and yellow peas; 豆沙糕; Y0.5-1), *jianbao* (尖包; fried pastry stuffed with herbs, garlic, and other fillings; Y0.5-2), and *jiangmiantiao* (starched noodles; 浆面条), made from mung bean milk, noodles, vegetables, and various other seasonings. *Tangmianjiao* (steamed dumplings; 汤面饺; Y0.5-1) in the shape of crescent moons were first prepared in Xinan County, Henan province, and are known for their thin wrappings and jade-like color.

One-of-a-Kind Restaurant (zhēn bù tóng fàndiàn; 真不同饭店), 359 Zhongzhou Zhong Lu (☎399 1404 or 395 5786), east of the Xiguan bus stop. Take bus #5 or 9 to Yuxi Binguan. We tend to agree with the name. After all, where else can you get a mini-Water Banquet for 2 for Y20, as well as so many other local specialties? Open daily 9:30am-9pm, or until the last guest leaves.

Fengwei Restaurant (fēngwèi lóu; 风味楼), on Xigong Qu Xiaojie. Exit through the back of the Luoyang Department Store; turn left and then make a right into the small alley. The restaurant is on the right, across from Big Mouth Fast Food. Ten *tangmianjiao* Y5. Open daily 8am-9:30pm.

SIGHTS

With the exception of Royal City Park and the Luoyang Museum, most major tourist attractions are outside the city center. All are within about an hour's ride via minibus or the public bus system, making independent daytrips from Luoyang a relatively simple endeavor.

LONGMEN GROTTOES

*South of Luoyang. Take **bus** #81 from Jinguyuan Lu in front of the train station or from Xigong at the intersection of Zhongzhou Zhong Lu and Jinguyuan Lu (30-40min., Y1.3). Get off at Longmen Qiao (Longmen Bridge); the entrance, about a 5min. walk, is down the steps immediately before the bridge. Visit in the morning when it's not as crowded. **Open** daily 6:30am-8pm; in winter 6:30am-7pm. **Admission** Y45.*

The site of the Longmen Grottoes (lóngmén shíkū; 龙门石窟) was once a large lake surrounded by hills. One day a young shepherd heard a mysterious voice and the words "*Kai bu kai* (shall I open)?" Perplexed, he sought out his mother, who counseled him to respond in the affirmative should he hear the same voice another time. When the boy heard the voice again, he shouted "Open!" to find the earth trembling. The hills split open and the lake flowed out all the way to the East Sea. In its place, small streams gurgled from cracks in the cliffs; the cliffs themselves contained caves that were miraculously filled with thousands of stone statues.

Impressive though it may be, today few people subscribe to this fascinating if unverifiable legend. Originally called Yi Que (in reference to the hills' resemblance to the column-like pillars at the entrances of some buildings), the area was renamed "Longmen" (Dragon Gate) during the Sui and Tang dynasties in honor of the imperial court at Luoyang. In AD 493, Emperor Xiaowen of the Northern Wei granted imperial patronage to the Guyang Cave in an effort to solidify his reign; emperors of nine dynasties subsequently followed his example, and construction continued for over 400 years.

Many of the 2100 niche shrines, 3600 tablets and inscriptions, and 100,000 sculptured figures are missing, limbless, or in disappointingly poor condition. What does remain inspires awe among the crowds of tourists who visit the site daily. Most of the largest caves and sculptures are found on the Western Hills, although a few temples and the possibility of a good panoramic view draw some visitors to the other side of the Yi River.

THREE CAVES OF BINYANG (bīnyáng sān dòng; 宾阳三洞). The caves were built by Emperor Xuanwu (AD 500-516) to honor his father and mother. The middle cave is generally considered the most significant. Relief sculptures formerly decorated the walls and depicted important Buddhist rituals and stories. In one such legend, the youngest prince of the ancient state of Maha Bodhi decided, after his two elder brothers refused, to sacrifice himself to save a dying tiger and its seven starving newborn cubs. Because the ailing tiger was too weak even to bite him, the unselfish prince pricked himself with a bamboo shaft before jumping off the cliff to land at the tiger's side, where he was then consumed.

OTHER CAVES. Ten Thousand Buddhas Cave (wàn fó dòng; 万佛洞) actually contains over 15,000 figurines, many only 4cm tall. According to records, the cave took six years to complete and was supervised by two female officials from the imperial court. The **Lotus Flowers Cave** (liánhuā dòng; 莲花洞) nearby houses the smallest statues of the Longmen Grottoes. **Fengxian Temple** (fèngxiān sì; 奉先寺) was financed by Empress Wu Zetian, who generously donated her entire annual cosmetics budget to the cause. The resulting shrine is the largest at Longmen and includes the 17m high Buddha Losana, who some suggest was modeled after the empress herself.

Medical Prescription Cave (yàofáng dòng; 药房洞) contains over 140 treatments and prescriptions, covering all things medicinal from herbal remedies to cures for esophagus cancer. Near the southern gate, the statue of the Buddha Sakyamuni presides over **Guyang Cave** (gǔyáng dòng; 古阳洞), the oldest and best preserved of the Longmen Grottoes. Numerous sculptures depict the process by which Siddhartha, the founder of Buddhism, attained enlightenment.

OTHER SIGHTS

WHITE HORSE TEMPLE (bái mǎ sì; 白马寺). The granddaddy of all Chinese Buddhist temples, the White Horse, built in AD 68, marks the site of the first Buddhist monastery in China. The two Indian monks who came to Luoyang to spread the Mahayana gospel carried their scriptures on a white horse, and the name remained. Many of the halls and statues are authentic works dating back hundreds of years to the Yuan or Ming dynasties. In the summer, venture to the back of the grounds to see the two ancient cypress trees in the courtyard garden of the Pavilion of Vairocana (田比卢殿); some tourist groups don't make it this far. *(About 12km east of Luoyang, a 45min.-1hr. bus ride. Take bus #5 from the train station (Zhongzhou Lu) to Xiguan; change to bus #56. Open daily 6:30am-6pm. Y25.)*

GUANLIN (guānlín; 关林). Nestled behind an alleyway and thick clouds of burning incense, this temple commemorates Guan Yu, a warrior said to have lived from AD 160 to 219. In the *Romance of the Three Kingdoms*, Guan Yu was defeated, captured, and executed by the ruler of the Kingdom of Wu. Fearing the wrath of Guan Yu's blood brother Liu Bei (ruler of Shu), the ruler of Wu sent Guan Yu's head to Cao Cao (ruler of Wei) in an effort to deflect responsibility for the death. Cao Cao, however, turned out to be an admirer of Guan Yu's loyalty and valor; he ordered that a wooden body be carved to accompany the head before Guan Yu was buried with full honors. The "lin" in the name of this site refers not, as is commonly assumed, to cypress trees but instead to the burial place of a sage or saint. Only the tombs of Confucius (see **Confucianism**, p. 31) and Guan Yu have received this designation. The ruddy-faced, long-bearded, green-robed figure of Guan Yu has been deified as a guardian of culture and is a popular Chinese opera character. *(At the end of Guanlin Nan Lu, on the left side if you are coming from the main road; about a 10-15min. walk from the bus #81 stop. Open daily 8am-6pm. Y20.)*

ROYAL CITY PARK (wángchéng gōngyuán; 王城公园). In the summer months, vendors selling overpriced ice cream and families with young children populate the park. During parts of April and May, the park really blooms; it is one of the best locations for viewing the famed Luoyang peonies. The small zoo in the northern section houses some tired-looking animals. *(On Zhongzhou Lu near Hedong Lu. Take bus #2, 102, or 103 from the train station sto Wangcheng Gongyuan. Open daily 5am-10pm. Y3.)*

LUOYANG CITY MUSEUM (luòyáng bówùguǎn; 洛阳博物馆). Displays of relics unearthed in the Luoyang region form the core of the museum's collections of bronzeware, ceramics, gold, silver, and jade. The museum also displays tri-color ceramics of everything from frogs to peonies to roosters. There are sometimes temporary exhibitions downstairs. *(298 Zhongzhou Zhong Lu, near Wangcheng Lu on the eastern edge of Royal City Park. Take bus #101 or 103 to Military Central Hospital; walk west for about 3min. Open daily 8:30am-5:30pm. Y10.)*

MUSEUM OF ANCIENT TOMBS (gǔmù bówùguǎn; 古墓博物馆). An ancient saying proclaims that Suzhou and Hangzhou are good places to live, and that Luoyang (Mangshan) is a good place to die. More than 20 ancient tombs, dating from the Han to Northern Song dynasties, prove that princes, generals, and other figures took this advice to heart. Many of the vividly painted murals have been restored, and a number of pottery figures and other relics are on display. Duck in and out of the dimly lit tombs in the museum's long corridors; the faint of heart may want to bring along a friend or a flashlight. *(About 25min. northwest of the city. Take bus #83 from Daonan Lu in front of the main bus station to Gumu Guan. Open daily 8:30am-7pm. Y15.)*

XIAOLANGDI DAM (xiǎolángdī shuǐlì shūnqǔ gōngchéng; 小浪底水利枢纽工程). At the mouth of the last gorge of the Yellow River's middle reaches, the dam, originally a World Bank-funded project, reaches a height of 154m. Plans are also in the works for the development of a major tourism zone in the area once construction is complete. *(About 1hr. north of Luoyang. Minibuses travel from the main bus station to Xiaolangdi several times per day, based on demand.)*

KAIFENG 开封 ☎0378

About a thousand years ago, Kaifeng was *the* place to have your dynastic capital. During the Five Dynasties period, four out of the five dynasties—the later Liang, the Jin, Han, and Zhou—all chose Kaifeng as their seat of imperial power. In 960, the Northern Song continued this trend, and Kaifeng soon became the most important commercial metropolis in all of Asia. For many centuries, the city also was home to a large Jewish community.

Today, unlike most of China's exploding cities, Kaifeng's population of 600,000 is less than the one million people who lived there in its heyday. Kaifeng is not the center of trade and industry that it once was, but from a tourist's perspective, this may be a good thing. Less developed than other Chinese cities, Kaifeng has retained some of that vague and elusive feeling often referred to as "character." All of this surfaces in the glare of light bulbs at the famed Kaifeng night markets, easily the most crowded and exciting of the city's sights. Traditional wooden-eaved buildings line the narrow backstreets; somewhat less authentic versions figure prominently in the most recently constructed tourist attractions, designed to recall Kaifeng's glory days as an imperial capital.

▐ TRANSPORTATION

Trains: Kaifeng Train Station (kāifēng huǒchē zhàn; 开封火车站; ☎565 3905), on Zhongshan Lu, about 1km south of the old city walls. Open 24hr. To: **Beijing** (8 per day, Y56); **Luoyang** (4hr., 2 per day, Y31); **Taiyuan** (13½hr., 1 per day, Y45); and **Zhengzhou** (1½hr., 11 per day, Y7-12).

Buses: Kaifeng Bus Station (kāifēng qìchē zhàn; 开封汽车站; ☎595 8053), near Xinmenguan Jie and Zhongshan Lu, a 3min. walk from the train station, on the other side of the street. The terminus for bus #3 is right outside. To: **Anyang** (4hr., 8 per day, Y27); **Beijing** (7-8hr., 3 per day, Y120); **Luoyang** (3hr., every 30min. 7am-5pm, Y30); **Taiyuan** (8-9hr., 1 per day, Y120); and **Zhengzhou** (1hr., every 20min. 5:30am-7pm, Y10). **Kaifeng West Bus Station** (kāifēng kèyùn xī zhàn; 开封客运西站; ☎393 3594), on Yingbin Lu south of Baogong Lake. Buses #1, 4, and 9 (all serving the train station and main bus station as well) stop outside at Xi Zhan. To: **Anyang** (5hr., 7 per day, Y19); **Luoyang** (3hr., every 40min. 7am-6pm, Y30); **Zhengzhou East Station** (1hr.; every 15min. 7am-7pm, Jinlong buses every 20min. 7am-5:40pm; Y7-10); and **Zhengzhou West Station** (1hr., 15 per day, Y6.5).

Local Transportation: Bus #1 goes from the train station up Zhongshan Lu and then northeast to Song Dynasty Street near the Iron Pagoda, and **#15** runs from the hospital in southeastern Kaifeng up to the northeast. Gulou Square, at the corner of Madao Jie, Sihou Jie, Shudian Jie, and Gulou Jie, is a major hub for buses.

Taxis: Base fare Y4.

Bike rental: There are small shops along the north side of Baogong Lake and on Shudian Jie, north of Gulou Square.

▟ ☍ ORIENTATION AND PRACTICAL INFORMATION

The heart of Kaifeng lies within old city walls, which are about 3km long on each side. **Zhongshan Lu** (中山路) runs north to south from Dragon Pavilion Park through the heart of the city and past the city wall to the long-distance train and bus stations. **Shengfu Jie** (省府街) turns into **Sihou Jie** (寺后街), then **Gulou Jie** (古楼街), and finally **Mujiaqiao Jie** (穆家桥街) as it moves east. The center of town is where **Shudian Jie** (书店街) crosses Sihou Jie.

Travel Agency: CITS, 98 Yingbin Lu (☎398 3410), inside the Tokyo Hotel, near the West Bus Station. Open M-F 8:30am-noon and 3-6:30pm. **Kaifeng Guesthouse Travel Ser-**

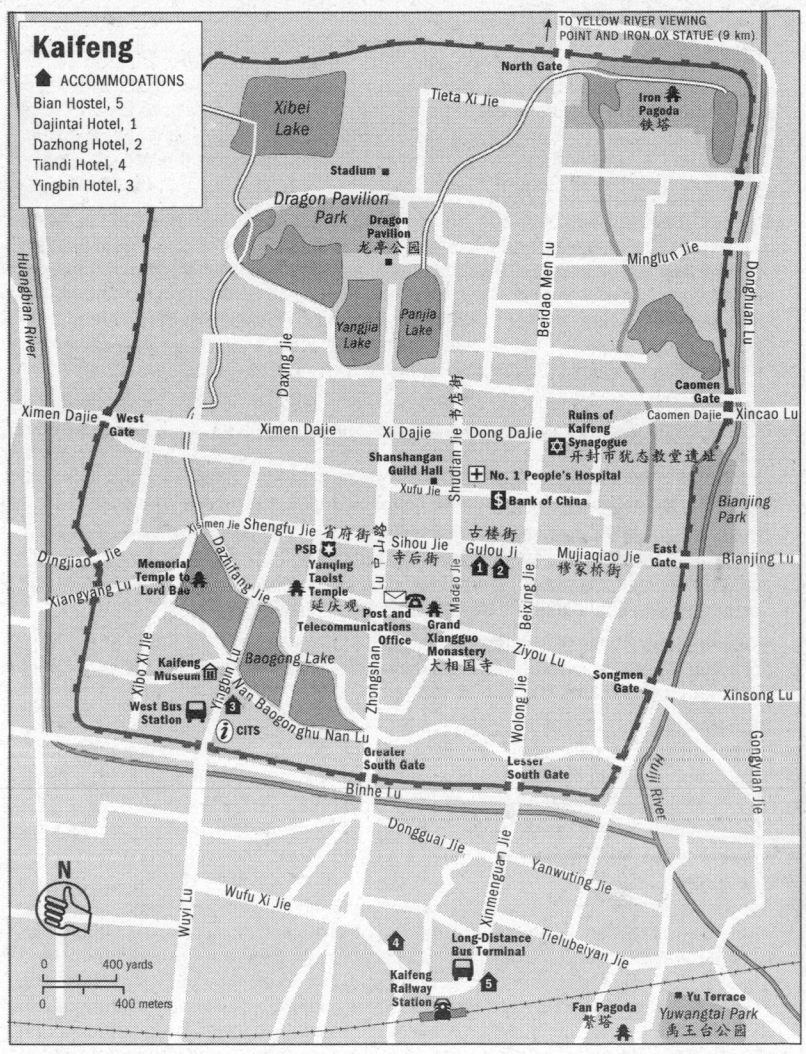

Kaifeng

⌂ ACCOMMODATIONS

Bian Hostel, 5
Dajintai Hotel, 1
Dazhong Hotel, 2
Tiandi Hotel, 4
Yingbin Hotel, 3

TO YELLOW RIVER VIEWING
POINT AND IRON OX STATUE (9 km)

North Gate

Xibei Lake

Tieta Xi Jie

Iron Pagoda 铁塔

Stadium

Dragon Pavilion Park

Dragon Pavilion 龙亭公园

Minglun Jie

Beidao Men Lu

Donghuan Lu

Yangjia Lake

Panjia Lake

Daxing Jie

Caomen Gate

Ruins of Kaifeng Synagogue 开封市犹态教堂遗址

Caomen Dajie

Xincao Lu

Ximen Dajie

West Gate

Ximen Dajie

Xi Dajie

Dong DaJie

Shudian Jie

Huangbian River

Shanshangan Guild Hall

Xufu Jie

No. 1 People's Hospital

Bank of China

Bianjing Park

Bianjing Lu

Ximen Jie Shengfu Jie 省府街

PSB

Sihou Jie

Gulou Ji 古楼街

Mujiaqiao Jie 穆家桥街

East Gate

Dingjiao Lu

Yanqing Taoist Temple 延庆观

Madao Jie

Beixng Jie

Xiangyang Lu

Dachitang Jie

Memorial Temple to Lord Bao

Post and Telecommunications Office

Grand Xiangguo Monastery 大相国寺

Ziyou Lu

Wolong Jie

Songmen Gate

Xinsong Lu

Xibo Lu

Kaifeng Museum

Zhongshan Lu

Baogong Lake

Yingbin Nan Baogonghu Nan Lu

West Bus Station

CITS

Greater South Gate

Lesser South Gate

Huiji River

Gongyuan Jie

Binhe Lu

Dongguai Jie

Yanwuting Jie

N

0   400 yards
0   400 meters

Wuyi Lu

Wufu Xi Jie

Xinmenguan Jie

Tielubeiyan Jie

Long-Distance Bus Terminal

Kaifeng Railway Station

Fan Pagoda 繁塔

Yu Terrace Yuwangtai Park 禹王台公园

CENTRAL CHINA

vice (kāifēng bīnguǎn lǚxíngshè; 开封宾馆旅行社; ☎595 1255), on Ziyou Lu, next to the hotel. Commission Y30.

Bank of China: 31 Zhongshan Bei Lu, on the west side of the street. Exchanges traveler's checks and major foreign currencies. Open daily 8am-6pm. The branch at 64 Gulou Jie, opposite and east of the Dajintai Hotel, keeps similar hours, but M-F only.

PSB: 16 Sihou Jie (☎595 5091), near Zhongshan Lu.

Post and Telecommunications: Post and Telecommunications Building, on Ziyou Lu, east of Zhongshan Lu. EMS available. Open daily 8am-6:30pm. **China Telecom,** in the same building, has IDD service. Open daily 8am-7pm. Another branch is at the corner of Gulou Jie and Wusheng Jiao. **Postal Code:** 475000.

ACCOMMODATIONS

Kaifeng, derived from the Chinese word for "open," is an apt description of the city's accommodation situation. Nearly every place in town accepts foreigners; even the cheap-looking hostels around the train station don't seem to be off limits to the occasional *laowai*. For easy access to the night market, Gulou Jie/Sihou Jie, Ziyou Lu, and Zhongshan Lu are the best places to stay. Several more expensive establishments are near Baogong Lake.

Dajintai Hotel (dàjīntái bīnguǎn; 大金台宾馆), 17 Gulou Jie (☎595 6677), a 3min. walk east of the intersection with Madao Jie/Shudian Jie. Buses #4 and 7 from the train station stop at Gulou. With the wooden traditional-style building behind you, walk east along Gulou Jie; the entrance is on the right, marked by an ornate red archway. The standard rooms have high-tech water heaters and hallucinogenic iridescent bow-tie wallpaper on the ceiling. There are no carpets or elevators, and A/C is Y5 per person per day. Breakfast included. Doubles Y40-60, with bath Y120.

Yingbin Hotel (yíngbīn fàndiàn; 迎宾饭店), 96 Yingbin Lu (☎393 1943), diagonally opposite and a short walk from the West Bus Station. Buses #1, 4, 7, and 9 from the train station stop nearby at Xi Zhan, and Baogong Lake is a 5min. walk to the north. Institutional atmosphere. No A/C, but some rooms have huge attached baths. Mosquito nets in most rooms. Doubles Y44, with bath Y76; triples Y60; quads Y64; quints Y75.

Tiandi Hotel (tiāndì dàjiǔdiàn; 天地大酒店), 317 Zhongshan Lu Nan Duan (☎391 2828, ext. 3666). A 3min. walk north of the train station, the Tiandi is somewhat out of range of the station pandemonium. In the summer, the clean, cool, A/C rooms may just be heaven on earth. Doubles Y50, with bath Y100; triples Y50/150.

Dazhong Hotel (dàzhòng bīnguǎn; 大众宾馆), 8 Gulou Jie (☎596 2796 or 598 1262), between Madao Jie and Wusheng Jiao. Rooms are small, but so are the prices. Doubles Y40, with A/C and bath Y68; triples Y45.

Bian Hostel (biàn dàlǚshè; 汴大旅社; ☎595 1893), at the far southern end of Xinmenguan Lu, at the terminus of bus #3. Look for large red characters at the top of the building. A quick jaunt from the train and bus stations; train whistles are a shrill reminder of the location. Facilities are basic, with common showers only. Deposit Y5. Singles Y25; doubles Y24-36, with A/C Y70; triples Y30-36; quads Y24-36.

FOOD

Kaifeng's **night market,** centered around the brightly lit intersection of Madao Jie/Shudian Jie and Sihou Jie/Gulou Jie, offers not only food but entertainment and adventure as well. The streets and sidewalks are precariously packed with stalls, leaving pedestrians to jostle for space with swerving bicycles and lurching minivan taxis. Eat your way through *shaguo*, noodles, wonton soup, dumplings, omelets, lamb skewers, meat-stuffed bread, almond jelly, and other delectable goodies that are served up piping hot for just a few *yuan*. The night market still takes place on rainy nights, albeit at a more subdued pace. In summer, ice cream stands are a popular stop.

No. 1 Dumpling Restaurant (dìyī lóu bāozi guǎn; 第一楼包子馆), 8 Sihou Jie (☎597 7480), between Zhongshan Lu and Madao Jie. *The* place to eat in Kaifeng, as proven by the ever-full tables, Di Yi Lou is a local landmark that serves up its pork-filled dumplings (xiǎolóng bāo; 小龙包) for Y5 per steamer. Open daily 11am-2am.

Tianli Cake Shop (tiānlì miànbāo xī bǐngwū; 天力面包西饼屋), on the southwest corner of Gulou Square. Let your nose guide the way to this small bakery under a red awning. Large selection of breads and pastries Y0.5-5, including excellent sponge cake. Open daily 6:30am-10pm.

 **SIGHTS**

Dotted with lakes and traditional-style buildings, Kaifeng is well suited to those who prefer sightseeing on foot. Many of the city's sights are within a 30-minute walk of the city center; of the more distant attractions, all but the Yellow River Viewing Point are conveniently accessed by public transportation.

■**IRON PAGODA** (tiě tǎ; 铁塔). The burnt brown of the tiles depicting the Buddha, ancient musicians, and other figures resembles the color of iron, hence the name. Built in AD 1049, the 13-story pagoda overlooks the surrounding park and portions of the Kaifeng city wall. In the summer, **Fusheng courtyard,** accessible through the first building on the left after the entrance, offers a lush, water lily-covered pond and a dazzling array of *bonsai* trees. *(210 Beimen Dajie, at Tieta Xi Jie. Bus #1 from Song Dynasty St. stops about 1 block away, and buses #3 and 18 also terminate here. ☎595 2279. Open daily 7am-7pm. Y15, pagoda additional Y3.)*

DRAGON PAVILION PARK (lóng tíng gōngyuán; 龙亭公园). The main hall of the Dragon Pavilion stands nearly 27m high, flanked by eight halls within the courtyard and by scores of private entrepreneurs and photographers outside. However, those who climb to the top of the main hall may be disappointed by the life-size wax figure reenactment of the "Founding Ceremony of Northern Song." Kitschy duck and dragon boats circle the lake (20-30min., Y10-20). **Song Dynasty Street,** (sòng dū jiē; 宋都街) just south of the main entrance, is lined with restaurants and souvenir shops. *(At the north end of Zhongshan Lu. Take bus #1 from the train station, or walk from the Gulou Square area. ☎566 0142. Open daily 6:30am-7pm; in winter 7am-6pm. Y25.)*

GRAND XIANGGUO MONASTERY (dà xiàngguó sì; 大相国寺). Built in AD 555, the monastery was later flooded, damaged by war, and rebuilt. At its proudest moments (during the Northern Song), it had 64 halls and over 1000 resident monks. Few of the buildings remain today; the Bell Tower and Drum Tower are the monastery's most recent 20th century additions. *(On Ziyou Lu, east of Zhongshan Lu. Open daily 8am-6pm. Y20.)*

TERRACE OF YU THE GREAT (yǔ wáng tái gōngyuán; 禹王台公园). First named the "Playing Terrace" in honor of the blind musician Shi Kuang, in 1522 the terrace was renamed to commemorate Yu the Great, the sage king who tamed the Great Flood (see p. 8). Tang poets Li Bai, Du Fu, and Gao Shi gathered in this shaded park to imbibe and compose in AD 744. *(Near Tielu Beiyan Jie. ☎595 4347. Open daily 7am-7pm; in winter 8am-6:30pm. Y5.)*

FAN PAGODA (fán tǎ; 繁塔). The oldest structure in Kaifeng, this pagoda dates back to AD 977. It originally stood nine stories tall, but only three stories remained by the Ming dynasty; now it has been rebuilt to a happy medium of six stories. The 7000 bricks feature 108 different designs. Those adventurous souls who want to make the brief but steep climb to the top should ask an attendant to come out and turn on the stair lights. *(Hidden in a neighborhood in southeast Kaifeng; once you're in the vicinity, get a local to show you the way. Fanta Bei Jie from Yu Terrace comes close; after about 5 min., turn left and follow the street to the sign painted in purple on the wall. Otherwise, take Fanta Xi Jie to Fanta Xi Er Jie or bus #15 to Yanchang stop. Open daily 8am-6pm. Y4.)*

MEMORIAL TO LIU SHAOQI (liú shàoqí chénlièguǎn; 刘少奇陈列馆). This museum is a tribute of sorts to Liu Shaoqi, Chairman Mao's heir apparent until he was purged during the Cultural Revolution (see p. 19); he died in Kaifeng in 1969. The architecturally and historically intriguing inner building was the Agricultural Bank of China before it was converted to government property. Early photos of a robust Liu Shaoqi touring Henan province contrast sharply with those of the ailing man at an interrogation session during the Cultural Revolution. In the inner build-

CENTRAL CHINA

EGGS-TREMELY GOOD NEWS In Henan Province, there are many rituals surrounding the birth of a baby—all revolving around eggs. Parents of newborn babies traditionally send red eggs to the baby's grandparents to share the good news. If the baby is a boy, a black spot is painted on top of each egg. An even number of eggs (often six or eight), imply that the boy will marry once he grows older. If the baby is a girl, an odd number of eggs (without black spots) are sent, implying that the girl will marry away. After receiving the eggs, the baby's grandmother bakes a cake for her son-in-law or for the man who brought the happy news. If the man meets a dog on the way home, he throws the cake to the dog; the dog then supposedly eats all the baby's misfortunes.

Also customary is the exchanging of gifts between the new parents and friends and relatives. When friends and relatives send gifts to welcome the baby, the baby's family must return the favor. The return gift of choice? Boiled red eggs. How many eggs are given is decided according to the value of the received gifts, with an even number for a boy and an odd number for a girl. Why the color red? It symbolizes luck.

---

ing is the former President's deathbed; his last days are detailed down to his last dose of medication, body temperature readings, and crematorium records (the bill came to Y33.78). *(On the west side of Beitu Jie.* ☎ *596 5306. Open daily 8:30am-5:30pm. Y4.)*

MEMORIAL TEMPLE TO LORD BAO (bāo gōng cí; 包公祠). Constructed in honor of Lord Bao, a famous officer of ancient China, this temple includes representations of events in his life and court in addition to historical records of his deeds. The rock gardens and lakeside views from the pavilion are nice, although not much more impressive than what can be enjoyed for free. *(At the corner of Xiangyang Lu and Xibo Bei Jie. Buses #8 and 10 stop nearby en route to Gulou Jie or the station.* ☎ *393 1595. Open daily 6:30am-7pm. Y20.)*

OTHER SIGHTS. All that remains of the **Kaifeng Synagogue** (kāifēng shì yóutài jiàotáng yízhǐ; 开封市犹太教堂遗址) is hidden in the boiler room of the No. 4 People's Hospital. Bus #3 stops at the Bianjing Hotel; the hospital is at 59 Beitu Jie, south of Dong Dajie. Walk straight through the hospital courtyard, then turn left into the alleyway; follow it for about 20m until it curves to the right. Bang on the large red doors to the boiler room; someone will usually let you in. **Yanqing Temple** (yánqìng guān; 延庆观), on Guanqian Jie northeast of Bao Lake, features the uniquely shaped Jade Emperor Hall and a photo exhibition detailing the temple's history. Buses #8, 9, and 16 stop outside. *(Open daily 7am-6pm. Y10.)* The **Yellow River Viewing Platform** (huánghé yóulǎnqū; 黄河游览区), about 10km north of the city, provides views of the surrounding fields but often not of the river itself. Relatively few visitors make the trip. *(Round-trip taxi about Y20. Open daily sunrise-sunset. Y2.)*

ANYANG 安阳   ☎0372

One of China's seven ancient capitals, Anyang was the site of the city of Yin, a fact confirmed by the oracle bones unearthed by local peasants over one hundred years ago. Subsequent excavations revealed tombs and ruins as well as bronzes, chariots, pottery, jade, and thousands of oracle bones, confirming that the legendary Shang dynasty had indeed existed in the 14th century BC (see p. 8). Although Anyang is of great interest to scholars and archeologists, the small city's charms may only hold visitors' attention for a day or two.

✴ 🛈 ORIENTATION AND PRACTICAL INFORMATION

Anyang is mostly to the south of the **Huan River** (huán hé; 洹河), near the border of Henan and Hebei provinces. **Jiefang Lu** (解放路), extending from the train station to People's Park, runs parallel to **Renmin Dadao** (人民大道). **Hongqi Lu** (红旗路), running perpendicular to Jiefang Lu and Renmin Dadao, becomes **Bei Dajie**

(北大街) and then **Zhongshan Jie** (中山街) as it enters the **Old City** (gǔ chéng; 古城) near the Drum Tower. The Yin Ruins and the Tomb of Yuan Shikai are in the northern part of the city; most hotels and other sights are easily reached by foot.

Trains: Anyang Train Station (ānyáng huǒchē zhàn; 安阳火车站), on Jiefang Lu. To: **Beijing** (5-6½hr., 21 per day, Y34-71); **Taiyuan** (5-6hr., 2 per day, Y25); and **Zhengzhou** (2-3hr., 27 per day, Y13-28).

Buses: Anyang Bus Station (ānyáng chángtú qìchē zhàn; 安阳长途汽车站; ☎591 3951, ext. 225), on Heping Lu. From the train station, go about 3 blocks south. Ticket office to the right of the waiting room. To: **Beijing** (6hr., 5 per day 9:30am-1am, Y92); **Jinan** (5hr., several per day 7:20am-3:20pm, Y45); **Shijiazhuang** (3-4hr., 6 Iveco minibuses per day, Y40); **Taiyuan** (6hr., 2 per day, Y80); and **Zhengzhou** (3hr., Iveco minibuses every 15min. 6:10am-6:30pm, Y30).

Local Transportation: Bus #2 runs from the train station along Jiefang Lu, up Hongqi Lu, and past Renmin Lu, while #11 goes from the train station up Zhangde Lu, down Renmin Lu, and down Dongfeng Lu past Renmin Park. Fare Y0.5 and up.

Taxis: Base fare Y4-5.

Bike Rental: Available on the south side of Jiefang Lu, just west of Zhangde Lu. Y2 per day, deposit Y100. Alternatively, from the train station, turn right and continue about 1 block to the stand in front of the Gonghang Hostel (工行招待所) on the right. Y1 per hr.; Y100 deposit.

Travel Agency: CITS, Anyang Hotel, Bldg. 3, 2nd Fl. (☎592 5650). Open M-F 8am-noon and 3-6:30pm.

Bank of China: On the west side of Bei Dajie, north of the Drum Tower. Open daily 8am-6pm. The Jiefang Lu branch, just east of the station, does not accept traveler's checks.

PSB: 35 Hongqi Lu (☎592 3461). Open M-F 8am-noon and 3-6:30pm.

Hospital: Anyang People's Hospital (ānyáng shì rénmín yīyuàn; 安阳市人民医院; ☎592 3331), on Jiefang Lu, about 1 block east of Hongqi Lu near the Anyang Hotel.

Internet Access: China Telecom, 2nd Fl., on the north side of Jiefang Lu, just east of Hongqi Lu. Y3 per hr. Open daily 8:30am-6:30pm.

Post and Telecommunications: Hongqi Lu Post and Telecommunications Building (hóngqí lù yóudiàn zhījú; 红旗路邮电支局), at the northwest corner of Dengta Lu. Open daily 8am-7pm. EMS available. The train station branch keeps the same hours. **Postal Code:** 455000.

ACCOMMODATIONS AND FOOD

Many lodgings are by **Jiefang Lu,** particularly around the train station. Most of the cheaper dormitory-style places, including those with English signs (such as the Jindi Hotel), are either closed for renovations or do not accept foreigners.

The night markets near the Drum Tower and in front of the Workers' Cultural Palace offer a wide variety of noodle and fried dishes (Y3-5), as well as lamb skewers (Y1), stuffed pitas (Y1.5), and other snacks. The **Kaifeng No. 1 Chain Restaurant** (kāifēng dì yī lóu tèxǔ liànsuǒ diàn; 开封第一楼特许链锁店), at the south corner of Jiefang Lu and Xianzhong Jie, dishes up Y6 steamers of dumplings, albeit it a bit removed from its famous Kaifeng counterpart. (Open daily 6:30am-11pm.) Ice cream lovers, take out your spoons: the **Little Swan Ice Cream Stand** (xiǎo qǐ'é bīngqílín wū; 小企鹅冰淇淋屋), on the north side of Jiefang Lu between the train station and Zhangde Lu, is marked by the cute penguins outside. Coffee, cold drinks, and ice cream delights include the Happy Welcome Boat (yíng lè chuán; 迎乐船; Y12), a variation on the banana split. (Open daily 10am-midnight.)

Anyang Guesthouse (ānyáng bīnguǎn; 安阳宾馆), 1 Youyi Lu (☎592 2219; fax 592 2244), just north of Jiefang Lu, a 15min. walk from the train station. An English sign indicates where to turn. Bus #2 from the train station stops at Hongqi Guangchang; from there, walk around the corner in the direction the bus came from, making a right on the 1st street after Hongqi Lu. This establishment is in the middle of a massive remodeling project, and the results are visible in the large, gleaming white bathrooms. All rooms have A/C, TV, and attached bath. Breakfast included. Doubles Y168-188.

Great Wall Hotel (cháng chéng bīnguǎn; 长城宾馆), 5 Xinxing Jie (☎591 0669), between Jiefang Lu and Heping Lu. Although only a 5min. jaunt from the train and long-distance bus stations, this hotel is somewhat quieter and definitely cleaner than its location suggests. All rooms have A/C and bath, but the cheaper, windowless doubles are often fully booked. Breakfast included. Check-out 2pm. Reservations recommended. Doubles Y160-280.

Flying Eagle Hotel (fēiyīng dàjiǔdiàn; 飞鹰大酒店), 119 Renmin Dadao (☎593 5888; fax 592 3037), west of Hongqi Lu. Bus #2 from the train station stops at Er Baihuo; from there it's a 5min. walk to the hotel. A taxi from the station area costs Y4-5. Rooms are equipped with standard amenities, although windowless rooms have a quaint penitentiary feel. Breakfast included. Deposit Y500-600. Doubles Y168-318; triples Y240.

👁 SIGHTS

By day, the sights are limited to a select few. By night, not too surprisingly, full-fledged entertainment options are also rather limited. For cheap food and free people-watching, try the night market south of the intersection of Jiefang Lu and Hongqi Lu. The **Workers' Cultural Palace** (gōngrén wénhuà gōng; 工人文化宫), five minutes east of the train station at Zhangde Lu and Jiefang Lu, has a movie theater and, when the weather is warm, a huge number of pool tables outside in front.

OLD CITY (gǔ chéng; 古城). Anyang's Old City begins on Bei Dajie just south of Jiefang Lu. The main alley is jam-packed with pedestrians, bikes, and vendors selling everything from fresh bread to mosquito netting. The small lanes near the **Drum Tower** (gǔlóu; 鼓楼) are not clearly marked with street names but are fascinating places to wander. Elderly residents playing *mahjong* and people selling snacks such as tofu on a stick (Y1) are common sights; foreigners definitely are not. **Wenfeng Pagoda** (wénfēng tǎ; 文峰塔), also known as **Tianning Temple Pagoda** (tiānníng sì tǎ; 天宁寺塔), materializes out of nowhere. From Bei Dajie and Jiefang Lu, walk four blocks south. Turn right onto Dasi Qian Jie and continue for a couple blocks; the pagoda is on the right. The 65m climb rewards visitors with a panoramic view of the city. *(Open daily 8:30am-6:30pm; in winter 8:30am-5pm. Y3.)*

MUSEUM OF YIN RUINS (yīnxū bówùyuán; 殷墟博物苑). This museum sits in a part of town that is dusty, barren, and of little interest to the average visitor. The collection itself is not particularly extensive, but the grounds are, with numerous excavation pits and flower gardens in the back. *(On Yinxu Lu north of Anyang Lu. Take bus #1 (Y1.2) to Yinxu Bowuyuan from Wenhua Gong on Jiefang Lu east of Zhangde Lu, on the north side of the street. Cross the train tracks and continue straight ahead, bearing to the left when the road splits; it's a 15-20min. walk. ☎393 2171. Open daily 8am-6:30pm. Y10.)*

MAUSOLEUM OF YUAN SHIKAI (yuán lín; 袁林). From the Museum of Yin Ruins, some visitors choose to continue the historical journey to the mausoleum by minivan taxi. Yuan Shikai's 1916 rule as self-proclaimed emperor of China lasted only one year (see p. 14), but the city seems determined to see the mausoleum last much longer; the bright red buildings and shiny green-tiled roofs indicate recent renovations. The mausoleum park features a small collection of photographs and relics toward the back of the courtyard. *(Bus #8 from People's Park stops at Shengli Lu; from there it's a 2min. walk. Open daily 8am-6:30pm; in winter 8am-6pm. Y20.)*

SHANXI 山西

The mountainous province of Shanxi has a history of resisting incursion. Bounded to the north by the Great Wall, Shanxi played a key role in protecting China from northern nomadic tribes to the north during the Qin and Han dynasties. Centuries later, during the Japanese occupation in the 1930s, Communist guerrillas hid among the caves and crevices in Shanxi's barren mountainsides, using the rugged natural formations as sites of resistance. Today, Shanxi's combination of rough roads, barren mountainsides, and unremarkable coal mining cities such as Taiyuan and Datong may keep away many visitors. However, Shanxi has some spectacular sights underneath the layer of smog that coats much of the province. These precious treasures are hidden well off the beaten path, but will reward those who are willing to spend a little time exploring. The ancient banking town of Pingyao and the lush valleys, monasteries, and spectacular views of Wutaishan shatter the dullness so often associated with central China. While the Yungang Grottoes and Hanging Monastery near Datong are not-to-be-missed sights, visitors who make these two places their first and only stop en route to Beijing, Xian, or Inner Mongolia will miss out on some of Shanxi's more remote but incredible offerings. The northern tribes who eventually broke through the Great Wall and set up base in Shanxi had the right mentality: Shanxi has a lot to offer, if you're willing to fight for it.

TAIYUAN 太原 ☎ 0351

Despite steel foundries, blast coke furnaces, and an overabundance of karaoke bars, Taiyuan can still sparkle. The glittering, brightly lit hotels and restaurants along Yingze Dajie culminate in May First Square, the place to go for romantic encounters or a quick snapshot in front of the large sculpture and fountains.

Taiyuan has long been a strategically important city. Founded in the ancient state of Zhao in 479 BC, Taiyuan later became the starting point for Tang founder Li Yuan's conquest of China and emerged as one of the Tang's military strongholds. However, many of the city's historical sights (including its walls) were destroyed in a bloody PLA siege during the struggle against the Nationalists. The capital of Shanxi province, Taiyuan is a crucial center of heavy industry and commerce, and sits on one of the richest iron and coal deposits in the world. Most travelers use Taiyuan as a starting point for tours to Wutaishan or skip it altogether.

▛ TRANSPORTATION

Airplanes: Taiyuan Airport (tàiyuán jīchǎng; 太原机场) is far from the city center. Shuttle buses (30min., Y10) generally leave daily at 6, 7am, and 3pm from the **China Eastern Airlines Ticket Office** (zhōngguó dōngfāng mínháng shòupiào chù; 中国东方民航售票处), 158 Yingze Dajie (☎ 404 2903), between Qingnian Lu and Dongzhou Lu. Open daily 8am-8pm. To: **Beijing** (1 per day, Y470); **Guangzhou** (2 per day, Y1140); and **Shanghai** (1-2 per day, Y960).

Trains: Taiyuan Train Station (tàiyuán huǒchē zhàn; 太原火车站; ☎ 418 2913), at the corner of Yingze Dajie and Jianshe Lu. To: **Beijing** (8-10hr., 5 per day 8:38am-9pm, Y77-131); **Datong** (7-9hr., 5 per day 3-11:17pm, Y65-104); **Guangzhou** (40hr., 8:30pm, Y279); **Shanghai** (22hr., 5:02pm, Y304); and **Xian** (11-12hr., 3 per day 6:55pm-1:29am, Y95-163).

Buses: Taiyuan Bus Station (tàiyuán qìchē zhàn; 太原汽车站; ☎ 404 2346), on the south side of Yingze Dajie between the train station and Bingzhou Lu. To: **Datong** (5hr., every hr. 7:30am-3:30pm, Y50); **Shijiazhuang** (3hr., every 30min. 6:30am-6:30pm, Y45); **Wutaishan** (4hr., every 15min. 6:15am-7:15pm, Y43); and **Zhengzhou** (8hr., 2 per day, Y120). Window #1 sells tickets to **Beijing** (6hr., every 20min. 7am-4pm plus another 10 departures 4pm-midnight, Y120). Minibuses to **Datong** (Y30), **Shijiazhuang** (Y45), **Wutaishan** (Y43), and other destinations congregate in the train station parking lot. Immediately west of the Electric Power Hotel is a small stand that handles several departures per day to **Beijing, Datong,** and **Wutaishan.**

Local Transportation: Most **buses** run from around 6am to 7 or 8pm, although bus **#103** to Shanxi University runs until 10pm. Fare Y0.5. Bus **#1** shuttles along Yingze Dajie past May First Square. **Electric buses** run up and down Wuyi Lu **(#2)** and Bingzhou Lu **(#3)** and cost the same as the bus. **Minibuses** (Y1-2) also troll the city streets.

Taxis: Base fare Y6, each additional km Y1.

✹ ⁊ ORIENTATION AND PRACTICAL INFORMATION

Yingze Dajie (迎泽大街) runs west from the train station through Taiyuan's main commerical district. Transportation and accommodation options sit at the eastern edge of the city, at the intersection of Yingze Dajie and **Jianshe Lu** (建设路). **May First Square** (wǔ yī guǎngchǎng; 五一广场) marks the busy intersection with **Wuyi Lu** (五一路) and **Bingzhou Lu** (并州路). Most of the tourist attractions and universities are near this area or in the southern portion of the city.

Travel Agency: CITS, 38 Pingyang Lu (☎ 723 2188). English-speaking staff member. Commission Y20. Open M-F 8am-noon and 2:30-6pm.

Bank of China: 288 Yingze Dajie (☎ 404 4027), a 1min. walk west of Yingze Park. Exchanges traveler's checks. Open M-F 8am-noon and 2:30-6pm. The branch 2 blocks west of the train station exchanges currency only. Open M-F 8am-noon and 2:30-7pm.

PSB: 9 Houjia Xiang (☎ 202 8550), northeast of May First Square. Open M-F 8am-noon and 2:30-5:30pm.

Hospital: Shanxi University No. 2 Hospital (shānxī dàxué dìèr yīyuàn; 山西大学第二医院; ☎ 307 3786), on Wuyi Lu near Bayi Mansion.

Telephones: China Telecom, across the street from the train station. A second branch at 213 Yingze Dajie, at Liugang Lu. IDD service available. Both open 24hr.

Internet Access: Global Internet Bar (huánqiú wǎngbā; 环球网吧; ☎ 701 9665), on Bingzhou Lu near Shanxi University. Take bus #103 from Yingze Dajie and Bingzhou Lu to Shanxi Daxue; cross the street and walk straight ahead for about 1min. Y4 per hr. **Microsoft Authorized Training Center** (wēiruǎn shòuquán péixùn zhōngxīn; 微软授权培训中心; ☎ 705 8891), in room 305 of the Shanxi University Chemistry Building (shānxī dàxué huàxué lóu; 山西大学化学楼). The building is to the right of the roundabout near the west gate. Y10 per hr. Open daily 8am-11pm.

Post Office: The post office opposite the train station, at the corner of Jianshe Lu and Yingze Dajie, offers EMS. Open daily 8am-8pm. The **May First Square Post Office** (wǔyì guǎngchǎng yóujú; 五一广场邮局), on the west side of Wuyi Lu, a 3min. walk north of May First Square, has Poste Restante (point to the small blackboard on the wall). Open daily 8am-7pm. **Postal Code:** 030001.

⌐ ACCOMMODATIONS

The cheaper places that accept foreigners are mostly around the train station. **Shanxi University Chinese Language Culture Center** (shānxī dàxué zhōngguó yǔyán wénhuà zhōngxīn; 山西大学中国语言文化中心; ☎ 701 0333) can provide travelers with accommodations near the northern entrance of the university, off Xuefu Lu. The university is a 30min. bus ride from Yingze Dajie on bus #103, so call first.

Yunshan Hotel (yúnshān fàndiàn; 云山饭店), 99 Yingze Dajie (☎ 404 1351, ext. 6116; fax 404 2294), just east of May First Square, about a 10min. walk from the train station or the first stop on any of the buses from the station area. Rooms are clean but a bit spartan. All rooms have TV and bath; A/C costs approx. Y10 extra. Singles Y90-118; doubles Y108-156; triples Y140-150.

Huayuan Hotel (huáyuàn bīnguǎn; 华苑宾馆), 9 Yingze Dajie (☎ 404 6201; fax 404 6980), 1 block west of the train station next door to the Bank of China. Although train station noise might disturb some guests, the large windows and rooms are quite pleasant. 10-15% discounts often possible. Singles Y168; doubles Y218; triples Y268.

Shanxi Electric Power Hotel (shānxī diànlì dàshà; 山西电力大厦), 39 Yingze Dajie (☎ 404 1784; fax 404 0777), a 5-10min. walk west of the train station. The rooms here are not exactly electrifying, particularly at the lower price ranges; the interior windowless rooms are somewhat claustrophobic. Rooms (some with A/C) are quite clean, though, and guests are thoroughly instructed in fire safety. Doubles Y120, with bath Y160-200.

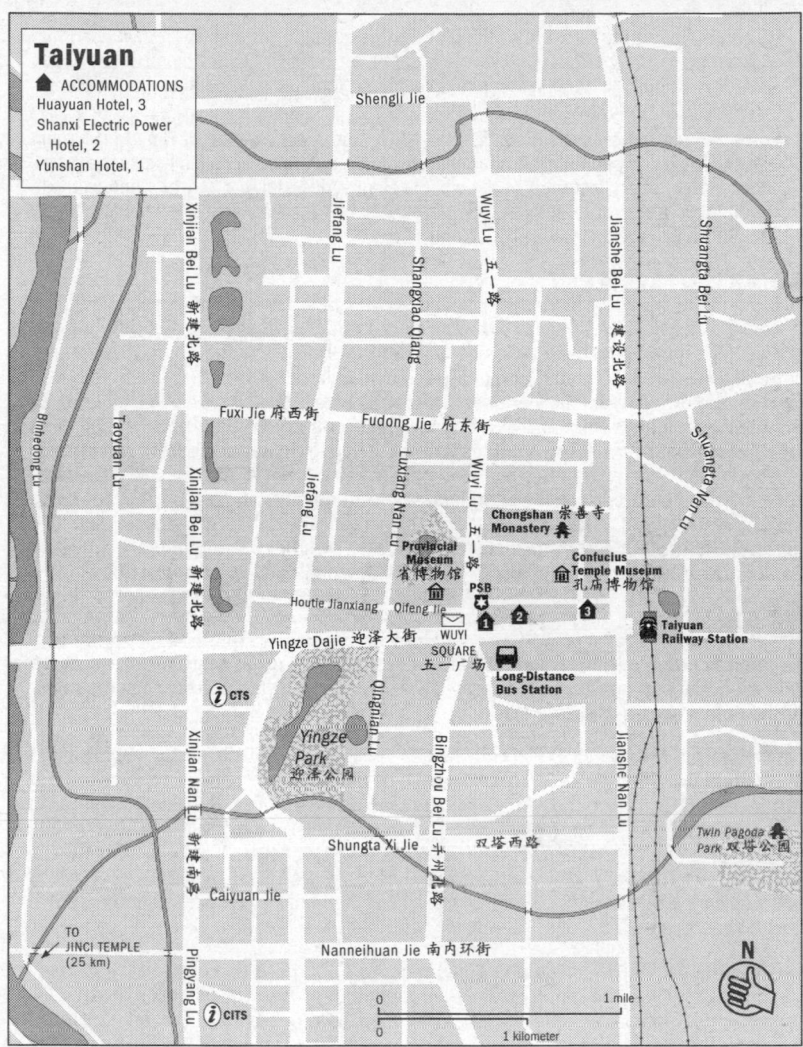

Taiyuan

▲ ACCOMMODATIONS
Huayuan Hotel, 3
Shanxi Electric Power
Hotel, 2
Yunshan Hotel, 1

CENTRAL CHINA

FOOD

Taiyuan is best known for its **knife-cut noodles** (dāo xiāo miàn; 刀削面), available for just a few *kuai* per bowl. If you're lucky, you'll get to see the knife-wielding chef in action. Street markets serve up a variety of noodles and fried dishes; hot-pot is also quite popular. Stands set up on summer nights along **Bingzhou Lu** south of Yingze Dajie and **May First Square,** and also much farther south along **Wucheng Lu,** near the Shanxi University campus (bus #103 from May First Square to Shanxi Daxue). **Liuxiang Nan Lu** runs north off Yingze Dajie and is lined with restaurants ranging from the trendy fast-food hangout **Dico's** (open daily 10am-11pm) to hole-in-the-wall noodle shops and lamb kebab stands. Go north from May First Square, take a left on the first street (Qifeng Jie), and go straight; most restaurants are to the right, while most of the clothing stalls are to the left.

Huayuan Restaurant (huáyuàn dàjiǔlóu; 华苑大酒楼), next to the Huayuan Hotel. Appearances can be deceiving: this restaurant's extensive English menu offers cheap standbys as well as more exotic fare. Everything from knife-cut noodles (Y3-5) to pig's brains (Y68). Open daily 11am-10pm.

Peter Burger (bǐdé hànbǎobāo; 彼得汉堡包), on the west side of Bingzhou Lu just south of Yingze Dajie. Considerably less crowded than the McDonald's across the street, Peter Burger offers fast food of the would-you-like-fries-with-that variety, complete with free plastic gloves for dainty eaters. Set meals Y14-20, including the specialty "Peter Burger" meal (Y18). Open daily 9:30am-10pm.

🎵 ENTERTAINMENT

It's harder to avoid karaoke bars than to find them, but otherwise, nightlife options are rather limited. **Wucheng Lu** south of Xuefu Lu bordering the Shanxi University campus (bus #103 to Shanxi Daxue) is lined with several bars that are frequented by the student crowd. **Friday Friday** (xīngqīwǔ xīngqīwǔ; 星期五星期五), about 10 minutes beyond the Shanxi Daxue bus stop (if you are coming from the city), is easily identifiable by its log cabin exterior. Closer to the city center, the **Chinatown "Disco Public"** (zhōngguóchéng dísíkē guǎngchǎng; 中国城迪斯科广场), 39 Bingzhou Bei Lu, features scantily clad dancers, loud music, candles (perfect for lighting cigarettes), and a dance floor that empties quickly during the slow songs. The nightly drawing for umbrellas, travel bags, and the like offers a chance to make back part of the Y20 cover charge. (☎408 4844. Open daily 8pm-midnight.)

👁 SIGHTS

Taiyuan is not generally considered to be much of a tourist destination, although several of the surrounding sights and towns are worth a visit. Within the city, many of the sights are near Yingze Dajie.

CHONGSHAN MONASTERY (chóngshàn sì; 崇善寺). Built during the reign of the Ming emperor Hongwu and ravaged by fire in 1864, the monastery is a small, quiet, fairly secluded compound. Guanyin, the goddess of mercy, dominates the main hall, and a number of impressive relics spanning several dynasties are also on display. *(East of Wuyi Lu and north of Yingze Dajie. From May First Square, walk north along Wuyi Lu to Shangguang Xiang, a small paved road running off to the right. Continue until the brick-colored wall is visible in front of what appears to be a dead end. Turn left; the monastery entrance is about 3min. ahead, accessed by a small lane to the right. Open daily 8am-5pm. Y4.)*

TWIN PAGODA PARK (shuāng tǎ gōngyuán; 双塔公园). Also referred to as **Yongzuo Monastery** (yǒngzuò sì; 永祚寺), the namesake twin pagodas were constructed during the Ming dynasty and have been renovated recently. The garden courtyard down below offers a more secluded setting. *(On a small street running east from Chuangta Bei Lu. Bus #19 from the train station stops at Xingyue Ge Xiecheng near the corner of Chaoyang Jie and Shuangta Bei Lu; turn right on the first street and take a left before the small stream. The entrance is another 10-15min. down the road, to the right. A taxi from the train station costs about Y5. Open daily 8:30am-5:30pm; in winter 9am-5pm. Y4.)*

YINGZE PARK (yíngzé gōngyuán; 迎泽公园). Notable more for its small amusement and water park than for its beautiful scenery, this is a popular hangout for local families and cuddling couples. Boat rentals Y10-30 per hour. *(On the southern side of Yingze Dajie between Jiefang Lu and Qingnian Lu. Buses #1 and 6 from the train station stop at Da Nan Men. Open daily 6am-9pm; in winter 6:30am-9pm. Y8.)*

JINCI TEMPLE (jìncí sì; 晋祠寺). This rambling complex (first constructed in AD 1023-1031) is filled with a diverse jumble of buildings from various dynasties, and, come the summer months, with plenty of tourists as well. Wandering may be more rewarding than trying to follow the twists and turns of the map; as always, you must run the gauntlet of souvenir stands and postcard hawkers outside the main entrance. *(25km outside the city. Take minibus #308 (1hr., Y2) from Yingze Dajie in front of the train station. Jinci Park open daily 7am-sunset. Y5. Jinci Temple open daily 8am-6pm; in winter 8:30am-5:30pm. Y15.)*

⚑ DAYTRIP FROM TAIYUAN: PINGYAO

*Easily accessible from Taiyuan. **Trains** #785 (departing Taiyuan at 7:13am) and 786 (departing Pingyao for Taiyuan at 4:14pm) cost Y6-8 and take about 2½hr. Buses from Taiyuan to Pingyao are more difficult to find, but minibuses (2hr., approx. Y10) leave frequently from the Pingyao Train Station for Taiyuan.*

Originally founded in the 8th century BC, Pingyao (平遥) flourished during the Ming and Qing dynasties as China's premier banking center. During the 20th century, coastal cities modernized, but Pingyao was left behind. As a result, the town is amazingly well preserved, full of outstanding examples of Ming and Qing architecture. In fact, Pingyao has retained so many of the features of a 19th century Han Chinese city that Zhang Yimou's film *Raise the Red Lantern* was shot here, and the town was recently named a UNESCO World Heritage Site.

The layout and scale of Pingyao make it easy to get around on foot. **Bei Dajie** (北大街), **Dong Dajie** (东大街), **Nan Dajie** (南大街; actually several hundred meters east of the intersection with Bei Dajie), and **Xi Dajie** (西大街) are the main thoroughfares. These main streets are surrounded by a 6km **city wall,** generally the first landmark that visitors encounter. *(Open daily 7:30am-7:30pm; in winter 8am-6pm. Y16.)*

To get to the city wall from the train station, continue straight down **Shuncheng Lu** (顺城路) to the first intersection with **Xiguan Dajie** (西关大街); make a left, and a 10-minute walk brings you to the west gate of the city wall, making a pedicab from the train station unnecessary. Visitors can only ascend the wall from the north and west gates. The city wall was built with rammed earth beginning in 827 BC, but the big, bad Song army set it on fire in AD 960. Savvier than the three little pigs, the residents of Pingyao learned their lesson after the first attack and rebuilt the wall with bricks in 1370 during the Ming dynasty. This sturdier version is still standing today. According to legend, the 3000 embrasures built into the wall represent the disciples of Confucius; his most venerated sages, an elite subset of that group, are represented by the 72 small watchtowers. The arrangement of the gates in the city wall—the north and south gates each have one opening while the east and west each have two—has led locals to call Pingyao the tortoise town. A walk around the top from the west gate to the small exhibition at the north gate takes about 30-45 minutes and affords a more leisurely glimpse into the courtyards of the traditional tile-roofed houses and narrow alleyways that define the city. Bicycle rental is available for Y5 per hour at the west gate.

To get to the center of the city from the west gate, walk straight for about 15 minutes along Xi Dajie to the intersection with Bei Dajie (distinguishable by a small wooden sign at the northwest corner). Along the southern side of the street, next door to 40 Xi Dajie, stands the **Chinese Financial House Museum** (rìshēng chāng piàohào; 日升昌票号). Housed in a now-defunct bank, it exhibits items dating back to its 1823 establishment. *(Open daily 8am-7pm; in winter 8:30am-5pm. Y10.)* The ornate traditional-style buildings that line **Ming Qing Street** (明清街) house various museums, antique shops, and other enterprises. From the **Town Tower** (shì lóu; 市楼), visitors can enjoy a bird's-eye view of the town and all its trademark red lanterns (Y5). Beyond this point, the streets become dustier, emptier, and of less interest to tourists.

Shuanglin Temple (shuānglín sì; 双林四), about 6km southwest of Pingyao, is accessible by pedicab (Y10-15 round-trip). The 10 halls contain 2058 colorfully painted Buddhist statues, some dating back as far as the Song dynasty. There are statues to suit any mood: some elegant, some farcical, some life-like, and in the case of the Palace of Kingdom of Hell, some downright creepy.

CENTRAL CHINA

WUTAISHAN 五台山   ☎0350

A galaxy of temples and monasteries dominates the landscape of the five peaks of Wutaishan, which constitute one of China's four sacred Buddhist mountains. The white-knuckle approach to **Taihuai** (太坏) winds through high alpine valleys, brightened by wildflowers and slowed by the progress of grazing livestock, and then gives way to the jangling bells and melodic Buddhist chants that fill the streets of the town. It may sound idyllic, but a constant stream of photo-crazed, souvenir-hunting tourists also hope to bask in the area's monastic glow, and the sounds of chanting monks actually emanate from cassette players. Despite the unholy number of visitors at times, most find that Taihuai's location, beautiful surroundings, and reasonably priced accommodations make it an ideal place from which to take in Wutaishan and other nearby attractions.

◾◾ ORIENTATION AND PRACTICAL INFORMATION

Taihuai is inside the Wutaishan Scenic Area. There are gates on the road at the edge of the scenic area; all vehicles going to Taihuai are stopped so that the passengers can pay the Y53 admission fee. Think of it less as the heavy hand of the tourist industry and more as a first step in the process of relinquishing all worldly possessions and living a spiritual life unfettered by material things.

Taihuai is a maze of narrow, hilly alleyways leading to the small hotels, restaurants, souvenir shops, and temples that give it its character. The **Qingshui River** (qīngshuǐ hé; 清水河), actually more of a small stream, runs roughly parallel to **Shiju Liangcheng Gonglu** (石咀凉城公路), the main highway running from north to south through town. Within Taihuai itself, most tourist attractions and services are clustered on the western side of the road; Dailuo Peak is a notable exception.

It is more convenient to take the bus to and from either Taiyuan or Datong. Several **trains** do serve Wutaishan, but the station is 48km from Taihuai village; minibuses (1-1½hr., Y20) leave the train station when full. Trains serve Beijing (6½hr., 1 per day, Y104) and Taiyuan (4-5hr., 2 per day, Y17-31). **Minibuses** to Taiyuan (4½hr., approx. every 30min. until 2-3pm, Y43) leave frequently from the bus station near Wutaishan No. 5 Hostel. **Buses** to Datong (5hr., 3 per day 6am-12:30pm, Y35) leave from the main road, opposite the bridge to Dailuo Peak and about three minutes south. The station is in a small courtyard with a red banner hanging over the entrance. Buses to Taiyuan also leave several times per day from a long-distance bus station at the southern end of Taihuai village, just beyond the Liangcheng Hotel, about a 15-minute walk from the center of town.

CITS, at 18 Mingqing Jie, has no English-speaking staff but can still arrange special foreigner-(over)priced tours to area sights. (☎654 2142. Open daily 8am-noon and 2:30-6pm.) **Bank of China**, just south of Wutaishan No. 5 Hostel, exchanges foreign currency only. (Open daily 8am-noon and 3-6:30pm; in winter 8am-noon and 2:30-6pm.) **China Telecom** (☎654 2666), on the road just north of CITS, has IDD service. The **post office** is on Yanling Jie parallel to and one block west of the main road. (Open daily 8am-8pm; in winter 8am-6pm.) The **postal code** is 035515.

◾◾ ACCOMMODATIONS AND FOOD

Small hostels compete with the larger "luxury" hotels south of town; most solo travelers gravitate toward the former. Prices, especially at the smaller places, may be flexible if rooms aren't full; mentioning the names and room rates of the competition doesn't hurt either. There are a number of small restaurants in the southern part of the village, near the departure point for local sightseeing minibuses.

Baoyin Hotel (bǎoyín bīnguǎn; 宝银宾馆; ☎654 2648), down the alley on the west side of the main road, across from and slightly south of the bridge leading to the parking lot for the Dailuo Peak cable car. The hotel is 1min. down the alley on the right, marked by a red sign with white lettering. Rooms, all with TV and bath, look clean and new, with brightly colored bedspreads and shiny yellow wood. Doubles and triples Y50.

Yaojin Hostel (yàojìn zhāodàisuǒ; 跃进招待所), 32 Yingfang Jie (☎654 2586), just before the Baoyin Hotel. The inconspicuous hostel entrance is on the right side of the street. Rooms are worn; you get what you pay for. 2-bed dorms Y30; 3-bed dorms Y20.

Honglou Hostel (hónglóu zhāodàisuǒ; 红楼招待所; ☎654 2520), on the east side of the main road. Doubles have fairly new bathrooms, but dorms have cement floors and grubby common bathrooms (no showers). 4-bed dorms Y20; doubles with bath Y100.

Jinjie Mountain Villa (jīnjiè shānzhuāng; 金界山庄; ☎654 2675 or 654 2568), on the east side of the main road near Dailuo Peak and the northern entrance to the village. Rooms in the main building and mid-range building have attached bath, carpet, and interior entrances. Doubles Y120, with bath Y200-240.

Liangcheng Hotel (liángchéng shānzhuāng bīnguǎn; 凉城山庄宾馆), 1 Mingqing Jie (☎654 2418; fax 654 2576), on the southern edge of town. The location is a bit more secluded; prepare to pay for privacy. All rooms have TV, phone, and attached bath. 20% discounts sometimes available. Doubles Y360-380; 30% surcharge June-Aug.

◉ SIGHTS

TAIHUAI VILLAGE. Within Taihuai Village, there are more than enough temples to keep most visitors occupied; wandering destination-less among them is most enjoyable, and certainly kept the 13th Dalai Lama happy when he came here in 1908 en route to Mongolia. Landmarks such as Big White Pagoda and Dailuo Peak make it relatively easy to get one's bearings. Admission to most sights is Y5 or less; some are free.

The most visually striking sight is the **Tayuan Temple** (tǎyuàn sì; 塔院寺), which houses the **Big White Pagoda** (dà bái tǎ; 大白塔), a Tibetan style, bottle-shaped pagoda topped off with a bronze cap. *(Open daily 7am-8pm. Y4.)* The small **Guangren Monastery** (guǎngrén sì; 广仁寺) is currently under construction, while **Xiantong Temple** (xiàntōng sì; 显通寺) is the proud owner of the oldest iron pot in the village. *(Open daily 6:30am-7pm. Y5.)* The small **Guangning Temple** (guǎngníng sì; 广宁寺) lies at the base of Pusa Hill. *(Open daily 6am-7pm. Free.)* Those who climb the 108 steps leading to **Pusa Hilltop** (púsà dǐng; 菩萨顶) will be rewarded with a panorama of the surrounding temples and countryside.

Dailuo Peak (dàilúo dǐng; 黛螺顶), east of the main road in the northern part of the village, offers glimpses of the fog-shrouded countryside or a spectacular panoramic landscape on sunnier days. The robust way to the top is via the 1080 steps, carefully planned to be a multiple of the lucky Buddhist number 108. A cable car also makes the trip. *(Open daily summer 6:30am-7pm. Y16 up, Y15 down.)* A visit to the temple grounds at the top costs an extra Y3.

OUTLYING SIGHTS. These sights, just like those in the village, include temples, temples, and more temples. As several of these temples are on the bus route from Wutaishan to Taiyuan, the cheapest option is probably to hop on a Taiyuan-bound bus or minibus and ask the driver to let you off at the temple (Y10-20). Half-day minibus tours depart in the morning from the stand on the east side of the main road near Wutaishan No. 5 Hostel. Prices vary wildly depending on destination, weather, and how many other tourists are around; expect to pay at least Y40-100. Alternatively, CITS arranges full-day tours (Y200 per person) usually visiting one sight in the morning and one in the afternoon, stopping for lunch in between.

The breathtaking ◼ **Nantai Temple** (nántái sì; 南台寺), 2485m high on the South Peak, looks out on beautiful alpine vistas. The equally impressive **Thousand Buddha Cave** (qiānfó dòng; 千佛洞), also known as **Fomu Cave** (fómǔ dóng; 佛母洞), takes about 1½hr. to climb. A round-trip taxi to the two sights should cost about Y120. To get to the more remote and seldom-visited **Nanchan Monastery** (nánchán sì; 南禅寺), take a bus bound for Taiyuan and get off at Dongyue (东岳). From Dongyue, a bumpy 20- to 25-minute taxi ride to Nanchan costs Y25-30. The most interesting thing here is probably its roof, constructed during the Tang dynasty entirely without nails. Some buses stop at **Foguang Temple** (fóguāng sì; 佛光寺), built in the 5th century and famous for its frescoes and statues.

DATONG 大同   ☎0352

Although Datong had quite a luminous past as the capital of the Northern Wei dynasty (AD 383-534), its current condition is distinctively dingy. In far northern Shanxi province near Inner Mongolia, Datong leads China in coal production and, unofficially, in household ownership of pet dogs. Known to some as "Dragon Wall City," Datong was the site of the legendary "dragon playing with the phoenix" exploits. Emperor Zhengde of the Ming dynasty (the "dragon") came on an imperial inspection tour and left having fallen in love with Li Fengjie, the "phoenix" and the daughter of a hotel owner. Today, outside the bustling commercial areas, the streets become a dusty maze of construction projects punctuated by horse- and mule-carts and lurching minibuses, surroundings that hold little appeal for most travelers. The reason most commoners venture out to the once imperial, now industrial Datong is for the awesome Yungang Grottoes and Hanging Monastery.

▐ TRANSPORTATION

Airplanes: Datong has no airport. **Datong Air Service Company** (dàtóng hángkōng fúwù zhōngxīn; 大同航空服务中心), 1 Nanguan Xi Lu (☎204 4039), can book tickets for flights between other cities. Open daily 8:30am-6pm.

Trains: Datong Train Station (dàtóng huǒchē zhàn; 大同火车站; ☎602 3458), at the intersection of Xinjian Bei Lu and Zhanqian Jie in the northern part of the city. Tickets may be hard to come by on trains that don't originate in Datong; some travelers resort to CITS for help. The ticket office is on the right as you face the station; in principle, both same day and advance tickets are sold. Open 24hr., although staff might not always be there. To: **Beijing** (6½-8hr.; 9-10 per day; seat Y27-52, sleeper Y63-104); **Hohhot** (4-7hr., 10 per day, Y20-37); **Nanjing** (30hr., 1 per day, Y234); **Shijiazhuang** (14hr., 1 per day, Y91); **Taiyuan** (7½hr., 5 per day, Y65-104); and **Xian** (18½hr., 1 per day, Y135). The Trans-Mongolian rail route from Beijing stops in Datong (Tu 2:15pm).

Buses: Datong Long-distance Bus Station (dàtóng chángtú qìchē zhàn; 大同长途汽车站; ☎281 4880), at Xinhua Jie and Xinjian Bei Lu, a 10min. walk from the train station. Open daily 6am-5pm; most people buy their tickets on the bus. To **Hohhot** (5hr., 7:20am, Y25) and **Taiyuan** (4½-5hr., 6 per day 6:30am-5pm, Y50). Minibuses to **Wutaishan** (4hr., multiple departures 6:10am 2pm). **Datong New Long-distance Bus Station** (dàtóng chángtú xīn kèzhàn; 大同长途新客站), 20 Yantong Xi Lu (☎602 0870), west of Xinjian Bei Lu, serves similar destinations. Bus #11 stops outside. Open daily 5am-6:30pm.

Local Transportation: Most **buses** run approximately 6am-7:30pm. Some, such as #15, run 5:30am-8:40pm. Base fare Y1. Bus **#11** follows a circular route that includes Xinkaili, the Datong Hotel, and the New Long-distance Bus Station; **#15** runs from the train station along Xinjian Lu to Yingbin Lu and the traditional tourist hotels; **#2, 4, 8, 14, 15, 16,** and **201** all originate at the train station.

Taxis: Base fare Y5, each additional km Y1.2. Train station to Yingbin Lu hotels Y10-12.

✴ ↗ ORIENTATION AND PRACTICAL

Datong's larger thoroughfares change names several times as they criss-cross the city. From the commercial center of town, **Da Xi Jie** (大西街; west), **Da Dong Jie** (大东街; east), **Da Bei Jie** (大北街; north), and **Da Nan Jie** (大南街; south) extend in the four cardinal directions. The **Drum Tower** (gǔ lóu; 鼓楼) lies just south of the traffic circle. **Xinjian Lu** (新建路) leads from the train station in the far northern part of the city to the southern reaches and the terminus of several bus routes.

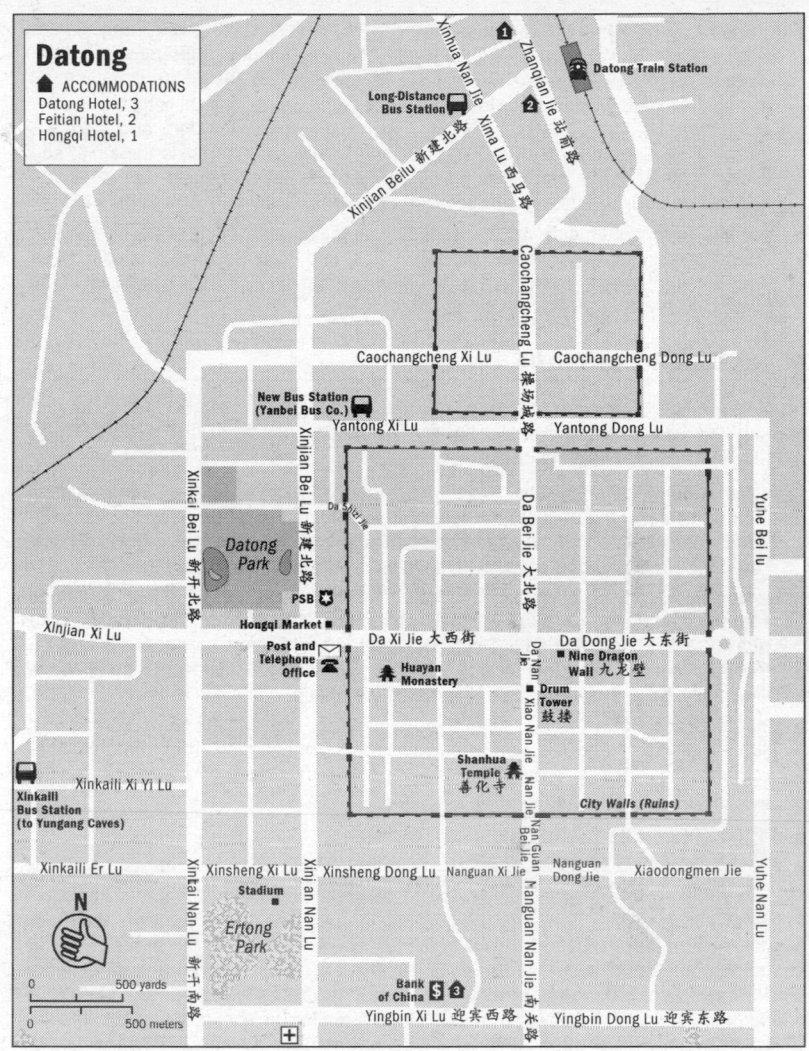

Datong

♠ ACCOMMODATIONS
Datong Hotel, 3
Feitian Hotel, 2
Hongqi Hotel, 1

Xinhua Nan Jie 新华南街
Xima Lu 西马路
Zhanqian Jie 站前路
Datong Train Station
Long-Distance Bus Station

Xinjian Beilu 新建北路
Caochangcheng Lu 操场城路

Caochangcheng Xi Lu   Caochangcheng Dong Lu

New Bus Station (Yanbei Bus Co.)
Yantong Xi Lu   Yantong Dong Lu

Xinjian Bei Lu 新建北路
Da Si Jie
Xinkai Bei Lu 新开北路
Da Bei Jie 大北街
Yune Bei lu

Datong Park
PSB
Hongqi Market
Post and Telephone Office
Xinjian Xi Lu
Da Xi Jie 大西街   Da Dong Jie 大东街
Nine Dragon Wall 九龙壁
Huayan Monastery
Da Nan Jie
Xiao Nan Jie
Drum Tower 鼓楼
Shanhua Temple 善化寺
City Walls (Ruins)

Xinkaili Xi Yi Lu
Xinkaili Bus Station (to Yungang Caves)

Xinkaili Er Lu
Xintai Nan Lu 新开南路
Xinsheng Xi Lu   Xinsheng Dong Lu   Nanguan Xi Jie
Nan Guan Bei Lu
Nanguan Nan Jie 南关南街
Nanguan Dong Jie
Xiaodongmen Jie
Yuhe Nan Lu

Xinj'an Nan Lu
Stadium
Ertong Park

N
0   500 yards
0   500 meters

Bank of China
Yingbin Xi Lu 迎宾西路   Yingbin Dong Lu 迎宾东路

Travel Agency: CITS (☎/fax 510 1326), in the train station between the two waiting rooms. Staffed by a friendly, knowledgeable, and mainly English-speaking contingent. Minibus guided tours of Yungang Caves and Hanging Monastery from Y100 per person (groups of 5 or more; not including admission). Sleeper ticket commission Y40. Open daily 6:30am-6:30pm.

Bank of China: 62 Yingbin Xi Lu (☎504 4114). Exchanges traveler's checks and major foreign currency. Open M-F 8am-6pm; in winter 8am-5:30pm.

PSB: On Xinjian Bei Lu north of Da Xi Jie, on the east side of the street (☎205 0778, ext. 2037). Open M-F 8:30am-noon and 2:30-5pm.

Hospital: No. 3 Hospital (dàtóng shì dì sān yīyuàn; 大同市第三医院; ☎502 1001), on the southwest corner of Xinjian Nan Lu and Yingbin Lu. Accessible by bus #15 from the train station.

Internet Access: Flying Internet Bar (fēiyáng wǎngbā; 飞扬网吧; ☎281 8499) on Xinhua Jie. From the train station, walk down Xinjian Beilu and turn right at the first intersection; the bar is about a 15min. ahead on the right. Y6 per hr. Open daily 8am-midnight. China Telecom's **Hengtong Computer Company** (dàtóng shì hēngtōng jìsuànjī gōngsī; 大同市亨通计算机公司), 6A Xinjian Bei Lu (☎204 4448), at Dashizi Jie. From the train station, take the bus to Datong Gongyuan, then cross the street and backtrack about half a block. The building's west side has a Compaq sign; the south side has an English "Internet Service" sign. Y10 per hr. Open daily 8am-7pm.

Post and Telecommunications: On the square on the southeast side of the intersection with Xinjian Lu and Da Xi Jie (☎202 3751). EMS and Poste Restante available. Open daily 8am-6:30pm; in winter 8am-6pm. **China Telecom** (☎202 2114), just east of the post office, has IDD service. **Postal Code:** 037004.

▚ ACCOMMODATIONS

Most of the hotels are near the train station or on Yingbin Lu. Many establishments still adhere to a dual pricing system for foreigners, although dorm beds (when available) are still relatively cheap.

Feitian Hotel (fēitiān bīnguǎn; 飞天宾馆), 1 Chezhan Qian Jie (☎281 3144), immediately to the left of the train station square upon exiting. Best for those who want cheap sleeps (and clean rooms) near the train station; be sure to sample the delicious hotpot next door. No A/C. 4-bed dorms Y40; doubles Y180-240; triples Y200.

Datong Hotel (dàtóng bīnguǎn; 大同宾馆), 8 Yingbin Xi Lu (☎203 2476), 10 stops from the train station on bus #15. Worn, not particularly clean rooms and dorms come with A/C, TV, phone, and bath. Dorm beds might be difficult for solo travelers to get if there are no other foreigners staying at the hotel. 30-50% discounts on doubles sometimes possible. 3-bed dorms Y80; doubles Y208 and up.

Hongqi Grand Hotel (hóngqí dàjiǔdiàn; 红旗大酒店; ☎205 6813 or 206 8405), straight ahead and to the right when you exit the train station. The Hongqi is more upmarket than its rail-side neighbors: rooms are clean and nicely furnished. 3 meals per day included. Doubles with bath Y170, with A/C Y190; triples Y170.

▐ FOOD

Datong folks are rough with their noodles. **Hand-pulled noodles** (lāmiàn; 拉面) and **knife-cut noodles** (dāoxiāomiàn; 刀削面) are among the most common. **Oat flour noodles** (yóu miàn; 右面) are also popular. They are usually served in a sauce and with vegetables during the summer; in the winter, they're served hot with meat. Food stalls set up around the intersection of Baibowa Dong Jie and the train tracks with Xinjian Bei Lu and Nanguan Dajie. Yingbin Lu, east of Nanguan Nan Jie and the Yungang Hotel, also has a decent selection of restaurants. Da Xi Jie and Da Dong Lu near the main square and drum tower are crowded with restaurants and Western fast-food joints, including the ever-popular **Dico's** on the corner of the square diagonally across from the post office.

■ **Madaha Restaurant** (mǎdàhā fàndiàn; 马大哈饭店), on Yingbin Lu, across the street from the Datong Hotel. This place is busiest in the mornings, when it cooks up piping hot bowls of knife-cut noodles (complete with hard-boiled egg) for Y2. Dumplings and other varieties of noodles are also available. Open daily from around 7:30am.

■ **Tonghe Hotpot** (tónghéyuán huǒguō chéng; 同和园火锅城; ☎280 3111), next to the Feitian Hotel. Offers all the amenities and atmosphere of an expensive hotpot restaurant. Cold appetizers and vegetable broth are free, ba bao cha Y1.5. Meat broth Y26, vegetables Y2 and up, meat Y8 and up. Open daily 11:30am-2:30pm and 6-9:30pm.

Da Huang Jia (dà huáng jiā; 大皇家; ☎207 0761), on the left side of the small alley across the street from Hangmeiqu Department Store on Da Xi Jie. Colorful decor includes hanging plastic vines and two levels of seating. The extensive selection of iced drinks, pastries, and ice cream makes this place popular. Try a shaved ice treat (Y4) while perched on one of the swings near the front door. Open daily 8am-11pm.

Yuguo Restaurant (yù guō diàn; 御锅店), on the west side of Xinhua Nan Jie. From the train station walk straight down Xinjian Bei Lu, turn right onto Xinhua Nan Jie at the first intersection, and walk straight for 10-15min.; the restaurant is on the left. The friendly owners will probably be surprised to see any *laowai* entering their restaurant; no English is spoken here, but pointing should get you what you want. *Shanshui doufu* (Y5) is very good, and draft beer is Y2.5 per mug. Open daily 8am-11:30pm.

Yonghe Hongqi Restaurant (yǒnghé hóngqí měishí chéng), 3 Yingbin Dong Lu (☎510 3008), east of Nanguan Nan Jie, near the Yungang Hotel. This place has become a bit of a tourist attraction in itself. Elegant surroundings and lots of variety on the glossy picture menu mean slightly higher prices. Open daily 11:30am-2:30pm and 5:30-9pm.

👁 SIGHTS

Datong's most famous attraction is Yungang Grottoes (p. 257), although several sights within the city itself are also worth a visit.

SHANHUA MONASTERY (shànhuà sì; 善化寺). Built in 713 during the Tang dynasty, this monastery was ravaged by war in 1122 and rebuilt under the supervision of a concerned monk a few years later. Inside the front gate, the four Heavenly Kings stand guard with a *pipa*, sword, serpent, and pagoda. Birds flutter about, and one of Datong's dragon walls, sits in a rather overgrown western courtyard. Some of the buildings are currently under construction; others are locked, but one of the friendly guards will generally let visitors in upon request. (*South of Hualin Department Store and west of Nanmen Jie. The entrance is down the small lane just north of the little park. Open daily 9am-6pm. Y5.*)

NINE DRAGON WALL (jiǔ lóng bì; 九龙壁). In imperial China, dragon walls served as screens to conceal palace and temple interiors from outsiders; Datong's Nine Dragons Wall was constructed in 1392 to hide the palace of Prince Zhugui, the 13th son of the founder of the Ming dynasty. The palace itself was destroyed by fire, but the sturdy wall still stands, although not in its original position (in 1954, the entire wall was moved 28m back so the road could be expanded). Most tour buses, in their allotted 5min. tour of the place, miss its majesty; the colorful teal-blue wall does have its charm. (*About 1 block east of Da Nan Jie and Da Dong Jie, on the south side of the street. Bus #17 stops at Jiulong Bi, and bus #4 from the station stops nearby at Sipailou. Open daily 8am-6:30pm; in winter 8am-6pm. Y3.*)

HUAYAN MONASTERY (huáyán sì; 华严寺). A large monastery in the Liao and Jin dynasties (907-1234), most of the original buildings are long gone. During the Yuan and Ming dynasties, the complex was divided into upper and lower portions. The lower portion houses some small displays of fossils, eggs, and relics of the dynastic period, in addition to the main **Bhagavan Stack Hall** where Buddhist *sutras* were kept. The upper monastery's **Daxiong Treasure Hall** features colorful frescoes and a number of statues. (*South of Da Xi Jie and west of Da Nan Jie. The Upper Monastery is off Shansi Bei Xiang; the Lower Monastery is on the next small lane to the east. Open daily 8am-6pm; in winter 9am-5pm. Y6. The Upper Monastery was closed for repairs at the time of writing.*)

🚌 DAYTRIPS FROM DATONG

YUNGANG GROTTOES
About 17km west of Datong. Bus #4 from the train station goes to Xinjiaili (Y1); from there, bus #3 goes past Yungang (Y1.5). Excellent Chinese and English descriptions. Open daily 8:30am-5:30pm. Y20.

The spectacular Yungang Grottoes (yúngǎng shíkū; 云冈石窟), dating back more than 1500 years, were carved out of the mountains west of Datong, the capital and spiritual center of the Northern Wei dynasty. The construction of the caves was ordered by the Northern Wei rulers as an act of atonement for their earlier persecution of Buddhism. Some 30,000 families of artisans living in Dunhuang (see p. 683) were forced to relocate to work on the caves. Carving from the top of the cliffs down, 40,000 sculptors took 50 years to complete the project, which now ranks among the finest examples of Buddhist art in China. All together, over 51,000 Buddhist statues, ranging in size from 17m to just a few centimeters, remain in the 20 or so caves. The sculptural style was primarily borrowed from Indian Buddhist art, which itself was created from a synthesis of various foreign styles, including Persian, Byzantine, and Greek. These sculptures differ from those of the later Longmen Grottoes (see p. 238), which feature a uniquely Chinese design.

Two hills divide the caves into three sections: east, middle, and west. The east and middle sections include caves 1-13. Cave 3 is the largest, 42m wide at the mouth, while cave 5 is home to the tallest Buddha at the site. The 17m tall statue is allegedly large enough for 120 people to stand on its knees, though testing this with 119 of your friends might not be appreciated by grotto staff. The statues and carvings in cave 6 are among the best preserved and most spectacular in the whole complex. The walls are covered with buddhas, *bodhisattvas*, *arhats*, and flying *apsaras*. The ceiling depicts the 33 Heavenly Kings replete with their royal regalia. Supporting the center of the cave is a two-tiered square pillar 15m high. Caves 9 and 10 house intricate and colorful carved niches. The western group of caves (16-20) are the oldest of the surviving works. Each contains a colossal Buddha intended to represent each of the dynasty's first five emperors. The remaining caves (21 and up) are not nearly as spectacular as numbers 1-20. There are excellent English descriptions, and, though you're bound to run into scads of tourists, the Yungang Grottoes are nothing short of stupendous.

HENGSHAN AND THE HANGING MONASTERY

*70km from Datong. Unscheduled **minibuses** (Y25-30) leave from the train and old bus station areas in Datong, generally in the morning. CITS tours often include the monastery. Taking a public bus from Datong's old bus station to Hongyuan, from where a taxi (Y25 one-way) will need to be hired, is more costly and time-consuming. ☎(0352) 832 2142. Open daily 6:30am-7pm; in winter 8am-5pm. Y27.*

One of the five sacred Daoist mountains, Shanxi's Hengshan (héngshān; 恒山) is often referred to as **Beiyue** (北岳) to distinguish it from Nanyue, the Hengshan of Hunan (see p. 390). Rising 2017m into the air, Beiyue showcases treacherous cliffs and calligraphy by Tang poet Li Bai on its boulders. The most dramatic of the Eighteen Scenes of Hengshan is the Hanging Monastery (xuánkōng sì; 悬空寺), suspended precariously under an overhanging precipice. Some of the 40 halls in this temple are held up by only a single support pillar. Signs indicate the proper pathway for visitors to follow as they wind their way up, then down, and around to reach the over 80 Buddha statues and other treasures. Looking down through the cracks of the flooring provides an exhilarating rush (or sheer terror for acrophobics). Hengshan Reservoir is up the stairs about five or 10 minutes beyond.

INNER MONGOLIA 内蒙古

The brazen exploits of Genghis Khan, Kublai Khan, and the roving Mongol armies are the most vivid and romanticized images of Inner Mongolia. However, the famous Khan leaders were dead and buried centuries ago, and things haven't been quite the same since. The unified Mongol Empire collapsed in the 14th century, and by the 20th China and Russia were busy haggling over how to split up the nation. Inner Mongolia (not to be confused with the independent country of Mongolia) became the PRC's first autonomous region in 1947.

Those who are tempted to associate Inner Mongolia with the word "hordes" are about 700 years too late. While some inhabitants maintain their traditional nomadic lifestyle, visitors are more likely to encounter Han Chinese on horseback than Mongolians. In fact, ethnic Mongolians make up only 10 or 20% of the region's population. Still, the region does have a different feel, and the grasslands (vast areas of endless prairie) near Hohhot delight visitors who head here from Beijing or Xian. Organized grasslands tours may seem somewhat contrived (concrete-floored yurts don't really jive with visions of "authentic" Mongol living), but most visitors who venture north find something with which to fall in love, whether it's the endless stretches of blue sky, the potent kick of local liquor, or the dashing Mongolian tour guides.

HOHHOT 呼和浩特 ☎ 0471

The name Hohhot is derived from Mongolian for "green city," but, for many visitors, the grass is greener on the other side: that is, on the grasslands about 100km away. True grass-loving prairie-seekers use Hohhot only as a convenient point of access for the surrounding plains, but the city itself, originally a frontier trading post, is a pleasant place to stay. The summer months are green and balmy, and parts of town have well-preserved architecture dating back to the early Ming dynasty, when Han Chinese first moved into the city. Today, Hohhot's population (hovering around one million) is predominantly Han, but shop signs featuring Mongolian script alongside Chinese characters suggest that, while the Mongol presence is outnumbered, it is not overshadowed.

▐ TRANSPORTATION

Airplanes: Hohhot Airport (hūhéhàotè jīchǎng; 呼和浩特机场), about 15km east of city center. The **CAAC ticket office**, 35 Xilinguole Bei Lu (☎ 696 4103), south of Zhongshan Lu and Xinhua Square, has airport buses (Y5) leaving 1½-2hr. before scheduled departures. Open daily 7am-10pm. To: **Beijing** (2-4 per day, Y400); **Guangzhou** (M and Th 8:10am, Y1500); and **Shanghai** (W and Su 7:20am, Y1080).

Trains: Hohhot Train Station (hūhéhàotè huǒchē zhàn; 呼和浩特火车站), at Chezhan Jie and Xilinguole Bei Lu, in the northern part of the city. Open 24hr. Although the ticket office supposedly sells tickets up to 6 days in advance, would-be passengers are often told to come back the day before they plan to leave, if not the day of. Sleepers to Beijing go very quickly. To **Beijing** (11½-14hr., 8-9 per day, Y95-163) and **Datong** (4-7hr., 10 per day, Y20-37).

Buses: Hohhot Bus Station (hūhéhàotè qìchē zhàn; 呼和浩特汽车站), on the west side of the train station, has 2 entrances, one facing the square and one off Chezhan Xi Jie. Open daily 6:30am-8:30pm. To: **Baotou** (2½-3hr., every 30min. 7am-6:30pm, Y14-25); **Beijing** (12hr., 3 per day, Y60); and **Datong** (6hr., 1 per day, Y32).

Local Transportation: Most local **buses** run from about 7am-7pm, with slightly shorter winter hours. Bus fare Y0.5 (drivers do not make change); minibus fare to most destinations Y1. Bus **#1** begins on the west side of the train station and travels down Xilinguole Lu, Zhongshan Xi Lu, and Gongyuan Xi Lu before reaching its terminus at Shiyangqiao Lu and Nanchafang Jie. Buses **#3** and **4** travel along the Zhongshan Lu and Xinhua Dajie corridor but do not directly serve the train station area.

Taxis: Base fare Y6, each additional km Y3.

Bike Rental: Cheap bike rental (Y3-5 per day) is available directly across from the train station at the southeast corner of Xilinguole Lu and Chezhan Dong Jie, and at the southeast corner of Hua'an Jie and Xilinguole Lu, about 5min. from the train station (Y1 for 4hr., Y2 per day, Y100 deposit).

✦♫ ORIENTATION AND PRACTICAL INFORMATION

Hohhot is compact and fairly easy to get around. The train and bus stations are in the north near the intersection of **Xilinguole Lu** (锡林郭勒路) and **Chezhan Jie** (车站街). East of the train station, **Hulunbeier Lu** (呼仑北尔路) is another major street. **Xinhua Dajie** (新华大街), which turns into **Xincheng Jie** (新城街), runs from east to west through the main shopping districts. **Zhongshan Lu** (中山路) runs slightly to the south. **Tongdao Jie** (通道街)/**Da Bei Jie** (大北街)/**Da Nan Jie** (大南街) runs from north to south through the older section of the city.

Travel Agency: CTS, Post Hotel, Rm. 208 (☎691 0118), just east of the train station. Open daily 8am-6:30pm. Branch in the Tourist Building, 95 Yishuting Nan Jie, 4th Fl.

Bank of China: 44 Xinhua Dajie, east of Xilinguole Lu and opposite the Zhaojun Hotel. Open M-F 8am-noon and 2:30-5:30pm; in winter 8am-noon and 2-5pm. Exchanges traveler's checks. The **Zhaojun Hotel,** at the intersection of Xinhua Dajie and Xilinguole Lu, generally exchanges traveler's checks on weekends, even for non-guests.

Market: Tianyuan Commercial Mansion (tiānyuán shāngshà; 天元商厦), 98 Zhongshan Xi Lu, near the Minzu Shangchang bus stop. Supermarket with some imported products. Open daily 9am-7:30pm. **Minzu Department Store** (mínzú shāngchǎng; 民族商场) has some traditional Mongolian items on sale on the 2nd floor. Open daily 9am-7:30pm; in winter 9am-7pm.

PSB: 39 Zhongshan Lu, on the north side of the street. To the left, just inside the gate, is the office of the **Division of Aliens Exit-Entry Administration.** Open M-F 8am-noon and 2:30-6:30pm.

Telephones: China Telecom, just east of the corner of Zhongshan Dong Lu and Renmin Lu. Open daily 8am-7pm; in winter 8am-6:30pm. 24hr. service about 50m east.

Internet Access: China Telecom Center Internet Bar (diànxìn yíngyètīng wǎngbā; 电信营业厅网吧), on the 2nd floor of the China Telecom building on Zhongshan Dong Lu. Y8 per hr. Open daily 8am-6:30pm; in winter 8am-6pm.

Post Office: On Zhongshan Dong Lu, west of Renmin Lu, about a 5min. walk from Shi Zhengfu bus stop (bus #1 from the station). EMS, IDD service, and Poste Restante available. Open daily 8am-7pm. The branch immediately to the left (east) as you exit the train station has the same hours. **Postal Code:** 010000.

▟ ACCOMMODATIONS

Many of the cheapest accommodations open to foreigners are around the train station. During the summer months, hotels are often filled to capacity. Try to avoid places with dual-pricing systems intended to gouge rich foreigners.

▧ **Tongda Hotel** (tōngdá fàndiàn; 通达饭店), 28 Chezhan Dong Jie (☎696 8731), across the street and slightly to the left when you exit the train station. Cheap and relatively clean. Only the 4th and 5th floors have guest rooms; no elevator. All rooms have fans and attached bathrooms; doubles have phones. Hot water 7-8:30am and 9-11:30pm. Free luggage storage. Deposit Y20. Singles Y58; doubles Y88, with A/C Y180.

Garden Hotel (huāyuán bīnguǎn; 花园宾馆), 83 Zhaowuda Lu (☎496 5478), at Wulanchabu Lu. From the train station, take bus #4 to the Inner Mongolia Hospital and backtrack half a block; a taxi costs about Y8. Friendly staff and clean rooms, plus lots of chubby costumed baby pictures. Breakfast included. Discounts sometimes available. Singles and doubles Y60, with bath Y120.

Hohhot Post Hotel (húshì yóuzhèng fàndiàn; 呼市邮政饭店; ☎696 6872), to the left as you exit the train station, marked by the green China Post symbol. More expensive rooms have TV, phone, and bath; staff generally do not place foreigners in the rooms without bath. Singles Y155; doubles Y204.

Xincheng Hotel (xīnchéng bīnguǎn; 新城宾馆), 40 Hulunbei'er Nan Lu (☎629 2288; fax 693 1141), north of Wulanchabu Xi Lu. Take bus #20 from the corner of Chezhan

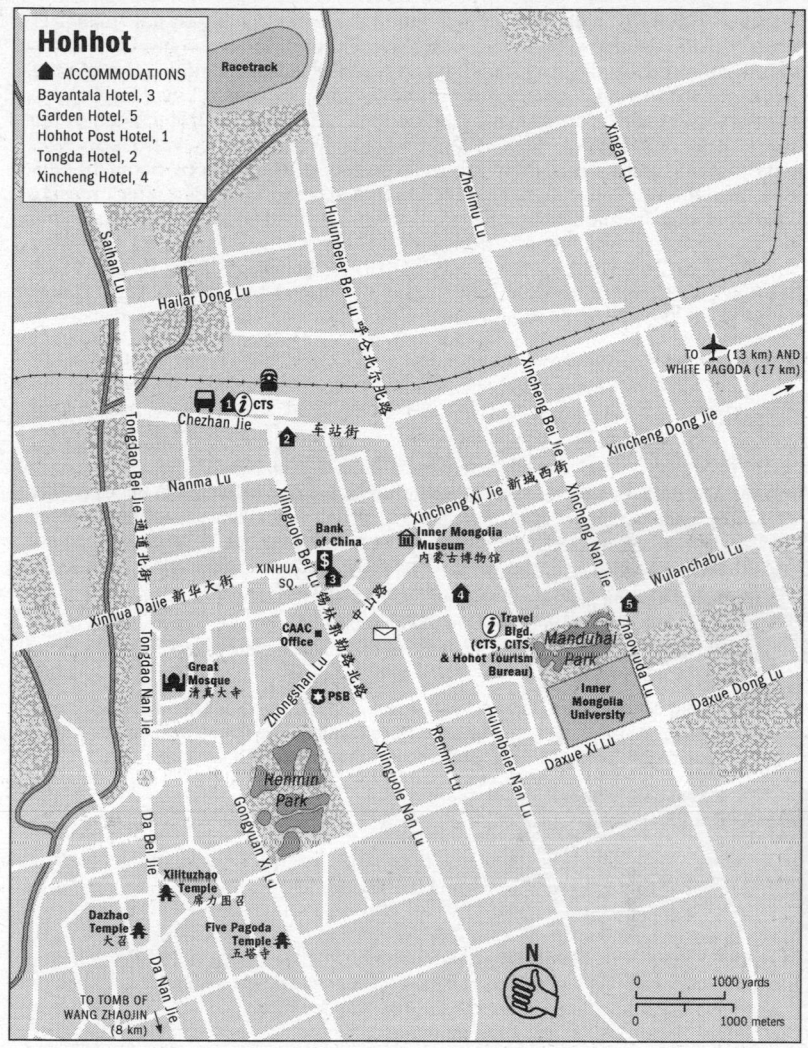

Hohhot

▲ ACCOMMODATIONS
Bayantala Hotel, 3
Garden Hotel, 5
Hohhot Post Hotel, 1
Tongda Hotel, 2
Xincheng Hotel, 4

Dong Jie and Hulunbei'er Lu (from the train station turn left, continuing straight until the traffic light, and then turn right) 2 stops to Erzhang. The cheapest rooms in this sprawling complex are the best all-around value; all rooms have large attached bath. Doubles Y120-260, with A/C and breakfast included Y430-600; triples Y120.

Bayantala Hotel (bāyàntǎlā fàndiàn; 巴彦塔拉饭店), 13 Xilinguole Bei Lu (☎696 3344), across the street from Xinhua Square. Bus #1 from immediately in front of the train station exit stops across the street at Xinhua Guangchang. Staff usually do not put foreigners in either the dorm beds or the rooms without A/C. Doubles with A/C Y200.

🍴 FOOD

Going to Mongolia and not eating hotpot would be like going to Italy and not eating pasta: a grievous culinary faux pas. **Mongolian hotpot** with sliced mutton (shuàn yángròu; 涮羊肉) is a specialty of the region. Though most people find the idea of boiling broth most appetizing in the winter, giant hotpot "palaces," hoping to do business year-round, turn their air-conditioners on full-blast in the summer to recreate that frigid feel. If the weather is warm and you tire of mutton, there are several good areas for outdoor dining. Stands selling *baozi* (Y2.5-3 per steamer) and other dishes set up outside the Bayantala Hotel south of the intersection of Xilinguole Lu and Xinhua Dajie. There are also various *shaguo* and dumpling restaurants along the western side of **Xilinguole Lu,** about 10 minutes from the train station. **Nanma Lu,** the first street on the right after crossing Chezhan Dong Jie and leaving the train station, is lined with indoor restaurants dishing up cheap noodles and dumplings. Some of the restaurants spill over onto **Xima Lu.** Just south of the Bayantala Hotel, **Wulanqiate Dong Jie** and **Guoziban Xiang** are filled with restaurants, many of which serve beef or lamb *jiaozi* for Y8 per 0.5kg (about 50 dumplings).

■ **Wangji Dumpling House** (wángjì jiǎozi lóu; 王记饺子楼; ☎629 6216), on the south side of Chezhan Dong Jie, between Xilinguole Lu and Hulunbei'er Lu. Although this crowded place is a convenient 10min. walk from the train station, most people come here because the food is actually good. Real good. Dumplings Y10-16 per 0.5kg. Open daily at variable hours. Ask the dumpling man.

■ **Wang Lao Hotpot** (wáng lǎo bàn shǐ guō; 王老扳史锅), 178 Xilinguole Bei Lu (☎692 1291), about a 3min. walk south from the train station, on the east side of the street. Although this place serves other dishes, most people come for the hotpot. Soup base Y10-15; vegetables Y3-6; meat Y6-16. Open daily 10:30am-2:30pm and 4:30-9:30pm.

Dairy Queen/Golden Skillet (guójì kuàicān chéng; 国际快餐城), 1 Gongyuan Dong Jie, at Zhongshan Xi Lu, across from the Minzu Shangchang. Golden skillet serves both Chinese and American fast food. Blizzards are tasty, but so small they should be called Chance of Flurries. For a change of pace, try a sesame and cashew Blizzard (Y10-16.50). Open 24hr.

Taiwan Beef Noodle Soup (táiwān niúròu miàn; 台湾牛肉面), 8 Chezhan Jie, just east of Xilinguole Bei Lu. Eerily reminiscent to the ubiquitous "California beef noodle kings," this place dishes up similar fare. Beef noodle soup Y6. Open daily 7am-11pm.

◉ SIGHTS

Most of the sights within Hohhot itself are in the southwest part of the city. For sights outside the city center, including the grasslands, it is possible to make most of the trip independently by bus.

■ **INNER MONGOLIA MUSEUM** (nèiménggǔ bówùguǎn; 内蒙古博物馆). This museum has exhibits, accompanied by both Chinese and English explanations, on everything from dinosaurs to yurts (see **Yearning for Yurts,** p. 273). The exhibition on the first floor to the right of the main entrance features colorful clothing, tools, and other items representing the minority nationalities living in Inner Mongolia, particularly ethnic Mongolians. *(2 Xinhua Dajie. Take bus #20 or minibus #33 from the train station to Bowuguan. The main entrance is on Hulunbeier Lu between Xinhua Dajie and Zhongshan Dong Lu. Open M and W-Su 9am-5pm; in winter 10am-4pm. Y8, students Y3.)*

DAZHAO TEMPLE (dàzhào; 大召). Dating back to the Ming dynasty, this large complex has since undergone numerous renovations. It houses a complete set (108 volumes) of Buddhist scriptures as well as a rare silver statue of Sakyamuni, and sometimes plays host to large prayer gatherings in the middle of the colorful decorations of the main hall. *(On Dazhao Qianjie off Da Nan Jie, the main south street; there is a large modern building nearby, close to the main road. Bus #6 from Tongda Bei Jie and Chezhan Xi Jie, west of the train station, stops nearby, from there walk straight ahead for 3 min. and then turn right onto Dazhao Qianjie; otherwise, take bus #1 from the station to its terminus and walk north on Nanchafang Jie/Xiao Nan Jie for about 15-20min. until the large building appears on the left. Open daily 8am-6:30pm. Y10.)*

FAREWELL, MY CONCUBINE
Times were tough for the Han in 33 BC. The fearsome Huns were menacing Xian, and the Han Emperor Xuandi decided to appease the Hun Chieftain Huhanxie Chanyu by offering him an imperial concubine. Sixteen-year-old **Wang Zhaojun,** who had been languishing at the bottom of the concubine hierarchy, decided it was better to get out than wait forever for the emperor's attention, so she volunteered to marry the Hun chieftan. The emperor consulted his catalogue of portraits and, noting that she was somewhat frumpy, consented. But when Wang Zhaojun entered the imperial palace to be handed over to the chieftain, the emperor and his entire entourage gasped, for the young concubine was the most beautiful woman they had ever seen. It turned out that the imperial portrait painter took bribes in exchange for creating flattering paintings. Poor Wang Zhaojun could not afford to pay off the greedy painter so he made her portrait unattractive, thereby ruining her chances to be chosen as a favorite of the emperor. Because the Hun chieftan was present at the hand-over ceremony, the Han emperor could not take back his offer and was forced to watch glumly as the ecstatic Hun swung Wang Zhaojun (whose tomb is in Hohhot; see p. 263) up onto his horse and rode off into the sunset. She must have been a real looker, because the Huns didn't try to attack for 50 years.

XILITUZHAO TEMPLE (xílìtúzhào; 席力图召). Situated off a maze of winding alleyways lined with squat adobe houses, this temple includes the largest stupa in Inner Mongolia. The dimly lit main hall is filled with imposing beams and brightly colored dragon carpets. This temple is also the home of the Living Buddha responsible for Buddhist affairs in Hohhot. *(On a small street just east of Da Nan Jie. From Dazhao, turn left onto Dazhao Qianjie to the main street and cross the road, continuing directly across to the lane on the other side. Open daily 8am-6:30pm. Y5.)*

GREAT MOSQUE (qīngzhēn dàsì; 清真大寺). The courtyards of this mosque are filled with bicycles and, often, old men chatting. Non-Muslim worshipers are not allowed inside the various worship halls. Outside the complex gate is a cluster of small, inexpensive Muslim restaurants and food stands. *(Just north of the intersection of Tongdao Jie and Zhongshan Xi Lu. Bus #3 from Xilinguole Lu on the southwest side of Xinhua Square terminates just beyond. Free.)*

FIVE PAGODA TEMPLE (wǔ tǎ sì; 五塔寺). Originally named *Tabun Suburga* in Mongolian, the remaining five pagodas are missing the Ci Deng Temple that was the original anchor of the site. On the back wall, the astronomical chart with Mongolian inscriptions is the only one of its kind in China. *(48 Wutasi Houjie, west of Gongyuang Xi Lu. Bus #1 from the train station stops at Wujing Yiyuan; from the stop, continue walking in the same direction (south) for a couple of blocks until the 5 pagodas become visible. Open daily 8am-6:30pm. Y5.)*

WHITE PAGODA (bái tǎ; 白塔). Originally known as the Ten Thousand Avatamska Sutras Temple, the pagoda towers more than 50m over the nearby fields. The white lime on the outside surface gives the structure a brilliant sheen, but the climb up the inside stairs can get a bit dark. *(About 15km east of Hohhot beyond the airport. Minibus #12 to Hexi from the eastern end of Dongfeng Lu goes past the site (approximately Y3); bus #3 from Xinhua Square stops at the terminus for bus #12. Open daily 8am-6pm. Y5, Y5 extra to climb the pagoda.)*

TOMB OF WANG ZHAOJUN (zhāojūn mù; 昭君墓). The final resting place of the Han dynasty imperial concubine offered to a Hun chieftain (see **Farewell, My Concubine,** p. 263) has now been turned into a money-making venture. From the top of the mound of earth there are decent views of the surrounding countryside; those with vivid imaginations would probably appreciate this sight more than most. *(About 10km south of the city. At the terminus of minibus #14 (Y1). Bus #1 from the train station* *terminates at the intersection of Shiyangqiao Xi Lu and Nanchafang Jie. Cross the intersection, continue in the direction the bus was traveling; the boarding point for minibus #14 is about a half block ahead on the right. Open daily 7am-7pm. Y10; extra to enter various exhibit halls.)*

NEAR HOHHOT: GRASSLANDS 草原

The grasslands in the Hohhot area feel simultaneously remote and touristy. You'll be spending a few days in seemingly endless prairie, but you'll probably be sharing the experience with loads of other tourists. Grazing flocks of sheep still roam the famed grasslands, but the only horses you'll see are the ones that cost Y40 per hour to ride. The dancing, singing, and wrestling all include a healthy dose of spectacle and, like the concrete-floored, electric-wired yurt accommodations, varying degrees of authenticity. Despite the summer camp-cum-club Med atmosphere, the yurt camps themselves are only small dots on an enormous landscape; a five-minute evening walk in any direction generally gives the impression that there is no one else around on the entire grasslands. All cautions aside, visiting the grasslands can be a fascinating experience.

GRASSLANDS AREAS. Of the three main grassland sites around Hohhot, **Xilamuren** (希拉穆仁; 80km from the city) is the most visited, **Huitengxile** (辉腾锡勒; 120km) is the most beautiful, and **Gegentala** (格根塔拉; 160km) just is. The best months to visit are July and August, when the grass is highest. In the winter, temperatures dip below -20°C; even in summer, the weather can get chilly, so bring a few layers of warm clothes. For more remote grasslands, head to the Hulunbeier Grasslands near Manzhouli (see p. 272).

GRASSLAND TOURS. Just about everyone who wants to visit the grasslands signs on with an official tour. Numerous tour operators, some extremely unscrupulous, solicit business all over Hohhot; so while it's certainly no trouble to book a tour, be cautious and keep your wits about you. It is most prudent to go yourself to the office of a reputable agency. Anyone who refuses to provide printed information and official permits is a potential scam artist. Do not pay for the tour until you return and are satisfied that conditions have been met. Likewise, keep in mind that some tourists have paid for tours to Huitengxile (easily identified by the large white windmills nearby) only to be taken to the less remote Xilamuren instead.

Tour prices depend upon where you want to go, how long you want to stay, the number of people going with you, and the tour agency itself. Individuals or small groups of travelers can be placed into larger tour groups to save money. Although almost every agency will quote prices from a list, these prices are negotiable, with discounts of over 50% possible. Stand your ground. Underbid drastically; mentioning the prices of competitor agencies doesn't hurt either. Prices usually go down Y30-50 per additional two or three people (2-day trip to Xilamuren Y200-300 per person; 2-day trip to Huitengxile Y250-350 per person.)

Most tours last two, three, or four days and include transportation, accommodations (in a yurt), food, and the opportunity to go horseback riding across the steppes (for a fee, of course). Food often includes the traditional mutton dish *shou ba rou*, and the evening meal culminates with the *hada* (哈达), in which local spirits are poured into goblets and passed around. After dipping your fingers and pointing first to the sky, then to the ground, and finally touching your forehead, it is time to imbibe. Try not to gag; this stuff is potent.

VISITING INDEPENDENTLY. Independent travelers can take a train from Hohhot to Jining (集宁) (one every afternoon, Y20) and hire a taxi (Y200-300) from Jining to take you to Zhongqi (中旗) near Huitengxile. Buses (daily at 11am, Y20) also travel from Hohhot to Zhaohe, the access point for the Xilamuren grasslands, but keep in mind there is no return bus to Hohhot. In both

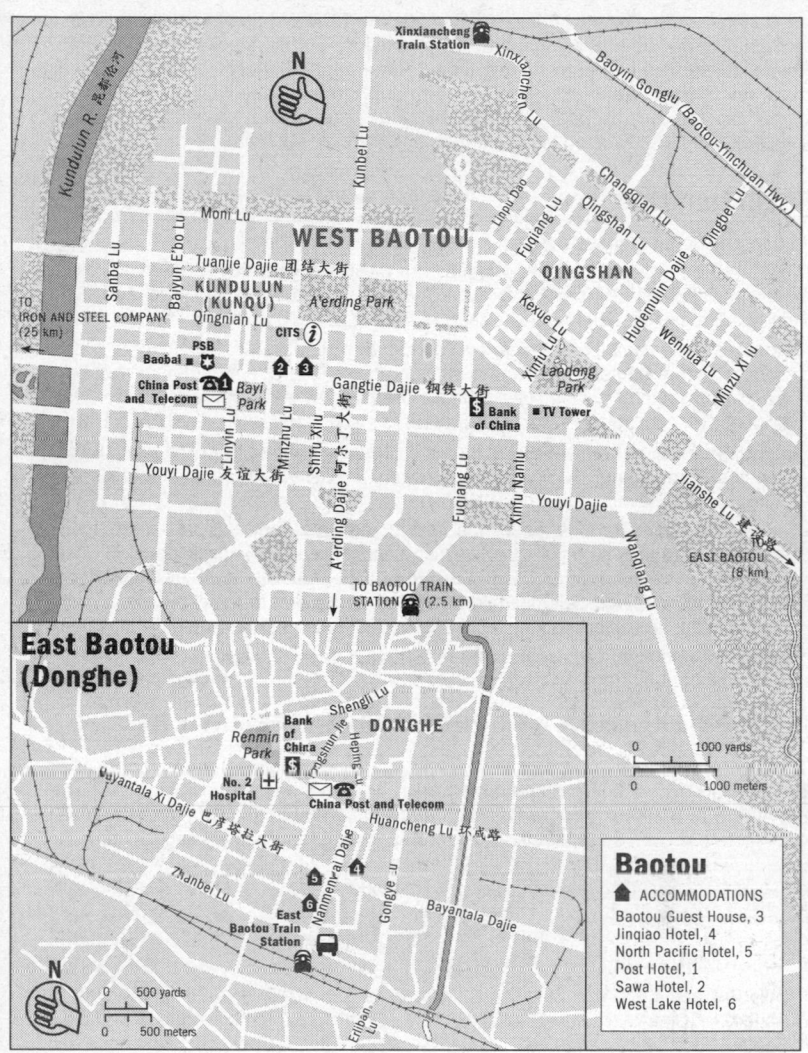

Zhongqi or Zhaohe, locals wait in the bus station and accost the newly arrived with offers of accommodation. Negotiate for a reasonable per day rate (Y20-30 per bed) and you can avoid tour groups altogether.

BAOTOU 包头   ☎ 0472

A tale of two cities...of East Baotou and West Baotou, separated by kilometers of grassy grazing land and industrial parks. Like many other industrial Chinese cities, East Baotou is a maze of streets and buildings under construction, which makes for a lively if somewhat noisy and bewildering atmosphere. West Baotou is the sleepy antidote; broad boulevards lined with neatly planted trees and bright summer flowers are the order of the day. The Baotou Iron and Steel Company, whose smokestacks rise up to the west of the city, provides employment for many of Baotou's residents, but it doesn't do much for tourist appeal. Apart from business purposes, few visitors have reason to venture to Baotou. Those who do usually use the city as a starting or ending point for trips to Singing Sands Gorge, Wudangzhao Monastery, or (less frequently) the Steam Locomotive Museum.

▐ TRANSPORTATION

Airplanes: Baotou Airport (bāotóu jīchǎng; 包头机场; ☎460 0160), is about 2km south of the Baotou East Train Station. The **CAAC ticket office,** 26 Gangtie Dajie, Kunqu (☎513 5492), is in the Aviation Building. Open daily 8am-6pm. CAAC shuttle buses Y10; call ahead to reserve a seat. To **Beijing** (2 per day, Y470).

Trains: Through-trains stop at **Baotou East Station** (bāotóu dōng zhàn; 包头东站), Donghe, and at **Baotou Train Station** (bāotóu zhàn; 包头站; ☎443 1011), West Baotou, 1.5km south of Kunqu. Open 24hr. To: **Beijing** (15-18hr., 7 per day, Y115-199); **Hohhot** (3hr., multiple departures daily, Y12-25); and **Xian** (26hr., 1 per day, Y188).

Buses: The most convenient bus station is in Donghe, just north of the train station. Buses to **Dongsheng** (2¾hr., every 15-20min. 7:30am-7:30pm, Y11) and **Hohhot** (3hr., every 15-45min. 7am-5pm, Y15-25).

Local Transportation: Most **buses** run from 6-7am to 7-8pm; bus **#5** runs 6:30am-10:30pm. Base fare Y0.5; East Baotou-West Baotou buses Y1.5, minibuses Y2.5. There is usually a fare collector on board. Be sure to hold on to the ticket until you exit the bus. Bus **#1** runs from Baotou Train Station up Aerding Lu to Gangtie Dajie. Bus **#5** runs from the far eastern parking lot of Baotou East Station to Gangtie Dajie in Kunqu.

Taxis: Base fare Y5-8, each additional km Y1.2.

▐✶▐ ORIENTATION AND PRACTICAL INFORMATION

Eastern Baotou, known as **Donghe** (东河), is the smaller and more compact of the two Baotous. The Donghe train station, long-distance bus station, and airport are all in the southern part of the city. **Nanmenwai Dajie** (南门外大街) leads north from the train station, intersecting **Huancheng Lu** (环城路) and forming the commercial center of the district. Western Baotou is composed of two districts, **Qingshan** (青山) and **Kundulun** (昆都仑), or **Kunqu** (昆区) for short. **Gangtie Dajie** (钢铁大街) runs from east to west through Qingshan and Kunqu. **Aerding Dajie** (阿尔丁大街) intersects Gangtie Dajie near the city government building and continues south to the train station.

Travel Agencies: CITS, 9 Qingnian Lu, 4th Fl. (☎515 4615; fax 515 1075), west of Shifu Xi Lu. Open M-Sa 8am-noon and 2:30-6:30pm. An easier to find branch inside the Baotou Guesthouse compound, 33 Gangtie Dajie, Kunqu. Open daily 8am-noon and 2:30-6:30pm. Both offer high-priced tours to Wudangzhao and Resonant Sands Gorge.

Bank of China: On Huancheng Lu near People's Park, Donghe, exchanges cash only. Open daily 8am-6:30pm; in winter 8am-6pm. 26 Gangtie Dajie (☎512 8888), Kunqu, exchanges traveler's checks. Open M-F 8am-noon and 2:30-6pm.

Market: Baotou Department Store, known as **Baobai** (bāobǎi; 包百), on Gangtie Dajie, Kunqu, west of Linyin Lu. Open daily 9am-8pm; in winter 9am-7:30pm.

PSB: Near the Baotou Department Store and Daliya Dasha, Kunqu (☎212 6212). Open M-Th 8am-noon and 2:30-6pm, F 8am-noon.

Hospital: No. 2 Municipal Hospital (shì dìèr yīyuàn; 市第二医院), also called **Central Hospital** (zhōngxīn yīyuàn; 中心医院), off Huancheng Lu facing People's Park, Donghe (☎417 2299).

Internet Access: Baotou Internet Company (bāotóu wǎng gōngsī; 包头网公司), 180 Bayantala Xi Dajie (☎442 8999). From the train station, walk north up Nanmenwai

Dajie, and turn left at the 1st major intersection onto Bayantala Xi Dajie; it's about a 15min. walk, on the left. Bus #4 stops at Tie Gong Xiao. The cafe is usually crowded with students from the nearby university. Y4 per hr. Open 24hr. Internet also available on the 4th floor of the **Youdian Hotel.** Turn left as you exit the elevator. Y5 per hr. Open daily 9am-9pm.

Post and Telecommunications: In Donghe, on Huancheng Lu, near the Shangmao Dasha bus stop. **China Telecom,** on the 2nd floor, is open daily 6:30am-midnight. In Kunqu, in the building on the southwest corner of Gangtie Dajie and Linyin Lu. EMS; no Poste Restante. Open daily 8am-7pm. **China Telecom,** on the 2nd floor, is open daily 8am-6pm. A night service booth next door is open daily 6pm-8am. **Postal Code:** 014000 in Donghe, 014010 in Kunqu.

▗ ACCOMMODATIONS

For those watching their wallets, Donghe is the more convenient and cheaper place to stay. Kunqu contains quieter surroundings that usually come with a higher price tag, catering to business people and travelers with plenty of money to spare.

DONGHE

West Lake Hotel (xī hú dàshà; 西湖大厦), 15 Nanmenwai Dajie (☎417 2288, ext. 8108), on the east side of the street, a 5min. walk from the train station. Clean dorms with common showers and bath on the 6th floor. Doubles have bright turquoise private bathrooms. 3-bed dorms Y30; doubles Y115, with A/C Y148.

Jinqiao Hotel (jīnqiáo bīnguǎn; 金桥宾馆), 84 Bayantala Dajie (☎417 1616), just east of Nanmenwai Dajie. The lobby entrance is hidden among the various furniture and repair shops. Rooms are clean and all have attached bath and fan. 5-bed dorms Y25; 3-bed dorms Y30-35; singles Y280; doubles Y88-180.

North Pacific Hotel (běi yáng fàndiàn; 北洋饭店), 23 Nanmenwai Dajie (☎417 5656, ext. 3110 or 3111), just south of Bayantala Dajie, a 10min. walk from the station. The hotel is on the left side of the street and identifiable by the constant call of bingo numbers just outside the elevator. Hallways are dark, but rooms are clean. Singles Y70; doubles Y80-90; triples and quads Y60 (generally sold by the dorm bed to Chinese guests).

KUNQU

Baotou Guesthouse (bāotóu bīnguǎn; 包头宾馆), 33 Gangtie Dajie (☎515 6655, ext. 5583), near Shifu Xi Lu. Bus #1 from Baotou Station and #5 from Donghe stop nearby. The newly renovated west building rooms, with soft carpets and sparkling new bathrooms, are cheapest. Registration in the west building. The high-rise building is probably not worth the extra money. West building doubles Y108, with A/C Y160.

Post Hotel (yóudiàn dàshà; 邮电大厦), 64 Gangtie Dajie (☎212 9988; fax 213 9988), at Linyin Lu opposite Bayi Park. Bus #1 stops at Bayi Gongyuan. The Post Hotel offers luxury-style rooms (with A/C) without the back-breaking prices. These rooms fill up quickly; reservations recommended. Breakfast included. Doubles Y160.

Sawa Hotel (sàwǎ fàndiàn; 萨瓦饭店), 37 Gangtie Dajie (☎210 6044; fax 210 6401), west of Minzu Xi Lu. Bus #5 from East Baotou's train station stops at Feilong Shangchang. From Baotou Station, take bus #1 or a taxi (Y10). Only 14 rooms available. Doubles Y120, with A/C Y200.

◖ FOOD

During the summer months, vendors set up street stands near the intersection of Huancheng Lu and Nanmenwai Dajie in Donghe. **Mr. Lee's California Beef Noodle King USA** (měiguó jiāzhōu niúròu miàn dàwáng; 美国加州牛肉面大王), at the intersection's southeast corner, dishes up its unoriginal signature fare for Y5.5 per bowl. (Open daily 7:30am-10:30pm; in winter 8am-9:30pm.)

In Kunhe, Minzu Lu just south of Gangtie Dajie and the small lane just west of the Sawa Hotel are lined with restaurants offering noodles, fried dishes, and more. During the day, small stands set up along the side streets near the Baotou Department Store, selling everything from noodles and shaved ice to Mongolian souvenirs. **Old Beijing Noodle Restaurant** (lǎo běijīng zhàjiàng miàn guǎn; 老北京炸酱面馆), is on 66 Gangtie Dajie, next to the post office in Kunhu. Although noodles (Y3-8 per bowl) are their specialty, the restaurant also offers a decent selection of other regional cuisine, and you might be lucky enough to bump into the occasional singing waiter. There is also a small bakery. (☎212 5425. Open daily 9:30am-10pm.) **Haide Burger** (hǎidé hànbǎo; 海德汉堡) is on the south side of Gangtie Dajie, west of the Kunhu post office. Haide serves the usual fast-food fare with unusual flair—try the sauceless "pizza" for Y9-12. (☎216 0968. Open daily 9:30am-9:30pm.)

👁 SIGHTS

BAOTOU IRON AND STEEL COMPANY (bāotóu gāngtiě gōngsī; 包头钢铁公司). A sprawling plant at the far western edge of Gangtie Dajie in West Baotou, the Iron and Steel Company can be visited independently, but this option is only feasible for decent Chinese speakers, and is difficult if visitors show up unannounced. CITS can generally contact the appropriate person or provide guidance. On the premises of the Company is a yard with some steam locomotives and newer engines. The roads west of the Kundulun River are in poor condition and are served only by the company buses, carts, and taxis hired from the city. It is not advised to tackle this part entirely by public transportation. A taxi costs Y20-30 and takes about half an hour to get there.

🎒 DAYTRIPS FROM BAOTOU

SINGING SANDS GORGE

*Arranging a tour through CITS (Y280) may be easiest, but making your way independently is feasible—especially if it hasn't rained recently. From Donghe Bus Station, **buses** to Dongsheng depart every 15-30min. The fare to the turn-off, recognizable by a white gate with "Singing Sands" written on it in red, should be Y8. From there it is an additional 8km over a dirt road; **taxis** and **minibuses** making the trip will usually stop and pick up travelers for about Y10, or go under the railroad bridge and start walking. Alternatively, get off the bus at Daqi (达旗) (Y5.5) before the turn-off and attempt to hire a taxi there (Y40). For the **return**, it is fairly easy to flag down a Baotou-bound bus from the side of the main road. **Admission** Y10.*

More refined tourists might cringe at the kitschy playground atmosphere of the Singing Sands Gorge (xiǎng shā wān; 响沙湾), but a walk or a camel ride (Y20 per 30min.) on the far side of the dunes provides a dazzling view of the surrounding sand, mountains, and cliffs. The gorge filled with sand dunes has only recently been turned into a money-maker, and it is still large enough for visitors to lose themselves among the dunes on the far side of the gorge. A chairlift (Y35 round-trip) runs from the parking lot across to the far side of the gorge where camel rides and sand-skiing (Y5) await. In the summer, colorful knee-high booties are worth the Y5 fee, as the sand gets unbearably hot.

WUDANGZHOU LAMASERY

*70km northeast of Baotou. Although a tour can be arranged through CITS, it is possible (though somewhat difficult) to go alone. **Minibuses** from the parking area between the East Baotou train and long-distance bus stations make the trip, usually leaving in the morning (2hr., Y15). A more reliable route is to take **bus #7** which leaves from the same point to Shiguai; from there, hire a **taxi** for the remainder of the trip (Y40-50 round-trip). **Open** daily 8am-6pm. **Admission** Y15.*

The largest lamasery in Inner Mongolia and one of the three most famous in China, this Yellow Hat sect monastery was built in 1749 (see **Coming of the Yel-**

low Hat Sect, p. 726). Likened by some to a small Potala Palace (see p. 735), Wudangzhao Monastery (wǔdāngzhào; 五当召) consists of six halls and originally housed some 1200 lamas. In total, there are eight temples that can be visited; the white Tibetan-style buildings extend up the hillside and contain some exquisitely detailed Buddhist statues and well-maintained, colorful frescoes. During the **Mani Fair** and other festivals, pilgrims flock to the area, but at other times, it is fairly deserted.

DONGSHENG 东胜   ☎ 0477

Dongsheng lies in the middle part of the Ordos Plateau, and like its northern neighbor, Baotou, coal production is this small city's leading industry. In fact, on windy days, a fine layer of coal dust often settles over the city, tinging the streets and the people of Dongsheng gray. Apart from an abundance of coal, the city has little to offer tourists. The few who choose to venture out to Dongsheng usually use it as a place to spend the night en route to the Mausoleum of Genghis Khan.

✳❷ ORIENTATION AND PRACTICAL INFORMATION

Dongsheng is small, with an urban area of just $8.6km^2$ and a population of about 72,000. The long-distance bus station is at the north end of **Hangjin Lu** (杭锦路), which runs the length of the city. Just north of the bus station is the dome-topped entrance to the **Jingyuan Ancient City.** Constructed for the purpose of bolstering tourism, this run-down street of traditional-style buildings is more a ghost town than a bustling tourist draw. **E'erduosi Jie** (鄂尔多斯街), which intersects Hangjin Lu, runs from east to west and houses many of Dongsheng's shops.

Buses: Dongsheng Bus Station (dōngshèng qìchē zhàn; 东胜汽车站), on the west side of Hangjin Lu, near Etuoke Jie. Open daily 5:30am-6pm. To **Baotou** (2½-3hr., every 30min. 6:20am-6:30pm, Y11.5) and **Hohhot** (4½-5hr., 10 per day, Y36).

Local Transportation: Given Dongsheng's size, walking is often the best way of getting around. **Minibuses** #1, 2, and 3 all stop at the train station. Minibuses **#1** and **3** serve the east and west parts of the city, respectively, while **#2** runs down Hangjin Lu to the Tianjiao Hotel. Fare Y0.2-1.

Taxis: Base fare Y5, but many cars are not metered.

PSB: On the northeast corner of the intersection of Etuoke Jie and Hangjin Lu.

Hospital: Meng Hospital (méng yīyuàn; 盟医院), on the north side of E'erduosi Jie, between Wenduer Lu and Hangjin Lu.

Post and Telecommunications: On the southwest corner of the intersection of E'erduosi Jie and Huaige'er Nan Lu (☎832 9957). EMS. Open daily 7:30am-4:30pm. **China Telecom** is across the street, on the southeast corner of the intersection. IDD service. Open daily 7:30am-6:30pm; in winter 8am-6pm. **Postal Code:** 017000.

♠◔ ACCOMMODATIONS AND FOOD

Most of Dongsheng's reasonably priced accommodations are on **E'erduosi Jie** between Hangjin Lu and Dalate Nan Lu. The overpriced Tianjiao Hotel, at the southern end of the city, caters primarily to businessmen and wealthy tourists.

There are some restaurants on Hangjin Lu and E'erduosi Jie. Those longing for Western fast food can try **Merry Holiday** (yínglè jiàn; 迎乐假日), on the southeast corner of the intersection of E'erduosi Jie and Dalate Nan Lu. A small **night market** also sets up in the courtyard just south of the train station.

Ih Ju League Hotel (yīkè zhāoméng bīnguǎn; 伊克昭盟宾馆), 3 E'erduosi Jie (☎832 1501), at Dalate Nan Lu, about a 10-15min. walk from the train station. Also known as the Yimeng Binguan, this is one of the few places that allows foreigners to have dorm beds. Both the smallish dorms and the rooms are clean. 3-bed dorms Y15; 2-bed dorms Y30; singles Y35; doubles with bath Y120, with bath and A/C Y160.

Mengjia Hotel (méngjiā bīnguǎn; 蒙佳宾馆), 1 Hangjin Lu (☎832 3699, ext. 2100), at E'erduosi Jie. Although the rooms are small, they come with TV, phone, clean tile floors, and fairly new attached baths. Singles and doubles Y86.

Dongsheng Hotel (dōngshèng dàjiŭdiàn; 东胜大酒店; ☎832 7333), on the northwest corner of the intersection of E'erduosi Jie and Hangjin Lu. Although the Dongsheng is slightly upmarket, the rooms in the newer central building are not worth the extra money. Cheaper rooms in the older west wing are large, with leaky bathrooms and carpets reminiscent of astroturf. Doubles Y98-186, with A/C Y238.

▌ DAYTRIP FROM DONGSHENG

MAUSOLEUM OF GENGHIS KHAN

50km from Dongsheng. From Dongsheng Long-distance Bus Station, **minibuses** *(2hr., approx. every hr. beginning at 7am, Y7) depart for Yulin (愉林), in Shaanxi province; ask to get off at the Mausoleum. It is also possible to take a* **bus** *from Baotou to Yulin. If you take an early morning bus, it might be possible to see the Mausoleum and make it back to Baotou by night.* **Open** *24hr.* **Admission** *Y25.*

The chances that the actual remains of Genghis Khan are housed in this so-called mausoleum (chéngjísī hán líng; 成吉思汗陵) are probably slim to none. However, those tourists who are tiring of the cult of Mao Zedong may be interested in seeing the almost godlike status to which Genghis Khan has been elevated here. During WWII, many relics of the great Khan were commandeered by a Japanese government intent on establishing a Mongolian puppet state. The Chinese retrieved them, and in 1955 took them out of safekeeping to build this gigantic shrine six years after the creation of the Inner Mongolia Autonomous Region.

Despite its being heralded as one of the "Forty Best Famous Tourism Scenic Spots" by the Chinese government, there is little to see. In fact, the mausoleum and the surrounding area can easily be seen in under an hour—less time than you might spend waiting on the side of the road for a Dongsheng- or Baotou-bound bus. The entrance is marked by a large bronze statue of the great man himself surrounded by—no, not galloping horses or waving grasslands—the gauntlet of nearly identical small souvenir shops. Three huge blue and gold tiled domes top the actual mausoleum. In the front part of the main hall sits a massive marble statue of Genghis Khan; behind him is a map showing the extent of his empire. The back room contains an altar behind which several yurts bear the "remains"; a typical offering is a bottle of fiery Mongolian spirits. Two side halls contain remains of relatives as well as some recovered pottery and metalwork. The walls of all the halls are covered with colorful murals depicting the life and exploits of the Khan.

To the left of the actual mausoleum visitors can pay their respects at the recently constructed **Sacrificial Altar to Suled** (sūlèdé jìtán; 苏勒德祭坛), which was the banner of the ancient Mongolian army. **Gandeli Obo** (gāndélì áobāo; 甘德利敖包) affords a nice view of the surrounding valley. Those with more time on their hands might prefer to make the half-hour trek to the **Reviewing Stand** (diǎnjiāng tái; 点将台), on the edge of the grasslands.

Accommodations are available for the 3am pilgrims among you in the **Genghis Guesthouse** (chéngjísī bīnguǎn; 成吉思宾馆), next to the parking lot on the right side of the entrance when facing the Mausoleum. Standard doubles have tile floors, TV, and attached baths, while the yurt accommodations are more rustic. (Yurt beds Y20-30; doubles Y100-160.)

MANZHOULI 满洲里　　　☎ 0471

In the far northeastern tip of Inner Mongolia, Manzhouli is near both the Russian border to the north and the Mongolian border to the west. The surrounding Hulun Buir grasslands further define the city's remoteness. Open since 1992 to border trade, Manzhouli has felt the tug of international influence; Russians dot its streets and stores, piling loads of Chinese goods into their vans.

✳ 🔋 ORIENTATION AND PRACTICAL INFORMATION

The center of Manzhouli is marked by the train tracks to the south and **North Lake Park** (北湖公园) to the north. The intersection of **Xinhua Lu** (新华路) and **Si Daojie** (四道街) marks the most lively commercial spot in town. Manzhouli is small enough for everything to be within walking distance.

Airplanes: The airport closest to Manzhouli is **Hailar Airport** (hǎiěrlā fēijīchǎng; 海尔拉飞机场). There are **CAAC ticket office** both in Manzhouli (☎ 622 1436) and Hailar (☎ 833 4404). To: **Beijing** (4 per day); **Dalian** (1 per day); **Hohhot** (1 per day); and **Qiqihar** (1 per day).

Trains: Manzhouli Train Station (mǎnzhōulǐ huǒchē zhàn; 满洲里火车站), on Yi Daojie, south of the train tracks. To: **Beijing** (1 per week, Y126-443); **Hailar** (3 hr., 2 per day, Y14-18); **Harbin** (14 hrs., 1 per day); **Moscow** (1 per week); and **Qiqihar** (11 hr., 1 per day, Y46-200).

Buses: The **Public Bus Station** (gōnggòng qìchē zhàn; 公共汽车站), 7 Shizheng Lu (☎ 622 1767), between Si Daojie and Wu Daojie, has buses to **Hulun Lake** (1 per day, Y10) and **Zhalainuo'er** (every 35min., Y3). The **Manzhouli Long-distance Bus Station** (mǎnzhōulǐ chángtú qìchēzhàn; 满洲里长途汽车站), on the corner of Yidao Jie and Shuidao Lu, has buses to **Hailar**.

Taxis: Taxis within town cost Y5. Crossing the railroad tracks to the train station costs Y10.

Travel Agency: CITS, 39 Er Daojie (☎ 622 2988; fax 622 2988), organizes tours to local sights, including: **Hulunbuir** (full-day trip, with Mongolian banquet lunch and horseback riding, Y600; two day trip, with yurt accommodations and a visit to the Sino-Soviet trade market, Y900); **Hulun Lake** (full-day trip, with Hulun Lake fish banquet lunch, Y450); and **Zhalainuo'er** (half-day trip, Y300). English-, Japanese-, and Russian speaking staff. Open daily 8am-noon and 2:30-5:30pm.

Bank of China: 16 Er Daojie. Open daily 8am-noon and 2:30-6pm; in winter 8am-noon and 2-5pm.

PSB: On San Daojie, at the corner of Shizheng Lu (☎ 622 2464). Processes day visas for Russia. Open daily 8am-11pm.

Hospital: No. 1 Hospital (dìyī yīyuàn; 第一医院), 10 San Daojie (☎ 622 2796; off-hours ☎ 622 6081). Open daily 8am-noon and 2-6pm.

Internet Access: Xinhua Bookstore, 2nd Fl., at the corner of Xinghua Lu and Si Daojie. Open daily 8:30am-6pm; in winter 8:30am-5pm.

Post and Telecommunications: China Post (☎ 622 9177), on Haiguan Lu, at Si Daojie. Open M-F 8am-6pm; in winter 8am-5pm; year-round Sa-Su 9am-4pm. **China Telecom,** 8 San Daojie. **Postal Code:** 021400.

📷 ⌘ ACCOMMODATIONS AND FOOD

Most travelers have no problem finding accommodations on the side of Manzhouli across the train tracks from the station. As for food, **Si Daojie** is lined with many affordable hole-in-the-wall restaurants. For a taste of traditional Mongolian life, try a cup of **milk tea** (naí chá; 奶茶): bricks of red tea are brewed with mare's milk, mare's fat, and salt. The **Mingzhu Hotel Western Restaurant** (míngzhū fàndiàn xī cāntīng; 明珠饭店西餐厅), on the corner of Yidao Jie and Xinhua Lu, serves some excellent Russian food.

Railroad Hostel (tiělù zhāodàisǔo; 铁路招待所; ☎622 2431), on the corner of Yidao Jie and Daokou Lu. Walk down the dirt road to the left of the train station; the hostel is on the right. Cleanliness and great prices make this place a budget traveler's dream. 4-bed dorms Y16.5.

Huanzhuang Central Hostel (huànzhuāng béixùn zhōngxīn zhāodàisǔo; 换装背训中心招待所; ☎622 1747), on Daokou Lu just across the train tracks. Not as well kept but livlier than the Railroad Hostel. Doubles with bath Y123; quads Y66.

Dianli Hotel (diànlì bīnguǎn; 电力宾馆), 1 San Daojie (☎622 2549), at Shulin Lu. One of the cheapest accommodations this side of the train tracks. Doubles Y70.

International Hotel (guójì fàndiàn; 国际饭店), 35 Er Daojie (☎622 2225; fax 622 2976), next to CITS. One of the fanciest places in town, this hotel—not surprisingly—often teems with international (mostly Russian) patrons. Doubles Y180.

👁 SIGHTS

A quick walking tour of Manzhouli soon proves that, other than shopping for souvenir trinkets of questionable Russian origin and admiring the occasional Russian-style wood buildings, the town's attractions lie elsewhere. The impressive open-pit coal mine and steam locomotive yards of **Zhalainuo'er** (zhálàinùo'ěr; 扎赉诺尔), 27km from Manzhouli on the same road to Hulun Lake, are open to the public. *(Buses from the Manzhouli Public Bus Station Y3. Round-trip taxi Y50-100.)* If grasslands, lakes, steam locomotives, and open-pit coal mines don't tickle your fancy, head for the border—**Russia** is only a 12km taxi ride away. The border crossing is at the **Sino-Soviet Trade Area** (zhōng é hūshì maòyì qū; 中俄互市贸易区). For more information on border crossings, see p. 78.

HULUN BUIR GRASSLANDS (hūlúnbùer dà cǎoyuán; 呼伦布尔大草原). From the outskirts of Manzhouli, the grasslands stretch as far as the eye can see. The sparsely populated grasslands are punctuated by lakes, ridges, rolling hills, and occasional settlements, some of the traditional tent-like yurts, others of baked brick or clay houses. Deep green grasses and vibrant fields of wildflowers are fanned by summer breezes, welcoming an increasing tourist population that peaks during the annual **Naadam** festival. The crackling of the icy, white ground marks the long winter season, in which horses and sheep roam the deserted grasslands, people retreat a bit farther into coal-heated homes, and the tourist trade all but comes to a halt. *(CITS runs tours to the grasslands most frequently June-Sept. Individual families also host visitors and may approach tourists arriving at the train or bus stations. Be sure to agree upon a set fee in advance; do not provide payment until you are satisfied that conditions have been met. Accommodations and bathing facilities are basic.)*

HULUN LAKE (hūlún hú; 呼伦湖). Hulun Lake, also known as **Dalai Lake** (dálài hú; 达赉湖), is the fifth largest lake in China. Numerous rare birds make their home on the protected wetlands and grasslands of the nature reserve surrounding this saltwater lake. During the summer, sunbathers, swimmers, and avid birdwatchers line the shores; a few short months later, ice fishermen battle the bitter cold. According to legend, Genghis Khan once tied his horse to the **Horse-tethering Stake** that stands over 20m high on the western bank of the lake. Many restaurants near the lake serve up Hulun Lake fish, the local specialty. *(45km southeast of Manzhouli. Buses from Manzhouli Public Bus Station Y10. A round-trip taxi costs Y100-150. Y10.)*

YEARNING FOR YURTS For those visitors who yearn to learn more about yurt construction, the concrete-floored yurts (ménggǔ bāo; 蒙古包) of the grasslands near Hohhot may provide little satisfaction. Even those who venture to the grasslands near Manzhouli could be left wishing they had traveled to Mongolia after all. Originally derived from *gert*, a Turkish-Mongolian term for a building which is transportable and easy to set up and take down, fully collapsible yurts have been traced back to the Northern Wei dynasty (AD 386-534). It is said that experienced yurt dwellers can put up a full-size yurt in under 30 minutes. Built to withstand the fierce winds that whip through the grasslands, the yurt is a sturdy, rounded structure. The traditional Mongolian yurt, or *ger*, is built of walls made from saplings braided together with leather ties. These walls, known as *khana,* can either open out or fold flat and are generally divided into two sections. Wooden rafters connect the top of the *khana* to the center roof ring to provide additional support. Two belly bands wrapped outside the *khana* prevent the rafters from pushing the *khana* farther open. Felt is often used for the walls and roof. No center poles are necessary to support modest-sized yurts (up to 10m in diameter), but smoke holes provide ventilation for cooking fires and hot summer days. Innovation strikes yet again: miniature sequined yurts (Y3 and up) can be found in some department stores, and web sites touting newfangled metal "yurt" structures make it possible to set up camp just about anywhere.

SHANGHAI
AND THE YANGZI DELTA

The region huddled around the mouth of the mighty Yangzi, comprised of Shanghai Municipality and Jiangsu and Zhejiang provinces, includes some of the most densely populated and prosperous land in the country. The river travels over 6000km from Tibet to get here, and rushing waters are by no means the only things drawn to the area. Money, tourists, traders, emperors, refugees, luxury goods, and novel ideas have been flowing into the Yangzi delta for centuries. North of the Yangzi, traffic thins out considerably as the scenery turns to smokestacks. South of the river, a complex network of waterways, at the center of which is the Grand Canal (see p. 5 for our suggested tour of the Grand Canal), meander through endless rice paddies. At the southern reaches of Zhejiang, the terrain turns rugged as it rumbles its way into neighboring Fujian province.

Parts of the region were inhabited as early as 5000 years ago, and cities like

---

HIGHLIGHTS OF THE YANGZI RIVER DELTA

RELAXED EVENING STROLLS along the **Bund,** the imposing colonial waterfront promenade in Shanghai (p. 290).

AFTERLIFE AND WILDLIFE among the ancient and 20th-century tombs on Nanjing's **Purple Gold Mountain** (p. 304).

WILLOW TREES AND PAVILIONS at Hangzhou's radiant **West Lake** (p. 335).

WESTERN PARADISE and fantastic sunrises on the magical monastic island of **Putuoshan** (p. 347), in the East China Sea.

SMOOTH AS SILK in the canal-lined, garden-crazy city of **Suzhou** (p. 308).

Suzhou, Wuxi, and Shaoxing were lively commercial and cultural centers by the 7th and 8th centuries AD. The attractions of the region's gentle, stately scenic beauty and strategic ports were not lost on the rulers of imperial China; the Song set up court in Hangzhou in the 12th century, and Nanjing served as the capital in the early Ming. In the early 20th century, Shanghai, a hub for intellectual activity, ushered in modern thought, technology, and temptation.

One would assume that very few remnants of the past would survive all this flow and flux. And it is true that today, only an occasional moat, city wall fragment, or tomb reminds the Yangzi delta's many residents of the sheer scope of their home's history. Revolution, rebellion, and the passage of time have destroyed the rest. Foreign missionaries and trading companies who emerged from the direction of the East China Sea left their unmistakeable mark on the region's architecture and economy. These days, outsiders still mob this well-established gateway to the Chinese mainland, but they come with different aspirations; camera-toting visitors crowd around the region's fabled scenic gems in the hopes of preserving, not altering, what remains of the ancient empire.

SHANGHAI 上海 ☎021

Cities with long histories often view progress with a certain sort of unease. Age hinders growth and innovation just as it slows a pianist's hands: the music still flows, but without the grace and ease of earlier days. One might assume that Shanghai would encounter just this problem, for Shanghai's colonial past still echoes strongly in the stately architecture of the Bund and in the elegant streets of the

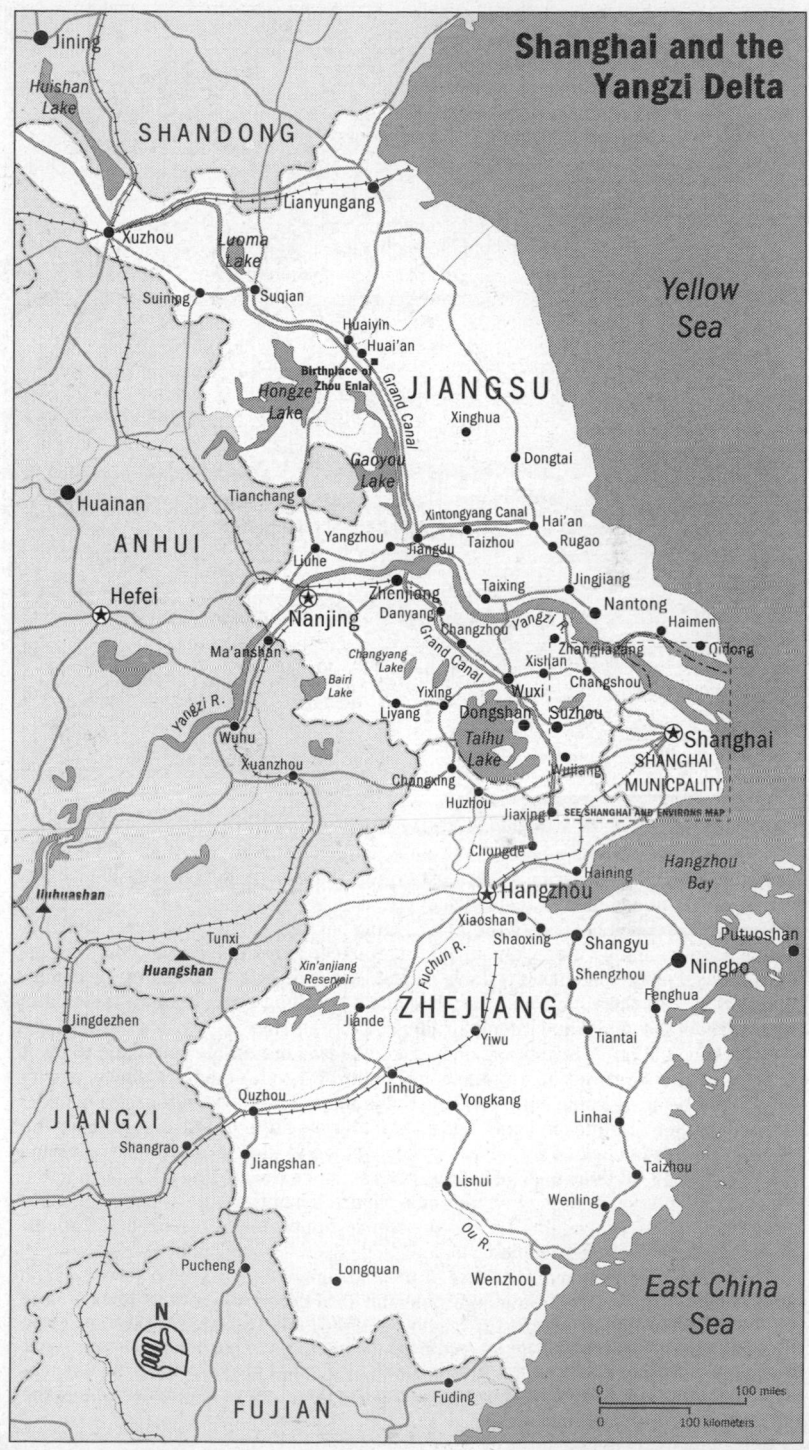

Shanghai and the Yangzi Delta

Jining

Huishan Lake

SHANDONG

Lianyungang

Xuzhou

Luoma Lake

Suining

Suqian

Huaiyin

Huai'an

Birthplace of Zhou Enlai

Hongze Lake

JIANGSU

Xinghua

Dongtai

Gaoyou Lake

Huainan

Tianchang

ANHUI

Yangzhou

Xintongyang Canal

Hai'an

Hefei

Liuhe

Jiangdu

Taizhou

Rugao

Zhenjiang

Taixing

Jingjiang

Nantong

Nanjing

Danyang

Changzhou

Yangzi R.

Haimen

Ma'anshan

Changyang Lake

Zhangjiagang

Qidong

Bairi Lake

Yixing

Xishan

Wuxi

Changshou

Wuhu

Liyang

Dongshan

Suzhou

Xuanzhou

Taihu Lake

Yangzi R.

Wujiang

Shanghai

Changxing

SHANGHAI MUNICIPALITY

Huzhou

Jiaxing

SEE SHANGHAI AND ENVIRONS MAP

Chongde

Hangzhou Bay

Jiuhuashan

Haining

Tunxi

Hangzhou

Xiaoshan

Shaoxing

Shangyu

Putuoshan

Huangshan

Xin'anjiang Reservoir

Fuchun R.

Shengzhou

Ningbo

Jingdezhen

Jiande

ZHEJIANG

Yiwu

Tiantai

Fenghua

JIANGXI

Quzhou

Jinhua

Yongkang

Linhai

Shangrao

Jiangshan

Lishui

Taizhou

Wenling

Pucheng

Longquan

Ou R.

Wenzhou

East China Sea

FUJIAN

Fuding

Yellow Sea

N

0   100 miles

0   100 kilometers

SHANGHAI

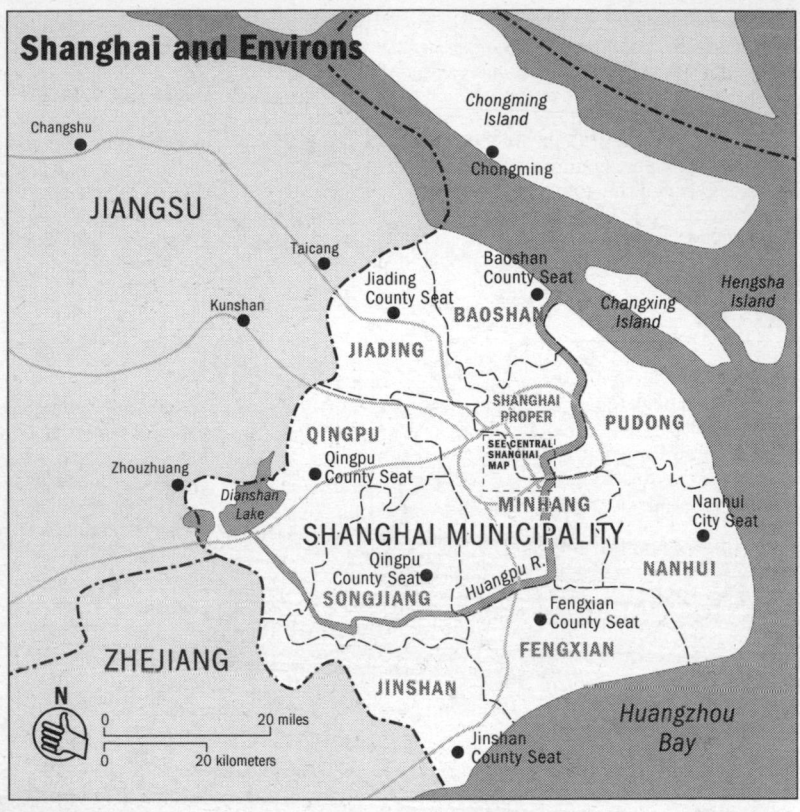

Shanghai and Environs

Changshu

Chongming
Island

JIANGSU

Chongming

Taicang

Baoshan
County Seat

Jiading
County Seat

Hengsha
Island

Kunshan

BAOSHAN

Changxing
Island

JIADING

SHANGHAI
PROPER

PUDONG

QINGPU

SEE CENTRAL
SHANGHAI
MAP

Zhouzhuang

Qingpu
County Seat

Dianshan
Lake

MINHANG

Nanhui
City Seat

SHANGHAI MUNICIPALITY

Qingpu
County Seat

Huangpu R.

NANHUI

SONGJIANG

Fengxian
County Seat

ZHEJIANG

FENGXIAN

JINSHAN

N

0   20 miles

0   20 kilometers

Jinshan
County Seat

Huangzhou
Bay

French Concession. Its Chinese tradition reveals itself in the pagodas of Yuyuan Gardens and the serene beauty of the Jade Buddha Temple. Yet of all of the cities in China, Shanghai is perhaps the most comfortable with change, still displaying the vibrance, mischief, and resilience of youth.

Until the imperial powers of the 19th century set their sights on China, Shanghai was a simple fishing village, unextraordinary except for the fact that many fishermen chose it as the place from which "to go to sea," or *shang hai*. After the Opium War (see p. 12), the village suddenly became a booming port, home to merchants and gangsters, scandal and iniquity, change and progress.

Even socialist policies couldn't depress Shanghai's inimitable spirit, and today it is again at the forefront of economic and cultural development. Business executives stroll beside kissing couples along the grand colonial waterfront promenade, beepers and cell phones in hand. Locals and tourists alike frantically preserve the moment with the click of a camera shutter, not a bad idea given the current pace of construction. Skyscrapers, albeit half vacant, grace the skyline of Lujiazui in the Pudong New Area, and cozy expat enclaves are sprouting up just beyond. Jam-packed shops along Nanjing Lu and the trendy boutiques of the French Concession showcase the latest fashions.

The narrow, densely packed lanes of the Old Chinese City, which served as the seat of the entire surrounding county in the 13th century, seem as if they can't have changed much in the last fifty years. A closer look, though, reveals that many residents peddle cell phones and watch television in their storefronts. Elsewhere, scores of locals cross Waibaidu Bridge, the first to span Suzhou Creek, en route to early morning tai chi in adjacent Huangpu Park. By night, caricaturists and knick-knack vendors barter to the music of a wistful violinist. The taxi long ago replaced the rickshaw, but chances are the driver still speaks *Shanghaihua*, a lilting, melodious dialect unintelligible to most Mandarin speakers.

However, Shanghai has not yet discovered its true character, still searching in its colonial facade and old world complexity for the city that it will become. The sights and sounds of Central Shanghai gradually recede into the farmland and villages of the outer counties of Shanghai Municipality. The muddy Huangpu River snakes through the countryside on its way to Shanghai Harbor and the mouth of the Yangzi River. Although this area offers a retreat from the hectic pace of life in Shanghai proper, few foreign tourists make it a stop on their itineraries. Dianshan Lake, a national forest, and numerous theme parks await those who do.

✈ GETTING THERE AND AWAY

BY AIR

In October 1999, Shanghai opened its second major airport, Pudong International Airport, on the east side of the Huangpu river in the Pudong district. Although both Pudong and Hongqiao International Airport currently serve foreign airlines, it is expected that all foreign airlines will operate out of Pudong by 2001. Both airports feature roughly the same design: arrivals are on the lower level and departures are on the upper level, with separate entrances for international and domestic travelers. Airline counters are generally on the upper level, while hotel, bus, and tourist information can be found on the lower level. For more information on international flights to China, see **Getting There: By Plane** (p. 72).

Airlines: Aeroflot (☎6415 6936). **Air France** (☎6360 6688). **Canadian Airlines** (☎6375 8899). **China Eastern Airlines** (☎6247 2255). **DRAGONAIR** (☎6375 6375). **Japan Airlines** (☎6472 3000). **Lufthansa** (☎6248 1100). **Northwest Airlines** (☎6279 8088). **Shanghai Airlines** (☎6255 1551). **United Airlines** (☎6279 8009). **Virgin Atlantic** (☎5353 4600).

TO	PER DAY	PRICE	TO	PER DAY	PRICE
Beijing	18-22	Y900	Changsha	2-3	Y710
Chengdu	6 8	Y1290	Chongqing	4-5	Y1190
Dalian	7-10	Y850	Fuzhou	8-9	Y620
Guangzhou	8-9	Y1020	Guilin	3-5	Y1040
Harbin	3-6	Y1410	Hefei	1-2	Y390
Hong Kong	6	Y1890	Kunming	4-7	Y1520
Lanzhou	1	Y1400	Lhasa	W, Su	Y2120
Qingdao	6-7	Y590	Sanya	2	Y1510
Shenyang	3-4	Y1040	Shenzhen	4-6	Y1120
Tianjin	2	Y820	Wuhan	5-8	Y650
Xiamen	7-8	Y770	Xian	6-8	Y1010

HONGQIAO AIRPORT. Hongqiao International Airport (shànghǎi hóngqiáo guójì jīchǎng; 上海虹桥国际机场), 2550 Hongqiao Lu (☎6268 3659), is about 10km west of Shanghai. The airport still handles more passengers than Pudong but most of its international flights are to other Asian countries. The **tourist center** in the international arrivals lounge offers free maps, brochures, and helpful advice in Chinese, English, and Japanese. (☎6268 8899, ext. 56750. Open daily 10am-9:30pm.)

A taxi ride to central Shanghai (45min.-1½hr., depending on traffic) will cost about Y50-70, but if you go far enough east, you'll have to pay an extra Y15 toll to take the Yanan Elevated Road. Buses line up outside the domestic arrivals area. Though most of the buses that run to Hongqiao only serve nearby areas, bus **#938** goes to the stadium. The **#1 airport shuttle** runs from Hongqiao to Pudong Airport (1hr., every 20min., Y30).

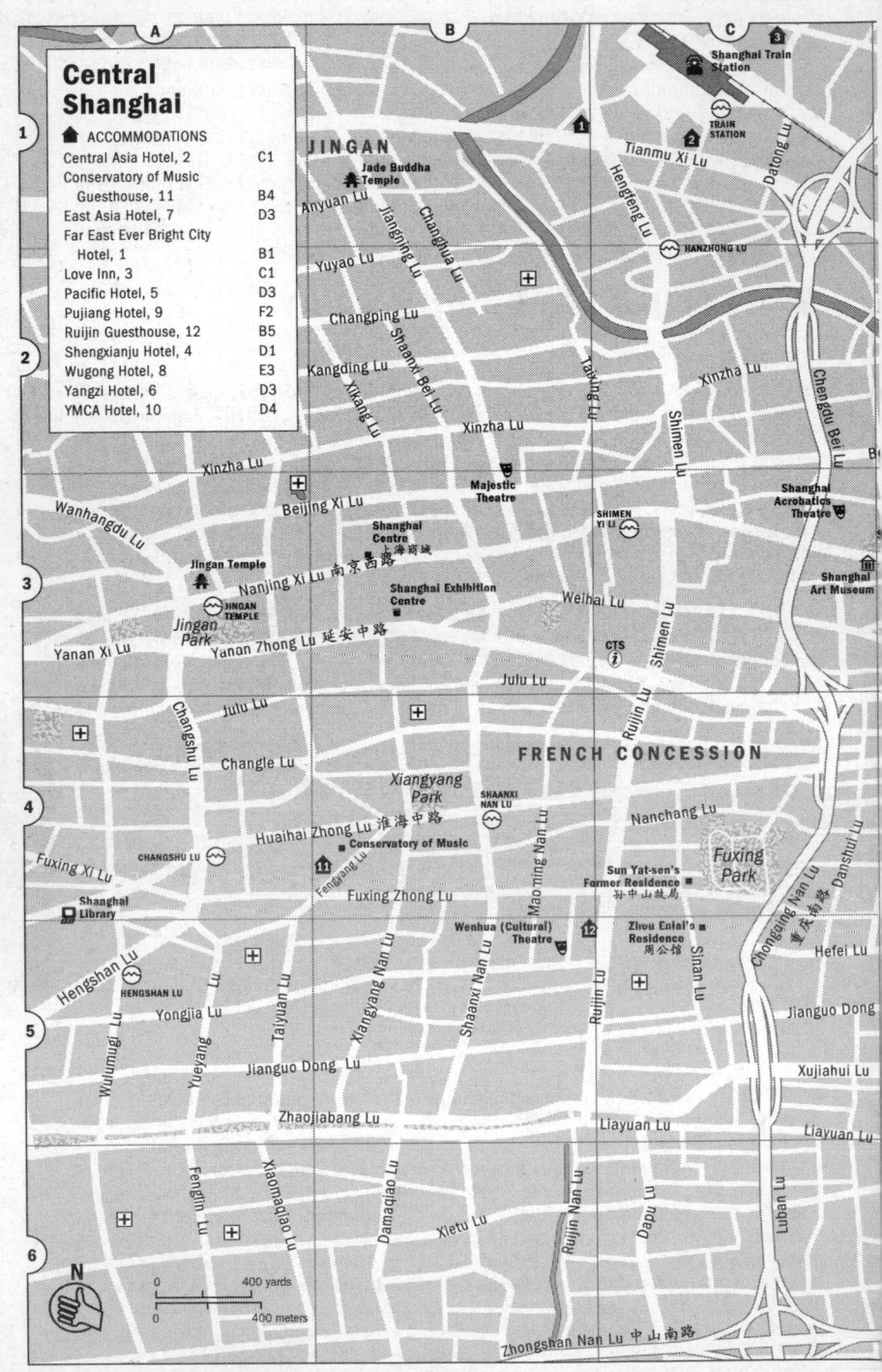

Central Shanghai

🏠 **ACCOMMODATIONS**

Central Asia Hotel, 2	C1
Conservatory of Music Guesthouse, 11	B4
East Asia Hotel, 7	D3
Far East Ever Bright City Hotel, 1	B1
Love Inn, 3	C1
Pacific Hotel, 5	D3
Pujiang Hotel, 9	F2
Ruijin Guesthouse, 12	B5
Shengxianju Hotel, 4	D1
Wugong Hotel, 8	E3
Yangzi Hotel, 6	D3
YMCA Hotel, 10	D4

JINGAN

Shanghai Train Station

TRAIN STATION

Jade Buddha Temple

HANZHONG LU

Majestic Theatre

SHIMEN YI LU

Shanghai Acrobatics Theatre

Shanghai Centre 上海商城

Shanghai Exhibition Centre

Shanghai Art Museum

Jingan Temple

JINGAN TEMPLE

Jingan Park

Nanjing Xi Lu 南京西路

Welhai Lu

CTS

Yanan Xi Lu

Yanan Zhong Lu 延安中路

Jufu Lu

FRENCH CONCESSION

Changle Lu

Xiangyang Park

SHAANXI NAN LU

Nanchang Lu

Fuxing Park

Fuxing Xi Lu

CHANGSHU LU

Huaihai Zhong Lu 淮海中路

Conservatory of Music

Sun Yat-sen's Former Residence 孙中山故居

Shanghai Library

Fengyang Lu

Fuxing Zhong Lu

Wenhua (Cultural) Theatre

Zhou Enlai's Residence 周公馆

Hefei Lu

Hengshan Lu

HENGSHAN LU

Yongjia Lu

Jianguo Dong

Jianguo Dong Lu

Xujiahui Lu

Zhaojiabang Lu

Liayuan Lu

Liayuan Lu

Fenglin Lu

Xiaomaqiao Lu

Damaqiao Lu

Xietu Lu

Ruijin Nan Lu

Dapu

Lupu Lu

Zhongshan Nan Lu 中山南路

N

0		400 yards
0		400 meters

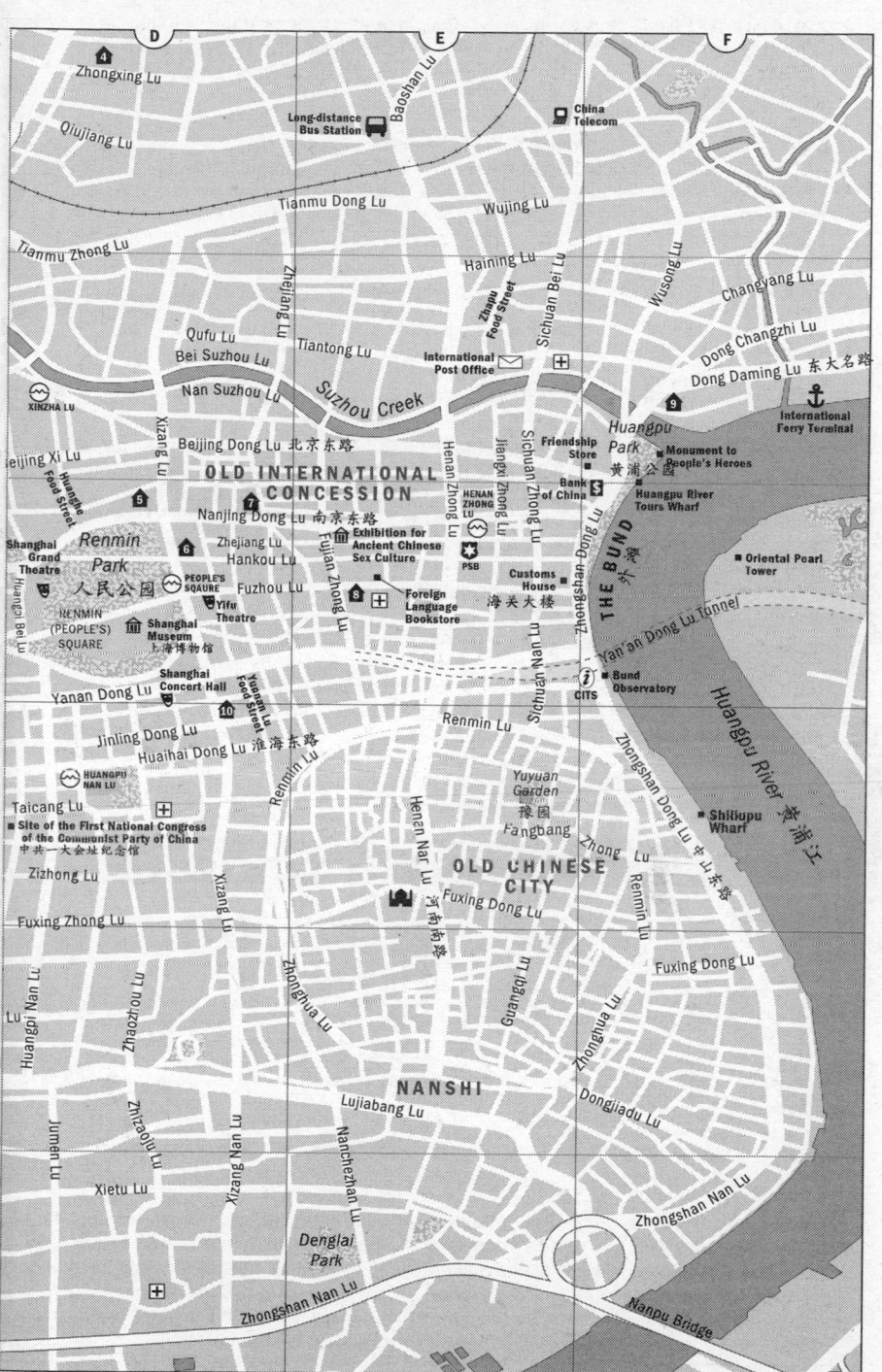

D

1 Zhongxing Lu

Qiujiang Lu

Long-distance Bus Station

China Telecom

E

Baoshan Lu

F

Tianmu Dong Lu

Wujing Lu

Tianmu Zhong Lu

Haining Lu

Changyang Lu

Zhapu Food Street

Sichuan Bei Lu

Wusong Lu

Qufu Lu

Zhejiang Lu

Tiantong Lu

International Post Office

Dong Changzhi Lu

Dong Daming Lu 东大名路

Bei Suzhou Lu

Nan Suzhou Lu

Suzhou Creek

9

International Ferry Terminal

XINZHA LU

Beijing Dong Lu 北京东路

Henan Zhong Lu

Jiangxi Zhong Lu

Friendship Store

Huangpu Park
黄浦公园

Monument to People's Heroes

Huangpu River Tours Wharf

Beijing Xi Lu

OLD INTERNATIONAL CONCESSION

5

7 Nanjing Dong Lu 南京东路

HENAN ZHONG LU

Sichuan Zhong Lu

Bank of China

Oriental Pearl Tower

Shanghai Grand Theatre

6 Zhejiang Lu

Exhibition for Ancient Chinese Sex Culture

THE BUND 外滩

Zhongshan Dong Lu

Renmin Park
人民公园

Hankou Lu

Fujian Zhong Lu

PSB

Customs House
海关大楼

Huangpu Food Street

PEOPLE'S SQUARE

Fuzhou Lu

Yifu Theatre

8

Foreign Language Bookstore

Sichuan Nan Lu

RENMIN (PEOPLE'S) SQUARE

Shanghai Museum
上海博物馆

Yan'an Dong Lu Tunnel

Shanghai Concert Hall

Yunnan Food Street

10

i CITS

Bund Observatory

Yanan Dong Lu

Jinling Dong Lu

Huaihai Dong Lu 淮海东路

Renmin Lu

Renmin Lu

Shiliupu Wharf

Zhongshan Dong Lu

HUANGPU NAN LU

Taicang Lu

Site of the First National Congress of the Communist Party of China
中共一大会址纪念馆

Renmin Lu

Yuyuan Garden
豫园

Fangbang

Zhongshan Dong Lu 中山东路

Huangpu River 黄浦江

Zizhong Lu

OLD CHINESE CITY

Henan Nan Lu

Zhong Lu

Renmin Nan Lu

Fuxing Zhong Lu

Fuxing Dong Lu

Fuxing Dong Lu

Huangpi Nan Lu

Zhaozhou Lu

Zhonghua Lu

Guangqi Lu

Zhonghua Lu

Xizang Nan Lu

NANSHI

Lujiabang Lu

Dongjiadu Lu

Zhizaoju Lu

Jumen Lu

Xietu Lu

Nanchezhan Lu

Denglai Park

Zhongshan Nan Lu

Nanpu Bridge

PUDONG AIRPORT. Pudong International Airport (pǔdōng guójì jīchǎng; 浦东国际机场; ☎3848 4500), 30km from downtown Shanghai, is bright and clean, and offers essentially the same transportation options as Hongqiao. For general flight inquiries, call ☎6268 8918. Information booths are scattered throughout the airport, and all maps, signs, and announcements are in both Chinese and English. An automated machine to pay departure tax is on the upper level.

A taxi to the Bund (45min.-1½hr.) averages Y120, not including the Yanan Elevated Road toll. **Shuttle buses** leave to Central Shanghai and Hongqiao Airport from outside the lower level (every 20-30min., Y30). Once the Metro is complete, it will offer a cheap and convenient way into the city.

BY TRAIN

The main train station is **Shanghai Train Station**, 330 Moling Lu (shànghǎi huǒchē zhàn; 上海火车站; ☎6354 3193; schedules ☎6317 9090), north of Suzhou Creek, near the intersection of Tianmu Xi Lu and Hengfeng Lu. Buses #64, 96, 104, 109, and 113 all terminate just east of the station's south square, across from the main Metro entrance. As of July 2000, the north side of the station was virtually impassable due to construction. The ticket office is a large building located just east of the main square on the southern side of the station, with at least some windows open at all hours. Foreigners and overseas Chinese can also buy tickets inside the quiet, air-conditioned office of the soft seat waiting room. (Open daily 7-11:30am, noon-5:30pm, and 6-7pm.) The Longmen Hotel just west of the station sells tickets with a commission of Y5-10.

Some trains depart from the **Shanghai West Train Station** (shànghǎi xī huǒchē zhàn; 上海西火车站; ☎6254 9500), 1 Taopu Lu, at the intersection of Jiaotong Lu and Caoyang Lu. Bus #106 goes here from the main train station.

The following table provides the departure station, number of trains per day, duration of travel (in hours), and the price (in *yuan*) for all major Chinese cities serviced by trains from Shanghai. Shanghai Main Train Station is indicated by "S," and Shanghai West Train Station is indicated by "W." Prices listed range from the cheapest hard seat to the most expensive sleeper. For more information on train types and train travel, see **Trains**, p. 81. For a helpful guide to reading your train ticket, see the ticket reader in the **Appendix**, p. 756.

TO	站	PER DAY	HR.	PRICE	TO	站	PER DAY	HR.	PRICE
Beijing	S, W	3	14	86-321	Changsha	S	1	19½	86-288
Chengdu	S	2	35-40	124-492	Chongqing	S	1	45	155-494
Fuzhou	S	1	21	83-280	Guangzhou	S	2	21-23	116-284
Guilin	S	2	33	180-388	Hangzhou	S	16	3-4	72
Hefei	S	3	10-11	38-165	Hong Kong	S	1	27½	127-420
Huangshan	S	1	12	51-177	Kunming	S	2	47-57	158-584
Nanjing	S, W	39	3-5½	18-111	Qingdao	S	1	18½	81-303
Suzhou	S	35	1½-2	45	Tianjin	S, W	7	17-18	79-294
Ürümqi	S	1	64	219-721	Wuhan	S	1	20	86-288
Xiamen	S	1	24½	98-326	Xian	S	2	21-23	88-343

BY BUS

Buses head to destinations along the east coast and beyond. However, this may not be the best way to travel because of the region's overly congested roads. There are two main long-distance bus stations, as well as several smaller ones spread throughout the city. Booths at the airport and main train station also handle departures for some destinations within the area. **North District Bus Station** (běi qū kèyùn zhàn; 北区客运站), 80 Gongxing Lu (☎6324 6464), at the intersection with Shijiang Lu, handles buses to Jiangsu, Zhejiang, Anhui, Fujian,

Hunan, Shandong, and Hubei provinces. **South District Bus Station** (nán qū kèyùn zhàn; 南区客运站), Longhua Xi Lu and Zhongshan Nan Er Lu, near the Shanghai Stadium Metro, and **Tianmu Dong Lu Bus Station** (tiānmù dōng lù kèyùn zhàn; 天目东路客运站), 100 Tianmu Dong Lu, serve similar destinations. **Shanghai Public Transportation Long-distance Bus Station**, 1015 Zhongshan Bei Lu (☎5653 8064), at Gonghexin Lu, serves Jiangsu, Zhejiang, and Anhui provinces. The **Shijiang Lu Bus Station** (shījiāng lù qìchē zhàn; 虬江路汽车站), 865 Shijiang Lu (☎5663 0230), also has buses to these provinces.

BY BOAT

The **Shiliupu Passenger Terminal** (shíliùpù kèyùn zhàn; 十六铺客运站), 111 Zhongshan Dong Er Lu, is a 10-minute walk south of the Diamond Restaurant. (☎6326 1261. Open daily 7am-11:30pm.) Bus #64 from the main train station terminates just south of here. Boats depart to: **Nanjing** (8½hr., 1 per day, Y30-200); **Wuhan** (33hr., 1 per day, Y60-300); **Chongqing** (60½hr., 1 per day, Y200-900); and other ports of call along the Yangzi River, as well as some closer destinations. Slow boats to **Putuoshan** depart daily at 6pm (13hr., Y40-300).

Boats going to **Dalian, Fuzhou, Guangzhou,** and **Qingdao** dock at the **Gongping Lu Passenger Terminal** (gōngpíng lù kèyùn zhàn; 公平路客运站), 50 Gongping Lu (☎6326 1261), a bit south of Daming Dong Lu. Bus #37 from Nanjing Lu stops nearby. The **International Passenger Terminal** (guójì kèyùn zhàn; 国际客运站), 1 Waihongqiao Lu, is not far beyond the point where Suzhou Creek empties into the Huangpu River. The **Passage Booking Office of the Port of Shanghai** (shànghǎi gǎng chuánpiào chù; 上海港船票处), 1 Jinling Dong Lu, just across the street from the main CITS office, sells tickets to boats sailing to **Hong Kong** as well as **Osaka** and **Yokohama, Japan.** (☎6323 8750. Open daily 7-11:30am and 12:30-5pm.)

■ ORIENTATION

Shanghai occupies the south portion of the Yangzi delta, bordered by the East China Sea to the east, Jiangsu province to the northwest, and Zhejiang province to the southwest. Although Shanghai Municipality is vast—almost 6000km² —most of Shanghai's sights and residents are found in the much smaller district known as Shanghai proper or **Central Shanghai.** In Central Shanghai, the Bund (wàitān; 外滩), a 1.5km waterfront promenade, runs parallel to **Zhongshan Dong Lu** (中山东路) and intersects **Nanjing Lu** (南京路) in front of the Peace Hotel. A veritable circus of shops, fast food restaurants, offices, and pedestrians, Nanjing Lu runs west for 6km before arriving at **Shanghai Centre** (shànghǎi shāngchǎng; 上海商场), the home of upscale shops and expats.

The former French Concession, anchored by **Huaihai Zhong Lu** (淮海中路) and lined with several Metro stops, runs west from the Bund and boasts trendy shops and clubs. Zhongshan Lu circles much of Central Shanghai, changing names as it slips across the river into the Special Economic Zone of **Pudong** (浦东). The **Old Chinese City**, circled by **Renmin Lu** (人民路) and **Zhonghua Lu** (中华路), is home to the Yuyuan Garden and Bazaar. Traveling in this area is best done on foot; the narrow, winding streets can confuse even the most navigationally gifted.

Western Shanghai contains considerably fewer places of interest to the average tourist; if, however, the stadium complex and surrounding industrial areas inspire particular curiosity, the first Metro line has several stops in the area. North of Suzhou Creek and beyond Hongkou Park, the surroundings become more industrial, much like the area around the main train station. Fudan University at **Wujiaochang** (五角场) is a good place to find cheap food and drinks. Chinese maps (Y3-8) are widely available; bilingual maps (Y6-15) can be bought from Tourist Information Centers, Foreign Language Bookstores, and many street vendors.

🖅 GETTING AROUND SHANGHAI

Although Shanghai Municipality spans a large area, the main tourist sights are clustered in Central Shanghai and are easily accessible by public transportation. Bilingual bus route maps are practically nonexistent. The situation with Chinese maps is slightly better, but most bus stops are not clearly indicated.

BY BUS. Using Shanghai's buses is a lot like programming a VCR: it's useful and something you'll probably have to try eventually, but damned if you actually understand what you're doing. It's impossible to find a bilingual bus map, and the buses only occasionally have English announcements, so unless you have a very good idea of where you're going and can read Chinese, riding the city buses can be a harrowing experience. Bus numbers are numbered according to the times at which they operate. Buses **#1-200** run from about 5am to 11pm, buses in the **200s** supplement peak hours, while buses in the **300s** run between midnight and 4am. Shanghai buses are crowded, and in bad weather or traffic conditions they tend to lurch to sudden halts. On the plus side, the system is fairly comprehensive, with service reaching all corners of the city proper. The chart below details some of the most important buses.

   Fares are usually flat: Y1 if the bus is not air-conditioned and Y2 if it is (indicated by a snowflake beside the route number). Fares on double-decker buses heading to more distant corners of the city (such as #910 to Wujiaochang) depend on the destination (Y1-5). There will be one circulating fare collector who can provide change; try proffering anything higher than a Y10 bill, though, and you might not receive a warm reaction. Tickets are sometimes sold near the main bus stops, including the Xizang Lu stop at the southern side of Nanjing Lu (near the entrance to People's Square Metro) and outside the main train station.

   Faster and more comfortable **minibuses** also ply many of the same routes as the buses. To catch one, wait at the regular bus stop and shout out your destination as the unmarked minibus slowly cruises past (often with a tout hanging out an open door). Prices vary, but Y2 to 5 is reasonable.

BUS #	ROUTE DESCRIPTION	BUS #	ROUTE DESCRIPTION
18	Lu Xun Park-People's Square	20, 37	Nanjing Lu-People's Square
64	Shiliupu Passenger Terminal-Bund-Main Train Station	917	Nanjing Lu-People's Square-Shanghai Centre

BY METRO. The Shanghai Metro offers clean, speedy trains, but has only two lines that serve a limited part of the city. Work on the Metro continues at an impressive pace—a third line is under construction, with a total of 11 Metro lines planned for completion by 2020. All stations have manned ticket booths. It's also probably one of the few subways in the world with velvet cordons. Announcements and most signs are in both Chinese and English.

   Line #1 runs south from the main train station, underneath People's Square, and along Huaihai Zhong Lu before terminating in Xinzhuang (open 5am-11pm). Fare is Y3 for a single journey. **Line #2**, when completed, will run from Hongqiao Airport to Pudong Airport (open 7am-8pm). Currently, it only runs from Longyang Lu, in the south of the Pudong district, to Zhongshan Park, west of the French Concession. Fare on this line is Y5. Trains run less frequently, but since fewer people use this line, you'll probably have a luxurious green plastic bench on the train all to your lucky self. Fares are line specific: if you try to switch from line #1 to line #2 at the People's Square, you'll have to buy a new ticket.

BY FERRY. Ferries regularly make the four-minute trip across the Huangpu River to Pudong New Area, dodging the barges and tugboats that clog the waterways. The departure area below the Diamond Restaurant on Jinling Lu and Zhongshan Lu sells the plastic tokens needed to cross. Round-trip fare is Y0.8 and boats operate from about 5am to 11:30pm.

BY TAXI. Taxis are a convenient and generally hassle-free alternative to public transportation. Base fare is Y10, and each additional kilometer costs Y2 (Y3 after 10km). From 11pm to 5am, base fare is Y13. Major cab companies operating 24hr. include **Dazhong Taxi** (dàzhòng chūzǔ qìchē; 大众出租汽车), which has just introduced new, larger taxis; **Friendship Taxi Service** (yǒuyì qìchē; 友谊汽车; ☎6258 1688); **Shanghai Qiangsheng Taxi** (shànghǎi qiángshēng chūzǔ qìchē; 上海强生出租汽车; ☎6258 0000); and **Tourist Taxi** (lǚyóu qìchē; 旅游汽车; ☎6464 7777).

🛈 PRACTICAL INFORMATION

TOURIST AND FINANCIAL SERVICES

Tourist Offices: The handy **Hotline for Tourist Consultancy** (☎6252 0000) gives advice and information in Chinese, English, and Japanese. Open daily 8am-10pm. For those looking for a face-to-face encounter, there are information desks scattered around the city, offering maps, brochures, and other information in Chinese and English. **People's Square Tourist Information Center** (rénmín guǎngchǎng lǚyóu wènxún zhōngxīn; 人民广场旅游问询中心; ☎6438 1693) is just inside entrance #5 of the People's Square Metro stop. Open daily 9am-5pm. **Yuyuan Commercial Building Tourist Information Center** (yùyuán shāngshà lǚyóu wènxún zhōngxīn; 豫园商厦旅游问询中心; ☎6355 4909), in the Yayi Gold Store on Fuyou Lu. Open daily 8:30am-5pm.

Tours: Various guided tours can be booked through CITS and CTS. Options include visits to family apartments and local schools as well as to the main tourist attractions. For those who want transportation between sights with more flexibility, **Shanghai Tour Bus Lines** (☎6426 5555), based at Shanghai Stadium, has 12 lines that travel to sights within the city proper as well as the outer counties.

Travel Agencies: CITS, Guangming Bldg., 2 Jinling Dong Lu (☎6323 8749), near the Bund's southern end, a block south of Yanan Lu. Open daily 8:30-11:30am and 1-5pm. **CTS,** 881 Yanan Zhong Lu (☎6247 7888). Open daily 8:30-11:30am and 1:30-5pm.

Consulates: See **Essentials: Consular Services in China,** p. 48.

Bank of China: 23 Zhongshan Yi Lu (☎6329 1979), on the Bund. Exchanges traveler's checks. Open M-F 9am-noon and 1:30-4:30pm, Sa 9am-noon.

ATM: Citibank has two ATMs (Cirrus, Visa/Plus, Diner's Club) in Shanghai, one conveniently close to the Bund at 19 Zhongshan Yi Lu, and one across the river in Pudong, in the Marine Tower at 1 Pudong Dadao. Most banks and hotels now have ATMs (Cirrus and Visa/Plus). In a pinch, the Bank of China will give cash advances on credit cards; be sure to bring your passport.

American Express: Shanghai Centre, 1376 Nanjing Xi Lu, Ste. 206 (☎6279 8082), provides traveler's checks, card replacements, and mail holding. Open M-F 9am-5:30pm.

LOCAL SERVICES

Bookstores: Shanghai Foreign Language Bookstore (shànghǎi wài wén shūdiàn; 上海外文书店), 390 Fuzhou Lu (☎6322 3200, ext. 231), a block east of Fujian Lu. Temporarily at 440 Fuzhou Lu. A good selection of travel books, maps, and greeting cards, and a floor of imported books, from just-published novels to computer manuals to cookbooks. The 1st floor also has CDs, VCDs, and Chinese language texts. Expat magazines may have 10% discount coupons. Open daily 9am-6pm. **Shanghai Book City** (shànghǎi shūchéng; 上海书城) has several locations around town, including at 465 Fuzhou Lu (☎6352 2222). This 6-floor megastore has mostly Chinese books, and an impressive section of imports (mostly in English). Classics Y20, bodice-rippers and sci-fi Y12, decorating books as much as Y300. Open M-Th 9:30am-6:30pm, F-Su 9:30am-9pm.

Library: Shanghai Library (shànghǎi túshūguǎn; 上海图书馆), 1550 Huaihai Zhong Lu (☎6445 5555). Over 13 million volumes. For foreigners, a peek at just one of these books will cost a cool Y25. Most collections open daily 8:30am-5pm; some (including social sciences) open until 7pm. Internet access also available.

Ticket Agencies: Shanghai Centre Theatre Ticket Office (shànghǎi shāngchéng jùcháng shòupiào chù; 上海商城剧场售票处), Shanghai Centre, 1376 Nanjing Xi Lu (☎6279 8663), just to the right of the main entrance. Sells tickets for performances at Shanghai Centre, the Music Hall, and other venues. Open daily 9am-8pm. The **Shanghai Grand Theatre** has several reservation offices around town that sell tickets for events. Main office on the lower level of the theater itself, at 300 Renmin Dadao (☎6372 8701), on the edge of People's Square. Open daily 9am-7:30pm.

Market: Lianhua Supermarket (liánhuá chāoshì; 联华超市), with a location at the corner of Fuzhou Lu and Zhejiang Lu, has a decent selection of Western food, but is a little pricey. Open daily 8am-9pm. **Kedi** (可的), a 24hr. convenience store, has locations on many corners in Shanghai, including at the corner of Henan Zhong Lu and Ningbo Lu. Here you'll find the usual chips, dried noodles, and soda, as well as an assortment of toiletries and essentials like laundry detergent. The **market** at 589 Jiangning Lu, about 15min. from the Jade Buddha temple, has a fine selection of fruits, plants, and animals, both dead and alive.

Weather Conditions: ☎121.

EMERGENCY AND COMMUNICATIONS

Crisis Lines: Al-Anon (☎6295 9551) accepts calls and holds weekly meetings. **Alcoholics Anonymous** (☎6433 6880, ext. 2244; open M, W, F) gets referrals from the US Consulate.

Pharmacies: Pharmacies in Shanghai are easy to spot: each one has a sign outside with a green cross on it. **Shanghai No. 1 Dispensary Co.** (shànghǎishì dì yī yīyào shāngdiàn; 上海市第一医药商店), 616 Nanjing Dong Lu (☎6322 4567), several blocks east of Xizang Lu, near the intersection of Zhejiang Lu and Nanjing Dong Lu. Several floors of Western and Chinese medicines and 24hr. emergency service. Open daily 9am-10pm. **Watson's,** the Hong Kong pharmacy chain, is all around town, including on the 1st floor of Shanghai Centre and in Pudong Airport. Open daily 9am-10pm.

Hospitals: Huashan Hospital (huáshān yīyuàn; 华山医院), 12 Wulumuqi Zhong Lu, 19th Fl. (☎6248 9999, ext. 1921). **No. 9 People's Hospital** (dì jiǔ rénmín yīyuàn; 第九人民医院), 639 Zhizaoju Lu (☎6377 4831). Both have joint-venture foreign sections. **WorldLink Medical Centers,** Shanghai Centre, 1376 Nanjing Xi Lu, Ste. 203 (☎6279 7688), specializes in non-emergency expat medical care. Open M and Th 8am-9pm, Tu-W and F 8am-7pm, Sa 9am-4pm, Su 10am-4pm. Call for an appointment. **New Pioneer International Medical Centre,** Geru Building, 910 Hengshan Lu, 2nd Fl. (☎6407 3898), provides 24hr. medical and dental services.

Telephones: China Telecom, 30 Nanjing Dong Lu, just west of the Peace Hotel, a half-block from the Bund. Open 24hr.

Internet Access: Internet cafes come and go; ask around or check out one of Shanghai's expat journals and you might stumble upon a speedy, cheap connection. **China Telecom Building,** 1761 Sichuan Bei Lu, 4th Fl., 1 block from bus #21's Hengbang Lu stop. Y10 per hr. Open daily 8:30am-8:30pm. **Shanghai Library,** 1550 Huaihai Zhong Lu. Take the elevator to the lower level, and take the hallway to the right. Passport required. Y6 per hr. Open daily 9am-6pm.

Post Offices: The **main post office** is at 395 Sichuan Bei Lu, between Tiantong Lu and Bei Suzhou Lu, just north of Suzhou Creek. Western Union desk. International service, including EMS (☎6356 6666), open daily 9am-5pm. For Poste Restante, head to counter #17 on the Tiantong Lu side of the post office. Open daily 7:30am-7pm. For basic services such as posting letters, there is another post office next door on the 2nd floor of the Bei Suzhou Lu building. Open daily 7am-10pm. **DHL Worldwide Express** has several locations around town, including one at Shanghai Centre, 1376 Nanjing Xi Lu, B02 (☎6536 2900). Open M-Sa 8am-6pm. **Postal Code:** 200085.

▛ ACCOMMODATIONS

Shanghai is self-consciously upscale. Many of the accommodations in the city cater to business travelers or tour groups, and rates tend to be high, especially along Nanjing Lu and in other central locations. A number of small places around the train station offer cheap rooms but almost always refuse foreigners. The current wave of construction in Pudong and Hongqiao, both some distance from the city center, may cause a few budget places to spring out from the rubble. A 10% surcharge applies to everything but dorm beds.

Pujiang Hotel (pǔjiāng fàndiàn; 浦江饭店), 15 Huangpu Lu (☎6324 6388; fax 6324 3179), just across Suzhou Creek from the Bund. Bus #64 from the main train station stops at the corner of Beijing Dong Lu and Jiangxi Zhong Lu. Continue along Beijing Dong Lu until you reach the Bund, then take a left and cross Waibaidu Bridge. The hotel is on the 1st street to the right. The Pujiang's high ceilings and etched glass windows whisper tales of its grander days as one of the first and most luxurious Western hotels in China. Though it has traded wealthy Europeans for "budgetary knapsack guests," the Pujiang remains a clean, well-kept, and very convenient hotel. Lockers. Laundry (Y10 self-serve). Deposit Y100. Reservations may be accepted for dorms. 5- to 12-bed dorms (many with bath) Y55; doubles with bath Y300-330; quads Y300; quints Y350.

Shanghai Conservatory of Music Guest House (shànghǎi yīnyuè xuéyuàn wàibīn; 上海音乐学院外宾), 20 Fenyang Lu (☎/fax 6437 2577), south of Huaihai Zhong Lu, between Changshu Lu and Shaanxi Nan Lu. A 15min. walk from the Changshu Lu or Shaanxi Nan Lu Metros, or take bus #45 to Xiangyang Gongyuan. From the campus gates, take the 2nd left, walk through the basketball court-cum-parking lot, and turn left again; look for the off-white building (with an English sign) on the right. The campus is alive with the sound of music. Really. Doubles with A/C Y80-150, with bath Y200.

Love Inn (héjiā huān jiàrì bīnguǎn; 合家欢假日宾馆), 1555 Zhongxing Lu (☎5672 2998; email happy@bonline.sh.cn), less than 5min. from the north entrance of the main train station, or take the Xinchuan bus 1 stop from the main entrance of train station and look for the hotel on the left. A lovely oasis in the northern Shanghai desert of dirt and dereliction. The rooms are as clean, attractive, and loving as the staff. Bath and IDD/DDD phones in every room. Bonus: remote-controlled air-conditioning! Y50-90 discounts possible. Singles Y129; doubles Y189; triples Y159.

Shengxianju Hotel (shèngxiánjū bīnguǎn; 圣贤居宾馆), 1032 Zhongxing Lu (☎5662 5001, ext. 100). Take bus #928 or 929 from the train station to the next stop. Continue down the street; the hotel is less than a block away on the right. The Shengxianju has clean, decent-sized rooms in fairly good condition. If the monochromatic color scheme has you down, take heart: it's better than anything you'll find outside. Standard singles Y380; doubles Y248-298; triples Y328.

East Asia Hotel (dōng yà fàndiàn; 东亚饭店), 680 Nanjing Dong Lu (☎6322 3223), a half-block from Zhejiang Lu. Don't be puzzled if the building seems to be a shopping mall—the elevators are on the right, and the reception is on the 2nd floor. The hotel apparently relies more on its fine location and friendly staff to draw customers than it does on closet space and classy bathrooms. Enjoy your glorified bookshelf and orange hand towels and keep telling yourself, "location, location, location!" Try bargaining. Singles Y457; doubles Y400-457.

Wugong Hotel (wúgōng dàjiǔdiàn; 吴宫大酒店), 431 Fuzhou Lu (☎6326 0303), at Fujian Zhong Lu, about halfway between the Bund and People's Square. Martha Stewart may not approve of the varied floral decorations in the rooms, but she couldn't fault the cleanliness and comfort. The hotel also offers a full range of amenities, including a sauna and Seafood World. Doubles Y280-500. Credit cards accepted.

Shizeyuan Hotel (shīzéyuán bīnguǎn; 师泽园宾馆), 999 Changyang Lu (☎6546 6008 ext. 102). Take bus #934 from People's Square to Huaide Lu. Decent rooms but a distant location. The signs may say no smoking in bed, but the round holes in the bedspread seem to say otherwise. Doubles Y200-330; triples Y380.

Pacific Hotel (jīn mén dàjiǔdiàn; 金门大酒店), 108 Nanjing Xi Lu (☎6327 6226), a block west of Xizang Lu. Guests at the Pacific enjoy well-kept, wonderfully decorated rooms, a full range of amenities, English-speaking staff, and very large closets. Doubles Y406-580 and up. Credit cards accepted.

Far East Ever Bright City Hotel (yuǎn dōng bú yè chéng dàjiǔdiàn; 远东不夜城 大酒店), 600 Hengfeng Lu (☎6317 8900), just south of the main train station, near Tianmu Xi Lu. Although this hotel offers an impressive range of facilities (including a bowling room and salon), the standard rooms are quite ordinary, with not a lot of space. Singles Y400; doubles Y300-400; triples Y300. Credit cards accepted.

Zhongya Hotel (zhōngyà fàndiàn; 中亚饭店), 330 Meiyuan Lu (☎6354 7804), near the main train station, at Tianmu Xi Lu. The Zhongya justifies its prices by offering tidy rooms with A/C, cable, IDD, and bath, as well as access to a salon, a night club, and a billiards room. Singles Y260-480; doubles Y260-500. Credit cards accepted.

YMCA Hotel (qīngnián huì bīnguǎn; 青年会宾馆), 123 Xizang Nan Lu (☎6326 1040; www.ymcahotel.com), between Jinling Lu and Yanan Lu. The dorms are spotless and have new furnishings, attached baths, and lockers; bunk beds lend a nice summer camp feel. The bathroom floors practically glitter. 4-bed dorms US$15; singles US$85. Credit cards accepted.

Yangzi Hotel (yángzǐ fàndiàn; 扬子饭店), 740 Hankou Lu (☎6351 7880; www.e-yangtze.com). Though they're close to People's Square and boast bathroom phones, the rooms here are not quite good enough for the price. The dental clinic right off the lobby could be a godsend for those worried about those pearly whites. 30% discount for Internet bookings. Singles Y360-450; doubles Y520-680; triples Y620-780.

Ruijin Guest House (ruìjīn bīnguǎn; 瑞金宾馆), 118 Ruijin 2 Lu (☎6472 5222, ext. 1000; www.shedi.net.cn/OUTEDI/Ruijin), south of Fuxing Lu in the former French Concession. If Huaihai Lu didn't quite convince you of Shanghai's colonial past, come here. Beautifully furnished rooms and sumptuous gardens await guests, but the colonial air is costly. Singles Y400; doubles Y650 and up. Credit cards accepted.

Honggang Hotel (hónggǎng dàjiǔdiàn; 虹港大酒店), 2550 Hongqiao Lu (☎6268 1019). Next to the domestic arrivals area at Hongqiao Airport (p. 277); head left past the taxi stand. Not so great for a honeymoon, but it is the place for those stuck on layovers. Singles Y300-360; doubles Y480-580. Credit cards accepted.

🍴 FOOD

It's almost possible to forget that you're in China when eating in Shanghai. The culinary options in this city tend toward the bland and uniform. Just kidding—this is Shanghai, after all.

Fast-food places (like McDonald's and Kentucky Fried Chicken) and Western-style restaurants abound, especially in the French Concession, the favorite haunt of expats. A Häagen-Dazs store tempts the chocolate lover, while the new Starbucks already serves hundreds of half-crazed caffeine addicts each day.

Though it may be nice to have a taste of home once in a while, travelers truly miss out if they don't sample the many kinds of Chinese regional cuisine around town. A walk down any side street or alleyway in Shanghai will find a number of street vendors selling noodles, steamed buns, or fried dumplings. A glance down any lane in the Old Chinese City, especially near Yuyuan Garden, will often reveal an open-air market offering cooked foods as well as the raw (and often still moving) materials from which they're made.

Shanghai also boasts several streets devoted entirely to food. **Zhapu Lu Food Street,** north of Suzhou Creek and just east of Sichuan Bei Lu, entices hungry souls with an explosion of neon lighting and a number of sit-down establishments. English language menus may be scarce, but rest assured that most owners will be happy to point out local favorites. Servings are large—a lone diner need not order more than two dishes to return home with a full stomach and a happy heart.

The easiest way to sample Shanghainese specialties is to go for a stroll along the Bund or near the Old Chinese City. The snack-like creations along the **Bund** involve no guesswork or menu interpretation—what you see is what you get. Most items are, just like all good snack food, on sticks; meat on a stick, corn on a stick, melon on a stick, ice cream on a stick, and all for Y1-3. In the Old Chinese City area, the Yuyuan Bazaar and surrounding neighborhoods are a diner's paradise. Small shops sells dumplings, steamed buns, and more for Y1-2. Outside the boundaries of the Yuyuan Bazaar area, not too far from People's Square, is **Yunnan Lu Food Street** (yúnnán lù měishíjiē; 云南路美食街), several blocks of pure, unadulterated food. Stretching from Yanan Dong Lu to Jinling Dong Lu, this area's restaurants stay open until nearly midnight. **Huanghe Lu** to the west has many restaurants offering Shanghainese fare. **Xizang Nan Lu,** off Yanan Dong Lu, is another good spot for gluttons. There is also, of course, Chinese fast food, like that found on **Shashi Food Street** (shāshì shíjiē; 沙市食街), which runs south from Jiujiang Lu.

Huaihai Zhong Lu cuts through the heart of the French Concession, where a mixture of trendy restaurants and hole-in-the-wall places attracts both Chinese locals and expats. Of particular note is **Yandang Lu,** running south of Huaihai Lu a block west of Chengdu Lu. Revelers can amble through the pedestrian-only zone and enjoy more *al fresco* dining than is available anywhere else in Shanghai.

NANJING LU AND ENVIRONS

Near People's Square, **Nanjing Lu** is crowded with fast food restaurants. **Huanghe Lu** (黄河路), between Nanjing Lu and Beijing Lu, north of People's Park, is also lined with restaurants. **Shanghai Centre,** farther along Nanjing Xi Lu, boasts several well-known Western imports in addition to smaller places serving typical Chinese fare.

Gongdelin Vegetarian Restaurant (gōngdélín sùshí chù; 功得林素食处), 445 Nanjing Xi Lu (☎6327 0218). Vegetarian dishes in the grand old Buddhist tradition. Most entrees (including "saute shaped hair vegetable ball") Y15-45. Yum. Open daily 6:30-9:30am, 11am-2pm, and 5-10pm.

Always Cafe (àowéisī; 奥微斯), 1528 Nanjing Xi Lu (☎6247 8333), a block west of the Shanghai Kerry Centre. Everything from Asian, Mexican, and French standards (Y50-80) to the "Good Old Bangers and Mash" (Y38). Set lunch includes an entree and free tea or coffee (daily 11:30am-5pm, Y20). Happy Hour 5-8pm (jug of beer Y80) and creatively named Lady's Drinks (try "Pussy Foot") average Y40. Open daily 11am-3:30am.

Sumo Sushi (yuánlù shòusī; 缘禄寿司), Lane 668, Huaihai Zhong Lu (☎5306 9136), opposite Sinan Lu. Sure, it's a chain restaurant, but the many branches do have their purpose: to serve up a Y58 all-you-can-eat sushi buffet (daily 11am-4pm and 9-11:30pm). This sashimi and nigiri paradise also has set lunches (Y28) and dinners (Y38) with sushi, tempura, salad, and drink. Open daily 11am-11:30pm.

Hard Rock Cafe, 1376 Nanjing Xi Lu, Shanghai Centre, Ste. 110 (☎6279 8133). Eating here is just like eating at the Hard Rock Cafe in London! Or Sydney! Or...Houston! Makes that soda worth the Y20, doesn't it? Burgers and other entrees Y65-85 and up. Drink prices subject to change after 10:30pm. Filipino band M-Sa beginning at 8pm. Open Su-Th 11:30am-2am, F-Sa 11:30am-3am; dining hours end at 10:30pm.

OLD CHINESE CITY AREA

▩ **Changan Dumpling Restaurant** (chángān jiǎozi guǎn; 长安饺子馆), 2-8 Yunnan Nan Lu (☎6328 5156), at Yanan Lu. Some 108 (hey, it's a lucky Buddhist number, after all) varieties of dumplings mean that any meal here is bound to be an adventure. Huge set meals on the first floor for 2-10 people (Y20 and up), with more stylish dining on the 2nd floor. 1st Fl. open daily 6am-2am; 2nd Fl. 11am-2pm and 5-9pm.

Old City God's Temple Mid-Lake Pavilion Tea Shop (shànghǎi lǎochéng húxīntíng chálóu; 上海老城湖心亭茶楼), 257 Yuyuan Lu (☎6373 6950), just outside the entrance to Yuyuan Garden. The most famous tea shop in town plays host both to world leaders paying tribute and to lazy tourists looking to enjoy extended teatime (one pot Y10-15). Lower level open daily 5:30am-noon and 1-6pm; upper level open daily 8:30am-6:30pm; nightly show until 9:30pm.

FRENCH CONCESSION

Gino Cafe (jìnuò yìdàlì xiūxián cāntīng; 季诺意大利休闲餐厅), 918 Huaihai Zhong Lu (☎6415 5245), in the Parkson Shopping Center, at Shaanxi Nan Lu. A casual atmosphere, excellent Italian food (starter salads and minestrone both Y15), and Coke floats make this place a worthwhile stop. Branches in Xujiahui and at 66 Nanjing Lu, 2nd Fl. Open daily 9am-11pm. Credit cards accepted.

Badlands (bǎilán; 百岚), 897 Julu Lu (☎6466 7788, ext. 8003), near Changshu Lu, about 10min. north of Huaihai Zhong Lu. Tex-Mex food (Y65 set meals), though quite good, appears to be only a secondary concern here. Look out back at the "Belgian Beer Garden" or check out the "Nutty Irish Man" (Y50) to discover this establishment's true passion. Y10 tacos on Tu, 2 tequila shots for Y30 on F. Open daily noon-1am.

The Gap Cafe (jǐntíng; 锦亭), 127 Maoming Nan Lu, 3rd fl. (☎6433 9028), a bit north of Huaihai Zhong Lu. A little slice of "Chuppie" (Chinese yuppie) heaven, strange phone booths and all. Most full meals here are expensive, but soups and cold appetizers are only about Y30. Order ahead for that Double Boiled Superior Shark's Fin with Yannan Ham (Y2800). Open daily 12:30-11:30pm.

Shenji Soup Restaurant (shěnjì tāng; 沈记汤), 41 Sinian Lu (☎5306 5777), at the corner of Fuxing Lu. You may not find your mother's chicken noodle soup here, but you're bound to find something good. Many dishes less than Y20; more exotic soups are far more expensive. Open daily 10am-2pm and 5-10pm. Credit cards accepted.

🎵 ENTERTAINMENT

Shanghai Acrobatic Theatre (shànghǎi shāngchéng jùyuàn; 上海商城剧院), 1376 Nanjing Xi Lu (☎6279 8606), in the Shanghai Centre Theatre. The current venue is relatively small, so even the cheapest seats provide a decent view. The theater showcases tons of tour groups, including teeterboard, various comic acts, and a funky surprise or two thrown in just for excitement. Performances are almost every night at 7:30pm. Box office open daily 9am-5pm if no show, 9am-7:45pm otherwise. Tickets Y30-60.

Shanghai Concert Hall (shànghǎi yīnyuè tīng; 上海音乐厅), 523 Yanan Dong Lu (☎6386 9153), near Xizang Lu. Primarily hosts classical music performances by local groups, but sometimes sees visiting orchestras or ensembles. Tickets generally sold at the Shanghai Centre Box Office (see **Ticket Agencies**, p. 284).

Yifu Theatre (yìfú wǔ tái; 逸夫舞台), 701 Fuzhou Lu (☎6351 4668), near People's Square. For those who've been craving the sweet sounds of Chinese opera, the Yifu shows traditional Beijing opera on Saturday nights and Sunday afternoons. Tickets available at the box office outside.

Majestic Theatre (měiqí dà xìyuàn; 美琪大戏院), 66 Jiangning Lu (☎6217 4409). Shanghai's oldest theater shows a variety of programs, including ballet and opera. Tickets available at Shanghai Centre (see p. 284).

Shanghai Grand Theatre (shànghǎi dà jùyuàn; 上海大剧院), 300 Renmin Dadao (☎6386 8686), on the edge of People's Square. Almost a sight in and of itself, this massive theater shows everything from Irish dancing to Russian ballet. Tickets available from the 1st floor box office and other locations around town.

⊠ NIGHTLIFE

Bars and clubs in Shanghai seem to disappear at precisely the moment they hit the peak of popularity. The intrepid party-goer is more than likely to find something of interest on Julu Lu, Maoming Nan Lu, or Huaihai Lu, all easily accessible from the Shaanxi Nan Lu Metro stop on line #1. **New York, New York** is a thing of the past, and new spots are popping up all over. *Shanghai Talk, That's Shanghai*, and the Shanghai edition of *Metrozine* are English-language monthlies with extensive listings of activities and establishments in addition to feature articles. Free copies are available at many hotels and at hangouts like the Hard Rock Cafe (see p. 287).

⊠**Time Passage** (zuótiān jīntiān míngtiān; 昨天今天明天), 1038 Huashan Lu, #183 (☎6240 2588). Lane 1038 is between Fuxing Lu and Xinguo Lu. Walk down the lane—the bar is a half-block away on the right. A warm, inviting interior combined with cheap food, drinks, and friendly locals who will just as soon offer you some ribs as they will a cigarette. Be prepared for large-scale singalongs and games of Indian poker. Drinks and shots Y25 and up, soups and sandwiches Y20. Hot chocolate to warm your soul Y15. Open Su-Th 11:30am-midnight, F-Sa 11:30am-2am.

Manhattan Bar, 905 Julu Lu (☎6427 7787), just east of Changshu Lu. Either people go here by habit or someone has convinced them that self-conscious trendiness can overcome stuffiness. Crowded, if not terribly interesting. Beer Y30-55, shots Y40, cocktails Y45. Open daily 8pm-late.

Tequila Mama (bāhāmá cūnzhuāng; 巴哈马村庄), 24A Ruijin Er Lu (☎6433 5086), half a block from Huaihai Zhong Lu. Don't be fooled by the game room and the loud music—most people come here to drink, not to dance. After a few of the margaritas (Y30), you too may find yourself striking a pose with this mainly international crowd. "Blow jobs" (the drink) optional (Y25). Cover Y30, foreign students (or those who look like they could be) free. Open daily until 1am.

Cotton Club, 1428 Huaihai Zhong Lu (☎6437 7110), at Fuxing Lu. This could be the perfect jazz bar. The lights are dim, the tables intimate, the drinks cheap, and the music sublime. Unfortunately, the mainly expat, middle-age, male crowd who flirts outrageously with the much younger local women tends to break the spell. Cocktails Y45, beer Y40, shots Y35; minimum tab Y25. Live music Su-Th 9pm-midnight, F-Sa 9:30pm-1:30am. Open daily 7pm-3am.

Shanghai Sally's, 4 Xiangshan Lu (☎5382 9551), a few blocks south of Huaihai Zhong Lu, at Sinan Lu. Don't be fooled by this lady's reserved exterior. Sure, the top floor may offer patrons the chance to sip a beer (Y35) in a pub-like setting, but don't miss the live music in the basement and the charmingly obscene graffiti on the walls. Happy Hour daily 6-8pm (buy 1 drink, get 1 free).

Babylon, 180 Maoming Nan Lu (☎6445 2330), just south of Huaihai Lu. Follow the insistent bass to the newest club in Shanghai. It remains to be seen whether or not it can sustain its mad popularity. Drinks about Y40, but you can get giddy on the crazed dancing alone. No cover—yet. Open W-Sa 8:30pm on, Su 4:30pm on.

Judy's Too, 176 Maoming Nan Lu (☎6473 1417). A ridiculously popular place, owing in part to the owner's reputation for throwing slightly scandalous parties for a mainly expat crowd. The scantily clad beauties grinding by the mirrors would probably agree. Reasonably priced drinks (beer Y35), if you can find your way through the maddening crowds to the bar. Ladies drink free on W. Open daily 5:30pm-2am.

Raise the Red Lantern (dà hóng dēnglóng; 大红灯笼), 5 Changshu Lu (☎6321 6888), just north of Julu Lu. Drink here and you can enjoy not only the lovely decor and pleasantly sedate atmosphere but also the super-fast Internet access. Go ahead and email that witty remark you've been saving to the girl or guy across the bar. You know you want to. Imperial concubine chicken Y28, drinks Y30 and up (20min. free computer access). Open daily 10am-5am.

SHANGHAI

O'Malley's Pub, 42 Taojiang Lu (☎ 6474 4533), between Hengshan Lu and Wulumuqi Lu. This would be the quintessential neighborhood bar–if it were in England. The mostly expat crowd seems to be having a good time, enjoying summertime patio seating and homestyle dishes like Cottage Pie (Y120) and Fish and Chips. Guinness flows freely–or, as freely as Guinness does flow (half-pint Y40, pint Y60). Happy Hour daily 6pm-2am. Open daily 11am-2am.

Peace Bar Jazz Band, 20 Nanjing Dong Lu (☎ 6321 6888), in the lobby of the Peace Hotel. If you'd like to listen to old jazz favorites with a bunch of other tourists who've been tricked into paying the Y50 cover, go ahead. This is an institution, after all. Two geriatric bands belt out tunes that haven't changed much since the 1930s–sit back and listen to "When the Saints Go Marching In," or request your favorite off the song list (Y30). Bar open daily 10am-2am; band performs nightly 8pm-1:30am.

📷 SIGHTS

Shanghai's main sights are architectural, from traces of the city's international settlements to modern wonders; plenty of religious sites, museums, and lively neighborhoods are thrown in for good measure. Within various quarters of the city, walking is often preferable to using the overcrowded public buses.

THE BUND AND PUDONG NEW AREA

THE BUND (wàitān; 外滩). This stately waterfront embankment stretches 1.5km along Zhongshan Dong Lu, all the way from Waibaidu Bridge to Jinling Lu. Tracing the path of the Huangpu River, the raised walkway passes some of Shanghai's oldest reminders of foreign influence. Back in Shanghai's heyday of international trade (after the Treaty of Nanjing effectively rendered the city a commercial colony of Britain, France, the United States, and later, Japan), the Bund was lined with European banks and trade houses. Today, many of these relics of economic imperialism still stand, treating passersby to a glimpse of colonial architecture.

At one end of the Bund, just north of Waibaidu Bridge, the towering and oddly shaped **Shanghai Mansions** (shànghǎi dàshà; 上海大厦), at various times the military headquarters for both Japan and the US, have been converted into a hotel. The looming and triangular **Monument to the People's Heroes** (shànghǎi shì rénmín yīngxióng jìniàn tǎ; 上海市人民英雄纪念塔) stands at the corner of Suzhou Creek and the Huangpu River, surrounded by various depictions of the glorious masses. The 1993 inscription on the tower pays tribute to the great people who, since 1840, have sacrificed their lives to the Socialist cause.

At the base of the tower lies the entrance to the **Bund History Museum** (wàitān lìshǐ jìniànguǎn; 外滩历史纪念馆), a good stop for an overview of Bund history, including an extensive collection of photographs of the Bund. Detailed captions chronicle events such as the opening of Shanghai as a treaty port, the introduction of gas lighting, and the upheaval of the 1920s and 30s, before moving on to more recent changes. *(Open daily 9am-4:15pm; last admission 4pm. Free.)* Just beyond the museum, **Huangpu Park** (huángpǔ gōngyuán; 黄浦公园) was the first park opened after the Opium War. It was then known as the British Public Gardens and closed to both dogs and Chinese. In 1928, the park was truly opened to the public, and it has since become a popular place to practice tai chi, talk on cell phones, and swat away the ravenous bugs. *(At the corner of Zhongshan Dong Lu and Beijing Dong Lu. Open daily May-Oct. 6am-10pm; Nov.-Apr. 6am-7pm.)*

The promenade along the Huangpu River is a prime spot for people-watching. A climb to the platform of the **Bund Observatory** (wàitān tiānwéntái; 外滩天文台) yields a panoramic view of the surrounding area. The building also houses the **Bund History Exhibition** (wàitān shǐchén lièshì; 外滩史陈列室), a small collection of documents and photographs from Shanghai's earlier days. *(1A Zhongshan Dong Er Lu. Open daily 9am-11:30pm. Y10, incuding the viewing platform and 5 postcards.)*

On the other side of Zhongshan Dong Lu are 52 buildings that represent various architectural styles. Among them are the former **English Consulate** (yuán yīngguó lǐngshìguǎn; 原英国领事馆) at 33 Zhongshan Dong Lu, the **City Government Building** (shìfǔ dàlóu; 市府大楼), and the **Customs House** (hǎiguān dàlóu; 海关大楼) at 13 Zhongshan Dong Lu, all of which date from the 1910s and 20s.

Frequent **boat tours** depart from a Bund-side dock. They provide an excellent means of escape from the Shanghai traffic, and the longer rides go all the way to the mouth of the Yangzi River. *(229 Zhongshan Dong Er Lu. Buy tickets along the Bund, just north of the Diamond Restaurant. Shorter tours (6 per day 9:15am-8pm, Y25-30) last 1hr. Longer tours (2-3hr., Y45-100) leave mainly in the afternoon.)*

ORIENTAL PEARL TV TOWER (dōngfāng míngzhū diànshì tái; 东方明珠电视台). Restaurants, KTV parlors, and several observation decks grace the 468m tower, the tallest in Asia. If the sky is overcast, however, be content with viewing it from the other side of the river—the admission fee is almost as high as the tower. *(On the Pudong side of the Huangpu. Buy tickets also along the Bund, north of the Diamond Restaurant. Y50-100, depending on how high you go. Ferry ride across the river free when you buy a ticket. From the ferry terminal in Pudong, continue straight for about 10min. Open daily 8:30am-10pm.)*

OLD CHINESE CITY

Seven main gates mark the boundaries of the Old Chinese City, in Shanghai's Southern City district. Narrow streets and labyrinthine alleyways make a trip to this area enjoyable only on foot. This part of Shanghai is still as densely populated as it once was, but it has lost its reputation as the dirtiest, dankest part of town. The **Yuyuan Bazaar** itself has both upscale stores and lone street vendors—chances are that they're both selling the same overpriced souvenirs or not-so-gold jewelry.

YUYUAN GARDEN (yùyuán; 豫园). The Garden is an oasis of greenery and relative calm amid the carnival atmosphere of the adjoining **Yuyuan Bazaar** (yùyuán shāngshà; 豫园商厦). Built between 1559 and 1577 by wealthy Ming dynasty officials, the gardens suffered during the Opium War and the Taiping Rebellion, but were eventually rebuilt in the traditional style. Contemplate the Tower of Happiness or the Hall of Observing Quietness as you make your way through well-preserved traditional Chinese buildings and assorted antique and art stalls. If serenity isn't your thing, no need to worry: the garden is also great for hide and seek. Outside, shops sell a variety of traditional products and refreshments to ensure that the many visitors leave with their hands and stomachs full. *(218 Anren Lu, in the northeast part of the district, bounded by Fuyou Lu. Open daily 8:30am-5pm. Y25, children Y10.)*

NANJING LU AND ENVIRONS

NANJING LU (nánjīng lù; 南京路). Shanghai's answer to Hong Kong's Golden Mile (p. 429) stretches across six upscale kilometers, from the Bund to Jingan Temple just beyond Shanghai Centre. The glamorous setting of the historic **Peace Hotel** (hépíng fàndiàn; 和平饭店), the road receives thousands of tourists and locals parading past every day. On Saturday afternoons the street is closed to all vehicles; even then, the sidewalks sometimes seem too narrow for the crowds, and the flow of people spills onto the street.

Back in 1850, this area formed the heart of the English Concession, and it was not shopping but horseracing that caught people's fancy. These days, **Shanghai No. 1 Department Store** (shànghǎi dì yī bǎihuò shāngdiàn; 上海第一百货商店) anchors the corner of Xizang Lu, and numerous other upscale establishments wait nearby. Just a few blocks south on Xizang Lu, **People's Square** (rénmín guǎngchǎng; 人民广场), the former site of the Shanghai Racecourse, invites tourists, locals, and groups of kite-wielding children to enjoy its greenery and fountains.

North of People's Square and People's Park, Nanjing Lu winds westward to the **Shanghai Centre** (shànghǎi shāngchéng; 上海商城). **Jingan Temple** (jìngān sì;

静安寺), the "Temple of Peace and Quiet," marks the official end of this raucous road and the beginning of industrial Shanghai. The temple is worth a peek, but not the Y5 admission. *(1686 Nanjing Xi Lu, at Wanhangdu Lu. Open daily 7:30am-4:45pm.)*

SHANGHAI MUSEUM (shànghǎi bówùguǎn; 上海博物馆). This modern building houses an impressive collection of ancient Chinese bronzes, ceramics, and calligraphy, as well as exhibits on jade, the artwork of ethnic minorities, and more. The exhibits are so extensive that they can become overwhelming, but those who take their time luxuriating in the air-conditioned bliss will find the trip rewarding. *(201 Renmin Dadao, in People's Square. ☎ 6372 3500. Open Su-F 9am-5pm, Sa 9am-8pm. Y20, students with ISIC Y5; free for students Sa 5-8pm.)*

SHANGHAI ART MUSEUM (shànghǎi měishù guǎn; 上海美术馆). Collections of modern art are normally interesting; this museum's collection, which features works by Shanghai artists, is no exception. The artwork ranges from mildly fascinating to utterly breathtaking, and the museum's newly renovated home only adds to the enjoyment anyone—art connoisseur or not—can take. *(325 Nanjing Xi Lu, just west of People's Square. Open daily 9am-5pm; last admission 4pm. Y20, students Y10.)*

EXHIBITION FOR ANCIENT CHINESE SEX CULTURE (huáxià wénhuà fāzhǎn gōngsī xìng bówùguǎn; 华夏文化发展公司性博物馆). If erotic pottery and wood carvings of rutting animals do it for you, then by all means see this frighteningly extensive collection of art, literature, furniture, and other sex-related paraphernalia. There are signs around, but come on, we all know that no one reads the explanations. *(479 Nanjing Dong Lu, 8th Fl., down the alley next to the Hotel Sofitel. ☎ 6351 4381. Open daily 10am-9pm; last admission 8pm. Y30.)*

FORMER FRENCH CONCESSION

The glitzy boutiques that line Huaihai Zhong Lu may lure masses of salivating shoppers each day, but much of the area's historical significance and atmosphere is best absorbed on side streets a few blocks away from the glitter. Once the haunt of gangsters and revolutionaries, the area now conveys a more proper image, particularly in the foreign diplomatic area west of Changshou Lu.

FORMER RESIDENCE OF ZHOU ENLAI (zhōu gōng guǎn; 周公馆). This building served both as the well-loved CCP premier's living quarters and as a meeting place for early Communist revolutionaries. As a residence, it's delightful, with a lovely interior and pleasant gardens. As a museum, it's a bit uninteresting. Free tours are in Chinese only. *(73 Sinan Lu, south of Fuxing Lu. Open W-Su 9-11:30am and 2:15-5pm; last admission 30min. before closing. Y2.)*

FORMER RESIDENCE OF DR. SUN YAT-SEN (sǔn zhōngshān gù jū; 孙中山故居). GMD founder Sun Yat-sen (see p. 15) lived here for six years, beginning in 1918; after Sun's death, his wife Song Qingling remained here until 1937. The two floors of the eerily well-preserved house contain many old portraits, a study with brushes and ink wells, as well as guest rooms frequented by visiting dignitaries. *(7 Xiangshan Lu, off Sinan Lu between Nanchang Lu and Fuxing Lu. Open daily 9am-4:30pm. Y8.)*

FORMER RESIDENCE OF SONG QINGLING (sòng qìnglíng gù jū; 宋庆龄故居). Sun's widow spent much of her time here in the years following 1948. A limo presented to her by Stalin and a painting by Chinese artist Xu Beihong are among the items on display. Don't miss the museum—it's one of the more interesting historical exhibits in town, with letters from Mme. Song to Stalin, Mao Zedong, and other less notorious figures. *(1843 Huaihai Lu, between Yuqing Lu and Wanping Lu. Take bus #920 from Xizang Lu to Wukang. Open daily 9-11am and 1-4:30pm. Y8, students Y6.)*

FIRST NATIONAL CONGRESS OF THE CHINESE COMMUNIST PARTY (zhōng gòng yīdà huìzhǐ jìniànguǎn; 中共一大会址纪念馆). On July 23, 1921, 11 representatives, including Mao Zedong and Chen Duxiu, initiated secret proceedings to found the CCP—secret, that is, until they were discovered by French police who forced the delegates to flee to a boat on South Lake in Zhejiang province. The building opened as a museum in 1952. *(76 Xingye Lu, at Huangpi Nan Lu. ☎6326 0664. Open daily 8:15-11am and 2-4pm, closed M and Th mornings. Y3.)*

FUXING PARK (fùxìng gōngyuán; 复兴公园). For a respite from sights of ponderous political and historical import, follow Huangpi Nan Lu to Fuxing Lu and take a right to head west toward **Fuxing Park,** a large park with shaded tables good for a leisurely cup of afternoon tea. Rent a fishing pole from a stand by the pond (Y0.8 per hr.) and spend a few hours mastering the art of fishing with a really long pole. *(316 Fuxing Lu. Open daily 6am-6pm. Y2.)*

WESTERN SHANGHAI

There are fewer obvious tourist attractions in this area of Shanghai than there are elsewhere in the city, and distances between them are comparatively greater. **Xujiahui Cathedral** (xújiāhuì tiānzhǔtàng; 徐家汇天主堂), 158 Puxi Lu (easily accessible from Xujiahui Metro, exit #3), was built in 1906. Daily mass begins at 6:15am, with several services open to all worshipers. The large **Shanghai Stadium** (shànghǎi tǐyùguǎn; 上海体育馆), at Tiyuguan Metro (one stop beyond Xujiahui), is part of a sports complex that includes a natatorium (yes, a natatorium), playing fields, and other training facilities. There is also a water park and go-kart racing, but it's more expensive and probably less fun than a pick-up game of basketball on one of the many outdoor courts.

LONGHUA MARTYRS' MAUSOLEUM (lónghuá lièshì língyuán; 龙华烈士陵园). The gardens here are lush and verdant, a soothing counterpoint to the industrial grime of the surrounding area. The prospect of lingering and enjoying the scenery amid the tombstones lying about, though, becomes slightly less appealing. An eternal flame in honor of those who died supporting the Communist cause burns in front of a giant sculpture emerging from the hillside. *(Open daily 6:30am-5pm; last admission 4:30pm. Y1.)* The **Longhua Martyrs' Museum** (lónghuá lièshì jìniànguǎn; 龙华烈士纪念馆) features exhibit after patriotic exhibit about the lives and achievements of those who supported the state against Imperialists and Nationalists. *(2887 Longhua Lu. Open daily 9am-4pm; last admission 3:30pm. Y5.)*

The Longhua complex continues on grounds close to the main building. The halls of the illustrious **Longhua Temple** (lónghuá sì; 龙华寺) are alive with the smell of incense and the occasional clanging of the large bell near the entrance—ring it yourself (Y10) and eliminate all worries. *(Temple open daily 7am-4:30pm. Vegetarian restaurant open daily 11am-2pm and 5-8pm. Y5.)* Across the street stands **Longhua Pagoda** (lónghuá tǎ; 龙华塔), a seven-story octagonal tower.

AROUND SUZHOU CREEK

HONGKOU PARK (hóngkǒu gōngyuán; 虹口公园). Hongkou Park, also known as **Lu Xun Park** (lǔ xùn gōngyuán; 鲁迅公园), is a pleasant place to spend an hour or two. Bridges and covered pathways wind past a tea house, and the **Tomb of Lu Xun** (lǔ xùn mù; 鲁迅墓) is open to visitors as well. *(Open daily 9am-5pm; last admission 4pm. Y5.)* Though the first floor is entirely in Chinese, the second floor offers signs in English, and provides a comprehensive overview of the life of the influential satirist and left-wing political activist (see **Modern Literature,** p. 36) who passed away here on October 19, 1936. *(2288 Sichuan Bei Lu, bordered by Dalian Lu on the north and Jiangbei Dong Lu on the west. Take bus #18 from People's Square. Open daily 6am-9pm. Y1.)*

OHEL MOISHE SYNAGOGUE (móxī huìtáng; 摩西会堂). Much of the area north of Suzhou Creek is part of Shanghai's International Settlement. Ohel Moishe Synagogue was a center for life in the "Designated Area for Stateless Refugees" during the 1930s and 40s. The museum features a few small exhibits, but its true

SHANGHAI

treasure is its curator, Mr. Wang. He is happy to share his near-encyclopedic knowledge and his poignant personal recollections of the area's history. *(62 Changyang Lu, 3rd Fl. ☎6512 1934. Open daily 9am-4pm. Y30.)*

JADE BUDDHA TEMPLE (yù fó sì; 玉佛寺). **Jade Buddha Temple** is renowned for a 2m tall white jade Buddha brought to China by a Burmese monk in 1822. The statue would not be around, however, were it not for a cunning abbot and a frighteningly strict law. During the Cultural Revolution, the abbot of the Jade Buddha Temple thought to close the gates and plaster them with pictures of Chairman Mao. As tearing down pictures of Mao was an offense punishable by death, the Red Guards were unable to enter and the temple was saved. The temple is far away, but if you're only going to see one Buddhist temple in Shanghai, this is the one to see. *(170 Anyuan Lu west of Jiangning Lu. Take bus #506 one stop from the train station. Open daily 7am-2pm and 4:30-9pm. Vegetarian restaurant open daily 11am-2pm and 4:30-7pm. Y10, additional Y5 to see the Jade Buddha himself.)*

❀ FESTIVALS

A number of smaller festivals take place throughout the year, and outdoor events are the norm during the summer. Ring in the **New Year** (literally) at Longhua Temple in southwestern Shanghai. Festivities begin on December 31 and last two days. Beverage connoisseurs, take heart: the **Shanghai International Tea Festival,** hosted by Zhabei district, features exotic and traditional blends of tea (begins on the last Saturday in April). Yandang Lu hosts the annual **international food festival** around the last weekend of June. For Y100 the curious can enter and eat. Those wishing to celebrate what is considered by some to be the second national drink of China should head to the **Shanghai Beer Festival.** The summertime revelry takes place at a designated city park beginning on the last Friday in July. For a tantalizing array of fresh seafood, the week-long **Shanghai Seafood Festival** in Xuhui district is the place to be (late Sept.-early Oct.). In the first week of November, the city gears up for the **Shanghai Tourism Festival.**

🚌 DAYTRIPS FROM SHANGHAI

The counties and districts that surround Central Shanghai are connected to the city proper by bus and minibus service; People's Square is a terminus for a number of these buses. Even the farthest townships are generally no more than 75km from the city center. The outlying areas themselves are a mixed bag; recently constructed amusement parks seem a bit out of place next to expanses of farmland and historical sites.

NANHUI COUNTY 南汇县

Southeast of the city center. A special tour bus departs from Shanghai's Shiliupu Passenger Terminal to Luchao Port. During the Peach Blossom Festival, buses (daily 7 and 7:30am) go from People's Square to Nanhui.

Nanhui County, in the southeastern part of the municipality, is part of the Pudong Area on the eastern bank of the Huangpu River. The northern part of the county is served by the outer ring road linking the two airports, and Luchao is an important port in the south.

Known locally as the "Land of Peach Blossoms," Nanhui boasts over 333 hectares of orchards that dress up in bold pastels at harvest time. In the spring, the area comes alive with the scent of ripening peaches; the **Peach Blossom Festival** runs from late March to early April. At the Peachland Folk Custom Village and the Fairy Land of Peaches in Shenxi, actors play out scenes of daily life past and present. **Luchao Port** (lúcháo gǎng; 芦潮港), on the northern coast of Hangzhou Bay, features a natural harbor and several miles of beach-bedecked coastline.

JIADING DISTRICT 嘉定区

In northwestern Shanghai, linked to the city center by the Shanghai-Jiading Freeway.
Buses *(M-F 6am-6pm, Sa-Su 6am-10pm) go to Jiading from Weihai Lu at Huangpi Lu,*
Yanan Lu at Weihai Lu, and Hengfeng Lu near the Shanghai Train Station. Buses (daily
*5am-8pm, Y6) to **Nanxiang** leave from the Shanghai North Station on Zhongshan Bei Lu.*

Remnants of China's dynastic splendor are the main draw here, although the recently constructed Shanghai Global Paradise and American Dreamland Park come heavily touted as high-class vacation and entertainment spots. Jiading's **Nanxiang Town** (nánxiáng; 南翔) features a collection of pagodas and temples that please both history buffs and casual tourists. The **Confucius Temple** (kǒngmiào; 孔庙), at 183 Nan Dajie, was built in 1219 and today houses the **Jiading Museum** (jiādìng bówùguǎn; 嘉定博物馆). Those with a penchant for poetic names will enjoy a stroll through this place; even the memorial archways bear such names as "Cultivating the Talents" and "Encouraging the Virtuous." The 72 carved lions outside the temple represent the 72 highly respected disciples of Confucius. *(☎5953 0379. Open daily 8-11am and 1:30-4:30pm.)*

Just east of the temple, the **Dragon Meeting Pond** (huì lóng tán; 汇龙潭) morphs into "five dragons snatching at a pearl." Five small streams (the dragons) run into a pond out of which Yingkui Hill (the pearl) rises. Visitors with tired imaginations can enjoy the pleasant scenery at the **Garden of Autumn Clouds** (qiū xiá pǔ; 秋霞圃), which evokes the style of the Ming dynasty. *(3144 Dongda Lu. ☎5953 1949. Open daily 8am-5pm.)* The **Garden of Ancient Splendor** (gǔ yī yuán; 古猗园) spreads splendidly over the eastern part of town. *(2 Minghu Dong Lu. ☎5912 1335. Open daily 7:30am-5pm.)*

QINGPU COUNTY 青浦县

In western Shanghai Municipality, bordered by Songjiang County to the south and Jiading
District to the north. Huqingping Lu (State Hwy. 318), a continuation of Yanan Lu, is the
*main thoroughfare. The **Qiangsheng Sightseeing Bus** (1½hr., 4 per day, Y12) goes to*
*Grand View Garden from the intersection of Jinling Lu and Yandang Lu in Shanghai. **Mini-***
***buses** (Y6) travel to the surrounding area from the Qingpu county seat. **Buses** (approx.*
5am-8pm) go from Shanghai West Station on Wuzhong Lu to the Qingpu county seat.

Activities in Qingpu County blend the old with the new, in case you haven't done enough of that in China already. **Grand View Garden** (dà guān yuán; 大观园), on Dianshan Lake, 65km west of Shanghai, reproduces the gardens in the classic novel *Dream of Red Mansions* (see **Ancient and Premodern Literature**, p. 36). Visitors can discuss the significance of buildings that are "Fraught with Favor, Basking in Kindness" or simply take in the pleasant scenery. *(Open daily 8am-4:30pm.)*

The ancient town of **Zhujiajiao** (zhūjiājiǎo; 朱家角) and the **Setting Free Bridge** (fáng shēng qiáo; 放生桥) also draw numerous visitors. This bridge, the largest stone bridge in the municipality, was originally built to set captive fish free; nets were prohibited in the surrounding area. In the northeastern part of the county, within Qingpu Town, the **Garden of Meandering Stream** sits near the Daying River. Built in 1745, the garden wins points for its lotus pond. *(Open daily 8am-4:30pm.)*

SONGJIANG COUNTY 松江县

In southwestern Shanghai municipality. The Huhang Gaosu Lu, an expressway linking
Shanghai with Hangzhou, extends to Songjiang city. Direct buses to Songjiang leave from
Songshan Lu, just across from Wusheng Lu and People's Square, or from Shanghai Stadium
*(1hr., every 20min. 6am-8pm, Y5). Take a **sightseeing bus** from Shanghai Stadium to*
*Sheshan or a **minibus** (30min., Y3.5) from the Songjiang county seat to Qingpu. Get off when*
*you see the large sign that says **Sheshan Tourist District.***

Sheshan certainly merits a trip, and if you're out in Songjiang county, it makes sense to see the Songjiang county seat as well, though it is mainly a dull, industrial place. Songjiang's attractive cathedral, the **Holy Mother Cathedral on Sheshan** (shéshān tiānzhǔ jiàotáng; 佘山天主教堂) was built in 1863 on top of a 100m hill. The slope leading up to the cathedral bears images of the 14 Stations

SHANGHAI

of the Cross, and the hillside fills with Christian pilgrims at festival times. *(Open daily until 3:30pm. Y2.)* The greenery of **Sheshan National Forest** soothes the soul, but bring a picnic, a book, and make a whole day of it to justify the steep admission. A cable car that runs up to the cathedral and the forest offers both spectacular views and heart-stopping experiences during brisk winds. *(Open daily 7:30am-4pm. Forest admission Y28, children Y22. Cable car Y15 round-trip to the cathedral, Y10 to the forest, Y20 combination cathedral and forest.)* **Sheshan Observatory,** next to the cathedral, records earthquakes and other natural phenomena. Pay a visit to the cathedral to count your blessings before receiving word about the latest natural disaster. *(Open daily 8am-4pm. Y6.)*

The Square Pagoda and Screen Wall stand inside **Square Pagoda Park** (fāngtǎ gōngyuán; 方塔公园), at 235 Zhongshan Zhong Lu, in the county seat. Take the bus that leaves from Zhongshan Zhong, by Renmin Lu across from the Industrial and Commercial Bank, to the fourth stop. The nine-story pagoda (Y5) has a history that spans over 900 years. For most people, climbing it is an enjoyable experience. For anyone over 6 ft. tall, though, it may turn into a perilous adventure. The large screen wall to the north was built in 1370 during the Ming. A huge, beastly animal called Tao is carved into the center of the wall; legend has it that the greedy animal swallowed all the treasures in the world but still craved the sun. The sun shone too high for Tao, so he fell into the sea and drowned. *(Open daily 7am-9pm.)*

The **Pond of the Drunken Bai** (zuì bái chí; 醉白池) is at 64 Renmin Nan Lu, in the county seat. Walk east from the bus station until you hit Renmin Bei Lu. Turn right and walk south for about 15 minutes, past the Drunken Bai Restaurant. The pond was originally the private residence of the famous Song painter Gu Dashen. Gu envied the relaxed lifestyle and enjoyed the work of Tang poet Bai Juyi so much that he designed a garden in honor of Bai. Empty and a little overgrown, the gardens are still a pleasant retreat. The abandoned children's amusement park is a bit scary, though; one expects an evil clown to emerge at any moment. *(☎5774 4559. Open daily 6:30am-4:30pm.)*

The **Songjiang Mosque** (sōngjiāng qīngzhēn sì; 松江清真寺), the oldest in the Shanghai area, was built in the mid-1300s. It is surrounded by houses and is difficult to find. From Zhongshan Zhong Lu, turn south onto Renmin Lu. Take the first right into an unmarked alley and continue straight until you find the mosque on your right. The entrance is around the corner. *(☎5781 1957. Open daily 8am-4pm.)*

JIANGSU 江苏

Hop a train cutting through Jiangsu province, which stretches along China's central-eastern coast, and your window becomes a lens onto the confrontation between ancient culture and modern industrial development that haunts most of China today. Throughout this "breadbasket" region, scattered among meandering rice paddies, fishing junks, and tiny cottages, smoke-belching, waste-puking factories push farmers away from their homelands—right toward the mouth of the beast, the region's already overstuffed cities.

The **Grand Canal,** that age-old trade route, traverses the province from north to south, but it has become outmoded in the face of modern, fast-paced transport. The canal epitomizes the region's current status, winding uselessly past the idyllic ancient city of Suzhou one day, then through sprawling modern ones like Wuxi the next: waiting, winding, wending onward through time toward Zhejiang province.

On the whole, though, things in Jiangsu aren't all bad. The region is spared the worst of the perennial flooding of the Yangzi, and the rich soil and temperate climate (apart from the sweltering summers) provide the area with abundant agricultural yields and the apt designation of "the land of fish and rice." Most of the industrial production is centered in Nanjing and Wuxi, which leaves many towns to reckon only with light industry and manufacturing. Indeed, while some of the cosmopolitan influence of Shanghai has spread to the southern cities (while the northern cities of Xuzhou and Lianyungang offer

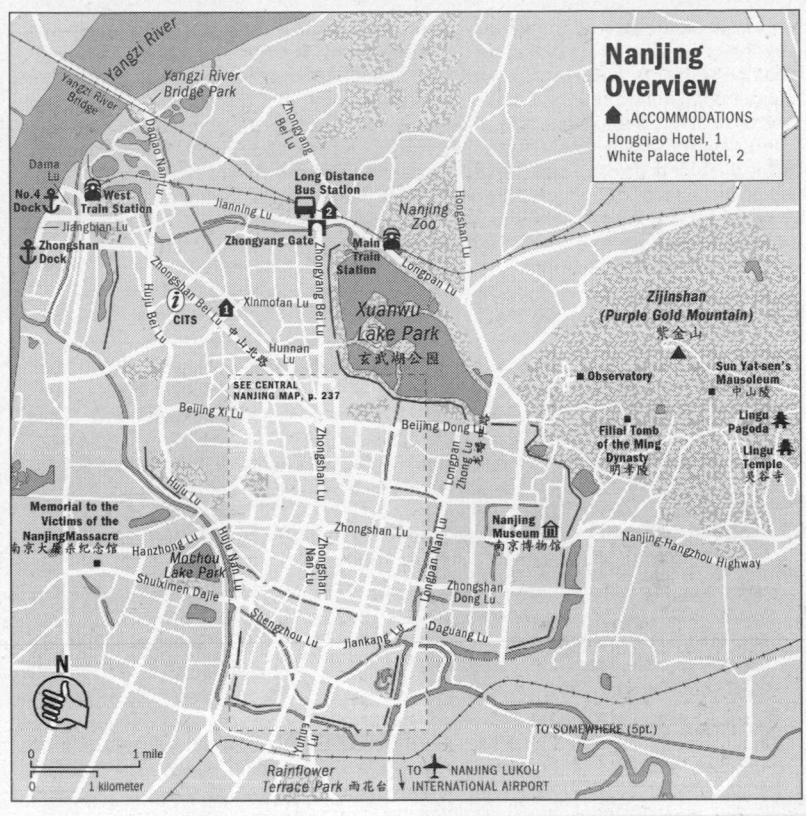

Nanjing Overview

⌂ ACCOMMODATIONS
Hongqiao Hotel, 1
White Palace Hotel, 2

considerably less altogether), a visit to Jiangsu province never fails to recall some of the good old days—or at least a slightly less hectic atmosphere in which to ponder histories lost.

NANJING 南京 ☎025

Legend has it that an ancient Chinese poet recorded his impressions of Nanjing (formerly Jinling, or "golden hills") with this verse: "Oh, what a beautiful place, ye Jinling! Deservedly the home for many a king." Nanjing ("southern capital") was the first city south of the Yangzi River to serve as the imperial seat of a united China; it served as the capital of the Ming dynasty for over 50 years. In the early half of the 20th century, it also acted as the capital for a frequently fragmented China, under Sun Yat-sen's brief government in 1912 and later during the Guomindang rule (1928-49). All told, Nanjing has served as the capital of 10 governments, and each one has left its mark on what is now the seat of Jiangsu province. Nanjing's historical sights and monuments illustrate how the history of one decade (the Nanjing Massacre of 1937-38) can change so drastically the events of another (the achievements of the Ming era). While Nanjing's history is continually in flux, it is never entirely lost: most of the 33km city wall, built between 1366 and 1386, still stands, and the larger-than-life Sun Yat-sen Mausoleum illustrates the ongoing reverence for past figures, ideas, and ways of life.

A booming economy has transformed Nanjing into a modern city that serves, with the completion of a double-decker bridge spanning the Yangzi River, as a gateway to the rest of China. Although it is not the historical fortress of Beijing or the scenic delight of Hangzhou, Nanjing exemplifies the evolution of a growing city (thin coat of dust included). While luxurious five-star hotels and decadent restaurants catering to pampered tourists and the business elite have sprung up around the city, Nanjing remains above all a city for the people who live in it; its lakes, parks, and museums are more local haunts than national tourist bureau treasures. City life in Nanjing is not led in glossy high-rises or behind closed doors, but on the streets that provide its livelihood: stroll through the small alleys off Xinjiekou past people doing laundry on traditional wooden boards or families setting up tables in front of shops for a dinner of *baozi* or noodles. Above all, Nanjing is promisingly, unabashedly regular—a regular city for regular folk.

▟ TRANSPORTATION

Airplanes: Nanjing International Airport (nánjīng lùkǒu guójì jīchǎng; 南京禄口国际机场; ☎248 0488; arrivals information ☎248 0531), operates frequent flights to most destinations in China. International flights are currently slim to none, with regular flights available only to Southeast Asia. Shuttle buses (40min.-1hr., every 30 min. 6am-6pm, Y25) run between the **CAAC ticket office**, 52 Ruijin Lu (☎449 9378), and the airport. Buses also run between Xin Han Mansion (180 Hanzhong Lu) and the airport. A taxi to the city center costs Y120. To: **Beijing** (6-7 per day, Y810); **Guangzhou** (5-6 per day, Y940); **Hong Kong** (2 per day, Y1480); **Kunming** (2-3 per day, Y1400); **Tianjin** (Tu, Th-F, and Su; Y700); and **Wuhan** (2-3 per day, Y580).

Trains: Nanjing Train Station (nánjīng huǒchē zhàn; 南京火车站), 264 Longpan Lu (☎582 2222), at the terminus for buses #1, 13, 32, and 33. To: **Beijing** (12hr., 5 per day, Y157-276); **Chengdu** (40½hr.; 2 per day; Y247, A/C Y405); **Shanghai** (3-5hr., 22 per day, Y44-82); **Xian** (20hr.; 2 per day; Y164, A/C Y265). Nanjing West Train Station tickets are also sold here.

Buses: Zhongyang Gate Long-distance Bus Station (zhōngyāng mén chángtú qìchē zhàn; 中央门长途汽车站), 1 Jianning Lu (☎562 5389), a 10min. walk west of Nanjing Train Station. Accessible via buses #1, 13, 32, and 33. Open daily 5:30am-5:30pm. To: **Changsha** (24hr., 1pm, Y213); **Guangzhou** (48hr., 4:40pm, Y323); **Hefei** (2-3hr., every 20-30min. 6:30am-7:30pm, Y38-54); **Jiuhuashan** (4½hr., 9am and 2pm, Y57); **Nanchang** (10hr., 4 per day, Y126-163); and **Shanghai** (3½hr., every 30min. 1am-5pm, Y82-88). **Hanfu Jie Long-distance Bus Station** (hànfǔ jiē chángtú qìchē zhàn; 汉府街长途汽车站), 25 Daxing Gong (☎454 0786), east of Xinjiekou off Zhongshan Dong Lu. Take bus #5, 9, 25, or 29 to Zhong Gong. To: **Hangzhou** (5-6hr., 5 per day, Y71); **Shanghai** (3½hr., 10 per day, Y75-88); **Suzhou** (2½hr., 12 per day, Y44-64); **Wuhan** (15hr., 8 per day, Y130); and **Wuxi** (2hr., 12 per day, Y37-54).

Boats: No. 4 Dock (nánjīng sì hào mǎtóu; 南京四号码头; ☎880 5501), on Xiaguan Jiangbian Lu, near the intersection of Jiangbian Lu and Dama Lu. Take bus #10 to the Sihao Matou. Ticket window open daily 8am-5pm. Buy tickets 1 day before departure. This scenic route less taken offers trips to **Shanghai** (8:30 and 10:30 pm, Y48).

Local Transportation: An extensive **public bus** system extends as far out as tourist areas like Zijinshan and the Yangzi River Bridge. Although buses #9W, 11W, 13W, and several others run 5am-11pm, most routes start around 6:30am and stop running by 8 or 9pm. Fare generally Y1, with A/C Y2. The price is marked on the outside of the bus near the door—drop the exact fare in the box. Street signs often have pinyin. Useful routes include **#9, 16,** and **34** (all of which run along Zhongshan Lu) and **#1, 13,** and **32,** which run along Fuzimiao and other tourist attractions. **Minibuses** (Y1-4) follow popular bus routes. A **subway** is scheduled to be completed in 2005; it will run north to south through the city center, with 13 stops, including Xinjiekou, Gulou, and the train station.

Taxis: Base fare Y7, each additional km Y2.1-2.4. Xinjiekou to the main train and bus stations Y20-25, to the airport Y120.

S H A N G H A I

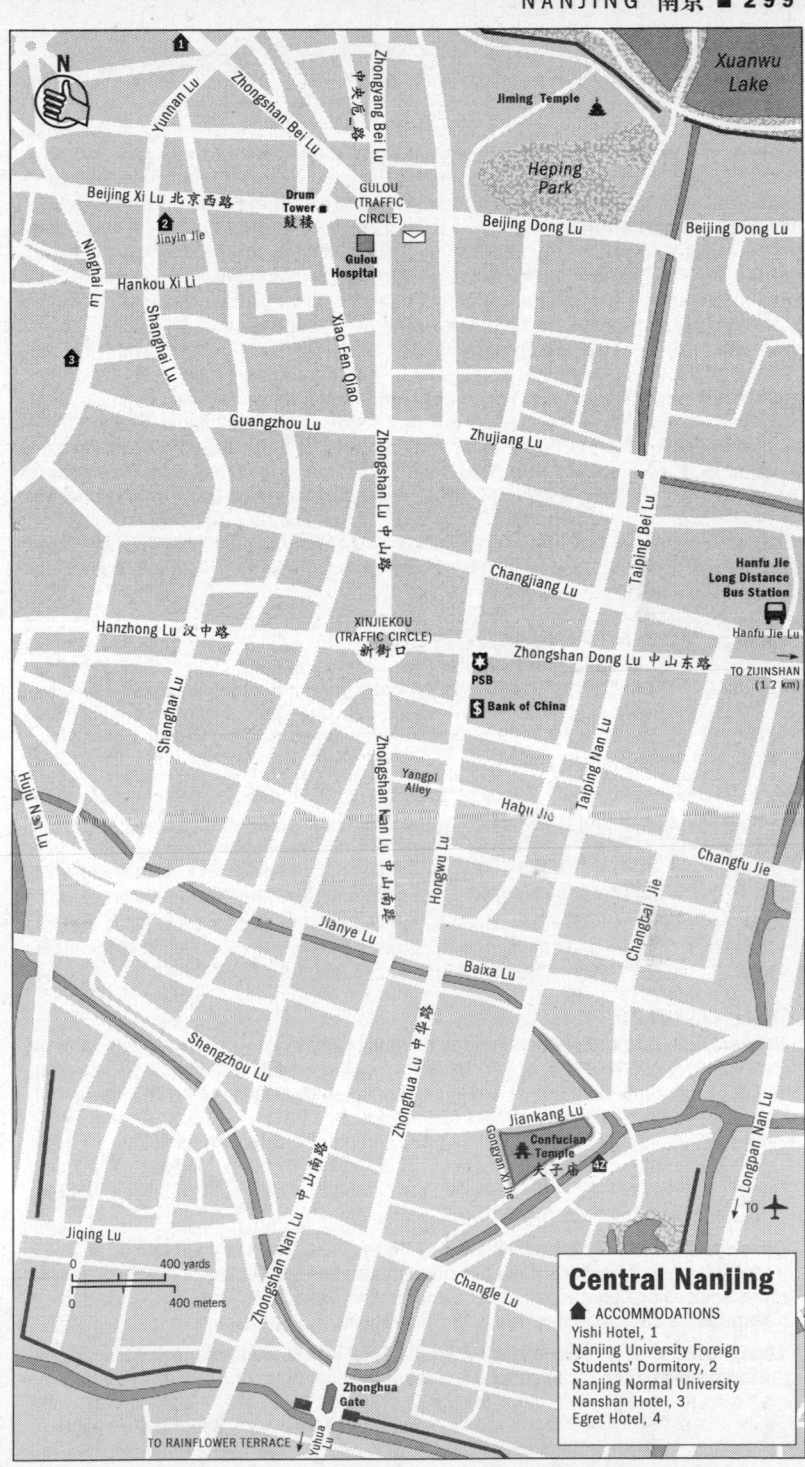

N

Xuanwu Lake

Yunan Lu

Zhongshan Bei Lu

Zhongyang Bei Lu 中央北一路

Jiming Temple

Heping Park

Beijing Xi Lu 北京西路

Drum Tower 鼓楼

GULOU (TRAFFIC CIRCLE)

Beijing Dong Lu

Beijing Dong Lu

Jinyin Jie

Ninghai Lu

Hankou Xi Li

Gulou Hospital

Shanghai Lu

Xiao Fen Qiao

Guangzhou Lu

Zhongshan Lu 中山路

Zhujiang Lu

Taiping Bei Lu

Hanfu Jie Long Distance Bus Station

Hanzhong Lu 汉中路

Changjiang Lu

Hanfu Jie Lu

Shanghai Lu

XINJIEKOU (TRAFFIC CIRCLE) 新街口

Zhongshan Nan Lu 中山南路

TO ZIJINSHAN (1.2 km)

Zhongshan Dong Lu 中山东路

PSB

Bank of China

Yangpi Alley

Hubu Jie

Taiping Nan Lu

Huju Nan Lu

Honghwu

Changbai Jie

Changfu Jie

Jianye Lu

Baixa Lu

Shengzhou Lu

Longpan Nan Lu

Jiankang Lu

Confucian Temple 夫子庙

Gongan Xi Jie

TO ✈

Jiqing Lu

Zhongshan Nan Lu 中山南路

Zhonghua Gate

Changle Lu

Yuhua

TO RAINFLOWER TERRACE ↓

0 — 400 yards
0 — 400 meters

Central Nanjing

🏠 ACCOMMODATIONS
Yishi Hotel, 1
Nanjing University Foreign
Students' Dormitory, 2
Nanjing Normal University
Nanshan Hotel, 3
Egret Hotel, 4

SHANGHAI

Bike Rental: Bike rental shops are few and far between, but explore the Nanjing University area for options. There is a bicycle rental stand on the corner of Taiping Bei Lu and Beijing Xi Lu (outside of Dongnan University). Y1 per hr. Open daily sunrise-sunset.

⚔ 🔂 ORIENTATION AND PRACTICAL INFORMATION

Nanjing's ten districts and five counties cover more than 6500km² on the south side of the **Yangzi River,** about 200km inland from Shanghai. The city is bounded on the east by **Zijinshan** (Purple Golden Mountain) and on the west by the river itself. Many of Nanjing's thriving commercial districts line the 10km stretch from Zhongyang Gate in the north to Zhonghua Gate in the south. Two large traffic circles are located at the heart of the city. The **Gulou** (鼓楼) traffic circle is at the intersection of **Zhongyang Bei Lu** (中央北路), **Zhongshan Bei Lu** (中山北路), **Beijing Dong Lu** (北京东路) and **Beijing Xi Lu** (北京西路). Zhongyang Bei Lu and Zhongshan Bei Lu continue south as **Zhongshan Lu** (中山路), and later as Zhongshan Nan Lu, on the south side of the **Xinjiekou** (新街口) traffic circle. This intersection lies approximately 2km south of Gulou, where Zhongshan Lu is met by **Hanzhong Lu** (汉中路) on the west and Zhongshan Dong Lu on the east. Other major streets in Nanjing include **Taiping Lu** (太平路), running roughly parallel to Zhongshan Lu, and **Jianning Lu/Longpan Lu.** The latter runs along the northern edge of the city, past the Nanjing Train Station and the Zhongyang Gate Bus Station and close to the West Train Station and the Yangzi River docks.

TOURIST AND FINANCIAL SERVICES

Tourist Office: Nanjing Municipal Tourism Bureau (nánjīng shì lǚyóuchù shìchǎng kāifāchù; 南京市旅游处市场开发处), 4 Nan Donggua Shi, 4th Fl. (☎336 2686; fax 771 1959). Take bus #13 or 65 north on Shanghai Lu 1 stop beyond the Foreign Students' Dormitory; Donggua Shi is the alley straight ahead, and the bureau is on the left. Open M-F 8am-noon and 2-6pm.

Travel Agencies: CITS, 202-1 Zhongshan Bei Lu (☎342 8999), near Xinmo Lu, north of the Hongqiao Hotel. Take bus #13 from the train station, or take #16, 26, or 34 heading northwest from Gulou for 5 stops and get off at the Nanjing Hotel stop. Average commission Y30. Open M-F 8:30am-5:30pm, Sa-Su 9am-4pm. **CTS,** 313 Zhongshan Bei Lu (☎343 1502). Average commission Y30. Open M-F 8am-5:30pm.

Bank of China: 29 Hongwu Lu. From the Xinjiekou traffic circle, walk 1 block east on Zhongshan Dong Lu and turn right on Hongwu Lu; the bank is on the left, 1 block down. ATMs (Cirrus, Visa, Plus). Open M-F 8:30am-noon and 2-5:30pm.

LOCAL SERVICES

Bookstores: Jiangsu Province Foreign Language Bookstore (jiāngsū shěng wài wén shūdiàn; 江苏省外文书店), 165 Zhongyang Lu (471 7422), At the corner of Hunan Lu and Zhongyang Lu, a 20min. walk from Gulou. Good selection of literary classics and more recent bestsellers at a fraction of the price. Open daily 9am-6pm. **Xinhua Bookstore,** 58 Zhongshan Dong Lu (☎664 5151), about 2 blocks east of Xinjiekou, on the right. Carries the mundane (Chinese and bilingual dictionaries) and the magnificent (English literary masterpieces), although the pickings are slimmer than those at the Foreign Language Bookstore. Open daily 8:30am-7pm.

Department Store: Xinjiekou Department Store (xīnjiēkǒu bǎihuò shāngdiàn; 新街口百货商店), 3 Zhongshan Nan Lu, is the grande dame of Nanjing department stores, with 8 imposing floors of just about every product imaginable. Open M-Th 9am-8pm, F 9am-9pm, Sa 8:45am-9pm, and Su 8:45am-8pm.

Supermarkets: SGCS (sūguǒ chāoshì; 苏果超市), with locations throughout the city, is a cornucopia of snackable goodies and ready-to-go dinners. One with a good selection is at 26 Hongwu Lu, one block east of Xinjiekou off Zhongshan Dong Lu, diagonally opposite the Bank of China building. Open daily 7am-10pm. **Zehong Supermarket**

(zéhóng chāoshì; 泽红超市), 67 Zhongshan Nan Lu, is reached by walking south along Zhongshan Nan Lu from Xinjiekou (the direction that the Sun Yat-sen statue faces) about 1 block past the Xinjiekou Department Store. Offers a good selection of Western and Chinese food as well as household items, basic medicines, and toiletries. Open 24hr.

EMERGENCY AND COMMUNICATIONS

PSB: 11 Hongwu Lu (☎442 0114), just south of the Xinjiekou traffic circle. The **Foreigners' Bureau** (chū rù jìng guǎnlǐ chù; 出入境管理处; ☎442 0004) has some English speakers on staff.

Pharmacies: Pharmacies are almost as easy to find in Nanjing as the ever present McDonalds and KFCs. **Baixin Pharmacy** has locations throughout the city (look for bright green and white signs), with everything from Tylenol to herbal elixirs. The Fuzimiao branch, 34 Gongyuan Xi Jie (☎662 3793), is open daily 8:30am-9pm.

Hospitals: Gulou Hospital (gǔlóu yīyuàn; 鼓楼医院), 321 Zhongshan Lu (☎330 4616). From Gulou traffic circle, walk a short distance down Zhongshan Lu; the hospital is on the right. Affiliated with Nanjing University Medical School, with English-speaking staff on call.

Internet Access: Lai Ba Cafe (láiba; 来吧;), is directly adjacent to the Nanjing University Foreign Students' Dormitory, at the corner of Jinyin Jie and Shanghai Lu. Y12 per hr., Y0.20 per min. Open daily 9am-1:30am. **Internet Impression** (yīngpàishēng wǎngluò; 英派升网络), 152 Shanghai Lu, on Shanghai Lu between Beijing Xi Lu and Hankou Xi Lu, with friendly English signs. Y8 per hr.; multiple-use cards offer substantial savings. The Internet club in the **Gulou China Telecom building,** 2 Zhongyang Bei Lu, 2nd Fl., offers fast connections at Y10 per hr. Open daily 8:30am-6pm.

Post Office: Nanjing Post Office, in the large high-rise building just south of Gulou traffic circle, at the corner of Beijing Dong Lu and Zhongshan Lu, with entrances on both sides. EMS and Poste Restante (send to the Gulou Post Office, 鼓楼邮局). Open daily 8am-6:30pm. **Postal code:** 210005 for regular mail, 210008 for Poste Restante.

Telephones: China Telecom, 2 Zhongyang Bei Lu, just off the Gulou traffic circle. To place IDD calls or send telegrams, look for the first counter on your right as you come in the main entrance (open M-F 8am-12:30pm and 1:30-10:30pm). A side office accessible via a separate entrance provides the same services from 11pm-8am daily.

▗ ACCOMMODATIONS

Aside from Nanjing's two university dormitories, most other establishments that accept foreign guests are expensive three-star hotels of variable quality. In many cases, if the room rates posted outside seem too good to be true, they are; chances are the place does not accept foreigners.

▨ **Nanjing University Foreign Students' Dormitory** (nánjīng dàxué xīyuàn; 南京大学西苑), 20 Jinyin Jie (☎359 3589), a block to the right (if you are coming from Gulou) of the intersection of Shanghai Lu and Beijing Xi Lu. Take bus #11W or 13W to Yunnan Lu. In a lively quarter, close to eateries and bars catering to foreign and Chinese students. While the mattresses aren't plush, the rooms and halls are clean and well kept. Dorms are no longer available. Deposit Y10. Doubles Y88, with bath Y140; triples Y120.

Nanjing Normal University Nanshan Hotel (nánjīng shīfàn dàxué nánshān jiā lóu; 南京师范大学南山家楼), 122 Ninghai Lu (☎371 6440, ext. 6060), off Ninghai Lu, about a block south of Hankou Xi Lu. Enter the campus through the main gate, continue straight until you reach the large flagpole, turn left and follow the blue signs around to the left. The hotel's campus location makes it a peaceful refuge from the traffic and noise elsewhere, although awakening to the shrilling arias coming from the nearby music students' building may not be terribly soothing. Summer 2000 renovations promise brighter and more spacious dorm rooms with A/C and the usual fixings. Internet access. Breakfast included with standard rooms. 2-bed dorms Y30; singles with bath Y100; doubles with bath Y170.

SHANGHAI

Yishi Hotel (jiāngsū yìshì yuán; 江苏议事园), 81 Zhongshan Bei Lu (☎332 6826; email YSHOTEL@Public1.ptt.js.cn), behind a yellow wall bordering Zhongshan Bei Lu and Yunnan Lu, off Sanxilu Square. One stop from Gulou on buses #16, 26, 31, and 34 northbound, or take bus #13 from the train and bus stations to Dafang Xiang. Built in traditional Chinese style, the Yishi's smaller size and attentive staff provide a welcome respite for those travelers who are tired of the usual high-rise hotel fare. Breakfast included. Currency exchange. Singles Y216; doubles Y260. Credit cards accepted.

Hongqiao Hotel (hóngqiáo fàndiàn; 虹桥饭店), 202 Zhongshan Bei Lu (☎340 0888), at Xinmo Lu. Take bus #13 or 32 from the train or bus stations to Hongqiao/Nanjing Binguan stop; the brightly lit English sign can be spotted from the intersection. Bright, and clean, this hotel sees more business deals struck over rounds of Tsingtao than the city's glossy skyscrapers do. Currency exchange. Doubles Y298. Credit cards accepted.

Egret Hotel, 68 Dashi Ba Lu (☎662 1999; fax 662 1895), off Gongyuan Jie in Fuzimiao. Overlooking the Qinghuai River, the Egret claims the same great location as its pricier neighbors. The newly renovated south building is chock-full of amenities, while the less expensive rooms in the north building show some wear and tear. Breakfast included. 40% discounts available for students. Singles Y231-354.

White Palace Hotel (bái gōng dàjiǔdiàn; 白宫大酒店), 2 Longpan Lu (☎550 9999, ext. 2200), opposite the Zhongyang Gate Long-distance Bus Station. Proximity to the train and bus station is its biggest draw; prices are as steep as some upmarket hotels of better quality. Doubles Y360. Credit cards accepted.

🍴 FOOD

According to a Chinese saying, Sichuanese food is like a hot woman, Beijing food a refined young lady, and South Yangzi food a humble farm girl. Nanjing's elaborate menu of age-old delicacies and mouth-watering *xiaochi*, however, is anything but plain, and opportunities to whet the appetite abound in small restaurants and family-run stalls that line city streets. The streets really reach their culinary apex at night, and an evening stroll can quickly become a scrumptious foodfest. The night market in **Xinjiekou**, on a small lane right behind the Xinjiekou Department Store off Zhongshan Nan Lu, specializes in grilled or fried Shanghai style chicken and beef (Y2) and smelly tofu (Y1), a delicacy whose potent odor earns it its name.

The stretch of **Ninghai Lu** between Hankou Lu and Beijing Xi Lu, near Nanjing Normal University, is crammed with street vendors serving everything from *baozi* (Y0.50-1) to salted duck's head (Y8). Carts carry Hong Kong style custard tarts, and vendors sell lychees and nectarines. This culinary main street turns into a night market after 5 pm, when locals buy fresh vegetables and fruits. To get there, take bus #11 or 13 to Yunnan Lu, walk on Shanghai Lu away from Beijing Xi Lu, and then take a right on Hankou Lu, the first large street that you come to.

Likewise, the area around Fuzimiao is teeming with vendors selling traditional Nanjing and South China favorites. Here you can sample the *bawei doufu nao* (八味豆腐脑; eight-flavored jellied bean curd pastries; 8 for Y2), or seek out even more flavors. The temple area can be reached by taking bus #1 east from Xinjiekou to the last stop, and then crossing the street toward the large gate.

🔲 **Jack's Place** (jiékè dìfāng; 杰克地方), 160-4 Shanghai Lu (☎361 5873), on the corner of Jinyin Jie and Shanghai Lu, opposite the Nanjing University Foreign Students' Dormitory. **Jack's Place II,** 195-4 Ninghai Lu (☎330 8737), opposite the main entrance of Nanjing Normal University; and **Jack's Place III,** 35 Wangfu Dajie, at Fengfu Lu. Bright red and yellow awnings and the chatter of students make this a cheery place to eat. Where else could you discuss American politics with a Brit in Chinese over french fries? Jack's french toast (Y6) gets rave reviews, as do many of the wide variety of Chinese and Western dishes, which range from chef's salad to Kungpao chicken. Lunchtime delivery. Book swap corner in Jack's Place II. All three open daily 9am-3am.

The Black Cat Café (hēimāo cānguǎn; 黑猫餐馆), 1 Cibei She (☎472 8973), on a small alley on the right of Hanzhong Lu as you head away from Xinjiekou, a block past the Jinling Hotel. A second restaurant on Hankou Lu, a 10min. walk from the main entrance to Nanjing University. Wood paneling and dim lighting combined with traditional window decorations and batik wall hangings provide an eclectic backdrop. Pizzas of both exotic and "just cheese" varieties (mini to 13 in., Y28-58) are excellent, and Black Cat's roast ribs are barbecued to perfection. Weekend pizza specials include medium 3-topping pizzas with free drinks (11am-2pm; Y48). Open daily 11am-11pm.

Swede and Kraut (yúnzhōngcān; 云中餐), 137 Ninghai Lu, 2nd Fl. (☎663 8020), about halfway between Beijing Dong Lu and Hankou Lu. Expensive pasta plates (Y40 and up) and submarine sandwiches (around Y20) earn high marks at this student-friendly restaurant owned by a German and a Swede, hence the English name. The Chinese name means "meal amidst the clouds." The connection? Damned if we know. Thursday pizza nights with individual pizzas and drinks (Y45). Open Tu-Su 5:30-10pm. Additional lunch hours Saturday 11:30am-1:30pm. Credit cards accepted. Hankering for salami on rye? **Skyways Bakery & Deli**, 3-6 Hankou Xi Lu (☎663 4834), is a newly opened Swede and Kraut venture that dishes up authentic German bread popular with students and locals alike. Open Tu-Su 5:30-10pm.

Wuzhou "Treehouse" Restaurant (wǔzhōu jiǔjiā; 五州酒家), 22 Xiaofenqiao (☎906 6066), off Guangzhou Lu near Zhongshan Lu, halfway between the Gulou and Xinjiekou traffic circles. Generous portions of Chinese dishes, English menus, and the occasional "ant crawling up a tree"—a platter, not a pest, Y8—make the "Treehouse" Restaurant popular with foreigners, even though it no longer has a tree sprouting through its roof. Open daily 11am-2pm and 4:30-10:30pm.

Maxiangxing Restaurant (qīngzhēn mǎxiángxìng càiguǎn; 清真马祥兴菜馆), 5 Zhongshan Bei Lu (☎330 5904), near Gulou Square. For a mouth-numbing experience, try a traditional favorite like *qingzhen lazi ji* (goldenrod spicy chicken, Y22), or splurge for one of Maxiangxing's famed crispy shrimp and fish dishes (Y85-112). Fast-food section open daily 6:30am-8pm. 2nd Fl. open daily 10:30am-1:30pm and 5-8pm.

Liu Feng Ju, 144 Gongyuan Jie (☎662 1593), in Fuzimiao. This cafeteria-style eatery has gained acclaim among locals for dishing up the best flat rice noodles, sticky rice meatballs, and beef kebabs this side of the Qinghuai River. Average meal Y20-30. Open daily 9am-9:30pm.

Tianming Tea House (tiānmíng chá lóu; 天明茶楼), 1 Dazhongting Lu (☎360 9578), in a small side street next to the China Telecom building opposite the Drum Tower. This teahouse serves up every mixture, variation, and concoction of tea imaginable in a traditional outdoor garden setting that is more *gu* than Gulou. Open daily 9am-1am.

🎵 ENTERTAINMENT

Nanjing's sizeable student population frequents a constantly changing nightclub and bar scene. New watering holes seem to open every few months, replacing those that have presumably lost their mojo. Because of this dizzying turnover rate, any news heard around the major universities is likely to be as reliable as what is below. The area near the Nanjing University Foreign Students' Dormitory offers options for casual drinks and fun: croon to karaoke favorites, do some jumpin' and jivin' to East-West hip-hop, or just do whatever your achy-breaky heart desires.

Blowing in the Wind (dáàn jiǔbā; 答案酒吧), 13 Jinyin Jie (☎323 2486), just down the street from the Nanjing University Foreign Students' Dormitory. The roomy atmosphere, painted walls, pictures of past shenanigans, and reasonable drink prices (Y10 and up) make this a lively hangout for students, foreigners, and jazz lovers alike. The owner, a bass guitar player, often joins in impromptu jam sessions, and monthly performances feature bands from around the city or student improvisations. Musical performances nightly at 9:30pm. Open daily 6pm-2am.

Italian Pizza Express Restaurant & Bar (yìdàlì bǐsà cāntīng; 意大利比萨餐厅), 19 Jinyin Jie (☎323 1353). Popular with students looking for late night snacks or weekend revelry, this dimly lit restaurant and upstairs bar feature communal red gingham covered tables and booths perfect for conversing, wining, and dining. Drinks Y10 and up. Big screen TV. Restaurant open daily 10:30am-midnight; bar open daily 8pm-5am.

Scarlet (luànshì jiārén yīnyuè xī cāntīng jiǔbā; 乱世佳人音乐西餐厅酒吧), 29 Chezhan Dong Xiang (☎335 1916), off the northwestern corner of Gulou behind Gulou Department Store. Party with the leather-clad, thong-strung, and tongue-pierced. A favorite with both locals and foreign students, who claim that, like the ultimate aphrodisiac, Scarlet leaves you begging for more. Drinks Y30 and up. Open daily 6:30pm-4am.

Danny's Irish Pub (dānní aiěrlán jiǔbā; 丹尼爱尔兰酒吧), Sheraton Kingsley Hotel, 169 Hanzhong Lu, 4th Fl. (☎666 8888, ext. 7776). Ritzy, kitschy, and over-the-top pricey, this pub is a hub for foreigners, ye of Irish blood or no, and anyone looking for a taste of Danny's authentic Irish brew. Drinks Y20 and up. Open daily 5pm-2am.

SIGHTS

Most of Nanjing's main attractions are scattered around the outskirts of the city. Places of reflection and remembrance, they are reminders of Nanjing's imperial, revolutionary, and war-torn past, as well as indications of its thriving future.

PURPLE GOLD MOUNTAIN

East of Nanjing. Take bus #9 from Xinjiekou to its last stop, Zhongshanling. The Argos bus company operates a bus route (#Y1) with stops just east of Gulou on Beijing Dong Lu, although it's a bit more difficult to flag this bus down. Bicycling is also a good option for those eager to avoid traffic and frequent stops; it's a 30-40min. ride from Xinjiekou. Bike storage available. A Zhongshan Fengjing sightseeing bus (with bright Fuji Film advertisements plastered on its sides) shuttles between the sights for Y1. Open daily sunrise-sunset. Admission free; separate admission to sights.

While neither purple nor gold, the lush, untarnished area that is Purple Gold Mountain (zǐ jīn shān; 紫金山) east of the city contains Nanjing's most renowned sights.

MAUSOLEUM OF DR. SUN YAT-SEN (zhōngshān líng; 中山陵). This grandiose mausoleum has become something of a pilgrimage site for the thousands of Chinese tourists who visit it each day. A plaque at the bottom of the 392-step memorial commemorates Sun Yat-sen's devotion to the revolutionary cause, and a small picture exhibit in the garden behind the mausoleum documents the building of the memorial (see **The Fall of the Qing & the 1911 Revolution,** p. 14). After the arduous climb to the top and a breathtaking view of Nanjing and its surrounding hills—most visitors will be convinced that the scale of this structure indeed does justice to Sun's memory. (☎444 5111. Open M-Sa 6am-6:30pm, Su 6am-7pm. Y25.)

LINGGU PARK (línggǔ gōngyuán; 灵谷公园). **Linggu Temple** (língǔ sì; 灵谷寺) Built in 514 and moved to its present site by Emperor Zhu Yuanzhang, this temple is smaller in scale than most temples, but makes up for its size with intricacy and numerous Buddhist relics. The **Beamless Hall** (wú liáng diàn; 无梁殿), the only remainder of the original structure, is constructed entirely of stone and brick, its arched ceiling supported only by paste and architectural ingenuity. **Linggu Pagoda** (línggǔ tǎ; 灵谷塔) commemorates the soldiers who fought in the revolution; a climb to the top offers a bird's-eye view of the park. (A 30min. walk or a 10min. ride east of Sun Yat-sen's Mausoleum. Open daily 6:30am-6:30pm. Park admission Y10; temple Y10.)

MING DYNASTY TOMB (míng xiào líng; 明孝陵). The Filial Tomb of the Ming Dynasty is the burial place of the first Ming emperor Zhu Yuanzhang, Empress Ma, and 46 sacrificed concubines. The **Sacred Avenue** (mínglíng shén dào; 明陵神道) leading to the tomb entrance is lined by six pairs of stone animals representing the leaders of the animal kingdom, and a nearby stone tablet features an inscription by Qing Emperor Kangxi himself. West of the tomb, and reached by the last stop on the sightseeing bus, a **chairlift** (Y35) goes to the top of the mountain. (Four stops from the mausoleum on the sightseeing bus. Open daily 6:30am-7pm. Y10.)

OTHER SIGHTS

GULOU SQUARE. (gǔlóu guǎngchǎng; 鼓楼广场). The heart of Nanjing before the city center shifted to Xinjiekou, the Gulou area remains the more aesthetically pleasing of the two traffic circles. The Drum Tower itself sits in the middle of a traffic island just west of the circle. Built in 1382, the drums were used to signal changes in the night watch. Today, you can climb to the second level to view the drums and enjoy refreshments in a tranquil tea house. (☎330 1101. Open daily 8am-midnight. Y4) A tea-and-snack package at **Gulou Tea House** (gǔlóu chá yì guǎn; open daily 8am-midnight) runs around Y24. Opposite the Drum Tower, on the other side of the traffic circle, **Gulou Park** (gǔlóu gōngyuán; 鼓楼公园) fills with families on Nanjing's balmy summer evenings, as adults read by small lamps and kids rush about waving neon armbands. *(On Zhongshan Lu, 2km north of Xinjiekou. Accessible via buses #1, 16, 26, and 34.)*

MEMORIAL TO THE VICTIMS OF THE NANJING MASSACRE (qìnhuá nánjīng dàtúshā yùnàn tóngbaō jìniànguǎn; 侵华南京大屠杀遇难同胞记念馆). This memorial is a somber and austere reminder of the hundreds of thousands of Nanjing residents terrorized and killed by Japanese troops in December 1937. Outdoor exhibits, an historical museum, and a building housing the remains of some of those killed are on display. The memorial sits on one of the former execution sites, a chilling homage to the victims of the massacre. English language audio tapes and documentary available. *(418 Shuiximen Dajie. Take bus #37 or 41 from Xinjiekou, 3 stops past Mochou Lake. ☎661 2230. Open daily 7:30am-5:30pm. Y10, Y8 students.)*

CONFUCIAN TEMPLE (fúzǐ miào; 夫子庙). Consisting of the entire area surrounding the site of an ancient temple built in AD 103, these northern shores of the Qinhua river where Confucian scholars once found inspiration are now where shoppers can find everything from parakeets to cheap clothing. The market is liveliest in the early evening, when lantern-lovers, dinner-goers, and die-hard shoppers all stroll along the lit banks of the river. *(Bus #1 heading east from Xinjiekou to the last stop stops directly opposite the main Fuzimiao gate. Open daily dawn-10pm.)*

ZHONGHUA GATE. (zhōnghuá mén; 中华门). The gate is one of the best preserved pieces of the old Nanjing city wall. It consists of four large archways, each with a double door and a 1000kg gate that used to shut automatically, trapping retreating enemy soldiers within the city. Luckily, it remains open today. It was built during the Yuan and Ming dynasties, between 1366 and 1386, and much of it has been restored to its original condition. The observation platform at the top provides the closest thing there is to a bird's eye view of Nanjing, and the bonsai garden in between the gates is worth a look, too. *(Bus #16 south along Zhonghua Lu to Zhonghua Men Nei (2nd to last stop). Open daily 8am-11pm. Y6.)*

NANJING MUSEUM (nánjīng bówùguǎn; 南京博物馆). The museum features a permanent exhibition on the "5000 Year Civilization of the Lower Reaches of the Yangzi River"—an ambitious choice of topic. Two rooms also house various short-term exhibitions. *(321 Zhongshan Dong Lu, just west of Zhongshan Gate. Take bus #9 east from Xinjiekou. Open daily 9-11:45am and 1:30-4:30pm; last admission 4pm. Y10, F-Sa Y5.)* The **Chaotian Palace** (cháotiān gōng; 朝天宫), a branch of the Nanjing Museum, has exhibits on coins, lanterns, drums, and other artifacts, all with English captions. *(Open daily 8:30-10:30am and 2-5pm. Y5.)*

PARKS AND VIEWS. Nanjing has its share of large parks offering recreational activities, scenic, and historical attractions. **Xuanwu Lake Park** (xuánwǔ hú gōngyuán; 玄武湖公园), at the Xuanwu Lake stop on buses #1, 3, 15, or 35, offers much to entertain kids and kids-at-heart, with a zoo, playgrounds, and plenty of space to roam around. Paddle boats are also available for a spin on the lake. *(Open daily 6pm-8pm. Y10.)*

SHANGHAI

Just beyond the Zhonghua Gate at the last stop on bus #16 from Gulou and Xinjiekou, Zhonghua Lu becomes Yuhua Lu as it leads to the entrance of the **Rainflower Terrace** (yǔhuā tái; 雨花台). A memorial to revolutionaries killed by Chiang Kai-shek in 1927, the gardens contain shaded pathways, rainflower pebble stands, and an elegant monument to the Revolutionary Martyrs. *(Open daily 6am-11pm. Y10.)*
Mochou Lake Park (mōchóu hú gōngyuán; 莫愁湖公园), in the triangle formed by Hanzhong Xi Lu, Shuximen Dajie, and Huju Lu (bus #13), is another park with a lake, a carousel, and local residents practicing *tai chi*. *(Open daily 6:30am-9pm. Y5.)*

Far from any of Nanjing's other tourist attractions is the **Yangzi River Bridge** (nánjīng chángjiāng dàqiáo gōngyuán; 南京长江大桥公园), off Daqiao Nan Lu (buses #12, 15, and 67 from Nanjing West Train Station). An elevator at the base of the bridge will take you straight to the top, where zooming cars and an expansive view of Nanjing awaits. *(Open daily 7:30am-11:30pm. Y5.)*

HUAIAN 淮安   ☎0517

North of Nanjing, the landscape changes from neat rows of industrial factories to sprawling flatlands, where the Grand Canal winds its way around largely unknown hamlets. Both the canal and State Highway 205 pass through the town of Huaian.

Huaian is a grab bag of neighborhoods. Donkey-led pushcarts clatter past old brick-and-mortar houses and imposing glass high-rises, and a frenzy of scooters and bicycles carry residents home for their daily afternoon siestas. This town thrives on its diversity; its remote location and barren exterior conceal the lively town center, where schoolchildren play hide-and-seek in the old city fort and shops sell framed pictures of hometown hero Zhou Enlai alongside carts piled high with *zhaicai* (a local lake-grown vegetable). With over 5000 years of history under its belt and a long list of locals who later graced the pages of China's history books, Huaian is an unexpected treasure trove of legends and stories, a living testament to its vibrant past. It is less a city of sights than one of atmosphere—it is practical, not glamorous, a city for those who enjoy the everyday.

◀▣ ORIENTATION AND PRACTICAL INFORMATION

Huaian is bounded on the east by the Grand Canal and on the west by **Huaijiang Gonglu** (淮江公路), which loops around the city. **Beimen Dajie** (北门大街) runs from north to south through the center of Huaian, parallel to Huaijiang Gonglu. Between the two lies the **Zhou Enlai Memorial Hall**, one of the city's main tourist draws. Perpendicular to both roads lie **Youyi Lu** (友谊路) and **Zhenhuailou Lu** (镇淮楼路). Huaian is small enough to navigate in half a day. Walking is a good bet, particularly since the number of bicycles, scooters, rickshaws, and carts crisscrossing each other makes bicycling or driving a rather hazardous affair.

Trains: Huaian Train Station (huáiān huǒchē zhàn; 淮安火车站) is scheduled for completion in November 2000. There will be service to Huayin and other nearby towns.

Buses: Huaian Long-distance Bus Station (huáiān chángtú qìchē zhàn; 淮安长途汽车站), 1 Huancheng Lu (☎591 2027). Follow Huaijiang Gonglu south past Zhenhuailou Lu; the station is on the right. Frequent buses go to **Nanjing** (3-5hr., 16 per day, Y24-41). There are also buses to **Hangzhou** (3 per day 6am-noon), **Shanghai** (3 per day 6:40am-4:30pm), and **Suzhou** (6:50am), but departures are more unpredictable.

Local Transportation: Buses #61, 62, and **63** service the Huaian area; however, buses are few and far between, as they are dispatched from the Huayin Bus Station. Fare Y1.

Taxis: Destinations within town cost Y5-10.

Bike Rental: Available from the Xiangyu Travel Development Company.

Travel Agency: Xiangyu Travel Development Company (xiángyǔ lǚyóu fāzhǎn gōngsī; 翔宇旅游发展公司), 92 Xicheng Jie (☎593 3501; fax 591 1412). Walk east on Zhenhuailou Lu to Xichang Jie; the office is 2 blocks south, on the left side of the street.

Take bus #62 2 stops beyond the hospital. Not much in the map or brochure departments, but staff can arrange car and bike rental. Open daily 8am-6:30pm.

Bank of China: 82 Zhenhuailou Dong Lu (☎591 3901). Walk west on Zhenhuailou Dong Lu from the Xichang Jie intersection; look for the huge, glass-paneled high-rise on the left. Exchanges traveler's checks and offers credit card advances. Open M-F 8am-5pm.

Hospital: Huaian Hospital (huáiān yīyuàn; 淮安医院; ☎591 2233), on Dongmen Dajie, just off Zhenhuailou Dong Lu. English-speaking staff. Open 24hr.

Post Office: Huaian Post Office, 2 Zhenhuailou Dong Lu (☎593 3209). Internet access available. Open daily 8am-6:30pm. **Postal Code:** 223200.

ACCOMMODATIONS AND FOOD

Huaian only has one hotel that accepts foreigners. **Huaian Hotel** (huáiān bīnguǎn; 淮安宾馆), 2 Youyi Lu, at Beimen Dajie, is a five-minute walk from the city center. This two-star establishment suffers from four-star envy, with A/C, TV, and bath in all rooms. (☎591 3700. Deposit Y15. Reserve at least 1 day in advance. Singles Y320; doubles Y160.)

There are very few restaurants and street stalls in Huaian; locals go to Xichang Jie's **Food Street** (měishí jiē; 美食街) in search of good food. Three delicacies are Huaian's claim to fame: yellow eel (shànyú; 鳝鱼), local vegetables (zhāicài; 择菜), and Pingqiao tofu soup (píngqiáo dòufǔ; 平桥豆腐). **Jinguchun Restaurant** (jīngǔchūn cāndiàn; 金谷春餐店), 10 Xichang Jie, about 15m south of the travel agency, serves Huaian specialties at an exceptional price. Garish orange chairs and minimal decor don't do much to whet the appetite, but the food (Y25-50) certainly does. (☎592 9179. Open daily 8am until whenever guests leave.)

SIGHTS

Most of Huaian's sights are homages to the people that came from the city, conveniently clustered around the city center.

FORMER RESIDENCE OF ZHOU ENLAI (zhōu ēnlái gùjū; 周恩来故居). Know Chairman Mao's right-hand man like you've never known him before: see the room where he was born on March 5, 1898, the room where he was nursed, and the room where he studied. Pictures of Zhou and an exhibition of his letters are housed in his old sitting room. (7 Fuma Xiang, at the intersection of Beimen Dajie and Zhenhuailou Lu. ☎591 2517. Open daily 7am-6pm; in winter 7:45am-5:30pm. Y10-50.)

ZHOU ENLAI MEMORIAL HALL (zhōu ēnlái jìniànguǎn; 周恩来纪念馆). A beautiful temple-like structure overlooking a lake in the center of Huaian, this memorial hall is a gentle respite from the crowded streets of the city. The museum of Premier Zhou's life and works highlights his achievements, with a few photos of his time in Huaian thrown in for good measure. (On Huancheng Lu. ☎591 3032. Open daily 8am-6pm. Y15 or Y28.)

ZHENHUAI TOWER (zhènhuái lóu; 镇淮楼). This imposing grey structure is a remnant of the city wall built around Huaian during wars with neighboring provinces. The interior has been transformed into a mini-museum on Huaian history. Among the exhibits are a soldier's corpse and a display on Huaian celebrities. (At the end of Zhenhuailou Lu. Y5.)

FORMER RESIDENCE OF WU CHENGEN (wú chéngēn gùjū; 吴承恩故居). The well-preserved home of Wu Chengen (1500-1582), author of the *Journey to the West* series, houses both original manuscripts and recent translations of his work (see **Literature: Ancient & Premodern,** p. 36). *Monkey Causes Havoc in Heaven* en français, anyone? Wu's kitchen, study, and living quarters are also open to the public. (12 Datong Xiang, at Beimen Dajie. ☎580 2897. Open daily 7:30am-6pm. Y10.)

SUZHOU 苏州 ☎0512

A famous Qing scholar once suggested that one should "stay away from the noise of town and imagine one's self amidst mountains and rivers." Visitors to Suzhou would do best to keep this advice in mind. As a town, Suzhou is filled with not just noise, but also grime, pollution, and traffic. In recent years, a surge in industrial development has smothered surrounding farmlands, dirtied the canals, and crowded (and clouded) city streets. Although Suzhou's famed canals are now garbage-strewn and many of the gardens that earned the city the name "Heaven on Earth" suffer from neglect or commercialization, with effort, one can still find in this outwardly uninspiring city evidence of Suzhou's more illustrious past.

One of China's oldest cities, Suzhou dates to 514 BC, when King Helu of Wu plopped himself down in the area. Old Helu gets credit for a lot in these parts: the canals were reportedly his idea, as were the gardens. But Suzhou really flourished about 2000 years later, when the construction of the Grand Canal enhanced the city's position on the route between Nanjing and Shanghai. Traders from as far as Europe came to pluck Suzhou's fruits, particularly those of its storied silk production. By the 12th century, Suzhou's fabrics were among China's top exports. Meanwhile, Suzhou scored intellectual treasures of its own, luring scholars and artists from Shanghai and Hangzhou and gaining renown as a center for high culture.

Although Suzhou can no longer boast of having the 280 private gardens it had in its heyday, the town still offers enough for the horticulturally inclined to go home happy. Rest assured the gardens will surely continue to lure visitors to the area for years to come. The discordant sights and sounds of construction, though, will just as surely provide a lesson in the fleeting nature of beauty.

⌐ TRANSPORTATION

Trains: Suzhou Train Station (sūzhōu huǒchē zhàn; 苏州火车站; ☎753 2831), on the north side of town, just west of Renmin Lu after you pass the moat. Bus #2 runs south from the station along Lindun Lu and Fenghuang Jie, to the Master of Nets Garden, just off hotel-heavy Shiquan Jie. **CITS** (☎753 0782) has an office on the east side of the station, in the soft seat waiting lounge. Open daily 8:15am-5:30pm. To: **Beijing** (15-22hr., 2 per day, Y68-457); **Hangzhou** (4½-5hr., 12 per day, Y16-266); **Nanjing** (3½-4hr., Y13-49) via **Wuxi** (30min., Y3-14); and **Shanghai** (30min.-1hr., Y5-24).

Buses: Most area destinations are served by the **Ping Men Long-distance Bus Station** (qìchē běi zhàn; 汽车北站; ☎752 4806), on the east side of the traffic circle at the head of Renmin Lu. Open daily 5am-6:30pm. To: **Hangzhou** (28 per day, Y24-41); **Nanjing** (2½hr., 36 per day Y46-64); **Shanghai** (1½hr., 31 per day, Y22-30); **Wuxi** (1hr., 11 per day, Y15-24); and **Yangzhou** (5 per day, Y51). Buses also leave from the **South Gate Long-distance Bus Station** (nán mén qìchē zhàn; 南门汽车站; ☎520 4867), on the east side of Renmin Lu, just before the southern part of the moat. Tickets are sold in the first building on your right as you walk down Renmin Lu. Ticket office open daily 5:30am-5pm. To: **Hangzhou** (12 per day, Y45); **Shanghai** (4 per day, Y20); and **Yangzhou** (6 per day, Y51). Farther south on Renmin Lu, about a 5min. walk past the moat, not far from where buses #14 and 313 terminate, is the **Wuxian Bus Terminal.** Minibuses leave frequently but at unpredictable intervals for Dongshan, Xishan, and other **Lake Taihu** spots. Just look for the buses with "Let Wuxian be China's most excellent tourist city!" in the back window.

Ferries: Suzhou Shipping Terminal (sūzhōu lúnchuán gōngsī; 苏州轮船公司), 8 Renmin Lu (☎520 6681), just south of the South Gate Bus Station, on the outer moat near the Renmin Lu bridge. Open daily 5:20am-5:30pm. A boat leaves daily for **Hangzhou** (14 hr., 5:30pm, Y47-95). The nighttime trip may not offer much in terms of river views, but it does feature on-board entertainment (read: alcohol and karaoke).

Local Transportation: Like everything else in town, the **buses** are geared to tourism, and so run to most popular sights. Most lines run 6am-8pm and have a flat fare of Y1. Some

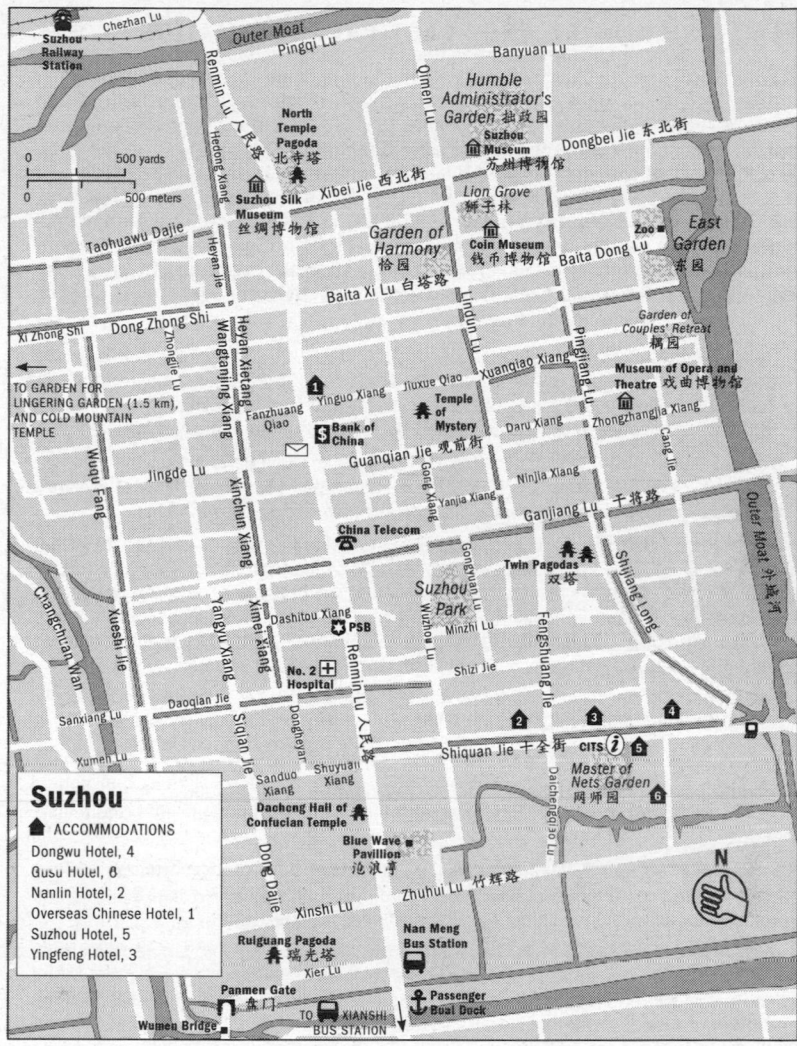

Suzhou

🏠 ACCOMMODATIONS

Dongwu Hotel, 4
Gusu Hotel, 6
Nanlin Hotel, 2
Overseas Chinese Hotel, 1
Suzhou Hotel, 5
Yingfeng Hotel, 3

SHANGHAI

useful buses include: **#1:** Renmin Lu from the train station to Wuxian city; **#4:** starting in the southeast, just outside the moat, it zigzags northwest, passing the Master of Nets Garden, the No. 1 People's Hospital, and the Twin Pagodas before terminating on Xizhong Shi; **#9:** east-west on Ganjian Lu through the center of town.

Taxis: Base fare Y10, each additional km Y1.8. A taxi from one of the Shiquan Jie hotels to the train station should cost Y15-20. For those who want their drivers to sweat for their money, cycle **rickshaws** (some with Y2 minimum), affectionately labelled "tourist pedicabs," can be found almost everywhere.

Bike Rental: A fine way to get from garden to garden to garden, traveling by bicycle in Suzhou can make the city's polluted air and rank alleyways seem a little sweeter. There are several stands on Shiquan Jie near the Suzhou Hotel. Look for crudely drawn signs in English and Japanese. Y15-30 per day, deposit Y200-300.

⚜ℤ ORIENTATION AND PRACTICAL INFORMATION

Getting your bearings in Suzhou is easy; the city's heart is still conveniently laid out along the original grid of canals, all of which are neatly confined within a rectangular outer moat. **Renmin Lu** (人民路), the major thoroughfare cutting north-south through the city, and **Guanqian Jie** (观前街) form the commercial heart of the city. Most of Suzhou's hotels are in the southeastern part of town, especially along **Shiquan Jie** (十全街), a tree-lined street that runs from east to west. Finding your way can be difficult due to construction, which makes through streets unreliable, and to the city's not so passionate commitment to posting street signs. If you keep cardinal directions in mind and remember that the **Grand Canal** flows west and south of the city, navigating the city shouldn't be too much trouble.

Travel Agency: CITS, 115 Shiquan Jie, 1st Fl. (☎522 2223; fax 522 4085), in the slightly hidden building on the right of the entrance to the Suzhou Hotel. Staff gladly look up from their board games to dish out quality information (in English) with a smile. Other CITS branches near the train station (☎753 0782) and in the Nanlin Hotel.

Bank of China: 490 Renmin Lu (☎720 1934), north of Guanqian Jie. Exchange services and two 24hr. ATMs (Cirrus, MC, Visa/Plus). Open daily 8am-5pm. Most of Suzhou's larger hotels also change currency, and non-guests rarely report difficulties.

Bookstores: Suzhou Foreign Language Bookstore (sūzhōu wài wén shūdiàn; 苏州外文书店), 44 Renmin Lu (☎/fax 519 7355), north of Zhuhui Lu. A good selection of foreign language dictionaries, but the classic *Nutrition for You and Your Dog and* maps of the US and Germany don't prove to be too useful. MC, Visa accepted. Open daily 9am-7:30pm. **Xinhua Bookstore,** 215 Shiquan Jie, sells some language primers and a few classic Chinese novels in English. Open daily 9am-10pm.

Emergency: For English-speaking assistance, call the CITS "tourist complaints" (☎522 3377) or information (☎522 3131) hotlines.

PSB: 7 Dashitou Xiang, at Renmin Lu north of Daoqian Jie.

Hospital: Suzhou No. 2 Hospital (sūzhōu dìèr yīyuàn; 苏州第二医院; ☎828 5295), half a block west of Renmin Lu on Daoqian Jie, or **No. 1 People's Hospital** (dìyī rénmín yīyuàn; 第一人民医院).

Telephones: Suzhou Renmin Lu Telecommunications Business Department, on Renmin Lu north of Daoqian Jie, on the east side of the street. IDD service Y8 per min. to most countries in Asia, Y15 per min. everywhere else. Open 24hr.

Internet Access: Internet Place (wǎngyǒu kōngjiān; 网友空间), 333 Renmin Lu (☎511 0115), in the north end of the China Telecom building, on the northwest corner of Renmin Lu and Daoqian Jie. Passport or driver's license required. Y6 per hr. **Suzhou Hotel's Business Center** has access for Y20 per 30min. Open daily 7:30am-10:30pm. A little building at the east end of Shiquan Jie offers rather speedy 24hr. access for Y3 per hr. Look for the blue sign that says "Internet Bar."

Post Office: China Post, 487 Renmin Lu, at Jingde Lu. A lovely branch with EMS (open daily 9am-5pm), Poste Restante, a newsstand, a detailed chart of postal rates...in English no less! Open daily 8am-8pm. **Postal Code:** 215005.

▟ ACCOMMODATIONS

Suzhou is as proud of its hotels as it is of its gardens, but truly inexpensive options are scarce. The east end of **Shiquan Jie** has something for everyone. Discounts will probably be offered even if you don't ask, but you might get larger ones if you do.

Dongwu Hotel (dōngwù fàndiàn; 东吴饭店), 24 Wuheng Chang (☎519 3681), across a bridge off the eastern end of Shiquan Jie. The rooms in the student residence are far and away Suzhou's best bargain, with TVs, clean Western-style common baths, and only a handful of mosquitoes. Other rooms are less spartan, with A/C and even fewer mosquitoes. Guests can try to decipher the Chinese instructions on the small (free) washing machine. Singles and doubles Y70-90, with A/C and bath Y150-240; triples Y310.

Yingfeng Hotel (yíngfēng fàndiàn; 迎枫饭店), 39 Huyang Chang (☎530 0907), just off Shiquan Jie. Cross the small bridge across from the Suzhou Hotel and look for the large rooftop sign. Take the 2nd right after the canal, and then go through the courtyard on your left. Rooms are unremarkable but have A/C, TV, and private bath. Doubles Y120.

Overseas Chinese Hotel (huá qiáo dàjiǔdiàn; 华桥大酒店), 518 Renmin Lu (☎720 2883), at Yinguo Lu, a block north of the Bank of China. It might not offer easy access to the beauty salons and souvenir shops of Shiquan Jie, but this hotel does have friendly, helpful staff, clean rooms in good condition, and frequently discounted rates. Singles and doubles Y180; triples Y230.

Suzhou Hotel (sūzhōu fàndiàn; 苏州饭店), 115 Shiquan Jie (☎520 4646), about 250m east of Fenghuang Jie—follow the tourist buses. Standard upscale fare: A/C, TV, tub, and 16 bars. Rooms in the new wing have bigger beds and newer furnishings (late 80s instead of late 70s) but are otherwise equivalent in quality. Doubles Y250-500.

Nanlin Hotel (nánlín fàndiàn; 南林饭店), 20 Gunxiu Fang, Shiquan Jie (☎519 4641 or 519 6333), 100m off the street just west of Fenghuang Jie. There must be something mysterious about the dorm rooms of the Nanlin. Sure, the brochure says they exist, but has anyone ever seen them? The only mystery surrounding the standard rooms is why these rooms cost so much. Maybe it's the Sauna Recreation Area. Dorms Y80-120; doubles in old building Y178, in new building Y270-450.

Gusu Hotel (gūsū fàndiàn; 姑苏饭店), 5 Xiangwang Lu (☎520 0566), 1 block south of Shiquan Jie. Some of the nicest rooms and baths around. "Summer specials" yield a more manageable Y288. Doubles Y480. Credit cards accepted.

⬛ FOOD

Many visitors stick to their hotels for effortless dining after long days of sightseeing. Like all good Chinese cities, though, Suzhou has its food streets, most notably **Tai Jian Fang** and **Jia Yu Fang**, two blocks of neon-illuminated excess north of the Garden of Harmony. The family-owned restaurants along Shiquan Jie serve heaping plates of dumplings and noodles. Across the canal on Fengmen Jie, restaurants offer long, exotic menus in nothing but Chinese characters. As for the Western alphabet, KFC restaurants seem to outnumber Suzhou's gardens (and if the restaurants don't, the signs certainly do). If you find yourself culinarily destitute, fear not—you can always find a Chupa Chup lollipop for Y0.5.

Yong He Soya Bean Milk (yǒnghé dòujiāng; 永和豆浆), 191 Shiquan Jie (☎510 5918), next to the entrance to the Master of Nets Garden. A friendly and convenient pit stop with a multi-page English menu. Wonton soup Y5, "intestines in fire pot" Y35, jellyfish salad Y18, and mmm-good, piping hot sweet bean milk Y3. Open 24hr.

Taipei Refreshments Centre (táiběi diǎnxīn chéng; 台北点心城), 29 Renmin Lu (☎529 5571), on the west side of the street, about 1½ blocks north of the moat. Not particularly enticing, save the English menu with dishes like dim sum (Y3-7 per plate), fried rice (Y6), and Taiwan Squid Soup (Y5). Open daily 7am-2am.

Suzhou Songhelou Restaurant (sōnghèlóu càifàn; 松鹤楼菜饭), 141 Guanqian Jie (☎727 7006), 1 block east of Renmin Lu. The preferred dining establishment for both emperors and tourists alike, this is Suzhou's famed restaurant, serving up expensive, banquet-style treats. Open daily 5:30am-1:30pm and 2-8pm.

🎵📺 ENTERTAINMENT AND NIGHTLIFE

Suzhou may be ruled by tourists during the day, but residents emerge at night for party-going and merry-making. Suzhou tourist authorities probably expect that visitors will wear themselves out enjoying all the daytime activities the city has to offer, but Suzhou's summer evenings are its finest time.

By far the best evening entertainment is the nightly **cultural performance** inside the **Garden of the Master of the Nets** (see p. 314), on Shiquan Jie. The multi-part concert provides a great chance to see one of Suzhou's natural masterpieces as it shimmers in the evening light, and also to indulge in the guilty pleasures of unadulterated tourism. From opera to flute to lute…to a stunning dance performance in the gift shop. Busloads of foreign and Chinese tourists are moved through this cultural assembly line every night, so just tag along with whichever group tickles your fancy. (May-Oct., nightly 7:30-10pm, Y60.)

Beyond that, one of the more bustling parts of Suzhou is the area just east of Renmin Lu between Guanqian Jie and Ganjiang Lu. Hordes of young, trendy, giggling locals flock here each night. The area features several discos, including the **Disco PTV** (jiāngshān DISCO guǎngchǎng; 江山DISCO广场), on the corner of Renmin Lu and Ganjiang Lu. Get up to the fourth floor and get funky on a huge, fluorescent dance floor, drink from multiple bars (beer Y15), or kick it with karaoke. (Cover Y5. Open daily 10am-2am.) For more good, clean fun, head northwest of here to the large plaza near KFC, home to the **Kai Ming movie theater.** Across the street from the Kai Ming is a multi-floor **entertainment complex** with a bowling alley, a live theater, a pool hall, and a disco.

Prices at Shiquan Jie night spots tend to be high, and few are ever full enough to be lively. Some places get busy at night, but in an entirely different way. When you see a photo of a couple enjoying a sumptuously decorated bedroom displayed next to the door of a "bar," it's time to be wary. You may be flattered to be chatted up by friendly, attractive women; start to buy them drinks and you'll pay dearly for the privilege. For a quiet drink, there are always the Suzhou Hotel's 16 bars. After all, nothing promises a good time more than a bar named "Morning Redness."

◉ SIGHTS

In Suzhou, ponds are seas, rocks are mountains, and nature's bounty lives harmoniously alongside classical Chinese architecture. A Suzhou garden is not just a pleasant expanse of ponds and greenery. Often, the grounds contain subtle allusions to art or literature, and are referred to as "silent poems" or "three-dimensional paintings." To understand these verdant treasures is also to understand Daoist, Buddhist, and Confucian ethic; they exist not only to please the eye, but also to please the mind.

To see just one of Suzhou's gardens would be a waste; many of the 70 or so formal gardens are worth a visit. A few hints: take your time, as contemplation's part of the game; arrive early in the morning or late in the day to beat the crowds; and if possible, tag along with a tour group or pick up extra readings to enjoy the entertaining anecdotes that accompany many of the garden's particular features.

If you're short on time, a **pedicab tour** (Y50) leaves each morning from the Nanlin Hotel (see p. 311). **Panda Tours** (☎522 3783, ext. 2403) also runs tours to a number of gardens, including distant Tiger Hill. The Y260 fee includes admission, a packed lunch, a map of the city, and five hours of fun. A better option for travelers too tough for tour buses might be to rent a bicycle. This gives you some flexibility throughout your trip—see as many (or as few) gardens as you find interesting. Take a breather from the bewildering number of sights by stopping at one of the town's museums, or simply use your cycling tricks to escape the crowds.

NORTH SUZHOU

HUMBLE ADMINISTRATOR'S GARDEN (zhuózhèng yuán; 拙政园). Despite the name, this sprawling garden is one of Suzhou's largest and possibly the most

SHANGHAI

famous. The garden was built by Wang Xianchen, a high-ranking, corrupt Ming dynasty official. After being cast out of his job, Wang sought solace in governing nature: "Building houses, planting trees, watering gardens, and growing vegetables," he wrote, "are a way for a humble man to manage administrative affairs." Three-fifths of the garden is covered by water, and the lush foliage overshadows the architecture here. *(On Dongbei Jie, 1km east of the North Temple. Open daily 7:30am-5:30pm; last admission 5pm. Y32.)*

SUZHOU SILK MUSEUM (sūzhōu sīchóu bówùguǎn; 苏州丝绸博物馆). Not your average stuffy picture gallery, this museum provides an enlightening, if somewhat esoteric, introduction to the fruit of the loom. Suzhou is still one of China's primary silk producers; the museum, which claims to be the only silk-centric museum in the world, uses well-presented exhibits (with English captions) to spin the yarn of the emergence of Suzhou's silk trade, from the Neolithic Age through the Tang and Song dynasties (AD 618-1279), right up to today. Check out the "weaving room" (including one loom you can try out) and the "Sericulture House," where you can witness silkworms at work. *(661 Renmin Lu. Across the street from the North Temple Pagoda and about a half-block north. Open daily 8am-5:30pm. Y7.)*

LION GROVE (shīzi lín; 狮子林). . This "kingdom of rockery" was built by a monk called Tianru in memory of his teacher, Zhong Feng, who lived in Lion Crag in Zhejiang province. Stones rule here—you can easily get lost in a labyrinth of scraggly rocks pulled out of Lake Taihu. Some are said to look like lions, but it could just be the power of suggestion. Many of the garden's buildings also contain paintings and etchings by famous calligraphers. *(About 250m south of the Suzhou Museum. Open daily 7:30am-5:30pm; last admission 5pm. Y10.)*

NORTH TEMPLE PAGODA (běi sì tǎ; 北寺塔). Supposedly Suzhou's first pagoda (the original main temple was built in AD 238-251), this 76m *Baoen* (Thanksgiving) Pagoda is the tallest south of the Yangzi. Climb up to the seventh floor, or pay an extra Y1 to go to the eighth; the kids at the top might let you use their telescopes. The top offers a fantastic 360° view of Suzhou and the rice paddies practically all the way to Shanghai. A small garden spreads out north of the temple, with a tea house that hosts occasional amateur musical performances. *(On Renmin Lu, about 800m south of the train station. Open daily 8am-6pm; last admission 5:30pm.)*

SUZHOU MUSEUM (sūzhōu bówùguǎn; 苏州博物馆). This collection isn't as focused or tourist-friendly as Suzhou's other museums, and few of the exhibits come with English captions. While the dioramas don't go beyond the usual ("primitive Suzhou caveman hunts wild beast!"), the small collection of Qing dynasty relics, silk, and an exampe of a classical stage is worth a peek—and the price is right. *(204 Dongbei Jie, just west of the Humble Administrator's Garden. Free group tours in Chinese and English every 30min. 10am-4pm. Open daily 8am-5pm; last admission 4:30pm. Y5.)*

OTHER SIGHTS. East of the Lion Grove, the **Garden of Couple's Retreat** (ǒu yuán; 耦园) is more than just a lover's lair, with gondola rides (Y10), local story-telling (Y5), and folk music. Built by a provincial governor who wanted a place to sit with his wife, today the garden is pleasantly free of tourist mayhem. *(Open daily 8am-5pm; last admission 4:30pm. Y10.)* **East Garden** (dōng yuán; 东园) and **Suzhou Zoo** (sūzhōu dòngwùyuán; 苏州动物园) join together at the end of Baita Dong Lu, near the Outer Moat. This large park offers visitors the chance to throw food or garbage at sad-looking animals in tiny cages—or, at the very least, to look on in horror. Grimy boats are available (Y10-15 per hr.), a sure treat for those who want to examine the dank pond in closer detail. *(Open daily 6am-5pm. Y5.)* To make every *kuai* count, head to the **Coinage Museum** (qiánbì bówùguǎn; 钱币博物馆) on Dongbei Jie, near the **Garden Museum** (yuánlín bówùguǎn; 园林博物馆).

SHANGHAI

CENTRAL SUZHOU

GARDEN OF HARMONY (qià yuán; 恰园). Also known as the Garden of Joy, this was the private residence of a feudal bureaucrat, Gu Wenbin, during the Qing dynasty. One of Suzhou's newer sights, the Garden of Harmony borrowed stylistic elements from other gardens in the area: caves from Lion Grove (p. 313), a stone boat like that in the Humble Administrator's Garden (p. 312), and so on. The plum groves make for a relaxing stop if you're in the area to send mail or change money. *(On Renmin Lu just south of Jiayu Fang. Open daily 7:30am-5:30pm; last admission 5pm. Y4.)*

TWIN PAGODAS (shuāng tǎ yuàn; 双塔院). Part of the Arhat Temple complex, the Twin Pagodas are all that's left of a Buddhist temple founded by three brothers in AD 1410. The site was ransacked during the mid-20th century, but the pagodas were restored in 1954. The garden, designed around the ruins of the former "Great Hall," evokes peaceful, monkish ghosts. Step back to the left from the sculpted steles (described in English) to find two large tea houses that serve tea and morning refreshments to ladies' social clubs and gabbing old men. *(Half a block east of Fenghuang Jie, just south of Ganjiang Dong Lu. Open daily 7:30am-5:30pm. Y4.)*

OTHER SIGHTS. To the east, north of Guanqian Jie, the **Temple of Mystery** (xuánmiào guān; 玄妙观) is a bonanza of kitschy tourist treats, with several temples besides. *(Open daily 7:30am-5pm; last admission 4:30pm. Main temple Y5; all temples Y7; children half-price.)* The **Museum of Opera and Theater** (xìqǔ bówùguǎn; 戏曲博物馆), farther east on Zhong Zhangjia Fang, hosts occasional performances.

SOUTH SUZHOU

GARDEN OF THE MASTER OF NETS (wǎng shī yuán; 网师园). During the 12th century, Shi Zhengzhi (better known as "Fishing Hermit") owned the **Hall of Ten Thousand Volumes.** About 200 years ago, a retired bureaucrat built the garden in its current form, declaring it his "Fisherman's Retreat." The Garden of the Master of Nets certainly knows how to net a lot—beautiful houses, a tranquil pond, a stone mountain, chambers for musical performances, Suzhou's tiniest stone bridge, even a large boulder that emits a ringing sound when struck—into a small space. Visit during the day and again at night, when the haunting melodies of Chinese folk music waft through the garden (see **Entertainment and Nightlife,** p. 312). *(On Shiquan Jie, near Fengshuang Jie. Enter through alleys off either street. Open daily 8am-5pm. Y10.)*

PAN GATE SCENIC AREA (pán mén jǐng qū; 盘门景区). The grounds of this scenic area have been newly renovated for a more enjoyable atmosphere. You can climb to the fifth floor of **Ruiguang Pagoda** (ruìguāng tǎ; 瑞光塔) for Y6. At the far corner, near a park filled with locals practicing *tai chi*, the **Tower of City Gates** displays (with rather satisfying English narration) the portcullises, cannons, stone walls, and "murder holes" used to fend off attackers. The semi-circular (and oft-photographed) **Wumen Bridge** (wǔmén qiáo; 午门桥) is on the southern edge of the park. *(At the far southwest corner of the old, moated city. Enter from outside the moat to the south or from just east of the massive Sheraton Hotel on Zhuhui Lu. Open daily 8am-5pm; last admission 4:30pm. Y15, children Y8.)*

BLUE WAVE PAVILION (cāng làng tíng; 沧浪亭). Also known as the Surging Waves Pavilion, this is Suzhou's oldest garden, built more than 1000 years ago. It is not as tidily kept than the others; some say the front facade is more impressive than what's inside. Notable features include the **Temple of 500 Sages,** which showcases prominent figures in Suzhou's history, and the **Green and Delicate Hall,** which lies enmeshed in several varieties of thick bamboo. *(East of Pan Gate, off the east side of Renmin Lu south of Shiquan Jie. Open daily 8am-5pm; last admission 4:30pm. Y8.)*

BEYOND THE OUTER MOAT

TIGER HILL (hŭ qiū gōngyuán; 虎丘公园). Song poet Su Shi once declared, "To visit Suzhou without seeing Tiger Hill will be a cause for regret." While not *quite* all that, the 20-acre park still merits a visit. The area's name derives from a legend surrounding Suzhou's founder, Helu of Wu, who was buried here by his son in 550 BC; three days after the burial, a white tiger was seen crouching by the tomb. Since then, the temple is said to have been destroyed seven times and to have been the site of an unbelievable number of strange and sordid tales.

Most striking is the 48m pagoda that rises—and tilts precariously—from atop the hill. Around the pagoda are rocks, springs, gardens, and buildings. Among the most visible are the **Sword-testing Rock,** with a huge cleft said to come from King Helu's swords; the **Thousand Man Rock,** site of a grisly massacre by King Fuchai, Helu's son; **Nodding Rock,** said to have bowed in agreement with the preachings of a monk cast out by his superiors; and **Sword Pond,** the supposed site of Helu's tomb. Tag along with a tour group or pick up a booklet for the legendary details.

The **Villa of Ten Thousand Scenes,** at the southeast foot of the hill, is an impressive garden of potted landscapes. If you're bored, rent a small boat (Y8-12 per hr.); boats also leave from just south of the complex for hour-long trips to Suzhou and back (Y100; try bargaining). If you're feeling extraordinarily lazy, some old ladies will tote you around like royalty atop a palanquin; a trip from the entrance to the hilltop costs a meager Y20. *(By bicycle, take Xizhong Shi Lu west from the city and turn right after the moat; then turn left on Shantang Jie, which follows a cobbled path directly to Tiger Hill. If you stop at the Lingering Garden, head west from the garden, and then take Huqiu Lu, the first major right off Liuyuan Lu. After about 3 blocks, bear left, and then cruise right up to Tiger Hill. Bus #5 from the train station stops outside. Open daily 7:30am-5:30pm; last admission 5pm. Y20.)*

LINGERING GARDEN (liú yuán; 留园). Another one of Suzhou's big draws, this 400-year-old garden attracts hordes of tourists and their megaphone-wielding guides en route to Tiger Hill. Despite its durability, most of the garden's three hectares were destroyed during the 1949 Japanese occupation. Since then, refurbishment has restored its original beauty. *(1km west of the city's outer moat. Follow Xizhong Shi Lu west until it turns into Fengqiao Lu; turn right on Guangli Lu, and then immediately left onto Liuyuan Jie. Open daily 7:30am-5:30pm; last admission 5pm. Y16.)*

COLD MOUNTAIN TEMPLE (hán shān sì; 寒山寺). 1300 years ago, Tang poet Zhang Ji, in typical Chinese poet style, eternalized this temple: "The moon is down, the raven calls, the cold frost fills the sky / Off Maple Bridge, with sleepless eyes I watch the fishing light / From far Cold Mountain near Gusu Town (Suzhou) as midnight passes by / The chiming of a temple bell comes to my boat tonight." Visitors can view the Maple Bridge (rebuilt), the bell (the Ming-era original is in Japan, but the replacement is also "Made in Japan"), and calligraphic inscriptions of the poem. Built in the 6th century, the temple is named after a Tang Buddhist monk known as Hanshan (Cold Mountain). Whatever hermetic asceticism is connoted in the name is drowned out by the throngs of incense-burning Chinese tourists who come to remember their grammar school days, when they learned the poem by heart. Although the **Maple Bridge Garden** is small and quite unremarkable, it provides a welcome respite from the strangely insistent street vendors outside. *(About 8km from Suzhou. Baita Xi Lu becomes Fengqiao Lu west of the Outer Moat; Cold Mountain Temple is next to the canal. Open daily 7:30am-5pm; last admission 4:50pm. Temple admission Y6; tower Y5; Maple Bridge Garden Y5; Maple Bridge Y2.)*

⚐ DAYTRIPS FROM SUZHOU: DONGSHAN AND XISHAN

*About 40km southwest of Suzhou. Getting there is simple enough, but finding reasonably priced transportation once you're out there can be a hassle. Catch a **minibus** from the train station (where bus #20 also leaves for the area) or from the Wuxian bus station* *(where you'll find buses to both Dongshan and Xishan). The buses should have their destinations in Chinese characters on the front. Buses cost Y7 and leave whenever they're full, operating during daylight hours. To make your trip more convenient, they'll let you take a bike on board for about Y5 extra. A warning: the roads on Dongshan are often steep, rocky, and not particularly well suited to low-quality rental bikes. Having a bike means you'll have to travel exclusively by land; the **motorboats** that cross the lake are usually too small to carry bicycles.*

The **Dongshan** (东山) peninsula stretches out into Lake Taihu; the island of **Xishan** (西山; also known as Xidongtingshan) sits not far off the coast. Far from the fume-belching industry of the city, these areas are home to fishermen, fruit farmers, fragrant countryside, and not a whole lot else—making them a worthwhile destination for tourists afflicted with that mysterious Suzhou creeping garden sickness.

Once in Dongshan, you'll be dropped near an intersection in the town proper. Head left at the intersection, and the road takes you around the hill past **Purple Gold Shrine** (zǐ jīn ān; 紫金庵). The beautiful nunnery is enshrouded in bamboos, pines, and wildflowers, and contains a shrine with some colored statues that are widely held to be ancient masterpieces. *(Open daily 8am-5pm; last admission 4:30pm. Y12.)* Head right at the crossroads, and the road passes a small boat dock that rents **motorboats** to Xishan (30min., Y80), eventually coming to the Dongshan Hotel.

Whichever direction you go, it's about 10km around the massive hill to the ferry dock to **Xishan;** taxis from Dongshan cost Y20-30. If the two scheduled ferries per day aren't running, it may be possible to hire a motorboat on the spot. Drivers will try to charge shamelessly high rates, offering to stop at various spots along the way. If you don't speak Chinese, be sure to indicate your desired destination on a map. Turn on the charm, though, and you might be able to jump onto one of the transport junks for the ride across.

Once on Xishan, make your way toward the large hill with the tower on top. A visit to the **Linwu Caves** can provide relief from the summer heat; the steps are slick and treacherous, though. From here, it's a short uphill hike to the **Jiatu Tower.** Once you climb past the souvenir and tea shops, you'll find spectacular views of the surrounding countryside, especially in spring when the plum blossoms are in bloom. *(Open daily 8am-4:30pm; last admission 4pm. Y18, higher during the annual Plum Blossom Festival.)* Minibuses to the main street in Donghe, Xishan's largest city, leave from the parking lot next to the tower. Buses back to Suzhou leave from a stop across the street from the Bank of China in Donghe.

WUXI 无锡 ☎ 0510

Just because there's little to do in Wuxi doesn't mean that there's little to love. Many consider the town to be an industrial wart on the beautifully scenic visage of Lake Taihu, one of China's largest freshwater lakes and domestic tourist draws. It's true that Wuxi has never been a center of culture or innovation. Early on, the city's glory lay in its tin deposits, but by the time the Han dynasty rolled around, the mines had been stripped, earning the town the name Wuxi, or "without tin." Since then, the city has functioned as a dull trade and transportation center. Now, the town's most important purpose is to offer quick, easy access to the lake, which lies below a misty haze just a few kilometers away. Wuxi has a lazy, resort town feel, an atmosphere only intensified by the wide, tree-lined avenues and verdant surroundings found across the river. Wuxi is well aware of its relative lack of excitement, but compensates nicely with its welcoming and friendly nature.

▐ TRANSPORTATION

Airplanes: Wuxi Airport (wúxī jīchǎng; 无锡机场), several kilometers outside the city, is accessible only by taxi and serves a very limited number of destinations. Book tickets at CTS for **Beijing** (3 per week, Y680) and **Fuzhou** (4 per week, Y450).

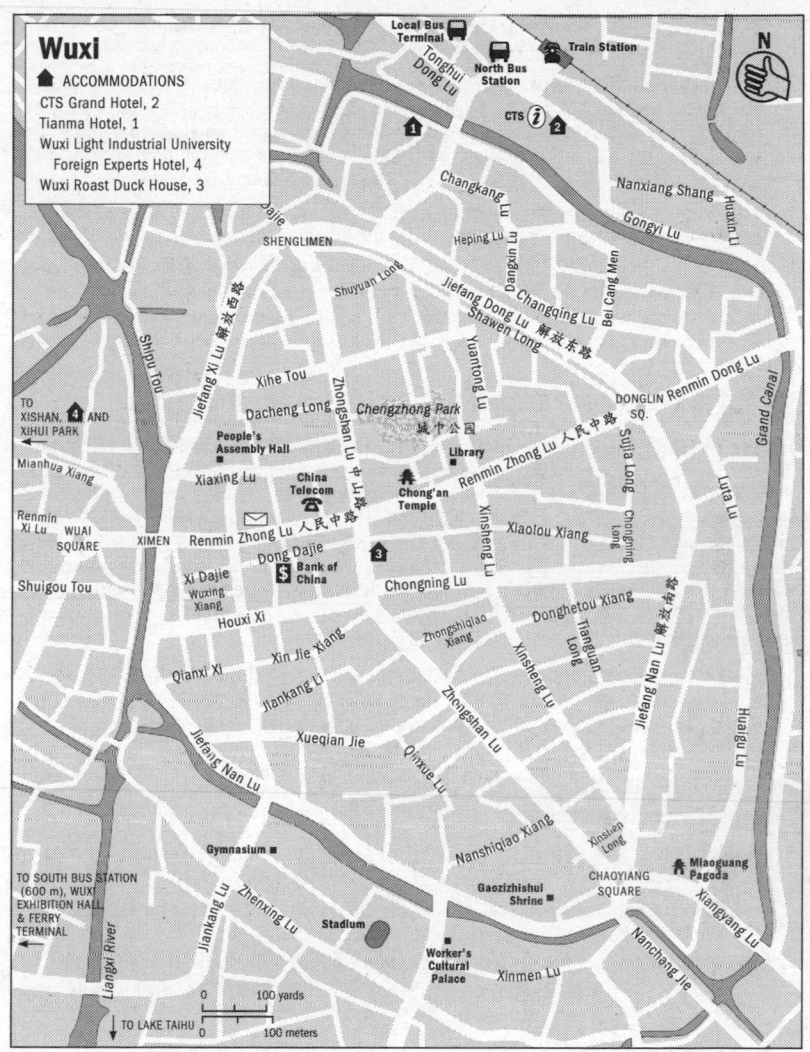

Wuxi

⌂ ACCOMMODATIONS
CTS Grand Hotel, 2
Tianma Hotel, 1
Wuxi Light Industrial University
  Foreign Experts Hotel, 4
Wuxi Roast Duck House, 3

Trains: Wuxi Train Station (wúxī huǒchē zhàn; 无锡火车站; ☎230 0426), at Tonghui Dong Lu and Wuhu Lu. Open daily 6am-9:45pm. A CITS branch is on the east end (near the soft seat waiting room). Over 30 trains per day to: **Nanjing** (2-3hr., Y10-39); **Shanghai** (1-2hr., Y36); **Suzhou** (30min., Y3-14); and **Zhenjiang** (2hr., Y7-27).

Buses: Wuxi Main Bus Station (wúxī qìchē zhàn; 无锡汽车站; ☎230 1633), just west of the train station. The ticket office is on the east side of the station. Open daily 5am-10:30pm. To: **Nanjing** (2hr., every 10-15min. 5:50am-6:30pm, Y37-52); **Shanghai** (1½-2hr., every 20-30min. 6:30am-6:30pm, Y37-43); **Suzhou** (1hr., every 10-20min. 6:50am-5:50pm, Y15); and **Zhenjiang** (1½hr., every 30min.-1hr. 7:20am-5:30pm, Y16). Buses from the rather deserted **West Bus Station** (qìchē xì zhàn; 汽车西站; ☎580 2297), on Hubin Lu, across Liangxi Bridge, go to **Nanjing** (11 per day, Y43-52) and **Shanghai** (4 per day, Y29-43). Some buses arrive across the canal at the **South Bus Station** (nán mén qìchē zhàn; 南门汽车站), near Liangxi Lu and Liangqing Lu.

Ferries: Boats run to **Hangzhou** (13hr., several per day, Y24-294) from the dock (☎586 5950) southwest of Liangxi Bridge.

Local Transportation: Buses in Wuxi are easy to use. Many lines terminate in an area just west of the train station and most run 6am-6pm. Fare Y1, with A/C Y2. Bus **#1** goes across Baojie Bridge to Turtle Head Island; **#4** cuts through town and heads to Liangxi Bridge, near the South Bus Station; **#11** goes into the city from the train station; **#20** links the North and South Bus Stations; **#820** shuttles around Lake Taihu tourist spots.

Taxis: You can't miss the taxis in Wuxi. Indeed, how could you miss anything painted so brightly in blue and yellow? Base fare Y7 for the first 2km, each additional km Y1.4-1.8. From the train station or either bus station to the city center, Y10-15.

Bike Rental: A few shops around the train station rent bikes, although none posts a sign in English; ask around, although it might be a bit of a useless wild goose chase, given Wuxi's convenient bus system.

ORIENTATION AND PRACTICAL INFORMATION

Jiefang Lu (解放路) forms an oval around downtown. The **Grand Canal** meanders along the west side of Wuxi, and several smaller canals run through the city. **Xihui Park**, visible from much of the city, is west of Wuxi, across the canal. Trains (and most buses) arrive in the northern end of town, across the **Gongyun Bridge** (工运桥) and just a few blocks from Jiefang Bei Lu. **Zhongshan Lu** (中山路) runs from north to south through downtown. Many businesses and top-end hotels are clustered around the junction of Zhongshan Bei Lu and **Renmin Lu** (人民路), which cuts across the city from east to west. **Liangxi Bridge** (liángxī qiáo; 梁溪桥) connects the area near the South Bus Station to the city proper.

Travel Agencies: CTS, 88 Chezhan Lu, 1st and 4th Fl. (☎230 0888, ext. 1725), across from the train station, next to the CTS Hotel. Look for the large "Wuxi Tourist Guide Center" sign. Booking services and an **automated information kiosk** with all sorts of practical info (and propaganda) in English are on the 1st floor. Open daily 7:30am-8:30pm. **CITS** (☎230 3329) is on the east side of the train station near the soft seat waiting room. Open daily 7:40am-8pm. The main office is at 8 Zhongshan Lu (☎270 5369). Open daily 7:30am-5:30pm.

Bank of China: 258 Zhongshan Lu (☎270 5888), just south of Renmin Lu, in a sparkling new building. Traveler's check exchange to the right. Open daily 7:45am-5:30pm.

Telephones: China Telecom is on Renmin Lu, down the street from the post office. 24hr. IDD service available on the western end. Open daily 8am-5pm.

Internet Access: The **Elite Information Technology Co.,** 196 Huaihe Lu (☎581 0417), across from the Light Industrial University Foreign Experts Hotel, is super-friendly, with super-friendly prices to match. Y4 per hr. Open daily 9am-midnight.

Post Office: China Post, 226 Renmin Lu, about 2 blocks east of Jiefang Lu. EMS. EMS branch next to the bus station. Open daily 8am-6pm. **Postal Code:** 214001.

ACCOMMODATIONS

Wuxi has gone hotel-crazy in the past few years, building several soaring hotels in the heart of downtown. It's hard to find good budget options; however, since supply exceeds demand, it's not too difficult to find great rooms at a good price.

Wuxi Light Industrial University Foreign Experts Hotel (wúxī qīnggōng dàxué zhuānjiā liúxuéshēng lóu; 无锡轻工大学专家留学生楼), 170 Huaihe Lu (☎586 1034), across the moat and down the road from Xihui Park. Take bus #2 from the train station to Wuxi Qingda (5th stop); the hotel is a half-block up the street on the left. Far from the city, but closer to what you want to see—the lake. Standard rooms are small and minimal. The best budget option around. Plus, you can eat super-cheap meals with foreign students. Breakfast included. Singles and doubles Y80-110.

Wuxi Roast Duck House (wúxī kǎoyā diàn; 无锡烤鸭店), 222 Zhongshan Lu (☎270 8222), 1½ blocks south of Renmin Lu. This mega-restaurant has spacious, well-kept rooms without a quacker in sight. Doubles Y150-220.

Tianma Hotel (tiānmǎ dàjiǔdiàn; 天马大酒店), 18 Liangxi Xi Lu (☎272 7668 or 272 7480). Walk south across the bridge from the train station, and turn immediately right; the Tianma is about a half-block ahead on the left. Open your door and listen to the lovely sounds of soprano sax piped throughout the building. Doubles Y168-218.

China Hotel (zhōngguó fàndiàn; 中国饭店), 90 Hanchang Lu (☎272 0041), across the bridge from the train station, about 3 blocks down on the left. Dorms do not have A/C, but the other rooms do. Dorms Y30; singles Y58-70; doubles Y58-70, with bath Y130.

CTS Hotel (zhōng lǚ dàjiǔdiàn; 中旅大酒店), 88 Chezhan Lu (☎230 0888), across from the train station. Not your average railway fare: clean, ultra-modern rooms, and amenities galore, with the local CTS right next door. Doubles Y480-628.

☐ FOOD

Wuxi's hotel restaurants (specializing in Jiangsu-style seafood dishes) are among the city's finest, serving up just about anything with gills, flippers, or shells. The area around the intersection of Zhongshan Lu and Renmin Lu is filled with fast food. Duck into a side street, though, and you're likely to find larger sit-down restaurants. In the summer, there's fresh produce on most smaller streets, and fresh, juicy peaches everywhere. There are a number of student-friendly cafes on Huaihe Lu around Light Industrial University, near Xihui Park.

China Restaurant (zhōngguó fàndiàn; 中国饭店; ☎270 7454), next to the China Hotel. A la carte delights from a point-and-eat display station, including dumplings (Y3), eel, snails (Y3-5), and more. Open daily 6:30am-8:30pm.

Jinxi Revolving Restaurant, 218 Zhongshan Lu (☎275 1688), at Renmin Lu. Round and round she goes, all atop the Jinjiang Hotel, serving up a whopping Chinese and Western buffet for just Y118. You'll find that you don't even notice the view outside, not when there's all you can eat sushi, shrimp, snake, eel, and some simply divine cream puffs. There's a Y20 ticket price for non-guests, but act clueless enough and staff might let it go. Afternoon tea Y38. Open daily 11am-2pm and 2:30-5pm (tea).

Wuxi Roast Duck House (wúxì kǎoyā diàn; 无锡烤鸭店), 222 Zhongshan Lu (☎270 8222). A multi-part, tourist-serving mega restaurant, dishing up duck, duck 'n' fish, and for dessert, "duck deluxe." It's high-grade Beijing- and Jiangsu-style food for rather reasonable prices (many entrees less than Y75). Open daily 11am-1pm and 5-9pm.

Wuxi Light Industrial University Foreign Experts Hotel (wúxī qīnggōng dàxué zhuānjiā liúxuéshēng lóu; 无锡轻工大学专家留学生楼), 170 Huaihe Lu. Large (sometimes buffet-style) meals for just Y5. Open daily 7-8am, 11am-1pm, and 5:30-7pm.

☐ SIGHTS

Likely because of the overwhelming amount of tourist junk lining nearby Lake Taihu, Wuxi itself has grown into a sizable city with almost no tourist offerings of its own. If you have a few hours to spare, **Chengzhong Park** (chéngzhōng gōngyuán; 城中公园), off Zhongshan Lu north of Renmin Lu, is a daytime getaway for legions of contemplative old men. Join them, or jump on the bumper cars (Y3).

XIHUI PARK (xīhuì gōngyuán; 锡惠公园). This small park is the site of **Xishan** (锡山), the large hill with the distinctive pink pagoda on top. You'll find a lot of forgettable attractions: gushing fountains, a zoo, an azalea garden, a sad amusement park with a dying carousel that they try to liven up with the name "turning luxury hobbyhorses." These are matched with unforgettable souvenirs—namely, the small clay figurines (usually of plump senior citizens or children cuddling fish, symbols of wealth and good fortune) that the park is famous for.

SHANGHAI

MY ENDLESS LOVE In AD 1000, amid warring states and imperial scandals, the Kingdom of Wu defeated the Kingdom of Yu, ending 10 years of angry skirmishes. The Emperor of Yu, ashamed of his defeat, became a eunuch for his conqueror, resolving to seek revenge by winning the trust of his enemy. He soon became a court favorite, gaining the coveted responsibility of emptying the Emperor of Wu's bedpan (as well as smelling it for signs of deadly diseases). In appreciation of his devotion, the emperor allowed Yu to return to his kingdom. Once there, the former emperor immediately set to rebuilding forts and training an army. At a loss for how to weaken the Kingdom of Wu, he took the advice of another eunuch and sent Xi She, a famed beauty, as a concubine for the Emperor of Wu. Apparently the ploy worked, for the Kingdom of Yu soon after demolished the Kingdom of Wu and sentenced the emperor (formerly his boss) to death. The victorious Emperor of Yu sent his eunuch to recover Xi She, but the eunuch, overpowered by her beauty, escaped with her to Lake Taihu. The emperor, hearing of the eunuch's disloyalty, ordered his death. Xi She, heartbroken and devastated, returned to Lake Taihu day after day to remember her lost love. The famous pearls of Lake Taihu thus came to be formed by Xi She's tears.

All that aside, two attractions stand out and nearly lift the whole place to mustsee status. The first is the ski lift style **cable cars** connecting this hill with **Huishan,** the other large hill visible from Wuxi. On clear days, the ride affords soaring views of the city and lake; beware of vertigo, though, as the trip is remarkably high and long. *(Runs daily 8:30am-5pm. Y22, children Y10.)*

Even more notable is the incomprehensible tunnel that cuts right through the middle of Xishan. The so-called **Dragon Light Cave** echoes with the digital whistles and roars of a hundred scattered robotic creatures, all lurking in dark rooms off an intimidatingly long, musty corridor. Walk from end to end, and marvel at surreal, six-foot singing carrots; fend off twitching Teenage Mutant Ninja Turtles, gasping dinosaurs, and motionless penguins; and most importantly, stay away from the huge, whistling, and highly dangerous fish-eating insects! *(Park open daily 5am-6pm. Y10-25, depending on how much you want to see.)*

DAYTRIP FROM WUXI: LAKE TAIHU

*By **bike,** follow either Liangxi Lu (toward Plum Garden) or Hubin Lu to the south, which then bends right and runs along the lake to Baojie Bridge. Otherwise, take **bus #1** or 820 from North Bus Station and get off either at Turtle Head Island or near Li Yuan, and then walk across. Bus #2's terminus is at the Taihu Amusement Park. **Accommodations** abound, although most tourists return to Wuxi for the night.*

Covering more than 2000km^2, Lake Taihu (tài hú; 太湖) is one of the largest freshwater lakes in China. The cooler air brings droves of Chinese tourists during the summer. With dozens of lush islands peering through frequent (albeit polluted) haze, coastlines graced with blossoming grapes, peaches, and plums, and shallow waters teeming with fish, the lake has reason enough to lure foreign travelers, too. And in case you need one more excuse: locals love to down their fresh seafood with cold bottles of **Taihu Shui** (太湖水), a tasty regional beer. Spring, with the fruit blossoms, and fall, with long, mellow days of harvest, are the best times to visit Lake Taihu. The summer months can be unforgivingly hot, despite the lake breeze. At any time, though, the folks who inhabit these misty coasts will throw out the welcome mat—just take the time to sample their seed-stuffed wares.

PLUM GARDEN (méi yuán; 梅园). If you bike to Taihu from Wuxi, ride along Liangxi Lu and you will come across Taihu Amusement Park on your left, followed by a bus terminal. Across the street is the middle gate for the Plum Garden, established in 1912 by two industrialists who planted 5000 plum trees to mark their retirement (and guilt?). Since then, additional features have been added, including the **"In Suddenly Enlightened Hole"** (a large, dank cave); a garage-like **perfumery** and greenhouse toward the back; the **Nian Qu Tower,** which after renovation should once again afford views from on high (Y2); and the **Kai Yuan Temple,** a Buddhist complex with several 20 foot statues of snarling deities (Y2). The garden sees occasional tourists, but mostly provides solitude and serenity—be careful not to disrupt the smooching couples. *(Open daily 6am-6pm. Y15.)*

TAIHU AMUSEMENT PARK (tàihú lèyuán; 太湖乐园). Across from Plum Garden, the amusement value of Taihu Amusement Park depends mostly on how you take to the names of the different attractions. Here's a quick sampling: "Joy River Rollercoaster," "Over Water World," "Profound Mystery World," "Swing and Drifting," "Shocking Car," and most mysterious of all, "Eight-Part Essay City." Chances are that you'll find more people painted on the map outside than wandering about inside. *(Open daily 8am-4:45pm; last admission 4pm. Y40, under 1.4m Y25, under 1m free.)* From there, follow the road alongside the amusement park toward the lake. At the intersection, turn left, and follow the rural path to the **Grand Dushan Bridge,** on your right, which heads past the fish ponds toward the island.

TURTLE HEAD ISLAND (yuántóu zhǔ; 鼋头渚). Perhaps the most renowned part of Lake Taihu is Turtle Head Island, a peninsula shaped like—guess what?—a turtle head, extending into the northwest part of the lake about 8km from Wuxi. This old reptilian noggin contains hidden natural gems for the daring explorer; to all others, it represents the unstoppable sprawl of pavilions and hokey tourist attractions. The island can also be reached via Baojie Bridge, which connects the head to land near the Li Yuan Garden. Near Turtle Head Island's east entrance is **Space City** (tàikōng chéng; 太空城), a surreal, ramshackle amusement center that seems to be on the verge of permanent retirement. Much farther east is the **East Aquarium,** with seven exhibition halls showcasing all sorts of sea-bound beasties. Especially cool is the "Sci-popularization video room." *(Open daily 8am-4pm. Y15.)*

Admission to Turtle Head Island includes ferry access to **Taihu Fairy Islands** (tàihú xiān dǎo; 太湖仙岛), also called **Three Hills Islands** (sān shān dǎo; 三山岛). While Turtle Head Island holds some natural treats (such as the "Sino-Japan Flowery Cherry Woods") to balance out the pavilions, the Fairy Islands are dominated by tourist-oriented statues, caves, and pagodas. Still, the trip out is a minor adventure, and there's no need to stay on the beaten path. *(Ferries run daily every 20-40min. 8.15am-5.50pm. Be sure to pick up a map (Y3) on your way in. Y35, children Y15. More expensive tickets (Y45, children Y22) also include a ride on a shuttle bus to the center of the island.)*

OTHER SIGHTS. For day-dippers, a **swimming park** of sorts spreads along the Lake Taihu shore on the mainland, east of Baojie Bridge. *(Open daily May-Sep. noon-10pm; ticket sales start at 8:30am. Y15-20.)* Beyond, the **Li Yuan Garden** packs in the crowds, but goes overboard on the manmade structures. *(Open daily sunrise-sunset. Y20.)*

ZHENJIANG 镇江 ☎0511

Some cities have distinctive landmarks or landscapes. Zhenjiang has a distinctive smell. Step a block or two away from Zhenjiang's stolid railway station, and you'll find yourself in a pickle. Or at least in the stuff pickles are made of. The sharp, pungent scent of vinegar drifts through the town, swirling about the jars sold at nearly every street corner and slinking about the doors of every local restaurant. The odor originates at the famed Heng Shun Sauce and Vinegar Factory, the home of a 1400 year-old recipe for China's most prized fragrant vinegar. In 1908, the recipe won the gold prize at the World Expo in Panama—a feat it repeated in Paris in 1985. The bottles of vinegar have since made their way around the world, and are as easy to find on the shelves of a grocery store in Chinatown as in China.

Zhenjiang's history certainly didn't begin with its 1908 culinary victory. The town's strategic position at the convergence of the Yangzi River and the Grand

SHANGHAI

Canal and between Nanjing and Shanghai has lured warlords, traders, and businessmen to the area. During the 19th century, imperialism and opium brought scores of Europeans to town. But the city proved to be saucy in more ways than one, and managed to trap the H.M.S. *Amethyst*, a British warboat, in 1949. Today, Zhenjiang lives in relative obscurity, attracting the occasional tourist who seeks nothing more than to stash away a few bottles of top vintage for the trip home. The city doesn't offer a whole lot else, and seems fairly content to remain that way. Indeed, residents often greet travelers with a slightly puzzled glance, wondering why their city merits a visit. The puzzlement fades quickly, though, replaced with an easy and welcoming friendliness.

✦❔ ORIENTATION AND PRACTICAL INFORMATION

Zhenjiang lies on the south bank of the **Yangzi River** and stretches more to the east and west than to the south. The **Grand Canal** runs north through town, cutting through the central part of the city before it makes its way to the river. Trains and many minibuses arrive near Zhongshan Lu, also in the west part of town, close to the Heng Shun factory and many hotels and restaurants. Most buses arrive at the bus station on Jiefang Nan Lu, a few blocks south of Dashi Kou.

The busiest part of town is in the southeast, centered around **Dashi Kou** (大十口), the large intersection of **Zhongshan Lu** (中山路), a major thoroughfare running from east to west, and **Jiefang Lu** (解放路), an avenue running from north to south. Almost all city buses pass through Dashi Kou, and a simple awareness of one's relative position to the intersection makes navigation infinitely easier. Here one can also find most of the city's useful tourist services. In the west, closer to the river, the streets become narrower and more closely packed in the oldest part of Zhenjiang, a maze of tiny shops and large-scale construction projects. **Jinshan Temple,** farther west, marks the end of the main city.

Trains: Zhenjiang Train Station (zhènjiāng huǒchē zhàn; 镇江火车站) is west of the city center. Buy tickets on the far right side of the station; hours vary, but windows #8 and 9 should be open all night. Zhenjiang is another one of those happy cities on the Nanjing-Shanghai line, with trains leaving frequently to: **Nanjing** (1hr., Y4-18); **Shanghai** (3-4hr., Y14-56); **Suzhou** (3-3½hr., Y9-36); and **Wuxi** (2-3hr., Y7-28). Trains also go to **Hangzhou** (5½-8hr., 6 per day, Y24-174) and **Hefei** (5-5½hr., 3 per day, Y25-161).

Buses: Long-distance buses leave from one of two stations across from each other on Jiefang Nan Lu, about 3 blocks south of Dashi Kou. The station on the east side serves: **Changzhou** (18 per day 6am-5:45pm, Y21); **Hangzhou** (5 per day 6:50am-2:40pm, Y33-60); **Hefei** (4 per day 7:40am-1:30pm, Y33-56); **Nanjing** (every 10min. 6am-7pm, Y10.5-21); **Shanghai** (11 per day 7:45am-5:15pm, Y56-77); and **Wuxi** (17 per day 7:15am-5:15pm, Y29-33). **Minibuses** leave from a station on Zhongshan Lu, a few blocks from the train station. To: **Hangzhou** (4hr., 3 per day, Y57-70); **Nanjing** (1hr., Y21); **Shanghai** (3hr., 11 per day, Y54-64); and **Wuxi** (1½hr., 17 per day, Y28-32). Buses to **Yangzhou** (40min.-1hr., Y7-12) are everywhere; catch one at the ferry terminal or at either bus station.

Local Transportation: City **buses** are useful for getting to the major tourist sites and transport hubs in town. Most run 6am-6pm, but some, like bus #2, run until 11pm. Fare usually Y1. Bus **#2** goes up Daxi Lu in the old neighborhood, stopping near the museum and ending at Jinshan Temple; **#4** goes to Beigushan and then out to Jiaoshan; **#10** goes to the ferry dock. **Ferries** cross the Yangzi regularly from a **dock** (dùkǒu; 渡口) in the northwest corner of town (Y8). A taxi from the center of town costs Y15-20. You also can hop on a minibus to Yangzhou as it waits in line to board the ferry.

Bike Rental: Bikes are ridden everywhere, but no decent bike rental places are to be found. If you're desperate, buy a cheapie (Y70-90), and resell it when you leave.

Travel Agencies: CITS, 92 Zhongshan Xi Lu (☎523 6361 or 523 7538), about 500m east of the train station. Don't expect a great deal of help here; if you need assistance, try the friendly English-speaking Assistant Manager at the Zhenjiang Hotel next door.

Open daily 8am-noon and 2-6pm. The **Zhenjiang China Culture Tourist Service** (zhèn-jiāng zhōngguó wénhuà lǚxíngshè; 镇江中国文化旅行社), 25 Jiankang Lu, Building 3 (☎523 1806), has brochures in Chinese only. Open daily 8am-noon and 2-6pm.

Bank of China: 235 Zhongshan Lu (☎502 6789), half a block west of Dashi Kou, on the south side of the street. Open daily 8-11:30am and 2-6pm. The **International Hotel Zhenjiang,** half a block to the west, is another option.

PSB: Off a small lane next to McDonald's near Dashi Kou.

Internet Access: Xuelu Bookstore (xuělú shūshè; 雪庐书舍), 17-27 Jiankang Lu (☎503 2143), a few blocks from Zhongshan Lu. From behind the Great Wall Hotel, walk west until the street dead-ends; turn left, and then take an immediate right. This mellow, hole-in-the-wall bookstore has a tiny cafe hidden on one side. A lone computer offers Internet access, so come during the day or be prepared to order a pot of tea (Y6) to sip while you wait. Y10 per hr. Open daily 9am-11pm.

Post Office: 423 Zhongshan Dong Lu has English signs. EMS (open daily 8am-6:30pm). Open daily 8am-6pm. A branch at 215 Jiefang Bei Lu, 1 block north of Dashi Kou, on the west side of the street. Open daily 8-11:30am and 2-6pm. **Postal Code:** 212000.

▚ ACCOMMODATIONS

Hotels cluster around Dashi Kou and the train station. Most post quite expensive rates, but in the off season (and in Zhenjiang, there really isn't a tourist season), hotels willingly grant discounts of up to 50%, and can be bargained to even lower rates. If you don't see a rate you like, just write your price on a sheet of paper, show it at the desk, and wait either for rejection, a room to meet the price, or, ideally, a big, fat discount on a big, fat room.

Jingkou Hotel (jīngkǒu fàndiàn; 京口饭店), 407 Zhongshan Dong Lu (☎522 4866). Look for a gate on the east bank of the Grand Canal; the hotel's about 100m down on the left. The staff may express disbelief when you ask for one of the cheaper rooms, but don't let it dissuade you; cheaper rooms may be old and crumbling, but they have A/C, TV, and bath. Newer rooms are bright and happy, and certainly worth it if you can wring out a discount. Doubles Y120, in new wing Y480.

Great Wall Hotel (cháng chéng dàjiǔdiàn; 长城大酒店), 59 Jiefang Nan Lu (☎523 6851), 2-3 blocks south of Dashi Kou, past the Yanchun Restaurant. The stone and marble lobby feels a bit like a subway station—only cleaner. Rooms are old, but in fair condition. Singles Y140; doubles Y200; triples Y240.

Zhenjiang Hotel (zhènjiāng bīnguǎn; 镇江宾馆), 92 Zhongshan Xi Lu (☎523 3888), 500m east of the train station. Views from the older rooms are dreary, but the rooms themselves are big and spotless. The friendly staff likes to bargain. Doubles Y300-510.

▟ FOOD

Zhenjiang is a veritable bonanza of food stalls and street markets. A walk down Zhongshan Lu reveals the pickled delights at the **Heng Shun Sauce and Vinegar Factory** (héng shùn jiàngcù chǎng; 恒顺酱醋厂). Since 1840, the factory has been pickling everything from turnips to cucumbers to "sacred pagoda vegetables." Not to be outdone, a few side streets off **Zhongshan Lu** just west of here have markets with pickled eggs, pickled vegetables, pickled pecks of pickled peppers, and other local delicacies—pickled, of course. Zhenjiang is also famous for its abundance of freshwater delicacies, including the long-tailed anchovy (huíyú; 回鱼), the rare Yangzi herring (shíyú; 鲥鱼), and another trout-like creature referred to by locals as knife fish (dāoyú; 刀鱼), known to ichthyologists as *leiocassis longirostris*. (We'll stick to "knife fish.") If seafood doesn't appeal, when **Dashi Kou** can soothe the fast food addict's soul, with McDonald's, KFCs, and a range of Chinese chains.

PEARL OF ZHENJIANG

Pearl S. Buck came to Zhenjiang from West Virginia when she was four months old, accompanying her Presbyterian missionary parents. Through the tutelage of her matron, Grandma Wang, and her fondness for Chinese snacks (especially the local sesame cakes), Buck became deeply enamored of Chinese life and, eventually, literature. After attending college in the US, Buck returned to the house in Zhenjiang and taught English at a nearby school.

Buck's prolific literary career spans nearly 30 novels and almost as many short stories, non-fiction works, and children's stories. She won the Nobel Prize for Literature in 1938 for *The Good Earth* (1931), *Sons* (1932), *A House Divided* (1935), and other works. *The Good Earth*, her best-known novel, narrates a rags-to-riches story set against the dramatic sweep of 19th-century China.

Yan Chun Restaurant (yàn chūn jiǔlóu; 宴春酒楼), 17 Renmin Jie (☎527 1615), about 2 blocks east of the museum. Arguably Zhenjiang's most famous restaurant, this place has been around since 1938. The raw pork (Y15) and plump dumplings are remarkably appetizing when dipped in that omnipresent sauce—Zhenjiang vinegar, of course. Open daily 6:15-10am, 11am-2pm, and 3-8:30pm. A newer location, on 87 Jiefang Lu (☎501 0477 or 501 0478), 2 blocks south of Dashi Kou, has numbing cowgirl and karaoke performances, presumably to disguise the blandness of the overpriced point-and-eat main dishes. Open daily 11am-1:30pm and 5-7pm.

▣ SIGHTS

Zhenjiang's sights could easily be ingested in the course of a long day. If you have more time to kill, dawdle in the **Daxi Lu** neighborhood near the museum, a part of town with labyrinthine alleys and street markets shaded by 100-year-old trees.

PEARL S. BUCK HOUSE (sàizhēnzhū jiùjū; 赛珍珠旧居). Pearl S. Buck (1892-1973), the Nobel-prize winning American author who astounded the world with her literary portrayals of Chinese men, spent a total of 18 years in Zhenjiang. The house where she grew up has since been wiped out by a factory, but the home in which she spent her later years in China still stands. In 1991, by the encouragement of Zhenjiang's American sister-city, Tempe, Arizona, the house was turned into a small museum, known as the "Zhenjiang Friendship Exchange Hall" or "Pearl S. Buck House." The museum contains original furniture from Buck's residence; photos and paintings with narration; a small collection of books; and two roomfuls of relics from Zhenjiang's sister-cities in America and Japan, including an assortment of Santa Clauses and "I Love Tempe" mugs. (*6 Runzhoushan Lu, not far from the train station. From the station, head down Zhongshan Lu toward Dashi Kou. Take the 1st left onto Daxi Lu, a narrow street near the Zijin Quan Hotel. At the 2nd left, head up the road going up the hill; the house is at the top. Open daily 8:30-11:30am and 2:30-5pm. Free.*)

JINSHAN TEMPLE (jīnshān sì; 金山寺). This temple and park complex in the northwest part of town has as much water as land space. The park area contains ponds (with those wacky dragon paddle boats), the "Number One Spring in China" (taste-tested by a monk), a slew of souvenir stands (with peeing plastic Buddhas galore), and, most impressively, a 1500 year-old Buddhist temple with a towering pagoda and a still-active community of monks. The main temple is lavishly stuffed with icons and Buddhas of all sorts (none of them peeing), and off to the right side, it's possible to catch the monks shoveling in the rice around mealtime.

Peer out from the top of the eight-sided, seven-storied, 36m tall **Ci Shou Pagoda** (cí shòu tǎ; 慈寿塔) for a view of Zhenjiang's other hilltop sights, an array of fish ponds and farmland, and the mighty Yangzi to the north. A temple was first built on this site 1400 years ago. The current pagoda was constructed in 1900 to mark the Empress Dowager's birthday, although the temple's abbot supposedly raised

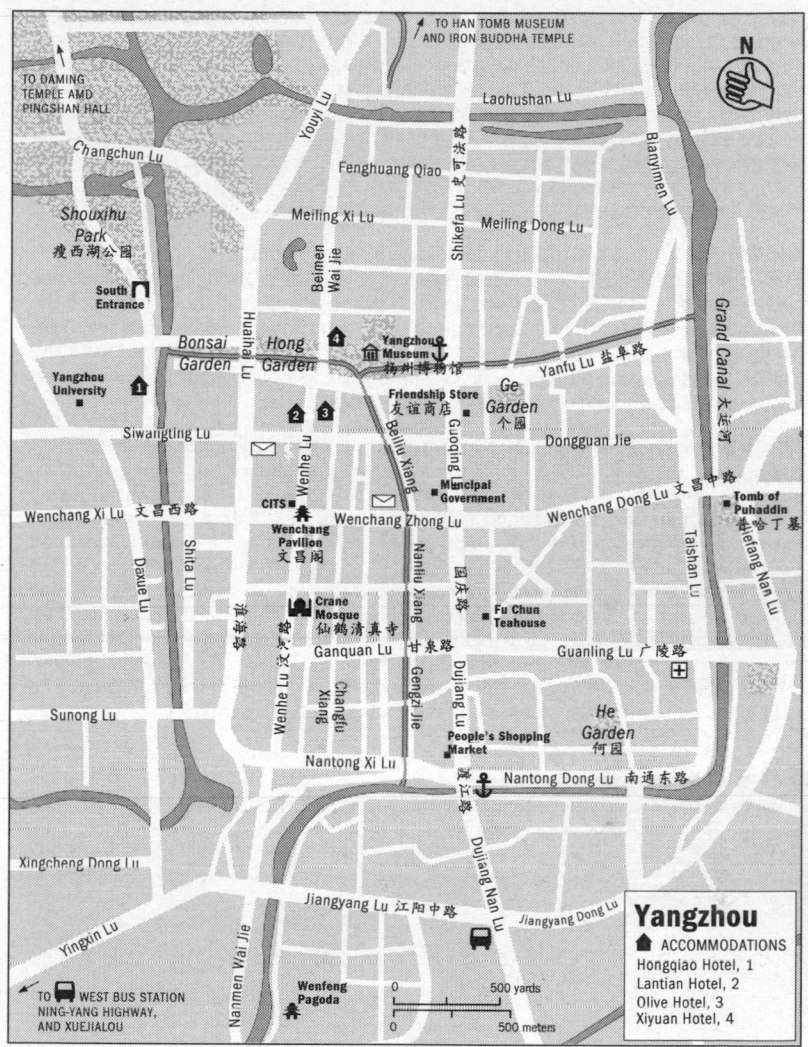

TO HAN TOMB MUSEUM
AND IRON BUDDHA TEMPLE

TO DAMING
TEMPLE AMD
PINGSHAN HALL

Laohushan Lu

Youyi Lu

Changchun Lu

Fenghuang Qiao

Meiling Xi Lu

Meiling Dong Lu

Bianyimen Lu

Shikefa Lu 史可法路

Shouxihu
Park
瘦西湖公园

South
Entrance

Beimen Wai Jie

Grand Canal 大运河

Bonsai
Garden

Hong
Garden

Yangzhou
Museum
扬州博物馆

Yanfu Lu 盐阜路

Huaihai Lu

Yangzhou
University

Friendship Store
友谊商店

Ge
Garden
个园

Siwangting Lu

Bailiu Xiang

Guoqing

Dongguan Jie

Wenhe Lu

Municipal
Government

Wenchang Dong Lu 文昌东路

Tomb of
Puhaddin
普哈丁墓

Wenchang Xi Lu 文昌西路

CITS

Wenchang
Pavilion
文昌阁

Wenchang Zhong Lu

Nanliu Xiang

Taishan Lu

Puhadetang Nan Lu

Shita Lu

Daxue Lu

Crane
Mosque
仙鹤清真寺

Ganquan Lu 甘泉路

Guoqing Lu

Dujiang Lu

Fu Chun
Teahouse

Guanling Lu 广陵路

Sunong Lu

Wenhe Lu 汶河路

Changfu Xiang

Gengzi Jie

People's Shopping
Market

He
Garden
何园

Nantong Xi Lu

Nantong Dong Lu 南通东路

Xingcheng Dong Lu

Dujiang Nan Lu

SHANGHAI

Yingxin Lu

Nanmen Wai Jie

Jiangyang Lu 江阳中路

Jiangyang Dong Lu

TO WEST BUS STATION
NING-YANG HIGHWAY,
AND XUEJIALOU

Wenfeng
Pagoda

0   500 yards

0   500 meters

Yangzhou

▲ ACCOMMODATIONS
Hongqiao Hotel, 1
Lantian Hotel, 2
Olive Hotel, 3
Xiyuan Hotel, 4

money for the project by collecting alms in his hands. *(At the terminus for bus #2.* ☎ *551 2992. Open daily 6am-6pm. Park Y18; Ci Shou Pagoda Y4.)*

JIAOSHAN (jiāoshān; 焦山). In the far eastern portion of the town hulks a jungly island with pavilions, historical remnants, and a large tower on top. The mainland side of this park has a few diversions of its own, including a waterfall, but the island is the main attraction. Free ferries shuttle visitors across the river (every 20min. 7:30am-5:30pm), or you can pay extra to ride a motorboat that will put you close enough to the river to spit in it—and for it to spit back (Y4 across the river, Y10 to Beigushan). The best way is to use the **cable car,** which lifts you far above the river, leaving you all alone to bear witness to the Yangzi's awesome flood potential. *(Cable car runs daily 8am-4pm. Y15 to the island, Y10 to the mainland.)*

The **pagoda** glistens after a recent restoration effort, which seems to be as much cause for pride as the existence of the pagoda itself. *(Y15, but the views from the base* *are just as lovely.)* Near the tower on the river side is a small **calligraphy museum** (Y2), and not far are some old gun batteries used during Zhenjiang's active stronghold days. On the mainland side is a cluster of buildings that includes the Buddhist **Din Hui Temple** and a tree-filled pavilion named after Jiao Guang, a sage hermit who lived here. You can also wander the island's winding paths, sucking in the fragrance of ancient trees rich with centuries of river dew, all the while relishing those final moments of sweet life before you get back on that big, scary cable car. *(Take bus #4, or head northeast on city streets until you hit Zhenjiao Lu, which winds out and around toward the front entrance. Open daily 7:15am-5:30pm; last admission 4:45pm. Y15.)*

ZHENJIANG HISTORY MUSEUM (zhènjiāng lìshǐ bówùguǎn; 镇江历史博物馆). The main attraction here is the weirdly angular red-brick building itself, an imaginative, woody old beast that once housed the British Consulate. If you have the time, fork over the cash and march up the hill, where you'll find several unexceptional cultural items from the area on display, including the anchor from the H.M.S. *Amethyst* and a silver coffin containing the ashes of a saint. *(85 Boxian Lu, at Daxi Lu. ☎ 527 7143. Open daily 9am-noon and 1:30-5pm. Y5.)*

BEIGUSHAN (běigùshān; 北固山). According to the *Romance of the Three Kingdoms*, the King of Shu Liu Bei was offered the hand of Sun Shangxiang, the sister of Sun Quan, King of Wu. As Liu Bei floated down the Yangzi for the wedding, Sun Quan and his treacherous advisors plotted to kill the bridegroom and annex the province of Hubei by ambushing butchers inside the **Ganlu Temple** atop Beigushan. But the girl's mother intervened and approved the marriage of her daughter to our hero; the royal hitch cemented the alliance against the Dark Side of Cao Cao's vast Kingdom of Wei to the north. Without the story, Beigushan would be just any old overgrown garden, with silly statues and an ancient temple with the irrevocably lightning-blitzed **Iron Pagoda,** and the **Qinghui Pavilion** overlooking the river. The rock in the courtyard with a gash in the middle is said to have been where the two kings swore their allegiance. *(Open daily 7am-5:50pm. Y10.)*

YANGZHOU 扬州 ☎ 0514

If Zhenjiang proved a brutish defensive stronghold through the centuries, then Yangzhou, the city across the river, was the brains behind the operation. Scholars, artists, and foreign merchants have flocked to this town to enjoy the meandering waterways, charming bridges, and breezy avenues. The city streets seem subdued and even peaceful–and not just because of the ordinances against honking. Residents here are sublimely easy-going and more than willing to chat. After all, vocal braggarts have a history here too: one of Yangzhou's cultural legacies is *ping hua*, a lively form of hyperbolic storytelling.

Even though modern Yangzhou is no longer the intellectual center it once was, it still has its pride: China's current president, Jiang Zemin, was born and raised in Yangzhou, something you'll hear mentioned often. Still, the city's plaintive, serene atmosphere inspires contemplation—a good thing, since there's little else to do. Stroll long enough, and you're bound to come across the city's few gardens, a monastery, and a small museum, all of which could easily provide distraction for a day.

✴ ❷ ORIENTATION AND PRACTICAL INFORMATION

Yangzhou is a relatively small city, tucked next to the **Grand Canal.** Like many cities along the Canal, the streets here are laid out on a grid, making navigation easy despite the fact that many streets often change their names as they go along. Most hotels and services are on **Wenhe Lu** (汶河路) and **Wenchang Lu** (文昌路), which intersect at the **Wenchang Pavilion** (wénchāng gé; 文昌阁) in the center of town.

Most buses arrive at a station in the south of town, just past the Grand Canal, on a major thoroughfare that has the gall to switch names three times, from **Dujiang Lu** (渡江路) in the south to **Guoqing Lu** (国庆路) and finally to **Shikefa Lu** (史可法路)

in the north. In the northwest part of town is **Shouxi Lake Park,** the town's most popular attraction. **Yanfu Lu** (盐阜路) runs east from the park, along a smaller canal where imperial boats used to dock—now the home to a thriving market of fruits, vegetables, and animals of all kinds.

Buses: Yangzhou Bus Station (yángzhōu qìchē zhàn; 扬州汽车站) is at the intersection of Dujiang Nan Lu and Jiangyang Dong Lu, about 1.5km south of town. Take buses #1 or 2 from the northeast part of town, or #5, 13, or 15 from Wenhe Lu or the northwest near Shouxi Lake Park. Ticket office open daily 5am-6pm. To: **Hangzhou** (6hr., 4 per day, Y78); **Hefei** (4hr., 6 per day 7:30am-3pm, Y53); **Nanjing** (1½hr., 36 per day 6:45am-5:45pm, Y22); **Shanghai** (4hr., 7 per day, Y40-69); and **Wuxi** (2hr., 16 per day 6:30am-5:30pm, Y42-51). Buses to **Zhenjiang** (40min.-1hr. with ferry, multiple departures per day, Y7-12) and other nearby towns leave from the **West Bus Station** (qìchē xī zhàn; 汽车西站), accessible via buses #8 (from Guoqing Lu) and 22 (from Wenhe Lu). Long-distance buses from the main station may also stop here.

Local Transportation: It's easy to walk to most places in Yangzhou, although some of the more popular tourist destinations are best reached by **bus.** Most buses run 7am-7pm, although they can be few and far between. Fare Y0.5-1. Bus **#15** runs from the far north of town, past Shouxi Lake and along Wenhe Lu to the main bus station; **#5** and **22** follow similar routes in the south, but after they pass Shouxi Lake, they continue to Daming Temple; **#4** and **12** run along Wenchang Lu. **Tourist buses** shuttle between the Imperial Dock, Shouxi Lake Park, Daming Temple, and other local tourist spots (6 per day 8:30am-3:30pm, Y5).

Taxis: Base fare Y5-7, each additional km Y1.2-1.4. Taxis are hard to find on the city outskirts, but **pedicabs** are everywhere. Drivers may try to charge high rates; be firm.

Travel Agencies: CTS, 10 Wenhe Zhong Lu (☎731 7188), on the west side of the street, just north of Wenchang Pavilion. Open daily 8am-6pm. **Yangzhou CYTS** (yángzhōu zhōngguó qīngnián lǚxíngshè; 扬州中国青年旅行社), 6 Siwangting Lu (☎735 3666). Open daily 8am-6pm.

Tourist Complaints: ☎732 5601.

Bank of China: 28 Wenhe Bei Lu. The exchange counter will make even the most paranoid traveler feel safe; be prepared for extensive examinations of your signature and documents. 24hr. ATM (Cirrus, MC, Visa/Plus).

Bookstore: Xinhua Bookstore, 65 Wenhe Lu (☎734 4427). Lots of maps, dictionaries, and well-thumbed English classics. Open daily 8-11am and noon-7pm. An even better place is at 10 Yanfu Xi Lu (☎734 3916), with piles of dictionaries and stacks of English novels and Chinese classics in translation. Open daily 8:30-11:30am and 2:30-6pm.

Internet Access: The **Xiyuan Hotel** business center has slow Internet access for Y20 per hr. Open daily 8am-10:30pm. **Jintu Computer Room,** 168 Siwangting Lu (☎736 9030), on the north side of the street, about a block west of the canal. Less than a block from the university, in a building with frosted glass doors. Noisy and dirty with a fast connection. Y2 per hr. Open daily 8am-11pm.

Post Office: China Post, 37 Siwangting Lu, just west of Wenhe Lu, on the south side of the street. EMS available. **Postal Code:** 225002.

▶ ACCOMMODATIONS

Yangzhou is high on high-end hotels, and there are few truly budget options. Anywhere in the center or north of town is convenient to tourist sights and amenities, so if you have time, wander this area and pressure proprietors to lower rates.

Hongqiao Hotel (hóngqiáo bīnguǎn; 虹桥宾馆; ☎736 5275). Pass through a gate on the west side of the street between Siwangting Lu and the south entrance to Shouxi Lake; the hotel is the white building on the right. With friendly staff, modest rooms with dying rugs, and primitive shower heads, this hotel passes the test. Singles and triples Y180; doubles Y160 (can be bargained to Y120).

Xiyuan Hotel (xīyuán dàjiǔdiàn; 西园大酒店), 1 Fengle Shang Jie (☎734 4888), north of Yanfu Xi Lu and 1 block east of Wenhe Bei Lu, behind the museum. Though the exterior of the Xiyuan may resemble a riot-proof monstrosity, the inside is fairly luxurious.

Rooms in an older building have big windows and plush carpets. A big bonus—complimentary detergent. Doubles Y256-620; triples Y238. Credit cards accepted.

Olive Hotel (aòlìwēi dàshà; 奥力威大厦), 36 Wenhe Bei Lu (☎736 1888). Apart from the temperamental keycards, this is a glossy newbie, with a friendly staff. Rooms sparkle and have remarkably powerful A/C. Bargain. Singles Y288; doubles Y328.

Lantian Hotel (lántiān dàshà; 蓝天大厦), 159 Wenhe Nan Lu (☎736 0000). Dark, claustrophobic hallways lead to surprisingly large, clean rooms with refrigerators. The view, both inside and out, can be a bit dreary. Practice your bargaining skills. Singles Y220-280; doubles Y280-420; triples Y360-420. Credit cards accepted.

FOOD

A Chinese city doesn't really deserve a visit unless it serves a decent dumpling. Luckily for Yangzhou, its dumplings and cakes are divine; they are best sampled in the southeast part of town, either at the **Fu Chun Tea House** or from nearby street carts. The bazaar-like area around the Imperial Dock features several sit-down places as well as a busy market with puppies and goldfish. In the evenings, small stalls and carts line **Wenhe Lu.** But this same street has also been afflicted by a festering fast food rash—you can find both **McDonald's** and **KFC** here.

■ **Fu Chun Tea House** (fúchūn cháshè; 富春茶社), 35 Desheng Qiao (☎723 3326), down an alley branching east off Guoqing Lu, between Guangling Lu and Wenchang Lu. The only thing better than tea and dumplings is more tea and more dumplings. Indulge in a fantastic 10-piece dumpling sampler and all the tea you can drink (about Y25). Open daily 6am-8:30pm. A second branch is at 10 Tonggong Bei Lu (☎784 4375).

White Art Original Pottery Bar (huáěrshí táobā; 华而石陶吧), 8 Fengle Xia Jie (☎734 7369), along the Imperial Dock, directly over the canal just south and about 1 block west of the Xi Yuan Hotel. Yangzhou's most high-concept bar/restaurant, an extension of a Shanghai bar: visitors sit in leaf-adorned rope-swing chairs and can try their hands with wet clay at one of three pottery wheels in the middle of the room. Singapore Sling Y20 and Coke Y8, although options for food are limited (dumplings Y16, fried eggs Y3). Open M-Th 1pm-1am, F-Su 9am-2am.

Wan Cheerful Department Store (wànjiāfú shāngchéng; 万家福商城, ☎973 7531), just south of McDonald's, on the west side of the street near Wenchang Lu. Never before have you seen so much plastic food—in the displays, that is. The **Taiwan Noodle Shop** (táiwān dànzì miàn; 台湾担仔面) on the top floor features a gigantic smorgasbord of dishes, almost all of which cost less than Y10. Just point, pay, and enjoy. Open M-Sa 8:30am-9:30pm, Su 8:30am-10pm.

Meixi Coffee Bar (méixì kāfēiguǎn; 梅茜咖啡馆), 26 Dahongqiao Lu (☎733 2653), half a block east of the south entrance to Shouxi Park. Look for the bizarre Greek columns and stone cherubs. One of the few coffee bars in the area, with funny, florid private sitting rooms in back, a super friendly owner, lots of booze, and an espresso machine. Open daily 1pm-midnight.

SIGHTS

If you don't have much time, Yangzhou offers one of the more unusual sightseeing tours in the region: **Emperor Qianlong's Boat Tour** (qiánlóng shuǐshàng yóulǎn; 乾隆水上游览) glides (via yellow dragon boat) along the route supposedly followed by the Qing dynasty ruler upon his visit to the city in 1757, past many of the sights constructed especially for him in Shouxi Lake Park. Catch this tour (2hr., Y200) near the Imperial Dock, just south of the Xi Yuan Hotel, or at the south entrance to Shouxi Lake Park.

SHOUXI LAKE PARK (shòuxī hú gōngyuán; 瘦西湖公园). This park's name means "Slender West Lake," an explicit comparison to the much more famous West Lake in Hangzhou (p. 335). Shouxi Lake is lush, sometimes overgrown, with willows and peach trees. The paths are pleasant, snaking past a canal and a vari-

THE LITTLE MONK WHO COULD As you're huffing and puffing to climb the stairs to the top of Qiling Temple (the large pagoda at the center of Daming Temple; see p. 329) bear in mind that your efforts are piddly compared to the hardship endured by Jian Zhan (688-763), the Buddhist monk to whom the structure and the nearby Jian Zhan Memorial Hall is dedicated. Jian, an 8th century scholar, was invited to Japan to share secrets of Chinese Buddhism and to reinject discipline into the Japanese branch of the religion. But as much as the monk tried to get to Japan, he was constantly forced to return. Finally, on his sixth attempt at age 66, he reached the island, where he and his followers dumped all sorts of knowledge (about Buddhism as well as medicine, architecture, and other liberal disciplines) on their Japanese colleagues. The monk died and was buried in Japan, but the Japanese hardly forgot him; instead, they have come to revere him for his wisdom (and persistence!). In 1974, Japanese benefactors, in joint commemoration with China, built the Quiling Temple, which was fashioned after the Toshodai Temple in Nara, Japan. The memorial hall houses a copy of a statue of the monk; the original is still a Japanese treasure.

ety of interesting structures, including Dahong Bridge, Lotus Pond, Southerly Breeze, "Long Loggie," and the usual playground and zoo. For a bit of high-flying fun (50m, to be exact), try the **hot air balloon** rides (Y30, 2 people Y50).

The vase-shaped **White Tower Pagoda** (bái tǎ; 白塔) was built by a salt merchant in 1784. Just past that, cross over **Five Pavilion Bridge** (wǔ tíng qiáo; 五亭桥), built by a local aristocrat to welcome Emperor Qianlong in 1757. This bridge has 15 "cavities," or roofed arches; as a sign declares, "When it's full moon, every cavity carries a moon, so the goldenness on the water sways and the moons contend for splendour, which is impossible to put into words." So we won't even try.

Beyond the bend at **Xi Chu Pavilion,** the path enters a less gimmicky, less crowded strip of the park, with pavilions spanning water all the way to the north entrance. Paddle boats cost Y10-16 per hour. *(On Liuhu Lu, off Siwangting Lu near the Hongqiao Hotel; also on Pingshantang Lu, near the Daming Temple. Accessible by buses #1, 4, 6, 16, and 18. ☎ 734 5111. Open daily 6:30am-5:30pm. Y20.)*

DAMING TEMPLE (dàmíng sì; 大明寺). Right across from the north entrance to Shouxi Lake stands the "Great Brightness Temple," named after the enlightened era in which it was built (AD 457-465). Among the highlights are **Pingshan Hall** (píngshān táng; 平山堂), originally built in 1048; a nine-story pagoda; and **Jian Zhan Memorial Hall** (Y5), built in 1973 to commemorate the monk Jian Zhan (see **The Little Monk Who Could,** p. 329). Says a sign at the front: "Monks, emperors, sages, poets, men of letters...all pious pilgrims who said their prayers [at Daming Temple], without exception, have had their prayers answered." So march up the stairs and start praying. *(Across from the north entrance to Shouxi Lake. Take bus #5, 21, or 22. Open daily 7:45am-5pm. Y12.)* The area northeast of the temple has a few ponds, the **Tang City Wall** (tángchéng yízhǐ; 唐城遗址), and the **Han Tomb Museum** (hàn mù bówùguǎn; 汉墓博物馆), built over an archeological site off Xiangbie Lu.

YANGZHOU MUSEUM (yángzhōu bówùguǎn; 扬州博物馆). The two exhibit halls house mostly pottery and porcelain wares, fans, and hairpins; more notable items include a spooky jade suit (worn by a dummy mummy) and a 14m long Tang-dynasty canoe dug out of a single tree trunk (and dredged out of the Grand Canal in 1960). The museum's Marco Polo Hall is by the entrance to the courtyard, near the many small antique stores. *(On Shikefa Lu, near the Friendship Store, in the northeastern part of the city. ☎ 734 5111. Open daily 8-11am and 2-5pm. Y8.)*

OTHER SIGHTS. On the canal, at the north end of Guoqing Lu, is the **Imperial Dock,** where Qianlong's tour boat is said to have docked during his visit 243 years ago. Thatch-roofed buildings line Yanfu Lu all the way to the Yangzhou Museum and the **Yangzhou Antique Store** (yángzhōu wénwù shāngdiàn; 扬州文物商店) across the street. Summer evenings, a plaza in front is converted into a rink for roller-skating. About 500m farther east at 10 Yanfu Lu, **Ge Garden** (gè yuán; 个园) is another leftover from the days when salt merchants were the fat cats in Yangzhou. It was built in 1818 by Huang Yin-tai, a big fan of bamboo; the garden is bursting at the seams with 40 species of the stuff. *(Open daily 7am-6pm. Y12.)*

On the south side of Yangzhou is the **Crane Mosque,** (xiānhè qīngzhēn sì; 仙鹤清真寺), one of the few mosques in this part of China. The stark courtyard is highlighted by a prayer room, with a large wooden wall covered in gilded Arabic inscriptions. Enter the building off an alley about 10m east of Guoqing Lu and one block north of Ganquan Lu. *(The gate is tended by a rather old man, so knock loudly. Open Sa-Th sunrise-sunset.)* Farther northeast (accessible by bus #12), on Wenchang Lu just across the Grand Canal, stands the **Tomb of Puhaddin** (pǔhādīng mùyuán; 普哈丁墓园), the resting place of a 16th-century descendant of Muhammad who served as a missionary in China. Look for the small, gold onion-domes; the tomb is through several gates beyond the garden and pond and atop the hill.

ZHEJIANG 浙江

Zhejiang's graceful scenic wonders have been the source of legends and the site of many landmark cultural and historical events over the centuries. Extending south from Shanghai municipality, most of the province's areas of fame and interest are clustered in the northern portion of the province, not far from Shanghai. The ancient provincial capital, Hangzhou, is the site of West Lake, whose beauty has been memorialized by painters and poets for more than a millennium. Nearby Putuoshan, an island sheltering one of China's four most sacred Buddhist mountains, is one of the can't-miss highlights of the province, infused with a sense of spirituality and magic that even the most diehard secular infidel can appreciate. Further inland and to the south, the province is dotted with densely populated towns, an occasional major city, and the fertile fields that yield some of the country's richest rice harvests. On the whole, the farther one goes from Shanghai, the fewer travelers (and attractions for travelers) there are. But the attractions of northern Zhejiang provide travelers with unmatched opportunities to experience the sites that have epitomized China's cultural achievements and natural beauty.

HANGZHOU 杭州 ☎0571

A now-famous saying declares that "above there is heaven, below there are Suzhou and Hangzhou." Indeed, at the other end of the Grand Canal from the "City of Gardens" (Suzhou), Hangzhou's famous West Lake has been fodder for artists and literati, inspiring calligraphy, paintings, and poetry, and leaving behind dozens of legends in its willow-tree scented wake. Blessed with over 57 scenic spots, Hangzhou's poetic beauty and idyllic landscapes make it not only a tourist beehive but a private retreat—Mother Nature did wonders for this city, and both locals and visitors make the most of its visual splendor.

Under the name Linan, Hangzhou served as the capital of the Southern Song Dynasty from AD 1127 to 1279, growing to become a cultural and political epicenter. These days, as the capital of Zhejiang province, Hangzhou balances its scenic beauty with thriving agricultural, industrial, and commercial districts. Tea and silk remain the region's most coveted local products, and their delicate refinement embodies Hangzhou's leisurely pace.

Hangzhou has not gone without the earthly changes of economic development, however; construction cranes tower over willow trees and large towers sprout up faster than spring blossoms. Thankfully, Hangzhou's attractions have stood their ground against the encroachment of urbanization, and the energy of the city center complements (rather than intrudes upon) the serenity of the lake.

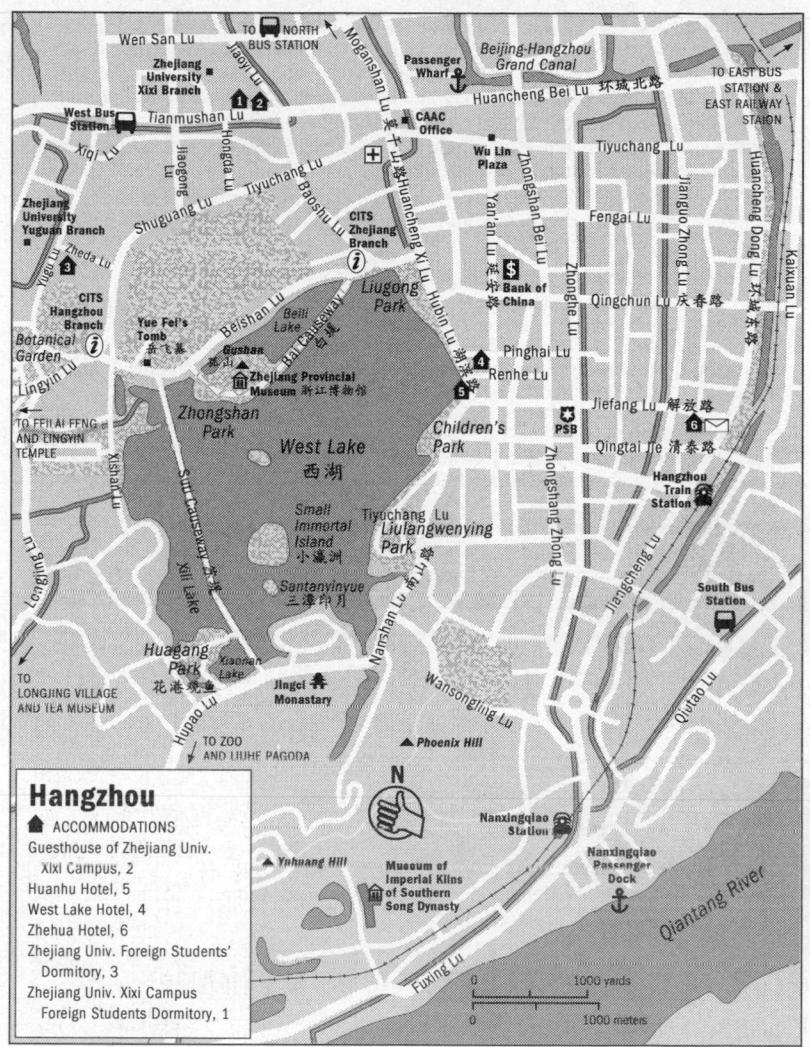

Hangzhou

🏠 ACCOMMODATIONS

Guesthouse of Zhejiang Univ.
Xixi Campus, 2
Huanhu Hotel, 5
West Lake Hotel, 4
Zhehua Hotel, 6
Zhejiang Univ. Foreign Students'
Dormitory, 3
Zhejiang Univ. Xixi Campus
Foreign Students Dormitory, 1

⬛ TRANSPORTATION

Airplanes: Hangzhou Airport (hángzhōu jīchǎng; 杭州机场; ☎514 1477 or 514 1010), northeast of central Hangzhou. A taxi to the city center costs about Y35-50 and takes about 30min. Shuttle buses (every 30-40min. 6:10am-6pm, Y5) run between the airport and the **CAAC ticket office,** 390 Tiyuchang Lu (domestic info ☎515 4259; international ☎515 2575), off Wulin Square. Open daily 8am-8pm. To: **Beijing** (4-5 per day, Y920); **Fuzhou** (8am, Y590); **Guangzhou** (5 per day, 8am-6:45pm, Y840); and **Hong Kong** (2 per day, Y1520).

Trains: Hangzhou Train Station (hángzhōu huǒchē zhàn; 杭州火车站; ☎702 3729), an ark-shaped building on Huancheng Dong Lu just south of Xihu Dadao. At the terminus of buses #7, 11, 39, and 151. To: **Beijing** (16hr., 9:25pm, Y200); **Fuzhou** (18hr., 5:25pm, Y125); **Guangzhou** (25hr., 10:16am, Y171); **Hefei** (11½hr., 8:07pm, Y106);

Nanchang (12hr., 6 per day, Y45); **Nanjing** (6-7hr., frequent departures, Y99); and **Shanghai** (2-3hr., 24 per day 9:05am-6:23pm, Y33). **Hangzhou East Train Station** (hángzhōu huǒchē dōng zhàn; 杭州火车东站; ☎645 0514), at the end of Tiancheng Lu and at the terminus of buses #5, 28, and 518, only has local service to nearby cities.

Buses: There are 4 bus stations with somewhat overlapping service. The East Station generally is a good bet, providing service to most neighboring areas except Huangshan.

East Long-distance Bus Station (chángtú qìchē dōng zhàn; 长途汽车东站), 215 Genshan Lu (☎694 8252), accessible by buses #19, 31, 56, 305, and 805. Currently fields more traffic than the other stations due to its size and proximity to the new expressway. Open daily 6am-7:30pm. To: **Fuzhou** (16hr., 8:20am, Y201); **Nanjing** (5hr., 8 per day 7:20am-4:40pm, Y67-113); **Ningbo** (2hr., every 10min. 6:20am-7:30pm, Y42-49); **Shanghai** (2hr., every 20min. 6:40am-7:10pm, Y47-54); and **Shaoxing** (1hr., every 20min, Y18.5).

North Long-distance Bus Station (chángtú qìchē běi zhàn; 长途汽车北站), 758 Moganshan Lu (☎809 7761), is far from the city center. Accessible via buses #155, 503, and 555. Open daily 6am-6pm. To **Hefei** (8hr., 3:40pm, Y67-171) and **Nanjing** (5hr., 1 per day, Y98).

West Long-distance Bus Station (chángtú qìchē xī zhàn; 长途汽车西站), 89 Tianmushan Lu (☎502 4220), at Yugu Lu. Accessible via buses #30, 152, and 502. Open daily 5:30am-7pm. To **Huangshan** (5hr., every 50min. 6:50am-2:40pm, Y54-76) and **Nanjing** (5hr., 7:50am and 2:50pm, Y98).

South Long-distance Bus Station (chángtú qìchē nán zhàn; 长途汽车南站), 417 Qiutao Lu (☎606 4914), at the terminus of bus #501 and accessible by bus #39. To smaller cities within Zhejiang, including **Dongyang** (3½hr., every 30min. 7am-7:30pm, Y20).

Boats: Passenger Wharf (kèyùn mǎtóu; 客运码头), 138 Huancheng Bei Lu (☎505 8458), north of Wulin Square, near the intersection of Huangshan Bei Lu and Zhongshan Bei Lu. Accessible via buses #52, 156, 502, and 806. Open daily 6am-6pm. The scenic route to the neighboring cities of **Suzhou** (13½hr., 5:30pm, Y55-95) and **Wuxi** (12hr., 6pm, Y51-82).

Local Transportation: Most **buses** run from around 6:30am to 8 or 9pm; hours for each route are marked on signs at designated stops. Base fare Y1, with A/C (denoted by a "K" in front of the route number) Y2. Bus **#K7** goes from the train station and then loops around the lake; **#27** shuttles between the northern edge of the lake and the Longjing tea village; **#152** and **32** run from east to west along the major commercial roads. **Mini-buses** (Y1.5) follow popular bus routes, and **tour buses** #1, 2, and 3 (Y2) service West Lake and the surrounding forest area.

Taxis: There are probably more cabs in Hangzhou than fish in West Lake. Base fare Y8-10, each additional km Y1. From Yanan Lu to the airport Y35-50, to the train and bus stations Y8-15. **Pedicabs** make short trips (under 1km) for Y5-8.

Bike Rental: The former Hangzhou University Student dormitory plans to rent bikes beginning in fall 2000.

✦🛈 ORIENTATION AND PRACTICAL INFORMATION

Hangzhou has built its reputation and tourist industry around **West Lake** (xī hú; 西湖), the approximate geographic center of the city. The major downtown area lies to the east. **Hubin Lu** (湖滨路) begins at the northeastern tip of the lake and hugs its banks as it continues south, becoming **Nanshan Lu** (南山路). East of and roughly parallel to Hubin Lu is the commercial **Yanan Lu** (延安路), which intersects **Qingchun Lu** (青春路), **Pinghai Lu** (平海路), and **Jiefang Lu** (解放路), all of which run from east to west. The area bounded by these four streets contains many of Hangzhou's more upscale hotels and stores. Most sights are accessible via public transportation. The main train station is on **Huancheng Dong Lu** (环城东路).

Travel Agency: CITS, 1 Shihan Lu (☎515 2888; email zjcitsat@mail.hz.zj.cn), on a small lane off the corner of Beishan Lu and Baoshu Lu, facing the lake. Average commission Y30-40. Separate "English Department" offers tours, interpreters, and tickets. Open daily 8:30am-5pm.

Bank of China: 320 Yanan Lu (☎707 7996), a half-block north of Qingchun Lu. Exchanges traveler's checks and issues credit card advances. ATM service. Open M-F 8am-noon and 2-5:30pm. Few other branches exchange traveler's checks.

Bookstore: Zhejiang Province Foreign Language Bookstore (zhèjiāng shěng wài wén shūdiàn; 浙江省外文书店), 34 Hubin Lu, just south of Qingchun Lu. Fair selection of English-Chinese tourist maps (Y4), plus good pickings in the English classics and translated Chinese literature section on the 3rd floor. Open daily 9am-8:30pm.

PSB: 155 Jiefang Lu (☎782 1114). Open daily 8am-noon and 2-5:30pm.

Hospitals: Hangzhou City Central Hospital (hángzhōu shì zhōng yīyuàn; 杭州市中医院), 453 Tiyuchang Lu (☎515 7591); **Hangzhou City No. 1 People's Hospital** (hángzhōu shì dì yī rénmín yīyuàn; 杭州市第一人民医院), 261 Wangsa Lu (☎706 5701); **Zhejiang Province No. 2 Hospital** (zhéjiāng dì èr yīyuàn; 浙江第二医院), 68 Jiefang Lu (☎707 7272). English speakers at all 3 hospitals.

Telephones: China Telecom, at the intersection of Yanan Lu and Tiyuchang Lu, in Wulin Square. IDD service at counter #1 (open 24hr). Open daily 8:15am-5pm.

Internet Access: Many of the newer university guesthouses and foreign student dorms offer on-site access. **WWW Internet Bar** (sāndá wǎngbā; 三达网吧), 218 Baoshan Lu (☎511 1823), near Hangzhou University off Tianmushan Lu, half a block south of Shuguang Lu. Y5 per hr. Open daily 9am-midnight. **China Telecom Internet Bar,** 10 Huxing Lu (☎708 0085), closer to the city center. Y5 per hr. Open daily 8:30am-5:30pm.

Post Office: Hangzhou International Post Office, 1 Jiefang Lu (☎780 0568), at Huancheng Dong Lu, 5min. north of the train station. Take bus #152 from the city center. EMS and Poste Restante available. Open daily 8am-6pm. **Postal Code:** 310000.

▌ ACCOMMODATIONS

University dormitories are the cheapest places to stay in Hangzhou for those who don't mind the slight trek to the city center. For just a bit more, it is possible to get a basic standard room at one of the city's lower-end hotels. Otherwise, big spenders have their pick of luxury hotels, including the historic **Shangri-La Hotel** (xiānggé lǐlā fàndiàn; 香格里拉饭店), 78 Beishan Lu (☎707 7951), where American President Richard Nixon met with Zhou Enlai during his historic 1972 visit to China.

Zhejiang University Foreign Students' Dormitory (zhèjiāng dàxué wàiguó liúxuéshēng lóu; 浙江大学外国留学生楼), ☎795 1386), a 10min. bus ride from the lake. Take either bus #16 from Hubin Lu or #21 west from Huancheng Xi Lu to the last stop, opposite the Zhejiang University main gate. Walk on Zheda Lu away from the university entrance, turn right at the first alley, and the dormitory will be on your left. Standard rooms are bare but practical with a not-so-lively surrounding area. Singles Y60; doubles Y100-120. If all rooms are full, try the **new dormitory** building on Xiqi Lu, scheduled to open in Sept. 2000. A 10min. walk through campus, or take bus #152 directly to Gudang and enter through the back gate of the university on Xiqi Lu. Rooms have A/C and bath. Reserve up to 1 week in advance. Singles Y50-100; doubles Y150-180.

Zhejiang University Xixi Campus Foreign Students Dormitory (zhèjiāng dàxué xīxī xiàoqū liúxuéshēng lóu; 浙江大学西溪校区留学生楼; ☎827 3784), at the corner of Hangda Lu and Tianmushan Lu, in Building 3. Take bus #152 from the train station or #21 from city center to Zhejiang Xixi. From the main gate, bear right along the main path, past basketball courts on the left. Dank common baths, poor lighting, and doors in various states of disrepair make for some aesthetic disappointment, but friendly service and fellow students provide solace for those who don't mind roughing it. Room availability limited during May and Oct. holidays. 3-bed dorms Y40; 2-bed dorms with A/C Y60.

Guesthouse of Zhejiang University Xixi Campus (zhèjiāng dàxué xīxī xiàoqū zhuānjiā lóu; 浙江大学西溪校区专家楼), 34 Tianmushan Lu (☎807 9996), at Baoshu Lu, 1 block east of the Zhejiang University main gate. An upgrade from humbler dorms, but rooms have dirty carpets and molding bathrooms. Doubles Y120-180; triples Y180.

Huanhu Hotel (huánhú dàjiǔdiàn; 环湖大酒店), 5 Hubin Lu (☎706 5491), between Renmin Lu and Jiefang Lu. Accessible by bus #7 from the train station. Facing the lake in all its opulent chandeliered splendor, the Huanhu offers amenities-stocked rooms with good views, plus a mini-arcade to the left of the main lobby. Breakfast included. Singles Y150; doubles Y208.

SHANGHAI

Zhehua Hotel (zhèhuá fàndiàn; 浙华饭店), 3 Jiefang Lu (☎780 2366), next to the main post office. Take bus #151 running east on Jiefang Lu. Attentive service and nicely furnished rooms make this hotel a pleasant option for those who must stay close to the train station or who want to steer clear of all the tourists in the West Lake area. Dorms Y50; singles with bath Y150; doubles Y138, with bath 180; triples with bath Y198.

West Lake Hotel (xī hú fàndiàn; 西湖饭店), 80 Renhe Lu (☎706 2630), at Hubin Lu, 1 block south of Pinghai Lu. Take bus #7 from the train station to Hubin. Dim halls, peeling bathrooms, and odors of smelly tofu, but take heart: the lake is near. 20% discounts Sept.-May. Singles Y80-140, with bath Y220; doubles Y100-170, with bath Y280.

🎌 🎵 FOOD AND ENTERTAINMENT

Hangzhou's scenic draws have long been touted as good for the soul, and its culinary specialties are enough to make your taste buds giddy. With an impressive list of dishes and enough history attached to rival West Lake itself, a routine meal can turn into an extravaganza. Most restaurants will serve these fabled delicacies (see **Food Heaven,** p. 335); pared-down versions of smelly tofu and crispy bean curd are readily available in street stalls around the city (Y1-4).

The side streets off **Zhonghe Lu** (east of and parallel to Yanan Lu), especially near the Jiefang Lu intersection, are lined with good, cheap restaurants. **Renhe Lu,** going east off of Hubin Lu, is home to some of the best *xiaochi* in the city. The take-out window of the famed **Zhiweiguan** sells almond paste cookies (Y1) and glutinous rice-covered meatballs (Y1), as well as roasted hind and front quarters of every kind of poultry imaginable. Even along the heavily commercial and touristed stretch of Yanan Lu, corner vendors sell steamed dumplings stuffed with pork, vegetables, or red bean paste (Y0.5-1.5). The restaurants along **Qingchun Lu,** between Hubin Lu and Zhonghe Lu, are ideal for larger groups wanting to sample some of Hangzhou's best. **Wahaha Restaurant,** 169 Qingchun Lu, serves snake, yellow eel, and other delicacies against a backdrop of gingham tablecloths and center fountains. (☎721 9898. Open daily 11am-3am.)

Touristy places and touristy prices are the name of the game along **Hubin Lu** south of Qingchun Lu. Teahouses are popular along streets north and northeast of the lake, particularly on **Beishan Lu** and Hubin Lu. **Paradise Bird Tea House** (tiāntáng pàomó hóngchá fǎng; 天堂泡沫红茶坊), 34 Hubin Lu, offers a selection of teas and beers (Y15-25) and noodle soups (Y15-20) in a sunken-level sanctuary. English-language menus and kitschy photographs of old Hollywood belles exude a Western air. (☎706 8883. Open daily noon-2am.) The **Lakeside Pavilion** (wànghú lóu; 望湖楼), 12 Beishan Lu, near CITS, commands a striking view of West Lake—and of chattering tourists enjoying the inexpensive teas (about Y10) and watermelon seeds. (☎515 5843. Open daily 8:30-11:30am, 12:30-4pm, and 6pm-midnight.)

Louwailou Restaurant (lóuwàilóu càiguǎn; 楼外楼菜馆), 30 Gushan Lu (☎796 9023), near the southern end of Solitary Hill Island. Opened in 1848 by a Qing noble, this is said to be the oldest restaurant in China. The quintessential Hangzhou experience (at least for tourist groups) with to-die-for views of the lake, Louwailou serves specialties like Dongpo Pork (Y7 per piece) and Beggar's Chicken (Y89). Open daily 11:30am-2:30pm and 4:30-8:30pm.

Zhiweiguan Restaurant (zhīwèiguān cāntīng; 知味观餐厅), 83 Renhe Lu (☎506 3055), between Hubin Lu and Yanan Lu. A local snack spot, meal spot, and fun spot, Zhiweiguan has fame without the pomp and circumstance. Known for its "cat's ear soup" (a tribute to a chef's noodle-making ingenuity), it serves an endless variety of *xiaolong bao,* peppered rice noodles, *jiaozi,* and sweet red-bean pancakes in a friendly cafeteria-style hall. Meals Y30. Open daily 6:30am-9:30am and 1:30-5pm.

Casablanca Bar (kāsàbùlánkǎ; 卡萨不兰卡), 23 Hubin Lu (☎702 5934). Nothing much to do with the movie, but trendy all the same. Long wooden tables and a high ceiling with exposed beams lend a relaxed country tavern feel that contrasts boldly with the hyped-up lake just outside. Weekend raffle prizes and live performances draw a young crowd. Appetizers Y8-15; drinks Y12 and up. Open daily 7pm-2am.

FOOD HEAVEN Hangzhou's famous 11 dishes are sensory master-pieces: visually stunning concoctions and creative exoticisms designed to satisfy both epicures and plain old food-lovers. They've been around and cooking for as long as West Lake itself. Happy feasting!

Dongpo Pork (dōngpō ròu; 东坡肉). Pieces of thinly sliced lean pork sandwiched between slices of roast pork, named for poet Su Dongpo, who wrote the poem, "In Praise of Pork."

West Lake Vinegary Fish (xī hú cù yú; 西湖醋鱼). Grass carp sauteed in vinegar and wine sauce to give it a sweet and sour flavor.

Beggar's Chicken (jiào huā tóng jī; 叫化童鸡). A whole chicken wrapped in lotus leaves, then paper and clay to seal in its flavors. Roasted to tender perfection, this dish is said to have originated when a beggar stole a chicken and, without ordinary cooking implements, developed this ingenious way of cooking it.

Dragon Well Shrimp (lóng jīng xiárén; 龙井虾仁). Baby shrimp cooked with Longjing tea leaves to give it a distinctive flavor.

Deep Fried Bean Curd Horse's Bells (gān zhài xiǎng líng; 干炸响铃). Paper-thin slices of pork wrapped in bean curd, deep fried, and dipped in sweet sauce.

West Lake Watershield Soup (xī hú chún cài tāng; 西湖纯菜汤). Soup made from an aquatic vegetable harvested from West Lake in mid-April.

Hangzhou Rolled Chicken (hángzhōu juǎn jī; 杭州卷鸡). Chicken wrapped in bean curd that is then fried.

Shrimp with Yellow Eel (xiá bào shàn bèi; 虾爆鳝背). Shrimp served with yellow eel that has been cooked in a wok.

Pine Nut Fish (sōngzǐ guì yú; 松子桂鱼). Fish from West Lake covered in pine nuts.

West Lake Pure Greens Soup (xī hú chún cài tāng; 西湖纯菜汤). Soup with greens harvested from West Lake.

Lakeside Tea House (húpàn jū chá lóu; 湖畔居茶楼), 23 Hubin Lu (☎702 1618), adjacent to Casablanca, on a dock overlooking West Lake. This traditional-style tea house offers over 100 varieties of tea (Y10-35); customers can watch the sun set over the lake with a cup of Hangzhou's own Longjing tea in hand. Open daily 7:30am-1am.

Tianwaitian Restaurant (tiānwàitiān càiguǎn; 天外天菜馆), 2 Tianzhu Lu (☎796 5450), outside Feilai Park. This so-called "heaven away from heaven" perches rather precariously on its laurels. With 2 levels of banquet-style tables, Tianwaitian is fine dining, fast-food tourist-group style. Seafood combination platter Y38, Beggar's Chicken Y85. Open daily 7am-9pm. The **Tianwaitian Snack Annex** (tiānwàitiān diǎnxīn bù; 天外天点心部), to the right of the main restaurant, serves skimpy wonton and noodle soups (Y4-16). Open daily 10:30am-1:30pm.

👁 SIGHTS

Hangzhou sights are easy to find and fairly easy to reach; the challenge is to find any not overrun by large tour groups.

WEST LAKE

Shimmering water at its full, sunny best.
Blurred mountains in a haze—marvelous even in rain.
Compare West Lake to the beautiful woman Xi Zi:
She looks just as becoming
Lightly made up or richly adorned.
—Su Dongpo, 1091

*Bordered by Beishan Lu to the north, Hubin Lu to the east, and Nanshan Lu to the south. **Bus #7** runs along Beishan Lu and the northern end of Hubin Lu; get off at any stop along that stretch. Numerous bus lines run along Hubin and Yanan Lu, including #16, 38, and 151; walk*

*1 block east from Yanan Lu to reach the eastern shore. Some individual sights around the lake require an **admission** fee.*

The famous beauty of West Lake (xī hú; 西湖) may well be Hangzhou's raison d'etre. For centuries, poets have compared the lake to beautiful women and beautiful women to the lake. Other bodies of water throughout China were named West Lake, in the hope that the mystique of the original could be stolen along with the name. It isn't difficult to understand why so many have been enchanted by its spell: surrounding hills carpeted by dense forests, a wide but intimate expanse of water, and air faintly perfumed by orchids and the memory of languid afternoons past combine to make this place as much paradise as earthly retreat.

Legend has it that West Lake originated with a pearl that was dropped out of the sky. Originally owned by a Jade Dragon and a Golden Phoenix, the pearl was coveted by a goddess in the heavenly palace. Having successfully stolen the pearl from the dragon and the phoenix, the jealous goddess brought it back to the privacy of her palace to admire it. When rumors of the pearl's whereabouts reached the dragon and the phoenix, though, they themselves stole into the palace to recover their precious stone. A struggle ensued, and the pearl tumbled out of heaven to earth and then morphed into West Lake, an accident that earth-dwellers have been gloating over for centuries.

Stroll along any portion of the West Lake shore or along **Bai Causeway** (bái tí; 白堤) and **Su Causeway** (sū tí; 苏堤) for views of the 3km long and 3km wide lake. Bai Causeway connects Solitary Hill to the north shore; Su Causeway, lined with willow trees, runs from the western end of the north shore to the southern shore, connecting the Tomb of Yue Fei to Huagang Park.

SOLITARY HILL ISLAND (gū shān dǎo; 孤山岛). Beautiful views draw almost every tourist who passes through Hangzhou. "**Autumn Moon on a Calm Lake**" (píng hú qiū yuè; 平湖秋月), is touted as the best location for twilight lake-gazing (Hangzhou's sport of choice), but there are plenty of other good spots with equally breathtaking views. This island also houses the **Zhejiang Provincial Museum** (zhèjiāng shěng bówùguǎn; 浙江省博物馆), with titillating collections of relics, gems, calligraphy, and coins. (☎798 0281. Open daily 8:45am-4:30pm; last admission 4:15pm. Y10, students Y5.) **Gushan Park** (gúshān gōngyuán; 孤山公园), also known as **Sun Yat-sen Park,** was established in 1752 as Emperor Kangxi's private resort, and boasts some of the best scenery and views of the lake (without the tourists). **Swan Pavilion** is perched atop a cluster of ornamental rocks that overlook the North Inner Lake. (Open daily sunrise-sunset. Y5.)

HUAGANG PARK (huāgǎng guānyú; 花港观鱼). South of Solitary Hill Island along Su Causeway, Huagang Park is reputedly the best place from which to check out the fish, which is why the second half of the park's name is *guanyu* (to view fish). Built as a private garden in the early Song dynasty, the park's main draws are its peony gardens, peacock farm, and **Red Carp Pond** (hóng yú chí; 红鱼池), whose hyperactive inhabitants are constantly leaping out of the water. (At the southwestern tip of West Lake. Enter off Nanshan Lu or the southern end of Su Causeway. Take bus #308 from Yanan Lu to Su Ti; the entrance is 50m ahead on the right. ☎796 7386. Open daily 6am-6pm. Y10, children under 1.4m Y5.)

ISLANDS. There's no need to linger on the banks—West Lake's waters see a lot of action. Two islands are only accessible by boat: **Mid-Lake Pavilion** (hú xīn tíng; 湖心亭) and **Small Immortal Isle** (xiǎo yíng zhōu; 小瀛洲). The serene forested grounds of the Mid-Lake Pavilion, not far from Solitary Hill Island, make for yet another peaceful stroll. (Open daily 8am-5pm. Free.) The Small Immortal Isle is called a "fairy islet," an island within a lake and a lake within an island. Manmade nature at its best, the island houses three stone towers farther out on the center of the lake. The waters are perfectly still, reflecting the **moon bridges** (sāntán yìnyuè; 三潭印月) that span the lake. Lit with lanterns during the Mid-Autumn Festival, they create three sparkling beacons on the water, giving them the name "three pools mirroring the moon." *(Y13, children Y7.)*

These islands may be reached, and the lake traversed, by one of several water vehicles. **Passenger ferries** leave from the eastern shore as well as from a dock between the Su and Bai Causeways on the northern shore, opposite the Tomb of Yue Fei. *(Every 30-40min. 7:50am-4:50pm. Y15, including Mid-Lake Pavilion and Small Immortal Isle Y25-33.)* **Night cruises** are also available, weather permitting. *(Tickets sold F-Su 6:50-9:30pm. Y20-25.)* **Private boats** can also be arranged (Y60-80 per hr.).

FEILAI PEAK

At the end of Linyin Lu, 15-20min. northwest of West Lake. Take bus #7 from Pinghai Lu or #507 from the train station to Lingyin Si, the last stop. ☎796 4426. Open daily 5:30am-6pm. Y20, children 1-1.3m Y10. Lingyin Temple Y15. English and Chinese introductions.

To the left of the entrance to Feilai Peak (fēilái fēng; 飞来峰), the **Chinese Park of Selected Grotto Carvings** (zhōnghuá shíkū jícuì yuán; 中华石窟集翠园) houses free-standing Buddhist sculptures and images culled from caves and temples, including from the Silk Road city of Dunhuang. Farther up the road on the left, signs point the way to the **Feilai Peak Grottoes** (fēilái fēng shíkū; 飞来峰石窟). According to legend, Feilai Peak came to existence when the Indian monk Hui Lai constructed Lingyin Temple in AD 326, and willed a well-loved peak from India to join him in his new home. The peak indeed "flew from afar," and houses a series of intricate statues, carvings, and etchings that bring to life the craggy limestone face and caves of the mountain. Visitors may clamber along the pathways of the mountain face and the stream that runs beside it to get a better view of the more than 470 Buddhist carvings, which date primarily from the 10th to 14th centuries. The almost pitch-black **Deep Dragon Cave** (lóng hóng dòng; 龙泓洞) is especially popular; it has a pinhole opening, allowing a tiny shaft of light (picturesquely termed the "thread of heaven") to pass through. The **Cave of Milky Icicles** contains carvings of the characters for peace, fortune, and love; tradition has led many a hopeful tourist to rub them for good luck.

The approach to **Lingyin Temple** (língyǐn sì; 灵隐寺), known as Monastery of the Soul's Retreat, is lined with two thousand-year-old Sutra Pillars and twin stone pagodas from AD 326, nicely interspersed with peddlers selling tea leaves, trinkets, and incense sticks. Its main **Mahavira Hall** houses China's largest wooden statue of the sleeping Buddha (Sakyamuni), towering 19.6m in height, a gorgeous statue of Guanyin, and thousands of buddhas carved into the wall.

OTHER SIGHTS

TOMB OF YUE FEI (yuè fēi mù; 岳飞墓). This tomb bears the phrase "endless loyalty and devotion to one's country," the characters that, according to legend, were tattooed onto Yue Fei's back by his mother when he joined the Song army. Yue Fei (1103-42) proved to be a brilliant general, but his loyalty to a corruptible court led to his demise; a Khitan conspiracy killed the zealous patriot. It took another 21 years, several disastrous defeats, and strong public sentiment to make the emperor give Yue Fei a ceremonial reburial. **Yue Temple** (yuè wáng miào; 岳王庙), constructed in 1221, memorializes Yue and his son. Murals recount the childhood bravery and kindness to peasants that earned Yue his popularity with common folk. Subsequent dynasties also contributed to the compound, and Qing merchants even brought in a giant bronze bell cast in Japan. During the Cultural Revolution, the tomb was ransacked by Red Guards. *(On Beishan Lu, near the northwest corner of West Lake. Take bus #7 to Yuewen. ☎797 2651. Chinese captions only. Open daily 7am-6pm. Y20, children 1-1.3m Y10, children under 1m free.)*

SIX HARMONIES PAGODA (liù hé tǎ; 六和塔). This eight-sided, seven-story pagoda is named after the six codes of Buddhism. It was built in 970 in an attempt to harness divine powers in order to prevent the destructive annual flooding of the Qiantang River. Ever since dikes were built along the banks, the pagoda has been officially retired, but its steep, mural-lined staircases continue to delight. The sur-

rounding **Liuhe Cultural Park** (liùhé wénhuà gōngyuán; 六和文化公园), with minia-
ture replicas of the "Who's Who among Pagodas," is worth a visit. *(16 Zhijiang Lu.
Take bus #308 to Liuhe Ta; the office is 1 block ahead. ☎659 1401. Open daily 6am-6:30pm.
Park Y15, children under 1.3m Y7.5; pagoda Y10, children under 1.3m Y5.)*

HIKING. About 20km southwest of West Lake, and remote enough to be only
accessible by car, bike, or on foot, lie some of the best-preserved forests in the
area. The **Bamboo Lined Path at Yunqi** (yúnqī zhújìng; 云栖竹径) is a sea of bamboo
lining a path that zigzags up into the hills. It is said that some clouds came flying
from a nearby hill and lingered there, hence the name Yunqi ("clouds lingering").
The main path leading east from the forest stops at **Five Clouds Hill** (wǔ yún shān;
五云山), nearly 345m tall, where thousand-year-old trees cluster about the trails.
Grottoed caves and pavilions make for exciting adventures.

HANGZHOU BOTANICAL GARDEN (hángzhōu zhíwù yuán; 杭州植物园). In addition to peaceful walkways and pavilions surrounded by exotic flowers and medicinal plants, the botanical garden is also home to a redwood tree that was a gift
from US President Richard Nixon. *(Bus #7 to the Lingyin Temple, #27 to Longjing, and others such as #15 and 28 stop at Quyuan Fenghe, near the corner of Beishan Lu and Lingyin Lu.
☎ 702 5793. Open daily 8:30am-4:30pm. Y10, children under 1.3m Y5.)*

▶ DAYTRIP FROM HANGZHOU: LONGJING

*Take bus #27 from Pinghai Lu downtown or from along the northern shore of West Lake to
Longjing Cha Shi, the last stop.*

Worlds apart from the pandemonium and commercialism of downtown and eastern lake shores, the Longjing tea plantations (lóngjǐng; 龙井) hidden in the hills
west of the lake are the source of China's most revered tea. The roads from Hangzhou to Longjing village follow a spectacular winding route through lush hills and
sprawling terraced tea fields. An hour-long stroll or a half-day spent sipping tea
and admiring the bird's-eye view of the city should be enough to convert anyone
into a tea enthusiast. The high-quality aromatic tea gets its name from the limestone **Longjing (Dragon Well) Spring,** past the central courtyard of **Longjing Tea Room**
(lóngjǐng chá shì; 龙井茶室), a few meters from the bus stop. According to popular
myth, a dragon with special powers inhabits the well, which explains why it never
dries up, even in drought. A short walk takes you past houses on hills, which double as business venues for residents eager to sell their fresh tea harvests. Many of
these individual homes make offers a bit too good to be true, and visitors may end
up paying more for less.

Two stops before Longjing village, at Shuangfeng, the beautiful **Chinese Tea
Museum** (zhōngguó cháyè bówùguǎn; 中国茶叶博物馆) features replicas of tea
houses, including a bamboo tea room in Yunnan and a Ming-era tea house, and
traces the history of tea from the Tang dynasty to the present. If reading about this
beverage is not your cup of tea, head over to the sampling room, where you can
taste-test several varieties for yourself. *(☎ 796 4221. Open daily 8:30am-4:30pm. Y10.)*

SHAOXING 绍兴   ☎0575

Shaoxing appears to have devoted many years of study to the fine art of taking it
easy. Here, amid thriving commercial avenues and bustling street markets, siestas
are taken, conversation made, and *mahjong* played in the small alleys whose sea
of gray-stone eaved houses, like Beijing's *hutongs*, form the heart of the city. In
stark contrast to many other cities, the streets here do not resemble a slice of traffic purgatory. In fact, Shaoxing's major thoroughfare allows only one lane of traffic each way, with special side lanes ensuring that the slow (bikes and pedicabs)
get equal billing with the fast and frantic. Like many cities in the South, Shaoxing
basks in its landscape; the waterways weaving across the city provide much of its

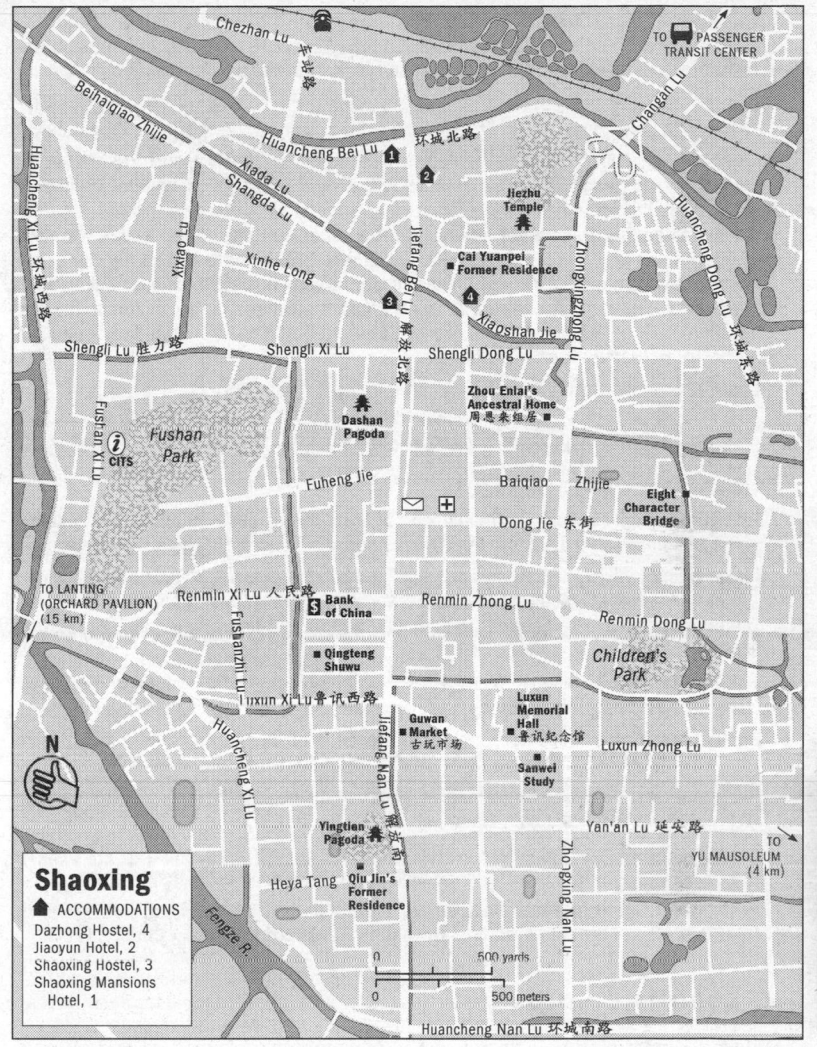

Shaoxing

▲ ACCOMMODATIONS
Dazhong Hostel, 4
Jiaoyun Hotel, 2
Shaoxing Hostel, 3
Shaoxing Mansions
    Hotel, 1

SHANGHAI

livelihood and its natural beauty. It is even possible to traverse the area in Shaoxing's unique *wupeng* boats, topped by round black awnings and operated by foot paddles. A history dating back to the 7th century BC sustains this languorous aristocrat of a city, the hometown of Lu Xun, China's greatest modern writer, and the birthplace of some of the nation's best rice wine.

✦ 7 ORIENTATION AND PRACTICAL INFORMATION

Jiefang Lu (解放路) runs north to south through the city, divided into Jiefang Bei Lu to the north and Jiefang Nan Lu to the south of the intersection with **Renmin Lu** (人民路). **Shengli Lu** (胜利路), **Dong Jie** (东街), **Luxun Jie** (鲁迅街), and **Yanan Lu** (延安路) all run from east to west. The city proper is ringed by **Huancheng Lu** (环城路). Most of Shaoxing's major sights lie outside the city proper, but are easily accessible by public transportation. The train station is slightly north of the city, connected to Jiefang Bei Lu by **Chezhan Lu** (车站路); the long-distance bus station is 10 minutes northeast of the city, accessible via **Zhongxing Bei Lu** (中兴北路).

Trains: Shaoxing Train Station (shàoxīng huǒchē zhàn; 绍兴火车站; ☎802 2584 or 802 2001), on Chezhan Lu, at the terminus of buses #1, 2, 3, and 4. Open daily 2-2:40am and 6am-9pm. To: **Hangzhou** (45min.-1½hr., 3 per day 8:50am-1:30pm, Y5.50-13); **Ningbo** (2hr., every hr. 7am-5:40pm, Y8-Y31); and **Shanghai** (3hr., 1:30 and 4:30pm, Y21-90).

Buses: Shaoxing Passenger Transit Center (shàoxīng shì gōnglù kèyùn zhōngxīn; 绍兴市公路客运中心; ☎801 8852, ext. 8004), 15min. northeast of the city center. Accessible via bus #12. One of China's most luxurious bus stations; buying tickets is a breeze. To: **Fuzhou** (18hr., noon, Y179); **Hangzhou** (45min.-1hr., every 20min. 6:30am-7:30pm, Y18.5); **Ningbo** (1½hr., every hr. 6:40am-5:40pm, Y38); and **Shanghai** (3hr., every hr. 6:20am-6:40pm, Y56.50-70).

Local Transportation: Public **buses** run roughly 6:30am-8pm (Y1-1.5). Bus #2 runs along Jiefang Lu to the Yu Mausoleum and #3 runs the length of Shengli Lu to Orchid Pavilion. A private minibus line, **Huanxian Bus** (huánxiàn bāshì; 还线巴士) runs along Jiefang Lu (Y1). A stroll between a few bus stops often takes the same amount of time as, if not less than, taking the bus.

Taxis: Base fare Y7, each additional km Y1. Most destinations under Y9-10. **Pedicabs** from Renmin Lu to the station area Y8-10, shorter distances Y3. Negotiate in advance.

Travel Agency: CITS, 360 Fushan Xi Lu (☎515 3454; English ☎515 1565), 2½ blocks south of Shengli Xi Lu. Accessible via bus #3 heading west from Jiefang Bei Lu. Average commission Y20. International Department on the 2nd floor. Open daily 8-11:30am and 2:30-5:30pm.

Bank of China: 201 Renmin Xi Lu (☎522 2888), 1 block west of Jiefang Lu. Exchanges traveler's checks. ATMs. Open daily 7:30am-8pm.

Bookstores: Xinhua Bookstore, on Jiefang Bei Lu, 1 block north of Shengli Xi Lu. One of the only places in Shaoxing to obtain a bilingual map. Open daily 8am-8:30pm.

Supermarkets: Gongxiao Supermarket (gōngxiào chāoshì; 供销超市), 219 Jiefang Bei Lu (☎513 4016). Open daily 8am-9pm.

Hospitals: Municipal People's Hospital (shì rénmín yīyuàn; 市人民医院), 61 Dong Jie (☎513 2419), about 200m from the post office. No official English speakers.

Post Office: Shaoxing Main Post Office, 1 Dong Jie (☎514 1024), at Jiefang Bei Lu. EMS and Poste Restante available. Open daily 7:30am-6pm. **Postal Code:** 312000.

▌ ACCOMMODATIONS

Budget accommodation is easy to find, especially in the northern end of town; staff members are usually generous about allowing foreigners to stay in cheaper rooms and establishments. An extra wad of cash (Y180-220) will secure more creature comforts at the upper-crust establishments closer to the city center.

Jiaoyun Hotel (jiāoyùn bīnguǎn; 交运宾馆), 12 Jiefang Bei Lu (☎802 3553), south of the northern local bus station, near Huancheng Bei Lu. Walk 15min. from the train station, or take buses #1, 2, 3, or 4 to Qiche Zhan. Low on dazzle: rooms are spacious but worn. Clean common baths and well-lit hallways make the stay worth it. 2-bed dorms with mosquito net Y31; singles with bath Y120; doubles with bath Y150.

Shaoxing Hostel (shàoxīng lǚguǎn; 绍兴旅馆), 213 Jiefang Bei Lu (☎513 2814), about 300m south of Shangda Lu. Take bus #2 from the train station. Not to be confused with the luxurious Shaoxing Hotel on Shengli Xi Lu. Dark, dank hallways and rickety doors lead to surprisingly clean rooms, although the constant chatter of the staff and paper-thin walls make peace and quiet next to impossible. Singles Y32; doubles Y50, with A/C Y66, with bath Y95-120; triples Y85, with bath Y120.

Shaoxing Mansions Hotel (shàoxīng dàshà bīnguǎn; 绍兴大厦宾馆), 498 Huancheng Bei Lu (☎513 6360), at Jiefang Bei Lu. Take bus #1, 2, 3, or 4 from the train station to Qiche Zhan. Comfortable, sunny standard rooms, but not-so-pleasant dorms. 3-bed dorms Y30; 2-bed dorms Y26; singles Y128; doubles Y148.

Dazhong Hostel (dàzhòng lǚguǎn; 大众旅馆), 43-45 Xiaoshan Jie (☎513 2118). Take bus #1, 2, 3, or 4 from the train station to the corner of Shengli Lu and Jiefang Bei Lu. Backtrack about 200m on Jiefang Lu and turn right at the street after the small bridge; the hostel is 1min. down the road, on the left. Dazhong Hostel offers the barest of bare necessities of life (a trek to the bathroom and no mosquito nets). The owner says the street might be torn down soon. 6-bed dorms Y10; 2-bed dorms Y14; singles Y20.

◖ FOOD

Local cuisine takes advantage of the wine that runs through the city's figurative veins: **Shaoxing Yellow Rice Wine** (shàoxīng huáng jiǔ; 绍兴黄酒). This cooking wine, produced from a special kind of glutinous rice, lends a potent and distinctive flavor. **Shaoxing Chicken** (shàoxīng jī; 绍兴鸡; Y15-30) is prepared by marinating the breast meat in the wine. Like its neighbor Hangzhou, Shaoxing is also a snack-lover's paradise. Most restaurants are arranged cafeteria style, so you can shop for everything from wonton soups to tapioca pearl drinks.

For cheap restaurants, look along **Luxun Lu** and on side streets off **Yanan Lu** (the next major street after Luxun Lu as you head south of Jiefang Lu). **Renmin Lu** even has a smattering of bakeries (individual pastries Y1.5-2.5, small breads and cakes Y5 and up). The **night market** on Dong Jie off Jiefang Bei Lu offers fresh vegetables and fried eggplant, spicy-hot tofu, and other entrees for Y8-10.

▨ **Grandma's Noodle Restaurant** (āpó miànguǎn; 阿婆面馆), 100 Luxun Zhong Lu (☎513 0826), near Lu Xun Memorial Hall. Grandma's noodles never tasted so good. Noodle dishes (Y6-10) and noodle soups (Y3-17) freshly made by *apo* herself are served in the downstairs dining area, while traditional restaurant fare is served in the evenings on the 2nd level. Cold noodle dishes and yellow eel soup are the house favorites. Open daily 7am-2am, 2nd Fl. 4:30pm-2am.

Jubilantly Cafe (jùnlěi měishí; 俊磊美食), 558 Jiefang Bei Lu (☎513 9718), close to Dong Jie. Popular with locals, Jubilantly dishes up noodle dishes (Y4-6), *jiaozi* (Y0.4 each), and a la carte dishes (Y3-7). The most popular counter, however, is the area where wonton soup (Y3) is made fresh while you wait. Colorful decor and an amusement park feel make for an all-around jubilant experience. Open daily 6:30am-midnight.

Xianheng Restaurant (xiánhēng jiǔdiàn; 咸亨酒店), 179 Luxun Zhong Lu (☎511 6666), across from Grandma's Noodle Restaurant. It is said that every Shaoxing native eats here at least once, and given its 100-year-old history and fame in Lu Xun's writings, most probably have. Serves authentic Shaoxing dishes in a circa 1890 tea house. Although most of the food is nothing to write home about, don't leave without trying the lima beans (Y6), Shaoxing chicken (Y15), and smelly tofu (Y6). Open daily 8am-8pm.

◖ SIGHTS

With the exception of the Lu Xun Memorial Hall in the south of the city, most of Shaoxing's major sights lie outside the city proper. The Yu Mausoleum and East Lake are a few kilometers to the east, and Orchid Pavilion lies much farther away.

ORCHID PAVILION (lán tíng; 兰亭). Built during the Han dynasty and named in honor of the orchids planted here by the emperor, the pavilion sits at the foot of Lanzhu Hill. While the pavilion is sacred to the cult of Chinese calligraphy, a visit to this rural locale may very well turn into a spiritual experience even for those who are less reverent about their brush and scroll. The array of calligraphic art gracing scrolls and monuments throughout the area is merely the very artful icing on the cake: craggy peaks and low mountains form a fantastic backdrop.

The pavilion first rose to cultural and historical significance in AD 353, when renowned calligrapher Wang Xizhi and 41 of his closest friends played a drinking game along a creek, near where the pavilion now stands; those who were unable to compose a sufficiently brief and witty poem on command were required to down three shots of wine. Wang's account of the 37 poems that the amusing game produced, the **Lanting Anthology Preface,** came to be revered as the quintessential example of lucid prose and superb calligraphic style. Indeed, scattered around the various pavilions and within the **Ancestral Shrine to Wang Xizhi** (wáng yòu jūncí; 王右军祠) are numerous copies of *Wang's Preface,* including one by Emperor Kangxi. The park also contains a tiny but smartly designed **Museum of Calligraphy** (shūfǎ bówùguǎn; 书法博物馆). *(On Shaoda Gonglu, 14km southeast of Shaoxing. Take bus #3 from the train station, Shengli Xi Lu, or Huancheng Xi Lu. The ride takes 35-40min., and the bus stops at Lanting, but the stop is unmarked; let the fare collector know your destination when you get on the bus. ☎460 9035 or 401 1035. Open daily 7:30am-5pm, although the gate-keeper often lets people in later. Y10, children under 1.4m Y2.)*

LU XUN MEMORIAL HALL (lǔ xùn jìniàn guǎn; 鲁迅纪念馆). Shaoxing was the birthplace and childhood home of Lu Xun (1881-1936), widely considered one of the best satirical fiction writers and essayists in modern China (see also p. 36). This complex is fitting homage. The memorial hall documents Lu Xun's life and works, from his decision to use literature as a form of "waking up the Chinese people" to a display of his handwritten autobiography. **Lu Xun's Former Residence** (lǔ xùn gù jū; 鲁迅故居), west of the memorial hall, displays his childhood home as it was when the tiny budding author lived there. **Baicao Garden** (báicǎo yuán; 百草园), a small vegetable garden (described as Lu Xun's "paradise") is on the grounds, as is **Sanwei Study** (sānwèi shūwū; 三味书屋; "three-flavor study"), the school that Lu Xun attended as a child. The school, diagonally across the street from the other sights, still houses Lu Xun's old desk; visitors ogle over the character for "early" (早) that Lu Xun carved when his teacher reprimanded him for being late. *(393 Luxun Zhong Lu. Take bus #2, 4, or 5 to the intersection of Jiefang Lu and Luxun Zhong Lu; the hall is a 5min. walk to the east. Bus #7 takes passengers to the front of the Memorial Hall. ☎513 2083. Open daily 8am-5pm; last admission 4:30pm. Guide Y50-100. All 3 buildings Y10, children under 1.4m Y3.)*

YU MAUSOLEUM (dàyǔ líng; 大禹陵). Unless you're a big fan of floods, the mausoleum is perhaps just a watered-down version of what you may have imagined it to be. A two-minute walk along a path lined with stone animals leads to the grounds dedicated to the "Great Yu," known as the "tamer of floods." Yu devoted 13 hard years to fighting the Yangzi floods (see p. 8). Although he passed his home three times, this hero never allowed himself to stop and greet his family. The mausoleum, a temple, and Yu's burial stones (he is said to have died doing his life's work during a routine inspection tour of the Yangzi River) are interspersed with pavilions and engraved steles. *(About 6km southeast of Shaoxing. Take bus #2 for 20-30min. to Dayu Ling, or take a 1hr. boat ride along the waterways from East Lake (Y40-50). Open daily 7:30am-5pm. Y15, children under 1.4m Y3.)*

EAST LAKE (dōng hú; 东湖). More a river than a lake and bisected by the **Long Causeway** (cháng tí; 长堤), East Lake is a pleasant excursion for those up for a little exploring. The spectacular rugged cliff faces that tower over the mirror-still water are a sharp contrast to the lake's prissier alter-ego, Hangzhou's West Lake. Caves, bridges, and pavilions wind away from the banks; restless visitors can hire a *wupeng* boat (wūpéng chuán; 乌篷船; Y30) to explore the length of the lake and admire the surrounding countryside. *(Take bus #1 to Dong Hu Fengjing Qu, or take a 45min. boat ride from Yu Mausoleum or the city itself. ☎864 9590. Open daily 7am-10pm.)*

OTHER SIGHTS. Zhou Enlai's Ancestral Home (zhōu ēnlái zǔ jū; 周恩来祖居) is at 369 Laodong Lu, near Zhongxing Zhong Lu. *(☎513 3368. Open daily 8am-5pm. Y10.)* A little bit southeast of here, running from Baziqiao Zhi Jie (which branches off

Zhongxing Zhong Lu), is the unique **Eight Character Bridge** (bā zì qiáo; 八字桥), so called because it has the same arched shape (八) as the Chinese character for the number eight. The home of **Qiu Jin,** a late 19th-century female revolutionary, is at the corner of Jiefang Nan Lu and Hechang Tang, near the Haigang Hotel. *(☎806 3369. Open daily 8:30am-4pm. Y3.)* Vendors of jade and bronze Buddha statues and other collectibles set up shop daily at the **Antiques Market** (gǔwán shìchǎng; 古玩市场), near Jiefang Nan Lu south of Luxun Zhong Lu and parallel to Fuhu Jie.

NINGBO 宁波   ☎0574

Things and people have been passing through Ningbo for centuries. An important trading port since the Tang dynasty, Ningbo has been instrumental in the exchange of goods between China and its neighbors. Portugal and Great Britain got involved in the action between the 16th and 18th centuries, when the colonial powers had a stake in the city's thriving commercial trade; these days, the neighborhood around the ferry terminal retains only a few vague architectural signs of their presence. By the mid-19th century, Ningbo's importance as a trading harbor had been eclipsed by Shanghai, which has a more direct link to the sea. Today, less romantic goods pass through Ningbo's port: mainly canned foods and ferry-loads of passengers headed to Shanghai and Putuoshan. Slick, fast-paced, and perpetually under construction, Ningbo is promising for those who have time to explore its borders, but its urban dash holds little appeal for visitors seeking a detour from the common cosmopolitan highway.

⊫ TRANSPORTATION

Airplanes: Ningbo Lishe Airport (níngbō lìshè jīchǎng; 宁波栎社机场; ☎742 7888), a 30min. taxi ride from Ningbo (Y40). Shuttle buses run to and from the **CAAC ticket office** (30-45min., approx. every 30min. 6am-3pm, Y5) on 91 Xingning Lu (☎731 2850). Open daily 8am-6pm. To: **Beijing** (2 per day, Y940); **Fuzhou** (3 per week, Y550); **Hong Kong** (1 per day, Y1870); and **Shanghai** (3 per day 8am-5:30pm, Y300).

Trains: Ningbo's train station, known as **South Station** (nán zhàn; 南站; ☎731 2084), is in a plaza at the terminus of Nanzhan Xi Lu, Ma Yuan Lu, and Gong Qing Lu, in the southwestern corner of the city. Accessible by bus #1 from downtown and buses #514 and 518 from Zhongshan Xi Lu. Ticket window open daily 6am-7pm. A confusing hierarchy of waiting rooms await. To: **Hangzhou** (2-3hr., 7 per day, Y14-Y49); **Nanjing** (10hr., 3 per day 4:56-7pm, Y46-Y94); and **Shanghai** (4½-6½hr., 5 per day 8:32am-4:56pm, express Y54-104, local Y27).

Buses: Although Ningbo has three bus stations, the **South Bus Station** (qìchē nán zhàn; 汽车南站; ☎713 1834), just west of the railway station in the same plaza, handles almost all long-distance traffic. Open daily 5:30am-7pm. To: **Hangzhou** (2hr., every 10-15min. 6am-4pm, Y42.4); **Nanjing** (6hr., 4 per day 7:50am-4pm, Y160); and **Shanghai** (3½hr., every 20min. 6:30am-6:30pm, Y90).

Boats: Ningbo Harbor Passenger Ferry Terminal (níngbō gǎng kèyùn mǎtóu; 宁波港客运码头), 142 Zhongma Lu (info ☎735 6332, tickets ☎769 1258), in the northeastern part of the city near where the Fenghua River branches into the Yong and the Yuyao Rivers. Known also as the **Lunchuan Dock** (lúnchuán mǎtóu; 轮船码头). Accessible by buses #1 and 10 from the station area to the Lunchuan Matou stop, just past Xinjiang Bridge. Ticket windows open daily 5:30am-6pm. To **Putuoshan** (2hr., every hr. 7am-5pm, Y55) and **Shanghai** (12-13hr., 5:30 or 6pm, Y39-132). More boats during the summer and on weekends.

Local Transportation: Buses #1 and **10** connect the bus and train stations with the ferry terminal in the north, and buses **#514** and **517** travel along Zhongshan Lu, linking the eastern and western parts of the city. Bus **#820** runs the length of Liuting Jie, passing the train station, Moon Lake, Chenghuang Miao, and the intersection with Jiefang Bei Lu. A few routes serve outlying areas subch as the main campus of Ningbo University (routes **#341** and **601**) and Baoguo Temple (**#332** from Renmin Lu just south of the passenger ferry terminal). Base fare Y1, with A/C Y2. Private **minibuses** offer direct services between the station area and the ferry terminal (daily sunrise to sunset, Y1-2).

Taxis: Base fare Y8, each additional km Y1.5. From the bus and train stations to the ferry terminal Y10-12, from the city center to the airport Y40. **Pedicabs** go most places for Y3-5, although many drivers refuse to go to the ferry area, as it is one long uphill climb.

ORIENTATION AND PRACTICAL INFORMATION

Ningbo city is split into three sections by the Y-shaped formation of the **Yuyao** (yúyáo jiāng; 余姚江), **Yong** (yǒng jiāng; 甬江), and **Fenghua** (fènghuà jiāng; 奉化江) **Rivers.** Travelers will most likely encounter only the western and northern thirds of the city, as the former is where the railway and bus stations and many sights lie, and the latter is where the ferry terminal is situated. These two sections of the city are connected by the **Xinjiang Bridge** (xīnjiāng qiáo; 新江桥). The western portion of the main east-west artery, **Zhongshan Xi Lu** (中山西路), is bookended by two significant junctions: the **East Gate** (dōng mén; 东门), at the intersection of Zhongshan Lu and **Lingqiao Lu** (灵桥路), and the **West Gate** (xī mén; 西门), at the intersection of Zhongshan Lu and **Changchun Lu** (长春路). The other major east-west street is **Liuting Jie** (柳汀路), also known as **Yaohang Jie** (药行街).

Travel Agency: Ningbo CITS (☎731 2890; fax 731 2831), immediately to the right past the main gate of Chenghuang Miao. Ticket commission 10%. Helpful International Department provides interpreters and tour guides. Open M-F 8:30am-5pm.

Bank of China: 139 Yaohang Jie (☎719 7174), between Moon Lake and the Fenghua River, 2 blocks east of the No. 1 Municipal Hospital. Accessible from the ferry terminal by bus #20 southbound. Exchanges traveler's checks at counter #10. ATMs (MC, Visa) and credit card advances available. Open daily 8-11:30am and 2-5pm.

Bookstores: Xinhua Bookstore, 99 Zhongshan Xi Lu (☎724 6719). A 4-level megastore selling just about anything in print. Open daily 8:30am-9pm.

PSB: In the municipal government's buildings complex (shì zhèngfǔ; 市政府), at the northeastern corner of the intersection of Zhongshan Lu and Jiefang Bei Lu (☎736 2934; visa extensions ext. 1923). Open daily 8am-5pm.

Hospitals: No. 1 Municipal Hospital (shì dìyī yīyuàn; 市第一医院), 90 Xingshu Jie (☎840 1412), off Liuting Jie between Moon Lake and Jiefang Nan Lu. English-speaking staff members. Open 24hr.

Post and Telecommunications: 258 Zhongshan Zhong Lu (☎736 5701), at the southeast corner of the intersection of Lingqiao Lu and Zhongshan Zhong Lu (Dongmenkou). EMS and Poste Restante available. International mail sent from counter #5. IDD and calling card service on 2nd floor. Open daily 7:30am-8pm. **Postal Code:** 315000.

ACCOMMODATIONS

While most of the hotels in Ningbo are mid-range, there are a few budget options available outside of the city center. Hotels in the immediate vicinity of the ferry terminal are reasonably priced and extremely convenient, but phone in advance to double-check addresses, since the pace of construction in Ningbo means short-lived existences for buildings outside of main commercial districts. Bargaining is possible virtually everywhere.

Huagang Hotel (huágǎng bīnguǎn; 华港饭店), 146 Zhongma Lu (☎769 1888), to the left of the ferry terminal ticket office. Newly renovated rooms (with A/C, TV, and bath), marble stairs, and floral centerpieces add a touch of class to this seedily situated establishment. Gotta love those early morning foghorn wake-up calls. Cheaper rooms are in a back building, but dorm beds are a no-no. Doubles Y120-280; triples Y250.

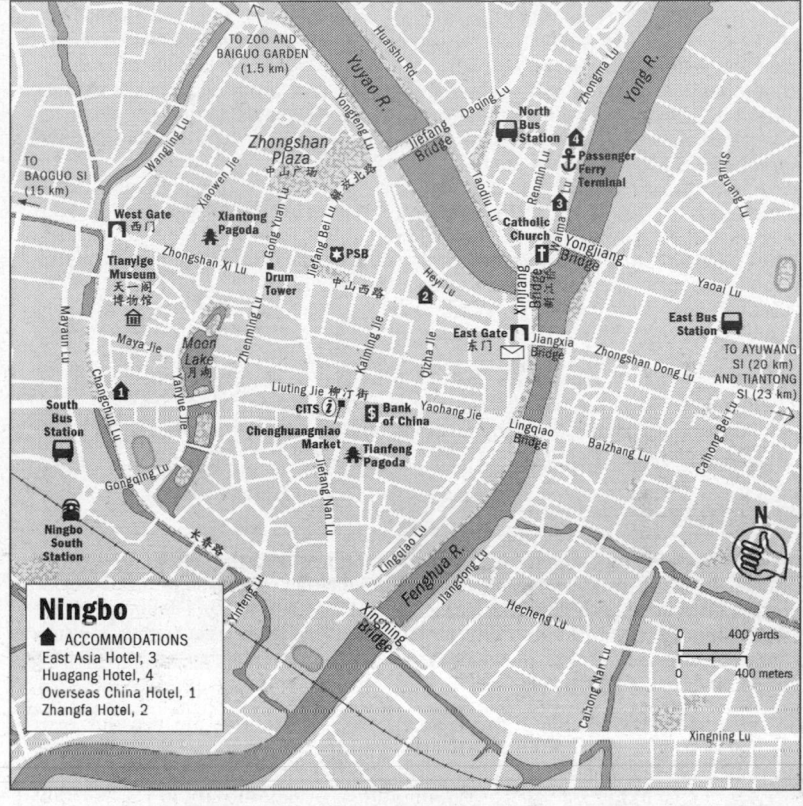

Ningbo
🔺 ACCOMMODATIONS
East Asia Hotel, 3
Huagang Hotel, 4
Overseas China Hotel, 1
Zhangfa Hotel, 2

Overseas Chinese Hotel (huá qiáo fàndiàn; 华侨饭店), 130 Liuting Jie (☎ 729 3175), at Changchun Lu, 2 blocks south of the Tianyige Museum. Sprawling grounds, high ceilings, and ornate design reminiscent of jazz-era Shanghai. A back building offers budget rooms, 3-star style. Rooms have all standard amenities. Singles and doubles Y98-198.

Zhangfa Hotel (zhāngfǎ jiǔdiàn; 长发酒店), 145 Zhongshan Dong Lu (☎ 725 1828), adjacent to the Ningbo Grand Hotel, in the city center. Take bus #518 going east on Zhongshan Dong Lu to Jiefang Lu; the hotel is 2 blocks east on the left. Rooms are clean and have all standard amenities, although the cheapest rooms are windowless. Breakfast included. Doubles Y198-228.

East Asia Hotel (dōng yà fàndiàn; 东亚饭店), 112 Zhongma Lu (☎ 735 6224), a few minutes south of the ferry terminal. Take bus #1, 601, or 811 from the station area to Lunchuan Matou. The wail of boat horns, the cramped rooms, and the worn sheets might make you think you're at sea. Breakfast included. Singles Y180-250; doubles Y188; triples Y270. Credit cards accepted.

🍴 FOOD

Ningbo serves up a wide variety of local seafood, both fresh and dried. Small restaurants offering exotic-looking creatures from the deep line **Renmin Lu** and **Zhongma Lu,** just south of the ferry terminal. For a good, cheap meal with generous portions, try **Rechao Fast Food** (rècháo kuài cān; 热炒快餐), on 142 Zhongma Lu, next to the ferry waiting room. Pick out your meal from a mini-aquarium in front; meals average Y8-10. Put on your raincoat before approaching the water-spouting clams. (☎766 5875. Open daily 5am-7:30pm.) Farther south, by the Moon Lake area, is another savory, not-to-be missed dining experience popular with locals. **Shipu Sea Flavor Restaurant** (shípǔ hǎiwèi fàndiàn; 石浦海味饭店), 60 Yanyue Jie, offers abundant seafood and vegetarian options, and about all the little dessert cakes, puffs, and twists you can handle. Order in a separate room lined with display dishes of sauteed crayfish (Y30), braised squid (Y12), custard puffs (Y4), and more. (☎730 7470. Open daily 10am-10:30pm.)

For more terrestrial options, try the **city temple** (chénghuáng miào shāngchéng; 城隍庙商城), at the southwest corner of the intersection of Yao-hang Lu and Kaiming Jie. Open-air stalls and stores sell everything from grand-father clocks to novelty stationery, in a setting of alleys and buildings designed to look like temples. Small eateries serve the usual noodle and fried dishes, as well as *ningbo tang tuan* (宁波汤团; balls of sweet glutinous rice paste filled with sesame or red bean paste and served in a sweet broth). In the summer, vendors also sell soothing desserts such as shaved ice with sweet toppings (bào bīng; 刨冰; Y4). In keeping with the bustling carnival atmosphere, **Gongyuan Lu,** off Zhongshan Xi Lu, looks like the old merchant districts of Ningbo's heyday with its specialty shops, fruit juice stands, and fast food vendors selling *nian gao* (年糕; glutinous rice cakes; Y1-2).

■ SIGHTS

For those looking for more to do in Ningbo than just pass through on the way to Putuoshan, there are some temples in the surrounding countryside that might be worth a visit, notably the **Baoguo Temple** (bǎoguó sì; 保国寺), in the Jiangbei District 15km northwest of Ningbo City, and the **Tiantong Temple** (tiāntóng sì; 天童寺), some 30km east of the city. Buses run from Ningbo East Bus Station to Tiantong Temple daily 6am to 5:30pm (Y4.7).

TIANYIGE MUSEUM (tiānyìgé bówùguǎn; 天一阁博物馆). Set amid a maze of streams, gardens, and meticulously arranged rock formations that beg to be climbed, the Tianyige Museum is built around the famed **Tianyige Library** (tiānyìgé bǎoshūlóu; 天一阁宝书楼), the oldest private library in China. Built between 1561 and 1566, the library was the collection of Defense Minister Fan Qing. Although the collection of more than 300,000 books is not open to the public, there are numerous other pavilions and exhibitions to explore: a **Painting and Calligraphy Hall** (tiānyìgé shūhuàguǎn; 天一阁书画馆), with displays of local art and stunning scrolls for sale; the **Former Residence of Fan Qing** (fànshì gùjū; 范氏故居), with books and printing woodblocks; and a small **Ningbo History Museum** (níngbō shǐ bówùguǎn; 宁波史博物馆), tracing the 7000-year history of the city. (*10 Tianyi Jie. Take bus #10 or 514 from the train station to Ximenkou, at the intersection of Zhongshan Xi Lu and Changchun Lu. Walk south on Changchun Lu for about 5min.; turn left on Tianyi Jie, a lane leading directly to the museum. ☎729 3526 or 729 2442. Open daily 8am-4:30pm. Y12.*)

OTHER SIGHTS. Near the Tianyige Museum is the oblong **Moon Lake** (yuè hú; 月胡), stretching from Changchun Lu in the south almost to Zhongshan Xi Lu in the north, and intersected by Liuting Jie and bordered on the west by Yanyue Jie. An atmospheric park on the western bank draws crowds that gather around chess players and makeshift barber shops. In mid-summer, Chinese opera performances take place in open-air pavilions surrounding the lake, drawing large crowds of locals. (*Open daily dawn-dusk. Free.*) The area north of **Xinjiang Bridge** is the site of the former Portuguese and British concessions. On Zhongma Lu, the 17th-century **Catholic Church** (tiānzhǔ jiàotáng; 天主教堂) stands proudly out of place among rows of residential houses and small storefronts. Dating from the period of Portuguese influence, it still holds daily and Sunday masses, with a congregation of 600 members. (*4 Zhongma Lu. From the ferry terminal, head south on Zhongma Lu for about 5min.; the church is in a gated area on the left. ☎735 5903. Free.*)

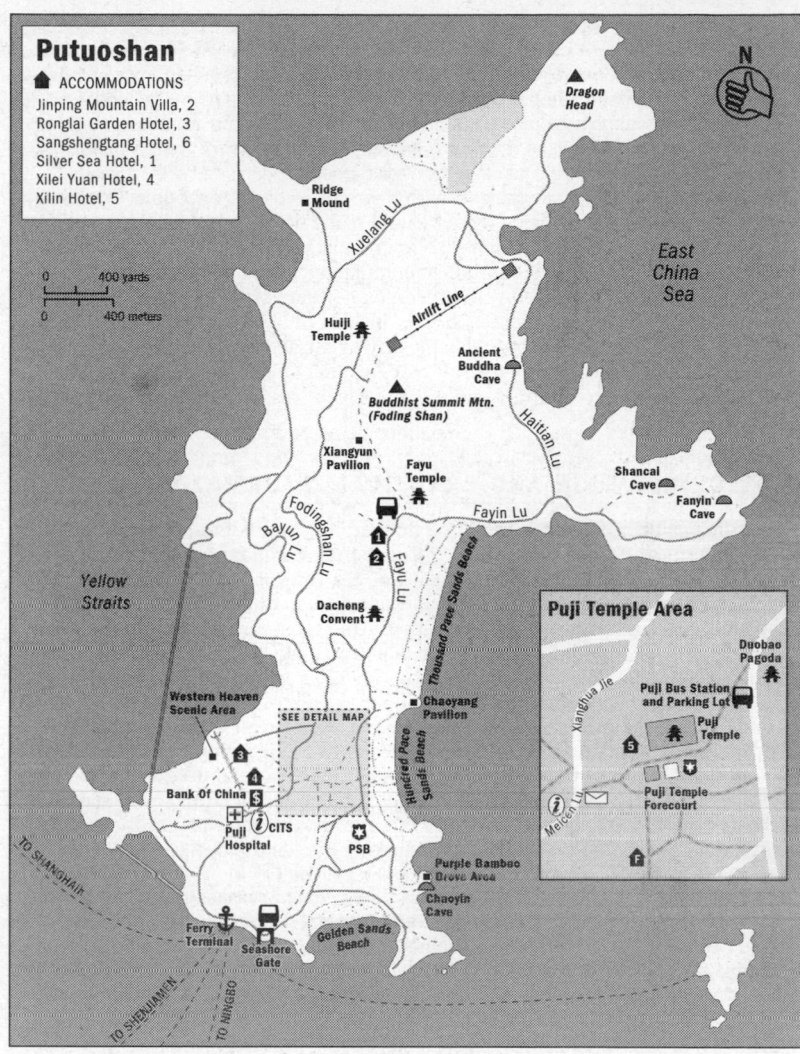

Putuoshan

⌂ ACCOMMODATIONS

Jinping Mountain Villa, 2
Ronglai Garden Hotel, 3
Sangshengtang Hotel, 6
Silver Sea Hotel, 1
Xilei Yuan Hotel, 4
Xilin Hotel, 5

The **Hemedu Site Museum** (hémǔdù guǐzhǐ bówùguǎn; 河姆渡贵址博物馆), north of Ningbo on the north bank of the Yaoying River, marks the site of Neolithic village ruins discovered in 1973. Various artifacts are on display, including skeletons, 7000-year-old cultivated rice, and even pottery pigs. (☎ 295 1731 or 295 1730.)

PUTUOSHAN 普陀山 ☎ 0580

Saturated with the fragrance of incense and strains of Buddhist chants while fanned by waves from the East China Sea, the air on the tiny island of Putuoshan is worlds away from the wafting exhaust fumes and din of auto horns that haunt many mainland cities. A mecca for both devout Buddhist pilgrims and wonder-struck tourists, the island's abundance of temples, shrines, and monasteries is set against a mist-covered expanse of sea. With rolling hills and rugged cliffside beaches, Putuoshan is indeed blessed with a touch of the sacred. It's easy to see why Guanyin herself chose it as her final resting place. Scores of temples are dedicated to this goddess of compassion and mercy, from the South Sea Guanyin on her welcoming perch overlooking the sea to the Thousand-Hand Guanyin, whose tangle of limbs represents her ability to offer a helping hand to those in need. Both seem to emanate a spirit of universal welcome that fills Putuoshan; its manifold spiritual and natural beauties make it a living place of worship with a power of enchantment that few other places in the world possess.

The serenity of Putuoshan is aged with years of religious devotion. Over 200 temples existed during the Ming dynasty, and many of the relics date to the late Song period. Even with its growing renown as a tourist hot spot, Putuoshan remains a vibrant and unspoiled Buddhist community, and most visitors who flood through its sanctified gates yearn to preserve its otherworldly rhythm, set to the beat of wooden gourds and chanted *sutras* instead of ticker-tape and the wail of car horns. Indeed, one of Putuoshan's mystifying attractions is its seeming timelessness; monks in flowing robes stroll along winding mountain roads as statues and temples continue to multiply, making the island less an historical monument than an evolving shrine.

✦❷ ORIENTATION AND PRACTICAL INFORMATION

Among the smallest islands in the Zhoushan archipelago off the coast of northern Zhejiang in the East China Sea, Putuoshan is compact enough to be traversed on foot in three or four hours. Longer than it is wide, most of the island's major roads run lengthwise, from north to south. The ferry terminal is at the southern tip of the island. From there, the most direct route to the center, where Puji Temple is located, is via **Meicen Lu** (梅岑路), which runs west and then north from the terminal. **Puji Lu** (普济路), which runs east and then northward along the eastern coast, completes the arc of roads along the southern edge of the island. From the Puji Temple area, several roads run northward, including **Fayu Lu** (法雨路), which leads to Fayu Temple at the base of Putuoshan's principal peak, **Buddhist Summit Mountain,** and **Foding Shan Lu** (佛顶山路), which scales the western side of the mountain and ends near the entrance to Huiji Temple. There are also many small footpaths running through the hills that serve as shortcuts linking the major routes.

Boats: The only way to arrive at the island is by ferry from Shanghai, Ningbo, or one of the larger islands nearby. The **Passenger Ferry Terminal** (lúnchuán mǎtóu; 轮船码头), 1 Puji Lu (☎609 1121), is at the southern tip of the island (also known as kèyùn mǎtóu; 客运码头; or kèyùn zhàn; 客运站). Tickets for Ningbo may only be purchased on the day of travel; tickets to other destinations may be purchased 1 day in advance. Ticket window open daily 6am-5pm. To **Ningbo** (2½hr., approximately 10 per day 6:40am-5:20pm, Y52) and **Shanghai** (5hr. or 13hr.; 2 fast boats per day, 1 slow boat per day; fast boats Y155-182, slow boats Y119-351). The most common route for passengers traveling between Ningbo and Putuoshan is the 2½hr., Y52 ticket, which consists of a 1hr. bus ride from the Ningbo Passenger Ferry Terminal to another dock nearer the island, and a 1½hr. ferry ride between the dock and Putuoshan.

Local Transportation: Walking is highly recommended. From the ferry terminal to Puji Temple takes 20-25min.; from Puji Temple to Fayu Temple 30-40min.; and the uphill climb from Fayu Temple to Huiji Temple another 45min.-1hr. **Minibuses** operate roughly from dawn to dusk, although service is erratic and it's often difficult to find minibuses willing to go to less-touristed attractions. Typical fares include: ferry terminal to the Puji Temple parking lot Y3; Puji Temple to Fayu Temple Y2.5; Puji Temple to the base of Buddhist Summit Mountain (near Huiji Temple) Y6. Some hotels rent vans for their guests.

Taxis: With only 5 **taxis** servicing Putuoshan and an asking fee of Y50, taking the taxi is best left as a last resort.

Tourist Office: Putuoshan Administrative Offices, Reception and Welcome Office (pǔtuóshān guǎnlǐ jú jiēdài chù; 普陀山管理局接待所), 115 Meicen Lu (☎609 1224 and 609 1104), opposite and a bit south of the post office, in a large courtyard overlooking a pond. No English-speaking staff, but this is still a good place to gather free maps and brochures introducing life on the island.

Travel Agency: CITS, 112 Meicen Lu, 2nd Fl. (☎609 1183), opposite the Bank of China, immediately to your left as you enter the courtyard. Arranges tours of Putuoshan (1-day tours Y300 and up) and books ferry tickets to Ningbo and Shanghai (commission Y10). English-, German-, Japanese-, and Korean-speaking interpreters available. Open daily 8am-5:30pm. Most hotels on the island also book plane, bus, and boat tickets (Y10-20 commission), with 1-day notice required.

Bank of China: 103 Meicen Lu (☎609 1591), opposite CITS. Exchanges traveler's checks. ATMs (MC, Visa) behind the counter. Open daily 8-11:30am and 1-5pm.

Markets: Several small **supermarkets** cluster on Xianghua Jie (also called Zhi Jie), the street east of Puji Si, and the alleys running off to the south from it. **Fruit vendors** abound on this street, sharing space with shops selling everything from dried seafood and seashells to miniature Guanyin statuettes and monastery garb.

PSB: 231 Puji Lu (☎609 2000), on the right side of the road when you head south from the Puji Temple parking lot. Open daily 8am-5pm.

Hospital: Puji Hospital (pǔjì yīyuàn; 普济医院), 95 Meicen Lu (☎609 2388), on the right, just past the Bank of China, when you head east from Puji Temple. No English-speaking staff. Open 24hr.

Telephones: Public pay phones are scarce. Calls may be made with IC phone cards; IDD service available.

Post and Telecommunications: 124 Puti Lu (☎609 1100), at the corner of Meicen Lu and Puti Lu, on a raised embankment to the left when you head south from Puji Temple. EMS, IDD service (to the right of the main entrance), and Poste Restante. Open daily 7:30am-4:30pm. **Postal Code:** 316107.

ACCOMMODATIONS

Most of Putuoshan's hotels are clustered on small alleys near the main temples, especially Puji Temple and Fayu Temple. Chinese (and often overseas Chinese) can generally find inexpensive lodging without too much trouble. Local residents make some extra pocket money by opening up their homes to Chinese tourists; a walk around the island reveals many signs painted on the walls of houses advertising "accommodation available inside" (nèi yǒu zhùsù; 内有住宿). However, this option is closed to foreigners, as are many of the cheaper hotels on the island. If all else fails, two middle- to top-end hotels that you can always fall back on are the **Xilei Little Villa Hotel** (xīlěi xiǎo zhuāng; 息耒小庄; ☎609 1505), at the corner of Puti Lu and Meicen Lu east of Puji Temple, and the **Putuoshan Grand Hotel** (pǔtuóshān dàjiǔdiàn; 普陀山大酒店; ☎609 2828), on Meicen Lu next to Puji Hospital. Because hotels often fill to capacity on weekends, during the summer, and over the May 1 and October 1 national holidays, reservations are suggested. Bargaining is possible except during peak season (July-Aug.), and the mind-boggling prices are often negotiable, especially for students.

■ **Xilin Hotel** (xílín fàndiàn; 锡麟饭店), 9 Xianghua Jie (☎609 1303; fax 609 1199), next to Puji Temple at its western end, bordering the alley leading to the Xilai Yuan Hotel. Humble surroundings and clotheslines crisscrossing the main courtyard are misleading: rooms are spotless and come fully equipped with minibar, A/C, TV, and bath. Two other benefits: a central location and friendly staff. Occasional 30% discounts available. Singles Y276; doubles Y258-416; triples Y245; quads Y408.

Sanshengtang Hotel (sānshèngtáng fàndiàn; 三圣堂饭店), 121 Miaozhuangyan Lu (☎609 1277; fax 609 1140), a 5min. walk along a footpath running along Haiyin Pond opposite Puji Temple, past the post office on your right. This vast monastery-turned-hotel offers a wide variety of rooms and caters to thrifty tourists and the backpacker scene. Arranged around a small central courtyard, with all standard amenities to boot, Sanshengtang is simply one of the best deals in town. Student discounts available. Singles Y200; doubles Y228-403; triples Y281. Off-season: Y160-240.

Silver Sea Hotel (yín hǎi fàndiàn; 银海饭店; ☎609 1114), on Fayu Lu between Jinping Mountain Villa and Fayu Temple. A minibus goes directly from the ferry terminal to the Fayu Temple parking lot, facing Fayu Lu; the hotel is to the right. While the rooms with balconies overlooking Thousand-Paces Sands Beach are airy and resort-like, some of the others aren't in tip-top condition, with ailing bathrooms and mosquito-frequented sheets. Singles Y380; doubles Y380-480; triples Y515.

Jinping Mountain Villa (jīnpíng shān zhuāng; 锦屏山庄), 107 Fayu Lu (☎609 1500; fax 609 1698), a few minutes south of Fayu Temple. With a tranquil location and semi-luxurious inner courtyards and pools, the Villa offers clean rooms near the Thousand-Paces Sands Beach. 50% discounts M-Th. Doubles Y300-550; triples Y390-650.

Ronglai Garden Hotel (rónglái xiǎoyuàn; 融来小院), 28 Xianghua Jie (☎609 1262), just east of Puji Temple. Walk into the market area to the right of the temple, facing the main gate, and take the lane to the left; the hotel is through an arched entryway after a few twists and turns. Not technically supposed to accept foreigners. Another in the procession of converted monasteries. Rooms here offer serene surroundings but are begging for renovation. 30-50% discounts possible. Doubles Y380; triples Y425; quads Y395.

Xilei Yuan Hotel (xílěi yuàn fàndiàn; 息耒院饭店), 5 Xianghua Jie (☎609 1119). Follow the alley on the western side of Puji Temple (to the left as you face the temple); signs point the way. Xilei Yuan's standard rooms are cramped and worn-down, not too far a stretch from its monastic days. Hot water 7-9pm. 20-30% discounts possible. Dorm beds may be available upon request. Doubles Y210-450; triples Y504; quads Y492.

FOOD

Like neighboring Ningbo, Putuoshan is famous for its seafood delicacies. One specialty is **Zhoushan Yellow Fish** (zhōushān huáng yú; 舟山黄鱼), served steamed or sauteed, with a side dish of tofu soup made with fish head. At Y100 per kg, though, it may as well be gold. Another well-known dish is **Zhoushan Snails** (zhōushān wōniú; 舟山蜗牛), stirred in a special vinegar sauce (Y20). Some places to look, especially for seafood, are the stretch of **Meicen Lu** opposite the Putuoshan Grand Hotel, with restaurants that allow guests to pick from a living "menu" of seafood and ready-made dishes, including dried squid (Y6) and deep fried fish (Y16), and **Puji Lu** east of the ferry terminal.

The market streets east of **Puji Temple** are crammed with stalls selling fresh fruit (both the mundane and the exotic), and **Xiangyun Lu,** the street between the Fayu Temple parking lot and the temple itself, with stalls selling everything from dried seafood and *baozi* to seashells. A small courtyard of restaurants specializing in seafood behind the Puji Temple area offers a good selection of cheap dishes. The **Wanghai Restaurant** (wànghǎi fàndiàn; 望海饭店), directly left of the main gate leading to Fayu Temple, has built a good reputation among locals for serving local specialties and doubling as a watermelon-seed cracking hangout. (☎609 1671. Open daily 6am-whenever guests leave.)

For vegetarians, Putuoshan is ripe for the eating, with vegetarian restaurants clustered around the main temples. **Baihua Tea House** (báihuá cháyè guǎn; 白华茶叶馆), 6 Xianghua Jie, serves its delicate creations, including radish pancakes (Y4.5), vegetarian fish (Y20), and vegetarian pork (Y30), made from fruit and glutinous rice, in an ornate dining hall tucked at the corner of Puji Lu and Meicen Lu. (☎609 1208. Open daily 6:30am-8:30pm.)

SIGHTS

There is a Y60 "admission fee" to enter the island, payable at the ferry terminal upon arrival. Think of it as "customs," for you are indeed entering something like a new country, one that moves to more relaxed rhythms than the mainland. The entire island can be considered a sight in itself—and a good one, at that. Strolling around the island, without even a glance at any of the "official" sights, is a treat, with vistas of the sea and emerald mountains, chickens and bamboo groves along some of the paths less trodden, and the occasional small temple or pavilion that does not charge admission. Putuoshan's three major temples—**Puji, Fayu,** and **Huiji**—are the main attractions for Buddhist pilgrims and lay visitors alike; some of the other sights may actually offer more variety and interest for non-Buddhists, though. All sights have kneeling stools in front of the Buddha statues.

PUJI TEMPLE (pǔjì sì; 普济寺). No one who knows anything goes through the main entrance of Puji. Legend holds that when Emperor Zhuang wanted to visit the temple, because he was dressed as a normal peasant, a monk wouldn't let him in the main door (which was closed) and let him in through the side instead. Furious, the emperor ordered that no one be allowed through, and three bridges were constructed over **Haiyin Pond** (hǎiyīn chí; 海音池)—the middle one for the emperor, the arched one for the nobles, and the plain one for the commoners.

The oldest of the three principal temples on Putuoshan and overflowing with people, Puji Temple is also the most central. The area around Haiyin Pond (also known as Freeing-the-Soul Pond) is a gathering place for tour groups, tai chi practitioners, and souvenir vendors. Built in 1080, the temple is not only the geographical heart of the island, but its devotional soul, housing the **Divine Guanyin** (shèng guānyīn; 圣观音), the only representation of Guanyin constructed by Putuoshan natives. In its main hall sits a magnificent grand Buddha, flanked by statues of the **Eighteen Mythical Disciples** (luó hàn; 罗汉). Other halls house lesser buddhas, including **Wen Shu Buddha**, the buddha of learning—and, for many of those who burn incense for him, the buddha of university entrance examinations. The traditional layout of Puji Temple is "typical" enough to serve as a good introduction to the island's other temples. *(15 Xianghua Jie. From the ferry terminal exit, follow Meicen Lu northward as it becomes Xianghua Jie; the temple is half a block down on the left. From the ferry terminal to the parking lot is a 5min. bus ride (Y3). Open daily 5:30am-6:30pm; shorter hours in winter. Y5, children under 1.4m and genuinely devout-but-penniless pilgrims free.)*

FAYU TEMPLE (fǎyǔ sì; 法雨寺). At the base of Buddhist Summit Mountain, this temple's terraced halls and buildings give it an expansive air that you won't find at the more dense and compact Puji Temple. Much of Fayu's beauty and opulence stems from its patronage by the Ming Emperor Zhu Yuan Zhuang. Built in 1580, the Fayu greets entering visitors with its unique **Nine-Dragon Screen** (jiǔ lóng bì; 九龙壁), carved from 60 stones pieced together in an interlocking jigsaw fashion. A miniature golden pagoda stands between the wall and the first of the temple's several halls, with five tiers of windows through which visitors toss coins for good luck. In one of the halls sits the (literally) **Open-Hearted Buddha** (kāixīn luóhàn; 开心罗汉), an image of the Buddha within his chest to symbolize his spiritual dedication and position as son of the great Buddha. The imposing statue of the **Thousand-Hand Guanyin** (qiān shǒu guānyīn; 千手观音) is so called because she gave up her hands in human form to heal her father's sickness; in return for her sacrifice, she was endowed with enlightenment. The highlight of the temple is the **Nine-Dragon Hall of Treasures** (jiǔ lóng bǎo diàn; 九龙宝殿), which was moved, by the orders of Emperor Kangxi, from Nanjing to Putuoshan during the Qing dynasty. *(1 Fayin Lu. Take a minibus from the Puji Temple parking lot, or walk north for 30min. Also accessible from Huiji Temple by descending the Buddhist Summit Mountain along a trail of a 1080 steps. ☎ 609 1317. Open daily 5:10am-6pm. Y5.)*

HUIJI TEMPLE (huìjì sì; 慧济寺). The smallest and least crowded of the three main temples, Huiji Temple is perched at the very top of Buddhist Summit Mountain. The surrounding area offers breathtaking vistas of the sea to the west and the mountainside and valley to the south and east. The long walkway leading to the temple, paved with ancient calligraphy and lotus leaves to represent Guanyin's presence, is believed to purify visitors of worldly sins. In 1794, a monk lit a candle and proclaimed it as Guanyin's presence, thus convincing workers to hike up to the summit bearing individual pieces of wood. The completed temple has only two main halls off an inner courtyard; the hum of praying monks emanates from side halls. Huiji houses the **Laughing Buddha** in its front hall; a Buddha in the main hall is flanked by Guanyin to the left and Four Heavenly Kings on either side. *(208 Xiangyun Lu. Take a minibus to the foot of Buddhist Summit Mountain and climb for 45min.-1hr. up the 1080 steps. Alternatively, take the chairlift (6:30am-5pm, Y35 round-trip) to the top. ☎609 1126. Open daily sunrise-sunset. Y5.)*

SOUTH SEA GUANYIN (nán hǎi guānyīn; 南海观音). A relatively new addition, the 33m tall South Sea Guanyin is set amid white limestone and marble, giving it a deservedly palatial air. The statue itself looms golden and impressive, a guiding light for tourists and sailors alike. The steps leading to it are lined with receptacles full of burning incense sticks and statues of some of the 18 mythical disciples.

Around the base of the statue are exhibition halls full of art and artifacts. Lower level walls are crammed with intricately detailed murals made of bronze, dark wood, and even colored jade. The murals illustrate scenes from the story of Putuoshan's origin as a Buddhist island, as well as familiar scenes of present-day Putuoshan. The second level exhibition contains hundreds of glass-encased icons of the goddess of mercy—including, most notably, the famous Thousand-Hand Guanyin—but these pale in comparison to the views of the sea and the island's green-carpeted mountains. *(Take Puji Lu south from the Puji Temple parking lot, and follow the left fork as it becomes Zizhu Lu. Continue straight as Zizhu Lu becomes a footpath leading uphill for another 5-10min.; the entrance is on top of the hill, to the right. Open daily 5:30am-6pm. Y6.)*

PURPLE BAMBOO GROVE (zǐ zhú lín; 紫竹林). Purple bamboo is the least of the many attractions in the grove. Inside a small temple flanked by a frieze of colorful miniature murals sits a statue of Guanyin carved entirely from a solid block of jade. Near the murals, intrepid visitors can climb to peer down into **Chaoyin Cave** (cháoyīn dòng; 朝音洞), a spine-tingling drop into which many devoted followers have plunged in their attempt to attain enlightenment; a stele erected next to the cave opening urges such devotees to reconsider. The small pavilion on the rocks, soothed by the drumming of breaking waves and the refreshing sea breezes, is where many visitors ooh-and-aah over **Luojia Mountain** (luòjiā shān; 洛迦山). The mountain is shaped like a sleeping Buddha; the rock depression on the beach is said to be the footprint Guanyin left when she stepped over to Putuoshan to admire its view. The focal point, however, is a tiny shrine to the left of Chaoyin Cave, known as the **Courtyard of the Cannot-Bear-To-Leave Guanyin** (bùkěn qù guānyīn yuàn; 不肯去观音院). It acquired its curious name from an episode in AD 916, when a Japanese monk begged to be able to take Guanyin back to Japan; the Putuoshan monks agreed, but Guanyin apparently did not, since the poor monk was shipwrecked not far offshore and returned to the island to build Guanyin a suitable temple. *(Minibuses (Y2) headed from the Puji Temple Parking Lot to the ferry will stop here if you ask. Otherwise, walk south along Puji Lu for about 10min.; when the road forks, go left onto Zizhu Lu. Turn left onto a little footpath just past a small parking lot a few minutes down Zizhu Lu.; this path leads to the entrance. ☎609 1221. Y5.)*

WESTERN HEAVEN SCENIC AREA (xī tiān jǐng qū; 西天景区). This area contains some of Putuoshan's most fabled natural sights, notably **Heart-Shaped Rock** (xīnzì shí; 心字石), **Pantuo Rock** (pántuó shí; 磐陀石), and the **Two Turtles Learning Buddhist Scripture** rock formation (èrguī tīngfǎ shí; 二龟听法石), apparently christened by some imaginative visitor. Pantuo Rock is something of a legendary curiosity because of its inexplicably stable position on a narrow and precarious rock ledge. *(On Puti Lu, the small lane that runs to the right off Meicen Lu just south of the Xilai Xiaoyuan Hotel. Open daily sunrise-sunset. Y8.)*

DACHENG CONVENT (dàchéng ān; 大乘庵). The primary attraction of this small convent is the impressive **Reclining Buddha** (wò fó; 卧佛) who takes it easy in the main hall, with carved symbols signifying peace hidden in the fringes of his robe. For those less enthused about seeing a reclining Buddha in the early stages of chippage, the hike it takes to get here may be more trouble than it's worth. *(39 Fayu Lu. Halfway up and off the left side of the road leading north from the Puji Temple parking lot to Fayu Temple. ☎609 1347. Open daily 6am-7pm; shorter hours in winter. Y2.)*

OTHER SIGHTS. Putuoshan is sprinkled with a host of lesser caves, temples, and pavilions, which are less frequented but just as stunning. The small **Hundred-Pace Sands Beach** (bǎi bù shā; 百步沙), opposite and a bit north of the Puji Temple parking lot, and the more spacious **Thousand-Pace Sands Beach** (qiān bù shā; 千步沙), with its entrance along a gardened path opposite Fayu Temple, are popular during the summer. These are regular, recreational beaches, yet Hundred-Pace Sands still maintains a touch of the sacred, in the form of a single pavilion at the top of a rocky promontory. Camping is possible on the Hundred-Pace Sands Beach, with tents rented out during the summer. Sunrise- and sunset-watching and tea sampling are popular hobbies among both locals and tourists, mixing the idyllic with the aromatic. For people who expect the scenic vistas to work magic, it doesn't disappoint. *(Both beaches open 8am-6:30pm for swimming, 7pm-midnight for moonlight strolls. Hundred-Pace Sands Y5, Y15 for swimmers; Thousand-Pace Sands Y12.)*

Putuoshan's eastern shores have some scenic spots that may yield moments of inspiration. **Chaoyang Pavilion** (cháoyáng gé; 潮阳阁), on the right side of Puji Lu, north of Hundred-Pace Sands Beach on the road leading to Fayu Temple, is a great place to watch the sun rise (Y6). At the far end of the peninsula, on 301 Fayin Lu (the road leading east from Fayu Temple), lies **Fanyin Cave** (fànyīn dòng; 梵音洞; Y5), accessible by minibus from the ferry terminal or Puji and Fayu Temples.

I LIKE TO BIKE

Traveling by bicycle can be a convenient and cheap way to get around, and it gives travellers the opportunity to see what they want, when they want, with minimum hassle. Rental stands can usually be found by looking for the long, orderly lines of bikes—parking areas are much more chaotic. You'll be asked to leave a deposit, usually Y100-200. If you're polite, you might be able to have the attendant add air to the tires or adjust the seat for you. Try to pick a bike that looks like it's in good condition—at the very least you'll want a reliable set of brakes.

When you're on the road, pay very close attention to the traffic around you—while cars and buses will honk to get your attention, other cyclists are unlikely to do the same and will sometimes appear rather suddenly next to you. To warn someone of your passing, you can either ring the bell (if it works) or just yell something. It doesn't really matter what you say, as long as it can catch someone's attention. Just make sure it's not offensive, as some bikers can be frighteningly aggressive.

The bicycle isn't likely to be top quality. Don't push the bikes too fast or too hard, and try to stand up at intersections unless you want your backside to be permanently sore. One good thing about cheap bikes, though, is that no one is likely to steal them. They're just that bad. The bike probably still has a built-in ring lock that closes around the back tire (basically useless, but it's the thought that counts). Take care, and you'll understand why so many people in China prefer to bike around town.

SHANGHAI

YANGZI BASIN

Like the Yellow River to the north, the Yangzi River (the third longest river in the world) has always dictated the fates of the countless people who have dwelt along its banks and looked to its waters for sustenance. Summer floods bring torrents of muddy water rushing down the river, threatening to overwhelm dikes and deluge even the most massive cities. In particularly bad years, the death toll reaches the thousands. Even in flood-free years, all that rushing water brings unbearably humid summers and damp, chilly winters to the riverside provinces of Anhui, Jiangxi, Hunan, and Hubei.

But the Yangzi is a gentler giant than the merciless Yellow River. The lands along its banks are among China's most populous and most productive, and the region's population has suffered less riverborne torment than that of Central China. The Yangzi has instead focused its energies on carving out dramatic scenery along its 6380km route from the Geladandong Glaciers of Tibet to the East China Sea. The pinnacle of the river's achievements, the towering Three Gorges in Hubei, gives way to sleepy hamlets and rapidly developing industrial parks as the waters widen on their journey eastward. Farther away from the Yangzi's all-powerful influence, mountains that have served both as retreats for the Chinese elite and as training grounds for revolution now attract tourists in search of the poetic splendor of times past. Local history is a several thousand-year-old tale of nature at its most sensational, woven together into the rich fabric of legends.

HIGHLIGHTS OF THE YANGZI RIVER BASIN

MOMENTOUS MAO MOMENTS in **Shaoshan** (p. 388), **Lushan** (p. 378), **Wuhan** (p. 394) and **Jinggangshan** (p. 381).

MONASTIC LIFE as lived on the sacred mountains of **Jiuhuashan** (p. 369) and **Wudangshan** (p. 403).

LIMESTONE SPIRES and caverns at **Zhangjiajie** (p. 392).

SUPERB SUNRISES over the "North Sea" in **Huangshan** (p. 363).

ANHUI 安徽

Often looked upon as the poor cousin to neighboring Jiangsu, Anhui province was first settled during the Han dynasty (202 BC-AD 220). Hefei, the provincial capital, perches far north of the Yangzi River, but most points of interest in the province are south of the waterway. Scattered in between are a number of flat, dusty cities, as well as river ports like Anqing and Wuhu.

While much of northern Anhui is unremarkable, the landscape to the south is spectacular. Take the time to join the chattering tourist groups that crowd the trails at Huangshan to catch a glimpse of the famed Beihai sunrise, or wander among the rice paddies and peasant huts that dot the idyllic countryside around Jiuhuashan, one of the four famous Buddhist mountains in China. Anhui's lush scenery and pastoral way of life tend to soothe the rattled nerves of travelers arriving from the frenzied coast.

HEFEI 合肥 ☎ 0551

The last time Hefei saw any *real* action was in AD 383, when the city was the staging ground for the Battle of Feishui; the brutal conflict ensured that north and south China would undergo cultural development independently of one another well into the future. Ever since the clash, the city has been waiting for some exciting gem to lure tourists. But even esteemed titles like provincial capital of Anhui and home of China's MIT (the University of Science and Technology of China) do little to add dazzle to this squarish, somewhat dull city. As such, it's mostly used as a transport hub either to Huangshan in the south, Jiangsu to the northeast, or simply to other, remotely more interesting destinations in Anhui. Still, some reminders of Hefei's legendary past remain: a temple here, a museum over there. And that Hefei, with its more than one million inhabitants, still runs at a less frantic pace than most cities its size, is surely to be commended, if not appreciated in person.

So what to expect? A pleasant, well-planned network of parks rings the city center, and the Nanfei River flows along the city's northern side; a number of universities, especially of science, engineering, and technology, are on the outskirts of town; and most generally, a typical Chinese population bustles through typical Chinese city streets, in a typical Chinese city: one unhampered by the dirty gold of tourism, and more than happy to sit and wait for something bigger to come along.

▐ TRANSPORTATION

Airplanes: Luogang Airport (luògǎng jīchǎng; 骆岗机场) is 7km south of town. Bus #11 runs from the train station to near the airport; taxis cost Y10-20. **China Eastern Airlines** (zhōngguó dōngfāng hángkōng gōngsī; 中国东方航空公司), 246 Jinzhai Lu (☎281 2768), doesn't provide airport transportation. Open daily 8am-10pm. To: **Beijing** (2 per day, Y790); **Chengdu** (1-2 per day Su-F, Y970); **Guangzhou** (2 per day, Y830); **Huangshan** (1-3 per day, Y330); **Kunming** (1-2 per day Tu-F and Su, Y1330); **Shanghai** (1-2 per day, Y390); **Wuhan** (1-3 per day, Y290); **Xiamen** (1 per day Sa-Th, Y690); and **Xian** (1 per day M, W, and Sa; Y690).

Trains: Even though Hefei's train station has been completed for some time, most residents (and bus lines) still refer to it as the **"new" train station** (xīn zhàn; 新站). Buses #1 and 119 run along Changjiang Lu to the station, and bus #101 links it to the southwest part of the city. The ticket office is just north of the bus parking lot, on the left side of the station. Ticket windows #6 and 7 are open all night. To: **Beijing** (11-12hr., 2 per day, Y68-399); **Guangzhou** (24hr., 1 per day, Y88-489); **Nanjing** (4-6hr., 5 per day, Y23-77); **Shanghai** (10hr., 3 per day, Y41-136); **Tianjin** (11hr., 1 per day, Y62-336); and **Zhenjiang** (4½-5hr., 3 per day, Y25-83).

Buses: Three or 4 long-distance bus stations are south of the intersection of Shengli Lu and Changjiang Lu, near the old train station. The **ticket office**, 168 Mingguan Lu, a few blocks west of Shengli Lu, sells tickets for all departures. The bus timetables, though, are just as chaotic as the station area. To: **Huangshan** (6hr., 4 per day 6:50am-12:30pm, Y60); **Nanjing** (2½hr., 33 per day 6am-6:20pm, Y23-55); **Shanghai** (6hr., 12 per day 6:40am-5pm, Y145); **Wuhan** (6½hr., 6 per day 7:30am-5:30pm, Y98-140); **Wuxi** (4½hr., 5 per day 7:10am-2pm, Y73-100); **Yangzhou** (3½hr., 6 per day 7:30am-3:30pm, Y33); and **Zhenjiang** (4½hr., 3 per day, Y83-100).

Local Transportation: The bus system is comprehensive, but traffic can be maddeningly slow, especially around the end of Changjiang Lu and Shengli Lu. There is both **bus** (buses #1-47) and **minibus** service (buses #101-202). Fare Y0.5-1.5, depending on destination. If you don't really know where you're going, just fork over Y1 and look hapless. Certain routes, such as **#1** (from the train station to the intersection of Wangjiang Lu and Jinzhai Lu), run from about 4:30am-11pm, but most have shorter service hours.

Taxis: Some taxis, particularly around the train station, are not metered. Base fare Y5-6, each additional km Y1.2; with A/C Y7, each additional km Y1.4. From the city center to the train station or airport Y15-20.

◼◪ ORIENTATION AND PRACTICAL INFORMATION

Hefei is in the northern part of Anhui province, about 80km north of the Yangzi River. The smaller **Nanfei River** cuts through the northern portion of the city, and, along with a handful of attached parks and ponds, it encircles the main part of the city. The industrial suburbs recede quickly into farmland.

YANGZI BASIN

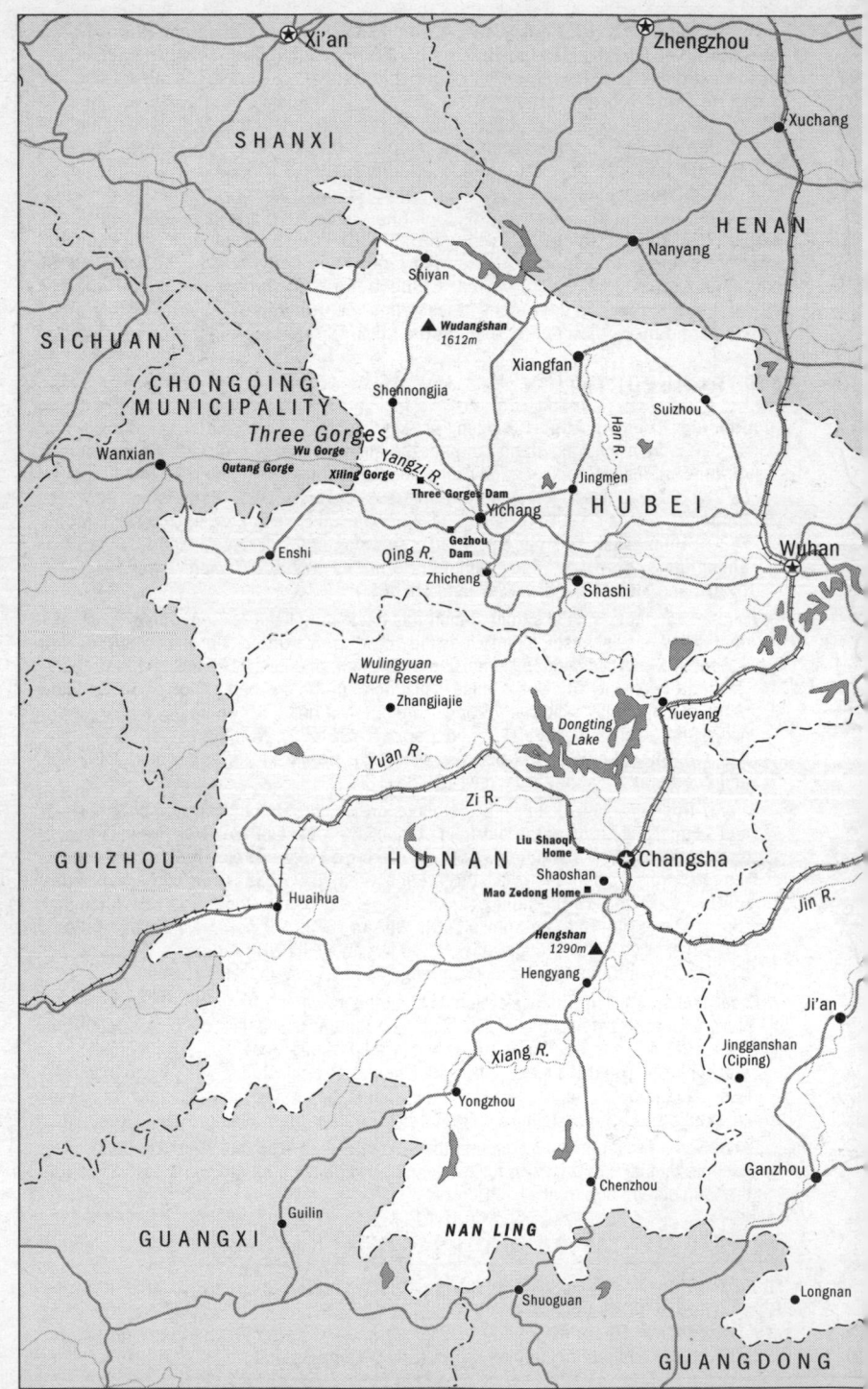

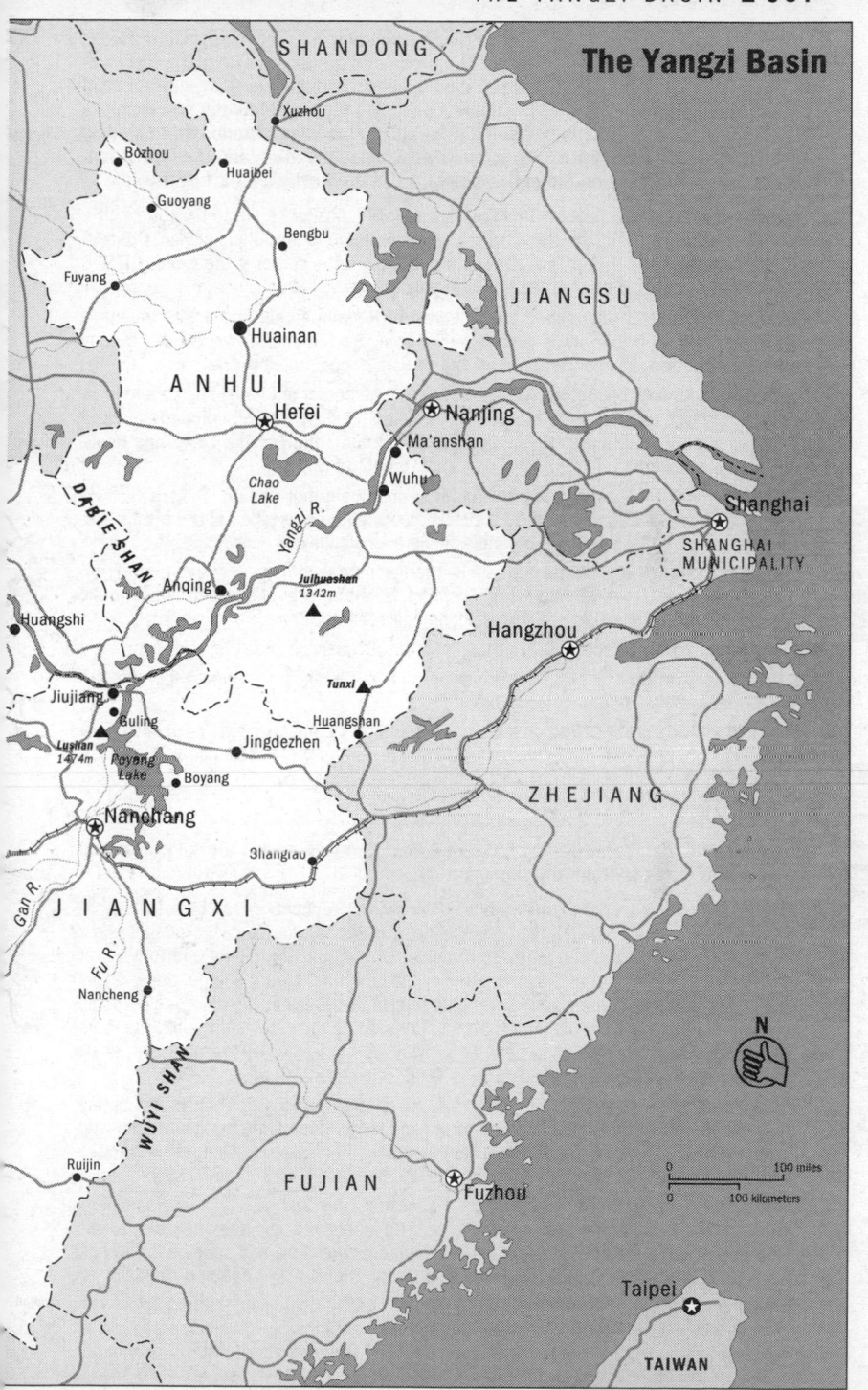

The Yangzi Basin

Hefei is largely navigable by foot. Three ring roads wind their way around Hefei, with **Huancheng Lu** (环城路) following the parks and waterways near the city center. **Changjiang Lu** (长江路) runs from east to west through the main commercial district. **Shouchun Lu** (寿春路), **Huaihe Lu** (淮河路), and **Meishan Lu/Wuhu Lu** (梅山路/芜湖路) run roughly parallel to Changjiang Lu, while **Jinzhai Lu** and **Meiling Dadao** cross the city from north to south. Both the train station and the main long-distance bus station are on **Shengli Lu** (胜利路), in the northeast part of the city.

Travel Agencies: CTS, Jiuzhou Building, 1st Fl., 381 Jinzhai Lu (☎264 6364 or 266 1223), near Lujiang Lu. Mrs. Jane Liu speaks English and readily offers advice. Open M-F 8:20am-noon and 2-6pm. Farther south and around the corner is the **Anhui CITS,** 8 Meishan Lu (☎282 2170). Open M-F 8:30am-5:30pm.

Bank of China: 313 Changjiang Lu, just west of Renmin Xiang. Exchanges traveler's checks. Open M-F 8am-noon and 2:30-5:30pm, Sa 8am-noon. Aggressive money changers out front give far better rates, but beware of counterfeit notes.

Bookstores: Xinhua Bookstore (☎265 2101), on the corner of Changjiang Lu and Meiling Lu, is large but has little more than the usual English learners' dictionaries and creased copies of *Treasure Island*. Open daily 8:30am-7pm. **Foreign Language Bookstore** (wài yú shūdiàn; 外语书店), 9 Jinzhui Lu (☎264 8910).

Hospital: Hefei Red Cross Hospital (héféi shì hóng shízìhuì yīyuàn; 合肥市红十字会医院; ☎363 4794; 24hr. ☎365 1919), near Anhui University. From the train station, take bus #119 to Jiuhu stop and walk up a small alley.

Pharmacy: Changjiang Pharmacy (ānhuī chángjiāng dàyàofáng; 安徽长江大药房), 315 Changjiang Lu, at Renmin Xiang. Three floors, with plenty of suspect homeopathic remedies, but few Western medicines. Open daily 8am-8:30pm.

Telephones: China Telecom, 99 Suzhou Lu. 24hr. IDD service.

Internet Access: On the 2nd floor of the Suzhou Lu/Changjiang Lu post office (☎262 0782). Y8 per hr. Open daily 8am-9pm.

Post Office: Hefei Post Office, at the corner of Suzhou Lu and Changjiang Lu, near Sipai Lou bus stop. EMS and Poste Restante. Open daily 8am-8pm. **Postal code:** 230001.

▚ ACCOMMODATIONS

Hotels in Hefei are primarily located along **Changjiang Lu,** near Yuhua Pond in the southwest, and by the train and bus stations.

Foreign Guesthouse of the University of Science and Technology of China (zhōngguó kējì dàxué zhuānjiā lóu; 中国科技大学专家楼), 96 Jianzhai Lu (☎360 2881), just south of the Keji Daxue bus stop. Go through the main university gate and turn left at the dead end; turn right, and then left again. The new hotel is past a large, beautiful lily pond, near the less conspicuous north gate to campus. The dorms (twin beds in rooms with TV and bath) are the best deal in town. They can be tough to get, though. The more expensive rooms are spanking new. Either way, you get to enjoy the pleasant, lively campus atmosphere. Dorms Y50; singles Y150; doubles Y240; triples Y290.

Xinya Hotel (xīnyà dàjiǔdiàn; 新亚大酒店), 18 Shengli Lu (☎429 2929). This option seems sad and worn when compared to the sparkling Holiday Inn, but it's friendly and a much better value. Aging rooms are kept neat and in good repair. Signs remind you to reuse towels and "make your mother proud." Doubles Y228-428; triples Y336.

Yinlu Hotel (yínlù fàndiàn; 饮路饭店), 9 Shouchun Lu (☎267 4554), near Huancheng Dong Lu. The kind of rooms only a mother could love: big and ugly. The straw bed covers and fake wood floors are unappealing, but the rooms are clean and spacious, with A/C and attached bath. Breakfast included. Singles and triples Y100; doubles Y55-100.

Changjiang Hotel (chángjiāng fàndiàn; 长江饭店), 262 Changjiang Lu (☎265 6441), near Tongcheng Lu. Buses #1, 3, 29, and 46 stop right outside. Relatively clean rooms and a central location more or less make up for any shortcomings. Most of the cheaper rooms are on the 2nd and 3rd floors. Deposit Y50. Singles Y150; doubles Y148-218.

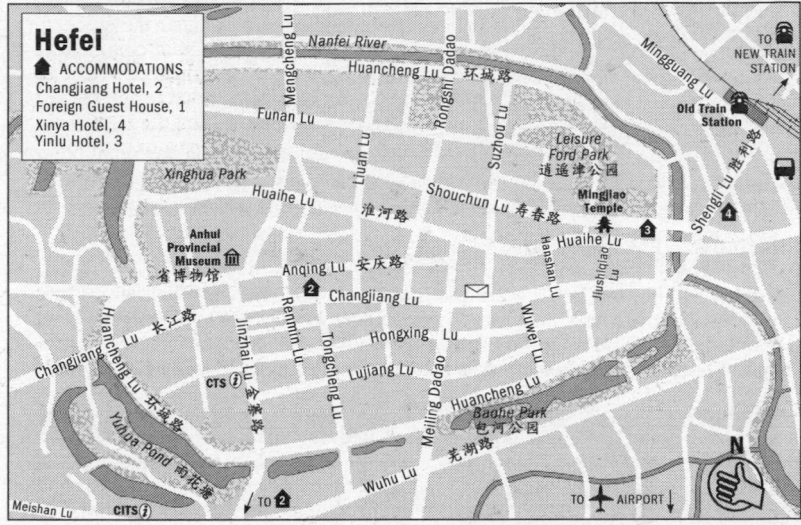

Hefei

🏠 ACCOMMODATIONS
Changjiang Hotel, 2
Foreign Guest House, 1
Xinya Hotel, 4
Yinlu Hotel, 3

🍴 FOOD

Hefei is a great place to sample regional specialities such as freshwater crab from Lake Chao, so good it will make you a devout crustacean convert at prices even an ascetic could afford. At the western edge of the city center, one block south of Changjiang Lu, small stands line the street from Jinzhai Lu almost to Gongwan Lu. With all the fresh ingredients close at hand, cooks toss everything into the frying pan as soon as the order is given. Prices here generally are no more than Y10. A bit east of Jinzhai Lu, **Renmin Xiang** stretches south from Changjiang Lu and features several blocks of excellent eateries and a lively atmosphere at night. Street markets are scattered throughout the city, with several right off Changjiang Lu.

The 24hr. **Haobangshou Supermarket** (hǎobāngshǒu chāoshì; 好帮手超市) on Renmin Xiang is a good bet. Then there are the usual bland Western options: expensive restaurant food, Big Macs, drumsticks, and mashed potatoes.

🍽 **Dalao Liu Restaurant** (dàlǎo liú xiǎochī bù; 大老刘小吃部), 16 Renmin Xiang (☎261 1461), serves up delicious, steaming-hot bowls of thick beef and noodle soup (Y3.5) to crowds of locals looking for good, cheap food. The friendly owners and cooks make dining here even better. Open daily 7am-10pm.

Anhui Minzu Restaurant (ānhuī mínzú fàndiàn; 安徽民族饭店), 8 Shouchun Lu (☎265 2865), northeast of city center. The entrance is just east of the main entrance to Leisure Ford Park; look for the Arabic inscription. Hefei may be a far cry from the Silk Road, but this restaurant dishes up decent Muslim cuisine, with soups starting at Y8 and heaps of food available for less than Y20. Open daily 9am-1pm and 5-9pm.

Mingjiao Temple Vegetarian Restaurant (míngjiào sì sù cāntīng; 明教寺素餐厅; ☎261 6179), just inside the temple entrance. The menu includes a few imitation meat dishes, soups (Y10), cabbage soaked in vinegar (Y5), and the old fried standbys. Open daily 11am-2pm and 5-9pm.

👁 SIGHTS

What Hefei lacks in tourist panache, it makes up for with its lush and lovely parks. In fact, the ring of parks surrounding the city center gave Hefei the honor of being named a "National Garden City" in 1992, and if you're here during the hot season, you'll quickly come to appreciate these areas' shaded retreat.

YANGZI BASIN

ANHUI PROVINCIAL MUSEUM (ānhuī shěng bówùguǎn; 安徽省博物馆). A cast of the skull of the ape-man unearthed in the county, inscriptions on blocks from Han dynasty tombs, a model of a Ming dynasty residence, and a study showcasing the "Four Scholastic Treasures" are some of the noteworthy sections. The examples of Huizhou architecture are similar to what remains in the old part of Tunxi (see p. 362) near Huangshan. A walk through the museum takes around 30 minutes, but if Donna, a polite, English-speaking tour guide joins you, tag on another 30 minutes. *(268 Anqing Lu, at the northern end of Jinzhai Lu. ☎ 282 3299. English captions. Open daily 8:30-11am and 2:30-5pm; last admission 4:30pm. Y4; special exhibitions Y2.)*

MINGJIAO TEMPLE (míngjiào sì; 明教寺). Cao Cao, an illustrious leader of the Kingdom of Wei, used the Archers' Training Terrace site to drill his troops during the early 3rd century, but the temple itself was not built until the early Tang dynasty. The current halls date from the 16th century, and were recently restored after being damaged during the Cultural Revolution. *(At the corner of Huaihe Lu and Jiushiqiao Lu, not far from the southern gate of Leisure Ford Park. Open daily 7am-6pm. Y5.)*

BAOHE PARK (bāohé gōngyuán; 包河公园). This park is a popular place for local families, who come to enjoy paddle boats and a few small temples. At night, lovers don't find it too bad either. The park contains the **Tomb of Lord Bao** (bāo zhěng mù; 包拯墓), a Song dynasty judge who was posthumously honored for honest and upright service; the fact that he became the protaganist of a wildly popular Taiwanese TV show is only incidental. *(Entrances at Ma'anshan Lu, south of Changjiang Lu, and at Huancheng Lu, off Meiling Lu. Open daily 24hr. Free.)*

OTHER SIGHTS. On the northeast side of town, **Leisure Ford Park** (xiāo yáojīn gōngyuán; 逍遥津公园), 18 Shouchun Lu, was the site of a famous battle between the Kingdom of Wu and the Kingdom of Wei. A statue commemorates General Zhang Liao (of the Kingdom of Wei), whose 10,000 man fight fighting force defeated an army 10 times its size. The park nicely combines a carnival atmosphere with more secluded lakeside trails. *(Open daily 5am-6pm. Y5.)* **Xinghua Park** (xìnghuá gōngyuán; 兴华公园) is bordered on the east by Mengcheng Lu, with an entrance between Shouchun Lu and Huaihe Lu. Other parks include **Yuhua Pond** (yǔhuā táng; 雨花塘), on the southwest side of the city, and **Apricot Blossom Park** (xìnghuā gōngyuán; 杏花公园), to the west. *(Open daily 5am-6pm. Y2.)* The small **Anhui Art Gallery** showcases the work of amateur artists on the 4th and 5th floors of a building at Changjiang Lu and Liuan Lu. *(Open daily 8:30am-noon and 2-5:30pm.)*

HUANGSHAN 黄山

After witnessing the Five Yue (Sacred Daoist Mountains), one looks not at any mere Shan (Mountain). After witnessing Huangshan, one looks not at any mere Yue.
  —Chinese Proverb

A trip to the spectacularly rugged landscape of Huangshan (Yellow Mountains) should be on the itinerary of every traveler in China. The peaks are also way up on the to-do lists of most Chinese tourists, who, with all the centuries-old calligraphy scrolls and national poetry dedicated to the place, practically breathe the Huangshan air before they've even been there.

The trails along Huangshan are crowded; apart from the luckiest off-season climbers, no one manages to escape the aggravating inertia of loud Chinese tour groups. And, yes, the area's rooms and food are priced higher than in other parts of China, mostly because tourism is Huangshan's greatest cash cow.

But hike for a while through the monolithic stone peaks—*watch* as the clouds roll in from a distant valley, up through caves and clusters of crooked pines, before smashing into your sweat-soaked, awe-filled face—and you'll understand in

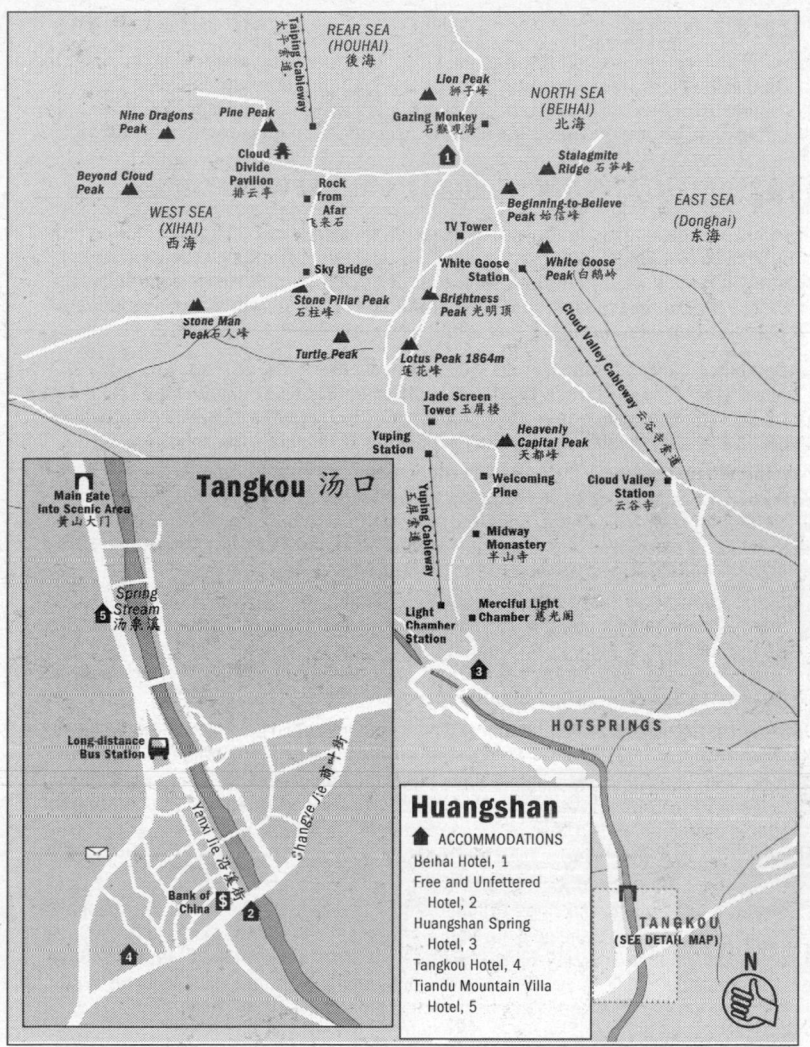

REAR SEA
(HOUHAI)
後海

Taiping Cableway
太平索道

Lion Peak
獅子峰

Gazing Monkey
石猴观海

NORTH SEA
(BEIHAI)
北海

Nine Dragons
Peak

Pine Peak

Cloud
Divide
Pavilion
排云亭

Stalagmite
Ridge 石笋峰

Beyond Cloud
Peak

Rock
from
Afar
飞来石

Beginning-to-Believe
Peak 始信峰

EAST SEA
(Donghai)
东海

WEST SEA
(XIHAI)
西海

TV Tower

White Goose
Peak 白鹅岭

Sky Bridge

White Goose
Station

Stone Pillar Peak
石柱峰

Brightness
Peak 光明頂

Cloud Valley Cableway 云谷索道

Stone Man
Peak石人峰

Turtle Peak

Lotus Peak 1864m
莲花峰

Jade Screen
Tower 玉屏楼

Yuping
Station

Heavenly
Capital Peak
天都峰

Tangkou 汤口

Welcoming
Pine

Cloud Valley
Station
云谷寺

Main gate
into Scenic Area
黄山大门

Yuping Cableway
玉屏索道

Midway
Monastery
半山寺

Spring
Stream
汤泉溪

Merciful Light
Chamber 慈光阁

Light
Chamber
Station

Long-distance
Bus Station

HOTSPRINGS

Yanxi Jie 沿溪街

Shangre Jie 商热街

Huangshan

⛰ ACCOMMODATIONS
Beihai Hotel, 1
Free and Unfettered
Hotel, 2
Huangshan Spring
Hotel, 3
Tangkou Hotel, 4
Tiandu Mountain Villa
Hotel, 5

Bank of
China

TANGKOU
(SEE DETAIL MAP)

N

a second why no one should miss this place. You'll see why Huangdi, an ancient sage king, is thought to have become a supernatural being here, living forever among the pines, stones, seas, and springs. And you'll likely agree that while other mountains' vistas elicit reverent sighs, Huangshan claws into your belly to pull out breathless, rolling moans of disbelief.

As another incentive, the main outposts for Huangshan hikes are spellbinding in their own right. Nestled in the foothills of the mountains, the towns of Tangkou and Tunxi are smoky mazes of narrow streets and alleys, many crowded with gritty markets and souvenir stands. Sure, they're tourist towns, and an amazing number of locals (i.e. everyone) seems to want to arrange your transport into the mountains. But the mellow and all-natural vibe of Huangshan promises more than a few gulps of fresh (albeit thin) air.

TUNXI 屯溪 ☎ 0559

Tunxi is also referred to as Huangshan City, not surprising given that the town's raison d'être is as a transportation hub for the mighty mountain. Because Tunxi is accessible by plane, train, and bus, most travelers will pass through it on their way to Huangshan, although some buses drive directly to the base town of Tangkou.

✈ 🏠 ORIENTATION AND PRACTICAL INFORMATION

The train station marks the far north of town. **Qianyuan Lu** (前园北路) runs south from here to the **Xinan River** (xīnān hé; 新安河). Several major east-west streets intersect Qianyuan Lu, including **Hehua Lu** (荷花路), which runs to the long-distance bus station in the east, and **Huangshan Lu** (黄山路), which runs to **Xinan Lu** (新安路) and the commercial heart of the city in the west.

Airplanes: Huangshan City Airport (huángshān shì fēijīchǎng; 黄山市飞机场), about 10km west of the city center. **CAAC ticket office** (☎ 953 4111). To: **Beijing** (1 per day T-Su, Y870); **Guangzhou** (1-4 per day Tu-Su, Y770); **Guilin** (W and Sa, Y730); **Shanghai** (2-3 per day, Y460); and **Wuhan** (2-3 per day M-Th and Sa-Su, Y500).

Trains: Huangshan City Train Station (huángshān shì huǒchē zhàn; 黄山市火车站; ☎ 251 2110), at the north end of Qianyuan Bei Lu, near the traffic circle at Guojing Lu. To: **Beijing** (21hr., 12:45am, Y88-489); **Fuzhou** (14hr., 6:32am, Y51-285); **Kunming** (57hr., 2:37am, Y139-798); **Nanjing** (7-11hr., 7 per day, Y21-161); **Shanghai** (12hr., 7:20am, Y44-263); and **Xiamen** (24hr., 9:01am, Y62-378).

Buses: Huangshan City Long-distance Bus Station (huángshān shì chángtú qìchē zhàn; 黄山市长途汽车站; ☎ 251 5949), at the eastern end of Hehua Dong Lu. To: **Hangzhou** (5hr., 6 per day 5:40am-4:20pm, Y36); **Hefei** (8hr., 5 per day 5:40am-10pm, Y42-57); and **Shanghai** (12hr., 5:40 and 10am, Y47). Minibuses go to **Huangshan Scenic Area** and **Tangkou** throughout the day (1hr., Y10-25).

Local Transportation: About 7 **minibus** routes run during daylight hours. Most, including bus **#4,** stop at both the train and bus stations and go along Huangshan Lu. Fare Y1.

Taxis: Taxis, pedicabs, and minibuses run throughout the region. Be careful about being overcharged—drivers have no qualms about ripping you off. From Tunxi to Tangkou should cost about Y50-100.

Travel Agencies: CITS, 6 Xizhen Jie, 3rd. Fl. (☎ 251 5295 or 251 2771), across from the Huaxi Hotel in the southwest part of town, just across the bridge from the Ancient Street; reach around and open the unlocked metal gate on the stairs. Exceptionally friendly and fluent English-speaking staff, with some maps and brochures to boot. Open daily 8:30am-noon and 2:30-6pm; in winter 8-11:30am and 2-5:30pm. **Huang Youjian** (huáng yǒujiàn; 黄有健; ☎ 139 0559) book tickets and arrange tours to some nearby sights. This self-proclaimed linguistic master speaks English and Japanese.

Tourist Complaint Line: ☎ 251 7464.

Bank of China: 9 Xinan Bei Lu, at Huangshan Lu. Open daily 8am-5:30pm.

Internet Access: Huaxi Xuefeng Internet Bar (huāxī wǎngbā; 花溪网吧), on the south side of Yanan Lu, just across the bridge from the end of the Ancient Street. Y10 per hr. Open daily 9am-11pm.

Post Office: Huangshan City Post Office, at the corner of Xinan Lu and Huangshan Lu. Open daily 8:30-10am and 2:30-4pm. **Postal Code:** 245000.

🏨 🍴 ACCOMMODATIONS AND FOOD

Tourism is the lifeblood of the Huangshan region. Finding a hotel room is easy. Finding a cheap room is not, leaving grotty dorm rooms as the only budget option. Prices listed here are for the high season (Mar. 15-Nov. 15); at other times, expect discounts (and bargaining leverage) to soar. The area around the train and bus stations is the best place to look for cheap sleeps, although the neighborhood near the Ancient Street is more interesting. The **Senlin Hotel** (sēnlín jiǔdiàn; 森林酒店), an old budget favorite, currently is closed for renovations, but is expected to reopen sometime in 2001.

Small food stands are clustered near the train and bus stations, especially along **Qianyuan Bei Lu** and **Hehua Dong Lu,** where giant bowls of *jiaozi* sell for as little as Y2. The street running to the west of the bus station also has loads of cheap noodle and dumpling stands. One of the primary nighttime activities is **karaoke,** but bad singers and early risers might prefer the hopping **morning market** near the bus station. And "hopping" doesn't just refer to the brisk atmosphere; frogs are Y3.

Yinlian Hotel (yínlián dàjiǔdiàn; 银联大酒店), 1-8 Xianren Dong Lu (☎252 7678; fax 252 7281). Walk west of the train station and take a left on Xianren Dong Lu; the hotel is about a block away, on the right. Enjoy TV, A/C, bath, a mini-bar, a pool, and your own ratty blue bathrobe. Singles Y288; doubles Y438; triples Y160.

Huangshan Jinwei Hotel (huángshān jìnwěi jiǔdiàn; 黄山缙纬酒店), 40 Huancheng Bei Lu (☎252 2383), the huge, glass cylindrical thing 1 block south of the train station. Big bucks, but it's ultra-convenient, and big rooms have curved walls and sweeping views. A truly unique bonus: your very own gas mask. Doubles Y360-480.

Huaxi Hotel (huāxī fàndiàn; 花溪饭店), 1 Xizhen Jie (☎251 4312; fax 251 4990), in the southwest part of the city, across the bridge at the western end of the Ancient Street. A modern, mid-market mega-monster, with restaurants and rooms galore. Rooms in the new building are more expensive, without a comparative increase in quality. Singles Y580; doubles Y280-480. Credit cards accepted.

◉ SIGHTS

Tunxi's **Ancient Street** (túnxī lǎojiē; 屯溪老街) begins near the bridge in the far western part of town and winds south toward the Xinan River. Many of the buildings lining the street date all the way back to the Song dynasty, and some of the tourist maps sold here can't be much younger. Tour leaders herd their groups through this narrow lane before taking them to the mountain, so expect to see plenty of kitschy, overpriced merchandise. Some shops, however, specialize in traditional local products, including medicine, tea, scrolls, and carved bamboo heads. Most unusual are the bottles of brandy (Y30-150) with large, dead snakes inside, a delicacy that puts every tequila worm to shame. Stop by one of these shops, and they'll give you a sample. Great taste *and* less filling.

TANGKOU 汤口　　　　　　　　　　☎0559

Tangkou, about 60km from Tunxi at the base of Huangshan, is the main outpost for hikes up the mountain. The town itself, built on the shoulders of the tourism industry, is not particularly remarkable, but Huangshan is. If you want to spend a few days traipsing up and down what is widely regarded as the most stunning mountain in China, you will probably end up staying here.

◼✴🛈 ORIENTATION AND PRACTICAL INFORMATION

Tangkou is a tiny cluster of hotels, shops, and restaurants, spread out next to a stream that comes down from the mountain. **Yanxi Jie** (沿溪街) runs along **Spring Stream** (quán xī; 泉溪) until it dead ends at **Shangye Jie** (商业街). The two-lane highway comes in from the southwest, drawing parallel to the stream as it heads north to the main gate into the Huangshan Scenic Area. Here Tangkou ends, and the highway continues up to the **Hot Springs Area** and the cable car terminal, the starting point for most mountain hikes.

Buses: Huangshan Scenic Area Long-distance Bus Station (huángshān fēngjǐng qū qìchē zhàn; 黄山风景区汽车站; ☎556 1550). Buses often go to the main gate before stopping here. Tickets sold in a small building on the highway, next to the bridge.

Open daily 6am-7pm. To: **Hangzhou** (7hr., 7 per day 6:20am-4:20pm, Y52-65); **Hefei** (8-10hr., 6 per day 6:05am-3pm, Y63); **Jiuhuashan** (4hr., 6am and 1:30pm, Y27); **Jiujiang** (6hr., 6:40am, Y85); **Nanjing** (6-8hr., 4 per day 6:30am-4pm, Y57-75); **Shanghai** (12hr., 6:20am, Y101); and **Wuhan** (12hr., 9am, Y146).

Taxis: Taxis circle like sharks waiting for fresh tourist blood. Fares are negotiable; as always, bargain, and do it hard and up front. Tangkou to the base of the Eastern Steps Y15-30, to the Hot Springs Area Y10-15.

Tour Guides: Mr. Wu, owner of the appropriately named Mr. Wu's Restaurant (p. 365), sells maps, provides quality information, and can help book bus tickets; all he asks is that you eat at his restaurant once or twice.

Bank of China: Directly across from the front gate of the Free and Unfettered Hotel. Open daily 8:30am-5pm. A branch in the **Beihai Summit Area,** across from the Beihai Hotel. Open daily 8-11am and 2:30-5:30pm. Most high-end hotels also change money.

Weather Conditions: ☎121. Weather is a crucial factor at Huangshan. Clear days can offer views of distant rock formations and cloudy weather creates seas of mist swirling around the mountain. While rainy days are the worst (slippery trails and poor visibility), after-rain conditions are considered optimal, with fleeting cloud formations giving way to sunshine and the occasional rainbow. For more information, contact the **Huangshan Meteorological Observatory** (☎251 2411). Open daily 8-11am and 2-5pm.

Hospital: Beihai Emergency Center (běihǎi jiùhù zhōngxīn; 北海救护中心; ☎556 2555), in the summit area, opposite the Beihai Hotel. Open daily 8:30-11:30am and 2-5:30pm. Just don't get hurt during lunch.

Internet Access: In the **Hot Springs Area** above Tangkou, the **Taoyuan Hotel**'s business center has access. Y60 per hr. Open daily 7am-11pm. A small store opposite and just west of the Free and Unfettered Hotel in Tangkou will let travelers use their computer to go online. Y20 per hr. Ask around or check with Mr. Wu.

Post Office: Tangkou Post and Telecommunications Office, on the highway toward the south end of town, just above and north of the Tangkou Hotel. Open daily 8am-noon and 2-6pm. **Postal Codes:** 242708 for Tangkou; 242709 for Huangshan Scenic Area, including Hot Springs Area.

ACCOMMODATIONS

TANGKOU

In hotels in Tangkou, as on the mountain, the major barrier for foreigners is huge Chinese tour groups, who clog dorm rooms and cause rates to soar. Still, the village is the best place to sleep if you're just hiking Huangshan in a day. If you're overnighting on the mountain, ask to leave your luggage (Y2-5 per day) at a Tangkou hotel, and then carry a daypack.

Tiandu Mountain Villa Hotel (tiāndū shān zhuāng bīnguǎn; 天都山庄宾馆; ☎556 2160), on the highway, about halfway between the bridge and the main gate to the mountains. Popular among foreigners, with a wide range of clean rooms. The cheaper rooms entail a stroll to the toilet and an epic trek to the shower. 3-bed dorms with bath Y60; singles Y180; doubles Y280.

Free and Unfettered Hotel (xiāoyáo bīnguǎn; 逍遥宾馆; ☎556 2533), at the south end of the market road along the stream. Often filled with free and unfettered Chinese tour groups, but still popular with individual travelers. The cheapest dorms are spartan, with concrete floors and patched walls. Doubles are fairly standard, with TV and A/C, and will probably be the only rooms available to foreigners. Rooms have attached bath. Deposit Y10. 4- to 5-bed dorms Y30; 3-bed dorms Y100-120; doubles Y283-320.

Tangkou Hotel (tāngkǒu bīnguǎn; 汤口宾馆; ☎556 2400), 500m past the Free and Unfettered Hotel, in a large blue building. Comparable to other mid-range options, but less frequented by foreigners. Dorms have fan, TV, and bath; some of the more expensive rooms have A/C. 3- to 4-bed dorms Y20-140; doubles Y100-280; triples Y60-360.

HOT SPRINGS AREA

If it's a hot tub party you're after, forget about it; the "springs" gurgle up far below expectations. There's very little to distinguish the "public springs" from a big swimming pool; they're no warmer or cleaner than your average YMCA. The "private springs" are even sillier: they're just bathtubs in a bathroom, complete with toilet and sink. Both cost Y50 for the privilege. This area's natural beauty is its best quality, but expect to pay big bucks for the mountain and riverside views.

Huangshan Spring Hotel (huángshān wēnquán dàjiŭdiàn; 黄山温泉大酒店; ☎556 2198), down the ramp from the road at the bridge, across the stream from the Huangshan Hotel. Basement dorms are stuffy, but have decent bathrooms. Slather on the bug repellent—no window screens here. Dorms Y100; singles Y280; doubles Y380.

Huangshan Hotel (huángshān fàndiàn; 黄山饭店; ☎556 2202), near Peach Flower Stream. Small standard A/C rooms have even smaller bathrooms. Hot spring swimming pool on site. Singles Y380; doubles Y300-420.

SUMMIT AREA

The same tour groups that clog the mountain trails also crowd into the dorms in the revoltingly overpriced hotels. Though the dorms are fairly basic, with woven mats for mattresses and distant, fetid bathrooms, remember that it's what's outside (the view) that counts. Pricier rooms aren't much different—the fetid bathrooms are just a bit closer, which probably isn't a good thing. For a decent, cheap room, get there early, or put your bargaining skills to the test. The following hotels are listed in the order in which they are positioned along the trail, assuming you walk from the Eastern Steps (White Goose Peak) toward the Western Steps.

Beihai Hotel (bĕihăi bīnguăn; 北海宾馆; ☎556 2555), Beihai Scenic Area, a 10min. walk from the White Goose Peak cable car. Musty rooms in the main building aren't even remotely worth the price. The dorms aren't any sweeter smelling, but are pleasantly rustic, with straw mattresses and a camp-like feel. Winter discounts. 4-bed dorms Y90-150; doubles Y240, with bath Y300-850; quads Y700; 6-person rooms Y420.

Xihai Hotel (xīhăi fàndiàn; 西海饭店; ☎556 3777), Xihai Scenic Area, 20min. past the Beihai Hotel. Far poorer standards than its prices and reputation suggest, although rooms are very clean. At least some of the dorm rooms have attached baths. Dorms Y150; doubles Y960 and up. Credit cards accepted.

Paiyunlou Hotel (páiyúnlóu bīnguăn; 排云楼宾馆; ☎556 1558), Xihai Scenic Area, about 2min. beyond the Xihai Hotel. In a mellow enclave along the trail, near the fork to the Taiping cable car. Dorms Y60, with shower Y150; doubles Y880-2000.

Brightness Peak Villa (guāngmíng dĭng shānzhuāng; 光明顶山庄; ☎556 2901), on top of Brightness Peak, near the television towers. Some rooms have dazzling views of the mountain; some rooms look out on the group of raucous tourists chugging beer in the courtyard. Try your luck, and remember that the views are the best part of these rooms. Dorm beds Y70; doubles Y300-680; triples Y180; quads Y160; quints Y140.

Yupinglou Hotel (yùpínglóu bīnguăn; 玉屏楼宾馆; ☎556 2317), in the complex at Yuping Peak, site of the Welcoming Tree. About the only option along the Western Steps, so it fills up quickly. Dorms Y180; standard rooms Y720 and up.

🗹🎶 FOOD AND ENTERTAINMENT

Often, restaurant owners takes care of all the work, by finding you, directing you to a table, and even choosing menu items. Be very careful to ask prices in advance; this village's economy thrives on milking visitors, and even Chinese tourists are charged exorbitant prices for mediocre fare.

Stroll down the road next to the stream, and you'll find an open-air market, selling everything from noodle and dumpling standbys to more exotic fare, including eels, snakes, and squirrels (all about Y3). Also here, tucked behind the first row of stalls, is **Mr. Wu's Restaurant.** Look for the sign in English, advertising coffee, toast, and advice. It may not be the most luxurious dining environment, but for break-

YANGZI BASIN

fast, nothing really beats a big plate of scrambled eggs and tomatoes (Y7). Save the cold beer (Y4) for later. If you're lucky, Mr. Wu might show you his pictures of Sweden. (Open daily approx. 6am-midnight.) And what would a Chinese mountain be without its tea leaves and dried fungi? Huangshan tea and mushrooms are everywhere, and make good, inexpensive souvenirs.

Up on the mountain itself, snack stands and freelance cookie-and-cucumber vendors can be found at every turn; don't be surprised to find that small bottles of water cost as much as Y10. Bargaining can still work; it's just not as effective when you're surrounded by tourists willing to fork over Y15 for a pack of beef jerky. Restaurants are mostly limited to the pricey offerings in the hotels, although the hotel just below **Brightness Summit,** as well as a stand at **Yuping Peak,** sell combo platters for about Y20. The market next to the Beihai Hotel sells dried noodles (Y4-10).

If waking before 5am to see the famous Beihai sunrise doesn't limit your sleeping hours enough, and if after a day's worth of hiking you're still rarin' to go, there is a dance floor and karaoke bar at the Beihai Hotel (and most other summit hotels). Billiard tables abound in the market along the stream in Tangkou.

⚠ CLIMBING HUANGSHAN

If you've come here, you've come to see only one thing. Admission to **Huangshan Scenic Area** (huángshān fēngjǐng qū; 黄山风景区) is Y82, for children Y57.

The trail is divided into three parts: the **Eastern Steps** (following the same path as the main cable car); the **Summit Area** (a variety of loop trails with relatively little up-and-down terrain); and the **Western Steps,** which are much longer than the Eastern Steps. Hiking Huangshan is hard business. Don't underestimate the physical toll of climbing several kilometers worth of non-stop steps, especially when you have to deal with maddening crowds. General wisdom holds that of the Yellow Mountains' 72 peaks, the most magnificent are the ones most difficult to reach. Maybe so, but the main trails reach plenty of vistas with breathtaking scenery. A heart-stopping view won't do you any good if your heart stopped halfway up.

Opt for the tried-and-true route: start at the base of the Eastern Steps (either hiking them or taking the cable car); follow the summit across to the west; then descend the Western Steps, which, even as a downhill run, are cartilage-crushing, knee-wrecking, and exhausting. Keep your head up: the stairs can be hypnotizing, almost enough to make you forget to look around at the views once in a while.

There's no shame in taking the easy way out of these hikes. (We're talking cable cars here; there is definitely shame in taking human porters.) There are a total of three cableways, including the one along the Eastern Steps (Cloud Valley line) and two in more obscure locations (Yuping and Taiping lines). Only two (Cloud Valley and Yuping) offer a logistically helpful way off the mountain; the Taiping makes a summit run from the Cloud Divide Pavilion. Expect long waits and exorbitant rates, at least along the Cloud Valley line. For whatever portion you do walk, the trails are in great condition, if often too narrow for the two-way traffic (particularly tour groups and porters with bulky loads). Guides are available to lead the way for the entire trip, but this only makes sense for those fluent in Chinese who want more detailed descriptions of the peaks and their legends.

SAY CHEESE Park rangers in Huangshan once reported finding a tripod abandoned near a cliff at the top of the mountain. Curious as to why anyone would simply discard valuable camera equipment, they developed the film left inside. The prints they got back were the usual assortment of vacation photos taken by a young couple as they enjoyed the climb up Huangshan. All, that is, except for the last shot. The duo had set the camera's timer before they posed for a shot near the edge of the cliff, and the last exposure, in their final ghastly Kodak moment, had caught the surprised pair as they fell backwards off the cliff. Huangshan's version of an urban myth? Perhaps. But the moral of the story remains: **stay on the trail.**

YANGZI BASIN

EASTERN STEPS

From the base town of Tangkou, minibuses (Y10) and taxis (around Y20) make frequent trips to the **Cloud Valley Cable Car Station** (yúngǔ sì zhàn; 云谷寺站), which marks the beginning of the climb for most hikers. *(Cable car runs daily 6:30am-4:30pm. Expect waits of several hours for the ascent. Up Y65, down Y50, children Y30.)* For those who choose the Eastern Steps route to return, the taxi fare from Cloud Valley Temple to Tangkou is about Y10, although ridiculous fare hikes are common. Put your foot down, if your muscles can move that much.

Much of the climb (ascent 1½-3hr., descent 2hr. or less) winds through forested areas; at the halfway point, hikers first catch glimpses of the spectacular peaks. Various lookout points, with names of the peaks in Chinese, offer time for necessary water breaks. In general, the scenery here is relatively unspectacular until you near the top. The path reaches the upper cable car station at **White Goose Peak** (bái é fēng; 白鹅峰) near the **Beihai Scenic Area** (běi hǎi; 北海; North Sea). The walk around the summit area is a popular and not-too-tiring route. On the sharp left, there is an obscure path that leads toward the television towers and to the Western Steps (as well as the last part of a good loop if you want to start and finish on the eastern path) beyond. If you're doing the east-west circuit, then follow the main path past the structures down to the right.

From here, there are two paths. The path upwards leads to two short hikes: **Beginning-to-Believe Peak** (shǐ xìn fēng; 始信峰) and the **Stalagmite Ridge** (shí sǔn fēng; 石笋峰) beyond. The path downward leads past the Beihai Hotel, near the viewing area for the famous Beihai sunrise. *(Daily sunrise and sunset times, as well as the weather forecast, are posted in the hotel lobby.)* From here, it's a 20- to 30-minute walk to the **Xihai** (xīhǎi; 西海; West Sea) area, a well-known stop for watching the sunset as clouds drift by in the early evening sky. The super-long **Taiping cable car** (tàipíng suǒdào; 太平索道), 3km long and with a 1km vertical drop, is supposedly the longest in Asia. A short walk from the Xihai Hotel, this cableway makes the run from the **Cloud Divide Pavilion** (pái yún tíng; 排云亭) to the distant **Songgu An** (sōnggǔ ān; 松谷庵), which leads to the north gate.

Beyond these hotels, the path runs over **Lotus Ridge** (fúróng lǐng; 芙蓉岭). For those setting out a bit earlier in the day, the main circuit continues past the **Rock Who Flew From Afar** (fēi lái shí; 飞来石), a precipitously positioned boulder on a cliff, and **Brightness Peak** (guāngmíng dǐng; 光明顶), the summit near the television towers. From here, you can head toward the towers and the trail loop back to the White Goose Peak cableway station, or drop over the other side of the mountain for the long roller coaster hike up and down…and up and down the Western Steps.

WESTERN STEPS

From Brightness Peak, the path continues for five to six hours along the steep Western Steps route down the mountain. The rock formations of **Turtle Peak** (biēyú fēng; 鳖鱼峰) on the right do the name justice. From this point, more steps lead to **Lotus Flower Peak** (liánhuā fēng; 莲花峰), the highest peak in the range. For a shortcut, head down to the right at the snack stand, instead of up to the left.

About halfway through the climb, the **Jade Screen Tower** (yù píng lóu; 玉屏楼) marks the terminus of the **Jade Screen cable car** (yù píng suǒdào; 玉屏索道). *(Runs daily 6:30am-5pm. Y55.)* The cable car soars by the **Moon-gazing Sky Dog** (tiān gǒu wàng yuè; 天狗望月) and the **Two Cats Capturing Mouse** (shuāng māo bǔ shǔ; 双猫捕鼠) formations en route to the **Merciful Light Chamber** (cí guāng gé; 慈光阁), which is in turn connected by road to Tangkou. The Jade Screen Tower is near the solitary **Welcoming Pine** (yíng kè sōng; 迎客松), among the oldest pines and an eternal symbol of Huangshan. Chances are you've seen it before, on hotel or restaurant walls around the country. Looming just beyond this, with an intimidating staircase but a worthy reward, stands **Heavenly Capital Peak** (tiān dū fēng; 天都峰). The bypass for this peak branches off at the Jade Screen Tower, but meets the main trail again at the Midway Monastery. The views from the top of Heavenly Capital Peak are divine—the best on the trail.

◪ DAYTRIP FROM HUANGSHAN: YIXIAN

*47km from Tunxi. Yixian County consists of a dozen villages in the basin, with the county seat in Yixian. From the Yixian Bus Station (on the main road in Yixian), **minibuses** go to Tunxi (1½hr., 7:30am-5:30pm, Y7) via Yuting, and Tangkou (1½hr., 2 per day, Y13) via Xidi. **Hongcun** (10km north of Yixian) and **Xidi** (3km east of Yixian), the two main scenic spots, are accessible by **minibus** (Y2) and **taxi** (Hongcun Y20, Xidi Y5-10). Because of its proximity to a PLA missile base, Yixian has no **accommodations** open to foreigners. **Food** specialties include "rock chicken legs," a gray-colored frog (shíjī; 石鸡), salted pork (làròu; 腊肉), and tea eggs (cháyè dàn; 茶叶蛋). **Admission** to Hongcun Y20; Xidi Y28.*

For centuries, the only way to reach Yixian (黟县) was through a cave. Hidden in a tiny basin ringed by the Huangshan Mountains, Yixian is one of the most isolated places in eastern China. For centuries, the only way to reach Yixian was through a cave. Yixian's name derives from Huangshan's ancient name, Yishan (黟山), a reference to black marble. Founded in 222 BC, Yixian was often a haven for refugees escaping conflicts on China's northern plains. During the Ming and Qing dynasties, residents of the county dominated commerce on the Yangzi delta and often were invited to perform opera for the emperors in Beijing. In the 1800s, devastating bouts of the plague put an end to the area's cultural and economic achievements, and Yixian receded into obscurity. Today, over 4000 well-preserved Ming- and Qing-era homes, shops, and bridges remain (and can be seen in Zhang Yimou's film, *Judou*), a testament to Yixian's heyday and to its ability to withstand the ravages of war and modernization.

While Yixian offers a quiet refuge from Huangshan's tour groups, those visitors mesmerized by the mist-shrouded mountains, sparkling streams, and bamboo groves should take note: the PLA has a ballistic missile base nearby, so don't stray too far off the beaten path.

HONGCUN (hóngcūn; 宏村). Locals claim that their village is built in the shape of a kneeling ox: a hill north of the village is the ox "head," with a pair of 400-year-old trees as the "horns," the village is the "body," and four bridges complete the "legs." From above, this may indeed be the case; from the ground, a bit of imagination is in order. According to legend, the village suffered numerous fires during the 1300s, so the local clan elders invited a *feng shui* master for advice. (For more on *feng shui*, see **Banking on Feng Shui**, p. 438.) The master proposed giving the ox a "digestive system" of reservoirs and canals, in order to cleanse the village of "flammable spirits." As a result, water from a nearby stream was diverted to fill a pool (the first "stomach") in the center village. Narrow curbside aqueducts still run along every cobblestoned alleyway, carrying water from the pool throughout the village. These "intestines" eventually lead to South Lake (the second "stomach"). The constant flow of water past every doorstep lends a serene quality to village life—that is, until the little kids start squirting each other with bamboo water guns.

Most of Hongcun's homes are inhabited by locals; only the **Inherit Dignity Hall** (chéng zhì táng; 承志堂) and a few smaller gardens officially are open to the public. Built by a Qing salt merchant in 1855, the Inherit Dignity Hall has over 60 rooms in seven buildings. Dubbed the "Forbidden City for Civilians," it is the largest and most elaborate example of Yixian architecture. Yixian merchants spent most of their time doing business abroad and feared that robbers would loot their homes; thus, most of the plain, whitewashed walls have few windows. Inside, the open courtyards, known as "sky wells," allow in natural light and rain. The walls are covered with ornate wood relief carvings, including two panels that depict battle scenes from the *Romance of the Three Kingdoms* (see **A True Romance Needs Three**, p. 37) and a New Year's celebration featuring over 100 boys. A carving in the master's parents' hall depicts a famous opera scene in which a daughter-in-law was beaten for not kowtowing during her mother-in-law's birthday party.

XIDI (xīdì; 西递). In AD 904, the oldest son of the last Tang emperor fled to southern Anhui after the Tang dynasty fell (see **Cosmopolitan Sui and Tang**, p. 10). Once there, he founded the Hu clan, now the biggest clan in town. Wealthy Xidi merchants, concerned about their social standing, donated generously to the imperial government. In return, the emperor awarded them various bureaucratic titles. Most of the houses display paintings of house masters dressed in mandarin attire, but few masters held any real power. Many masters had window panes carved depicting window frost (symbolizing bitterness and hard work in winter) alongside bats and grapes (symbolizing good fortune) to remind their sons that success required sacrifice. At the village entrance, the **Governor's Arch** (cìshǐ páifǎng; 刺使牌坊), a massive stone arch with 16 lions and six crocodiles, was commissioned by the Ming emperor Shenzong to honor a Xidi native who served the Ming court for 32 years. Visitors will find more traditional homes and mansions open to the public in Xidi than they will find open in Hongcun.

JIUHUASHAN 九华山 ☎0566

Jiuhuashan is just 50km from Huangshan, but it's about four hours away by bus, and a whole world apart in atmosphere. One of China's four sacred Buddhist mountains, Jiuhuashan attracts as many pilgrims as tourists, and greets travelers with a serene, spiritual beauty that is less spectacular but no less rewarding than that of Huangshan. Monks and pilgrims have flocked to the area for centuries, ever since a young Korean named Kin Kiao Kak stopped by the mountain and proceeded to devote the next 75 years of his life to Buddhism. This was no lowly monk: after his death he became known as Dizang Buddha, and Buddhists honor him each year on the last day of the seventh lunar month.

Today, over 80 temples hide in the densely wooded slopes of Jiuhuashan, and the Buddhist chants that fill the air cast an otherworldly glow about the place. The tiny village that feeds and houses most travelers, though, has no illusions about having a higher purpose. Nearly every building makes its living off visitors, and each is determined to milk every last *jiao*. Don't let this strike too sour a note, though—there's no better way to recover from the town's desire for money than to appreciate nature and one of the world's least materialistic faiths.

▓ 🛈 ORIENTATION AND PRACTICAL INFORMATION

Jiuhuashan is in the southern part of Anhui province, about 30km (1hr.) from Qingyang. The town sits cradled in a small valley, with the mountain wrapping around its south and east sides. To enter the village, buy a ticket at the main gate, in the northeast corner of town. **Admission** from March 1 to November 30 is Y60, Y45 for students. In the winter, admission is Y40, Y30 for students, but keep in mind that snow regularly renders the roads impassable. From the entrance, the main road in town, **Jiequ Gonglu,** runs south along the side of town before it curves to the west along the foot of the mountain. Narrow streets and uneven steps run from the main road throughout town, although few have names or useful services. Anything that tourists need is along Jiequ Gonglu or on **Jiuhua Jie** (九华街), a road that branches off the main road in the western part of town.

The nearest **airport** is in Anqing, 125km to the northwest, and the most regular nearby **train** depot is Tunxi, four hours away. The **Jiuhuashan Bus Station** (jiǔhuáshān qìchē zhàn; 九华山汽车站), about 100m before the main village gate, runs buses to: Hangzhou (7hr., 6 and 9am, Y55-70); Hefei (5hr., 5 per day 7am-2:30pm, Y50); Huangshan (Tangkou, not Tunxi; 4hr., 7am and 2:50pm, Y25); Nanjing (5hr., 7am and 1pm, Y54); Shanghai (9hr., 3 per day 6am-2:30pm, Y80); and Wuhan (7hr., 11am, Y90). (☎501 1440. Open daily approx. 5:30am-8pm.) Tickets can also be bought at a kiosk inside the gates, visible from the main road. Turn right at the bridge after you enter the village; the booth is on the right. (☎501 1283. Open daily 5:30am-6:30pm.) Many of the buses require you to transfer in **Qingyang.** **Minibuses** for various destinations depart throughout the day on a variable schedule. They regularly make the run to the Tiantai cable car (Y5). Don't worry about finding one; they'll find you. Within Jiuhuashan, there isn't much need for **taxis,** as the town takes about 10 minutes to cross on foot.

CTS, 135 Jiuhua Jie, 3rd floor (☎501 1588), provides service that is about as ramshackle as the building. Follow the main road around to the west part of town. When you see the pond, cross over and look for the sign on the left. **Maps** can be bought at any stand, and most locals will be happy to help out if you need directions or help buying bus tickets. Many might also offer to act as guides, taking you to a restaurant or finding you a room; as always, be wary of scams. **Bank of China,** 65 Furong Lu, about half a block west of the main plaza, just down the steps across from the Zhan Tan temple, exchanges traveler's checks and offers credit card advances. (☎501 1270. Open daily 8am-6pm.) A **PSB** (☎501 1331) is on the southeast corner of the main plaza, with six officers on call 24hr. a day. The **post office,** on the southwest corner of the main plaza, has EMS. (Open M-F 8am-6pm.) **China Telecom,** in the same building, has IDD calls 24hr. The **postal code** is 242811.

▟ ACCOMMODATIONS

It's not hard to find a small, inexpensive hotel in Jiuhuashan; whether it will accept foreign guests that day or suddenly double the rates, only the owner can say. Few hotels offer anything unique. For a more memorable room, try the hotel in the Zhiyuan Temple—Buddhist monks tend to be extremely friendly, and if you are able to communicate your interest, you might be able to persuade one of the mountain temples to put you up for a night or two.

Shangketang Hotel (shàngkètáng bīnguǎn; 上客堂宾馆; ☎501 2071), in the Qiyuan Temple, just south of the bus station, up through a small store and off to the left. Offers outsiders a taste of monastic life, with simple but spotless rooms, and convenient access to the Buddha himself. Most rooms Y100-200 during the peak season.

Longquan Hotel (lóngquán fàndiàn; 龙泉饭店; ☎501 1320), on the main road near its southwest corner, on the right side just before the street turns right. Nothing luxurious here except the strange velvet curtains—and the concrete floors, of course. Fortunately, rooms are clean and a good value. Dorms Y40; doubles Y180, with A/C Y200.

Dongya Hotel (dōngyà bīnguǎn; 东亚宾馆; ☎501 1370), a few blocks inside the main Jiuhuashan gate. Walk down the main road; the hotel is set off to the right. The decor may be old and well-used, but rooms are clean and comfortable. And besides, you just don't see colorful vegetable prints on all hotel blankets. Doubles Y240.

Julong Hotel (jùlóng dàjiǔdiàn; 聚龙大酒店; ☎501 1368), on the right side of the main road, not far beyond the main gate to the village. Don't be fooled by the hotel's upscale facade: bright green carpets, tiny bathrooms, and cracked walls and ceilings do not a luxury hotel make. A/C and TV. Doubles Y280-398.

Fo Guyuan Hotel (fó gǔyuán bīnguǎn; 佛古园宾馆; ☎501 1379), on Jiuhua Jie just south of the CTS office, next to the sports field in the east part of town. Large rooms with A/C, TV, lots of free bathroom products, and window screens, a godsend in insect-filled Jiuhuashan. Singles and doubles Y320-400. MC, Visa accepted.

◐ ♫ FOOD AND ENTERTAINMENT

Many restaurants line the main road in Jiuhuashan, and a whole slew of eateries are in the southeast part of town, where the main road turns west. Here, a two-story building sells souvenirs and Buddhist paraphernalia on the lower level, and cheap rice and noodle dishes on the upper level. Some hotels have more upscale restaurants, or you can make friends with a villager or a monk and get some good home (or temple) cookin'. The **Zhan Tan Buddhist Temple** (zhàn tán chánlín; 旃檀禅林; ☎501 1225), on the left side of the main road, serves vegetarian meals nightly at 6pm. Although some places may attach a "specialty of Jiuhuashan" label to certain menu items, Jiuhuashan's most famous products (mushrooms and Jiuhuashan tea leaves) come already dried and packaged.

As for entertainment: near the main plaza, there are billiard tables, archaic video games, a target shooting game, and a ping-pong table. And don't forget karaoke. Bring it on, my friend.

🔍 SIGHTS

Nearly all the tourists who journey to Jiuhuashan come to worship at (or simply admire) the area's many Buddhist temples. The village itself has a few large temples (and shrines are tucked into nearly every corner), but if you've got a day, a more interesting tour (including plenty of nature worship) follows the trails through the hills surrounding the village.

Conveniently close to the gate, the **Tend the Land Monastery** (zhǐ yuán sì; 祇园寺), an imposing, yellow-tiled building just inside the village, is a good place to start. Off to the left after you enter, the Buddhist trinity sits inside the Mahavira Hall, which is the setting for the annual celebration held in Dizang's honor. *(Open daily 6am-8pm. Y2.)* On the north side of this temple complex, a long staircase leads up the mountain to **Hundred Year Palace** (bǎisuì gōng; 百岁宫), the white hilltop building visible from the village. *(Open daily sunrise-sunset. Y5.)* Beyond the entrance hall here, often occupied by monks meditating or chanting scriptures, is a second room containing the mummified body of Ming priest Wu Xiam. In life Wu Xiam was known to use gold dust and his own blood in his work on the Huayan sutras; in death, his gilded body is seated in prayer. A cable car runs to the palace from the village. *(Runs daily 6am-6pm. One-way Y18, round-trip Y28.)*

Walk south along the ridge, and you'll come across the **Bell Tower** (zhōng lóu; 钟楼), which is lit up at night, then **Huacheng Temple** (huāchéng sì; 化城寺) back in Jiuhua Village, where a new temple is under construction. From here, the trail branches off to the west toward **Small Heavenly Platform** (xiǎo tiāntái; 小天台). On the way, an especially atmospheric temple includes various depictions of Buddhist hell: hell-arious renderings of demons stewing the unfaithful in boiling cauldrons, sawing them in half, or goring their bodies with a spiked seesaw.

The eastward, uphill trail heads toward the **Phoenix Tree** (fēnghuáng sōng; 凤凰松), an ancient, jagged Huangshan pine thought to look like—surprise!—an ascending phoenix. It was praised by Li Keran as "The Best Pine in the World." In theory, from here you could also hike up to the summit. Few people do, though, and judging from the state of the trail, few people have in a long time. If you do brave the path, you'll proceed past the **Huiju Temple** (huìjū sì; 慧居寺), **Fuxing Nunnery** (fùxìng ān; 复兴庵), and **Chaoyang Nunnery** (cháoyáng ān; 潮阳庵). Near the Phoenix Tree, a **cable car** whisks travelers up to Mt. Jiuhua's 1342m summit. *(Cable car runs daily 6am-5pm. Y30 up, Y20 down, children Y10 less.)* Once at the **Golden Chicken Yelling to Heaven Gate** (jīnjī jiàotiān mén; 金鸡叫天门), take a moment to join in the heavenly chorus of poultry, and admire the view.

JIANGXI 江西

Jiangxi has always been a well-kept secret. Nearly uninhabited for thousands of years, the province didn't really come to life until the Han dynasty, when an influx of migrants created a population explosion. During the Six Dynasties period, refugees fled south to escape foreign invaders and ended up settling on the plains around Lake Poyang, China's largest freshwater lake. The construction of the Grand Canal clinched Jiangxi's status as an unspoiled up-and-comer, suddenly thrusting the provincial capital of Nanchang into the limelight as an important stop on the internal trade route between north and south. The mild-mannered province chugged happily along, enjoying a period of unprecedented but unflamboyant prosperity, until the opening of treaty ports and the increase of coastal trade in provinces to the east left Jiangxi high and dry.

The first half of the 20th century brought hard times. Years of battling warlords were finally brought to an end by Chiang Kai-shek, only to be followed by years of struggle between the Guomindang and the Communists. But when the dust settled and the Communists came to power in 1949, Jiangxi entered a period of stability and growth, and also came to be remembered fondly as a cradle of the Chinese revolution. With the largest number of revolutionary memorial sites in the country,

Jiangxi is a can't-miss destination for those interested in the history and development of the CCP. The green hills in the summer resort of Lushan and the colorful ceramics of Jingdezhen offer alternatives for those tired of seeing red.

NANCHANG 南昌   ☎ 0791

Lying 70km north of Lake Poyang, the capital of Jiangxi province is a busy trade and commerce center on the Gan River between Shanghai and Changsha. Its hotels are filled with businessmen who make deals and exchange money during the day and frequent flashy bars and shady massage parlors at night. Vendors crowd city streets lined with billboards, plying their wares to anyone (and everyone) who passes.

And yet, ironically enough, this free-market capitalism loving town is also cherished in China for its role in the development of the Communist Party. On August 1, 1927, Zhou Enlai and Zhu De, a pair of GMD officers with Communist inclinations, organized a mutiny and seized control of the city after Chiang Kai-shek's Shanghai massacre (see p. 16). The revolutionaries soon fled to the mountains, but they had left their mark on the city. The foundation of the People's Liberation Army is celebrated each August 1 as visitors celebrating the event flood the city's museums and monuments. Most visitors to Jiangxi pass right through Nanchang en route to Lushan or Jinggangshan, but those who stick around for a while get to see a city that shows both sides of the strange, ever-changing coin that is China.

◪ TRANSPORTATION

Airplanes: Nanchang Airport (nánchāng jīchǎng; 南昌机场) is 30km away from the city. **China Eastern Airlines ticket offices** (zhōngguó dōngfāng hángkōng gōngsī; 中国东方航空公司), 67 Beijing Xi Lu (☎623 1351), off Bayi Dadao; 15 Zhanqian Lu (☎622 3656), near the train station; and 87 Minde Lu (☎628 2654), just west of the Jiangxi (Binguan) Hotel. To: **Beijing** (3-5 per day, Y1040); **Chengdu** (1-2 per day, Y960); **Guangzhou** (2-3 per day, Y580); **Haikou** (1-2 per day Sa-Th, Y950); **Nanjing** (Th and Sa-Su, Y530); **Shanghai** (3-5 per day, Y570); and **Xian** (1-2 per day, Y810).

Trains: Nanchang is one of southern China's main rail hubs. **Nanchang Train Station** (nánchāng zhàn; 南昌站), on Zhanqian Lu, is beneath a huge square arch on Zhanqian Lu, about 1km east of Fushan Traffic Circle. To: **Beijing** (22hr., 3 per day, Y84-485); **Guangzhou** (15½hr., 2 per day, Y64-364); **Hefei** (8hr., 2 per day, Y27-166); **Jingdezhen** (6hr., 1:20pm, Y20-155); **Nanjing** (18hr., 1:20pm, Y53-315); **Shanghai** (14hr., 3 per day, Y53-315); **Xiamen** (22hr., 3 per day, Y44-315); **Xian** (22½hr., 7:34pm, Y84-485); and **Wuhan** (7hr., 6 per day, Y26-161).

Buses: Nanchang Long-distance Bus Station (nánchāng chángtú qìchē zhàn; 南昌长途汽车站) is in a long, shiny building on the east side of Bayi Dadao, a few blocks south of August First Square. The ticket office is past the luggage storage room. Open daily 5:30am-7pm. To: **Hefei** (8-10hr., 2-3 per day 7:20am-3:20pm, Y125); **Jingdezhen** (5hr., every hr. 6:50am-5:50pm, Y46); **Jinggangshan** (6-8hr., 2 per day, Y60-74); **Jiujiang** (2½hr., every 30min. 6am-7pm, Y35); **Lushan** (2½hr., every 30min. 6am-4:35pm, Y37); and **Wuhan** (5hr., 6 per day 7am-4pm, Y59). Buses to **Jiujiang** also leave from a large parking lot northwest of the train station (2½hr., every 30min., Y35).

Ferry: Nanchang Ferry Terminal (nánchāng mǎtóu; 南昌码头; ☎681 3068), about 1km north of Tengwang Pavilion; buy tickets just north of Bayi Bridge. Open daily 6am-7:30pm. Travel times vary greatly, depending on the boat. To: **Botao** (3-12hr., 4 per day 6:30am-6pm, Y26-56); **Duchang** (3-8hr., 4 per day 6:40am-7:30pm, Y15-38); and **Ruihong** (2-5½hr., 4 per day 7:30am-4pm, Y10-31), on Lake Poyang.

Local Transportation: Most **buses** run 7am-7pm. Fare Y1. Buses **#1** and **#2** run along Bayi Dadao, and you can transfer to other routes along any major intersecting street. Bus **#2** connects the train station to the heart of downtown, and **#3** heads south toward Qingyun Pu, a suburb. Bus **#20** runs along the river.

Taxis: Base fare Y6, each additional km Y1.4. Motorcycle taxis are also an option.

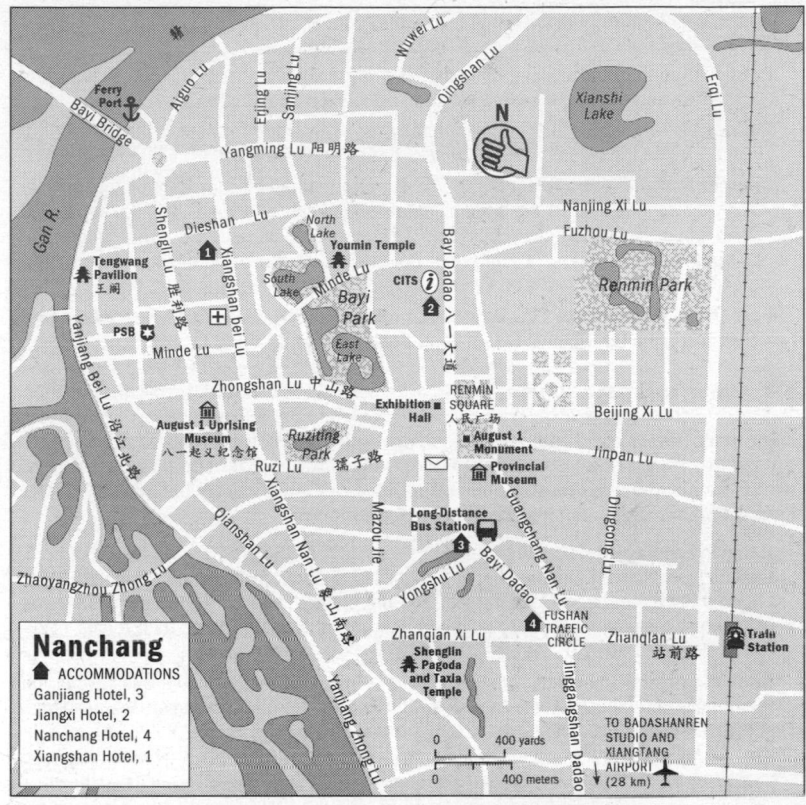

Nanchang

▲ ACCOMMODATIONS
Ganjiang Hotel, 3
Jiangxi Hotel, 2
Nanchang Hotel, 4
Xiangshan Hotel, 1

✴ ⚡ ORIENTATION AND PRACTICAL INFORMATION

Nanchang is roughly ovular and ample in girth, with the **Gan River** (gàn jiāng; 赣江) stretching along its west side. **August First Square** (bāyī guǎngchǎng; 八一广场), though not the geographic center, is the spiritual and commercial center of town. Running along the west side of the square is **Bayi Dadao** (八一大道), the major north-south thoroughfare in Nanchang. Bayi Dadao continues south to the **Fushan Traffic Circle,** another service- and hotel-filled area. From here, **Zhanqian Lu** (站前路) extends east to the train station.

In the northwest part of town, Bayi Bridge crosses the Gan River just next to the ferry port on **Yanjiang Bei Lu** (沿江北路). **Minde Lu** (民德路), **Ruzi Lu,** and **Zhongshan Lu** (中山路) run east from Yanjiang Bei Lu to Bayi Dadao. **Shengli Lu** (胜利路) and **Xiangshan Lu** (象山路) both run north-south through the district.

Travel Agencies: CITS, 78 Bayi Dadao (☎622 4396 or 628 5014), in an unmarked office off the southeast side of the parking lot behind the Jiangxi (Binguan) Hotel; the door is by some chalkboards. Open daily 9am-5:30pm. **China Youth Travel Service** (zhōngguó qīngnián lǚxíngshè; 中国青年旅行社), 614 Fuzhou Lu (☎626 2452), about 2 blocks east of Bayi Dadao, on the south side of the street. The very friendly (although uniformly unilingual) staff can book tickets. Open daily 8am-8pm.

Bank of China: 1 Zhanqian Xi Lu (☎647 1688), on the west side of Fushan Traffic Circle, across from the Nanchang Hotel. Currency exchange at counter #17. 3% processing fee for credit card advances. Open daily 8am-7:30pm; in winter 8am-7pm. Otherwise, try either of the Jiangxi Hotels.

Bookstore: Xinhua Bookstore, 3-4 blocks north of the Fushan Traffic Circle, on the west side of Bayi Dadao. Open daily 8:30am-7pm.

PSB: Just north of the Jiujiang bus plaza in front of the train station. Another branch is 1½ blocks northwest of the intersection of Shengli Lu and Minde Lu.

Pharmacy: Huangqing Renzhan Pharmacy, on Bayi Dadao, about 2 blocks north of Fushan Traffic Circle, sells mainly Chinese products. Open 24hr.

Internet Access: China Telecom, 38 Ruzi Lu, about a half-block west of the post office. Slow net connection. Y4 per 30min., Y6 per hr.; each additional hr. Y5. The **Jiangxi Hotel**'s business center has access for Y0.8 per min. Open daily 7:30am-midnight. The **Zhineng Internet Bar,** 371 Xiangshan Bei Lu (☎664 6285), is bright and cool, with speedy connections. Y4 per hr. Open M-F 1pm-midnight.

Post Office: China Post, 262 Bayi Dadao (☎626 2498). EMS, Poste Restante, and a "Philately" counter. Open M-F 8am-8pm. **Postal Code:** 330003.

▌ ACCOMMODATIONS

Nanchang hotels cater almost exclusively to business travelers; you'll be hard-pressed to find a hotel without a bellhop and karaoke bar. The large number of rooms means that mid-range hotels often have openings, so try bargaining. Hotels have a 3% tourist tax and a 0.5% city construction tax.

Jiangxi (Fandian) Hotel (jiāngxī fàndiàn; 江西饭店), 356 Bayi Dadao (☎621 2123), about 1 block south of Minde Lu, and south of the other, nicer Jiangxi (Binguan) Hotel. Rooms have amazingly clean carpets and big closets, and are especially good if you can wrest a shared-bath room from a yellow-hatted tourist. Shared-bath rooms Y120-320; singles Y180-240; doubles Y210-280.

Nanchang Hotel (nánchāng bīnguǎn; 南昌宾馆), 16 Bayi Dadao (☎627 1281), off Fushan Traffic Circle. Rooms have A/C and TV, and some bathrooms have huge windows. Discounts. Doubles Y148-228.

Xiangshan Hotel (xiàngshān bīnguǎn; 象山宾馆), 222 Xiangshan Bei Lu (☎678 1402), through a gate on the west side of Xiangshan Lu, 3 blocks north of Minde Lu. A good location and a pleasant staff almost compensate for the plain rooms and decaying decor. Singles Y160; doubles Y160-220; triples Y156. MC, Visa accepted.

Ganjiang Hotel (gànjiāng bīnguǎn; 赣江宾馆), 138 Bayi Dadao (☎622 1159). Stalactites in the lobby are the best part of this place, which usually doesn't let foreigners stay in shared-bath rooms. Dorms Y100-160; doubles with bath Y200-320.

◖▐ FOOD AND ENTERTAINMENT

Super-cheap eats are found on the south end of the railway plaza; a number of stands and restaurants offer plates of food with rice for just Y3. In the north part of town, Xiangshan Lu has stir-fry stalls, as does the area around Tengwang Pavilion. For another link in a most unusual chain, sip tea (Y10 in the afternoon, Y12 in the evening) in a rope-swing chair, then scoop some clay and get down and dirty on one of three pottery spinning wheels at the **Tea and Pottery Bar,** 88 Minde Lu, two blocks west of the Jiangxi (Binguan) Hotel. (☎623 6202. Open daily 1pm-1am.) The **Wall Street International Club** (huáěrjiē guójì jùlèbù; 华尔街国际俱乐部), 48 Chengde Lu, is a strange beige edifice about two blocks west of the Jiangxi (Binguan) Hotel. This bar serves beer (Y20) and cocktails to wealthy youngsters and old men. (☎627 8463. Open daily 7pm-midnight.)

Haoxianglai Steakhouse (háoxiǎnglái niúpáiguǎn; 豪享来牛排馆), 175 Minde Lu (☎625 1678), on the north side of the street, about 3 blocks west of the Jiangxi (Binguan) Hotel, east of Youmin Temple garden. The "Plate of Steak" and the "Plate of Pork Chop" Y18; beer Y10-25. A great place for carnivores who crave western food in a diner-like atmosphere. Open 24hr.

Mintaofang Cottage (míntáofǎng; 茗陶坊), on the south side of Ruzi Lu, about 2 blocks west of Yanjiang Lu. There's no English sign; look for the green, smiling, tear-shaped logo. A solid low-budget fast-food style eatery with point-and-choose pictures of various dishes on the wall (Y3-10). Open daily 10am-2am.

Peace Hotel (hépíng dàjiǔdiàn; 和平大酒店), 215 Ruzi Lu (☎ 663 3777), on the north side of the street, about 3 blocks east of Bayi Dadao. From the exotic (snake Y58) to the just plain expensive (raw asparagus Y22), this upscale restaurant has something for everyone—that is, everyone who doesn't mind spending exorbitant amounts of money. Open daily 11:10am-2pm and 5:10-9pm.

◉ SIGHTS

The few tourist sights in Nanchang revolve around that revolution one hears so much about, and the whole lot of them can be enjoyed in a day.

TENGWANG PAVILION (téngwáng gé; 腾王阁). Nanchang's most popular tourist attraction is this decidedly apolitical pavilion overlooking the Gan River. The area is packed with souvenir shops and tourist services, and the pavilion, built in 1989, is definitely worth a peek. Inside are more shops, a small theater, a museum, and other tourist-oriented features, but it's the view—back over Nanchang's squat, gray downtown—that brings most people to the top. *(Off Yanjiang Lu, north of Minde Lu. Open daily 7:20am-6pm; in winter 8am-5:30pm; last admission 30min. before closing. Y30.)*

MUSEUM OF THE AUGUST 1 UPRISING (bāyī qǐyì jìniànguǎn; 八一起义纪念馆). This interesting exhibit concerns the nighttime attack on Nanchang by the upstart Communist army. The first floor has a roomful of guns, a dining hall (with rifles in a nearby cabinet), and a display of heavy artillery (who'd have known what these guys had in mind?). The second and third floors show the progress of the attack, with a rough English narrative to accompany full Chinese text. Included are maps, a few brutal massacre photos, and a scale model of Nanchang. *(380 Zhongshan Lu, on the south side of the street, 3 blocks east of Yanjiang Lu. Open daily 8:30am-6pm. Y15.)*

PEOPLE'S SQUARE (rénmín guǎngchǎng; 人民广场). This large, grassy plaza can safely be viewed from the comfort of a city bus; the towering, stone flag-and-rifle monument is the most notable thing here. In typical Nanchang fashion, the green lawns dedicated to communism are off limits to the masses, and the Exhibition Hall's former Eastern Bloc-inspired glory is obscured by advertisements and CD peddlers. *(Just north of the intersection of Bayi Dadao and Ruzi Lu.)*

BADASHANREN STUDIO (qīngyún pǔ bādàshānrén jìniàntáng; 青云谱八大山人纪念堂). This immaculate complex, with gardens, courtyards, and various pavilions, displays the work of the late Ming/early Qing hermetic painter Badashanren, also known as Zhu Da. The site was formerly used as a temple and, during the Eastern Jin, was inhabited by Xu Shen, a high achiever responsible both for defending against floods and for introducing Daoism to the region. Even if you're not into the art, the surroundings provide some fresh air away from the clatter of Nanchang. *(In Qingyun Pu, 5km south of Nanchang. Take bus #20 from along Yanjiang Lu to the Badashan stop. You'll see a large pond along the road; the studio is just across the footbridge. ☎ 521 2565. Open daily 8:30am-5pm; last admission 4:30pm. Y10.)*

JINGDEZHEN 景德镇　　☎0798

Back in the Northern Song dynasty (AD 960-1127), Emperor Zhengzhong stumbled across a city capable of producing porcelain just the way he wanted: "White as jade, lustrous as mirror, thin as paper, resonant as a chime." With that, the city's destiny was sealed. With a seemingly ceaseless supply of *kaolin* (clay used in porcelain) from nearby Mt. Gaolin, Jingdezhen still cranks out the ceramics: gaudy vases, teacups by the boatload, figurines both tacky and wacky. While a certain cosmopolitan feel has touched the city, the skyline—a string of smokestacks belching the sooty residue of so many kiln-baked teacups—can obscure the artistic impulses that are its real heart and soul.

Only hard-core potheads will want more than a day to see the city's many porcelain factories, museum displays, and shops. Good souvenirs abound, though: after all, it was Jingdezhen that put the china in China.

◢◣🗐 ORIENTATION AND PRACTICAL INFORMATION

Jingdezhen is bisected by the **Chang River** (chāng hé; 昌河); the old city east of the river has nearly everything a traveler would want. **Zhushan Lu** (珠山路) runs east from the river, through the middle of town to the city center, a rotary with a large silver sculpture. From here, **Ma'anshan Lu** (马鞍山路) runs southeast to the train station, and **Lianshe Bei Lu** (莲社北路).

Airplanes: Luojia Airport (luójiā jīchǎng; 罗家机场), 10km northwest of the city, off the road to Jiujang. **CAAC ticket office,** 5 Lianshe Bei Lu (☎/fax 822 3458). Open daily 8am-5pm. To: **Beijing** (M and F, Y1000); **Guangzhou** (M and F, Y690); and **Shanghai** (1-2 per day Tu-Th and Su, Y400).

Trains: Jingdezhen Train Station (jǐngdézhèn huǒchē zhàn; 景德镇火车站), 1km southeast of the city center. The ticket building (at the south end) frequently keeps only 1 window open, so either go at off-hours or book through CITS or a hotel. To: **Beijing** (24hr., 1 per day, Y96-553); **Huangshan** (3-3½hr., 7 per day, Y10-39); **Nanchang** (6hr., 12:39am, Y17-161); **Nanjing** (11hr., 4 per day, Y30-214); and **Xiamen** (19hr., 2 per day, Y46-325).

Buses: The **bus station** (☎822 8708) across from the train station mainly serves destinations in Jiangxi, including **Jiujiang** (6hr., frequent departures 6:30am-2:50pm, Y38) and **Nanchang** (5-6hr., frequent departures 7:30am-11pm, Y45). Ticket office open daily 6am-5:30pm. Other buses leave from a dingy, poorly organized station across the river on **Xinfeng Lu.** To: **Guangzhou** (7:40am, Y222); **Hangzhou** (10hr., 6:40am and 3:50pm, Y80); and **Hefei** (9hr., 6:15am, Y53).

Local Transportation: City **buses** are few and far between in Jingdezhen, with a handful of lines running during daylight hours (Y1). Good luck trying to read the bus stop signs; they seem to have been painted by a grade school penmanship class. **Motorcycle taxis** cruise everywhere. A trip across town shouldn't cost more than Y7.

Travel Agencies: CITS, 21 Lianshe Bei Lu (☎822 3925 or 821 0672), a small, hidden office. Arranges factory tours. Open M-F 8am-noon and 2:30-6pm.

Bank of China: On Cidu Dadao, across from the Porcelain Museum. Open daily 7:30am-6pm.

PSB: In a tall building just north of the main Bank of China, in the southwest part of town (☎852 1001 or 852 5354).

Telephones: China Telecom, next to the post office. 24hr. IDD service. Open daily 8am-6pm; in winter 8am-5:30pm.

Internet Access: The **Jingdezhen Joint-Venture Guesthouse** has connections for Y12 per hr. Open daily 8am-10pm. Also, one of the computer stores along Lianshe Bei Lu might be persuaded to let you check your email.

Post Office: Zhushan Post Office, on the north side of Zhushan Lu, about 250m west of the city center. Open daily 8am-7pm. **Postal Code:** 333000.

◤◥ ACCOMMODATIONS AND FOOD

Jingdezhen would be a perfect town for a daytrip, but the gods of transportation have placed a curse on the city, and chances are you're going to have to spend the night here. There are few hotels in town, and even fewer that accept foreigners. As of July 2000, the **Jingdezhen Guesthouse** (jǐngdézhèn fàndiàn; 景德镇饭店) on Zhushan Lu was being renovated.

At least one thing in Jingdezhen is free of kiln grit and grime: the cooking. An usually large number of streetside vendors, especially around the train and bus stations, whip up tasty stir-fried dishes from a variety of fresh ingredients. To satisfy your sweet tooth, head to the **No. 1 Bakery** on Ma'anshan Lu and feast on sweet breads and birthday cake. For a mellow drink afterwards, the **Gardens for Art Tea House** (yìyuán cháguǎn; 艺园茶馆), across from the CITS on Lianshe Bei Lu, is a dark bar with garden decoration and a piano. *(☎823 1332. Open daily 8am-midnight.)*

Wenyuan Hotel (wényuàn dàfàndiàn; 文苑大饭店; ☎853 1227), on Qinghua Lu, a half-block north of the train station. Most hotels of this kind offer the usual transients' fare: hallway stench, functional rooms, and a fume-spewing smokestack out back. The Wenyuan does them one better: this stench extends all the way into the rooms. More expensive rooms are no different, so don't let them put you in one. Doubles Y50-90.

Jingdezhen Hotel (jǐngdézhèn bīnguǎn; 景德镇宾馆), 60 Fengjing Lu (☎822 4927), directly behind the Joint Venture. Rooms have A/C, TV, bath, and lots of space. Doubles Y128-188; triples Y150-180; quads Y220.

Jingdezhen Joint Venture Guesthouse (jǐngdézhèn hézī bīnguǎn; 景德镇合资宾馆), 60 Fengjing Lu (☎822 5010), about 1km north of town around a pair of ponds. It's sweet repose, with a garden, a sauna center ("Box for Honoured Gentleman" Y238), and a quality restaurant. The standard rooms are fresh and airy, with garden views—no smokestacks in sight. Singles and doubles Y280-580. Credit cards accepted.

▒ SIGHTS

It would be a shame to pass through Jingdezhen and not learn a little about the porcelain and ceramics trade. As chance would have it, the city has several factory tours and museums, all dedicated to the explanation and promotion of the region's tradition of churning out urn after urn's worth of shiny clay. CITS-arranged **factory tour,** where you'll stop at local porcelain factories, as well as a porcelain-oriented research center, 1000-year-old kiln site, and museum. Seeing the city this way can be pricey, but you can bargain down the price to suit your budget (full-day tour Y160, 2 people Y240).

If you're just in town to **buy** the stuff, the **Jingdezhen Arts and Crafts Corporation** (jǐngdézhèn gōngyì měishù gōngsī; 景德镇工艺美术公司), 27 Zhushan Zhong Lu (☎/fax 822 4063), about half a block east of the post office, sells pieces by certain renowned artists. For bargain prices, hop onto a bus heading out toward Jiujiang; about 3km outside the city is a mind-boggling row of shops hawking plates, vases, and more. Whether you are in museums, hotels, or tiny street markets, ceramics shopping is never far away; make sure you know what you're buying.

CERAMIC HISTORY MUSEUM (táocí lìshǐ bówùguǎn; 陶瓷历史博物馆). If have time to see only one sight, head out to the Ceramic History Museum. More a lazy man's garden than an exhibition space, the Ming- and Qing-era restored buildings bestow ample old-school charm. Walk back past the pond and bridges toward the main display hall, which features examples of porcelain and pottery through the ages. There are no English captions, but as they say, a piece of porcelain's worth a thousand words. *(On the far west end of Xinfeng Lu. Accessible by bus #18. ☎852 1594. Open daily 8am-5pm. Y5.)*

ANCIENT PORCELAIN FACTORY. This factory, constructed in Ming and Qing styles, is the only place in town that still employs traditional techniques. There's a Buddhist shrine and a shop right inside, but past that you can wander along several long assembly lines guided by skilled human hands. Watch as pieces are thrown from raw clay (using a manual wheel driven by a cane), baked in the cavernous, multi-story wood kiln next door (which you can walk inside), and then honed and painted in one of the other shops. The craftspeople here are reserved, but will demonstrate their skills if asked politely. *(Next door to the Ceramic History Museum. Open daily 8am-5pm. Y10.)*

LUSHAN 庐山   ☎0792

There's no question that Lushan is a resort town. The immaculate paved streets and footpaths and the lazy, laid-back atmosphere speak for themselves. But this isn't just any resort town: this was *Mao*'s resort town. Lushan was actually developed as a vacation spot by Europeans and then taken up by the Chinese during the early 20th century. Chiang Kai-shek and the most powerful early Communists considered Lushan to be their "summer capital," meeting here regularly.

Picturesque though they may be, the sights and scenery possess none of Huangshan's breathtaking splendor. Lushan's beauty is soft and subdued, with cool mountain breezes that soothe the frantic nerves of the wealthy Chinese families who flock here to escape the stifling summer heat. Lushan sees hordes of tourists each summer, but nature remains accessible and mellow. The area has also developed a broad collection of museums and restored buildings dedicated to early Communist history, which, together with the paintings and poems abundantly displayed nearly everywhere, create an interesting mix of culture and nature.

▐ TRANSPORTATION

Obviously, **trains** don't travel up the mountain. However, **buses** regularly shuttle passengers back and forth from the Lushan Train Station to the mountain (Y7). Many trains that stop at Nanchang also stop at Lushan. **Trains** travel to: Beijing (21hr., 12:30pm, Y66-457); Chongqing (30hr., 2 per day, Y66-457); Nanchang (2½hr., 12 per day, Y7-28); Shanghai (14hr., 5:16pm, Y50-351); and Wuhan (5hr., 7 per day, Y16-155). To buy **long-distance bus** tickets, walk up Hexi Lu and through the tunnel. Turn left; the small office is about 30m ahead on the left. (☎828 0199. Open daily 7am-9pm.) From Jiujiang (30min., 8 per day 7:50am-4:30pm, Y7), you can catch buses to more distant places. Tickets to Wuhan (5hr., 2 per day, Y72) can also be booked at this ticket office, but you'll still need to change buses in Jiujiang. The Nanchang bus depot is on the other side of the tunnel, just past the fork in Hexi Lu (2½hr.; every 30min. 6:51am-6:21pm; Y30, with A/C Y35.) **Minibuses** for Jiujiang and other Lushan destinations leave frequently from just outside Guling, on the road to Jiujiang. **Taxi** and minibus rides generally cost Y10 along Hexi Lu, and Y15-25 for other sights in Guling.

✦▐ ORIENTATION AND PRACTICAL INFORMATION

The largest gateway to the Lushan area is **Jiujiang** (九江), a city on the mouth of Lake Poyang, which spreads to the north of the mountains. Between Jiujiang and **Guling** (牯岭), the main town within the Lushan region, buses (Y7) and taxis (Y30) cruise up a winding highway with fantastic views of the city and lake, right up to the entrance gate. **Admission** is Y51, plus Y10 to take a taxi inside. (Open 24hr. ☎828 3627.) Guling lies just a few kilometers beyond, wrapping around the mountain. Buses enter the town through a tunnel in the northeast. From here, **Hexi Lu** (河西路) runs south, past hotels, restaurants, and sights. Branching off to the east is **Guling Jie** (牯岭街), a pedestrian street that continues on to **Jiexin Park**, a small shady area that overlooks the valley.

The **CITS office**, 443 Hexi Lu, just north of the Lushan Hotel, is well organized, and helpful staff speak English and French. (☎828 2497. Open daily 8am-6pm.) **Bank of China**, on Guling Jie, about a block past Hexi Lu, exchanges traveler's checks. (Open daily 8am-noon and 2:30-6pm.) The **post and telecommunications office**, across from the Bank of China, has 24hr. IDD service and slow **Internet access** for Y0.1 per minute. (Open daily 7am-9:30pm.) The **postal code** is 332900.

▐▐ ACCOMMODATIONS AND FOOD

Few foreigners stay in Lushan, and most tour groups make the mountain a daytrip from Jiujiang. It seems that the government would be happy to keep it that way, protecting Lushan's sleepy atmosphere for its higher party officials. Few hotels accept foreigners, and those that do have high prices, mediocre rooms, and a habit of arbitrarily closing their doors. That said, sometimes the extra money is worth it, especially for a small villa or bungalow, which will put you right in the middle of Lushan's impressive wilderness. The following rates generally reflect high-season prices, so expect discounts (or bargain hard) during winter months.

The unique atmosphere of Lushan extends to eating as well: unlike most Chinese cities, the main part of Guling boasts nary a street vendor. Restaurants in town are almost all of the sit-down variety. Most meals cost Y20-30, but don't expect anything fancy unless you head to a hotel. Luckily, there's plenty of ice cream around to beat the heat.

Guling Hotel (gūlíng fàndiàn; 牯岭饭店), 104 Hedong Lu (☎828 2435 or 828 2780), just south of the bus station. The rooms here are unspectacular and the staff can be slightly ornery, but it's your best bet for a reasonably priced bed, and you can bargain if you're lucky. Those cursed tour groups often steal away all of the cheap rooms here. Doubles Y200, with bath Y300-480; triples Y420.

Lushan Hotel (lúshān bīnguǎn; 庐山宾馆), 446 Hexi Lu (☎828 2060), about 1km south of the bus station. Rooms here are in removed villas with pleasant views and cool summer breezes. Don't be surprised to find some multi-legged friends waiting in your room—this is nature, after all. Singles and doubles Y260 and up.

Lengthwise and Crosswise Hotel (jīngwěi bīnguǎn; 径纬宾馆), 4 Jinglong Lu (☎828 2080), across the stream at the south end of the pond, next to the People's Museum. Nice setting, but dingy rooms. Check out the mysterious "4 in 1 toothbrush" in the small bathroom. Doubles Y360; triples Y480; quads Y600.

Jiaxiu Hotel (jiǎxiù bīnguǎn; 甲秀宾馆), 458 Hexi Lu (☎828 8218), across and just down the street from the Guling Hotel. Sure, the rooms are big and clean, but an extra Y20 for A/C? Sheesh. Singles Y190-249; doubles Y380-480.

🧭 SIGHTS

Countless Chinese ancients have spent long, contemplative chunks of their lives in Lushan, resulting in some legend or gushing poem associated with every cave, tree, and waterfall on the mountain. With that in mind, no single sight stands out here; whether you have a day or a week, wandering the trails and soaking in the oft-extolled surroundings is still the best way to explore the area.

In general, the sights closer to Guling draw larger crowds. The Lushan area is expansive, and some of the most spectacular waterfalls and cliffs are hours away from Guling. The lofty **Sandiequan Falls** (sāndiéquán pùbù; 三叠泉瀑布), with a three-step drop of more than 150m, is 12km to the east, accessible by an elevated tourist tramway. **Dahanyangfeng Peak** (dàhànyán fēng; 大汉阳峰), at 1474m, is the tallest point on Lushan, in the remote south, near the town of **Xiufeng** (秀峰). Another cluster of attractions is in the nearby foothills, including **Yellow Cliff Falls** (huángyá pùbù; 黄崖瀑布) and **Incense Burner Peak** (xiānghú fēng; 香炉峰), which inspired the poet Li Bai. Getting there by taxi or minibus is costly (Y30-50), but you're bound to find unparalleled solitude.

For a good day hike combining both cultural and natural sights around Guling, walk down the trail along the stream southwest of Guling, stopping in at Meilu Villa and People's Hall, and eventually moving along to Lake Lulin, the Three Ancient Trees, and Dragon Pools. Cross over to the other side of Lake Lulin, passing the Mao Zedong Poetry Memorial and Lushan Museum. From there, it's a good one-hour walk beyond to the Botanical Gardens and Hanpokou. Alternatively, join the masses at Hanpokou for the famous sunrise, and follow this same route in reverse. Another one-day, single-trail hiking option is to head to the area 2.5km west of Guling, accessible from a trail near the Lushan Hotel. **Xianren Cave** (xiānrén dòng; 仙人洞), where folk hero Lu Dongbin became immortal, and **Dragon Head Precipice** (lóngshǒu yá; 龙首崖) are the main sights to see here.

Organized tours for Chinese groups run frequently throughout the day during the tourist season; to join in, inquire at CITS, flag down one of the tour buses on the road, or just ask a driver at one of the sights if you might tag along.

YANGZI BASIN

LUSHAN MUSEUM (lúshān bówùguǎn; 庐山博物馆). Established in 1957, this is the best museum in Lushan, combining all the elements that make the mountain interesting: culture, communism, and natural history. Highlights include Buddhist paintings, a *papier mâché* model of the Lushan region, photos of some of the dignitaries who visited Lushan, and a room full of impaled insects to help you identify that monstrous beetle in your bathroom. Limited English captions. *(On Huanhu Lu, southwest of Lake Lulin. Open daily 7:45am-6pm. Y10.)*

LAKE LULIN (lúlín hú; 庐林湖). This small lake with an attached pavilion, halfway between Guling and Hanpokou, is a good starting point for short jaunts to the Three Ancient Trees, the Dragon Pools, and the Lushan Museum. On the lake's north end is the **Monument of Mao Zedong's Poems,** a group of huge granite slabs inscribed with Mao's own poetry and some of his personal favorites.

MEILU VILLA (měilú biéshù; 美庐别墅). An unusual range of political styles found comfortable refuge in this complex. Built at the turn of the 20th century by a British lord, this villa was sold during the early 30s to Song Meiling, the vampish wife of Chiang Kai-shek. After the ruling couple's untimely exile, the villa passed unscathed into the hands of Communists; Chairman Mao even came to stay here several times between 1959 and 1961. On display are roomfuls of ghostly photos of Chiang Kai-shek, as well as of Mao and his entourage. There's also a dining hall, a cavernous bathroom, an American kerosene refrigerator, and other relics of upper-class leisure. *(Across the stream from Hexi Lu. Open daily 8am-6pm. Y15.)*

THREE ANCIENT TREES (sān bǎo shù; 三宝树). Standing behind fences in front of a Buddhist temple, these three old guys were supposedly planted by Tan Shen, a monk of the Eastern Jin dynasty. Don't be fooled—in reality they are only about 500 years old. Still, the trees are massive, and the on-site explanation tells you just how it can feel to stare up such towering trunks: "Sense quietness first, then darkness, and finally coldness." Just down the hill from the Ancient Trees are the **Dragon Pools** (lóngchí; 龙池), at the confluence of two streams. This is a good place for a picnic, with fruit sold nearby. *(3.5km from Guling. A 10min. walk from Lake Lulin, on the trail along the stream in Guling.)*

PEOPLE'S THEATER (rénmín jùyuàn; 人民剧院). Also known as the **Lushan Conference Site** (lúshān huìyì huìzhǐ; 庐山会议会址), this is where the Camelot camaraderie among Long March cadres wilted (see **Camelot Period,** p. 17). During an important get-together here in 1959, Chairman Mao overruled the objcetions of his defense minister Peng Dehuai and steamrolled ahead with the Great Leap Forward (see p. 18). The large auditorium has a stage set up as it might have been during Party meetings, with videos (in Chinese) that feature Mao, in all his fleshy glory, enjoying a swim in the Lushan lakes. In the front rooms of the hall is a small, unimpressive photo exhibit; many of the same shots are on display in the Lushan museum. *(504 Hexi Lu. At a right fork in the road, in front of a pond. Open daily 8am-6pm. Y10.)*

HANPOKOU (hánpókǒu; 含鄱口). One of the few sweeping vistas readily accessible from Guling, Hanpokou ("the mouth sucking on Lake Poyang") overlooks a valley vast enough to swallow the lake. Visitors can take the **Dakou cable car** to one of Lushan's many waterfalls. *(One-way Y21, round-trip Y41; children half-price.)* Perched at 1210m, on the Hanpoling Ridge, the small pavilion fills to the brim with Chinese tourists. The eastern-facing spot is famous for its glimmering, misty views at dawn; come at any other time, and you're likely to find yourself enshrouded in a foggy soup. *(6km from Guling on Hanpokou Lu, south of the Botanical Gardens. Walking here would monopolize the better part of a day.)*

BOTANICAL GARDENS (zhíwùyuán; 植物园). Built in 1934, this complex houses thousands of poorly labeled plants. Unless you're truly interested in potted specimens, you're probably better off skipping the greenhouse in favor of the eastern half of the gardens, which has more nature trails. *(5.5km from Guling. From Lake Lulin, take Hanpokou Lu, following the left (north) fork. ☎828 2542. Open daily 7am-5:30pm. Y10.)*

JINGGANGSHAN 井冈山 ☎0796

Dense, wet forests blanket most of the Jinggangshan mountains, which spread nearly 700km between Hunan and Jiangxi provinces. The craggy cliffs and bare, jutting peaks familiar to other Chinese mountains don't exist here—or, if they do, they too are cloaked in the rolling felt of trees. Seemingly anything could hide in these forest valleys, which is precisely why the battered Communist army convened here before breaking through the GMD blockades and retreating on the Long March (see **United Front & Civil War,** p. 16).

Because of this brief but hugely significant historical congregation, Jinggangshan is known to most Chinese as "the cradle of the Chinese Revolution." Mao Zedong brought his Autumn Harvest Uprising troops here in 1927, joining forces with the remnants of Zhu De's troops from the Nanchang Uprising, as well as Peng Dehuai's up-and-coming legions of soldiers. The leaders and their armies established residence in Jinggangshan's main village, Ciping, and other nearby towns. While most of their homes and outposts were subsequently destroyed by GMD reactionaries, the Chinese government has since resurrected the most important sites. These landmarks—combined with the cool, wet air and miles of mountain hiking—are why tourists come so far out of their way to get here.

ORIENTATION AND PRACTICAL INFORMATION

The small town of **Ciping** (茨坪), sometimes called **Jinggangshan City,** is small enough to be traversed in 30 minutes. At the middle of the village is **Yicuihu Park** (挹翠湖公园), containing a large pond with an island pavilion in the middle and a pagoda on the south side. The large, gold **Monument to the Martyrs of the Revolution** (gémìng lièshì jìniàntǎ; 革命烈士纪念塔) stands atop a hill at the north end of town, useful for getting your bearings, unless the mist is so thick you can't see it.

From the long-distance bus station in the northeast corner of town, a commercial street runs south down the hill, forking east and west along Yicuihu Park. As you face the pond near the bus station, a right and then a left turn will bring you to **Hongjun Lu** (红军路), which runs from north to south along the west side of the park. Going straight west of the park from the bus station brings you past the bank and post office. Between the north side of Yicuihu Park and a playing field is **Zhongyang Dajie** (中央大道), which crosses the park from east to west and runs parallel to **Wujing Lu** (五井路), which runs toward the bus station. Between Wujing Lu and Zhongyang Dajie is **Shangpin Lu** (商品路), the heart of the village.

Trains: Jinggangshan Train Station (jīnggāngshān huǒchē zhàn; 井冈山火车站) is actually in Taihe, a 3hr. minibus ride from the mountain. From Taihe to Jinggangshan, buses leave approx. every hr. 6:30am-2 or 3pm; flag one down on the main street. From Jinggangshan to Taihe, the last express bus leaves around 12:30pm, the last regular bus around 2pm. Fare is Y25.

Buses: Jinggangshan Long-distance Bus Station (jīnggāngshān chángtú qìchē zhàn; 井冈山长途汽车站), at the corner of Zhongxin Dadao and Nanshan Lu. To: **Changsha** (8-9hr., 12:15pm, Y69); **Hengyang** (8-9hr., 11:30am, Y50); and **Nanchang** (6-7hr., 6:30am and 7pm, Y61.5).

Local Transportation: Minibuses and **tour buses** await customers at a station 1 block south of the bus station. One-day tours of Jinggangshan (8am-5pm) cover the bulk of the sights for under Y50 per person. A *miandi* **taxi** costs Y80-150; bargain, bargain, bargain. Within Ciping, walking is always an option.

Travel Agencies: CTS (☎655 2504), off Hongjun Lu at the end of Shangpin Lu, next to the gate leading to the Jinggangshan Guesthouse. Staff members speak some English and might give you free maps and brochures, but mostly they'll refer you to the tourist information office next door. Arranges guided tours (Y100, including transportation). Open daily 8am-noon and 3-6pm. **Qiu Shuigen,** 29 Ciping Xin Cun (☎655 5669), doesn't speak English, but is friendly and helpful, and also gives Y100 tours.

Tourist Hotlines: Complaints ☎655 2626. **First aid** ☎655 2595. **Info** ☎655 6777.

Bank of China: 6 Nanshan Lu, near the southwest tip of Yicuihu Park. Exchanges traveler's checks. Open M-F 8am-6pm.

Telephones: China Telecom, in a towering office about 100m south of Yicuihu Park. Open daily 7:30am-7:30pm.

Post Office: About 200m north of the Bank of China alongside the park, across from the pagoda in the pond and near the Jinggangshan (Fandian) Hotel. EMS available. Open daily 7:30am-6pm. **Postal Code:** 343600.

▓◐ ACCOMMODATIONS AND FOOD

Surpisingly enough, humble Jinggangshan doesn't come cheap, and almost all hotels charge above Y200 range, but as always, bargaining is possible throughout the year. Most hotels are lined up along Hongjun Lu; upon leaving the bus station, turn right, go up the hill and around the bend until you run into a tree-lined road.

As for dining, inexpensive restaurants can be found on nearly every corner. You can live like the Red Army, subsisting only on tiny portions of red rice and pumpkins that once fed Communist troops. Otherwise, there's a **fresh food market** down the hill to the left of the China Telecom office selling raw meat and veggies. The road leading downhill from the bus station has a few small places, and a number of quick-fry stands are congregated near the post office and at the east end of Zhongyang Dajie. The street running perpendicular to Shangpin Lu is crammed with outdoor eateries that cook up Jinggangshan specialties, including just-picked wild vegetables with mint (Y15), roasted pheasant (Y45), and sauteed frog (Y65).

Jinggangshan Mansion (jǐnggāngshān dàshà; 井冈山大厦), 31 Hongjun Bei Lu (☎655 2251). This self-touted "Jinggangshan Baosteel Mountain Villa" is a cavernous stone hotel with little pretense, gorgeous high ceilings, comfy rooms, and helpful service. 12hr. hot water. The Mansion plans to upgrade to three-stardom next year, so prices may be jacked up along with the facilities; bargain. Dorms Y120 and up; doubles (many with balcony) Y240 and up.

Jinye Hotel (jīnyè dàshà; 金叶大厦), 30 Hongjun Bei Lu (☎655 8188). The pristine lobby earns the Jinye points for cleanliness and upkeep. The old building is a massive Gothic cobblestoned structure. Doubles Y240-490; triples Y300; quads Y360.

Jinggangshan Guesthouse (jǐnggāngshān bīnguǎn; 井冈山宾馆), 10 Hongjun Bei Lu (☎655 2221 or 655 2272), above a long stone wall and accessible by a ramp leading up from the road. Service can be a bit lackluster, but get staff to show you Rm. 115 in the main building. Kept just as it was when the Chairman paid a visit in 1965, the room contains the small selection of books he left behind. The rooms in the villas (including the "Nuclear Power Villa") are comparable to those in the main building, just farther away. Doubles Y320-380, in main building Y680.

Jinggangshan Hotel (jǐnggāngshān fàndiàn; 井冈山饭店), 1 Xinshichang Lu (☎655 2328). From the bus station, walk south down the hill; it's about 600m down the hill, on the left. The hotel is unmarked in English except for a "Foreign Nationals" plaque. The rooms are puny with squat bathrooms. Dorms Y20; doubles Y180.

◉ SIGHTS

Outside the immediate area lie many of Jinggangshan's most renowned natural beauties, which can all be taken in a day if you've got a taxi and a map.

CITY SIGHTS

MONUMENT TO THE JINGGANGSHAN REVOLUTIONARY MARTYRS (jǐnggāngshān gémìng lièshì jìniàntǎ; 井冈山革命烈士纪念塔). The monument is a shimmering, angular sculpture representing a torch. Within the same complex is the **Revolutionary Martyrs' Cemetery,** a Memorial Hall inscribed with 15,744 names; a **Forest of Ste-**

les, with slabs of poetry inscribed in calligraphy by national leaders and celebrities; and a **sculpture garden** featuring 19 statues of early CCP leaders, including an especially virile-looking Mao Zedong. The entrance to the Monument is just up the hill to the west of the bus station; follow the loop trail to see all the sites. *(At the northern end of Ciping, towering atop a hill. Open daily 7am-7pm. Y15.)*

JINGGANGSHAN REVOLUTIONARY MUSEUM (jǐnggāngshān gémìng bówùguǎn; 井岗山革命博物馆). This museum houses a large, impressive collection of papers, eerie photographs, maps, scale-models, old uniforms, books, and weapons. English narrations are nowhere to be found, but the photos and relics speak for themselves. *(In the southwest part of Ciping. ☎655 2449. Open daily 8am-5:30pm. Y8.)*

COMRADE MAO ZEDONG'S RESIDENCE (máo zédōng tóngzhì gùjū; 毛泽东同志故居). For a peek into the stark, primitive living conditions of the early revolutionaries, head here. Their one-time living quarters (rebuilt) make a budget dorm look like the Shangri-La, with threadbare uniforms folded neatly over rock-hard mattresses. A plaque across from Mao's quarters explains the "traditions of Mt. Jinggang," a list of the CCP commandments of mass toil and struggle. It takes some imagination to picture chunky Mao living the hard life here, but the site certainly merits a visit. *(About 50m north of China Telecom. Open daily 8am-6pm. Y8.)*

OUTSIDE JINGGANGSHAN

HUANGYANGJIE (huángyángjiè; 黄洋界). Originally an army post in the Mao era, this lookout point is now a favorite spot with sunrise watchers and landscape lovers. Perched 1343m above sea level, it looks out over precipitous terrain and offers a spectacular view of the surrounding terrain. Because Huangyangjie hovers over a valley, on foggy days the entire area turns into a sea of clouds, thus earning the spot the name "sea border." Huangyangjie is not to be missed—just take care not to lean too far over the edge. *(A 20min. drive northwest of Jinggangshan. Open 24hr. Y7.)*

FIVE DRAGON POOLS (wǔ lóng tán; 五龙潭). The Five Dragon Pools are a series of drooping valleys with five gushing waterfalls and winding paths through mystical water curtains. Poetic names like "fairy waterfall" and "rainbow curtain" grace these spots, and a half-day hike through the mountainous and rocky area may provide you with poetic discoveries of your own. For those short on time or eager to see the whole thing up front, a steep cable car ride (Y50) goes past some of the main waterfalls and sights. *(7km from Jinggangshan City. Open daily 5am-6pm. Y30.)*

FIVE FINGERS PEAK (wǔ zhí fēng; 五指峰). The Five Fingers Peak, plastered on the back of the Y100 bill, can be seen life-size here, but requires a little imagination all the same. Still, it makes for some gorgeous panoramic views of the mountainous terrain. *(☎655 7667. Open daily 6am-7:30pm. Y10.)*

HUNAN 湖南

Mild-mannered and lackluster at first glance, Hunan has fire in its blood—white-hot local cuisine and red-hot home-grown ideological zeal have both set the province's inhabitants ablaze at one time or another. The much-lauded birthplace of China's greatest cult icon, Mao Zedong, Shaoshan is one of several sights in Hunan that retrace the steps of the Great Helmsman. Any Mao pilgrimage done right also passes through Hunan's capital, Changsha, where the CCP founder learned the ABCs of communism, both as a student and as a young revolutionary.

Aside from stops along the well-beaten Mao pilgrimage path, Hunan lays claim to the eerie, fog-shrouded stone outcroppings of Wulingyuan Scenic Area in far northwestern Hunan and the northeastern lakefront city of Yueyang. Several ethnic minorities, including the Miao, Tujia, Dong, and even Uighur (See **Ethnic Composition,** p. 23), inhabit the border regions of the province.

CHANGSHA 长沙 ☎0731

These days, ongoing massive reconstruction fills the air in Changsha fills with yellow dust. While embracing modernity, this provincial capital still wears its 3000-year-old history proudly on its sleeve. Perhaps its best attraction is the 2100-year-old corpse of a Western Han era woman and the contents of her tomb. Mummies aside, Changsha boasts many Mao pilgrimage sites, for it was here that the Chairman spent the early years of his life. Changsha also lays claim to the Yuelu Mountain Scenic Area and other natural sites on the banks of the Xiang River.

▐▔ TRANSPORTATION

Airplanes: Huanghua International Airport (chángshā huánghuā guójì jīchǎng; 长沙 黄花国际机场; ☎444 9500), is 25km east of Changsha. Buses (every 30min. 6am-9pm, Y13) connect the **CAAC ticket office**, 75 Wuyi Dong Lu (☎411 2222 or 415 5777), with the airport. Open daily 7:30am-10:30pm. A taxi from the airport to town costs Y120. To: **Beijing** (2-5 per day, Y970); **Chengdu** (2-4 per day, Y730); **Chongqing** (2-5 per day, Y590); **Fuzhou** (1-2 per day, Y550); **Guangzhou** (1-3 per day, Y550); **Haikou** (2-5 per day, Y880); **Hong Kong** (1 per day, Y1600-2100); **Kunming** (1-3 per day, Y760); **Nanjing** (1-2 per day, Y670); **Shanghai** (1-3 per day, Y710); and **Xian** (1-2 per day M-Th and Sa, Y710).

Trains: Changsha Train Station (chángshā huǒchē zhàn; 长沙火车站; ☎229 6421), at Wuyi Dong Lu and Chezhan Lu, in the eastern part of town. Open 24hr. To: **Beijing** (15hr., 11 per day, Y191); **Guangzhou** (9-11hr., 25 per day, Y99); **Guilin** (9-11hr., 7 per day, Y76); **Kunming** (7 hr., 3 per day, Y191); **Shanghai** (20hr., 1 per day, Y154); **Shenzhen** (13hr., 2 per day, Y147); **Tianjin** (11hr., 1 per day, Y201); **Wuhan** (3-5hr., 13 per day, Y50); and **Xian** (20hr., 2 per day, Y175).

Buses: The **East Bus Station** (qìchē dōng zhàn; 汽车东站; ☎461 1731), on the eastern end of Bayi Lu, accessible from the train station by bus #26. To **Wuhan** (7hr., Y75) and **Yueyang** (3hr., Y33). Departure times vary widely; ask at the station. The **South Bus Station** (qìchē nán zhàn; 汽车南站; ☎228 2816), considerably south of the city on Shaoshan Nan Lu; take bus #107 from the train station. To **Guangzhou** (18hr., Y73) and **Hengyang** (3hr., Y42). Buses for **Zhangjiajie** (10hr., Y90) leave from the **West Bus Station** (qìchē xī zhàn; 汽车西站), on Fenglin Er Lu (bus #312 from the train station).

Local Transportation: Most **buses** run 6am-8pm, although some minibuses and buses serving the train station have extended hours. Fare Y1, with A/C Y2. Very few bus stops are east of the main train station.

Taxis: Base fare Y8, each additional km Y1.6.

✚▮❷ ORIENTATION AND PRACTICAL INFORMATION

Most of Changsha lies on the eastern edge of the flood-prone **Xiang River**. The main train and bus stations are east of the city center. From the train station area, **Wuyi Lu** (无一路) is the main east-west thoroughfare, eventually becoming **Fenglin Lu** (枫林路) west of the Xiang River. **Cai E Lu** (蔡鄂路) is an important north-south boulevard that intersects Wuyi Lu. Aside from the Yuelu Mountains and Hunan University, most points of interest are located in the eastern half of the city.

Travel Agency: CITS Ticket Center (zhōngguó guójì lǚxíngshè piào wù zhōngxīn; 中 国国际旅行社票务中心), 114 Wuyi Dong Lu (☎446 5885; fax 446 7867), next to the Lotus Hotel (fúróng bīnguǎn; 芙蓉宾馆). Open daily 8:30am-6:30pm. **CITS**, 8 Wuyi Dong Lu (☎229 6270), on the 11th floor of the Xiǎoyuán Building (哓园大厦). Open daily 8am-5:30pm.

Bank of China: 71 Wuyi Dong Lu (☎411 9424). Open M-F 8:30am-noon and 2:30-5pm.

Bookstore: Foreign Language Bookstore (húnán shěng wài wén shūdiàn; 湖南省外文书店), 124 Cai E Lu, between Bayi Lu and Wuyi Lu. Open daily 8am-6pm.

PSB: 445 Huangxing Nan Lu (☎222 6241), at Jiefang Lu. Open 8am-noon and 2:30-6pm.

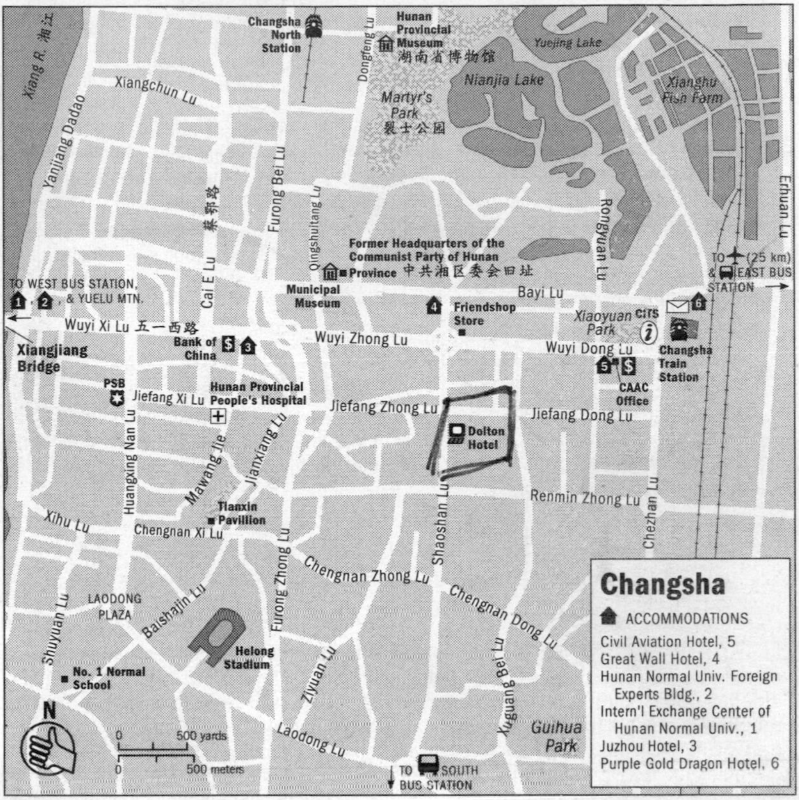

Map of Changsha with the following labels:

Xiang R. 湘江
Yanjiang Dadao
Xiangchun Lu
Changsha North Station
Dongmeng Lu
Hunan Provincial Museum 湖南省博物馆
Yuejing Lake
Nianjia Lake
Xianghu Fish Farm
Martyr's Park 烈士公园
Furong Bei Lu
Qingshuitang Lu
Rongyuan Lu
Erhuan Lu
TO (25 km) & EAST BUS STATION →
Former Headquarters of the Communist Party of Hunan Province 中共湘区委会旧址
Municipal Museum
Bayi Lu
Xiaoyuan CITS Park
TO WEST BUS STATION, & YELU MTN.
Cai E Lu
Wuyi Xi Lu 五一西路
Bank of China
Wuyi Zhong Lu
Friendshop Store
Wuyi Dong Lu
Changsha Train Station
Xiangjiang Bridge
PSB
Jiefang Xi Lu
Hunan Provincial People's Hospital
Jiefang Zhong Lu
Jiefang Dong Lu
CAAC Office
Huangxing Nan Lu
Mawang Jie
Jianxiang Lu
Dolton Hotel
Renmin Zhong Lu
Chezhan Lu
Xihu Lu
Tianxin Pavilion
Chengnan Xi Lu
Chengnan Zhong Lu
Chengnan Dong Lu
Shaoshan Lu
Furong Zhong Lu
Shuyuan Lu
LAODONG PLAZA
Baishajin Lu
Helong Stadium
Ziyuan Lu
Kuguan Bei Lu
Guihua Park
No. 1 Normal School
Laodong Lu
TO SOUTH BUS STATION
N
0   500 yards
0   500 meters

Changsha

ACCOMMODATIONS
Civil Aviation Hotel, 5
Great Wall Hotel, 4
Hunan Normal Univ. Foreign Experts Bldg., 2
Intern'l Exchange Center of Hunan Normal Univ., 1
Juzhou Hotel, 3
Purple Gold Dragon Hotel, 6

Hospital: Hunan Provincial People's Hospital (húnán shěng rénmín yīyuàn; 湖南省人民医院), 28 Dongmao Jie (☎222 4611), on the southern side of Jiefang Xi Lu before reaching Cai E Lu. Take bus #2 or 141.

Internet Access: Jintian Yulecheng (jīntiān yúlèchéng; 金天娱乐城; ☎222 1310), on Jianxiang Lu, at the big intersection of Wuyi Lu and Furong Lu. Recognizable by the big Mario cartoon character on the outside; computers downstairs on the right. Y6 per hr. Open daily 9:30am-11pm.

Post Office: Changsha Post Office, on the north side of the train station square. EMS. Open daily 8am-8pm. **Postal Code:** 410001.

▐ ACCOMMODATIONS

Restrictions on foreigners are still imposed at many of Changsha's cheapest establishments. Accommodations near the train station and around Wuyi Lu and Bayi Lu are convenient, though often expensive. Cheaper hotels can be found across the river at the university.

International Exchange Center of Hunan Normal University (húnán shīdà guójì xuéshì jiāolíu zhōngxīn; 湖南师大国际学士交流中心; ☎887 2188). Bus #202 from the train station (Hunan Shida stop). Some of the only eye candy in the city, this redder-than-thou building provides respite from its gray surroundings. Sits proudly at the foot of the Yuelu Mountain Scenic Area. A/C, heating, and 24hr. hot water. Singles Y100; doubles Y120; triples Y150.

Hunan Normal University Foreign Experts Building (húnán shīfàn dàxué wàiguó zhuān-jiā lóu;湖南师范大学外国专家楼; ☎887 2211). Just up the hill behind the International Exchange Building. A/C and heating. Hot water 7-8am and 8-9:30pm. Deposit required. Doubles Y160; triples Y180.

Juzhou Hotel (jùzhōu jiǔdiàn; 巨州酒店), 1 Wuyi Xi Lu (☎222 9148; fax 444 6685), at Jianxiang Nan Lu. The rooms aren't spectacular, but the location puts you close to the commercial areas and chaos of the western part of town. Singles Y150-170; doubles Y150-200; triples Y150-160. 10% service charge. MC, Visa accepted.

Great Wall Hotel (chángchéng bīnguǎn; 长城宾馆), 28 Shaoshan Bei Lu (☎446 2888; fax 446 2321), at the corner of Bayi Lu. A luxurious feel with rooms and facilities to match. KFC, a Friendship Store, and a grocery across the street. Singles and doubles Y280; triples Y300. Visa accepted.

Purple Gold Dragon Hotel (zǐjīn lóng dájiǔdiàn; 紫金龙大酒店), 1 Wuyi Dong Lu (☎229 3366, ext. 9688; fax 229 3366, ext. 9668), located next to the post office in the train station square. Singles Y298; doubles Y223; triples Y238.

Civil Aviation Hotel (mínháng dàjiǔdiàn;民航大酒店), 7 Wuyi Dang Lu (☎417 0288; fax 414 8014), creatively takes its name from the CAAC office in the same building. A relatively cheap escape from the din of the eastern end of Wuyi Dong Lu. Singles Y226; doubles Y218.

◖ FOOD

The unofficial slogan to dining in Changsha should read "If you can't stand the heat, step out of the fire." Before even sitting down to read a menu, visitors to Changsha should be sure they have an ample supply of tissues and something cool to drink. The local cuisine is flavored with enough spices and hot peppers to make anyone's nose run. Legend has it that Chairman Mao liked it that way. Spicy chicken (all parts included) is a favorite, and in Changsha, every year is the Year of the Snake, at least for more adventurous diners. These Hunanese favorites can be easily found across the street west of the train station along **Chezhan Zhong Lu** and are also concentrated one block further west along **Chaoyang Lu.** Another hot spot for food is **Yanshan Jie,** one block south of Bayi Lu near Shaoshan Lu. The narrow lane is lined with fresh fruit stands and restaurants serving stir-fried vegetables and noodle dishes; a meal is rarely more than Y10. Farther west along **Huangxing Lu,** stretching for blocks south of Wuyi Dong Lu, restaurants specialize in everything from wonton soup to *doupi* (stuffed bean curd).

Huo Gong Restaurant (huǒ gōng diàn jiǔjiā; 火宫殿酒家), 46 Pozi Jie (☎581 4896). Walk toward the river; it's off Huangxing Nan Lu to the right. A traditional red gate temple facade guards the entrance to its courtyard. The *chou doufu* (smelly beancurd) served here garnered praise from Chairman Mao during his historic visit in 1958. A second branch at 105 Wuyi Dong Lu. Tea Y2, appetizers Y4-10, meals Y12-38. Open daily 7:30am-8:30pm.

Do Do Fun Cafe (dòudòufāng kāfēi; 豆豆坊咖啡), 398 Jiefang Dong Lu (☎415 0059), right before the Huatian Hotel at the corner of Shaoshan Lu and Jiefang Dong Lu. The airy, relaxed atmosphere makes this cafe an ideal place for an afternoon breather. Mainly "chuppie" (Chinese yuppie) clientele. Double the "do" means double the fun. Specialty coffee Y18-25. Chinese and Western set meals Y20-30. Open daily 8am-1am.

De Yuan Snack Shop (dé yuán bāodiǎn diàn; 德园包点店), 313 Huangxing Nan Lu (☎581 7732), on the right just past Pozi Jie when you walk south on Huangxing Nan Lu. Offering finger foods like *baozi* (Y1-3) and other traditional favorites, this place is best for a late lunch or a heavy snack. Open daily 5am-6:30pm.

Mona Lisa Restaurant (méngnà lìshā zhōngxī cāntīng; 蒙娜丽莎中西餐厅), 458 Furong Zhong Lu (☎516 3222), near Renmin Zhong Lu. Despite the Grecian urns and Corinthian columns, the Mona Lisa remains a rowdy Chinese restaurant. Serves a wide variety of Western and Chinese cuisine (entrees Y20-40). The restaurant is a town hotspot, featuring an open bar at all hours (imported beer Y20, cocktails Y28) and live bands starting at 8pm. Open daily 7am-2am.

🔘 SIGHTS

While many of Changsha's attractions revolve around the Chairman and the early years of his life spent in the city, Changsha does have a few worthwhile pre-Maoist historical sights and scenic areas as well.

YUELU MOUNTAIN RANGE (yuèlù shān; 岳麓山). Yuelu is the main scenic spot of Changsha, with two universities nestled at its base. A trip to this picturesque park is part nature and part cultural history lesson. Famous ancients such as Pei Xiu of the Tang dynasty and philosopher Zhu Xi of the Song lived here, and modern revolutionaries Huang Xing and Cai E are buried in the park as well. *(Take bus #202 from the train station and get off at the Hunan University stop with the Mao statue. Y2.)*

Just before the East Gate entrance to the park is **Yuelu Academy** (yuèlù shūyuàn; 岳麓书院), established in AD 976 as one of the four most outstanding institutions of the period. The traditional architecture and calligraphy inscriptions bear witness to its important position. *(Open daily 7:30am-5:40pm. Y14.)*

Inside the park, one of the first sites on the right side path is the famous **Aiwan Pavilion** (àiwǎn tíng; 爱晚亭), which features a stone tablet inscribed by Mao Zedong, after a well-known verse by Du Mu. Those hardy enough to make it to the top can ride down the mountain to the North Gate by cable car, which shuttles tourists up and down the mountain. Those who wish to take a walk on the wild side can careen down the mountainside on a bobsled (Y30). *(Take bus #202 from the train station to the Yue Lu stop right outside the North Gate. Cable car Y15 one-way, Y25 round-trip. Open daily 9am-5:30pm.)*

HUNAN PROVINCIAL MUSEUM (húnán shěng bówùguǎn; 湖南省博物馆). Though its most famous showpiece—the 2100-year-old corpse of a Han dynasty woman unearthed from Mawangdui in 1972—has been recently shipped to Beijing, a replica of her preserved body remains on display. Evidence and observations regarding her final moments (she died soon after consuming musk melon) decorate the walls. The exhibition halls also hold other fascinating relics, including numerous embroidered silk tapestries, paintings, and lacquerware. *(28 Dongfeng Lu. ☎ 451 3123. Open M-Sa 8am-noon and 3-6pm, Su 8:30am-5pm; in winter 8am-noon and 2:30-5:30pm, Su 8:30am-5pm. Y15.)* The **Mawangdui Han Dynasty Tomb**, the site of the Han woman's discovery, is open to visitors. Most of its treasures are preserved in the museum, however, which essentially makes the tomb an empty excavation site. *(Buses #10 and 14 go to Mawangdui from the train station. Open daily 8am-5pm. Y2.)*

MARTYRS' PARK (lièshì gōngyuán; 烈士公园). Bordering the Provincial Museum, the park offers lakes, pagodas, and shaded walks—a perfect place for a breath of fresh air after visiting the more macabre parts of the museum. Inside, the Martyr's Memorial pays homage to revolutionary heroes of the Republican era. *(Take bus #112 or 113 to the park. Otherwise, the west entrance is a short walk from the Provincial Museum along Dongfeng Lu. Park open 24hr., memorial open daily 8:30am-4:30pm. Free.)*

CHANGSHA MUNICIPAL MUSEUM (chángshā shì bówùguǎn; 长沙市博物馆). A lesser version of the Provincial Museum, the city museum still offers some unique exhibits, notably the Three Kingdoms writings inscribed on bamboo strips and Shang dynasty bronze percussion instruments. The **Former Headquarters of the Communist Party of Hunan Province** (zhōnggòng xiāngqū wěihuì jiùzhǐ; 中共湘区委会旧址), where Mao and his first wife Yang Kaihui once lived, is at the same location. *(480 Bayi Lu. Take bus #1 from the train station to the Qingshuitang stop. ☎ 222 3498. Open daily 8am-noon and 2:30-5:30pm. Y10 covers both sights.)*

OTHER SIGHTS. On the southeastern bank of the Xiang River sits the **Tianxin Pavilion** (tiānxīn gé; 天心阁), one of the last remnants of the old city walls. Located on the corner of Jianxiang Nan Lu and Chengnan Xi Lu, the fortress provides a nice view of Changsha. *(Take bus #9 from the train station. ☎ 222 2404. Open daily 6am-11pm. Park admission Y2; pavilion Y5.)* Mao's alma mater, **No. 1 Normal School** (dìyī shīfàn; 第一师范), where he studied from 1913 to 1922, is nearby. *(From Tianxin Pavilion, follow Baishajin Lu past the intersection with Laodong Lu. ☎ 513 1786. Open daily 7am-7pm. Y6.)*

SHAOSHAN 韶山 ☎0732

Terraced hillsides and rice paddies line the tracks between Changsha and the hamlet of Shaoshan, the exalted birthplace of Mao Zedong and probably the most important Communist pilgrimage site in the country. At the height of Mao's personality cult in the 60s, more than 8000 Mao groupies a day paid homage to the CCP founder's hometown. As the fanaticism surrounding the Chairman fizzled in the aftermath of the Cultural Revolution, so too did tourism to Shaoshan, but these days Mao-mania is undergoing something of a revival. In China, 60s retro meant Mao. Mao suits, Mao badges, and buttons are all collectors' items, and Shaoshan vendors hawk oodles of plastic kitsch bearing the Chairman's face; perhaps his perpetually stern demeanor is an expression of displeasure at his increasingly wayward proletarian flock.

■🗗 **ORIENTATION AND PRACTICAL INFORMATION.** Shaoshan is divided into two parts: the **new town,** including the train station just south of the Mao statue at town center and the bus station just north of it, and **the village,** also with a Mao statue at its center, a few kilometers away, harboring most of Shaoshan's important Mao-related sights. Minibuses (Y2) shuttle between the two halves from the area near the Mao statue in the new town.

A daily **train** leaves Changsha at 6:50am and makes the return trip from Shaoshan at 5:25pm (3hr., Y11-17). **Buses** leave for Shaoshan from Changsha's South Bus Station (2½hr., every hr., 8am-5pm, Y20) and West Bus Station (2½hr., 4 per day), returning every hour until late afternoon.

Changsha's **Huatian Hotel** (huátiān jiǔdiàn; 华天酒店), 380 Jiefang Dong Lu (☎444 2888; fax 444 2270), offers daily **guided tours** of Shaoshan that include transportation and admission to sights (leave at 8am, return at 6pm; Y140).

🗗🖸 **ACCOMMODATIONS AND FOOD.** Should you choose to stay overnight, village accommodations are generally preferable to those in town, as they put you closer to Shaoshan's sights. **Shaoshan Hotel** (sháoshān bīnguǎn; 韶山宾馆) is more of a guesthouse than a hotel, and the second most visible landmark in Shaoshan village. A lot of the tour groups overnight here, so you won't be lonely. Private baths available. (☎568 5080. Singles Y328; doubles Y240-280; triples Y248-280.) **Postal Guesthouse** (yóuzhèng xiǎobīnguǎn; 邮政小宾馆) is directly to the left of the Shaoshan Hotel. A/C, TV, private bath, and 24hr. hot water are provided, as is a restaurant downstairs. (☎568 5488. Doubles and quads Y160; triples Y180.) **Restaurants** line the streets near the Mao Statue. One local favorite is *hong shao rou* (红烧肉) or "soy braised pork," which tastes much better than it sounds.

🗺 **SIGHTS.** Minibuses from the new town to the Dripping Water Cave pass **Mao's childhood home** (máo zédōng tóngzhì gùjū; 毛泽东同志故居), on the left as you enter the village. Furniture, threshing tools, and pictures of the Great Helmsman clutter the small house's interior. A plaque (much like the ones dotting nearly every other sight in Hunan) resting near the pond in front of the house commemorates Mao's love of swimming. (☎568 5125. Y6.) Next door is **Nanan school** (nánàn; 南岸), where Mao studied as a child. (☎568 5121. Open daily 7:30am-5:30pm. Y6.)

A couple hundred meters into the village is the large Mao statue that marks the center of town. Directly opposite the statue is the **Mao Zedong Geneaology Museum** (máo shì zōngcí; 毛氏宗祠). Those whose Chinese is up to the task can check out Mao's family history dating back to his ancestral patriarch, who joined the Ming revolution to kick out the Mongols. (☎568 5364. Open 8:30am-5:30pm. Y6.) Next door on the left is the **Museum of Comrade Mao** (máo zédōng tóngzhì jìniànguǎn; 毛泽东同志纪念馆). Although it's all in Chinese, the museum has enough audiovisual materials to spark interest—even for those who don't read the language. (Y7.)

Buses run from outside the Shaoshan Hotel to **Dripping Water Cave** (dī shuǐ dòng; 滴水洞), approximately 3km from the village. Although taking the bus is probably easier, by foot, follow the road past the village for about 2km, turn right at the sign, and follow the winding path to the site. Dripping Water Cave is not so much a cave as it is yet another shrine to Mao, who came here in June 1966 for a retreat. The only thing that can be considered a "cave" is the drippy war bunker (built to protect Mao) that you pass through at the end of the tour. Toward the exit, a path on the right leads to Mao's ancestral tombs. *(Open daily 7am-6:30pm. Y18.)*

Tourists on organized tours of Shaoshan often find **Liu Shaoqi's Childhood Home and Former Residence** (liú shàoqí jìniànguǎn; 刘少奇纪念馆), halfway between Changsha and Shaoshan, on their itineraries. Another Hunanese native, Liu Shaoqi, was the second-in-command under Mao in the 1950s and 60s, although he was never as popular as his superior. More architecturally impressive than any of the Mao sights in Shaoshan, this place is really a large park encompassing several museums, of which Liu's former residence and the memorial hall are particularly worth visiting. *(Open daily 7:30am-7pm. Y12.)*

HENGYANG 衡阳 ☎0734

It is no surprise that Daoist ancients made Hengshan (also known as Nanyue) a center for spiritual enlightenment; the harmony of nature is visible when wind eases foggy clouds between pine trees and into the faces of wild mountain goats. The nearby city of Hengyang transports visitors in an entirely different way; it is a major junction for rail lines lumbering on to Guilin and Guangzhou.

✳🛈 ORIENTATION AND PRACTICAL INFORMATION

Hengyang is bisected by the Xiang River (湘江). The train station is on the eastern side of the river, but most accommodations and points of interest are on the western side. On the western bank, Zhongshan Lu (中山路) and Zhongxiang Lu (中湘路) intersect Jiefang Lu (解放路), the commercial center of the city.

Trains: Hengyang Train Station (héngyáng huǒchē zhàn; 衡阳火车站), on Guangdong Lu. Buses #1 and 18 go to the station. To: **Beijing** (23hr., 6 per day, Y270); **Changsha** (4hr., 10 per day, Y19); **Guangzhou** (7hr., 33 per day, Y100); and **Guilin** (8hr., 10 per day, Y120).

Buses: West Bus Station (qìchē xī zhàn; 汽车西站), at the junction of Jingyuan Lu and Jiefang Lu. Purchase tickets in the **High Speed-Direct Waiting Hall** (gāosù zhídá hòuchēshì; 高速直达候车室; ☎821 8742), to the right of the main entrance. Take a bus to Nanyue (not Hengshan) to reach the Hengshan Daoist mountains. To **Changsha** (3hr., every 30min. 7:30am 6pm, Y40) and **Nanyue** (1hr., every 30min. 7am-6pm, Y8).

Local Transportation: Bus #1 runs from the Xindu Hotel across the river and down Jiefang Lu on the other side (Y1). **Taxis** sputter about town as well; base fare Y5, each additional km Y1.4.

Tourist Office: Hunan Nanyue China Travel Company (húnán shěng nányuè zhōngguó lǚxíngshè; 湖南省南岳中国旅行社; ☎834 9229), on Guangdong Lu in the Xindu Hotel. Open daily 8am-6:30pm.

Bank of China: 351 Huancheng Nan Lu (☎814 4675), off Jiefang Lu. Open daily 8am-noon and 3-6pm.

PSB: At the corner of Chuanshan Lu and Zhongshan Bei Lu (☎823 3171).

Hospital: People's Hospital (rénmín yīyuàn; 人民医院; ☎827 9000), on Zhongshan Bei Lu, north of Chuanshan Lu.

Internet Access: The **International Internet Club** (gúo jì hù lían wǎng jù lè bù; 国际互联网俱乐部), 13 Heping Nan Lu. Y5 per hr. Open daily 9am-9pm.

Post Office: Directly to the right of the train station exit (☎833 4742). IDD phones. Open daily 7:30am-11:30pm. **Postal Code:** 421000.

🏨🍴 ACCOMMODATIONS AND FOOD

If you visit Hengshan, it's best to stay in Hengyang, since Nanyue has little in terms of lodging. Hengyang's accommodations offer similar amenities at uniformly high prices. Many small shops and restaurants line the streets of Hengyang, but few stay open past 8pm. Vendors on **Yancheng Lu** serve lunchbox-type Chinese fast food during the day. The night market on **Renmin Lu** offers cheap, tasty desserts.

Xindu Hotel (xīndū dàjiǔdiàn; 鑫都大酒店; ☎839 7935), on Guangdong Lu. Walk out of the train station's main exit and go past the bridge; the hotel is identifiable by the bright red neon lights on your left. If you're just in town for one night, this is the most convenient place to stay. All rooms have TV, telephone, and 24hr. hot water. Singles Y168; doubles Y198; triples Y225.

Zhongjian Hotel (zhōngjiàn dàjiǔdiàn; 中建大酒店), 57 Jiefang Lu (☎826 6288), in the commercial district. Comfortable rooms with A/C and 24hr. hot water. Singles Y188; doubles Y168; triples Y178.

Huatian Hotel (huátiān dàjiǔdiàn; 华天大酒店), 20 Renmin Lu (☎828 8888; fax 828 8688). Take Jiefang Lu to Zhongshan Lu and turn right; turn left at Renmin Lu, and the hotel is on your right. This place is the best Hengyang has to offer. Dance club downstairs. Rock on. Doubles Y228; triples Y298.

Sanding Fast Food Restaurant (sāndǐng měishí kuàicān guǎngchǎng; 三鼎美食快餐广场), at the corner of Zhongshan Bei Lu and Renmin Lu. A great place for a fruity concoction from the juice bar or a Cantonese-style breakfast. Open daily 7am-2am.

Meixin Ice Cream Bar (měixīn bīngbā; 美心冰吧), 4 doors from the Sanding Restaurant. Sidle up to this ice cream joint, where you can cool down on Hengyang's popular summertime specialty: *bing dousha*, a cold soup made from ground sweet red beans. Open daily 8am-midnight.

◪ CLIMBING HENGSHAN

The main sight in Hengyang is Hengshan itself, located 45km outside the city. The Hengshan mountain range actually stretches from Hengyang in the south all the way north to Yuelu Mountain in Changsha, but Hengshan (1290m) is the highest and most famous of the 72 peaks. Hengshan is known not only for the scenic beauty of its natural surroundings, but also for the poetry and calligraphy engravings that adorn its steles. Each season endows Hengshan with a special quality: in spring, it's flowers; in summer, clouds; in autumn, the moon; and in winter, snow.

Buses with A/C from Hengyang to the mountain cost Y8 and take about one hour to reach the base. The bus stops on Highway 107, before the intersection with Zhunan Lu; the last bus back to Hengyang leaves at 6pm. From the bus stop, you can reach the mountain's main gate by walking up **Zhunan Lu**, which is dotted with vendors selling Buddhist trinkets. The ticket office is farther up the road in the foothills, past the **Nanyue Great Temple.** *(Open 24hr. Y40.)* Climbing the mountain is moderately difficult and takes about 4hr. Minibuses make the trip for Y10-26. From the halfway point at **Xuandu Daoist Temple,** cable cars also ascend to the foothill of the highest peak; from here, it is a 30min. hike to the **Zhurong Palace.** *(Cable car Y30 up, Y25 down; Y50 round-trip.)* Those seeking an escape from the crowds should climb the left side of the mountain up to **Tianzhu Temple.** This is a more strenuous hike than the conventional route, with fewer sights along the way; however, the journey is quicker and more isolated.

The **Water Curtain Cave** (shuǐ pù dòng; 水瀑洞), near Zhunan Lu at the eastern edge of Nanyue village, can provide a refreshing post-climb break. However, don't expect any saunas or hot tubs here; it's waterfall all the way. The new **China Construction Bank Hotel** (nányuè yínyuè bīnguǎn; 南岳银岳宾馆), on the left side of the main road into town, provides comfortable rooms. (☎566 2245. Singles Y288; doubles Y188-208; triples Y208.)

YUEYANG 岳阳   ☎0730

As a wayside stop between Chongqing and Wuhan, Yueyang feels like a soft-spoken fishing village biding its time in cadence to the slow-moving ferries that pass by. Thanks to Tang and Song poetry, Yueyang has two claims to fame: the Yueyang Tower on Dongting Lake (the second-largest freshwater lake in the country) and Junshan Island, known for its fragrant and expensive "silver needle" tea.

▐ TRANSPORTATION

Trains: The **Yueyang train station** (yuèyáng huǒchē zhàn; 岳阳火车站), on Zhanqian Lu, in the northern part of the city. Trains run to **Changsha** (2hr., every hr., Y16-24).

Buses: The long-distance bus station is south of the train station, close to the traffic circle. To **Changsha** (2½hr., Y20-30) and **Wuhan** (4hr., 3 per day, Y50).

Ferry: Yueyang Ferry Wharf, on Dongting Bei Lu, just north of the Yueyang Tower. Boats go up the Yangzi River to **Chongqing** (36 hrs.; 2 per day; 3rd class Y200, 2nd class Y476) and downriver to **Wuhan** (8 hrs.; 1 per day; 3rd class Y46, 2nd class Y98).

Local Transportation: Bus #15 runs from the train and bus stations down Baling Lu and up Dongting Bei Lu, passing the Yueyang Pavilion and dock areas (Y1). **Taxi** base fare Y5, each additional km Y2.5.

▟ ❷ ORIENTATION AND PRACTICAL INFORMATION

There are two main roads. **Baling Lu** (巴陵路) runs east-west past the bus station through the main part of the city and ends at the lakeside, where it intersects with Dongting Lu. **Dongting Lu** (洞庭路) runs north-south from the Yueyang Tower to the Old Town area. **Bus #15** stops within walking distance of many major sights.

Tourist Office: CITS, 25 Chengdong Lu (☎826 2010), next to the Yunmeng Hotel. Take bus #15 toward the lake and get off right before the Baling Bridge. Turn left down Chengdong Lu; the Yunmeng Hotel and CITS are on your right. Offers tours to Junshan Island and Yueyang Pavilion. Open daily 8am-noon and 2:30-5:30pm; in winter 8am-noon and 3-6pm. A CITS booking office for Yangzi River cruises and ferries is at the entrance to the Yueyang Ferry Wharf.

Bank of China: On Dong Maoling Lu, off Baling Xi Lu (☎822 2964). Open daily 8am-noon and 2:30-5:30pm; in winter 8am-noon and 3pm-6pm. The **Zhongyin Hotel** (zhōngyín dà jiǔdiàn;中饮大酒店), next to the train station, also exchanges money.

PSB: Next to the Yueyang Tower Hotel (☎861 9026).

Hospital: Yueyang Tower People's Hospital (yuèyáng lóu rénmín yīyuàn; 岳阳楼人民医院), 39 Dong Maoling Lu (☎822 1211).

Internet Access: Internet Bar (☎821 3313), on Baling Xi Lu, next door to the post office. Y6 per hr. Open daily 8am-6pm.

Post Office: To the right as you exit the train station (☎826 6287). Another post office is about 100m west of the intersection of Baling Xi Lu and Dong Maoling Lu, across from the China Telecom building. **Postal Code:** 414000.

▛▟ ACCOMMODATIONS AND FOOD

The best places to stay in Yueyang are away from the bustle of the train station, near Dongting Lake and the Yueyang Tower. As for food, a fresh day's catch in Dongting Lake makes a sumptuous meal in the restaurants that line **Dongting Bei Lu.** About 200m west of Baling Bridge, the alleys of **Miaoqian Jie district** are a popular place for a late night dinner or snack, from duck (all parts of it) to traditional fried sweets.

Xuelian Hotel (xuělián bīnguǎn; 雪莲宾馆; ☎832 1633), on Dongting Bei Lu, across from the Yueyang Ferry Wharf. Curious odor and squat toilets aside, the Xuelian is one of the best bargains in town. All rooms have A/C and private bath. Singles Y60; doubles Y100; triples Y120.

Yueyang Tower Hotel (yuèyáng lóu bīnguǎn; 岳阳楼宾馆), 57 Dongting Bei Lu (☎832 1288; fax 841 4000), just opposite the Yueyang Tower. Take bus #15 from the train station to the Yueyang Tower stop, backtrack about 60m, and turn left; the hotel is on the right, recognizable by its traditional front gate. A rather average place in the most interesting part of Yueyang. Doubles Y158; triples Y198.

Yunmeng Hotel (yúnmèng bīnguǎn; 云梦宾馆), 25 Chengdong Nan Lu (☎822 1115). Take bus #15 toward the lake and get off just before the Baling Bridge. Turn left down

Chengdong Lu; the hotel is on the right. Rooms have all standard amenities. Singles Y228; doubles Y198; triples Y208.

Zui Ming Lou Restaurant (zuìmíng lóu jiǔjiā; 醉名楼酒家; ☎832 6326), on Dongting Bei Lu across from Yueyang Tower, with an English sign above the door. Both the wait-staff and the kitchen sparkle. Be sure to try the house specialty, *hongshao haigui* (braised turtle), or one of the hotpots. Open daily 8:30am-8pm.

Xiuyu Tea House (xiùyù hóngchá fáng; 秀玉红茶房;☎831 5456), down the steps underneath the Garden Hotel, just past the Baling Bridge (when you come from the west). The interior of this place meshes the feel of an Italian villa, Old English manor, and Roman bathhouse. Western and Chinese entrees Y10-20. Open daily 9:30am-1am.

👁 SIGHTS

Yueyang Tower (yuèyáng lóu; 岳阳楼), inside Yueyang Tower Park, was originally a naval watch station built during the Three Kingdoms Period (AD 220-280). The entire structure, over 20m tall, was built without a single nail. Several famous Chinese poets have composed odes to the tower; the *Notes on the Yueyang Tower*, by Song poet Fan Zhongyan, have been drilled into the memories of generations of Chinese students. *(On Dongting Bei Lu, along the riverfront. ☎831 9349. Open daily 7am-6pm. Y23, additional Y5 to climb the tower.)*

A short boat ride away lies **Junshan Island** (jūnshān dǎo; 君山岛), described by Tang poet Liu Yuxi as a sumptuous green conch in a silvery plate. The chance to see how tea is cultivated and to sample Junshan's famous silver needle brews is worth the trip. Be sure not to miss **Monkey Mountain** (hóuzi shān; 猴子山), tucked away in the island's hilly interior, where indigenous monkeys playfully vie for your attention. *(Early morning ferries leave from Yueyang Ferry Wharf and make a late afternoon return trip; Y15 round-trip. Speedboats leave Yueyang every hr. 7:30am-5pm (Y30). Last boat from Junshan Island to Yueyang leaves at 5pm. Y33.)*

ZHANGJIAJIE 张家界   ☎0744

Part of the Wulingyuan Scenic Area that has been declared a UNESCO World Heritage Site, Zhangjiajie is named for a Han lord, Zhang Liang, who according to local legend lived here in seclusion and was buried under Qingyan (now Zhangjiajie) Mountain. The entire Wulingyuan landscape is dominated by quartzite sandstone pillars, and underground brooks and streams flow for long distances between enormous caves. Zhangjiajie is one of China's most beautiful nature reserves, offering lush scenery, wonderful hiking trails, and the chance to get off the beaten path to do some exploring on your own.

🚍 TRANSPORTATION

Airplanes: Zhangjiajie Airport (zhāngjiājiè jīchǎng; 张家界机场; ☎823 8294), southwest of the city center. Buses (Y5) go to and from the Daqiao Lu airport ticket office (fēijī shòupiàotīng; 飞机售票厅), across from the post office. Beware of frequent flight cancellations. To: **Beijing** (Tu, Th, F, and Su; Y1020); **Changsha** (2 per day, Y460); **Chengdu** (1 per day, Y640); **Chongqing** (Tu, W, F, and Su; Y460); **Guangzhou** (2 per day, Y690); and **Shanghai** (1 per day, Y1060).

Trains: The **Zhangjiajie Train Station** (zhāngjiājiè huǒchē zhàn; 张家界火车站) has service to: **Beijing** (27hr., 1 per day, Y380); **Changsha** (8hr., 4 per day, Y120); and **Guangzhou** (23hr., 1 per day, Y317).

Buses: Zhangjiajie Long-distance Bus Station (zhāngjiājiè chángtú qìchē zhàn; 张家界长途汽车站), at the intersection of Renmin Lu and Huilong Lu. To: **Changsha** (11hr., 5 per day, Y49-83); **Guangzhou** (25hr., 1 per day, Y181); **Guilin** (1 per day, Y160); and **Wuhan** (14hr., 1 per day, Y101).

Local Transportation: A **public minibus** shuttles between the train station and the center of Zhangjiajie city, with a stop at the entrance of the long-distance bus station. Runs daily 6am-8pm. Fare Y1. A minibus also runs from the long-distance bus station to the park entrance (1hr., every 10min., Y8). **Private minibuses** from the train station to the city Y30; to the park entrance Y80.

🛈 PRACTICAL INFORMATION

Tourist Office: Dragon International Hotel (xiánglóng guójì jiǔdiàn; 祥龙国际酒店), 46 Jiefang Lu (☎822 6888; fax 822 2935), arranges white-water rafting trips and tours to the cave for a hefty surcharge. Luggage storage Y5. English-speaking staff. **CITS,** 37 Jiefang Lu (☎830 0011; fax 830 0022), is across the street. In Zhangjiajie Park, **Zhangjiajie Travel Service Company** (zhāngjiājiè guójiā sēnlín gōngyuán lǚxíngshè; 张家界国家森林公园旅行社; ☎571 2162), in the lobby of the Jinbianyan Hotel, organizes tours and private drivers. The manager is especially helpful.

Bank of China: On 1 Xinmatou Jie (☎822 3383). Open daily 8am-5:30pm.

PSB: On Ziwu Lu (☎822 5050). Open daily 8am-6pm.

Internet Access: Hong Cheng Internet Center (hóngchéng wǎnglù zhōngxīn; 洪诚网路中心), 3 Bei Zheng Jie, across from the China Construction Bank. Y4 per hr., and a chance to play computer games with the owner. Open 24hr.

Post Office: In Zhangjiajie City, the **post office** (☎822 4757) is on Huilong Lu, just east of the long-distance bus station. Open daily 8am-8pm. In Zhangjiajie Park, it is on the main street outside the park entrance on the right (when you are facing the park), about 100m past the Pipaxi Hotel. Open daily 8am-6pm. **Postal Code:** 427000.

🛏 ACCOMMODATIONS

Zhangjiajie's nature reserve is its chief attraction, and most tourists head straight for the park on arrival. A few hotels border the main road leading to the park. There are also some pricier hotels inside the park; arrange a reservation to be guaranteed a room. If you are stuck in Zhangjiajie City overnight, try the **Doule Hotel** (dōulè bīnguǎn; 都乐宾馆), 1 Renmin Lu, opposite the long-distance bus station. (☎822 2921. Singles Y120; doubles and triples Y240.) At most Zhangjiajie hotels, bargaining is a possibility—test your luck.

Zhangjiajie Hotel (zhāngjiājiè bīnguǎn; 张家界宾馆; ☎571 2388; fax 571 2816), on the left side of the road about 100m before the last bus stop. 3-bed dorms Y15; singles and doubles Y420.

Jinbianyan Hotel (jīnbiānyán fàndiàn; 金鞭岩饭店; ☎571 2362), closer to the park entrance than the Zhangjiajie Hotel. The hotel has a good Cantonese breakfast and is one of the best places in the park area to book rafting or sightseeing tours. Doubles Y120, with bath Y240; triples Y270.

Pipaxi Hotel (pípāxī bīnguǎn; 琵琶溪宾馆; ☎571 8888; fax 571 2257), on the right side of the road as you enter the park area. Quieter and more comfortable than most other accommodations in the park. Singles and doubles Y280-548; triples Y300.

🍴🎵 FOOD AND ENTERTAINMENT

Although there are some ethnic Miaos in the area, Tujia restaurants predominate in Zhangjiajie. The restaurants near the Golden Rice Bowl Restaurant serve a variety of foods, ranging from Mao's family tofu to dumplings.

🏮The Comrade Bar (tóngzhì bā; 同志吧), on Bei Zheng Jie. Despite China's turn toward market capitalism, the Comrade Bar does its best to keep socialism sexy. With its Communist chic theme and a vast selection of drinks and snacks, this place is packed every night with wanna-be pop stars singing their favorite Chinese tunes. The staff is superfriendly, too. Open daily 11am-2am.

Golden Rice Bowl Restaurant (jīn fàn wǎn jiǔlóu; 金饭碗酒楼; ☎571 2688), in a 2-story bamboo building overlooking the stream opposite the Zhangjiajie Hotel. This place specializes in Tujia food, but the best item is the *tudou bing* (potato croquettes; 土豆饼). Also a great place to sip a cup of tea or coffee and to snack on melon seeds. Entrees Y8-40. Open daily 8am-midnight.

🏔 HIKING ZHANGJIAJIE

Zhangjiajie National Forest Park (zhǎngjiājiè guójiā sēnlín gōngyuán; 张家界国家森林公园), the realm of the Zhang family, is a surreal world. On the surface, a forest of tree-covered sandstone pillars towers above mist-shrouded ravines, pristine mountain pools, and thundering rapids, while underneath another forest of stalagtites fills palatial caverns fed by underground rivers and waterfalls. *(Park ☎571 2229. Y62; you can remain in the park for several days without paying an additional fee.)* Travel agencies arrange half- and full-day whitewater rafting trips (generally Y120-160, plus Y35-40 for transport to the rapids) and cave tours (Y35-40) in the northeastern part of the park.

Hiking trails begin just beyond the main entrance, or hop on a free minibus to **Huangshizhai Mountain** (huángshízhài; 黄石寨). At 990m, Huangshizhai is the highest point in Zhangjiajie, and on a good day offers spectacular views of the forests that dot the rugged landscape. Huangshizhai and **Jinbianxi** (金鞭溪) are the most popular scenic areas, which means two things: the best scenery and the most tourists. Walking up and riding the cable car down is a good way to avoid the throngs of tourists who tend to do it the other way around. *(Cable car runs daily 8am-6pm. Y47 up, Y37 down, Y74 round-trip.)* Many scenic spots are surrounded by "temples" that charge an additional fee—don't bother unless you've got plenty of spare change, as most of the temples at Zhangjiajie are really just souvenir shops in disguise. Maps (Y3) point out the major hiking paths, but the more obscure trails usually make for more thrilling treks. Be forewarned that wild animals do roam the forests of Zhangjiajie, most notably the infamous "five-step snake." After being bitten, victims take five steps and...well, you get the idea.

If you have some time to spend in Zhangjiajie City, the **Cengguang Temple** (céngguāng chánsì; 曾光禅寺), on Jiefang Lu between Bei Zheng Jie and Lingyuan Lu, is a hidden treasure. Talk to the Daoist fortune teller for a glimpse into your future (Y40) or relax to strains of traditional Tujia music. Antiques and traditional furniture are also sold here. *(☎ 822 2824. Open daily 8am-6pm. Y10.)*

HUBEI 湖北

Deep in the heart of the Yangzi River region, Hubei province has long been at the mercy of the river and its many tributaries. Even as the river brings yearly flooding and occasional disaster, it is also the source of livelihood for those living along its banks, bringing trade, industry, and now tourists from the wealthier coastal provinces to the interior of the country. The Yangzi meets the Han River at Wuhan, the capital and cultural center of the province. Farther upstream near Yichang, the Three Gorges form a magnificent backdrop for the ferries that cruise down the river. As one moves toward the northwest, the scenery turns wild and rugged, while much of the region south of the Yangzi is given over to industrial production and high tech zones. As the "Gateway to Nine Provinces," Hubei is central China's transportation hub; most travelers to the area are bound to spend some time here. Summer weather can be brutal, but fortunately, a plentiful supply of watermelon and heaps of local hospitality temper the stifling summer heat.

WUHAN 武汉 ☎027

Situated at the confluence of the Han and Yangzi rivers in the heart of China, Wuhan owes much of its development to its position halfway along the shipping

lanes of the Yangzi. The area has a history over 3000 years old and figures prominently in the colorful novel *Romance of the Three Kingdoms* (see p. 37), but it is
probably best remembered for the events of the last two centuries. In 1842, the
Treaty of Nanjing opened the district of Hankou to foreign trade, and the city's
European architecture is a visible reminder of its five foreign concessions. During
the 1911 Revolution, bombings and uprisings marred Wuhan's prosperous facade,
nearly leveling several parts of the city, and periodic upheavals wreaked havoc in
the city until the end of the Cultural Revolution. During the hot, humid summer
months, torrential rains and the threat of flooding test the manpower and
resources of this city of nearly five million. Thus far, Wuhan has continued to blossom, and today an increasing number of foreign and Chinese visitors are coming in
search of the financial and cultural riches that this crucial city has to offer.

◢ TRANSPORTATION

Airplanes: Tianhe International Airport (tiānhé guójì jīchǎng; 天河国际机场; ☎581
8222) is about 30km northwest of central Hankou. Buses (35-45min., 10 per day
6:30am-5pm) leave from the **China Southern Hubei Airlines office** (zhōngguó nánfāng
hángkōng húběi gōngsī; 中国南方航空湖北公司), 1 Hangkong Lu (☎8361 1756).
Open daily 8am-9pm. The **CAAC Booking Service Center** (wǔhàn tiānhé jīchǎng
shòupiào fúwù zhōngxīn; 武汉天河机场售票服务中心), 1087 Jiefang Dadao,
Hankou (☎8360 2228). MC, Visa accepted. Open 24hr. **Wuhan Airlines Booking
Office** (wǔhàn hángkōng gōngsī shòupiào chù;武汉航空公司售票处;☎8364
6425), farther down Jiefang Dadao. Open daily 8am-8pm. To: **Beijing** (3-4 per day,
Y860); **Chengdu** (3-6 per day, Y730); **Chongqing** (1-4 per day, Y630); **Guangzhou** (6-
7 per day, Y740); **Guilin** (1-3 per day, Y620); **Hefei** (1-3 per day, Y290); **Kunming** (2-
5 per day, Y1050); **Nanjing** (2-3 per day, Y580); **Shanghai** (6-9 per day, Y650); and
Xian (2-5 per day, Y550).

Trains: Almost all trains passing through and most originating in Wuhan stop at both
Hankou and Wuchang, about 30min. apart. In general, more trains pass through
Wuchang. Prices listed are for A/C trains. **Wuchang Train Station** (wǔchāng huǒchē
zhàn; 武昌火车站; ☎8887 1161), along Zhongshan Lu and not far past Ziyang Lu. To:
Beijing (12-16 hr., 13 per day); **Chengdu** (27hr., 10:30pm); **Changsha** (4hr.); **Chong-
qing** (24hr., 2 per day); **Fuzhou** (22hr., 2 per day); **Guangzhou** (16hr., 11 per day);
Kunming (44hr., 2 per day); **Nanchang** (9hr., 6 per day); **Shanghai** (19hr., 11:52am);
Shiyan (9hr., 2 per day); **Xian** (14-16 hr., 3 per day); and **Xiangfan** (5-6hr., 3 per day).
Hankou Train Station (hànkǒu huǒchē zhàn; 汉口火车站; ☎8585 0932), at the
intersection of Fazhan Dadao and Qingnian Lu. To: **Beijing** (12-16hr., 10 per day);
Chongqing (24hr., 2 per day); **Fuzhou** (22hr., 1:37pm); **Guangzhou** (16hr., 6 per day);
Harbin (10:58am); **Hefei** (10hr., 8:16pm); **Kunming** (44hr., 2 per day); **Nanchang**
(9hr., 4 per day); and **Shiyan**.

Buses: Wuchang Long-distance Bus Station (wǔchāng chángtú qìchē zhàn; 武昌长途
汽车站), 519 Zhongshan Lu (☎8804 4703), 1 block from Ziyang Lu in the opposite
direction from the train station. To: **Hefei** (Iveco minibuses: 9-11hr., 6 per day, Y140;
regular buses: 2 per day; seat Y63, sleeper Y96); **Nanjing** (14hr., 4 per day, Y135-
160); and **Yichang** (4-5hr., every hr. 7am-6pm, Y90; 5 Iveco minibuses per day, Y61).
Wuchang's **Fujiapo Bus Station** (fùjiāpō qìchē zhàn; 付家坡汽车站; ☎8789 8687),
on Wuluo Lu near Da Dong Men and Zhongshan Lu has buses to **Yichang** (every 30min.
6:30am-8pm) as well as less frequent departures to destinations such as: **Guangzhou**
(24hr., 3 per day, Y120); **Guilin** (24hr., 1 per day, Y160); and **Shanghai** (20-22hr., 1
per day, Y160). In Hankou, long-distance buses leave from all over the place, but a
good number depart from the ferry terminal on Yanjiang Lu for Hefei, Jiujiang, Nanjing,
Shanghai, and Yichang, among other places.

Boats: Wuhan Passenger Ferry Terminal (wǔhàn kèyùn gǎng; 武汉客运港; ☎8283
9546), on Yanjiang Dadao, Hankou. As you enter the ticket hall, an inquiry booth will be
on your right; timetables and ticket windows are against the back wall. Open daily 7am-
10:30pm. Prices ranges are for 3rd-1st classes. To: **Chongqing** (62hr., 1-5 per day,

Y229-1082); **Jiujiang** (9-10hr., 3-4 per day, Y48-200); **Nanjing** (33-36hr., 2-4 per day, Y112-476); and **Shanghai** (43hr., 11am and 7pm, Y163-698).

Local Transportation: Most **buses** run from around 6am to 9pm. Fare Y1. **Bus #10** links the train stations in Wuchang and Hankou, and other routes extend far beyond the main commercial districts. There are also three tourist bus lines (Y1), which run to sights and nearby scenic areas. **Ferries** link Hankou and Wuchang, with frequent departures from the **Hankou docks** along Yanjiang Lu and the **Zhonghua Lu** and **Hanyangmen docks** in Wuchang (10-15min., every 20min. 6am-11pm, Y1-4).

Taxis: Base fare Y8, each additional km Y1.4. Fares in Wuhan can be quite high, and taxis don't get you to your destination much faster than city buses—indeed, often the traffic is slow enough that pedestrians seem to fly by. From either train station to central Hankou around Zhongshan Dadao Y20-30.

✳🛈 ORIENTATION AND PRACTICAL INFORMATION

Wuhan is divided into three main districts, all linked by bridges: **Hankou** (汉口) and **Hanyang** (汉阳) north of the Yangzi River, separated by the Han River, and **Wuchang** (武昌) to the southeast. The city, originally three separate towns, is composed of the three districts of Hankou, Hanyang, and Wuchang. Hankou, a bustling commercial center, lies just across the Han River from Hanyang, the smallest of the three, a quiet center of light industry. On the southern banks of the Yangzi, Wuchang has been transformed from an ancient walled city into a sprawling settlement that eventually recedes into greener pastures and the East Lake Scenic Area. Hanyang's main commercial streets are **Yingwu Dadao** (鹦鹉大道) and **Hanyang Dadao** (汉阳大道), which runs roughly perpendicular to the Yangzi. Hankou is full of shops and offices, especially along **Zhongshan Dadao** (中山大道) and **Jiefang Dadao** (解放大道), parallel to each other and about 1km apart. The train station is in the northern part of the Hankou district, and the main docks line the Yangzi along **Yanjiang Dadao** (沿江大道). In Wuchang, **Zhongshan Lu** (中山路), which goes past the train station, and **Wuluo Lu** (武珞路) are important thoroughfares. The **East Lake Scenic Area** covers much of the southeast portion of the district.

Travel Agencies: Wuhan is chock-full of travel agencies, especially in the area around the ferry passenger terminal and on Jiefang Dadao in Hankou, and around the train and bus stations in Wuchang. **CITS,** 26 Taibei Yi Lu, 7th Fl., Hankou (☎8578 2124), 5min. east of Xinhua Lu, opposite the Marriott Hotel. Open daily 8am-5pm. **CTS,** 142 Yanjiang Dadao (☎8285 5259), Hankou, across from the ferry terminal. Open daily 8:30am-7:30pm. The **Hubei CITS Ticketing Center** (húběi shěng zhōngguó guójì lǚxíngshè hángkōng fúwù zhōngxīn;湖北省中国国际旅行社航空服务中心), 27 Jianghan Lu, Hankou (☎8283 1494 or 8280 4814), a few blocks from Yanjiang Dadao, is currently closed due to construction.

Bank of China: 1021 Zhongshan Dadao, Hankou (☎8283 5605), at Jianghan Lu. Exchanges traveler's checks and major foreign currencies at counters #11 and 12 (M-F 9am-noon and 2-5pm). Open daily 8am-5:30pm. Most expensive hotels will also change money, but often not traveler's checks.

Bookstore: Xinhua Bookstore, 896 Zhongshan Dadao (☎8278 4963), Hankou, at Jianghan Lu. A large selection of books, including a decent stock of English-language novels and translations of Chinese classics, plus *X-Files* in Chinese. Open M 9:30am-5pm, Tu-Su 9am-7pm.

PSB: 206 Shengli Jie, Hankou.

Internet Access: You can hardly throw a rock in Wuhan without hitting an Internet club. **Wuhan Window Trade Information Club Internet Club** (wǔhàn zhīchuāng wàimào xìnxī jùlèbù;武汉之疮外贸信息俱乐部), Xinminchong Leyuan, 608 Zhongshan Dadao, 3rd Fl., Hankou (☎8754 3890), across from Qianjin Er Lu. F-Sa 7pm-midnight "English and Internet" gathering. Y5 per hr. Open daily 10am-midnight. **Minzu Internet Bar** (mínzú wǎngbā; 民族网吧), on Zhongshan Lu about 100m east of the Wuhan Window Internet Club, on the 2nd floor. Y4-12 per hr. Open 24hr. **Youbang Internet Bar**

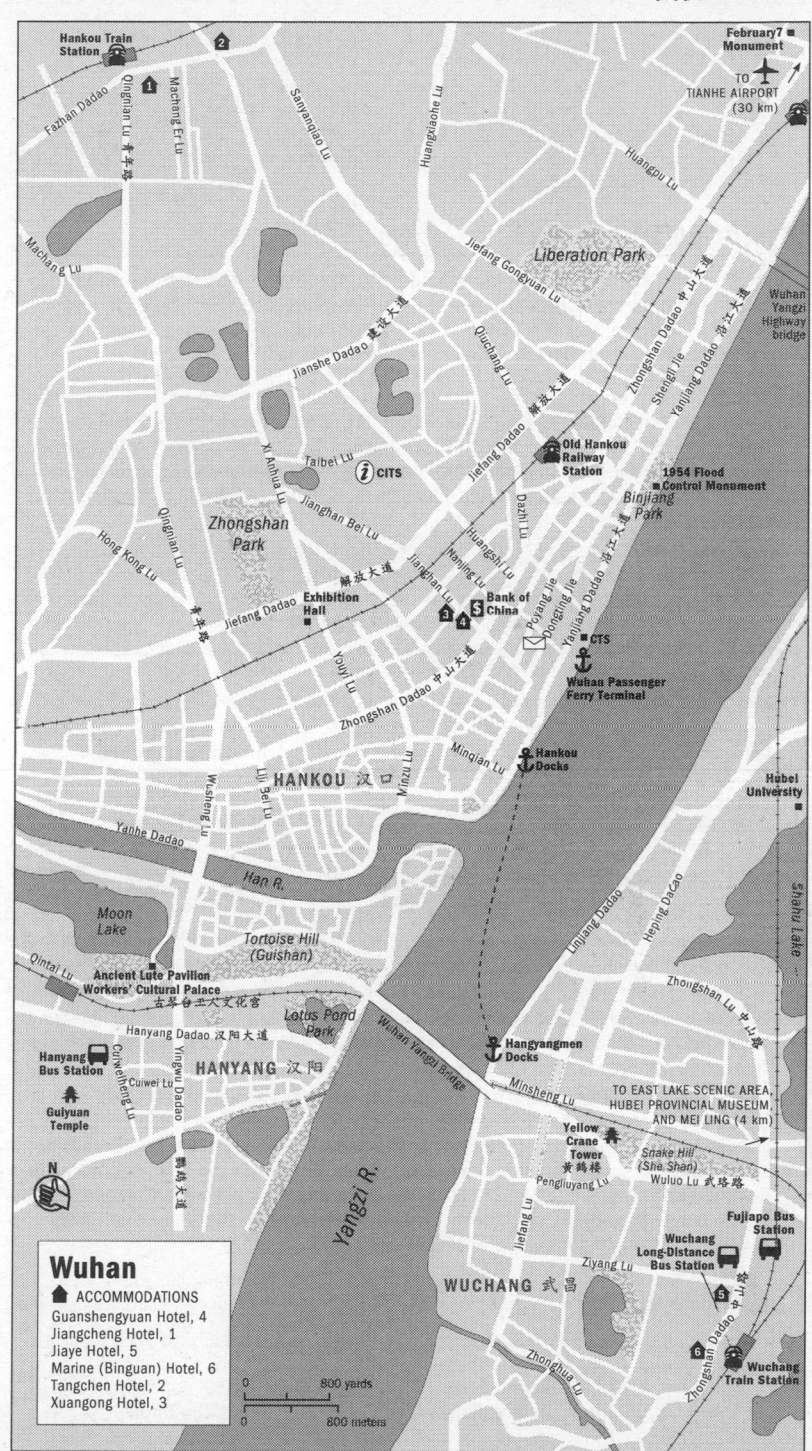

Wuhan

⬆ ACCOMMODATIONS
Guanshengyuan Hotel, 4
Jiangcheng Hotel, 1
Jiaye Hotel, 5
Marine (Binguan) Hotel, 6
Tangchen Hotel, 2
Xuangong Hotel, 3

0   800 yards
0   800 meters

YANGZI BASIN

(yǒubāng wǎngbā; 友邦网吧), 258 Ziyang Lu, Wuhan (☎ 8873 0059), across from the restaurant with the large red sign saying "555." Y4 per hr. Open 24hr.

Post Office: The **International Department** (guójì yíngyè tīng; 国际营业厅; ☎ 8283 0766) is in the post office at the corner of Shanghai Lu and Dongting Jie, Hankou. EMS and Poste Restante (windows #12 or 13) available. Open daily 8am-6pm. In Wuchang, there is a branch immediately to the right upon exiting the train station. Open daily 8am-6:30pm. **Postal Code:** 430014.

ACCOMMODATIONS

Most of Wuhan's cheapest hotels are still off limits to foreigners, but promotions during the summer and other times—and the fact that the city isn't too heavily touristed—help to bring the prices down. Accommodations are plentiful in the **Zhongshan Dadao** area in Hankou and near the Wuchang Train Station.

HANKOU

Guanshengyuan Hotel (guānshēngyuán dàjiǔdiàn; 冠生园大酒店), 109 Jianghan Lu (☎ 8277 9069, ext. 8200), about 1 block beyond Zhongshan Dadao in the direction away from the Yangzi. In the heart of Hankou's main shopping district, this establishment offers nothing particularly special to go with that attached bath. Singles Y138; doubles Y168; triples Y188.

Xuangong Hotel (xuángōng fàndiàn; 璇宫饭店), 57 Jianghan Lu (☎ 8281 0365; fax 8281 6942). From Zhongshan Dadao, head up Jianghan Lu 2 blocks, moving away from the river; the hotel is on the left. The classical European facade leads to modestly-sized yet well-appointed rooms, pleasant staff, and cheap room service. Try not to get a room that looks out over the construction site outside. Breakfast included. 10% service charge. Singles Y228; doubles Y288; triples Y680.

Jiangcheng Hotel (jiāngchéng dàjiǔdiàn; 江城大酒店, ☎ 8587 6508; fax 8587 8583), immediately to the left as you exit the train station. Although this hotel is undeniably convenient for travelers, its prices reflect its 3-star status. Rooms are pleasant but not spectacular. Try bargaining. Singles and doubles Y398.

Tangcheng Hotel (tángchéng bīnguǎn; 唐城宾馆), 1 Guangchang Dong Lu (☎/fax 8588 6689). From the train station exit, turn left and walk to the end of the street, and then turn right; the hotel is a block away on the left. Although the Tangcheng is not officially open to foreigners, Chinese-speaking foreigners might snag a clean room with A/C. 6-bed dorms Y40; singles with bath Y188; doubles with bath Y168-228; triples Y218.

WUCHANG

Jiaye Hotel (jiāyè bīnguǎn; 嘉叶宾馆), 426 Zhongshan Lu (☎ 8807 4679, ext. 8118), at Ziyang Lu, not far from the train station. The bright lights outside make the place look like the Moulin Rouge, but there's little inside to make hearts race. Rooms are fairly clean. Proximity to the station means that rooms often fill up by 9 or 10pm, if not earlier. Reserve ahead. Singles Y128; doubles Y168; triples Y158.

Marine (Binguan) Hotel (hánghǎi bīnguǎn; 航海宾馆), 460 Zhongshan Lu (☎ 8804 3396, ext. 8375), across the street and about a block to the left after you exit the train station. Pay attention to the characters, as the nearby Marine (Fandian) Hotel does not accept foreigners. The carpets in the rooms and the uniforms of the floor attendants are blue, keeping with the nautical theme. The spacious, newly refurbished rooms and baths, however, should leave guests with no reason to turn the same color. Singles Y128; doubles Y138-148; triples Y168-180.

FOOD AND ENTERTAINMENT

Although Wuhan doesn't claim a distinctive taste as its own, catfish from East Lake is a popular treat. Floating restaurants line **Bayi Lu,** near East Lake. Also in Wuchang, several of the side streets off **Ziyang Lu** feature dense concentrations of street stands. In Hankou, **Jiefang Dadao** and especially **Zhongshan Dadao** feature a mixture of stylish establishments and local and international fast food. **Jianghan Lu, Nanjing Lu,** and nearby alleyways are crowded with people day and night.

The nightlife in Wuhan isn't as happening as one might expect in such a large city. A stroll down **Zhongshan Dadao** or **Xianggang Lu** leads to a few bars and clubs, and a walk up **Jianghan Lu** leads to a karaoke lover's pot of gold. More interesting are the **night markets,** centered around Jianghan Lu and Nanjing Lu, where many residents while away their evening hours. Vendors peddle clothing, footwear, food, jewelry, and more to anyone who's interested. You may see some locals heading to beauty parlors in the late hours--be aware, though, that many such establishments don't just cater to women, and don't give more than facials.

■ **Four Seasons Dumpling House** (sìjì jiǎozi guǎn; 四季饺子馆), 241 Pengliuyang, Wuchang (☎8886 7023). Not far from the Pengliuyang bus stop, about 5min. from either Jiefang Lu or Wuluo Lu. This well-known spot offers almost every kind of dumpling imaginable, including mushroom-pork and tomato-garlic. 8 scrumptious dumplings, an individual pack of napkins, and a toothpick Y1.6-6. Open daily 10:30am-10:30pm.

Laotongcheng Restaurant (lǎotōngchéng dòupí dàwáng; 老通城豆皮大王), 1 Dazhi Lu, Hankou, at the corner of Zhongshan Dadao across from Tianjin Lu. Try food for the masses in one of Mao's old haunts. The Pepsi ads might make him roll over in his mausoleum, but the food's affordable. Stuffed bean curd (dòupí; 豆皮) Y3-6, dim sum Y0.5-5, and Peking duck Y40. Open daily 6am-10pm, 2nd floor 7am-9pm.

STL, 1130 Zhongshan Dadao (☎8279 5278), at the corner of Huangxing Lu, Hankou. The tables at this bar are full of Wuhan's 20- and 30-somethings chatting away over milk pearl tea (Y11), exotic juices, or a spectrum of beers. Open daily 9am-1:30am.

👁 SIGHTS

Although Wuhan is famous for happenings of the Three Kingdoms period (AD 220-280), most present-day sights are related to 20th-century events.

HANKOU

Zhongshan Dadao served as the center of the foreign concessions in the early 20th century; now the swarming shopping district is the navel of consumer culture. Closer to the Yangzi River, Yanjiang Dadao leads past the old **Customs House** and several open-air markets (including one filled with carrier pigeons) before reaching the hulking **Yangzi Ferry Terminal. Binjiang Park** (bīnjiāng gōngyuán; 滨江公园), at the intersection of Yiyuan Lu opposite the city government building, contains the towering **1954 Flood Control Monument.** While summer rains are a perennial threat and the floods of 1998 brought destruction to much of China, the toll was not nearly as great as that of the floods several decades before.

HANYANG

GUIYUAN TEMPLE (guīyuán sì; 归元寺). The cavernous, incense-filled halls of this large Buddhist monastery are often crowded with visitors filing past to admire hundreds of smaller sculptures in the **Arhat Hall** or the white jade statue of Sakyamuni. A vegetarian restaurant is also on the premises. (*At the corner of Cuiwei Lu and Cuiweiheng Lu. Take bus #61 from the train station to Zhongjiacun. From Yingwu Dadao, turn right on Cuiwei Lu and walk for several blocks. Open daily 8am-5pm. Y3.*)

ANCIENT LUTE PAVILION WORKERS' CULTURAL PALACE (gǔ qín tái gōngrén wénhuà gōng; 古琴台工人文化宫). A nice setting for a peaceful walk, even if the imaginative lute-playing mushrooms always seem to be broken. Part of the palace overlooks the nearby **Moon Lake.** (*☎8483 4187. Open daily 7:30am-4pm. Y5.*) **Tortoise Hill** (guī shān; 龟山) marks the spot where the heroic efforts of Yu (see p. 8) saved the people from flooding 4000 years ago. (*Just beyond the intersection of Guishan Bei Lu, Qintai Lu, and Yingwu Dadao. Tourist bus #1 and buses #507 and 701 stop at Guqintai. Open daily 8am-10pm. Y5.*)

WUCHANG

YELLOW CRANE TOWER (huáng hè lóu; 黄鹤楼). Just beyond the **Great Yangzi Bridge** (chángjiāng dàqiáo; 长江大桥), this park affords an impressive view. Built by Huang Wu in AD 223, it has been the subject of over 1000 poems and numerous landscape paintings. Gardens, ponds, pagodas, and inscriptions contribute to the setting's natural beauty, although the sun beats down on visitors like a fly-swatter on a mosquito. *(On Wuluo Lu. Tourist bus #1 stops outside. ☎8887 7330. Open daily 7am-6pm; in winter 7:30am-5:30pm. Y30, children Y15.)*

HUBEI PROVINCIAL MUSEUM (húběi shěng bówùguǎn; 湖北省博物馆). This museum's collection is devoted to the objects unearthed from the 2400-year-old tomb of Marquis Yi of the Zeng State. With over 7000 tomb artifacts on display, it's no wonder there's little room for other exhibits. Chime bells, zithers, and other musical instruments are among the finds, although the only sounds you'll actually hear here are those of the plastic booties given to each visitor. *(On Donghu Lu. The entrance is hard to miss if backtracking from the East Lake entrance. Tourist bus #1 stops at Sheng Bowuguan. Good English narration. Open daily 9am-5pm; tickets sold 9-11:30am and 1:30-4:30pm. Y20, students Y12.)*

EAST LAKE (dōng hú; 东湖). A watery respite from the hurried pace of downtown, East Lake and its surrounding greenery offer city-weary travelers a chance for boating, hiking, and even swimming, though the rather rank waters might dissuade some would-be athletes. *(In the eastern part of Wuchang. Bus #14 from the Zhonghua Lu docks terminates here; tourist bus #1 also stops here. Open 24hr. Y10, children Y5.)*

MAO ZEDONG'S VILLA (méilǐng biéshù; 梅岭别墅). Unlike the steady stream of dignitaries that the Chairman once received, today only the occasional slipper-clad visitor disturbs the dust at Mei Ling Villa, one of Mao Zedong's favorite haunts. It was here that Mao composed his oft-quoted ode to "Swimming." Plenty of photographs bear witness to the era. *(10min. beyond the Provincial Museum. Backtracking from the terminus of buses #14, 701, and 710 for about 10min. leads to the turnoff; look for the large billboard. ☎8679 6106. Open daily 8am-7pm. Y10.)*

YICHANG 宜昌   ☎0717

The giant Gezhou Dam rumbles in the distance and the gargantuan Three Gorges Dam construction project looms farther upstream from this hydroelectric town. Yichang marks the end of the Yangzi canyonlands and the first disembarkment point for most river cruise passengers. Other than a few colonial-style buildings from the foreign concession established in 1877, the city holds little of interest to travelers; most press on to Chongqing or Wuhan or journey to Wudangshan. For more on the Three Gorges, see p. 646.

▐ TRANSPORTATION

Airplanes: Three Gorges Airport (sānxiá jīchǎng; 三峡机场) has flights to about 10 domestic destinations. The airport bus (Y20) picks up passengers approximately 2hr. in advance from the International and Three Gorges Hotels. To: **Beijing** (1-2 per day, Y1040); **Chengdu** (1 per day W-M, Y630); **Chongqing** (1-3 per day Su-F, Y390); **Guangzhou** (M, W-Th, and Sa 8:20am; Y770); **Nanjing** (M, W, and Sa 8:30am; Y650); and **Shanghai** (1-2 per day Tu-Su, Y860).

Trains: Yichang Train Station (yíchāng huǒchē zhàn; 宜昌火车站; ☎644 5242) is at the intersection of Yunji Lu and Dongshan Dadao. The stairs up to the station are on Dongshan Dadao, on the right side of the construction around the tunnel at the head of Yunji Lu. Tickets are sold on the left side of the station daily 5am-10pm; be prepared to push your way to the window. To: **Beijing** (21½hr., 1-2 per day, Y298); **Guangzhou** (25½hr., 1 per day; Y330); and **Xian** (20hr., 1 per day, Y172).

Buses: Yichang Bus Station (yíchāng qìchē zhàn; 宜昌汽车站; ☎644 5314), on Dongshan Dadao, about 1½ blocks from the train station. Open 24hr. The "English and Dumbness Window" is especially helpful for those who need to know departure times and ticket prices. To: **Hefei** (3 per day 11am-9:20pm, Y162); **Shiyan** (several per day 8am-6pm, Y83-90); **Wuhan** (every 30min.-1hr. 7am-8pm, Y88-108); **Xiangfan** (several per day, Y45); and **Xingshan** (every 20min. 6:30am-6pm, Y29-35). Buses to Wuhan also leave from the docks and from some hotels and travel agencies.

Boats: Dagongqiao Amphibious Passenger Terminal (dàgōngqiáo shuǐlù kèyùn zhàn; 大公桥水陆客运站; ☎622 2714), off Yanjiang Dadao near Shengli Si Lu. Also sells tickets to cruises of the Three Gorges and the Little Three Gorges. To **Chongqing** (7 per day 7am-9pm) and **Jiujiang** (9pm) via **Wuhan**.

Local Transportation: Buses run 6am-8pm. Fare Y0.5. From the dock, bus **#2** zips along Yanjiang Dadao, and **#3** and **4** run past the train station. Buses **#6** and **11** run from Gezhou Dam and the Three Gorges Hotel, respectively, to the long-distance bus station. **Taxi** base fare Y5, each additional km Y1.2. Most trips Y5-10, but be wary of drivers who try to avoid turning on the meter to charge a higher fare.

■✻🛈 ORIENTATION AND PRACTICAL INFORMATION

Yichang's compact city center occupies the northeast Yangzi bank, the edge of which is traced by **Yanjiang Dadao** (沿江大道). The docks are in the south, and the rail and bus stations are several blocks away from the river, off **Dongshan Dadao** (东山大道) roughly parallel to Yanjiang Dadao. Perpendicular to the river is **Yunji Lu** (云集路), the downtown street lined with stores, hotels, and entertainment options that spill onto **Jiefang Lu** (解放路) and **Yiling Dadao** (夷陵大道). The town's construction boom can make navigating a bit tricky, but since there really aren't a lot of places to go, it's not a major problem.

Travel Agencies: CITS, 18 Longkang Lu (☎622 0915; email yctgcits@public.yc.ht.cn). A few members of the helpful, courteous staff speak English. Open daily 8:30-11:30am and 2:30-5:30pm. **CITS Ticketing Center,** 2 Erma Lu (☎623 4567), is open 24hr. A number of travel agencies are also bunched along Yanjiang Dadao near the docks.

Bank of China: 10 Shengli Si Lu (☎623 6217), at Longkang Lu. Open M-F 8-11:30am and 2-6pm. The Taohualing and International Hotels have currency exchange counters, although the Taohualing does not exchange Australian or Canadian dollars.

PSB: Near the intersection of Xueyuan Jie and Huancheng Dong Lu. Open M-F 8:30am-noon and 2:30-5pm.

Hospital: No. 2 People's Hospital (dì èr rénmín yīyuàn; 第二人民医院; ☎673 2452), on Xiling Lu near Huancheng Lu.

Telephones: The main **China Telecom** (☎646 6999) is on Fusui Lu, next door to the post office. IDD service and pay phones available. Open daily 8am-10:30pm. Another branch is next to the post office at Yunji Lu and Yiling Dadao. Open daily 8am-5:30pm.

Internet Access: The main China Telecom on Fusui Lu has a room with about a dozen computers, on the right side of the office. Y3 per hr. Open daily 8am-10:30pm.

Post Office: The post office on Fusui Lu has EMS and Poste Restante. Open daily 8am-8pm. Another branch is at the northeast corner of the intersection of Yiling Dadao and Yunji Lu. Open daily 8am-6pm. **Postal Code:** 443000.

■▮🛈 ACCOMMODATIONS AND FOOD

The wealthy clientele that the Three Gorges attracts has jacked up Yichang's hotel rates; the best deals are along Yunji Lu, near the docks, or near the train station.

The lively riverfront restaurants and night market on **Taozhu Lu,** west of Yunji Lu, serve point-and-choose stir-fry platters for Y5-10 per person. A few hotpot restaurants also bubble up in the area. Around the train station, cheap food stands are strewn along **Dongshan Dadao** near the base of the steps with only a few restaurants directly in front of the station itself. The street just east of Fusui Lu and south of Yunji Lu, near the No. 1 City Hospital, is filled with fruit and vegetable stands, meat shops, and steamers of *mantou* and buns.

Yichang Railway Hotel (yíchāng tiělù dàjiǔdiàn; 宜昌铁路大酒店; ☎644 2980), in the train station square, immediately to the left of the station entrance. Do not take the steps down to Dongshan Dadao. Rooms have A/C, and some are quiet given the location. The bathrooms are a little grimy, so don't waste money on a private one. 3-bed dorms Y40; singles Y208; doubles Y168-188; triples Y210. MC, Visa accepted.

Taohualing Hotel (táohuālíng fàndiàn; 桃花岭饭店), 29 Yunji Lu (☎623 6666), east of Longkang Lu about halfway between the train station and the Yangzi River. Buses #3 and 4 stop at nearby Jiefang Lu. The cheapest rooms are a bit claustrophobic and not too pretty, but A/C keeps things cool. More expensive rooms have been renovated recently. All rooms have attached bath and use of indoor swimming pool (for a fee). Internet access and currency exchange. Breakfast included with more expensive rooms. Doubles Y120, in new building Y328-398.

Sunshine Hotel (yángguāng dàjiǔdiàn; 阳光大酒店), 1 Yunji Lu (☎644 6075, ext. 8181), across from the steps to the train station. Rooms have A/C and bath; the usual unattractive decor is in unusually good condition. Doubles Y118-230; triples Y135-225.

◐♬ SIGHTS AND ENTERTAINMENT

Yichang's main point of interest is the **Gezhou Dam** (gězhōu bà; 葛洲坝), north of the city and accessible by bus #8 from the corner of Jiefang Lu and Yunji Lu. Built in 1989 and soon to be dwarfed by the behemoth upriver, the 2.5km-wide, 70m-tall wall across the mouth of the Xiling Gorge is currently China's largest dam. Locals turn the nearby riverbanks into an informal swimming hole. The riverside heights provide for leisurely strolls and vistas of the grand, murky Yangzi, laden with river traffic. Closer to the city center, **Binjiang Park** (bīnjiāng gōngyuán; 滨江公园) stretches along the waterfront from Shengli Lu to Xiling Lu, and has a number of places to sit and watch the powerful Yangzi current.

On **Yunji Lu** close to the waterfront and on **Erma Lu,** a number of small bars with poorly spelled menus and overpriced drinks cater primarily to tourists.

XIANGFAN 襄樊　　　　　　　　　　☎0710

Few foreigners travel to Xiangfan. The city is devoted mainly to transport, building cars and shuttling passengers throughout the country by way of train, plane, and bus. If you're heading to Wudangshan, chances are you'll have the chance to spend a few hours or even a night in this pleasant (if unexciting) town.

✴🛈 ORIENTATION AND PRACTICAL INFORMATION

Xiangfan is a small city, made even smaller by the fact that most travelers don't need to venture very far away from the train or bus stations. The train station is in a large square just off **Qianjin Lu** (前进路), at the head of **Zhongyuan Lu** (中原路). About two blocks down Zhongyuan Lu, on the right side of the street, is the main bus station, and several other bus and minibus stations are scattered about. The entire area is filled with markets, restaurants, ticket agencies, and hostels.

Airplanes: The **airport** has a limited number of flights to: **Beijing** (Th and Su 3:50pm, Y 710); **Guangzhou** (W and Su 8:40pm, Y920); **Shanghai** (M and Th 2:35pm, Y860); and **Shenzhen** (Tu and Sa 3:30pm, Y870). **CAAC ticket office,** 44 Qianjin Lu (☎323 9213 or 325 6492), at Zhongyuan Lu. Open daily 7am-9pm.

Trains: Xiangfan Train Station (xiāngfán huǒchē zhàn; 襄樊火车站) is off a square at the intersection of Zhongyuan Lu and Qianjin Lu. The main ticket hall is on the right. Buy your tickets early, as sleepers can be extremely difficult to get even a couple of days in advance. Hard seat travelers, be forewarned: passengers line up at the station gates 30min. before departure, and then run en masse for the trains at frightening speeds. To: **Beijing; Chengdu** (22 hr.); **Chongqing** (18hr.); **Shanghai;** and **Wuhan.**

Buses: Xiangfan Bus Station (xiāngfán qìchē zhàn; 襄樊汽车站; ☎322 3345) is on Zhongyuan Lu, about 2 blocks from the train station. Ticket office open 24hr. Luggage storage available in the ticket hall, to the left of the entrance. To: **Changsha** (5½hr., 5:30pm, Y108); **Shiyan** (5hr., frequent departures 7am-6pm, Y29.5-38); **Wuhan** (5hr., 13 per day 6am-5:30pm, Y54); and **Yichang** (4hr., frequent departures 6am-5:40pm, Y45). **Minibuses** to Yichang and Shiyan also leave frequently from nearby depots.

Currency Exchange: None of the Bank of China branches exchanges foreign currency. The **Railway Grand Hotel** usually assists non-guests.

Post and Telecommunications: The train station branch (☎322 3457) is down the alley that runs next to the luggage storage office. EMS on the 1st floor; IDD service on the 2nd floor. Open daily 8am-6pm. **Postal Code:** 441003.

ACCOMMODATIONS AND FOOD

Although plenty of hostels on **Qianjin Lu** near the bus and train stations have rooms for Y20, foreigners risk being laughed out of the lobby if they try to get one. Still, for such a cheap deal, it probably doesn't hurt to try.

The streets around the train stations are filled with small stores selling snack foods. There are also a few restaurants with outdoor seating, as well as some dumpling houses and a Muslim restaurant. **Tiege Dumpling House** (tiěgē jiǎozi guǎn; 铁哥饺子馆), down to the right as you exit the train station), serves eight dumplings for Y1-3. (☎322 0043, ext. 6833. Open daily 11am-2pm and 5-10pm.)

Post and Telecom Hotel (yóudiàn bīnguǎn; 邮电宾馆), 111 Qianjin Lu (☎321 2878). From the train station, turn right past the luggage storage; the entrance is on the left side, just beyond the post office. This hotel has just about everything a traveler could want: clean rooms with bath, gleaming tile floors, charming service, and an excellent location. Singles Y148-168; doubles Y128-218. Credit cards accepted.

Aeolus Hotel (fēngshén bīnguǎn; 风神宾馆), 36 Qianjin Lu (☎322 3483 or 322 4035; fax 322 4968), across the street and about a block to the right from the train station. The fake plastic-wood floors and orange bedcovers are surprisingly inoffensive, as is everything else in this clean, if slightly run-down and unexciting, option. Rooms have all standard amenities. Singles Y198; doubles Y168; triples Y180.

Railway Grand Hotel (tiělù dàjiǔdiàn; 铁路大酒店), 46 Qianjin Lu (☎322 0043 or 322 0454; fax 322 1774), across from the train station. This upscale option has French-speaking staff, an ornate lobby fountain, and comfortable rooms with plenty of amenities and spacious bathrooms. Doubles Y228-388; triples Y368. Credit cards accepted.

WUDANGSHAN 武当山　　　　☎0719

Wudangshan is one of Daoism's most holy mountains, with a stealthy, precise beauty. The fog curls its way about craggy cliffs, slipping around trees and rocks as it moves steadily forward, creating an almost haunted atmosphere. Its temples and palaces are scattered about, built more vertically than horizontally to accommodate the mountain's steep slope. Primarily famed as the birthplace of one of Daoism's deities, the Great Emperor Zhen Wu, the mountain is also known as the birthplace of Wudang boxing. Many schools around the village teach this art, and even more souvenir stands sell various instruments and teaching manuals. One is never far away from evidence of war, be it in the exhibits on Wudang boxing, the fortress-like temples, or the dark forests. Wudangshan is a beautiful place, if unsettling at times, and is certainly worth a visit.

ORIENTATION AND PRACTICAL INFORMATION

The Wudangshan range stretches across northwestern Hubei between Xiangfan and Shiyan. Most travelers to Wudangshan stay in the city, which is about 25km from the main peak. One main street runs through town, going east to Xiangfan and west to Shiyan. Up on the mountain, the road ends at a plaza, where most of the hotels and restaurants are.

Trains: Wudangshan Train Station (wŭdāngshān huŏchē zhàn; 武当山火车站) is about 1km south of the main road, past the bus station. The ticket office is rarely manned; to catch a train, just check the timetable, go to the platform to wait for your train, and buy a ticket once on board. If trains arrive early and no one is there, they often do not stick around, and if they're late, they tend not to stop at all. To: **Beijing** (11:31am, Y66); **Shiyan** (3 per day, Y2); **Xiangfan** (4 per day, Y8); and **Wuhan** (9:59pm, Y27).

Buses: A bus either to **Shiyan** (Y10) or **Xiangfan** (Y30), where train connections may be made more easily, might be the best bet. Once again, the ticket office is rarely manned. Buses run up and down the main road, trolling for passengers.

Bank of China: Just west of the bridge, on the main road (☎ 566 6154). Exchanges cash only. Open daily 9am-5pm.

Bookstore: Sanwei Bookstore (sānwèi shūdiàn; 三味书店), down the street opposite the Laoying Hotel, on the left, has an English corner with a small selection of English novels and language texts. Owners Mr. Shiyi (Victor) Gu and his wife both speak English and are happy to offer advice or tours around town.

Internet Access: Xiangkeji Internet Bar (xiăngkèjī wăngbā; 想科技网吧; ☎ 566 8181), on the main road, about 25m east of the Xuanwu Hotel, across from the movie theater. Y4 per hr. Open daily 7am-11pm.

Post and Telecommunications: ☎ 566 0414. From the bridge, go 2 blocks west along the main road and turn right. Continue about 200m; the office is on the left. IDD service available. Open daily 7:30am-6pm; in winter 8am-5pm. **Postal Code:** 442714.

ACCOMMODATIONS AND FOOD

Hotels on the mountain tend to be a little more expensive and a little more rustic than those in town. Travelers will have to switch from a long-distance bus to a local minibus to get there, though. Staying amid the dirt and mess of the town makes it easier to drop off packs and make a quick daytrip of the mountain.

A number of restaurants and stalls line the streets that run off the main road, selling scallion pancakes (Y0.5), vegetable stir-fry (Y5-10), and small loaves of sweetbread (Y2). Some hotels also have restaurants that offer sit-down meals for under Y20. At night, the normally mild air has a habit of turning chilly, and most residents turn in early—although there are a few arcades around for the kid in you.

Laoying Hotel (lăoyíng fàndiàn; 老营饭店; ☎ 566 5349 or 566 5347), on the left side of the main road, across the bridge. Rooms range from ornate (3-room singles with desks, huge beds, and large bathrooms with jets in the tub) to ordinary (slightly musty rooms with stained carpets and grotty bathrooms); most have A/C and all have 24hr. hot water. 3-bed dorms Y105; singles Y140-180; doubles Y120-140; triples Y150-180.

Baihui Hotel (☎ 568 9111), about 500m before the end of the mountain road, on the left. The views might not be spectacular, but the spiral staircase isn't bad. Rooms are clean and in good condition, with TV, phone, and large bathtubs. 4-bed dorms Y40; singles Y160-200; doubles Y68-100; triples Y70.

Xuanwu (Binguan) Hotel (xuánwŭ bīnguăn; 玄武宾馆; ☎ 568 1975), just across from the Baihui Hotel, near the end of the mountain road. Perfect for Big Bird: rooms are big, clean, and ever so yellow, with decent bathrooms and 24hr. hot water. Doubles Y120-200; triples Y120-240.

Xuanwu (Dajiudian) Hotel (xuánwŭ dàjiŭdiàn; 玄武大酒店; ☎ 566 5347), in the city, across from the road leading to the train station, on the north side of the street. Large groups of loud tourists often congregate here, which you'll quickly discover through the paper-thin walls. Lucky foreigners may be able to share rooms with friends, too—if your friends are ants. The hotel equivalent of a hard seat. Bargain. Doubles Y100.

◤ CLIMBING WUDANGSHAN

The main gate to the **Wudangshan Scenic Area** (wǔdāngshān fēngjǐng qū; 武当山风景区) is just east of town. *(Open daily 7am-5:30pm. ☎556 5396. Y51.)* Minibuses from town to the trailhead cost Y20-30. On rainy days, though, drivers may try to charge up to Y60, simply because they have a tidy monopoly. From the main gate, it's a good 30-minute drive along narrow, sharply curving roads to the parking lot, the starting point for most hikers. Minibuses can also take you around to the other side of the mountain, where a cable car goes directly to the summit by way of a long, lazy ride through mist and trees. *(Runs daily 8am-4:30pm. Up Y45, down Y35, round-trip Y70; children half-price.)* The hike to the top of Wudangshan isn't too difficult; paths have plenty of level parts, and the trail is in good condition. Large numbers of souvenir stands and maddeningly temperamental weather can frustrate even the most well-intentioned climber, though. When it rains on Wudangshan, it pours, and the staircases can turn into mini-waterfalls. In good weather, a climb to the top takes about two hours.

PURPLE HEAVEN HALL (zǐxiāo gōng; 紫霄宫). Purple Heaven Hall clings to the side of the mountain, about 10 minutes before the end of the road. Built in 1413, this temple contain shrines, a shop selling traditional Chinese herbal remedies, and Daoist monks who float down the frighteningly steep staircases with uncanny ease. Two trails lead from the edge of the parking lot: the one to the right goes to South Crag Hall and Dragon Head Rock, while the one to the left goes past Yellow Dragon Cave on its way to the summit. *(Open daily 7am-6pm. Y10.)*

SOUTH CRAG HALL (nányán gōng; 南岩宫). South Crag Hall is about a 10-minute walk from the parking lot. From the large stone arch, go down the steps; heading up leads to views of the surroundings and a couple of somewhat uninteresting temples. The hall is a simple structure that, much like Purple Heaven Hall, consists of several buildings along the mountain connected by staircases. *(Open daily 7am-6pm. Y10.)* At the top, walk around back and turn left; follow a narrow trail for a few meters until you reach another, smaller temple. Here is **Dragon Head Rock** (lóng tóu shí; 龙头石). a narrow rock extending beyond the mountain face. Although it now has guardrails and is off limits to the public, incense still burns at the end, as it has for centuries.

TEMPLE OF BETEL PALM AND PLUM (láng méi cí; 榔梅祠). This temple was built during the Six Dynasties period to honor the Black Warriors, famous in Daoist legend for grafting a plum branch onto a betel palm. Much of the temple is devoted to Wudang boxing, developed by Zhang Sanfeng after he was inspired by a magpie's victory over a snake. The diagrams and pictures inside depict techniques for overcoming strength with flexibility. From time to time, there are martial arts demonstrations (Y5) in the courtyard.

YELLOW DRAGON CAVE (huánglóng dòng; 黄龙洞). Continue through the temple to the halfway point on the trail, the Yellow Dragon Cave, a small shrine with a yellow wooden dragon and—you guessed it—a cave! A very pleasant and outgoing monk here might offer you a sip of water from the gurgling stream as he grabs your hand to offer an analysis of your future. *(Free; donation requested.)*

TO THE SUMMIT. From here, it's onward and upward to the summit. You can get rid of your chopsticks at the fork in the road. To the right are the **Three Gates of Heaven** (sān tiān mén; 三天门), a difficult trail with little to offer but the promise of sore muscles. To the left is a less strenuous and more pleasant path. The top of the mountain (tiānzhù; 天柱) yields some spectacular views, both of the rugged landscape and of the impressive temples that crown Wudangshan. Here, **Golden Peak Hall** (jīn dǐng gōng; 金顶宫) includes a room dedicated to Zhen Wu, provided that your legs can manage the final walk. *(Y10.)* To head back to civilization, take the cable car back to the lower station or climb back the way you came.

YANGZI BASIN

HONG KONG 香港
AND MACAU

In July 1997, Hong Kong returned to mainland China after being under British rule for nearly a century. Macau followed suit, returning from the Portuguese in December of 1999. Though they have interacted with mainland China over the years because of physical proximity, socially and economically the two could not have been further removed. After being under European influence for so many years, Hong Kong and Macau have a character to them that is best and obviously described as unique; how their cultures will morph because of the takeovers remains yet to be seen. Full of the old, the new, the East, and the West, Hong Kong and Macau escape all introductions.

HIGHLIGHTS OF HONG KONG AND MACAU

SHOPPING in Hong Kong's crowded alleys and chic malls for electronic goods, jewelry, clothes, and souvenirs (p. 427 and p. 440) .

FOOD, GLORIOUS FOOD from caldo verde, gazpacho, and African chicken in Macau, to dim sum, snake, shark fin's soup, and much more in Hong Kong.

THE VIEWS of Hong Kong's skyscraper skyline from atop Victoria Peak (p. 437).

A RIDE across Victoria Harbour on the Star Ferry (p. 418), in operation for over a century, and get a spectacular view for only HK$1.70-2.20 .

RUINS OF ST. PAUL set against a backdrop of Portuguese Old World charm spiced up by Far Eastern flair (p. 458).

RENTING A MOKE (and puttering around Macau's islands (p. 460).

HIKING along the MacLehose Trail through the lush lowlands, demure beaches, and misty mountains of Hong Kong's New Territories (p. 444).

HONG KONG ESSENTIALS

MONEY

HONG KONG DOLLAR	
US$1=HK$7.799	HK$1=US$0.128
CDN$1=HK$5.235	HK$1=CDN$0.191
EUR€1=HK$7.073	HK$1=EUR€0.141
Y1=HK$0.942 (CHINESE YUAN)	HK$1=Y1.062
MP1=HK$0.98 (MACAU PATACA)	HK$1=MP1.02
UK£1=HK$11.731	HK$1=UK£0.0852
IR£1=HK$8.981	HK$1=IR£0.1113
AUS$1=HK$4.569	HK$1=AUS$0.219
NZ$1=HK$3.557	HK$1=NZ$0.281
SAR1=HK$1.119	HK$1=SAR0.892

Legal tender is the **Hong Kong dollar** (HK$), divided into 100 **cents.** Bronze-colored, government-issued coins come in 10¢, 20¢, and 50¢ denominations; silver-colored come in $1, $2, $5, $10, and $100. Three private banks issue notes in denominations of $10, $20, $50, $100, $500, and $1000 for those wild mornings of dim sum bacchanalia. Currency can be exchanged at banks, hotels, money changers, or 24hr. automatic currency exchange machines, called **EA$YXCHANGE,** at a few Wing Lung banks (HK$30 handling fee), although banks usually have the best rates.

Anyone with a passport can open a **bank account.** Hang Seng Bank requires a minimum initial deposit of HK$10, no service fees. All major **credit cards** (AmEx, Diner's Club, JCB, MC, and Visa) are generally accepted in Hong Kong, although some shops may charge extra for their use. ATMs hooked up to international money networks such as Cirrus, Plus, Mondex, and NYCE can be found around the city and dispense money in Hong Kong dollars only. All HongkongBank ETC machines accept Cirrus, Plus, Visa, and MasterCard. Look for machines that specifically say 'For International Cards.'

Tipping is not common, so don't feel obligated to tip waiters, bellhops, or other attendants. Most restaurants automatically levy a 10% service charge, and expect to keep the change. For taxis, round the fare up to the nearest dollar.

HISTORY

Named for its wonderful plethora of smells, Hong Kong (from the Cantonese *Heung Gong* or "Fragrant Harbor") was believed to have been originally inhabited thousands of years ago by the **Yue,** a tribe of boat people and fishermen whose descendents, the Tanka, still live in the area. The region came under Chinese control in the first century AD, but little was written about it until 1000 years later, when it served as a garrison town and the pearl harvesting center for Tanka divers.

QING DYNASTY

In the 17th century, the Qing dynasty evacuated the area to control piracy, an experiment that was short-lived. The sparsely populated region became a haven for the ethnic minorities known as Hakka ("guests"), and Cantonese families began to consolidate control over the area's commerce. In the late 17th century, European merchants began trading opium for Chinese goods, converting the handful of small fishing villages into a thriving commercial base. As the Chinese government saw capital leaving the country in exchange for a population of addicts, they restricted British trade. Drug smugglers persevered, however, and by the beginning of the 19th century, opium trade multiplied. In 1821, the British established themselves in Hong Kong. Threatened with a full-scale ban on drug trafficking, they attempted negotiations and then struck with their navy, setting off the Opium Wars in 1841 (see p. 13) by claiming Hong Kong Island as a British territory and invading the mainland. Beginning with the Treaty of Nanjing, the Chinese were forced to cede the area known as "Hong Kong." Hong Kong Island and its waters were taken in the First Opium War (1842), Kowloon in the Second (1860), and the New Territories for a 99-year lease in 1898.

20TH CENTURY

The Japanese invasion of China, the establishment of the People's Republic of China, and the Korean War drove millions of Cantonese (many of them professionals) and others to Hong Kong, which prospered economically. During the late 1960s, China's Cultural Revolution kept Hong Kong on edge, as its citizens realized that it would take little effort for China to subsume the tiny island. Instead, China became Hong Kong's largest trade partner. The British and Chinese eventually questioned how useful a split colony would be to either power once the New Territories and much of Kowloon reverted to China. To simplify things, Britain signed the Sino-British Joint Declaration in 1984, stipulating that all of Hong Kong would return to China on July 1, 1997.

POST-HANDOVER

At the stroke of midnight on July 1, 1997, Hong Kong citizens erupted in the singing of the Chinese national anthem as the city was returned to the People's Repub-

HONG KONG

lic. Dazzling fireworks lit up the sky and illuminated the reveling thousands amid countless policemen and journalists. As China-appointed governor Tung Chee-hwa prepared to take office, Prince Charles and the last British governor, Chris Patten, sailed ceremoniously out of the harbor.

Hong Kong's first few years as a **Special Administrative Region (SAR)** of China were surprisingly uneventful. When 60 politicians hand-picked by Beijing were installed as an interim government in 1996, detractors feared the worst for the future of Legco (short for Legislative Council), Hong Kong's elected legislature. But the May 1998 elections restored many Democratic Party members to the government, resulting in a near even split between them and pro-Beijing party members. The **Asian financial crisis** of summer 1997 hit Hong Kong much harder than it did the Chinese mainland, and Tung Chee-hwa's administration used the economic slump that followed in 1998 to push through a series of highly interventionist (and not always popular) economic reforms. Another potential pitfall of the **"one country, two systems"** policy by which China governs Hong Kong came to light early in 1999. A ruling by Hong Kong's highest court that would have allowed the mainland-born children of Hong Kong residents to reside in Hong Kong was overturned by the central government in Beijing. Skeptics took this as evidence that China would not keep their promise to leave Hong Kong's democratic institutions intact. They also said the same of the **2000 Legco elections,** which allowed residents to elect only 24 of the 60 legislative seats, leaving six to be decided by committee and the remaining 30 to be chosen by "special interest" groups such as big businesses. The debate over whether Legco is a real "watchdog" of the administration or just a "poodle," rages on.

LIFE AND TIMES

PEOPLE

Chinese constitute about 95% of Hong Kong's population of 7 million, the majority of whom are of Cantonese descent and born and bred in the city. The remaining 5% consists of Filipinos, Indians, Pakistanis, Brits, Australians, and others. The fishing population of aboriginal islanders, the **Tanka,** makes up a small percentage of the population as well.

LANGUAGE

Chinese and English are the official languages of Hong Kong. **Cantonese** is the most widely spoken dialect of Chinese in Hong Kong, although the use of Mandarin is on the rise. Like Mandarin, Cantonese is a tonal dialect; but, unlike Mandarin with its mere four tones, Cantonese has six or seven different inflections to differentiate between the same set of consonant and vowel sounds. Several of the tones sound very similar, and even native Cantonese speakers are sometimes hard-pressed to distinguish between them. Cantonese also has the unique habit of adding an "ah" sound to the end of most of its phrases, and Cantonese speakers will tell you a sentence feels incomplete without it. English and other foreign words have crept into Cantonese to such an extent that you might take a "teik si" or a "bas si" from the airport or buy a "fon kad" at the 7-Eleven. Cantonese uses standard Chinese characters but since Hong Kong was under British rule when simplified characters were introduced (see also p. 26), the former colony persists in its use of **traditional characters.** When standard Chinese characters have proved inadequate to express in writing some homegrown Hong Kong expression or word, the city has invented its own characters, which have been incorporated into common local writing.

Most people who work in the tourist industry speak English, but many shopkeepers, vendors, and restaurant owners do not; learning to count and say a few key phrases in Cantonese can prove very useful.

NUMBERS			
0 ling	5 mm	10 sap	22 yee sap yee
1 yat	6 luk	11 sap yat	100 yat pak
2 yee	7 chat	12 sap yee	200 yee pak
3 sam	8 pak	20 yee sap	10,000 yat man
4 sei	9 gau	21 yee sap yat	100,000 sap man

USEFUL PHRASES			
Hello	nei hou	Goodbye	bai bai
How are you?	nei hou ma?	I'm sorry	doi mm chi
Thank you	do je/mm goi	You're welcome	mm sai mm goi
What's your name?	nei giu meh meng?	My name is ...	ngo giu ...?
yes	hai	no	mm hai
I don't speak Chinese.	ngo mm sek kong kong tong wa.	Do you speak English?	nei kong ying man ma?
I don't understand.	ngo mm meng.	Where is ... ?	... hai bin tou?
How much does it cost?	gei chin ah?	too expensive	tai gwai lah

ARTS AND ENTERTAINMENT

FILM

If the words "Hong Kong cinema" make you think of kung fu kicks and furious fists, you've got another thing coming. Though *Enter the Dragon, Drunken Master,* and *Once Upon a Time in China* are Hong Kong movie classics, there is also Hong Kong cinema that has considerable depth and variation outside the scope of kung fu films. In the past decade, a large number of filmmakers such as Stanley Kwan, Tsui Hark, Ann Hui, and **Wong Kar-wai** have begun to grapple with more thorny issues such as nationalism, Westernization, cultural modernism, and technology. Movies like Wong Kar-wai's *Chungking Express* wrap vexing issues in a visually hypnotic package that is downright sexy, offering something that is both intellectually and viscerally satisfying. Die hard kung fu fans need not despair—the Hong Kong action flick is still alive and kicking. The man himself, **Jackie Chan**, is known as the Buster Keaton of kung fu, thanks to his devotion to sight-gags and death-defying stunts. The success of movies like *Rumble in the Bronx, Replacement Killers,* and *Romeo Must Die* in recent years has helped make Chan, **Chow Yun-fat**, and **Jet Li**, hugely popular in Hong Kong, into international stars.

MUSIC

While Hong Kong has two world-renowned orchestras, one specializing in Western fare (the Hong Kong Philharmonic) and one playing Chinese classics (the Hong Kong Chinese Orchestra), the city has also popularized its own indigenous form of music: a bubble-gum-esque sound called **Canto-pop** (see p. 43). The **"Four Heavenly Kings"** of Canto-pop world are Jacky Cheung, Andy Lau, Leon Lai, and Aaron Kwok, superstars who have been drawing screaming, adoring audiences to the Hong Kong Coliseum and the Hong Kong Stadium for years. Increasingly popular in Taiwan, Japan, and on the mainland, some artists are even gaining renown in the West—although usually for their acting, since many Hong Kong pop stars also dabble in film. The "Queen of Asian Pop" herself, **Faye Wong**, is best known outside Asia for starring in Wong Kar-wai's classic *Chungking Express* (see above), while Cheung, Lau, Lai, and Kwok have also appeared in a Hong Kong flick or two.

MUSEUMS

Hong Kong is home to countless museums, scattered across its countless barrier islands, mainland drags, and outlying towns.

HONG KONG

ENTERTAINMENT INFORMATION. Hong Kong is on the cutting edge of Chinese culture, and the opportunities for artistic and cultural enrichment can at times be overwhelming. The following are some great resources:

bc Magazine event listings (☎2976 0876; www.bcmagazine.net).
HKTA events calendar (☎2508 1234; www.hkta.org).
HK Magazine event listings (☎2850 5065; email asiacity@asia-city.com.hk).
Hong Kong Academy for Performing Arts (☎2584 8500).
Hong Kong Arts Centre (☎2734 2820; Bulletin Box ☎2824 5355; www.hkac.org.hk). Free guide to monthly program available at Centre.
URBTIX hotline (☎2734 9009).
Hong Kong City Hall (☎2921 2840; www.lcsd.gov.hk/hkch).
Hong Kong Coliseum box office (☎2895 1347). Open daily 10am-6:30pm.
Hong Kong Cultural Centre (☎2734 2009; www.lcsd.gov.hk/hkcc).
Hong Kong Stadium box office (☎2895 7895). Open daily 9am-5pm.

KOWLOON

MUSEUM NAME	☎	DESCRIPTION
Hong Kong Museum of Art	2721 0116	Major art from around the world. Free on W.
Hong Kong Space Museum	2734 2722	Um, out of this world. Free on W. Amazing Space Theater show HK$24-32.

HONG KONG ISLAND

MUSEUM NAME	☎	DESCRIPTION
Flagstaff Museum of Tea Ware	2869 0690	Exactly what it says. One lump or two?
Hong Kong Arts Centre Pao Galleries	2582 0200	Contemporary art with rotating exhibits.
Hong Kong Museum of Coastal Defence	2569 1500	Dedicated to HK's ancient coastal defense.
Hong Kong Racing Museum	2966 8065	The story behind the passion.
Law UK Folk Museum	2896 7006	A restored Hakka home.
Police Museum	2849 7019	An account of how the police battled triads.
University of HK Museum and Art Gallery	2975 5600	The university's premier collection.

NEW TERRITORIES

MUSEUM NAME	☎	DESCRIPTION
Chinese University of HK Art Museum	2609 7416	Enjoy the view on the way up.
Hong Kong Heritage Museum	2180 8107	Opened in 2000. Cantonese opera and more.
Hong Kong Railway Museum	2653 3455	They've come a long way, baby.
Sheung Yik Folk Museum	2792 6365	Recreation of a Hakka village.

SPORTS AND RECREATION

RUGBY. The **Hong Kong Rugby Sevens,** held annually in the Hong Kong Stadium, are the city's biggest international sporting event. In 2001, the dates of the three-day rugby extravaganza at the Hong Kong Stadium are March 30-April 1. Call the HKTA or the **Hong Kong Rugby Football Union** (☎2504 8311; fax 2576 7237) or visit www.hksevens.com.hk for details.

SOCCER. Soccer fever, taking the world by storm, has also lured Hong Kong onto the playing field. To watch or to play, which is the most exhilarating? Hong Kong bar managers, tapping into *la joie de* "spectatorship," vie for clientele by offering bigger and more screens, and by splashing the starting times of exciting matches outside their doors. Lager in hand, soccer-loving souls beside, and the drama of a game in front of you—what makes a better mix? **Carlsberg Cup 2001** runs January 24-27 at the Hong Kong Stadium (www.carlsberg.com.hk).

SURFING. Surfing has gained popularity ever since the charismatic wind-surfer, Lee Lai-Shan, a native of **Cheng Chau Island** (see p. 449), won Hong Kong's first Olympic medal in the 1996 Atlanta Games. Windsurfing in Hong Kong requires certification of training. Boards are available for rent at most watersports centers for HK$16-22/hr. on weekdays, HK$20-24/hr. on weekends and public holidays. Call the Hong Kong Windsurfing Association at 2504 8255 for information on the watersports center closest to you and for information on training classes.

TAI CHI. Many Hong Kong residents are avid tai chi practitioners. Developed in the 12th century, tai chi is a slow, repetitive martial art which, although useless against knife-wielding assailants in a dark alley, is nonetheless an increasingly popular way of keeping physically and spiritually fit. The **HKTA** (see also p. 419) organizes free tai chi classes, taught in English, at the Middle Rd. Playground off Nathan Rd. in Tsim Sha Tsui. (Classes Tu, Th, Su 7:15-8:15am. Call 2508 1234 to confirm.) For an intellectually stimulating pursuit, try *mahjong* (see also p. 43), the classic Chinese game of memory and strategy. Its popularity is confirmed by the constant clicking heard in Chinese hangouts.

HOURS AND HOLIDAYS

Business hours are 9am to 5pm on weekdays (many offices take a lunch break from 1 to 2pm) and 9am to noon on Saturdays. Most shops open every day at 10am, except during the Lunar New Year, when almost everything shuts down for a few days. Public holidays and festivals for 2001 are as follows:

January 1: New Year's Day.

January 5-29: City Festival (Alternative Art Festival). More info at www.hkfringe.com.hk.

February 5-7: Lunar New Year, a 15-day festival. Most businesses close for at least 3 days. Fireworks over Victoria Harbour.

February 10-March 10: 29th Hong Kong Arts Festival. www.hk.artsfestival.org.

April 4: Easter Monday and Qingming Festival. Families visit graves and make offerings to ancestors.

April 16: Tin Hau Festival, celebrated at temples to Tin Hau, Goddess of the Sea.

April 30: Lord Buddha's Birthday. Buddhist temples hold special ceremonies.

June 6: Dragon Boat (Tuen Ng) Festival. "Dragon boats" race to drums.

July 1: SAR Establishment Day.

August 14: Hungry Ghost Festival. Offerings are burned in the streets, and various locations stage Chinese opera.

August 28: Liberation Day.

September 12: Mid-Autumn Festival. Mooncakes, mooncakes, and more mooncakes.

October 1: National Day.

December 25: Christmas Day.

December 26: Boxing Day.

HONG KONG, SAR 香港 ☎852

Despite Britain's flight from Victoria Harbour and Hong Kong's status as a Special Administrative Region of China, business is as usual in the former colony—lightning-fast and devil-may-care. Capitalism is the name of the game, and everybody's playing. Suzie Wong has become a corporate boss, and the *taipan* of Hong Kong's mythical past are eager, Armani-clad moguls. Beneath all the ultra-modern clothes and haircuts and the glossy building exteriors, however, beats the heart of old Hong Kong. CEOs head home to light joss sticks and pay homage to Buddha in front of ancestral shrines. The gliding junks and incense-clouded temples of Hong Kong's past endure, somewhat obscured by Victoria Harbour's neon lights and the

HONG KONG

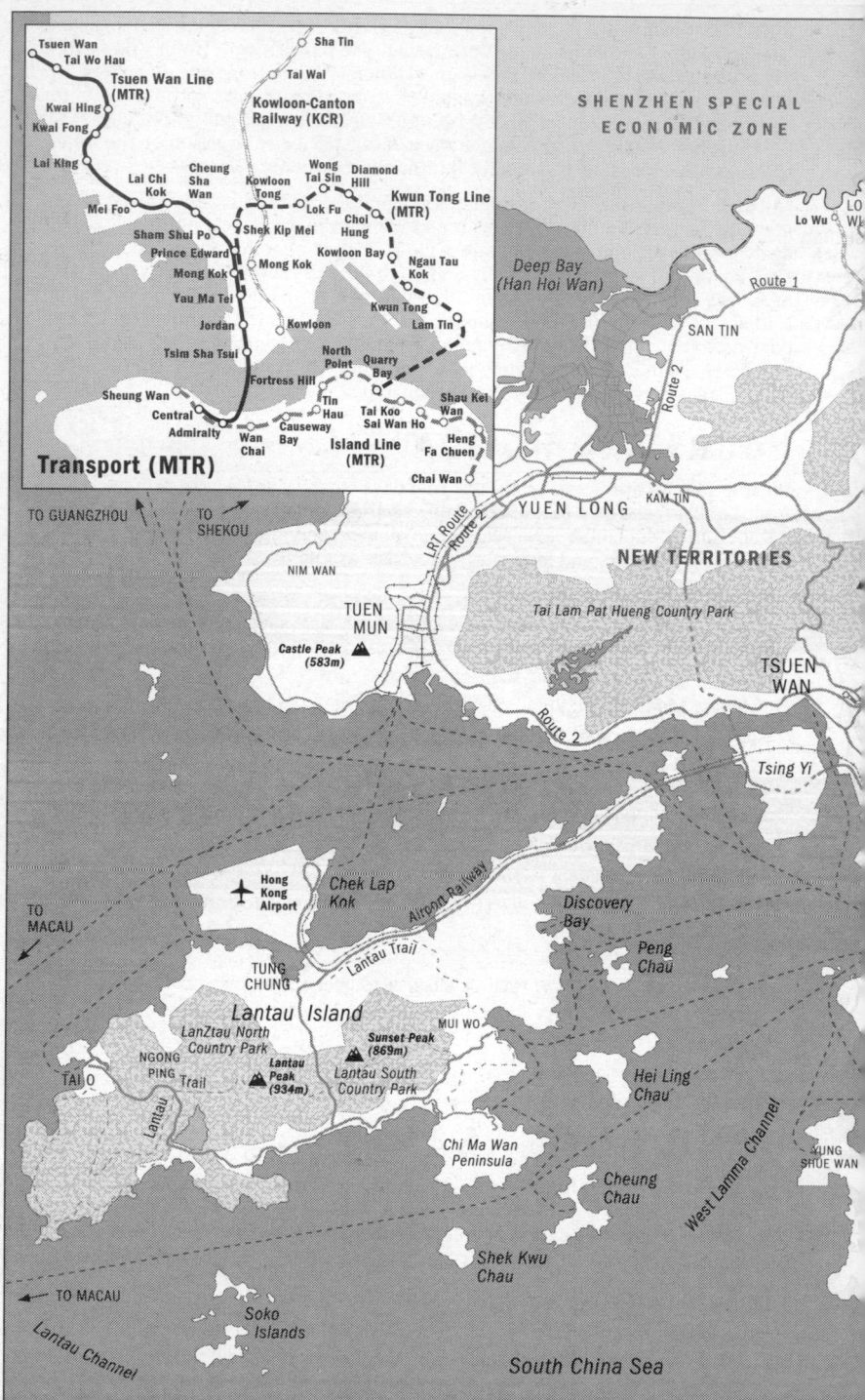

Transport (MTR)

Tsuen Wan
Tai Wo Hau
Tsuen Wan Line
(MTR)
Kwai Hing
Kwai Fong
Lai King
Lai Chi Kok
Cheung Sha Wan
Mei Foo
Sham Shui Po
Prince Edward
Mong Kok
Yau Ma Tei
Jordan
Tsim Sha Tsui

Sha Tin
Tai Wai
Kowloon-Canton Railway (KCR)
Wong Tai Sin
Diamond Hill
Kowloon Tong
Lok Fu
Kwun Tong Line (MTR)
Shek Kip Mei
Choi Hung
Mong Kok
Kowloon Bay
Ngau Tau Kok
Kowloon
Kwun Tong
Lam Tin

Sheung Wan
Central
Admiralty
Wan Chai
Causeway Bay
Island Line (MTR)
North Point
Quarry Bay
Fortress Hill
Tin Hau
Tai Koo
Sai Wan Ho
Shau Kei Wan
Heng Fa Chuen
Chai Wan

SHENZHEN SPECIAL ECONOMIC ZONE

Deep Bay (Han Hoi Wan)

Route 1
Lo Wu
W

SAN TIN

Route 2

TO GUANGZHOU
TO SHEKOU

LRT Route
Route 2

YUEN LONG
KAM TIN

NEW TERRITORIES

NIM WAN

TUEN MUN

Tai Lam Pat Hueng Country Park

Castle Peak (583m)

Route 2

TSUEN WAN

Tsing Yi

TO MACAU

Hong Kong Airport

Chek Lap Kok

Airport Railway

Discovery Bay

Peng Chau

TUNG CHUNG

Lantau Trail

Lantau Island

LanZtau North Country Park

MUI WO

Sunset Peak (869m)

Hei Ling Chau

NGONG PING

Lantau Trail

Lantau Peak (934m)

Lantau South Country Park

TAI O

West Lamma Channel

Chi Ma Wan Peninsula

Cheung Chau

YUNG SHUE WAN

TO MACAU

Shek Kwu Chau

Soko Islands

Lantau Channel

South China Sea

Hong Kong, SAR

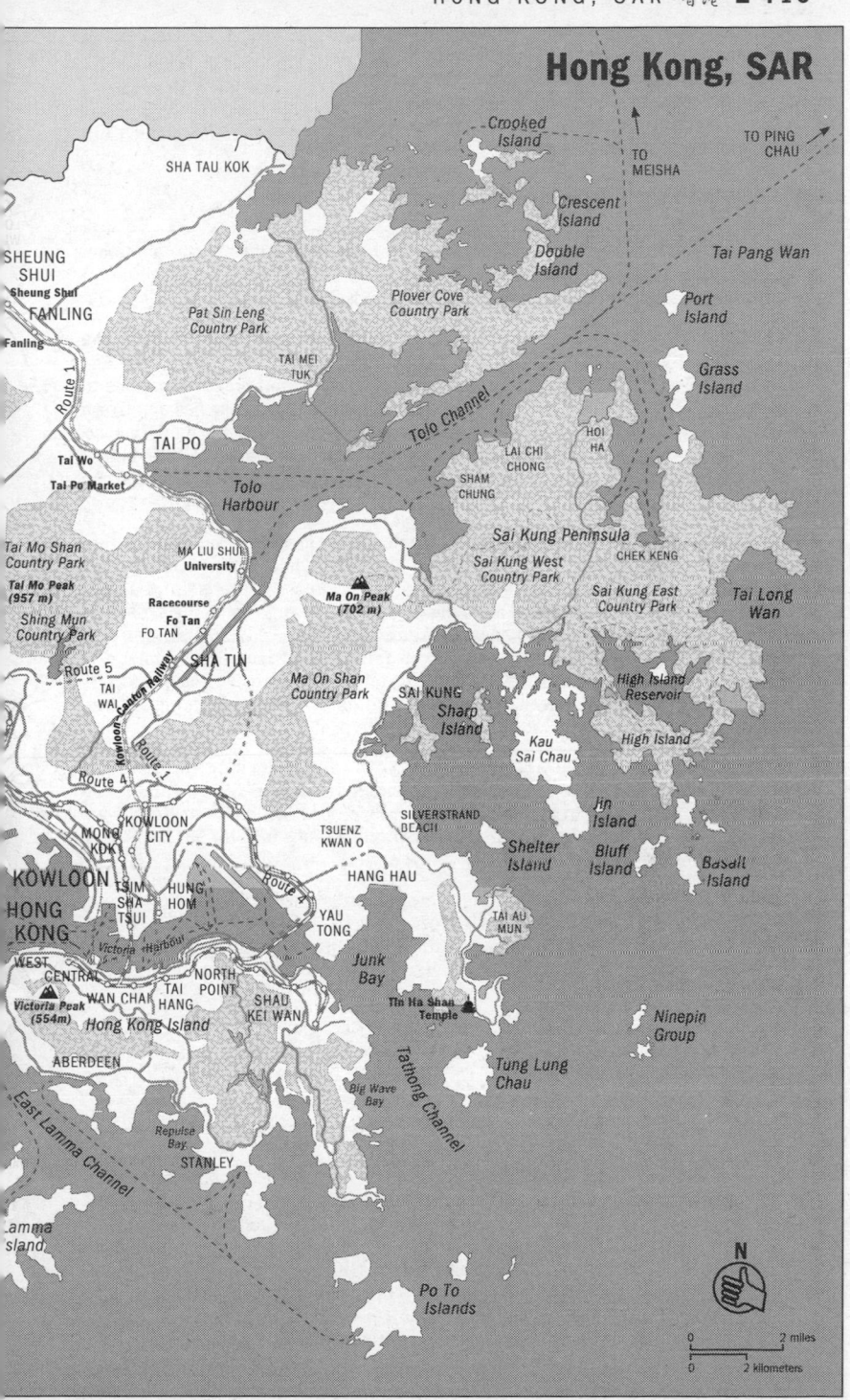

SHA TAU KOK

Crooked
Island

TO
MEISHA

TO PING
CHAU

Crescent
Island

SHEUNG
SHUI

Double
Island

Tai Pang Wan

Sheung Shui

FANLING

Port
Island

Fanling

Pat Sin Leng
Country Park

Plover Cove
Country Park

Grass
Island

TAI MEI
TUK

TAI PO

HOI
HA

Tai Wo

LAI CHI
CHONG

Tolo Channel

Tai Po Market

Tolo
Harbour

SHAM
CHUNG

Sai Kung Peninsula

Tai Mo Shan
Country Park

MA LIU SHUI
University

Sai Kung West
Country Park

CHEK KENG

Tai Mo Shan
(957 m)

Racecourse
Fo Tan

Ma On Peak
(702 m)

Sai Kung East
Country Park

Tai Long
Wan

Shing Mun
Country Park

FO TAN

SHA TIN

High Island
Reservoir

Route 5

TAI
WAI

Ma On Shan
Country Park

SAI KUNG

High Island

Sharp
Island

Route 4

KOWLOON
CITY

Kau
Sai Chau

SILVERSTRAND
BEACH

MONG
KOK

TSUENZ
KWAN O

Jin
Island

Shelter
Island

Bluff
Island

Basalt
Island

KOWLOON

TSIM
SHA
TSUI

HUNG
HOM

HANG HAU

Route 4

HONG
KONG

YAU
TONG

TAI AU
MUN

Victoria Harbour

Junk
Bay

WEST

CENTRAL

NORTH
POINT

WAN CHAI

TAI
HANG

SHAU
KEI WAN

Tin Ha Shan
Temple

Ninepin
Group

Victoria Peak
(554m)

Hong Kong Island

ABERDEEN

Big Wave
Bay

Tung Lung
Chau

Repulse
Bay

STANLEY

Tathong Channel

East Lamma Channel

Lamma
Island

Po To
Islands

N

0   2 miles

0   2 kilometers

all-too-ubiquitous golden arches. Chinese opera and Canto-pop duke it out in the streets with the Spice Girls and the Beatles. Indeed, Mr. Rolex, Ms. Rolls-Royce, and little Rémy Martin lead a peaceful cheek-by-jowl coexistence with seahorse aphrodisiacs and roast-duck banquets. A city in search of free trade nirvana, Hong Kong works hard but plays harder, leaving many visitors stunned and slightly out of breath, but invigorated nonetheless.

✈ ORIENTATION

Sandwiched between the **Kowloon Peninsula** and **Hong Kong Island, Victoria Harbour** is the heart of Hong Kong. Hong Kong's trademark skyline of neon lights, glimmering buildings, and big business billboards lights up the harbor at night.

KOWLOON. North of the harbor, at the tip of the **Kowloon** peninsula, is **Tsim Sha Tsui (TST)**, the city's tourist center. Along the eastern banks of the harbor, **Tsim Sha Tsui East (TST East)**, with its more upscale shopping malls and hotels, struggles to compete with Tsim Sha Tsui proper for tourism business. **Hung Hom** lies quietly on the other side of Tsim Sha Tsui East, and, with the exception of the Whampoa Gardens, is seldom frequented by tourists. **New Kowloon,** north of Tsim Sha Tsui, marks the frontier between the waterfront districts and the New Territories. For more on Kowloon's layout, see p. 422.

HONG KONG ISLAND. Across Victoria Harbour from Kowloon, Hong Kong Island is accessible by three harbor tunnels, the MTR's island line, and the Star Ferry. To the west, **Sheung Wan** is a honeycomb of cluttered streets and alleys. Right in the thick of things, **Central** and **Admiralty** sprout vertigo-inducing skyscrapers. Infamous **Wan Chai** is one stop east of Admiralty on the MTR. **Causeway Bay** is the next stop. The predominantly rural southern part of Hong Kong Island is marked by the expat haven of **Stanley** and the talcum beaches at **Repulse Bay.** A short skip to the west is **Aberdeen,** to which the grandiose Jumbo Floating Restaurant is moored. For more on Hong Kong Island, see p. 430.

NEW TERRITORIES. The New Territories stretch to Shenzhen, at Hong Kong's border with mainland China. In the New Territories, **Tsuen Wan, Sha Tin,** and **Tai Po** are fast-developing "new towns" that house a large portion of Hong Kong residents, while the **Sai Kung Peninsula** has sparkling beaches and hiking trails. For more on the New Territories, see p. 441.

OUTLYING ISLANDS. The Hong Kong archipelago is not limited to Hong Kong Island. Scenic **Lamma Island** (see p. 445), off the coast of Aberdeen, has walking trails, caves, and beaches inviting exploration. **Lantau Island** (see p. 448), the site of the international airport, also houses the giant Tian Tan Buddha and the Po Lin and Po Lam Zen Monasteries.

✈ GETTING THERE AND AWAY

BY AIR

Amid great fanfare, the **Hong Kong International Airport** at **Chek Lap Kok** opened on July 6, 1998. Dubbed "the biggest construction project since the Pyramids" by the press, the endeavor cost US$20 billion and took nine years to complete. The airport sits just off Lantau Island's northern rim, some 30km from central Hong Kong. New arrivals enjoy all the latest airport perks, including 54 moving walkways, a 30,000m^2 sky mall, and a high-speed rail link between the airport and Victoria Harbour. (The new airport levies a departure tax of HK$50 per person aged 12 and over, which is sometimes included in the price of the plane ticket.)

A direct **Mass Transit Railway Airport Express Line (AEL)** jets from the airport to Kowloon (20min., single journey or same-day return HK$60, round-trip valid for 1 month HK$100) and to Hong Kong Island (23min., single journey or same-day return HK$70, round-trip HK$120). All airport trains run 6am-1am and depart every 10min. There are free in-town check-in counters at both Hong Kong and Kowloon Stations.

Airbuses run from the airport to Hong Kong Island, Kowloon, and the New Territories. **A11** goes to Causeway Bay (every 15min., HK$40); **A12** to Siu Sai Wan (every 15min., HK$45); **A21** to the Hung Hom KCR Station (every 10min., HK$33); **A22** to the Lam Tin MTR Station (every 15min., HK$39); **A31** to Tsuen Wan (every 15-20min., HK$17); **A35** to Mui Wo (every 30-40min., HK$14, Su HK$23); **A41** to Sha Tin (every 20min., HK$20); and **A43** to Fanling (every hr., HK$28).

Less expensive conventional **bus** routes include **E11** to Causeway Bay (every 10-20min., HK$21); **E22** to Kowloon City (every 6-20min., HK$18); **E33** to Tuen Mun (every 11-20min., HK$13); **E41** to Tai Po (every 12-20min., HK$13); and **E42** to Sha Tin (every 15-20min., HK$13).

Taxis wait outside the airport terminal. A ride from the airport to TST runs about HK$270; to Causeway Bay HK$335; to Central HK$330; and to Tsuen Wan HK$235. There is a HK$5 surcharge per piece of luggage.

Numerous carriers fly passengers between Hong Kong and major Chinese cities, most destinations in Southeast Asia, and points beyond.

Asian Airlines: Air China (CAAC), CAAC Bldg., 10 Queen's Rd., Ground Fl., Central (☎2973 3666); 54-64B Nathan Rd., Mirador Mansions, Ground Fl., TST (ticketing ☎2739 0022); United Centre, 95 Queen's Way, 34th Fl., Admiralty (☎2973 3733). **All Nippon,** Pacific Place Two, 88 Queensway, Rm. 2512, Admiralty (☎2810 7100, ticketing ☎2810 7100). **Asiana,** Gloucester Tower, 11 Pedder St., Landmark, Rm. 3407, Central (☎2523 1358, ticketing ☎2523 0855). **Cathay Pacific,** New World Shopping Centre, 20 Salisbury Rd., Basement, Shop 53, TST East. Also at Swire House, 9 Connaught Rd., 4th Fl., Central (☎2747 1888, ticketing ☎2747 1577). **China Airlines,** St. George's Bldg., Ice House St. and Connaught Rd., 3rd Fl., #2, Central (☎2843 9800, ticketing ☎2843 9800). **Dragon Air,** Cosco Tower, 183 Queen's Rd., 46th Fl., Sheung Wan (☎2868 6777). **Garuda Indonesia,** Henley Bldg., 5 Queen's Rd., 7th Fl., Central (☎2840 0000, ticketing ☎2216 1088). **Japan Airlines,** Gloucester Tower, 11 Pedder Landmark, 20th Fl., Central (☎2523 0081). **Japan Asia,** Gloucester Tower, 11 Pedder Landmark, 20th Fl., Central (☎2521 8102, ticketing ☎2847 4573). **Korean Air,** South Seas Cetre II, 75 Mody Rd., Ground Fl., TST East (☎2368 6221, ticketing ☎2369 7151). **Malaysia Airlines,** Central Tower, 28 Queen's Rd., 23rd Fl., Central (☎2521 8181). **Myanmar Airlines,** Shun Tak Centre, 168-200 Connaught Rd., #2206, Central (☎2526 0100). **Philippine Airlines,** East Ocean Center, 98 Granville Rd., Ground Fl., TST East (☎2301 9300, ticketing ☎2301 9350). **Singapore Airlines,** United Centre, 95 Queensway, 17th Fl., Admiralty (☎2520 2233, ticketing ☎2769 6387). **Thai Airways,** United Centre, 95 Queensway, 24th Fl., Admiralty (☎2876 6888).

European Airlines: Air France, Alexandra House, 20 Chater Rd., 21st Fl., Central (☎2769 6662, ticketing ☎2524 8145). **British Airways,** Jardine House, 1 Connaught Pl., 24th Fl. (☎2882 9000, ticketing ☎2822 9090). **KLM Royal Dutch,** World Trade Centre, 280 Gloucester Rd., Rm. 2201, Causeway Bay (☎2808 2111 or 2808 2188). **Lufthansa,** Winghan Tower, 173 Des Voeux Rd., 11th Fl., Rm. 1109, Sheung Wan (☎2868 2313). **Swissair,** Admiralty Centre, 18 Harcourt Rd., Tower II, 8th Fl., Admiralty (☎2529 3670). **Virgin Atlantic,** Kinwick Centre, 32 Hollywood Rd., 27th Fl., Central (☎2532 6060).

North American Airlines: Air Canada, Wheelock House, 20 Pedder St., Rm. 1002, Central (☎2522 1001, ticketing ☎2769 6032). **American Airlines,** New World Tower, 18 Queen's Rd. Central, Tower 1, 16th Fl., Central (☎2826 9269; ticketing ☎2826 9102). **Northwest Airlines,** Alexandra House, 20 Chater Rd., 29th Fl., Central (☎2810 4288). **United Airlines,** Gloucester Tower, 11 Pedder St., Landmark, 29th Fl., Central (☎2810 4888, ticketing ☎2801 8688).

Other Airlines: Air New Zealand, Lipo Chun Chambers, 189 Des Voeux Rd., 17th Fl., Central (☎2524 9041). **Ansett Australia,** Lipo Chun Chambers, 189 Des Voeux Rd., 17th Fl., Central (☎2527 7883, ticketing ☎2842 3642). **Qantas,** Jardine House, 1 Connaught Place, 37th Fl., #3701, Central (☎2822 2900, ticketing ☎2842 1400).

HONG KONG

FLIGHTS FROM HONG KONG TO MAJOR CHINESE DESTINATIONS:

DESTINATION	FREQUENCY	PRICE (HK)	DESTINATION	FREQUENCY	PRICE (HK)
Beijing	5 per day	2450	Changsha	M, Tu, Th-Sa	1550
Chengdu	1 per day	2390	Chongqing	M, Tu, Th- Sa	2150
Dalian	1 per day	2600	Fuzhou	3 per day	1560
Guiyang	M, F	1500	Haikou	2 per day	1370
Hangzhou	1 per day	1560	Harbin	W	3070
Hefei	M, F	1530	Jinan	Tu, F	2320
Kunming	1 per day	1640	Nanchang	Tu, F, Su	1650
Nanjing	2 per day	1750	Ningbo	1 per day	1630
Qingdao	1 per day	2190	Guilin	3 per day	1440
Shanghai	6 per day	1730	Shenyang	M, W, Th, Sa	2910
Tianjin	1 per day	2450	Wuhan	1-2 per day	1730
Xiamen	2 per day	1270	Xian	1 per day	2080

BY LAND

TRAINS. Hong Kong is connected to the Chinese mainland by the **Kowloon-Canton Railway (KCR)** (☎ 2947 7888 or 2602 7799; fax 2690 3705), which runs from **Hung Hom (Kowloon) Station** to **Lo Wu Station** (every 3-10min.; HK$33, half-price ages 3-12 and 65 and over). Passengers can cross the Chinese border at Lo Wo into **Shenzhen** (see p. 484). Trains leave from Hung Hom 5:45am to 10:19pm and return from Lo Wu 6:01am to 12:20am. Tickets to Lo Wu can be purchased at any KCR station. The KCR also has a through-train service to the mainland. Tickets can be purchased at any KCR station or from **CTS** (see p. 419). Trains depart from Hung Hom (Kowloon) Station to: **Beijing West** (30hr., 3pm, upper hard sleeper HK$574); **Dongguan** (1hr.; 9:25am, 1:25, and 2:30pm; 1st class HK$135-145); **Foshan** (3hr., 2:30pm, HK$210); **Guangzhou** (1½-2hr., 7 per day, premium class HK$180-230); **Shanghai** (29¼hr., 3pm, upper hard sleeper HK$508); and **Zhaoqing** (4¼hr., 2:30pm, HK$235). For through-train service, children aged 5-9 travel for half-price. Prices rise during peak tourist season and on public holidays or festivals.

BUSES. Buses also make the journey between Hong Kong and Guangdong province. **Citybus,** 33 Canton Rd., China Hong Kong City, TST (☎ 2736 3888) provides service to **Shenzhen** (1½hr., several daily 7am-2:30pm, HK$65-85) and **Guangzhou** (3½hr.; M-Sa 7:30, 9:45am, and 2:30pm; one-way HK$80, round-trip HK$150) leaving from China Hong Kong City, TST. These trip durations are driving times only—expect an hour's delay crossing the border on holidays. **CTS** (see p. 419) can reserve Citybus tickets in advance for no surcharge.

Even destinations as distant as London or Moscow can be reached overland from Hong Kong, via China and the **Trans-Siberian Railroad** (see p. 76). **Moonsky Star,** 36-44 Nathan Rd., Chungking Mansions, Block E, 4th Fl., Flat 6 (☎ 2723 1376; fax 2723 6653; email MonkeyHK@compuserve.com; www.monkeyshrine.com), is the best place to book packages and tickets for the Trans-Siberian Railway. (Open M-Sa 10am-6pm.) Started in Beijing as a company that does the "monkey business" for clients wishing to travel hassle-free, Moonsky Star can arrange passage from Hong Kong, Guangzhou, or Beijing to **Moscow, St. Petersburg,** and beyond. Russian and Mongolian visas are available to those who book with them. Prices vary depending on the number and length of stopovers and class of train (US$395-2790). Cruise by their website for up-to-date information. **Time Travel Services Ltd.** (see p. 419) also books tickets for the Trans-Siberian Railroad.

BY SEA

Travel from Hong Kong to **Macau** is easiest by boat. Most boats depart from the **Macau Ferry Terminal,** Shun Tak Centre, 200 Connaught Rd., Sheung Wan (MTR: Sheung Wan), although some leave from the **China Ferry Terminal,** 33 Canton Rd.,

TST, behind Kowloon Park. The **Macau Government Tourist Office,** Shun Tak Centre, 200 Connaught Rd., Sheung Wan, Rm. 336 (☎ 2857 2287; open daily 9:30am-5:45pm) and the **Hong Kong Tourist Association** (see p. 419) provides detailed schedules and fare information. For more information about other services provided by the Macau Government Tourist Office see **Macau: Tourist Offices** (p. 452). All ferries from Hong Kong arrive at the **Macau Maritime Ferry Terminal.**

Independent ferry companies go to **Guangzhou** and **Shenzhen. CTS** (see p. 419) can also arrange passage to: **Shantou** (14hr.; leaves W and Sa 5pm, returns F and Tu; 1st class HK$212, 2nd class HK$202); **Xiamen** (18hr.; Tu 2pm, 1st class HK$478, 2nd class HK$428); and **Zhuhai** (1¼hr.; 10 per day; 1st class HK$186, 2nd class HK$176). A HK$26 departure tax is included in all ferry tickets, and prices are HK$5-10 more on the return trip from Macau.

> **Hongkong & Yaumati Ferry Co., Ltd.** (☎ 2736 1387 or 2516 9581). Catamaran service from China Ferry Terminal to Macau (1hr.; HK$113, weekends and holidays HK$134, daily after 6pm HK$154). Hoverferry service (50min., 5 per day 7:45am-6:50pm, HK$105) from the China Ferry Terminal to Shekou (Shenzhen port).

> **Far East Jetfoil Company** (☎ 2859 3333), Shun Tak Centre, Macau Ferry Terminal. From the Macau Ferry Terminal to Macau (1hr.; every 15min. 24hr., but fewer at night; economy HK$112, weekends and holidays HK$141, after 6pm HK$161).

⌐ GETTING AROUND HONG KONG

MASS TRANSIT RAILWAY (MTR). The MTR (information ☎ 2881 8888) is Hong Kong in a nutshell: super-efficient, automated, and lightning-fast. Five MTR lines connect Kowloon, Hong Kong Island, the New Territories, Chek Lap Kok Airport, and most points in between. Tickets (HK$4-13; maximum HK$26) are valid for 90 minutes of travel on the day of issue. You can also purchase a long-term, multiple-use ticket called an **Octopus** (hotline ☎ 2993 8880) in increments of HK$70 (for ages 3-12 and the elderly), HK$100 (for Hong Kong students), or HK$150 (for adults); the card can be used on the MTR, KCR, AEL, most KMB and Citybus cross-harbor buses, Hongkong & Yaumati Ferry routes to the outlying islands, and even in the photo booths in subway stations. For short-term visitors, it is probably not worth the extra HK$50 refundable deposit on the card. Information centers in MTR stations sell Octopus cards, give change, and answer questions. Most tickets cost more during **rush hour** (7:30-9:30am and 5:30-7:30pm). The system runs from 6am 1am, although individual stations may open later and close earlier by an hour.

KOWLOON-CANTON RAILWAY (KCR) AND LIGHT RAIL (LR). The KCR (☎ 2602 7799), an older version of the MTR, runs from Kowloon Station in TST East, through the New Territories, to the old Chinese border at Lo Wu (HK$3.50-9, children and seniors half-price). Passengers can change from the MTR to the KCR at Kowloon Tong Station. Trains run every three minutes 5:30am-12:20am. The KCR also operates a through-train service to the mainland (see p. 416).

The LR (☎ 2468 7788) joins the towns of Yuen Long and Tuen Mun in the New Territories. Tickets are HK$4-5.80 and can be purchased at vending machines along the route. Trains run daily 5:40am-12:30am.

BUSES. Hong Kong's five-star bus system (HK$1.20-$45) ventures into any area worth visiting (and even some places better left alone). Schedules and fares are posted at bus stops and available at any tourist office. Buses with numbers ending in M go to MTR stations; those with numbers ending in K go to KCR stations, and those ending in X indicate express routes. On Hong Kong Island, **New World First Bus** (☎ 2136 8888) runs cream-and-blue buses and **Citybus** (☎ 2873 0818) operates orange buses. In Kowloon, cream-and-red caravans are run by **Kowloon Motor Bus** (☎ 2745 4466). Air-conditioned buses cost extra.

Red-and-cream **minibuses** stop anywhere along their routes except at busy intersections and city bus stops. Just let the driver know your stop and pay as you disembark. Green-and-cream minibuses called **maxicabs** only stop at marked maxicab stops; pay as you get on. In both cases, destinations are marked on the front of the bus, but the English is often small and hard to read. All buses accept only the exact fare (HK$1.50-20), so keep loose change handy.

TAXIS. Taxis are **red** in Kowloon and Hong Kong Island, **blue** on Lantau Island, and **green** in the New Territories. Base fare for red taxis is HK$15, and each additional 200m is HK$1.40. Red taxis will take you to Hong Kong Island and vice versa, but there are surcharges for the Cross-Harbour Tunnel (HK$20), the Eastern Harbour Tunnel (HK$30), and the Western Harbour Tunnel (HK$45) to cover the cab's round-trip tunnel toll. Base fare for blue taxis is HK$12 and each additional 200m is HK$1.20. Base fare for green taxis is HK$12.50 and each additional 200m is HK$1.20. Green taxis only pick up and drop off passengers within the New Territories. Taxi drivers may also charge HK$5 per piece of luggage. Most major thoroughfares have taxi stands. Taxis are not allowed to pick up or set down passengers in areas marked with yellow lines. It is often helpful to have addresses written in Chinese. To file a complaint against a driver, copy down the taxi number displayed on the dashboard and call the **police hotline** (☎2527 7177).

TRAMS. The aging tram system has lumbered along northern Hong Kong Island since 1904. The tram follows a route from Kennedy Town to Shau Kei Wan, past Central, Admiralty, Wan Chai, and Causeway Bay. Trams run 6am-1am. Fare is HK$2 (children and seniors half-price). Board at the rear and pay with exact change as you exit. The tram's last stop is written in English on the front. Contact **Hong Kong Tramways** (☎2118 6338) for more information.

TRANSPORT INFORMATION. For the most up-to-date information on all types of transportation into, out of, and around Hong Kong, contact one of the following companies. If all else fails, contact the **Hong Kong Tourist Association hotline** (☎2508 1234).

Hong Kong International Airport (☎2181 0000).
To and From the Airport: Try **Airbus Coach** (☎2745 4466) or **Airport Express** (☎2881 8888).
Trains: MTR (☎2881 8888). **KCR:** East Rail (☎2602 7799); Light Rail (☎2468 7788); and West Rail (☎2684 8833).
Buses: New World First Bus (☎2136 8888). **Kowloon Motor Bus** (☎2745 4466). **City Bus** (☎2873 0818). **Lantao Bus Co.** (☎2984 9848).
Taxis: Hong Kong Island (☎2861 1008), Kowloon/New Territories (☎2397 0922). **Taxi Union Loss Report Hotline** (☎2385 8288).
Peak Tramway (☎2522 0922).
Hong Kong Ferry (☎2815 6063).

BOATS. The **Star Ferry** (☎2366 2576) has been in operation for over 100 years. The Star Ferry Terminal in TST is at the end of Salisbury Rd. Ferries glide between TST and Central (every 5-10min. 6:30am-11:30pm; lower deck HK$1.70, upper deck HK$2.20) and between TST and Wan Chai (every 8-20min. 7:30am-11pm, HK$2.20). There is also service to Hung Hom from the Star Ferry pier in Central, in front of Jardine House and the post office in Exchange Square (7am-7pm, HK$5.30).

Ferries to the outlying islands leave from the **New Ferry Piers,** off the Exchange Square in Central, to: **Lamma** from Pier 5 (30min.; every hr. 6:30am-12:30am; M-Sa HK$10, Su HK$14); **Cheung Chau** from Pier 6 (48min.; every hr. 6:20am-11:15pm; M-Sa HK$10, deluxe class HK$16; Su and public holidays HK$15, deluxe class HK$24); **Lantau** from Pier 7 (48min.; every 1½-2hr. 6:10am-10:30pm; M-Sa HK$10-16; Su HK$15-24); and **Peng Chau** (38min.; every 30min. 7am-11:30pm; M-Sa HK$10-16; Su HK$15-24). For schedules, fares, and fast ferry options, contact the tourist office or the **Hongkong & Yaumati Ferry Co. Ltd.** (☎2736 1381 or 2516 9581).

HONG KONG

⁊ PRACTICAL INFORMATION

TOURIST SERVICES

TOURIST OFFICES

▨ **Hong Kong Tourist Association (HKTA),** The Center, 99 Queen's Rd. Ground Fl., Central (☎2807 6543; fax 2806 0303; email info@hkta.org; www.hkta.org), Hong Kong Island. MTR: Central, D exit. Turn left on Pedder St., and then turn left onto Des Voeux Rd. Central. Walk about 10min. until you reach a set of escalators on your left. Take the escalator one level up and walk through the maze of steel mirrors between the two water pools until you reach another set of escalators. Take the escalator down into the basement, turn left and voilà! Representatives are very eager to help. Open daily 8am-6pm. Other HKTA offices at **Star Ferry Concourse,** TST (open daily 8am-6pm) and **Hong Kong International Airport** in Buffer Halls A and B in the transit area (open 24hr.). All HKTA offices have maps, subway, bus, and ferry route maps and schedules, and the official guides to shopping, dining, and sightseeing. Weekly *Hong Kong Diary* lists current festivals and events. Visitors with foreign passports who plan to do some shopping can also ask for a free **Hong Kong VIP card** that offers special discounts at many upscale stores. Self-guided **walking tour** guides with portable CD-ROM player and headphone HK$50, HK$500 refundable deposit. *Exploring Hong Kong's Countryside* by Edwards Stokes (HK$80) serves as an excellent reference for walks, hikes on Hong Kong Island, Lamma, Lantau, and New Territories.

Multilingual HKTA Visitor Hotline (☎2508 1234). Open daily 8am-6pm.

24hr. Infofax Facsimile Information Service (☎(900) 6077 1128). Local calls HK$2 per min. 8am-9pm, HK$1 per min. all other times.

TRAVEL AGENCIES

▨ **Time Travel Services Ltd.,** 40 Nathan Rd., Chungking Mansions, Block A, 16th Fl. (☎2366 6222; email timetrvl@hkstar.com; www.home.hkstar.com/~timetrvl). Friendly staff can recommend nightclubs, dim sum restaurants, and even kung fu venues. Books Trans-Siberian Railway tickets. Arranges visas to Cambodia, China, Laos, Russia, Taiwan, Thailand, and Vietnam. Open M-F 9am-7pm, Sa 9am-2pm.

▨ **Sincerity Travel,** 835A Star House East Block (☎2730 3269), next to the Star Ferry pier. Offers discounts for ISIC holders (ISIC HK$100). Open M F 9:30am-7:30pm, Sa 9:30am-6:30pm. Credit cards accepted (2.25% surcharge).

CTS, CTS House, 78-83 Connaught Rd., 4th Fl., Central (☎2853 3888; fax 2541 9777; email ctsdmd@hkstar.com). Open M-Sa 9am-5pm. Branch offices in Alpha House (27-33 Nathan Rd., 1st Fl.; ☎2315 7188), Central (77 Queen's Rd., China Travel Bldg., Mezzanine; ☎2522 0450), Mong Kok (62-72 Sai Yee St., 2nd Fl.; ☎278 9582), and Wan Chai (138 Hennessy Rd., Southern Centre, 1st Fl.; ☎283 2388).

Shoestring Travel Ltd., Alpha House, 27-33 Nathan Rd., 4th Fl., Flat A (☎2723 2306; email shoetvl@hkstar.com). Enter from Peking Rd. Student discounts available. Open M-F 8:30am-7pm, Sa 8:30am-5pm. All credit cards accepted (except JCB).

Travel-Net Services, Hong Kong Pacific Centre, 28 Hankow Rd., 1st Fl., G11 (☎2723 7138; email trvl_net@HK.super.net). Visas to Burma, Cambodia, Nepal, Taiwan, Thailand, and Vietnam. Open M-F 9am-7pm, Sa 9am-4pm.

Sunflower Travel Service, Prestige Tower, 23-25 Nathan Rd., 6th Fl. (☎2721 1682). Enter from the basement stairs below Joyce Cafe. Tours into mainland China by bus, train, car, ferry, and air. Visas for customers who book with them. Specify if you're looking for low prices. Open M-Sa 9am-8pm, Su 10am-6pm.

Traveller Services, Silvercord Tower 1, 30 Canton Rd., 10th Fl., #1012 (☎2375 2222; www.traveller.com.hk). This agency was started in Chungking Mansions for backpackers; inquire about cheap air and boat fares. Open M-F 9am-6pm, Sa 9am-1pm.

Armaan Travel Service, Alpha House, 27-33 Nathan Rd., 5th Fl., Flat C (☎2723 3330; email atsl@armaantravel.com). Mostly deals with air travel. One of the few places that can arrange visas for India. Open M-F 9:30am-6pm, Sa 9:30am-1pm. Credit cards accepted (3% surcharge).

HONG KONG

CONSULATES, VISAS, AND IMMIGRATION

The Chinese consulate is on 26 Harbour Rd., Lower Block, 5th Fl., Wan Chai (☎2827 1881). For an extensive listing of other consular offices in Hong Kong, see **Essentials: Consular Services in China** (p. 48).

British citizens can stay in Hong Kong visa-free for six months; US, Canadian, Australian, New Zealand, Western European, and most Central and South American citizens can stay for three. Eastern European and African citizens usually require a visa. The Hong Kong Immigration Department handles **visa extensions**.

Most travel agents and some guesthouse owners can arrange **Chinese visas** (see p. 50). This may take 1-5 days, and prices vary (HK$100-200 for single entry, 1 month tourist visa). Photo machines in every subway station (HK$35) and in the CTS office (HK$30) provide fast visa and passport photos.

Hong Kong Immigration Department, Immigration Tower, 7 Gloucester Rd., Wan Chai (24hr. ☎2824 6111; www.info.gov.hk/immd). For **visa extensions,** bring your passport, airplane ticket, and HK$135 and fill out form ID91. Work and study visas require an ID card, passport, a completed ID91 application form, and a letter from the appropriate company or school. Open M-F 8:45am-4:30pm, Sa 9-11:30am.

The Visa Office of the Ministry of Foreign Affairs of the People's Republic of China in Hong Kong, China Resources Bldg., 26 Harbour Rd., Lower Block, 5th Fl., Wan Chai (☎2827 1881). The entrance is off Gloucester Rd.; look for the red and white building. Issues single-entry tourist visas (1 month, HK$100); dual-entry visa (1 month, HK$150); multiple-entry visa (HK$400). Visas take 1 working day to process. Express 1hr. service HK$150. Photos HK$30 for 4. Open M-F 9:30am-12:20pm and 2-5:30pm.

CTS. See p. 419. Bring HK$160, a passport, and a recent photo, fill out a visa application at the office, and in 3 working days, a 3-month visitor visa is magically issued. Express visas in 1 (HK$380) or 2 (HK$220) working days. Open daily 9am-5pm.

LOCAL SERVICES

Banks: Hang Seng Bank (☎2825 5111, hotline 2822 0228), at every subway station. Open M-F 9am-5pm, Sa 9am-1pm. **HongkongBank** (☎2822 1111, hotline 2749 3322). Open M-F 9am-4:30pm, Sa 9am-12:30pm. **Bank of China** (☎2826 6888). Open M-F 9am-5pm, Sa 9am-1pm.

Currency Exchange: Banks usually offer the best rates, but there are several avenues for currency exchange. In **Chungking Mansions,** 36-44 Nathan Rd., stalls on the 1st Fl. (not the very first booth at the entrance) have competitive rates and are usually open daily 9:30am-6pm. AmEx cardholders can use Jetco **ATMs** for cash advances in Hong Kong currency. MC and Visa holders can use HongkongBank's "Electronic Money" ATMs.

American Express: Henley Bldg., 5 Queen's Rd., 1st Fl., Central (☎2277 1010, 24hr. hotline 2528 3247). MTR: Central Station, Landmark exit. Provides foreign currency exchange, cashes AmEx traveler's checks at no fee, and handles credit card payments. Open M-F 9am-5pm, Sa 9am-12:30pm. Cheung Lee Commercial Bldg., 25 Kimberly Rd., TST (☎2315 9198). Exchanges traveler's checks. Open M-F 9am-5pm, Sa 9am-12:30pm. Taikoo Place, Somerset House, 979 King's Rd., 18th Fl., Quarry Branch (☎2811 6888). Offers client mail services, mail held 30 days at no fee for members and holders of AmEx traveler's checks. Does not cash traveler's checks. Open M-F 9am-5pm, Sa 9am-12:30pm.

Thomas Cook: ☎2854 4938.

Western Union: ☎2528 5631.

Bookstores: P.O.V. Bookstore, 137-147 Lockhart Rd., Hong Kong Mansion, Shop A, 1st Fl., Wan Chai (☎2865 5116). Fiction, gay and lesbian literature, and a small selection of Chinese and foreign CDs. Open M-F 11am-10pm, Sa 11am-midnight, and Su 1-10pm. Another branch in Prosperous Garden, Shop 112, Cinema Block, 3 Public Square St., Yau Ma Tei. **Swindon,** 13-15 Lock Rd., TST (☎2366 8001). Branches in Ocean Terminal, Ocean Center, and Star Ferry Pier. **Times,** Golden Crown Court, 66-70 Nathan Rd., Basement, TST (☎2367 4340 or 2367 0644). Writing supplies, maps, travel guides, and fiction 20-30% off list price. Open daily 10:30am-8:45pm. Branches in Central and Causeway Bay.

Library: City Hall Library (☎2827 2833 for libraries in Hong Kong Island and Kowloon; ☎2698 0002 for libraries in New Territories; www.lcsd.gov.hk), next to City Hall. From the Star Ferry in Central, turn left to Edinburgh Place. The library is in a white and black building, and the entrance is next to Maxim's Express. Branch libraries in Kowloon, Sha Tin, Tuen Mun, Tseun Wan, and Hong Kong Island. Visitors can check out a maximum of 5 books for HK$130 each (refundable). English and Chinese books. Free **Internet access.** Open M-Th 10am-7pm, F 10am-9pm, Sa-Su 10am-5pm.

Weather and Local Information: Time and Temperature in English (☎18501). **Weather Conditions** in English (☎187 8066). **Special Weather** such as typhoons (☎2835 1473). **English Newsline** (☎(900) 0038 7177).

Gay Organizations: HORIZONS, Winning Commercial Bldg., 46-48 Hillwood Rd., TST (☎2815 9268; fax 2542 3714). Information on gay nightlife and events around town as well as support and counseling. Open Tu and Th 7:30-10:30pm.

EMERGENCY

Emergency: ☎999.

Police: Crime Hotline and Taxi Complaints (☎2527 7177). To locate the nearest police station, call 2860 2000.

Medical Services: Hong Kong Island: **Queen Mary Hospital** (☎2855 3111); Kowloon: **Queen Elizabeth Hospital** (☎2958 8888); New Territories: **Prince of Wales Hospital** (☎2632 2211). **Free ambulance service:** Hong Kong Island (☎2576 6555); Kowloon and New Territories (☎2713 5555).

Lost or Stolen Credit Cards: American Express (☎2811 6122); **Citibank** (☎2823 2323); **JCB** (☎2366 7211); **Mastercard** (☎2511 6387); **Visa** (☎2810 8033).

COMMUNICATIONS

Internet Access: All public libraries have free Internet access (see **City Hall Library,** above). Also, universities such as the Hong Kong Polytechnic University on Yuk Choi Rd., Hung Hom, often have many computers with Internet access.

■ **Cafe Online** (☎2366 0060), on Nathan Rd. just before Peking Rd., TST (MTR: Tsim Sha Tsui, Hong Kong Museum of Art exit.). 20min. of Internet access with the purchase of a beverage. Fruit juice HK$8, grande cappuccino HK$30. Open daily 8:30am-10pm.

Shadowman Cyber Cafe, Karlock Building, 7 Lock Rd., Ground Fl., TST (☎236 6262). Artistic black and pink color scheme. 20min. free Internet use for customers. Otherwise, HK$15 for first 15 min., each additional 15min. HK$10. Open daily 8:30am-midnight.

Pacific Coffee House Company, Queensway Plaza, 1st Fl., Shop C34 (☎2861 2302). MTR: Admiralty. Relax with a cup of coffee (HK$20) and check your email free for 15-20min. Open daily 7:30am-9pm. Since it's a chain joint, you might run into the other 20 branches around Hong Kong. The **New Territories branch** is at Festival Walk, Kowloon Tong (☎2265 8600). MTR: Kowloon Tong. Open M-Sa 7am-10pm Su 9am-9pm.

Maxim's Fast Food, Newtown and Grand Central Plaza, Shop 240-244, phase 1 (☎2697 3405). KCR: Sha Tin. Has an impressive wall of 10 terminals. Menu of Chinese fast-food HK$7.50-$28.50. 20min. free internet use for customers. Open 7am-10pm. Branch in Central MTR station also has internet booths (☎2140 6689).

Post Offices: GPO, 2 Connaught Pl., **Central** (☎2921 2333). MTR: Central, Jardine House exit. Immediately to the right of Star Ferry and in front of the Jardine House. Poste Restante held for 2 weeks. Open M-Sa 8am-6pm, Su 8am-2pm. Hermes House, 10 Middle Rd., Ground Fl., **TST** (☎2366 4111). MTR: TST, Nathan Rd. exit. Pass Chungking Mansions, walking toward the harbor, and turn left onto Middle Rd.; Hermes House is at the end of the street on the left. Poste Restante held for 3 months. Open M-F 8am-6pm, Sa 8am-2pm, Su 8am-6pm.

Telephones: HK$70 or HK$100 IDD phonecards sold at Hong Kong Telecom Service centers, HKTA offices, or 7-Eleven and Circle K stores. Hong Kong Telecom sells cards in denominations of HK$200, HK$300, and HK$500. The office on 10 Middle Rd. is open

24hr. Local calls HK$1 for 5min. For home country operators, call the **HCD number** for your country: Telecom Australia (☎80096-0161); British Telecom (☎80096-0044); Canada Direct (☎80096-1100); Telecom Eireann (☎80096-0353); New Zealand Telecom (☎80096-0064); Telekom South Africa (☎80096-0027); AT&T (☎80096-1111); MCI (☎80096-1121); Sprint (☎80096-1877).

Telephone Information: Directory Assistance (☎1081). **Operator assistance** (☎10010) for IDD inquiries, collect calls, and/or phonecard inquiries.

KOWLOON 九龍

Kowloon, the jam-packed little peninsula coming off the New Territories, is the quintessential postcard picture of Hong Kong. Kowloon (*gau lung* in Cantonese) is named for the nine mythical dragons that are said to inhabit the 11km^2 peninsula—a dragon for each of the peninsula's eight mountain peaks and one extra for Ping, an ancient child emperor elevated to the status of dragon because of his royal station. Today, the color and fury of these legendary winged beasts remain. Apartment blocks, hotels, restaurants, and plazas encroach on their traditional turf, adorned in neon lights and wired placards of Chinese characters. The fiery breath of these beasts of old still pours through Kowloon, propelling crowds along Nathan Rd. Some linger in front of jewelry stores; some inhale the subtle hue of saffron in restaurants; others appear in their 3-inch dancing shoes at night to paint the town various shades of red.

Unsatisfied with building upwards and unconvinced that a shoreline imposes a limit on development, the Hong Kong government has created land where there was none, gaining over 21km^2 of new land under the Hong Kong Land Reclamation Project. In West Kowloon, this has led to more land for developers to fight over. All the while, the dragon's fiery breath blows throughout the land—a pulsing heat that travelers to Hong Kong simply cannot avoid.

■ ORIENTATION

At the southernmost tip of Victoria Harbour are **Tsim Sha Tsui (TST)** and **Tsim Sha Tsui East (TST East)**, separated by **Chatham Rd. South** and held in from the south by **Salisbury Rd.** Along the waterfront are some of Kowloon's most recognizable landmarks, including the Star Ferry Pier, the Cultural Centre, the Hong Kong Space Museum, and the New World Centre. **Nathan Rd.** begins at Salisbury Rd. and runs north into the smaller districts of **Yau Ma Tei** and **Mong Kok,** famous for their crowded street markets. The red line of the **MTR** subway system runs along Nathan Rd. and under the harbor to Hong Kong Island. To the east, past the **terminus of the KCR** and the **Hong Kong Coliseum,** lies **Hung Hom.** North of all the bustle, **Boundary Rd.** demarcates the border between Kowloon and the New Territories. Kowloon also extends to former border areas such as **New Kowloon,** once considered part of the New Territories.

▶ ACCOMMODATIONS

Tsim Sha Tsui is the place for those who want to live in the midst of the chaos, the dirt, the noise, the decadent luxury of Hong Kong. The accommodation options are numerous, the location central, and all services are readily accessible.

CHUNGKING MANSIONS 重慶大廈
The notorious Chungking Mansions, at 36-44 Nathan Rd. (MTR: Tsim Sha Tsui, Hong Kong Museum of Art exit), is a run-down 16- to 17-floor building that has been subdivided into six- to eight-room independent guesthouses on the upper floors, with food stalls and shopping arcades on the lower levels. The elegant dark marble and gold lettering are incongruous with Chungking's chaotic interior; it is legendary for its dim labyrinth of hallways and dank staircases, its disreputable inhabitants, and its racial and ethnic diversity. You should be wary of individuals

NEW KOWLOON

Cheung She Wan Rd.

Ki Lung St.
Tai Nan St.
Lai Chi Kok Rd.
Tong Mi Rd.

Boundary St.

TO NEW TERRITORIES

Boundary St.

Yuen Po St.
Bird Garden

Flower Market Rd.

PRINCE EDWARD

Prince Edward Rd. W

Hung Shing Temple

Bute St.
Canton Rd.
Reclamation St.
Shanghai St.

Aquarium Market

Fa Yuen St. Market

Mong Kok Rd.

MONG KOK

Mong Kok KCR

Kadoorie Av.

Waterloo Rd.

Kowloon Central Library

Pui Ching Rd.

Fat Kwong St.

Chung Hau St.

Chi Man St.

Argyle

MONG KOK

Nelson St.

Shantung St.

Soy St.

Nathan Rd.

Fa Yuen St.
Tung Choi St.
Sai Yeung Choi St. S

Yim Po Fong St.

Ho Man Tin St.

Ho Man Tin Hill Rd.

Ladies' St. Market

Dundas St.

Hamilton St.

Pitt St.

YAU MA TEI

Waterloo Rd.

YAU MA TEI

Man Ming Ln.

Tung Kun St. Lung Ln.

King's Park Rise

Welle Rd.

Public Square St.

Tin Hau Temple

Queen Elizabeth Hospital

TO WEST KOWLOON EXPWY. & WESTERN HARBOUR CROSSING

Jade Market

Kansu St.

Saigon St.

Battery St.

Ning Po St.

Shanghai St.

Temple St.

Parkes St.

Woosung St.

Jordan Rd.

Jordan Rd.

Nanking St.

Temple Street Night Market

JORDAN

Gascoigne Rd.

Bowring St.

Tak Shing St.

Austin Rd.

Austin Rd.

TO HUNG HOM (200 m)

Jordan Rd. Ferry Terminal

Canton Rd.

Ferry St.

Hillwood Rd.

Austin Av.

Hong Kong Museum of History

Hong Kong Polytechnic University

Hong Tai Rd.

Cheong Wan Rd.

Yuk Choi Rd.

Hung Hom (Kowloon) Station

Coliseum

China Hong Kong City

Kowloon Park

Observatory Rd.

Kimberly Rd.

Granville Rd.

Hong Kong Science Museum

Science Museum Rd.

Hong Chong Rd.

Salisbury Rd.

China Ferry Terminal

TSIM SHA TSUI

Nathan Rd.

Park Lane Shopping Blvd.

American Express

Cameron Rd.

TSIM SHA TSUI EAST

TO CHINA

Kowloon Mosque and Islamic Centre

Harbour City

Haiphong Rd.

TSIM SHA TSUI

Humphrey's Ave.

Hart Av.

Hanoi Rd.

Cornwall

Mody Rd.

Mody Rd.

Minden Av.

Hong Kong Tourist Association

Tsim Sha Tsui West Ferry Pier

Ocean Terminal

Hong Kong Tourist Assoc.

Star House

Ashley Rd.

Lock Rd.

Harlow Rd.

Canton Rd.

Kowloon Rd.

Peking Rd.

Park Crt Rd.

Hong Kong Cultural Centre

Clock Tower

CTS

Middle Rd.

Hong Kong Space Museum

Hong Kong Museum of Art

Peninsula Hotel

Sheraton Hotel

New World Centre

Salisbury Rd.

Promenade

Cross Harbour Tunnel

Star Ferry Concourse

TO HONG KONG CENTRAL

TO HONG KONG CENTRAL

TO HONG KONG CENTRAL

Victoria Harbour

TO HONG KONG CENTRAL

HONG KONG

Kowloon

ACCOMMODATIONS

Chungking Mansions, 5
Golden Crown Mansions, 3
Mirador Mansions, 4
STB Hostel (HK) Ltd., 1
Victoria Hostel, 2
YMCA, 6

N

0   400 yards
0   400 meters

who aggressively tout their "very clean, very quiet, very cheap" rooms, or who offer to show you the way to the guesthouse you are looking for. Chungking Mansions actually does have very quiet, very clean rooms, but it is unlikely that these people on the ground floor are affiliated with such establishments. Additionally, women travelling alone may find themselves the object of unwanted attention from some long-term Chungking residents.

Chungking Mansions is divided into five blocks, unimaginatively called A, B, C, D, and E block. From the entrance to the arcade, the A, B, and C elevators are on the left, while D and E are on the right. A and B blocks have the most guesthouses, but C and E blocks are somewhat cleaner. Each block has a pair of elevators, one that services even-numbered floors and the other odd-numbered ones. Quality varies more than price, so choose guesthouses carefully; ask to look at a room before agreeing to spend the night. All guesthouses accept cash only.

■ **Mandarin Guesthouse,** E5, 13th Fl. (☎2366 0073). With kitchen cabinets stocked with snack foods, free bottles of boiled water in the fridge, paintings of tulips on the lilac walls, and ultra-clean rooms, the Mandarin seems more like a home than a hostel, and Mrs. Lida Li takes great pride in keeping it that way. Every room has A/C, TV, phone, and private bath, as well as towels, toilet paper, and even sandals. IDD phone available. Prices very negotiable. Singles HK$130-150; doubles HK$200.

■ **Travelers Hostel,** A Block, 16th Fl. (☎2368 2505 or 2368 7710; digand@hotmail.com). Spacious, fairly clean dorms popular with backpackers. Cable TV in common room. Free lockers for guests, but no padlocks provided. Luggage storage HK$5-10 per day. **Internet access** HK$10 per 15min., and IDD phone. Posted reminders that we all share the planet and the hostel and to be neat and responsible. Groovy. 6-bed dorms with A/C HK$65; singles HK$100, with A/C HK$130.

■ **Peking Guesthouse,** A1-A2, 12th Fl. (☎2723 8320 or 2366 6215). A friendly proprietor runs 2 sections of the Peking Guesthouse, Old Peking and New Peking. New Peking is exceptionally clean. Large rooms have A/C, TV, fridge, and private baths; some even have real bathtubs. Singles HK$120-160; doubles HK$180-250; triples HK$260-320.

Welcome Guesthouse, A5, 7th Fl. (☎2721 7793 or 2721 7436; email gloriak@netvigator.com). Run by a father-son team that readily offers travel advice, it rents out clean but aging rooms with large windows, towels, A/C, TV, and fridge. In July prices rise 10-20%. 10-15% student discount available. Singles HK$100, with bath HK$130-150; doubles with twin beds and bath HK$200-220.

Pay-Less Guesthouse, A2, 7th Fl. (☎2723 0148 or 2368 0920). Think pretty in pink. Rooms are small but cheerful. All rooms have private bath, TV, and A/C. 10% discount for students staying 2 or more days. Singles HK$100; doubles HK$120 and up; triples HK$180 and up.

Harbour Guesthouse, B8, 4th Fl. (☎2721 2207 or 2367 2777). All rooms have A/C and TV. Discounts for longer stays; rates increase by about HK$10 in summer. Singles HK$110, with bath HK$150; doubles HK$160-200.

Kyoto Guesthouse, A8, 15th Fl. (☎2721 3574 or 9077 8297). A small guesthouse with colorful rooms give this place a homey feel. HK$10 discount for individual travelers. Singles HK$100, with bath HK$120, with A/C and bath HK$130; doubles with A/C and bath HK$150-160.

MIRADOR MANSIONS

Marginally more upscale than the Chungking, Mirador Mansions, at 54-64 Nathan Rd., also has a shopping gallery on lower floors and guesthouses on the rest. Unlike Chungking, it is relatively clean, quiet, and uncrowded.

■ **Cosmic Guesthouse,** A1, A2, and F1, 12th Fl. (☎2721 3077 or 2369 6669). Open for just over 2 years, and run by a friendly mother-daughter pair, the Cosmic Guesthouse is, um, out of this world. A/C, TV, and phone. IDD available. Check-out 11am. Deposit HK$100. 8-bed dorms HK$60; singles HK$110-130, with bath HK$150; doubles with bath $200-220; triples with bath $240-270.

Man Hing Lung Hotel, F2, 14th Fl. (☎2311 8807 or 2722 0678; email mhlhotel@hkstar.com). This fairly clean guesthouse even meets government safety standards, unusual for guesthouses in Mirador. A/C, TV, and phone. Singles HK$100, with private bath HK$150; doubles HK$150-220; triples HK$220-270.

Garden Guesthouse, F4, 3rd Fl. (☎2311 1183). Somewhat dingy and drab, Garden's saving grace is its large outdoor balcony. A/C, TV in the common room, and phone. 6-bed dorms HK$60; singles with bath HK$160; doubles with bath HK$180.

GOLDEN CROWN MANSIONS

The Golden Crown Mansions, at 66-70 Nathan Rd., are yet another imitation of the famed original. With only five guesthouses on the premises, Golden Crown is not as crowded, noisy, or interesting as its competitors. Room rates tend to be more expensive than in other TST mansions.

Wah Tat Guesthouse, 5th Fl. (☎2366 6121 or 2191 9960). The tile, walls, and linens are all blue. The Australian manager heats up the cool decor with easy, laid-back warmth. A/C, TV, and phone. IDD phone available. Arranges airport pickups (HK$50) for guests. 4-bed dorms HK$90; singles HK$150, with bath HK$250; doubles HK$200; 1 triple with bath HK$300.

BEYOND THE MANSIONS

YMCA, 41 Salisbury Rd. (☎2268 7000; email room@ymcahk.org.hk), next to the Peninsula Hotel and opposite the Hong Kong Cultural Centre. MTR: Tsim Sha Tsui. In Hong Kong, even the Y is posh, with its swimming pool, squash courts, and indoor climbing walls. IDD service and **Internet access** available. Wheelchair accessible. Closet-sized lockers with personal safes. Deposit HK$150 room deposit. 7 night max stay; dorm guests must have a visa showing that they have been in Hong Kong 10 days or fewer. 10% discount for YMCA associates. 4-bed dorms with A/C and bath HK$190 plus 10% service charge. Credit cards accepted.

Victoria Hostel, 33 Hankow Rd., 3rd Fl. (☎2376 0621; email vhostel@hkstar.com). Just 2 blocks from Nathan Rd. MTR: Tsim Sha Tsui, Hong Kong Museum of Art exit. Walk onto Middle Rd., turn right, walk ahead until Hankow Rd., turn right and walk until you see the blue and white sign for the hostel. Don't worry—the building's grimy outside is not indicative of its interior. A/C, TV, phone, and common baths. Deposit HK$100. 10-bed dorms HK$60; 4-bed dorms HK$140; singles HK$220; doubles HK$280.

STB Hostel (HK) Ltd., 255-261 Reclamation St., 1st-3rd Fl. (☎2710 9199). MTR: Yau Ma Tei. Despite the crumbling exterior, the STB is hospitable, and the information counter is downright useful. The international ambience makes it a compelling place to say, although the neighborhood is not as picturesque as Tsim Sha Tsui proper. A/C, TV, phone, and bath. **Internet access** HK$1 per min. IDD phone available. Luggage storage HK$5 for same day pickup, HK$20 per bag overnight. Deposit HK$20. 8-bed dorms (men-only) HK$100; 4-bed dorms (women-only) HK$100. 10% discount for international students, teachers, and card-carrying ISIC members. MC, Visa accepted.

⚡ FOOD

Hong Kong is a self-acclaimed cuisine heaven, with restaurants and food stalls lining every road. The *Official Dining and Entertainment Guide* (available at HKTA offices), the *HK Magazine*, and *bc Magazine*, free and widely available, all offer restaurant listings and rankings.

Dim sum is the soul of Hong Kong. Meaning "to touch the heart," dim sum is positive proof that the fastest way to someone's heart is through their stomach. Enjoyed in the late morning or early afternoon, dim sum is a selection of bite-sized morsels shared among three or four people along with pot after pot of tea. Most Cantonese restaurants serve dim sum from 11am to 2pm, although some establishments devoted solely to dim sum continue on through the evening. The usual pro-

HONG KONG

cedure for ordering dim sum involves either checking off a desired dish on a slip of paper or pointing as waiters wander by with rolling carts.

Some of the best culinary bargains are found in decrepit, no-name shops and stalls. Food vendors come out in the late evening (after 11pm) to refuel eager shoppers along **Nathan, Carnarvon,** and **Mody Rds.** Try also the small streets west of Nathan Rd. While many **Indian** restaurants have members-only rules, the first and mezzanine floors of Chungking Mansions host a number of jam-packed but dirt-cheap stalls serving delectable South Asian dishes (often under HK$20).

Small cafes along **Haiphong** and **Canton Rds.** post menus listing Cantonese and Western food items outside their windows (HK$30-40). For those seeking Western food, **Ashley Rd.** features restaurants and pubs that serve up hearty portions of Australian, Italian, and English food at mid-range prices. **Kimberly Rd.,** which branches off Nathan Rd. farther inland, is packed to the brim with restaurants. The area bounded by **Hart Ave.** and **Prat Ave.,** on the opposite side of Nathan Rd. to Kowloon Park, has an exciting selection of both Western and Asian fare—and nightlife venues to work away the extra pounds.

▨ **The Sweet Dynasty,** 88 Canton Rd., Ground Fl., TST (☎2375 9119), opposite the Harbour City shopping plaza. Famed for its *tong shui*, sweet soups traditionally served after meals. Flour and peanut balls, paste glue pudding soups, and even more curiously named dishes such as stewed snow frog fat are also on the menu. You may want to start off with a delicious bowl of almond soup (HK$15) and then plunge into a bowl of fresh pork kidney and pig's tripe congee (HK$36). Diners sit on barrel-shaped chairs among strangers. The ancient phone by the cashier actually works. Open Su-Th 7:30am-midnight, F-Sa 7:30am-1am.

▨ **Cheerful Ginseng Congee,** Fullcorp Centre, 53-55 Chatham Rd. South, TST East (☎2368 9203), near Cameron Rd. True to its name, this restaurant serves up delicious bowls of hot congee for a palatable HK$16-30. Some meat congees run slightly higher, at HK$38-88. Health-friendly, vegetarian-friendly, and people-friendly. English and Chinese menu. Take out available. Open daily 7:30am-4am.

Jade Court Seafood Restaurant, Pacific Centre, 16-38 Hankow Rd., 2nd Fl., TST (☎2723 1823). A festive atmosphere prevails in this local favorite. Light dim sum for 3 people (3-4 dishes) costs a reasonable HK$200. Top it off with mango pudding. Chinese language ability helps here. Credit cards accepted. Open daily 7am-midnight.

Flower Lounge Restaurant, World Commerce Centre, 11 Canton Rd., Harbour City, TST (☎2730 2200). Customers can point to the tastiest looking creature in the Flower Lounge's fish tanks, and greet their choice again when it emerges from the kitchen on a plate—it's the magic of flower power. Dim sum 11am-4pm (dishes HK$12-32). Credit cards accepted. Open M-Sa 11am-11:30pm, Su and public holidays 10am-11:30pm.

Her Thai Restaurant Shop 1, Promenade Level Tower 1, on Canton Rd. (☎2735 8898), in China Hong Kong City, TST. Outdoor tables and a stunning view of the harbor. On your way down the escalator, check out the time-telling fountain. Entrees HK$50-70, seafood dishes HK$100-120, and drinks HK$27-30. The longan drink is a sweet refreshment. Stick with the less expensive set menus (HK$138-298). Credit cards accepted. Open daily noon-11pm, happy hour 3-7pm.

New Little Flying Elephant Portuguese BBQ Restaurant, 1 Hillwood Rd., 2nd Fl., TST (☎2782 1325). MTR: Jordan. The cute flying elephant logo emblazoned on the napkins, menus, walls, and waiters offsets the slightly spooky interior, with its low lights and loud A/C. Meals are good-sized; dishes HK$60. Drown in your sins; the deep-fried ice cream (HK$30), seeped in whipped cream and chocolate is to die for. MC, Visa accepted. Open daily noon-3pm and 6pm-midnight.

Han Wo Korean Restaurant, Multifield Plaza, 3-7A Prat Ave., Ground Fl., Flat 9, TST (☎2739 7798). Open atmosphere, and open to all budgets, with prices ranging from HK$15 to HK$550. Credit cards accepted. Open daily 11am-1am.

Hard Rock Cafe, 30 Canton Rd., TST (☎2735 1323). Which has achieved greater fame—John Lennon's music or Hainanese chicken (HK$95)? Dip into both and decide.

Eat in the company of huge black and white prints of those who rocked the world, then leave your own legendary imprint on the dance floor. Open daily 11am-midnight.

Wing Fat Restaurant, 448 Nathan Rd., Ground Fl., Yau Ma Tei (☎2385 8167). The unpretentious fare, cheap prices, long hours, and plastic-vinyl decor are as down-to-earth as you can get. Dishes HK$30-45, french toast HK$15. Open daily 7am-4am.

 SHOPPING

There is no need to go looking for good shopping in Hong Kong—it's everywhere. Serious shoppers may want to pick up *The Official Shopping Guide* from HKTA offices (see p. 419). It has shipping and insurance advice, bargaining and bargain-hunting hints, and the hours and addresses of almost every store in the city.

Bargaining is inappropriate in large boutiques and department stores, where prices are indicated. In many smaller shops and especially in street market stalls, it's expected—don't hesitate to ask for a "special price."

For short shopping sojourns near any of TST's "mansions," head to Nathan Rd.'s **Golden Mile,** the road's final stretch leading to Victoria Harbour. **Granville Rd.,** off Nathan Rd., is also lined with shops selling clothing at incredible discounts. Street-side vendors emerge with their carts along **Salisbury Rd.** and Nathan Rd. and beside major hotels most evenings. Watches and shirts (from "Rolax" and "Tammy Hill-finger") cost about half what they do in the more crowded street markets. As always, prices are negotiable.

STREET MARKETS. Kowloon's street markets are an experience beyond compare. While you might find some good deals, prices that seem too good to be true probably are. Most designer labels are cheap—albeit good—imitations.

You'll find the best deals on clothing at **Fa Yuen St. Market** (MTR: Prince Edward, B2 exit). From Prince Edward Rd. West, walk against traffic (on the pedestrian sidewalk, of course); Fa Yuen St. is two blocks ahead on the right. Walk one block along Fa Yuen St. away from Prince Edward Rd. and turn right onto the street parallel to Fa Yuen St. to arrive at the Tung Choi St. **Aquarium Market.** Shops have walls lined with water-filled plastic bags housing departing fish. Goldfish, said to bring good luck, are always in high demand. *(Open daily 10am-6pm.)*

Off Sai Yee St. is **Flower Market Rd.,** (MTR: Prince Edward, B3 exit). Turn left on Prince Edward Rd. West, and walk along this road until Sai Yee St. is on the left; keep walking and you will hit Flower Market Rd. on the right. Hong Kong's best-smelling street sells nothing but blooms of all types. Petals give way to feathers at the end of the road, where you will see the entrance to **Yuen Po St. Bird Garden.** Built recently to replace the old Bird Street Market on Hong Lok St., the Bird Garden houses vendors selling birds, cages, and live grasshoppers. Old men also come here daily to "walk" their birds. *(Open daily 10am-6pm.)*

Mong Kok and **Yau Ma Tei** also bustle with street markets. **Mong Kong Market** is on Tung Choi St. (MTR: Mong Kok, D2 exit). Walk straight ahead for one block. At the traffic light, turn right and cross the street. Otherwise known as **Ladies' Street Market,** this is the place for handbags, shirts, dresses, and even underwear. *(Open daily 10am-10:30pm.)* To reach **Temple St. Night Market** (MTR: Jordan, Temple St. exit), walk three blocks from the station before turning right on Temple St. Imitation designer shirts, watches, and handbags are all for sale, while palm-readers and fortune-tellers prophesize outside the temple. Shoppers can also sample snacks from stalls or enjoy performances of Chinese opera. *(Open daily 7-10pm.)* From Temple St., turn left on Kansu St. and walk three blocks to reach the **Jade Market,** where vendors hawk jade trinkets and souvenirs, as well as sunglasses, nail clippers, and other odds and ends. *(Open daily 10am-3:30pm.)*

SHOPPING MALLS. The western side of Canton Rd. from the Star Ferry Pier to Kowloon Park is essentially a string of malls and department stores. Beginning with **Ocean Terminal** (open daily 10am-8pm) and **Harbour City** (open daily 8am-9:30pm) next to the pier, and ending with **China Hong Kong City** (open daily 7am-8pm), many of these malls are joined by underground tunnels, allowing for a long,

HERE, KITTY, KITTY

Glance across the train and you'll see the black and white figure of her face on a small white T-shirt. Look further and you'll see her discreet pink bow peeking out from a mobile phone case in the hands of a 20-something female business executive. You'll catch her blank stare from the bottom of a pink electronic hand-held fan cooling the perspiring face of a middle-aged man. Look around once more and you'll see her face on the hairpieces of every other woman—and on their watches, handbags, keyrings, pencil cases, filo-fax covers, socks, and hats.

Say hello to Hello Kitty, the femme feline who seems as ubiqitous as cellphones. A bright third-grader hailing from London, she's got the purr-fect life: supportive parents, a sister named Mimmy, and even a boyfriend named *Dear Daniel*. Her favorite pastime? Making friends.

With such a friendly persona, Hello Kitty couldn't help but capture the hearts of Hong Kong's residents. When McDonald's Hong Kong (in a joint endeavor with Japan-based Sanrio, the creator of Hello Kitty) made Hello Kitty one of their toy offers in 1999, long lines of Hong Kong residents converged at the golden arches on the eve of the release in order to be first ones to cradle Hello Kitty in their arms the next morning. Supposedly, these dolls were so much in demand that many who had waited all night to buy the 12cm doll alongside their Happy Meals swiftly resold them at 10 times their initial value. Neighboring Singapore demanded not to be left out of the excitement, and McDonald's Hong Kong sent 500 pairs of *Hello Kitty* and *Dear Daniel* (sporting McDonald's uniforms, of course) to Singapore in September of 1999.

air-conditioned hike through a retail world. The **Palace Mall,** next to the Space Museum at the corner of Salisbury and Nathan Rd., is another monument to the well-appeased gods of shopping.

CHINESE MEDICINE. Throughout Hong Kong, **Chinese medicine** emporiums beckon passersby with their bitter odors and jars of antlers, seahorses, and other oddities. Since the staff at most stalls generally speaks little or no English, try visiting **Eu Yan Sang (Hong Kong) Limited,** Eu Yan Sang Tower, 11-15 Chatham Rd. South, Ground Fl., for an overview of herbal remedies and other Chinese cures in English. En Yan Sang displays samples of a whole array of Chinese medicinal plants, rocks, and animal parts, all with tags identifying the maladies each one cures. Call the central office hotline (☎2544 3268) to inquire about the location of other branches. (☎2366 8321; www.euyansang.com. Open daily 10am-8:30pm.)

⭐ NIGHTLIFE

Bars and pubs pack the odd quadrilateral formed by Carnarvon, Cameron, Chatham, and Mody Rds. Try also the area bounded by **Hart Ave.** and **Prat Ave.** Bars in Tsim Sha Tsui often have a dance floor, so bring your dancing shoes.

Ned Kelly's Last Stand, 11A Ashley Rd. (☎2376 0562). A horseshoe door handle marks the entrance to this Aussie saloon that immortalizes a hanged outlaw. For jazz lovers, this is the place to be. Live jazz band 9pm-2am. Happy hour 11:30am-9pm. Menu items HK$48-130. All day breakfast of fried eggs, bacon, sausages, chips, toast, and tea/coffee/juice HK$64. Open daily 11:30am-2am.

Felix (☎2315 3188), at the Peninsula Hotel. The rooftop bar and restaurant offer a glimpse into the elegance of Hong Kong's elite and spectacular night views of Victoria Harbour. Coffee HK$40, dessert HK$85. Don't miss the bathrooms; they're the talk of the town. Proper dress required. Credit cards accepted. Open nightly 6pm-2am.

Grammy's Lounge, Supreme House, 2A Hart Ave., 1st Fl. (☎2368 3833). A favorite hangout for locals with its multicolored lights, shimmering gold curtains, and Canto-pop performances. Karaoke M-Sa 5-9pm and all day Sunday. Live band M-Th 2-5pm, F-Sa 1-5pm. Happy hour 3-10pm with most drinks HK$18. Cover HK$15, HK$10 during happy hour. Credit cards accepted. Open M-Th 1pm-2am, F-Sa 1pm-1am, all day Su.

Rick's Cafe, 4 Hart Ave. (☎2367 2939). Sporting a palm tree design and a Casablanca theme, this popular nightspot bars men with shorts and anyone with sandals. The DJ has a penchant for love songs. Happy hour 5-10pm (mixed drinks and bottled beer HK$22). Open M-Th 5pm-3am, F-Sa 5pm-5am. Play it again, Sam—there's another branch on 53-59 Kimberly Rd. (☎2311 2255).

K.K. Pub & Cafe, 45-51 Chatham Rd., Shop B, Basement (☎2312 2808). Hearts begin thumping around 9pm when the DJ arrives, and techno keeps them that way (M-Sa 8pm-3am). This large establishment has many, many, many screens to watch soccer—as if watching the dancers were not diversion enough. Drinks HK$32-50, HK$18-40 during happy hour (daily 3-9pm). Open M-F 11am-5am, Sa 11am-6am, Su 4:30pm-5am.

👁 SIGHTS

TSIM SHA TSUI 悸沙咀

NATHAN ROAD. Dubbed "Nathan's Folly" after the imprudence of the British governor who designed the wide road nearly 100 years ago, TST's most important thoroughfare is also its greatest tourist attraction, with countless gaudy shrines to capitalism, from banks to boutiques. The distinguished **Peninsula Hotel** marks one end of Nathan Rd. A few minutes away are the legendary **Chungking Mansions,** which have gained celebrity status since the film *Chungking Express*.

Covering the vast space between Nathan and Canton Rd., **Kowloon Park** (MTR: Tsim Sha Tsui, A1 exit) is an oasis of greenery amid Hong Kong's endless concrete. The park melds lush foliage and wildlife (flamingos and rare Asian birds share an open-air aviary) with postmodern sculpture. If it gets crowded with lovers and tai chi devotees, go get lost in the maze. The footbridge to the Royal Pacific Hotel offers great views of the harbor. *(Open daily 6am-midnight.)* Near the park's Nathan Rd. entrance sits the majestic **Kowloon Mosque and Islamic Centre.** *(105 Nathan Rd. ☎2724 0095. Visitors must wear pants or long skirts. Open daily 4:30am-10pm. Free.)*

ON THE WATERFRONT. Removed from the neon lights and bargain-hunting bustle of Nathan Rd., many of TST's ultra-modern museums and landmark attractions are clustered along the waterfront near the Star Ferry Pier. From the **Clock Tower,** a lonely remnant of the old KCR station, a concrete walkway known as the **Promenade** stretches along the northern banks of Victoria Harbour and into TST East. The Promenade passes by the **Hong Kong Cultural Centre,** the city's prime venue for Cantonese opera, Andrew Lloyd Weber musicals, and symphony concerts.

Directly adjacent to the Cultural Centre is the **Hong Kong Space Museum.** Shaped like a giant silver golf ball, the museum attracts science enthusiasts with its hands-on exhibits. *(10 Salisbury Rd. ☎2734 2722. Open M, W-F 1-9pm, Sa-Su 10am-9pm. Cantonese, English, Japanese, and Mandarin recorded tours. HK$10, students and seniors HK$5, free W.)* Inside, one of the world's largest **Planetariums** and the **Omnimax Theater** each have at least three shows a day. *(Shows usually start every hr. 11:30am-8:30pm. HK$32, students and seniors HK$16.)* Behind the Space Museum, the **Hong Kong Museum of Art** houses large and well-maintained exhibits of ancient and modern Chinese art. The quiet, air-conditioned lobby on the second floor offers good views of the harbor. *(☎2721 0116. Open daily 10am-6pm. HK$10, students and seniors HK$5, free W.)*

TSIM SHA TSUI EAST 悸沙咀東郡

The waterfront **Promenade** begins in Tsim Sha Tsui and ends in Tsim Sha Tsui East. Fishermen dangle their makeshift lines in Victoria Harbour, but they seem to catch more oil cans, boots, and rubbish than fish. Couples often cuddle in corners of the second-level walkway (open daily 7am-11pm) behind the Cultural Centre, a popular lookout point. Farther down, the Promenade runs past the **New World Centre,** near an artificial waterfall and a gigantic watch embedded in a rock.

Chatham Rd. South, the boundary between the two Tsim Sha Tsuis, veers off Salisbury Rd., away from the waterfront, just after the New World Centre. Noodle, rice, and dim sum restaurants line one side of the street, while parks and covered rest areas proffer benches for tired sightseers on the other. At the intersection of

Chatham Rd. and Austin Rd. is the brand-new **Hong Kong Museum of History.** (☎ 2724 9042. Open Tu-Sa 1-6pm. HK$10; students, seniors, and handicapped HK$5.)

NEW KOWLOON 新九龍

Squeezed between Mong Kok and the New Territories, New Kowloon has neither the glamour of Kowloon nor the seclusion of the New Territories. Nonetheless, **Cheung Sha Wan** (MTR: Cheung Sha Wan) is a good neighborhood for seafood restaurants and other eateries, especially around **Pratas St.,** near the minibus #94 stop. **Sham Shui Po** (MTR: Sham Shui Po), a local shopping district, is New Kowloon's other sizable locale, connected to Cheung Sha Wan by Cheung Sha Wan Rd. These areas are accessible by MTR or by bus #2 from the Kowloon Star Ferry pier to So Uk (every 6-10min. 6am-midnight; HK$3, with A/C HK$4.30).

CHI LIN NUNNERY. Reputedly built without a single nail over the course of 10 years, Chi Lin Nunnery is the latest architectural wonder of Hong Kong. This newly opened Tang dynasty-style Buddhist complex is visually very impressive, with 16 halls and a beautiful rock garden. Its elegant grandeur in the midst of such an urban setting is rather bizarre—as is the aura of newness for a building perfectly constructed as a monastery would have been a thousand years ago. (5 Chi Lin Dr. MTR: Diamond Hall, C exit. Follow the yellow signs. ☎ 2354 1604 or 2354 1882. Open Tu-Th 9:30am-3:30pm; Western Lotus Pond Garden open daily 6:30am-7pm.)

WONG TAI SIN TEMPLE COMPLEX. This complex is named after a legendary healer and dedicated to Daoist and Buddhist deities, as well as to Confucius. Old ladies sell incense sticks to temple-goers; while tourists look on, the devout come to bow and pray in this active place of worship, bearing offerings of fruit and whole cooked chickens. Homage is also paid at smaller temples in the complex. Donations go to support education and temple maintenance. (2 Chuk Yuen Village. MTR: Wong Tai Sin, B exit. ☎ 2327 8141. Open daily 7am-5pm. Free.)

The peaceful **Good Wish Garden** stretches behind the main temple. Artificial rock formations, marred only by lovers' graffiti, offer shade from the sun. As you exit the garden, Kowloon's nine coiled dragons bid you farewell. (Open Tu-Su 9am-4pm.)

HONG KONG ISLAND 香港島

✈ ORIENTATION

When viewed from across the harbor, Hong Kong Island's impressive skyline looks like an unbroken string of high-rises. From left to right (east to west), Hong Kong Island divides into the districts of Sheung Wan, Central, Admiralty, Wan Chai, and Causeway Bay; further south lies Stanley. The island's center is dominated by mountains like Victoria Peak, which are still largely pristine and undeveloped.

SHEUNG WAN (上環). At the end of the MTR Island line, Sheung Wan is also the launching ground for the Macau Ferry Terminal. Following the edge of the harbor past the terminal is the main thoroughfare, **Connaught Rd. Central.** Moving away from the coast, **Des Voeux Rd. Central** and **Queen's Rd. Central** run parallel to Connaught Rd. Central. Roughly three blocks south of Queen's Rd. Central, **Hollywood Rd.** marks the edge of SoHo district.

CENTRAL (中區) AND ADMIRALTY. Most of Central's major landmarks and sights are easily reached using the **Star Ferry Pier** as a reference point. The silver rectangle with glass peepholes cutting a dramatic outline on the sky is the **Jardine House.** Parallel to the Star Ferry Concourse is **Connaught Rd. Central/Harcourt Rd.,** which runs past Jardine House. A 10-minute walk from the Star Ferry following an imaginary vertical line would lead to the merge between Queen's Rd. Central and Des Voeux Rd. Central. The two become **Queensway,** with the intersection serving as host to the bold gaze of the austere black **Cheung Kong Centre,** the gleaming blue **Bank of China Tower,** and the beige pillar and dome structure of the **Legislative Council (Legco) building.** Three blocks beyond Queen's Road Central is the infamous expat playpen **Lan Kwai Fong.**

Northern Hong Kong Island

ACCOMMODATIONS
Fairview Mansion, 1
Wonderful Garden, 2

Typhoon Shelter

CAUSEWAY BAY

Victoria Park Rd.
Victoria Park
TO TIN HAU TEMPLE (400 m)
Gloucester Rd.
Paterson St.
Pennington St.
Caroline Hill Rd.
Leighton Rd.
Yee Wo St.
Jardine's Bazaar
Jardine's Crescent
Yun Ping Rd.
The Excelsior
Sogo
CAUSEWAY BAY
Lee Garden Rd.
Neon Day Glo
Caroline Hill Rd.
Wong Nai Ch
Russell St.
Times Square
Happy Valley Racecourse
Canal Rd.
Canal Rd.
Gloucester Rd.
Gloucester Rd.
Marsh Rd.
Jaffe Rd.
Tonochy Rd.
Hennessy Rd.
Wood Rd.
Hung Hing Rd.
Wan Chai Swimming Pool
WAN CHAI
Wan Chai Sports Ground
Museum of Chinese Historical Relics
Stewart Rd.
Wan Chai Rd.
Fleming Rd.
Lockhart Rd.
Lockhart Road Market
WAN CHAI
Ship St.
Johnston Rd.
Queen's Rd. E.
Expo Dr.
Expo Dr. C.
HKCEC Extension
Hong Kong Convention and Exhibition Centre
Harbour Rd.
Hong Kong Immigration Tower
Central Plaza
O'Brien Rd.
Hong Kong Arts Centre
Luard Rd.
Fenwick St.
Fenwick Pier St.
Jaffe Rd.
Gloucester Rd.
Hong Kong Academy for Performing Arts
Arsenal St.
Queensway
VICTORIA HARBOUR

WAN CHAI
TO DISCOVERY BAY
HIGH SPEED STAR FERRY
WAN CHAI-TSIM SHA TSUI FERRY
CENTRAL-TSIM SHA TSUI EAST HOVERFERRY
CENTRAL-TSIM SHA TSUI FERRY
CENTRAL-HUNG HOM FERRY
WAN CHAI-HUNG HOM FERRY
CENTRAL-TSIM SHA TSUI FERRY

ADMIRALTY
Harcourt Rd.
Queensway Plaza
Pacific Place
Tamar St.
Drake St.
ADMIRALTY
Cotton Tree Dr.
Hong Kong Park
Queensway
Queen's Pier
City Hall Complex
Murray Rd.
Chater Garden
Flagstaff House Museum of Tea Ware
Star Ferry Pier
Main Public Library
Bank of China Tower
Hong Kong and Shanghai Bank
Garden Rd.
Star House Rd.
Jackson Rd.
Chater Rd.
STATUE SQUARE
Legislative Council Building
The Landmark
Cotton Tree Dr.
Upper Albert Rd.
US
Victoria Peak Tram
Lower Albert Rd.
Ice House St.

CENTRAL
Jardine House
GPO
Exchange Square
HONG KONG STATION
Harbor View Rd.
Jordan Rd. Ferry Terminal
Pier 7
Pier 6
Pier 5
Pier 4
Pier 3
Pier 2
Pier 1
TO TUEN MUN, TO LAMMA ISLAND, TO CHEUNG CHAU, PENG CHAU
TO TSING YI, TB LEI WAN, TAI O
CENTRAL
Connaught Rd. C.
Des Voeux Rd. C.
Queen's Rd. C.
Pedder St.
LAN KWAI FONG
Wyndham St.
D'Aguilar St.
Upper Albert Rd.
Zoological and Botanical Gardens
KENNEDY TOWN & MOUNT DAVIS
TO VICTORIA PEAK TOWER (300 m)
Old Peak Rd.

HONG KONG ISLAND

SHEUNG WAN
Man Wa Ln.
Wing Wo Low St.
Bonham Strand
Central Market
The Center
Wellington St.
Hollywood Rd.
Cat St.
Aberdeen St.
Old Bailey St.
Wing Wah Ln.
Wyndham St.
Peel St.
SOHO
Mid-level Escalator
Cache Rd.
HK Macau Ferry Terminal
SHEUNG WAN
TO WESTERN MARKET

Victoria Harbour

N

TRAMS

500 yards
500 meters

WAN CHAI (灣仔). The **Hong Kong Convention and Exhibition Centre** juts out into the harbor, dominating the Hong Kong Island waterfront when viewed from afar. Farther inland from the harbor, behind the Convention Centre and **Harbour Rd.**, stands **Central Plaza.** Along with the **Hong Kong Revenue Tower** and the **Immigration Tower,** it makes up a family of sleek, gleaming black triplets. **Gloucester, Hennessy,** and **Johnston Rds.** run east-west roughly parallel to one another, and are intersected by **Fenwick, Luard, O'Brien,** and **Fleming Rds.**

CAUSEWAY BAY (銅鑼灣). Causeway Bay is divided roughly into northern and southern sections by the broad swath of **Hennessy Rd.**, which becomes **Yee Wo St.** and then **Causeway Rd.** as it runs eastward. **Gloucester Rd.** runs parallel to and north of Hennessy until it hits **Victoria Park** and makes a sharp right-angle turn, eventually crossing Yee Wo St./Causeway Rd. The tightly packed **Jardine's Bazaar** and **Jardine's Crescent** streets are parallel to Yee Wo St.

STANLEY (赤柱). Most of Stanley's attractions (including its famous market) are on **Stanley Main St.,** an intricate thread of connected lanes. The frenzy of shopping stalls and restaurants that make up this street make it difficult to find a site by following an address number.

▐ ACCOMMODATIONS

The accommodations on Hong Kong Island are usually at least twice as expensive as the guesthouses on the Kowloon peninsula. A few semi-affordable options are in Causeway Bay, but you'd still be better off in Tsim Sha Tsui.

Ma Wui Mt. Davis Youth Hostel (HI) (☎2817 5715 or 2788 1638) is far, far away on top of Mt. Davis Path, off Victoria Rd., in Kennedy Town. A shuttle runs to the hostel from the Macau Ferry Terminal in Sheung Wan (20min.; 9:30am, 7, 9, and 10:30pm; HK$10). Call ahead to ensure there are vacancies. The only inexpensive option on Hong Kong Island, Ma Wui has large, clean dorm rooms and an upbeat communal atmosphere. A/C and linen provided. Common kitchen, bathrooms, and phones. Simple chores required daily. Lights out 11pm, curfew midnight. Dorm beds (single-sex) HK$65, non-members HK$95; 4-person rooms available at HK$75, non-members HK$105. A reservation for Ma Wui Mt. Davis Youth Hostel can be made internationally from your nearest HI hostel.

Jetvan Traveller's House, Fairview Mansion, 51 Paterson St., Flat 4A, Causeway Bay (☎2890 8133 or 2984 8539). A nondescript establishment with a large TV and a spacious reception area. Rooms come with towels and sheets, A/C, TV, and phone. Singles HK$250, with bath HK$300; doubles with bath HK$350; triples HK$450.

Payless Inn, Fairview Mansion, 51 Paterson St., Flat 5A (☎2808 1030 or 2808 1004; fax 2890 7798). The smell of ginseng greets guests of this clean guesthouse. IDD phone in lobby. Expect a 20% increase during peak tourist season. Singles with towels, A/C, TV, phone, and bath HK$250; HK$50 for an additional person.

An Zhang Hang, Fairview Mansion, 51 Paterson St., Flat 2A (☎2895 0626 or 2577 5758; fax 2895 2895). Bizarre cherubs grace the doors opening onto the common area. For cleanliness and pleasant atmosphere, this is probably the best bet on the island. One-bed doubles with A/C, TV, phone, and bath HK$350-400; triples HK$450.

Wonderful Garden, 70 Lee Garden Rd., Phoenix Apartment, 2nd Fl., Flat I, Causeway Bay (☎2577 7306). The manager speaks just enough English to rent rooms. One-bed doubles with A/C, TV, phone, and bath HK$220.

▐ FOOD

SHEUNG WAN

Hankering for a taste of Russian caviar, Argentinian steak, or Japanese *sashimi?* If so, head to **SoHo** ("South of Hollywood Rd."). A couple of flights up the Mid-Level E escalators, SoHo is an uneasy collection of expensive international restaurants on otherwise lackluster streets. Most of SoHo's restaurants open for dinner

(6-11pm) and sometimes for lunch (noon-3pm). **Staunton St.**, parallel to Hollywood Rd., and **Elgin St.**, which begins slightly south of the intersection of Staunton St. and Peel St., are the two live wires of this culinary vibe.

A little off the well-beaten path, **La Piazetta**, 5 Tsun Wing Ln., is a classy Italian restaurant that serves up pizza (HK$38-78), pasta (HK$37-60), and specials like deer *ragout* (HK$31-48). (☎2522 9505. Open daily noon-11:30pm.) The **Singapore Restaurant**, 130-131 Connaught Rd., in the Alliance Building, offers an extensive menu with low-end prices. The menu includes chicken *a la portuguese* (HK$55), shredded beef stroganoff (HK$38), and 10 kinds of ice cream sundaes (HK$22-28). (☎2815 1566. Open daily 11am-11pm.)

CENTRAL

▨ **Midnight Express**, 3 Lan Kwai Fong (☎2525 5010 or 2523 4041). Serves generous portions of Greek, Indian, and Italian dishes for under HK$55; the kebabs (HK$35-55) are tasty and filling. On weeknights, the small eating booth is a refreshing space amid the glitz and sparkle of Lan Kwai Fong. On weekends, this place draws a thick crowd of business-suited individuals enjoying cool beer straight from the bottle (HK$20-30). Free delivery in Central and Wan Chai. Open M-Sa 10am-3am, Su 11am-3pm.

Dai Pai Dong, 128 Queen's Rd. (☎2851 6389). Choose from more than 10 noodle combination meals (Y38). Those with a sweet tooth may want to try the Dai Pai Dong toast (HK$13) or a sweet Chinese pancake (HK$26). Scrambled egg on toast HK$26. 10% service charge. Open M-Sa 8am-10pm, Su 9:30am-7pm.

South East Garden Vietnamese Food, 8 Queen Victoria St. (☎2525 3953). Sit at a small glass table and enjoy the unique ambience created by dark wooden furniture and plastic flowers. Barbecued pork HK$20; sandwiches HK$8-11. No English or Mandarin is spoken in this local hangout. Open daily 7am-5:30pm.

Déli France, Pacific House, 20 Queen's Rd. 1st Fl. (☎2810 5941). Take the escalator on the left of Bookazine Bookstore. The cool interior of this delicatessen, complete with soothing French music, is a welcome change from the hustle-bustle of Queen's Rd. Even the hearty sandwiches (HK$25) are somewhat of an anomaly for Hong Kong. Open M-Sa 7:30am-8pm, Su 8am-8pm.

Bravo. Le Cafe, 34-37 Connaught Rd. Central (☎2104 7129). The black roof, varnished wood tile and scattered fruit baskets make think you're in Europe. Hong Kong Chinese chefs deftly serve up buttered French toast (HK$16), Indian samosa platters, Chinese-style chicken, and other sumptuous orders from an open kitchen. Open M-Sa 7am-9pm.

WAN CHAI

▨ **Kublai's**, 1 Capital Plaza, 18 Luard Rd., 3rd Fl. (☎2529 9117). Other locations at 55 Kimberley Rd., TST (☎2722 0733) and 1 Keswick St., **Causeway Bay** (☎2882 3282). Fill a bowl with an assortment of noodles, rice, vegetables, and meat, top it off with sauces from Korea, India, and China, and hand it to an army of cooks who will return a hot, tasty meal to you in 10min. All-you-can-eat dinner buffet after 5pm HK$138, children HK$98; lunch buffet HK$98, children HK$78. Reservations recommended. Open daily noon-3pm and 6:30-10:30pm.

▨ **Banana Leaf Curry House**, 440 Jaffe Rd., 1st Fl. (☎2573 8187). Other locations in TST, Mong Kok, Whampoa Garden, and Causeway Bay. Waitresses in traditional costume scoop rice from a large wooden bucket onto a banana leaf. A comfortable setting for families. Pork satay appetizer HK$48, curry HK$24-48, and vegetables HK$20. Credit cards accepted. Open M-F 11:30am-3pm and 6pm-midnight, Sa-Su and public holidays 11am-11:30pm.

Healthy Vegetarian Restaurant, 51-53 Hennessy Rd., Ground Fl. (☎2527 3918). Using the culinary marvels of bean curd, the Healthy Vegetarian allows customers to experience the taste and texture of meat (entrees HK$38-138). The strict vegetarian can even try shark's fin (HK$68). Takeout available. Diner's Club, MC, Visa accepted. Open M-Sa 10:30am-11pm, Su 5pm-11pm.

CAUSEWAY BAY
Laurel Noodle, 462 Lockhart Rd. (☎2904 7867). Eat spare ribs in pineapple sauce (HK$28) off porcelain dishes and propose a toast with mineral juice (HK$8) to the gods of great value meals. Open daily noon-11pm.

Fantasy Vegetarian Restaurant, 66 Electric Rd. (☎2887 3886 or 2807 0569). MTR: Tin Hau Electric Rd. exit. One of the few vegetarian restaurants with an English menu and a friendly, English-speaking staff. The lineup includes noodles (HK$17-29), congee (HK$48-60), vegetables with mock kidney (HK$52), and a dozen other veggie dishes (HK$48-60). Open daily 11am-10pm; dim sum stalls open 9am-11:30pm.

STANLEY
Pepperoni's, 18B Stanley Main St., Ground Fl. (☎2813 8605), resembles an Italian bistro with tables that spill out onto the sidewalk. Delicious pizza is available in small (HK$50-65), medium (HK$65-85), and large (HK$80-100) sizes; ask for the special secret sauce. Open daily 10am-10pm.

Al Fresco's, 30A Stanley Main St., Ground Fl. (☎2813 2520), is a colorful eatery with a varied menu, including Mexican tacos (HK$65). Open daily 10am-10pm. Same management as Pepperoni's; both have branches throughout Hong Kong Island.

Ga Luck Kitchen, 14 Stanley Main St. (☎2813 9787), next door to Pepperoni's. One of the few Cantonese restaurants in the area. Small dim sum combo HK$68. Open daily 7am-8pm.

The King of Pasta, 928 Stanley Main St. (☎2813 7313). Create your own dish from a choice of 10 pastas, 24 ingredients, and 8 sauces (HK$60 and upwards). Breezy Mediterranean atmosphere to enjoy your work of art. Open daily 11am-midnight or 1am. AmEx accepted.

🛍 SHOPPING

Unlike Kowloon, Hong Kong Island has few cheap street markets where budget travelers can haggle for discounts on rip-offs of brand-name goods. Older, more upscale tourists flex credit cards in boutiques selling Yves St. Laurent, sparkling gold jewelry, and other 24-carat emblems of conspicuous consumption.

STREET MARKETS
 Li Yuen St. Market, in Central. Li Yuen St. East lies between Des Voeux Rd. and Queen's Rd. Excellent bargains for traditional Chinese dresses. Open daily 7am-10pm. Li Yuen St. West is parallel to and 1 block left of Li Yuen St. East if you are standing with Jardine House behind you. More shops than its sister street and a selection of shoes that will make the shoe-lover delirious. Open daily 7am-10pm.

Central Market, at the intersection of Queen Victoria St. and Queen's Rd., Central. Three floors packed with produce, meat, and customers. Trade the fierce smells and questionable cleanliness for low prices and undeniably fresh food. Open daily 6am-8pm.

Graham Street Fruit and Vegetable Market, on Graham St., off Queen's Rd., Central, between the Union Bank of Hong Kong and the V. Heun Building. This open-air market—a fruit connoisseur's fantasy—is very clean and well stocked. Nuts, corn on the cob, and fresh tofu also available. Open daily 6am-8pm.

Jardine's Bazaar and **Jardine's Crescent,** in Causeway Bay. MTR: Causeway Bay, Jardine's Crescent exit. The Crescent is the small tunnel of clothing stalls to the right of the Giordano store. The Bazaar is the next street on the left. Peddlers sell traditional herbal medicines, preserved bean curd, and tea. Open daily noon-10pm.

SHOPPING MALLS
Pacific Place (☎2801 4197), connected to Queensway Plaza by a pedestrian overpass, on Queensway, Admiralty. MTR: Admiralty, Queensway Plaza exit. Its motto, "a world of delights under one roof," fits this shopping cavern to a T. Information counter on L2. Most stores open daily 10:30am-7pm.

Sogo (☎2833 8338), at the intersection of Great George and Paterson St., Causeway Bay. MTR: Causeway Bay. With 10 floors of everything, Sogo promises to keep even the most jaded shoppers entertained. Sogo! Open daily 10am-10pm.

Times Square (☎2118 8900), Causeway Bay. MTR: Causeway Bay, Times Square exit. Showcases designers like Gucci and Versace. Open daily 10am-10pm.

Western Market (☎281 3586), on New Market St., which runs between Des Voeux Rd. and Connaught Rd. Shop inside a quiet Edwardian building to escape the outdoor humidity. Open M-Sa 10am-7pm, Su 9:30am-7pm.

 NIGHTLIFE

Before heading out for a night on the town, pick up a free copy of *HK Magazine* or *bc magazine*, two English-language weeklies with up-to-date entertainment listings. Find them at many restaurants, bars, hotels, and newsstands.

CENTRAL AND ADMIRALTY

The L-shaped **Lan Kwai Fong** area overflows with trendy restaurants and bars. During the day, the area is packed with mild-mannered eateries catering to a mellow clientele (see **Food**, p. 435). As dusk falls, Lan Kwai Fong becomes *the* happening hot spot for Hong Kong's expats. The city-slicker material girl regulars often provide enough entertainment to justify the upwardly mobile cover charges and bar tabs. Credit cards are accepted in most bars and clubs.

■ **Oscar's**, 2 Lan Kwai Fong (☎2804 6561). Amid high ceilings and elegant decor, Oscar's caters to a cosmopolitan crowd. Tasteful style, good music, and a great bar manager who might even buy you a drink. Happy Hour daily 4-8pm (Budweiser HK$30). Open M-F 11am-1am, Sa-Su 11am-3:30am. Check out the Australian restaurant (☎2861 1511) in Causeway Bay, run by the same management.

Club 64, 12-14 Wing Wah Ln., Ground Fl. (☎2523 2801), off D'Aguilar St. Popular with both expats and backpackers, this laid-back bar is normally packed on weekends. Happy Hour daily 11am-9pm. Drinks normally HK$40-60; during Happy Hour a Carlsberg goes for HK$15. Open M-Th noon-2am, F-Sa 10am-3am, Su 6pm-1am.

Post 97, 9-11 Lan Kwai Fong (☎2810 9333), part of the elite 97 group that includes **Club 97** (which bars non-members from entering) in the same building. Bottled beer HK$47. Happy Hour daily 3pm-7pm, dinner served until 11pm. Open M-Th 10am-12:30am, F Sa 10am 3am, Su 10am-midnight.

LA Cafe, Lippo Centre, 89 Queensway, Ground Fl., Shops 2-3 (☎2526 6863). Conjures up every stereotype of Los Angeles and Hollywood possible, from its neon to its palm trees. Mexican dishes HK$75-125, burgers HK$90-95, and pasta HK$85-105. Happy Hour daily 2-8pm with 2 for 1 drinks. Bottled beer HK$24. Open M-F 11am-12:30am, Sa-Su 10am-12:30am.

Sherman's, California Entertainment Bldg., 34-36 D'Aguilar St., Ground Fl. (☎2801 4946). Sophisticated patrons blow smoke rings from long, thin cigarettes in this dim bar and restaurant. Pastas HK$40, soups HK$55-60, sandwiches HK$80-110, and desserts such as tiramisu HK$55. Open M-Th noon-2am, F-Sa noon-4am, Su 4pm-1am.

Yeltsinn, 42 D'Aguilar St., Ground Fl. (☎2524 7790 or 2523 4448). Think hammers, sickles, and jocular Russians on the walls; think expats. Happy Hour (2 for 1 drinks) daily 5-9pm. Drinks normally about HK$45. Open daily 5pm-4am.

Zip, 2 Glenealy St. (☎2523 3595). Around the corner from The Noodle Box and opposite St. Paul's Church, a subtle black door opens into an inferno of pink curves and artsy decor. Caters to international gay men. Drinks HK$40-50. Open daily 7pm-2am.

The Fringe Club, 2 Lower Albert Rd. (☎2521 7251 or 2868 4415). An art gallery and bar in one. Lunch buffet noon-2:30pm HK$75 (M-F vegetarian). Drinks HK$35-55. Happy Hour daily 5-8pm. Open M-Th noon-midnight, F-Sa noon-2am.

WAN CHAI

As the setting of Richard Mason's novel *The World of Suzie Wong* (the film was actually shot in Sheung Wan), Wan Chai will never shake its associations with brothels, bars, and furloughed sailors. While Central's nightclubs are posh and upscale, Wan Chai's are flashy and sometimes sleazy. Pubs and bars cluster on **Jaffe** and **Luard Rds.**, their neon signs lighting the path to drunken revelry.

The Wanch, 54 Jaffe Rd. (☎2861 1621). MTR: Wan Chai, Lockhart Rd. exit. An intimate ode to Hong Kong pop culture, this spot is designed like a Star Ferry. This jack-of-all-trades has set lunches (HK$65-80), pub grub dinner, and Hong Kong souvenirs. Live music nightly beginning at 10pm. Happy Hour daily 11am-10pm (drinks HK$24-30); "madness hour" M-Sa 6-7pm (drinks HK$19). Open M-Sa 11am-2am, Su noon-2am.

Carnegie's, 53-55 Lockhart Rd. (☎2866 6289). This popular pub heats up at night and goes wild on weekends. Cocktails HK$40-150. "Crazy hour" daily 6-7pm (drinks HK$19). Specials every night of the week. DJ every night except Th and Su, when local groups show their stuff. Open M-Sa 11am-5am, Su 5pm-2am.

Joe Bananas, 23 Luard Rd. (☎2529 1811), at Jaffe Rd. Despite the many rules—no furs, t-shirts, or shorts—this is a swinging nightlife spot. Tropical, sunny feel with palm trees and tin foil on the walls. Asian, European, and New World food served until midnight. Unplugged every Friday. All drinks 2 for 1 during Happy Hour 7-10pm. 21+ after 6pm. Open M-Th 11am-5am, F-Sa 11am-6am, Su 5pm-5am.

Nickleby's, 57-73 Lockhart Rd. (☎2862 1023). In the basement of the Wharney Hotel, amid suspended model airplanes and clouds on the ceiling, a Filipino band plays English and Tagalog pop songs nightly (M-Th 6:15pm-12:15am, F-Sa 6:15pm-1:15am). Very mellow, relaxed atmosphere with a devoted following of regulars. Big screen broadcasts live soccer games. Cocktails HK$60. Happy Hour M-Th all day, F-Sa 4:30-9pm (all drinks 2 for 1). Open M-Th 4:30pm-1am, F-Sa 4:30pm-2am.

Cinta-J, 69 Jaffe Rd., Shop G-4, Malaysia Bldg. (☎2529 6622). A Malaysian-Filipino-Indonesian restaurant and lounge. Lunch sets M-F 11am-3pm HK$43. Happy Hour M-F 3-9pm (half-pints HK$15-16, pints HK$25-27). Live music M-Sa 5pm-1am, Su 11am-1am. Credit cards accepted; HK$200 min. charge. Open daily 11am-5am.

Beer Castle, 15-19 Luard Rd. (☎2527 7211). The big TV and red vinyl bar stools don't make it much of a castle, but there's certainly enough beer to keep things afloat. A healthy mix of expats and locals. Imported beers HK$31-40, snacks HK$30. Happy Hour Su-Th 11am-5pm, F-Sa 11am-9pm (2 for 1 drinks). Open daily 11am-6am.

Delaney's, 18 Luard Rd., 2nd Fl., One Capital Pl. (☎2804 2880). To get there, supposedly all you need to say to a taxi driver is "Jay Faye Doe." The manager greets clients with a genuine brogue. HK$59 for a pint of Guinness. Happy Hour daily 3-9pm. Open Su-Th noon-2am, F-Sa noon-3am. Another branch in **Kowloon** (☎2301 3980). To get to this one, just tell the driver "Buck King Doe."

CAUSEWAY BAY

Most of the bars in Causeway Bay are joined to hotels and close early, but there are a few tucked away with relatively late hours.

▧The China Jump Bar and Grill, Causeway Bay Plaza 2, 463 Lockhart Rd., 7th Fl. (☎2832 9007 or 2832 7122). Emerge from the elevator onto the deck of the Jump, and head to the starboard side to the bar. This place will make you jump with its joltin' decor (sit in a glass booth or up in a dimly lit loft), upbeat waitstaff, decadent food at mid-range prices, and a dance floor. Happy Hour M-Sa 4-8pm, all night Su. Open M-Tu, Th noon-2am, W-F, Su noon-3am.

Dickens, The Excelsior Hotel, 281 Gloucester Rd., Lower Ground Fl. (☎2837 6782). Sports buffs will appreciate the autographed pictures of tennis, soccer, and marathon champions. Very classy—don't underdress. Beer HK$50. Happy Hour 5-8pm, dinner menu 6-10pm. Open Su-Th 11am-1:30am, F-Sa 11am-2:30am.

STANLEY

Smuggler's Inn, 90A Main St. (☎2813 8852), is boarded with heavy, wooden beams. Happy Hour M-F 6-10pm, bottled beer HK$25. Open M-F 9am-late.

Lord Stanley's Sports Bar, 92A Main St. (☎2813 0993). Open Su-Th 10am-1am, F-Sa 10am-2am.

 **SIGHTS**

SHEUNG WAN

When the Royal Navy dropped anchor and raised the Union Jack to claim Hong Kong for the British in 1841, it was here that they did it. Ironically, this area is rich in local character. Missing the glitz characteristic of much of Hong Kong Island, this district overflows with little shops, streetside markets, and mildewing apartments. The **Macau Ferry Terminal** reigns over the northern edge of the district. Farther south, on the corner of Ladder St. and Hollywood Rd., looms **Man Mo Temple,** where the lovelorn shake fortune-telling sticks to check on the state of their star-crossed destinies. Dedicated to the ancient gods of *Man* ("Literature") and *Mo* ("Warfare"), the temple also houses shrines to the city god and the 10 divine judges. *Feng shui* advice and palm-reading is available. *(☎2540 0350. Open daily 8am-6pm. Free.)*

Curving across the center of Sheung Wan is **Hollywood Rd.,** where antiques and Chinese artwork is laid out for sale (daily 10am-6pm). Following Hollywood Rd. to the eastern edge of Sheung Wan, on Cochrane St. and Shelley St., run the **Central Mid-Level Escalators,** the longest covered escalator in the world. Over 800m of moving stairs (and a total of 20 exits) transport residents down the hill (6-10am) and up again (10am-11pm). Bars and restaurants are constantly sprouting up on the hillside along the Escalators, and toward the top is Hong Kong's own **SoHo.**

CENTRAL

VICTORIA PEAK. The quintessential Hong Kong experience is a trip to Victoria Peak. At 396m above sea level, the Peak provides a spectacular view of Hong Kong; binoculars (HK$2 per 5min.) are available on levels two, four, and five of the Peak Tower. Entertainment options on the Peak (shopping, motion simulator, theme gallery, and daily movie) are expensive and crowded with tourists. Sitting quietly and absorbing the panoramic view from the Level Four terrace is free, as is a walk around the trails at the top. The **peak tram** offers an exhilarating ride up a 45° incline, at a speed leisurely enough for you to take in the view. *(33 Garden Rd., behind the Murray Building. A double-decker bus (Y3) departs from the Central Star Ferry pier to the tram station daily every 15min. 7am-midnight. Alternatively, walk the 600m by following Garden Rd. away from the Harbor. ☎2522 0922. Tram departs every 10-15min. 7am-midnight; HK$20, round-trip HK$30; children 3-11 HK$6/HK$9; seniors over 65 HK$7/HK$14.)*

HONG KONG PARK. For a park, Hong Kong Park boasts an impressive amount of cement, and in spite of its eight hectares, it has an air of being cramped. Perhaps the park's most worthwhile site is the **Flagstaff Museum of Teaware.** Constructed between 1844 and 1846, the Flagstaff House was both home and office to the Commander of the British forces in Hong Kong. The museum offers a comprehensive and innovative study of British and Chinese tea and tea customs. *(☎2869 0690. Video at 11:30am, 1:30, and 3:30pm; groups of 10 or more can inquire about additional screenings. Open Th-Tu 10am-5pm.)* The Edward Youde Aviary, Forsgate Conservatory, K.S. Lo Gallery, and the Visual Arts Centre are also on the premises, and there is a small but lovely *bonsai* and rock garden hidden behind the aviary. *(Park ☎2521 5041; open daily 6:30am-11pm. Aviary and Conservatory open daily 9am-5pm. Gallery ☎2869 6690; open Th-Tu 10am-5pm. Visual Arts Centre ☎2521 3008; open W-M 10am-9pm. Wheelchair accessible. All free.)*

H
O
N
G

K
O
N
G

BANKING ON FENG SHUI Belief in the ancient practice of *feng shui*, or wind-water geomantic principles, still inspires modern-day engineers and architects in Hong Kong. Prime examples are the **Bank of China** and the **Hong Kong & Shanghai Banking Corporation** buildings in Central, both of which rank as internationally recognized architectural marvels. Made of titanium, the Hong Kong & Shanghai Banking Corporation building was the most expensive building in the world at the time of its construction, while the 70-story Bank of China building earned its acclaim as the tallest building in Hong Kong until Central Plaza snatched the title a few years ago.

When the Bank of China Tower, designed by I.M. Pei to resemble a budding bamboo shoot, was finally completed in 1990, occupants of the surrounding structures complained of the bad *feng shui* generated by their newest neighbor. Indeed, the Hong Kong & Shanghai Banking Corporation registered a loss in profits that very year. As a defensive measure, the Hong Kong & Shanghai Banking Corporation employed a *feng shui* expert who advised the company to board up the windows of the transparent tower and to erect two arms to jut out from the side of the building closest to the rival bank. With red blinking lights and round barrels, the arms look more like guns trained on the Bank of China than manifestations of an ancient faith. In any case, business for the Hong Kong & Shanghai Banking Corporation did improve the following year.

ZOOLOGICAL AND BOTANICAL GARDENS. The Zoological and Botanical Gardens sit just off Garden Rd., a 10-minute walk from the Hong Kong Hilton past St. John's Cathedral. The main entrance is at the intersection of Garden Rd. and Upper Albert Rd. Stick to the maze of pedestrian walkways and keep your eyes alert for signs pointing to the Gardens. The Gardens are a pleasure for flora and fauna enthusiasts. Jaguars, reptiles, monkeys, and butterflies call this their home, but like Hong Kong residents, space constraints are a sad reality for some of these animals. (☎ 2530 0153. *Open daily 6am-7pm; greenhouse open 9am-4:30pm.*)

OTHER SIGHTS. Businessmen pound the pavement in this financial and government watershed. Ebel clocks grace street corners and bus and train stations, showcasing not only the time, but Hong Kong's time consciousness. Long-standing beliefs about the placement of buildings in accordance with the harmony of nature, and precise attention to detail and *feng shui* (see **Banking on Feng Shui**, p. 438), have created one of the most beautiful cities in the world.

Some of the most tranquil gardens found anywhere in Hong Kong are in the midst of Central's gleaming urban landscape. **Statue Square** (a three-minute walk from the Star Ferry through the pedestrian underpass) sprouts a crop of picnic-goers on Sundays and public holidays. In the center of the square, the statue of Sir Thomas Jackson, one of Hong Kong's beloved capitalists, surveys the ever-thriving business district with approval. Farther inland, the **Chater Garden** is a shady vantage point for observing Central's most famous buildings. The concrete pavilion that embraces the garden, well camouflaged in green creepers, is a subdued break from the busy streets around it.

WAN CHAI

In keeping with Wan Chai's fascination for lights, **Central Plaza**, the tallest building in Hong Kong, is easily spotted from most locations on Hong Kong Island. Its color beams serve as a clock: the color of the bottom light indicates the hour (red 6pm, white 7pm, purple 8pm, yellow 9pm, pink 10pm, and green 11pm); if the top light is a different color, it's a quarter past; if the top two and bottom two lights differ, it's a half past; if the top three match, it's 45min. past the hour; and when all four lights match, it is on the hour.

HONG KONG CONVENTION AND EXHIBITION CENTRE (HKCEC). This grand waterfront building stands as an impressive testament to Hong Kong's ability to put on a good show. Opened in 1997 for the handover ceremonies, the Centre is a quiet, sprawling marvel of glass, sunlight, and expansive floor-to-ceiling windows with romantic views of the Kowloon shore. It was supposedly constructed to look like a bird on the brink of takeoff, but many claim that it slightly resembles the Sydney Opera House. Exhibits, cafes, and restaurants keep the HKCEC active at night. (☎ 2582 8888. Open 24hr. No slippers or shorts.) The outdoor garden and waterfront promenade come as a welcome surprise in this otherwise urban desert. The **Hong Kong Arts Centre**, to your right as you leave the HKCEC, sells tickets for shows in its auditoriums. Brochures and posters in front of the box office on the ground floor advertise upcoming performances. (Program inquiries ☎ 2582 0202; URBTIX hotline ☎ 2734 9009. Box office open daily 10am-6pm.)

CAUSEWAY BAY

▨ **VICTORIA PARK.** At dawn and dusk, this haven of sprawling green lawns and leafy boulevards is peppered with tai chi devotees. Sports facilities include tennis courts, a roller-skating rink, a bowling green, and a swimming pool (all for a fee). Free jogging trails wind through spacious lawns, an aviary, and a topiary garden. The park is home to a large flower fair during the Chinese New Year, and during the Mid-Autumn Festival, local families come here to eat lotus-seed cakes and gaze at the moon. (Enter on Gloucester Rd., opposite the Park Lane Hotel. ☎ 2890 5824. Park open 24hr. Roller-skating rink open daily 9am-11pm; HK$16 per hr. Swimming pool open daily 6:30am-noon and 1-10pm; HK$19, children HK$9.) A single footbridge in the northwest corner of the park, along the path from the Model Boat Pool, leads to **Causeway Bay Typhoon Shelter**, where floating homes bob next to sleek yachts.

NOON-DAY GUN. This famous gun, featured in Noel Coward's 1924 satire *Mad Dogs and Englishmen* ("In Hong Kong they strike a gong and fire a noon-day gun"), squats on the waterfront across from the Excelsior Hotel. In 19th-century Hong Kong, the famous Jardine Matheson company had their own private artillery as protection against pirates. Guards fired the gun to hail their *taipans*. This unlicensed show of military might finally angered a new naval officer so much that he demanded the company be punished. Jardine Matheson was forced to fire the gun every day at noon to signal the time—a tradition that continues today. (Take Jaffe Rd. toward Victoria Park; walk straight toward the alley near the Excelsior Hotel car park. Just after you pass the 7-Eleven on your left, look ahead and follow the red-letter sign to the gun. Open daily 7am-midnight.)

OTHER SIGHTS. Past Victoria Park, on Tin Hau Rd., is the small **Tin Hau Temple**. Take the tram or MTR to Tin Hau MTR station, and take exit B onto King's Rd. Cross the street, turn right and go around the block onto Tin Hau Temple Rd. An air of hushed stillness extends from the main altar to the courtyard garden. Next to the Tin Hau Temple, on Dragon Rd., the **Raja Yoga Meditation Centre** helps teach the art of blessed repose with free classes in meditation, vegetarian cooking, and positive thinking for a new and improved you. (☎ 2806 3008; fax 2887 0104. Call ahead; registration required. Open M-F 9am-1pm and 2-9pm, Sa-Su and holidays 9am-1pm and 2-7pm.)

Back toward Wan Chai, **Times Square** (see also **Shopping**, p. 434), bounded by Canal Rd., Russell St., Matheson St., and Sharp St., comes alive at night. The large dome clock that gives the square its name lights up, as do the giant TV and building exterior. Rest here after shopping all day or come simply to watch people.

STANLEY

Stanley's main attraction is **Stanley Market**. Stanley Main St. charters a journey through clean stalls and petite shops full of every garment known to man, from snake-skin boots to the street's specialty, silk pajamas. This is a good place to buy a chop (stone stamp) carved with your name. **Stanley Main Beach**, just east of the market along Stanley Beach Rd., is often packed on weekends. **St. Stephen Beach** is a 10-minute walk south along Wong Ma Kok Rd., away from the market and toward the hills. From the bus station terminus on Stanley Village St., turn left and follow the signs in pink print all the way to the beach entrance. In the opposite direction from the bus station, follow the signs for **Stanley Plaza** to reach the new shopping mall. Beside it is Stanley's **Tin Hau Temple,** which provided shelter to villagers during WWII Japanese bombings. *(Market open daily 9am-6:30pm. Beaches open 24hr. Shower facilities available at Stanley Beach.)*

▟ WALKS ON HONG KONG ISLAND

Perhaps one of the most intriguing aspects of Hong Kong is that its dense urban fabric is nestled in a topography of sweeping, unspoiled hills and mountains. Over 40% of the territory has been preserved in public parks, most of which are tattooed with an intricate network of extremely well-maintained trails. The "Magic Walks" series (HK$45-85), available in major bookstores and at the HKTA, covers most hiking options. The HKTA (see p. 419) also distributes pamphlets about specific trails. Happy trippers should bring sunscreen, proper shoes, and plenty of water.

The **Wilson Trail,** named after an ex-governor and inveterate hiker, starts in Stanley and ends in the New Territories. The entire trail takes 27 hours to complete. The **Shing Mun Jogging Trail,** the **Sai Kung Coddle Stones** path, and the southern valley of **Mount Butler** are some of the trail's highlights. The **Wan Chai Green Trail** specializes in urban flora. It begins at the Wan Chai Old Post Office on Queen's Rd. East and ends at Stubbs Rd. Eleven educational stations along the trail point out plants of interest. The **Hong Kong Trail** passes through five country parks on Hong Kong Island, offering scenic views of some of the island's most beautiful areas.

▨ SOUTHERN HONG KONG ISLAND

A few kilometers from the hubbub of northern Hong Kong Island, Southern Hong Kong Island's shores flow serenely, with clear waters, beaches, and good hiking.

KENNEDY TOWN 堅尼地城
Although it is a long trek to get to **Hong Kong University,** hidden on the side of a mountain in Kennedy Town, on Hong Kong Island's western edge, the **University Museum and Art Gallery** is definitely worth a visit. The museum houses permanent exhibits of bronzes and ceramics that date back to the Shang (1600-1066 BC) and Zhou (1066-221 BC) dynasties. Relics from the Yuan dynasty (AD 1279-1368) also grace the display shelves. To get to Hong Kong University, take bus #7 from Pier 7 in Central (every 10-15min., HK$5.30) or bus #5A from along Des Voeux Rd., Queensway, or Queen's Rd. East (every 10-12min., HK$3.40). Ask a student to point out the building upon arrival at the University. *(☎ 2241 5500. Open M-Sa 9:30am-6pm, Su 1:30-5:30pm. Free.)*

SHEK O 石澳
On the southeast coast of Hong Kong Island, not far from Stanley, lies the lovely Shek O Beach. Crowded with oiled-up bodies chasing tanning rays, but fanned by breezes filtering down from the mountains, this long, well-maintained stretch of shore is one of the most popular beaches on Hong Kong Island. Stake out a spot and rent an umbrella tent for the day (HK$30). Several shops rent bikes (HK$15-20 per hr., HK$35-40 per day) for exploring the surrounding hillside. Bus #309 goes to Shek O from Central (50min., Su every 30min., HK$11). On weekdays, ride the tram to its last stop and board bus #9 for Shek O at the Shau Kei Wan MTR Station (A1 or A2 exits; every 15-30min. 6am-11pm; HK$4.20, A/C HK$6.20); wander around the markets in Shau Kei Wan if you have time on your hands before getting on the bus. Allow at least two hours to get to the beach if you're going this way.

DEEPWATER BAY 胸水環 AND REPULSE BAY 淺水環
Deepwater Bay beach has a long coast, a beautiful view, and powdery soft sand. Take bus #6 from Central Exchange Square to the Deepwater Bay stop (every 10-30min., HK$5.30). Repulse Bay is Hong Kong Island's gem. Take bus #6 to the Shell station stop on Repulse Bay Rd. Sturdy nets anchored offshore ensure that no unwanted sea life comes in for a morning snack. Two large statues of Gwan Tum

and Tin Mau, traditional protectors of local fishermen, guard the shores. Bus #73 connects Aberdeen, Repulse Bay, and Stanley (every 15-25min., HK$5.80).

ABERDEEN 香港仔

Once just a small fishing village with a harbor full of floating *sampan*, Aberdeen and its pricey floating restaurants are now a must-see for many tourists. The **Aberdeen Promenade,** a smaller version of the TST walkway, passes junks, *sampan*, and teenagers fishing in waters clearly marked with pollution signs. The **Jumbo Floating Restaurant,** self-proclaimed as the "most luxurious floating restaurant in the world," offers overpriced seafood. Little old ladies waylay tourists near the bus stop for *sampan* cruises around the harbor (HK$40-50 for 30min.). Bus #70 runs between Central and Aberdeen (every 6-15min. 6am-midnight, HK$4.70).

Ocean Park declares itself "the largest and most spectacular theme park in Southeast Asia," and deserves the title with its nerve-wracking, stomach-dropping roller coasters, goldfish pagoda, shark aquarium, dolphin university, and Hong Kong's two Giant pandas, An An and Jia Jia. The Giant pandas occupy a 2000m^2 habitat that is within walking distance of **Atoll Reef,** where 400 species of fish can be viewed through a glass gallery. The **Middle Kingdom,** a meta-park showcasing 17 Chinese dynasties, is near the back. Next door is **Water World,** a giant aquatic play-pen, full of slides, pools, and tanned teenagers. *(A Citybus shuttle runs from the Aberdeen bus terminal to Ocean Park and Water World (HK$12). Take bus #70 from Exchange Square in Central (every 6-15min., HK$4.70) or bus #72 from Causeway Bay (every 10-20min., HK$4.70); get off at the stop after the Aberdeen Tunnel and follow the blue signs to Ocean Park.* ☎2552 0291. *Ocean Park open daily 10am-6pm. HK$140, ages 3-11 HK$70 with purchase of adult ticket, 1 child age 3-11 free. Water World* ☎2552 0291. *Open daily May 29-July 9 and Sept. 1-Oct.3 10am-6pm; July 10-Aug. 31 9am-9pm. Day admission HK$65, evening HK$44.)*

NEW TERRITORIES 新界

The New Territories, quiet, rural and somewhat reserved, stretch over 794km^2 of rugged mountains and unexplored beaches, rough-hewn by forces older than man. Rich in temples, rock carvings, and cultural relics, there is a sense of loss in the fact that the wide open spaces of the New Territories make it a natural site for development as Hong Kong's population and demand for cities grows.

ORIENTATION

The best way to navigate around the New Territories is by KCR and MTR stops. Each stop has a bus station with buses, minibuses/maxicabs, and the green New Territories taxis. The KCR East Rail runs from south to north, beginning at Hung Hom and zigzagging through **Mong Kok, Sha Tin, Fotan,** the **Chinese University,** and **Tai Po,** ending at **Lo Wu** on the Chinese border. From Central, the MTR red line runs northwards, finishing at **Tseun Wan.** Accessible by ferry or bus, **Tuen Mun,** a residential center in the far west, is connected to **Yuen Long** in the northeast by KCR Light Rail (LR). The beaches of **Sai Kung Peninsula** and **Clearwater Bay,** in the southeast corner, are accessible by bus #299 from University KCR Station.

FOOD

After spending a day exploring **Sai Kung**'s tropical forests and spectacular views (see p. 444), eating and unwinding in Sai Kung town can be the perfect nightcap. Sai Kung town overflows with seafood restaurants, many of which boast live specimens in tanks. **Fuk Man Rd.** runs to the left of the bus station (if you stand with your back to the waterfront). Little English is spoken in the local bars, but music proves to be the universal language—in other words, karaoke is everywhere.

■ **Pepperoni's,** 1592 Po Tung Rd. (☎2792 2083). If you enjoy the Gipsy Kings, a warm ambience, and fine apple crumble mounted with vanilla ice cream, this is the place to be. Expect to wait for a table. Famed pizzas range from HK$55 for a small margherita to

HK$70 for a small pepperoni special. Delivery to New Territories. Credit cards accepted. Open daily 9am-11pm.

Indian Curry Hut, 64 Po Tung Rd. (☎2791 2929 or 2791 2333). Serves tandoori specialties, including tandoori squid (HK$66) and chicken tikka (HK$48). Rice, bread, mutton, and vegetarian plates are also available. Open daily 11:30am-11:30pm.

Tapas Tree, 10A Po Tung Rd. (☎2792 6608). Upbeat music, classy decor with flowers on every table, and attentive service. *Tapas* live up to their exotic names. *Souvlakis*—lamb and lemon kebabs with minted tomato sauce—go for HK$40. Open M-Th noon-midnight, F-Su noon-2am.

Susannah's Seafood, 76 Po Tung Rd. (☎2792 2139). The friendly staff humbly admits that people come for miles around to sample the baked lobster with cheese, chili crab, and salt-fried prawns (seasonal prices). Chinese dishes include beef, vegetables, and chili beef or chicken (HK$48-60). English menus. Open M-F noon-2:30pm and 6-10:30pm, Sa-Su noon-3:30pm and 6-10:30pm.

Duke of York, 42-56 Fuk Man Rd. (☎2792 8435). Comfortable and social. Snacks HK$25-30. A live rock band plays some nights. During Happy Hour (all day M, Tu-F 2-9pm), beer is HK$30 a pint. Open daily noon-2am.

Steamers, 82-83 Chan Man St. (☎2792 6991). With its glass windows and open space, Steamers has a more airy atmosphere than most bars. Happy Hour M-F 2-9pm (Carlsberg HK$22). Open daily 9am-2am.

Beach Resort Hotel Beach Pub, 1780 Tai Mong Tsai Rd. (☎2791 0550). Known as the "Surf Hotel" by those in the know. Live music Sa 10pm-3am. Happy Hour M-F 5-9pm, Sa-Su 3-7pm. Open M-F 5pm-3am, Sa-Su 3pm-3am.

 # SHOPPING

In the past, Hong Kong Island and Kowloon were fierce competitors in the race to construct bigger and glassier malls, while the New Territories looked on in dazed bewilderment. Today, the New Territories are being drawn into the fray, with every major stop on the KRC (East Rail) boasting an impressive mall complex. Two noteworthy malls are:

Festival Walk, 80 Tat Chee Ave., Kowloon Tong (☎2520 8028). MTR: Kowloon Tong; KCR: Kowloon Tong. A gleaming work of massive glass floors and windows ribbed by interwoven steel elevators. With more than 200 shops, this is not the place for the faint-hearted shopper.

New Town Plaza and Grand Central Plaza, (☎2683 9175). KCR: Sha Tin. For those prepared to argue that Festival Walk is in Kowloon, this massive mall in Sha Tin is proof that the New Territories can do it too. At 12:45pm, make your way to the central fountain on the 1st floor and watch the crowds ooh and aah as water shoots upwards in a choreographed dance to classical music.

 # SIGHTS

TSUEN WAN 全環

At the end of the red Tsuen Wan MTR line is a major cultural and spiritual bedrock, the fast-expanding city of Tsuen Wan. Its temples have more continuous prayers and incense burning for the dead than anywhere else in Hong Kong. This is to be expected, as this town is the most expensive place to deposit the ashes of the departed. **Tai Mo Shan,** the biggest mountain in Hong Kong, is also in Tsuen Wan.

The **Sam Tung Uk Museum,** 2 Kwu Uk Lane, is a five-minute walk from the Tsuen Wan MTR station (B3 exit). A restored, walled Hakka village dating to 1786, the museum has period rooms furnished with tools and items. A small exhibition hall also houses a rotating exhibit. (☎2411 2001. Open W-M 9am-5pm. Free.)

Western Monastery holds religious ceremonies on the 2nd Fl. that are open to tourists on special days. It's aesthetically impressive, as is its neighbor, the famous

Yuen Yuen Institute. The temple complex is dedicated to Confucianism, Buddhism, and Daoism, featuring the Arches of the Three Religions and the Great Temple of the Three Religions. A stroll around the complex reveals a bronze statue of Confucius, a *bonsai* garden, and a temple blessed with 60 statues of deities, one for each year in the Chinese 60-year cycle. Yuen Yuen shelters three of Hong Kong's largest "Precious Buddha" statues inside its walls, and vendors sell incense sticks and flowers by the gold and silver chariot outside. *(Take green minibus #81 to Lo Wai Village. From B3 exit at Tseun Wan MTR Station, follow pedestrian overpass until the end. On emerging on the street below, with your back to the MTR station, walk left. Make a right turn at Chung On Street. Walk up the block, turn right at the corner, and minibus #81 will be on your right. Monastery ☎2411 5111. Institute ☎2429 2220. Both open daily 9am-5pm. Free.)*

Chuk Lam Sim Yuen, translated as "Bamboo Forest Monastery," is one of Hong Kong's most elaborate Buddhist monasteries. *(Green minibus #85 runs to the monastery from the same station as minibus #81. See above for directions. Open daily 7am-4pm. Free.)*

TAI PO 大浦 AND PLOVER COVE RESERVOIR
Take the KCR to Tai Po Market, then exit for Uptown Plaza, take the pedestrian underpass, and hop on bus #75K at the far back corner of the bus station (50min., HK$3.60). The reservoir is the last stop on the bus line.

Tai Po is a typical New Territories town—a mess of construction, a marvel of tall, identical apartments, and a stone's throw away from stunning panoramas of land and sea. Plover Cove Reservoir is a favorite of both hikers and picnickers. Visitors can barbecue by the water's edge and rent boats on the weekends. A family walk that begins next to the Bradbury Lodge tours the surrounding area in under an hour and numerous side trails await exploration by the more adventurous.

Bradbury Lodge (HI), on Tai Mei Tuk Rd. (look for the sign and trail at the back of the bus terminal), puts up guests who wish to stay at the Plover Cove Reservoir for the night. The lodge has a communal atmosphere with A/C, a large, shared kitchen and dining area, a TV in the common room, and a rooftop balcony with a splendid view of Plover Cove. The drawbacks are the six shared showers and non-Western toilets for up to 48 guests, and some cleaning duties. Reservations are recommended on weekends. (☎2662 5123. Reception open daily 7-10am and 4-11pm, with a 10am-noon lockout. Lights-out at 11pm. Dorms HK$55, non-members HK$80; doubles HK$200.)

CHINESE UNIVERSITY 香港中文大學
A shuttle bus (☎2609 7990) runs from the University KCR station to the central campus at the top of the hill (every 30min. M-F 9am-5:15pm, Sa 9am-1am; HK$1). Take the exit for the university campus, turn right and walk toward the bus station. Art museum ☎2609 7416. Open M-Sa 10am-4:45pm, Su 12:30-5:30pm. Free.

One stop south of Tai Po Market on the KCR, Chinese University's lovely campus is built into the side of a mountain in Ma Liu Shui. Its location means beautiful surroundings dotted by green parks and peaceful lakes, but also landslides during the monsoon season. A visit to the art museum, next to the university library and miniature hedge maze, is worth the risk.

SHA TIN 沙田
Sha Tin's **Shing Man River** is a popular venue for dragon boat racing at the time of the annual **Dragon Boat Festival,** or **Tuen Ng.** At the time of Tuen Ng, people eat dumplings wrapped in bamboo leaves as teams race colorful dragon boats to the beat of drums (see **Dragon Boats Galore,** p. 535, for the legend behind the festival). Sha Tin is also home to the **Bo Fook Ancestral Worship Halls** on Tai Po Rd. These are beautifully situated in the mountains, their pristine tranquility a dramatic contrast to the industrial sprawl below. Use the escalator at the base of the building to access the halls easily. For the more hardy, the **Ten Thousand Buddhas Temple** is a strenuous 450-odd steps to the top. The climb is steep, and winds its way through heaps of rusting iron and the poorer New Territories residences. Turn left at the entrance to the Worship Halls and ask for directions; stay alert for the little yellow

placards. The rewards for reaching the top are cooler temperatures and the company of many, many, little gold Buddhas. *(Exit through the left entrance of the Sha Tin KCR station and follow the yellow signs. Both Halls and Temple open daily 9am-5pm.)*

Sha Tin's greatest claim to fame is its **racecourse,** which draws thousands on race days (W late Sept.-late June). To get there, take the KCR to Fo Tan Station; from the C exit (Jubilee Garden), cross the street, turn left, and walk until Jubilee Garden is on your right. Soon after, enter the garden, and before the Jubilee Wet Market, go into the tunnel (on the left) and follow it until you reach the horse-racing stadium. Bus #888 also leaves from the Sha Tin KCR to the racecourse. There is an old Chinese proverb that cautions, "When you win, you win a particle of sugar. When you lose, you lose the whole factory." In spite of this ancient wisdom and the general perception that gambling is evil, horse-racing continues to thrive. Horse-racing fervor suffered a temporary setback when the Asian economic crisis led to individuals losing huge sums of money on the stock market. But progress and prosperity are the names of the game in Hong Kong—and all is back on track. On losing large sums of money, many individuals have begun donating to charity (appeasing the spirits, perhaps?*).*

SAI KUNG 西貢
Sai Kung town has the perpetual aura of an old fishing village on late Sunday afternoon. It is relaxed, foreigner-friendly, and a bonding territory for hikers, campers, beach-lovers, and those who deeply appreciate natural beauty.

The area is scattered with temples over 300 years in age. Ask a local to point the way to a place of worship, and they may share the fascinating thread of history and myth that has been spun around those holy relics. The **Tin Hau Temple,** built in honor of the Goddess of the Sea, is the place of worship for fishermen whose lives are inextricably bound to her will. *(With the waterfront behind you, walk left from the bus station.* ☎ *2461 5725.)* For a spiritual connection to the great outdoors, explore Sai Kung's **Country Park** and the famous **MacLehose Trail,** which begins in Pak Tam Chung, (take bus #94 from Sai Kung station). The HKTA provides a free booklet outlining a walk in Sai Kung that includes a visit to **Sheung Yiu Village Museum,** a restored Hakka village in Pak Tam Chung. *(*☎ *2792 6365. Open W-M 9am-4pm.)*

Sai Kung's Clearwater Bay Beaches No. 1 and 2 are famed for their high water quality. From Diamond Hill MTR, take bus #91 and disembark at the terminus. There is also a country park in Clearwater Bay. To windsurf, canoe, row a *sampan,* or kayak, contact the **Chong Hing Water Sports Centre** (☎ 2792 6810).

CLEARWATER BAY 清水灣
To reach the beach, take the MTR to Diamond Hill station, and take bus #91 from exit B to the end of the line (every 12-18min. 6am-10pm; HK$4.70, with A/C HK$6.50).

Clearwater Bay, one of Hong Kong's more popular beaches, has pristine white sand and turquoise water. But beware of the ominous fins that may circle offshore; the shark attack warnings plastered all over the beach are serious. Clearwater Bay comes fully equipped, with showers, changing rooms, a first aid station, and lifeguards who may one day stand between you and Jaws's jagged teeth (only 9am-6pm, however). The bus route winds through thickly wooded slopes and offers glimpses of the ocean.

LANTAU ISLAND 大嶼山
Lantau Island, larger than Hong Kong Island and breathtaking in its natural grandeur, is Hong Kong's Eden. Lantau's craggy mountains, isolated monasteries, giant Buddha statue, and wide open skies give the island an otherworldly feel. On weekends, Hong Kong residents descend upon Lantau to dine on fresh seafood, visit temples, and picnic in the mountains. When the daytrippers have left, quiet descends, and residents and hikers camping in the wilderness can marvel at the simple beauty of the night sky.

✦? ORIENTATION AND PRACTICAL INFORMATION

Lantau Island is essentially comprised of small towns that span the island's coastal perimeter. On the northeast coast, **Discovery Bay** is a tightly knit community of high-income individuals who can afford to maintain a picture-perfect neighborhood. Moving down along the eastern coast is Lantau's ferry arrival port, **Mui Wo,** also known as **Silvermine Bay.** Along the Southern coast is **Pui O,** a residential area that eventually leads to **Tong Fuk Village,** famous for its gorgeous Cheung Sha beaches. **Tai O** is an old fishing village on the west coast that is home to the Tanka people, descendants of the Yueh. **Ngong Ping,** in the inner Western region of Lantau, is surveyed by the immense Tian Tan Buddha atop Po Lin Monastery. Now the fast developing central town of Lantau Island, **Tung Chung** was previously the remote site of an old fort to keep out opium traders. **Chek Lap Kok,** the site of the new airport, was once an insignificant appendage on the northwest coast, hanging onto Lantau by a thin thread of land. The newly constructed 2.2km road and rail suspension bridge, **Tsing Ma Bridge,** the longest in the world, effectively links Chek Lap Kok, Lantau Island, and Hong Kong.

Government and financial services are concentrated in **Mui Wo** and **Tung Chung.** In **Mui Wo,** banks with **ATM** machines, chain grocery stores, and 7-Elevens are available immediately upon arrival as components of the square that surrounds the bus station. Mui Wo police station, clinic, and post office are all in the same government services complex. To reach it, walk toward Silvermine Bay beach on **Ngan Kwong Wan Rd.** Just after the bridge to the beach (Mui Wo Chung Hau St.) branches off Ngan Kwong Wan Rd., you will see gray complex labeled "Government Offices" on your left. The **police** force (☎2721 2486) is in Rm. 215. The **clinic** (☎2984 2178) and **post office** are on the ground floor. (Open M-F 9am-4:30pm, Sa 9am-12:30pm.) **Tung Chung MTR Station** has a small bank with **ATM** machines, and **Citygate Mall,** attached to the station, has a large grocery store.

▐ TRANSPORTATION

Trains: Trains travel the yellow Tung Chung line, beginning at Hong Kong station and ending in Tung Chung MTR Station (HK$23).

Buses: Mui Wo, Tung Chung, Pui O, Tong Fuk, Tai O, and Ngong Ping all have easily visible bus stations with fares and schedules posted for each. Journeys tend to be long (averaging an hour), and bumpy, but offer spectacular views of Lantau. Buses are run by the New Lantau Bus Co. (☎2984 9848). Blue **taxis** are available at all bus stations (☎2984 1328), but since all the major routes spiral up mountains in a leisurely fashion, taking a taxi is not recommended.

Ferries: Ferries depart from Pier 7 at the Central Star Ferry to Mui Wo port (daily, every 30min. 1:30am-11:30pm). Free schedules are available on request from HKTA offices and the Star Ferry ticket office.

Local Transportation: Bus E31 leaves from Tseun Wan, Discovery Park to Tung Chung MTR; **E32** leaves from Kwai Fong MTR on the Red line via Tung Chung MTR en route to the Chek Lap Kok airport terminus. Both buses run every 10-20 min. and cost HK$10.

Bicycles: Friendly Bicycle Shop (☎2984 2278), behind McDonald's in Mui Wo. HK$10 per hr., weekdays HK$30 per day, weekends HK$40 per day. HK$5 student discount on weekdays. Open daily 10am-8pm. **King of Bicycle** (☎2984 7704), two stores down from Friendly Bicycle. HK$10 per hr., HK$30 per day (overnight included). Discounts available for large groups. Open daily 10:30am-8:30pm.

▐ ACCOMMODATIONS

S.G. Davis Hostel (HI), Ngong Ping (☎2985 5610). From Mui Wo bus station at the ferry port, take bus #2 to Po Lin Monastery, Ngong Ping. Follow the sign to the left of the

Buddha statue; the hostel is a 10min. walk farther. Quite, serene, and run by an exceptionally friendly couple. Dorms soon to be converted into singles. Simple chores required. Curfew 11pm. Dorms HK$35 for HI members, HK$55 for non-member accompanied by member, HK$180 for non-member (comes with a membership card valid for a year). May-Oct. HK$10 extra per adult, HK$5 per child. Bargain.

Jockey Club Mong Tung Wan Hostel (HI), Pui O (☎2984 1389). From Mui Wo bus station, take bus #7 to Pui O terminus. Signs for the hostel are on Chi Ma Wan Rd., which loops around the bus station. Follow the signs; it's about a 45min. walk. Alternatively, take the ferry from Pier 6 (Central Hong Kong Island) to Cheung Chau Island. Hire a *sampan* to the jetty at Mong Tung Wan (HK$100). The hostel is a few minutes walk away and within walking distance (45min.) of Pui O beach. Prices and curfew time same as at the S.G. Davis Hostel.

Mui Wo Inn, 24 Tung Wan Tau Rd., Silvermine Bay/Mui Wo (☎298 7225 or 2984 8597). From Mui Wo bus station, walk toward Silvermine Bay beach. Tung Wan Tau Rd. runs along the length of the beach. With a swimming pool surrounded by Greek statuettes and a view of the beach, this is the perfect place to spoil yourself after roughing it. A/C, refrigerator, TV, VCR, and private bath. Singles HK$280, waterfront singles HK$450. On weekends, singles HK$450, waterfront singles HK$550.

◪ FOOD

MUI WO. Upon arriving at Mui Wo, travelers are greeted with a choice of restaurants. The **Mui Wo Square** surrounding the bus station has a few small Chinese restaurants tucked between stores. By the ferry terminal, the golden arches of **McDonald's** beckon just-docked guests, and just behind it is the **China Bear Bar and Restaurant.** Feast on nachos (HK$45), bangers and mash (HK$55), and an all-day breakfast platter (HK$58). The local *gwailo* community comes here to enjoy the great waterfront view and laid-back atmosphere. (☎2984 9720. Open M-F noon-11pm, Sa-Su 11am-11pm.) The **Mui Wo Cooked Food Market,** also by the ferry terminal, contains small blocks of restaurants that share an outdoor seating area. (Open daily 6am-midnight.) On the road to the beach from the Cooked Food Market is a small cluster of local seafood restaurants to your left. The large, outdoor pavilions and view of the beach make this a compelling venue for seafood enthusiasts. Those who like to keep it fresh should visit the **Mui Wo Food and Vegetable Market,** on the first floor of the Mui Wo complex. Walk from the ferry pier toward Silvermine Bay beach. At the junction that leads to the beach on your right, walk straight until you reach a large gray building on your right.

PUI O AND TAI O. Apart from Mui Wo, **Pui O** is your best bet for a selection of good restaurants in the midst of rural Lantau. From Mui Wo bus station, take bus #7 to Pui O bus terminus. A string of restaurants, mostly Chinese, line the street opposite the bus station. If you want to eat as the Chinese eat, take bus #1 from Mui Wo bus station and get off at **Tai O.** This small and densely populated fishing village is famous for its seafood restaurants. Unfortunately, restaurants are hard to find, which is made worse by the fact that the village is hard to navigate.

OTHER OPTIONS ON LANTAU ISLAND. For devout vegans, **Po Lin Monastery** in **Ngong Ping** is the place to be. On arrival at Po Lin (take bus #2 from Mui Wo station at ferry pier), walk straight from the Buddha statue through the stone gateway to the main hall. The cafeteria is on the left (Arhan temple). A meal ticket costs HK$60, but light snacks are available. (Noodles or tofu HK$20, desserts HK$10. ☎2985 5248. Open daily 11:30am-5pm.) The **Tea Garden Restaurant** is a five-minute walk from the entrance to the statue. Follow signs leading from the large red banner to the right of the statue. (☎2985 5161. Open daily 10am-6pm.)

The **Tung Chung** MTR station exits into the new Citygate Mall. There is a **McDonald's,** with **Delifrance** beside it. On the other side of Delifrance is the ▧ **Cat-street Cafe.** With its outdoor seating, upscale decor (sleek, long-stemmed water glasses), and budget prices, this joint is a rare find. The menu caters both Western and Chinese dishes, with sumptuous fried rice noodles with satay beef (HK$40) and grilled steak with black pepper sauce (HK$48). (☎2109 1131. MC, Visa accepted. Open daily 11am-10pm.)

👁 SIGHTS

NGONG PING. Perhaps Lantau Island's most popular sight is the giant ▨ **Tian Tan Buddha statue,** the largest outdoor seated bronze Buddha in the world. Completed in October 1989, the statue is 33.95m tall and covers an area of 3284m^2. Be prepared to walk up 260 steps to view the Buddha statue up close. High atop his altar, Buddha raises his right hand as if greeting visitors and peacefully surveying the lives of those down below at the **Po Lin Monastery.** His left hand, with palm upturned, is in the "mudra of sfulfilling wishes" (that is, granting blessings). Every feature of the statue is religiously symbolic. Buddha's broad forehead and elongated ears signify virtue, wisdom, and perfection. Viewing the bronze giant is free, but the museum beneath it requires a snack or meal ticket to enter. Be forewarned: a stream of visitors crowd the complex during the weekends. (☎ 2985 5248. Open daily 10am-6pm.)

The beauty of the surrounding mist-covered mountains makes for inspirational hiking. The **Lantau Trail** goes by **Sunset Peak,** the second highest mountain on Lantau. Early birds who catch the sunrise from the mountain take in an unforgettable sight. Although it can be dangerous when wet, tourists can still walk the paved roadway to **Po Lam Zen Monastery** (45 minutes from Po Lin Monastery), winding up and down through incredible scenery. In the morning, the usually closed-off monastery may permit visitors, but beware of stray dogs.

OTHER AREAS. Just a short walk from the ferry terminal in **Mui Wo,** the **Silvermine Waterfall** is a hidden treasure, unknown even to many of the residents of Mui Wo. Like many of Lantau's natural wonders, the falls are tucked behind much greenery, accessible by a path lined with homes. To get to the waterfall, take a right out of the ferry terminal. Continue down the road and turn right on Ngen Shek St. Follow Ngen Shek St. as it curves to the right, then turn left onto Wong Tong Rd. Keep to the left at the two forks, and you'll soon hear the falls in the distance. The walk from ferry to falls takes about 25 minutes.

Pui O beach, accessible by bus #7, is popular with locals. The **Cheung Sha Upper beach,** accessible by bus #4 (specify to the driver that you are going to Cheung Sha *Upper* beach), has lovely views and high water quality. (Beach hotline ☎2414 5555. All beaches in Lantau open daily 9am-6pm.)

Maritime Square is an "ocean-liner" that houses an immense mall. The Old Market on the first floor uses computer technology, lighting, and sound effects to recreate Hong Kong in the past. (MTR: Tsing Yi Station. ☎2449 9013 or 2186 7284.)

⚠ HIKING

Lantau is rich in country parks and hiking terrain. A large map pointing out walking trails, campsites, and country parks often greets visitors to each town. For the dedicated hiker, E. Stokes's book *Exploring Hong Kong's Countryside* is highly recommended (HK$80, available at HKTA main office and major bookstores). The HKTA (see p. 419) also publishes a free guide to five walking trails, one of which is on Lantau. **Mui Wo** is a good starting point, with a **Country Parks Information Post** in the ferry station. (Open M-F 8:30am-noon, Sa-Su 8:30am-4pm.)

LAMMA ISLAND 南丫島

Though Hong Kong Island is only one island away from Lamma, it might as well be one planet away. On one island, life never stands still; on the other, life is in a perpetual state of stupor. Lamma shuns cars, business suits, and stress, glorying instead in the beach. Needless to say, it is an escapist haven for expats in search of *la vie bohème.*

✦⃰ ⁊ ORIENTATION AND PRACTICAL INFORMATION

Roughly, Lamma has a northern and southern half, held together by a strip of land. The port of arrival for the Northern region is **Yung Shue Wan;** for the south, **Sok Kwu Wan.** A ferry shuttles from the port to Pier 5 in Central. Lamma is so small that a walk from Yung Shue Wan to Sok Kwu Wan takes under an hour.

As there are no cars on the island, most people walk or ride bikes. **Bikes** can be rented at Hoi Nam bicycle store in front of the Shai Po New Village street sign. (☎2982 2500. HK$15 per hr. Open daily 7am-11pm.) There are two public **Internet** facilities, both in Yung Shue Wan. **Scorpio,** on Back St., has four terminals with net access for HK$1 per minute (15min. minimum). (☎2982 4121. Open M-Th 9am-8pm, Su noon-6pm.) The **Bookworm Cafe,** 79 Yung Shue Wan Main St., has one terminal available for HK$1 per minute. A small selection of books is also available for loan or purchase. (☎2982 4838. Open Sa-M and W 10am-10pm; Tu, Th-F 10am-6pm.) The **website** www.lamma.net has invaluable information on Lamma Island.

█ ACCOMMODATIONS

Hoi Yee Holiday Resort, 32 Yung Shue Wan Main St. (☎9028 6846). Spacious, clean, decorated rooms, some with balconies opening out onto the bay. A/C, TV, VCR, phone, bath, and fridge. Weekly and monthly rentals available. Rooms Su-F HK$200-350, Sa HK$400-550.

Man Lai Wah Hotel (☎2982 0220 or 2982 0600), right off the ferry terminal at Yung Shue Wan. A/C, TV, phone, and bath. Rooms are clean and many have balconies. Doubles HK$350-400, weekends HK$500 and up.

Lamma Vacation House, 29 Yung Shue Wan Main St., Ground Fl. (☎2982 0427). A/C, TV, and fridge. Rooms HK$150-400, weekends HK$300 and up.

◖◗ ⬛ FOOD AND ENTERTAINMENT

Lamma's undisputed specialty is seafood. The docks and walkways along the bay in **Sok Kwu Wan** are lined with seafood restaurants showcasing aquariums of edible fish. In **Yung Shue Wan,** seafood restaurants cluster around the ferry terminal. Not a seafood fanatic? Don't worry—there are plenty of alternatives. All listed establishments are in Yung Shue Wan.

▩ Bookworm Cafe, 79 Yung Shue Wan Main St. (☎2982 4838). Cool your body with a pineapple smoothie or warm your heart by chatting with the friendly proprietor. Pricey but very tantalizing salads. Open M, W, Sa-Su 10am-10pm; Tu, Th-F 10am-6pm.

Deli Lamma, 36 Main St. (☎2982 1583). Serves hefty and high-quality portions of both Western and Indian delights. Open daily 9am-11pm.

Lamma Seaview Man Fung Restaurant, 5 Main St. (☎5982 0719). Vegetable dishes and open air dining tables complete with fresh roses gracing each table top. Plenty of seafood, plenty of sea view. Credit cards accepted. Open daily 11am-10pm.

Diesels Sports Bar, at 51 Main St. (☎2982 4116). With no service charge and bottled Heineken HK$20 during Happy Hour, Diesel has a good thing going. Open M-F 6pm-late, Sa-Su 2pm-late.

Fountainhead, along Yung Shue Wan Main St. (☎2982 2118). This place woos crowds with its screens. If you don't like the red-brick interior, there's always the pleasure of sitting outside. Happy Hour M-Sa 6-8pm, Su noon-6pm. Open M-F 6pm-2am, Sa-Su noon-2am.

The Islander, (☎2982 1376), on Main St. Unabashedly prides itself on being Lamma's *true* bar (they do not serve snacks) and subsequently draws a mixed crowd. Happy Hour daily 6-8pm. Open M-F 6pm-late, Sa-Su noon-late.

⚡ HIKING

The trail from Yung Shue Wan to Sok Kwu Wan touches upon breathtaking beaches and caves (although tarnished en route by reckless garbage disposal) before emerging near the ferries bound for Central. From Yung Shue Wan, turn onto Yung Shue Wan Back St. and follow the concrete path through tiny villages until you hit the countryside. The trail veers past the fully equipped and staffed **Hung Shing Ye Beach** (a 25min. walk) before continuing over and around **Kamikaze Cave.** In Sok Kwu Wan, you can catch a ferry back to Central or continue on to **Mo Tat Wan** or **Lo So Shing** beaches. From Sok Kwu Wan, the trail follows the curve of the mini-bay. Walking the entire trail takes under one hour. Watch for signs for the trail in both cities.

⚡ CHEUNG CHAU 長州

Tiny in landmass but abundant in character, Cheung Chau Island, perhaps the most buoyant of the outlying islands, is small enough to easily stroll around. It has certainly given rise to flamboyant characters, from Lee Lai-Shan, Hong Kong's first Olympic gold medalist, to Cheung Po Tsai, a legendary pirate who supposedly hid in a cave that now bears his name. Ride the ferry from Pier 6 in Central and cruise through stunning portraits of mountain and sea. The Cheung Chau ferry pier has **ATM** machines, **grocery stores,** and the **police** station. Wander down **Pak She St.,** which runs between the waterfront and the procession of restaurants, bars, shopping stalls, and numerous ice cream stalls. The island is a colorful collection of three-tiered buildings that host restaurants and bars on the lower floors and sun-loving islanders on the third.

MACAU 澳門   ☎853

The first European colony in Asia, Macau soaks in the colorful and vibrant history that permeates its architecture and cuisine. Every pastel colonial building or crumbling Tin Hau temple, every order of *zarzuela* (Spanish seafood casserole) or spicy African chicken, has a story to tell—a story of conquest, trade, and hybridization. When Portuguese traders dropped anchor on the peninsula in 1513, Macau flourished on trading Oriental silks and spices. A procession of Jesuit missionaries made their way to Macau to ensure it remained true to its given name, "City of the Name of God, Macau," leaving a scattering of elegant churches behind. Today, spices and silks no longer flow through Macau, but people—tourism accounts for half of Macau's income. A good number of these are Portuguese; most, however, are giddy Hong Kong weekenders, whisked over by round-the-clock jet foils. They spend their time (and money) gambling in Macau's casinos or partaking in its notoriously racy nightlife. On December 19, 1999, residents had red stars instead of red lights on their minds. Following in Hong Kong's footsteps, this prodigal son was returned to the Motherland after an absence of more than 400 years.

MONEY

Gambler-friendly Macau takes its money seriously. The **pataca** (MP), divided into 100 **avos,** is the official unit of currency of Macau. Coins come in 10, 20, and 50 avos and 1, 5, and 10 patacas; bills come in 20, 50, 100, 500, and 1000 patacas. All Macau businesses accept HK dollars; public pay phones only take patacas. If you change HK dollars into patacas, be careful not to have any patacas left over at the end of your trip—the exchange rate is disadvantageous. **Banks** exchange currency and traveler's checks; they can be found around every corner. **ATMs** hooked up to Plus, Cirrus, Visa, and Jetco networks can be found all over Macau. Most hotels and restaurants accept credit cards. Some may add a 10% service charge and 5% government tax to all bills. **Tips** are not usually expected.

MACAU PATACA (MP)	US$1=MP7.958		MP1=US$0.126
	CDN$1=MP5.384		MP1=CDN$0.186
	Y1=MP0.961		MP1=Y1.040
	HK$1=MP1.02		MP1=HK$0.98
	EUR€1=MP8.393		A=EUR€0.119
	UK£1=MP13.024		MP1=UK£0.077
	IR£1=MP10.653		MP1=IR£0.094
	AUS$1=MP5.199		MP1=AUS$0.192
	NZ$1=MP4.256		MP1=NZ$0.235
	SAR1=MP1.309		MP1=SAR0.764

✈ GETTING THERE AND AWAY

VISAS AND CUSTOMS. Citizens of EU countries, Australia, Canada, New Zealand, South Africa, the US, and other nations can enter Macau with only a passport or travel document and stay for 20 days. Permanent residents of Hong Kong and Portuguese passport holders can stay visa-free for 90 days. For those who need single-entry individual visas, head to any Portuguese consulate, or obtain them upon arriving at the Macau Ferry Terminal. Visas are valid for 20 days and cost MP100, MP200 for families, and MP50 for members of a group of 10 or more.

Macau does not levy export duties, but Hong Kong limits the quantities of dutyfree cigarettes (100) and wine (1 liter) that travelers can carry back with them.

BY AIR. Completed in 1995, the **Macau International Airport** (24hr. ☎861 111), on the eastern coast of Taipa Island, has regular flights to Beijing, Shanghai, and other cities in China, as well as to Bangkok, Brussels, Kaohsiung, Kuala Lumpur, Lisbon, Seoul, Singapore, and Taipei. More flights and carriers will be added in coming years. The government levies a departure tax on all flights (destinations in China MP80, ages 2-12 MP50; all other destinations MP130, ages 2-12 MP80). No departure tax is charged for stays under 24hr. The AP1 bus (MP6) runs every 15 minutes from the airport to all major hotels. Taxis also cover the short distance.

BY SEA. Boats depart from Hong Kong's **Macau Ferry Terminal,** 200 Connaught Rd., Shun Tak Centre, Sheung Wan (MTR: Sheung Wan), although some leave from the **China Ferry Terminal,** 33 Canton Rd., TST, behind Kowloon Park. A departure tax is included in the price of ferry tickets (HK$19 to Macau, MP19 to Hong Kong).

The **Hongkong & Yaumati Ferry Co. Ltd.** (☎726 301) has catamaran service (70 min., 12 per day) from the ferry terminal in Macau to the China Ferry Terminal in **Kowloon, Hong Kong** (☎2516 9581). Ferries run from **Macau to Kowloon** (10:05am-11:30pm; M-F HK$119, Sa-Su and holidays before 6pm HK$140, daily after 6pm HK$160) and from **Kowloon to Macau** (8:30am-8pm; M-F HK$113, Sa-Su before 6pm HK$134, daily after 6pm HK$154).

Turbojet (Macau ☎285 9333; Hong Kong ☎790 7039) has boats from the ferry terminal to **Sheung Wan, Hong Kong** (1hr.; every 15min., less frequent in early morning; HK$112-176, HK$15 discount for adults 60 or above and children below 12). Make advance reservations for weekend tickets from Hong Kong to Macau. **Yuet Tung Shipping Company** has a daily ferry from Macau Pier 14, beside the Peninsula Hotel (2:30pm; MP100, children MP57), to **Shekou** and **Shenzhen.**

✦ ORIENTATION

The Macau Peninsula occupies the western portion of the Pearl River Delta guarding the gateway into China's Guangdong province. **Taipa Island** and **Coloane Island** are linked to Macau by the Friendship Bridge. The Zhuhai Special Economic Zone

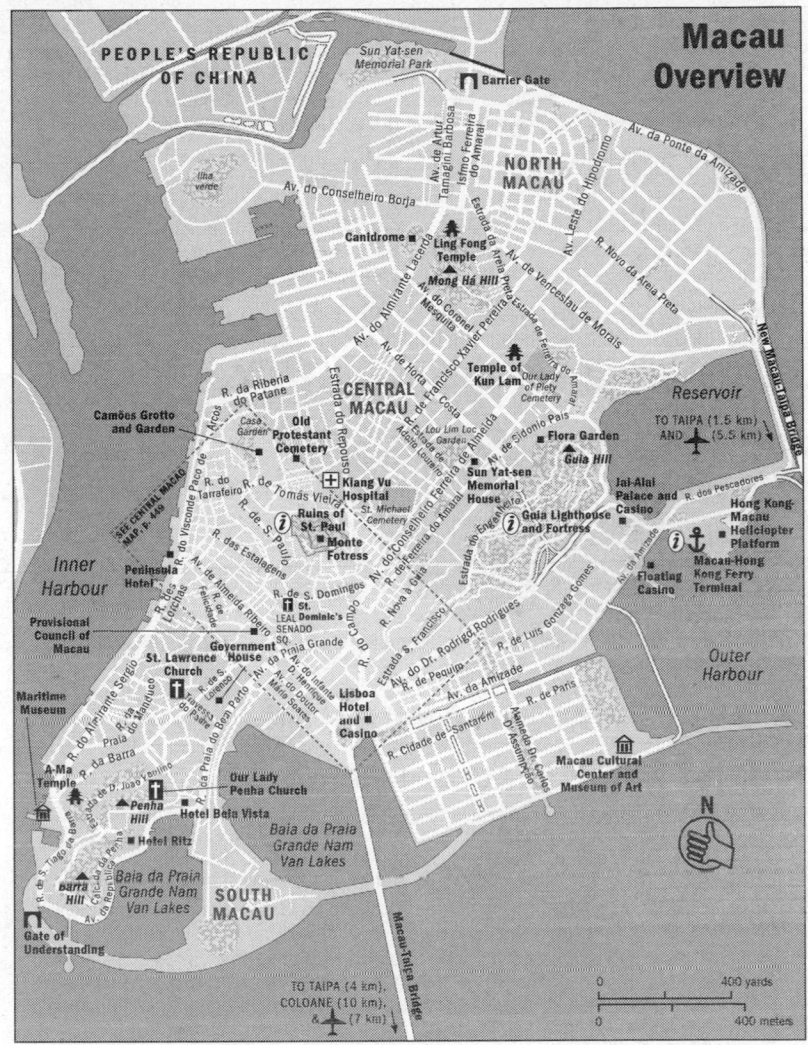

Macau Overview

PEOPLE'S REPUBLIC OF CHINA

Sun Yat-sen Memorial Park

Barrier Gate

Av. da Ponte da Amizade

Av. de Artur Tamagnini Barbosa
Isfino Ferreira do Amaral

NORTH MACAU

Av. do Conselheiro Borja

Ilha verde

Av. do Almirante Lacerda

R. Nova da Area Preta

Av. de Venceslau de Morais

Estrada da Areia Preta

R. Novo da Area Preta

New Macau-Taipa Bridge

Canidrome

Ling Fong Temple

Mong Há Hill

Av. do Coronel Mesquita

Av. de Horta

Av. de Francisco Xavier Pereira

Estrada de Ferreira do Amaral

Temple of Kun Lam

Our Lady of Piety Cemetery

CENTRAL MACAU

Estrada do Repouso

Camões Grotto and Garden

Casa Garden

Old Protestant Cemetery

R. da Riberia do Patane

R. de Tomás Vieira

Lou Lim Loc Garden

Flora Garden

Reservoir

TO TAIPA (1.5 km) AND (5.5 km)

Guia Hill

Kiang Vu Hospital

St. Michael Cemetery

Sun Yat-sen Memorial House

Guia Lighthouse and Fortress

Jai-Alai Palace and Casino

R. dos Pescadores

Hong Kong-Macau Helicopter Platform

Ruins of St. Paul

Monte Fotress

R. de Ferreira do Amaral

Estrada do Engenheiro

Floating Casino

Macau-Hong Kong Ferry Terminal

Inner Harbour

Peninsula Hotel

R. de S. Domingos

St. Dominic's

LEAL SENADO

Government House

Praia Grande

R. de Pequito

Estrada S. Francisco

R. de Dr. Rodrigo Rodrigues

R. de Luis Gonzaga Gomes

Outer Harbour

Provisional Council of Macau

St. Lawrence Church

Lisboa Hotel and Casino

Av. da Amizade

R. de Paris

Maritime Museum

A-Ma Temple

Praia da Barra

Our Lady Penha Church

Penha Hill

Hotel Bela Vista

Hotel Ritz

Baia da Praia Grande Nam Van Lakes

Baia da Praia Grande Nam Van Lakes

SOUTH MACAU

Macau Cultural Center and Museum of Art

Barra Hill

Gate of Understanding

Macau-Taipa Bridge

TO TAIPA (4 km), COLOANE (10 km), (7 km)

N

0   400 yards
0   400 metes

borders **North Macau,** which has sharper-angled streets and few casinos; luckily, bars and clubs offer enough nightlife to compensate.

Most of Macau's casinos are in **Central Macau.** Twisting, narrow streets criss-cross this area, curving around Guia Hill, the Ruins of St. Paul, and St. Dominic's Church. Macau's main road, **Avenida de Almeida Riberio,** commonly known as **San Ma Lo (New Street),** runs from the Peninsula Hotel on the West Coast to the Hotel Lisboa on the South Coast. The southern half of this road bears the name **Ave. de Infante D. Henrique.** Running from the Macau-Hong Kong ferry terminal to the Hotel Lisboa is **Ave. de Amizade.** Major landmarks in Central Macau include: Camões Grotto and Garden near the district's western edge; Largo de Senado, the central square where street markets and shops meet 16th century colonial government buildings; the infamous Lisboa Casino to the south; the ferry pier at the eastern fringe; and the highly visible Guia Lighthouse.

In hilly **South Macau,** Our Lady of Penha Church, A Ma Temple, and the Macau Maritime Museum huddle together. The large thoroughfare **Ave. de Praia Grande** turns into a new street (as roads in Macau are apt to do), the **Rua de Praia do Bom Parto.** Rua de Praia do Bom Parto passes by the historic Bela Vista Hotel and the Hotel Ritz before changing again into **Ave. de República** near Barra Hill.

⎚ GETTING AROUND MACAU

Local Transportation: The Macau Peninsula is small enough to walk across under an hour. **Transportes Colectivos de Macau (TCM)** and **Transmac** operate frequent A/C buses. Within Macau proper MP2.5, to Taipa MP3.3, to Coloane MP5.

Taxis: Base fare MP10, each additional 250m MP1, waiting time MP1 per min., luggage MP3. There are surcharges for trips to, but not from, the islands (MP5 to Coloane, MP2 from Taipa to Coloane) and from the airport (MP5). **Pedicabs** wait outside the ferry terminal and Hotel Lisboa; rates are negotiable (around MP100 per hr., MP15-20 for a ride around the bay).

Car Rental: The only reason to rent anything might be to drive a *moke*—a cute, small cousin to the jeep. Drivers must be at least 21 and have a valid driver's license. **Happy Rent A Car** (☎726 868), on the ground floor of the Macau Ferry Terminal, rents *mokes*. All Hong Kong, Canadian, Japanese, Indian, and Singaporean citizens need an IDP (see **Essentials: Getting Around,** p. 84), valid for at least 2 years. M-F MP480 per day, Sa-Su MP500 (cost of gas extra). 20% discount for same-day returns. MP4000 credit card deposit. Open daily 9am-5:30pm. **Avis** (☎726 571), also in the Macau Ferry terminal. International Driver's license for customers not from Australia, the US, or UK. M-F MP450 per day, Sa-Su MP500. 20% discount for same-day returns. MP3000 credit card deposit. Open daily 9am-5:30pm.

⁊ PRACTICAL INFORMATION

TOURIST AND FINANCIAL SERVICES

Tourist Offices: In Hong Kong, the **Macau Government Tourism Office (MGTO),** Shun Tak Centre, 168-200 Connaught Rd., Ste. 336, Sheung Wan (☎2857 2287 or 2559 0147). MTR: Sheung Wan, D exit. Has lots of information, including the comprehensive *Macau Guide Book.* Open daily 9am-1pm and 2:30-5:30pm. In Macau, the **MGTO,** 9 Largo de Senado (☎315 566; www.macautourism.gov.mo), provides information in Chinese, English, Japanese, and Portuguese. The *Official Map and Guide* is particularly useful for the islands. Free local calls. Open daily 9am-6pm. Other offices at the **Macau Ferry Terminal,** near customs (open daily 9am-10pm); **Macau International Airport** (open daily 9am-10:30pm); **Guia Lighthouse** (open daily 9am-5:30pm); and the **Ruins of St. Paul** (open daily 9am-6pm). **MGTO hotline:** ☎340 390. Daily 9am-6pm.

Travel Agencies: CTS (☎700 888), on Rua de Nagasaki, Xinhua Building, 1st Fl., opposite the World Trade Center. Chinese single-entry visas MP150; arrive before noon for pickup after noon the next day. Bring a photo or buy it there (MP30). Open daily 9am-9pm. **Branch** at the Macau Ferry Terminal, 3rd Fl., shop 1027 (☎726 756), near the MGTO. Makes hotel reservations. Open daily 9am-8:30pm.

Consulates: Portugal provides consular services in Macau; most other countries have offices in Hong Kong (see **Essentials: Consular Services in China,** p. 48).

Currency Exchange: Bank of China, on Ave. Dr. Mário Soares. Open M-F 9am-5pm, Sa 9am-1pm. **Banco Nacional Ultramarino (BNU),** 22 Ave. de Almeida Ribeiro. Open M-F 9am-5pm, Sa 9am-noon. **Hongkong Bank,** 73-75 Rua da Praia Grande. Open M-F 9am-5pm, Sa 9am-12:30pm. The **Macau Ferry Terminal** has a currency exchange counter near the tourist office. Open daily 9am-6pm.

American Express: 23B Rua de S. Paulo R/C (☎363 262), near the Ruins of St. Paul. Traveler's checks, credit card advances, and AmEx payments. Open daily 9am-5:30pm.

Central Macau

■ **ACCOMMODATIONS**

Hotel Man Ya, 1
Vila Universal, 2
Ko Wah Hotel, 3
San Va Hotel, 4
Vila Men Men, 5

Pensão Nam In , 6
Hotel Nam Tin, 7
Wai Lee Guest House, 8
Vila Jing Jing, 9

Inner Harbour

Av. de Demetrio Cinatti
Rua do Visconde Paco do Arcos
Rua do Tarrafeiro
Rua Colonos
Rua dos Faitiões
Rua de Cinco Outubro
Rua Nova do Comercio
Rua das Lorchas
Rua da Caldeira
Rua Guimarães
Travessa Caldeira
Travessa Auto Matadouro
Travessa da Mastro
Rua da Felicidade
Travessa Atero Novo
Rua Cules
Calcada do Tronco Velho
Rua do Pagode
Rua da Madeira
Rua das Estalagens
Travessa Amazem Velho
Rua Camilo Pessanha
Rua Nossa Sentora do Amparo
Rua da Tercena
Rua des Mercadores
Rue de S. Paulo
Rua San Antonio
Largo da Commanha
Camões Grotto and Garden
Orient Foundation Museum
PRACA LUIS DE CAMÕES
Old Protestant Cemetery
Rua do Patane
Rua Coelho do Amaral
Church of St. Anthony
Ruins of St. Paul
Calcada de S. Paulo
Rua de D. Balchior Carneiro
Rua de Tomás Vieira
Monte Fort & Museum of Macau
Estranda do Repouso
LEAL SENADO SQUARE
Government Tourism Office
Largo de Senado
CTT
CTM
Rua Monte C. Roche
Church of São Domingos and Treasure of Sacred Art Museum
Church of St. Augustin
Rua Central
Rua Central
Courthouse
Statue of Jorge Alvares
Hongkong Bank
Cathedral
Largo da Se
Rua Palha
Rua da S. Domingos
Rua Padro Nolasco da Silva
Travessa Dos Anic
Travessa do Pato
Calcada do Gaio
Rua do Campo
Rua Formosa
Avenida da Praia Grande
Rua Dr. Pedro Jose Lobo
Travessa de Praia Grande
Avenida Dom Joao IV
Avenida Dr. Mário Souares
Avenida do Infante D. Henrique
Bank of China
Library
Rua Santa Clara
Rua Noronha
Rua Novo à Guia
San Francisco Gardens
Callada dos Quarteis
Military Club
Estrada do Visconde de Januano
Government Hospital
Estrada dos Parses
Avenida de Lisboa
Estrada de S. Francisco
Lisboa Hotel and Casino
Avenida da Amizade
Rua de Foshan
Rua de Cantao
Avenida do Dr. Rodrigo Rodregues
Rua de Pequim
Rua de Xangai

0 100 yards
0 100 meters

LOCAL SERVICES

Grocery: Yaohan Department Store, 1579 Ave. da Amizade. Follow the pedestrian walkway from the Macau Ferry Terminal. Open daily 11am-10:30pm.

Library: At Jardine de S. Francisco on Rua Do Campo, in a Chinese-style building. Open daily 9am-12pm and 7-10pm. The **Provisional Municipal Council of Macau Building** on Ave. de Almeida Ribeiro (opposite the fountain) is open daily 1-7pm.

Bookstore: Plaza Cultural Macau, 32-G Ave. do Conselheiro Ferreira de Almeida. Open daily 11am-9pm.

Weather: English ☎1311.

EMERGENCY AND COMMUNICATIONS

Emergency: ☎999. **Fire:** ☎572 222. **Ambulance:** ☎577 199 or 378 311.

Police: ☎919 or 573 333.

Hospitals: Government Hospital (☎313 731), Estrada do Visconde de S. Januário. **Kiang Vu Hospital** (☎371 333), Rua de Coelho do Amarel. Both open 24hr.

Pharmacies: Farmacia Popular, 16 Largo de Senado (☎573 739 or 566 568). Open M-F 9am-9pm, Sa-Su 9am-8pm. **Watson's,** at the intersection of Ave. da Praia Grande, Rua do Campo, and Rua de Santa Clara.

Telephones: Companhia de Telecomunicações de Macau (CTM) offices and the snack shops on the 2nd Fl. of the Macau Ferry Terminal sell MP70 and MP100 phone cards. For international calls, dial 00 and then the country code. For Hong Kong, dial 01. **International Directory Assistance:** ☎101. **Collect calls:** ☎191. **Local Directory:** English and Cantonese ☎181, Portuguese ☎185.

Internet Access: CTM, Long Cheon Com Bldg., 22 Rua S. Domingos, 2nd Fl. (☎833 833). Look for the red ribbon logo. Free unlimited access. Open daily 10am-8pm.

Post Office: CTT de Macau, Largo do Senado, in Leal Senado Square. EMS and Poste Restante (counter #1; mail is held for 1 month). Open M-F 9am-6pm, Sa 9am-1pm.

▛ ACCOMMODATIONS

Macau abounds with guesthouses to suit any taste. Although some still rent rooms by the hour, most are respectable, modern establishments. The staff at most guesthouses does not speak English, but this does not usually impede the business of renting rooms to foreigners. Almost all are in central Macau, clustered on side streets branching off **Ave. de Almeida Ribeiro,** near the harbor, or off **Ave. de Infante D. Henrique.** Many of the low-budget rooms were carved out of a single apartment; the vast majority have dim lighting and let in little natural light. Consider yourself lucky to have a room with a view. There are two **youth hostels** (*pousada de juventude*) on Coloane Island (see **Hostels** below).

Anyone planning to spend more than MP200 should first check out the travel agencies at the ferry terminal; they typically offer up to 50% discounts on larger hotels. Some packages include ferry tickets to or from Hong Kong.

HOTELS AND PENSIONS

▨ **Vila Jing Jing,** 998 Ave. da Praia Grande (☎715 037), across from the pink colonial building known as the Military Club. Run by a very friendly woman, this place has carpeted, slightly musty (but very pretty) rooms with A/C, TV, rooftop balcony, and plenty of sunlight. Discounts for stays over 1 week. Singles MP100, with bath MP130; doubles MP180; triples MP230.

▨ **Pensão Nam In,** 3 Travessa da Praia Grande (☎710 024 or 710 008). Make sure you are on Travessa da Praia Grande, not Rua da Praia Grande. Clean, airy rooms with A/C, TV, phone, couch, and natural light. Singles MP150; doubles MP180.

San Va Hotel, 67 Rua da Felicidade (☎573 701; email sanva@hongkong.com), off Rua dos Mercadores from Ave. de Almeida Ribeiro. Heaven for those who like bright green.

Hollow walls make for free evening entertainment. A lovely balcony, dirty wicker chairs, and two semi-outdoor toilets and showers play home to many backpackers. Singles MP60; doubles MP70.

Wai Lee Guest House, 38 Ave. de Dom João IV, 1st Fl. (☎710 199). Clean rooms with A/C, TV, and bath. The friendly Malaysian proprietor speaks English. Check-out 1pm. There are only 5 rooms; reservations recommended. Singles MP110; doubles MP150.

Vila Men Men, 24 Rua Dr. Pedro Jose Lobo, 3rd Fl. (☎715 241), at Rua da Praia Grande. Part of a family home, this guesthouse has 5 dimly lit, grungy rooms with A/C, TV, sinks, and large beds. Singles MP90; doubles with showers MP120.

Ko Wah Hotel, 71 Rua da Felicidade (☎375 599 or 375 452). Reception on 4th Fl. Spacious rooms have A/C, TV, and private baths. Discounts for long-term stays. Singles MP150; doubles and triples MP160.

Vila Universal, 73 Rua da Felicidade (☎573 247 or 375 742). Clean, well-maintained rooms have A/C, TV, phone, bath, and large windows. Singles MP146; doubles MP216.

Hotel Nam Tin, 4 Travessa da Praia Grande (☎711 212), off Ave. de Dom João IV. Lucky guests may get leopard-skin duvet covers, curtains, and couches. Singles MP200; doubles and triples MP250. Credit cards accepted.

Hotel Man Va, 30 Travessa da Caldeira (☎388 655), off Ave. de Almeida Ribeiro. Large, clean rooms with all the standard amenities. MP30 deposit. Reception on 4th Fl. Singles MP173; doubles MP230.

HOSTELS

Although both hostels are on Coloane Island, hostel bookings must be paid for in advance in Central Macau at the **Youth Hostel Booking Office,** Rue de Santiago da Barra. (☎988 0712. Open M-F 9am-5:45pm.) Both hostels have a fairly comprehensive list of regulations: HI/IYH members only, midnight curfew, no cooking, and beds made by 10am. The 30-bed dorms cost MP40-100 for foreigners (MP20-80 for locals). In the summer, hostels are often fully booked by Hong Kong youth groups.

Hac Sa Beach Youth Hostel (☎882 701), in a gray building opposite the Water Sports Centre. Take bus #25 from the station in front of Hotel Lisboa to the 2nd to last stop; Hac Sa Beach is on the right. Has the feel of a beach resort: less than two years old, rooms are spotless and homey, with colorful sheets, yellow lockers, and couches.

Cheoc Van Beach Youth Hostel (☎882 024), off Estrada de Cheoc Van, on the way down to the beach. From the Cheoc Van bus station, walk ahead a few meters towards Taipa. Turn left and walk down Rua de Antonio Francisco; the hostel is the blue and white building on your right.

◘ FOOD

While there may not be as many restaurants here as in Hong Kong, Macau's eateries more than make up for any scarcity in quantity with impressive quality—at low cost. Macau's Chinese origins have melded with Portuguese influences to create a savory local cuisine. Many restaurants serve Chinese favorites like noodles and dim sum alongside German roasted pig knuckle, *caldo verde* soup, and *tiramisu*. Vendors around **Senado Square** sell skewered chicken, shish kebabs, and fish balls, and cafes and *sopa de fitas* abound.

Rua do Almirante Sérgio, running past A Ma Temple and the Macau Maritime Museum in South Macau, has a mixture of cheap Chinese eateries and slightly more expensive Portuguese restaurants. **Alameda Dr. Carlos D'Assumcao,** which runs from the Kun Lam statue off Ave. Dr. Sun Yat Sen to the Macau Landmark on Ave. de Amizade, has a few restaurants serving more upscale Portuguese and international cuisine. It eventually arrives at **Rua Cidade da Sintra,** a street full of outdoor international restaurants. **Rua Com. Mata Oliveira,** off Ave. de Dom João IV, has colorful outdoor seating and a cluster of cafes.

CENTRAL MACAU

⛻ **Dili Deli,** Edf. Kam Lok, 96 Rua Com. Mata Oliveira, Ground Fl., Block 3 (☎713 177), off Ave. de Dom João IV. Run by an exceptionally hospitable mother-daughter set, this deli makes you want to dilly-dally. Scrambled eggs, toast, and freshly squeezed fruit juice MP15; blueberry or raspberry pancakes MP10. Open daily 8am-8pm.

⛻ **Coffeeworks,** 201 Rua Com. Mata Oliveira, Ground Fl. (☎711 7771), off Ave. de Dom João IV. Soak up sunshine on the outdoor tables or sit in a home-style loft. How does 2 eggs (sunny side up), a curl of bacon, 2 pieces of toast, and a potent cup of coffee sound? Like a good deal for MP13. The menu boasts 17 blends of coffee, like Jamaica Blue Mountain coffee (MP18) and Indian Monsoon Malabar (MP10). Chinese meals available. Open daily 8am-6:30pm, closed every other Sunday.

Kam Pou Café e Casa de Pasto, 21-23 Largo de Senado, Ground Fl., Sobre-Loja (☎573 986 or 572 338), tucked behind the bakery stall on Largo de Senado. With the fountain behind you, it is on your left. A local treasure; the extensive menu (in Chinese, English, and Portuguese) includes both Portuguese and Chinese fare. Top the shredded chicken macaroni (MP16) with mango ice cream (MP8.5). Open daily 7am-9:30pm.

B+ Café, Edf. Kai Fu Centro Comercial, Rua Leste Mercs Domingos, 3/5 A (☎356 778). Unusual decor includes hanging flowers, a sack of coffee beans at the door, and a large poster of Clark Gable and Vivien Leigh. Ham and cheese sandwich special 3-6pm (MP5), Sichuan-style filet of fish with rice noodles (MP10), and *fusilli bucati* salad (MP15) give this place more than a B+. Open M-F 11am-10pm, Sa-Su 11am-midnight.

The Haven, Travessa São Domingos, Jardim Lok Wa, Bk A, Ground Fl. (☎335 080). With the fountain at Largo de Senado behind you, turn right at McDonald's onto Travessa São Domingos; outdoor tables are ahead, to the left. Portuguese portions of wickedly good food: try the Thai-style clams (MP40), Mexican salad (MP34), chicken cordon bleu (MP45), or New England clam chowder in a bread bowl (MP26).

Ali Curry House, 4K Ave. da República (☎555 865). Curry everything, plus Portuguese stewed beef (MP38) and soups (MP13-16). Cocktails MP28. JCB, MC, Visa accepted. Open daily 12:30-11:30pm.

Henri's Galley, 4G Ave. da República (☎556 251). You really can't go wrong: Henri will beam with pride at whatever you order. African chicken MP85. Credit cards accepted. Open daily 11am-11pm.

A Vencedora, 264 Rua do Campo (☎355 460). The accommodating manager speaks Chinese, English, and Portuguese. Try *costeleta panada* (pork chop cutlet; MP20) or, for the more daring, *iscas de vaca froto* (fried cow's liver; MP38). All dishes come with bread, in true Portuguese style. Open daily 11:30am-10pm.

Pizzeria Toscana, 1 Ave. de Amizade (☎726 637), in the Grand Prix Stand opposite the Maritime Terminal, behind the bus station. The pizzas (MP43-66), pastas (MP55-70), and Gypsy Kings make up for whatever this pizzeria lacks in location. Credit cards accepted. Open M-Sa 8:30am-11pm, Su 9:30am-11pm; closed 1st Tu of every month.

Hotel Sintra Restaurant (☎710 170), Ave. de Dom João IV, 1st Fl. Buffet M-Sa noon-2:30pm Y55, Sa 7-9:30pm MP118, Su noon-2:30pm.

TAIPA ISLAND

Rua da Cunha ("Food Street") cuts through the village and lives up to its name. The wooden furniture and painted leaves at **Satay Court,** at the corner of Estrada Nora and Rua Fernão Mendes Pinto, create a breezy, smart interior that goes well with menu items such as chicken with coconut and curry (MP48). (☎827 751. Open daily noon-11pm. MC, Visa accepted.) **Panda Portuguese,** 4-8 Rua Carlos Eugenio, in Taipa Village, cooks up charcoal eel (MP78), African Chicken (MP48), and other Portuguese and Mecanese favorites. (☎827 338. Open daily 11am-11pm.) **Tai Lei,** near the tourist information booth at the western edge of Taipa village, dishes up its famous rice noodles for MP15. (☎827 150. Open daily 6am-6:30pm.)

COLOANE ISLAND

The selection of restaurants in Coloane village is rather limited. **Nga Tim Cafe,** 8 Rue Caeteno, in front of the Chapel of St. Francis Xavier, is a local favorite serving up Portuguese and Chinese fare for under MP50. (☎882 086. Open daily 1pm-1am. MC, Visa accepted.) **Fernando's Restaurant,** 9 Praia de Hac Sa, next to the main bus stop, is famous for its clams (MP98). You may have to wait an hour for a table, but it's worth it. (☎882 264. Open daily noon-9:30pm.) **La Torre,** Praia de Cheoc Van, on the beach, has predictable Italian cuisine. Pastas (MP50-60), seafood (MP55-165), and good music entice customers to linger. (☎880 156. Open daily 11am-11pm. MC, Visa accepted.)

🏛 CASINOS

In Macau, gambling is very serious business; there are no show girls in skimpy sequined dresses and very little flashing neon. Dealers and gamblers keep their eyes glued to the cards and numbers, rarely smile, and almost never laugh. Macau residents under 21 and visitors under 18 are prohibited. **Slot machines,** known as "hungry tigers" by the locals, devour HK$/MP1 and HK$/MP2 coins. Other ways to get rich quick include **baccarat, blackjack,** and **big and small,** a game in which players try to predict which numbers will show up on three dice—if the total is at least 12, it's "big"; otherwise, it's "small." Minimum bets are MP100-500 at most casinos.

Lisboa, Ave. de Amizade. The grande dame of Macau's casinos, Lisboa fills with the clamor of activity on all 5 floors, 24hr. a day. Distinguished by yellow walls and a pin-head cupola, this casino is for those in the "no": no cameras, no caps, no guns, no shorts, no singlets for men, no smoking (1st floor). Baccarat, big and small, blackjack, and *pai.* Slot machines (MP2) on 1st and 2nd floors; VIP rooms on the 5th floor.

Casino Macau Palace, Ave. de Amizade, Outer Harbour, by the ferry terminal. Also known as the **Floating Casino.** The casino does actually float; in fact, it recently floated over from its previous location in the Inner Harbour. Lisboa's closest competitor in terms of atmosphere, this giant palace on the water devotes an entire floor to slot machines.

Jai-Alai Palace and Casino, Outer Harbour, near the ferry terminal. The playing cards and dominoes on Jai-Alai's sign greet new arrivals to Macau. To avoid the layer of smoke hanging in the air, try the health spa.

Mandarin Oriental, Ave. de Amizade, next to the World Trade Centre. This sophisticated, plush red velvet casino offers slot machines, baccarat, and blackjack tables.

Kingsway Casino, Kingsway Hotel, 1st Fl., across from the Mandarin Oriental. One of the smaller casinos. Those sick of losing can head to the spa, club, and karaoke bars.

New Century Casino, Taipa Island, with a flashing neon exterior. All buses to Taipa stop first at the New Century Hotel. Baccarat, big and small, blackjack, and roulette.

Taipa Casino, in the Hyatt Regency Taipa Island. A few slot machines line the entrance to small parlors of baccarat and blackjack.

🏮 NIGHTLIFE

After emptying your pockets in the casinos, head to one of Macau's happening **nightclubs** and **bars.** Pick up a copy of the *Macau Magazine* (available at many restaurants, hotels, and newsstands) for weekly entertainment listings. Many locals in search of newer, racier dance clubs go to Zhuhai for a wild weekend.

Macau is home to at least one pub whose reputation extends to Hong Kong. 🍺 **Oskar's Pub,** 82-86 Rua de Pequim, on the ground floor of the Holiday Inn, is a popular meeting place for expats who enjoy its live music and relaxed, jovial atmosphere. For the **Crazy Paris Show** at the Hotel Lisboa, one needs only to follow the neon sign of a voluptuous woman in front of the Eiffel Tower. (18+. MP 300. Shows at 8 and 9:30pm.) Taipa Island is not the round-the-clock disco-dancing hive that Macau proper is, but there is a small concentration of bars, some with pool tables, near the Macau Jockey Club. Cross Estrada Governado Albana Olivera and walk down Ave. de Kwong Tong; the courtyard is under the pastel cinder blocks on the right. Buses #22, 28A, and 33 stop across from the Jockey Club.

Irish Pub, Jardim Nam San, Taipa. Neon shamrocks and black leather couches. Drinks MP20 and up. Happy Hour 6-8pm (buy 1, get 1 free). Open daily 5:30pm-3am.

Bar dos Namorados, across from the Jockey Club, Taipa. This bar has "heartfelt" (or "heart-full") decor, with TV and darts for the less lovey-dovey. Draft beer MP13-28. Happy Hour 4-8pm (buy 1 glass of wine, get 1 free). Open daily 4pm-2am.

Hugo's Pub, across from the Jockey Club, Taipa. Check out the wall of graffiti. Drinks MP30. Happy Hour 5-8pm (half-price drinks). Open daily 5pm-2am.

🔳 SIGHTS

CENTRAL MACAU

This part of the peninsula harbors Macau's biggest and busiest neighborhoods.

LEAL SENADO SQUARE. The fountain, pastel buildings, bakeries, and evening performances add a fairy tale quality to the square. The **Leal Senado** (Municipal Council) building is classic colonial Portuguese architecture at its finest. The gray stone building, built to resemble a similar edifice in Coimbra, Portugal, houses the Senate Chamber and library. It received its name (meaning "Loyal Senate") for keeping close ties to its mother country when Spain occupied Portugal in the 17th century. Once a powerful oligarchy, the Senate now functions as a conventional political body with limited powers. *(A 10min. walk from either the Hotel Lisboa or the Floating Casino on Ave. de Almeida Ribeiro. Open T-Su 9am-9pm. Library open Tu-Su 1-7pm. Free.)*

The large clock tower of the **Post Office** stands watch across the street. Walking from the fountain with the Municipal Council building behind you leads to the **Church of São Domingos;** the white stucco moldings and green shutters belie the building's long, raw history. Built at the turn of the 16th century by Dominican friars, the church witnessed the murder of a Spanish-allied military officer at its altar during Mass in 1644. Today, the graceful and airy interior inspires hushed reverence. Some of the works in the **Treasure of Sacred Art Museum** date to the 17th century. *(Open daily 10am-6pm. Donations accepted.)*

RUINS OF ST. PAUL. The winding path behind the Church of São Domingos leads to Rua da Palha and the Ruins of St. Paul, once dubbed the "greatest monument to Christianity in all the Eastern lands." A devastating fire in 1835 left only the front facade (accessible by a wrought-iron staircase) and a few cornerstones standing. **The Museum of Sacred Art** under the site of the old church contains the bones of Japanese and Vietnamese Christian martyrs; a side hall filled with relics adds to the store of curiosities. *(Open W-M 9am-6pm. Free.)*

MONTE FORT. Visible from the Ruins of St. Paul, Monte Fort can, with a little imagination, evoke images of the stronghold's glory days, when it repelled a Dutch takeover in 1622. The newly opened **Macau Museum,** with entrances at both the top and bottom of the fort, is built into the excavated citadel. *(Fort open daily 7am-6:30pm. Museum open Tu-Su 10am-6pm. MP8; children under 11, students, and seniors MP4.)*

CAMÕES GROTTO AND GARDEN. In the opposite direction of the Ruins of St. Paul from Monte Fort, the Camões Grotto and Garden sprawls behind the intersection of Rua do Terrafeiro, Rua de Tomás Vieira, and Rua de S. Paulo. Named after the Portuguese poet Luis de Camões, the park has cool, shady trails and relaxing pavilions. The **Old Protestant Cemetery** to the right of the mural-covered entrance is the final resting place of 150 residents of old Macau. Inside, a small Anglican chapel still holds services on Sundays. *(Buses #8A, 17, 18, 19, and 26 stop at the garden. Garden open daily sunrise-sunset. Free. Cemetery gates usually open during the day; if not, knock or ring the bell. Free.)* Between the Camões Garden and the Old Protestant

Cemetery lies the **Cosa Garden.** Once the home of the president of the British East India Co., it now houses the Orient Foundation. *(Open daily 10am-7pm.)*

GUIA LIGHTHOUSE AND FORTRESS. Built in 1638, Guia Fort hosts both the lighthouse and a small chapel. Although visible from most of the Macau Peninsula, the best vantage point for the Guia Lighthouse and Fortress awaits on Ave. de Amizade. A walk up from Hotel Lisboa along this street allows a sudden vista of the lighthouse atop a seemingly impenetrable wall of greenery. The lighthouse, built in 1865, has a light that can supposedly be seen for over 30km. Although the lighthouse is closed to the public, visitors can see the mountains across the border from the coffee bar on the grounds. *(Walk up Estrada do Engelheiro Trigo from the Guia Hotel. Open daily 9am-5:30pm. Free.)*

OTHER SIGHTS. West of Guia Hill, between Ave. do Conselheiro Ferreira de Almeida and Ave. de Sidonio Pais, the **Sun Yat-sen Memorial House** rests in Moorish splendor. Relatives built the house in the 1930s, after Sun's death. *(Open W-M 10am-5pm. Free.)* On the opposite side of Ave. de Conselheiro Almeida, off the narrow Estrada de Adolfo Loureiro, the **Lou Lim Loc Garden** offers open-air pavilions and several lakes. *(Open W-M 10am-5pm. Free.)* Not far away, **St. Michael Cemetery,** bound by Rua do Almirante Casta Cabral, Rua de Alfonso de Albuquerque, and Estrada do Cemiterio, is crowded with elaborate tombs. *(Open daily 8am-6pm. Free.)*

NORTH MACAU

At the foot of Mong-Há hill (home to a fort from 1866 to 1960) on Ave. General Castelo Branco, greyhounds race and chase metal bunnies at the **Canidrome.** *(☎ 221 199. Races M-Tu, Th-Sa 8pm.)*

The **Temple of Kun Lam,** on Ave. do Coronel Mesquita, is dedicated to the Goddess of Mercy. Fortune tellers and joss stick vendors surround the three altars inside. The table where the Chinese government and US Ambassador Cushing signed their 1844 treaty of friendship is on display in a side room. There are several interesting *bonsai* trees in another room; one in particular garners fame because it is bent into a 寿, the Chinese character for long life. *(Open daily 7am-6pm. Free.)* **Our Lady of Piety Cemetery,** right beside the temple, is filled with row after row of stone tombs with black and white photographs of the deceased. *(Open daily 8am-6pm. Free.)*

SOUTH MACAU (PENHA PENINSULA)

AVE. DA PRAIA GRANDE. A good walking tour of Southern Macau starts on Ave. da Praia Grande at the **Statue of Jorge Alvares,** the first Portuguese man to set foot on Chinese lands. Farther along Ave. da Praia Grande is the pink, colonial **Government House,** a masterpiece of architect Thomaz de Aquino. Travessa do Padre Narciso, off Ave. da Praia Grande, leads to **St. Laurence Church,** constructed in the 1560s. A side entrance allows visitors to view the stained-glass windows and intricate artwork of the main and side altars. *(Open M 10am-1pm and 2pm-6pm, Tu-Su 10am-6pm. Donations accepted.)* Ave. da Praia Grande becomes Rua da Praia do Bom Parto, and a side street off the main thoroughfare splits into two. To the left, the road leads to Bela Vista and Hotel Ritz; to the right, Calcada da Penha takes a steep climb to Penha Church. Compared to its sister church, São Domingos in Senado Square, **Our Lady of Penha Church** is unremarkable, but the view from the grounds takes in the nearby bridges and even Taipa Island. *(Open daily 9am-5:30pm. Free.)* Rounding the tip of the southern peninsula around Barra Hill, there is a curious bronze metal sculpture named the **Gate of Understanding;** double interlocking arches memorialize the friendly relations between China and Portugal.

MACAU MARITIME MUSEUM. This museum overlooking the waterfront is devoted to the long history of maritime activities in Macau, with a special exhibit on the neighboring A Ma Temple. Electronic intercoms and telephones connect to Cantonese, English, Mandarin, and Portuguese tape guides. A small aquarium allows close-up views of life under the sea. Visitors can also tour the harbor on a junk. *(1 Largo do Pogode da Barra, at the northern end of Rua de S. Tiago de Barro. ☎ 595 481. Open W-M 10am-5:30pm. MP10, ages 10-17 MP5; Su MP5, ages 10-17 MP3. 30min. junk tours F-M 10:30, 11, 11:30am, noon, and 2pm. MP10, children under 10 free.)*

A MA TEMPLE. According to legend, the goddess A Ma led a group of storm-tossed, weary sailors to what was to become Macau. The grateful survivors named the place A Ma; A Ma became A Ma Gao, which the Portuguese changed to Macau upon their arrival. Shrines to A Ma and rock paintings of the first fateful ship dot the temple landscape. *(Open daily sunrise-sunset. Free.)*

SOUTHEASTERN COAST. Ave. Dr. Sun Yat Sen provides a scenic stroll, past the **Ecumenical Centre** and a 32m bronze statue of the Goddess Kun Lam atop a lotus flower. The **Macau Cultural Centre,** Ave. Xian Hai S/N NAPE, offers free programs in Chinese, English, and Portuguese. *(☎ 797 7418. Guided tours are available in English on Fridays. Open Th-Tu 9am-7pm.)* In the adjoining building is the excellent **Art Museum.** *(Open Tu-Su 10am-7pm. MP5, students and children MP3. Certain exhibits free.)*

TAIPA ISLAND

Buses #11, 22, and 33 run through Taipa from the Hotel Lisboa (10min., MP3.30). There is a tourist information booth on Rua Direita de Carlos Eugenio, at the western edge of Taipa village. (☎ 827 882. Open M-F 9am-1pm and 2:30-5:30 or 5:45pm.) Bike rental (MP12-16 per hr.) is available from the shops at the western end of Taipa Village.

Most of the island lies along broad, new cement streets, and tiny Taipa village huddles in the shadow of its neighbors, the pink **Taipa Stadium** and the **Macau Jockey Club.** *(1st Fl. free, 2nd Fl. MP20. Proper clothing required; cell phones prohibited. 18+.)* The Jockey Club puts a new twist on Macau's favorite pastime. On race days, the area buzzes with excitement, and people boost their luck by lighting incense to the **Four Faces Buddha** outside. **Macau International Airport** juts out from the island's east coast, and two thin bridges anchor Taipa to Macau proper. Most city buses use the older, more dramatic **Macau-Taipa Bridge** instead of the new **Friendship Bridge.**

The large, white **Taipa Monument** on the hillside greets visitors. Following the shoreline, the road passes pastel-colored houses on the way to **Carmel Church** and the lovely, if tiny, **Carmel Garden.** At night, beautifully lit steps lead up to the church; the steps below lead to the mud flat. The last blue-green house is now the **Taipa House Museum,** arranged as a middle-class Portuguese family might have had it in the early 20th century. *(Open Tu-Su 9:30am-1pm and 3-5:30pm. Free.)* Several colorful temples cluster around the main bus station in Taipa village. **Tin Hau Temple** stands on Rua Governador Tamagnini Barbosa, while the slightly larger **Pak Tai Temple** is close by on Rua do Legedo.

COLOANE ISLAND

Bus #21 runs from A Ma Temple on Macau proper to Coloane village (MP4); #21A runs from A Ma Temple to Hac Sa Beach (MP4.5); #25 runs from Hotel Lisboa to Hac Sa Beach (MP4.5). The trip takes 10-15min.

For the most part, Coloane is a sleepy holiday island. The village itself is tiny; its city limits quickly peter out, merging with Seac Pai Van Park to the north and Cheoc Van Beach to the east. Most visitors head to Hac Sa Beach, on the eastern coast, for the sports complex and barbecue facilities. The thin string of the **Taipa-Coloane Bridge** turns into a winding road that follows the coastline, changing from Estrada de Seac Pai Van, to Estrada de Cheoc Van, to Estrada de Hac Sa, to Estrada do Altinho de Ka-Ho.

Seac Pai Van Park, on the western side of the island, uneasily merges the qualities of an amusement park with access to the 25km **Trilho de Coloane hiking trail,** which leads to **Alto de Coloane,** the island's highest point. *(Open daily 9am-7pm. Aviary open Tu-Su 10am-4pm. Free.)*

Tiny **Coloane village,** in the southwest, is the next stop of interest. The **Chapel of St. Francis Xavier** is the town's claim to fame. Previously home to a piece of St.

Francis Xavier's arm bone, it now serves as a testament to the harmony of Buddhism and Christianity. Street stalls and cafes line the picturesque square outside; giant trees grow in the middle of the eating areas and shoot through the canopy roofs. Near the pier, right of the chapel and facing the water, is the very red **Sam Seng Temple.** To the left is **Tin Hau Temple,** and, beyond it on Ave. de Cinco de Outubro, the larger **Tam Kung Temple** boasts a four-foot dragon boat carved from a whale bone. *(Chapel and all three temples open daily sunrise-sunset. Donations accepted.)*

Buses #21A and 25 continue to **Cheoc Van Beach** and eventually **Hac Sa Beach.** Silt from the Pearl River makes the water muddy. There are a few walking trails (30min.-3hr.) that meander through Coloane; all are clearly marked.

SOUTH COAST

The coastal provinces of Guangdong, Fujian, and Hainan came into their own in the late 20th century. In no small part because of these provinces' links (geographically and culturally) to Hong Kong and Taiwan, many of the South Coast's cities have barreled ahead in the race for development. In 1979, China's first four Special Economic Zones (SEZs) were established in Shantou, Shenzhen, Xiamen, and Zhuhai, and the money has been virtually growing on trees ever since.

China's "gold coast" has plenty to interest savvy entrepreneurs. The region has long had ports-of-call all along the coast and up and down the Pearl River. Exports of tea, silk, ceramics, and spices flowed out of centers of maritime trade like Guangzhou (formerly Canton), as foreign peoples and goods flowed in. Early Arab and Muslim traders paved the way for the Portuguese to initiate trade in the 16th century; the Dutch and British followed close on their heels, and later, the French and Americans came to have commercial interests in the region. Seafaring locals eventually realized migration could go both ways, and the Cantonese (inhabitants of Guangdong) and Fujianese now constitute the vast majority of overseas Chinese, both in Hong Kong and Taiwan and farther ashore.

Blanketed by factories churning out "Made in China" goods, the South Coast's tourist attractions are, for the most part, more manmade than natural, and more modern than ancient. But between Shenzhen's theme parks and Sanya's beach resorts, hidden scenic wonders and magnificent temples pop up.

HIGHLIGHTS OF THE SOUTH COAST

SURF'S UP at **Sanya** (p. 520), the sunny, sandy "Hawaii of the Orient."

SUNNY BEACHES at Xiamen's **Gulangyu** (p. 515), with a mix of architectural styles and breezy, oceanside charm.

BAMBOO RAFTS and mammoth nature along **Wuyishan**'s Nine-Bend River (p. 504).

NAVY SEALS and other vestiges of maritime history at **Quanzhou** (p. 506).

'ROUND AND 'ROUND WE GO at the roundhouses near **Meizhou** (p. 490).

MAN'S BEST FRIEND at Guangzhou's **Qingping Market** (p. 472), proof that the Cantonese will eat *anything*.

GUANGDONG 广东

A ride on the Guangshen Expressway through Guangdong is a ride through time, from the Middle Pleistocene bones of Maba Man discovered outside Shaoguan to the skyscraper skeletons under construction in Shenzhen. Somewhere in the middle, Guangzhou, the capital of the province, has nearly uprooted itself trying to build a modern subway system under more than 2800 years of history. Guangdong sprawls across the fertile Pearl River basin, rich with natural resources and people. Amid the rapid economic development, trains race past farmers who live as they have for centuries, brand new highways stretch alongside rice paddies, and everywhere the marks of human labor and time are apparent.

GUANGZHOU 广州 ☎ 020

Elderly Guangzhou locals tell stories of how their ancestors moved in 2800 years ago; their grandchildren are far more interested in telling visitors about version 2800 of the latest electronic gizmo X. This odd combination has set Guangzhou apart from its made-from-scratch industrial neighbors, Zhuhai and Shenzhen. It may not be a shiny, industrial metropolis—in its desperate hurry to modernize, lit-

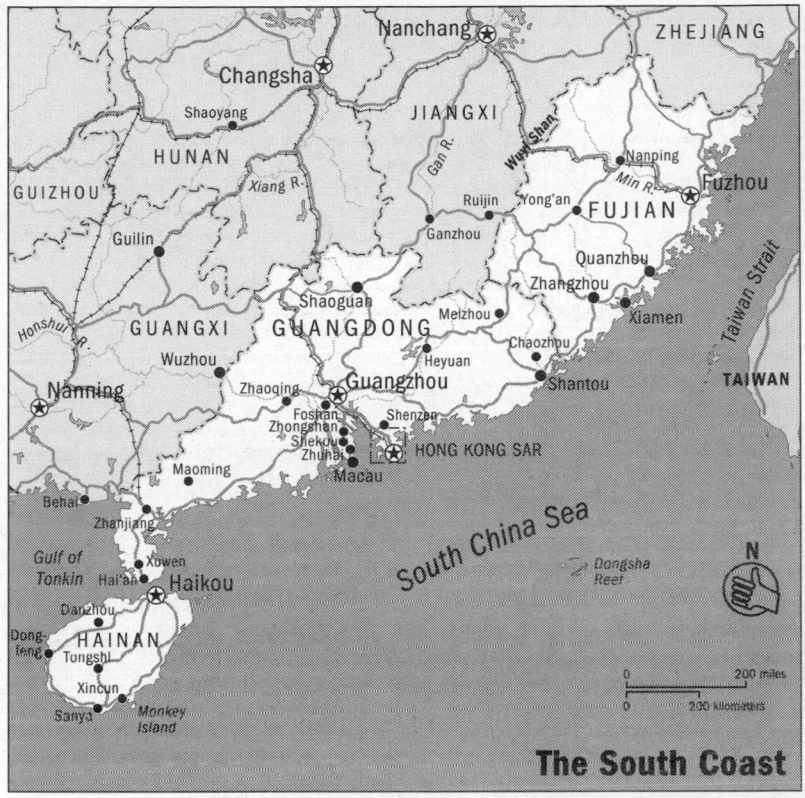

The South Coast

tle effort was put into design or landscaping—but Guangzhou derives its charm from its vibrant, bustling markets and the people that fill them. Despite the new subway, the center of Guangzhou is crowded, polluted, and dirty—but alive. Classic tourist venues like the pagoda- and palace-rich Beijing elegantly march China's past into the present, but Guangzhou is in a mad rush to China's future.

★ ORIENTATION

Guangzhou seems to lack any apparent city planning. Fortunately, most major streets are labeled according to direction, and the new subway system helps with orientation. **Huanshi Lu** (环市路), the city's busiest road, runs from central Guangzhou westward into **Tianhe Lu** (天河路) in Tianhe district. **Zhongshan Lu** (中山路) runs from east to west, cleaving the city in two. The subway follows most of the length of Zhongshan Lu before making a right angle northward at **Tiyu Xi Station** (体育西站), running alongside **Tianhe Dong Lu** and terminating at Guangzhou East Train Station. The newly constructed and more organized **Tianhe district** makes up the eastern part of Guangzhou, north of the Pearl River. Four-lane **Dongfeng Lu** (东风路), the widest street in Guangzhou, runs parallel to Zhongshan Lu. **Jiefang Lu** (解放路) and **Guangzhou Lu,** divide Tianhe district from Dongshan district. Backpacker headquarters, a.k.a. **Shamian Island**—no longer an island due to land reclamation—sits at the southwest fork in the **Pearl River** (珠江).

Each of the large thoroughfares, as well as many of the smaller streets, are divided into north (*bei*), central (*zhong*), and south (*nan*) sections, or east (*dong*), central, and west (*xi*) sections. Only the long stretch of Zhongshan Lu is divided into eight numbered sections from east to west.

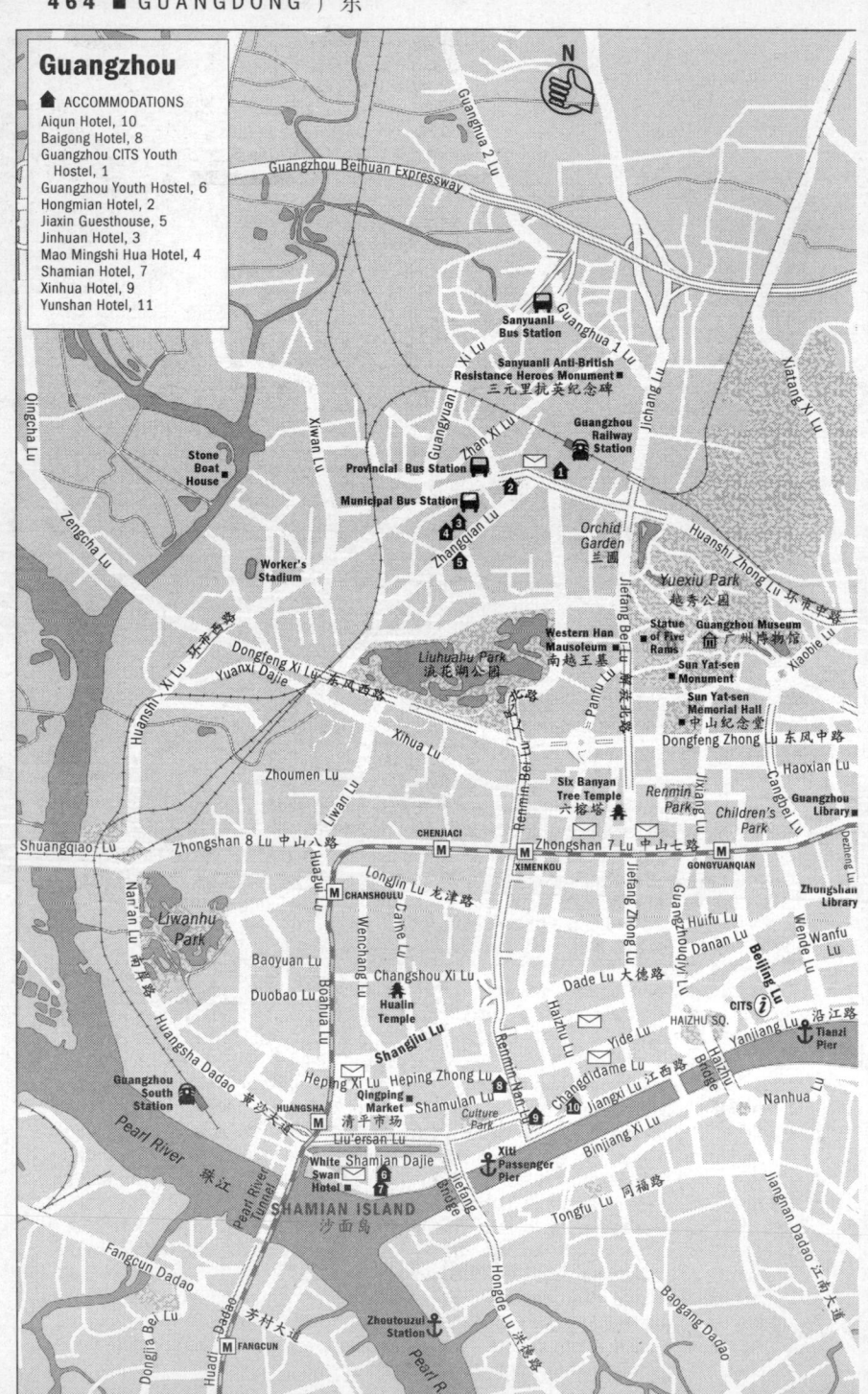

Guangzhou

ACCOMMODATIONS
Aiqun Hotel, 10
Baigong Hotel, 8
Guangzhou CITS Youth
   Hostel, 1
Guangzhou Youth Hostel, 6
Hongmian Hotel, 2
Jiaxin Guesthouse, 5
Jinhuan Hotel, 3
Mao Mingshi Hua Hotel, 4
Shamian Hotel, 7
Xinhua Hotel, 9
Yunshan Hotel, 11

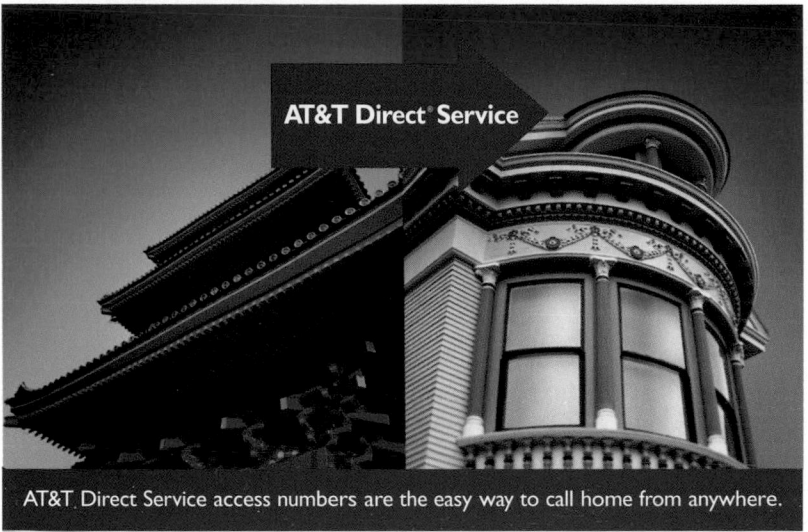
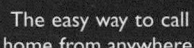

The best way to keep in touch when you're traveling overseas is with **AT&T Direct®** Service. It's the easy way to call your loved ones back home from just about anywhere in the world. Just cut out the wallet guide below and use it wherever your travels take you.

For a list of AT&T Access Numbers, tear out the attached wallet guide.

AT&T

Macao...............0800-111	Reunion Isl.....0800-99-0011
Malaysia●▲...1-800-80-0011	**Saipan●.....1-800-2255-288**
Marshall Isl....1800-225-5288	Singapore......800-0111-111
Micronesia..................288	Solomon Islands.........0811
Nepal●▲........0800-77-001	**Spain............900-99-00-11**
Netherlands●...0800-022-9111	Sri Lanka..............430-430
New Zealand●.......000-911	**Switzerland●..0800-89-0011**
Pakistan▲......00-800-01001	**Taiwan..........0080-10288-0**
Palau.....................02288	Thailand◄....001-999-111-11
Papua New Guinea...0507-12880	**U.K..............0800-89-0011**
Philippines●...........105-11	Vietnam➤........1-201-0288

FOR EASY CALLING WORLDWIDE

1. Just dial the AT&T Access Number for the country you are calling from.
2. Dial the phone number you're calling.   *3.* Dial your card number.

For access numbers not listed ask any operator for **AT&T Direct®** Service.
In the U.S. call 1-800-331-1140 for a wallet guide listing all worldwide AT&T Access Numbers.

Visit our Web site at: **www.att.com/traveler**

Bold-faced countries permit country-to-country calling outside the U.S.

- ● Public phones require coin or card deposit to place call.
- ▲ May not be available from every phone/payphone.
- ✔ Use U.K. access number in N. Ireland.
- ✚ Available from payphones in Phnom Penh and Siem Riep only.
- ➤ Available in select hotels in Ho Chi Minh City, calling centers in Hanoi, post offices in Da Nang, Ho Chi Minh City and Quang Ninh.
- ◄ When calling from public phones, use phones marked "Lenso."

When placing an international call *from* the U.S., dial 1 800 CALL ATT.

AP   © 8/00 AT&T

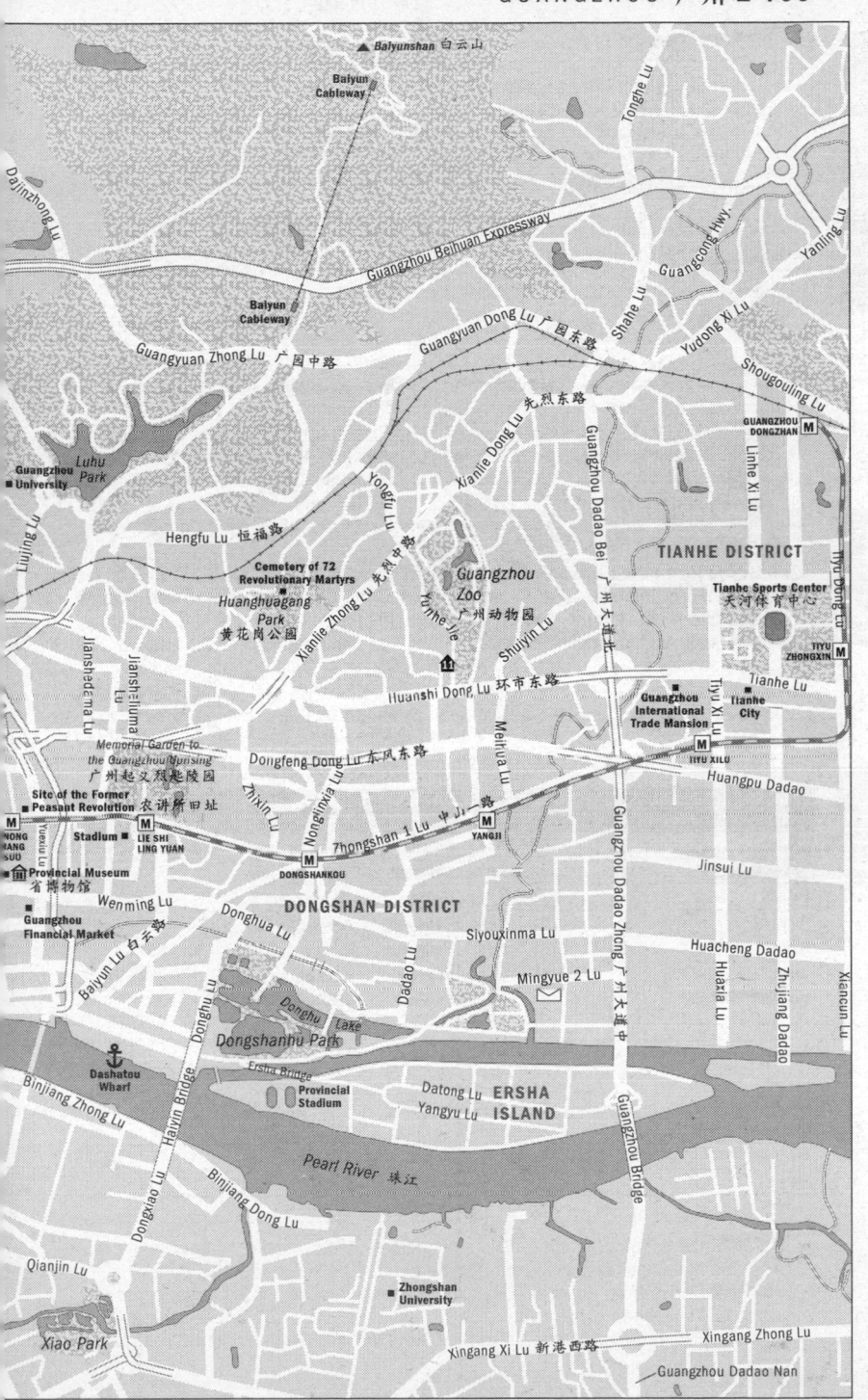

▲ Baiyunshan 白云山

Baiyun
Cableway

Dajinzhong Lu

Tonghe Lu

Guangzhou Beihuan Expressway

Baiyun
Cableway

Guangyuan Zhong Lu 广园中路

Guangyuan Dong Lu 广园东路

Guangcong Hwy.

Shahe Lu

Yudong Xi Lu

Yanling Lu

Xianlie Dong Lu 先烈东路

Shougouling Lu

GUANGZHOU
DONGZHAN Ⓜ

Linhe Xi Lu

Liuhua Lu

Luhu
Park

Guangzhou
University

Hengfu Lu 恒福路

Yongfu Lu

Cemetery of 72
Revolutionary Martyrs

Huanghuagang
Park
黄花岗公园

Xianlie Zhong Lu 先烈中路

Guangzhou
Zoo
广州动物园

Yunhe Jie

Shuiyin Lu

Guangzhou Dadao Bei 广州大道北

TIANHE DISTRICT

Tianhe Sports Center
天河体育中心

Thyu Dong Lu

TIYU
ZHONGXIN Ⓜ

Jianshedama Lu

Jiansheliuma Lu

Huanshi Dong Lu 环市东路

Meihua Lu

Guangzhou
International
Trade Mansion

Tianhe Lu

Tianhe
City

Thyu Xi Lu

Memorial Garden to
the Guangzhou Uprising
广州起义烈士陵园

Site of the Former
Peasant Revolution 农讲所旧址

Dongfeng Dong Lu 东风东路

Zhixin Lu

Nongjiang Lu

Huangpu Dadao

TIYU XILU Ⓜ

Jinsui Lu

NONG
JIANG
SUO Ⓜ

Yuexiu Lu

Stadium ■ LIE SHI
LING YUAN

Provincial Museum
省博物馆

Zhongshan 1 Lu 中山一路

YANGJI

DONGSHANKOU Ⓜ

Guangzhou Dadao Zhong 广州大道中

Huacheng Dadao

Wenming Lu

Guangzhou
Financial Market

DONGSHAN DISTRICT

Donghua Lu

Baiyun Lu 白云路

Donghu Lu

Dadao Lu

Siyouxinma Lu

Mingyue 2 Lu

Huaxia Lu

Zhujiang Dadao

Xiancun Lu

Donghu Lake

Dongshanhu Park

Hainin Bridge

Ersha Bridge

Dashatou
Wharf

Provincial
Stadium

Datong Lu

Yangyu Lu

ERSHA
ISLAND

Guangzhou Bridge

Binjiang Zhong Lu

Dongxiao Lu

Binjiang Dong Lu

Pearl River 珠江

Qianjin Lu

Xiao Park

Zhongshan
University

Xingang Xi Lu 新港西路

Xingang Zhong Lu

Guangzhou Dadao Nan

SOUTH COAST

☐ TRANSPORTATION

Airplanes: Guangzhou's **Baiyun Airport** (báiyún jīchǎng; 白云机场; ☎8612 0000) is west of White Cloud Mountain. In reasonable traffic, a taxi from central Guangzhou to the airport costs Y30-40. A **shuttle bus** leaves from the gray building next to CITS on 179 Huanshi Xi Lu (30min., every 30min. 7am-7pm, Y3-4). Major airlines that fly to Guangzhou are:

Air China (zhōngguó mínháng gōngsī; 中国民航公司), 980 Jiefang Bei Lu (☎8668 1399). Open daily 8am-5pm.

China Southwest Airlines (zhōngguó xīnán hángkōng gōngsī; 中国西南航空公司), 181 Huanshi Xi Lu (☎8612 0449, ext. 477). Open daily 8am-5:30pm. To: **Chengdu** (8-9 per day, Y1300); **Chongqing** (3 per day, Y1150); **Guilin** (7-8 per day, Y530); **Harbin** (1-2 per day, Y2580); **Kunming** (3-4 per day, Y1200); and **Xiamen** (2-3 per day, Y630).

Hainan Airlines (hǎinán hángkōng gōngsī; 海南航空公司), Overseas Chinese Hotel, 99 Zhanqian Lu (☎8669 9999). Open M-F 8:30am-6pm, Sa-Su 8:30am-5:30pm. To **Haikou** (5 per day, Y560).

Malaysian Airlines, Garden Hotel, 368 Huanshi Dong Lu, 2nd Fl., Shop M-04-05 (☎8335 8838). Open M-F 8:30am-5:30pm, Sa 8:30am-12:30pm. To **Kuala Lumpur, Malaysia** (Tu-Th; Y2500, round-trip Y3550).

Shanghai Airlines (shànghǎi hángkōng gōngsī; 上海航空公司), Liuhua Hotel, 194 Huanshi Xi Lu, Rm. 2832 (☎8666 8800, ext. 1248). Open daily 8am-8pm. To **Shanghai** (Y1020, but ask for a Y200 discount).

Singapore Airlines, Dongshan Plaza, 69 Xianle Zhong Lu, 28th Fl., Rm. 2807-2808 (☎8732 0600). Open M-F 9am-1pm, Sa 9am-noon. To **Singapore** (Tu-Th; Y3500, round-trip Y4700; prices rise during July and August).

Trains: The **Guangzhou Train Station** (guǎngzhōu zhàn; 广州站; ☎8715 7222) is on the western end of Huanshi Lu—look for the crowds. The **Guangzhou East Train Station** (guǎngzhōu dōng zhàn; 广州东站; ☎8755 0917 or 8755 8714) is considerably cleaner, safer, and less harrowing than the notorious main station. It is also easily accessible by subway line #1. Tourist information center open daily 6:10am-10pm (☎8714 6164 or 8714 6222). Fast and efficient service to the Kowloon KCR station in **Hong Kong** (1½-2hr., 12 per day 8:30am-8:45pm) and to **Shenzhen** (1hr., every 25-45min. 7am-11:17pm). Trains to destinations other than Shenzhen and Hong Kong are listed in the table below; all run from the main station, although many also stop at Guangzhou East.

TO	TRAVEL TIME	PER DAY	PRICE	TO	TRAVEL TIME	PER DAY	PRICE
Beijing	24	4	366-396	Changsha	8-10¼hr.	at least 10	158-164
Chengdu	44	2	392-424	Chongqing	46-47	2	350
Fuzhou	32	1	276-294	Guilin	12-13	3	150
Guiyang	33	5	254-275	Hangzhou	25½	1	194
Hefei	24	1	183	Hengyang	4-5	at least 20	114
Jinan	34½	1	350-378	Kunming	44	1	282-305
Lanzhou	44	1	491	Liuzhou	16¼	1	247
Luoyang	28½	1	217	Nanchang	15½-18	4	171-183
Nanjing	33½	1	341-370	Nanning	17½	1	171-183
Ningbo	30	1	305-329	Shanghai	24-27	3	377
Shantou	7-10	2	140-149	Shaoguan	3	at least 20	159
Shenyang	35	1	576	Tianjin	33¼	1	383
Taiyuan	38	1	392-424	Wuhan	14-14½	9	147-255
Xian	28	2	428	Yueyang	12	at least 10	140
Zhangjiajie	23	1	317	Zhengzhou	20	3	144

Long-Distance Buses: Guangzhou has an inordinate and confusing number of bus stations. The **Municipal Bus Passenger Station** (shì qìchē kèyùn zhàn; 市汽车客运站; ☎8227 9825) is down Huanshi Xi Lu from the train station, on the left at the pedestrian overpass. To: **Foshan** (1hr., every 15min. 7am-10:30pm, Y12) and **Zhaoqing** (2hr., daily every 25min. 7am-10pm, Y30). The **Provincial Bus Station** (shěng qìchē kèyùn zhàn; 省汽车客运站; ☎8666 1297), 145 Huanshi Xi Lu, opposite the Municipal Station, provides service to **Guilin** (8hr., 9:30pm, Y130) and **Haikou** (12hr., several per day 9:45am-6pm, Y250). Buses to **Hong Kong** and **Macau** board from major hotels, such as the Garden Hotel, China Hotel, Hotel Landmark, and Liuhua Hotel.

Boats: Turbo Jet (☎8222 2555) offers 4hr. boat trips from the **East River Guangzhou Ferry Terminal** (dōng jiāng suìkèlián mǎtóu; 东江穗客连码头) to the Hong Kong China Ferry Terminal (10am and 4:30 pm; HK$189 or HK$284).

Subway: Guangzhou's newly opened subway system (☎8755 3460, inquiries ☎8667 3366, ext. 1703) is a sure sign of efficiency to come. One line currently runs along Zhongshan Lu between Xilang Lu in the southwest and the Guangzhou East Train Station in the northeast. Stops are marked by a yellow sign with two red stripes. Single-ride tickets can be bought from vending machines (accepting only Y1 coins) at every stop. Fare is Y2 for 3 stops traveled and Y1 for every additional 3 stops, with a maximum of Y6 per ride. The subway runs approximately 6am-11pm. Another line connecting to the Guangzhou Train Station is under construction.

City Buses: Buses are still the most common system of travel in Guangzhou. Double-digit buses range over the city center (Y1, A/C Y2); triple-digits travel to the far ends of the city (Y1-2). To board a bus, wave one down at designated stops and pay with exact change. The most important bus routes for backpackers, buses **#5** and **31**, shuttle between Shamian Island and the main train station (30min.-1hr., Y1).

Taxis: Base fare Y7, each additional km Y2.2. Taxis are not allowed to stop on Huanshi Xi Lu opposite the bus and train stations; if seeking a taxi in this area, walk onto a side street off the main road. **Motorbike** drivers provide short rides for around Y5.

🛈 PRACTICAL INFORMATION

TOURIST AND FINANCIAL SERVICES

Tourist Office: Guangzhou Tourism Bureau (guǎngzhōu shì lǚyóu jú; 广州旅游局), 180 Huanshi Xi Lu (☎8668 7051 or 8669 8043). English-speaking staff consists of enthusiastic recent college graduates who know their city and take great pleasure in sharing it with tourists. Free brochures and pamphlets. Open daily 8am-5:30pm.

Tourist Complaint Hotline: ☎8668 7042.

Travel Agencies: CITS, 10 Qiaoguang Lu (☎8339 9038), next to the Hotel Landmark off Yanjiang Lu. Open M-F 8:30am-6pm. **GZL International Travel Service Ltd.** (guǎng zhī lǚ guójì lǚxíngshè; 广之旅国际旅行社), 155 Huanshi Xi Lu (☎8638 4156 or 8383 5477), to the right as you exit the train station. English speakers. Open M-F 8:30am-noon and 2-5pm, Sa 8:30am-noon and 2-4pm. **Guangzhou Travel Agency,** 2 Huale Lu, behind the Garden Hotel, staffs a 24hr. hotline (☎980 7798). Open M-F 9am-5:30pm, Sa-Su 10am-5pm. **Holiday Inn Ticket Office,** 38 Huanshi Dong Lu (☎8776 6999, ext. 69). Open daily 8am-8pm. **White Swan Hotel Ticketing Office** (bái tiān'é bīnguǎn piàowù zhōngxīn; 白天鹅宾馆票务中心; ☎8188 6968, ext. 14), on Shamian Nan Jie, Shamian Island. Although intended for guests only, the hotel's ground floor ticketing office rarely asks for identification. English speakers. Open daily 7:30am-10pm.

Consulates: See **Essentials: Consular Services in China,** p. 48.

Bank of China: Main branch ☎8190 7077. The small branch on Shamian Dajie between Shamian Yi Jie and Shamian Er Jie, on Shamian Island, has English-speaking staff. Open M-F 9am-6pm, Sa-Su 9am-5pm. Two Bank of China **ATMs** on Chandidama Lu accept international ATM cards: one is opposite the Huxia Department Store and the other is opposite McDonald's. Closer to the bus and train stations is the Bank of China **branch** in Guangdong International Hotel (广东国际大酒店), 339 Huanshi Dong Lu. 2 ATMs. Open M-F 9am-noon and 2-5pm, Sa 9am-6pm. All Bank of China branches issue credit card advances. There is a **Western Union,** 4 Zhanghai Zhannan (☎185), off Huanshi Xi Lu close to the train station. Open daily 8-11:30am and 1:30-7pm.

LOCAL SERVICES

Bookstores: The **Foreign Language Bookstore** (wàiwén shūdiàn; 外文书店), on Beijing Lu, near the pedestrian street, has 2 floors of foreign language books. Open daily 9am-8pm. The largest bookstore in town, **Guangzhou Book Center** (guǎngzhōu gòushū zhōngxīn; 广州购书中心), in Tianhe District, takes up 4 floors of a complex opposite the Trem Plaza (subway: Tiyuxi, D exit). Buses #33, 183, and 194 boarded from the Guangzhou Train Station also go to the Tianhe District. Open daily 9:30am-9pm. **Guangzhou Book and Map Store** (guǎngzhōu dìtúshūdiàn; 广东地图书店), 468 Huanshi Dong Lu. Open M-F 8am-5pm.

Libraries: Guangzhou Library (guǎngzhōu túshūguǎn; 广州图书馆; ☎8333 3885), on Zhongshan Lu, near Dezheng Lu. A statue of Lu Xun marks the entrance. Open daily 9am-9pm; English section open daily 9-11:30am and 2-5:30pm. **Zhongshan Library** (zhōngshān túshūguǎn; 中山图书馆; ☎8382 5710), on Wenming Lu, near Dezheng Lu, has a bigger, better English book section on the 3rd floor. Open F-W 9:30am-4:30pm, Th 8:30am-noon. Foreigners with an ID card or passport can obtain library cards and borrow books at no cost at both libraries; refundable Y20 deposit (Zhongshan) or Y200 deposit (Guangzhou).

Supermarkets: JUSTCO is a huge, recently opened supermarket that dominates the 2nd floor of the 7-floor shopping mall, **China Plaza** (subway: Lei Shi Ling Yuan; follow signs for China Plaza). Open daily 10am-10pm.

Weather: ☎121.

EMERGENCY AND COMMUNICATIONS

Hospital: Guangzhou No. 1 People's Hospital (shì yī rénmín yīyuàn; 市一人民医院), 602 Renmin Bei Lu (☎8108 3090). Open M-F 8am-noon and 2-5pm, Sa 8am-noon, Su emergencies only. No English spoken.

Internet Access: Sport Bar (☎8666 6888, ext. 3161), on Jiefang Lu, in the basement of the China Hotel. Y30 per hr. Open daily 11am-1am. **Jinan University** (jìnán dàxué; 济南大学; ☎8522 0114), Nanhai Bldg., 4th Fl., Tianhe. Take bus #243 from Shamian. Unlimited access Y5 for students only; staff will probably assume you're one a foreign student at the university. **Internet e bar** (☎8188 6353), 18 Shamian Jie, between the Catholic Church and the Victory Hotel. English-speaking staff and a backpacker bent. Y20 per hr. Open M-F 7pm-2am. **Henan.net e-business Service Center,** 3 Shamian Jie (☎8818 87651 ext. 8006). Y15 per hr. Open daily 10am-11pm.

Shipping: United Parcel Service, Guangzhou World Trade Center, 371-375 Huanshi Dong Lu, South Tower, Rm. 2107 (☎8775 5778). Open M-F 9am-6pm, Su 9am-1pm.

Post Office: Liuhua Post Office, on the right side of the train station parking lot as you exit the train station, directly adjacent to the local bus lot. EMS and unreliable Poste Restante. Open daily 8am-5:30pm. **Postal Code: 510010.** On Shamian Island, the **Shamian Post Office,** on Shamian San Jie, has EMS services. Open M-F 9am-5pm. **Xiti Post Office** (guǎngzhōu shì xītí yóujú; 广州市西堤邮局), just east of the island next to Culture Park. EMS and Poste Restante. Open daily 8:30am-7pm. **Postal Code: 510130.**

■ ACCOMMODATIONS

Most budget places are in the Shamian Island area. During the two trade fair periods (the end of April and September), prices rise significantly and rooms are scarce. In the vast majority of hotels, including five-star establishments, bargaining is expected, and a standard discount is typically available on weekdays. Most places accept credit cards. There is a 5-10% service charge in most hotels.

SHAMIAN ISLAND AND PEARL RIVER

To get to Shamian Island from Huanshi Lu near the train station, take bus #5 headed south to the end of the line, go left out of the parking lot, and cross over the canal. Bus #31 also runs to Shamian. The last stop is in front of Culture Park, and the eastern edge of Shamian Island is across Liuersan Lu and to the right.

■ **Baigong Hotel** (báigōng jiǔdiàn; 白宫酒店), 13-17 Renmin Nan Lu (☎8188 2313; fax 8188 9161). The Baigong offers clean rooms with all standard amenities. For an impressive discount and an exuberant welcome, ask for Jenny, who speaks excellent English. Singles Y238; doubles Y318.

Guangzhou Youth Hostel (guǎngzhōu qīngnián zhāodàisuǒ; 广州青年招待所), 2 Shamian Si Jie (☎8188 4298 or 8188 7912, ext. 3102). Bored-looking staff answer questions in English and Chinese. High quality rooms have towels, soap, and even toilet paper. The communal showers bear a sign saying "no shitting, no pissing." Deposit Y50. The dorms are usually full; call ahead. 8-bed dorms with A/C Y50; 3-bed dorms Y70, with bath Y80; singles Y100; doubles Y170, with bath Y190-210. Cash only.

Shamian Hotel (shāmiàn jiǔdiàn; 沙面酒店), 52 Shamian Nan Jie (☎8191 2288, ext. 3123). Very friendly English-speaking staff rent out well-maintained rooms. The dim lighting gives a romantic feel. Singles Y215; doubles Y235-295.

Xinhua Hotel (xīnhuá dàjiǔdiàn; 新华大酒店), 2-6 Renmin Nan Lu (☎8188 2688). Rooms and bathrooms are clean, though the paint is peeling a bit. 30% discount possible. Singles Y198-228; doubles Y248-288.

Aiqun Hotel (àiqún dàjiǔdiàn; 爱群大酒店), 113 Yanjiang Xi Lu (☎8186 6668). A 3-star hotel, the Aiqun is perfect for travelers who want to avoid Shamian Island but not stray too far; it's a 15min. walk east along the river. Rooms are well furnished, with spotless bathrooms. 20% discount on weekdays. Singles Y250; doubles Y260-320.

ZHANQIAN LU (NEAR THE TRAIN STATION)

Amid the chaos of the station area, touts carrying hotel brochures and claiming to have special discounts approach anyone with a suitcase or backpack. Sometimes the claims may be true: many of the larger hotels in town give the touts a small commission, and they can offer up to 50% discounts. Ask for a business card and insist on paying the hotel, not the tout.

■ **Guangzhou CITS Youth Hostel** (guǎngzhōu guójì xuéshēng lǚguǎn; 广州国际学生旅馆), 179 Huanshi Xi Lu (☎8666 6889; fax 8667 9787), inside the Guangdong Tourist Hotel, just left of the long-distance train station as you exit. Rooms are well-kept and serene—a dramatic contrast to the frenzy outside. Staff speaks excellent English. Deposit Y50. 2- and 4-bed dorms and singles Y50-75 for HI members.

Jinhuan Hotel (jīnhuán jiǔdiàn; 金环酒店), 103 Zhanqian Lu (☎8622 0510). Do not be too dismayed by the dingy condition of the building—the rooms are fairly pleasant, though not much can be said for the bathrooms. Doubles Y160.

Jiaxin Guesthouse (jiāxìn bīnguǎn; 嘉信宾馆), 92 Zhanqian Lu (☎8666 7888), to the right of the Overseas Chinese Hotel. Rooms are large and clean, but baths aren't. The stairs are *really* grungy; there is no escalator. Doubles Y150; triples Y210; quads Y240.

Maoming Shihua Hotel (màomíng shí huà bīnguǎn; 茂名石化宾馆), 101 Zhanqian Lu (☎8622 0388, ext. 2128). Very friendly English-speaking staff will check you into clean, standard rooms that are comfortable but in need of retouching. 30% discount available. Singles (1 per floor) and doubles Y238.

Hongmian Hotel (hóngmián dàjiǔdiàn; 红棉大酒店), 184 Huanshi Xi Lu (☎8666 3989, ext. 1188). Exceptionally well-kept rooms with a possible 15% discount. The usual hotel jazz. Singles Y385; doubles Y325-337.

DONGSHAN DISTRICT (XIANLIE LU)

Yunshan Hotel (yúnshān dàjiǔdiàn; 云山大酒店), 8 Yunhe Bei Jie (☎8776 5259). At the roundabout where Huanshi Dong Lu meets Xianlie Lu, walk along Xianlie Lu towards the direction of Huanghuagang Park. After a 30min. walk, Yunhe Bie Jie is on the right, 1 block beyond the bus station. Rooms are fairly clean but old, bathrooms are stained, and halls dimly lit. Few English-speaking staff. 20% discount possible. Singles Y258; doubles Y260.

BON APPETIT! On sitting down to a meal in Guangzhou, the sky's the limit. Menus here boast meats as rare as Australian Farm Kangaroo Steak, but these pale in comparison to such sweet sensations as Double-boiled Crocodile with Sea Coconut or Double-boiled Turtle with Snake and Dates. Deterred by the price of the aforementioned dishes? Take heart—cheaper alternatives beckon, like the pink, hot, fat-dripping, deep-fried Octopus Legs that dangle from skewers at street booths. Those who like to savor their meals can take a seat in a local food stall and plunge into a steaming bowl of Pig Heart and Intestines Congee. Having stirred that appetite, you may want to slice into the Cooked Goose Intestines. For a heartier meal, take a crunchy bite on steamed claws, but remember: you are what you eat!

🍴 FOOD

Guangzhou reigns as the (albeit disputed) seat of Chinese cuisine. Residents take great pride in their world-famous dim sum and snake dishes, often quoting the Chinese saying that a perfect life is "to be born in Suzhou, live in Hangzhou, eat in Guangzhou, and die in Liuzhou." Guangzhou dining certainly counts as adventure, and those who enjoy unusual dishes will find exquisitely prepared, delicious meals for a pittance. Undoubtedly, the best meal deals in Guangzhou are at the government-owned food stalls on almost every street corner. At these places, a ticket for Y5 entitles you to rice, a choice of three or four (rather normal) side dishes, and sometimes a soup.

SHAMIAN ISLAND

Shamian Coffee Shop (shāmiàn kāfēi wū; 沙面咖啡屋; ☎8190 7062), at the intersection of Shamian Nan Jie and Shamian Si Jie, behind the White Swan Hotel. Look for glass windows plastered with large red characters. Most backpackers in Shamian stop here at least once. The menu (in both English and Chinese) has entrees like pig heart and intestines congee (Y6), pan-fried Italian noodles (Y6.5), steamed claws (Y8), and deep-fried tentacles (Y10). Open daily 7:30am-1am.

Kiumei Restaurant (qiáoměi shíjiā; 侨美食家), 52 Shamian Nan Jie (☎8188 4168). Kiumei dishes up a culinary menagerie of Cantonese delicacies such as spiced pig's ear (Y28), fried stone frog in pot (Y68), and fried sliced snake. The double-boiled crocodile with sea coconut (Y188) may not be available the day you visit, but there are certainly enough live specimens to keep things interesting. English menu. Open daily 11:30am-3pm and 5:30pm-4am.

Lan Kwai Fong (lán guì fáng; 兰桂坊), 5 Shamian Nan Jie, Shamian Island (☎8191 9733 or 8192 1523). Hard to find, but not to worry—hostesses wait on Shamian Nan Jie to escort customers to this delicious Thai restaurant and bar. The food ranges from green curry (Y28) to prawns in leaves (Y38) to vegetable medleys (Y16-28). Try the *roti* with either pineapples or bananas. Much of the cooking takes place outdoors. Open daily 11am-3pm and 5pm-4am.

DOWNTOWN GUANGZHOU

🏮 Black Swan Dumpling Restaurant (hēi tiāné jiǎozi guǎn; 黑天鹅饺子馆; ☎8767 5687), on Jiefang Lu. On the converted 2nd floor of a warehouse, hot, plump dumplings are dished up by the dozen to happy customers. No English menu, but *jiaozi* will get you as far as you need to go. Y8-15 for a heaping plateful (vegetarian dumplings available). Open daily 9am-11pm.

🏮 Gaoyuan Moslim Restaurant (gāoyuán qīngzhēn lín fàndiàn; 高原清真林饭店), 6 Xiatang Xi Lu (☎8350 6633). Feast like kings on the wonderful-smelling food. Spicy eggplant, hot lamb, chicken dishes, and oven-baked bread prepared according to Muslim law, as the misspelled restaurant name boasts. Open daily 9:30am-11pm.

🏮 Monte Carlos, Yin Zheng Bldg., 338 Huanshi Dong Lu (☎8387 9146). The light-brown stone walls, candlelight, and earthy music exude a warm, rustic feel. Serves Russian borscht (Y10), African chili chicken steak (Y26), chicken curry and rice (Y16), congee, and pizza in the same breath. Set meals Y26. The more daring can try a pot of frog with oyster sauce and rice (Y28). Open daily 9am-1:30am. Dance floor and performance space. Another **branch** at 6 Siyou Xin Lu, 2nd Fl. (☎8767 6136).

Lotus Restaurant (liánxiāng lǎobǐngjiā; 莲香老饼家), 67 Dishi Nan Lu (☎8181 3388). The famous dim sum is worth the wait. Wander around the 2 floors until you see an open table. The waitresses are usually too busy to help you; prepare to jostle around other customers to order dishes. Try to avoid the busiest hours (mid-morning to early afternoon). Dim sum Y5-10 per dish. 10% service charge. Open daily 6:30am-midnight.

Shengji Restaurant (shèngjì hǎixiān yěwèi fàndiàn; 胜记海鲜野味饭店), 228 Chang-didama Lu (☎8332 8318). Who needs to go to a zoo when you can see reptiles, mammals, amphibians, and even the occasional peacock on display here? Conventional dishes, such as soups (Y28) or shrimp (Y28-60), and some more exotic ones, such as steamed snake (Y38). Open daily 11am-6am.

NIGHTLIFE

At night, you can either drink and dance or drink and sing (karaoke, of course). Cross Renmin Bridge from Shamian and turn right as you come off the island; impromptu riverside stalls sell beer and soft drinks for customers lucky enough to grab a table. Vendors selling fried squid or chicken satay make the rounds, as do aggressive beggars and flower sellers. Restaurants line the waterfront for a mile or so and stay open approximately 8pm to 3am. Alternatively, the more OK-oriented Panfu Lu scene, dominated by D&D Disco Two, keeps 'em singing all night long. The free magazine *Clueless in Guangzhou*, available at hotels and stalls, has extensive nightlife listings.

Windflower Music Pub, 387 Huanshi Dong Lu (☎8358 2446), next to the Holiday Inn. With a choice hillside location and a manager named Tonic, the Windflower is *hip*. The decorating alone garners kudos. Live Filipino band 4 times a week 10pm-1am. Drinks Y30-35, snacks Y20-25. Open daily 6pm-6am.

D&D Disco Two, Li Kam Center, 13 Panfu Lu (☎8136 0481). Black-clad staff serves drinks (beer Y35) amid swirling lights, velvet bar stools, and pulsating music spun by a live DJ (all night, every night). Open daily 8pm-6am.

Top Show Disco, 109 Yanjiang Xi Lu (☎8188 8489). See all those lights and golden palm trees? You can't miss Top Show, a place where the ultra-chic can sing karaoke and sip cocktails. Y50 drink minimum. Open daily 8:30pm-5:30am.

Rock Disco, 101 Yangjiang Xi Lu, 4th-5th Fl. (☎8190 8088), the silver-gray building across the street from Top Show. Mirrors and lights heighten the sense of crowding. Open Su-Th 8:45pm-2am, F-Sa 8:45pm-3am.

Peace Road Music Bar and Restaurant (hépíng lù jiǔbā; 和平路酒吧), 2 Heping Lu (☎8358 1720), just off Huanshi Dong Lu next to the Holiday Inn. A small, friendly bar with live music downstairs (9:30pm-midnight) and burgers and pastas upstairs (Y15-28). Happy Hour 4-9pm and midnight-3am. Open daily 7pm-3am.

SIGHTS

PEARL RIVER 珠江

Locals sigh that the Pearl River was beautiful before industrialization and pollution set in. In the morning, elderly men and women intently practice tai chi exercises; in the evening, fishermen doze or wait beside their lines; and at night, neon signs and billboards flash frantically. The **Guangzhou Passenger Ship Tourism Company** (guǎngzhōu shì kèlún lǚyóu fēn gōngsī; 广州市客轮旅遊分公司), at **Xiti Wharf** (☎8190 8190 or 8188 8932), and **Tianzi Wharf** (tiānzì mǎtou; 天字码头;☎8333 0397), on Yanjiang Lu, sells cruise tickets for tours of the river (6:30am-10:45pm, Y38). One-hour trips leave daily at 3pm from both wharfs; tickets can also be bought at most travel agencies.

Shangjiu Lu (shàngjiǔ lù; 上九路), which turns into **Xiajiu Lu** (下九路), is lined with shop after shop selling stationery, souvenirs, jewelry, shoes, and clothes. Companies hand out samples, hold contests for prizes, and put on zany shows. Weekends are the best time to visit; the street is closed to traffic, making it every pedestrian shopper's heaven. From Shamian Island, head north past Qingping Market, away from the river for about 10 to 15 minutes.

■ **SHAMIAN ISLAND** (shāmiàn dǎo; 沙面岛). At the beginning of the century, Shamian used to house all the foreigners in Guangzhou, who built European-style customs and government buildings on the island. These days, Shamian's wide, shaded streets are spared the incessant traffic that plagues the rest of Guangzhou. The displaced grace of Shamian architecture, its cobbled streets, and its elegant footbridge has an old-world, almost intoxicating charm. **Shamian Park** (shāmiàn gōngyuán; 沙面公园), the area directly overlooking the river, is especially popular at night. A stroll through the small park demands threading your way through old men and women playing dominoes, chess, or *mahjong.*

QINGPING MARKET (qīngpíng shìchǎng; 清平市场). Guangzhou's Qingping Market is basically an edible zoo, and a walk through it takes patience and morbid curiosity. Some parts, like the innocuous herb and roots section, close in the late afternoon, but the poultry, fish, and meat markets farther north rage against the dying of the light. The market, with 60,000 patrons visiting every day, is a 2000-stall testament to the idea that the Cantonese will eat anything—snails, roaches, beetles, fish heads and guts, freshly killed chickens, and meat carcasses. The most disturbing soon-to-be-dim sum ingredients sold, however, are the dead or dying rabbits, kittens, and foxes, lumped and crammed together in cages, awaiting their final moments. While the apparent lack of concern about animal suffering is shocking, Qingping's varied selections demonstrate that the Chinese have gotten through many a lean year by eating whatever nature could offer. (*At the corner of Qingping Lu and Tiyun Lu, just north of Shamian Island. From Shamian, walk over the canal via the footbridge. The medicine section is at the outer fringe; the meat section lies farther in, along Shanmulan, Shibafu Nan Lu, and Tiyun Dong Lu. The wild game section is opposite the poultry street.*)

HUANSHI LU 环市路

WHITE CLOUD MOUNTAIN (bái yún shān; 白云山). A popular escape from Guangzhou's pollution, this tidy hill draws nearly 1000 trekkers a day to make the strenuous two-hour climb to the top. From the radio tower at the top, visitors can gasp their way past Qing dynasty officials' tombs, bamboo groves, and fragrant foliage. A concrete road leads to the entrance of a mountaintop **park** (Y5), with views of the airport, amusement park, and surrounding countryside. Side attractions include a **temple** (Y5), **Mingchun Bird Valley** (Y10), and a mountain **toboggan ride** (Y20-30) at the foot of the mountain. (*Accessible by bus #46.*)

YUEXIU PARK (yuèxiù gōngyuán; 越秀公园). The park guards the **statue of the five rams** (wǔ yáng shíxiàng; 五羊石像), which Guangzhou residents have long seen as their city's emblem—a close look costs Y3. The **Guangzhou Museum** (guǎngzhōu bówùguǎn; 广州博物馆) is housed in the beautiful **Zhenhai Tower**, dating from 1380. (*Open daily 9am-5pm. Y10, children Y5.*)

In the northwest corner of the park, the **Orchid Garden** (lán pǔ; 兰圃) is full of over 10,000 pots and 200 varieties of orchids. (*Open daily 8am-9pm. Y8, includes tea in the central house near the ponds.*) The flowers bloom in fall and spring; in the dead of winter or summer, you may end up staring at pots of dirt. (*On Huifu Xi Lu, near the main train station. Take bus #202 or 219 from the bus stop opposite the Xiti Wharf on Yanjiang Lu to the stop nearest to the huge crag or boulder on Jiefang Lu. Open daily 6am-9pm. Y3.*)

WESTERN HAN DYNASTY MAUSOLEUM (xī hàn nányuè wángmù; 西汉南越王墓). This little 2000-year-old anachronism houses the tomb of the Nanyue King, who ruled over what is now Guangzhou in 137 to 122 BC. The tomb is unremarkable, but the building beyond holds some impressive finds, including a jade full-body shroud. (*867 Jiefang Bei Lu. Open daily 9am-5:30pm; last admission 4:45pm. Y12.*)

OTHER SIGHTS. The **Guangzhou Zoo** (guǎngzhōu dòngwùyuán; 广州动物园), one of China's biggest zoos (with over 4500 animals), and **Ocean World** (guǎngzhōu hǎiyángguǎn; 广州海洋馆) are between Xianlie Zhong Lu and Huanshi Dong Lu. *(Zoo open daily 8am-5:30pm; last admission 4:30pm. Y8, children Y4. Ocean World open daily 9am-5:30pm. Y100, weekends Y120; children half-price.)* The **Cemetery of the 72 Revolutionary Martyrs in Huanghuagang** (huánghuāgǎng qīshíèr lièshì mù; 黄花岗七十二烈士墓), on Xianlie Lu, near the zoo, commemorates the dead and provides some green relief; tree-lined walkways lead to the tombs of the martyrs—all 72 of them. *(Open daily 9am-5pm. Y2.)* South of Yuexiu Park, the sprawling **Sun Yat-sen Memorial Hall** (zhōngshān jìniàn táng; 中山纪念堂) honors the founder of modern China. *(Open daily 8am-5:30pm. Park Y5; hall Y10.)*

ZHONGSHAN LU 中山路

Following the route of the subway east along Zhongshan Lu leads to a few interesting sights in the heart of Guangzhou. **Six Banyan Tree Pagoda** (liù róng tǎ; 六榕塔) houses a multi-tiered pagoda surrounded by numerous statues in temples. *(Park Y1, pagoda Y6.)* The next stop, Gongyuanqian, is in the middle of a shopping bonanza that centers around the **Beijing Lu** (北京路) pedestrian street. Every night at 7pm, hundreds of stalls appear on **Xihu Lu** (西湖路) and the neighboring streets.

The **Site of the Former Peasant Movement Institute** (nóngjiǎng suǒ jiùzhǐ; 农讲所旧址), on Zhongshan Lu next to the Guangzhou Library, celebrates revolutionary peasants. The government has preserved dormitory and study rooms and hung up old photographs of famous students and leaders on the walls. The exhibits are accompanied by a few English captions. *(Open daily 8-11:30am and 2-5pm. Y2.)* A block south, the **Provincial Museum** (shěng bówùguǎn; 省博物馆), on Wenming Lu, next to the Guangzhou Library, offers a tiny slice of Guangdong history and culture, but is barely worth the admission fee. *(Open Tu-Sa 9am-5pm. Y8.)*

A giant statue of a hand clenching a gun casts a shadow over tourists at the **Memorial Garden to the Guangzhou Uprising** (guǎngzhōu qǐyì lièshì língyuán; 广州起义烈士陵园). The garden on Zhongshan Er Lu (subway: Lieshi Lingyuan) and tomb commemorate those who died during the Guangzhou Uprising of December 11, 1927. *(Open daily 6am-9pm. Y3.)*

FOSHAN 佛山   ☎0757

After the incessant noise and bustle of Guangzhou, Foshan's quieter, more organized streets and cleaner air are a refreshing change.

◪⁊ ORIENTATION AND PRACTICAL INFORMATION. Most transportation to and from Foshan is via Guangzhou. **Trains** run from the Foshan Train Station (fóshān huǒchē zhàn; 佛山火车站), north of town, to Guangzhou East (40min.; 8 per day; HK$180, 1st class HK$230) and Hong Kong/Hung Hom Station (3hr., 1 per day, HK$210) as well as to Shenzhen and Zhaoqing. **Buses** from the Foshan Bus Station (fóshān qìchē zhàn; 佛山汽车站; ☎228 6700), on Fenjiang Lu, at the northern end of town, run to Guangzhou (1hr., every 20min. 6:50am-6:25pm, Y11); Huizhou (3hr., 3 per day, Y55); Shenzhen (every 30min. 8am-7pm); and Zhongshan (14 per day, Y14). Buses from the Zumiao Bus Station (zǔmiào qìchē zhàn; 祖庙汽车站; ☎222 0557 or 225 5409), on Chengmentou Lu, go to: Guangzhou (1hr., every 15-20min. 7:30am-6:30pm, Y8-14); Shenzhen (2½-3hr., 2 per day, Y58); and Zhuhai (2 per day, Y42). **Local buses** (Y2) #1, 4, 6, 9, 11, and 12 run from the Foshan Bus Station to the Ancestral Temple. There is another local station on Zumiao Lu, just opposite the Ancestral Temple. Base fare for **taxis** is Y7, each additional km Y2.2-2.6. **Pedicabs** or **motorbikes** cost about Y5.

Visitors to Foshan will find almost all of their needs satisfied within a two-block quadrangle bordered by **Qinren Lu** (亲人路) in the north, **Zumiao Lu** (祖庙路) in the east, **Chengmentou Lu** (城门头路) in the south, and **Fenjiang Lu** (汾江路) in the west. The **Bank of China** has two branches: one at 236 Qinren Lu (open M-F 8am-5:30pm, Sa-Su 8am-noon and 2:30-5:30pm) and another on Zumiao Lu (open M-F 8am-5:30pm, Sa-Su 9am-5pm). The **post office,** at 4 Qinren Lu, has EMS and Poste Restante. *(Open daily 8:30am-9pm.)* The **postal code** is 528000.

⌐⌐ ACCOMMODATIONS AND FOOD. For those who fall in love with Foshan (or miss the last bus), the cheapest and most convenient place to stay is the **Foshan City Huasheng Hotel** (fóshānshì huáshèng jiǔdiàn; 佛山市华盛酒店), 3 Fenjiang Lu, to the right of the Foshan Bus Station, has old but decent rooms. (☎228 7950. Singles and doubles Y55-150.) Outside, a collection of *dai pai dangs*, street-side cafes, and restaurants presents a range of fried foods, meats, and pastry snacks. While KFC, Pizza Hut, and McDonald's all cluster around the intersection of Zumiao Lu and Chengmentou Lu, the **Mingren Cafeteria** (míngrén cāntīng; 名人餐厅), has Chinese fast food in a clean, brightly lit environment. (Open daily 8am-10pm.) The 24hr. **DJWL** (dòujiàng wáng; 豆浆王), at Qinren Lu and Fenjiang Lu, serves soy milk (Y2-3) and other dishes. Look for the big yellow drooling face. The romantically lit **Rosery Coffee Shop** (méiguī yuán kāfēi tīng; 玫瑰园咖啡厅), 32 Zumiao Lu, serves rather small portions of everything from fried rice (Y15-18) to Holland cowboy steak (Y15). Ask for the daily buffet special of the four-course lunch set; an English menu is available. (Open daily 10am-midnight.)

▣ SIGHTS. Foshan myth holds that a Daoist god, the Northern Emperor, rules the world's waters, therefore holding considerable sway over the denizens of the flood-prone Pearl River region. Inside the **Ancestral Temple** (zǔmiào; 祖庙), a weapons collection guards the altar of this all-important emperor. The temple grounds display iron cannons from the 1840s, examples of wooden architecture, a life-size carriage and boat, and an incredible collection of *bonsai* trees. Inside the grounds across from the temple itself, the **Wanfu Stage,** decorated with beautiful and intricate gold inlay, is famed as the birthplace of Guangdong opera. *(21 Zumiao Lu. Open daily 8:30am-7pm; last admission 6:30pm. Museum open daily 9:30am-4:30pm. Y20.)*

At the **Renshou Temple** (rénshòu sì; 仁寿寺), on Zumaio Lu, a small but attractive tower is surrounded by a few classical Chinese-style walkways. The complex accepts donations and prayers at any of its three altars. *(Take bus #1, 5, or 11. ☎225 3053. Open daily 8am-5pm.)* Just north of the temple, the **Folk Arts Studio** (mínjiān yìshùshè; 民间艺术社) is more shop than museum. Enter through the paper lantern store, proceed to the stairs on the left, and head to the 2nd floor. The studio displays and sells handicraft items from all over China, including clothes, scarves, and jade, stone, and bone carvings. Near the exit, intricate paper cuttings are for sale and can be viewed in progress. *(Open daily 9:30am-4:30pm.)*

ZHONGSHAN 中山 ☎0760

The Sun shines brighter in Zhongshan. Yet another rapidly developing city, Zhongshan derives its more unique elements from a strong connection to the early 20th-century reformist Sun Yat-sen. Most of the sights in this city involve the venerable leader; even the name Zhongshan is a transliteration of Yat-sen. The Sun Yat-sen Memorial Hall and Sun Yat-sen's residence, in Cuihengcun about an hour to the east, both draw visitors from afar.

✳❷ ORIENTATION AND PRACTICAL INFORMATION

On the west side of the **Shiqi River** (shíqí hé; 石歧河), **Zhongshan Lu** (中山路) runs from north to south. **Sunwen Lu** (孙文路), running roughly perpendicular to Zhongshan Lu, miraculously transforms beyond the Fuhua Hotel into a beautifully paved pedestrian street that winds past pastel buildings, glossy shops, and pinewood benches. On the opposite end of Sunwen Lu is the commercial center.

> **Buses: Zhongshan International Hotel Bus Station** (zhōngshān guójì jiǔdiàn shíjiān; 中山国际酒店时间; ☎863 2149) has buses to: **Guangzhou** (2hr., every 25min. 6:15am-6:30pm, Y30); **Hong Kong-Kowloon** (3hr., 4 per day, Y130); **Shenzhen** (2hr., every 30min. 7:40am-7:40pm, Y70); and **Zhuhai-Gongbei Station** (50min., every 20min. 7am-7:20pm, Y15).

Local Transportation: The main bus stop (☎183 9831 or 183 9811) is on Sunwen Lu. Most **buses** run roughly 6am-10pm. Fare Y2-5. Aggressive **sampan** and **motorbike** drivers also wait impatiently to grab tourists (fares Y5 and up).

Taxis: Base fare Y7-8, each additional km Y0.5. A hotel taxi (available at Zhongshan International Hotel, on Zhongshan Yi Lu) to the Sun Yat-sen Residence costs Y30.

Travel Agencies: CTS, in a wing of the Fuhua Hotel, sells bus tickets to Guangzhou, Hong Kong, and Shenzhen. Credit cards accepted. Open daily 8am-5:30pm. **Zhongshan Traffic Travel Ltd.** (zhōngshān jiāotōng lǚxíngshè; 中山交通旅行社), directly across from the Zhongshan International Hotel on Zhongshan Lu. Friendly staff. Private car and driver to the Sun Yat-sen Residence Y70. Open daily 8am-6pm.

Bank of China: Zhongshan International Hotel, 1st Fl., on Zhongshan Yi Lu. Exchanges traveler's checks. Open daily 8:30am-5:30pm.

Post and Telecommunications: On Sunwen Lu, way past the Shiqi River. EMS and IDD service. Open daily 9am-5:30pm; may be closed 12:30-2pm. **Postal Code:** 528400.

▌ ACCOMMODATIONS

Zhongshan accommodations tend not to be budget traveler-oriented, but discounts are often available. Most hotels accept major credit cards.

Tiecheng Hotel (tiěchéng jiǔdiàn; 铁城酒店), 107 Zhongshan Yi Lu (☎863 3803), at Sunwen Lu. Rooms are old but comfy. Deposit high. Singles Y140-185; doubles Y168.

Xiangshan Hotel (xiāngshān jiǔdiàn; 香山酒店), 113 Zhongshan Yi Lu (☎863 4567). Standard rooms are clean and well furnished, but the musty odor is not too fragrant. Doubles Y160-260; triples Y350 and up.

Zhongshan Jinyue Hotel (zhōngshān jīnyuè jiǔdiàn; 中山金悦酒店), 111 Zhongshan Yi Lu (☎862 2888), across the street from the Zhongshan International Hotel. Clean, perfumed rooms and easy access to Prince's Grill. "Special offer" rooms begin at Y268. Ask for that discount! Doubles Y460 and up.

◖ FOOD

The **Xiangshan Hotel Luncheonette** beside the Xiangshan Hotel hides its identity as a branch of the fast food chain **Timmy's**, but the food's all the same. Hamburgers (Y6-7), Chinese and Western meals (Y12-18), and beer (Blue Girl Y8-18, Heineken Y10) are available. (Open daily 8:30am-1:30am.) Along **Sunwen Lu,** across the river, cheap noodle shops and fast food restaurants keep great hours. Noodle-weary appetites might appreciate the **McDonald's** and **Pizza Hut.**

▨ **I Love You Cafe** (xī qū guǎngchǎng; 西区广场), 139 Sunwen Lu (☎862 6970). Large windows overlooking the street provide an abundance of light. The pine tables, tie-dyed bench covers, and fresh atmosphere are a perfect complement to the 40 kinds of tea, coffees, and floats. Open 10am-1am.

▨ **Fuzhou Hotel** (fùzhōu jiǔdiàn; 富洲酒店), 131 Fuhua Dao, 14th Fl. A breakfast buffet (7:30-10:30am) that is not to be missed. For Y20, it's all the dim sum, eggs (sunny-side up?), sausages, croissants, porridge, freshly squeezed fruit juices, and coffee you can eat. The friendly staff is eager to practice English. Open daily 7:30am-1am.

No No Cafe (nóngnóng dòujiāng; 浓浓豆浆), 139 Fuhua Dao (☎862 2666). The fruit juices and floats (Y10-16), waffles (Y6), and dumplings (Y10) will have you saying Yes Yes. A store-length window overlooks Sunwen Lu. Canto pop—groovy. Open 24hr.

◉ SIGHTS

SUN YAT-SEN RESIDENCE (sūn zhōngshān gùjū; 孙中山故居). Sun Yat-sen's Residence is the pride of Zhongshan. Born in this village in 1866, Sun Yat-sen went on to head the movement that overthrew the last remnants of the Qing dynasty in 1912 (see p. 14). Visitors can gaze at the library that educated this future revolutionary, the kitchen that clothed him, and the bed that cradled him. While certain objects on display are rather obscure—like a list of the building materials written by the house's architect in 1892—the exhibition hall provides some truly fascinating insights into the history of Chinese nationalism and Chinese national perception of the character of Sino-Western relations. *(In Cuihengcun (翠亨村). Bus #23, from the main bus stop on Sunwen Lu, and bus #12 from the Fuzhou Hotel stop outside (approx. 1hr., Y3.5). Otherwise, take a taxi from the Zhongshan International Hotel (30min., Y30). Y20.)*

OTHER SIGHTS. An alleyway to the right of Sunwen Lu, with your back to the river, leads to **Zhongshan Park** (zhōngshān gōngyuán; 中山公园), which has walking paths and clearings perfect for kite flying. *(Open 24hr. Free.)*

While the western bank of the Shiqi River is fairly tame, crossing the bridge and walking down the pedestrian thoroughfare of Sunwen Lu leads into a glamorous display of Zhongshan's new-found wealth. Construction has given the area an elegant look, and motorcycle drivers zoom around pedestrians while Chinese music, hip-hop, and funk-pop urge people to move at an ever faster pace. The riverbank area opposite the Fuhua Hotel becomes an impromptu **night market.** A little farther east on Sunwen Lu (about a 30min. walk from the Fuhua Hotel), **Sun Yat-sen Memorial Hall** (zhōngshān jìniàn guǎn; 中山纪念馆) pays homage to this city's most famous Sun. The hall hosts a number of local and international dance and music performances. *(☎882 2014. Open daily 8am-5pm. Y1.)*

ZHAOQING 肇庆   ☎0758

According to legend, the Seven Star Crags, Zhaoqing's primary attraction, formed when seven stars fell to earth from the heavens. For hundreds of years, the dramatic crags have inspired moving poems and essays. Unfortunately, the once-natural phenomena are now dressed in flashing light bulbs, kitschy cartoon characters, and silly rides that cost an exorbitant amount of money to ride. The outer fringes of the crags, however, remain free for all to walk or cycle through, and no one can charge for the stunning beauty of the crags as seen from afar.

✴🛈 ORIENTATION AND PRACTICAL INFORMATION

Zhaoqing is fairly small: Seven Star Crags and the train tracks define Zhaoqing's north border, and the **Xi River** (xī hé; 西河) marks its southern end. **Tianning Lu** (天宁路) houses tourists and their hotels, and **Gongnong Lu** (工农路) houses locals and their shops. **Jianshe Lu** (建设路), parallel to **Duanzhou Lu** (端州路), connects Tianning Lu and Gongnong Lu. The long-distance bus station is on Duanzhou Lu.

Trains: Zhaoqing Train Station (zhàoqìng huǒchē zhàn; 肇庆火车站; ☎283 5114), north of town, a Y15 taxi ride from Duanzhou Lu. To **Guangzhou** (2-3hr., 11 per day, Y25) and **Hong Kong** (4½hr., 9:17am, Y300).

Buses: Zhaoqing City Bus Station (zhàoqìng shì qìchē zhàn; 肇庆市汽车站; ☎223 3629) is on Duanzhou Lu, between Wenming Lu and Gongnong Lu. To: **Guangzhou** (2hr., at least every 30min. 6:20am-8pm, Y140); **Shenzhen** (3½hr., every 1-2hr. 8:20am-6:30pm, Y65); **Zhongshan** (2½hr., 3 per day, Y40); and **Zhuhai** (3½hr., 2 per day, Y36-50). **Minibus** competition is intense for the Guangzhou route—do some comparison shopping.

Ferry: Zhaoqing Passenger Ferry Terminal (zhàoqìng gǎng kèyùn zhàn; 肇庆港客运站; ☎283 3231 or 226 9713), on Jiangbin Lu, not clearly visible from the street's raised surface. Walk or take bus #4, 5, 8, or 11 to the corner of Jiangbin Lu and Renmin Lu. Instead of taking the incline, stay on the level ground and head for the underpass. The road curves to the right as you're facing the river; the ferry terminal is on the right just after the bend. To **Guangzhou** (7hr., 1am) and **Wuzhou** (10hr., 9am and 11pm).

Local Transportation: Fare on **buses** Y1-2 within the city center, Y3 on the outskirts. Aggressive **motorbike** drivers are always on hand; look for the colored helmets. Short trips approx. Y5; negotiate. **Taxi** base fare is Y7, each additional km Y2.2-2.6.

Travel Agencies: CITS, 46 Renmin Nan Lu (☎228 6038). On the corner of Duanzhou Lu and Tianming Lu, the **Star Lake International Travel Service** (xīnghú guójì lǚxíngshè; 星湖国际旅行社; ☎225 2033 or 223 5813), not to be confused with the Star Lake Travel Service opposite the memorial arch. Sells bus tickets to Guangzhou and Shenzhen (no commission). English-speaking staff. Open daily 8am-8pm.

Currency Exchange: The bank inside the **Star Lake Hotel** (xīnghú dàjiǔdiàn; 星湖 大酒店), 37 Duanzhou Lu, exchanges traveler's checks. Open daily 7:30am-midnight.

Hospital: People's Hospital (rénmín yīyuàn; 人民医院; ☎283 3612).

Post and Telecommunications: On Jianshe Lu near its intersection with Wenming Lu. EMS available. Open daily 7:30am-9:30pm. **Postal Code:** 526040.

ACCOMMODATIONS AND FOOD

Zhaoqing has plenty of hotels with plenty of fancy amenities; most offer discounts, but many also increase prices during the summer and on weekends and holidays.

Bakeries and tiny rice and noodle shops line **Gongnong Lu,** while KFC and other fast food restaurants are on **Jianshe Lu.** Across from the Star Lake Hotel, the **Precious Star Food Street** (bǎoxīng shí jiē; 宝星食街) consistently packs in the crowds. (Open daily 10am-3am.) Farther west, along Duanzhou Lu, past the memorial arch, a **food court** contains several small eateries.

Mount Dinghu International Youth Hostel (zhàoqìng dīnghú shān guójì qīngnián lǚxíng-guǎn; 肇庆鼎湖山国际青年旅行馆; ☎262 1668; fax 262 1665), at Dinghushan. Take bus #3 from the bus stop on Duanzhou Lu. From the bus terminus, bear left (with the park entrance behind you); it is a 10min. walk. Run by an exceptionally friendly staff. Hike endless hours through the mountain's rugged terrain; if that doesn't suffice, check out the winning pool and table tennis facilities. Dorms Y38.

The Seven Star Crags International Youth Hostel (HI) (☎222 6688; fax 222 4155), at the Seven Star Crags Park. Take bus #1 to the Park; the hostel is outside the middle gate (zhōng mén; 中门). Dorms Y30, non-HI members Y50.

Zhaoqing Friendship Guesthouse (zhàoqìng shì yǒuyì lǚguǎn; 肇庆市友谊旅馆), 45 Gongnong Lu (☎223 9298 or 223 2214). Large, clean rooms with TV, fan, and phone; attached baths not well maintained. Deposit Y50. Doubles Y60-118; triples Y90-138.

SIGHTS

The **Seven Star Crags** (qī xīng yán; 七星岩), Zhaoqing's prime attraction, are said to mirror the pattern of the Big Dipper. The center of the crags has become a **park** with fishing and cave exploring opportunities. Despite the unfortunate amount of kitsch, the park allows strolls along or even hikes up the crags. Romantics can hire a pedicab for a turn around the park (Y10), and walkers and cyclists abound. Take bus #19 from the stop near the memorial arch, right below the Star Lake International Travel Service sign. (☎227 7724. Open 24hr.; tickets sold 7:30am-6pm. Y30.) Boats speed across the lake between the park and the dock near the memorial arch (Y4-8). At the corner of Duanzhou Lu and Tianning Lu, the **Seven Star Crags Memorial Arch** frames the crag scenery from afar.

At the eastern terminus of Zheng Lu, where it intersects with Yuejiang Lu, **Yuejiang Temple** (yuèjiāng lóu; 阅江楼) overlooks the river. Closer to the water's edge, the graceful nine-tiered **Chongxi Pagoda** (chóngxī tǎ; 崇禧塔) is worth a visit.

HIKING DINGHUSHAN

18km east of Zhaoqing. Take bus #3 (30min.-1hr., every 20min., Y3) from the bus stop on Duanzhou Lu, on the same side of the street as the Star Lake Hotel. Bus #3 (every 7min. 7am-10pm) to Zhaoqing leaves from the bus stop inside the park. Avoid going on weekends, when the park is crowded and bus tickets are hard to come by. Y30.

SOUTH COAST

Dinghu Mountain (dǐnghú shān; 鼎湖山) beckons as a challenge to hikers and makes for a worthwhile daytrip from Zhaoqing. Inside **Dinghushan Park** (dǐnghúshān gōngyuán; 鼎湖山公园), a concrete trail winds up the mountain, opening onto some truly spectacular views of the farmland. Side routes farther up the mountain or through the woods lead to small clearings, beautiful waterfalls, and ponds. The main road passes fancifully named lakes such as **Leaping Dragon Pool** and **White Goose Pond**. Snack stands dot the road irregularly, and those who tire halfway can always hop on a motorbike (Y5-10). Most visit Dinghushan for its lovely **White Cloud Temple** (bái yún sì; 白云寺), a two-hour walk up the mountain from the bus stop. *(Open daily 8am-5pm.)*

Some travelers, enthralled by the highly touted clean air (famed for being "rich in anions") and gorgeous scenery, choose to stay a little longer at Dinghushan. The **Mt. Dinghu International Youth Hostel** (see p. 477) is a 10-minute walk into the park from the bus stop; take the road on the left. The **tourist office** sells maps (Y5). The **restaurant** across the tourist office offers an English menu with dishes such as pork dumplings (Y8 for 6) and vermicelli. (Open daily 7am-2pm and 5-8pm.)

SHAOGUAN 韶关   ☎0751

The select few who choose to stop in Shaoguan on their way north out of Guangdong province will encounter a down-to-earth city—not a single McDonald's on the horizon. The surrounding area holds some of the most impressive natural and historical treasures in Guangdong, namely Danxiashan and Nanhua Temple.

■ ? ORIENTATION AND PRACTICAL INFORMATION

Shaoguan straddles a peninsula where the **Wu River** (wǔ jiāng; 武江) and the **Zhen River** (zhēn jiāng; 浈江) flow together to form the **Bei River** (běi jiāng; 北江). **Fengdu Lu** (风度路) runs north to south, dividing the peninsula in half; **Fengcai Lu** (风采路) and **Jiefang Lu** (解放路) run perpendicular to Fengdu Lu. Fengcai Lu is a busy shopping street, streaming past a thick offering of boutiques, *dai pai dangs*, and restaurants. Jiefang Lu leads to the train station just off the peninsula to the east.

Trains: Shaoguan Train Station (sháoguān huǒchē zhàn; 韶关火车站), on Nanshao Lu at the Qujiang Bridge, just across from the terminus of Jiefang Lu on the peninsula. To: **Foshan** (3hr., 1 per day, Y39); **Guangzhou** (2½-3hr., 6 per day, Y36); **Shantou** (14½hr., 2 per day, sleeper Y102-129); and **Shenzhen** (5hr., 1 per day, Y52).

Buses: Shaoguan Bus Station (sháoguān qìchē zhàn; 韶关汽车站), on Gongye Xi Lu, just east of the peninsula. To **Zhuhai** (8hr., 1 per day, Y80) via **Guangzhou** (4hr.).

Local Transportation: Most **buses** stop at the train station square. **Taxi** base fare is Y4. **Motorbike** and **sampan** drivers charge about Y3.

Travel Agency: Guotai Travel Agency (guótài lǚxíngshè; 国泰旅行社; ☎822 3993), in the Guotai Hotel, on the north side of the train station. Train ticket commission Y5. Open daily 8:30am-noon, 2:30-5:30pm, and 7-10pm.

Bank of China: 158 Jiefang Lu (☎888 8338, ext. 212). Exchanges traveler's checks (daily 3-5pm). The branch to the right of the train station exchanges currency only. Both open daily 8am-5:30pm.

Internet Access: Head for the Shaoguan Hotel (162 Jiefang Lu, across the bridge from the train station) and ask the friendly porter to point the way to the "e bar" with over 100 terminals. Y3 per hr. Free tea may be provided.

Post and Telecommunications: On the north side of the train station square. The **post office** has EMS and Poste Restante. Open daily 8am-9:30pm. **China Telecom** has IDD service half-price after 9pm. Open daily 8am-10:30pm. **Postal Code:** 512023.

■ ⌂ ACCOMMODATIONS AND FOOD

Finding a hotel in Shaoguan is easiest for those arriving by train. In the station area, be prepared to contend with the noise of arriving trains and passengers.

The ubiquitous Y5 *dai pai dangs* are out in full force around the peninsula and north of the train station. **Shaoguan Restaurant Fast Food** (sháoguān jiǔjiā kuàicān; 韶关酒家快餐), 2 Xunfeng Lu, just off Jiefang Lu, serves dishes for Y5-13. (Open daily 10:30am-8:30pm.) Other fast-food joints as well as smaller, pricier Chinese and Japanese restaurants cluster around the mall on **Fengcai Lu**. Many hotel restaurants offer surprisingly good deals.

Gangdu Hotel (gǎngdū jiǔdiàn; 港都酒店; ☎812 2223), next to the train station. Best for those on a tight budget; cleanliness is not a virtue here. 8-bed dorms Y15; 2-bed dorms Y25; singles Y40-68; doubles Y60-98; triples Y120-128.

Guotai Great Hotel (guótài dàjiǔdiàn; 国泰大酒店; ☎888 8999), to the left as you exit the station. Clean rooms have all standard amenities. 20% or more discount available. 6% tax. Doubles Y190-248; triples Y288-328.

Shaohua Hotel (sháohuá jiǔdiàn; 韶华酒店), 162 Jiefang Lu (☎888 1870, ext. 3888), across the bridge from the train station. The Shaohua provides a warm welcome to Shaoguan, with English-speaking staff and clean, well-organized rooms with A/C, TV, bath, and refrigerator. An excellent Chinese restaurant and a gym on premises. Just 3min. away from the largest Internet cafe you may see in your life. 20% discount. Singles Y260; triples Y350. Credit cards accepted.

👁 SIGHTS

Short afternoon- and day-long trips out of the city reward the visitor with dramatic yet unpretentious sights. Travel agencies around the train station organize one- or two-day trips to surrounding sights. Shop around; cost varies quite a bit.

DANXIASHAN (dānxiáshān; 丹霞山). Danxia Mountain features some of the most stunning scenery in the Pearl River basin. Cliffs are mist-covered in the morning, and their red sandstone walls blaze all day. The park admission price includes access to hiking trails and temples. You can also ride a cable car (Y35) to the top. *(About 1 hr. north of Shaoguan. Take the pink buses (Y10) that depart from Jiefang Lu just beyond the Shaohua Hotel. The last minibus back to Shaoguan leaves around 6pm (Y15); if you miss it, take a minibus to Yunhe city and negotiate a taxi ride back to Shaoguan (Y50-100). Y43.)*

NANHUA TEMPLE (nánhuá sì; 南华寺). Despite its fame as the nexus of Zen Buddhism (see p. 33), the temple, or "Southern Flower Temple," retains a peaceful atmosphere. Built in AD 502, the temple has acquired a rather impressive collection of relics, including the 2m wide "one-thousand man pot" cast in AD 191 that is still used to feed the monks on occasion. Also on display is a 1.2m drum that causes the enormous 10,000kg bronze bell in the bell tower to resonate. The temple is best known for its sixth patriarch, Huineng, an illiterate monk whose teachings later developed into Zen Buddhism; a statue of Huineng supposedly cast from his body sits in the back hall. The temple is also famed for a more secular patron, the scholar Su Dongpo. In 1093, when he was demoted by the court, Su Dongpo went into exile in northern Guangdong. While there, he used a kitchen broom to write the calligraphy on two of the header boards in the temple. *(Minibuses (30min., the empty promise of "every 5min.," Y10) and taxis (around Y50) leave from Shaoguan Train Station. Buses return to Shaoguan daily until 6pm. Open daily 8am-5pm. Y10.)*

LION CRAG (shīzi yán; 狮子岩). The crag's claim to fame is Maba Man, the bones of an early *Homo sapiens* that dates to the middle Pleistocene (600,000 BC). The admission price includes a brief walking tour of the caves with a guide who describes (in Chinese) Maba Man's use of tools and division of labor. The actual bones and artifacts have been moved from the cave to a run-down **museum** on the grounds, and poorly proportioned clay statues don't fill the void. Nevertheless, Lion Crag is a quick trip, and the crag itself, if not the anthropological find inside, is picturesque. *(South of Shaoguan, outside the town of Qujiang (曲江; known as Maba). From the Shaoguan Train Station, cross the bridge to the peninsula; the bus stop is just past the pedestrian overpass on the left. Blue buses (30 min., every 15min., Y3) go to Maba. From Qujiang, motorbikes cruise the 5min. drag (Y3). For a more comfortable ride, take one of the cyclo-motorbike hybrids (Y4). Open daily 8am-7:30pm; last admission 5:30pm. Y10; museum Y5.)*

ZHUHAI 珠海 ☎0756

For many tourists crossing the China-Macau border at Zhuhai, the city is but a brief stopover. Those who stay longer come to understand why this is the stomping ground of choice for wheelers and dealers, whether at work or at play. The privileges bestowed on Zhuhai as a Special Economic Zone make it a hub of free and unfettered enterprise: Zhuhai's streets are filled with bargain-basement-priced electronics, food stands, and young women, all hoping to catch the eye of a visiting businessman. Few residents seem to notice the setting of the sun as restaurants, karaoke bars, and hotels field a steady stream of customers all night long.

⌐ TRANSPORTATION

Airplanes: Zhuhai Airport (zhūhǎi jīchǎng; 珠海机场; ☎889 5494), on the peninsula southwest of Gongbei. Airport buses leave from the Zhangzhou Bldg. near Gongbei Market, or from the Xiangzhou Bus Station (40min., every 30min., Y20). A taxi to the airport costs Y100; ask for a flat rate. **Zhuhai Airlines** (zhūhǎi hángkōng gōngsī; 珠海航空公司), 34 Yuehai Dong Lu (☎889 7881), is friendly. Smiley Kong speaks excellent English. Open 24hr.; after 10pm, call first. To: **Beijing** (1-2 per day, Y1550); **Kunming** (1-3 per day, Y900); and **Shanghai** (1-3 per day, Y1120).

Buses: The best way to leave Zhuhai is by bus. **Gongbei Bus Station** (gǒngběi qìchē zhàn; 拱北汽车站; ☎888 8554), adjacent to the Yongtong Hotel, has buses to **Zhongshan** (1hr.; every 30min. 9:10am-7pm; Y16, weekends Y18). **Xiangzhou Long-distance Bus Station** (xiāngzhōu chángtú qìchē zhàn; 香洲长途汽车站; ☎222 5637), on Shuiwan Lu, next to the Gongbei Palace Hotel, has buses to **Guangzhou** (3hr.; every 30min. 7am-7pm; Y35, A/C minibus approx. Y50).

Boats: Jiuzhou Ferry Terminal (jiǔzhōu gǎng kèyùn zhàn; 九州港客运站), in Jida. Take bus #4 from the border crossing. To: **Hong Kong** (1hr., 5 per day 8am-5pm, info ☎333 2113); **Jiuzhou Island** (1½-2hr., 1-2 per day); and **Shenzhen** (1hr., approx. every 15min. 7:50am-6pm., info ☎333 3359).

Local Transportation: Buses are cream with red lettering. Stops are marked by signs or a large orange pagoda roof; most routes serve **Gongbei Bus Station** near the Macau border. Fare Y1, A/C buses Y2. Bus **#2** runs along Yingbin Nan Lu and Jingshan Lu, from Xiangzhou to Lianhuashan to Gongbei.

Taxis: Base fare Y10, each additional km Y2.40. **Taxi Complaints:** ☎226 2628.

✴❓ ORIENTATION AND PRACTICAL INFORMATION

Zhuhai is divided into three districts. **Gongbei** (拱北), the main tourist district, borders Macau; **Jida** (吉大) is the site of the ferry terminal and the famed mermaid statue; and **Xiangzhou** (香洲) is to the north. **Shuiwan Lu** (水湾路) and **Yingbin Nan Lu** (迎宾南路) run through Gongbei and Jida. Two very good maps (about Y5), the *Zhuhai Tourist Map* and the *Tour and Transportation Map of Zhuhai*, are available at the border crossing and in most hotels and bookstores.

Travel Agency: CTS (☎888 5777), at the corner of Yingbin Lu and Lian'an Lu, next to the Overseas Chinese Hotel. More a ticket office than a travel agent. Open daily 8am-7pm.

Visas: Foreign travelers to Zhuhai need Chinese visas. Visas can be obtained abroad before departure (see p. 50), in Hong Kong (see p. 420), or in Macau (see p. 452).

Bank of China: At the corner of Yingbin Lu and Yuehai Dong Lu. US or Hong Kong dollars are easiest to exchange. Also exchanges traveler's checks. Open M-F 8:30am-noon and 2-5pm, Sa-Su 9am-noon and 1:30-4pm. Many hotels charge exorbitant exchange fees.

Bookstore: Xinhua Bookstore, on Yingbin Dadao in Gongbei, sells 3 maps of Zhuhai, but a limited selection of English literature. Open daily 9am-9:15pm.

Hospitals: People's Hospital (rénmín yīyuàn; 人民医院; ☎222 2571) and **Gongbei Hospital** (gǒngběi yīyuàn; 拱北医院; ☎888 5463) are open 24hr.

Post and Telecommunications: **Yuehai Post and Telecom,** on Yuehai Dong Lu, a few blocks east of the Guangdong Hotel. EMS and IDD service available. Open daily 8am-8pm. **Postal Code:** 519020.

ACCOMMODATIONS

Most accommodations in Zhuhai cater to businesspeople. Discounts of 10-40% are often available. Unless otherwise noted, major credit cards are accepted. Be fore-warned that most hotels demand a deposit that is at least 200% of the room fee.

Zhuhai International Youth Hostel (zhūhǎi guójì xuéshēng lǚguǎn; 珠海国际学生旅馆; ☎333 3838; www.zhuhai-holitel.com), on the luxuriant grounds of the Zhuhai Holiday Resort Hotel on Shihua Mountain. Bus #4 runs from central Zhuhai to the hotel; a free shuttle runs from the hotel to the hostel. Exceptionally clean and comfortable rooms have A/C and bath. 5-bed dorms Y50, non-HI members Y60.

Overseas Chinese Hotel (huá qiáo bīnguǎn; 华侨宾馆; ☎888 6288), on Yingbin Nan Lu, past Lianan Lu. Clean, comfortable rooms with dark wood paneling, plus about everything else you could need, including friendly staff, a Tang-dynasty restaurant, a gym, and a CTS office next door. If you can squeeze out a discount, this is certainly the best value for your money. 10% increase on weekends, 30% on holidays. 13% service charge. Singles Y286-338; doubles Y438.

Gongbei Hotel (gǒngběi jiǔdiàn; 拱北酒店), 36 Lianhua Lu (☎888 5260). Do not be misled by the simple lobby—rooms are elegant and airy, generously brushed with sunlight. Deposit Y300. 60% discounts possible. Singles Y300; doubles Y320.

Yongtong Hotel (yǒngtōng jiǔdiàn; 永通酒店; ☎888 8887), on Youyi Lu. From the border crossing, head toward the bus station, and turn right on Youyi Lu; the hotel is the smaller gray building with the luminous orange symbol. Standard rooms come with electronics galore. 10% service charge. Singles Y289-318. MC, Visa accepted.

FOOD

Most hotel restaurants serve dim sum and are home to "Western-style cafes" or "coffeehouses." At night, food vendors set up makeshift tables and chairs and serve simple but tasty meals (Y10-20, beer Y7-10). *Dai pai dangs* are numerous, particularly along the Xiangzhou coastline and in Gongbei on **Yuehai Dong Lu** and **Yingbin Lu.** In the evening, cooks wheel carts down the streets, serving tea and snacks for Y2-3. Some stalls and restaurants may be unwelcoming to foreigners.

Chinese Restaurant (zhōngguó dàshíjiā; 中国大食家), on the 2nd floor of the Overseas Chinese Hotel. Waiters in Tang-dynasty clothes pour jasmine tea and guide newcomers around the buffet (Y30) of over 80 delicious dishes. Open daily 11am-9:30pm.

Cup (bēizi hóngchá guǎn; 杯子红茶馆), on Yuehua Lu. This 24hr. coffee and juice bar caters to card players and young couples. Lots of country music. Impressively authentic European cafe decor; no English menu. Drinks Y15-22.

Haili Seafood Restaurant (hǎilì hǎixiān cāntīng; 海利海鲜餐厅; ☎888 9813), on Yuehua Lu, near McDonald's. Around 6pm, plastic tables and chairs come out and the sidewalk is transformed into a crowded outdoor restaurant. Open 24hr.

ENTERTAINMENT

Zhuhai almost never sleeps. Most of the night action is contained in the triangular region of Gongbei, between Yingbin Lu and Shuiwan Lu; a generous selection of discos and clubs thrill revelers from nearby Macau. Every night around 6pm, **Gongbei Market** (gǒngběi shìchǎng; 拱北市场) emerges from the woodwork. Tents filled with everything from watches to lingerie materialize alongside stalls hawking sound systems; the occasional unabashed karaoke singer will give an unsolicited concert. When the market shuts down around 10pm, business picks up at the numerous karaoke clubs on the second floor of every hotel in town. **Lianhua Lu** is filled with small shops and maze-like corridors of tiny boutiques.

SOUTH COAST

SIGHTS

Hopping on bus #9 from the Gongbei Bus Station at the Macau border and riding it to Jida district brings you near Zhuhai's famed **mermaid statue,** a representation of a fishing girl handling a pearl. The palm trees and lake at nearby **Seaside Park** (hǎibīn gōngyuán; 海滨公园) make for pleasant ambience, but the brightly painted amusement rides detract from overall elegance. *(Open 24hr. Y1.)* To the west, near the intersection of Haijing Lu, Haibin Lu, and Lingshan Lu is **Shijingshan Tourist Centre** (shíjǐngshān lǚyóu zhōngxīn; 石景山旅游中心). Climbing the stone steps up Mt. Shijing affords magnificent views of Xianghu Bay.

The **New Yuan Ming Palace** (yuánmíng xīn yuán; 圆明新园), complete with its own lake, is a "replica" of the Old Summer Palace in Beijing (see p. 126) that was destroyed in 1860 during the Opium War (see p. 13). Expensive "activities," the scarcity of real artifacts, and the ubiquitous souvenir shops make for a somewhat contrived atmosphere. *(Take bus #13 to Lanpu Jiuzhou Dadao. Open daily 9:30am-10pm; tickets sold 9am-9pm. Y100.)* The **Lost City Water Park** (mènghuàn shuǐchéng; 梦幻水城), visible from the New Yuan Ming Palace, has a wave pool, waterfall, and torrent river. *(Open daily noon-9pm. Y80, Y40 when purchased with admission to the palace.)*

SHENZHEN 深圳   ☎0755

Other Chinese cities enjoy Special Economic Zone (SEZ) status, but none takes the title quite as seriously as Shenzhen. The well-tended city jets ahead of the rest of China in the quest to be just like Singapore, Seoul, Tokyo, and most of all, its neighbor, Hong Kong. The streets are straight and clean, the buildings tall and shiny, and the general atmosphere bustling and rich. Hong Kongers in pursuit of entertainment flock to the region on weekends and holidays to spend time and money in the colossal theme parks nearby. Unfortunately, all this prosperity has left some people behind and jarringly out of place; gaunt beggars and entire families of bare-bottomed children try their hardest to tweak the heartstrings of even the city's most hardened capitalists.

BORDER CROSSING: SHENZHEN AND HONG KONG

The border is open daily 6:30am-11:30pm. Trains leave Hung Hom Station in Hong Kong daily 5:45am-10:19pm and return from Lo Wu KCR Station to Shenzhen daily 6:01am 12:20am.

Into Hong Kong (p. 406): Trains from Shenzhen (p. 483) head to Kowloon Tong (in Tsim Sha Tsui East, p. 422), Hung Hom Station (p. 416), and cities in the New Territories (p. 441). The customs office abuts the Lo Wu KCR station on the Hong Kong side.

Into Shenzhen: All destinations on the mainland, including Shenzhen, require a valid Chinese visa; obtain a visa at the Hong Kong CTS office (p. 419). When entering Shenzhen County by **bus,** visitors must show valid travel documents. Chinese citizens disembark briefly to go through inspections. Foreign passport holders will usually stay on the bus, showing passports to an official, but sometimes they, too, must accompany the official to the inspection counter.

TRANSPORTATION

Airplanes: Shenzhen International Airport (shēnzhèn guójì jīchǎng; 深圳国际机场; ☎777 6555), in the northwestern Baoan district. Take bus #330 from Hualian Mansion on Shennan Zhong Lu, west of Lizhi Park, or minibuses #501 and 507. **CAAC ticket office,** Huachang Sanyo Bldg., 1007 Huachang (☎377 9800), sells domestic tickets 20% discounts available. Open M-F 8am-6pm, Sa-Su 9am-4:30pm. To **Beijing** (3 per day, Y1400) and **Tianjin** (4 per week, Y1290). **Shanghai Airlines,** 18 Shandu Lu (☎3240 1431), is open daily 8am-5pm. To **Chengdu** (5-6 per day, Y1130) and **Shang-**

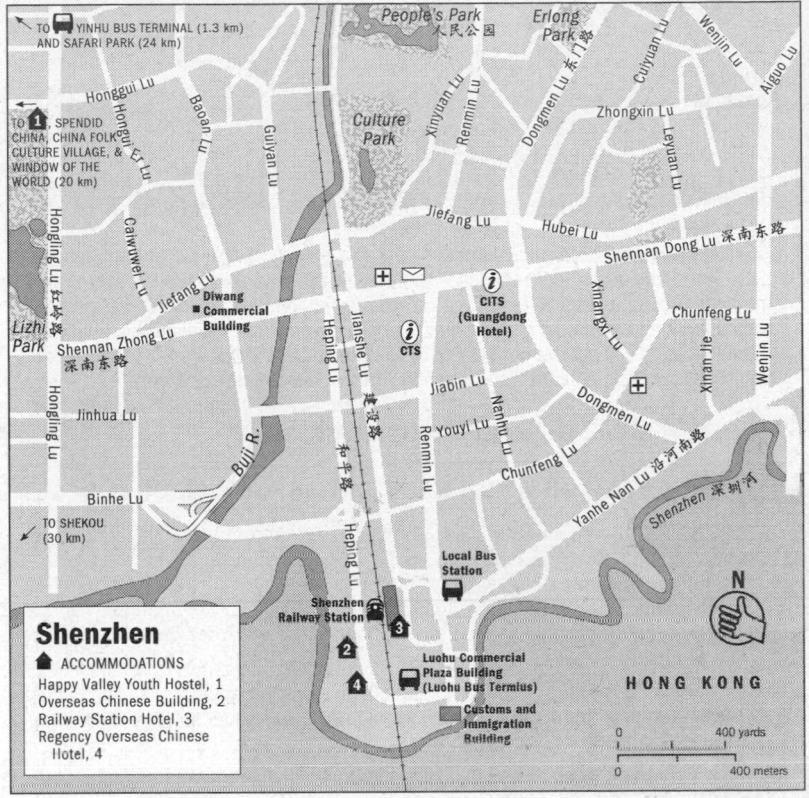

Shenzhen

■ ACCOMMODATIONS
Happy Valley Youth Hostel, 1
Overseas Chinese Building, 2
Railway Station Hotel, 3
Regency Overseas Chinese
Hotel, 4

hai (9-10 per day, Y1120). **Eastern Airlines** (zhōngguó dōngfāng hángkōng gōngsī; 中国东方航空公司; ☎322 7740), in the Chinese Airlines Building, 1st Fl., at Huaqian Lu and Hongli Lu. Open daily 8:30am-5pm. Several flights per day to **Beijing** (Y1400) and **Shanghai** (Y1120).

Trains: See also **Border Crossing: Shenzhen and Hong Kong,** p. 482. **Shenzhen Train Station** (shēnzhèn huǒchē zhàn; 深圳火车站; ☎232 8647, ticket office ☎232 5043), on Jianshe Lu, a giant building attached to the customs and immigration office and the bus station by covered walkways. Electronic information kiosks in Chinese and English. Open daily 5:50am-10pm. To: **Beijing** (24hr., 2 per day, Y616); **Changsha** (10hr., 4 per day, Y291-354); **Guangzhou** (1-1½hr., every 10-35min. 6am-9pm, Y40-70); **Guilin** (14½hr., 1 per day, Y358); **Shaoguan** (5hr., 1 per day, Y89); **Shanghai** (26½hr., 1 per day, Y541); and **Shantou** (9¾hr., 1 per day, Y300).

Buses: See also **Border Crossing: Shenzhen and Hong Kong,** p. 482.

Luohu Bus Terminus (luóhú qìchē zhàn; 罗湖汽车站; ☎233 7378 or 232 1670), in the same complex as the train station. Most buses to **Guangzhou** depart from the basement level of the station (2hr., every 4min. 6am-10pm, Y60). Tickets sold on the 2nd floor. Open daily 7am-6pm. To: **Chaozhou** (4½hr., 3 per day, Y160); **Huizhou** (1½hr., every 15min. 7am-7pm, Y30-35); **Foshan** (2½hr., every hr. 8am-7pm, Y75); **Shantou** (4hr., every 30min. 8am-8pm, Y150); **Xiamen** (9½hr., 4 per day, Y187); and **Zhaoqing** (3½hr., every hr. 8am-6pm, Y90).

Shenzhen City Bus (☎540 9465 or 541 5107) services **direct Hong Kong-Shenzhen** routes. The Qiaoshe Bus Station between the Overseas Chinese Building and the Regency Overseas Chinese Hotel on Heping Lu has long distance buses to most destinations in Guangdong Province and buses to Fuzhou, Xiamen, Quanzhou, Zhangzhou, and Sishi in Fujian Province.

An **A/C double-decker bus** runs from the Shenzhen Bay Hotel to **China's Hong Kong City** (3:45, 4:45, and 5:15pm). The same bus stops by the Shangri-La Hotel, near the border crossing (every 30min. 4:30-6pm). Ticket prices vary (M-F HK$65-150, children HK$45-110, depending on embarkation point; weekend prices rise HK$20). Credit cards accepted.

Boats: The nearest port to Shenzhen is **Shekou Port** (shékǒu gǎng; 蛇口港; ☎669 5600). From Shenzhen, take bus #113 heading west along Shennan Lu (Y6) or buses #204 and 217. From here, boats go to **Haikou** (16hr., Su-F 4pm, Y218-458) and **Zhuhai** (1hr., every 15-30min. 7:30am-6pm). The **ticket office** (☎669 1213), in the domestic ferry building, sells tickets 10 days in advance to **Hong Kong** (50min., 10 per day 7:45am-9:30pm, HK$90-125) and **Macau** (1½hr., 11am, HK$87).

Local Transportation: Many local **buses** stop at the parking lot near the train station and the Luohu Commercial Plaza. Buses within the city usually bear single- or double-digit numbers (Y1-3); buses with triple-digit numbers go far from the center (Y2-12). Bus **#3** runs down Shennan Lu, and **#101** and **113** (7am-7pm) follow Shennan Lu past the theme parks to Shekou. **Minibuses** (Y2-5) post the destination in the front window; red minibuses stay within the SEZ and green minibuses go beyond the border.

Taxis: Base fare Y12.5, each additional 250m or 45 seconds of waiting time Y0.6. 30% surcharge 11pm-6am. **Taxi service complaints:** ☎322 8111.

✈❓ ORIENTATION AND PRACTICAL INFORMATION

Shenzhen county covers a broad area; Shenzhen proper comprises the southeastern corner. Most of the tourist attractions lie a few kilometers to the west of the city center along **Shennan Lu** (深南路), which runs from east to west past many of Shenzhen's hotels. **Renmin Lu** (人民路) runs perpendicular to Shennan Lu. **Jianshe Lu** (建设路), roughly parallel to Renmin Lu, leads to the border crossing (see p. 482). The Shenzhen Train Station and the Luohu Bus Terminus, adjacent to the customs and immigration center, are at the southern end of Jianshe Lu.

Travel Agency: CTS, 3023 Renmin Lu (☎225 5888), usually has an English-speaking staff member on hand. Open daily 9am-6pm.

Currency Exchange: Bank of China, 23 Jianshe Lu. Open daily 8:30-11am and 2-5pm. The train station branch, 1009 Renmin Lu, has international **ATMs.** Open M-F 8:30-11:30am and 2-5pm, Sa-Su 9:30am-3:30pm. **HongkongBank,** 1015 Renmin Lu, beside the Century Plaza Hotel, also has **ATMs.** Hong Kong dollars are accepted in the city, but change is given in *yuan.* Most bank ATMs service Cirrus, Plus, and NYCE.

Police: Shenzhen Police Office (☎557 6355). **Shekou branch** (☎669 1011).

Hospitals: Liuhua Hospital (liúhuā yīyuàn; 流花医院; ☎223 8826), on Chunfeng Lu, a little bit northeast of Dongmen Lu.

Internet Access: Most hotel business centers have access for approx. Y20 per 15min.

Post and Telecommunications: At the intersection of Jianshe Lu and Shennan Lu, to the right of the hospital. For international service and telephone calls, take the outside staircase to the 2nd floor. Open daily 8am-7pm. The post office on the mezzanine level of the train station has EMS. Open daily 8am-8pm. **Postal Code:** 518000 or 518001.

▌ ACCOMMODATIONS

Shenzhen's special economic status means that the hotels are geared toward the rich; forget your budget, or head elsewhere. If you stay, expect a high level of comfort, with A/C, TV, and private bath.

■ **Regency Overseas Chinese Hotel** (huá qiáo jiǔdiàn; 华侨酒店), 1009 Heping Lu (☎559 6688; fax 558 3779). Behind the train station, follow the pedestrian overpass to the left of the Hong Kong Immigration building (facing Shangri-La). The Overseas has slightly small, elegant rooms, and equally welcoming bathrooms. 30% discount may be available. 10% service charge. Singles Y258; doubles Y298. Credit cards accepted.

Happy Valley Youth Hostel (HI) (☎694 9443; fax 694 9046). From the train station, take minibus #473 (Y3) to the last stop or take bus #101 (40min., Y4) to Window of the World Theme Park, and then take a taxi to the Happy Valley Parking Plaza. The English-speaking manager, Liu, is extremely friendly. 6-bed dorms Y50, non-HI members Y55; doubles Y170/180.

Overseas Chinese Building (huá qiáo dàshà; 华侨大厦), 1043 Heping Lu (☎556 4762), across from the Regency Overseas Chinese Hotel. People fresh off the bus constantly stream across the lobby. Standard rooms are fairly clean. 20% discount may be available. 4-bed dorms with shared bath Y45; singles Y238; doubles Y138-268.

Railway Station Hotel (huǒchē zhàn dàjiǔdiàn; 火车站大酒店; ☎232 1168), in the New Railway Station Bldg. on Jianshe Lu. Rooms are large and well furnished. Alas, there are no bathtubs. 10% service charge. Singles HK$238; doubles HK$268.

⬛ FOOD

Visitors to Shenzhen who join the crowds at the **theme parks** will be rewarded with exotic dining experiences for reasonable prices. In the city center, most establishments are either fast-food joints or expensive restaurants (identifiable by the pretty young women standing at the entrance). One mid-range restaurant, **Sandra** (xiānlè dū; 仙乐都), 1068 Heping Lu, has Asian-style Western food, from steaks (Y30-48) to "french frices." (Open daily 8am-2am.) Along **Jianshe Lu,** McDonald's and **Cafe de Coral** join the fray. **Diwang Commercial Building,** on Shennan Zhong Lu, midway between Jianshe Lu and Hongling Lu, brings together several fast-food or Western restaurants, including the **Hard Rock Cafe** (for those hoping to augment their t-shirt collections). Cheap eateries and cafeterias abound at the **train station.**

⬛🎵 SIGHTS AND ENTERTAINMENT

Shenzhen, boasting no natural attractions of its own, has decided to usurp those of the rest of China and the world. Although Splendid China, the China Folk Culture Village, and Window of the World are all within walking distance of one another, they are connected by the **Happy Line,** a monorail that circles the three sights and the Shenzhen Bay Hotel (Y35 between any 2 of its 7 stops).

▨ **CHINA FOLK CULTURE VILLAGE** (zhōngguó mínsù wénhuà cūn; 中国民俗文化村). Not surprisingly, this village was set up to teach visitors about China's many minority nationalities. Surprisingly, it does a good job of it. The Bai, Dai, Dong, Mongolian, and other villages highlight the different techniques and materials used in building homes, furniture, and farming tools. Some of the other displays, such as the "Guanyin Buddha Making Her Presence," tend to be more hokey. Mini-cars with drivers run between villages (10min. drive HK$10/Y10, 1hr. drive with stops HK$150/Y150). Frequent minority drumming and dancing shows culminate in a large evening performance that most feel is well worth the extra money (7:30 and 8:30pm, Y15-20). Visitors can dress up in ethnic costumes (Y10-20) and participate in staged wedding rituals or create handicrafts. A food street offers a taste of Sichuanese, Dai, Cantonese, and Northern Chinese cuisines (Y5-10). *(Accessible by bus #101 or 113. Free wheelchairs and baby carriages. Open M-F 10:30am-9pm, Sa-Su 10:30am-11pm. M-F Y85, Sa-Su Y80; children 1.1-1.4m tall and ages 65-69 half-price. Combination ticket with Splendid China M-F Y145, Sa-Su Y155.)*

WINDOW OF THE WORLD (shìjiè zhī hù; 世界之户). Wildly popular among Hong Kongers and Chinese, this theme park toes the line between tastefully cultural and garishly tacky. Colorful flags from the all over the world wave to the beat of international music. View miniature versions of the famous landmarks, including the Golden Gate Bridge, the Louvre, the Eiffel Tower, the Pyramids, and the Grand Canyon, or settle down for a snack of Viennese cafe, Chinese shark fin, Turkish *kebaps*. *(From Shekou or Shenzhen, take bus #101 or 113 (45min., Y4) to near the Eiffel Tower or the Golden Gate Bridge. Open daily 9am-10:30pm; last admission 9pm. M-F Y100, Sa-Su Y110; children 1.1-1.4m tall and ages 65-69 half-price.)*

SAFARI PARK (yěshēng dòngwùyuán; 野生动物园). Touted as a park that allows wild animals to roam free, this drive-through zoo is in fact a vast collection of animals put on display for the unique benefit of tourists. If watching bears in tutus or posing with chained ostriches doesn't appeal to you, skip this park. *(Take the blue city bus #206 (Y3) or bus #101 (Y7) to the end of the line. Open daily 8:30am-6:30pm; last admission 5:50pm. M-F Y80, Sa-Su Y90; children 1.1-1.4m tall and ages 65-69 half-price.)*

SPLENDID CHINA (jǐnxiù zhōnghuá; 锦绣中华). In the words of President Jiang Zemin, Splendid China hopes "to make the world get close with China." The Great Wall, Terracotta Warriors, Forbidden City, Seven Star Crags, and the Yangzi's Three Gorges all grace the premises. The costumes, festivals, and houses of the Bai, Dai, Hakka, and Northern Shanxi peoples are also on display. *(Take bus #101 or 113 from the train station to Shenzhen Bay Hotel. Open daily 8:30am-6pm. M-F Y70, Sa-Su Y80; children 1.1-1.4m tall and ages 65-69 half-price. Combination ticket with China Folk Culture Village M-F Y130, Sa-Su Y150.)*

SHANTOU 汕头 ☎0754

Although Shantou has a colorful history, the city today has little to show for it, save the old-town quarters in the western peninsula area. Prior to the 19th century, this part of Guangdong province was regarded as an untamed frontier, a place of exile for criminals and disgraced officials. British commercialists and colonialists, who entered the area in 1858, are generally credited with putting Shantou (which they knew as "Swatow") on the map by developing it as a trading port. After the sun set on the Empire, the Chinese residents of Shantou developed their home into a prosperous and ever-expanding urban center, especially since its designation as the first of China's Special Economic Zones in 1980.

Unfortunately, SEZ status has just about leveled the old city, leaving behind bare avenues of glass-and-steel monstrosities. A prototype of the modern metropolis, Shantou is a pot of gold for aspiring investors, but leaves most visitors empty-handed (often literally). Travelers who do end up here are likely to find the atypical part of Shantou, the older sliver near the water, to be of the most interest.

⌐ TRANSPORTATION

Airplanes: Shantou Airport (shàntóu jīchǎng; 汕头国际机场; ☎579 9678), 15km northeast of central Shantou. The **CAAC ticket office,** 83 Jinsha Lu (☎825 1915), 3 blocks west of the main Bank of China, operates a shuttle bus to the airport (30min., every hr. 6:30am-5:30pm, Y4). A taxi costs about Y50. To: **Beijing** (11:20am and 6:50pm, Y1460); **Guangzhou** (3-4 per day, Y530); **Hong Kong** (8:40am and 4:55pm, Y1050); and **Shanghai** (10am and 12:10pm, Y490).

Trains: Shantou Train Station (shàntóu huǒchē zhàn; 汕头火车站; ☎881 6487), on Taishan Lu, at the eastern edge of the city. Open daily 7:50am-9:40pm. To **Guangzhou** (7½hr., 3 per day 8:10-10am, Y125-341) and **Shanghai** (12hr., 6:54pm, Y216-398). Trains no longer run to Chaozhou.

Buses: Shantou Passenger Transit Station (shàntóu qìchē kèyùn zhàn; 汕头汽车客运站; ☎811 1359), on Chaoshan Lu, north of Huoche Lu, 7km from the train station. Connected to Jinsha Lu by bus #4 and to the old town center by bus #7. Open daily 6am-1am. To: **Fuzhou** (10hr., 3 per day 9:20am-3:40pm, Y120); **Guangzhou** (6hr., every 30min. 7am-1am, Y180); and **Xiamen** (4-5hr., 6 per day 9am-8pm; Y45, express Y90). Minibuses run to **Chaozhou** (1hr., every 20min. 6:30am-7:30pm, Y10).

Local Transportation: Most **buses** run approx. 6am-9pm. Fare Y2, A/C buses Y3. Buses **#2, 4, 6, 8, 11,** and **12** terminate at the train station in the far east of the city. Bus **#11** runs from the old city dock area and along the commercial thoroughfare of Jinsha Lu. Private **minibuses** run the same routes (Y2), but are often in worse condition.

Taxis: Base fare Y8-10, each additional 250m Y1.4-1.8. **Pedicabs** to most destinations within the city center Y5-8; negotiate prices in advance.

✈🏠 ORIENTATION AND PRACTICAL INFORMATION

Shantou is vast, sprawling on the northern bank of its very own **harbor** (shàntóu gǎng; 汕头港) in the far north of Guangdong province. The old town center is in the southwestern end, around a tiny peninsula, and consists of several small streets that converge at tiny traffic circles, the most important of which is fed by **Shengping Lu** (升平路), **Minzu Lu** (民族路), and **Anping Lu** (安平路). From the old town, the larger streets of **Waima Lu** (外马路) and **Zhongshan Lu** (中山路) run eastward into the newer parts of town. The new areas seem to have spread north and east at such a rapid pace that there is no well-defined city center. **Jinsha Lu** (金砂路) runs from east to west through the city.

Travel Agency: CTS, 41 Shanzhang Lu (☎862 9888), in the Overseas Chinese Hotel. The 1st floor office books local tours (Y30 per day; English speakers available) and tickets.

Bank of China: 98 Jinsha Lu, just east of the Golden Gulf Hotel. Take buses #2, 4, or 6 to Jinhaiwan Dajiudian. Counters #8 and 9 (around the corner on the right) exchange traveler's checks. Issues credit card advances. Open M-F 8:30-11:30am and 3-5:30pm.

PSB: 11 Yuejing Lu (☎827 2275), off Nanhai Lu, which runs south from Waima Lu, west of the No. 2 Hospital in the old part of town.

Hospitals: People's No. 2 Hospital (dì èr rénmín yīyuàn; 第二人民医院), 28 Waima Lu (☎827 2765, ext. 4211), east of Shengping Lu. Take bus #1 to Shengping Lu.

Post Office: Shantou Post and Telecommunications Office (☎829 4330), on the south side of Zhongshan Dong Lu, near Longyan Nan Lu. **Postal Code:** 515000.

🏠 ACCOMMODATIONS

Shantou ain't cheap. Off-season discounts are possible, but keep in mind that prices are usually exorbitant to begin with. Budget travelers should consider spending the night in Shantou's more affordable neighbor, Chaozhou (see p. 488).

🏨 Xinhua Hotel (xīnhuá jiǔdiàn; 新华酒店), 141 Waima Lu (☎827 3710). Take bus #10 from Zhongshan Lu or #1 from Changping Lu to Xinhua. The Xinhua has sparkling rooms and shiny lacquer furniture, plus matronly service and a prime location in the old city area. Discounts available. Doubles Y98-130; triples Y138-220.

Overseas Chinese Hotel (huáqiáo dàshà; 华侨大厦), 42 Shanzhang Lu (☎862 9888), at Changping Lu. Take bus #2 from the train station to Jinsha Gongyuan or #3 from the main bus station to Shanzhang Lu. Rooms are overpriced and underkept, and service is grudging at best; the only perk is a good location by the city center. Cheaper rooms on the lower floors. 20% discounts. Singles Y228-340; doubles Y228-380; triples Y360.

Swatow Peninsula Hotel (tuódǎo bīnguǎn; 鸵岛宾馆), 36 Jinsha Zhong Lu (☎831 6668). Take bus #4 or 11 from the bus station or #2, 4, 6, or 11 from the train station to Jinsha Gongyuan. Good views, sterile baths, and luxurious wet bars make this a worthwhile splurge. 40% discounts possible Sept.-May. Singles and doubles Y388.

🍴👁 FOOD AND SIGHTS

Shantou city has no official sights, and even the local CTS seems to have resigned itself to that fact. But the old town area is an interesting, aging neighborhood, whose small streets crammed with tatami mat vendors and vegetable stalls give it an entirely different feel from unabashedly modern Shantou. The local food is distinctive and good, and a half-day walking-eating tour of the waterfront has no admission fee. From the train or bus stations or from anywhere on Jinsha Lu, take bus #11 to **Xiti Harbor** (xītí gǎng; 西堤港); buses #1, 3, and 10 also go in the right direction. On all buses, get off at the last stop. **Xiti Lu** (西堤路) leads north from here and is lined with crumbling wooden European buildings left over from the British treaty port days. **Anping Lu** and, farther north, **Shengping Lu,** run eastward off Xiti Lu, and are brimming with local markets selling fresh cilantro and bamboo shoots. Any of the little streets around here are good places to sniff out small restaurants serving flat white rice noodles and delicious boiled pork and cabbage dumplings. Closer to the center of the city, a row of small restaurants lining **Jinhuan Zhong Lu,** immediately north of Jinsha Lu, offers clean, cheap and bounteous Shantou fare, including Chaozhou-style seafood and sliced beef noodle soup.

CHAOZHOU 潮州 ☎0768

Just 39km north of Shantou, Chaozhou may be for all practical purposes a mere satellite of its more businesslike neighbor. But where such matters as charm and character are concerned, Chaozhou proves that more people and more money are not always *more*. What it lacks in gleam and *nouveau riche* glamor, Chaozhou makes up for with crusty alleyways and mind-bending food markets lined with racks of sliced-and-diced poultry and clumps of fresh green tea leaves brought in from the countryside. Businessmen howling pop tunes in karaoke bars are replaced by hollering vendors and early-morning revelers who take full advantage of the somewhat grotty snack stands open until dawn.

Massive urbanization hasn't missed Chaozhou, but visitors and locals both shy away from the sterile, bare, modern thoroughfares for the intimate, motorcycle- and pedicab-crammed streets of old. Stately Chaozhou preserves a distinctive feel, with its ancient city wall and its famed Kaiyuan Temple. However, the best taste of Chaozhou's history comes free of charge in the maze of streets leading to the two sights. They are full of tatami mat and rocking chair specialty stores and Y0.2 sweet bun bakeries tucked under the awnings of crumbling prewar buildings. Chaozhou, with its fabled cuisine, is certainly a city to be savored.

■✱🛈 ORIENTATION AND PRACTICAL INFORMATION

Chaozhou is small enough to be explored at leisure, with the more interesting old city crammed into the eastern portion of the city. The old city walls stretch along the entirety of Chaozhou's eastern border, right along the **Han River** (hán jiāng; 韩江), between **Huancheng Bei Lu** (环城北路) in the north and **Huancheng Nan Lu** (环城南路) in the south (both extend west from the wall). **Kaiyuan Lu** (开元路) also runs west from the wall, about halfway between Huancheng Bei and Nan Lu. **Xima Lu** (西马路) runs just north of and parallel to Kaiyuan Lu. **West Lake** (xī hú; 西湖) and the sprawling **West Lake Park** (西湖公园) are not far west of the northern portion of the wall, bordered to the east by **Huancheng Xi Lu** (环城西路).

Trains: Chaozhou Train Station (cháozhōu huǒchē zhàn; 潮州火车站; ☎685 3708), off Xinfeng Lu 7km southwest of the city. Open daily 8:30am-9:30pm. Train ticket stands throughout the city sell tickets for a Y5 commission. To **Guangzhou** (11hr., 3 per day 8:38am-7:27pm) and **Meizhou** (2hr., 5 per day 6:58am-1:58pm, Y29).

Buses: Chaozhou Long-distance Bus Station (cháozhōu chángtú qìchē zhàn; 潮州长途汽车站; ☎220 6052, ext. 3128), on Chaofeng Lu, southwest of West Lake and 1km west of the city wall. Open daily 6am-11:30pm. To **Guangzhou** (6½hr., 5 per day 8:20am-11:30pm, Y190) and **Shantou** (1hr., every 20min. 6:30am-7:30pm, Y10).

Travel Agency: CITS, 77 Chaofeng Lu (☎228 4177), 2 blocks west of the bus station. The staff always seems to be out to lunch or in a meeting; look to private travel agencies for help. Open M-F 8-11:30am and 2:30-5:30pm.

Hospital: Central Hospital (zhōngxīn yīyuàn; 中心医院), 84 Huancheng Xi Lu (☎222 4092), just north of Xima Lu. Open 24hr.

Postal Code: 521000.

▌ ACCOMMODATIONS

Overnighting in Chaozhou is a good bet; nice rooms go for relatively low prices and foreigner-friendly places are plentiful. Discounts and bargaining are possible year-round at virtually all establishments, except during the May and October national holidays. The long-distance bus station is an easy walk to the old town. Immediately adjacent to the bus station are a few hostels that normally don't accept foreigners, but may be convinced when business is slow.

Chaozhou (Binguan) Hotel (cháozhōu bīnguǎn; 潮州宾馆; ☎226 1168), on Chaofeng Lu, opposite the front entrance of the long-distance bus station. Inviting and well-kept rooms, pagoda-style buildings, and lush tropical grounds keep this place pleasant. 50-60% off-season discounts. Doubles Y328.

Chaozhou (Dajiudian) Hotel (cháozhōu dàjiǔdiàn; 潮州大酒店), 26 Xihe Lu (☎220 2128). This place offers a slew of clean, newly renovated standard rooms. Some members of the helpful staff have been here as long as the hotel. Cheaper rooms on lower floors. Ask about student discounts. Singles and doubles Y120-160; triples Y150-Y220.

Chunguang Hotel (chūnguāng dàjiǔdiàn; 春光大酒店; ☎226 1211), adjacent to the Chaozhou Hotel. Slightly dingier than its neighbors, but the rooms have a view. A/C, TV, and bath. Doubles Y180; triples Y210.

⬛ FOOD

Chaozhou, home of one of China's famed regional flavors, gets creative with its food. The flour-and-vegetable staples of the North have been traded for the tasty tripe and cow-tongue exoticisms of the coast. Chaozhou also offers delicacies such as smoked pigeon and lake-grown vegetables, local specialties gathered from the neighboring mountain area. Two items certainly worth experiencing are the goose with plum sauce and a post-meal tea, served in tiny porcelain tea cups. **Yonghu Lu**, the road leading south from Chaofeng Lu, past the Chaozhou Hotel and adjacent to the long-distance bus station, is full of everything from cheap eateries dishing up wonton soup to trendy Western-style drinkeries. **Chengxin Lu**, running south of and parallel to Chaofeng Lu, comes alive after dusk, with fruit, blackgrass jello, and clothing vendors.

⬛ SIGHTS

The stretch of Kaiyuan Lu near the Kaiyuan Temple features the best shopping in town; electronics stores sit comfortably alongside merchants selling Buddhist silk brocades, banners, bronze Buddhas, wooden and gilded sculptures, and precious jewelry and jade. Stock up on lanterns and dragon costumes for the New Year's festival, and strum a few bandolinos in the music stores lining the street.

KAIYUAN TEMPLE (kāiyuán sì; 开元寺). One of Chaozhou's quiet gems, this spacious temple is almost hidden along the older, narrow section of Kaiyuan Lu. The relaxing, soothing atmosphere is enhanced by the background chanting of the monks at service and worshipers clutching incense sticks as they quietly make their way across the shaded stone courtyard to the halls and pavilions. Visitors come primarily to worship, not to buy postcards and gawk, and the deep mahogany of the intricate wooden latticework is an elegant contrast to the brighter, gaudier color schemes of other Buddhist temples. Not to be missed is the **Guanyin Pavilion** (guānyīn gé; 观音阁), to the left of main courtyard; dedicated to the Buddhist "goddess of mercy," it features 18 different iconographic representations of her. (*32 Kaiyuan Lu, about 5min. west of the city walls. From the long-distance bus station, take Huancheng Xi Lu south from the southern tip of West Lake, and take a left at Kaiyuan Lu, the first major street. Kaiyuan Lu becomes a smaller lane; the temple is on the left about 200m beyond. Open daily 6am-6pm. Y5.*)

CITY WALL. The ancient mortared stone wall that runs along the eastern edge of the city, at the end of Huancheng Bei Lu, Huancheng Nan Lu, and Xima Lu, is not very high but is thick, impressive, and atmospherically run-down, with grass and wildflowers growing out of the top. Visitors can make their way to the little back alley that runs the length of the wall and enjoy a quiet stroll. Equally impressive are the wall's several small gates, through which you can pass to the outside of the city for splendid views of the Han River. **Guangji Gate** (guǎngjí mén; 广济门), reached by following **Shuiping Lu**, the street leading north past Kaiyuan Temple, is surrounded by stone steps leading to the top of the wall. From here, the top of Kaiyuan Temple is visible to the south.

MEIZHOU 梅州   ☎ 0753

A homonym for Meizhou translates into "beautiful county," and it is a fitting tribute to this mountainous city, land of tea plantations and Chinese football, where clambering across overgrown paths and scoring goals are second nature to local children. Accordioned tea fields line the valley in perfectly manicured form against the glow of mild dusks and fertile shades of green. Monks in newly constructed temples high up on hills call these mountains *xian shan*, mountains endowed with the divine. Sacred or no, these mountains are as good as it gets, and their natural beauty provide the livelihood that their inhabitants have come to depend on. Bleating goats, sauntering cows, and a sea of capped straw hats show the labor that goes into the upkeep of this landscape.

Enveloped by a shroud of mountains, the city of Meizhou itself is taking several great leaps forward, rushing to widen streets and build resort areas in the hopes of bringing tourists and the accompanying *yuan* to its still virtually unknown districts. The big bucks of overseas Chinese eager to preserve their roots have ensured the hands-off approach to many of the old city streets, so don't be disheartened at the lack of official sights; tree-lined boulevards, quiet intersections, and busy alleyways where you can taste everything from rice-noodle cakes to fried taro root may prove just as worth exploring as museums and thousand-year-old temples. Locals are willing to explain the intricacies of *kejia cai*, the local cuisine, or to discuss routes to far-off sights. Indeed, a local proverb captures Meizhou's easygoing warmth with the story of a poor family that gave its last egg to a stranger seeking shelter. Rising from its humble origins as Guangdong's poorest region, Meizhou continues to preserve a small town hospitality and relaxed pace of life.

✈ ⓘ ORIENTATION AND PRACTICAL INFORMATION

Meizhou city proper is divided by the **Mei River** (méi jiāng; 梅江), forming the **Jiangnan** (江南) and **Jiangbei** (江北) districts, south and north of the city, respectively. Jiangnan is arranged in grids, with the major commercial avenue of **Jiangnan Lu** (江南路) running perpendicular to **Meijiang Dadao** (梅江大道) and **Binfang Dadao** (彬芳大道), which run from north to south from the train station to the city center. The pedestrian **Mei River Bridge** (méi jiāng qiáo; 梅江桥) runs north off Meijiang Dadao, connecting Jiangnan with the old city district of Jiangbei. **Yuancheng Lu** (元城路) and **Taikang Lu** (泰康路), which run west of **Cultural Park** (wénhuà gōngyuán; 文化公园), form the center of the old city, and the spanking new commercial **Jiangbian Lu** (江边路) branches east towards the development area.

Trains: Meizhou Train Station (méizhōu huǒchē zhàn; 梅州火车站; ☎ 231 1774), on Binfang Dadao at the southernmost edge of the city. Accessible by bus #6 from Jiangnan Lu. Ticket window open daily 8:20am-noon and 2-8pm. To: **Ganzhou** (6-7hr., 11:15am and 5:10pm, Y55-114); **Guangzhou** (11hr., 3:38 and 5pm, Y58-Y190); and **Shenzhen** (13hr., 9:10am and 11:29pm, Y97-Y286).

Buses: Meizhou Main Bus Station (méizhōu qìchē zǒng zhàn; 梅州汽车总站), 1 Meishe Lu, Jiangbei (☎ 222 2137). Accessible by buses #2 and 3. Ticket window open daily 8am-8pm. To: **Dongguan** (8:30am and 7:20pm, Y95); **Guangzhou** (4 per day 8:20am-7:30pm, Y120); and **Shenzhen** (9:10am and 4:30pm, Y120). **Jiangnan Bus Station** (jiāngnán qìchē zhàn; 江南汽车站; ☎ 226 9568), on Binfang Dadao. Accessible by bus #6. To **Dapu** (3hr., every 30min. 6am-6pm, Y20).

Local Transportation: Meizhou's bus service is erratic and infrequent, with service roughly every 30min. on most routes. It's often more convenient to hop on the **pedicabs**

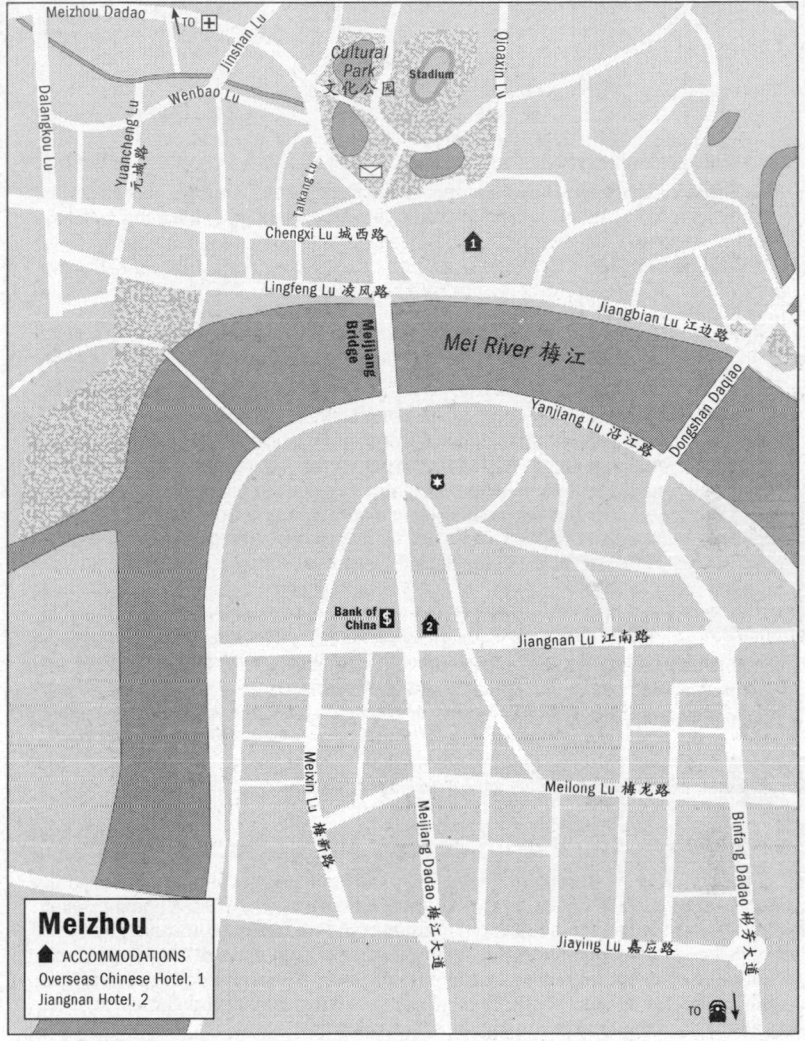

Meizhou

⌂ ACCOMMODATIONS
Overseas Chinese Hotel, 1
Jiangnan Hotel, 2

or **motor-cabs** whizzing around the city (most destinations Y5 or less, to outlying sights Y20 or less). **Taxis** are few and far between, with a base fare of Y10.

Tourist Office: Meizhou Tourism Bureau (méizhōu lǚyóu jú; 梅州旅游局), 28 Binfang Dadao, 5th Fl. (☎224 3687), 3 blocks south of Jiangnan Lu. Guide Mr. Yao is well traveled and eager to share tips. Brochures and maps of far-off sights available. Open M-F 8-11:30am and 2-5:30pm.

Travel Agency: CTS, 105 Jiangnan Lu (☎226 1089; email gdmzets@pub.meizhou.gd.cn; www.meizhou.gd.cn), near Dongshan Daqiao. Arranges full-day tours for Y50. Not much friendly advice available, though. Open M-F 8:30-11:30am and 2:30-5:30pm.

Bank of China: 53 Meijiang Dadao (☎225 0778), north of Jiangnan Lu. Exchanges traveler's checks. Open M-F 8-11:30am and 2:30-5:30pm.

PSB: 1 Fazheng Lu (☎216 9332), the 1st street off Meijiang Dadao, as you backtrack south from the river. The **Division of Exit and Entry** (chūrù jìng guǎnlǐ chù; 出入境管理处) is to the left as you walk in. Open daily 8-11:30am and 2-5:30pm.

Hospital: Meizhou No. 3 People's Hospital (méizhōu shì dì sān rénmín yīyuàn; 梅州市第三人民医院; ☎235 4244; emergency ☎235 5963), at the terminus of Dalangkou Lu. Take bus #6 from the bus station to the last stop.

Internet Access: There is an **Internet bar** (☎236 7333) on Jiangbian Lu, 1 block to the right of the Overseas Chinese Hotel; look for the red 上网 sign. Painfully slow connection. Y2.5 per hr. Open daily 9am-midnight. Also try the old city area, particularly along Ruancheng Lu, where you can surf while sipping wildgrass tea.

Post Office: 5 Gongruan Lu, off Jiangbian Lu, near Cultural Park. EMS and Poste Restante. Open daily 7:30am-7:30pm. **Postal Code:** Jiangnan 514021; Jiangbei 514011.

ACCOMMODATIONS

Meizhou's limited tourism industry means more than just cheap admission tickets and freedom from cacophonous tour groups; for relatively low prices, you can get a room at one of the city's upper crust hotels, which suffer from a depressing lack of business and are usually willing (after some seasoned wheeling and dealing) to let their rooms go for as little as half the list price.

Overseas Chinese Hotel (huá qiáo dàshà; 华侨大厦), 12 Jiangbian Lu (☎223 2388), just east of Meijiang Bridge. This former hostel turned 3-star hotel offers all the trimmings—mahogany furniture, marble baths, and balconies—for rock-bottom prices. The service is impeccable and the ornate, gold-plated lobby might be enough to send shivers down your budget-bed sore back. 10% service charge. 40% discounts often possible. Doubles Y300; suites Y380. Credit cards accepted.

Meizhou Hotel (méizhōu bīnguǎn; 梅州宾馆; ☎223 3530), in a small alley 2 blocks north of Meijiang Bridge near the old city. From the main entrance of Cultural Park, go straight down the street facing the gate across the plaza. Follow this winding road; the hotel is on the right. A CTS-run hotel, the Meizhou offers clean, somewhat weathered rooms with all standard amenities. Doubles Y60; triples Y100; suites Y143.

Jiangnan Hotel (jiāngnán dàshà; 江南大厦), 35 Jiangnan Lu (☎224 8489, ext. 8001), at Meijiang Dadao. Despite the central location and clean-looking standard rooms, some insect residents may have guests itching to leave these tiny rooms for good. 30% discounts available. Singles Y138; doubles Y158; triples Y198.

FOOD

As befitting a city in Guangdong province, Meizhou seems to dish up everything that moves, crawls, slithers, and flies. The dizzying array of stews, sautés, and broths—some boiled for a full day before serving—is believed to provide both a tasty, feel-good meal and essential healing powers. Often, though, with ingredients such as snakeskin and dried scorpions, it might be just as well *not* to know exactly what's swimming in your broth. Even those unwilling to try certain crawling members of the food chain shouldn't go hungry in Meizhou.

The local cuisine is *kejia cai* (客家菜), named for present-day locals whose ancestors moved here from northern China. Because Meizhou hails from a mostly rural tradition, *kejia cai* is saltier and more flavorful than that served by its tamer neighbors, and includes such specialties as roasted pork and mountain-harvested wild vegetables, fresh, melt-in-your-mouth soul food gathered from the surrounding countryside. **Hakka wine** (kèjiā jiǔ; 客家酒), famed for its sweetness, is mixed with ginger to produce the signature Hakka sauce, especially delicious with chicken. Another Hakka chicken dish is the **salt-baked whole chicken**, wrapped in butcher paper (Y25-30; enough for two). You can ask the cooks to chop up the meat into more manageable chunks, passing on the beak and claws if you'd prefer.

Meizhou is brimming with establishments eager to share their age-old recipes with curious visitors. A stroll along **Meijiang Dadao** near Jiangnan Lu after 10pm yields late night "soup kitchens" that specialize in *xiao ye* (夜宵), night snacks of broths brewed from morning. **Yuan Long Dongping**, near Jiangnan Lu, is a popular place to try frogs' legs stew (Y5) or the more classic chicken broth. (☎225 9616.

Open daily 7pm-2am.) Along **Yuancheng Lu** are smaller snack stands that dish up complete meals of blackgrass jello (Y0.5), a sweetened drink, and bowls of rice noodles mixed with soy, pepper, and other spices. The restaurant at **Yearning Tea Plantation** (see p. 493), although definitely more upscale and pricier than ones in the city, is the most authentic place to try traditional *kejia cai*, with ingredients gathered every morning from the mountains and served in a spectacular setting overlooking the tea plantation. (Open daily 8am-10pm.)

And there's always the ◳ **Noodle King Restaurant** (miàndiàn wáng; 面店王.), at the end of Wenhua Lu off Jiangnan Lu, one block east of the Jiangnan Hotel., which boasts authentic food from the Northeast, pink plastic tablecloths, dumpling hawkers, and a friendly, plodding owner. Dumplings of every variety (Y5 for 20), sugar-coated yams (Y6), and delicious vermicelli dishes are worth a taste at this small but constantly full establishment. (☎226 7861. Open daily 8am-9pm.)

▣ SIGHTS

Most of Meizhou's sights, consisting of temples, new resort areas, and whitewater rafting in scenic areas, are outside the city center. The **Thousand Buddha Pagoda** (qiān fó tǎ; 千佛塔), a 15-minute drive northeast from Jiangbian Lu, is a gaudy complex worth seeing only if you've got time to spare. Overseas Chinese have donated mind-boggling amounts to this temple, resulting in a crazed frenzy of building and rebuilding that overshadows the real draw of the place: a Tang-dynasty steel pagoda (engraved with 1000 steel buddhas) that has weathered wars, revolutions, and even a stint in a water-pumping factory. Now sheltered by a bigger stone pagoda, a climb to the top offers good views of Meizhou and the surrounding area. Be thankful you don't adhere to the same schedule as the monks: to bed at 9pm, up at 3am can get awfully tiring after a while. *(Open daily 8am-6pm. Y5.)*

▧ DAYTRIP FROM MEIZHOU: YEARNING TEA PLANTATION

*30km from the city center. No public buses come here and **taxis** cost about Y300 round-trip. Ask at **CTS** or other travel agencies if you can hop on one of their tour buses or join one of the full-day tours (Y100) to the area. Visitors receive tickets to spend in the tea houses and swimming pools in the complex. **Villas** cost as much as Y1098-7000. ☎282 8888; fax 282 6898. **Open** daily 8am-10pm. **Admission** Y30.*

The Yearning Tea Plantation (yànnán fēi chá tián; 雁南飞茶田) resort is a tea-lover's paradise. Lush tea plantations sprawl over panoramic mountains, dotted with the red-tiled roofs of villas ready for guests to splurge on opulent but exorbitantly priced rooms. Rows of budding tea plants spread neatly over hills and valleys, and far-off buildings contain some of the most advanced tea production machinery in China. Well-maintained grounds, winding roads, and animal-like hedges show the care that has gone into every inch of the place, making it ideal for nature lovers craving a little cultural pampering. Mountain spring pools gush by glassed-in tea houses where visitors sip on free cups of freshly harvested tea; the intricacy of the orchestrated tea ceremonies makes this a veritable shrine to tea. Numerous tea houses next to the entry to the **Hill of Amorous Feelings** serve every variety of tea under the sun, and the resort restaurant dishes up wild mountain vegetables (yě cài; 野菜), red mushroom fried rice, and roast pork slices smoked with mountain herbs.

DAPU 大埔

From Meizhou, a grueling and bumpy three-hour minibus ride takes you to the small town of Dapu, about 60km to the east. Hidden by jagged mountains on all four sides and called a "mountain within a mountain" by locals, Dapu has seen very little of the massive-scale industrialization that's hit other towns in the area: many roads are still unpaved, and the town center consists of three or four small streets bustling with vegetable and fruit peddlers. Small enough to be navigated on

TEA E-TEA-QUETTE

According to legend, tea was discovered over 500 years ago when some tea leaves accidentally blew into a pot of boiling water. Upon drinking the result, Emperor Nong Sheng was thrilled with its flavor. People say that on some days, the emperor would eat 72 poisonous plants, then drink some tea and miraculously be cured. It's not surprising that tea is the beverage of choice here in the land of tea plantations, but this drink has evolved to become more of a social custom than a thirst-quencher. Tea etiquette is a sign of social know-how: knowing how to pour tea correctly for guests is as important as the kind of tea served. A faux pas might mean anything from a fallen deal to grumpy visitors.

First, tiny porcelain cups are arranged in a close circle. Fresh tea leaves are sprinkled in the teapot, which is then filled with boiling hot water. Tea is poured into the first cup, which is then used to wash the second up, and so on, until all the cups have been washed with hot tea. Finally, the teapot is refilled, and tea is poured into each cup in succession without breaking the line of water. When you're done sipping your tea, place your cup face down on the serving tray, and you've got it down to a tea.

Some tea lingo:

guanxi shangjiao ("the Buddha steps into the sedan chair"): picking up tea from the box with tea pincers

wulong rugong ("the oolong enters the palace"): putting tea into the pot

wenxiang bei: fragrance-smelling cups

pinming bei: tea-tasting cups

yi pin: first, tasting sip

er pin: second, drinking sip

san huiwei: third, recollection sip

foot in two hours, the town is a great place to get a taste for daily life—workers drinking tea in the town's grassy plaza, and families bringing TVs out onto streets to catch their favorite soaps while taking in the balmy night air. Intimate in scale and quiet in character, Dapu also positions you smack in the center of gorgeous mountain countryside, as wild, bare, and untouched as it was years ago.

ORIENTATION AND PRACTICAL INFORMATION

Transportation to and around Dapu is a huge hassle and may leave you too out-of-breath or frustrated to enjoy the natural scenery or old architecture; be ready for some extra running around. Take some extra cash, as banks are scarce and taxi fares are high. The **Dapu Bus Station** (dàpǔ qìchē kèyùn zhàn; 大埔汽车客运站) is on Hushan Lu in the center of town. (☎552 2486 or 552 2387. Ticket window open daily 8am-4pm.) Buses go to: Chaozhou (4½hr., 7:50am, Y34); Guangzhou (12hr., 3 and 3:30pm, Y90); Meizhou (3hr., every 20min. 7am-4pm, Y20); Shantou (5hr., 8:30am, Y52-62); Shenzhen (10hr., 1:30 and 3pm, Y85); and Zhuhai (14hr., 3 and 3:30pm, Y140). **CTS**, on the first floor of the Overseas Chinese Hotel, offers full-day tours (Y30) of Dapu; these are difficult for solo travelers to arrange. (☎552 2933; fax 552 2520. Open M-F 8-11:30am and 2:30-5:30pm.)

ACCOMMODATIONS AND FOOD

From the bus station, a walk down **Hushan Lu** (虎山路), heading straight to Tiger Mountain Park, leads past low-end hotels catering to overnight bussers. Immediately across from the bus station, on the corner of the street, is the **Dapu Hostel** (dàpǔ lüshè; 大埔旅社), which is mostly dark, damp, and deserted. (☎552 2246. Singles Y15; doubles Y20; rooms with A/C and bath Y45-50.) A walk down Hushan Lu until you hit the faded Wenhua Lu sign leads to the **Overseas Chinese Hotel** (huá qiáo dàshà; 华侨大厦), which has standard rooms and gas-heat showers. (☎552 2933. Doubles Y80.)

There are few formal restaurants in Dapu; the best and cheapest food is from the food stalls lining the side streets near Hushan Lu. **Rat's noodles** (lǎoshǔ miàn; 老鼠面; Y2), a local specialty, taste better than they sound; they actually are just rice noodles shaped like rats' tails.

👁 SIGHTS

As for things to see and do, there's actually not much in Dapu itself unless you're hankering to buy rocking chairs and popsicles; most of the sights are in the outlying area. A place that merits a look-see just for the breathtaking drive there is the **Ten Thousand Buddha Temple** (wàn fó sì; 万佛寺), 40km from Dapu and halfway up **Yingya Mountain** (yīngyǎ shān; 英雅山). The sight itself, a barren relic of a Ming-dynasty temple, is still actively trying to build new worship halls with money from Singapore. The ascent to the temple is half the spiritual experience, with staircase-like tea plantations rising and falling with the curves of the mountain, clusters of stone houses, children leading bulls to pasture, and secret mountain pools that trickle softly below the rocky road. Indeed, the monks at the temple compare sitting on Yingya Mountain to sharing the embrace of the mountain, admiring the unspoiled and fertile landscape and its sense of grandiose wilderness. A hike uphill finally leads to the temple itself, where monks greet you at any time of day and may even provide a steaming dinner. The monks will proudly show you around their expanding complex. Even the din of construction doesn't diminish the grandeur of this place—its beauty is an eyeful.

🚌 DAYTRIP FROM DAPU: DADONG

About 30km from Dapu, Dadong is even smaller and more remote than Dapu. Minibuses travel from Dapu to Dadong (approx. every hr. 7:30am-3pm, Y10).

Dadong (大东) itself is simply a block's worth of small dirt buildings, with tiny villages across the river in the distance. Getting here is a bit of an adventure; if you do end up in the area, Dadong may prove one of the most memorable experiences of your trip. Most anyone who comes here comes to see the famed **mud roundhouses** (tǔ fáng; 土房), which date from the Ming dynasty and are still used. Villages in the town are entirely self-sufficient, with farmers living much as they have been for the past hundred years—winnowing fresh wheat, gathering well water, and sharing sweetened rice and buns with visitors. To see the roundhouses requires a treacherous climb up a mountain from Dadong proper (40min., approx. Y80), as the roads are so rocky and narrow only motorcycles or very skilled taxi drivers can navigate them. The roundhouses, one of the best representations of Kejia culture and one of the world's four famous kinds of peasant dwellings, date back to 1608. One of the largest is 11.9m high and has 210 rooms. Each roundhouse houses about 30 to 40 families who plant and harvest together.

FUJIAN 福建

Running down the southeast coast of the country and staring across the straits at Taiwan, Fujian province has nurtured an intimate relationship with the sea and the lands that lie beyond. Arab and European traders have been docking in the ports of Fujian for centuries, and an overwhelming majority of China's fabled mariners (and many present-day Taiwanese) were also native Fujianese. However, these strong connections to the world outside of China, and particularly to Taiwan, put Fujian in a delicate position. While the province joins the rest of the mainland in expressing displeasure over Taiwanese independence, the flow of funds and friendship across the straits (most evident in the ostentatious riches of the provincial capital, Fuzhou) seems unlikely to slow because of mere politics.

The lush hillsides and craggy peaks of Wuyishan beckon to those exploring the more rugged interior, and the architecture of spectacular port cities like Quanzhou and Xiamen spells out very clearly the intriguing history of cosmopolitan Fujian. These attractions, and the Sha county-style snacks for which the province is famous, deserve (and are increasingly getting) the attention of visitors.

FUZHOU 福州   ☎ 0591

Founded during the Tang Dynasty in 202, Fuzhou was baptized with its present name when a mountain discovered on its outskirts resembled the Chinese character for fortune, *fu*. Fuzhou has certainly lived up to its name.

An eclectic mix of languages, foods, and traditions simmers in a heterogeneous melting pot that nearly spills over Fuzhou's dense and expanding borders. Here you will find *Minnanhua*-speaking locals of Portuguese descent, migrants from the poverty-stricken countryside eager to start anew in a wealthy provincial capital, Shanghainese expats bringing their entrepreneurial ventures into the far South (peddling their *xiaolong bao* and glutinous rice cakes), and cell phone toting businessmen paying their respects at Buddhist temples. The voluntary repatriation of Taiwanese riches to the mother province has only added to the wealth. Struggling to preserve its identity in the face of booming industrialization and commercial success, Fuzhou is filled with striking contrasts, from decaying European colonial architecture and broad high-rise-lined avenues to healing hot springs and small, curving alleys filled with the smells of Sha county-style cooking. All things considered, Fuzhou has certainly lived up to its name. For those seeking the good life, Fuzhou is chock-full of possibility.

▛ TRANSPORTATION

Airplanes: Fuzhou Changle International Airport (fúzhōu chánglè guójì jīchǎng; 福州长乐国际机场; ☎801 2888), south of Fuzhou city. **Shuttle buses** (40min., every 15min. 8am-8pm, Y20) run to and from the **CAAC ticket office,** 185 Wuyi Zhong Lu (☎334 5988 or 331 4957), a bit north of the South Long-distance Passenger Bus Station, on the opposite side of the street. Open daily 8am-8pm. To: **Beijing** (3 per day 11:25am-3pm, Y1240); **Changsha** (11 per day 9:45am-5:45pm, Y560); **Guangzhou** (6 per day 8:05am-6:10pm, Y660); **Hong Kong** (3-4 per day 10:05am-3:30pm, Y1720); **Nanchang** (6pm, Y360); and **Shanghai** (6 per day 8:05am-8:30pm, Y620).

Trains: Fuzhou Train Station (fúzhōu huǒchē zhàn; 福州火车站; ☎759 3294), at the terminus of Hualin Lu as it curves northward, 5min. north of the North Long-distance Passenger Bus Station. To: **Beijing** (23hr., 10pm, Y253-Y705); **Changsha** (22hr., every other day 10:40pm, Y210) via **Guangzhou** (9hr., Y98); **Hangzhou** (9hr., 2:23pm, Y125); **Nanchang** (14hr., 5:58pm, Y81-274); and **Shanghai** (9hr., 1:54pm, Y150-230).

Buses: North Long-distance Bus Station (chángtú qìchē běizhàn; 长途汽车北站; ☎758 0118), on Hualin Lu at Beihuan Lu, 5min. south of the train station. Open daily 5:30am-10:30pm. To **Guangzhou** (12hr., 4 per day 5:10am-7:40pm, Y210-260) and **Shanghai** (25hr., 10:20am, Y247) via **Hangzhou** (22hr., Y215). **South Long-distance Passenger Bus Station** (chángtú qìchē nán kèyùn zhàn; 长途汽车南客运站; ☎332 2874), on Wuyi Zhong Lu at Guohuo Xi Lu in the southern part of the city, a few minutes south of the CAAC ticket office. Bus #51 runs to the train station and North Bus Station, and #8 runs to May First Square. Open daily 6am-9pm. To **Guangzhou** (15-16hr., 6 per day, Y259-287) and **Hong Kong** (16hr., 2 per day, Y312-332).

Local Transportation: Fuzhou's **bus** system stretches from the train station in the north to the neighborhoods south of the Min River, as well as to districts east and west of the city proper and to Drum Mountain. Most routes run 5am-10 or 11pm. Fare Y1, with A/C Y2. Bus #1 runs down Bayiqi Lu and along the north bank of the Min River, and then crosses over to the south bank; #5 goes from the train station down Wusi Lu to Dong Jie; #8 heads up Wuyi Lu to the area around West Lake and Zhuhai Park; #20 and 821 continue down Bayiqi Lu from the train station; #51 runs the length of the city from Wusi Lu to the end of Wuyi Lu. A special "**ya-si-ya**" (亚细亚) bus plies a useful route north from Guangda Lu, passing Yushan Park, going north on Bayiqi Bei Lu to Dongjiekou, and terminating at the train station (Y2).

Taxis: Base fare Y7-8, each additional km Y1.4-1.8. **Pedicabs** are plentiful; fares should be settled in advance. From the train station to city center about Y7.

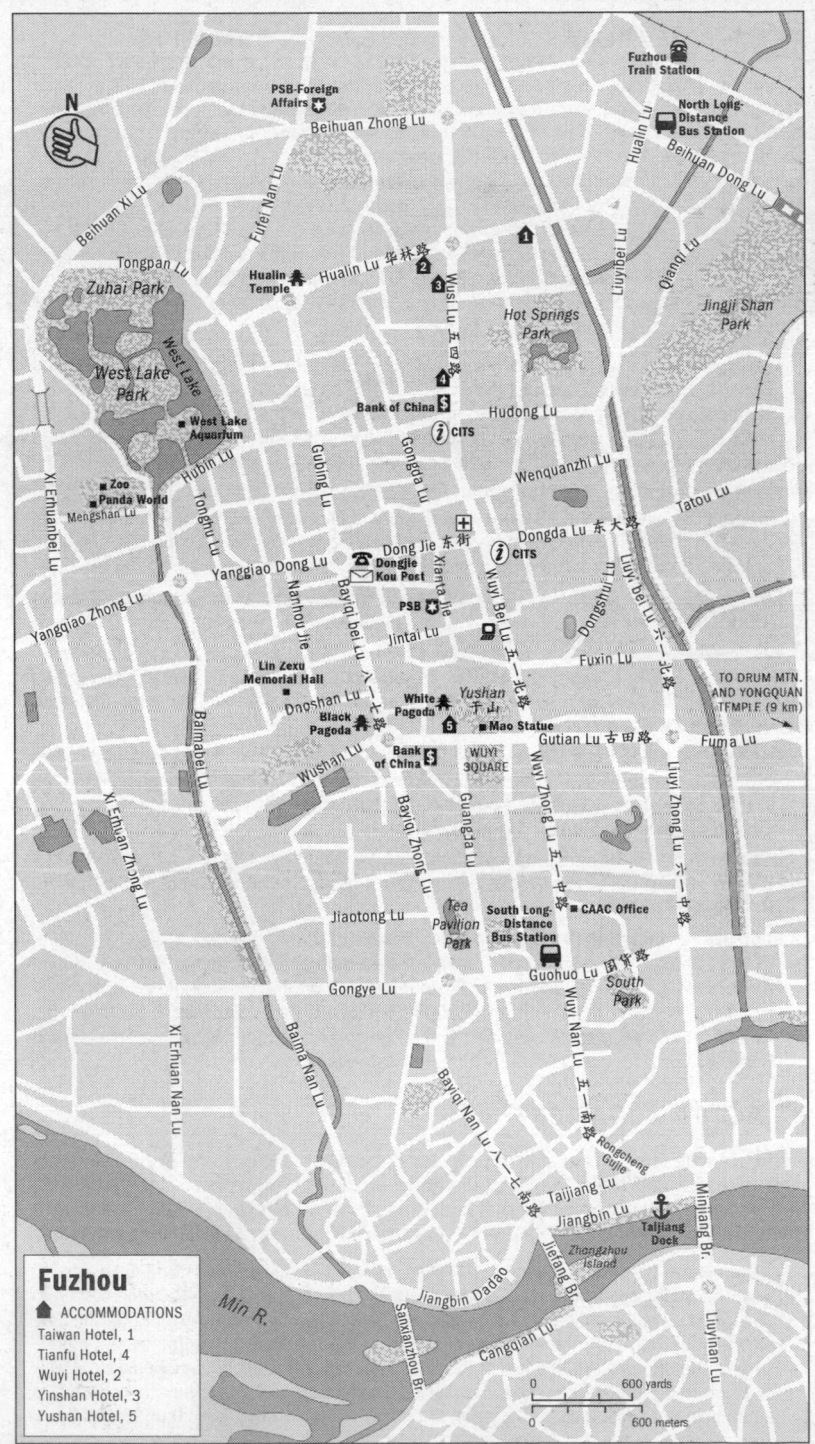

N

PSB-Foreign Affairs ✚

Fuzhou Train Station

North Long-Distance Bus Station

Beihuan Zhong Lu

Beihuan Xi Lu

Fufei Nan Lu

Beihuan Dong Lu

Hualin Lu

Liuyibei Lu

Qianqi Lu

Tongpan Lu

Zuhai Park

Hualin Temple 寺

Hualin Lu 华林路

Wusi Lu 五四路

1

2

3

Jingji Shan Park

West Lake

Hot Springs Park

West Lake Park

West Lake Aquarium

4

Bank of China $

Hudong Lu

Hubin Lu

Xi Erhuanbei Lu

Tonghu Lu

Gubing Lu

Gongda Lu

ℹ CITS

Wenquanzhi Lu

Tatou Lu

Zoo ■ Panda World

Mengshan Lu

Yangqiao Dong Lu

Nanhou Jie

Bayiqi bei Lu

Dong Jie 东街

☎ Dongjie Kou Post

✉

PSB ✚

Xianta Jie

✚

Dong Jie 东街

ℹ CITS

Dongda Lu 东大路

Wuyi Bei Lu 五一北路

Dongshu Lu

Liuyi bei Lu 六一北路

TO DRUM MTN. AND YONGQUAN TEMPLE (9 km)

Yangqiao Zhong Lu

Jintai Lu

Fuxin Lu

Lin Zexu Memorial Hall ■

Baimabei Lu

Daoshan Lu

Black Pagoda 寺

White Pagoda 寺

5

Yushan 于山

■ Mao Statue

Gutian Lu 古田路

Fuma Lu

Wushan Lu

Bank of China $

Bayiqi Zhong Lu

Guangda Lu

WUYI SQUARE

Wuyi Zhong Lu 五一中路

Liuyi Zhong Lu 六一中路

Xi Erhuan Zhong Lu

Jiaotong Lu

Tea Pavilion Park

South Long-Distance Bus Station

■ CAAC Office

Gongye Lu

Guohuo Lu 国货路

South Park

Xi Erhuan Nan Lu

Baima Nan Lu

Bayiqi Nan Lu 八一七南路

Wuyi Nan Lu 五一南路

Taijiang Lu

Rongcheng Gujie

Jiangbin Lu

Taijiang Dock ⚓

Minjiang Br.

Liuyinan Lu

Min R.

Jiangbin Dadao

Sanzanzhou Br.

Jiefang Br.

Zhongzhou Island

Cangqian Lu

Fuzhou

🏠 ACCOMMODATIONS

Taiwan Hotel, 1
Tianfu Hotel, 4
Wuyi Hotel, 2
Yinshan Hotel, 3
Yushan Hotel, 5

0 ————— 600 yards
0 ————— 600 meters

▃▮ ORIENTATION AND PRACTICAL INFORMATION

Fuzhou is a vast city, spanning from the train station in the northeast to the lower bank of the **Min River** (mǐn jiāng; 闽江) to the south. **Wusi Lu** (五四路) runs from north to south to the Min River. Two other major streets running from north to south are **Bayiqi Lu** (八一七路) to the west and **Liuyi Lu** (六一路) to the east. Running from east to west, **Hualin Lu** (华林路) curves northward to the train station and North Bus Station; **Dong Jie** (东街), between Bayiqi Lu and Wusi Lu, becomes **Dongda Lu** (东大路) east of Wusi Lu; and **Gutian Lu** (古田路) roughly marks the heart of the city, sandwiched between **May First Square** (wǔ yī guǎngchǎng; 五一广场) to the south and **Yushan Scenic Area** and a huge **statue of Mao Zedong** to the north. The South Long-distance Passenger Bus Station is at the intersection of Wuyi Zhong Lu and **Guohuo Xi Lu** (国货西路).

Travel Agencies: There are 2 **CITS** offices near the intersection of Wusi/Wuyi Lu and Dong Jie/Dongda Lu. **Tianma CITS** (☎337 0073), on the 7th floor of the large high-rise at the corner of Wuyi Bei Lu and Dongda Lu. English and Japanese interpreters available. 1-day tours of Fuzhou Y70. Ticket commission Y50. Open daily 9:30am-noon and 3-5:30pm. Numerous plane and train ticket booking offices line Wuyi Lu and Wusi Lu.

Bank of China: On Gutian Lu between Bayiqi Lu and Guangda Lu, west of KFC. Exchanges traveler's checks (counter #6). Open daily 8am-6pm. Another branch at 136 Wusi Lu exchanges currency and issues credit card advances. ATMs. Open M-F 7:40am-5:30pm, Sa 8:30-5pm. Avoid the money changers loitering on Wusi Lu.

PSB: 1 Jingmen Lu (☎755 7705), off Jintai Lu. For visa extensions, contact the **Foreign Affairs Department** (wài guǎn kē; 外管科), 109 Beihuan Zhong Lu (☎782 1000), west of Wusi Bei Lu. Open M-F 8am-noon and 3-6pm.

Hospitals: Fujian Provincial Hospital (fújiàn shěng lì yīyuàn; 福建省立医院; ☎755 7768), on the northwest corner of the intersection of Dong Jie and Wusi Lu. The emergency entrance is off Dong Jie.

Bookstores: Antai Book City (āntài shūchéng; 安泰书城, ☎755 2619), at the corner of Jintai Lu and Bayiqi Lu. A bustling book market that's home to VCD vendors and map stores, as well as a **Foreign Language Bookstore** with a not-too-shabby map and English classics department. Open daily 8am-9pm.

Internet Access: Hongru Internet Club, Hongru Bldg., 96 Jingtai Lu, 2nd Fl. (☎337 3117), at Wuyi Bei Lu. Super-fast connections. Passport or other ID required. Y4 per hr. Open daily 8am-11pm.

Post Office: Dongjiekou Post and Telecommunications (dōngjiēkǒu yóudiàn dàlóu; 东街口邮电大楼; ☎755 6580), a high-rise at the southeast corner of Dong Jie and Bayiqi Bei Lu, opposite Juchunyuan Restaurant. EMS on the 1st floor; Poste Restante at counter #4. Open daily 7:30am-7:30pm. **DHL Worldwide Express,** 203 Hualin Lu (☎781 1111), off a small alley next to the Taiwan Hotel. Open M-Sa 8am-6pm. **Postal Code:** 350000 for city center, 350001 for Poste Restante.

▞ ACCOMMODATIONS

Filthy-rich Fuzhou offers few options for dirt-poor backpackers. Establishments near the train and bus stations to the north of the city may prove to be your best budget option, but don't rule out high-end places altogether, which sometimes lower their prices during the summer season to entice amenities-seeking travelers.

Yushan Hotel (yúshān bīnguǎn; 于山宾馆), 10 Yushan Lu (☎335 1668). Take bus #8 from the South Bus Station to Yushan on Gutian Lu or bus #51 from the train station to Wuyi Bei Lu (keep walking and then take the first right onto Gutian Lu). Facing the Mao statue on Gutian Lu, take the stairs that run up the left side; the entrance is across a small street. Rooms exude a feel of the old Orient, with low to the ground beds and a view of the inner garden. Cheaper rooms have dim lighting and aging furniture. Standard amenities. Breakfast included. Singles Y120-150; doubles Y180-370; triples Y250-370.

Taiwan Hotel (táiwān fàndiàn; 台湾饭店), 197 Hualin Lu (☎781 8666), at Shutang Lu. Take bus #20 from the train or North Bus Station to Shutang Lu. This 3-star breakaway Nationalist hotel offers spacious rooms and standard amenities. Currency exchange. Summer deals and off-season discounts make this one of the best deals in town. 10% service charge. Doubles Y310-385.

Wuyi Hotel (wǔyí dàjiǔdiàn; 武夷大酒店), 169 Hualin Lu (☎784 3038), just past Wusi Lu. Accessible by bus #20 from the station area to Pingdong, or #51 from all stations to Hualin Lu. Gorgeous, newly renovated rooms with silk coverlets and wooden furniture (9th floor and up) make the hassle worthwhile. Cheaper, older rooms are none too shabby, but staff usually puts foreigners in newer rooms only; negotiate. 30% summer discounts. Singles Y300-338; doubles Y198-338.

South Pacific Hotel (nán yáng fàndiàn; 南洋饭店), 346 Hualin Lu (☎757 9699), near Liuyi Bei Lu, a 5-10min. walk south from the North Bus Station. Clean if slightly worn facilities in unpretentious surroundings. Breakfast included. Currency exchange. Singles Y228; doubles Y168-248; triples Y258.

Yinshan Hotel (yínshān dàjiǔdiàn; 银山大酒店), 254 Wusi Lu (☎781 8688, ext. 2106), at Hualin Lu. Accessible via bus #51 going in either direction along Wusi Lu; get off at the Hualin Lu stop. Facilities are slightly shoddier than most, but this is one of the cheapest options available, even if beds are lumpy, some rooms are cramped, and the croon of pop tunes continues late into the night. Rooms have all standard amenities. Breakfast included. Reservations recommended. Doubles Y100-178.

Tianfu Hotel (tiānfú dàjiǔdiàn; 天福大酒店), 138 Wusi Lu (☎781 2328), just north of the main branch of the Bank of China. Take bus #51 from the train or either bus stations to Huaqiao Dasha. Walk north on Wusi Lu, across Hudong Lu; the hotel is on the left. Up to 30% discounts during the summer make this glammed-up place affordable, but beware: weathered rooms, stained walls, sheets, and carpets abound. Currency exchange. Singles Y240-259; doubles Y325-390.

FOOD

In addition to the street vendors near the South Bus Station and the train station, Fuzhou has a number of popular restaurants that have morphed into chains, with branches throughout the city.

You needn't look too hard to find a glossy **McDonald's, KFC,** or **Pizza Hut.** Those in need of more cultural diversity in their grease should look out for **Dico's** (dékèshì chǎojī; 德克士炒鸡), a Chinese fried chicken chain with branches on the southeast corner of Hualin Lu and Wusi Lu, opposite the McDonald's, and on the corner of Gutian Lu and Wuyi Lu, east of the Mao statue. Fruit juice parlors, tea houses, and coffee shops are popular among the youth of Fuzhou, who can now establish themselves as both health-conscious *and* chic; any doubts about the city's upscale credentials should fade instantly upon entrance into any of these refreshment stations (although relatively few young people can actually afford them).

Sha County Snacks (shā xiàn xiǎochī; 沙县小吃), in a little alley near the South Bus Station. From the station, walk east on Guohuo Xi Lu and turn left at the first alley; the eatery is on the left. The holy grail of budget travel, Sha County is ideal for the thrifty and hearty. This amazing little kitchen has only a partially written menu serving specialty dishes from Sha county in Fujian province—ask for the mixed noodles (bàn miàn; 拌面), and you shall receive a plate of thin noodles with an intriguing mixture of peanut, sesame, soy, and other sauces that you personally mix to taste, along with a bowl of wonton soup broth (Y1). Other meatball soups and noodle dishes Y1-3. The *baozi* and vegetable dishes are also a must-try, and at Y2, they'll be sure to fill you up without wearing you (or your wallet) down. Open daily until around midnight-2am.

Shanghai Restaurant (shànghǎi xī cāntīng; 上海西餐厅), 155 Bayiqi Lu (☎755 3620), on Taijiang Lu near Wuyi Nan Lu. Other branches on Yushan Lu, and on the western edge of the scenic area. Eclectic, efficient, and everywhere, the Shanghai chain stands poised to take over the world. Dim sum Y2-5 each, noodle dishes Y5-10, and full-fledged dinners Y10-15. A Western-style menu dishes up somewhat dubious set meals of fried chicken and pork chops (Y10-12). The Bayiqi Lu branch has Chinese and Western bakeries as well. Open daily 11am-1:30pm and 5:30-9:30pm.

Juchunyuan Restaurant (jùchūnyuán cāntīng; 聚春园餐厅), Juchunyuan Hotel, 2 Dongjiekou, 2nd Fl., across the street from the post office. This hundred-year-old establishment has garnered well-earned fame from its **Buddha Jumping over the Wall** (see **Buddha Business,** p. 501), a pricey seafood concoction (Y200 per person) served in a traditional banquet-style setting. Its other dishes have less breath-stopping prices but are just as delectable. Open daily 5-8:30pm.

Farmer's Family Restaurant (nóngjiā fànzhuāng; 农家饭庄), 7 Wenquan Zhi Lu (☎756 4612). Take bus #51 to Wusi Lu, walk north, and take the 1st right; the restaurant is on the right after crossing the street. A second branch is at 77 Baima Bei Lu, south of Yangqiao Dong Lu. Rusticity is all the rage: "peasant" décor includes wooden tables and chairs, red paper lanterns, and waitresses in green smocks and simple dress. Flavorful dainties such as xiaolong bao (Y3 per serving) or glutinous sweet cakes stuffed with sesame seed and other delectables (nián gāo; 年糕; Y1) are delicious. The "authentic" experience involves heartier entrees, like "Peasants' Braised Beef" (nóngjiā hóngshāoròu; 农家红烧肉; Y12). Open daily 10am-1:30pm and 5pm-3am.

TEA AND JUICE HOUSES

Zhengzai Fresh-Squeezed Juice Hut (zhèng zài zhàzhī wū; 正在榨汁屋), 172 Bayiqi Bei Lu, just north of a Bank of China and 10min. south of Dongjiekou Department Store. Customers should find satiation at minimum expense (Y3-8) at this tiny place. Large cups of fresh-squeezed, every-fruit-imaginable juice and a friendly mother-son team make this a cozy spot to get your mango-banana twist. Open daily 8:30am-11:30pm.

Luck Tea House (lèkè pàomò hóngchá diàn; 乐客泡沫红茶店; ☎753 0850), in the Jiangxing Department Store, on Yangqiao Dong Lu a block west of the corner of Bayiqi Bei Lu and Dong Jie. This tea house specializes in Taiwanese-style "foaming ice tea" (pàomò hóngchá; 泡沫红茶). A proud brainchild is the foaming milk pearl tea (zhēnzhū nái chá; 珍珠奶茶; Y14) made with tapioca pearls; the "foaming" effect is created by vigorously shaking the tea in a special canister. Lunch and dinner items also available. Open daily 9:30am-midnight; delivery 9:30am-8pm.

Lan Fang Coffee and Tea House (kāfēi hóngchá fáng; 咖啡红茶房), 56 Shengfu Lu (☎751 9733), just off the 1st lane north from Yangqiao Lu, west of Bayiqi Bei Lu. An avant-garde atmosphere for the cool, young, hip, and caffeine-addicted: espresso and tea (Y15-20), trippy sunflower decorations, and a magazine corner. Open daily 10am-2am; food service until 11pm.

SIGHTS

With the exception of **Drum Mountain** to the east of the city, the sights in Fuzhou are pleasant but not significant. A much more worthwhile activity is to stroll through Fuzhou's various neighborhoods, particularly the ones bordering the city center. West of Dongjiekou off Yangqiao Dong Lu, beginning with Nanhou Jie, is the neighborhood of **"three lanes and seven alleys,"** a well-preserved cross section of old Fuzhou, with street stalls, festival lanterns, and *mahjong* groups. Among this maze of streets lie **Pagoda Alley** (tǎ jiē; 塔街) and **Literary Scholar Lane** (wénrū lù; 文儒路), both of which date back to the Ming and Qing Dynasties.

DRUM MOUNTAIN

*9km (about 20-30min.) east of Fuzhou. Several public **buses** run regularly to the foot of the mountain: #7, 36, or 37 from the Chating stop on Guangda Lu, west of the South Bus Station, next to the Children's Park; #49 from the train station; and #60 from West Lake. The mountain is at the terminus for all but routes #36 and 37: in those cases, get off at the Xiayuan stop (30-40min, Y1.5). **Taxis** go from the base up the mountain (Y5). Minibuses from downtown Fuzhou (Nan Men stop, off Gutian Lu one block east of Yushan, to your* *left) also offer direct services to the summit (20-30min.; one-way Y5, round-trip Y8).* **Cable car** *rides (daily 8am-4:45pm) one-way Y25, children Y10; round-trip Y30, children Y15.* **Admission** *Y6, payable near the summit.*

Drum Mountain (gǔ shān; 鼓山) is Fuzhou's finest. Rising 900m above sea level, the summit offers unbeatable panoramas of the city and the outlying maze of rivers and mountains. The climb along the sloped stone steps will definitely put you in the best company, with elderly couples who make the ascent slowly but surely, and energetic powder kegs of children who barely break a sweat charging up the mountain. The 1800m climb takes about an hour, with markers every 200m, and will get your heart pumping loudly enough to make up for the silence of the drum.

The largest temple, **Spring Gushing Temple** (yǒng quán sì; 涌泉寺), houses a Guanyin statue, goldfish pond, shops selling wooden artwork and wax-paper umbrellas, a vegetarian restaurant, and an impressively restored main hall containing three big Buddhas. *(Open daily 6am-5:30pm. Y6.)* Bear right through some hallways once you enter the complex to reach a small side hall exhibiting Buddhist *sutras* from the Ming and Qing dynasties, some written in Tibetan, Burmese, and Cambodian scripts. Others are written in plain old Chinese—but with blood. The large copper pot in **Heavenly King Hall** (tiān wáng dian; 天王殿) to the right of the main hall is said to have cooked food for a thousand people. The remainder of the mountain area makes for a pleasant ramble, with the possibility of happening upon a fresh spring or an unoccupied pavilion, but all in all it's not that impressive.

OTHER SIGHTS

FORMER FOREIGN CONCESSION. Although very few visitors to Fuzhou have any practical reason to venture south of the South Bus Station, the banks of the Min River, and the neighborhood to the south, offer tangible glimpses of Fuzhou's past. A walk across one of the three main bridges that span the Min River—from west to east, the wire-suspension **Sanxianzhou Bridge** (三县洲桥), the short, cute, and light-bedecked **Jiefang Bridge** (解放桥), and the heavily trafficked **Minjiang Bridge** (闽江大桥)—will reveal barges and larger junks traveling through the swirling waters below, as well as a panoramic view of the southern reaches of the city, which used to house the foreign concession. Among the houses built into the hills, a few church spires and clock towers are visible, as are the ramparted roofs, arched windows, and brick exteriors of some colonial buildings that still stand in the cobblestoned streets of this neighborhood. Several of the churches still in use today are marked with red crosses—the one on **Zhongzhou Island** (zhōngzhōu dǎo; 中洲岛) can be reached via the stairs descending from Jiefang Bridge. Retired old men gather around on the city sidewalks, masses of bikes block walkways, and random decrepit buildings neighbor newly built ones, mirroring Fuzhou's eclectic mixture of foods, dialects, and accents. *(The terminus of bus #51 is on Taijiang Lu, just a block away from the north bank of the river; the Jiefang and Minjiang Bridges are nearby. Bus #1 from Bayiqi Lu crosses the Minjiang Bridge to the south side of the city; bus #20 does the same across the Jiefang Bridge.)*

BUDDHA BUSINESS The ultra-famous "Buddha Jumping Over the Wall" is a steamed-then-aged-then-stewed-then-served-in-a-ceramic-pot dish that contains over 20 types of seafood, including shark fin, fish maw, sea cucumber, abalone, and scallops. Ingredients are selected for taste and shape, making the final steaming pot more an artistic creation than a seafood broil. First created by an aristocrat's chef, Zheng Chunfa, the dish had such success that Zheng shed his chef's hat for entrepreneurship, opening the Juchunyuan Restaurant in the 1860s. One day, he decided to invite a group of scholars to sample the dish. When he took off the lid, the room was filled with the dish's intoxicating scent, drawing forth floods of praise and impromptu poems. One verse read, "The flavorful scents are flowing around the neighborhood. Buddha smelled the food and abandoned his temple and jumped over the wall." The excitable name stuck.

YUSHAN SCENIC AREA (yúshān fēngjǐng qū; 于山风景区). Following the gently sloping curved path up the hill takes you past old buildings with stone archways and groups of elderly folk playing cards and *mahjong* to a rather insignificant **Fuzhou Municipal Museum** detailing the city's 700-year history. *(Open daily 8am-5pm. Y3.)* The **flower nursery** nearby houses hundreds of varieties of orchids (Y3). The **White Pagoda** (bái tǎ; 白塔) marks the western edge, and affords a bird's-eye view of the city. *(Open daily 8:30am-5:30pm. Y2.)* Yushan has some historical significance of its own; at the summit are the crumbling remains of the old city walls. *(There are 2 entrances to the scenic area: one from a path to the left of and behind the Mao statue as you face it, the other off Wuyi Bei Lu just north of its intersection with Gutian Lu. Free.)*

WEST LAKE PARK (xī hú gōngyuán; 西湖公园). Hangzhou's West Lake it's not, but the park makes for a pleasant outing. The park consists of a few islands in the middle of the manmade West Lake and offers such delicate delights as garden paths, paddle boats (Y20 per hr., 4 people max.), and a sprinkling of amusement park rides (typically Y5 per ride). The only other possible point of interest, besides a park fountain shaped as a mountain being attacked by dozens of clambering monkeys (illustrating a scene from *Journey to the West*), is the **West Lake Aquarium** (xī hú hǎiyáng shìjiè; 西湖海洋世界), which features a small selection of tropical fish. *(Main entrance is on Hubin Lu, where it meets Tonghu Lu, near the southern end of the lake. Take bus #1 from Bayiqi Lu or #60 from Dongda Lu to Hubin and walk forward; the park entrance is to the right. Y4. Aquarium open daily 8:30am-10pm. Y25, children under 1.2m Y15.)*

WUYISHAN 武夷山 ☎ 0599

Mammoth nature at its best—winding rivers, looming cliffs, and sprawling mountains tower over the tiny resort town of Wuyishan, in the northwest corner of Fujian province. Hailed as the most beautiful mountain in southeastern China, Wuyishan's craggy peaks and secluded waterfalls appeal to thrill seekers and dreamy nature-lovers alike. Locals like to tell stories of the mountain's legendary beginnings, when an immortal, Peng Zhu, descended from heaven and ordered two of his sons, Peng Wu and Peng Yi, to stop a flood. As the water receded, the lush fields and rocks that appeared grew famous for their unique beauty, and so Wuyishan emerged triumphant from its deserted, anonymous, and soggy roots.

Anonymous no longer, Wuyishan is slowly lumbering its way up China's mountain hierarchy; it was recently designated 22nd in a list of national must-see scenic spots. Wuyishan's long untouristed trails are beginning to be infiltrated with marching processions of tour groups, eager to savor the region's famed Big Red Robe tea or to float down the Nine-Bend River in a bamboo raft. A dream come true for sentimentalists itching to live life as it was, get here *now* before you have to wait in line to hike up King's Peak, and muse over life as it must have been. Visitors can take part in a favorite local pastime, joining in the imaginative effort to christen individual peaks with enamored epithets. While you're floating down rivers so clear you can count the rocks at the bottom, sipping tea brewed with mountain spring water, craning to see ancient boat coffins in the nooks of massive cliffs, and trying to decipher the monkey's face in a series of rocky towers, you might just have to agree that wonderlands really do exist.

◼ ⁊ ORIENTATION AND PRACTICAL INFORMATION

Most visitors bypass Wuyishan proper for the resort town bordering the scenic area, 30-40 minutes south of the city. Just three roads run through the resort town. Sights border **Chongyang Stream** (chóngyáng xī; 崇阳溪), the sometimes-creek, sometimes-rapids river that winds its way through the Wuyishan mountain range. The resort town lies to the east of the river, spanning a small stretch divided into a hotel and market area by the **Huang Hua** intersection. Crossing **Lantang Bridge** (lántāng dàqiáo; 兰汤大桥) to the west of the river leads to the scenic area, which divides into the **Nine-Bend Stream** south of the bridge, and **Water Curtain Park** and **Big Red Robe** tea plantation north of it. **Wuyishan Scenic Area** spans a whopping 60km. **Shanguxin Jie** (山姑新街) is the main road in the resort town.

Airplanes: Wuyishan People's Airport (wǔyíshān mínyòng hángkōng zhàn; 武夷山
民用航空站; ☎530 6513), on Wuyi Dadao north of the resort town, accessible by
miandi (15min., Y2) from the city center. To: **Beijing** (Su-Tu and Th, Y1080); **Fuzhou**
(Tu-Th and Sa, Y380); **Guangzhou** (M-Sa, Y690); and **Shanghai** (Su-Tu and Th-F, Y530).

Trains: Wuyishan Train Station (wǔyíshān huǒchē zhàn; 武夷山火车站; ☎510 2688),
on the outskirts of Wuyishan city. From the resort area, take bus #2 (Y1.5) or share a
miandi (Y3). Open daily 8-11:30am and 2-5pm. To: **Fuzhou** (6hr., 10:45am, Y46);
Quanzhou (15hr., every other day 4:36am, Y81); and **Xiamen** (15hr., 3:10am, Y81).

Buses: Wuyishan Bus Station (wǔyíshān qìchē zhàn; 武夷山汽车站; ☎531 1446), in
Wuyishan city, accessible by bus #2 from the resort town. Open daily 5:30am-6:50pm.
To: **Fuzhou** (11hr., 6 and 6:50pm, Y87); **Hangzhou** (15hr., 12:30pm, Y110); and **Xia-
men** (20hr., 2:30pm, Y145).

Local Transportation: Only 2 **bus** routes service the Wuyishan area. Bus **#2** shuttles
between the train and bus stations and the resort area, and **#6** runs between the resort
area and the city center. Neither runs regularly within the scenic area.

Taxis: Cheery yellow *miandi* taxis replace the old red taxis of most urban areas. From the
resort town to Wuyishan city center Y3, resort town to Wuyishan Scenic Area Y1-2.
Within Wuyishan Scenic Area, **scootered pedicabs** take tourists from sight to sight (Y6-
7 each trip, Y60-70 per day); some drivers may also informally serve as tour guides.

Travel Agencies: CTS (☎525 1888), on Nanwu Lu, on the foot of the sloped path leading up to the Wuyishan Mountain Villa. From the Scenic Area side of Lantang Bridge,
take a left on the tree-lined path; walk straight for 5min., and turn right at the 2nd path
toward the guard station. Although unaccustomed to individual travelers, CTS generously hands out nifty bilingual brochures and maps and arranges tours (Y100 per person) and interpreters. Open daily 8am-5:30pm.

Bank of China: 2 Wujiu Zhong Lu (☎530 6617). Exchanges traveler's checks. ATMs
available. Open daily 7:40am-6pm. Most large hotels (like the Wuyishan Mountain
Villa) exchange currency for a small fee.

PSB: In the Wuyi Palace area of the resort town (☎525 2483).

Hospitals: No hospital exists as of yet in the resort town; the closest one is in the city
center. **Wuyishan Hospital** (wǔyíshān yīyuàn; 武夷山医院), 65 Wengong Lu (☎530
2782; emergency ☎531 0463). Open 24hr.

Bookstore: Wenyou Bookstore (wényóu shūdiàn; 文友书店; ☎525 2002), in the San-
guxin Jie market area, off the 3rd alley to the left. Bilingual maps and brochures. Open
daily 8am-6pm.

Post Office: Wuyishan Resort Town Post Office (☎525 2875), off Shanguxing Jie,
marked by a large arched gate to the west of the Huang Hua intersection. The office is
2 blocks down this road, in an alley on the left. EMS and Poste Restante. Open daily
8am-6pm. **Postal Code:** 354302.

ACCOMMODATIONS

Wuyishan's resort town is full of nearly identical two- and three-star hotels. The
area near the Huang Hua intersection is closest to the market area. Most of the
budget options are directly across Lantang Bridge from the main resort town. Proprietors of these mostly family-owned inns, however, often tend to be unwilling to
bend the rules for foreign travelers—although overseas Chinese are in luck. Prices
are rock-bottom (beginning at Y10); when all else fails, beg.

Wuyi Mountain Villa (wǔyí shān zhuāng; 武夷山庄; ☎525 1888), at the end of the
sloping path off Nanwu Lu. From Lantang Bridge, turn left and walk straight along
Nanwu Lu, the tree-lined path bordering the western bank of the Chongyang River; the
hotel is on the 2nd path to the right, past CTS. Bus #6 stops in front of the villa. Villa's
the magic word at this luxurious mountain hideaway. The combination of award-winning
architecture, landscaped gardens, idyllic views, and equally stunning rooms means that
this place has seen its share of visiting royalty and CCP premiers. Join the ranks budget-

style; the Y100 economy doubles have everything but the view. Currency exchange. Doubles Y480, off-season Y240.

Aihu Hotel (ăihú bīnguăn; 矮胡宾馆; ☎525 2268), directly across Lantang Bridge in the Scenic Area, at the top of a small set of stairs visible from the bridge. The oldest hotel in Wuyishan, the Aihu's aged wooden furniture and intimate courtyards create a personal atmosphere that makes this the best budget has to offer. Clean, comfortable rooms have A/C, TV, and bath. Dorms Y40; singles Y80; doubles Y100.

Yulin Hotel (yùlín jiŭdiàn; 郁林酒店; ☎525 2206), west of the Huang Hua intersection, on the left side of the road leading to Lantang Bridge. A small driveway winds around the entrance. The Yulin is newly built and offers rooms with TV and bath; it draws in guests with its impeccable location across the street from the main market and restaurant area. The cheapest doubles are in a separate building across the bridge. Doubles Y20, with A/C Y90; triples Y110.

FOOD

Visitors don't come to Wuyishan for the food, but you can eat your fill at the lively street markets that line the resort area. Wuyishan's culinary claim to fame is its **Snake Banquet**—not yellow eel or other snake-like creatures—but the real, slithering thing, which come a dime a dozen in Wuyishan's forests and mountains. Those adventurous enough to sample this delicacy should do so in large hotel restaurants rather than in small street shops. It's fun going down the food street for the first time, when it seems that every other person wants you to go into the kitchen and try some fabulous dish; however, when you start noticing the half-dead animals and coiled snakes sitting in molding cages outside and in formaldehyde inside, it can be quite jarring. Most cheap options are on **Yinshe Yitiao Jie** (银蛇一条街), directly opposite the gate leading to **Shanguxin Jie.** It is liveliest from sunset to 2am, and features small restaurants offering generous portions of basic dishes like tofu (Y6), noodle soups (Y10), and *baozi* (Y3).

◉ SIGHTS

Immortals are said to live in the mountains
A clear winding stream runs at the foot.
  —Local Ballad

Wuyishan isn't a scenic spot for nothing, and virtually everywhere you turn can qualify as a sight. Listed below are not-to-be-missed main attractions, but Wuyishan itself is a piece of paradise for hikers, who can discover rock scaling opportunities and off-the-beaten path trails. In particular, the narrow mountain passes and steps leading to the summit of King's Peak and Heavenly Tour Peak provide a good workout and an even better view. Indeed, one of the best ways to get a feel for the breathtaking Wuyishan is to climb its peaks, from which you can admire the sea of mountains set within a spreading sea of clouds. Main trails are well maintained and safe, even in the wee hours of the morning, when falling mountain dew, glimmers of sunrise, and safety from chaotic tour groups provide ideal conditions for solitary rambles. Admission fees are charged separately for individual sights; an all-inclusive ticket (Y80) can be purchased at any scenic spot.

NINE-BEND RIVER

*Bamboo **rafts** (zhú fàn; 竹泛) are the most popular way to traverse this winding creek, and provide a mellow introduction to the famed sights along the riverbanks. Rafts leave from **Xingcun village,** in the southwestern corner of the Wuyishan Scenic Area. Each raft seats 6 people; fixed **price** per raft is Y425 for the 1½hr. ride. Boats run daily 7am-5pm, with several going out every 30min. Ticket office ☎526 1752.*

Winding its way through 9.5km of gorges and bends in the southern portion of Wuyishan, the Nine-Bend River (jiŭ qŭ xī; 九曲溪) is one of the most justifiably hyped sights in the area. Zigzagging through rugged canyons and peaks, the river's mirror-like waters and rushing rapids are pristine and unspoiled, with a serene beauty that embodies all the natural wonder Wuyishan has to offer. Indeed, brochures and tour guides often compare rafting down the river to entering a Chinese landscape painting—an incredibly, almost flawlessly idyllic atmosphere. Bamboo chairs are wound onto the body of simple bamboo rafts, so you can dip your feet in the river the entire way. The rafts themselves are usually manned by families, with one person in front and one in back.

Main sights center around the nine bends of the river. From **Xingcun Village** (xīngcūn zhèn; 星村镇) and the ninth bend, the raft goes by **White Cloud Rock** (bái yún yán; 白云岩), a former gathering place for scholars and worshiping pilgrims. The eighth bend takes you past **Pinzi Rock** (pǐnzì yán; 品字岩), also known as **Wusha Rock** (wūshā yán; 乌纱岩), named and shaped after the black gauze caps that imperial officers used to wear. Look for two flat rocks—two turtles, one might say—on the left side of the river, and a large peak immediately to the right, which has the shape of a walking elephant. Downstream at the sixth and fifth bends, the river flows by **Heavenly Tour Peak** (tiān yóu fēng; 天游峰) and **Cloud's Lair,** named for the view from atop the Immortal Pavilion, and **Draper's Rock** (shàibù yán; 晒布岩), a cliff face whose fanlike folds give it its name. At the third bend, the boat passes an **ancient boat coffin,** high up on the cliff to the right. Burial customs in the area consisted of the dead being put into boat tombs and then placed into small caves in the riverside cliffs. The second bend passes one of the most photographed sights in Wuyishan, **Jade Goddess Peak** (yù nǔ fēng; 玉女峰). The first bend goes by **King's Peak** (dà wáng fēng; 大王峰), one of the most spectacular summits of the 36 peaks. Curiously wider at the top, with only one crevice leading up its steep ascent (see **Rock-Steady,** p. 506), it resembles a crown.

The raft tour wraps up at **Wuyi Palace** (wǔyí gōng; 武夷宫), a small complex of hotels, souvenir shops, and restaurants. The area also houses the **Museum of Wuyi Mountain** (wǔyí shān bówùguǎn; 武夷山博物馆), a short but lovingly designed tour introducing the mountain's role as an ecological reserve, rich in biodiversity and natural resources. An admission-charging counterpart to the museum has an exhibit explaining the intricacies of boat coffin burials, including a display of a boats acquired from an archeological dig. It's worth a look even if the coffins don't really float your boat. (☎ 525 2729. *Open daily 8-11:30am and 2-5:30pm. Y3.*)

OTHER SIGHTS

A five-minute drive past Lantang Bridge north in the scenic area will take you to the **Big Red Robe Tea Mountain** (dà hóng páo; 大红袍), which houses the **Nine Dragons Nest,** a stunning group of towering rock formations that resemble nine coiled dragons. Farther up the mountain, past myriad mountain pools and waterfalls, you come to a small tea pavilion overlooking the famed tea plantation, where you can sip this revered beverage while admiring the view. (*Open daily 6am-6pm. Y12.*) Close to the summit is **Ever-happy Temple** (yǒnglè chánsì; 永乐禅寺), the biggest Buddhist temple in the Wuyishan area. A spectacular view awaits those willing to clamber up (1½hr.) to the elysian, mist-shrouded summit of **Heavenly Tour Peak.** Locals call this area **Cloud's Lair,** since the steam from geysers in winter turns the park into a sea of clouds. (☎ 525 2827. *Open daily 6:30am-6pm. Y40.*) A pricey but unique alternative to climbing the peak is to go via *hua jiao,* manned sedan chairs (Y160 roundtrip, available in front of the ticket office).

THREAD OF SKY (yī xiàn tiān; 一线天). Farther south of the Nine-Bend River, this mind-bending, neck-craning, hair-raising work of nature far surpasses the pleasant but mundane landscapes of rolling hills and brooks. The highest and narrowest of its kind, this fissured cave is formed by a split in the stone linking the Fuxi and Feng Caves. At 3m wide, it lets in only a beam of light—a thread of sky, for the poetically inclined. The dark and steep climb through this narrow seam is an adventure, involving a bit of creative sideways maneuvering and hands-included footwork, giving new meaning to the phrase "seeing the light at the end of the tunnel": avoid the bats. (*Open daily 6:30am-6pm. Y18.*)

ROCK-STEADY Perching over the last two bends of the Nine-Bend River, on opposite banks, sit **King's Peak** and **Jade Goddess Peak,** two cliffs that resemble a king's crown and a svelte lady (this requires a healthy dose of imagination). Legend has it that when the Jade Goddess descended from heaven against the Jade Emperor's wishes, she came to Wuyishan and fell in love with a good-natured king. A Daoist monk, Tieban, who wanted to curry favor with the Emperor, gleefully reported the whereabouts of the Jade Goddess to the Jade Emperor. In order to capture the lovers, Tieban turned them into stones and himself into a rock standing between them. Buddha took pity on the lovesick pair and placed a mirror stage, known as **Dressing Table Rock** (gèngyī tái; 更衣台), so the two could see each other. Ah, true love.

WATER CURTAIN CAVE (shuǐ lián dòng; 水帘洞). This so-called water curtain is less of a curtain than a tempermental waterfall, a trickle on dry days and a gushing spout during the rainy reason. The long trek to get here, plus a seemingly endless staired ascent, are well worth it. Tourists flood the area until late afternoon. Endowed with a mystical tranquility left here by the legendary sages that once inhabited the cave (now marked by the **Hall of Three Sages**), the shroud of mountain water that rains into the pond at the foot of the cave is a testament to the area's almost sacred quality. From the top of the first set of stairs leading to the cave, there is a spectacular view of **Eagle's Peak** (yīng zuǐ yán; 鹰嘴岩), shaped like an eagle about to soar into flight. *(North of Lantang Bridge. Open daily 7am-6pm. Y12.)*

QUANZHOU 泉州 ☎ 0595

Pull up to Quanzhou's seaside today and the remnants of its naval heyday during the Song and Yuan dynasties—scores of discarded fishing boats, a stone bridge, and long stretches of rocky coastline—make it hard to believe that this was once a bustling cosmopolitan city. At the time, Quanzhou was one of the largest ports in the world; its harbor packed off silk and porcelain to the Middle East and shepherded to shore the spices and ivory that flowed in. Large merchant ships and a colorful group of sailors, missionaries, and wheeler-dealers frequented the lively wharf area, where religions, languages, and architectural styles mixed as easily as the teas and spices that were traded.

Today, the port's significance has diminished into memories of a bygone era, and the Arab and Persian traders of yesteryear have either scattered to the winds or disappeared into the local population. Hints of Quanzhou's romantic past still stand their ground, though, turning up in places like the display of a Song-era trading ship or in the 900-year-old Ashab Mosque. Aside from these official sights, this pint-sized city is full of curved doorways, stone carvings, and tucked-away steles that remind it of its past.

⊠ ☷ ORIENTATION AND PRACTICAL INFORMATION

Quanzhou is bordered by the **Jin River** (jìn jiāng; 晋江) to the west. The downtown area is bounded to the north by **Xi Jie** (西街) and **Dong Jie** (东街). Xi Jie and Dong Jie are bisected by **Zhongshan Lu** (中山路), which runs from north to south. Running parallel to the east, **Wenling Lu** (温陵路) terminates in the south near the long-distance bus station at the intersection with **Quanxiu Jie** (泉秀街). **Tumen Jie** (涂门街) and **Jiuyi Jie** (九一街) both run between Zhongshan Lu and Wenling Lu. The latter continues east of its intersection with Wenling Lu as **Fengze Jie** (丰泽街), into the newest part of town.

Buses: Quanzhou Bus Station (quánzhōu qìchē zhàn; 泉州汽车站; ☎ 228 4141), at the southeast corner of Wenling Lu and Quanxiu Jie, connected to the northern part of the city via by #2. Most Quanzhou buses have restrooms and a stewardess who serves tea and cookies. To **Fuzhou** (2hr., approx. every 30min. 7am-7:30pm, Y52-60) and **Xiamen** (1½hr., 26 per day 6:40am-7:30pm, Y32).

Quanzhou

🏠 ACCOMMODATIONS
Great Wall Hotel, 2
Jian Fu Hotel, 3
Overseas Chinese Hotel, 4
Zhonglou Hostel, 1

Local Transportation: Many destinations within the city can be reached on foot, and most locals get around by moped. Quanzhou **buses** have comprehensive service, but certain routes can get frighteningly crowded—keep an eye on your belongings. Most routes run 6am-10pm. Base fare Y1, farther destinations Y1.5. Bus **#2** runs from the bus station up Wenling Lu, passing Dong Jie, Xi Jie, and Kaiyuan Temple, and **#15** travels the length of Wenling Lu, continuing north to Qingyuan Mountain.

Taxis: Base fare Y8-10, each additional km Y1.4-1.8; *miandi* taxis Y6, each additional km Y1.4. **Pedicabs** within city center Y3-5, bus station to Kaiyuan Temple Y8-10.

Tourist Office: Quanzhou Municipal Tourism Bureau (quánzhōu shì lǚyóu jú; 泉州市旅游局; ☎227 4888), in the Jingweige Bldg., 3rd Fl., on Dong Jie next to the PSB. Take bus #2 to Zhonglou and backtrack 1 block. Welcoming and helpful staff have a small selection of English-language brochures. Open M-F 8-11:30am and 3-6pm.

Travel Agency: CTS (☎298 5940), in the Huaqiao Building, on Baiyuan Lu next to the Overseas Chinese Hotel. Private bus to Fuzhou with daily 9am departures (Y55). English- and Japanese-speaking staff. Ticket commission Y10. Open daily 8:30am-6pm.

Bank of China: 1 Jiuyi Jie, at Wenling Lu. Take bus #18 to Wenling Lu; there is a big sign atop the high-rise. Exchanges traveler's checks and issues credit card advances. Open daily 8-11:30am and 3-6pm.

Bookstore: Xinhua Bookstore/Foreign Language Bookstore (wài wén shūdiàn; 外文书店), on Wenling Lu at Yinjing Lu, a block south of the Great Wall Hotel. Open daily 8am-9pm.

PSB: 62 Dong Jie, a few minutes east of Zhongshan Zhong Lu. From the bus station or Wenling Lu, take bus #2 to Zhonglou and backtrack a block. For visa extensions, the

SOUTH COAST

Division of Entry and Exit (chūrù jìng guǎnlǐ chù; 出入境管理处; ☎218 0308) has a separate entrance around to the right of the building as you face it. Open daily 8-11:30am and 3-6pm.

Hospital: Quanzhou Municipal People's Hospital (quánzhōu shì rénmín yīyuàn; 泉州市人民医院), 54 Daxi Jie (☎228 3490; emergency ☎228 5221), near Zhongshan Zhong Lu.

Internet Access: Once on the "maritime silk route," now on the information superhighway, Quanzhou is full of high-speed Internet bars. **Webfanroom** (wǎngmí zhī wū; 网迷之屋), off Dong Jie near Xianggong Xiang, 1 block east of the police station. Look for the blue and white sign. Y4 per hr. Open daily 9am-midnight. **Xiaokan Luohua Internet Bar** (xiàokàn luòhuā wǎngbā; 笑看落花网吧; ☎219 4414), 8 Wenhua Jie, immediately off Tumen Jie, south of the Guandi Temple. Super-fast connections and new computers. Y3 per hr. Open daily 8am-11pm. The **Multimedia Communications Center** (duō méixiū tōngxìn zhōngxīn; 多媒休通信中心), on the 2nd floor of the post office. Y10 per hr., deposit Y100. Open daily 8:30am-6:30pm.

Post Office: A high-rise at the corner of Jiuyi Jie and Wenling Bei Lu. EMS and Poste Restante. Open daily 8am-8pm. **Postal Code:** 362000.

ACCOMMODATIONS

Mid-range accommodations in Quanzhou are not hard to find, but jaw-droppingly cheap options are few and far between. Some hotels are clustered on Wenling Lu between the bus station and Jiuyi Jie; the city center is mostly a dry well for the budget traveler. Fledgling tourism and a slim peak season make prices negotiable, even in some higher-end establishments.

Zhonglou Hostel (zhōnglóu lǚshè; 钟楼旅社), 1 Zhongshan Bei Lu (☎237 3343), at Xi Jie. Take bus #2 from the long-distance bus station. Where else can you live close by the Kaiyuan Temple, trade stories with well-traveled backpackers, and be cared for by generous staff? Seafood restaurant on 2nd floor. Rooms without A/C have mosquito nets. Dorms Y25; singles Y50; doubles Y70; triples Y75. With A/C: dorms Y40; singles Y60, with bath Y100; doubles with bath Y100; triples Y120, with bath Y150.

Overseas Chinese Home (huá qiáo zhījiā; 华侨之家), 149 Wenling Lu (☎228 3559), a few minutes north of the bus station. Call this Home your home: a serene inner courtyard set back from the street plus views of the city (without the noise). Rooms have all standard amenities. 2-bed dorms (Y80) may be available. Reserve up to 1 week ahead for singles. 20-30% discounts possible. Singles Y235; doubles Y195; triples Y235.

Jianfu Hotel (jiàn fú dàshà; 建福大厦; ☎228 3511; fax 298 6041), on Wenling Lu next to the Overseas Chinese Home. Added glitz, luxurious rooms with fridges, and gimmicky floral centerpieces don't come with added *yuan;* this is a good break from threadbare budget rooms. Year-round discounts. Singles Y100; doubles Y138-158; triples Y150.

Great Wall Hotel (cháng chéng bīnguǎn; 长城宾馆), 23 Wenling Lu (☎228 7938), just north of Tumen Jie. Take buses #2, 5, 8, or 9 from the bus station. Shabby but centrally located, this hotel offers old, clean rooms and not-so-perky service. Cell phone barking businessmen and *anmo* girls are the name of the game. And no, the Great Wall does not extend this far south. Singles Y80-100; doubles Y88-120; triples Y120.

FOOD

Quanzhou is a snack-lover's haven, and its popular fast-food joints and street stalls assemble a gratifying collection of flavors from neighboring regions. Definitely try the **steamed sponge cakes,** snowy white rice cakes slightly fermented for a subtle sweet flavor. The **glutinous rice** steamed with either chicken, pork, or red bean paste and wrapped in bamboo leaves in a pyramid shape (zòngzi; 综子) are as fun to unravel as they are to eat. The colorful small streets in the older, northwest section of town—on and around **Dong Jie, Xi Jie,** and **Zhongshan Bei Lu** in particular—harbor a treasure of small eateries offering these snacks, as well as those featuring

Sha County-style treats (shā xiàn xiǎochī; 沙县小吃), small family-owned ventures cooking up *ban mian* and wonton soups for under Y5. The alleyways hung with advertising banners behind the Post and Telecommunications building, along the north portion of **Wenling Lu,** are lined with shops selling bowls of appetizing beef noodle soup for Y5-6. At night, the street parallel to and directly west of Wenling Lu (between Tumen Jie and Jiuyi Jie) comes alive with fruit stands, sesame cake (Y1) vendors, and neon-lit seafood restaurants.

> **Anji Baozai Restaurant** (ānjì bāozǎi fàndiàn; 安记煲仔饭店; ☎298 2699), on the corner of Wenling Lu and Tumen Jie. The Anji rocks its snacks (Y3-5) and entrees (Y8-15) 'round the clock. Its specialty is an oven-roasted rice platter served piping hot with various side dishes, including pork chops and roast duck (Y12). Watch chefs through the glassed-in kitchen. For breakfast, try their porridges (zhōu; 粥; Y6-8). Open 24hr.

> **Yonghe Soy King** (yǒnghé dòujiāng dàwáng; 永和豆浆大王; ☎228 0199), on Wenling Lu, 2 blocks north of the Great Wall Hotel. This hangout dishes up generous helpings of sweet or salty soy milk along with deep-fried crispy dough sticks for Y4. Steamed custard buns (Y1) provide satisfaction for the sweet-toothed. Open 24hr.

▨ SIGHTS

Quanzhou's sights reflect its colorful religious and cultural heritage. Museums pay homage to Quanzhou's weathered past as the starting point of the ancient maritime silk route, while its position as the birthplace of many illustrious soon-to-be Overseas Chinese appears in sleek new memorials to these figures.

Spirituality has also held its own against the secular currents of trade and commerce in Quanzhou, thanks to those who brought religion as well as silk, jewels, and perfumes onto Quanzhou's open shores. Long known as an exhibition of world religions, Quanzhou has a wealth of Muslim and Buddhist relics to show for the city's devoted past. Buddhist temples, including four along the length of Zhongshan Lu alone, are scattered throughout the city. The Islamic tradition keeps a lower profile but is still visible in **Qingjing Mosque,** the one remaining mosque of the six or seven that stood during the Yuan dynasty. **Ling Mountain** (líng shān; 灵山), to the east of the city, is the site of graves of Muslims who lived in Quanzhou during the Tang, Song, and Yuan dynasties. Perhaps the best way to get a feel for Quanzhou's religious and maritime history is to stroll through its old city streets, particularly along **Jubao Jie** (聚宝街), which used to house markets where jewelry was traded, and **Xiaomen Xiang** (小门巷), where the crumbling remains of the Maritime Administration of Foreign Trade sit.

QINGYUAN MOUNTAIN (qīngyuán shān; 清源山). Looming over Quanzhou and its surrounding environs lies Qingyuan Mountain. Not yet overpopulated by tourists, it's easy to get lost in this place, so prepare to bushwhack your way to the summit. Dotted with shrines, temples, and statues dating back to the Tang dynasty, as well as Islamic tombs from the Ming dynasty, this scenic area has become a bit of a living relic in itself; covering every waterfall, stone inscription, or sculpture might well take the bulk of a day. Before all the shrines begin to blur into one ornate jumble, don't miss the massive stone statue of **Laozi** (lǎojūn yán; 老君岩), the founder of Daoism. A climb uphill from the statue leads to **Mituo Rock** (mítuó shí; 弥陀石), the sometimes-waterfall, sometimes-rock cavern whose cool hollows between giant rocks provide respite from the elements. Near the summit, the **Rock Hundreds of Meters High** (bǎi zhàng píng; 百丈坪) actually is the flat expanse of rock where Yu Dayou, a Ming dynasty general, resisted invading Japanese troops. The summit offers fantastic views of the surrounding area. *(3km north of the city. Take bus #3 from Zhongshan Lu or #15 from Wenling Lu to the last stop (30min., Y2). Laozi and Qianshou Yan gates both lead to the scenic area. ☎279 7606. Open daily 7am-6pm. Y25, including all sights.)*

KAIYUAN TEMPLE (kāiyuán sì; 开元寺). The largest of Quanzhou's Buddhist temples, Kaiyuan Temple is also the primary tourist attraction of the city. The temple itself is prefaced by an airy, stone-paved courtyard, and flanked by the impressive

East and **West Pagodas.** Sculpted on all sides with Buddhist icons, the pagodas are unique for their Chinese and Indian artistic styles. Although the temple dates back to AD 686, the pagodas were not constructed until more than 500 years later. The ceiling of the main hall is lined with 24 flying *apsaras*, which resemble a cross between Catholic angels and traditional Chinese figurines.

To the east of the temple proper (to the right as you face it), behind the garden containing the East Pagoda, is a small but very worthwhile exhibit on the history of navigation and foreign contact in Quanzhou, especially during the Song and Yuan dynasties. There is something uncannily enticing about very old boats: in this case, it's a partially reconstructed 13th-century sailing ship, discovered in Quanzhou Bay in 1973 during the dredging of an irrigation channel. *(27 Xi Jie, in the northwest part of the city. Take bus #2 from the bus station or Wenling Lu to Kaiyuan Si. Open daily 7:30am-6pm. Y4, children 1.2m and under Y2.)*

QINGJING MOSQUE (qīngjìng sì; 清净寺). Also known as the **Ashab Mosque,** the Qingjing Mosque has beaten the forces that destroyed its counterparts to emerge as Quanzhou's only mosque. Though it is fairly run-down and suffers a dwindling number of visitors, the mosque retains its splendor and has a certain wildness found in hidden, intricate gems. Overall, the mosque is more a monument to a forgotten era than an active museum. The open-air worshiping hall, to the left of the entrance and set back from the bustling avenue outside, has an otherworldly feel. The exhibition room to the west (left as you enter) presents a history of "Islam in Quanzhou," with photos and complete English translations, discussing both the mosque (built in AD 1009) and the burial sites tucked away in the hillsides to the north and southeast of the city. *(On Tumen Jie, west of a minor Buddhist temple and near Baiyuan Lu. Take bus #18 from the bus station to Guandi Si. Open daily 8am-6pm. Y3.)*

XIAMEN 厦门   ☎ 0592

Beware: this city may spoil you. Other Chinese cities, and even your beloved hometown, may never look the same once you've sunk your teeth into the sweet delights of Xiamen, including a mild climate, a mixture of architecture, some of the best sights in Fujian province, title of "cleanest city in China," fresh sea air, gracious residents...well, you get the idea. Locals take full advantage of their city: leisurely strolls, afternoon swims, and evening feasts are staples of life in Xiamen. Those seeking a fast-paced life must look elsewhere.

Over the past four centuries, Xiamen has seen a succession of foreign influences, as Portuguese, British, French, and Japanese all settled here (calling it "Amoy") to take advantage of the city's port and strategic location on maritime and overland trade routes. Xiamen took well to cosmopolitan influence. Even today, proudly renovated colonial facades face storefronts and residences in the western waterfront district, and numerous restaurants around the city serve authentic cuisine from all over the world. Enjoying the perks of foreign investment and its status as a Special Economic Zone, Xiamen has made quite a bundle in recent years, but the city has made a point of laying the fruits of development *beside* the relics of its past, not over them.

▄▀ TRANSPORTATION

Airplanes: Xiamen Gaoqi International Airport (xiàmén gāoqí guójì jīchǎng; 厦门高崎国际机场; ☎ 602 2936), about 10km and a 30-45min. drive northeast of downtown Xiamen city at the northern end of the island, near the causeway to the mainland. Bus #37 goes from the airport to the Gulangyu ferry pier (opposite the Lujiang Hotel). Taxis to the airport cost Y40-50. The **Xiamen Airlines ticket office** (xiàháng shòupiào zhōngxīn; 夏航售票中心), 931 Xiahe Lu (☎ 515 3601), is outside the long-distance bus station. Open daily 8am-6pm. To: **Beijing** (3-4 per day 10:40am-2:20pm, Y1370); **Guangzhou** (7 per day 7am-6:10pm, Y530); **Hong Kong** (3 per day 10am-7:15pm, Y1460); and **Shanghai** (5-6 per day 7:10am-8pm, Y770).

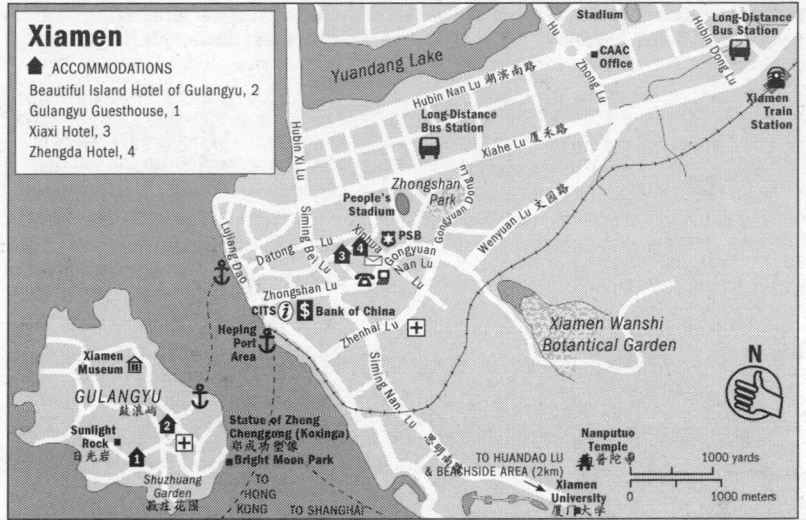

Xiamen

↑ ACCOMMODATIONS
Beautiful Island Hotel of Gulangyu, 2
Gulangyu Guesthouse, 1
Xiaxi Hotel, 3
Zhengda Hotel, 4

Trains: As with most cities in Fujian province, trains are not the best way to leave and enter Xiamen, as buses are faster and more frequent. **Xiamen Train Station** (xiàmén huǒchē zhàn; 厦门火车站; ☎505 4338 or 582 2442), on Xiahe Lu at the southern end of Hubin Dong Lu, east of the waterfront area. Buses #3, 4, 28, and 30 connect to the pier area. Open daily 7:50am-9:40pm. To **Shanghai** (26hr., 4:30 and 8:20pm, Y170-472) via **Hangzhou** (23hr.).

Buses: Xiamen Long-distance Bus Station (xiàmén chángtú qìchē zhàn; 厦门长途汽车站), 931 Xiahe Lu (☎505 5525), a 2min. walk west of the train station. Open daily 5:30am-10:30pm. To: **Fuzhou** (3½hr., approx. every 20min. 6:25am-10:05pm, Y50-87); **Guangzhou** (9hr., 7 per day 8:50am-10pm, Y110-220); and **Hong Kong** (10hr., 8am, Y350). Several of the luxury bus lines have ticket offices scattered around the western district, allowing you to buy tickets and board buses at more central locations such as the ferry pier and in front of Xiamen University/Nanputuo Temple.

Local Transportation: English transportation maps (Y10) are available in Xinhua Bookstore. Most **buses** run 6am-10pm. Fare Y1. **Buses #1** and **21** head south to Nanputuo Temple and Xiamen University; **#10** connects the bus station to the ferry pier; **#12** runs up Zhongshan Lu; **#31** runs from the pier and up along Hubin Bei Lu; and **#38** connects the pier with the airport.

Taxis: Base fare Y7-8, each additional km Y2; all taxis should be metered. Most western district destinations (near the waterfront and Gulangyu) Y8-10; from the bus station to the waterfront Y12-14, from the train station Y20-30, and from the airport Y35-50.

✹ 🕐 ORIENTATION AND PRACTICAL INFORMATION

Xiamen Island juts out from the mainland off the coast of southern Fujian, connected by the **Xiamen Causeway**. **Xiamen city** occupies the southwestern portion of the island. The most visited portion of the city is confined to a 10km² chunk along the island's western shores, facing **Gulangyu** (鼓浪屿), Xiamen's satellite islet and its biggest tourist attraction. This compact western district, eminently navigable on foot, is dominated by a 1km long stretch of **Zhongshan Lu** (中山路), which runs from east to west to the waterfront. North of the western end of Zhongshan Lu is the passenger terminal for ferries to Gulangyu. **Siming Lu** (思明路) runs from north to south, intersecting with Zhongshan Lu. Visitors will most likely only see the rest of Xiamen Island while in transit. In the eastern part of the city, the main long-distance bus station is on **Hubin Dong Lu** (湖滨东路), near **Xiahe Lu** (厦禾路), where the train station is located.

Tourist Office: Xiamen Municipal Tourism Bureau (xiàmén shì lǚyoú jú; 厦门市旅游局), Xinye Bank Bldg., 78 Hubin Bei Lu, 6th Fl. (☎531 8858). Maps and travel brochures available, but staff is not used to individual travelers.

Travel Agencies: Plane, train, and bus ticketing offices abound along Zhongshan Lu, Siming Lu, and near the waterfront. **CITS,** 2-3 Zhongshan Lu (☎202 0658), off a small alley around the corner from the Bank of China, in front of the Hong Kong Bank. English-speaking staff and no commission on airline bookings. Open M-F 8:30am-5:30pm. The main CITS office (☎504 1180) is in Zhenxing Mansion, 15th Fl., on Hubin Bei Lu, a block east of the tourism bureau. Take bus #31 from the pier to Te Mao. Arranges tours of Xiamen (Y100 per day). English-speaking staff. Open daily 9:30am-5:30pm.

Bank of China: 6-10 Zhongshan Lu, opposite the Lujiang and East Ocean Hotels, near the harbor. Exchanges traveler's checks, and issues credit advances at counter #19. ATMs (Chinese bank cards only) available. Open daily 8:30am-noon and 3-5:30pm.

Bookstores: Xinhua Bookstore/Foreign Language Bookstore (wài wén shūdiàn; 外文书店), 151-153 Zhongshan Lu (☎202 4059; foreign language dept. ☎513 7768), on the north side of the road just a bit west of Siming Bei Lu. Carries dictionaries, guidebooks, and a fair selection of literature. The area near Xiamen University, especially along its northwestern edge on Yanwu Lu, around the corner from Nanputuo Temple, houses some bookstores with substantial English-language sections.

PSB: 43 Xinhua Lu (☎202 5505), near Gongyuan Nan Lu, opposite the Xinhua Lu Post Office. For visa extensions, go to the **Division of Exit and Entry** (chūrù jìng guǎnlǐ kē; 出入境管理科; ☎202 2329), in a separate building in the far back corner of the compound, close to Gongyuan Nan Lu. Open daily 8-11:30am and 3-6pm.

Hospitals: Xiamen No. 1 Hospital (xiàmén shì dì yī yīyuàn; 厦门市第一医院; ☎213 7275; emergency ☎213 7101), on Zhenhai Lu, parallel to and south of Zhongshan Lu, a 10-15min. walk east of the Holiday Inn. On Gulangyu: **Xiamen No. 2 Hospital** (xiàmén shì dì èr yīyuàn; 厦门市第二医院), 60 Fujian Lu (☎206 2449; emergency ☎206 3549), off Longtou Lu, a 10min. walk from the ferry pier.

Internet Access: Internet Cafe (yīntè kāfēi wū; 因特咖啡屋), 12-13 Yanwu Lu, 2nd Fl. (☎209 7778), opposite and around the corner from Nanputuo Temple. Y8 per hr, deposit Y100, funky 80s soundtrack free. Open daily 10am-11pm. **Zizai Internet Bar** (zìzài wǎngbā; 自在网吧), 260 Zhongshan Lu (☎210 1472). Y5 per hr. Open daily 9am-midnight. **Internet Pub** (yángyǔ wǎngbā; 洋宇网吧), 349 Zhongshan Lu (☎207 6300). Look for psychedelic blue signs leading you off the street. ISDN speed connections at Y4 per hr. Open 24hr.

Post Office: 54 Xinhua Lu (☎202 2549 or 203 8277), just north of Zhongshan Lu at its eastern end. Open daily 7:30am-9pm. **Haihou Lu Post and Telecommunications Office** (hǎihòu lù yóudiàn jú; 海后路邮电局), 58 Haihou Lu (☎202 3486), on Lujiang Dao opposite the Gulangyu ferry pier and a few minutes' walk north from the western end of Zhongshan Lu. Poste Restante. Open daily 7:30am-7:30pm. EMS and IDD service at both branches. **Postal Code:** 361001 for western district and Poste Restante, 361002 for Gulangyu.

■ ACCOMMODATIONS

While Xiamen has many options for high rollers, budget travelers will find a few pleasant surprises, even on Gulangyu. Indeed, staying on Gulangyu for at least one night is an experience that no one should pass up: being able to stroll along the sea late into the night and catch the sunrise early the next morning does wonders. A few of the aging colonial villas overlooking Gulangyu's shores are now inhabited by families or adopted by *mahjong*-playing retirees who may be convinced to rent out some of these gorgeously unkept, zero amenities rooms for a small fee, but this option may take time and patience. The off season is from September to May.

XIAMEN CITY

Xiaxi Hotel (xiáxī fàndiàn; 霞溪饭店), 30 Xiaxi Lu (☎202 4859 or 202 7139). Xiaxi Lu runs north off Zhongshan Lu near its eastern end, between Xinhua Lu and Siming Lu; the hotel is on the right, about 5min. up the road. The faded mint-green facade and open, curved staircase hint at the stately elegance in this colonial building's past. This grand presence has gone downscale, but the basic rooms still reap the benefits of high ceilings, good views, eclectic antique furniture...and mosquito nets. Communal bathrooms are poorly maintained. 24hr. hot water. 20% discounts available. Dorms Y25; singles Y35; doubles Y60; quads Y100. With A/C: singles Y55, with bath Y85; doubles Y80, with bath Y130-160; triples with bath Y165; quads with bath Y168.

Zhengda Hotel (zhēngdà jiǔdiàn; 正大酒店), 30-38 Xinhua Lu (☎203 1288, ext. 100), at Zhongshan Lu, opposite the PSB. Take bus #3 or 4 from the train station to Wenhua Gong. Exuberant service and spacious rooms, plus 3 meals per day, full-day tours of Xiamen, and a ticket to the hotel's sauna. 30% discounts. Doubles Y350; triples Y450.

GULANGYU

Beautiful Island Hotel of Gulangyu (lìzhīdǎo jiǔdiàn; 丽之岛酒店), 133 Longtou Lu (☎206 3309). From the ferry pier, follow Longtou Lu, the main road leading inland, to the right. Take a left at a crossroads; this is *still* Longtou Lu. The hotel is on the right. Standard rooms are good enough and staff is great. Perks include discounted admission to sights and assistance with dragging luggage to and from the ferry. Cheaper rooms go fast; reserve in advance. 15% discounts during the off season. Singles Y208-218; doubles Y120, with windows Y168-218; triples Y210.

Gulangyu Guesthouse (gǔlàngyǔ bīnguǎn; 鼓浪屿宾馆), 25 Huangyan Lu (☎206 6050 or 206 3856). Follow the signs toward Sunlight Rock; the road leads past a grassy stadium area and then to the hotel on the left. The atmosphere and ambience cannot be beat, with shady paths and gardens connecting the impressive colonial-style buildings. In the central building, the dark wood furniture and oriental rugs in the parlor and a curved marble staircase lead to some pricey suites, including one where US President Richard Nixon stayed in 1972. 20% year-round discounts, up to 50% off-season discounts. Doubles Y200-240; suites Y500-800.

◖◗ FOOD

Xiamen is as eager to share its local specialties and culinary assets with visitors as it is to share in the flavors of others. The northern end of Xiamen University, south of Nanputuo Temple, is one of the best places to go for variety. You'll find a few restaurants specializing in the **handmade noodles** (xīběi lāmiàn; 西北拉面) of the Northwest, a couple **Taiwanese** restaurants around the corner from a McDonald's, and **Korean** restaurants farther down. The **wharf** and **western districts** near the waterfront also have streets teeming with cosmopolitan cuisine. On **Siming Dong Lu** are a couple of restaurants specializing in the Fujian **Sha-county** (shā xiàn fēngwèi; 沙县风味) style. At 26 Zhongshan Lu, a tiny entrance leads to a **Xinjiang** (新疆) noodle restaurant, where a windowed kitchen reveals white-capped chefs molding perfect stringlets of noodles. Try the spicy wonton soup with a platter of Muslim-style mixed noodles *(ban mian)* for Y5. (☎203 1985. Open daily 8am-11pm.) Narrow **Jukou Jie**, running north from Zhongshan Lu just west of Siming Bei Lu, has a string of **Sichuanese** restaurants.

As for local specialties, **seafood** tops the list, especially on Gulangyu. The more adventurous can seek out rarities such as **turtle soup** and **grilled crayfish**, a popular dish in summer for its golden shell and light flavor. Seafood restaurants line **Longtou Lu,** the commercial market road leading inland from the pier. Xiamen's specialties also include snack foods such as sweet fried pastries stuffed with peanut crumblies, a sweet "soft peanut soup" (huāshēng tāng; 花生汤), and a savory vegetable-filled pastry called *jiu cai he* (酒菜盒). Two other famous dishes native to Xiamen are a jelly (tǔsǔndòng; 土笋冻) made with wasabi, soy and fragrant oil sauces, and a special seaworm that's more appetizing than it sounds, and paper-thin rice noodles with vegetable and seafood delicacies (miànxiànhū; 面线糊).

SOUTH COAST

XIAMEN CITY

■ **Huangzehe Peanut Soup Shop** (huángzéhé huāshēng tāngdiàn; 黄则和花生汤店), 22-24 Zhongshan Lu (☎212 5825), between McDonald's and the Bank of China. This wildly popular family-owned restaurant and bakery (going strong for 50 years) is the best place to sample the special snacks said to have originated in Xiamen. Definitely try the peanut soup (Y1) and shaved green bean ice (Y3). Open daily 6am-9:50pm.

Haoxianglai Chinese Western Restaurant (háoxiānglaí zhōngxī cāntīng; 豪享来中西餐厅), 5 Haihou Lu (☎203 5212), next to the back entrance of the Lujiang Hotel and opposite the front of the East Ocean Hotel. Haihou Lu is the 1st street running north off Zhongshan Lu as you head inland from the waterfront. A popular family chain, this is the perfect place to satisfy those uncontrollable cravings for "Western food" that won't turn your paper plate transparent. House specialty is tender, juicy Western-style steak, but stay away from the salad with ketchup sauce. Y25 set menu includes soup, vegetables, bread or rice, entree, and drink. Open 24hr.

Outer Limits Pub (yīnyuè chúfáng; 音乐厨房), 34-36 Datong Lu (☎213 4023). Datong Lu runs inland 1 block to the right of the Haihou Lu Post Office as you face it; the restaurant is a 5min. walk, on the right. Advertising "music and culture," the Pub will take you to the outer limits of coolness—with live music nightly 7:30-10pm, lots of young couples, and even more khaki—provided you come at night. Although the extensive drink list is translated into English (soft drinks Y8-15, cocktails Y15-19), the food menu is only partially so, but never fear—the special set meals of rice dishes plus side helpings of roast duck and pork dishes (Y10-20) are a good deal. Open daily 9am-2am.

GULANGYU

■ **Haijiang Restaurant** (hǎijiāng dàpáidǎng; 海江大排档; ☎239 0460), perched on a dock opposite Gulangyu. Fishing boats from Pier No. 1 (dì yī mǎtóu; 第一码头), west of the Gulangyu ferry dock, shuttle patrons back and forth. This open-air seafood spot with sea on all four sides (indeed, many locals eat while their poles balance on chairs off the dock into the water below) makes dinner scenic, balmy, and good. A local hot spot that patrons claim serves the best, cheapest seafood around—and the food doesn't disappoint. Pick out your marine maties from the aquarium and then sit back and admire the sunset while peeling crayfish and inhaling scalloped shrimp. *Tusundong* Y5 per bowl. Open daily 10am-midnight.

■ **Gulong Pie House** (gǔlóng bǐngjiā; 鼓龙饼家), 21 Longtou Lu (☎206 0721). From the pier, the Pie House is 1 block down, on the left. Paris has its croissant, New York its bagel, and Gulangyu its *xian bing,* a pastry with sweet green bean paste filling (Y1)— made fresh only at this longtime establishment. Open daily 8am-8pm.

Gulang Prestige Restaurant (gǔlàng xìnyù jiǔlóu; 鼓浪信誉酒楼), 4 Zhonghua Lu (☎206 3073 or 206 1996). From Sunlight Rock, walk down Huangyan Lu past the turf area and take a right; the restaurant is on the left half a block down. The food doesn't come cheap, but the pearl fish (jīn zhū yú; 金珠鱼;Y90 per kg), steamed to tender perfection, and eight-treasure tea (Y10), a concoction of chrysanthemum leaves and herbs, are delicacies you (and your taste buds) won't forget. Open daily 10am-11pm.

👁 SIGHTS

Although Xiamen is most famous for Gulangyu, "Drum Wave Island," the neighborhoods along the southwestern shore of Xiamen Island (including some renovated colonial facades along Zhongshan Lu) are also worth seeing. The beach area by the southern part of Xiamen proper, along the stretch of **Huandao Lu** (环岛路), is mile upon mile of rollicking, frolicking good fun, with uninterrupted, swimmable coastline, bike rental shops, and rows of vendors selling everything from fruit drinks to Pokémon life jackets. Perhaps more sobering is the view of Jinmen Island, under Taiwanese control, a mere 1km from shore.

GULANGYU

Boats for Gulangyu leave from a busy passenger terminal just a few minutes north of the western end of Zhongshan Lu (15min., every 10-15min. 5:30am-12:20am). From Xiamen to Gulangyu, the primarily standing-room only lower deck is free, while the upper deck— where you might be able to snag a seat if you're lucky—is Y1; pay on board. From Gulangyu to Xiamen, the cost is Y3 for the lower deck, and Y4 for the upper deck; pay at the ticket kiosk. Speedboats (seating 6 people) offer island cruises for Y80; tickets are available from the small fishing pier opposite the Underwater World.

Those lucky enough to set foot on the multicolored cobblestoned streets of Gulangyu (gǔlàngyǔ; 鼓浪屿) may come away convinced that this tiny 1.78km^2 island is the stuff of which legends are made. Long known as the "Garden on the Sea" and "Piano Isle," Gulangyu's grand assemblage of colonial-style European architecture, winding gardens, and rocky, windswept beaches have made coming here a pilgrimage for resort-seeking vacationers and culture-craving aesthetes alike. No cars mar the island's streets, reserved for pedestrians and the occasional electric golf cart (Y20-30). Balmy breezes and puffs of salty sea air blow past red-shuttered colonial buildings, domed roofs, and the occasional church spires. Hidden speakers and tea houses waft vague airs of Bohemian rhapsodies and Viennese waltzes, providing the slow, rolling rhythms to which Gulangyu abides.

Sensual pleasures aside, a great deal of historical significance lies within Gulangyu's sunny shores. From the Xiamen waterfront, two of Gulangyu's most recognizable sights are clearly visible: the colossal **Statue of Zheng Chenggong** (郑成功), a national military hero and native of Fujian, at the island's southern end, and the stark grey protusion of **Sunlight Rock** (rìguāng yán; 日光岩), capped by military battlements, near the center of the island. Not only was the island a base for Zheng Chenggong's resistance against foreign invaders during the 17th century, but it has also been the home base and concession area of foreigners— Portuguese, British, French, and Japanese—who came to Xiamen to capitalize on its strategic commercial location. Ghosts from this checkered past live on, in the form of an eclectic jumble of **colonial architecture,** ranging from terraced patios and red brick structures to stone mansions with yellow-shuttered windows. Many of these buildings are still used as residences; a stroll along **Fujian Lu,** leading off from the Beautiful Island Hotel, is a showcase for these crumbling but still impressive villas, and many families are willing to open their doors and let visitors look around. Gulangyu has also produced many of China's greatest pianists, and the ratio of pianos to families here is the highest in the nation. The music school on the island strives to keep up the tradition, and the melodies of students hard at practice leak out through open kitchen doors and windows.

■ **SUNLIGHT ROCK** (rìguāng yán; 日光岩). One of the most popular sights on the island is the park containing Sunlight Rock, a 100m boulder that grants views of the entire island, the shores of mainland China, and the East China Sea in the distance. Named for being the first spot on Gulangyu to catch glimmers of the sun, the summit is a great place to watch the sun rise and to join groups of tai chi practitioners. Zheng Chenggong stationed troops on this "peak" to fight the Dutch colonialists who were occupying Taiwan in 1612, capitalizing on the strategic value of the spectacular view. Beyond a Buddhist temple near the base of the hill and near the Koxinga Memorial Hall, several paths head upward toward the peak—climb the last few steep steps to the "naval command post" at the top for a bird's-eye experience similar to that of Koxinga's men more than 300 years ago. The **Koxinga Memorial Hall** (zhèng chénggōng jìniàn guǎn; 郑成功纪念馆), in a stately three-story colonial building, is dedicated to this national hero. *(Open daily 8am-5pm. Free.)* From the foot of the iron-wrought stairs leading to the summit, a cable car will string you along to **Hundred Bird Park** (bǎi niǎo yuán; 百鸟园), a massive net-enclosed area where rare birds roam somewhat freely, and where you can watch hourly shows that showcase parrots grooving to disco tunes. *(Off Huangyan Lu, in the interior of the island beyond Gulangyu Guesthouse. Signs (some in English) from the ferry pier will direct you. Open daily 8am-6pm. Y40, children free; includes cable car and entrance to Hundred Bird Park.)*

SHUZHUANG GARDEN (shūzhuāng huāyuán; 菽庄花园). Shuzhuang Garden sits on the far southeast side of the island, past rows of dried seafood, trinket, and photo vendors, and next to a pristine beach. The garden, previously the private retreat of an overseas Chinese businessman, now opens its Nine-Bend Bridge, Listening-to-the-Tide pavilion, rocks, rare plants, and other scenic wonders to the public. Shuzhuang's intricate manmade structures contrast with the wild expanse of sea beyond. On Tianwei Lu at the end of Nine-Bend Bridge is the **Gulangyu Piano Museum** (gǔlàngyǔ gāngqín bówùguǎn; 鼓浪屿钢琴博物馆), which features over 40 different pianos from all periods and countries. *(Follow signs that lead off to the left from the main road after you disembark from the ferry. Open daily 8am-6pm. Y20, children 1-1.3m Y5, under 1m free.)*

BRIGHT MOON PARK (hào yuè yuán; 皓月园). From this point, visitors can view the **Statue of Zheng Chenggong** (zhèng chénggōng shídiāoxiàng; 郑成功石雕像) up close and personal—all 16m, 1400 tons, and 625 granite pieces of it. According to legend, Zheng threw his sword into the sea before leaving for Taiwan, and was subsequently transformed into a huge rock. Made to withstand a typhoon of scale 12 and an earthquake of over 8 on the Richter scale, chances are dear Koxinga isn't going anywhere anytime soon. The 150 peacocks in the **Peacock Park** (kǒngquè yuán; 孔雀园) aren't shy about begging visitors for food. *(From Shuzhuang Garden, follow the coastline east until you reach the park. Open daily sunrise-sunset. Y15.)*

XIAMEN UNDERWATER SEA WORLD (xiàmén hǎidǐ shìjiè; 厦门海底世界). This aquarium features over 10,000 denizens of the deep. Several hundred fresh- and sea-water species are represented, ranging from Amazon piranhas to Australian sea dragons. Visitors can view these animals from all sides by walking through an 80m long transparent tunnel. Better yet, they can hand-feed small fish to an open pond of turtles and baby sharks. *(2 Longtou Lu. On the main road leading off to the right from the ferry pier, after a grassy park; look for a golden octopus statue. ☎206 7668 or 206 7825. Open daily 8:30am-7pm. Y60, children and students Y30.)*

XIAMEN CITY SIGHTS

NANPUTUO TEMPLE (nánpǔtuó sì; 南普陀寺). A huge, impressive complex of multicolored halls, a golden Buddha statue, vast ponds and pavilions, and rock formations and mountains, Nanputuo Temple is one of the most active and best-kept monasteries in China. A Tang-dynasty construction, the temple is also now the site of the **Buddhism College of South Fujian** (mǐnnán fó xuéyuàn; 闽南佛学院). The temple is named after **Putuoshan** (see p. 347), the island off the coast of Zhejiang province to the north, which is dedicated to the *bodhisattva* Guanyin, the "goddess of mercy." Nanputuo Temple also takes Guanyin as its sacred deity. Indeed, the Guanyin statues are perhaps the most impressive aspect of the temple, with three **thousand-hand Guanyins** facing three sides of an elevated rotunda behind the main hall. Guanyin is often presented with a multitude of arms to symbolize her ability to help many people at once. Behind the Guanyin Pavilion, people gather around the **Making Money Grotto**, a rock engraved with characters for fortune on which visitors throw coins for luck. *(South of the city, immediately north of Xiamen University. The eastern gate and entrance is next to the bus station at the terminus for buses #1 and 21, both of which run south along Siming Nan Lu. Open daily sunrise-sunset. Y3, children under 1m free.)*

XIAMEN UNIVERSITY (xiàmén dàxué; 厦门大学). The lovely campus of Xiamen University contains buildings that manage to be both modern and tasteful. The student dormitories flanking the northern ends of the campus lake are a combination of red brick, curved archways, and pagoda towers, which, in typical Xiamen fashion, somehow manage to turn clash into genuine class. The grounds are covered in construction, but word has it that the red brick buildings will remain. To the left of the main Yanwu Lu entrance is Lu Xun Memorial Hall, built in honor of this scholar and author who used to be a professor at the university. *(South of Nanputuo Temple. Buses #1 and 21 running south along Siming Nan Lu terminate at a parking lot outside of the north entrance. Bus #2 from the western end of Zhongshan Lu stops at Xiada Bei Cun (夏大北村) on the western edge of the campus; on Yanwu Lu there is an entrance on your right.)*

HAINAN 海南

Hainan is China's dainty southern belle, the country's smallest, southernmost, and newest province. Part of Guangdong until it became a Special Economic Zone in 1988, Hainan province encompasses the isle of Hainan and the South China Sea archipelagos of Nansha (Spratly), Xisha (Paracel), and Zhongsha, although China's claim on all but Hainan is hotly disputed by a host of Southeast Asian neighbors. The rest of the islands may be reef beds that barely peek out from beneath the ocean's surface, but Hainan has some 1500km of something truly rare in China: beaches stretching as far as the eye can see. China's southernmost city of Sanya—so far south that the Chinese dub it "the end of the earth"—attracts Chinese tour groups galore with its promise of sandy bliss.

While about two-thirds of Hainan's residents are Han Chinese, the island is home to two large minority groups, the Li and the Miao, who collectively number over a million people. Many Li continue to live in the thatch-roofed, mud-walled cottages that dot the highlands around Tongza. The Miao (or Hmong) belong to the same ethnic group whose members blanket much of southern and southwestern China (see p. 608). With such a colorful collection of cultures and a brilliant stretch of coastline, Hainan Island is what some people call paradise.

HAIKOU 海口 ☎ 0898

Breezy, balmy Haikou is the unofficial gateway to Hainan. The port was originally established to provide ocean access to the ancient capital of Qiongshan, but Haikou outstripped its sister city soon after the area was opened to foreign trade under the Treaty of Tianjin in 1876. Most people pass through Haikou on their way to Sanya or Tongza, and few stay for very long. The happy-go-lucky tropical spirit that visitors from Hong Kong and Guangzhou find so soothing is tempered by a rash of crime. Prostitution and local gangs thrive, and tourists are often the target of pickpockets, especially along Haixiu Lu in Haikou's shopping district.

★ ⚡ ORIENTATION AND PRACTICAL INFORMATION

Haikou sits at the northern tip of Hainan Island, across the Qiongzhou Strait from Haian on the Leizhou peninsula in Guangdong province. **Haikou Park** (hǎikǒu gōngyuán; 海口公园) marks the central reference point in the city: from here, **Haixiu Lu** (海秀路) runs to the southwest; **Datong Lu** (大同路) runs to the northwest; **Haifu Dadao** (海府大道) runs to the southeast. One of the most important landmarks is the **Hainan International Commercial Center** (hǎinán guójì shāngyè dàshà; 海南国际商业大厦) on 38 Haixiu Lu, at Datong Lu.

Airplanes: Haikou International Airport (hǎikǒu guójì jīchǎng; 海口国际机场) southwest of the city. Free CAAC shuttle buses run between the CAAC office and the airport (every 30min. 5:30am-6:30pm); buses to the city from the airport wait outside the lower level of the airport terminal (30 min.; free with a plane ticket, Y15 without). Taxis cost about Y50; bargain to Y30. **CAAC ticket office,** 9 Haixiu Lu (☎670 3306), behind the International Commercial Center. Open daily 8am-10pm. To: **Beijing** (5-6 per day, Y1800); **Guangzhou** (16 per day, Y560); **Guilin** (2-3 per day, Y620); **Hong Kong** (2 per day, Y1150); **Shanghai** (4-5 per day, Y1300); and **Xian** (2-3 per day, Y1380).

Buses: Regular and long-distance buses run from **Haikou Bus Station** (hǎikǒu qìchē zǒngzhàn; 海口汽车总站), on Nanbao Lu, between Haixiu Dong Lu and Daying Lu. To: **Changsha** (60hr., 1 per day, Y252); **Fuzhou** (72hr., 1 per day, Y322); **Guangzhou** (10hr., 1 per day, Y202); and **Guilin** (10hr., 1 per day, Y192). The **East Bus Station** (qìchē dōng zhàn; 汽车东站), accessible by bus #217 heading toward the Five Figures Temple, has luxury buses to **Sanya** (3½hr., every 20min. 7am-11pm, Y71).

Boats: Haikou New Port (hǎikǒu xīn gǎng; 海口新港), north of the city center and accessible by bus #218. To: **Beihai** (12hr., 1 per day, Y43.5-50); **Haian** (1½hr., every hr. 6:30am-6:30pm, Y27.5-31.5); and **Zhanjiang** (3½hr., 2 per day, Y101). **Xiuying Haikou Port** (xiùyīng hǎikǒu gǎng; 秀英海口港), on Binhai Lu, is east of the city. The **ticket office,** 7 Haifu Dadao (☎535 1557), is across from the East Lake Hotel. Open

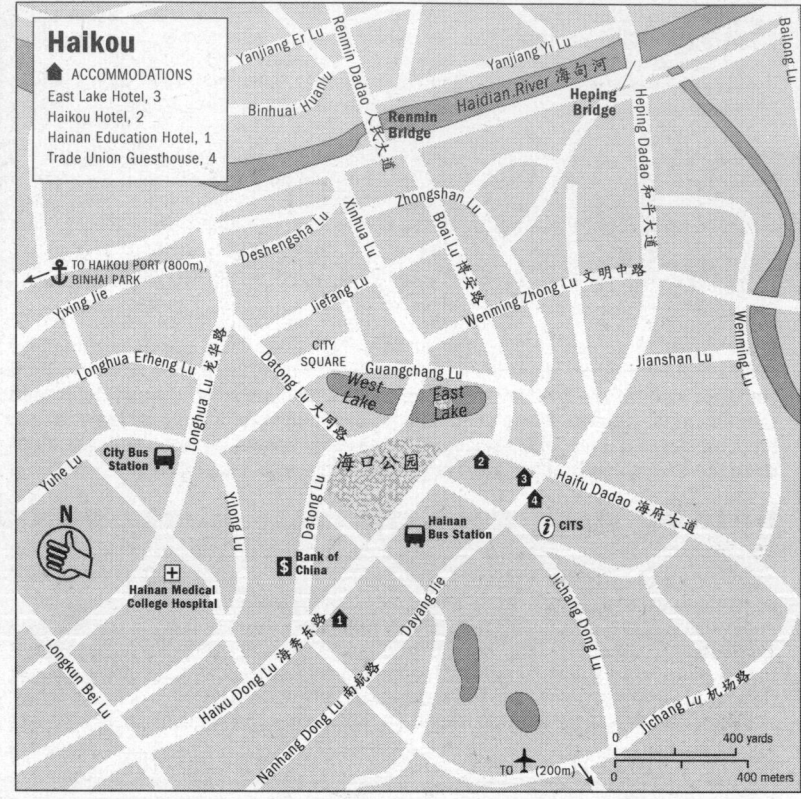

SOUTH COAST

Haikou

🏠 ACCOMMODATIONS
East Lake Hotel, 3
Haikou Hotel, 2
Hainan Education Hotel, 1
Trade Union Guesthouse, 4

daily 7am-5:30pm. To: **Guangzhou** (19hr.; M, W, and F; Y96-450); **Shenzhen** (20hr., Sa-Th, Y113-453); and other destinations similar to those served by Haikou New Port.

Local Transportation: Bus #217, a cross between a minibus and a full-sized bus, covers all tourist destinations, including CAAC, CITS, the main hotel strip, the International Commercial Center, and East Bus Station (Y2). **Bus #15** travels down Renmin Dadao, Heping Lu, and Haixiu Lu, before heading down Longkun Nan Lu (Y1).

Travel Agency: CITS, 8 Haifu Dadao (☎535 7999 or 537 9966), in front of the Donghu Hotel. Best for arranging Hainan Island tours, starting at Y180. Open daily 8am-10pm.

Bank of China: 33 Datong Lu (☎677 8001), in the International Commercial Center. Exchanges currency and traveler's checks and provides credit card advances. Open daily 8:30am-noon and 2:30-5pm.

Internet Access: The 2nd floor of the **Huabao Building** (huábǎo dàshà; 华宝大厦; ☎675 4802) has an Internet bar. Walk down Haixiu Lu toward Haikou Park until you see the Happy Tom Fast Food Restaurant on the right; the building is at the end of the alley adjoining it. Y12 per hr., Y5 initial fee. Open 24hr.

Post and Telecommunications: 28 Haifu Dadao (☎533 5840), in the China Telecom Building. Open daily 8am-7pm. **Postal Code:** 570203. A second branch, 46 Haixiu Lu, at Longkun Lu. Open daily 8am-6:30pm. **Postal Code:** 570206. EMS, IDD service, and Poste Restante available at both offices.

🏠 ACCOMMODATIONS

Budget accommodations in Haikou are scarce; bargain for cheaper rates, especially during the summer. Be careful not to exchange goods for services, though. Prostitution is rampant on Hainan, and hotel guests may receive repeated phone calls offering *sangna* (local terminology for a prostitute's services).

Hainan Education Hotel (hǎinán jiàoyuàn dàshà; 海南教苑大厦), 18 Haixiu Lu (☎677 2998), opposite the CAAC ticket office and the International Commercial Center. Rooms are shabby but clean. Doubles Y50, with bath and A/C Y140.

East Lake Hotel (dōnghú jiāfēng dàjiǔdiàn; 东湖嘉丰大酒店), 8 Haifu Dadao (☎535 3333), at Haixiu Lu, next to CITS. Fairly nice, with discounts possible. Singles and doubles Y550, off-season Y220; try bargaining to as low as Y160.

Trade Union Guesthouse (gōnghuì zhāodàisuǒ; 工会招待所), 2 Donghu Nan Lu (☎533 6125), about 50m into the alley to the left of the East Lake Hotel. A row of fruit and food stalls stretches right outside the hotel. Rooms have all standard amenities. Singles Y90; doubles Y120; triples Y150.

Haikou Hotel (hǎikǒu bīnguǎn; 海口宾馆), 4 Haifu Dadao (☎535 1234). Rooms are a bit overpriced, but there is a good Chinese restaurant and a decent Western cafe on-site. 60% off-season discount. Singles and doubles Y588. Credit cards accepted.

FOOD

Haikou's streets are lined with vendors selling mangos, coconuts, bananas, and other tropical delights. **Yilong Lu** (义龙路), parallel to Haixiu Lu, near Longkun Lu, has a market filled with rows of colorful fruit. Surprisingly, seafood does not dominate the local cuisine, and Hainan has few local specialties to distinguish it from mainland destinations.

Kuaihuolin Delicious Food Town (kuàihuólín měi fàn chéng; 快活林美饭城), 2 Jichang Lu (☎678 1645), off Haixiu Lu. A smorgasbord of Chinese cuisine, with Cantonese dim sum breakfast, Taiwanese food stand favorites, and local flavors. Noodle dishes Y3-8; set meals Y15. Open daily 7am-2am.

Greenfield Restaurant (tián yuán cāntīng; 田园餐厅), International Commercial Center, 38 Haixiu Lu, 1st. Fl. (☎679 6999). Enjoy sandwiches and drinks (Y16 and up) and set meals (Y25-52)—including a wonderful set curry meal (Y25)—in this congenial, relaxed setting. English menu. Open daily 7am-10:30pm.

Haikou Hotel Coffee Shop (hǎikǒu bīnguǎn xī cāntīng; 海口宾馆西餐厅), in the Haikou Hotel. Good Chinese and Western breakfast set meals for Y30, with a selection of coffee, sandwiches, and snacks available later in the day. Open daily 8am-midnight.

FRUITFUL HAINAN   Hainan Island, in all its tropical splendor, is home to many succulent and delicious fruits. Next time you're at a fruit stand, overlook the usual fruits like pineapples and bananas in favor of something more special.

One favorite is **sugarcane** (gān zhè; 甘蔗), a snack with the appeal of beef jerky; you'll have to gnaw at it for some time. Vendors cut its long stalks into sections about a foot long and shave off the dry brown covering with a machete. Hold the golden baton and chew away, but make sure you're in a place where you can spit out the sawdust remains after sucking out all the sugary juice.

The **lychee** (lìzhī; 荔枝), native to southern China, has been praised by successive generations of emperors for its sweetness. The bumpy reddish-brown skin peels away to reveal a translucent white fruit that many say is best eaten chilled. Lychees are sold in strands, and can be popped in the mouth one after another like grapes. The **Dragon Eye** (lóngyǎn; 龙眼), named after its shape, is a brownish ball the size of a nickel and tastes somewhat like the lychee. Another variation of lychee-like fruit is the **Hong Mao Dan** (hóng máo dān; 红毛丹), possibly the ugliest edible displayed on the fruit stand. Don't shy away—the red shiny shell that makes the whole thing look like an electrocuted mouse actually hides a tender and succulent inside.

In Chinese culture, a gift of mangoes has long been symbolic gesture of love and goodwill. The **Chicken Egg Mango** (jīdàn mángguǒ; 鸡蛋忙果) is the size of a kiwi, colored dull beige like a chicken egg, and found only on Hainan Island. Great demand for this fruit means that supplies last only two months after its harvest in late March and April; a chance to sample this mango's sweet-and-sour texture is a rare treat.

👁 SIGHTS

Despite the city's picturesque surroundings, there is little to see or do in Haikou. The two sights of interest, **Five Figures Temple** and **Hai Rui's Tomb**, are accessible by bus #217 from the city center.

FIVE FIGURES TEMPLE (wǔ gōng sì; 五公寺). Erected in 1889 to commemorate five Tang and Song dynasty officials who were banished to Hainan Island, this temple houses lifelike stone sculptures of these gentlemen. Exiled to paradise? Perhaps. The temple and halls are famous for the exquisite architecture, and the grounds are beautifully manicured. Some high-quality and high-priced calligraphy and art shops are in the exhibition hall. *(Open daily 7:30am-6:30pm. Y5.)*

HAI RUI'S TOMB (hǎi ruì mù; 海瑞墓). Local Hainan boy Hai Rui (1514-1587), revered as an honest and well-loved Ming statesman, is interred here. A famous play by contemporary writer Wu Han about Hai Rui's dismissal by a tyrannical emperor provoked the wrath of Mao Zedong, who saw allegorical parallels to his own purges (see **Cultural Revolution,** p. 19). The Chairman unleashed the nation's youth to purge "corrupting elements" from Chinese culture and consequently the tomb was a prime target for the Red Guards during the Cultural Revolution. Now restored, the tomb is displayed with its original stone tablets. The park grounds resemble Guilin's karst formations. *(On Hairui Lu. Take bus #217 to Fucheng; a motorcab or motorcycle from here to the tomb costs Y2-4. Open daily 8am-6pm. Y5.)*

OTHER SIGHTS. The now dormant volcano that created Hainan Island is about 2km southwest of town. Trek up the volcano and descend into its massive mouth, now certainly more green and inviting than when it was spewing lava and ash. *(Not accessible by public transportation, so bargain with a taxi driver; Y150 is reasonable. Y35.)*

SANYA 三亚   ☎ 0899

Sanya is known as the "Hawaii of the Orient," and the moniker is appropriate. Fringed by kilometer after kilometer of sublime white sand that fades into crystal-clear turquoise ocean, it is a top tourist destination. Many visitors come to bask in sunny weather (even in the dead of January) as they listen to the pitter-patter of coconuts falling from palm trees. All the trappings of resort living are here: golf courses, tennis courts, saunas, and swimming pools, not to mention scuba diving, deep sea fishing, windsurfing, and parasailing—and the high prices that come with them. Try hard enough, though, and you can escape—or ignore—the sun-seeking crowds and enjoy poor man's pleasures like snorkeling and swimming. Sanya just might be the perfect place to sink your toes into some toasty white sand, kick back, and kowtow to the sun.

✈ ℹ ORIENTATION AND PRACTICAL INFORMATION

Sanya is divided into two main sections: **Sanya City** (三亚市) and **Dadonghai** (大东海), the beach resort area just east of the city. **Yuya Dadao** (榆亚大道) runs from Dadonghai across the bridge, where it turns into **Gangmen Lu** (港门路) and finally veers right to the main thoroughfare of Sanya City, **Jiefang Lu** (解放路), which runs all the way out to Sanya Airport.

Airplanes: Sanya Phoenix International Airport (sānyà fènghuáng guójì jīchǎng; 三亚凤凰国际机场), is on Jiefang Xi Lu, 16km northwest of town. **CAAC ticket office** (☎821 4646) is off Yuya Lu, across from the Hawaii Hotel. Open daily 7:30am-11pm. To: **Beijing** (1-2 per day, Y1850); **Guangzhou** (2-3 per day, Y640); **Haikou** (1 per day, Y100); **Hong Kong** (2 per day, Y1150-1440); and **Shanghai** (1 per day, Y1510).

Buses: Sanya Bus Station (sānyà qìchē zhàn; 三亚汽车站; ☎827 2440), on Jiefang Lu. Take minibus #2 from Dadonghai or bus #2 or 4 from Sanya City in the direction of the airport; the station is on the left. To: **Haikou** (5hr., 2-3 per day, Y41); **Lingshui** (1½hr., every 20min. 7:10am-6:40pm, Y12); and **Tongza** (2½hr., every 30min. 6:40am-5:30pm, Y13).

Local Transportation: Minibuses regularly run from Dadonghai to Sanya City. They are not always numbered, but always post the destination in the front. Fare Y1.

Travel Agency: CYTS (zhōngguó qīngnián lǚxíngshè; 中国青年旅行社; ☎821 4688), Jinling Holiday Resort, 2nd Fl., off Luling Lu, Dadonghai. Open daily 8am-9pm.

Bank of China: 31 Yuya Lu, Dadonghai, across from Southern Chinese Hotel. Exchanges traveler's checks and issues credit card advances. Open daily 8:30am-5:30pm. A branch at 7 Jiefang Lu, opposite the Sanya Hotel, is open daily 8am-5:30pm.

Internet Access: Computer World (wànxiáng diànnǎo; 万翔电脑), 7 Xinjian Lu (☎827 7130), opposite the post office. Y10 per hr. Open daily 8:30am-10pm.

Post Office: 8 Xinjian Lu (☎827 2143). Take a minibus into Sanya City and get off at the beginning of Jiefang Lu; Xinjian Lu is on the left. EMS and Poste Restante available. Open daily 7:30am-7:30pm. **Postal Code:** 572001.

ACCOMMODATIONS

Even in China, beachfront property doesn't come cheap. Hotels in Sanya are almost exclusively budget-busting luxury resorts. Although there are places to stay in Sanya City, the lodgings in Dadonghai put you within spitting distance of Sanya's raison d'être: the beach. Sand and surf in a more isolated setting at Yalong Bay may cost you more than the budget of a small country, but it is the only way to escape the droves of tourists at Dadonghai. Peak season (Nov.-Feb.) and off season (Mar.-Oct.) rates are indicated for the places listed below.

Seaside Holiday Inn (bīnhǎi dùjià cūn; 滨海渡假村; ☎821 3898), off Haihua Lu on the first road to your left, Dadonghai. This hotel has clean, spacious, breezy rooms with all standard amenities. Singles and doubles Y260, off-season Y160.

Hawaii Hotel (xiàwēiyí dàjiǔdiàn; 夏威夷大酒店; ☎821 3666), at the corner of Yuya Lu and Haihua Lu, Dadonghai. More upscale than the Seaside—the prices show it. 50% off-season discount. Singles Y488; doubles Y568; triples Y658.

Hainan Sanya Hotel (hǎinán sānyà bīnguǎn; 海南三亚宾馆), 2 Jiefang Lu (☎827 4819), in Sanya City. Minibus #2 to the beach stops in front of the hotel. Well kept, spacious, and almost affordable. 50% off-season discount. Singles Y130; doubles Y180; triples Y240; quads Y300; quints Y580.

Mountain Water Hotel (shān shuǐ bīnguǎn; 山水宾馆), 13 Hedong Lu (☎826 0554), past Ganghua Jie. Some rooms have a great view of the tranquil Sanya River. 60% off-season discount. Singles and doubles Y330; triples Y408.

FOOD

Sanya is justifiably famous for its seafood. **Yuya Dadao, Luling Lu, and Gangmen Lu** are lined with small restaurants serving up denizens of the deep (but not for cheap!), including Hainan specialties like **Hele crab.** Seafood is typically sold by weight; the standard unit of measurement is the *jin* (斤), about half a kilogram.

The less culinarily adventurous can always turn to hotel restaurants, many of which have English-language menus. The **Seaside Holiday Inn Western Restaurant** (bīnhǎi dùjià cūn xī cāntīng; 滨海渡假村西餐厅) offers a mixture of Chinese and Western dishes, from fried noodles to crepes (Y10-20).

Northeast Porridge King (dōngběi zhōu wáng; 东北粥王), 3 Hedong Lu (☎826 3684). This shop makes even a bland thing like porridge sexy—if you don't like one kind, try one of the 14 other varieties. The all-you-can-eat buffet (Y12) makes this breakfast dish an all-day treat. Porridge-haters, don't despair: *baozi, jiaozi,* and vegetable dishes abound. Open daily 9am-9pm.

Donghai Seafood Restaurant (dōnghǎi yú cūn; 东海鱼村; ☎821 3148), right behind the Jinling Holiday Resort, Dadonghai. This open-air restaurant on the beachfront is the perfect place to enjoy the sunset and the balmy breeze. Serves a variety of lobster, fish, and crab (Y30 and up). Open daily 11am-2pm and 6-11:30pm.

Hailai Seafood Restaurant (hǎilái hǎixiān chéng; 海来海鲜城; ☎821 0987), behind the Hawaii Hotel, Dadonghai. Meet and greet your dinner, with 5-6 different species of crab, clams, and even sea cucumbers. Open daily 11am-2am.

Nanshan Hotpot City (nánshān huǒguō chéng; 南山火锅城; ☎825 3265), on Hexi Lu near Yuejin Lu. People come here to warm up with lamb hotpot (Y20)—a local specialty—and the lively nighttime atmosphere. Hotpots Y30-60. Open daily 9am-9pm.

SIGHTS

The non-sandy parts of Sanya are an afterthought for most visitors. **Luhuitou Park** ("Deer Turning Its Head Park"; lù huí tóu gōngyuán; 鹿回头公园), near the intersection of Yuya Lu and Luling Lu, is named after a legend. A young Li boy was chasing a deer when it turned and looked at him; it then metamorphosed into a young girl and the couple fell in love. The walk to the top takes about 30 minutes. Atop the mountain abutting Dadonghai is a statue of the young girl emerging from the deer. The statue itself is not terribly interesting, but the views from the mountain are spectacular, especially at sunset or at night, when the city lights twinkle beneath you. *(Open daily 7am-10pm. Y23.5.)*

BEACHES

Water sports and sunbathing are the order of the day in Sanya.

ASIAN DRAGON BAY (yà lóng wān; 亚龙湾). The beach here is 7km of glistening, alabaster wonderland. The **Hainan Asian Dragon Bay Underwater World** (hǎinán yàlóng wān hǎidǐ shìjiè; 海南亚龙湾海底世界) offers a variety of activities, including parasailing (Y160 per 5min.), deep-sea fishing (Y300 per hr.), boating (Y170 per 30min.), and scuba diving (Y350 per trip). There is also an underwater excursion in a submerged viewing deck. *(☎827 3400. Open daily 8:30am-4:30pm.)* The beach itself is extraordinary, and the best option is just to wander off until the crowds get thin. *(4.5km east of Sanya. Board a bus or minibus (Y2) anywhere along Yuya Dadao heading to Tiandu (出独), getting off at Asian Dragon Bay. The bus stop is at the beginning of the long road to the water; a motorcar costs Y5-10. Free.)*

DADONGHAI (dàdōnghǎi; 大东海). Dadonghai's 3km of angel dust may not be Sanya's best beach, but it is undoubtedly its most crowded and convenient. Water sports are cheaper here than at Asian Dragon Bay; try bargaining down to Y200 for a scuba diving trip. *(3km southeast of Sanya. Accessible by numerous minibuses (Y1) that ply the route between the beach and the city. Free.)*

TIANYA CORNER (tiānyá hǎijiǎo; 天涯海角). Take out your wallet. See that Y2 note? Now look up. Dubbed the "End of the Earth and Corner of the Sea," the southernmost point of China is a popular destination for tourists who come to have their pictures taken at the same spot that appears on the back of the Y2 note. It's not the best beach around, but it makes a pleasant excursion outside the city limits. *(30km west of Sanya. Take a bus or minibus from the western part of Jiefang Lu. Y46.5.)*

DAYTRIP FROM SANYA: XINCUN AND MONKEY ISLAND

*About 62km northeast of Sanya City. **Minibuses** from the Sanya Bus Station to Lingshui deposit travelers to Xincun at a fork in the road 3km from town. Jump on a sidecar (Y3) for the ride along Xincun's main road, Zhongshan Lu, to the waterfront. **Buses** returning from Lingshui to Sanya (every 30min. until 6pm) stop right outside Xincun. From the Xincun waterfront, **motorboats** (5min., Y20) wind through the maze of houseboats linked by precarious boardwalks, dropping visitors at the beginning of a 2km road to the Visitors Center, accessible by foot or on a **motorcab** (Y5). A **cable car** (8am-5pm; one-way Y28, round-trip Y68, including admission) from the Xincun waterfront takes people directly to the Visitors Center on Monkey Island. Open daily 8am-5pm. Y20.*

Xincun (新村) provides access to nearby South Bay Monkey Island (nán wān hóu dǎo; 南湾猴岛), which is actually a small peninsula jutting out into the ocean. The town itself is populated by the Hakka and Danjia minorities, many of whom earn their living from fishing and pearl cultivation; the nets and posts marking each family's pearl farm and fishery are clearly visible. However, furry creatures are Xincun's main tourist draw, a situation that allows some monkey business.

On this small green crag live over 3000 wild macaques, personable golden-brown monkeys with red behinds. Legend has it that during the Tang dynasty, a plague left residents of this seaside port blind and near death. Local hero Yanan set sail in search of the black pearls that provided the cure, but the young boy was shipwrecked during a fierce storm. A group of compassionate fairy monkeys saved him and returned with the boy and the black pearls, saving the town and finding a new home, which the grateful villagers vowed to protect forever. Legend is strangely silent on how the monkeys' rumps turned crimson.

Folklore aside, Monkey Island offers a great chance to see these wild animals up close. Visitors can buy a pack of peanuts (Y10) and watch monkeys frolic around their feet, or undertake the 30-minute climb to the highest point on the island for an impressive view of the surrounding countryside.

TONGZA 通什   ☎ 0899

Tongza (often pronounced Tongshi), a small, laid-back Li and Miao autonomous prefectural seat, is best known for its museum. Aside from this attraction, the city rarely belies its ethnic heritage; to fully appreciate Tongza's hidden treasures, one needs to patiently search below the surface of the minority villages that dot the surrounding countryside.

■■▓ ORIENTATION AND PRACTICAL INFORMATION. Tongza is divided into two parts by the **Nansheng River** (nánshèng hé; 南圣河), with the downtown area on one side and the museum and bus station on the other. **Haiyu Lu** (海榆路) is shaped like a "T," with one branch splayed across the bridge over the river and the other running past the bus station and museum, in the direction of Haikou.

The **Tongza Bus Station** (tōngzā qìchē zhàn; 通什汽车站) is on Haiyu Bei Lu. Cross the bridge, go around the traffic circle, and turn left; the station is 50m ahead on the right. To: Haikou (luxury buses: 4hr., 4 per day, Y40; regular buses: 5½hr., every 30min.-1½hr. 5:30am-2:30pm, Y30); Lingshui (2hr., 3 per day, Y12.5); and Sanya (2hr., every 30min. 6:30am-5:30pm, Y12). The **Bank of China,** 8 Jiefang Lu, near Xinhua Lu, exchanges traveler's checks and offers credit card advances. (☎ 662 3642. Open daily 8am-6:30pm.) The **China Telecom Internet Bar** (zhōngguó diànxìn yīntèwǎng bā; 中国电信因特网吧), at the end of Xinhua Lu just before the river, offers access for Y6 per hour. (☎ 662 7773. Open M-F 9am-11:30pm, Sa-Su 8:30am-11:30pm.) The **post office** at the intersection of Haiyu Nan Lu and Hebei Xi Lu also provides IDD service. (Open daily 7:30am-8pm.) The **postal code** is 572200.

▛▞ ACCOMMODATIONS AND FOOD. Tongza has few accommodations and restaurants, but those that do exist are cheap and relatively clean. The best budget accommodations are south of the river. The **City Supply and Marketing Hostel** (shì gōngxiāo zhāodàisuǒ; 市供销招待所), 21 Hongqi Lu, in the alley across from the Industrial and Commercial Bank of China, is steps away from the market. (☎ 662 2457. Singles Y15; doubles Y15; triples Y20; quads Y24.) The **Feicui Hotel** (fěicuì bīn-guǎn; 翡翠宾馆), 1 Hongqi Lu, at Xinhua Lu south of the river, is clean and well kept. All rooms but the dorms have attached bath. (☎ 662 3125. Dorms Y20-30; singles Y40, with A/C Y120; doubles Y55/160; triples Y65.)

Tongza's best eateries are the outdoor restaurants near the bus station (dishes Y3-8). Li foods such as **bamboo-steamed rice** and **rice wine** are served in some of the minority restaurants in the Li villages surrounding Tongza.

▓ SIGHTS. The main sight in Tongza is the **Hainan Province Minority Nationalities Museum** (hǎinán shěng mínzú bówùguǎn; 海南省民族博物馆), directly past the bus station if you are heading north from the town center. Turn right at the sign and climb up a steep hill, following the signs. The museum has an interesting collection of minority tools, exceptional handwoven tapestries, and descriptions of Li and Miao festivals, although its most beautiful part is probably the view of the surrounding countryside. (☎ 662 2336. Open daily 8am-5:30pm. Y15.) **Qiongzhou University** (qióngzhōu dàxué; 琼州大学) is a fine example of traditional Li architecture. As you exit the museum, head down toward the bus station; the structure is on the right. The Li village of **Lizhai** (lízhài; 黎寨), on Haiyu Nan Lu 3km outside of Tongza, contains numerous traditional boot-shaped houses with pyramidal huts. *(Accessible by motorcab, Y3.)*

THE SOUTHWEST

China's southwest is a region with diversity to spare. Encompassing some of the country's richest land and some of its poorest, the landscape varies from the shivering Tibetan highlands in northwestern Yunnan to the limestone pinnacles of Guangxi to the steamy jungles of Xishuangbanna. Guangxi, Yunnan, and Guizhou provinces are blanketed with a colorful patchwork of least three dozen ethnic groups (see also **Southwestern Minorities,** p. 24), including the **Bai** (see p. 561), **Dai** (see p. 584), **Dong** (see p. 610), **Miao** (see p. 608), and **Naxi** (see p. 565). Some are almost completely assimilated with the Han. Others, aware of the revenue to be had from cultural tourism, are marketed to visitors in contrived settings, uncharitably dubbed "ethnic circuses" or "human zoos." Still others live traditional lives in isolated locales and are stunned to discover travelers' interest in their lifestyles.

The government's apparent tolerance of minority peoples today hides a long history of discrimination and forced sinicization. Far from China's ancient capitals, the region was long dismissed by rulers as the home of fractious "southern barbarians." A closer peek at the history of the southwest reveals the cultural dynamism that resulted when the Miao-Yao peoples, originally from the Yangzi region, interacted with Tibetans from the west, the Burmese, Thai, Khmer, and Vietnamese from the south, and even Hui Muslim traders, lured by the promise of riches from the silk and spice trade along the ancient Southern Silk Road.

Caravans of elephants and peppers no longer wend their way along the well-trodden roads of the southwest, but lots of tourists do. Amid idyllic landscapes of rice paddies, rushing streams, it seems that little could ever go wrong. Even the ugliest socialist concrete-block cities are stunned to find themselves amid breathtaking scenery and rowdy backpacker enclaves like Dali and Yangshuo, a rare blitz of banana pancakes, espresso, and English speakers silenced by the beauty around them.

HIGHLIGHTS OF THE SOUTHWEST

TROPICAL TREKKING between **Xishuangbanna**'s (p. 584) minority villages.

KARST CRUISES near **Guilin** (p. 531) and its backpacker-friendly alter-ego, **Yangshuo** (p. 536).

MOUNTAINS AND MOCHA in **Dali** (p. 557), a hopping backpacker mecca.

PADDY-HOPPING and market-shopping around off-the-beaten-path Miao and Dong villages near **Kaili** (p. 604).

FOOD, FOLKS, AND FUN in **Kunming** (p. 545), the congenial "city of eternal spring."

GUANGXI 广西

To the Chinese, the name "Guangxi" is almost synonymous with the term "karst rock formation." The distinctive limestone pinnacles, arches, bridges, and caverns are the big tourist draws in Guilin and nearby Yangshuo. Over and above bizarrely shaped rocks, Guangxi's topography also has its share of terraced rice fields, misty mountains, and even a seaside resort or two. Much of the area's character derives from its diverse peoples, ranging from the Zhuang, who are almost indistinguishable from the Han, to minorities such as the Yao and the Miao, who still wear traditional dress in villages tucked away from mainstream tourist eyes. In recognition of the Zhuang people, the largest minority group in the region, Guangxi province became the Zhuang Autonomous Region of Guangxi in 1958. Presently, cities like Guilin, Yangshuo, and the provincial capital of Nanning are pockets of affluence amid the continued impoverishment of the Guangxi countryside. Given the stark urban-rural economic divide, the striking serenity of the karst rock formations and apparent contentment of Guangxi's minority peoples tell only half the story.

NANNING 南宁 · ☎0771

Tucked away on China's southern fringe, a few hundred kilometers from the Vietnamese border, Nanning is a city that travelers have few reasons to visit but even fewer reasons not to like. An insignificant market town just a century ago, Nanning has ridden a wave of foreign influences and national regimes into modernity. When foreign trade was allowed into the city in 1907, the city flowered so quickly that it became too big for its britches and spilled past the old city walls. From 1912 to 1936 it beat out big, bad Guilin as the capital of Guangxi province, and was transformed by warlord Li Zongren into a modern, spacious city. During WWII it oscillated between being occupied by the Japanese and serving as a US air base supplying Chinese resistance forces. In the decades following the war, Nanning provided supplies and military support to the Vietnamese in their struggle against the French, and later, the Americans. Despite all these changing allegiances, Nanning has always remained true to one goal: to be a contender in China's rat race to prosperity and modernity. It has frantically built rail connections to Vietnam (via Pingxiang), the coast (via Fengchang), central China (via Guilin, Hengyang, and points north), and, most recently, Kunming. A plucky, can-do kind of city, Nanning regained its status as provincial capital of Guangxi province in 1949, and still heads the re-named Zhuang Autonomous Region of Guangxi. Nanning today is fresh-faced, subtropical, and about as modern as cities come in southern China.

▛ TRANSPORTATION

Airplanes: CAAC ticket office, 82 Chaoyang Lu (☎243 1459; 24hr. ☎242 8418), about a 10min. walk from the train station on the left, next to the Yinhe Hotel. The center also sells tickets for the **bus** from the center to the airport (45min., making the trip starting 3 hours before each departure, Y15). Buses from the arrival terminal leave for Nanning (approx. every 30min. 7:30am-7pm, Y15). Taxis to the airport cost Y80 and up. To: **Beijing** (1-2 per day, Y1640); **Chengdu** (1 per day, Y710); **Guangzhou** (3 per day, Y580); **Guilin** (Su-M and F, Y460); **Hong Kong** (Tu, F, and Su, Y1080); **Kunming** (2-3 per day, Y500); and **Shanghai** (1 per day, Y1330). Nanning also has twice weekly connections to **Hanoi, Vietnam** (M and Th, Y890).

Trains: Nanning Train Station (nánníng huŏchē zhàn; 南宁火车站; ☎243 2468), is at the northern end of Chaoyang Lu. Open 24hr. To: **Beihai** (4hr., 2 per day, Y20); **Beijing** (33hr., 2 per day, Y487); **Changsha** (15hr., 1 per day, Y229); **Guangzhou** (17hr., 2 per day, Y252); **Guilin** (7hr., 3 per day, Y63); **Kunming** (19hr., 3 per day, Y195); **Shanghai** (36hr., 1 per day, Y399); and **Xian** (36hr., 1 per day, Y267). There are direct train links to **Fangcheng** (5hr., 1 per day, Y10) and **Pingxiang** (4hr., 2 per day, Y13), two cities on the Vietnam border.

Buses: Nanning Bus Station (nánníng qìchē zhàn; 南宁汽车站), 80 Chaoyang Lu (☎243 7420), about 10 stores past the CAAC ticket office, on the same side of the street. Ticket office open daily 5:30am-10pm. To: **Beihai** (3hr., every hr. 7:30am-6pm, Y50); **Guangzhou** (14hr., 8 per day, Y180); **Guilin** (6½hr., every hr. 8am-7pm, Y80); and **Wuzhou** (7hr., 4 per day, Y80). Buses also go to **Fangcheng** (2½hr., 8 per day, Y30) and **Pingxiang** (5hr., 2 per day, Y45) on the Vietnamese border. Buses depart from the **Bus Transport Center** on Youai Nan Lu to **Wuming** (every 10-15min., Y5) and other local destinations.

Local Transportation: Several **buses** travel the main drag of Chaoyang Lu, including buses **#6** and **10**. Bus #6 also travels across Minzu Dadao, while bus #10 heads farther south down Taoyuan Lu, passing Nanhu Lake on its way to the base of the Blue Mountain Scenic Area. Bus **#13** begins west and cuts through Renmin Xi Lu and Minzhu Lu, heading south down the town center's Xinmin Lu and finally to Qixiu Lu. Bus **#21** heads from the train station down Chaoyang Lu and then across the river. Bus **#23** also makes the trek south down Baisha Dadao and Nan Lu, first cutting across Chaoyang Square through Minzhu Lu and Gucheng Lu. **Minibuses** from Chaoyang Square go directly to destinations such as Nanhu Park and the Blue Mountain Scenic Area.

Taxis: Base fare Y6. **Pedicab** rides average Y4-5.

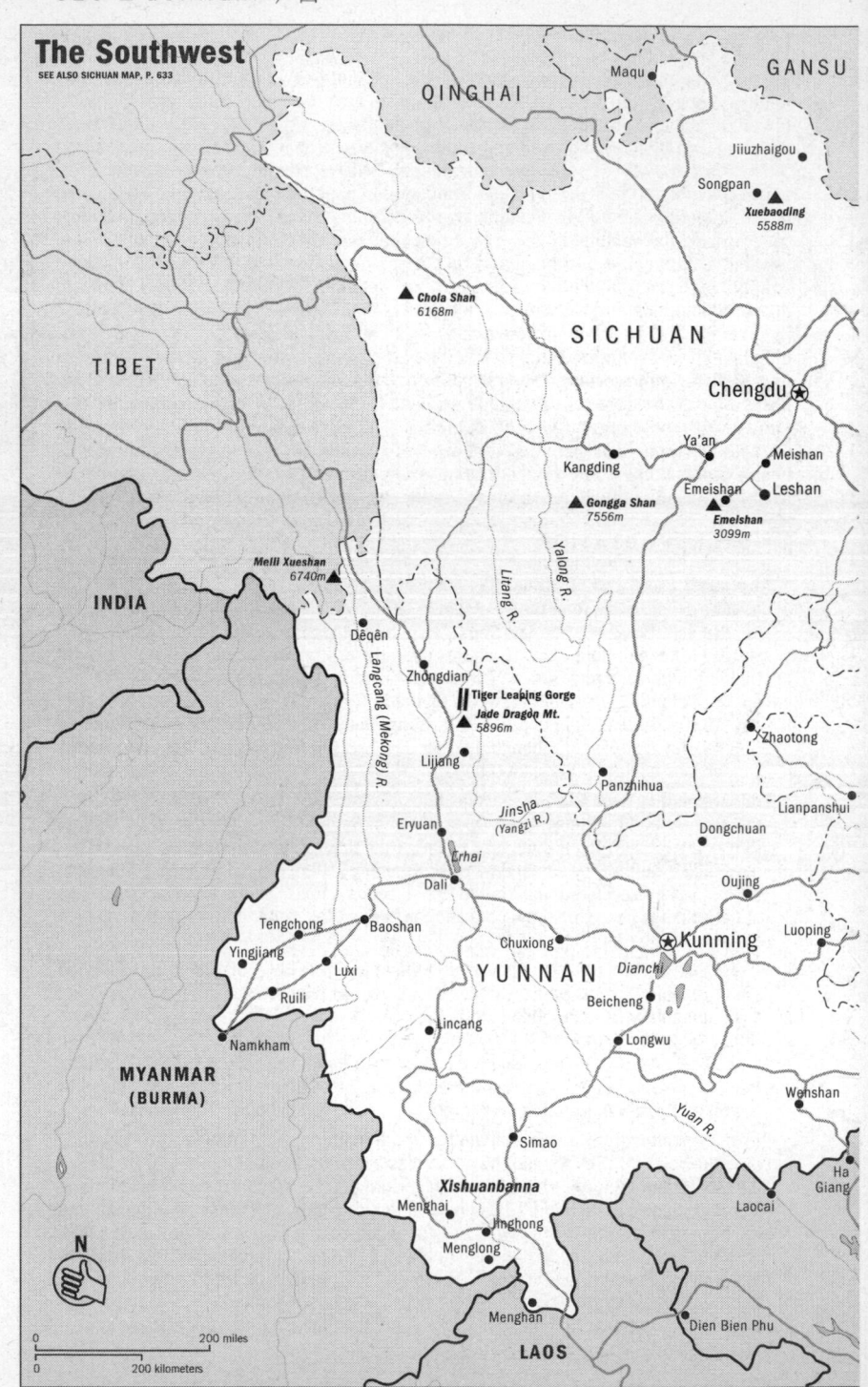

The Southwest
SEE ALSO SICHUAN MAP, P. 633

QINGHAI

GANSU

Maqu

Jiuzhaigou

Songpan

▲ Xuebaoding
5588m

▲ Chola Shan
6168m

SICHUAN

TIBET

Chengdu ◉

Ya'an

Meishan

Kangding

Emeishan

Leshan

▲ Gongga Shan
7556m

▲ Emeishan
3099m

Meili Xueshan
6740m ▲

INDIA

Dêqên

Langcang (Mekong) R.

Litang R.

Yalong R.

Zhongdian

Tiger Leaping Gorge

Jade Dragon Mt.
5896m

Zhaotong

Lijiang

Panzhihua

Lianpanshui

Eryuan

Jinsha
(Yangzi R.)

Dongchuan

Erhai

Dali

Oujing

Luoping

Tengchong

Baoshan

Chuxiong

Kunming ◉

Yingjiang

Luxi

YUNNAN

Dianchi

Ruili

Beicheng

Namkham

Lincang

Longwu

MYANMAR
(BURMA)

Wenshan

Yuan R.

Simao

Ha
Giang

Xishuanbanna

Laocai

Menghai

Jinghong

Menglong

N

Menghan

Dien Bien Phu

LAOS

0   200 miles

0   200 kilometers

⚓ 🔁 ORIENTATION AND PRACTICAL INFORMATION

Nanning's railroad tracks slice the city in half, and there are definitely right and wrong sides of the tracks. The north, especially toward the northeast, is the underbelly of Nanning, with roads full of potholes, shantytowns, and gun-toting Chinese soldiers completing military maneuvers. The southern half of the city, however, presents a bustling picture of commercial affluence; stores burst with gleaming imported goods, and new office buildings scream prosperity. The central part of Nanning's southern half is bound by the railroad to the north and east, by department store-studded **Chaoyang Lu** (朝阳路) to the west, and by broad, highway-like **Minzu Dadao** (民族大道) to the south.

Travel Agency: CITS, 40 Xinmin Lu (☎262 4736 or 282 2514), offers great suggestions for visiting local tourist sites. Vietnam visas take 10 working days and cost Y650; get one in Beijing, Hong Kong, or Bangkok if possible. Open daily 8am-noon and 3-6pm.

Bank of China: 45 Minzu Dadao (☎283 0419), just beyond Chaoyang Lu. Exchanges traveler's checks and issues credit card advances. Open M-F 8:30am-noon and 2:30-5:30pm; in winter 8:30am-noon and 2:30-5pm.

PSB: 67 Donghe Lu, near Minzu Dadao. The **Foreign Affairs Department** (wàishì chù; 外事处) is to the left of the main entrance. Open M-F 8am-noon and 2:30-6pm.

Hospital: People's Municipal Hospital (rénmín shì yī yīyuàn; 人民市一医院), 89 Qixin Lu (☎280 4290).

Department Stores: The area around the intersection of **Chaoyang Lu** and **Minzu Dadao** is known for its high concentration of boutiques and department stores. Specifically, **Nanning Department Store** (nánníng bǎihuò dàlóu; 南宁百货大楼)—the new one, not the old one—stands proudly on Chaoyang Lu at the intersection with Xinhua Lu. Don't be fooled by the same-name game; choose the brightly lit, air-conditioned building. Basement grocery store with Western products. Both department stores open around 9am and close around 9:30pm.

Bookstore: Xinhua Bookstore (xīnhuá shūchéng; 新华书城), 15 Xinhua Lu, has a large English-language section on the 4th floor. Open daily 9am-9:30pm.

Internet Access: Nanning Department Store (see Department Stores, p. 528) on the 7th floor of the new store. Y8 per hr. Open daily 9am-9:30pm. The **China Telecom** Internet bar is on the 5th floor of the same building. Y10 per hour. Open daily 9am-9:30pm.

Post Office: On the corner of Xinmin Lu and Minzu Lu. EMS, IDD, and Poste Restante available. Open daily 8am-10pm. There is a smaller branch office in front of the train station. **Postal Code:** 530012.

⚑ ACCOMMODATIONS

Except those visitors who are in transit to Vietnam, few foreigners actually spend the night in Nanning. Budget options are fairly limited—check out Chaoyang Lu near the train station. Bargaining is a must in Nanning. With skill and a little luck, you might even end up staying in a four-star hotel for half the price.

Yingbin Hotel (yíngbīn fàndiàn; 迎宾饭店), 71 Chaoyang Lu (☎241 2299), across the street and to the right when you exit the train station. Rooms aren't exactly luxurious, but they'll do. All but the dorm rooms have attached bath. 4-bed dorms Y30; 3-bed dorms Y35; 2-bed dorms Y40. Singles Y80, with A/C Y100; doubles Y80, with A/C Y120; triples with A/C and bath Y150.

Phoenix Hotel (fēnghuáng bīnguǎn; 凤凰宾馆), 63 Chaoyang Lu (☎243 9833; fax 243 9309). Rooms in the South building are a bit run-down, but they come with all the standard amenities. Singles and doubles Y80; triples Y128.

Yinhe Hotel (yínhé jiǔdiàn; 银河酒店), 84 Chaoyang Lu (☎243 8223), near the station. This hotel appears to be making a conscious attempt to become upscale (i.e., a Western-style coffee shop in the lobby). Singles Y250-280; doubles Y380; triples Y300.

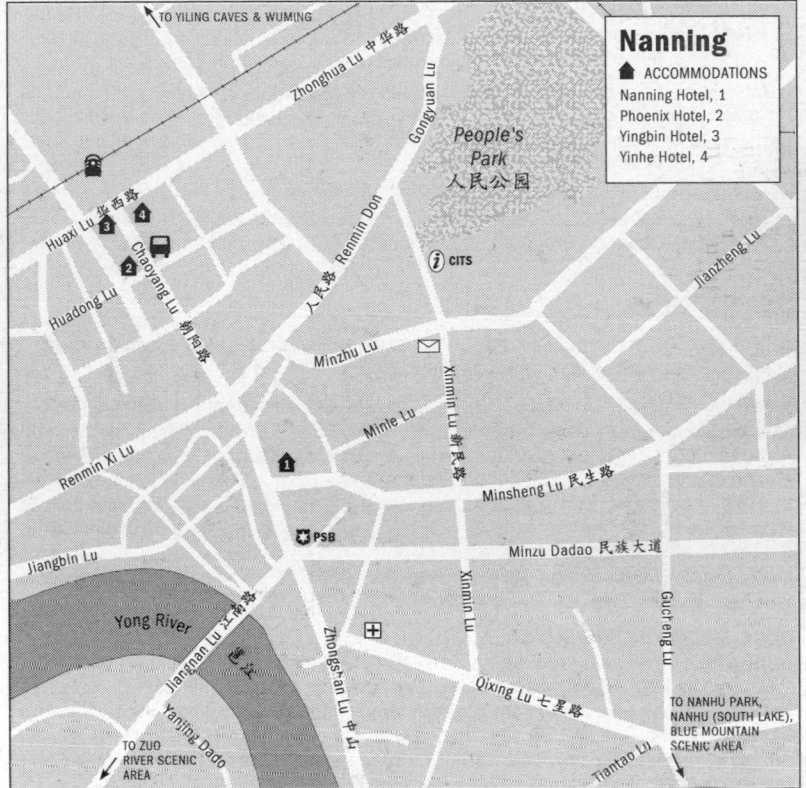

Nanning Hotel (nánníng fàndiàn; 南宁饭店), 36 Minsheng Lu (☎261 8138), off Chaoyang Lu, in the middle of the city's entertainment and commercial areas. The rooms in the East building are cheaper. Singles Y265; doubles Y250; triples Y195.

🍴🎵 FOOD AND ENTERTAINMENT

Nanning is not a culinary powerhouse. It is, however, a hot spot of sorts—and by spot we mean the "Spot" that was your childhood dog. **Guangxi dog hotpot** rules Nanning's culinary world, and the area south of Chaoyang Lu, just off Chaoyang Stream, is famous for its canine creations. Those who'd prefer to play catch and not to eat their best friend can opt for fresh seafood. The **Zhongshan Lu night market** (open daily approx. 7:30pm-midnight or 1am) is the place to go for fish festivities galore. For the basics, cheap noodle and dumpling restaurants (Y3-5) line **Zhonghua Lu** and **Chaoyang Lu,** near the train station.

■ **Meilihua Taiwanese Ice Palace** (měilìhuá bīngchéng; 美丽华冰城), 51 Minzhu Lu, at Xinhua Lu. Can't read Chinese? No worries. Just point to the window picture that appeals to you. Cool down with tropical drinks (Y6-9) and one of the all-time Taiwanese favorites, shaved ice desserts (Y5-9). Rice dishes Y10-15. Open daily 9:30am-5pm.

Nanning Ethnical Park Restaurant (nánníng wénwùyuàn jiǔlóu; 南宁文物苑酒楼; ☎281 5792), at the corner of Minzu Dadao and Gucheng Lu (see **Sights, p. 530**). Not surprisingly, this restaurant serves a variety of Guangxi's minority cuisines. It's a good place to pass the time sipping tea on the pleasant upstairs terrace. Entrees average Y18-35. Open daily 9am-1am.

Yinhe Hotel Coffeeshop (yínhé jiǔdian; 银河酒店), 84 Chaoyang Lu (☎243 8223). Night owls and Anglophones top the customer list here. The English menu includes many kinds of coffee (Y25-28), as well as ice cream, salads, and sandwiches. Open 24hr.

JJ's Disco (JJ dísīkē; JJ迪斯科), 62 Taoyuan Lu (☎282 3333), near Tiantao Lu. Techno music, disco dancing, and an amusing Chinese opera intermission show make JJ's *the* place to spend hours bumping and grinding with Nanning's young trendsetters. Cover Su-Th Y20, F-Sa Y30. Open daily 8pm-late.

Minzu Cinema (mínzú yǐngchéng; 民族影城), 28 Dongyang Lu, off Binjiang Lu, near the river. Missed that blockbuster hit three months back? Catch the much-delayed Chinese version of Hollywood flicks here. Admission Y15. Open daily noon-midnight.

🔆 SIGHTS

Although not famous for any major historical or cultural sights, Nanning and the surrounding countryside can fill a couple days of relaxed sightseeing.

GUANGXI PROVINCIAL MUSEUM (guǎngxī shěng bówùguǎn; 广西省博物馆). This museum houses some interesting artifacts from the Taiping Rebellion, as well as a wealth of information about the Miao, Dong, and Zhuang minorities living in Guangxi province. A huge second floor exhibit displays colorful, elaborately sewn minority costumes. Exit through the back of the museum to the **Ethnical Park of Nanning** (nánníng wénwùyuàn; 南宁文物苑) to relax in its shaded gardens amid examples of traditional minority architecture. *(On Minzu Dadao. Bus #6 runs from the train station and stops in front of the museum. Open W-F 8:30am-noon and 3-5:30pm, Sa-Su 9am-5pm. Y2. Park open daily 8:30am-6pm. Y2.)*

BLUE MOUNTAIN SCENIC AREA (qīngxiù shān fēngjǐng qū; 青秀山风景区). The rolling hills offer plenty of pathways to explore, each rewarding visitors with great views of the surrounding countryside. Take time to feed the overeager goldfish in the pond at the base of **Dragon Pagoda** (lóngxiàng tǎ; 龙象塔), or venture to the **Phoenix Pagoda** (凤凰塔) on the other end of the park. **Lion Temple** (shī lín; 狮林), one of several on the mountainside, is not far from the cable car to the **Monument to Martyrs of the Sino-Japanese War** (kàng rì lièshìbēi; 抗日烈士碑). *(10km southeast of Nanning. Bus #10 stops at the foot of the mountain, or take a direct minibus that leaves every 10-15 min. 8am-5pm from Chaoyang Square. Y8.)*

PEOPLE'S PARK (rénmín gōngyuán; 人民公园). Known before as White Dragon Park, People's Park sits at the very heart of Nanning. The densely wooded areas with boulevard-like paths wind around sculptured gardens and a lake (paddle boats Y12 per hr). In the afternoon, many of the city's elderly residents congregate to sing their favorite Chinese operas, play *mahjong*, or sip tea. *(The main entrance is on Gongyan Lu, near to where Renmin Lu branches off to the right; a side entrance is on Xinmin Lu. Open daily 8am-6pm. Y2, admission to the formal garden an additional Y2.)*

OTHER SIGHTS. Nanhu Park (nánhú gōngyuán; 南湖公园) is accessible by bus #10, and makes a good stop on the way to or from Blue Mountain Scenic Area. The Nanning skyline forms a nice backdrop for the city's largest lake. *(Open daily 5am-midnight. Y2.)* A covered passageway built high above the docks on **Jiangbin Lu** serves as Nanning's **pet shop alley**—live scorpions for sale! Animal-lovers should probably avoid **Shui Jie** (shuǐ jiē; 水街), a small side street running perpendicular to the pet shop alley. At this open-air market, everything from seafood to man's best friend is destined for eventual consumption.

🗺 DAYTRIPS FROM NANNING

YILING CAVES AND WUMING
50min. north of Nanning. Buses head to both destinations (To the caves 40min., Y3; to Wuming 50min., Y5). ☎602 0420. Open daily 8am-5pm; gate entrance Y6, cave fee Y15.

The biggest attractions around Nanning are the **Yiling Caves** (yílíng yán; 伊岭岩) and, along the same road, the village of **Wuming** (武鸣). Yiling is one of the largest and finest caves in Guangxi and fortunately, the caves' light displays do not overwhelm any natural features. The walkways are spacious, and the tour (1hr.) is an easy walk-through. The park grounds are also home to wild monkeys, which mostly can be heard and not seen chattering in the trees. The village of **Wuming,** north of the caves, is known for its natural spring swimming pool. During the summer, Nanning residents go to Wuming to relax in the huge pool, which is the size of a small lake. **Ling Shui** (líng shǔi; 灵水), as it is locally known, has a gate fee of Y6 for a day of swimming, and inner tubes can be rented for Y5 per day. There are no lifeguards or closing hours, but novice swimmers will have fun hanging out near the natural spring channel watching the clear water flow into the pool.

ZUO RIVER SCENIC AREA

Another attraction is the Zuo River Scenic Area (zuǒjiāng fēngjǐngqū; 左江风景区). From the nearby town of Ningming (宁明), a 2½hr. train ride away, take a cruise down the Zuo River (boat ride Y30) to view karst rock formations, or to tour neighboring minority villages. Take a 40-minute boat ride from Ningming to see the **Huashan wall paintings,** emblazoned on the cliff rocks by the Zhuang (Y15).

GUILIN 桂林 ☎ 0773

For centuries, Guilin was deemed the most beautiful place on earth by tourists and poets alike. Even today, the two syllables of its name give rise to romanticized images of greenery, misty caverns, and peaceful boat rides down the winding Li River. On clear days, a climb up the city's hills affords a view of the patchwork of karst formations and industrial warehouses that claim shares of Guilin's spirit. Commercial areas abruptly end at the entrances to the numerous parks, which are packed with as many tourist groups as locals. Guilin's reputation is clearly one built upon its craggy peaks and riverbends. One cannot help wonder if one day the ever-present "under construction" will obscured by another, more menacing sign: "warning: tourist trap."

▣ TRANSPORTATION

Airplanes: Lijiang International Airport (líjiāng guójì jīchǎng; 漓江国际机场). A **shuttle bus** leaves from the CAAC office to the airport (30min. 6:30am-7:30pm, Y20) and also plies the route from the airport to either the train station or the CAAC office for all arriving flights (board the mini-van on the bottom floor of the airport right outside the gate area). Taxis will be glad to give you a lift from downtown Guilin to the airport (Y80-100). The **CAAC ticket office** (☎384 3922), on Shanghai Lu and Minzhu Lu, books domestic tickets; **CITS** (see p. 532) books tickets for Dragon Air flights to Hong Kong. **Airport Information** (☎284 5304) provides detailed departure and arrival info. To: **Beijing** (Y1430); **Changsha** (Y360); **Guangzhou** (Y530); **Hong Kong** (Y1640); and **Wuhan** (Y620).

Trains: Guilin Train Station (guìlín huǒchē zhàn; 桂林火车站; ☎383 3124), at the intersection of Zhongshan Nan Lu and Shanghai Lu. The ticket office is on the 1st floor, on the left when facing the front of the station. Tickets go on sale 3 days in advance. Book early, especially for hard sleeper tickets. To: **Beijing** (33hr., 2 per day, Y400); **Guangzhou** (13hr., 2 per day, Y180); **Kunming** (30hr., 3 per day, Y300); **Nanning** (6½hr., 5 per day, Y50); **Shanghai** (26hr., 2 per day, Y350); and **Xian** (30hr., 1 per day, Y300). Most trains through Guilin also pass through the **Guilin North Train Station** (guìlín běi huǒchē zhàn; 桂林北火车站), on Zhongshan Bei Lu north of Huancheng Lu.

Buses: In general, it's cheaper to buy tickets at bus stations than from hawkers. **Guilin Long-distance Bus Station** (guìlín chángtú qìchē zhàn; 桂林长途汽车站; ☎382 0600), on the northern section of Zhongshan Nan Lu, a 10min. walk north of the train station, almost to Nanhuan Lu. To: **Longsheng** (4hr., every 20min. 6am-5pm, Y10.5); **Nanning** (8hr., every 1-2hr. 6:30am-8:30pm, Y75); **Sanjiang** (6hr., 8 per day, Y17);

and **Yangshuo** (1½hr., every 20 min., Y6-10). Direct buses to **Guangzhou,** Longsheng, and Nanning are more expensive but make the trip in half the time. The **Guilin South Bus Station** (guìlín nán zhàn; 桂林南站), behind the train station, also has buses to Yangshuo and Longsheng. Buses to Yangshuo usually continue on to farther destinations, and prices to Yangshuo depend on the bus's ultimate destination. To **Fuli** (1hr., 1 per day, Y8) and **Longsheng** (5hr., every 20min. 7am-5pm, Y9.5).

Local Transportation: Most **buses** leave from the train station. Fare Y1-2. Bus **#1** runs to the North Train Station from the intersection of Shanghai Lu with Zhongshan Nan Lu; **#2** from Guilin Train Station, past Nanmen Bridge, Elephant Trunk Hill, Fubo Hill, Folded Brocade Hill, over west toward Reed Flute Cave; **#3** from Guilin Train Station, past Nanxi Park toward Yangshuo; **#5** from Guilin Train Station, past Wayan Crossroad and Yanshan Zhen, to Yangshuo; **#11** from Seven Star Park, past Crossroad Circle, the Guilin Train Station, and the South Stream Park, to Pingshan; **#13** from Seven Star Park, up Zhongshan Zhong Lu past Solitary Peak Park and Folded Brocade Hill, to Reed Flute Cave; **#14** from West Hill Park, past Jiefang Bridge and Sanlidian Circle, to Wulidian.

✦❼ ORIENTATION AND PRACTICAL INFORMATION

Guilin covers an area of 4195km^2 and comprises four urban districts, one suburban district, and two counties. Parks, karst pinnacles, and lakes are scattered throughout the city center, which is ringed by **Shanghai Lu** (上海路), **Lijiang Lu** (漓江路), and **Cuizhu Lu** (翠竹路) to the south, and **Huancheng Lu** (环城路) and **Putuo Lu** (普陀路) to the west, north, and east. The **Li River** (漓江) runs from north to south through the city. The urban center lies west of the river, while **Seven Star Park** lies to its east. **Binjiang Lu** (滨江路) runs along the river's western shore. The main road, **Zhongshan Lu** (中山路), runs parallel to and farther west of the river. **Jiefang Lu** (解放路), **Nanhuan Lu** (南环路), and Shanghai Lu run from east to west, intersecting with Zhongshan Lu.

Travel Agency: CITS, 41 Binjiang Lu (☎282 8314 or 282 8304; fax 280 5303), a short walk from where Nanhuan Lu ends at the Li River. There is an English- and Japanese-speaking staff, but most of their suggestions are aimed at big spenders. The office books city tours, cruises down the Li, and airline tickets on the ground floor. Open M-F 8:30am-noon and 3-6:30pm.

Bank of China: 5 Ronghu Bei Lu (☎283 1147). Exchanges traveler's checks and provides credit card advances. Open daily 8am-noon and 3-6pm. The **Lijiang Hotel** and the **Sheraton Guilin Hotel** will exchange currency for non-guests.

Department Store: Guilin Niko Niko Do Plaza (guìlín wēixiào táng; 桂林微笑堂), 187 Zhongshan Zhong Lu (☎281 5390), at Jiefang Lu. A behemoth 6-floor department store, with a pharmacy, a grocery store, and a selection of English-language books. Credit cards accepted. Open daily 9am-9pm.

Hospital: People's Hospital (shì rénmín yīyuàn; 市人民医院; ☎282 3767), on Wenming Lu, which curves off Zhongshan Zhong Lu and Nanhuan Lu.

Internet Access: The **Xinhua Bookstore** (☎283 0947) on 150 Zhongshan Zhong Lu has a 24hr. Internet bar. Deposit Y20. Y6 per hr.

Post and Telecommunications: 249 Zhongshan Lu (☎383 6836), 2 blocks north of Jiefang Lu, toward Solitary Peak Park. EMS, IDD service, and Poste Restante available. The only place where you can place collect and calling card calls. There are 2 other post offices along Zhongshan Lu. All open daily 8am-8pm. **Postal Code:** 541000.

▌ ACCOMMODATIONS

Guilin is packed with ritzy tour groups, so accordingly, budget accommodations are few and far between. Most are clustered on Zhongshan Nan Lu. Many budget travelers opt to head directly to Yangshuo for the night.

Overseas Chinese Mansions (huáqiáo dàshà; 华侨大厦), 39 Zhongshan Nan Lu (☎383 5753). From the station area, take bus #4 or 11 to Nanxi Park stop, and back-

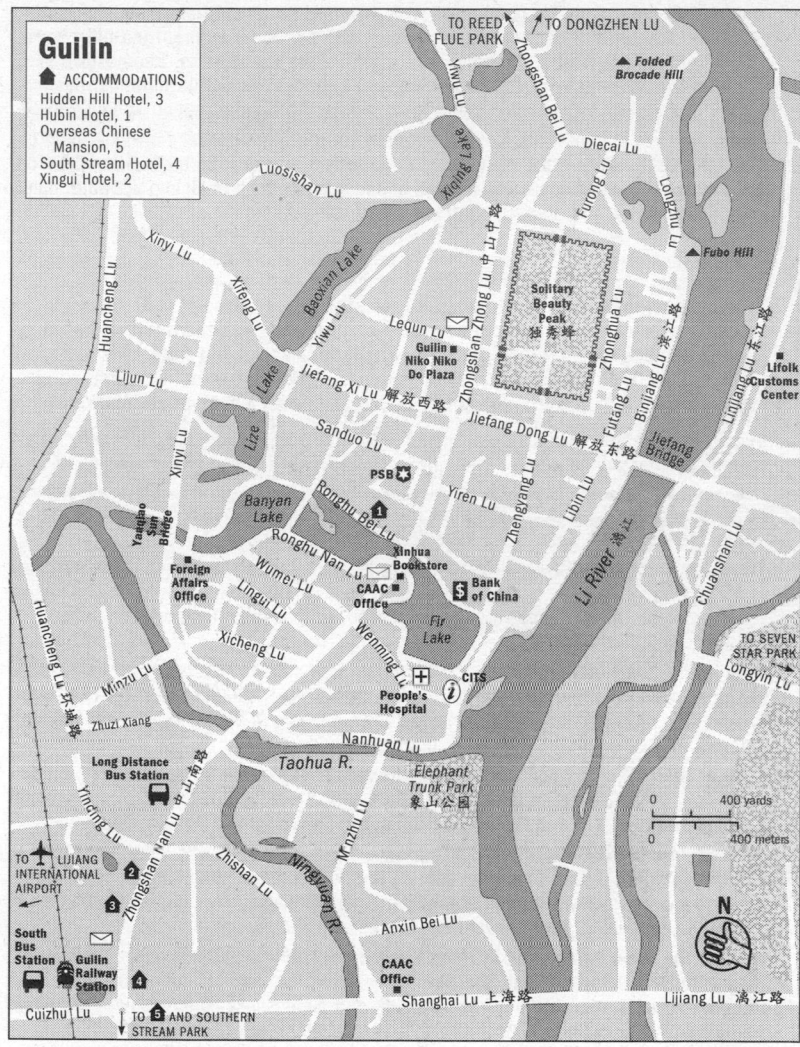

Guilin

🏠 ACCOMMODATIONS
Hidden Hill Hotel, 3
Hubin Hotel, 1
Overseas Chinese
   Mansion, 5
South Stream Hotel, 4
Xingui Hotel, 2

TO REED
FLUE PARK

TO DONGZHEN LU

Zhongshan Bei Lu

Folded
Brocade Hill

Diecai Lu

Furong Lu

Ywu Lu

Qiping Lake

Longzhu Lu

Fubo Hill

Luosishan Lu

Xinyi Lu

Xifeng Lu

Baoyian Lake

Ywu Lu

Lequn Lu

Zhongshan Zhong Lu 中山中路

Zhonghua Lu

Lijiang Lu 东江路

Lijun Lu

Huancheng Lu

Lize Lake

Jiefang Xi Lu 解放西路

Guilin
Niko Niko
Do Plaza

Futang Lu

Binjiang Lu 东江路

Lijiang Lu 东江路

Lifolk
Customs
Center

Sanduo Lu

Jiefang Dong Lu 解放东路

Jiefang
Bridge

Xinyi Lu

PSB ✚

Yiren Lu

Libin Lu

Ronghu Bei Lu

Banyan
Lake

Zhengyang Lu

Li River 漓江

Chuanshan Lu

Yangqiao
Sun
Bridge

Ronghu Nan Lu

Xinhua
Bookstore

Bank
of China

Foreign
Affairs
Office

Wumei Lu

CAAC
Office

Lingui Lu

Fir
Lake

TO SEVEN
STAR PARK

Xicheng Lu

Wenming Lu

Longyin Lu

Minzu Lu

Huancheng Lu 环城路

✚ People's
Hospital

ℹ CITS

Zhuzi Xiang

Nanhuan Lu

Yinding Lu

Taohua R.

Long Distance
Bus Station 🚌

Zhongshan Nan Lu 中山南路

Elephant
Trunk Park
象山公园

0   400 yards
0   400 meters

TO 🛪 LIJIANG
INTERNATIONAL
AIRPORT

2

3

Zhishan Lu

Ninguan R.

Minzhu Lu

N

South
Bus
Station

Guilin
Railway
Station

4

Anxin Bei Lu

CAAC
Office

Cuizhu Lu

TO 5 AND SOUTHERN
STREAM PARK

Shanghai Lu 上海路

Lijiang Lu 漓江路

track a few minutes. Alternatively, turn right as you exit the train station and walk down Zhongshan Lu. Despite its somewhat remote location, this hotel is some of the best Guilin has to offer the budget traveler. Standard rooms have A/C, TV, phone, and bath. 10% service charge. Dorms Y44; doubles Y280-350.

Hubin Hotel (húbīn fàndiàn; 湖滨饭店), 2 Ronghu Bei Lu (☎282 2665), on Banyan Lake. Accessible by bus #2 from the station area to Yang Qiao (the corner of Ronghu Bei Lu and Zhongshan Lu). Turn left on Ronghu Bei Lu and look for the giant bowling pin in front. Once inside, be sure to relax with your pin pals in the bowling alley. Hot water 8:30-11pm. Singles Y80, with A/C Y150; doubles Y120, with A/C Y150; triples 130.

South Stream Hotel (nánxī fàndiàn; 南溪饭店), 84 Zhongshan Nan Lu (☎383 4943), opposite the train station. Only those who find the location appealing should bother to check in, as the place is bombarded by tour groups. Hot water 7:30-11:30pm. Singles Y52; doubles Y84; triples Y120.

Hidden Hill Hotel (yǐnshān fàndiàn; 隐山饭店), 97 Zhongshan Nan Lu (☎383 3540), halfway between the bus and train stations. There's no hiding from the noise here; rooms are predictably noisy, given the proximity to the transit hubs. Rooms have A/C, TV, phone, and bath. 24hr. hot water. Singles Y120; doubles Y150; triples Y180.

Xingui Hotel (xīnguì dàjiǔdiàn; 新桂大酒店), 229 Zhongshan Nan Lu (☎383 7905). From the train station, walk along Zhongshan Lu; the hotel is past the Hidden Hill, on the left. Set back from the main road, Xingui offers respite from the racket of station traffic. Sweet dreams come with inflated prices, though. Try bargaining. Hot water 6pm-midnight. Singles and doubles Y200; triples Y240.

🍴 FOOD

Going up **Zhongshan Lu** from the train station, the area to the left of Nanhuan Lu is lined with riverfront restaurants; here you can observe your seafood and poultry in their prime before chowing down. The locals rave about **Linjiang Lu** (临江路), on the eastern bank of the Li River, as *the* place to grab favorites like stir-fried rice noodles (mǐfěn; 米粉). In the evening, **Nanhuan Lu** hosts a lively night market.

Yiyuan Restaurant (yíyuàn fàndiàn; 怡園饭店), 106 Nanhuan Lu (☎282 0470), may be the best restaurant around. With no meet-what-you'll-eat, living food displays, Yiyuan instead has huge windows behind a classy patterned wood design. Tasty Sichuanese dishes such as Gongbao chicken attract a humming evening crowd. English menu available. Entrees Y6-30. Open daily 11am-2pm and 4:30-9pm.

The Pizzeria at the Universal Hotel (huánqiú dàjiǔdiàn; 环球大酒店), 1 Jiefang Lu (☎282 8228), near the bridge. English menu with unbeatable sandwiches and pizzas made to order. A set Chinese menu offers bread, soup, entree, fruit, and coffee for Y28. Open daily 6:30am-midnight.

Zhengyang Soup City (zhèngyáng tāng chéng; 正杨汤城), 60 Zhengyang Lu (☎285 8553), behind the Sheraton. Terrific English menu offers standard favorites like sweet and sour pork (Y20) and fried Guilin noodles (Y15), as well as snacks like fried *mantou* (Y2 each). Open daily 11:30am-11:30pm.

Cafe at Niko Niko Do (guìlín wēixiào táng de kāfēitīng; 桂林微笑堂的咖啡厅), on the 2nd floor of the Niko Niko plaza (see **Department Store,** p. 532). A little cafe offering set lunches (Y12-15) and even sundaes. English menu. Open daily 9am-9pm.

Arirang Korean Restaurant (yá lǐng láng; 雅里朗), Golden Elephant Hotel, 36 Binjiang Lu (☎280 8888), down the street from CITS. This restaurant offers everything from *bulgogi* to *bibimbap*, a whole page of *kimchee*, and a make-your-own-Korean BBQ. Entrees Y30-60. Open daily 11am-2:30pm and 5-10:30pm.

Roof of the Town Restaurant at Hong Kong Hotel (xiāngjiāng fàndiàn; 香江饭店), on the 19th Fl. of the Hong Kong Hotel. While it may be the roof, it is not exactly the talk of the town, but it offers scenic views of Guilin and good drinks all the same. Cantonese breakfast is a bargain at Y22, served 7:30am-10:30am. Open daily 7:30am-10pm.

🎵🎭 ENTERTAINMENT AND NIGHTLIFE

Stunning scenery seems to have dampened Guilin's desire for a nightlife. Expect a short-lived night out on the town, since most places shut down by 11pm. What nightlife there is packs into the large karaoke places between Zhongshan Zhong Lu, Jiefang Lu, the Li River, and Shanhu Bei Lu. A couple of pricey bars and coffee shops line the alleys behind the Universal and Sheraton Hotels, as well as a few bizarre discos spinning live music and catering to lingering night owls.

King David Bowling (dàwèi wáng; 大卫王), 1 Zhengyang Lu (☎286 2810). Strike the discos off your list and spend your spare time as kingpin of the lanes. Bowling 9am-3pm Y7 per hr., 3-7:30pm Y9 per hr., 7:30-11pm Y15 per hr., after 11pm Y9 per hr. Prices slightly higher on weekends. Shoe rental Y5. Open daily 9am-2am.

E.T. Bar, 10 Ronghu Nan Lu (☎285 4963), next to the Holiday Inn. Nothing to phone home about, but popular with locals, tourists, and other extraterrestrials. Indoor and

outdoor tables overlooking Banyan Lake. Beer, cocktails, and coffee drinks Y20-45.
Open daily 2:30pm-about 2am.

Dixieland Cafe (dèxīlán jiǔbā; 德希兰酒吧; ☎280 8888), in the Golden Elephant
Hotel on Binjiang Lu. Late night crooners are welcome to jam with the live band. Cocktails Y30; draft beer Y15-20. Open daily 7pm-1am.

⚆ SIGHTS

Guilin is blessed with parks, caves, and stunning river vistas that attract nature
buffs and other scenery-seekers from far and wide. At times, especially during the
summer, it is also plagued with swarms of camera-toting tourists with money to
burn. Despite inflated admission prices and mushrooming park crowds, Guilin still
warrants a few days' stay. Most of the peaks and attractions lie around the central
and northern parts of town. Taxis offer full-day city tours for about Y100, usually
bargainable to about half the price.

An interesting time to visit Guilin is during the Chinese Dragon Boat Festival
(duānwǔ jié; 端午节), which falls on the fifth day of the fifth lunar month on the
Chinese calendar. During this festival, the Li River churns with the slapping oars of
Dragon Boat Races, and the shores are lined with spectators chanting the rowers
on to the rhythm of loud Chinese drums.

REED FLUTE PARK (lúdí gōngyuán; 芦翟公园). Named for the legendary musical
qualities of its reeds, Reed Flute Park is home to some of Guilin's best scenery and
caves. In an attempt to control the flow of people through the subterranean wonderland, the Guilin tourist authority has built a 500m long trail with garish neon
lights. All tours are conducted in Chinese, allowing visitors who do not look Chinese greater freedom to putz around by themselves. The peak across from the
cave entrance offers a lovely view of the countryside. Nearby Fragrant Lotus Pond
(fāng lián chí; 芳莲池; ☎260 2473) has bamboo rafts available for rent (Y2); it's not
whitewater rafting, but it's an exciting trip nonetheless. *(A 25min. ride from the center
of Guilin. Accessible by buses #2 and 3. Open daily 7:30am-5pm. Y45.)*

ELEPHANT TRUNK PARK (xiàng shān gōngyuán; 象山公园). Pack your trunk and
head to the site of **Elephant Trunk Hill** (xiàng bí shān; 象鼻山), Guilin's most famous
peak. The thirsty pachyderm stands at the meeting point of the Li River and the
Peach Blossom River (táo huā jiāng; 桃花江). On top of the hill stands the **Puxian
Pagoda** (pǔxián tǎ; 普贤塔), built during the Song dynasty as an offering to calm
the flood-prone river. Visitors can also make the climb up to the **Elephant Eye Cave**
(xiàng yǎn yán; 象眼岩). Those not content with just looking can dress up in
ancient-style clothing for a souvenir photo (Y6), watch cormorant fishing from a
boat (Y20), or simply relax on the little island (sān xīng dǎo; 三星岛) across the
crooked bridge. *(On Nanhuan Lu, across from CITS. Open daily 6:30am-11:30pm. Y10, but try
getting in free around twilight when there are fewer visitors.)*

DRAGON BOATS GALORE
Duan Wu Jie (duàn wū jié;
端午节), or the "Dragon Boat Festival," is an annual Chinese celebration involving the
racing of long dragon-shaped vessels in waters all around China, most notably in the
Hong Kong harbor and the edges of the Li River. This holiday was first celebrated to
commemorate Qu Yuan, a minister during the Warring States period who committed
suicide in the Mi Lo River to protest the corrupt government. His death, which fell on
the fifth day of the fifth month of the lunar calendar, was greatly mourned by the peasants whom he taught while travelling throughout the country. Legend has it that after
his suicide, fishermen got in their boats banging drums and throwing in dumplings to
keep the fish from eating Qu Yuan's body. Today, Duan Wu Jie, which falls in late May
or early June according to the western calendar, is celebrated by the eating of *zongzi*, a
triangular-shaped dumpling made of glutinous rice wrapped in bamboo leaves, and the
racing of dragon boats to the cadence of large drums. This vibrant spectacle is an
enduring demonstration and symbol of the commitment to the community.

SEVEN STAR PARK (qī xīng gōngyuán; 七星公园). Across the Li River from the central part of the city, Seven Star is Guilin's largest park and quite popular with locals. **Seven Star Cave** (qīxīngyán; 七星岩) and the appropriately named **Camel Hill** (luòtuó shān; 骆驼山) are among the attractions. In recent years, the place has seemed more like an amusement park (complete with a kiddie roller coaster) than a nature park, but one can still take a pleasant afternoon stroll. *(Open daily 6am-11pm. Cave hours 8am-5:30pm. Park Y20; cave Y20; Y25 for both.)*

XIONGSEN BEAR AND TIGER VILLAGE (guìlín xióngsēn xióng hǔ shānzhuāng; 桂林雄森熊虎山庄). As its name suggests, this zoo attempts to protect some of the most endangered animals in Asia, including the South China and Siberian Tigers (both numbering a couple dozen in the wild) and the Black Bear, with an assortment of crocodiles, monkeys, and ostriches added to the mix. Skip the guided three-hour Chinese tour to roam the premises on your own, and don't forget to check out the cute monkey performance show and the petting zoo. *(On Cuizhu Lu, halfway to the airport. ☎280 9257. Open daily 9am-5pm. Y80.)*

SOUTHERN STREAM PARK (nánxī shān gōngyuán; 南溪山公园). At the park, two distinct peaks shelter the **Buddha Cave** and the **White Dragon Cave**. The former has a bunch of Buddha statues, mainly of interest to those who enjoy religious relics; the White Dragon Cave is a quirky little hole containing a stalactite/stalagmite "Three Gorges." *(On Zhongshan Nan Lu, beyond the train station. ☎384 4714. Open daily 7am-7pm. Park Y12; White Dragon Cave Y15; Buddha Cave Y8; all Y26.)*

LI RIVER FOLK CUSTOMS CENTER (guìlín líjiāng mínsù fēngqíng yuán; 桂林漓江民俗风情园). The closer you get to China's borders, the more likely you are to come across minority cultures. Guilin has capitalized on this fact by setting up the Folk Customs Center. As the province's largest venue created expressly for entertainment, the park showcases the culture, architecture, and art of Guangxi's minorities. At night, the park is lit up in vivid neon lights—how that justifies the inflated nighttime admission prices, we're not quite sure. *(On Lijiang Lu, at Lijiang Kou. ☎581 5678. Daytime Y30, nighttime Y50.)*

OTHER SIGHTS. Solitary Beauty Peak (dú xiù fēng; 独秀蜂) rises pillar-like from the center of Guilin, soaring more than 150m and offering a stunning panoramic view. The Guangxi Teacher's University's red and white traditional architecture dots one area of the park's premises. *(On Zhongshan Zhong Lu, past Jiefang Lu. ☎280 9217. Y20.)* **Fubo Hill** (fúbō shān; 伏波山), on the Li River's western bank and near Solitary Beauty Peak, rises between the Li River and the point where Binjiang Lu turns into Longzhou Lu. The Tang and Song dynasties left their mark in **Thousand Buddha Cave** (qiānfó dòng; 千佛洞), which cuts into Fubo Hill's southern slope, by carving Buddhist statues and frescoes into the walls. *(Open daily sunrise-sunset. Y10.)* To visit **Folded Brocade Hill** (dié cǎi shān; 叠彩山), continue up Longzhou Lu, take a left at Diecai Lu, and then a right. The hill, amid a stunning setting, resembles a stack of fabric at a Chinese silk market. *(Open daily sunrise-sunset. Y13.)*

  Banyan and **Fir Lakes,** on either side of Zhongshan Zhong Lu and Ronghu Bei Lu (accessible by bus #2 to Yang Qiao), are dotted with several small islands connected by roads to the shore. Paddle boat rides are a far better way of crossing the water; both lakes can be circumnavigated in about an hour. Best of all, in the middle of tourist-trampled Guilin, these attractions don't cost a single *mao*.

YANGSHUO 阳朔   ☎0773

Yangshuo has all of Guilin's comely charms but none of its death-by-tour-group distractions. Like its much larger cousin, Yangshuo is set amid the craggy limestone pinnacles that are the region's hallmark. The Li River snakes its way between the two, and many expensive package tours cruise to Yangshuo from Guilin, stopping only long enough to buy a cheap trinket. Many backpackers spend a night (or two or three or 10) here, finding the town as arresting as the surrounding scenery. Yangshuo's main streets are an oasis of faux familiarity to visitors who

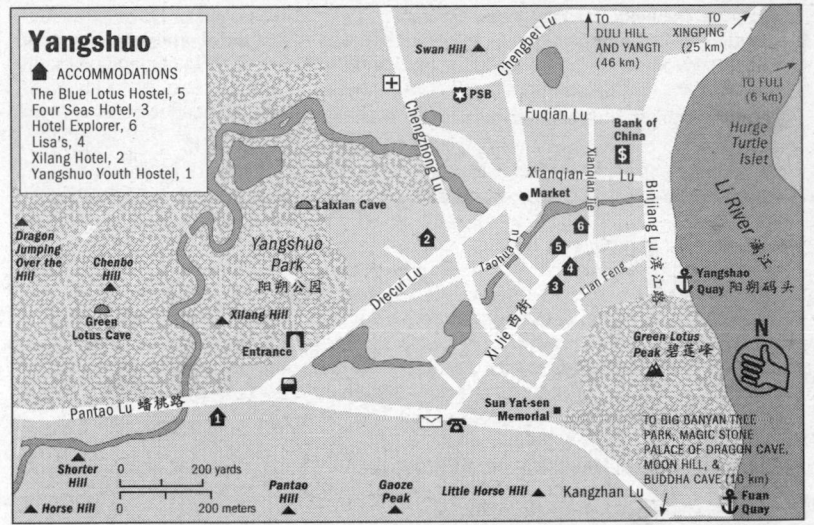

Yangshuo

▲ ACCOMMODATIONS
The Blue Lotus Hostel, 5
Four Seas Hotel, 3
Hotel Explorer, 6
Lisa's, 4
Xilang Hotel, 2
Yangshuo Youth Hostel, 1

chuckle at its "Fawlty Towers Hotel," "Twin Peaks Cafe," and "Planet Yangshuo." Travelers pass the days exploring the natural wonders of the nearby countryside, and while away the evenings in the eateries along Xi Jie, sipping coffee and swapping stories to the sounds of Jimi Hendrix and Britney Spears.

✦🛈 ORIENTATION AND PRACTICAL INFORMATION

Yangshuo is 65km by road or 83km by river southeast of Guilin. Central Yangshuo lies between the **Li River** and **Green Lotus Peak** to the east and **Yangshuo Park** to the west. The bus station is just beyond the park walls along the town's main road, **Pantao Lu** (叛逃路). From the bus station, walk up Pantao Lu toward the city center, and take a left on **Xi Jie** (西街) at the post office to reach most of Yangshuo's guesthouses, cafes, and restaurants. Visitors arriving by boat at the **Yangshuo Dock** (yángshuò mǎtóu; 阳朔码头), on **Binjiang Lu** (滨江路), can walk along the river toward Green Lotus Peak to find Xi Jie running away from the river on the right.

Buses: The **bus station,** on Pantao Lu near Yangshuo Park, services both long-distance and local traffic. Most buses to non-Li River region destinations depart from Guilin. To **Guangzhou** (14hr., 1 per day, Y80) and **Zhuhai** (15hr., 3 per day, Y100).

Minibuses: Minibuses make the trip to **Guilin** (1½hr., every 10-15min. or whenever the bus fills to 110% capacity, Y6), leaving from in and around the bus station. Beware of overcharging. Minibuses go to **Xingping** (1hr., every 20min., Y5) via **Fuli** (15min., Y2).

Boats: See the Li River description in **Sights**, p. 539.

Bike Rental: Many hotels and vendors along Xi Jie near Pantao Lu rent bikes for Y5-10 per day. No deposit required.

Travel Agencies: Travel agencies, backpacker cafes, and self-proclaimed tour guides crowd Xi Jie and Pantao Lu. Perhaps the most congenial CITS independent agent is ▨ **Uncle Bob** (email unclebobyangshuo@hotmail.com), who speaks excellent English and has attained the status of a local celebrity. Look for his sign along Xi Jie.

Bank of China: 11 Binjiang Lu (☎882 2329), near the river. Walk to the end of Xi Jie and turn left at the river; the bank is 100m down on the left. Open daily 8am-5:30pm; in winter 8am-5pm.

PSB: 39 Chengbei Lu (☎882 0778), on the right side of the building. Officer **Bin Yao** is in charge of crimes against foreigners.

Hospital: People's Hospital (rénmín yīyuàn; 人民医院) has a doctor for emergencies: **Dr. Lee** (☎882 0505, pager 127 159 8929), who is **SOS International**'s Yangshuo doctor. For minor problems, go to the **foreigners' clinic** (☎882 2461) in the back of Xilang Hotel. Open daily 9am-6pm.

Internet Access: Several Internet cafes line Xi Jie, charging Y10-20 per hr.

Post and Telecommunications: Yangshuo Post Office, 28 Pantao Lu, at Xi Jie. IDD service (no calling card or collect calls) and Poste Restante available; fax 2 doors down, in the business services department. Open daily 8am-10pm. **Postal Code:** 541900.

ACCOMMODATIONS

Finding a cheap room, even one outfitted with toilet seats, is usually no trouble in Yangshuo. Many of the best bargains boast not only a place to lay your head, but travel agencies, cafes, laundry services, and more. Bargaining hard may yield almost 50% savings during colder months, although room prices may be double to triple their going rate at certain times of the year, especially Chinese New Year. Guests staying for extended periods of time may also garner discounts.

The Blue Lotus Hostel and Cafe, 62 Xi Jie (☎882 7873). Charming rooms extend a homey, log cabin feel, and the friendly owners earn praise from travelers. Dorms Y20; singles Y20; doubles Y30; triples Y45.

Lisa's (lǐshā jiǔdiàn; 李莎酒店), 71 Xi Jie (☎/fax 882 0217). Proves that it's not what you know, but whom. Lisa (email lisa@public.glptt.gx.cn), the grande dame of this establishment, is almost as famous as Uncle Bob for travel advice and tips. 24hr. hot water. Dorms with bath Y30; singles with A/C Y80; doubles with A/C Y150; triples Y60.

Four Seas Hotel (sì hǎi fàndiàn; 四海饭店), 73 Xi Jie (☎882 2013; email sihai@hotmail.com). Four Seas' halls are spacious and well lit. 24hr. hot water. 4-bed dorms Y10-20; singles Y20-30; doubles Y30-50, with bath Y30-60, with A/C and bath Y70-200.

Yangshuo Youth Hostel (qīngnián zhāodàisuǒ; 青年招待所), 85 Pantao Lu (☎882 2347), 1 staggering step from the square outside the bus station. 5-bed dorms with bath Y15; 3-bed dorms Y10; doubles Y30, with bath Y40-60, with A/C Y40-60 extra.

Hotel Explorer (wénhuà fàndiàn; 文化饭店), 11 Xianqian Jie (☎882 8116; fax 883 7816). This establishment has sparkling facilities and is a bit removed from the hubbub of Xi Jie. Singles, doubles, and triples Y120-140.

Xilang Hotel (xīlángshān fàndiàn; 西郎山饭店), 31 Diecul Lu (☎882 2312). Dorms have fan, TV, and attached bath; the other rooms have all standard amenities. Hot water 7:30pm-midnight. Foreigners' medical clinic behind hotel. 2- to 3-bed dorms Y25; doubles and triples Y120-150.

FOOD AND ENTERTAINMENT

In a town where the main attraction is the surrounding countryside, visitors typically pass the evening hours and an occasional rainy day in the small cafes and restaurants that line both sides of Xi Jie. Not just eateries, these establishments double as the town's nightlife and information nerve center. Make arrangements for the week's excursions, get some free advice, sip coffee, knock back a couple beers, play a little pool, or boogie down to disco.

Red Star Express (hóng xīng tèkuài; 红星特快), 66 Xi Jie (☎882 2699). Best pizza in town, as well as the biggest selection (16 toppings, Y15-20). The kitchen is the cleanest around, and Charlie, the personable owner, keeps the joint open into the wee, wee hours. A mixed crowd of backpackers and locals makes for great socializing and story swapping. Beer and cocktails Y12-16. Open daily 8am-midnight (or whenever the last straggler wanders home).

Meiyou Cafe (méiyǒu fàndiàn; 没有饭店), 80 Xi Jie (☎882 1167). Meiyou is a bit of a misnomer—unless it's short for *meiyou wenti* (no problem). The snake dinner even comes with a photo and free t-shirt (Y70-90). Organizes cormorant fishing trips (Y25) and daytrips to Xingping and Fuli. Open daily 7am-late.

Minnie Mao's, 83 Xi Jie. The oldest restaurant on Xi Jie, this place proves it is still with the times, thanks to daily showings of recently released movies. Entrees Y8-15. Open daily 6:30am-late.

Susannah's Cafe (sūshānnā kāfēi diàn; 苏珊娜咖啡店), 81 Xi Jie (☎882 7090). Susannah's immense, 34-page English-language menu and delicious breakfast specials (Y18) earn lots of praise. Open daily 6:30am-late.

MC Blues Cafe (líshì jiǔdiàn; 黎士酒店), 101 Xi Jie (☎882 0095). Whistle while you work, listen while you eat.... MC Blues has the best selection of music around. The small borrowing library (Y2 per book) with copies of *China Daily* and other English publications attracts Anglophones from far and wide. Open daily 7am-midnight.

Le Votre French Restaurant (lèdè fǎshì cāntīng; 乐得法式餐厅), 79 Xi Jie (☎882 8040), across the street from Minnie Mao's. A bit more expensive than the average Xi Jie restaurant, but the classy atmosphere and authentic French cuisine is worth it. The grilled tenderloin (Y80) and *creme brulee* (Y25) come highly recommended. Most entrees Y20-30. Open daily 7:30am-late.

SHOPPING

Another timeworn pastime in Yangshuo is shopping for cheap souvenirs. Although most of the bric-a-brac isn't as cheap as it used to be, the town is still one of the best places in China to buy souvenirs; you just need to bargain. **Forrest**, the "Chinese Picasso" as the locals call him, designs cute t-shirts ("no beer, no happy") in his shop directly opposite Red Star Express. Many visitors also have custom silk clothing made in Yangshuo. Yangshuo tailors can accommodate unusual requests (like brocade overalls) and are quick with custom orders (same-day to one-day service). Prices run around Y35 for a skirt, Y25-30 for a shirt, and Y80 for pants. There are also batik products to peruse, as well as a variety of Chinese antiques, including old puppets and door carvings.

SIGHTS

Yangshuo's raison d'être is its striking scenery, easily explored on foot, by bike, or by boat. The countryside is overflowing with venues for lazy bike rides, but more gung ho cyclists may choose to take to the hills outfitted with mountain bikes, muscular legs, and a little determination. Even visiting couch potatoes should take the chance to explore Yangshuo's fantastic slice of the great outdoors.

LI RIVER (漓江). Marking the eastern border of town, the Li River is Yangshuo's main attraction (and same for Guangxi province). It winds for miles around fantastically shaped limestone peaks bearing names such as **Camel Crossing the River** (luòtuó guòjiāng; 骆驼过江) and **Yearning for Husband Rock** (wàng fū shí; 望夫石).

Most travelers explore the river by boat or by bike, although at times inner tubes are permitted. The most popular method is to take a one-way boat ride, returning by bike to Yangshuo. Tickets for the boats, which leave daily around 10am, are on sale at the Yangshuo Dock and at practically every other cafe, restaurant, and hotel along Pantao Lu and Xi Jie. Prices are fixed at Y60 to **Fuli** (1hr. by boat, 40min. back by bike), Y70 to **Xingping** (3hr. by boat, 2hr. back by bike), and Y100 to **Yangdi** (5hr. by a boat that then takes you back the 1½hr. to Xingping). Bikes can be thrown in the cargo hold of the boat. Going to Yangdi is well worth the extra time and money, as the most impressive scenery is between Xingping and Yangdi.

Cormorant fishing is a popular evening activity. Li River fishermen have long trained cormorants to dive into the river and catch fish in the light of a flaming torch. These days, some enterprising locals allow small tourist boats to tag along after them to see them practice their trade—for a price, of course (1-1½hr., daily around 7:30pm, Y25).

MOON HILL (yuèliāng shān; 月亮山). Named for the crescent-shaped hole through its center, Moon Hill is a 50-minute bike ride from Yangshuo proper. The 800 steep steps to the top are no leisurely stroll, but they're worth it: the view of the countryside from the top is outstanding. Beware of the aggressive hawkers along the way, but do take the time to enjoy the photo scrapbooks and travel logs of a sprightly septuagenarian who occupies a midway point in the climb. Tours of the hill and parts of the surrounding villages cost about Y50—touts will look for you along Xi Jie and at other major tourist sights. *(Ride along Pantao Lu past Green Lotus Peak, and then take Kangzhan Lu to your right when the road forks; look for the English sign. Minibuses or small trucks from around the Yangshuo Bus Station to Gaotian can drop you off at the entrance (Y2). Open daily sunrise-sunset. Y9.)*

BUDDHA CAVE (fó dòng; 佛洞). Used as a refuge by local villagers from the invading Japanese army during WWII, the cave draws its name from a tiny stalagmite resembling the Maitreya, a short distance inside the cave. It's easy to see why the locals thought the cave secure from the Japanese and why portions are still off-limits to visitors—it's full of narrow, maze-like, and sometimes dangerous passages. Even in the areas open to the public there have been injuries during the cave's 10 years as a tourist attraction. A guide and a flashlight are necessary, as is an urge to crawl through muddy holes, climb up and down stalagmites, and sidle in between stalactites, all with the most rudimentary aid of rope and ladders. The cave is the most extensive, unaltered subterranean microcosmos in the area, complete with stalactite "drums" and an underground waterfall pool where you can bathe and swim. Bring your suit and towel, perhaps a change of clothes, and be prepared to sacrifice your crummiest rags to the grubby climb in. *(Down the road from Moon Hill, in the direction of Yangshuo. There are three tours open: the shortest takes about 1hr. for Y40, a second takes around 1½ hr. for Y50, and exploring all of the cave open to the public takes 3hr. for Y120. Groups of 8 or more can bargain.)*

OTHER SIGHTS. Yangshuo Park (yángshuō gōngyuán; 阳朔公园) does not quite justify its admission fee, but some advise to wait to go after 6pm, when they most likely will let you in for free. *(Main entrance is across the square from the bus station. Open daily 7:30am-8pm. Y5.)*

The Big Banyan Tree Park lies halfway on the road to Moon Hill (½hr. bike ride or Y2 by the minibus to Gaotian), home to an ancient tree with an over-1400-year history and a Zhuang minority cultural showcase. Those who balk at the Y18 admission just to see a tree may content themselves with a good glimpse by the roadside as you pass by on a bicycle. A little farther across the street stands the **Magic Stone Palace of Dragon Cave** (qíshígōng; 奇石宫), a museum collection of over 1000 strange and exotic geological formations found in nearby **Dragon Cave**. *(Open daily 9:30am-6pm. Y23.)*

DAYTRIPS FROM YANGSHUO

About 25km from Yangshuo, **Xingping** (兴坪) is primarily a connecting point for those who bike back to Yangshuo after their boat trip up the Li River. The bike ride to Yangshuo takes about two hours. It's easy to find the road back to Yangshuo; take the only paved road in town from the quay, and when the road forks just outside the town, turn right. There is also a bus from Xingping to Yangshuo (Y6). For those not just passing directly through the village, Xingping is best visited on market days. There are markets on the 3rd, 6th, 9th, 13th, 16th, 19th, 23rd, 26th, and 29th of each month, the same as in Yangshuo. **Fuli** (福利) is a similarly small stop on the bike path. For bikers coming from Xingping, take a right on the main road to get to Fuli. You can also rent a sidecar to Fuli (Y30 round-trip) or Xingping (Y90-100 round-trip) if the bike ride doesn't interest you or if the weather is bad. Fuli also has markets similar to those in Xingping where one can find an assortment of goods, including frogs, snakes, firecrackers, fishing baskets, and woven hats. Fuli also specializes in fans and calligraphy; the street perpendicular to the river on the left is lined with calligraphy shops. Market days are the 2nd, 5th, 8th, 12th, 15th, 18th, 22nd, 25th, and 28th of each month.

LONGSHENG 龙胜   ☎ 0773

High in the mountains and in one of the poorest counties in China, Longsheng serves as a base for exploring nearby Dong, Miao, and Zhuang minority villages. The traditional stilt houses sit against the stunning backdrop (and the physical challenge) of the steepest rice terraces in the country. Trekking around Longsheng and the surrounding areas can be tough, but the scenery is brilliant.

📧 **TRANSPORTATION.** Longsheng is 100km northwest of Guilin, its main **bus** link. From the Guilin Bus Station (see p. 531), buses go to Longsheng (regular 4hr., every 20min. 7am-5pm, Y10.5; express 2½hr., every hr., Y15). Buses go from Longsheng to **Guilin** (every 10-15min. 6am-5:50pm, Y10) and **Sanjiang** (every 30min. 6am-5pm, Y8.3).

🍴 **ACCOMMODATIONS AND FOOD.** The **Riverside Hostel** (kǎikǎi lǚshè; 凯凯旅社), 5 Guilong Lu, is about a five-minute walk uphill from the Longsheng Bus Station. Turn left out of the station, take an immediate right down Guilong Lu; the hotel is up ahead on the left. Owner and English teacher Ms. Li will draw maps of Longsheng's sights upon request, and there is an inexpensive hotel restaurant with an English-language menu. Ask for a room with a river view to watch the cormorant fishing at dusk. *(☎ 751 1335. 24hr. hot water. 2- to 3-bed dorms Y10-20; singles Y20.)* For the most enchanting places in the area, though, head directly to the village of **Pingan** (píngān; 平安) at the top of the Dragon's Backbone Rice Terrace.

As for Longsheng's food, well, its unremarkable. The **Jinhui Restaurant** (jīnhuī fànjiā; 金徽饭家; ☎ 751 2493), about a five-minute walk after you cross the bridge and turn left at the first intersection, serves overpriced, mediocre food. Your best bet is to sample the food stalls lining the market sandwiched between the river and **Xinglong Zhong Lu.** Most food there is under Y5 per item.

🏯 **SIGHTS.** There's not a whole lot to do within Longsheng itself. To get out of town, walk uphill from the bus station, taking a left opposite the first bridge you encounter; the Xun River is to the right. About 40 minutes later, you can cross another bridge over the river. After reaching the other side, take a left; a small bridge is 10 minutes up ahead on the right. Alternatively, turn right at the bridge and navigate your way up and down the terraced paddies. A two-hour walk will bring you to another bridge, which leads back into town.

The 5km bike ride to **Dong Bridge** (dòng qiáo; 侗桥), the historic symbol of the Dong minority, is another popular sightseeing choice. *(Open daily sunrise-sunset. Y20.)* Bicycles (Y5 per day) are available for rent from the Riverside Hostel.

📷 **DAYTRIP FROM LONGSHENG: DRAGON'S BACKBONE TERRACE AND PINGAN.** Peeking through and rising above the mists that cling to it like wispy white veils, the 800m high **Dragon's Backbone Terrace** (lóngjǐ tì tián; 龙脊梯田) is an amazing testament to the power of rice cultivation. The view from the top, with rice terraces snaking about the mountain, is breathtaking. *(Take a minibus (1½-2hr., every 20min. 8am-5pm, Y5) from the Longsheng Bus Station in the direction of Shuanghekou; the terrace is on the way.)* The one-hour climb involves many stone steps, about one foot wide and carved along a sheer drop of a 100m down the slope. The path ends at the bridge that marks the entrance to the Zhuang village of **Pingan** (píngān; 平安).

Pingan is a good base town: you can hike to and swim in a small lake about 30 minutes to the right of the village, see a gold mining site, or spend a day exploring the minority villages on the mountain ridge to the left. From the path at the bridge, take a right up to the stone steps. In one minute you will come to the **Silver Terrace Hotel** (yíntì lǚguǎn; 银梯旅馆), a large wooden Zhuang house on stilts. It has beautiful views—and the scent from its wooden floors and walls smells nice, too. (☎ 758 2050. On-site restaurant. Doubles Y40; quads Y80.) Farther up the steps, the **Li Qing Hostel** (lìqīng lǚshè; 丽晴旅社) is named after the two sisters, Liao Yen Li and Liao Yen Qing, who run the place. The friendly service, delicious food, English menus, inexpensive dishes (Y6-15), and tours make up for the more limited view. (☎ 758 9008 or 758 2012. Singles Y15; doubles Y30; triples Y45.)

DILING 地灵

The Dong village of Diling is about halfway between Longsheng and Sanjiang. The village, close to natural attractions such as rice terraces and waterfalls, has only recently opened its doors to visitors. As such, it does not yet feel like a carefully organized parade of "model minorities." The friendly villagers open up their homes, providing tours of the architectural wonders and samples of traditional Dong cuisine. All of this deserves a stay of two to three days. As there are no marked hiking trails to Diling, hiring a local guide from Longsheng is advised.

SANJIANG 三江

Minibuses to Sanjiang from Longsheng (2½hr., every 30min. 6am-5pm, Y8.3) drop you off down the street from the Sanjiang Bus Station (☎861 2202). Minibuses return to Guilin (5hr., every hr. 7:10am-2:30pm, Y18); Long'e (1 per day, Y10); and Longsheng (2½hr., daily 6:30am-5pm, Y7).

Capital of the Sanjiang Dong Autonomous County, Sanjiang is 167km northwest of Guilin and 66km from Longsheng. Chaotic, dusty, and not particularly pleasant, its saving grace is that it offers access to the marvelous scenery on the outskirts of town. Dotted with the brown-black wooden houses of the Dong people, who comprise more than half the population, the rest of the county is utterly disarming.

The biggest attraction of the area is the **Chengyang Bridge** (chéngyáng yǒnglíu qiáo; 程阳永流桥),built by the Dong between 1912 and 1924. The bridge is 78m long, 4m wide, and 20m high, and made entirely of wood without the use of a single nail. *(Open daily sunrise-sunset. Y10.)* Such "wind and rain" bridges served as gathering places where villagers could relax during inclement weather. Aside from presenting a beautiful view of the surrounding countryside, Chengyang Bridge is also a good starting point from which to explore nearby Dong villages and architecture. The village **drum tower** (gǔ lóu; 鼓楼), about 3km farther down the road and recognizable by its distinctive, multi-layered, pagoda-like roofs, often hosts traditional Dong festivals.

There is nothing to experience in Sanjiang itself beyond the echoing sounds of karaoke that mingle with the smell of foodstalls wafting through the night air. The best place to stay, if you absolutely must crash for the night, is the **Department Store Hotel** (báihuò zhāodàisuǒ; 白货招待所), near the bus station. (☎861 3528. 4-bed dorms Y8; singles Y15-18; doubles Y24-30; triples Y20 and up.) For lodging or just a quick bite (Y5 and up), the **Chengyang Bridge Hostel** (chéngyáng qiáo lǚshè; 程阳桥旅社) is to the left of the bridge. (☎858 2091. Singles and doubles Y20.) The government-run **Chengyang Guesthouse** (chéngyáng zhāodàisuǒ; 程阳招待所), across the bridge to the left, is housed in a former Dong residence. Enjoy a riverfront view on the balcony sipping a cup of oil tea, a Dong specialty. (☎858 2468. Singles Y20; doubles Y40; triples Y45.)

BEIHAI 北海   ☎0779

Beihai is a city with a split personality. On the northern shore, blue collar workers live by the call of the freight vessels that dock next to fishermen's weatherbeaten canoes. On its southern shores, visitors to Silver Beach swear by another kind of boat—the speed cruisers that scream carefree fun and fancy. Beneath all this, Beihai remains a pleasant and serene stop on the way to neighboring Hainan. The balmy climate wouldn't have anything to do with it now, would it?

▌ TRANSPORTATION

Airplanes: Beihai International Airport (běihǎi guójì jīchǎng; 北海国际机场; ☎207 2511), 25km northeast of the city. **Buses** (Y10) shuttle back and forth from the airport to the **CAAC ticket office,** on Beibuwan Xi Lu near Yunnan Lu. Open daily 8am-10pm. To: **Beijing** (1 per day, Y1650); **Changsha** (1-2 per day, Y710); **Chengdu** (Tu and F,

Y950); **Guangzhou** (1-2 per day, Y550); **Haikou** (4 per day, Y310); **Hong Kong** (M, W, and F-Sa; Y1380); **Guilin** (2-3 per day, Y420); **Kunming** (Tu-W, F, and Su; Y620); **Shanghai** (Tu-Su, Y1270); and **Wuhan** (W and Su, Y850).

Trains: Beihai Train Station (běihǎi huǒchē zhàn; 北海火车站; ☎320 9898), at the southern end of Beijing Lu. To **Chengdu** (45hr., 1 per day, Y141) via **Liuzhou** (12hr., Y41) and **Nanning** (4hr., 2 per day, Y15). All other trains connect through Nanning. Buy tickets from **Beihai Tourism Transportation Ticket Center** (běihǎi lǚyóu jú piàowù zhōngxīn; 北海旅游局票务中心; ☎202 8618 or 203 3196; fax 203 2690), 10 Beibuwan Lu, a few minutes walk west of the bus station. Open daily 8am-6pm.

Buses: Beihai Main Bus Station (běihǎi qìchē zǒng zhàn; 北海汽车总站), on Beibuwan Lu. **Express buses** to: **Fangcheng** (2hr., every 1½hr. 7:40am-6:10pm, Y25); **Guangzhou** (9½hr., 2 per day, Y180); **Guilin** (7hr., 2 per day, Y138); **Liuzhou** (5hr., 2 per day, Y100); and **Nanning** (3hr., every 30min. 6:60am-7pm, Y50).

Ferries: Beihai Passenger Ferry Terminal (beíhǎi hǎiyùn kèyùnzhàn; 北海海运客运站), 22 Haijiao Lu (☎390 2542), near Yunnan Lu. Tickets must be bought at least 1 day before departure. Open daily 8:30am-6pm. To **Haikou** (12 hr., 6pm, Y59-194).

Local Transportation: Most buses depart from Jiefang Lu. Walk west on Beibuwan Lu until it forks; go down Woping Lu until Jiefang Lu. Bus **#1** runs east along Beibuwan Lu; **#2** runs west to the Ferry Station; **#3** goes along Sichuan Lu to Silver Beach; **#5** runs along Sichuan Lu to the train station.

PRACTICAL INFORMATION

Travel Agency: CITS, on Sichuan Lu about 500m north of the train station. Come here for helpful suggestions for touring Beihai and nearby cities. A more centralized place for in boat, train, bus, and airplane tickets is **Beihai Tourism Transportation Ticket Center.**

Bank of China: On the corner of Beihai Dadao and Guizhou Lu. Exchanges currency and traveler's checks and gives credit card advances. Open daily 8am-noon and 3-5:30pm; in winter 8am-noon and 2:30-5pm.

Hospital: The **People's Municipal Hospital** (rénmín yīyuān; 人民医院), 83 Woping Lu (☎202 2245).

PSB: 213 Zhongshan Dong Lu (☎209 1114).

Internet Access: Holiday Internet Bar (jiàrì wǎngbā; 假日网吧), on Beibuwan Lu past Sichuan Lu, in the alley opposite the Mindu Hotel. Y2 per hr. Open 24hr.

Post Office: On Sichuan Lu, about 300m south of Beibuwan Square, on the right side of the street. EMS and Poste Restante available. Open daily 8am-8pm. The **Business Services Center** next door offers 24hr. fax and IDD services. **Postal code:** 536000.

ACCOMMODATIONS

No-name hostels right on the shoreline of Silver Beach provide cheap accommodations, but put guests hair-raisingly close to noisy karaoke restaurants nearby. The hotels lining the road by the beach entrance offer more choice lodgings; alternatively, try the hotels within Beihai city, which offer the best bang for your buck.

Taoyuan Hotel (táoyuán dàjǐudiàn; 桃源大酒店; ☎202 0919, fax 202 0520), is slightly removed from the main thoroughfare in an alley just opposite the bus station. Amenities and cleanliness by far better than any other accommodation in its price range. Offers a delicious congee breakfast special (7:30-10:30am, Y3). Singles Y128; doubles Y158; triples Y188.

Ocean Hostel (hǎiyáng zhāodàisuǒ;海洋招待所), 224 Haijiao Lu, a few doors to the left of the ferry docks. Not much in terms of aesthetics, but one of the best deals in Beihai. 4-person dorms Y18. Rooms with private bath: doubles Y35; triples Y30; quads Y25. With A/C and bath: singles Y60; doubles Y100; triples Y120.

CAAC Hotel (mínháng dàjiǔdiàn; 民航大酒店; ☎305 1899), on Beibuwan Lu, on your right as you pass Guizhou Lu. Offers very clean accommodations and a convenient place to book your plane tickets. Singles and doubles Y168; triples Y210.

Silver Beach Hotel (yíntān dàjiǔdiàn; 银滩大酒店; ☎388 4141), across the street from the main entrance to the Silver Beach. A stone's throw away from Beihai's main attraction, but still far enough removed for some nighttime peace and quiet. One of the more affordable hotels along the strip. Singles and doubles Y198; doubles with bath Y126; triples Y238.

◐ FOOD

Being close to the sea, Beihai offers a variety of affordable, fresh ocean catches. A cluster of restaurants can be found on the sidewalk outside the entrance to the Silver Beach; all follow the same photocopied menu (Y25-40 seafood dishes, Y8-15 vegetable dishes). For more options, try the row of restaurants that lies on **Waisha,** the islet off the western end of Haijiao Lu. Waisha also hosts the daily fish market, where one cay buy a pound of fish jerky and a variety of other exotic dried goods.

▨ Waisha Danjia Restaurant (wàishā dànjiā pèng; 外沙蛋家埘; ☎202 6889), on the far right hand side of the row of restaurants on Waisha Islet. The restaurant has a fresh seafood display that rivals an aquarium theme park. Pick and choose your own dinner up front, then relax in an open-air cabana setting with an unobstructed view of the ocean horizon. Seafood Y20 and up, most regular dishes Y5-15. Open 9-2am.

Dexing Restaurant (déxīng shíjiē; 得兴食街), 1 Sichuan Lu, behind Beibuwan Square (☎303 6178). Choose between Cantonese-style dim sum served all day (Y2-8 per dish), or the regular entrees-and-rice menu (Y8-25 per entree). Be like the locals and make this your hometown favorite. Open 7-2am.

Red House (hóngfángzi; 红房子), from Beibuwan Xi Lu, turn left onto Guizhou Lu and walk about 50m. This establishment looks like an American colonial house, with a friendly panting watchdog terrier to match. Wash down fried rice dishes (Y8) and vegetable entrees (Y12-18) with a variety of teas (Y10-20). Open 10-2am.

◉ SIGHTS

SILVER BEACH (yíntān; 银滩). As its name suggests, most of the worthy sights of Beihai ("Northern Sea") involve the ocean, including its centerpiece attraction, Silver Beach. Touted as the "world's best beach," Silver Beach is a 16km stretch of glistening white sand. Its beauty, however, is marred by the visual blotch of Chinese tourists who bask in droves underneath multicolored umbrellas, and the annoyance of beachware hawkers who are as ubiquitous as the sandcrabs. The best way to enjoy Silver Beach is to cruise by motorboat away from the crowds (Y20 per hr., negotiable), or to walk along the beach and plop down where there aren't so many people. *(Take minibus #3 (Y2) from Jiefang Lu for the 20min. ride from the city center, or bargain for a taxicab ride (Y20-25). Open 6am-7pm. Y15.)*

BEIHAI AQUARIUM (běihǎi suǐzúguǎn; 北海水族馆). Amuse yourself with the underwater world of the Beihai Aquarium, in Haibin Park (hǎibīn gōngyuán; 海滨公园). This aquarium is one of the leading marine research institutes in China. One can even glimpse the endangered and protected sea cow. The surrounding park grounds provide a more leisurely stroll than the overpopulated parks and public areas along Beibuwan Lu. *(Along Chating Lu close to the northern waterfront, at the intersection with Guangdong Lu. An easy walk from the bus station. ☎206 2089. Park Y2, open daily 6:30am-6pm. Aquarium Y12, open daily 8am-6pm.)*

YUNNAN 云南

It won't take much tongue-wagging to persuade those backpackers lucky enough to step onto Yunnan's red soil that they are as close to heaven as humans possibly can get. Tucked away in the far southwest, China's fourth largest province is blessed with much to love. There is, quite honestly, no bad destination in Yunnan. Few places in the world offer more or better reasons for venturing off the beaten path, and traveling in Yunnan is not about the destination; the journey justifies itself. Yunnan's landscapes range from the high mountain passes and snow-capped peaks of the north to the luxuriant tropical rainforests of the south.

Yunnan has had plenty of time to adjust to its role as a cultural crossroads. The lesser-known Southern Silk Route, which connected Southeast Asia to the better known Eurasian Route, passed right through the region; Myanmese, Thai, Khmer, and Tibetan people and goods flowed into the area, very often settling in to stay. The aboriginal tribes who were the original inhabitants of Yunnan acknowledged Han Chinese rule as early as the Qin and Han dynasties but never completely fell under the mantle of Chinese culture. During the Tang, the independent Nanzhao kingdom, led by the ancestors of the present-day Bai people, ruled the region from the city of Dali. The Mongols conquered Nanzhao in 1253, gave the province its current name ("south of the clouds"), and incorporated it into the Yuan empire. Many of the Hui Muslims in the area date to this time.

Ming leaders promoted Han Chinese migration to Yunnan, hoping to sinicize the local population. They failed miserably. Stopping the influx of foreign influence and weakening the hold of indigenous cultures would have been as difficult as emptying the Yangzi with a thimble. Minority groups with populations in the millions include the Yi, Dai, and Bai; smaller nationalities include the Hani and Lahu and some groups whose ranks are so thin, such as the Ake, that they do not receive national recognition. The provincial government long ago realized that ethnic diversity holds plenty of appeal for curious visitors, and has vigorously pumped money into the tourist industry. In some cases, this has resulted in a rather tasteless and insensitive marketing of minority cultures to visiting urbanites hungry for something quaint and primitive. At least the government's heart appears to be in the right place; efforts to preserve minority cultures, including the creation of autonomous counties and more bilingual schooling, are being made.

KUNMING 昆明 ☎0871

Kunming, "city of eternal spring," fulfills both its name and its role as Yunnan's provincial capital. Year-round blooms and mild weather aside, the city moves with an energy that belies its pride and sense of responsibility at being both the heir to amazing ethnic traditions and a leader in China's determined march through the 21st century. It's a precarious balance that Kunming maintains with surprising grace. But the city has had a long history of dealing with clangs and clashes. The rugged cityscape, at an elevation of almost 200m, bears witness to millennia of tectonic tumult, and the Han, Dai, and Muslim influences in local architecture and cuisine only hint at the cultural clash that has shaped the surrounding area for centuries. Part of the Dali-centered Nanzhao kingdom in the 8th and 9th centuries, Kunming was not integrated into the bulk of China until Mongols swarmed down the Southwest Silk Route in 1253. Come 1911, Kunming was the first city to heed Sun Yat-sen's call to secede from Manchu rule.

The 1999 International Horticultural Exposition as well as domestic and international investment transformed large parts of the city infrastructure, including many of Kunming's historic neighborhoods and narrow *hutongs*. Kunming's push for modernization seems more bedecked with flowers than with the dreary pollution plaguing other cities. The city is lively, clean, and bursting at the seams with character—a fleeting visit makes you wish for a longer one, and a longer one makes you wonder what it would be like to call this place home.

▟ TRANSPORTATION

Airplanes: Kunming Airport (kūnmíng jīcháng; 昆明机场; ☎717 9113 or 711 3229) is a few kilometers outside town. Accessible via buses #52 from Huguo Bridge, 78 from Qingnian Lu, and 67 from North Train Station. A shuttle bus (Y5) from the airport to the

Numerous thefts have been reported on buses serving Kunming. Passengers should guard valuables with particular vigilance on long-distance buses, especially on sleeper buses. Travelers also have reported incidents of robbery and fraud involving tickets sold at a Kunming's bus stations. Readers are advised to purchase tickets only from official sources; if someone offers you a ticket at a cheaper than advertised price, be suspicious.

Worker's Palace usually takes passengers to any central destination they request. Different airlines sometimes offer different "discount" prices to the same destination. To: **Baoshan** (M, W, F, Su; Y440); **Dali** (3 per day, Y360); **Jinghong** (17 per day, Y520); **Lijiang** (6-7 per day, Y420); and **Mangshi** (3 per day, Y530). Other domestic flights to: **Beijing** (7-10 per day, Y1450); **Chengdu** (at least 10 per day, Y560); **Chongqing** (1 per day); **Guangzhou** (6-10 per day, Y1010); **Guilin** (4-6 per day, Y670); **Guiyang** (2-5 per day, Y350); **Hong Kong** (1 per day); and **Shanghai** (4-6 per day, Y1520). To **Bangkok** (1hr., M-Su 3:20, 3:50 and 7:15pm).

Air China (zhōngguó mínháng; 中国民航; ☎351 1591), by the main train station, left of the main ticket office. Open daily 8am-8pm.

China Southern Airlines (zhōngguó nánfāng hángkōng gōngsī; 中国南方航空公司), 433 Beijing Lu (☎310 1831 or 310 1832), near Dongfeng Lu. Credit cards accepted. Open daily 8am-8pm.

China Southwestern Airlines (zhōngguó xīnán hángkōng gōngsī; 中国西南航空公司; ☎353 1222), on Huancheng Nan Lu opposite the Bank of China. Open daily 8am-6:30pm.

Shanghai Airlines (shànghǎi hángkōng gōngsī; 上海航空公司), 46 Dongfeng Dong Lu (☎ 351 1534), east of Beijing Lu.

Yunnan Airlines (zhōngguó yúnnán hángkōng gōngsī; 中国云南航空公司), 24-28 Tuodong Lu (☎316 4270; reconfirmation ☎316 4415). The manager in the top left corner of the office often seems to find seats that other staff can't. Credit cards accepted (4% charge). Open 24hr.

Trains: Kunming Train Station (kūnmíng zhàn; 昆明站; ☎351 1534 or 302 2122) is at the southern end of Beijing Lu. The ticket office is on the left when you are facing the station. Open daily 6:30am-11pm. Tickets are sold 3 days-1 week in advance, starting at 8:15am. To: **Beijing** (46hr., 1 per day, Y319-889); **Chengdu** (24hr., 2 per day, Y105-322); **Chongqing** (24-25hr., 2 per day, Y95-345); **Dali** (8hr., 1 per day, Y30 or 70); **Guangzhou** (34hr., 1 per day, Y170-515); **Guiyang** (13hr., 1 per day, Y75-233); **Shanghai** (57hr., 2 per day, Y179-553); and **Xian** (42hr., 1 per day, Y218-612). For travel to **Guilin**, go to **Nanning** (16hr., 2 per day, Y98-301) first. **North Train Station** (kūnmíng běizhàn; 昆明北站; ☎515 3506), at the northern end of Beijing Lu, is to the right after walking up the road beside the underpass. Open daily 6am-10:40pm. Trains only go to **Hekou** (16-17hr., 1 per day, Y37 or 77).

Buses: Kunming has 3 main bus stations.

Kunming Passenger Station (qìchē kèyùn zhàn; 汽车客运站; ☎354 3325), to the right as you face the train station. The ticket office is to the right, down the row of shops before the fence demarcating the bus area. Open daily 7am-10pm. To: **Jinghong** (24hr., 6 per day, Y150); **Lijiang** (10hr., 3 per day, Y130); **Ruili** (24hr., 4 per day, Y150); **Xiaguan/Dali** (5hr., 6 per day, Y100); and **Zhongdian** (16hr., 1-2 per day, Y200).

Kunming Bus Station (kūnmíng qìchē zhàn; 昆明汽车站; ☎351 0617), a 5min. walk up Beijing Lu from the train station, on the left. Open daily 6:40am-9pm. To: **Guiyang** (15hr., 1 per day, Y130); **Hekou** (9hr., 1 per day, Y101); **Lijiang** (10hr., 4 per day, Y156); **Xiaguan** (6hr., 10 per day, Y110); and **Zhongdian** (12hr., 1 per day, Y197).

Yunnan Express Bus Station (yúnnán gāosù gōnglù kèyùn zhàn; 云南高速公路客运站), in the same place. The ticket office is to the left. Open daily 6:30am-9pm. To **Dali** (5hr., 1 per day, Y103) and **Lijiang** (8hr., 2 per day, Y130).

Local Transportation: The extensive **bus** system has announcements in both English and Chinese. Fare Y1. Buses **#50, 64, 67,** and **68** ply Beijing Lu from the South to North Train Stations; **#5** runs along Dongfeng Dong Lu; **#101** goes around Cuihu Park; **#52, 67,** and **78** go to the airport.

Taxis: Base fare Y7-8, each additional km Y1.6-1.8.

Bike Rental: Camellia Hotel. Y2 per hr., Y15 per day; deposit Y200-300. **Kunhu Hotel,** 3rd fl. The best shop for foreign bike parts is at 33 Tieju Jie, just off Cuihu Nan Lu. There are a number of bike shops on Renmin Dong Lu.

◢✳🛈 ORIENTATION AND PRACTICAL INFORMATION

Kunming's downtown area is surrounded by **Huancheng Lu** (环城路), the first ring road. **Beijing Lu** (北京路) links the North Train Station marking the north end with the Kunming Train Station and the main long-distance bus station at the south end. **Dongfeng Lu** (东风路) runs from east to west, bisecting Beijing Lu at the Worker's Cultural Palace near the **Panlong River** (pánlóng jiāng; 盘龙江). Most of the parks, bite-sized eateries, and coffee shops are found around **Cuihu Park,** near **Yunnan University,** and to the north of the city.

Travel Agencies: CITS, 287 Huancheng Nan Lu, after the overpass. The very helpful pair Ma Tongchun (☎353 3276) and Wang Ping (☎355 5890) both speak English, or try the North America and Europe bureau (☎353 5448). Open M-F 8:30-11:30am and 2-5:30pm. **Camellia Travel Agency** (cháhuā lǚxíng shè; 茶花旅行社), 96 Dongfeng Dong Lu (☎316 6514). Open daily 8am-8pm. **Kunhu Travel Agency** (kūnhú lǚxíng shè; 昆湖旅行社), 202 Beijing Lu (☎313 3737). Supposedly open 24hr.

Consulates: Kunming is a good place to stock up on visas for Southeast Asian countries. There is no **Vietnamese consulate.** Traveler accounts differ as to the possibility of obtaining one through CITS; contact Ma Tongchung (see Travel Agencies) for details.

Laos, Camellia Hotel, 96 Dongfeng Dong Lu, Bldg. 3, 2nd Fl. (☎317 6623; fax 317 8556). Issues 15-day transit visas (US$35 for German, Japanese, and US citizens; US$30 for Australian, New Zealand, and most Western European citizens); visas take 3 working days to process. No visas are issued at the Lao border. Open M-F 8:30-11:30am and 1:30-4:30pm.

Myanmar, Camellia Hotel, Bldg. 3, 3rd Fl. (☎317 6609; fax 317 6309). Issues 1-month tourist visas (Y165; no extensions). Visas take 3 working days to process (rush fee: 3hr. Y100; 12hr. Y50). Officially, entry into Myanmar is permitted only via Yangon airport; tourists must change US$300 into Foreign Exchange Certificates (FEC). Open M-F 8:30am-noon and 1-4:30pm.

Thailand, Kunming Hotel, 145 Dongfeng Dong Lu, South Bldg., 1st Fl. (☎316 8916 or 314 9296; fax 316 6891). Issues max. 30-day transit visas (Y70; must have proof of plane tickets from China to Thailand and from Thailand to a 3rd country), 60-day tourist visas (Y110; up to 1-month extension permitted), and 90-day "non-immigrant" business visas (Y180; with invitation letter). Visas take 2 working days to process. Open M-F 9-11am.

Currency Exchange: Bank of China, 515 Beijing Lu (☎318 8974), at Renmin Dong Lu. Open daily 9-11:45am and 1:30-4:45pm. **Industrial and Commercial Bank of China** (zhōngguó gōngshāng yínháng; 中国工商银行), 275 Beijing Lu (☎317 0614). Exchanges traveler's checks. V/MC ATM. Open daily 9am-5pm. Many major hotels also have currency and traveler's check exchange counters.

Bookstores: Xinhua Bookstore (xīnhuá shūdiàn; 新华书店), 90 Yuantong Jie. A very limited selection of English books. Open M-Tu 10am-8pm, W-Su 9am-9pm. **Journey to the East Cafe** (p. 552) and **Wei's Pizzeria** (p. 551) have a better selection.

Market: Sakura Shopping Center (yīnghuā gòuwù zhōngxīn; 樱花购物中心), 27 Dongfeng Dong Lu (☎314 0429), next to the Holiday Inn. The *pièce de resistance* is the **grocery section** on the 1st floor. You'll pay for those cravings: box of cereal Y45, small jar of peanut butter Y23, and a measly Dove chocolate bar Y12. Open daily 9:30am-10pm. Credit cards accepted. **Paul's Shop** (bǎolì shāngdiàn; 保利商店), 40 Wenlin Jie (☎535 4210), stocks imported foods and drinks. Open daily 8:30am-9pm.

PSB: 94 Beijing Lu (☎316 1021 or 316 3585), in the big municipal building between Dongfeng Lu and Xiangxi Jie. The **visa office** is in a small building at the side (☎301 7585). Open daily 8-11:30am and 1-4:30pm.

Internet Access: China Telecom, 12 Dongfeng Dong Lu (☎317 7875), at Beijing Lu, with 24 computers. Y10 per hr., deposit Y20. Open M-F 8am-5pm, Sa-Su 9am-5pm. **Holiday Inn,** 25 Dongfeng Dong Lu (☎316 5888), at Baita Lu. Y20 for 2hr. Open daily 8am-10pm. **Dove Email** (xìn'gē diànnǎowū; 信鸽电脑屋), 47 Wenlin Jie (☎536 9789), toward Dongfeng Xi Lu. Y8 (expected to be Y6 soon) per hr. Open M-Sa 10am-8pm, Su noon-6pm. **Technology Service Center** (jìshù fúwù bù; 技术服务部), 221 Baita Lu, near Mama Fu's 2. Y10 per hr. Open daily 9am-10pm. Several backpacker restaurants and hotels also have access.

Post Office: 231 Beijing Lu (☎318 4132), just above Heping Lu. EMS and Poste Restante available. Open daily 8am-8pm. **Postal Code:** 650011.

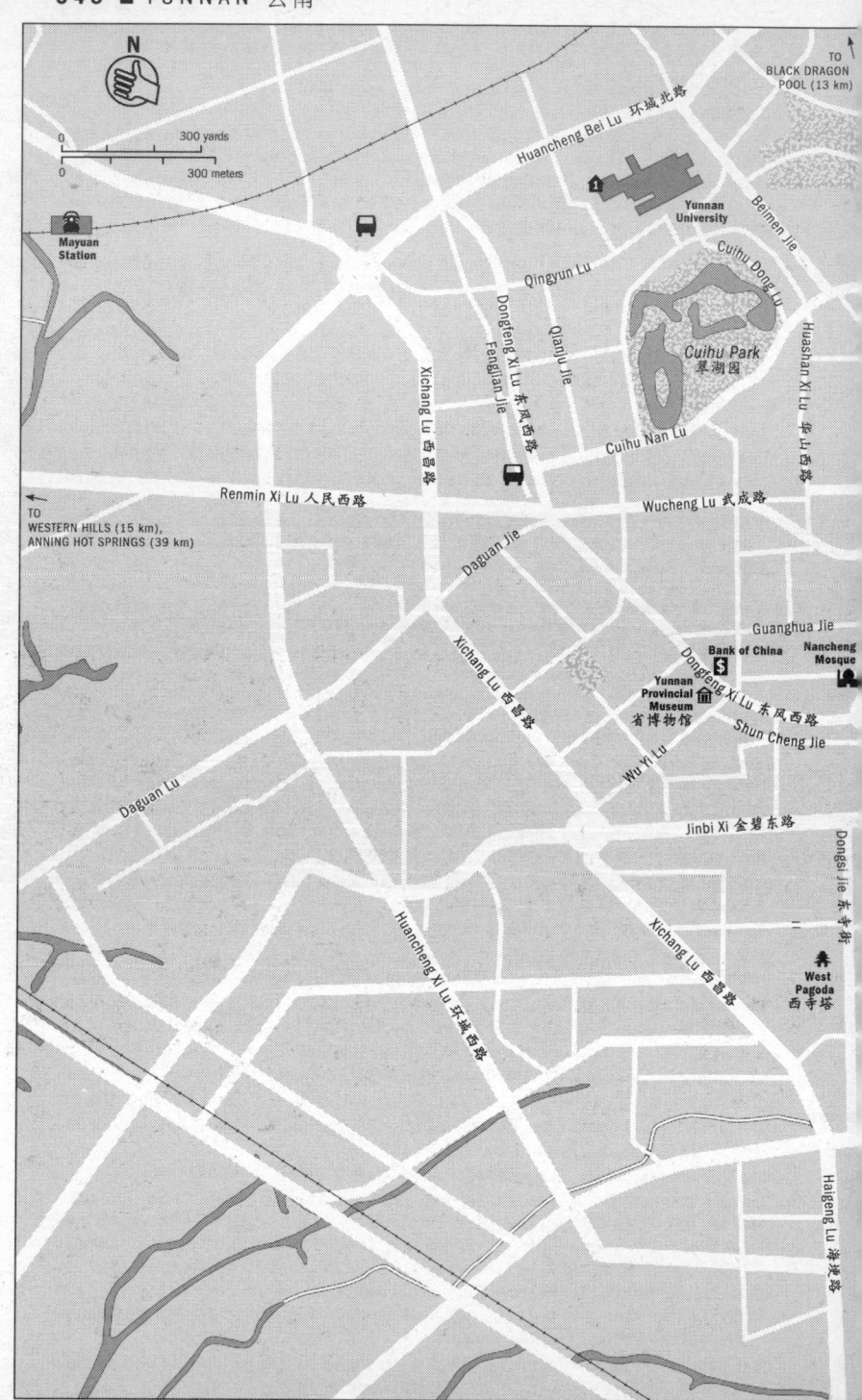

N

0 ____ 300 yards
0 ____ 300 meters

Mayuan
Station

Huancheng Bei Lu 环城北路

TO
BLACK DRAGON
POOL (13 km)

Beimen Jie

1

Yunnan
University

Qingyun Lu

Cuihu Dong Lu

Dongfeng Xi Lu 东风西路

Fengjian Jie

Qianju Jie

Cuihu Park
翠湖园

Huashan Xi Lu 华山西路

Xichang Lu 西昌路

Cuihu Nan Lu

Renmin Xi Lu 人民西路

Wucheng Lu 武成路

TO
WESTERN HILLS (15 km),
ANNING HOT SPRINGS (39 km)

Daguan Jie

Xichang Lu 西昌路

Guanghua Jie

Bank of China

Dongfeng Xi Lu 东风西路

Nancheng
Mosque

Yunnan
Provincial
Museum
省博物馆

Shun Cheng Jie

Daguan Lu

Wu Yi Lu

Jinbi Xi 金碧东路

Dongsi Jie 东寺街

Huancheng Xi Lu 环城西路

Xichang Lu 西昌路

West
Pagoda
西寺塔

Haigeng Lu 海埂路

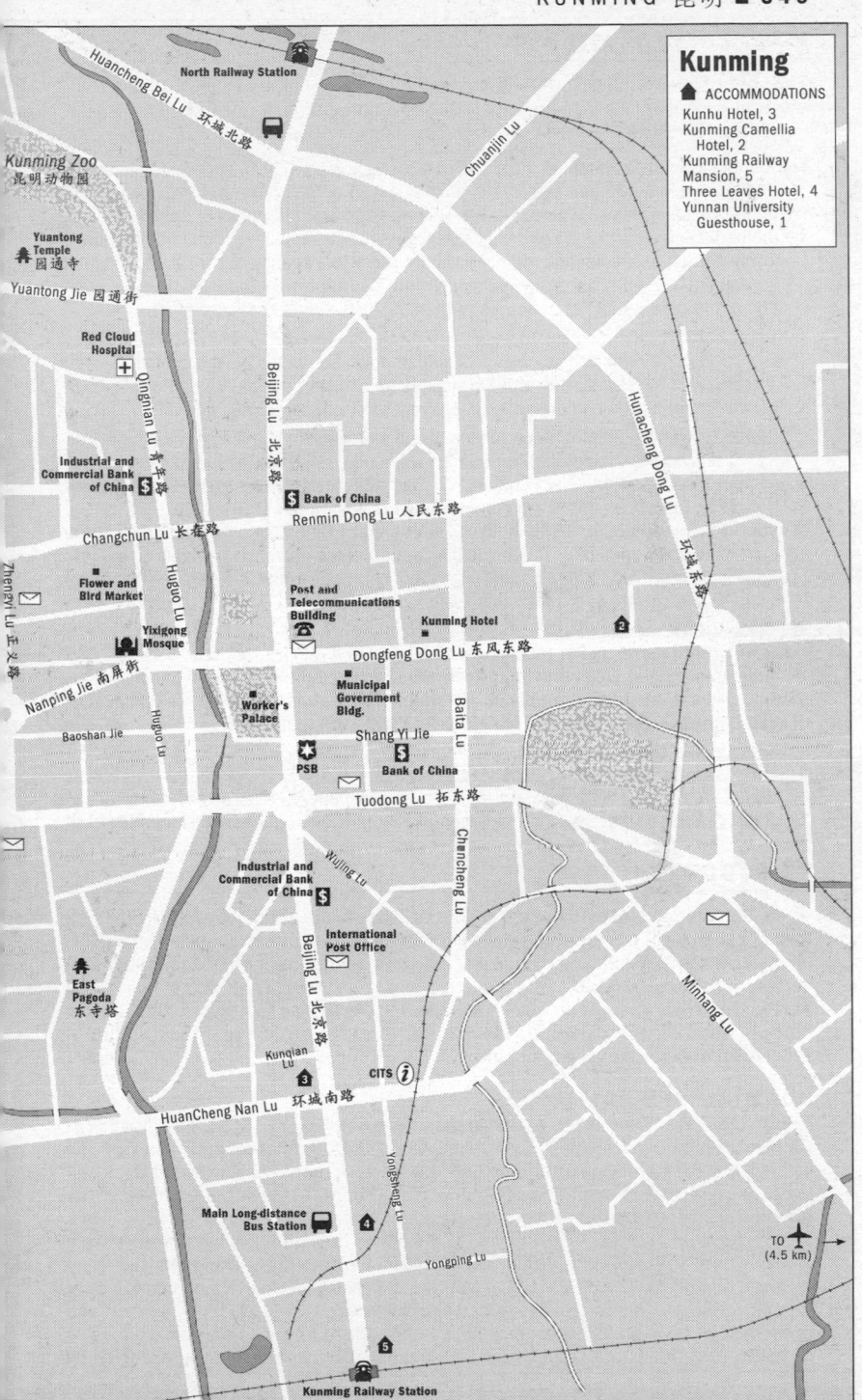

Huancheng Bei Lu 环城北路

North Railway Station

Chuanjin Lu

Kunming

🏠 ACCOMMODATIONS

Kunhu Hotel, 3
Kunming Camellia
  Hotel, 2
Kunming Railway
  Mansion, 5
Three Leaves Hotel, 4
Yunnan University
  Guesthouse, 1

Kunming Zoo
昆明动物园

Yuantong
Temple
圆通寺

Yuantong Jie 圆通街

Beijing Lu 北京路

Red Cloud
Hospital

Qingnian Lu 青年路

Hunacheng Dong Lu 环城东路

Industrial and
Commercial Bank
of China

$ Bank of China 人民东路

Changchun Lu 长春路

Renmin Dong Lu 人民东路

Huguo Lu

Zhengyi Lu 正义路

Flower and
Bird Market

Post and
Telecommunications
Building

Kunming Hotel

Yixigong
Mosque

Dongfeng Dong Lu 东风东路

Nanping Jie 南屏街

Municipal
Government
Bldg.

Baita Lu

Baoshan Jie

Worker's
Palace

Shang Yi Jie

PSB

Bank of China

Tuodong Lu 拓东路

Chuancheng Lu

Industrial and
Commercial Bank
of China

Wujing Lu

East
Pagoda
东寺塔

Beijing Lu 北京路

International
Post Office

Minhang Lu

Kunqian
Lu

CITS ⓘ

HuanCheng Nan Lu 环城南路

Yongsheng Lu

Main Long-distance
Bus Station

Yongping Lu

TO ✈
(4.5 km)

Kunming Railway Station

SOUTHWEST

 ACCOMMODATIONS

The cost of accommodations in Kunming has been rising over the last few years, often inducing shock and sorrow in those arriving from more rural areas. All hotels provide 24hr. hot water unless otherwise specified.

 Kunming Camellia Hotel (kūnmíng cháhuā bīnguǎn; 昆明茶花宾馆), 96 Dongfeng Dong Lu (☎316 3000 or 316 2918). Take bus #23 or 67 from either train station, get off at Dongfeng Dong Lu; switch to bus #5 heading toward Huancheng Dong Lu. This is the undisputed favorite of Kunming backpackers, with cheap beds, bona fide service, a lovely garden, and chandeliered hallways. On-site travel agency, 2 consulates, Internet access (Y10 per hr.), currency exchange, and free airport shuttles. 3-, 4-, and 7-bed dorms (foreigners only) Y30; doubles with bath Y140. Credit cards accepted.

Kunhu Hotel (kūnhú fàndiàn; 昆湖饭店), 202 Beijing Lu (☎313 3737), by Huancheng Lu. The lobby is dank and the corridors dim; happily, the rooms are much nicer. Next to 3 cafes, with travel agencies and 100 telephone stalls on the premises. Go ahead, ET phone home. 3- to 4-bed dorms Y25-26; singles Y60; doubles Y68, with bath Y128.

Yunnan University Guesthouse (yúnnán dàxué zhāodàisuǒ; 云南大学招待所; ☎503 3557; email ccfs@ynu.edu.cn), on Tian Jun Dian, off Yieryi Dajie, on the western edge of campus. From the North Train Station, take bus #22 down Huancheng Bei Lu to Yunnan University, near Dongfeng Xi Lu. From the main station, a taxi (Y14) is easier. If coming from Wenlin Jie, turn up Wenhua Xiang about halfway along the street, turn right at the end of the road, and left at Journey to the East Cafe; the university center is on the left. Technically reserved for foreign language students, but anyone is welcome. TVs, bright lighting, and private bath make this guesthouse's popularity well deserved. Hot water possibly 24hr. soon. Singles Y70; doubles Y100; triples Y150.

Kunming Railway Mansion (kūnmíng tiělù dàshà; 昆明铁路大厦; ☎351 1996), next to the train station. Noisy and far from anywhere you actually would want to spend time, unless you're into boxcars and axles. Hot water 8:30-9:30am and 8-10pm. Singles Y50, with bath Y160-190; doubles Y60, with bath Y160-190; triples Y75.

Three Leaves Hotel (kūnmíng sānyè fàndiàn; 昆明三叶饭店), 83 Beijing Lu (☎351 2543), across from the long-distance bus station and about 200m from the main train station. You'll need more than just three leaves over your ears to sleep at night—try earplugs. Ask to see the small standard room (Y68). Singles and doubles with bath Y138.

📷 FOOD

While there's much to salivate over, Kunming cuisine is not quite as varied as visitors might expect. Cheap snacks as well as more expensive tea houses and coffee shops encircle **Cuihu Park.** Just north of the park, restaurants offering heartier fare surround **Yunnan University,** asking only Y2-5 for everything from dumplings to Hui Muslim food. Another prime place for cheap food is **Beijing Lu,** toward the long-distance bus station and Kunming Train Station. There is a fruit market in the alley to the left upon entering the train station.

KUNMING SPECIALTIES

Kunming is most famous for its **Across-the-Bridge Noodles** (see p. 551). **Across Bridge Garden** (guò qiáo yuán; 过桥园) is in an alley off Dongfeng Dong Lu, across the street from the Camellia Hotel. The third floor decor, with dark artificial trees and awkward tea servers in Manchu costume, is a triumph for tackiness; however, the noodles (Y20-180) are nothing but pure, unadulterated pleasure. (☎316 9135. Open daily 8am-9pm.) The restaurant at 161 Qingnian Lu, midway between Renmin Dong Lu and the zoo, on the right as you come from Renmin Dong Lu, dishes up gigantic bowls of Across-the-Bridge Noodles for just Y5. (Open daily 8am-8pm.)

Another local Kunming dish is **Steampot Chicken** (qìguō jī; 汽锅鸡), cooked and presented in brown earthenware pots. Chopped into chunks and still clinging to the skin and bone, the tender meat comes floating in broth. **Chuncheng Hotel**

BRIDGE OVER TROUBLED WATERS Kunming's most famous local dish is Across-the-Bridge noodles (guò qiáo mĭ xiàn; 过桥米线), named for a medieval myth from Southern Yunnan. A diligent scholar preparing for the imperial examinations did his cramming on an isolated island, accessible by a lone wooden bridge. His devoted wife brought him food everyday, but everyday he grumbled that it was cold by the time it reached him. Intent on pleasing her beloved, the woman tried various experiments. One day she discovered that she could keep the soup hot by adding a layer of oil on the top. After crossing the bridge, she would quickly mix all the other ingredients together in the soup, making the perfect meal. This same basic method of preparation continues today. Across-the-Bridge restaurants start patrons off with a selection of finger foods; they are then given bowls of boiling soup, with raw meat and vegetables placed in bowls on the side. It is up to the diners to oversee the cooking of the meat and vegetables in the soup. Prices for Across-the-Bridge Noodles range from reasonably cheap to exorbitant, according to the amount and variety of ingredients spicing up the soup. Even the cautious backpacker watching every *mao* should try at least the mid-priced savory noodles.

(chūnchéng jiŭlóu; 春城酒楼), 11 Dongfang Xi Lu, diagonally opposite a Bank of China as you head away from Beijing Lu, serves this dish for Y30-35 per pot. (☎363 3271. Open daily 7:30-11am, 11:30am-2pm, and 5-8pm.)

MUSLIM CUISINE

Kunming's pockets of Hui, or Chinese Muslims, have long maintained a presence in the neighborhood bounded by **Wuyi Lu, Dongfeng Xi Lu,** and **Jinbi Lu. Shuncheng Jie** (顺城街), parallel to Dongfeng Xi Lu, is a vibrant Hui restaurant alley overflowing with green store fronts with Arabic inscriptions. From Dongfeng Xi Lu, turn at Wuyi Lu, which intersects the road at the Yunnan Provincial Museum, and take the first left. For those not averse to point-and-eat pantomimes, stalls offer spicy noodle soups at fire-sale prices (Y2-3). Interspersed among the stalls are a couple of flatbread and pastry vendors worth checking out. The pastries, often filled with nuts and cream, go for Y10-20 per kg. **Kunming Muslim Special Flavor Restaurant** (kūnmíng qīngzhēn fēngwèr chéng; 昆明清真风味儿城), 76 Shuncheng Jie, near Wuyi Lu, is the only restaurant in the area with an (albeit minimal) English menu. Skinned white duck (Y18), spiced lamb shish kebab (Y20), and flaky, round, sesame-covered sweet pastries (Y4) are among the favorites. (☎316 8806 or 313 0898. Open daily 11:30am-2pm and 5-9pm.)

DAI CUISINE

One of the few Dai restaurants in town, the **White Pagoda Dai Flavor Restaurant** (bái tă dài wèi tīng; 白塔傣味厅), 127 Shangyi Jie, showcases heavily spiced food, often wrapped in banana leaves, grass, or bamboo, including the house favorite, sticky black rice cooked in pineapple (Y8). Go south on Baita Lu from the intersection with Dongfeng Dong Lu, taking the first right; the restaurant is a three-minute walk on the left. (☎317 2932. Open daily 5am-9pm.)

WESTERN FOOD AND BACKPACKER HANGOUTS

Despite the good Chinese food (and good Chinese prices), backpackers inevitably flock to higher-priced cafes in search of the holy steak and chocolate cake grail.

■ **Wei's Pizzeria** (hāhā fàndiàn; 哈哈饭店), 400 Tuodong Lu (☎316 6189), a 10min. walk from Beijing Lu. If coming from the Camellia Hotel, turn right, take a left at the Holiday Inn, down Baita Lu, then turn right at the Green Lands Hotel to get to Wei's, which is just up the road on the right, before the China Insurance Company. Wei's has great pizza (Y20-30) but an even better atmosphere—the clientele is a refreshing mix of locals and foreigners. Open daily 7:30am-midnight.

SOUTHWEST

Golden Bay Western Restaurant (jīnhǎiàn xīcāntīng; 金海岸西餐厅), 60 Cuihu Bei Lu (☎537 9584), behind Cuihu Park's North Gate. An impressive selection of Western food (Y8-30) and drinks, a wonderfully relaxed air, friendly staff, and the best pizza this side of the Great Wall (Y15-36). Added perks include: M 8-10pm buy 2 beers get 1 free; W-Th free fruit platter with orders over Y80; and Su free cup of beer with pizzas Y20 and up. Open daily 10am-midnight.

Louise Bar (lòuyì cānbā; 露易餐吧), 90 Dongfeng Dong Lu (☎313 5018), before the Camellia Hotel, beyond Baita Lu. Has replaced Camel 2 as the most popular bar in town. Most dishes Y4-15; pizzas Y20-35; beer Y10-30. It's amassing an English book collection and a traveler's notebook; Y2 per day per book. Open 24hr.

Journey to the East (dōngfāng zhīlǚ; 东方之旅), 15 Tian Jun Dian (☎531 7451), near the Yunda Hotel. Turn right out of Yunnan University Guesthouse and walk up the slope. More like a journey to Kunming's expat community than "to the East." Entrees Y5-15, Internet access Y12 per hr., and the largest international book collection you'll find in Kunming (book rentals Y1 per day). Open daily 8am-late.

Teresa Pizza House (bǐsà fáng; 比荫房), 40 Wenlin Jie (☎537 6725). Pizzas Y15-40, free garlic bread or peanuts, depending on the stock. Internet access Y20 per hr. "English speakers' corner" Sa 2-5pm, frequented mainly by Yunnan University students and local business people. Open daily 9am-11:30pm.

Mama Fu's 2, 219 Baita Lu (☎311 1015). Turn north at the intersection with Dongfeng Dong Lu, away from the Holiday Inn and toward the Kunming Hotel. Run by Mama Fu's niece, this spin-off of the Lijiang Mama Fu's offers Naxi and Western food (Y5-15). While the Chinese food is good, only true devotees will find the goat-cheese flavored pizza (Y12-40) and extra-dry "brownie" (Y8) worthwhile. Open daily 8:30am-11pm.

🎵 ENTERTAINMENT

Nightlife happens in Kunming, but guessing just when and where it will happen is a gambler's enterprise. In order to render the city more "presentable" for Flower Power Expo '99, local police shut down many of the city's nightspots; some others are frequented by prostitutes. Currently, the most popular places are the discos of a few major hotels, with most of the clientele in their late teens or early 20s.

Camel Bar (luòtuó jiǔbā; 骆驼酒吧), 274 Baita Lu (☎317 6255). A long trek down Baita Lu, but there's live music and plenty of other thirsty revelers. They don't call this place the Camel Bar for nothing—most visitors drink like camels, soaking up all the liquid they can before moving onto the hot dance floor. Drinks Y12-15. Open 24hr.

Top One Disco, 329 Baita Lu, in the Bolan Hotel (bólán jiǔdiàn; 博兰酒店; ☎316 2118), and 98 Beijing Lu, in the King World Hotel (jīnhuá dàjiǔdiàn; 锦华大酒店), before the main bus station. The cutest Kunmingers around come to dance to loud techno. The one in the Bolan Hotel is currently at the top of the popularity contest. Beer Y35 and up. Dress smart-casual. Open daily 10:30pm-6am.

👁 SIGHTS

Too many misguided travelers wrongly assume that Kunming is just another typical provincial capital and only stop for a night or two. Indeed, Kunming has plenty of spirit and enough attractions to occupy twice that amount of time. Kunming's charms stem as much from the general atmosphere as from specific sights. In preparation for the 1999 International Horticultural Exposition, one of Kunming's proudest moments, much of the city was razed, and many of the older *hutongs* no longer exist. However, enough old edifices remain to provide an intriguing contrast to the dizzying scale and speed of Kunming's latest additions. Though many of the traditional Vietnamese and Cantonese commerce centers along **Jinbi Lu** (jīnbì lù; 金碧路) were torn down, a few sections remain.

EAST AND WEST PAGODAS (dōng sì tǎ; 东寺塔; and xī sì tǎ; 西寺塔). These twin relics from the Tang dynasty, the oldest standing structures in Kunming, are still hanging on by bare threads. Preserved in small parks, these timeworn gray towers provide a nice backdrop for the timeless art of relaxation. The West Pagoda is in an alley just off the main street, but easily visible and down a street flanked by old red walls. Opposite a small library, the pagoda courtyard is frequented by *mah-jong* players and other gamblers. *(The East Pagoda is halfway along Shulin Jie, going from either Jinbi Lu or Huancheng Nan Lu. The West Pagoda is directly opposite the East Pagoda on Dongsi Jie, the parallel street, going away from Beijing Lu. Both open daily 7am-8pm. Y0.5 each.)*

MUSLIM NEIGHBORHOOD. There are approximately 40,000 Hui Muslims in Kunming. The best remaining examples of Islamic architecture line Shuncheng Jie, which runs parallel to and one road south of Dongfeng Xi Lu, just opposite the Provincial Museum. Most older mosques are no longer standing. Among the new places of worship is **Nancheng Mosque** (nánchéng qīngzhēn gǔsì; 南城清真古寺), on the corner of Zhengyi Lu and Chongyun Jie. Turn up the large intersection of Zhengyi Lu, going north; the mosque is in an alley just past the Giordano shop. The green minarets and gold Arabic rooftop blaze bright and clear from afar. The first floor is occupied by a canteen; the prayer hall is on the second floor. Worshipers come at around 1:30pm daily, though mostly on Fridays. **Yixigong Mosque** (yìxīgōng qīngzhēn sì; 迤西公清真寺), near the corner of Qingnian Lu and Nanping Jie, just opposite the Bank of Communications, is very different from typical, delicate Hui mosques. Its impressive scale demonstrates the size and role of Kunming's Muslim community, and a life much beyond the streetside beef shish kebab stands.

FLOWER AND BIRD MARKET (huā niǎo shìchǎng; 花鸟市场). Plants and rare birds are just the tip of the iceberg. Stalls in this sprawling market offer myriad other creatures you might want to own and love, from carved wooden animals to gerbils, maggots, and plastic cockroaches. Even if you don't join in the pet accumulation, plan to spend at least an hour or two if you want to cover the entire market. The edges of the market, particularly toward the back, are lined with some fine examples of traditional Kunming architecture. Surrounding side streets, such as Jingxing Jie and Wenming Jie, are also dotted with old wooden structures; if you can tear your eyes away from the goods at street level, a glance upwards will reveal a very different world. The shopping mall opposite the market entrance, on Jingxing Jie, has some stunning photographs of Yunnan on the third floor. *(Between Jingxing Jie and Guanghua Jie. Walk north up Zhengyi Lu from the large intersection with Dongfeng Xi Lu, and turn left where a large sign advertises "Jingxing antique and jewelry center." This market blends into the flower and bird market on the right.)*

YUANTONG TEMPLE (yuántōng sì; 圆通寺). Built over 1000 years ago during the Nanzhao kingdom, this Buddhist temple represents the Mahayana, Theravada, and Tibetan sects. The best time to go is in the early morning or late afternoon, when the ratio of serious worshipers to idle visitors is greatest. *(30 Yuantong Jie, about a 10min. walk from Qingnian Lu, in the opposite direction of the stream running parallel to Qingnian Lu. ☎ 517 2881. Open daily 8am-5:20pm. Y4.)*

CUIHU PARK (cuìhú yuán; 翠湖园). Cuihu is a complex of four twisting lakes, the remnants of swampland that Emperor Kangxi had drained in the 17th century. Today, sculpted gardens, restaurants, and an amusement park are all fighting for space to breathe between the lakes. Even on weekdays, the tree-shaded stone benches overflow with elderly *mahjong* players and kids clamoring for rides on the lake's car-shaped boats (Y20-30 per hr.). More tranquil grounds can be found near the east entrance or directly to the north, across Wenling Jie, on the cool, shady campus of **Yunnan University,** the province's most prestigious university. The classroom buildings range from classical French to modern minimalist. *(Take bus #5 up Dongfeng Lu and get off at Xiaoxi Gate. Keep walking in the direction the bus is moving and turn right up Cuihu Nan Lu; from there, it's a 10min. walk to the south entrance. There are also entrances on the east, north, and west sides. ☎ 363 2081. Open daily 7am-10pm. Y2.)*

YUNNAN PROVINCIAL MUSEUM (yúnnán shěng bówùguǎn; 云南省博物馆). This grand beige building with a gold star on top is an extravagant testament to provincial pride in Yunnan's minority ethnic groups. The third floor exhibit on textiles, costumes, handicrafts, and artifacts, along with life-size mannequins of minority people in costume and a Yunnan map showing ethnic distributions, is the museum's main draw. The second floor has Neolithic Yunnan bronzeware and Buddhist art, going farther back in time with each ascent of the stairs. *(At the intersection of Dongfeng Xi Lu and Wuyi Lu. Take bus #5 along Dongfeng Lu to Jinre Gongyuan (近日公园). Continue walking in the same direction; the museum is on the left. ☎ 361 1551. Open Tu and Th-Su 9am-4:30pm. Y5, students Y2.5.)*

WORLD HORTICULTURAL EXPOSITION GARDEN (shìjiè yuányì bólǎnyuán; 世界园艺博览园). Kunming's 1999 International Horticultural Exposition closed over a year ago, but the Expo remains a prime tourist attraction. There are small gardens representing each Chinese province, Taiwan, as well as 34 foreign countries (the US garden is a "Texas ranch," complete with cacti and spicy chicken). Unless you really enjoy contrived cultural moments and specimens of unusually large garlic, squash, and plums, the steep entrance fee is probably not worth it. *(In the northeast part of Kunming. Take bus #47, 68, 69, or 72 (Y1). From Beijing Lu, you can also walk up to the intersection with Renmin Lu, turn right onto Renmin Lu, left on Baita Lu, and follow Baita Lu around to the right as if becomes Bailong Lu. Go to the end of Bailong Lu; the entrance is on the right where the road forks. ☎ 501 2367. Open daily 8am-9pm. Y100, after 2pm Y50; students and teachers Y50.)*

BAMBOO TEMPLE (qióngzhú sì; 筇竹寺). Bamboo Temple is a Zen Buddhist temple dating from the late 13th century and famous for its art and architecture. Legend has it that two princes, led by a magical rhinoceros, encountered a group of strange monks on the site of the future temple. The monks left behind walking sticks, which eventually organized into a bamboo grove. The temple's 500 quirky, life-size depictions of *luohans* are to the right of the main courtyard. In the 1880s, the master Sichuanese sculptor Li Guangxiu modeled (some would say caricatured) these statues after real-life personalities. Li met with a rather mysterious demise—a glance at the wonderfully expressive but often highly unflattering clay figures makes it easy to entertain suspicions. *(12km northwest of Kunming. Take the bus (30min., leaves when full, Y5) from outside the Yunnan Hotel.)*

GOLDEN TEMPLE PARK (jīndiàn míngshèng qū; 金殿名胜区). The main attractions here are the **Bell Tower,** which contains China's largest ancient bell, and **Golden Temple** itself—China's largest bronze temple. Over 300 years old, the temple was commissioned by Wu San Gui, a military genius who helped the Qing dynasty and was later named the King of Yunnan. There is also a combined Daoist and Buddhist temple. *(Take bus #10 or 71. Alternatively, walk toward the Expo Garden, but turn left instead of right (into the Garden) when Bailong Lu forks; turn right again at Cuanjin Lu. The park is a 15min. walk on the right. You can also enter the park via cable car from the Expo Garden (Y10 one-way, Y25 round-trip). Open daily 8am-8pm. Y15.)*

HAIGENG PARK AND YUNNAN MINORITIES VILLAGE (hǎigěng gōngyuán; 海埂公园; and yúnnán mínzú cūn; 云南民族村). Haigeng Park is a local resort and another source of scenic views of Lake Dian. The park is now dominated by the **Yunnan Minorities Village.** Young minority couples have been invited by the government to stay in their traditional-style houses, wear traditional clothing, and occupy themselves with traditional work, such as weaving or cultivating crops. Critics have called it an "ethnic Disneyland" or even a "human zoo." It presents a more representative display of minority culture than the Yunnan Provincial Museum, but still retains a bit of a disturbing circus feel. *(Take bus #44 from the main train station. Buses to the Minorities Village (Y10) also leave from the platform around the Western Hills' Tomb of Nie Er. A cable car (Y20) also goes from the village to the Western Hills.)*

OTHER SIGHTS. Kunming Zoo (kūnmíng dòngwùyuán; 昆明动物园), once China's second largest, has gone a bit downhill as of late. If live animals aren't enough, you can always pose next to a stuffed peacock while donning the minority costume of your choice. *(92 Qingnian Lu. Open daily 6:30am-8pm. Y6.)*

About 16km from Kunming, accessible by bus #9 or 79 from North Train Station, is **Black Dragon Pool** (hēi lóng tán; 黑龙滩). This restored Ming-dynasty Daoist temple is named for a legendary little black dragon whose life was spared by a Daoist immortal in return for its promise to aid mankind. The grounds contain cypresses and flowering trees that bloom in April and May; the botanical garden has even more plant life. *(Open daily sunrise-sunset. Y5.)*

Grand View Park (dàguān gōngyuán; 大观公园), on the northernmost tip of Lake Dian, is yet another construction commissioned by the demanding Emperor Kangxi. Inside the three-story pavilion, Qing scholar Sun Ranweng inscribed a famous 180-character poem praising the lakeside scenery. *(Bus #4 from the Kunming Zoo, by way of Nanping Jie and Huancheng Jie, stops here.)*

With waters streaming forth at temperatures of around 38°C, **Anning Hot Springs** (ānníng wēnquán; 安宁温泉) has been a favored bathing spot for Chinese since it was discovered during the Han dynasty. Foreigners have given it lukewarm reviews, though. Across the river and 2km south of the hot springs is **Caoxi Temple** (cáoxī sì; 曹溪寺), a Song-era monastery. A bus leaves from the bus station by the main train station for Anning.

▪ DAYTRIPS FROM KUNMING

STONE FOREST

*In Lunan Yi Autonomous County, 126km outside Kunming. Express **trains** from Kunming Main Station (90min.; 8:28 and 8:47am, returning at 3:18 and 3:54pm; Y30 round-trip) are the best bet. **Minibuses** (Y2) run to the forest from the station. Minibuses from the Camellia Hotel (30min., Y40 round-trip) depart at 8:30am, stop several times along the way, and return at 3pm; you won't actually arrive at the forest until 1-1:30pm. Minibuses also depart from outside the King World Hotel, on the corner of Beijing Lu and Yongan Lu, but the stopping problem also haunts this option. From the forest, minibuses (Y15) return to Kunming frequently. **Open** 24hr. **Admission** Y55, students Y30.*

A self-designated "wonder of the world," the Stone Forest (shí lín; 石林) covers 11.92km², of which only one portion—the Big and Little Stone Forests—is open to visitors. The forest is a gigantic labyrinth of jagged karst (limestone) pillars, some over 30m high, lashed and split by ice and rain, and eroded to their present form. Formed more than 200 million years ago, some rocks were lucky enough to end up distorted into shapes that resemble "a 1000-year-old tortoise," "a baby elephant," or "a stone buffalo," thrilling the not insubstantial community of connoisseurs of rocks-that-look-like-something-else.

A tragic Yunnan tale of love and adventure provides inspiration for those same rock experts. Ashima, a beautiful maiden and the beloved of the dashing and daring Aheige, was kidnapped by the son of a nasty rich man. Aheige came to the rescue, but the villain sent a flood to drown Ashima. The animalesque rocks all play their part in the saga; Ashima is immortalized as yet another big rock, a woman carrying a bamboo basket with a flower in it, near the end of the Big Stone Forest.

The Stone Forest's status as a tourist attraction means that it usually harbors dangerous packs of tour groups. Paths are narrow, making exploration slow and exhausting, and it is difficult to find any place in the main forest that is not crawling with people. For the less harrowing company of stones and some relief from the human circus, take the path to the right at the main fork, which leads to a small and quiet pavilion. Although the forest can be visited as a daytrip, perhaps the most pleasant way is to arrive in late afternoon, stay overnight, and wander around in the morning before the tour bus invasion. The surrounding area is populated by the **Sanyi** minority group, a subgroup of the Yi; many locals sell their wares or are employed as tour guides.

To stay overnight at the forest, there are two main options. The **Yunlin Hotel** (yúnlín bīnguǎn; 云林宾馆), inside the forest, is a good choice. From the main path, turn right, left, and left again; signs point the way. (☎771 1410 or 771 1058. 6-bed dorms Y30; doubles with bath Y250; triples with bath Y200-250.) The **Shilin Hotel** (shílín bīnguǎn; 石林宾馆) is just past the entrance to the forest, on the left. (☎771 1401. Singles Y200, with A/C Y300; triples Y210, with A/C Y350.)

SOUTHWEST

LAKE DIAN AND THE WESTERN HILLS

*A **minibus** (8am, Y10) runs from the Yunnan Hotel, 128 Dongfeng Xi Lu; to get to the Hotel, take bus #5 along Dongfeng Lu to the stop after the Yunnan Provincial Museum. Alternatively, take **bus** #5 all the way to the end of the line, where you can squeeze onto a crowded #6 to the base of the hills; from here, minibuses run to the Tomb of Nie Er (Y4). Buses also run back down the hill (Y6); many of these will go all the way to the beginning of bus #5. To bike to the Western Hills (1½-2hr), take Renmin Xi Lu; bear left when the road forks. The road should lead directly to the Western Hills. Take the cable car up, and the ride down should be a breeze. Western Hills Dragon Gate area **open** daily 7am-8pm. **Admission** Y15.*

Lined with small fishing hamlets, **Lake Dian** (diān chí; 滇池) is the largest lake in Yunnan and the sixth largest in China. Many of the "sights" around Kunming are in fact spots that afford the finest views of the lake. By far the most spectacular view of Lake Dian is from the **Western Hills** (xī shān; 西山), nicknamed **Sleeping Beauty Mountain** because of its resemblance to a woman reclining. Carved into the craggy cliff faces are Yuan, Ming, and Qing dynasty temples, with a series of grottoes thrown in for good measure. Near the summit, even the most perilous passageways and stone paths have chest-high walls with guard rails.

The area between the Tomb of Nie Er and the top of the mountain is officially known as **Dragon Gate** (lóng mén; 龙门). A chairlift runs from the tomb to the top. *(Runs daily 8:30am-3:30pm. Y20.)* In 1781, the Daoist monk Wu Laiqing, aided only by a hammer, a chisel, and a dream, determinedly chipped a long corridor up the face of the mountain. Legend has it that the tip of his chisel broke as he neared the end of his work (a good 14 years later), throwing him into a fit of despair; in turn, he threw himself into the waters below. Over 50 years later, the monk's followers finally reached a natural cliff-top platform, now called Dragon Gate. Over 2400m high, it commands a breathtaking vista of Lake Dian. A 15-minute climb from Dragon Gate leads to the top of one of the hills, covered with rocks known as the Small Stone Forest, and home to a large pagoda. A 10-minute descent leads to **Sanqing Pavilion** (sānqīng gé; 三清阁). Built in the 14th century as a country retreat for a Yuan dynasty prince, the pavilion was later reincarnated as a Daoist shrine.

The **Tomb of Nie Er** (niè ěr mù; 聂耳墓) is 20 souvenir vendor-filled minutes down from Sanqing Pavilion. A native of Yunnan, Nie Er (1912-1936) composed China's national anthem before drowning en route to the Soviet Union. From the Tomb of Nie Er, buses run to the base of the hills or back to Kunming. However, walking down the hills leads to two more temples. **Taihua Temple** (tàihuá sì; 太华寺) is the next temple down the mountain, about a 30-minute walk from Nie Er's tomb. A Yuan dynasty temple rebuilt during Qing Emperor Kangxi's reign, Taihua is known for its camellia blossoms. *(Open daily sunrise-sunset. Y5.)* **Huating Temple** (huátíng sì; 华亭寺) sits another 30-minute walk down the main road. Beyond the ornamental lake and garden, the main temple contains lavishly painted statues of Buddha. *(Open daily sunrise-sunset. Y5.)* The mountain base is yet another 30-minute walk.

The **Taihua Mountain Hotel** (tàihuá shān zhuāng; 太华山庄) is about 150m from the entrance. (☎841 1893. Singles Y96; triples Y110. Special group rates available.)

JIUXIANG SCENIC AREA (jiǔxiāng fēngjǐng qū; 九乡风景区)

Transportation options are limited. The East Bus Station, accessible by buses #11, 50, and 63, might have minibuses to Jiuxiang soon. Renting a minibus costs about Y220. Otherwise, try to catch a ride from Transfer International Travel Service (yúnnán shěng jiāotōng zǒng gōngsī; 云南省交通旅行游总公司), 60 Beijing Lu (☎351 4274). Y68.

Not nearly as well known as the Stone Forest but definitely just as amazing a natural wonder, Jiuxiang contains 66 caves, of which only a few are open to the public. Human and other mammalian remains from the Paleolithic Age were discovered in the 1980s, and the caves became a scenic spot in 1989, though the main sites are still unfinished. Despite quite a heavy human presence (eerie neon lights, camera toting vendors, and exhibits), the Jiuxiang caves maintain a primeval feel. Main attractions include a series of rock terraces that have been dubbed **Magic Fields** (神田) and a spectacular underground river and waterfall. We recommend that you discover this place before tour groups do.

HOLY SMOKES Many travelers come to China with their olfactory systems all geared up for the fragrance of incense smoke in temples. They will find some of that, but not before they encounter plenty of China's other sacred smoke. Cigarette smokers light up any time, any place, and in front of anyone. In the past, the only women who dared to smoke in public were prostitutes, and even today, smoking remains predominantly a male activity. Non-smoking areas in restaurants are practically unheard of; the posted "no smoking" signs on trains often seem more decorative than anything. Non-smokers with weak lungs or allergies can find daily life quite harrowing. On the other hand, foreign smokers often delight in the unfettered social legitimacy that Chinese culture grants all brave knights of the nicotine order.

The government is beginning to realize the dangers of smoking and the potential health costs, but the economy speaks otherwise. Yunnan, China's number one tobacco producer, draws 70% of its revenues from tobacco farming and cigarette sales. The popular Yunnan Red Pagoda Mountain (yúnnán hóng tǎ shān; 云南红塔山) brand goes for twice the price of imported Marlboros.

✠ BORDER CROSSING INTO VIETNAM: HEKOU

Hekou (hékǒu; 河口) is the small town at the Chinese border with Vietnam; on the other side of the border is **Sapa,** an old French hill station populated by Hmong people. The border crossing is actually a small bridge across a river, and the respective border formalities take place on either side. Border officials rarely speak much English, but tend to be friendly on the Chinese side, though many travelers have to pay a small "handling fee" on the Vietnamese side. **Vietnamese visas cannot be obtained at the border crossing.** Some travelers have been able to get them from CITS in Kunming (p. 547), but it is best not to count on that possibility.

Buses to Kunming run from the bus station on the main road, Renmin Lu, ten times per day (16-18hr., Y100-120). Chinese time is one hour ahead of Vietnamese—be careful to not the miss the bus. **Trains** to Kunming's North Station leave in the early afternoon (16hr., Y33-77). The first thing most people need to do once in China is change money. The **Bank of China** is at the end of the main road, on the left side on the corner. The bank will not exchange Vietnamese currency for Chinese, but many locals will do so.

Hekou has plenty of **hotels.** One cluster is up the main road, and another cluster is left out of the border office and left again. Dorms go for Y10-40, but many places only have standard rooms (Y100 and up). Key deposit tends to be high. Both the **Tourism Administration of Hekou County** (☎/fax 0873 342 1259) and the **CITS** (☎0873 342 2256; fax 342 1252) are at 9 Renmin Lu.

OLD TOWN DALI 大理古城   ☎0872

Dali's location between lake and mountains makes it one of the most beautiful and relaxing spots in China. Old Dali lies on the Yunnan-Myanmar and Yunnan-Tibet trade routes and served as the capital of the Nanzhao Kingdom from AD 739 to 937. Today, the economic and political activity of the prefecture lies to the south around the city of Xiaguan (also called Dali City), so Old Dali has none of the bustle and pollution of so many other Chinese cities. Old Dali is home to the Bai people, a branch of the Yi minority present in Yunnan province. The town is a mixture of authentic history and contrived "tradition," a haven for both foreign and Chinese visitors (4.3 million tourists passed through last year). Despite the flow of people, Dali is rarely crowded, and solitary moments are easy to experience on an excursion through the back streets or a bicycle ride through the countryside. Travelers eager for the "real" China, a mythical place free of the damages of tourism, may be disappointed by Dali's easy expatriate air and keen lookout for colorful pieces of *yuan.*

SOUTHWEST

✴ ❼ ORIENTATION AND PRACTICAL INFORMATION

Dali is between **Lake Erhai** (Ear Lake) and the **Cangshan Mountains**, 1940m above sea level. Its historical role as a defense-worthy administrative center is evident from the remnants of stone walls that mark the outer boundaries of the old, square-shaped town. **Fuxing Lu** (复兴路) runs between **North City Gate** (běi mén; 北门) and **South City Gate** (nán mén; 南门). **Huguo Lu** (护国路), the coffee- and pizza-laden "foreigner street," branches off from Fuxing Lu.

Buses: The **Dali Long-distance Bus Station** (dàlǐ chángtú qìchē zhàn; 大理长途汽车站) is on Dianzang Lu about 30m from Huguo Lu, and right past the No. 4 Guesthouse. Most travel agencies, hotels, and restaurants along Huguo Lu sell tickets and take people to the station. To **Kunming** (4½-5hr.; 11 per day; Y50-105, express Y100-110) and **Lijiang** (2½-3hr.; 34 per day; Y30-35, express Y55). More buses to these and other destinations leave from **Xiaguan** (see p. 563).

Local Transportation: While Old Town Dali itself can be navigated entirely on foot, local buses cover the distance between Dali and Xiaguan. **Buses** (Y1.2) and **minibus #4** (Y1.5) to **Xiaguan** stop frequently along Boai Lu (30-40min., every 10min.), or flag down a minibus (Y2) on Dianzang Lu. For either of these, turn left off Huguo Lu with Dali behind you, and you will be heading in the correct direction.

Bike Rental: Michael's, 44 Boai Lu, next to Michael's Miao Art. Turn left off Huguo Lu with Fuxing Lu behind you. Y3 per hr., Y10 per day. Open daily 8am-8pm. The **No. 4 Guesthouse** on Huguo Lu and the **No. 5 Guesthouse** on Boai Lu have a small selection of bikes. Y10-15 per day.

Travel Agencies: It's not hard to find travel advice or information in Dali. **Dali Travel Information Service Bureau** (dàlǐ lǚyóu xìnxī zīxún fúwù bù; 大理旅游信息咨询服务部; ☎267 1890; mobile 13508 724 012), on Huguo Lu before the Tibetan Cafe. Open daily 7am-9pm. **Dali Travel Centre** (dàlǐ gǔchéng kèchē zhōngxīn; 大理古城客车中心; ☎267 1890; mobile 13508 724 197), on the corner of Fuxing Lu and Huguo Lu. Open daily 7am-10pm.

Bank of China: 304 Fuxing Lu (☎267 0171). Exchanges traveler's checks and issues credit card advances. Open daily 8am-7:30pm. Also on Fuxing Lu (facing the post office) is the **Industrial and Commercial Bank of China** (zhōngguó gōngshāng yínháng; 中国工商银行; ☎267 0231). Exchanges US currency and traveler's checks. Open daily 8am-8:30pm.

PSB: 4 Huguo Lu (☎267 0016), next to the No. 4 Guesthouse. Open M-F 2-5:30pm. Visa extensions available from **Dali PSB Foreign Affairs Office,** on Cangshan Lu in Xiaguan.

Internet Access: Tim's Internet Shop, 82 Boai Lu (☎207 1572), next to Cafe de Jack. Y3 per 10min., Y16 per hr. Open daily 8am-1am. Several shops along Huguo Lu also offer Internet access.

Post and Telecommunications: On the corner of Fuxing Lu and Huguo Lu (☎267 0111). EMS and IDD service; no collect calls. Open daily 8am-9pm. **Postal Code:** 671003.

▌ ACCOMMODATIONS

Most of the cheapest places in backpacker-friendly Dali are around Huguo Lu and Boai Lu, close to the tourist cafes. All have dormitories (often co-ed) as well as individual rooms, and offer laundry services and luggage storage.

Old Dali Inn No. 5 Guesthouse (dàlǐ sìjí kèzhàn; 大理四季客栈), 51 Boai Lu (☎267 0382). Attractive rooms and a garden courtyard create an inviting atmosphere. Toilet cleanliness may be the sole complaint. Bike rental Y15 per day. Hot water 8am-11pm. 4-bed dorms Y15; singles Y30; doubles Y50, with TV and bath Y110-115; triples Y20.

No. 4 Guesthouse Yuan Garden Hotel (yú'ān yuán huāyuán lǚshè; 榆安园花园旅社), 4 Huguo Lu (☎267 2093), above Boai Lu and several steps below the intersection with Dianzang Lu, a common stop for minibuses. The guesthouse contains a pretty courtyard

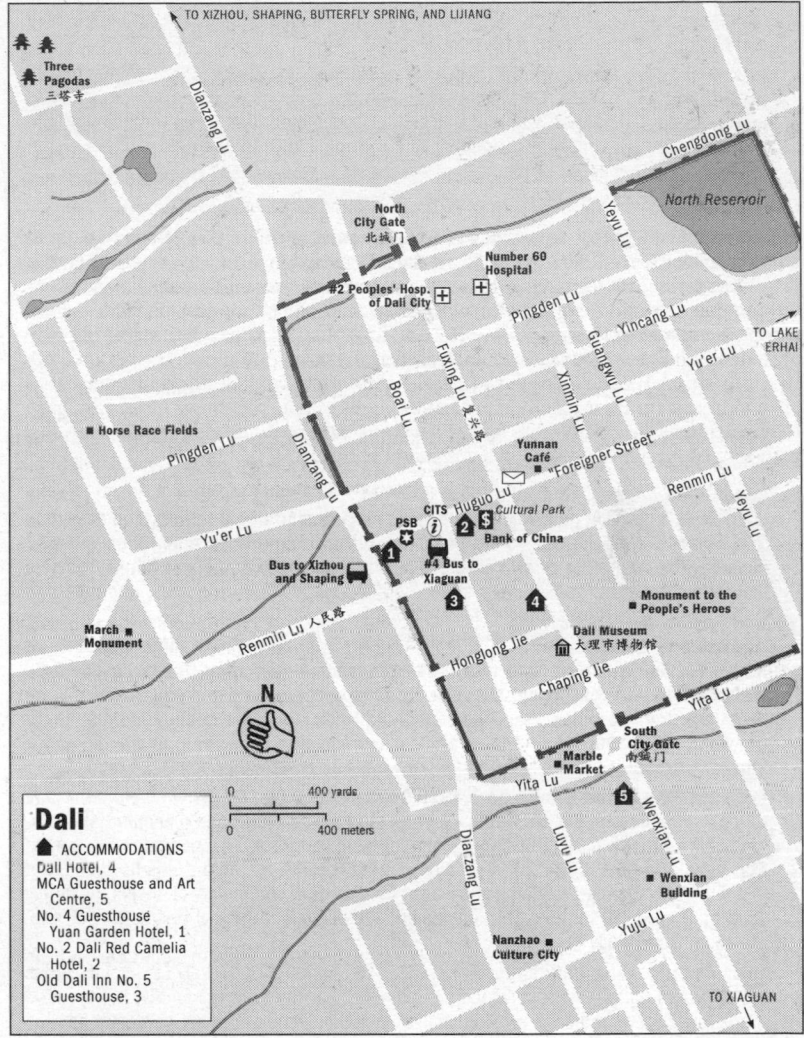

TO XIZHOU, SHAPING, BUTTERFLY SPRING, AND LIJIANG

SOUTHWEST

Dali

🔺 ACCOMMODATIONS

Dali Hotel, 4
MCA Guesthouse and Art
Centre, 5
No. 4 Guesthouse
Yuan Garden Hotel, 1
No. 2 Dali Red Camelia
Hotel, 2
Old Dali Inn No. 5
Guesthouse, 3

with fellow backpackers lounging about. Hot water 24hr., and some of the cleanest bathrooms in Dali. Free washing machines. Bike rental Y10 per day. 5- to 6-bed dorms Y10; 3- to 4-bed dorms Y15; singles Y30, with bath Y100; doubles Y50, with bath Y100.

MCA Guesthouse and Art Centre, 7000 Wenxian Lu (☎267 3666 or 267 1999), a 5min. walk out of Dali from the South Gate, about 7-8min. from the center of town. No Chinese name; ask for "MC" if you need directions. Run by artists affiliated with the Yunnan School of Art; the 10-bed dorms have been converted into a studio and gallery. Although the remote location can be inconvenient, the MCA seems to have it all, including an outdoor pool (sometimes functional), cafe, book rental (Y2 per day), pool tables, Internet access (Y18 per hr.), bike rental (Y10 with deposit), and more. 4- to 5-bed dorms Y10; singles Y50; doubles Y50, with bath Y150; triples Y100.

Dali Hotel (dàlǐ bīnguǎn; 大理宾馆), 277 Fuxing Lu (☎267 0386 or 267 1604). The Dali has elegant Bai architecture, a maze of connected courtyards, and decent modern facilities. The more expensive rooms are clean and spacious; unfortunately, the cheaper rooms are not nearly as nice. Hot water 6-9am and 7pm-midnight. 3-bed dorms with TV and bath Y40; 2-bed dorms Y40; doubles Y140-240.

No. 2 Dali Red Camellia Hotel (dàlĭ hóng shān chá bīnguǎn; 大理红山茶宾馆), 32 Huguo Lu (☎267 0423). Dark hallways and a noisy karaoke place next door make this hotel less appealing than some of Dali's other accommodations. Hot water 6-9:30pm. 5-bed dorms Y10; singles and doubles Y30, with bath Y80; triples Y36.

◗ FOOD

The majority of Chinese restaurants are on Renmin and Yuer Lu. Most locals grab a *baozi* (meat or red bean paste filled bun) for breakfast, but many also head to ■ stands selling *er quai* (fried dough and various—usually spicy hot—sauces wrapped in a grilled rice pancake) or *er si* (rice noodles). Marvelous Muslim food can be found along Fuxing Lu and Renmin Lu; look for Arabic writing or the Chinese characters for Islam (清真). Many foreign visitors pounce on the opportunity to enjoy good Western food and head to the cafes and restaurants clustered around **Huguo Lu**. Bearing colorful English signs and menus, these places are hard to miss. Some Chinese visitors have even come to treat them as tourist attractions, places to observe the *laowai* in a simulated native habitat.

■ **Yunnan Cafe** (yúnnán kāfēiguǎn; 云南咖啡馆), 151 Huguo Lu (☎267 0083). On the left side of Huguo Lu, near Fuxing Lu. Small and peaceful, with a relaxing sun deck, this is a reprieve from the upper end of Huguo Lu. Consistently excellent food (Y8-18), including the best pizza in town (Y10-20) and a wide range of alcoholic drinks. The cafe also offers imported books, Internet access (Y18 per hr.), board games, and massage (Y60). Open daily 8am-midnight.

Cafe de Jack (jiékè kāfēiwū; 杰克咖啡屋), 46 Boai Lu (☎267 1572), just left off Huguo Lu. Run in conjunction with Tim's Internet Cafe next door. The atmosphere de Jack is warm and welcoming, although the food quality is variable and customers are encouraged not to order "complicated dishes" when the place is busy. Dishes Y8-15. Don't miss the clean bathroom—check out the clever verse written on the door by a former customer. Open daily 8am-1am (or whenever everyone is done).

Xian Yuan Restaurant (xián yuán; 闲园), 369 Fuxing Lu (☎267 0451), before the Dali Cinema. A small door and narrow alleyway lead to the Xian Yuan's enchanting court-yard. The owner is putting up more stone tables in his backyard, beneath a canopy of fruit trees and next to the 200-year-old main house. The restaurant has no menu, but instead offers to cook "anything you want." Play cards or *mahjong* with locals, or simply slurp up a bowl (Y2) of cold chicken rice noodles (*liangji mixian*) or traditional rice noo dle soup. Open daily 8am-8pm.

Sunshine Cafe (yángguāng kāfēi; 阳光咖啡), 16 Huguo Lu (☎267 0712). Comfy chairs and a great location make for good people-watching. The staff is friendly, but the food tends toward the mediocre, although some customers rave about the homemade bread (Y4-5) and the chocolate brownies. Dishes Y5-15. Open daily 7:30am-12:30am.

Mr. China's Son (☎267 8234), on Boai Lu. Although its namesake is no longer alive, the cafe has an excellent guidebook for travelers and an interesting collection of Bai "relics" on the side wall. 5- or 6-course Bai meals Y12-14. Open daily 8am-midnight.

Ancient Music Teahouse (gǔyuè cháshì; 古乐茶室), 53 Huguo Lu (mobile 1350 882 2849), next to Old Wooded House Restaurant. Try the famous Bai 3-course tea (三道茶), served with complimentary pickled fruits (Y10). Excellent Yunnan coffee (Y5) tops off the meal. Open M-F 8am-midnight, Sa-Su 9am-midnight.

◗ SIGHTS

Old Town Dali's relaxed atmosphere, unique architecture, and people-watching opportunities are far more impressive than its actual sights. For some non law-abiding tourists, a certain locally grown herb (dàmá; 大麻) is one of the greatest attractions of Dali; possession of marijuana is illegal in China. *Let's Go* just says no. The **North** or **South City Gate** along the Old Town Wall affords good views of the

THE BAI PEOPLE The Bai minority live in northwestern Yunnan, clustered around Dali prefecture. Their language is part of the Yi group of the Tibeto-Burmese family and, until recently, had no written form. Although many Bai words are borrowed from Mandarin Chinese, Bai itself is a non-Chinese tonal language with a very different grammatical structure.

The religion of the Bai is similar to that of the southern Chinese, emphasizing local deities and ancestral spirits. Although the Bai maintain their distinct language and dress, their daily practices bear the influence of a long history of contact with the Han Chinese. In the Yuan dynasty, Kublai Khan conquered the Dali kingdom, and the Bai were encouraged to model themselves on Chinese literati. Today, many Bai, even those who are extensively assimilated into Chinese society, make a point of stressing their Bai ancestry in order to obtain exemptions from the one-child policy, which does not apply to non-Han ethnic groups. The Bai today number between 1.4 and 1.7 million.

town and Lake Erhai. *(Open daily 9am-7pm. Y2.)* From up here, a visitor can get a sense of what it was like back when Dali's strategic importance was not tied up in Internet cafes and pizza joints. The **Dali Museum** (dàlǐshì bówùguǎn; 大理市博物馆), 111 Fuxing Lu, is housed in a noteworthy Bai-style building. Unfortunately, appearances may be deceiving: a rather bland collection of historical relics and marble artifacts awaits. *(☎ 267 0196. Open daily 8:30am-6:30pm. Y8.)* **Dali Cultural Park** (dàlǐ wénhuà yuán; 大理文化园) is really just a regular old park, where visitors can watch old men playing *mahjong* and cards. With your back to the mountains, turn right off Huguo Lu; the park is on the right. *(Open 24hr. Free.)*

THREE PAGODAS (sān tǎ sì; 三塔寺). The oldest standing structures in Yunnan, the pagodas have come to symbolize Old Dali. With Cangshan in the background, these majestic towers stand on a hill an hour beyond the North Gate and are visible from almost any vantage point within Dali and the surrounding area. Erected over 42 years during the Nanzhao era, the original pagodas were destroyed in a fire in the 19th century, and a replica was built in 1997. They rest on the foundation of the Chongsheng Temple, patronized by the Nanzhao royal families. The central **Qianxun Pagoda** stands at 69m and is flanked by twin 42m pagodas on either side. The towering landmarks are just as impressive from a distance as from up close, because from far away you can't see the numerous trinket vendors. A better bet is the nearby **Reflection Park** (dàoying gōngyuán; 倒映公园), where you can see the pagodas reflected in the lake. *(Turn right off Huguo Lu onto Dianzang Lu; follow Dianzang Lu for approx. 1hr. ☎ 267 0179 or 267 1847. Horse tours Y90. Open daily 8am-8pm. Y20; Jianyi Bell Tower Y5. Reflection Park Y5.)*

OTHER SIGHTS. The ride to the avant-garde construction of **Butterfly Spring** (húdié quán; 蝴蝶泉) is beautiful. Star-crossed lovers once threw themselves into the waters in despair. Their spirits turned into butterflies and the transformed lovers return each spring to frolic at the site of their last union. Despite the romantic (or somewhat schmaltzy depending on your point of view) legend surrounding the sight, the spring itself is not terribly interesting. *(Buses make the 35min. trip every 20min. starting at 7:30am for Y6. By bicycle, follow Dianzang Lu all the way the way to the spring; the trip will take about 2½hr. each way. Y20.)* For those who want to go shopping in Shaping (shāpíng; 沙坪), the **market** takes place every Monday. By bike, the trip takes about two and a half hours each way; turn right off Huguo Lu onto Dianzang Lu. *(Public buses leave Dali Bus Station on Dianzang Lu every 20min. for the 20min. ride to Shaping and cost Y6. Travelers can also book tickets on a tour bus; tours leave at 9am, return at 1:30pm, and cost Y15)*

🛍 SHOPPING

Shopping is a major Dali pastime. **Huguo Lu** is lined with tailors selling all manner of striped or tie-dyed clothing; if you don't like what they have, many will make items to suit a custom order. Batik shops are also abundant; most batiks (blue tie-dyed or colorfully painted clothes), are made in Guizhou, but Dali is one of the best places in Yunnan to buy them. Peddlers at street stalls push jewelry and small potteries, while Bai women selling silver and embroidery often follow people from restaurant to restaurant. It is a bonanza for knick-knacks of varying charm and uselessness. Just outside the South City Gate is the sprawling **Marble Market,** which has tons of small stalls selling cups, animal figurines, and jewelry made of Dali's famous marble. In fact, the Chinese word for marble, *dalishi* (大理石), literally means "stone of Dali." The pieces of marble are mesmerizing; the rivulets of different colors looking like mountains or seascapes tempt visitors (mostly Chinese tourists) to schlep home with the heavy rocks.

⚡ DAYTRIPS FROM OLD TOWN DALI

Half the joy of the sights around Dali is in getting to them. Whether cycling, taking the bus, walking, or horseback riding, visitors cannot miss this region's stunning scenery. The blazing green rice fields and the vivid Bai dresses are brilliant against the clear blue of Lake Erhai and the mist-shrouded Cangshan slopes.

CANGSHAN

*Cangshan Temple can be reached by **cable car** for Y35, or on horseback for about Y70. A cheaper alternative to the cable car is to take **bus** #4 (Y5) on Boai Lu going toward Xiaguan to Gantong Temple. From there, take one of the many horse carriages or small vans (30min., Y5) to the foot of the mountain; to Gantong Temple. **Hiking** from Gantong Temple to Zhonghe Temple takes 6-8hr. walk, and the path is not clearly marked. Ask at a travel agency in Lijiang for a more detailed map. **Admission** to the temples is free; other sights Y6-10.*

The Cangshan Mountains (cāng shān; 苍山) surrounding Dali offer more than just pleasant scenery. For the many monks and nuns who reside on these spectacular hills, they are also a place of religious worship and retreat. The most popular place for tourists to view the daily worship of these monks and nuns is **Cangshan Temple,** which offers a stunning view of Lake Erhai and the surrounding area. From Cangshan, visitors can walk along a flat road north (the left, facing away from the mountains) to **Zhonghe Temple** (zhōnghé sì; 中和寺), or head off in the opposite direction to **Gantong Temple** (gǎntōng sì; 感通寺). If you arrive around noon, you can join the residents for a vegetarian meal. The very lucky might even witness the monks and nuns in an elaborate ceremony performed on behalf of worshipers. From the Gantong Temple it is a 10-minute trek to **Jizhao Monastery** (jízhào ān; 寂照庵), a lovely, utterly peaceful place where eight nuns and monks reside.

WASE

A tourist boat (leaves 9:30am, returns 4pm; Y20) leaves Dali for Wase. If you want to leave later in the day, many local Dali street merchants will offer to take you; it will cost more (Y30-50), but there will be fewer foreigners at the market. For tourist boats exploring other parts of Lake Erhai, try the Yuxing Tourist Office. Most trips take 6hr. and cost Y20-50.

The **market** in Wase (wāsè; 挖色), held every five days from the 5th to the 25th of each month, is your "typical" Bai market—teeming with life, confusion at its best and most exciting. The area near Lake Erhai's shore is the market square, where Bai merchants in traditional dress ply their peaches, *er si* (rice noodles), household goods (including rat poison), and even live fowl. A walk into the town offers a great opportunity to explore the small streets and local architecture. The public ferry no longer runs, but tourist boats ply the route across Lake Erhai, usually taking in sights such as **Minor Putuo Island** (xiǎo pǔtuó; 小普陀), **Tianjing Pavilion** (tiānjìng gé; 天境阁), and **Sea Island** (hǎi dǎo; 海岛). It is possible to bike to Wase in just over four hours, meandering through lakeside Bai villages. If you get stuck in Wase, stay in the **Wase Hostel** (wāsè zhāodàisuǒ; 挖色招待所). Turn left out of the market square with your back to the lake and go as far along the road as you can, following it as it turns right; the hostel is the last building on the right, before the PSB. (Dorms Y7.) If you miss the Wase market, you can still take a trip on **Lake Erhai** that visits some of the major sites around the lake.

BAI-BAI, MR. NICE TEA The Bai three-course tea is named for its three flavors. The first cup (called "lightning tea" because of the process used to make it) is bitter, symbolizing the harsh moments in life. The second cup (stewed with Bai cheese) is sweet and represents all of life's goodness. The last cup (containing ginger, pepper, honey, and an herb called *guipi*) is a cup of bittersweet remembrance, completing the trilogy that is meant to represent each person's life. When Bai men bring a potential wife home to meet the family, the first cup of tea she is served is crucial: if it's sweet, the girl has been approved of; if it's bitter, she is deemed unsuitable.

XIZHOU VILLAGE

Buses (30min., every 30min., Y4) leave from the Dali Bus Station. Many buses go along this route; ask to be dropped at Xizhou when you get on the bus or when buying your ticket. There are 2 attractive routes for **biking** to Xizhou (2hr. one-way). To take the low road, follow Fuxing Lu out through North Gate. If it's hot, take the high road along Dianzang Lu; the road is a little uneven, but the trees offer some shade. Both taking the bus and cycling along Dianzang Lu will land you at a large sign (in English) pointing to Xizhou. After a bumpy 5min. cycle ride or a 15min. walk along this cobbled path, cross the road and continue in the same direction. Arrows direct you to the main square.

Xizhou (xǐzhōu zhèn; 喜洲镇), a military stronghold during the Nanzhao Kingdom, retained enough wealth to build huge Bai houses whose crumbling remains remind visitors of the town's glorious past. The road to Xizhou, surrounded by the fresh green of rice paddies and the majestic Cangshan Mountains in the background, can be more of an attraction than the rather contrived (but entertaining all the same) display of Bai culture in the town itself. The special sight here is **Yan's Big Courtyard** (yán jiā dà yuàn; 严家大院), in the main square. The Yans were rich industrialists who left China during the Cultural Revolution. Now their massive house offers a Bai cultural experience of traditionally-clad dancers and singers performing while the "trilogy tea of the Bai clan" (named for its three flavors: bitter, sweet, and spicy) and Bai bread are served. Performances start once enough people show up, so the cultural experience is usually "enhanced" by an encounter with Chinese tour groups at play, an important contemporary phenomenon. *(Open daily 8am-6pm. Y4; Y20 for meal and performance.)*

From Xizhou main square, a 20-minute walk through the rice fields, following the sign to Shiping Jie (市坪街) leads to the **Haixin Pavilion** (hǎixīn tíng; 海心亭). *(Open daily 8am-midnight. Free.)* While the pavilion itself is unspectacular, the walking route is picturesque. The **Xizhou Tianzhuang Hotel** (xǐzhōu tiánzhuāng bīnguǎn; 大喜州田庄宾馆), on Shiping Lu, is housed in a grand Bai building, with rooms arranged around a lush courtyard. (☎245 1515. 24hr. hot water in good weather, 8-11pm otherwise. 5-bed dorms Y30; doubles Y60.)

XIAGUAN 下关 ☎0872

At the mouth of Lake Erhai and at the foot of the Cangshan mountains, Xiaguan should have been named China's "windy city." The combination of mountains and lake make the wind literally howl in this capital of Dali Bai Autonomous County, especially at night. Xiaguan is a town for drifters, and the large floating population has more than its share of itinerant (and homegrown) pickpockets—so keep a tight hold onto your hat and your wallet. Most use Xiaguan as a base for exploring nearby Jizushan, a sacred Buddhist site.

ORIENTATION AND PRACTICAL INFORMATION

Xiaguan is often referred to as **Dali City** (dàlǐ shì; 大理市) and should not be confused with Old Dali (dàlǐ gǔchéng; 大理古城), the intended destination of many travelers who pass through Xiaguan. Virtually all major establishments in Xiaguan are on **Jianshe Lu** (建设路).

Airplanes: The new **Dali Airport** (dàlǐ jīchǎng, 大理机场; ☎216 6771 or 216 8288) is 16km outside Xiaguan and accessible only by taxi (Y20-30). To **Jinghong** (1 per day, Y520) and **Kunming** (3 per day, Y340). Purchase tickets in Old Dali, or in Xiaguan at the **Dali Travel Ticket Center** (dàlǐ lǚyóu piàowù zhōngxīn; 大理旅游票务中心), Dali Hotel, 1 Jianshe Xi Lu, 1st Fl. (☎216 6588; fax 216 6578), at Renmin Lu.

Trains: Dali Train Station (dàlǐ zhàn; 大理站; ☎219 1660), is 2 km away from the intersection of Jianshe Xi Lu and Renmin Lu. Take bus #1 from Jianshe Lu (going away from the Cangshan mountains). To **Kunming** (9hr., 1 per day, Y60-70).

Buses: Xiaguan has three bus terminals, all on Jianshe Lu within 10min. of each other. For information on buses to Jizushan, see p. 564.

Dali Long-distance Bus Station (dàlǐ qìchē kèyùn zhàn; 大理汽车客运站; ☎218 9330), a modern building near the intersection of Jianshe and Renmin Lu. To: **Baoshan** (5½hr., 5 per day, Y19-26); **Kunming** (express: 4½hr., every 30min. 7:30-9:30am and every hr. 10:30am-8pm, Y89-100; regular: 7hr., every hr. 7:30am-5:40pm, Y50-70); **Lijiang** (4hr., 4 per day, Y25-50); **Ruili** (sleeper bus 20hr., 1 per day, Y109); and **Zhongdian** (8hr., 2 per day, Y85).

Bus Station of Dali Prefecture (dàlǐ zhōu kèyùn zhàn; 大理州客运站; ☎217 4621), the only station with an English sign, is diagonally across from the Dali Long-distance Bus Station. To: **Baoshan** (5hr., 2 per day, Y25); **Jinghong** (24hr., 1 per day, Y140); **Kunming** (4hr., 12 per day, Y70); **Lijiang** (3hr., 6 per day 7-11:30am, Y25-50); and **Ruili** (12hr., 2 per day, Y69-90).

Xiaguan Long-distance Bus Service Station (xiàguān qìchē kèyùn fúwù zhàn; 下关汽车客运服务站), 50 Jianshe Lu (☎212 5631, ext. 202), opposite the 35108 Military Service Station, the former Nanzhao Hotel. To: **Baoshan** (6hr., 5 per day; Y26); **Kunming** (4½hr., 27 per day, Y50-80); **Ruili** (20hr., 3 per day, Y65-90); and **Zhongdian** (7hr., 2 per day, Y42-55).

Local Transportation: To get to Old Dali, take **bus #4** from the main station at the corner of Renmin Lu and Jianshe Lu (30-40min., every 10min., Y1.2). Bus stops along Jianshe Lu are marked with yellow signs. **Minibuses,** also marked #4, ply the same route for Y1.5 or more; they are also slower and often have more pickpockets on board. Avoid **Wenhua Lu,** where minibuses congregate with drivers attempting to dupe tourists and pickpockets lie in wait.

ACCOMMODATIONS AND FOOD

It is usually better to take the bus to Old Dali than to put up in Xiaguan's relatively expensive accommodations. If circumstances necessitate a night in Xiaguan, there are two fairly cheap hotels near the bus stations. **Xiaguan Hotel** (xiàguān fàndiàn; 下关饭店), 1 Renmin Lu, on the corner of Jianshe and Renmin Lu, has basic rooms with 24hr. hot water. (☎217 4933; fax 216 8889. Doubles Y80; triples Y60.) **Keyun Hotel** (kèyún fàndiàn; 客运饭店), 24 Jianshe Lu, next to Dali Long-distance Bus Station, has hot water available from noon to midnight. (☎212 5286. 4-bed dorms Y6; singles Y14-26; doubles Y25; triples Y24.) The side streets winding around Xiaguan feature tiny cubicled resturants serving up savory local specialties.

HIKING NEAR XIAGUAN: JIZUSHAN

Towering 3240m over northwestern Binchuan County in the Dali Prefecture, with nary a chicken foot in sight (jizu means "chicken foot"), Jizushan (jīzúshān; 鸡足山) has been a sacred Buddhist site since Jiaye, a famed disciple of the Sakyamuni Buddha, took up residence there. By the Qing dynasty, 36 temples and 72 nunneries were flourishing on the mountain. Now recovering from the devastation of the Cultural Revolution, the mountain and its ancient structures offer breathtaking views to hardy hikers or hard-nosed transportation hagglers. While simply trekking about the mountain is rewarding in itself, there are also several sights, including **Zhusheng Temple** (zhùshèng sì; 祝圣寺), historically the most prominent of the temples, and **Jinding Temple** (jīndǐng sì; 金顶寺), at the very peak of Jizushan. The trip to the top is costly. Admission is Y40, and most shell out Y25 for horses to get to the **cable lift** (Y22) at **Huideng Nunnery** (huìdēng ān; 慧灯庵), and more still if the cable car isn't working. The best month to visit is March. In the rainy summer months, the ascent takes about two hours by horse and cable car; on foot it takes 30 minutes more.

Basic dorm accommodations are available at **Jinding Temple Zonghe Hostel** (jīndǐng sì zōnghé lóudài; 金顶寺宗合楼待), next to Jinding Temple. (☎935 0060. 4-bed dorms Y15.) If you don't make it to the top before nightfall or before the frequent rainstorms, there are cheap rooms (Y10 per bed) above many restaurants in the triangle near the Jizu Shan Hotel, next to four gold cranes preening in a pool.

Buses go from Xiaguan's Dali Bus Station (dàlǐ kèyùn zhōngxīn, 大理客运中心) on Huangcheng Dong Lu to **Binchuan** (2½hr., last bus 7pm, Y20) and from Binchuan to the foot of Jizushan (1hr., last bus 6:30pm, Y10). The last bus to Xiaguan from Jizushan leaves at 7pm. The **Guesthouse of Binchuan No. 12** (bīnchuān bīnguǎn; 宾川宾馆) is the main hostel for foreigners in Binchuan. Turn left out of the bus station and left again at the intersection; the hotel is up the road on the left. (☎714 1323. 3-bed dorms with TV Y12.)

LIJIANG 丽江   ☎0888

The topography of Lijiang Naxi Autonomous Prefecture (population 1,069,200) ranges from gently rolling plains to the highest mountain ranges south of the Yangzi. The area's inhabitants are just as varied; 22 minority nationalities, of which the most populous is the Naxi, have made their homes in Lijiang. The distinctive blue and black aprons worn by Naxi women, the Dongba religion with its synthesis of sorcery, medicine, and philosophy, and the ancient Naxi pictographic script that still graces many landmarks render this area culturally distinctive. Activity centers around the prefectural seat, also called Lijiang, set at an elevation of 2400m. The city is distinguished by an intricate system of narrow waterways and canals. In 1996, an earthquake measuring 7.2 on the Richter scale devastated Lijiang, leveling the old part of town. Since then, for better or for worse, a replica of the original old town has been built, and Lijiang has become a UNESCO World Heritage Site. Some decry the faux antique, tourist trap atmosphere of the old town, but for most, the well-worn cobblestone back alleys still seem to have the musty air of centuries past, and the traditional Naxi-style houses that line the rebuilt canals prove just as enchanting as ever.

TRANSPORTATION

Airplanes: Lijiang Airport (lìjiāng jīchǎng; 丽江机场; ☎517 0987 or 512 8088), 26km from the city. Buses leave from next to the **Yunnan Airlines ticket office** (zhōngguó yúnnán lìjiāng shòupiào chù; 中国云南丽江售票处;☎516 1291), at the intersection of Yunshan Zhong Lu (known as Xueshan Zhong Lu by the locals) and Fuhui Lu. **CAAC ticket office** (☎512 0280), on the corner of Xin Dajie as you walk into the new town. Open daily 8:30-11:30am and 2:30-5:30pm. To **Jinghong/Xishuangbanna** (1-2 per day, Y610) and **Kunming** (3 -4 per day, Y420).

Buses: Neither of the 2 main bus stations serve the destinations of Baoshan and Chengdu. To get to **Baoshan,** take the bus to Xiaguan and then catch another bus. To get to **Chengdu,** take the bus to Jinjiang/Panzhihua and then take a train.

North Bus Station (běi qìchē zhàn; 北汽车站; ☎518 9141), on Xin Dajie just past Mao Square, on the same side as the Lijiang International Ethnic Cultural Exchange Center. Buses leaving from this station have "Guluwan" (古路湾) written on them. Bus tickets can be bought opposite the train station. Ticket office open daily 6am-7pm. To: **Daju** (3hr., 3-5 per day, Y23); **Jinjiang/Panzhihua** (8hr., 5 per day, Y43-62); **Kunming** (11hr., 6 per day, Y115-155); **Xiaguan** (3hr., 12 per day, Y30-50); and **Zhongdian** (5hr., 5 per day, Y21-29) via **Qiaotou** (2½hr., Y15).

South Bus Station (lìjiāng kèyùn zhàn; 丽江客运站; ☎512 2187 or 512 1106), at the far end of Minzhu Lu. Turn left out of the old town, and left again on Minzhu Lu, past the post office. To: **Jinjiang/Panzhihua** (8hr., 7 per day, Y43.5); **Kunming** (11hr., 9 per day, Y105.5-115.5); **Xiaguan** (3hr., 20-30 per day, Y31.5 or Y50.9); and **Zhongdian** (5hr., 7 per day, Y27).

Local Transportation: Several local **buses** crisscross the new city. From Xin Dajie, near Mao Square, bus **#7** (every hr. 8am-6pm) heads to Baisha (Y6) and Jade Dragon Mountain (Y8). Bus **#1** (every 15min. 7am-9 or 10pm, Y0.8-1) stops at the South Bus Station and on Fuhui Lu and Xin Dajie, near the entrance to the Old City.

Bike Rental: The best place to rent bikes used to be under Mao's watchful eyes. The Square was under construction during summer 2000; upon its completion, the bikes may again come streaming in. In the meantime, try the **Ju Yi Yuan,** a painting shop on Mishi Alley opposite Mama Fu's restaurant. Y20 per day. Open daily 8:30am-11pm. **Prague Cafe** has a small selection. Y8 per day.

▗★❷ ORIENTATION AND PRACTICAL INFORMATION

Lijiang is divided into two distinct entities: the New and Old Towns. The **New Town** (xīn chéng; 新城) is still under construction. Most visitors encounter the stretch of **Xin Dajie** (新大街) from the entrance of the Old Town to Black Dragon Fountain Park, via **Mao Square** (Red Sun Square as the Chinese call it) and the bus station. **Minzhu Lu** (民主路) runs from the Old Town to the South Bus Station. The **Old Town** (gǔ chéng; 古城) tries just as hard to preserve (or commercialize) history as the New Town tries to disregard it. Stores, cafes, and trinket galleries line **Dong Dajie** (东大街) and **Xinyi Jie** (新义街). These two thoroughfares diverge at the northern tip of the old city and then meet again at **Sifang Jie** (四方街), the central meeting point, known as **Market Square.**

Travel Agencies: Lijiang CITS Reception Center (☎512 3508), on Xin Dajie, just past Mao Square on the right. Very friendly and helpful staff. Open daily 7:30am-10pm. **Blue Sky Travel Agency** (zhōngguó lìjiāng mínháng lántiān guójì lǚxíngshè; 中国丽江民航蓝天国际旅行社; ☎516 1018), at the intersection of Fuhui and Yunshan (Xueshan) Zhong Lu. Open daily 8am-6pm.

Bank of China: Opposite and to the left of the South Bus Station. Exchanges traveler's checks. Open daily 8am-5:30pm. More convenient is the branch on Xin Dajie at Fuhui Lu, just opposite the Chinese Construction Bank. Open daily 8:30am-7:30pm. **Industrial and Commercial Bank,** on Dong Dajie, near the entrance to Market Square, exchanges traveler's checks and US, Hong Kong, and Japanese currencies. ATM available. Open daily 8am-5pm; in winter 8:30am-5pm.

Bookstores: Xinhua Bookstore, on Xin Dajie, at the turn into the Old Town. Small supply of English books, plus some maps of Lijiang and Yunnan. Open daily 8:30am-9:30pm.

PSB: Near the South Bus Station, up the 1st right alley on Nanguojing Lu (☎512 1567). Grants up to 2 visa extensions (1 month). Open daily 8-11:30am and 2:30-5:30pm.

Hospital: Lijiang District Hospital (lìjiāng dìqū yīyuàn; 丽江地区医院; ☎512 1545; emergency ☎512 2393 or 512 2335), on Fuhui Lu. Minimal English spoken. **Lijiang County People's Hospital** (lìjiāng xiàn rénmín yīyuàn; 丽江县人民医院; ☎512 2871), on Changshui Lu, near the South Bus Station.

Internet Access: Many hostels and cafes in the Old Town offer access. All except the **Old Town Square Inn** (Y15 per hr.) charge Y18 per hr.

Post and Telecommunications: The main **post office** is on Minzhu Lu. Turn left out of the Old Town, and then left again; the post office is on the right. EMS. IDD service and Internet access (Y18 per hr.) on the 2nd floor. Open daily 8am-8pm. The branch on Dong Dajie also offers IDD service. Facing the Old Town, follow the street on the right; the post office is on the left, opposite the Industrial and Commercial Bank. Open daily 8am-10pm. **Postal Code:** 674100.

▛ ACCOMMODATIONS

Prices are roughly the same in the Old and New Towns; most travelers prefer to stay in the Naxi-style Old Town, a five-minute walk from North Bus Station. Most guesthouses have 24hr. hot water, and prices usually begin around Y20 per bed; expect price hikes of Y10-20 during peak season (generally May, Aug., and Oct.).

Prague Cafe Guesthouse, 80 Xinyi Jie, Mishi Xiang (☎512 3757), diagonally across from Mama Fu's. The closest thing to a "home away from home," the Prague isn't too far from home itself, as it offers Internet access, a good restaurant, luggage storage, bike rental, and travel information. Friendly English-speaking staff. 4-bed dorms Y15; singles Y60; doubles Y25; triples Y20.

Sakura Cafe Guesthouse (☎512 5179 or 518 7619). Go to the Sakura Cafe on Xinhua Jie and ask to be taken to the guesthouse. An excellent deal. 4-bed dorms Y10; doubles Y40; triples Y45.

MCA Guesthouse (☎517 5431 or 518 7630; email dongba@hotmail.com), on Xinyi Jie. Also known as Dongba House (dōngbā háosí; 东巴豪斯). Take the left lane when you enter the Old Town. We haven't got a clue what the name means, but with friendly staff and clean rooms, who really cares? Check out the barbecued piglet specialty at the restaurant across the street. 8-bed dorms Y20; 3-bed dorms Y30; singles Y50.

First Bend Inn (dì yī wān jiǔdiàn; 第一湾酒店), 43 Mishi Xiang (☎518 1688 or 518 1073), off Xinyi Jie. As you go into the Old Town, veer left onto Xinyi Jie, and keep going past Lamu's House of Tibet and the MCA Guesthouse. First Bend has a beautiful courtyard and comfortable beds, along with excellent maps and information for Tiger Leaping Gorge trekkers. 4 days free luggage storage. Hot water 8-10am and 7-10pm. 4-bed dorms Y25; 3-bed dorms Y30; singles Y80; doubles Y40.

Yizhou Inn (yízhōu kèzhàn; 怡舟客栈), 3 Wuyi Jie (☎512 7439). Follow Xinyi Jie past Mama Fu's until the bridge on the right. Turn left; the inn is 3min. ahead, on the left, marked by the blue and white banner on the right. This small, quiet guesthouse is about as close as you can get to living with a Naxi family. The owners speak minimal English. 4-bed dorms Y15; singles Y25-30.

Huang Family Flower Inn (huáng jiā huāyuán kèzhàn; 黄家花园客栈), 29 Xinyi Jie, Jishan Xiang (☎512 8679; mobile 1390 888 3030). At the courtyard in front of the MCA, follow the road around the grilled piglet restaurant until you see the red and white banner about 1min. ahead. A lovely and clean Naxi home, away from the tourist rush. Non-English speaking owners. 4-bed dorms Y20-30; doubles Y50-70; triples Y25-35.

Old Town Square Inn (sìfāng kèzhàn; 四方客栈), 307 Huangshan Xia Duan (☎512 7487). From the Old Town, take Dong Dajie all the way to Market Square and turn onto the road by CC's Bar; take the first left. It's a steep climb to the communal baths, but the friendly staff and clean rooms make up for it. One of the 2-bed dorms has a whopping 3 windows. 4-bed dorms Y20; 3-bed dorms Y40; off-season Y20; 2-bed dorms Y30.

◖◗ FOOD

Vendors in the Old Town steam, fry, and grill an inviting selection of local delicacies, including **baba** (fried Naxi flatbreads), noodle soups, and hotpot pork and rice dishes. Anyone craving travel advice and the company of foreigners—or just the company of steak and chocolate cake—can head to the gaily marked cafes that line **Jishan Xiang, Mishi Xiang,** and **Market Square.**

▨ **Sakura Cafe** (yīnghuā kāfēi; 樱花咖啡; ☎518 7619), on Minzhu Lu. Upon entering Market Square, take the first right, and the first right again; walk parallel to the way you came. Run by an eager local and his Korean wife, this comfy spot has great Korean food (Y5-18), apple pie (Y5), and travelers' notebooks that rave about the place (free advertising?). Internet access (Y18 per hr.) and free movies. Open daily 7am-1am.

▨ **Laosan Zashi Restaurant** (lǎosān záshí diàn; 老三杂食店). Follow the stream out of the Old Town; Laosan's is the 2nd door on your right, opposite the Gelan Hotel just after the small bridge. This is a wonderful Naxi restaurant—clean and friendly (both the establishment and the staff), tasty and cheap (the food, not the staff). There is no menu, but the chefs will cook up whatever you want. Try the stir-fried er si (rice noodles, Y3) or stir-fried red and green peppers with homemade sausage (Y8). Open daily 7am-2am.

Lamu's House of Tibet (xīzàng wū; 西藏屋; ☎518 9000), on Xinyi Jie, not far past the entrance to the Old Town. Fabulous Tibetan food (Y6-15), especially the momos (Y8), served in a lovely bamboo structure with a garden. A favorite with many travelers—check out the notebooks for anecdotes. Open daily 7am-midnight; in winter 8:30am-midnight.

Longevity Restaurant (chángshòu cāntīng; 长寿餐厅), 166 Dashiqiao (☎512 0184), on the right side of the 1st street to the left out of Market Square. Look for low tables with marble tops. You might wish you could live forever, after eating here. Excellent hotpot (Y6) and cold noodles (Y3). Open daily 7:30am-10:30pm.

#69 Cafe, 69 Mishi Xiang (☎518 5206), down the street from First Bend Inn, toward Market Square. A vegetarian restaurant with friendly, English-speaking staff and Internet access. Some locals say the food is less tasty under the new owners. Decide for yourself; we say the Chinese vegetable burger (Y12) is worth it. Open daily 8am-midnight.

Mama Fu's Restaurant (māmā fù cāntīng; 妈妈傅餐厅), 76 Xinyi Jie, Mishi Xiang (☎512 2285), with outdoor tables overlooking the canal. Reportedly better at making Chinese food than Western, but the apple pie (Y7) still keeps the kids coming back for more. Open daily 9am-12:30am.

CC's Bar, 55 Sifang Jie (☎512 1459), in the far right corner of Market Square as you approach from Dong Dajie. Buffet (Y8) and Happy Hour (drinks 25% off) daily 5-8pm and "Ladies Night" F-Su 8pm-midnight (1 free drink). The honey and ginger tea is a good remedy for an evening of too much fun. Open daily 9am-late.

Big Stone Bridge Restaurant (dà shí qiáo huǒtuǐ chǎofàn fàndiàn; 大石桥火腿炒饭饭店; ☎512 9866), on Xin Dajie, next to Xinhua Bookstore. Locals flock here for the *shaoguo fan* (hotpot; Y6) and *mixian* (rice noodle soup; Y3). Open daily 7am-10pm.

🔲🎵 SIGHTS AND ENTERTAINMENT

The old town's winding cobbled streets, traditional Naxi houses with intricate wooden facades, and women in Naxi dress make wandering at will through Lijiang a legitimate activity in its own right. Head away from the main streets to get away from the gift shops; getting lost can be quite rewarding. Be forewarned; admission to tourist sights has risen sharply in the past two years.

▓ DAYAN NAXI MUSIC ASSOCIATION (dàyán nàxī gǔyuè huì; 大研纳西古乐会). Research shows that this "authentic Naxi music" is actually very similar to ancient Han music, as the Naxi minority has historically appropriated Han styles as part of attempts at assimilation. The music is haunting, and the charismatic director of this association, Xuan Ke, spices up his introduction of the orchestra, the music, and himself with provocative social commentary (although these witticisms are rarely translated into English). The performance also features wonderful displays of folk songs. For a more folk-flavored show, many tourists choose to go to the **Dongba Music House** (Y35), directly across the street. *(On Dongda Jie. Don't worry about missing the place—there's a large sign right outside the door, and every night you'll see countless people waiting. ☎512 7971 or 4559. Performances nightly 8pm. Y30-50.)*

BLACK DRAGON FOUNTAIN PARK (hēi lóng tán gōngyuán; 黑龙潭公园). Here you will find numerous Dongba art galleries, temples, and gardens along with the small lake that is the park's namesake. Most pictures of Jade Dragon Snow Mountain are taken from here. Some consider the entrance fee too high for a park, but it can be a worthwhile way to spend a relaxing day. For a little adventure, you can make the one-hour climb up **Elephant Hill** (xiàng shān; 象山), where a spectacular view awaits. It is recommended that women do not visit here alone, even during daylight hours; at least one rape is rumored to have occurred here. *(Take a left out of the Old Town, and then a right onto Xin Dajie; follow Xin Dajie 15min. to its end. For a more scenic route, follow the stream out of the Old Town. Cross the bridge on your left just before the small waterfall; bear left when the road forks, and follow it to the end. The museum entrance is 20m to the right. Open daily 7am-9pm. Y20; some travelers report being able to get in free before 7am.)*

LION HILL (shīzi shān; 狮子山). Both the hill and the wooden structure called **Wangulou** (wàngǔlóu; 万古楼) provide good views of the Old Town and the surrounding countryside. Few travelers find the trip worthwhile, though. *(Walk up the street to the right of CC's Bar and look for signs to take a left to Wangulou. The round-trip walk takes under 1hr. Open daily 8am-6pm. Climbing Lion Hill is free; Wangulou admission Y15.)*

LAND OF THE SUN AND MOON "Shangri-La" in a

Zhongdian dialect of Tibetan means "the slope leading to the land of the sun and moon in my heart." British author James Hilton based his novel *The Lost Horizon* (1933) on this mysterious, hidden Eden in Southeast China. The fanciful have long sought this surreal utopia, supposedly tucked away in forbidding mountains near a flourishing, horse- and tea-trading town between Tibet and Yunnan. Part of Shangri-La's magic is that it is a place of eternal youth; natives who left quickly aged and died.

In 1997, a team of investigators sent by the Chinese government officially declared Deqin Prefecture (the area around Zhongdian, see p. 572) to be the lost Eden described by Hilton. More recently, Lijiang (p. 565) and Daocheng (in Sichuan) have both been contending with Zhongdian for the title of the "true Shangri-La." A debate has ensued between cynics and romantics; the former search for physical evidence of such a place, while the latter insist that Shangri-La is not a specific place but rather a paradise in the heart that could exist anywhere. To find Shangri-La for yourself, consider adding our three-week-long "Shangri-La" itinerary through Southwest China to your travel plans (see p. 6).

◪ DAYTRIPS FROM LIJIANG

JADE DRAGON SNOW MOUNTAIN

35km north of Lijiang. Take bus #7 (30min., every hr., Y8) from Baixin Department Store on Xinda Jie. Open daily 8:30am-4:30pm. Admission to National Park Y40.

Jade Dragon Snow Mountain (yù lóng xuě shān; 玉龙雪山) is the dramatic 5596m peak that appears in virtually every postcard of the area. After staring at the peak every day that you've spent in Lijiang, it would be a shame to miss it. Two cable cars ascend the mountain, one to a meadow halfway up and the other to 4506m. The shorter lift (Y40) ends at **Donkey Meadow**, where you may get to see pretty shrubbery and Naxi maidens dancing. More worthwhile, however, is the longer lift (Y110), one of China's longest cable car rides. At the top is a short but exhausting walk to a viewing platform; those who suck up the financial and physical abuse of the trip are rewarded with utterly spectacular views. The fact that hawkers at the peak sell oxygen pillows (Y20-30) instead of tacky trinkets is a bit alarming, but some climbers have no difficulty with the altitude and even manage to get some mileage out of the karaoke machine in the tea house. At least they have an excuse for sounding like strangled monkeys. For information on trekking in Tiger Leaping Gorge, across the Yangzi from Jade Dragon Snow Mountain, see p. 570.

BAISHA

*About 8km north of Lijiang. From Fuhui Lu or from the market right outside the Old Town, take a **farm truck** (Y2) marked 龙泉 (lóngquán) or 白沙 (báishā). There are two **biking** routes. For both, cycle along Xin Dajie and take a left where the road forks. Follow this flat road until you come to the sign that says "Shabai" in Roman letters, which points you down a dirt path leading right to the village; alternatively, turn left down any of the dirt paths off the main road and right onto another dirt path, which will lead to Baisha.*

The small village of Baisha (báishā; 白沙) is best known for its frescoes. **Fuguo Monastery** (fùguó sì; 福国寺) holds scores of large frescoes of Tibetan-Buddhist, Daoist, and Han origins. The damage to the frescoes is more often due to violence during the Cultural Revolution than to natural decay. Naxi girls sometimes dance and sing in the courtyards. *(Open daily 7am-8pm. Y8.)* The old house around the corner, with Mao quotation wall graffiti still visible, is one of the few unrenovated area buildings that visitors are allowed to enter. Baisha is also the home of **Dr. Ho**, the "Daoist physician" made famous by travel writer Bruce Chatwin. You'll probably encounter him near his office, in a slightly dirtied white coat, strolling along the main street of Baisha. For a small sum, he will show you newspaper cuttings documenting his international fame as you sip his special blend of herbal tea.

To reach the nearby **Dragon Springs** (lóng quán; 龙泉) and grab a peek into a typical Naxi village, follow the main road (identifiable by the newspaper clippings proclaiming Dr. Ho's fame) for 25 minutes by bike or for 45 minutes on foot. Go through a village and across some fields, cross the river, and look out for a small building at the end of the road.

TIGER LEAPING GORGE 虎跳峡

The hike through Tiger Leaping Gorge (hǔ tiào xiá) has become a sort of backpacker's rite of passage—a ready source of conversation and the topic of innumerable entries in travelers' notebooks. Indeed, Tiger Leaping Gorge deserves all the attention it gets. The gorge lies at the point where **Haba Snow Peak** (hābā xuě shān; 哈巴雪山) shoots up to face the Jade Dragon Snow Mountains over the swift waters of the fledgling Yangzi River. Still known as the Jinsha (Gold Sand) River this far west, it chiseled out one of the deepest and most breathtaking gorges in the country. The 35km long and 12km wide gorge, the southernmost glacial mountain in China, marks the northern boundary of Lijiang Prefecture. Shanzidou, the summit of the surrounding peaks, stands a lofty 5600m above sea level. At its narrowest point, the gorge spans barely 30m; it is said to be named for a hunted tiger that leaped across the stone abyss to escape its pursuer.

🔏 TREKKING AROUND THE GORGE

The hike is challenging and not for the fainthearted or the out-of-shape. Leave large packs in Lijiang, and bring water and snacks. During the rainy season, the trek can be particularly treacherous; flooding and mudslides are not uncommon. The situation for gorge trekkers is in constant flux. Ask other travelers what they have done and talk to locals in cafes before setting off. Do know that many local guesthouses and restaurants may underestimate the length of time it will take to get to the next stopping point; whether this is because they are super-fit or because they want you to linger and spend money before making the "quick jaunt" to the next stopping place is debatable. The best places to get information include **MCA Guesthouse, Prague Cafe,** and **First Bend Inn** (see **Lijiang**, p. 565). The best **trekking map** of the gorge, by Scottish engineering mapper Neil McLean, is available at First Bend Inn (Y1). Tiger Leaping Gorge is bounded on one side by the town of **Qiaotou** (qiáotóu; 桥头) and on the other by **Daju** (dàjù; 大具). **First Bend Village** (běndìwān; 本地湾) and **Walnut Grove** (hétáo yuán; 核桃园) villages lie in between. Admission to the gorge is Y30.

DAJU TO WALNUT GROVE. Buses (3hr., 3 per day, Y20-24) to Daju leave from Lijiang North Station (see p. 565). Buses from First Bend Inn also make the trip almost every day (leave 7:30am-1:30pm, return 8am-2:30pm; Y23.5). Dorms (Y10) are available at the **Snowflake Hotel,** next to the Daju Bus Station.

From Daju, it is an hour's walk or a short taxi ride (Y5) to a lake. If you don't see a ferry man, call out for him. The new **ferry** takes only two minutes to cross the lake, but in the rainy season, it is much safer to take the old ferry. Taking the old ferry often means an overnight stay in Walnut Grove for a night; the new ferry often means an overnight in First Bend Village. The walk from the ferry crossing to **Walnut Grove** takes about four hours. If you are short on time, you can get a ride along the road between Daju and Walnut Grove and start your trek at Walnut Grove. At Walnut Grove there are two places to stay, five minutes apart: **Chateau de Woody** (báiliǎn lǚguǎn; 白脸旅馆) and **Stan's Spring Guesthouse** (shān quán kèzhàn; 山泉客栈). Both have dorm beds (Y10-20), restaurants, and showers. Another 30- to 45-minute walk along the road leads to **Tina's House,** at the point where the low path leaves the road to join the high path (dorms Y10-20).

WALNUT GROVE TO FIRST BEND VILLAGE. The walk from Walnut Grove to First Bend Village takes three to four hours, encompassing the most gorgeous scenery of the whole gorge. Sporadic yellow or red arrows mark most of the trails; if in doubt, head for the power lines to keep on track. At **First Bend Village,** you will see another guesthouse; from there, head straight up the steep slope. Don't despair over the climb—there is a waterfall at the top to revive you. The **Halfway Guesthouse** nearby has dorms with showers (Y15-20). Mr. Feng, the owner, is a specialist in natural medicine who offers tours to other local spots.

FIRST BEND VILLAGE TO QIAOTOU. Halfway Guesthouse is most people's last place of rest before the six- to eight-hour hike to Qiaotou. There is a farmhouse in the last village before Qiaotou that advertises "bowel and lodging"—who knows what that really means. **Qiaotou** is a dusty, concrete and pavement town, so try to avoid having to stay overnight. If you must stay in Qiaotou, try the **Tiger Leaping Gorge Hotel,** right next to the bus station and opposite the Backpacker's Cafe (dorms Y15-20). From Qiaotou, the last bus (Y15) leaves for **Lijiang** or **Zhongdian** at 6pm. Inquire at the Backpacker's Cafe.

QIAOTOU TO DAJU. Buses (Y13) to Qiaotou leave Lijiang's First Bend Inn starting at 6am. From Qiaotou, take a left out of the Backpacker's Cafe and follow the sign to the gorge, which will point you to a tall gate. Walk 100m past the gate and take a left. When you come to the basketball court, walk across and turn right, then walk along the base of the hill until you pick up the trail on your left. Always bear left when the trail looks like it is forking; trails to the right usually lead to private houses. If you want to do the trek in two days, plan carefully. The last **ferry** across the lake to **Daju** leaves at 6pm.

LUGU LAKE 泸沽湖 ☎ 0888

The nearly eleven-hour bus ride from Lijiang keeps many would-be visitors away from Lugu Lake, an utterly beautiful piece of water and countryside at the Yunnan-Sichuan border. Those who do make the trip often find it hard to leave the serenity of the lake and the hospitality of its people. Lugu Lake is surrounded by tiny Tibetan, Yi, Pumi, and Mosuo villages and is best known for the unique Mosuo culture. The Mosuo, a subgroup of the Naxi, is a matrilineal society whose members engage in traditional "walking marriages;" partners remain in their maternal homes and often have more than one partner.

According to locals, the lake is gorgeous in all seasons, but most visitors prefer to visit in late spring or fall when the sky is usually a clear blue and the weather is mild. In winter, Lugu Lake is very cold and often snowy; wild geese and seagulls congregate on its icy shores. There are frequent rains during the late summer.

▟ TRANSPORTATION

A new road to **Ninglang** (宁蒗), the Lugu County seat and stopover point for the lake, is still under construction. Once completed, it will likely shorten the seven-hour trip on the old road from Lijiang to about three hours. **Buses** (7am and 2pm, Y34) leave from Lijiang South Station for Ninglang (see p. 565). It is fairly easy to get a bus from Ninglang Bus Station or the main street to Lugu Lake (3hr., Y15-20). The last buses usually leave around 6 or 7pm. From Lijiang, a 9am bus (Y54) goes all the way to Lugu Lake via Ninglang.

Buses from Lugu Lake to Ninglang leave from the **Mosuo Hotel** (7:30 and 8am, Y20). From Ninglang, buses go to **Lijiang** (every hr. 7am-1pm, Y34), **Kunming** (1 pm, Y105), and **Xiaguan** (7 and 7:30am, Y48).

▟▢ ACCOMMODATIONS AND FOOD

Ninglang is noisy, dirty, and not a terribly pleasant place to stay. The **Bus Station Guesthouse** (kèyùn zhāodàisuǒ; 客运招待所), in the bus station, has rooms for Y10-15. The nearby **Ninglang Jiamei Hotel** (nínglāng jiāměi bīnguǎn; 宁蒗佳美宾馆) has hot water from 5 to 10pm. Turn right out of the bus station and walk about 100m; look for the words "Jia me hote" on black marble to your right. (☎ 552 4489. Doubles and triples Y15.)

SOUTHWEST

SOUTHWEST

The bus to Lugu Lake drops off passengers at the **Mosuo Hotel,** in the village of **Luoshui.** Turn right out of the Mosuo Hotel; you'll see the guesthouses on your right. The guesthouses all have dorm beds (Y15) and no showers. There is a **village bathhouse** (cūnzhuāng línyù; 村庄淋浴; Y3); ask a villager and you'll be pointed the way. The best places to stay are **Cloud Pagoda Inn** (cǎi tǎ jiā; 彩塔家; ☎588 1123) and **Xingzhe Inn** (xíngzhē wū; 行者屋; ☎588 1021), where students can bargain rooms down to Y8-10. Another good bet is the **Husi Teahouse** (☎588 1170), with a restaurant, guesthouse, Internet access (Y20 per hr.), and extremely friendly staff. Although the manager does not speak English, the Husi Teahouse is still a great place to get information about trips around the lake.

Most visitors choose to eat where they stay; expect to pay Y15-20 per day for food. The food is simple and delicious, consisting of fish (surprise, surprise), bread, and potatoes. The Husi Teahouse's hot cola and ginger drink (Y6) has soothed many a traveler's queasy stomach. They also have Western dishes (Y8-20).

👁️ 🅰️ SIGHTS AND HIKING

The key to visiting Lugu Lake is to get away from the inn-cluttered and tourist-laden Luoshui village. **Boats** (Y35 per person) go from the Luoshui Dock to **Tusi** and **Liwubi,** two small islands with lamaseries. There's not much to see on either of them, but the boat ride is delightful; ask the rowers to sing for you. Hiring a guide at the dock area costs about Y100 per day. It is best to arrive around 7 or 8am to arrange this. **Horserides** (Y40) leaving from the dock stop at a nearby meadow for tourists to wrestle with local champions. Beware: a "local tradition" is to split the opponent's pants in these wrestling matches.

The smaller, more tranquil Mosuo villages of **Lige** (里格), **Xiao Luoshui** (小落水), and **Dazui** (大咀) have remained almost untouched by the ever-expanding tourism frenzy. It is here that the local Mosuo culture is at its most inviting and inspiring. Some Mosuo families offer **accommodations** and **food** for Y10-20 per night. It takes more than 12 hours to walk around the entire lake, and about six to seven hours to get to the three villages listed above.

The majority of the Mosuo live in **Yongning** (永宁), about a one-hour bus ride from Lugu Lake. Yongning is worth a visit for further insight into Mosuo culture. It is also possible to visit **Yongning Monastery** (yǒngníng sì; 永宁寺), although the local **hot springs** *(wenquan)* have been converted to a public bathhouse. **Accommodation** is available in Mosuo homes. The **bus** from Ninglang to Yongning (Y5) passes by Luoshui daily at 10am; ask the manager of the Husi Teahouse to take you to the bus or to arrange for alternate transportation to Yongning.

The **trek** from Yongning to Lijiang is said to be gorgeous, and a few backpackers have done it, camping or staying at villagers' homes along the way. It is difficult to get information about this hike once in Lugu Lake. Instead, while in Lijiang, ask other backpackers, check out travelers' notebooks, or talk to travel agencies.

ZHONGDIAN 中甸 ☎0887

Part of Diqing Tibetan Autonomous Prefecture (known as Gyelthang in Tibetan) in the far north of Yunnan, Zhongdian is the name of both a county and its capital. It is impossible to travel onward to Tibet from this area at the moment, but Zhongdian county is a reasonable substitute. Tibetan villages dot the valleys, and you're bound to catch a glimpse out your bus window of at least one saffron-robed monk sitting by the roadside. Ranging in elevation from 1480m to 6740m, the prefecture covers some breathtaking and precarious scenery. Zhongdian, atop the Tibetan highland, is the major town in the region. Despite its resplendent setting, however, the town itself has more dust than atmosphere. A few traditional-style buildings, gaudy and pretentious, are being built, no doubt to entice more tourists into the city. For those who moan at the thought of this, or decry the gray shades and rect-angular shapes of China's cities, a tour through the poverty of the old town is a reminder that the untouched past is not always "quaint" and appealing.

✴🔒 ORIENTATION AND PRACTICAL INFORMATION

There are two distinct areas within Zhongdian. The rough-hewn, construction-crazed center around **Changzheng Lu** (长征路), the main shopping street, constitutes modern Zhongdian. The old town is a muddled series of narrow lanes and dilapidated houses, with dogs barking from within and pigs wandering the streets.

Airplanes: Diqing Airport (díqìng jīchǎng; 迪庆机场; ☎822 9916) is 3km out of town. A taxi from town costs Y30-40. Open daily 8:30am-noon and 2-5:30pm; in winter 9am-noon and 2-5:30pm. The **CAAC ticket office** (☎822 9901) is on Changzheng Lu, a couple of doors down from 2 stone lions. To **Kunming** (8:45am, Y560).

Bus: Zhongdian Central Bus Station (zhōngdiàn kèyùn fúwù zhōngxīn zhàn; 中甸客运服务中心站; ☎822 2972) is on Changzheng Lu. The ticket office is inside the waiting room. Ignore the large timetable on the wall; the small one by the ticket booth has more up-to-date information. Open daily 6am-8pm. To: **Deqin** (6hr., 2 per day, Y27-35); **Kunming** (14hr., 5 per day, Y176); **Lijiang** (5hr., 5 per day, Y29-35); **Sanba** (4hr., 1 per day, Y20) via **Baishuitai;** and **Xiaguan** (7hr., 11 per day, Y56).

Local Transportation: Bus #3 runs from outside the Tibet Hotel down Changzheng Lu, past the bus station and bank, and on to Songzanlin Monastery. Bus **#2** travels the length of Changzheng Lu. For shorter distances, you can also take a **pedicab** (Y2-3). Those who find a ride with a private car have found that it is customary to pay the driver.

Travel Agency: CITS (☎823 1935 or 822 2238), on Sifang Jie in the old town. At the end of Changzheng Lu, take the 1st street leading in to the old town, walk to the end, and turn right; the office is on the right. The office of an English-speaking staff member is on the 2nd floor.

Tourist Complaints: ☎822 5390.

Currency Exchange: People's Bank (zhōngguó rénmín yínháng; 中国人民银行), on Changzheng Lu, opposite the Bita Hotel. Exchanges traveler's checks and issues credit card advances. Open M-F 8:30-11:30am and 2-5pm.

PSB: On Changzheng Lu (☎822 6834), just right of the CAAC ticket office, 2 buildings past the Kodak shop. Go through the metal gates on the 3rd floor of the building on the right. Issues **visa extensions** and provides information on travel conditions for most routes out of Zhongdian, except those to Sichuan. Open M-F 8:30-11:30am and 2:30-5:30pm.

Medical Assistance: Foreigner's First Aid Center (☎822 9979).

Internet Access: China Telecom has access for Y8 per hr. The **Tibet (Yongsheng) Hotel** has 1 computer (Y10 per hr.), as does the **Tibet Cafe** (Y12 per hr.).

Post and Telecommunications: China Telecom, on Changzheng Lu, to the left of the bus station. IDD service and Internet access (Y8 per hr.). Open daily 8:30am-10pm; in winter 9am-8pm. You can also make IDD calls from the Tibet Hotel. **China Post** is to the right of the bus station. Poste Restante. **Postal Code:** 674400.

🏠🍴 ACCOMMODATIONS AND FOOD

Although the trickle of backpackers through Zhongdian is increasing, the place still suffers from a lack of pleasant budget accommodations.

Food in Zhongdian consists mostly of Chinese standards flavored with heavy Sichuanese spices. Local favorites include hotpot and cured beef. Restaurant stalls line **Changzheng Lu** and **Heping Lu** (dishes Y5-8), and there are some dumpling stalls along **Hongqi Lu.** A produce and meat **market** is just left of the bus station.

Restaurants with English menus are few and far between. Of these, the best is the **Long Life Tibetan Hotel Cafe. AAA Cafe,** toward the end of Heping Lu, parallel to Changzheng Lu, has mediocre food. (Open daily 8am-midnight.) **Tibet Cafe,** on the right side of Changzheng Lu toward the old town, also has average fare. Stay away from the stuffed tomatoes (Y10), but try the Tibetan flower tea (Y4), and be sure to read the travelers' notebook. (Internet access Y12 per hr. Open daily 8am-11pm.)

Long Life Tibetan Hotel (yŏng shēng fàndiàn; 永生饭店), 106 Tuanjie Lu (☎822 2448). Turn right out of the bus station, then turn left at the end of the road; continue 5-10min. If there are any foreigners in Zhongdian, you'll likely find them here. The hotel doesn't live up to the elaborate lobby kitschfest, but the staff is friendly and there is bike rental (Y15 per day), a cafe with an English menu, and terraces. Some travelers have complained about being denied the cheapest rooms. Currency exchange and IDD service. Hot water 8pm-midnight. 6-bed dorms Y20; 4-bed dorms Y20; 3-bed dorms Y25; doubles Y50.

Old Town Guesthouse (gŭ chéng lǚshè; 古城旅社; ☎822 3629), in the old town. Walk onto the 1st street of the old town (at the end of Changzheng Lu); the guesthouse is on the left, marked by a bright yellow sign and an iron fence. Run by a Tibetan family. Public showers nearby (Y5). 2- to 4-bed dorms Y8; singles Y10; standard doubles Y170.

Diqing Hotel (díqìng bīnguǎn; 迪庆宾馆), 11 Changzheng Lu (☎822 7599), next to the PSB, guarded by 2 stone lions. Zhongdian's only 3-star hotel; cheap, clean rooms are in back. IDD service. Hot water 6:30-11pm. 4- to 5-bed dorms Y30.

Jian Hotel (jiān jiǔdiàn; 季安酒店), 6 Changzheng Lu (☎822 7299), to the right of the bus station. With a richly ornamented, Tibetan-style restaurant on the 1st floor and a lounge on the 2nd, this hotel is a pleasant place to stay, if the bathroom odor and late-night singing don't spoil things. Hot water 6pm-midnight. 2- to 3-bed dorms Y30.

Transport Hotel (jiāotōng fàndiàn; 交通饭店), 21 Changzheng Lu (☎822 3612), next to the bus station. Rock bottom prices and rock hard beds. Join the men in the lounge for a game of *mahjong*. Hot water only when there are more than 15 guests. 5-bed dorms Y10; 4-bed dorms Y15-20; 3-bed dorms Y25-30.

◉ SIGHTS

Zhongdian itself is not much to look at, but it is a useful launchpad for exploring more scenic surrounding areas. The old part of town around the Long Life Tibetan Hotel makes for interesting walks, but beware of dogs. **Big Turtle Park** (dà guīshān gōngyuán; 大龟山公园) provides a good view of the old town. From Changzheng Lu, go straight instead of turning left toward the Tibetan Hotel, then turn left, and then right; from here you should be able to see the base of the small hill and a monastery. Toward the end of April or beginning of May, entire Tibetan families trek up to the monastery to burn incense and pray for a good farm year. *(Open daily 8am-6pm. Y3.)* There are also two small **monasteries** near the upper end of the old town. *(Open daily sunrise-sunset. Y3 and Y5.)*

RIDE 'EM COWBOY The annual Horse Racing Festival in Zhongdian injects a bit of life, both human and equine, into an otherwise uneventful town. The festival falls at the same time as the lunar Dragonboat Festival, usually in late May or early June. Although the festival lasts only three days, preparations begin early, as tents are repaired, special foods cooked, and traditional costumes brought out.

In a tradition dating back centuries, the gathering takes place in a flat meadow. All the horses are specially decorated for the occasion; the jockeys' dress depends on the race in which they are competing. Those in the "Jog Race," a trotting contest, wear short tunics trimmed with silver and gold, overcoats, fox fur hats, Tibetan boots, and broad swords. Participants in the "Galloping Race" wear silk racing clothes. The first 10 to 20 riders to complete the races win prizes, often of more than Y1000 (US$120).

In addition to the conventional races, there are competitions in just about everything else one can do on horseback, such as picking *hada* (white prayer scarves) off the ground and archery on horseback. Horseplay of all stripes entertains the hordes of eager spectators who flock in from the surrounding area and further afield. This is a wonderful time of year to visit Zhongdian, but book your hotel room early, before the mounted hordes invade all available accommodations.

SONGZANLIN MONASTERY (sōngzànlín sì; 松赞林寺). This monastery is the most worthwhile sight in Zhongdian. Affiliated with the Yellow Hat sect (see p. 726), the Songzanlin is the largest Tibetan Buddhist monastery in Yunnan. The temple was first approved in 1679, but was almost completely demolished during the Cultural Revolution. It has since been reconstructed (though some construction is still underway) and is active again, with many monks in residence. Be sure to walk around to the back, where you will find another prayer hall and, on a good day, some of the younger monks at play. Local Tibetans suggest visiting the monastery very early in the morning to escape the swarm of tourists—with the added benefit of getting to hear (and even to see) the monks in their morning prayers. *(5km northwest of Zhongdian. Take bus #3 (15min., 1 per day between 6-8am, Y1) from outside the Long Life Tibetan Hotel. Open daily sunrise-sunset. Y10.)*

NAPA LAKE (nāpā hǎi; 纳帕海). This "lake" only exists from July to September; at other times of the year, it is a large, idyllic meadow. The surrounding hills are blanketed with patches of wild blossoms in May and June, creating a nearly perfect place for a picnic and a nap. Watch out for muddy patches and for what the Chinese call "landmines" (hint: there are many cattle and horses grazing in the area, and they eat a lot of food). During winter, the rare black neck cranes visit here. *(5km from Songzanlin Monastery. Take bus #2 (Y5) from Changzheng Lu; ask before you board, as not all of them go to Napa Lake. Lake Y10. Horse rides Y40.)*

BITA LAKE (bìtǎ hǎi; 碧塔海). Bita Lake is 3540m above sea level, but hiking in the surrounding mountains can take you up to 4500m. It is 3km from the west entrance of Bita Lake to the lake itself; it is also possible to ride a horse (Y25). From the south entrance, it's about a 2km hike down a log-covered path, a killer for weary feet. Most of the hike around the lake is not grueling, but sooner or later the altitude, the swampy patches, and the immense animal droppings will get to you. The lake is nothing spectacular, but the woods surrounding it are lovely, with long strands of moss hanging from the trees and wildflowers sprouting up in the most precarious of places. Accommodation is available in white shingled wood cabins (Y15-30 per person) or in campgrounds on the premises. Bring plenty of water. Visiting **Shudu Lake** (shǔdū hǎi; 属都海), also west of Zhongdian, costs a similar amount to Bita Lake. *(About 45min.-1hr. west of Zhongdian. There is no regular public transportation. Hire a taxi and driver (Y150 for 3-4 people) from Zhongdian. Bita Lake Y30, students Y15. Canoe rental Y20; speedboat Y25 per person. Shudu Lake Y10.)*

BAISHUI TERRACE (báishuǐ tai; 白水台). The white stepped terraces of Baishui, the second largest natural terrace of its kind in the world, make their way along a valley whose water source is thought to be a holy spring. In the fall, red and pink wildflowers dot the land around the terraces. Try to avoid visiting during the pilgrimage month of March. *(Take the bus to Sanba from Zhongdian, which leaves at 8:30am (summer) and 6:30am (winter) for the 4hr. trip (Y30). You can stay overnight here, at guesthouses right by the road for Y20-30 per bed; try to bargain. It is also possible to hire horses in Baishuitai and trek to the Tiger Leaping Gorge (Y400-500 per day); ask at the Long Life Tibetan Hotel for details.)*

DEQIN 德钦

Deqin Tibetan Autonomous County is Yunnan's northernmost region, situated in the Hongduanshan Mountains on the southern edge of the Tibetan plateau. The population of the entire county is just over 55,000, of which 80% is Tibetan. The county seat, also called Deqin, is a ramshackle little mountain town, tantalizingly close to the Tibetan border. The trip between Zhongdian and Deqin passes a tributary of the Yangzi, traditional Tibetan-style villages, fields of summer wildflowers, and, toward the end, glacier-capped mountains, a spectacular vision that makes up for the bumpy ride. Deqin's setting lends it a certain mystique and excitement, but to those who aren't mountain lovers, the town does not merit more than a couple of days. It is mostly a spring and summer destination; roads are impassable during the winter months. **Deqin Bus Station** (déqīn kèyùn fúwù zhàn; 德钦客远服务站; ☎841 2115) is on Nanping Jie, Deqin's main road. Buses go from Deqin to **Zhongdian** (8hr., 2 per day, Y31).

ACCOMMODATIONS AND FOOD

There is a decent selection of accommodations in Deqin. Although there are several "tourist designated restaurants" on the main street, none of these, and in fact no restaurant in town, has an English menu. Go into the kitchen of your chosen restaurant and pick the ingredients of your meal yourself. Food is standard Chinese cuisine. A produce and meat **market** is at the end of Nanping Jie.

Dexin Hotel (déxīn lóu; 德薪楼), 86 Nanping Jie (☎841 2031). Walk downhill from the bus station; the hotel is on the right. With graceful Tibetan-style floral patterns on the walls and a glassed-in patio, Dexin is a congenial place to spend a couple of days. A friendly Tibetan family runs the place; the son is an excellent tour guide. While the thin mattresses on the dorm beds in the basement don't provide much comfort, the 2nd floor rooms have comfy mattresses and TVs. Almost-warm showers are available on request, and there are even toilet seats on the premises. 7-bed dorms Y10-15; 2- to 3-bed dorms Y20-30; singles Y20, with bath Y50; doubles with bath Y80.

People's Government Guesthouse (qí rénmín zhèngfǔ zhāodàisuǒ; 其人民政府招待所; ☎841 2118), 25 Nanping Lu, next to the bus station. Much noisier than the Dexin. Hot water 6-10pm. 3- to 4-bed dorms Y10, with TV Y20-25; singles with bath Y30-40; doubles with bath Y40-60.

Adunzi Hotel (ādūnzǐ jiǔdiàn; 阿墩子酒店; ☎841 3378), on Nanping Jie. Turn right out out of the bus station. Travel agency on-site. Hot water 5:30pm-10am. 4- to 7-bed dorms Y20; standard rooms also available.

SIGHTS

Deqin's stunning surroundings are its main attraction. Although some of the nearby sights are somewhat inaccessible, the trip is well worth it.

MEILIXUE SHAN (méilǐxuě shān; 梅里雪山). Meilixue Shan, literally "Plum in Snow Mountains," lies just beyond the banks of the Mekong River on the Yunnan-Tibet border. The mountain range contains Yunnan's highest peak, **Mt. Kagebo**, at 6740m. In 1991, 17 Chinese and Japanese mountain climbers died in an attempt to conquer the peak. A fair amount of mystique surrounds these mountains; many locals say that whether you see the snow-covered peaks depends solely on Kagebo's mood and your fate. The closest most travelers come to scaling Kagebo is the fantastic hike up to **Mingyong Glacier** (míngyǒng bīngchuān; 明永冰川), which at 2700m is the world's lowest altitude glacier. *(West of Deqin. A bus (leaves daily 3pm, returns next day 7 or 8am; Y10) to Mingyong Glacier leaves from Nanping Jie near the bus station. A taxi to Mingyong costs Y250-400 round-trip. Accommodations are available in the hotel near the glacier (Y15 per person). It takes about 2hr. to hike up the glacier. Horses are also available (one-way Y60, round-trip Y80). Y60.)*

FEILAI MONASTERY (fēilái sì; 飞来寺). Feilai Monastery is the name given both to the small monastery and a viewing area 1km away. Ask to have the prayer hall opened for you. The viewing terrace is a sight in itself, with a line of bright white *stupas* and piles of Tibetan prayer flags, raised at the Tibetan New Year and left up throughout the year. On clear days, the terrace affords stunning views of the surrounding mountain landscape. *(11km from Deqin. A bus (Y4) leaves daily from Nanping Jie (near the bus station) around 7am. You can also walk or take a taxi (Y30-50); roads are almost deserted, making other means of transportation almost impossible. Terrace open daily 8am-8pm. Y10. Monastery free; donations accepted.)*

DONGZHULIN MONASTERY (dōngzhúlín sì; 东竹林寺). Like Songzanlin Monastery near Zhongdian, this monastery was destroyed in the Cultural Revolution and has since been rebuilt. Towering mountains and breathtaking precipices keep watch over the monastery. Weary walkers can stay the night; dilapidated beds with thin blankets and mattresses cost Y10. Bring your own provisions. *(On the bus route between Deqin and Zhongdian; tell the bus driver to drop you off at the monastery. You can either return to Deqin or continue on to Zhongdian the next day.)*

BAOSHAN 保山 AND DEHONG 德宏

Baoshan Prefecture and Dehong Dai Jinpo Autonomous County, in far western
Yunnan, are one of the least visited and wildest areas of the province. A large number of Dai, Jingpo, Achang, and other minority peoples live in the area, and
Dehong County's long border with Myanmar throws a strong international flavor
into the already potent ethnic mix of the region. The area has been the site of cultural and economic transition for centuries; since the middle of the first millennium, it has been a crucial stretch of the Southern Silk Road, linking China,
Southeast Asia, and India. Trade, both legal and illegal, continues today; prostitutes, drugs, and disease flow across the border alongside machinery and clothing,
injecting a note of suspicion and danger into the region's heavy subtropical air.
Relations between China and Myanmar are contentious, and the authorities close
the border sporadically.

BAOSHAN 保山 ☎ 0875

More prosaic than the lively towns of Tengchong and Ruili, Baoshan city is the
seat of Baoshan Prefecture. Baoshan has a prominent bourgeois air, nicely
flaunted in a fountain of gold dragons at the city center. In the 4th and 5th centuries, silk, gold, precious stones, and elephants would pass through on their way to
India and Southeast Asia. Remnants of this glorious past are hardly apparent, but
Baoshan is a convenient stopover on the way to the southwestern frontier.

ORIENTATION AND PRACTICAL INFORMATION

Most hotels and many high-end shops are on **Baoxiu Lu** (保岫路), **Shangxiang Jie**
(上巷街), and **Xiaxiang Lu** (下巷街); the latter two run parallel to one another a
block apart. These thoroughfares are bounded by the long-distance bus station on
one side and **Taibao Park** on the other.

Airplanes: Baoshan Airport (bǎoshān jīchǎng; 保山机场; ☎212 1666) is not far out of
town. Shuttle buses (20min., Y2) leave 2hr. before departure from in front of the **CAAC
ticket office** (☎216 1737), at the corner of Longquan Lu and Taibao Nan Lu. Open
daily 8:30-11:30am and 2:30-5:30pm. A more convenient branch (☎212 1888, ext.
660) is in the Landu Hotel, the largest hotel on Baoxiu Xi Lu. Open M-F 8-11:30am and
2:30-6pm, Sa-Su 8:30-11:30am and 2:30-5:30pm. To **Kunming** (daily, Y440).

Buses: Baoshan Long-distance Bus Station (bǎoshān kèyùn zhàn; 保山客运站;
☎212 2311), where Baoxiu Dong Lu meets Huancheng Dong Lu. The best place to buy
maps. Open daily 6am-9pm. Sleeper buses to **Kunming** (24hr., 7 per day, Y80-110).
Hard seaters to: **Ruili** (7hr., approx. every hr., Y35); **Tengchong** (5hr., approx. every hr.,
Y25); **Xiaguan** (7hr., 10 per day, Y25); and **Yinjiang** (8hr., 3 per day, Y37).

Bank of China: 1 Baoxiu Dong Lu, next to the Yindu Hotel. Exchanges traveler's checks
and issues credit card advances. Open daily M-F 8-11:30am and 12:30-6pm.

PSB: On Lujia Jie. From Baoxiu Xi Lu, take the 2nd left after passing the Landu Hotel on
your right. The staff is not terribly cooperative. As of June 2000, this office grants **visa
extensions;** in the future, this capacity may be moved to the **regional PSB** (☎212
2445), on Zhuxi Jie, the 2nd street on the left after Zhengyang Bei Lu.

Internet Access: Landu Hotel, on Baoxiu Xi Lu. Y15 per hr. Open M-F 8am-1pm, Sa-Su
9am-5pm. Tiny computer shops around town expect to be wired soon. All charge Y4-6
per hr. Try **Lancheng Computer,** 34 Mali Jie (☎212 6910). Take the first road on your
left after passing Landu Hotel on the right. Open daily 8:30am-9pm. **KL,** 15 Shangxiang
Jie (☎212 7775). Open daily 8:30-6pm.

Post Office: China Post, 21 Xiaxiang Jie, at Xiaoci Jie. EMS and Poste Restante available. **Postal Code:** 678000.

SOUTHWEST

ACCOMMODATIONS AND FOOD

Accommodations in Baoshan are fairly basic; the only thing that puts Baoshan accommodations in a class of their own is the ever-friendly staff. No hotel is more than 10 minutes by foot from the bus station, and all have 24hr. hot water unless otherwise specified.

Food is cheap—a large bowl of rice with three dishes goes for Y3—and delicious. Stalls setting out their edible bonanza for inspection cluster around the long-distance bus station and the market on **Xiashuihe**. For Muslim food, go to the corner known as **Qingzhen Jie**, at the intersection of Shangxiang Jie and Huancheng Xi Lu. Along Shangxiang Jie, the coffee and tea shops in bamboo stalls adorned with plastic hanging plants are a pleasant surprise. The **Cold Rice Cafe** (lěngfàn kāfēi; 冷饭咖啡), 189 Baoxin Xi Lu, opposite the Yongchang Hotel, fortunately serves more than just cold rice. (Coffee Y8. Open daily 10am-11:30pm.)

Yongchang Hotel (yǒngchāng bīnguǎn; 永昌宾馆), 7 Baoxiu Xi Lu (☎212 2802 or 212 2595). Turn right out of the bus station and right again at the traffic circle; the hotel is 10min. up the road on the left. Friendly and informative staff. 4-bed dorms Y10; singles Y30; double and triples with bath Y120-150.

Shengyang Hotel (shēngyáng fàndiàn; 昇阳饭店; ☎216 0660). Turn right out of the bus station and left at the traffic circle; the hotel is on the right. Rooms are basic by most standards but impressive for the price. Hot water 7-11:30pm. Singles Y25; doubles Y30, with bath Y40; triples Y36/45.

Huacheng Hotel (huāchéng bīnguǎn; 花城宾馆), 16 Huancheng Dong Lu (☎212 2037), across the street from the bus station. Clean rooms with TV. Singles Y22, with bath Y40; doubles Y24/50; triples Y30.

Lanhua Hotel (lánhuā bīnguǎn; 兰花宾馆), 23 Baoxin Xi Lu (☎212 2803 or 212 0835), next to the Yongchang Hotel. The lobby's attempt at chandeliered grandeur sets a chintzy tone for the rest of the hotel. Singles Y30, with bath Y50; doubles with bath Y80; triples with bath Y75; quads with bath Y125.

SIGHTS

The countryside around Baoshan is beautiful and tempting, but unfortunately there is no bike rental place in town. Within the city, all sights are concentrated on the western edge. Walk along Baoxiu Lu away from the bus station, past the Bank of China and the Landu Hotel, until the road stops at an incline with steep steps going upward and ending in a fork. To the right, **Yuhuang Pavilion** (yùhuáng gé; 玉皇阁) offers a good view of the city, especially at night. To the left is the entrance to **Taibao Park** (tàibǎo gōngyuán; 太保公园), a wooded area interspersed with pagodas. *(Open daily 7am-9pm. Y3.)* As with all Chinese parks, go early (around 6am) or late (after 6:30pm) to avoid the entrance fee and to mingle with locals at rest and play, a soothing and often amusing experience. From the paths that run through the park, the 13-tiered **Wenbi Pagoda** (wénbǐ tǎ; 文笔塔) is visible just to the south; unfortunately, the pagoda looks its best from a distance. **Yiluo Pond** (yìluó chí; 易罗池) is just below the hill on which the Wenbi Pagoda rests; the pagoda at the center of the pond is a good place to relax and breathe some of that fresh Baoshan air. *(Free unless you go in an obvious tourist pack.)*

TENGCHONG 腾冲   ☎0875

Set in a wilder landscape than Baoshan, with more lushly covered and higher mountains, extinct volcanoes, and still-bubbling hot springs, Tengchong reflects its rougher surroundings. The main streets, unlike those of Baoshan, are dismal thoroughfares filled with scurrying vehicles and lined with dirty mechanics' shops, but the side streets are delightfully (and surprisingly) labyrinthine, lined with traditional buildings that invite and reward independent exploration.

✴ 🛈 ORIENTATION AND PRACTICAL INFORMATION

Although there is no distinction between an old town and a new town, Tengchong certainly seems divided between the maze of its narrow side streets and the wide main roads that encircle them. Running vaguely northeast to southwest, **Huancheng Dong Lu** (环城东路) is where Tengchong's two bus stations are; **Fengshan Lu** (风山路) runs parallel to it. Intersecting those two are **Yingjiang Lu** (盈江路), the larger street of **Guanghua Lu** (光华路), and **Huancheng Nan Lu** (环城南路), also known as **Feicui Lu** (翡翠路).

Buses: Tengchong's two **bus stations** are opposite each other on Huancheng Dong Lu; they offer comparable prices and destinations and differ only in departure times. The **bus station** (qìchē zhàn; 汽车站; ☎518 1450), on the same side of the street as the Tonglida Hotel, has a ticket office open daily 6am-9pm. Sleeper buses to **Kunming** (16hr., 4 per day, Y100). Non-sleeper buses to: **Baoshan** (4hr., 7 per day, Y25); **Ruili** (6hr., 3 per day, Y30); **Xiaguan** (10hr., 2 per day, Y70); and **Yingjiang** (3hr., 9 per day, Y18). **Tengchong Passenger Station** (téngchōng kèyùnzhàn; 腾冲客运站; ☎518 1363) is across the street. Ticket office open daily 6am-8:30pm. To: **Baoshan** (9 per day, Y25-30); **Kunming** (3 per day; Y130-140); **Ruili** (4 per day, Y30); **Xiaguan** (1 per day, Y70); and **Yingjiang** (10 per day, Y18).

Bank of China: At the intersection of Fengshan Lu and Yingjiang Lu. Exchanges traveler's checks and issues credit card advances. Open daily 8-11:30am and 2:30-6pm; in winter 8-11:30am and 2-6pm.

PSB: In a yellow-tiled complex on an alley off Yingjiang Xi Lu, going toward Guanghua Lu (☎513 6602). **Foreign bureau** for visa extensions open daily 8-11:30am and 2:30-5:30pm.

Post and Telecommunications: China Post, a 3min. walk down Fengshan Lu, just past the intersection with Yingjiang Xi Lu in the opposite direction from Guanghua Lu (☎512 3192). EMS and Poste Restante available. Open daily 8am-6pm. **China Telecom,** next door to China Post, offers international phone calls. Open daily 8am-9:30pm. **Postal Code:** 679100.

▮◌ ACCOMMODATIONS AND FOOD

Hotels in Tengchong are rather spread out, and the budget accommodations are none too inspiring. Most hotels have standard amenities, including the ever-present TV, phone, and 24hr. hot water.

In addition to the usual Chinese fare, Tengchong has a significant number of Muslim restaurants and the occasional Myanmar-influenced menu. Most eateries are street stalls where customers can choose from ingredients to create their own culinary masterpiece (or pale approximation thereof). A speciality of Tengchong is the steamed buns *(baozi)* normally found only farther east; the round bamboo steamers in front of restaurants are a dead giveaway that buns are near.

Tonglida Hotel (tōnglìdá bīnguǎn; 通利达宾馆), 50 Huancheng Dong Lu (☎518 7787), in a prominent white building. Tonglida's proximity to the bus station makes it a good stop. 2- to 3-bed dorms Y25. With bath: singles Y110; doubles Y80; triples Y100.

Tengchong Guesthouse (téngchōng bīnguǎn; 腾冲宾馆; ☎518 1044), 12 Guangting Xiang, a Y5 pedicab ride or a 20min. walk from the bus station. Take Huancheng Dong Lu in the direction of the Tonglida Hotel to the major crossroads and turn right on Huancheng Nan Lu; the hotel is on the left with an English sign. The staff is friendly and professional, but the rooms are basic and the bathrooms far away. Singles have hot water during the day only. Singles Y30; doubles Y128-168; triples Y80.

Postal Service Training Center (yóudiàn fúwù péixùn zhōngxīn; 邮电服务培训中心), 2 Fengshan Jie (☎513 1418), next to the post office. 3-bed dorms Y20; singles Y180; doubles Y60.

Tengyun Hotel (téngyún bīnguǎn; 腾云宾馆; ☎518 3553), on Yinjiang Dong Lu. The prominent sign says "Jinlin Fandian" (jīnlín fàndiàn; 金林饭店), but everyone calls it Tengyun. Uninspired staff and dark hallways. Booked solid during early July. Hot water 8am-11pm. Dorms Y5; singles with bath Y40; doubles with bath Y50.

Taian Hotel (tàiān bīnguǎn; 泰安宾馆; ☎518 3382), on the corner of Huancheng Dong Lu and Huancheng Nan Lu. From the bus station, walk past the Tonglida Hotel toward the major intersection for about 15min.; a large sign marks the hotel. Clean rooms have all standard amenities. Singles, doubles, and triples with bath Y100-120.

👁 SIGHTS

Tengchong itself packs all the satisfaction of a sight. Strolls around the old wooden shops and houses of **Yingjiang Dong Lu** (盈江东路), which turns into **Shangxi Jie** (上西路), can prove highly rewarding.

Tengchong's markets tend to be vivid affairs. On **Guanghua Xi Lu** (光华西路), there is a daily market for produce and meat; around the corner on **Huancheng Xi Lu** (环城西路), heftier items like horses and beds are traded. Another food-oriented market is just off **Fengshan Lu,** as you walk toward **Yinjiang Xi Lu.**

About 2km west of town, **Laifeng Temple** (láifēng sì; 来风寺) is set inside **Laifeng Mountain National Park** (láifēng shān guójiā gōngyuán; 来风山国家公园). The attraction here is more the journey than the destination itself. From Tengchong, walk along Fengshan Lu (toward Guanghua Lu) to Yinjiang Lu; when the road forks, bear right. *(Open daily sunrise-sunset. Y20.)*

🏞 DAYTRIPS FROM TENGCHONG

HESHUN VILLAGE

A few kilometers southwest of Tengchong. Take bus #3 (15min., every 20min., Y1.5) from the intersection of Huancheng Nan Lu and Fengshan Lu, heading away from the Tongchang Hotel. Yuanlong Pavilion open daily 8am-8pm. Y2. House of Ai Siqi open daily 8am-7pm. Y10.

Heshun village (héshùn xiāng; 和顺乡) is a well-preserved Qing-dynasty village that is the ancestral home of many members of the Chinese diaspora. The narrow cobblestone streets, set amid undulating hills and rice fields, beckon to visitors with the prospect of real, untempered relaxation. Anyone who spends a half-day or more here is bound to be a saner person in the long run. Sights include Heshun's **ancient library** (túshūguǎn; 图书馆), straight ahead from the arch that serves as the village entrance; **Yuanlong Pavilion** (yuánlóng gé; 元龙阁), a small lakeside temple; and the **House of Ai Siqi** (ài sìqí gùjū; 艾思奇故居), a museum idolizing one of the great Communist educational reformers. The latter two are on the path that runs from the village entrance around the left edge of the village, a 15-minute walk past a manmade lake on the left.

SEA OF HEAT HOT SPRINGS

12km south of Tengchong. **Minibuses** *(25min.; 8am-6pm; Y5 per person for groups, Y10 for individuals) with the characters for "Rehai" (热海) leave from the traffic circle along the road between the Taian and Tengchong Hotels. You can also wait at the minibus "station" on the road opposite the orange PICC sign near from the traffic circle.* **Taxis** *cost Y20-30.* **Open** *daily 8am-midnight.* **Admission** *Y20; special commemorative "tourist coin" comes as a bonus.*

Tengchong lies in the middle of a once-active tectonic region; the surrounding landscape consequently has some rather unusual features, 80 geysers among them. Most of these are clustered in an area known as the "Sea of Heat" (rè hǎi; 热海). Geyser names conjure up images of nightmarish amusement park rides ("Toad Eruption Spring," "Pregnant Spring," "Big Boiler"), the fragrance of sulfur fills the air, and a naturally heated pool gets Buddha-bellied local men into bathing suits to test the waters. Through all the human absurdity, though, the springs themselves still manage to impress. The waters are rumored to have healing qualities, and dips in the steaming pool might cure a stress-induced ailment or two.

TENGCHONG VOLCANOES

Minibuses run to Mazhan (马站) from Tengchong. Follow Guanghua Lu around the corner to the right and up Huancheng Xi Lu to the West Gate. When the road forks, bear right. Take the bus labeled Diantan (滇滩), which goes through Mazhan (40min., 7:30am-7:30pm, Y5). In Mazhan, continue down the main road and turn right onto a flat road. After 20min., turn left onto another flat road. Steps lead to the summit, a 20min. walk. *Admission* free.

Along with the hot springs, another remnant of Tengchong's explosive past lies in the more than 60 extinct volcanoes (huǒshān; 火山) nearby. The most accessible are north of the town of **Mazhan** (mǎzhàn; 马站). These fire-mountains-no-more are most definitely extinct; the craters are skeletal and grown over with grass. But the hike up the slopes is pleasant and not too grueling, and there is a good view of the surrounding countryside from the top.

YINGJIANG 盈江

A connecting point for travel between Tengchong and Ruili, the bustling town of Yingjiang already reflects the tropical culture found farther south. Palm trees grace the roadsides and sarong-wrapped locals take part in a rollicking nightlife scene. Although some buses from Tengchong to Ruili now bypass Yingjiang altogether, this town still makes for a quick, pleasant stop.

🔁🔀 ORIENTATION AND PRACTICAL INFORMATION. The **Yingjiang Bus Station** (yíngjiāng qìchē zhàn; 盈江汽车站) is on **Yongsheng Lu** (永胜路), the main road. (☎ 818 0766. Open daily 5:30am-9pm.) Sleeper buses go to Kunming (21hr., 4 per day, Y140), and non-sleeper buses head to: Baoshan (8hr., 5 per day, Y36); Ruili (4hr., 10 per day, Y21); and Tengchong (3hr., 10 per day, Y21). The **post office** is on Zhengxing Lu, the road farthest to the right from the traffic circle, next to the area **hospital. Bank of China** is near the bus station, across the street and a few minutes' walk to the left.

🔁🔀 ACCOMMODATIONS AND FOOD. Budget accommodations in Yingjiang are sparse; the cheapest and most convenient place to spend a night is in the **Bus Station Hostel** (qìchē zhàn zhāodàisuǒ; 汽车站招待所). This all but completely drab place does have 24hr. water. (3-bed dorms Y5; 2-bed dorms Y7; singles with bath Y35; doubles with bath Y20.) Most other hotel rates in the area start at Y120. Two **food markets** are on streets off Yongsheng Lu; one is just after the Agricultural Bank of China, diagonally across the street from the bus station, and the other one is farther up the road just before another Agricultural Bank.

RUILI 瑞丽   ☎ 0692

The last major town in Yunnan before the border, and a famous stronghold of free trade and dubious morals, Ruili is equally dedicated to its megalithic markets and its slightly naughty nightlife. Traders and sarong-wearing Burmese crowd the streets by day, and well-amplified karaoke resounds from every other building once the sun goes down. In recent years, Ruili's "openness" has ushered in the attendant problems of heroin addiction, HIV/AIDS infection, and prostitution. While the city itself offers little in the way of conventional sights, visitors with an eye for human drama are likely to find plenty here: Ruili has all the life and grit of a border town.

🔲✳🔀 ORIENTATION AND PRACTICAL INFORMATION

Ruili's major street, **Nanmao Jie** (南卯街), runs from east to west. The street's eastern portion is called **Ruihong Lu** (瑞宏路), which forks into highways going to the villages of Wanding and Nongdao, to the left and the right respectively. The Ruili market complex spills out of **Bianmao Market** (biānmào shìchǎng; 边贸市场), parallel to and a block above Nanmao Jie.

SOUTHWEST

Airplanes: Flights leave from **Mangshi Airport** (mǎngshì jīchǎng; 芒市机场). Tell the Mangshi minibus driver to drop you off along the way. A shuttle leaves from the **Yunnan Airlines Booking Office** (yúnnán hángkōng lǚyóu bāo gōngsī; 云南航空旅游包公司; ☎414 8275), on Renmin Lu, next to the Yongchang Hotel, 3hr. before the 1st flight of the day. Open daily 8:30am-5:30pm. To **Kunming** (2 per day, Y530).

Buses: Ruili Bus Station (ruìlì kèyùn zhàn; 瑞丽客运站), 9 Nanmao Lu (☎414 1423). Open daily 5:40am-9pm. To: **Baoshan** (8hr., 8 per day, Y35); **Kunming** (20hr., 8 per day, Y147); **Nongdao** (45min., Y8); **Tengchong** (6hr., 4 per day, Y30); **Xiaguan** (10hr., 3 per day, Y90); **Yinjiang** (4hr., 8 per day, Y20); and **Zhangfeng** (1hr., 15 per day, Y10). The local **minibus "station"** is opposite the bus station. Minivans leave when full for: **Jiegao** (15min., Y4); **Mangshi** (2hr., Y20); and **Wanding** (40min., Y10).

Bike Rental: The **Limin Hotel** rents bikes for Y10 per day.

Bank of China: On Nanmao Jie, down the street from the bus station, on the other side. Exchanges traveler's checks and offers credit card advances. Open M-F 8am-6pm.

PSB: 10 Jinshe Lu (☎414 1690). Pass the Ruili Guesthouse and take the 1st right up the hill; bear left when the road forks. Issues Chinese **visa extensions.** They are a suspicious crowd at this branch; non-emergency affairs are probably best handled in another town. Visas to Myanmar must be obtained in Kunming (see p. 547).

Telephones: China Telecom, on Mengmao Lu, past the post office and around the corner to the left, a few doors down from the branch of China Telecom that has Internet service. IDD service. Open daily 8am-9pm.

Internet Access: China Telecom, on Mengmao Lu. Y18 per hr. Open daily 8am-6pm.

Post Office: China Post, on Renmin Lu, across the street and up from the Yongchang Hotel. EMS and Poste Restante. Open daily 8am-8pm. **Postal Code:** 678600.

ACCOMMODATIONS

The hotel situation in Ruili changes often, and many of the good hotels that used to accept foreigners no longer do. Most hotels have 24hr. hot water.

Taihe Hotel (tàihé bīnguǎn; 泰和宾馆; ☎414 4333), just off Nanmao Jie, across the street from the bus station and up the 1st alley to the right. You can luxuriate in one of the spacious rooms in the hotel proper. The side building has less comfortable but cheaper rooms. 3-bed dorms Y15; singles Y35, with bath Y45-80; doubles and triples with A/C and bath Y100.

Tiandu Hotel (tiāndū jiǔdiàn; 天都酒店; ☎414 4835), on Mengmao Lu opposite and to the left of the street coming from the China Telecom, beside Ruili No. 1 Nationality Middle School. Beds are beautifully clean. Hot water when there is sunlight. 4-bed dorms Y15; doubles Y40; triples Y60.

Limin Hotel (lìmín bīnguǎn; 利民宾馆), 2 Nanmao Jie (☎414 2249). Turn left out of the bus station; the hotel is 500m down the road, on the left. The Limin has clean rooms but is otherwise not all that exciting. Hot water 6am-11pm. 3-bed dorms Y20; 2-bed dorms Y25; doubles with A/C and bath Y120; triples with bath Y150.

Post and Telecommunications Hotel (yóudiàn gōngyù; 邮电公寓), 5 Renmin Lu (☎411 8889), opposite the Yongchang Hotel. All but the dorms have A/C, phone, and bath. 2-bed dorms Y40; 3-bed dorms Y30; singles and doubles Y120; triples Y150.

Yongchang Hotel (yǒngchāng dàjiǔdiàn; 永昌大酒店; ☎414 1808 or 418 0008), on Renmin Lu. Turn left out of the bus station and then right at the intersection. A good choice for those with cash to spare—all others should hold their wallets and stand clear. Singles Y200; doubles Y120-168; triples Y148.

FOOD

Small restaurant stalls featuring Chinese, Burmese, and Dai cuisine are a dime a dozen in Ruili. The surfeit of Burmese signs at restaurants is misleading—they exist for the benefit of Burmese speakers and do not indicate that the restaurant serves Burmese cuisine. While there's plenty to sink your teeth into during the day, most of the local flavor comes out at night, when all sorts of delectables vie for the chance to please your palate. Visitors might need some guts to try *sapi* (sápī; 撒丕), a Dai noodle dish made of fried cow small intestine and boiled cow ears and tail—it's supposed to have a cooling effect. Don't ask and we won't tell.

Fruit stalls offering fruit and freshly squeezed citrus juices abound; look for the glasses with limes on top. Many stalls offer **edible lotus flowers** (liánzi; 莲子), an exquisite local specialty that looks vaguely like green mushrooms and has a slightly nutty flavor. The **Old Tree Coffee Shop** (lǎo shù kāfēi; 老树咖啡), between the bus station and the Limin Hotel, has a phenomenal staff, comfortable seats, an English menu, a few snacks (Y6-12), and a range of teas and coffees (Y5-15). The thirst-quenching iced coffee (bīng kāfēi; 冰咖啡; Y10) garners high marks. (☎412 0627. Open daily 9:30am-1:30am.) Next door, the **'97 Ice Restaurant** (jiǔqī bīng fàndiàn; 九七冰饭店; ☎414 8233) serves soft drinks, alcohol, and desserts.

SIGHTS AND ENTERTAINMENT

Ruili offers very few sights of note; this town is more about doing (or buying or selling or partying) than looking. More conventional sights, most with a Buddhist flavor, are clustered along the palm-lined road that runs between the villages of Nongdao and Wanding, passing Ruili on the way. If nothing else, they serve as an excuse to get out of town to explore the local countryside.

RUILI MARKET. The real heart of Ruili is its colossal market. Within this complex, there are special sections for jade and jam. Pay attention: not all products are quite what they seem. While mango jam is probably the genuine article, "real" jade may well be something else. Jade bracelets, depending on their quality, range from Y80 to Y4000 per pair. Brightly colored Burmese sarongs make good purchases. Ruili's other pride surfaces at night, when the neon is bright, the drinks (Y20-35) are stiff, and the stage is set for virtual orgies of karaoke. Those whose vocal cords or eardrums can't take the heat may find Ruili's fabled nightlife less than magical. *(Between the minibus station and Jianshe Lu.)*

TEMPLES. Leixian Zhuang Temple (lěixiān zhuāng sì; 雷仙奘寺) is Ruili's oldest *stupa*. The temple is somewhat out of the way, and barely frequented by tourists. Legend has it that about 10 years ago, a gold Buddha fell from the sky into one of the villages near the temple. To get to Leixian, take the Nongdao-bound minibus and ask to be dropped off at *Leixian zhan*. Walk away from the road toward the fields and you'll soon be in a Dai village; any villager can lead you to the temple. On the left side of the road to Nongdao, heading away from Ruili, a mud trail veers left toward **Denghannong Temple** (děnghǎnnòng zhuāngsì; 等喊弄奘寺), a red-painted wood edifice with yellow markings to distinguish it from the woven wood local houses. After you get off at the stop for the temple, walk a few minutes toward a small bridge, after which you'll see the temple; a sign points the way.

Back on the road going to Ruili, near the town of Tiexiang, the **Hansha Temple** (hǎnshā zhuāngsì; 喊沙奘寺) is up another dirt road to the left. The gray wooden temple, with small carved animals guarding the steps, is slightly larger than the Denghannong Temple; a small market sets up next door. The **Nongan Golden Duck Temple** (nòngān jīn yā tǎ; 弄安金鸭塔) complex is just southwest of town. One of the temples has elaborate white decorations and golden duck carvings on its red roof, and the other has two blue dragons carved onto its walls. Past Ruili in the direction of Wanding, just past the village of Jiele, lies the popular **Jiele Golden Pagoda** (jiělè jīn tǎ; 姐勒金塔), which takes its name from the gold paint on top of the central *stupa*. Seven smaller *stupas* represent the seven days of the week. *(Take a pedicab (15min., Y3) from the minibus station. Y3.)*

DAYTRIPS FROM RUILI

Another of Ruili's selling points is its proximity to Wanding and Jiegao, checkpoints along the Myanmar border. Jiegao (15min., Y4) and Wanding (40min., Y10) are both accessible by minibus from Ruili. In **Jiegao** (jiěgaò; 姐告), a huge jade market sets up next to the bus stop. **Wanding** (wǎndīng; 畹町) is China's smallest open border town, distinguished by a bridge connecting it with Myanmar. Foreigners cannot cross into Myanmar from here, but it is possible to gaze at the hills from just across the border. People interested in testing their luck can contact the **PSB** at the Wanding border bridge. (☎ 515 1541 or 515 3043. Open daily 7:30am-5pm.)

XISHUANGBANNA 西双版纳

Xishuangbanna Dai Autonomous Prefecture, in far southern Yunnan, is one of the most engaging regions in China. The Lancang River, also known by its Vietnamese name, the Mekong, cuts through the old-growth tropical rainforest. Biology buffs will salivate over the 5000 or more species of flora and fauna that thrive here, and even the most exhausted travelers grudgingly admit that the area is breathtaking. Bordering Laos and Myanmar and sitting firmly in the tropics, Xishuangbanna has a unique, not terribly Chinese feel. Even the name, with its whopping four syllables, rings with the resonance of foreign influence. In fact, "Xishuangbanna" (often shortened to "Banna") is the sinicized version of the region's Thai name, *Sip Sawng Panna*, which means, rather mundanely, "twelve rice-growing districts." The name does little justice to Xishuangbanna's elysian "districts."

The prefecture is composed of three counties: Jinghong, Menghai, and Mengla. Jinghong, the capital and largest city, is the base for most travelers to the region. Members of the Dai minority group, closely related to the Thai, make up one-third of the area's population. Other minorities include the Lahu, Hanii, Bulong, Yao, and Jinuo. In other parts of China, one sometimes gets the impression that minority peoples are dressed in those exotic costumes only for the sake of curiosity-hunting tourists. Not so in Xishuangbanna. Jinghong is pretty thoroughly sinicized, but the rest of Banna provides a superb opportunity to catch a glimpse of minority peoples who are not quite so aware of what gawking audiences want to see. A majority of the local people are Buddhists of the Southeast Asian Theravada school, and as a result, the local monasteries, *stupas*, and statues more closely resemble those of Thailand and Laos. Monks wear bright saffron orange robes, not the dark red of Tibetan monks.

OUT, OUT, DAMNED SPOT! The Dai, the largest and best-established minority group in Yunnan, comprise more than a third of Xishuangbanna's population. During April, tourists flood the region to celebrate Dai New Year. Among the most popular events is the Water Splashing Down Dance, in which the Dai splash huge amounts of water on each other, washing away dirt and sin. Legend has it that an evil demon set his sights on the beautiful Princess Nanzongbu. He captured her, forced her to be his seventh wife, and then invited her to celebrate New Year's Day with him. In desperation, the princess drank, danced, and flattered him shamelessly, telling him that he deserved to be master of the three worlds: heaven, hell, and humanity. The demon modestly agreed but admitted his (soon-to-be) fatal flaw: were someone to pull even a single hair out of his head and tie it around his neck, the demon's head would detach from his body. Soon, the stealthy princess had secured the hair, sending the unsuspecting demon's head tumbling to the ground. Every drop of blood that dripped from its gory base turned into fire, and war spread to the human world. The only way to stop the destruction was to turn the head upside down. Wishing to save the young ingenue from a life spent holding a severed head, the demon's other wives volunteered to take turns. The princess returned to the human world, where she rushed to wash the demon blood off her hands—hence the Water Splashing Down Dance. An epic hand-washing, to say the least.

The story of Xishuangbanna's ethnic stew has not always been a pleasant one, though. Once part of an independent Dai kingdom, the region was not absorbed into imperial China until the 12th century, and was largely ignored until the 20th century. In the 1950s and 60s, the CCP made a serious attempt to reshape minority culture and lifestyles, most likely out of fear that the area's population might demand more autonomy. Nowadays, if there is anything unpleasant about Banna, it is probably related to the region's startlingly irresponsible, often sickening domestic tourism industry, one in which minority cultures seem to be preserved for the sake of tourists willing to pay dearly for the experience. Xishuangbanna is now promoted to domestic tourists as a slice of Thailand closer to home.

It is strongly recommended that you do not join a Chinese tour group of any sort when in Banna, or else your exposure to this lovely region will probably be in the form of knick-knack shops and more methods of squeezing *yuan* out of you than you'd think possible. Even those who derive their livelihoods from the gears and pulleys of the tourism machine lament that this machine has gone too far. Since the mid-90s, warned off by the horror tales of friends, fewer and fewer people have ventured into Banna, and a sense of desperation and helplessness seems to pervade those who depend on the influx of travelers. However, as long as you wander off the trodden path, chances are that all these distressing matters will be far, far away from your mind, and the only thing that will really matter is how glorious these twelve rice-growing districts truly are.

⚠ TREKKING IN XISHUANGBANNA

Trekking is the single best way to experience Xishuangbanna's vast natural and cultural richness. The rainy season is from June to September, but the skies tend to be clear in the mornings. October to May is said to be the best time to visit; temperatures remain warm but not swelteringly so.

Many travelers to Xishuangbanna take **guides** arranged in Jinghong. Although more expensive than going alone, guides can be invaluable on twisting country roads hemmed in by dense jungle. Guides often speak both Mandarin and Dai, highly important in a region where English speakers are almost nonexistent and a striking number of adults do not speak Mandarin, at least not in any way comprehensible to foreign ears. They are also often capable of scouting out less-traversed routes and are almost always more effective diplomats in isolated villages than your average funny-looking foreign giant. If you do decide to venture out without a guide, try to pick up a few phrases of Dai beforehand, and remember that younger people are more likely to know Mandarin than older ones. Those who forgo the guide are advised to find a traveling companion for the trek. Bring **food** and **bottled water** or **iodine tablets,** as well as a sizable stash of **toilet paper.** Take care to dispose of your plastic and paper waste as responsibly as possible. You may need to ford a few small rivers; **matches** can help to rid yourself of leeches.

Many people spend the night in villagers' homes along the way. This can be the highlight of a trek, but sensitivity is important. Do not assume that you and your party are welcome in a home unless you have what is indisputably an invitation, and do not abuse the kindness of the hosts. It is customary to pay for any food that you consume in private homes. If possible, try to arrange a price before you have eaten or spent the night, and aim to pay slightly more than the market price. Most guides advise paying Y10-15 per person for an overnight stay and a more varied amount (usually under Y20) for food, depending on the quantity and quality. A few people have reported being shouted at the next morning for not paying enough, but these cases are rare; a more common complaint is the hangover produced by too much hospitality. Bewitching though the area may be, the same etiquette should be observed here as in the rest of China. Always ask (or pantomime) before taking anyone's picture, and be especially careful with monks and in temples. It's important to remember that though you may be going through the area only once, all your actions will affect the way in which future travelers will be treated.

Before setting off, scour the **travelers' notebooks** for advice, anecdotes, or vendettas. Those at Mei Mei's and Forest Cafe in Jinghong are most useful, and Mekong Cafe is also starting a notebook legacy.

JINGHONG 景洪   ☎0691

As the gateway to a region filled with enchantment, Jinghong is a bit of a disappointment. Dilapidated buildings or scaffolding line the outskirts of the city; within the city center, luxury hotels overshadow the luxuriant Banna palms. Despite the wave of construction, Jinghong still moves at the pace of a small town; streets are crowded with locals sitting in the afternoon sun, people-watching. The uninspiring atmosphere does not detract, though, from Jinghong's role as a convenient staging point for more remote and promising reaches of the prefecture.

■✦? ORIENTATION AND PRACTICAL INFORMATION

Jinghong lies southwest of the **Lancang River** (láncāng jiāng; 澜沧江), which flows into Laos and Vietnam; the new **Lancang Bridge** (láncāng qiáo; 澜沧桥) is just east of town. The city is oriented around **Peacock Lake** (kǒngquè hú; 孔雀湖), from which **Jinghong Lu** (景洪路) stretches in the four cardinal directions. **Jingde Lu** (景德路) runs south of the lake, parallel to **Jinghong Xi Lu** and **Jinghong Dong Lu.** Most restaurants and some backpacker accommodations lie on **Manting Lu** (曼听路), at the end of Jingde Dong Lu. The town is easily navigable on foot.

Airplanes: A bus (Y2) goes from the **airport** to the Xishuangbanna Hotel (the expensive one); ask to be dropped off near your chosen destination. To get to the airport, take bus #1 (Y3) from outside the Yunnan Airlines Office. Taxis cost Y30. **Yunnan Airlines Office** (yúnnán hángkōng gōngsī; 云南航空公司; ☎212 4774), on the corner of Jingde Xi Lu and Minhang Lu. Follow Jingde Lu toward the Nationalities Park. To **Dali** (1 per day, Y520) and **Kunming** (5-30 per day depending on the season, Y520).

Buses: Long trips, like those to Dali and Kunming, can take up to 10hr. longer, especially if roads are washed out during the rainy season. The prices below all apply to the trip out of Jinghong; many return trips along the same routes vary somewhat in price.

Jinghong Banna Main Bus Station (jīnghóng bǎnnà kèyùn zhàn; 景洪版纳客运站), 5 Minzu Bei Lu (☎212 4427 or 212 3348), at Jindong Bei Lu. Known to locals as **Fantai Chang** (fāntái chǎng; --Ī¥³§). Open daily 6am-8pm. To: **Hekou** (26hr., 1 per day, Y145); **Kunming** (22hr., 9 per day 8am-6:30pm, Y119.5); and **Xiaguan/Dali** (28hr., 2per day, Y150). Minibuses run to: **Menghai** (2hr., every 20min. 7am-6pm, Y8); **Menghan/Galanba** (45min., every 20min. 7am-7pm, Y7); **Mengla** (5hr., every 30min. 7am-5pm, Y25-29); **Menglong** (2hr., every 10min. 6:30am-7pm, Y11); **Menglun** (2hr., every 30min., Y12); **Mengyang** (1½hr., every hr. 8am-6:30pm, Y6); **Puer** (3hr., 3 per day, Y42); and **Simao** (5hr., every 30min. 7am-5pm, Y26).

Jinghong Bus Station (jīnghóng qìchē kèyùn zhàn; 景洪汽车客运站), 23 Jinghong Bei Lu (☎212 3570). Stay on Jinghong Lu as it turns from Jinghong Nan Lu into Jinghong Bei Lu; the station is on the right. Open daily 6am-9pm. Sleeper buses to **Kunming** (18hr., about 5 per day (whenever there are 15 passengers), Y146) and **Xiaguan/Dali** (1 per day, Y152). Minibuses run to: **Menghai** (Y9); **Menghan** (Y7); **Mengla** (Y26.5); **Menglun** (Y12.5); and **Mengyang** (Y6.5).

Local Transportation: Bus #3 (Y1) runs along Manting Lu. Jinghong is small enough to get around by foot, but **pedicabs** will go anywhere; arrange the price before embarking.

Bike Rental: Banna Guesthouse rents standard bikes (Y8 per day) and mountain bikes (Y18 per day). **Mekong Cafe** rents standard bikes for Y10 per day.

Travel Agencies: CITS, 6 Galan Zhong Lu (☎212 6783), opposite the Banna Guesthouse. Offers 1-day all-inclusive bus tours for about Y160, with some English-speaking tour guides. **Mengyuan Travel Service** (mèngyuán lǚxíngshè; 勐苑旅行社), Mengyuan Hotel, 3 Jinghong Nan Lu, Rm. 224 (☎212 5214; email myluke@bn.yn.cninfo.net). Standard treks about Y200 per day. 3 English-speaking guides, including the highly recommended **Luke Liu** (刘诗军). Open daily 8:30-11:30am and 3-5:30pm. James **(Jame's Cafe),** Sarah **(Forest Cafe),** and Vicky **(Mekong Cafe)** arrange and guide custom treks.

Bank of China: On 1 Jinghong Nan Lu, on the corner opposite Peacock Lake. Traveler's checks and credit card advances. ATM. Open M-F 8am-5:30pm, Sa-Su 8-11am and 3-5pm. **Agricultural Bank of China** (zhōngguó nóngyè yínháng; 中国农业银行), 15 Jinghong Dong Lu, opposite the Jingyong Hotel. Traveler's checks. Open daily 8am-8pm.

Bookstore: Mei Mei's, Mekong Cafe, and the **Forest Cafe** have book exchanges.

PSB: 5 Jinghong Dong Lu (☎212 2676), with an English sign. Visa extensions possible. Open daily 8-11:30am and 3-5:30pm. For more extensive visa services, go to the **main PSB** (☎212 2778, ext. 2259), on Jinde Lu next to Mei Mei's. Open daily 7am-1am.

Post and Telecommunications: 2 Jinghong Xi Lu, opposite Peacock Lake. EMS and Poste Restante. Next door, **China Telecom** has IDD service and Internet access (Y18 per hr.). Both open daily 8am-8pm. **Postal Code:** 666100.

▗ ACCOMMODATIONS

Jinghong's lodgings offer a reprieve from rougher village nights. Most hotels have 24hr. hot water.

▨ Banna Guesthouse (bǎnnà bīnguǎn; 版纳宾馆), 11 Galan Zhong Lu (☎212 3679; fax 212 6501). From Peacock Lake, follow Jinghong Dong Lu, and turn left at the end; the Banna is 5min. away, on the right. Lovely landscaped grounds and a shaded courtyard. Rooms and dorms have TV, phone, and bath. Bike rental, travel agency, and medical clinic on-site. 3-bed dorms (foreigners only) Y30; doubles Y80-390.

Dai Building Hotel (dàijiā huāyuán xiǎolóu; 傣家花苑小楼), 57 Manting Lu (☎213 2592). From Peacock Lake, go down Jinghong Nan Lu, turn left onto Jingde Dong Lu, and turn right at the end of the road; the hotel is 5min. ahead, on the right, just past the White Elephant Dai Restaurant. Rooms are small Dai-style bamboo huts on stilts, each with a narrow balcony and charm to spare; however, the cleanliness may suffer a bit. Fans and mosquito nets provided. Solar-heated water supposedly 10am-midnight, but only if Mr. Sun is happy. Deposit Y5. 2- to 4-bed dorms Y25; doubles Y50.

Jingyong Hotel (jǐngyǒng fàndiàn; 景永饭店), 12 Jinghong Dong Lu (☎/fax 212 3727), right of Peacock Lake. Clean, comfortable rooms with attached bath. 2- to 3-bed dorms Y30; doubles Y168-248; triples Y198.

Mengyuan Hotel (měngyuán bīnguǎn; 勐苑宾馆), 3 Jinghong Nan Lu (☎212 3028 or 212 4573). Walk 2min. away from Peacock Lake; the hotel is on the right, on a nicely shaded street. Rooms are clean, with TV and bath. Staff is typically receptive to bargaining. Singles Y120; doubles Y150-200; triples Y230.

Xishuangbanna Traffic Hotel (xīshuāngbǎnnà jiāotōng fàndiàn; 西双版纳交通饭店), 23 Jinghong Bei Lu (☎212 4043), next to Jinghong Bus Station. Rooms are decent, with A/C, TV, and bath. Doubles Y80-150; triples Y180.

🎨🎵 FOOD AND ENTERTAINMENT

Dai cuisine infuses a note of adventure into Jinghong's restaurants, in the form of dishes like the rather lurid green "pungent vegetables with egg," which tastes far better than it sounds. Dai food is distinguished by its emphasis on vegetables and the use of unique ingredients such as oil-fried river moss. Pineapple is often combined with salty foods or rice, which is eaten with your hands. Mint leaves straight from the plant itself make a refreshing addition. The Dai version of *shao kao* (a type of Chinese barbeque) consists of whole fish and half of a chicken drenched with a delicious sour-spicy sauce.

The Dai restaurants along **Manting Lu** are instantly recognizable by the brightly clad women who stand in front, enticing customers with clashing cymbals and eye-catching dances. These restaurants are also the main source of Jinghong's evening entertainment. Beginning around 6pm, Dai dancers perform while food is served. The ruckus breaks up around 9pm. **Mekong Cafe** and **Jame's Cafe** have English menus, but dishes (Y10-20) are less of a bargain than at other Dai places.

Many small restaurants serve "Myanmar-" and "Thai-style" noodles (Y5-8). Perhaps those with discerning tastebuds can savor the subtle difference. Stalls by the bus stations and along **Galanba Lu** and **Jingde Lu** dish up standard Chinese fare. **Pastry shops** cluster on northern Jinghong Bei Lu. For imported goods and trekking supplies, try the swell **supermarkets** on Jinghong Nan Lu, just before Peacock Lake. Mouth-watering fruits, including mango, melon, and jackfruit, are sold everywhere; the highlight is sweet, abundant, and obscenely cheap pineapple (Y0.5-1). The listings below are for those with a hankering for the flavors of the West.

▨ Mei Mei's (měiměi kāfēidiàn; 美美咖啡店, ☎212 7324), on Jinde Xi Lu opposite the entrance to Manting Lu, near the top left corner of the traffic triangle when you're walking out of Manting Lu. Good Western and Chinese food (Y8-16) and a great BLT sandwich (Y7). The best thing about Mei Mei's is the bounty of travelers' notebooks. English book collection (deposit Y100). Open daily 8:30am-10:30pm.

The Forest Cafe (sēnlín kāfēi; 森林咖啡; ☎213 6957), on Galanba Nan Lu diagonally across from Mei Mei's. Loaves of homemade bread (Y13-17; order a day in advance) and Western and Chinese dishes (Y5-18). Not much atmosphere, though, and the food is mediocre. The Forest is distinguished by its surprisingly large English book collection (deposit Y200). Also check out the travelers' notebooks here. Open daily 9am-11pm.

Jame's Cafe (jiémǔsī kāfēi; 杰姆斯咖啡), 153 Manting Lu (☎212 2937). Also known as **Wanli Restaurant and Guesthouse**, although the guesthouse portion is long gone. One of the few places in town that attracts both Chinese and foreigners. Good Dai, Chinese, and Western food (Y10-20). Try the *peroda* (Y6), a sweet Myanmar drink made of jello, bread, ice, milk, and peroda (a type of fruit) juice. Open daily 8am-10:30pm.

Mekong Cafe, 111 Manting Lu (☎212 8895), before the White Elephant Dai Restaurant. Atop a Dai-style building, Mekong is the youngest and prettiest of the backpacker cafes; it's also quickly becoming the most popular. Frequent Banna downpours are a welcome excuse to stay longer, and longer, and longer... Trekking info, bike rental, limited book collection, and Internet access (Y10 per hr.). Open daily 8:30am-late.

◼ SIGHTS

Many visitors bust out of Jinghong on their way to the surrounding villages, but the city itself is not altogether lacking in sights.

XISHUANGBANNA TROPICAL FLOWERS AND PLANTS GARDEN (xīshuāngbǎnnà rèdài huā huì yuàn; 西双版纳热带花卉苑). Organized around a chain of lakes and ponds, the garden provides ample opportunity to ramble off the predetermined route. The over 1000 species of flowering friends here would make any botanist green with envy. Two monuments commemorate Premier Zhou Enlai's 1961 visit to Jinghong; he came to the garden, proudly stroked a rubber tree, and ponderously declared, "This is our own rubber tree." *(28 Jinghong Xi Lu. The main entrance is just past the Yilan Resort and a floating restaurant on the right; pass under the arch and head toward the end of the road. Open daily 7:30am-6:30pm. Y15.)*

MANTING PARK (mántīng gōngyuán; 曼听公园). No mantises, no mating, just the oldest park in Xishuangbanna, originally known as Chunhuang Park, or "Garden of the Soul." A beloved of one of Banna's ancient rulers suddenly became sick and died after spending a nice day at the park, leading the court physician to conclude that after leaving her soul in the gardens, the lady's body could no longer survive. Chances are a similar fate won't befall you, but it's always wise to be careful. The vast area includes a monument to Zhou Enlai, a Bodhi tree, 400 peacocks, and a garishly painted temple, complete with resident monks. At certain times of day, Dai people perform death-defying tightrope maneuvers across the Lancang River. The **Dai Water Splashing Dance** (see **Out, Out, Damned Spot!,** p. 584) a traditional dance at the Dai New Year in April, is performed daily at 2:30pm. *(1 Manting Lu, a 10min. walk out of town; Manting Park is on the right, marked by English signs. Open daily 7am-7pm. Y10, students with ISIC Y5.)*

NATIONALITIES PARK (mínzú fēngguāng yuán; 民族风光园). Contrived but informative, this is Jinghong's somewhat dubious tribute to the minority peoples of Xishuangbanna and to the wildlife of the region. Six small houses are dedicated to the Dai, Jinuo, Hani, Lahu, Yao, and Bunan. Minorities in traditional garb lead visitors inside to view photographs and artifacts and to learn about each group's distinctive characteristics. Cock-fighting, dancing, music, and elephant performances are staged throughout the day. Of particular interest is the "Dance of the Lights"—look out for the women in gold body suits and extended gold fingers. *(4 Minhang Lu. Follow Jingde Lu to Minhang Lu and turn left; the park is on the right. Open M-Tu, Th-F, Su 8:30am-7:30pm, W and Sa 8am-10pm. Y30.)*

PEACOCK LAKE (kǒngquè hú; 孔雀湖). The lake is not so much a "sight" as an important town landmark, attracting morning tai chi practitioners and fishermen. It is also a reverent tribute to Xishuangbanna's many peacocks; peacock feathers are among the most popular local souvenirs. On Jinghong Dong Lu, on the right side of the lake, a path leads to some small snack shops and pleasant places to sit. *(On the edge of Jinghong Dong Lu, stretching up the right side of Jinghong Bei Lu. Free.)*

XISHUANGBANNA PRIMEVAL FOREST PARK (xīshuāngbǎnnà yuánshǐ sēnlín gōngyuán; 西双版纳原始森林公园). As the closest tropical forest to Jinghong, the park offers a feel of what the region was like before the big buildings and becapped tourists came. Parts of the forest are extremely slippery, especially the bamboo path and bridges that you can take instead of the beaten way through the undergrowth. The park also offers the usual ethnic dances and staged "marriage ceremonies" of audience members and blushing (or heavily rouged) minority brides. Be prepared for never-ending bands of Chinese tourists. *(8km north of Jing-hong. You can either bike along the highway from Jinghong to Mengyang and then turn left into the park (very visible entrance) after about 1hr., or take the bus to Mengyang and ask to be dropped off at the park. Open daily 8am-10pm. Y25.)*

MONASTERIES. Jinghong's two largest active Buddhist monasteries, both on Manting Lu, are cool, dark, and wonderfully ornate. Young boys come here to study Buddhism and to learn the Dai language and script. Respectful observers are welcome: shoes should be removed before entering the prayer hall and photography is not permitted. Even outside the prayer hall, please ask before taking any pictures; many monks dislike having their photos taken. **Manjing Temple** (mànjǐng fósì; 曼景佛寺), known in Dai as *Wat Chienglarn*, is just past the Dai Building Guesthouse on Manting Lu, on the left when facing out of town. Golden dragons and lions guard the entrance. *(Open daily sunrise-sunset. Free.)* A 10-minute walk down the road, just before Manting Park, is the dragon-guarded **Manting Temple** (màntīng fósì; 曼听佛寺), also known as *Manting Wat. (Y1.)*

MARKETS. Jinghong's main **produce market** (jímào shìchǎng; 集贸市场), between Jingde Xi Lu and Nonglin Lu, sells edible goods, household items, and other local products. There is a vegetable market directly opposite the Jinghong Bus Station. The **Minority Crafts Market** (mínzú gōngyìpǐn shāngchǎng; 民族工艺品商场), on Zhuanghong Lu across from the Banna Guesthouse, consists of tourist-oriented outfits selling jade, "authentic minority dress," carved wooden animals, peacock-feather fans, and other objects fit to entice the acquisitional instinct. Another place to buy minority cloth and clothing is the market on Jingde Dong Lu.

DAYTRIP FROM JINGHONG: MANTING

A 10-minute walk down Manting Lu from Jinghong. It takes 15min. to traverse Manting by foot. A ferry crossing, down a dirt path in the same direction, consists of a small hut by the river and a simple, long, narrow boat (Y1). Bicycles can be carted along. The boat stops at 7pm; a shout should be sufficient to call it over from the other side.

The quiet and splendid scenery of (mǎntīng; 曼听) belies its proximity to dusty Jinghong. On the other side of the river, a clear path winds between the rice paddies. Shortly after the crossing, it veers slowly to the right, and a smaller trail leads off to the left toward an **animal reserve** (dòngwù yuán; 动物园), empty but for a few peacocks and monkeys. Continuing on the path, a white *stupa* is visible to the right. Although various paths appear to approach it, the best option is to go as far as possible (about 15min.) on the main path, and then turn right where it forks. A 10-minute walk in this direction leads to **Manyangguang Monastery** (mànyǎngguǎng sì; 曼养广寺), an intimate temple with a few monks, a wooden prayer hall, and a gleaming *stupa. (Open daily sunrise-sunset. Free.)* Following the path to the left of the fork will bring you to Dai villages. When the road forks again, the upper road leads to the hamlet of **Manhena** (mànhènà; 曼贺纳), which has a small supply stall but no restaurants; some visitors have been invited into local homes for a meal. From Manhena, paths lead deeper into the countryside.

MENGHAN (GALANBA) 勐罕

Menghan, also known by its Dai name, **Galanba** (gǎnlǎnbà; 橄榄坝), is 27km southeast of Jinghong. Dai rice growers inhabit the area; the surroundings are overflowing with rice, palms, and flowers. The town itself is very small and offers little in the way of non-practical attractions, but the flat roads that radiate out from it make for easy biking through the countryside.

PRACTICAL INFORMATION

Buses stop at an indentation off the main road. Tickets to Jinghong (45min., every 20min. 7am-6pm, Y7) should be bought at the office inside. To go to Mengla (5hr., every 20min., Y25) or Menglun (1½hr., every 20min., Y10), stand on the road and hail any bus going in the direction leading away from Jinghong. To **bicycle** to Menghan from Jinghong, turn right out of Jinghong's Banna Guesthouse. When the road forks, bear right toward the river. At the bottom of the hill, follow the traffic right, past the ponds, and onto a large new road. Go left, and follow this road all the way to Menghan. The ride should take about four hours. **Bike rental** is available opposite the Dai Bamboo House; bikes are kept in a courtyard at the end of the path. (Standard bikes Y10 per day, mountain bikes Y20. Deposit Y300.) No **bank** exchanges foreign currency, so go armed with plenty of cash.

ACCOMMODATIONS AND FOOD

The **Dai Bamboo House** (dǎijiā zhúlóu lǔshè; 傣家竹楼旅社), on the main road, is the first building past the furniture shop; look for the small yellow sign. There are thin mattresses on a bamboo floor and cold showers. (6- to 7-bed dorms Y10.) The **Galanba Guesthouse** (gǎnlǎnbà bīnguǎn; 橄榄坝宾馆) is on a small street parallel to the main street. Turn right down any of the side streets running off the main street, going away from Jinghong, and then left onto the next street; the guesthouse is on the right. Amenities include actual bed frames, mosquito nets, TV, and attached baths. (☎241 1216. Singles Y80; doubles Y100; triples and quads Y120.) Fruit sellers are scattered along the road. A **market,** off the main road about halfway along, joins the two largest streets in town.

DAYTRIPS FROM MENGHAN

The enticing countryside around Menghan—flat, cultivated, gentle, and inviting—begs for casual and meandering exploration by foot or by bike. It is hard to give particular recommendations, since one would have to try very hard to end up anywhere unappealing and since the emerald backdrop of rubber plantations and rice fields is enough to justify any trip. Those who stray from the routes outlined below are all but guaranteed to stumble upon something quite marvelous.

The Mengyuan Travel Service in Jinghong offers a two-day casual **trekking** tour of area villages and monasteries suitable even for elderly or less fit travelers. For the more ambitious, a popular route is the road to **Menglun** (see p. 592). The Mengyuan Travel Service runs a four-day trek between the two towns, running through Dai, Hani, and Ahe minority villages. This trek is slightly easier than the route from Damenglong to Bulangshan.

MANCHUNMAN SCENIC PARK (mànchūnmǎn fēngjǐng yuán; 曼春满风景园). A trip to the Manchuman Scenic Park (the name given to an area that encloses a cluster of temples and monasteries), can make for an enjoyable half-day jaunt. The first temples were built here in AD 538, though they have since been restored countless times. Water and film can be bought along the trail. From Menghan, walk away from Jinghong down the main street, past the Dai Bamboo House. When the road forks, turn right down a slight slope, cross the river, and turn left at the end, toward a yellow arch announcing the park. *(The park is apparently always open. Y20, but ticket sellers are sometimes sleeping.)*

MENGBALA KINGDOM PARK (mèngbālā wángguó yuánlín; 勐巴拉王国园林). After entering the park, head right when the road splits, toward the park. Mengbala Kingdom Park is on the right, visible for an unusual monastery set amid painted statues of peacocks and lions, typical white *stupas*, and a Buddha nearly buried in lotus leaves. At the back of the temple are more statues and a small bridge ringed by forest. These are some of the most distinctive monastery grounds in all of Xishuangbanna and are well worth a visit. *(Open daily 8am-8pm. Y7.)*

MENGHAN CHUNMAN TEMPLE (mènghàn chūnmǎn sì; 勐罕春满寺). The path from Mengbala Kingdom Park continues to Menghan Chunman Temple, also known as *Wat Ban Suan Men*, set slightly back from the road among modest Dai residences. The fantastic, resplendent gold *stupa* sits in the center of the courtyard, surrounded by smaller *stupas* and a temple building—colors are dazzlingly bright. On July 21st, the temple celebrates its birthday with Dai dancing, a Dai pop group, and enthusiastic crowds from the surrounding area, with all ages well represented, rounded out by the delicious Dai snacks on offer; the large, round, semi-sweet puffed rice cakes are especially good (Y1).

MANZHA VILLAGE (mànzhà; 曼乍). From Menghan Chunman Temple, the road veers around to the right to reach the small village of Manzha. Just opposite the stone marker for this village is a small monastery, a humble wooden structure that is a good staging ground for shade-hunts and a pleasant contrast to the garish spectacles at other area monasteries. There is no sign, but the monks hanging out in the gardens should clue you in. From the monastery, the road goes straight and then veers to the left; 10 minutes beyond is the last monastery in this complex, **Manting Buddhist Temple** (màntīng fósì; 曼听佛寺). A giant white *stupa* dominates the temple area; inside the monastery is an enormous gold Buddha whose head reaches so high it cannot be seen. It's a 30-minute direct walk from the temple to Menghan. The return trip traverses gorgeous landscapes and Dai villages; many people wander off the path and explore.

MENGLUN 勐仑

Menglun, southeast of Jinghong, is another zero-horse town with luscious attractions nearby. But very few other tiny townlets can boast sights as major as Menglun's enormous Chinese Academy of Science tropical arboretum.

ⓘ PRACTICAL INFORMATION

Buses go to Menglun from Jinghong (1½hr., every 30min., Y12), Menghan (1hr., every 20min., Y12), and Mengla (5hr., when full). From Menghan, take the bus labeled "Mengla" and ask to be dropped off at Menglun; vice versa coming from Mengla. In Menglun, buses wait at the traffic circle back along the main street. It's possible to ask cafe owners in Jinghong (many of whom speak English) or other friendly folk to write your intended destination on a piece of paper to show the driver. The **PSB** is a small, laid-back office on an alley off the main road. Walk about seven minutes past the Sinodec gas station and Wantong Inn, and turn left into the alley; the office is three minutes ahead, on the left. (☎ 871 5094. Open daily 8am-5pm.) **China Post** is on the left, a few minutes past the alley with the PSB, opposite the Luosuojiang Restaurant (逻梭江饭店). (Open daily 8am-5pm.)

⌂ ACCOMMODATIONS AND FOOD

The **Cuixinyuan Hotel** (cuìxīnyuán jiǔdiàn; 翠馨园酒店), on the road where the bus stops, has rooms with A/C, bath, and 24hr. hot water. (☎ 871 5737 or 871 5711. Doubles and triples Y100.) Rooms in the **Scientists' Activity Center** (kēxuéjiā huódòng zhōngxīn; 科学家活动中心) have attached bath and hot water after 6pm. When entering the garden, turn left after the bridge; follow the signs. (☎ 871 5043. Singles Y180; doubles Y150; triples Y200.) **Wantong Inn** (wàntōng lǚshè; 蔓通旅社), on the main street next to the Sinodec gas station, about 4km from the botanical gardens, has clean rooms and hot water during the day. (☎ 871 6318. 3-bed dorms with bath Y50; 2-bed dorms Y20.) Small, bland **restaurants** line the main street. There are also snack stalls within the garden. In the morning **market**, *baozi* (Y0.5) abound; they are slightly sweet, made of rice, and utterly delicious.

⌕ DAYTRIPS FROM MENGLUN

CHINESE ACADEMY OF SCIENCE TROPICAL BOTANICAL GARDENS (zhōngguó kēxuéyuàn xīshuāngbǎnnà rèdài zhíwùyuán; 中国科学院西双版纳热带植物园). The sublime gardens here fulfill every botany buff's horticultural fantasies. Even the less horticulturally savvy should be humbled in the presence of over 120 species of bamboo and palm trees, many native to Xishuangbanna. Especially famous

Pack the Wallet Guide
and save 25% or more* on calls home to the U.S.

It's lightweight and carries heavy savings of 25% or more*
over AT&T USA Direct and MCI WorldPhone rates. So take this
YOU wallet guide and carry it wherever you go.

To save with YOU:
- Dial the access number of the country you're in (see reverse)
- Dial 04 or follow the English voice prompts
- Enter your credit card info for easy billing

Service provided by Sprint

Hmm, call home or eat lunch?
With **YOU**ᴿᴹ
you can do both.

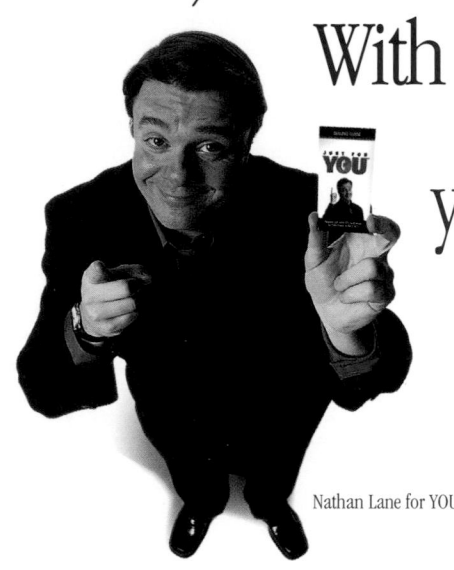

Nathan Lane for YOUᴿᴹ.

No doubt, traveling on a budget is tough. So tear out this wallet guide and keep it with you during your travels. With YOU, calling home from overseas is affordable and easy.

If the wallet guide is missing, call collect 913-624-5336 or visit www.youcallhome.com for YOU country numbers.

are the "stranglers," parasites that cling on to other trees and grow over their trunks before squeezing the life out of them, and the much friendlier "dancing plant," which moves its tender leaves when you sing to it. A dusty little museum inside the gardens commemorates visits by Deng Xiaoping and Zhu Rongji. The tropical gardens are worth a visit and then some, but it is advisable to get there before midday, when Chinese tour groups flood in and take their sweet time to stop and smell the flowers. *(Continue walking in the direction in which the bus goes and turn right by the market; the gardens are at the end of the road. To return to Menglun, either backtrack through the park, or take the much longer route (5-6hr. on foot) out of the East Gate and through the countryside back to town. ☎871 5071. Open daily 8am-11pm. Y35.)*

DAI GARDEN (dǎizú yuán; 傣族园). Sometimes, in the happy world of travel, a sight sticks out so much that it needs to be listed if only to direct tourists to mock it. And, unless you have a major masochistic streak or a special itch to see men decked out in gold crowns and glittery pink robes, this grotesque exploitation of Dai culture will probably send you hurling toward the nearest vomitorium. After half an hour of melodramatic "ethnic" dancing, seven Dai "princesses" fall madly in love with seven audience members, egged on by a raucous, drum-beating parade. In return, all they ask from these audience members is a Y100-300 token of affection. *(43km from the Botanical Gardens, on the left side of the main road. Open daily 8am-10pm. Y10.)*

MENGHAI 勐海

Menghai, the largest town in western Xishuangbanna, is often used as a stepping-stone to more interesting areas nearby. The Menghai region is prime tea-growing country and an important source of **pu-erh tea,** a black, earthy brew favored by dieters. The town also has a sizable Muslim population, rare in Xishuangbanna. There is a **mosque** (qīngzhèn sì; 清真寺) on the main street going back toward Jinghong. Menghai's Sunday market attracts an ethnic mélange of peoples from around the area. About 10 minutes down the main road to Jinghong are some small **Dai villages** and a gold **pagoda.** A path to the left leads to another small hilltop **pagoda** and attached **temple,** with commanding views of vast tea fields. Recovering caffeine-aholics should beware.

Just about everything a visitor could need is on the main street, **Xiangshan Xinjie** (香山新街). **Menghai Bus Station** (měnghǎi qìchē zhàn; 勐海汽车站) is just past the Muslim section of the main street, on the right as you head toward Jinghong; look for a large yellowish arch. The other **bus station** (kèyùn zhàn; 客运站) is across the street. Both stations run buses to: Daluo (2hr., every 30min., Y17); Jinghong (2hr., Y8); Kunming (24hr., 4 per day, Y142); and Ruili (28hr., 1 per day, Y120).

The **Banna Hotel** (bǎnnà lǚshè; 版纳旅社), with an English sign, is past the bus stations on the way to Jinghong and opposite the Industrial and Commercial Bank of China and the market. Dorm beds (Y10) are dingy but have mosquito nets; try not to get a room facing the noisy street. Opposite the Menghai Bus Station, the **Customs Hostel** (hǎiguān zhāodàisuǒ; 海关招待所) has clean rooms with attached bath and mosquito nets. (Singles and doubles Y80.) For plates of dumplings and steamed buns (Y4), try the small row of wooden open-fronted **restaurants** just up from the Banna Hotel, down the small alley to your left. For Muslim food, go back in the direction of Jinghong, five minutes up the street; look for the Arabic script.

🎫 DAYTRIPS FROM MENGHAI

MENGHUN (勐混). Menghun, southwest of Menghai, is a tiny blip on the map. The surrounding area is populated by a lively mix of Dai, Bulang, and Ahe people, and Menghun's **Sunday market** is a wonderful technicolor affair. It is best to stay in Menghun or nearby Menghai the night before, since the market is most active in the morning; tour groups sometimes bus in to rain on the parade around 11am. **Buses** overflowing with people, animals, and goods run from Jinghong (3½hr., Y15) and Menghai (1½hr., Y10) to Menghun. To reach a non-descript guesthouse (dorm beds Y10), turn right from where the bus stops and walking up the hill through the tiled arch. After passing two basketball courts, turn left in front of a brownish-gray building onto a gravel path. Follow the path as it curves, past a brick building; the entrance is right behind a gate.

XIDING (西定). Xiding, directly west of Menghai, is a tiny town that comes alive for the **Thursday morning market.** Market visitors should plan to spend the night before in Menghai and take an early bus (1hr., every 20min., Y7).

JINGZHEN (景真). Jingzhen is 20km west of Menghai, near the town of Mengzhe (勐遮). The primary attraction is the well-worn **Jingzhen Octagonal Pavilion** (jǐng-zhēn bājiǎo tíng; 景真八角亭), modeled after the shape of Sakyamuni's golden headgear and topped by a silver umbrella surrounded by small bronze bells. The 22m wooden pavilion was built in 1701 (year 1063 by the Dai calendar). *(Jingzhen can be reached from Menghai (45min., Y6) or Jinghong (3hr., Y15).)*

DALUO (打洛). Daluo is in the southwestern corner of Xishuangbanna, right on the border with Myanmar. Crossing the border is illegal; the main attraction here is the **Tree That Looks Like a Forest,** a prized 900-year-old fig tree (Y3). There is also a small **border fair.** *(Buses go to Daluo from Jinghong's main bus station (4hr., every hr., Y22).)*

DAMENGLONG 大勐龙

Damenglong, usually listed on bus timetables as **Menglong** (勐龙), is basically just a single street but a fine base for a trek. Two marvelous temples stand at either end of town. The **Manfeilong Bamboo Temple** (mànfēilóng sǔntǎ; 曼飞龙笋塔), several kilometers back toward Jinghong, lies at the base of a hill. A 15-minute walk up the hill leads to the *stupa;* when the road forks, go up the stairs to the *stupa* instead of following the path onwards. The white pagoda, built in AD 1204 (year 565 of the Dai calendar), was named for its resemblance to bamboo shoots. The whole complex is awash with carvings of plants, animals, and Buddhas. *(Y5.)* At the other end of town, just before the road bends to the left, a path branches off to the right, leading to the **Black Pagoda** (hēi tǎ; 黑塔). A monastery fronted by a silver *stupa* sits about 50m up the hill. Another 10 minutes of scrambling gets you to the main *stupa,* shining gold amid the overwhelming green of the countryside. There is a **small market** just before the path up to the Black Pagoda.

 Buses to Damenglong depart from Jinghong Main Bus Station (3hr., every 10min. 6:30am-7pm, Y11). There's little room for luxury on Damenglong's one street. The **Bus Station Hostel** (qìchē zhàn zhāodàisuǒ; 汽车站招待所), next door to the bus station, has run-down dorms (Y10). The noisier **Damenglong Hostel** (dàménglóng zhāodàisuǒ; 大门龙招待所) is up the road and to the right, at the end of the street, in the top left corner of the government building courtyard. The Damenglong has **bike rental** (Y3 per hr., Y15 per day).

TREKKING AROUND DAMENGLONG

The surrounding area is populated by one of Xishuangbanna's most colorful ethnic mixes, including the Dai, Han, Lahu, and Bulang peoples. The 50km stretch between Damenglong and **Bulangshan** (布朗山) usually takes two to four days. This route is fairly populated; if you have walked more than two hours without seeing anyone, chances are that you're lost. This route covers some steep terrain and is definitely more rigorous than the Menghan to Menglun circuit. Water and snacks can be bought in most villages between Manpo and Bulangshan, but you should consider carrying some with you just in case. Beware of dogs; some travelers have reported vicious canines roaming around the villages. In the rainy season, the geography looks different, so you need to be extra observant.

DAMENGLONG TO BULANGSHAN. The following is a rough description of the trek. Check travelers' notebooks in Jinghong and ask around before you head out. The first village after Damenglong is **Manguanghan.** Follow the road south toward Myanmar, and turn right when the border guards are visible. It is also possible to grab rides in motorbike sidecars. After Manguanghan, follow the tractor trail for 20 minutes to **Guanmin**, a small Hani village. From there, it is a 5km walk to **Manpo**, a Bulang minority village.

Leave Manpo for the walk to **Nula** (1½-2hr.) from the trail starting at the back of the town. After you've climbed a steep hill and within five minutes of beginning the trail, there will be a plateau where the trail splits. The branch that forks left is quickest. The scary bamboo bridge just past Nula is an awesome test of courage and agility. After braving the bridge, take the trail to your left which runs along the edge of some rice paddies. You'll soon cross a fence made of branches and within 20-25 minutes will see a somewhat trodden path that descends to the river. The winding path may make it seem like you're backtracking, but this is the way to **Songer**, a Lahu village (1hr.).

From Songer, take the path that heads downward for about 30 minutes to a clearing near cornfields. Follow the path toward the stream; with the cornfields on your right, bear left. The more obvious path to your right is the wrong (or harder) way, leading to muddy rice paddies with several paths up a hill. It takes about two hours to reach **Weidong**, a Hani village. It is best to look for housing with local families here, since some travelers have reported problems finding accommodation in Bulangshan. From Weidong, follow the broad tractor trail to **Bulangshan** (3hr.). Buses run from Bulangshan back to Menghun.

BULANGSHAN TO DAMENLONG. The road from Bulangshan to Weidong forks after about an hour or slightly more. Bear left to go directly to **Weidong;** to the right is a village. When the road forks again (about 1¾hr. after leaving Bulangshan), bear left again. The first sign that you are in Weidong is a basketball court outside a school; continue, following the descending path. After 10 or 15 minutes, a gold *stupa* should be visible.

From Weidong to **Bannakan** takes about 30 minutes. A village on the other side of the valley has a very similar name, and you may be mistakenly directed to that one; pay attention. At the fork in the road past Bannakan, bear left. After a while, the road crosses a stream; once on the other side, proceed left to **Songer**. About 500m after Songer, head toward the right. About one-and-a-half hours later, **Nula** will appear on the right side of the valley; head toward the river and cross the rickety bamboo bridge. Continue up through and then alongside the village for about an hour to **Manpo**; much of this portion is uphill. From Manpo to Damenglong takes five hours; some trekkers grab a ride on a motorbike sidecar instead.

BITTEN BY THE LOVEBUG

In the more remote stretches of Xishuangbanna, the courtship traditions of the Dai and the Hanii (Xishuangbanna's two largest minority groups) still continue today. During the annual Dai **Water-Splashing Festival,** the first bucket of water is poured over one's object of affection, who returns the favor if the attraction is mutual. Dai maidens also carry **perfumed pouches** that they throw at the lucky (or unlucky) man who catches their eye. If the man accepts the pouch, it means he likes her. If he flings it back, it's rejection at its most obvious. Another Dai courtship ritual involves **barbequed chicken.** The man heads towards the poultry-seller who has stolen his heart (or stomach); if she doesn't like him, she'll charge an exorbitant price. Unfortunately, bargaining isn't an option here.

Even after the bucket of water, the silk pouch, or the chicken, the courtship phase is far from over. Most Dai families require a future son-in-law to donate at least two years of "hard labor" before they'll consider him serious marriage material. **Hanii** men have a much quicker (though perhaps more acutely painful) way of catching a bride. While a Hanii maiden goes to fetch water or firewood, her Romeo "kidnaps" her, throwing the girl on his back and running as fast as he can to his house. She usually has already expressed that she likes him, but she still has to scream and cry for her parents, who come scurrying out to hurl various objects, such as tools and vegetables, at the bandit. To prove to her lover that she really does like him, the girl must **bite** him several times on the neck and shoulder. The harder she clamps down, the more she loves him—Hanii men wear these scars with pride.

MENGLA 勐腊

Mengla's main draw is its proximity to **Mohan,** site of the border crossing to Laos. Due to the increasing flow of people and goods across the border, Mengla is growing like a weed, but most tourists pass through quickly.

Buses run to Jinghong (5hr., Y27) and Menghan (5hr., Y26) from the bus station (qìchē zhàn; 汽车站; ☎812 2773). **Bank of China,** outside the bus station, on the left corner of the next intersection, exchanges traveler's checks and foreign currency, including Lao *kip.* The **postal code** is 666300.

Mengla Xumushou Medical Technology Support Center (měnglà xùmùshòu yīkèjì péixùn zhōngxīn; 勐腊畜牧兽医科技培训中心) accepts foreigners. From the bus station, turn right and keep on going. The hotel is on the left; if you can see the river, you have gone too far. (☎812 2240. Doubles Y60; bargain to Y50.)

BORDER CROSSING INTO LAOS: MOHAN

Buses (2hr., Y10) go from Mengla to **Mohan** (磨憨), the small town where China ends and Laos begins. Minibuses (Y60) also ply the route. There is no Bank of China in Mohan; other banks will change US dollars, but usually only in amounts over US$100. Small notes can be changed on the black market.

Laos **visas** are not issued at the border. All visas must be obtained at the embassy in Beijing (see p. 48) or the consulate in Kunming (see p. 547). The Lao entry checkpoint is a 20-minute walk from the border.

GUIZHOU 贵州

No one discusses Guizhou without making reference to the saying "In Guizhou, the sky is never three days clear, the land does not have three feet that are flat, and the people haven't three cents worth of money." In other words, Guizhou is drizzly, hilly, and poor. More accurately, Guizhou challenges any attempt to dismiss it with an easy characterization. The landscape, strewn with jagged and soft-peaked karst hills, is undeniably evocative, but Guizhou's defiant beauty is also its sorrow; the mountainous topography and low-grade soils have always made agriculture difficult and prosperity elusive. In many ways, the province is something of a Chinese Appalachia: the site of wretched material poverty, gentle mountain beauty, and great cultural wealth.

Guizhou is, and always has been, the home of many minority nationalities; today, Han Chinese comprise 70% of the population, but the remainder includes a full 30 minority groups, clustered mainly in the south. The history of this ethnic mix has been tumultuous. The province was not brought under full Chinese control until the Ming dynasty, and, in the Qing, major ethnic conflict broke out, mainly between the Miao, the predominant minority group, and Han Chinese. In the infamous Battle of Mount Leikong in 1726, more than 10,000 Miao were beheaded, and another 40,000 starved to death. In 1856, Guizhou Miao joined the Taiping Rebellion (see p. 56) and were defeated only in 1871. Even in the 20th century, relations between minorities and Han were tense; only recently has the government begun to make efforts to protect minority cultures.

Chinese tourists visit Guizhou with two things in mind: the famed scenic sights near the town of Anshun (see p. 601), which foreign visitors may find less inspiring, and the province's most acclaimed export, *maotai* liquor, a heart-pounding, sorrow-drowning experience. Yet Guizhou has much more to offer. Restful, welcoming hamlets of Miao, Dong, and other minorities snuggle in valleys and by riversides, offering windows into a life both difficult and enchanting, like the province itself.

GUIYANG 贵阳   ☎0851

Guiyang, the capital of Guizhou, is a curious beast; it is both the major urban center in a province that is overwhelmingly rural and the wealthiest corner of one of China's poorest areas. Like most of the province, the city was originally populated entirely by non-Chinese peoples. Both the Sui and Tang dynasties had official posts here, but it wasn't until the Mongol invasion of southwest China in 1279 that Chinese settlement began, and only in the Ming and Qing dynasties was Chinese cultural dominance of the area ensured. In recent years, Guiyang has been the site of rapid economic development, and today it is a city of haunting differences, with buoyant commercial districts sitting uncomfortably alongside the crumbling buildings that typify much of Guizhou. The poverty is heartbreakingly prominent, but the city never quite succumbs to its sorrows. Great parks, superb food, and more shops than there are bicycles in Beijing provide plenty to do, while the whole of the city provides plenty to ponder.

▛ TRANSPORTATION

Airplanes: An airport bus (Y10) runs to and from the **CAAC ticket office,** 304 Zhonghua Bei Lu. **China Southern Airlines** (zhōngguó nánfāng hángkōng gōngsī; 中国南方航空公司), 70 Zunyi Lu (☎582 8429), is open daily 8am-8pm. To: **Beijing** (3-4 per day, Y1380); **Chengdu** (2 per day, Y500); **Chongqing** (1-2 per day, Y310); **Guangzhou** (5 per day, Y690); **Guilin** (F and Su, Y520); **Kunming** (4 per day, Y350); and **Shanghai** (3 per day, Y1280).

Trains: Guiyang Train Station (guìyáng huǒchē zhàn; 贵阳火车站; ☎698 1222), at the southern end of Zunyi Lu. The ticket booth is in the center-right of the station. Staff at the soft seat ticket office (off to the side) speak a little English. Few trains originate here and tickets can be hard to obtain; express trains are the emptiest. To: **Beijing** (36½hr., 2 per day, Y500); **Chengdu** (20hr., 4 per day, Y160); **Chongqing** (15½hr., 9 per day, Y80); **Guangzhou** (33hr., 7 per day, Y300); **Kaili** (3½-4½hr., several per day, Y14); **Kunming** (12-14hr., 10 per day, Y150-160); **Shanghai** (37hr., 4 per day, Y240); and **Zunyi** (5hr., several per day, Y16).

Buses: There are 2 main bus stations in Guiyang. **Guiyang Long-distance Bus Station** (guìyáng chángtú kèyùn zhàn; 贵阳长途客运站; ☎682 4224), near the train station. Buy tickets on the bus. To: **Anshun** (1½hr., depart when full 7am-7pm, Y21-35); **Guangzhou** (30hr., 1 per day, Y176-284); and **Zunyi** (2½-3½hr., depart when full 7am-7pm, Y21-34). The **Bus Service Station** (kèyùn zhàn; 客运站; ☎687 1116) is on Yanan Xi Lu. Turn left at the intersection of Ruijin Lu and Yanan Lu, away from the main shopping area; the station is 10min. down the road on the right. Open daily 5:30am-9pm. To: **Anshun** (every 20min. 6:30am-8pm, Y14); **Huangguoshu Falls** (depart when full 7am-8pm, Y65); **Kunming** (15hr., 1 per day, Y120); and **Zunyi** (2½-3½hr., every 20min. 7am-9pm, Y25.5).

Local Transportation: The most useful **buses** are **#1** and **2,** which run from the train station up Zunyi Lu, along Ruijin Lu past the Jinqiao Hotel, and then around the city along Beijing Lu and back down Zhonghua Nan Lu (Y0.5).

Taxis: Base fare Y10.

▛▟ ORIENTATION AND PRACTICAL INFORMATION

Although sizable, Guiyang is easy to navigate. The city sits along the **Nanming River** (nánmíng hé; 南明河), a tributary of the Wu River, which eventually joins the Yangzi in Sichuan. **Yanan Lu** (延安路), Guiyang's main shopping thoroughfare, runs from east to west through the city center. **Beijing Lu** (北京路) runs parallel to and north of Yanan Lu, and **Zhongshan Lu** (中山路) runs south of it. **Zhonghua Lu** (中华路), which turns into **Zunyi Lu** (遵义路) at its southern end and terminates at the train station, runs from north to south, intersecting with Yanan Lu. West of Zhonghua Lu, **Ruijin Lu** (瑞金路) has a cluster of budget accommodations.

Travel Agencies: CITS, 20 Yanan Zhong Lu (☎825 5873), opposite the large ICBC Bank. Knowledgeable and helpful English-speaking staff members.

Bank of China: 30 Dusi Lu, a 10-15min. walk from Yanan Lu down Zhonghua Lu. Turn right on Dusi Lu. Exchanges traveler's checks and issues credit card advances. Open M-F 8-11:30am and 2:40-5:30pm, Sa-Su 9:30-11:30am and 2:40-4pm.

Bookstores: Foreign Language Bookstore (wài wén shūdiàn; 外文书店), 31 Yanan Dong Lu, has the usual classics in English. Open daily 8:30am-6pm.

PSB: On the corner of Zhonghua Lu and Zhongshan Xi Lu (☎582 3189), a 10min. walk down Zhongshan Lu from Yanan Lu.

Telephones: China Telecom, 68 Zhonghua Nan Lu, just below Dusi Lu. IDD service in the central hall. Open daily 8am-7pm.

Internet Access: China Telecom, to the left of the IDD phone office. Y5 per hr. Open daily 8am-noon and 2:30-6pm. The **geology department of Guizhou University,** 116 Baoshan Bei Lu. Walk through the gates toward the tall building directly in front of you; the geology department is on the right a little before the building. The computers are at the end (last room on the left) of the main hallway. Y3 per hr. Open daily 9am-11pm.

Post Office: China Post, 1 Zhonghua Bei Lu, at Yanan Lu. EMS and Poste Restante. Open daily 8:30am-7pm. **Postal Code:** 550001.

ACCOMMODATIONS

Hotels abound in Guiyang, but keep your expectations for budget choices low. Most hotels do offer up to 20% discounts during some parts of the year. Expect price hikes during the first week of May and October. All hotels listed provide 24 hr. hot water.

Coal Guesthouse (méitàntīng zhāodàisuǒ; 煤炭厅招待所), 57 Beijing Lu (☎683 2447). All rooms have TV, phone, and bath. Compared with the rest, it remains the best. Doubles Y100; triples Y120.

Caizhen Guesthouse (cáizhèntīng zhāodàisuǒ; 财政厅招待所), 346 Zhonghua Bei Lu (☎689 4100). Conference participants often stay here; rooms may be hard to get at times. Newer rooms are worth it, though. Doubles Y125-168.

Tongda Hotel (tōngdá fàndiàn; 通达饭店; ☎579 2327), right next to the train station. Don't expect any peace and quiet when you're this close to Guiyang's transportation hubs. Singles and doubles with bath Y198-207.

Zhilin Hotel (zhílín bīnguǎn; 絷林宾馆), 110 Yanan Zhong Lu (☎586 4000), near the center of town. Clean rooms have matching comforters and curtains. Book through CITS to get a Y200 rate. Singles and doubles Y268.

Golden Bridge Hotel (jīnqiáo bīnguǎn; 金桥宾馆), 34 Ruijin Zhong Lu (☎582 9951 or 581 4872). Take bus #1 or 2 from the train or main bus stations. Come here to see how the other half lives; the lobby is a grand mess of chandeliers and marble. Currency exchange. Singles Y238-280; doubles Y248-288; triples Y276.

FOOD

Food is one of the best things about Guiyang, where making masterpieces out of the sparest ingredients is a finely honed art. Most of the food is very spicy, but you can order it in less throat-burning, eye-watering incarnations.

Snacks are the real centerpiece of Guiyang cuisine. Guiyang's official **"snack alley"** (dàinán báishā xiǎochī xiàng; 大南白沙小吃巷) is on **Zhonghua Dong Lu,** just before Nanhua Lu, in the direction away from Yanan Lu. **Kebabs** (sháokǎo; 烧烤) and all manner of unlikely but edible items can be found grilled on a stick. Guizhou is known for its very sour dishes, and pickled vegetables turn up by the bushel. Particularly worth trying is the **sour radish** (suān lóbō; 酸萝卜), which looks like a tongue on a stick—are you licking the radish, or is the radish licking you? Most popular are the stalls that line the road leading to Qianling Park during the day; customers fill small crepes with a variety of foods laid out on the table, creating a do-it-yourself spring roll.

To reach the **night market** on Ruijin Nan Lu in front of Hebin Park, turn left out of the Golden Bridge Hotel and continue about five minutes. Other night markets, offering the same delicious edibles, line Yanan Lu. There are a host of hotpot stalls opposite the night market, and another group on Feishan Jie; turn right out of the

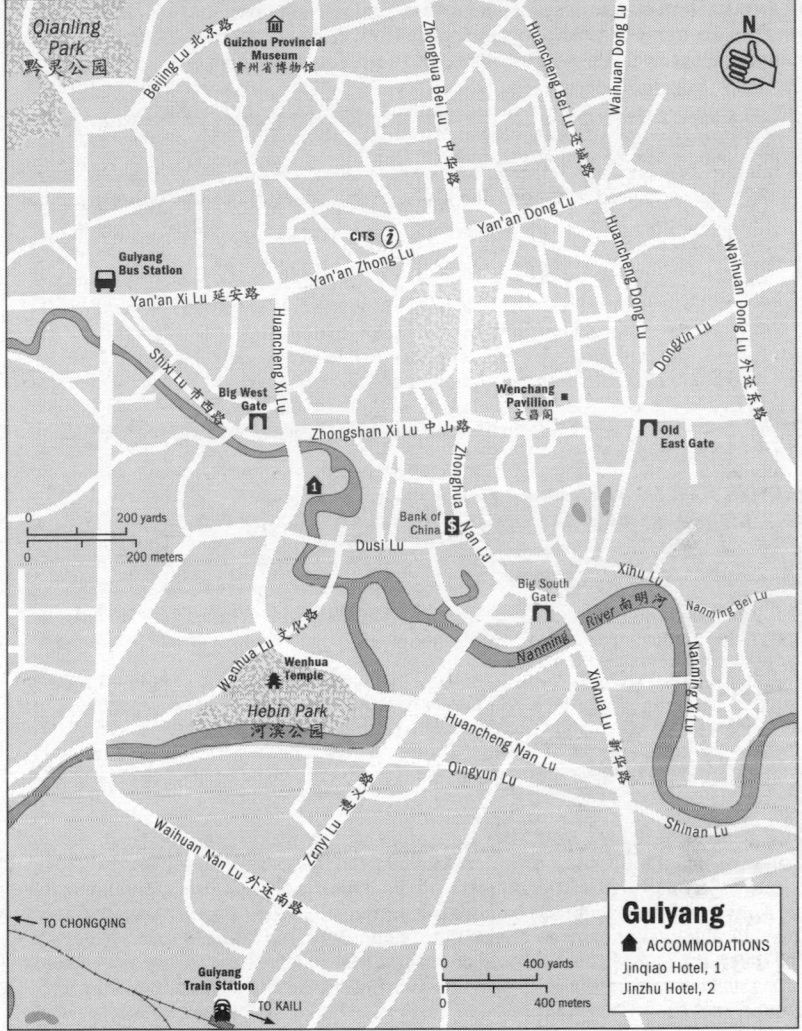

Guiyang

⌂ ACCOMMODATIONS

Jinqiao Hotel, 1
Jinzhu Hotel, 2

Golden Bridge Hotel, and take the second street on the right. The base price for hotpot tends to be Y2-3, with each additional ingredient Y3-8. **Dog hotpot** (gǒuròu; 狗肉) is quite common in Guiyang. The prime place for trying one of Guiyang's special **noodle soups** is at 1 Yanan Dong Lu, near Guizhou University. Big bowls of beef rice noodles (niúròu fěn; 牛肉粉; Y3-5) attract big crowds during meal times. (Open daily 5:40am-7:30pm.) Many restaurants and bars are on Baoshan Bei Lu, near the Guizhou University campus.

SIGHTS

Guiyang deserves a second look—and a third, and a fourth. The contrast between new wealth and obviously timeworn poverty are among the city's most striking aspects. Guiyang also has some of the best parks in China; the maze of old houses and infinite paths create prime ground for unfettered exploration.

QIANLING PARK (qiánlíng gōngyuán; 黔灵公园). The biggest of Guiyang's parks, this area offers a fantastic mixture of natural forests, temple solemnities, and amusement park madness. The 383 steps to the top of Mt. Qianling, known as the "nine-winding path," lead to fabulous views of the city and surrounding Guizhou scenery. Monkeys set up shop along many of these paths; they won't try to sell you souvenirs, but some can be vicious (particularly those with newborns). The highlight is **Hongfu Temple** (hóngfú sì; 弘福寺), built in 1672 by Master Chi Song (1634-1706). After 32 years of construction, 100 monks took up residence, and the temple became a regional center for Buddhist teachings. In classic Cultural Revolution style, all the monks were evicted, and some damage was done to the temple. Today, monks have moved back in, including a few from Henan province's Shaolin monastery (see p. 233), recognizable by the nine dots imprinted on their upper foreheads. A vegetarian restaurant is in the courtyard. *(Open daily 11am-4pm.)*

Some people choose to swim in **Qianling Lake** (qiánlíng hú; 黔灵湖), although it's not necessarily advisable. Amusement park prices are usually listed, but foreigners are often charged more; bargaining is possible. *(Take bus #1 or 2 to the corner of Beijing Lu and Zaoshan Lu, or walk all the way up Ruijin Lu, past Yanan Lu, and turn left onto Beijing Lu. The park is up a shaded path leading away from the city. Open daily 6:30am-10pm. Park Y5. Hongfu Temple Y1.)*

FLOWER STREAM PARK (huāxī gōngyuán; 花溪公园). Most visitors go to the park grounds to swim in the river or water reservoir right outside the park. Spring brings an inordinate amount of blossoms, hence the park's name. The distinctive villages surrounding the park make for a great half-day of exploration. One of them has houses made of stone slabs, and another one rests beside a mountain that looks as though it was sliced straight down the middle. *(Take the bus from Dashizi. Open daily 8am-6pm. Y5; outside park hours free.)*

PAPER GORGE (xiāngzhǐ gōu; 香纸沟). This scenic sight offers unspoiled woodlands of bamboo and birch, small ponds, waterfalls, and most of all the chance to see ancient methods of paper-making. The products of this unmechanized process are thin, yellowish pieces of paper that most people buy to burn as spirit money in commemoration of ancestors. *(Take the bus (1½hr., Y1.5) from Guiyang Long-distance Bus Station. Open daily 8am-6pm. Y10.)*

GUIZHOU PROVINCIAL MUSEUM (guìzhōu shěng bówùguǎn; 贵州省博物馆). Not surprisingly, the museum focuses most of its exhibitions on Guizhou's 48 minority peoples, with visual displays on festivals, traditional dress, and minority art. Only a few descriptions are in English, but much of the pictoral message filters through. Permanent exhibits are on the second floor. *(On Beijing Lu. Take bus #1 or 2 and ask to stop at the museum, or walk up Zhonghua Bei Lu from Yanan Lu, and turn left onto Beijing Lu; the museum is 10min. down on the right. Open Tu-Su 9am-4:30pm. Y10, students Y5; ISIC may work.)*

ZUNYI LU. The road forks as you walk down Zhonghua Nan Lu; **Zunyi Lu** is the right side of the fork. Parts of Zunyi Lu are a walled walkway. Following its left side leads to a small **flower and bird market.** The market twists around to the left along the river and is positively blooming with character. Plants and flowers are interspersed with adorable talking mynah birds that can say such amusing expressions (in Chinese) as "have you eaten yet?," "buy some eggs," and "please buy me." **Qianming Temple** (qiánmíng gǔsì; 黔明古寺) is near the end of the market, just off Zunyi Lu, to the left. *(Open daily 7:30am-5:30pm. Y0.5.)* Back on Zunyi Lu, past the temple area, is **People's Square** (rénmín guǎngchǎng; 人民广场). Elderly Chinese linger to play *mahjong* or sit and talk in the mid-sized park area around where the Chairman stands in all his stone splendor.

QINGYAN ANCIENT TOWN (qíngyán gǔ zhèn; 青岩古镇). This well-preserved Ming dynasty Han village provides a relaxing stroll through grounds steeped in traditional architecture. Relive those school days in the **Scholar's House.** *(Take the bus (1hr., Y1.5) from Guiyang Long-distance Bus Station. Village free. Scholar's House Y5.)*

BUILT TO LAST Guizhou may be poor, but it certainly produces some tough specimens of humanity. In November of 1998, Li Guanghai and his wife Wang Fangzhan were officially registered by the Guinness Book of World Records as the world's oldest couple and the progenitors of the biggest extended family (perhaps setting another record for most records set by a single couple in one year). The couple, ages 101 and 102, have been married for 83 years and have 140 offspring spanning five generations. They are cared for by Li Rong, a great-grandson, but still help to prepare their own meals. They have no advice to offer aspiring centegenarians, but their favorite dish, apparently, is sticky rice.

OTHER PARKS. Wenchang (wénchāng gé; 文昌阁) and **Huajia** (huájiā gé; 华家阁) **Pavilions,** on Huancheng Dong Lu near Zhonghua Lu, are not especially remarkable, but still offer attractive opportunities to retreat from the hefty human drama of Guiyang. Wenchang Pavilion has a small display of coins from around the world, and a produce market sits on the other side of Huancheng Dong Lu. The swimming pool at **Riverside Park** (hébīn gōngyuán; 河滨公园), on Ruijin Nan Lu about five minutes from the Golden Bridge Hotel, is where locals go to escape the sweltering summer heat. *(Open daily 6:30am-10:30pm. Park Y3. Swimming pool Y8.)*

ANSHUN 安顺 ☎0853

Anshun is a rough-and-tumble town in western Guizhou, on the rail line between Guiyang and Kunming. Anshun presents visitors with an uncensored picture of the imbalances in China's current economic "boom." The city is a harsh depiction of Guizhou's extreme poverty, complete with pitted streets, beggars, and illustration after illustration of the supreme effort that so many must go through simply to subsist. Anshun sees tourists because of its proximity to **Huangguoshu Falls** and **Longgong Caves,** Guizhou's best-known tourist attractions. It is also a base for visits to **Zhijin Caves,** Asia's largest karst caves.

◼ 🛈 ORIENTATION AND PRACTICAL INFORMATION

Nanhua Lu (南华路) runs from the train station in the southeast up through town to a traffic circle at **Guihuanggong Lu** (贵黄公路), and past Anshun's only large modern buildings, including the Bank of China, the post office, and China Telecom, all at the corner of **Tashan Lu** (塔山路). Anshun is small enough to navigate on foot.

> **Trains: Anshun Train Station** (ānshùn huǒchē zhàn; 安顺火车站; ☎322 3295), at the south end of Nanhua Lu. Open 24hr. To: **Chongqing** (12hr., 2 per day, Y100); **Guiyang** (1½hr., 3 per day, Y14); **Kunming** (11hr., 8 per day, Y100-130); and **Shanghai** (39hr., 2 per day, Y300).

> **Buses:** Prices and destinations are similar. **Anshun Passenger Bus Station** (ānshùn kèchē zhàn; 安顺客车站; ☎322 3111), on Nanhua Lu, a block before the train station, by the traffic circle. Open daily 6:30am-7pm. To: **Guiyang** (1½hr., every 20-30min. 6:30am-6:20pm, Y12); **Huangguoshu Falls** (1½hr., when full 7am-6pm, Y10); and **Kunming** (12hr., 2 per day, Y100). A small van goes to **Longgong Caves** (1hr., when 5-7 people show up, Y10). **Anshun West Bus Station** (ānshùn xī zhàn; 安顺西站; ☎322 3839), on Tashan Xi Lu. Head toward the large buildings on Nanhua Lu and turn left at the Bank of China; the station is a few minutes down on the left. Buy tickets on the bus. To: **Guiyang** (1½hr., every 20min. 7am-7pm, Y12); **Huangguoshu Falls** (1½hr., every 20min. 7am-5:40pm, Y10); and **Longgong Caves** (1hr., 2 per day, Y4).

> **Local Transportation: Buses #3** and **4** go up Nanhua Lu and turn right on Nanhua Dong Lu, while **#7** and **8** run from the train station up Nanhua Lu and turn left on Tashan Xi Lu.

> **Taxi:** Base fare Y5.

> **Travel Agencies: CITS** (☎322 3173), on Tashan Dong Lu. Turn right off Nanhua Lu; CITS is a 15min. walk, on the left. **Family of Workers Hotel Travel Service** (☎322 4377) has a friendly staff (see **Accommodations**).

Bank of China: 1 Nanhua Lu. Exchanges traveler's checks and issues credit card advances. Open M-F 8am-6pm.

PSB: On Tashan Xi Lu (☎350 2242). Turn left off Nanhua Lu at the Bank of China; the PSB is a 10min. walk, on the left. For visa extensions, go to the **Foreigners' Bureau** on the 5th floor. Open M-F 8am-noon and 2:30-6pm.

Post and Telecommunications: China Post and Telecom, 2 Nanhua Lu, opposite the Bank of China. Poste Restante. **Postal Code:** 561000.

ACCOMMODATIONS

Anshun has few cheap accommodations, but those that do exist tend to be of good quality. Hotels listed have 24hr. hot water unless noted.

Family of Workers Hotel (zhígōng zhījiā; 职工之家), 48 Nanhua Lu (☎322 5376), halfway between Tashan Lu and Guihuanglong Lu, next to the "Wholesale Market of Small Goods in Anshun." Welcome to the family. Rooms are clean and bright, with mosquito nets and attached baths. 3-bed dorms Y30; doubles Y100-180.

Xixiu Shan Hotel (xīxiù shān bīnguǎn; 西秀山宾馆), 63 Nanhua Lu (☎332 1641), opposite the Family of Workers Hotel and up toward the traffic circle. Very friendly staff and excellent rooms with attached bath. Rooms can be rented by the hour. 20% off-season discount. Singles Y138-258; doubles Y98-258.

Nationalities Hotel (mínzú fàndiàn; 民族饭店), 67 Tashan Dong Lu (☎322 2621). Turn left off Nanhua Lu at the post office, and the hotel is a 10min. walk on the left; a large bowling pin marks the spot. The inconvenient location and high prices won't bowl you over. Hot water 7pm-9:30am. Doubles Y180; triples Y220.

FOOD

Those looking for gourmet thrills among the survival food of Anshun will be barking up the wrong tree. **Dog,** known as a hearty, warming staple, is immensely popular here. There is a small selection of restaurants near the traffic circle on Nanhua Lu. Street stalls line the road, and the main **market areas** are near the intersection with Tashan Lu. **Fruit sellers** are all over the city, clustered in the market just up from the post office on Nanhua Lu. **Guiyang Chicken Chang Wei** is on Guihuanggong Lu near Nanhua Lu. Slurp up one of their filling bowls (Y3-5) of noodle soups, including Guizhou specialty Hunan noodles (húnán miàn; 湖南面) and the spicier *changwei* noodles (chángwèi miàn; 肠胃面). If you really want to know what you're gulping down, *changwei* means intestines. Yes, it tastes better than it sounds. (Open daily 7am-7pm.)

If you find yourself getting seriously depressed after more than a night's stay in Anshun, you might want to head out to ■ **Farm Family Love** (nóngjiā qíng; 农家情), on Guihuang Xi Lu. The straw and bamboo structure is about a 30-minute walk or 10-minute taxi ride along the road to Huangguo Falls, on the right. This place is exactly as it sounds—all farm, all family, all love, and lots of Miao and Chinese food (Y6-15). Try the scrumptious *hema* and egg pancake (Y12). *Hema*, a local poison ivy that induces an extreme allergic reaction if met in the uncooked wild, makes an extremely tasty and nutritious dish once stir-fried. Waitresses also bear wine-filled tubes of bamboo to toast you with Miao drinking songs. After leaving, the world seems a friendly place, at least for a little while.

SIGHTS

The main attractions of Anshun are the thunderous natural wonders outside of town, although the old part of Anshun can be intriguing. The same **Xixiu Mountain Pagoda** (xīxiù shān tǎ; 西秀山塔) that lends its name to so many local institutions is set on a small hill overlooking Nanhua Lu. Follow Nanhua Lu away from the Guihuanglong traffic circle, past the modern buildings, and then turn left. The narrow, winding streets are lined with peddlers trying to eke out a living. Sellers seem to vastly outnumber buyers, and the whole phenomenon, like much of Anshun, is simultaneously troubling and intriguing.

Anshun is also famous for its **batik**. Batik sellers clog the tourist sights outside town, but the best prices are usually in Anshun. Shops line Nanhua Lu between the traffic circle and the Bank of China. Hard bargaining is the order of the day.

🏃 DAYTRIPS FROM ANSHUN

ZHIJIN CAVES

About 150km (2½-3hr.) from Anshun. Buses may leave from Anshun's bus stations (Y30-40) and from Guiyang Long-distance Bus Station (Y60), but don't count on it. Minibuses (Y5) go from Zhijin to the caves. The Family of Workers Hotel in Anshun can arrange daytrips (Y300-400 per vehicle). Open daily 8am-6pm. Y60.

The spectacular ▓ Zhijin Caves (zhījīn dòng; 织金洞), the largest series of karst caves in Asia, is touted with increasing fervor as the "number one cave in the world." There are currently 12 "rooms" open to the public, with more—one reportedly the size of a soccer field—still under preparation. The immense scope of the caves and the awe-inspiring formations of stalactites and stalagmites is mind-boggling. Floor lights and guides with flashlights do their job of preventing stumbles, but the inky darkness of some spots reminds visitors that they are deep within the earth. **Zhijin Caves Hotel** (zhījīn dòng bīnguǎn; 织金洞宾馆) is next to the cave entrance. (☎ (0857) 781 2046 or 762 7181. 4-bed dorms Y20; singles with bath Y120.)

HUANGGUOSHU FALLS

The path of least resistance is to take a minibus (departs 7:30am, returns 5-7pm) from one of the hotels in Anshun, combining a visit to the falls with a stop at the Longgong Caves. Open daily 6am-7pm. Y30.

Huangguoshu Falls (huángguǒshù pùbù; 黄果树瀑布), Guizhou's biggest tourist attraction, are doubtlessly imposing at 81m wide and 74m high. The heavy publicity surrounding them at times can make the blasts of water a mite disappointing, but after heavy rains (generally in summer), the falls are truly sublime. The area suffers from being recognized all too well as an attraction; batik shops, drink stands, and quantities of tourists overwhelm the pastoral effect. Still, there is a winning surreal effect to the whole scene; the sight of sizable tour groups sidling along a cliff face, outfitted in silver-gray ponchos and looking like a procession of space troopers, has a certain appeal. Various viewing platforms surround the crashing waters, and it is possible to go behind the falls themselves (Y10). This latter option provides an irreplaceable opportunity to hear and feel the force with which the water descends. This location is also one of the best from which to catch the frequent rainbows arching over **Rhinoceros Pool** below the falls. To make the most of the trip, continue along the path by the river to some beautiful spots farther downstream. The small **railway** on the far right side of the area, beyond the bridge, is but a mediocre tourist gimmick (Y5).

The only hotel that officially takes foreigners is **Huangguoshu Hotel** (huángguǒshù bīnguǎn; 黄果树宾馆), on Huangguoshu Lu, just before the park entrance, to the left. (☎ 359 2111. Doubles Y140-580; triples Y380-480.) The cheap places downhill from the Huangguoshu Hotel may be willing to bend the rules. Try the **Chuanji Hostel** (chuānjì zhāodàisuǒ; 川记招待所), on your right as you head away from the falls. (☎ 359 2663. 2-bed dorms Y15, with bath Y20, July-Aug. Y60-80.)

LONGGONG CAVES

South of Anshun. Tour buses from Anshun hotels usually visit the caves after a morning trip to Huangguoshu Falls. Buses from Anshun West Bus Station (2 per day, Y4) and minibuses from Anshun Passenger Bus Station (depart when full, Y10) make the 1hr. trip. Y30.

The Dragon Palace Caves (lónggōng dòng; 龙宫洞), along with Huangguoshu Falls, form the backbone of any tourist jaunt through the area. These caves are among the most extensive karst caves yet discovered, and they house the longest underground river in China. All visitors must set sail on small yellow boats that glide into the caves, traffic jams permitting, accompanied by a Chinese-speaking guide. The 30-minute trip is something like a third-rate carnival haunted house, with bits of the caves lit up by red, green, and purple lights to highlight the prominent karst features. Creepiness aside, the caves are magnificent, with stalactites and stalagmites sharp enough to put out an eye. The viewing platform in the large park near the entrance allows visitors to look down onto the thundering water of **Guanputai Waterfall** (guānpùtái pùbù; 观瀑台瀑布), or "Watch the Waterfalls Platform Falls," and grin in the face of watery death.

HEAVENLY STAR BRIDGE SCENIC AREA

*A few kilometers downstream from Huangguoshu Falls. Most **tour buses** to Huangguoshu Falls and Longgong Caves also stop here. Otherwise, motorcycle taxis or pedicabs ply the route from the falls; don't pay more than Y8 one way. **Minibuses** go from the scenic area to Anshun (10); to return to Guiyang, you must first return to the Huangguoshu Falls area. **Open** daily 8am-6pm. **Admission** Y30.*

Heavenly Star Bridge Scenic Area (tiān xīng qiáo fēngjǐng qū; 天星桥风景区) is comprised of three "sights" that meld nicely together. It begins with a series of expansive ponds traversed by paths of stepping stones, and a pavilion—just lovely enough to be a prime target for assembly-line tourist processing. This where most tour guides end their Y10 tour, leading their unknowing band of picture-hungry travelers out of the area and leaving the rest of the place (now truly celestial) to those who've decided to strike out on their own. Clusters of curious tree roots seem to grow from the karst formations, and a truly lovely series of little waterfalls and one awesome stone bridge that formed when a boulder just happened to drop between a crevice await. A cable car (Y10) goes to the exit. It is possible to find pleasant and peaceful spots by leaving the main pathways, but visitors must struggle hard to avoid being herded along a pre-assigned route. If in doubt about where to go, one of the many souvenir sellers will point you in the right direction.

KAILI 凯里 ☎0855

Kaili, a small, largely Han Chinese town in eastern Guizhou seems to be nothing remarkable. This drab, dusty little city is surrounded by resplendent countryside, where local life is set against spiky karst hills and rice patties that glimmer like jewels in the damp morning sunlight. Villages heavily populated by minority nationalities temper the celestial beauty of the landscape with the earthy tones of pastoral life. The Miao and Dong are the predominant groups, but the area also counts Yao, Shui, Buyi, Mulao, and Gelao peoples among its population. Kaili itself has convenient accommodations and the necessary facilities for exploration farther afield, in a region that remains largely untapped by tourists.

◼◼▌ ORIENTATION AND PRACTICAL INFORMATION

Kaili is easy to navigate. With the exception of the train station, most important places and attractions lie within a small area around the city center, easily accessible on foot. **Beijing Lu** (北京路) runs from east to west, intersected by **Shaoshan Lu** (韶山路), which runs from north to south. The crossroads of town, this intersection is known as **Dashizi** (大十字). North of and parallel to Beijing Lu is **Yingpan Lu** (营盘路), lined with craft shops, restaurants, and budget accommodations.

Trains: Kaili Train Station (kǎilǐ huǒchē zhàn; 凯里火车站), on Qingjiang Lu, at the far northern end of town. Take bus #2 or a taxi (Y10). The ticket office is on the left. Sleeper tickets are best bought in Guiyang. To: **Guiyang** (4½hr., 6 per day, Y14); **Shibing** (1½hr., 2 per day, Y5); and **Zhenyuan** (2hr., 3 per day, Y8).

Buses: Kaili Long-distance Bus Station (kǎilǐ qìchē kèyùn zhàn; 凯里汽车客运站; ☎822 3794), on Wenhua Bei Lu. From Dashizi, go east on Beijing Dong Lu and take the 2nd left up Wenhua Lu. The station is on the left, past Yingpan Dong Lu. Ticket office open daily 5:30am-10pm. Most tickets are bought on the bus. To: **Duyun** (every 40min. 6:30am-4:20pm, Y10-15); **Guiyang** (6hr., every hr. 6:30am-10:30pm, Y25-35); **Huangping** (3hr., 3 per day, Y15); **Leishan** (1½hr., every 30min. 7am-6pm, Y15); **Rongjiang** (6hr., every hr. 7:40am-7pm, Y20-30); and **Sanhui** (4hr., every 40min., Y20). **Kaili Society Bus Station** (kǎilí shèhuì kèchē zhàn; 凯里社会客运站), next to the Kaili Hotel, in the southern part of town. Sleeper buses to **Guangzhou** (24hr., Y180-240) and buses to **Guiyang** for about the same price as at the other station.

Local Transportation: Bus #2 (Y0.5) runs from the train station to Dashizi.

Taxi: Base fare Y5.

Travel Agencies: CITS, 53 Yingpan Dong Lu (☎822 2547), on the grounds of Yingpan Hotel, behind the tennis court. Friendly and helpful staff members speak excellent English and can provide information on local events. Open M-F 8am-noon and 2:30-6:30pm; staff is sometimes also there on weekends.

Bank of China: 6 Shaoshan Nan Lu. Exchanges traveler's checks and issues credit card advances. Open daily 8am-noon and 2:30-5:30pm. A branch on 11 Beijing Dong Lu also exchanges currency. Open daily 8am-6:30pm.

PSB: On Beijing Xi Lu. Turn left at the intersection with Shaoshan Lu; it's 5min. down on the left. Open M-F 9:30am-noon and 2:30-4:30pm.

Post and Telecommunications: 1 Beijing Lu, at Shaoshan Lu. EMS and Poste Restante available. **China Telecom** is on the 2nd floor. **Postal Code:** 556000.

ACCOMMODATIONS

Kaili offers some dirt-cheap accommodations, although the ranks of cheap hotels that accept foreigners seem to be slimming every day. Hotels are clustered around **Beijing Lu** and **Yingpan Dong Lu.** All hotels listed will store luggage for travelers striking out for surrounding villages, and most have 24hr. hot water.

Blue Sky Hotel (lántiān dàjiǔlóu; 蓝天人酒楼), 1 Beijing Xi Lu (☎/fax 823 4600), right by Dashizi. Rooms are clean and cool, with overhead fans to chase those clouds away. 4-bed dorms Y30; doubles with bath Y168; triples with bath Y228.

Yingpanpo Hotel (yíngpánpō mínzú bīnguǎn; 营盘坡民族宾馆; ☎823 4600), on Yingpan Dong Lu. From Beijing Lu, walk up Shaoshan Lu and take the 1st right; the hotel is 5min. down on the left, with an English sign. The hotel itself is up a slope and to the right. Staff is friendly, but rooms are dim sum and bathrooms are in poor condition. Singles Y20; doubles with bath Y60-80; triples Y30, with bath Y75; quads Y32/120-160.

Petroleum Guesthouse (shíyóu bīnguǎn; 石油宾馆; ☎823 4331), on Yingpan Dong Lu, just before Wenhua Lu. From the intersection with Beijing Lu, walk up Zhongshan Bei Lu and turn right onto Yingpan Dong Lu; the hotel is on the right. 5-bed dorms Y12, with bath Y23; 2-bed dorms with bath Y34.

FOOD

Cuisine in Kaili is fairly uninspiring. Sour is the flavor *du jour* every *jour*, and pickled vegetables are an important part of local diets. Kaili's pride and joy is its **Sour Fish Soup** (suān tāng yú; 酸汤鱼), a type of hotpot where the fish is cooked to tender perfection. The place to try this delectable meal is at **Kuaihuolin Restaurant** (kuàihuólín jiǔjiā; 快活林酒家), 54 Huancheng Xi Lu. Ask to go down to the kitchen to select your scaled treat from the multitude thrashing away. The Y16 per *jin* fish yields a Y38 meal. (☎821 0200. Open daily 8am-10pm.) **Guan Guan Chicken Food Store** (guànguàn jī shípǐn diàn; 罐罐鸡食品店) is at 11 Yingpan Dong Lu. Turn right off Shaoshan Dong Lu and the store is on the left, with a raised seating area. Portions (Y10-20) are small, but staff will be able to tell you which are local delicacies and which are, well, just chicken feed. The caramelized fruit dishes (básī shuǐguǒ; 拔丝水果; Y12) are excellent. (☎825 2559. Open 24hr.)

Those saving their stomachs for puppy chow can head to the row of **dog hotpot** restaurants on Beijing Dong Lu. Turn right off Shaoshan Lu and the restaurants are down the road on the left, just past Wenhua Lu. The pick of the litter is the **Zhangjia Dog Restaurant** (zhāngjiā gǒuròu diàn; 张家狗肉店), serving hotpot for Y30 per person. (Open daily until 10pm.)

There is a small **night market** on Beijing Lu near Dashizi, with stall after stall of *bingfen*, a type of jello with ice, pickled fruits, and nuts (Y1-3 per bowl). Before ice cream, this is what people screamed for (and still do). The stall run by a woman in her mid-thirties right in front on the Industrial and Commercial Bank of China is especially good.

SIGHTS

Most visitors to Kaili head elsewhere to sightsee. In town, the **Grand Pavilion** (dà gé; 大阁) is a small temple and pagoda perched atop a hill, an active site of worship and an attractive spot from which to observe local life. To get there, walk to the end of Shaoshan Bei Lu, turn right, and then take the first left up Dage Xiang, which leads to the base of the hill. On special occasions, the temple is open at night for worship ceremonies; those who catch one of these should consider themselves many times blessed. *(Open daily 8am-6:30pm. Y1.)*

SHOPPING

Every Sunday, the **Kaili Market** sets up along Men Jie, north of and parallel to Beijing Lu. Some serious mercantile action happens here, although it pales in comparison to the spectacular Sunday markets in the outlying villages. **Shopping**, especially for crafts from various Guizhou minorities like the Miao and Dong, is one of the best things to do in Kaili. During the weekend, across the street and to the right of the Yingpanpo Hotel, minority goods (mainly embroidered clothes and bags) are sold along a small alley. Bargaining is of the essence. At other times, individual craft sellers linger around the entrance of the hotel.

🎒 DAYTRIP FROM KAILI: LANGDE

*South of Kaili, on the road into the Leigong Hills. Take the Leishan-bound **bus** (45min., every 30min., Y5) from Kaili and ask to be let off at Langde. There is a small **guesthouse** (zhāodàisuǒ; 招待所) in Langde and one in Upper Langde (Y6 per person). Every villager will know the way and will probably show you; you're unlikely to find it in the twists and turns of identical-looking streets and houses.*

Langde (lǎngdé; 朗德) is one of Guizhou's more accessible minority villages. The wooden houses linked by narrow, winding cobblestone streets create a delightful labyrinth filled with snapshots of daily village life—pigs and chickens chomping away at lunch, tanned youngsters at play, and adults carrying out domestic cleaning chores or sitting on their verandas. Waterwheels rest alongside a slow-moving river and water buffalo submerge in the deeper places. More than in most area villages, locals here are beginning to realize that their culture could be quite lucrative, and visitors are often greeted with people rushing out of their houses to offer greetings and traditional jewelry and handicrafts. This is a rather strange twist on typical Miao hospitality, but still makes for an extremely warm reception. Accommodations are available with Miao families. Accommodations are basic but acceptable; wooden beds (Y6) with thin mattresses are the order of the night, and bathing is in male- and female-designated parts of the river. Most meals cost Y5.

Langde itself is not far from the main road out of Kaili; 3km up the path, on the other side of the river but the same side of the road, is **Upper Langde** (lǎngdé shàng; 朗德上). There is little obvious difference between the two villages, but the walk between them, especially up the distinctive double-tiered wooden bridge next to Upper Langde, is truly beautiful. The views from Upper Langde will take your breath away, as will the uphill trek to get there. When tour groups visit Upper Langde, you can hop on the festive wagon. Villagers get decked out in gorgeous traditional costume. The men bring out their *lushengs* (reed flutes) to greet the guests, while the women stop visitors 12 times before the hamlet gates to toast them with small bowls of homemade liquor. Traditional dancing follows, including a performance called "climbing the knife mountain and entering the burning sea." This involves, true to its name, a smiling young man who climbs barefoot up a pole stuck with rusty but still sharp knives and then walks across a burning piece of wood (twice). It's useless to ask how he does it—villagers don't seem to know either. The tour group usually will have paid for the performance; individual visitors standing with the villagers along the sides (instead of sitting at the wooden tables with the guests) do not have to pay; if you do, though, Y30-50 is standard.

KAILI MINORITY VILLAGES

The area around Kaili may well contain the single richest and most diverse concentration of minority peoples in all of China. The two dominant groups are the Miao in the north, south, and west, and the Dong in the southeast, but a potpourri of Gelao, Mulao, Gejia, Yao, and Shui peoples ensures that nothing about this area's culture is the slightest bit uniform. Thanks to the sluggish rate of tourist traffic through the region, no one has yet thought to market the culture of these peoples to curious tourists hankering after exotica. Minority life is lived without embellishment; the sights and smells of everyday life have not been sterilized or forced to conform in the interest of audience expectations. The terrain erupts into spiky green karst peaks at every turn, making any journey a magnificent exercise in scenic drama. So much natural beauty is more than enough compensation for the long, bone-rattling bus rides along the region's bumpy, ill-kept roads. Trips require quite a bit of planning and coordination, since most buses back to Kaili stop running by early afternoon and bus trips often will take longer than expected. Kaili is the central point from which most roads radiate.

MARKETS

Village life is at its most lively and urgent in the local markets. People trade all manner of goods: live, dead, and occasionally inanimate. Buyers and sellers are usually so busy with economic strategy and maneuvers that the stray foreigner wandering through the fray may get next to no attention. Most markets start when the day is still in its infancy and wind down by noon. On Sunday, markets are held in **Kaili** (p. 604), **Shibing** (p. 609), and **Zhenyuan** (p. 610). Markets are held every five days in **Chongan** (p. 609) and every six days in the villages of **Leishan** (p. 608), **Xijiang** (p. 608), and **Zhouxi**. The above list of area markets is by no means comprehensive. Check with the Kaili CITS for exact dates.

FESTIVALS

Local festivals offer opportunities to see minority cultures at their most expressive and vivid. Festivals are occasions for mass gathering, singing, and dancing; for many young people, they are also a prime opportunity to mingle with and consider potential spouses. For the most part, locals tend to welcome the participation of outsiders; respectful behavior on the part of visitors will ensure that this continues to be the case. Festivals follow the lunar calendar; therefore, the dates in the Roman calendar vary from year to year. Most festivals are annual events, but some are far rarer; the **Miao Guzang** festival, held on November 6-7, 2000, is held only once every 12 years.

A small selection of the festivals in 2001: the **Miao Reed Flute Festival** (miáozú lǔshēnghuì; 苗族芦笙会), February 21-24; the **Miao Hill-Leaping Festival** (miáozú tiào huāpō; 苗族跳花坡), February 20; the **Miao Dragon Boat Festivals** (dòngmiáozú lóng chuán jié; 苗族龙船节), June 25 and July 15; and the **Shui Dragon Boat Festival** (shuǐzú duān jié; 水族端节), September and October.

KAILI MINORITIES: THE MIAO苗

Most villages in this part of Guizhou are Miao strongholds. With over seven million members dispersed throughout Hunan, Sichuan, Guangxi, Yunnan, and (predominantly) Guizhou, travelers to the southwest would probably have to try hard to avoid encountering this important ethnic group. The Miao ethnicity, a branch of the better-known Hmong tribes of Southeast Asia, is actually a Miao mix, comprised of seventy or more sub-groups, distinguished by fine variations in dialect, dress, and custom.

The Miao language, the closest relative of which is that of the Yao people, has nearly as many dialects as Chinese. The Miao cluster in mountainous regions and build simple, single-story houses out of wood or thatch. Agriculture and forestry keep Miao villages afloat, though in the past the Miao were known as prime producers of opium. Some Miao were converted to Christianity by 19th-century missionaries, but their traditional religion is profoundly polytheistic, involving a range of gods and demons, with a stronger emphasis on ancestor worship than that of other area minorities (like the Dong). Traditional Miao society also afforded an unusual degree of sexual freedom to young women, who were permitted by their parents and by public opinion to become intimate with as many men as they liked in their search for a husband; it was not uncommon for a young Miao woman to have a child or two by the time she married.

Miao traditional dress varies according to age and occasion; after marriage, women adopt a whole new wardrobe. Across the board, though, Miao traditional dress is elaborate; young women don unwieldy headdresses and neckwear. The Miao are known for their intricate embroidery and handicrafts and, in particular, for elaborate baby carriers. Mounds of silver jewelry are worn at festivals.

The reed flute (lúshēng; 芦笙) is the foundation of Miao music, the necessary accompaniment of Miao dances, and the symbol of Miao culture. Visitors who cannot attend the annual Reed Flute Festival (see **Festivals,** p. 607) should ask around to see if they can persuade a local reed flute virtuoso to stage an impromptu performance.

LEISHAN 雷山

Leishan (south of Kaili) has little to recommend it as a destination, but it is a useful mini-hub for travel farther south or northwest to Xijiang. Leishan has two main roads. The bus stops at one end of town, and from there the road marches straight through town and across the river. The other major road branches off to the right of the first one and leads to the Leigongshan Hotel, on the south side of the river.

Buses go to Leishan from Kaili (1½hr., every 30min. 7am-6pm, Y7), returning to Kaili whenever full; the last bus leaves for Kaili at 4pm. Buses to **Xijiang** (1½hr., 8:30am-2:30pm, Y6) leave earlier and sometimes more frequently on market days (see **Markets,** p. 607).

The **Post Office Hostel** (yóudiàn zhāodàisuǒ; 邮电招待所), beside the bus station, has uninspiring rooms. (☎323 1426. Singles Y25; doubles Y36; triples Y36.) The **Leigongshan Hotel** (léigōngshān bīnguǎn; 雷公山宾馆) is a more attractive but less convenient alternative. From the bus stop, bear right whenever possible; the hotel is 10 minutes down on the right. (☎323 1921. Hot water 6-10pm. Singles Y45; triples Y75.) The **Electric Energy Guesthouse** (diànlì zhāodàisuǒ; 电力招待所) is on the left side of the road to Xijiang, 200m away from the crossroads. Rooms are in good condition. (☎333 1519. Singles and doubles Y70-80, with A/C Y100.) Streetside food stalls, small restaurants, and fruit vendors cluster around the bus stop.

XIJIANG 西江

Xijiang, southwest of Kaili, is said to be the biggest Miao village in the region, though a booming Miao-tropolis it definitely is not. Set in the Longgong Hills, this is one of the loveliest villages in the area. To get to Xijiang, take the **bus** from Kaili to Leishan, and then hop on another bus from Leishan (1½hr., every 30min. 7am-6pm, Y6). The last bus leaves Xijiang for Leishan fairly early, so staying the night is usually necessary. Fortunately, in endearing Xijiang, this should be no hardship. The **Government Guesthouse** (zhèngfǔ zhāodàisuǒ; 政府招待所) is just off the main drag. Turn right from where the bus stops and then right again at the first road; the guesthouse is on the right. (☎334 8030. Dorms Y20; bargaining may be possible.)

CHONGAN 重安

Tiny Chongan is infused with life every five days, when the local market sets down by the river, drawing mostly Miao and a few Dong traders. The market spreads into local alleyways and produces human traffic jams; snorting pigs and screaming chickens add to the pandemonium of buying, selling, auctioning, and haggling. An antidote to all the commercial chaos, the area around Chongan offers some wonderful hiking options. A short walk along the river leads to pleasant vistas of the limpid, sluggish waters. To venture out of Chongan, walk up the main road in the direction away from Kaili and turn right at the end; the path leads to a Gejia minority village several hours away. Guides (Y20) can be arranged at area hotels, including the Xiaojiangnan Guesthouse. The guesthouse has a list of suggested routes but is flexible. One of their special trips is a 10-hour trip through Mulao minority villages, with a stop for lunch. The guesthouse can also arrange bus tours of the area (6-10 people, Y100 per day), 10km trips by horse cart (3-4 people, Y30), 10km outings in a fishtail boat (10-15 people, Y80), and, for the proud and the brave, 5km trips in an "armored wooden boat" (Y30).

To get to Chongan, take the **bus** (2hr., Y8) heading straight to Chongan from Kaili or get off on the way to Huangping (黄平) or Shibing (施秉). **Chongan Jiang Holiday Resort** (chóngān jiāng lǚyóu tíngcūn; 重安江旅游停村) is on the road back to Kaili, a 10-minute walk from the bus stop, on the left with an English sign. Staff will bend over backward for you. (☎245 1069. Dorms Y30.) The **Xiaojiangnan Guesthouse** (xiǎojiāngnán zhāodàisuǒ; 小江南招待所) is in a two-story brick building just before the Chongan Jiang Holiday Resort. Hot water is available when there's enough sun to heat up the solar panel. (☎245 1208. Breakfast Y4-6; lunch Y15-18; dinner Y20-25. 3- to 5-bed dorms Y20; 2- to 3-bed dorms Y40.) The **Tourist Vacation Village** (lǚyóu dùjià cūn; 旅游渡假村), next door to the Xiaojiangnan, has similar accommodations, if a step up. (☎235 1069. Singles with bath Y60-70; doubles Y30-35, with bath Y60-70.)

SHIBING 施秉   ☎0885

The town is an excellent base from which to explore the **Wuyang** (wǔyáng hé; 舞阳河) and **Shamu** (shāmù hé; 杉木河) **Rivers. CITS** (☎422 1177), in the Minfu Hotel on Dong Jie, can arrange cruises, rafting, and tubing trips. From Shibing, it is also possible to walk up the **Yuntai Mountains**, which offer stunning views of the karst landscape and more opportunities to punish your leg muscles.

Shamu River is a smaller river than Wuyang, with generally calmer waters and less spectacular scenery, though the surrounding karst mountains are still awesome, and the mostly slow-paced meandering allows you to stop and swim at deeper waters and to pull your raft to shore to savor barbecued fish, chicken, corn, and the occasional frog or crab that locals hold out enticingly. *(Try to join a CITS group already heading out to the Yantai Mountains. Buses from town (round-trip Y15) and from the train station (Y100) go to the Shamu River. River admission Y100. Raft rental Y100.)*

It is possible to travel between Shibing and Zhenyuan by boat. Three kilometers down the road toward Zhenyuan lies the village of **Caizawan;** catch the bus running to Zhenyuan and ask to be let off early, or ask someone (perhaps at CITS) to write on a piece of paper where you want to go, and show this to the bus driver. Once in Caizawan, walk down through the village and then turn left toward the hydroelectric power station, so that the village is to the right and a gorge is in front of you. Scramble over the rocks; available boats are at the dock. The trip should cost about Y50 per person, although it will take bargaining to get it to that price. All boats follow a fairly similar route through river gorges, waterfalls, and mineral formations along the lines of Peacock Rock. The one-hour trip ends about 17km from

Zhenyuan. Once off the boat, walk along the paved mountain path and go through the gate to reach the **Buddhist Green Dragon Temple** (Y10). To get to Zhenyuan, walk up the hill and wait for the bus; buses to Zhenyuan (Y6) should be going in the direction that leads uphill.

ZHENYUAN 镇远

North of Kaili is Zhenyuan, a "minority village" of sorts: a predominantly Han town in an area where Han Chinese are most definitely in the minority. By the Wuyang River, one of the region's major arteries, Zhenyuan has an interesting **Old Town** (gǔ chéng; 古城), although some of the oldest buildings, including parts of the old city walls, are now under attack from earnest renovators. Within Zhenyuan, follow the road and river away from the train station to reach the **Green Dragon Cave Temple** (qīng lóng dòng; 青龙洞), a cluster of Daoist and Buddhist pavilions, pagodas, and temples on the right. *(Open daily sunrise-sunset. Y10.)* The hills nearby make for memorable walking: slightly challenging and infinitely rewarding. Buses (round-trip Y15) run from Zhenyuan to the **Wuyang River.** *(River admission Y10. Boat rental Y30.)* Boat cruises run to Shibing (see p. 609).

Zhenyuan has a vibrant **market** every Sunday and several annual festivals. The **Dragon Boat Festival** (lóng chuán jié; 龙船节), held in the 5th lunar month, will be on June 24, 2001 (see **Dragon Boats Galore,** p. 535).

To get to Zhenyuan, take the **train** from Kaili (2hr., 3 per day, Y5) or the **bus** from Shibing (1½hr.; when full, about 1 per hr.; Y10). The **Lerong Hotel** (lèróng bīnguǎn; 乐容宾馆) has fairly unappealing dorms (Y12) and doubles (Y30). The **Zhenyuan Hotel** (zhènyuǎn bīnguǎn; 镇远宾馆) is by the municipal government building, a five-minute walk from Green Dragon Temple. (☎(0855) 572 2592. 3-bed dorms Y20-30; doubles with bath Y90-100.)

DONG VILLAGES 侗村

This region, on the formidable road between Guizhou and Guangxi provinces, is said to be one of the singlemost stunning areas in China. Roads are bad, transport links are spotty, and tourists are rare tidbits of exotica indeed. The outlay of time and patience should be compensated many times over by the chance to experience, amid blindingly beautiful scenery, a culture virtually unknown to most.

KAILI MINORITIES: THE DONG侗 Numbering over two and a half million, over half of whom live in Guizhou and the rest of whom sprawl through Guangxi and Hunan, the Dong are a significant presence in the region. Historians trace the evolution of Dong culture back to the Qin and Han era. They do not make an appearance in Chinese records, however, until the Song, when the entire Dong people, originally based in Hunan, picked up and moved south, lock, stock, and barrel, to avoid the invading Mongols. Loosely related to the rest of the languages in the Sino-Tibetan family and more closely resembling the languages of the Zhuang and Shui peoples, the spoken Dong language is unique, though they use Chinese characters for writing, and speak over 15 tones. Dong religion is based around a complex and little-understood pantheon of spirits and demons.

Those not well acquainted with the differences in China's minority cultures can distinguish a Dong village from a Miao village, first and foremost, by architecture. The Dong tend to live in foothills, and their houses are built on pilings, unlike Miao houses, which sit flat on the ground. The Dong are, in fact, known best and widely respected in China for their distinctive architectural achievements. Most Dong villages of note will have at least one pagoda-like wooden drum tower, the signature feature of the Dong landscape, some of which reach a height of 30m. The Dong are also known as master bridge-builders, and examples of their "wind and rain bridges" span rivers all over Dong country. The traditional Dong costume consists of an earth-tone tunic, brightened up by colorful sleeves, a waist sash, and shoes.

Buses (6hr., every hr. 6am-5:30pm, Y20-30) rumble and bounce from Kaili to **Rongjiang** (榕江). From Rongjiang, more buses huff and puff on to **Xiajiang** (下江) via **Tingdong** (停洞). Some buses go directly to **Congjiang** (从江), at the Guangxi border; others terminate at Xiajiang, making it necessary to take another bus to Guangxi. In general, Xiajiang is a better place to spend the night than the more expensive, less charming Congjiang. If coming from Guangxi, the last bus from Congjiang to Xiajiang leaves in the early afternoon; if you miss it, taking a taxi to Xiajiang may be worthwhile, since no one who puts forth the effort to make the arduous trek in the first place should even think of missing this remarkable town. **Gaozhen** and **Xiaohuang**, two tiny villages near Congjiang, as well as **Basha**, 7km from Congjiang, are all excellent places to explore. However, the road is difficult and transportation scarce. The Kaili CITS recommends hiring a taxi (half-day Y100). Betwen Rongjiang and Congjiang lies **Zengchong**, a village famous for its 311-year-old drum tower.

ZUNYI 遵义   ☎ 0852

Zunyi lies in rugged and remote northern Guizhou, along the road from Guiyang to Chongqing. The surrounding area was brought under Chinese control in the 7th century, but was thoroughly ignored until the Ming dynasty. It wasn't until 1935 that this backwater-to-end-all-backwaters finally made its way onto the map, when the desperate, bedraggled Red Army Long Marched into town (see p. 15). In its darkest hours, the central committee of the CCP held a meeting here, at which they decided to hand the chairmanship to a Hunanese peasant partisan by the name of Mao Zedong. The site of this famous agreement is Zunyi's only attraction worth gushing over; the city itself is over-industrialized and quite run-down. As with other semi-major towns in Guizhou, Zunyi can also be used as a base for greater adventures in the marvelous countryside.

◼🛈 ORIENTATION AND PRACTICAL INFORMATION

The train and bus stations and the only cheap accommodations are bunched together off **Waihuan Lu** (外环路). This leads to the main shopping street, **Zhonghua Lu** (中华路). On the other side of **Phoenix Hill** (fēnghuáng shān; 凤凰山), which marks the center of town, is **Zijun Lu** (子君路), the fabled conference sight, and entrances to Zunyi's park.

Trains: Zunyi Train Station (zūnyì huǒchē zhàn; 遵义火车站; ☎ 883 2074), just off Waihuan Lu. It is particularly difficult to book hard sleepers here. The ticket office is in the middle facing the station; an information window is on the left. Open 24hr. To: **Chengdu** (15hr., 3 per day, Y122); **Chongqing** (6-7hr., 9 per day, Y37); **Guiyang** (2½-4hr., 4 per day, Y10); and **Kunming** (15hr., 2 per day, Y130).

Buses: Zunyi Bus Station (zūnyì qìchē zhàn; 遵义汽车站; ☎ 885 8084), just off Waihuan Lu, in front and to the left of the train station. Buses are prone to epic delays. Buy tickets on the bus. To: **Chishui** (10-12hr., 1 per day, Y50); **Guangzhou** (36hr., 1 per day, Y200-400); and **Guiyang** (2½hr., every 30min. 5am-7pm, Y25).

Local Transportation: Bus routes are shown on the tourist maps available at the Jinhong Hotel. Bus **#3** leaves from Waihuan Lu, runs around the edges of town, and then heads down Zhonghua Lu (Y0.5).

Taxi: Base fare Y5.

Travel Agencies: CITS (☎ 883 2917), in the Xiangshan Hotel, 2nd floor, near Dingzikou. Open M-Sa 9:30am-6pm. The **Zunyi Hotel Travel Service** (☎ 822 8249) also arranges tours and treks.

Bank of China: On Xinhua Lu. Take bus #3 and get off past the conference site, just over the bridge. If walking, turn right off Zhonghua Lu at the large traffic circle; the bank is on the right, 5min. down the road, in a huge building. Exchanges traveler's checks and issues credit card advances. Open daily 8am-5pm.

Internet Access: Louzhuang Computer City (lóuzhuāng diànnǎo chéng; 楼装电脑成),
a computer store on Louxiang Gong Lu. Y4 per hr. Open daily 8am-7pm.

Post and Telecommunications: On Xinhua Lu, at the far end of Zhonghua Lu in the direction away from the train station. Take bus #2 or 3 and get off at the large traffic circle
with a monument in the middle of it. EMS and Poste Restante available. Open daily
8am-10pm. **China Telecom** is next door. Open daily 8am-6pm. **Postal Code: 563000.**

▓▓ ACCOMMODATIONS AND FOOD

Cheap rooms are sadly lacking in this birthplace of the workers' paradise, but
what budget accommodation there is is very budget indeed. **Jinhong Hotel** (jīnhóng
dàjiǔdiàn; 金红大酒店), 134 Beijing Lu, is the tall building to the left of the train
station with "hotel" written on it. (☎822 2925. 5-bed dorms Y10; 4-bed dorms Y12;
3-bed dorms Y15; singles Y30-40; doubles Y25, with bath Y35-60.) Live in style at
the **Zunyi Hotel,** 3 Shilong Lu—just be sure to check with CITS first. (☎822 4902.
Singles and doubles Y388; with CITS discount, Y40 plus Y40 per night to CITS.)

Restaurants, snack stalls, and fruit vendors are concentrated around the train
and bus stations and in small alleys off **Zhongshan Lu.** Hotpot is available in restaurants just up the road from the train station.

▓ SIGHTS

Zunyi itself is short on scintillation but long on the Long March (see p. 15); the biggest and best sights honor the biggest and best of the Marching martyrs.

ZUNYI CONFERENCE SITE (zūnyì huìyìzhǐ; 遵义会议址). Once driven out of their
guerrilla stronghold at Jinggangshan (see p. 381) in Jiangxi province, the rapidly
dwindling forces of the Red Army played a deadly game of hide-and-seek with
their GMD pursuers across the Guizhou countryside. The leadership was divided
between Moscow-trained Chinese Bolsheviks who favored a Russian-style urban-
oriented revolution, and Mao Zedong's faction, which maintained that the Communists must focus on the country's peasantry. As defeats mounted, the balance of
power began to shift. When the Army stopped off in Zunyi midway through the
Long March, the top CCP leaders spent three days and nights (January 15-17, 1935)
engaged in acrimonious arguments over future strategy. At the end of the meeting,
a popular vote handed the chairmanship of the Party to Mao Zedong.

The conference site is a mansion that belonged to a GMD-affiliated warlord,
who was kicked out for the occasion. The house itself is nothing much, but just
picturing Zhou Enlai, Zhu De, and other CCP big-shots-to-be settling down in the
various rooms is exciting enough. A museum and an old coin collection have been
added recently. If you've come to Zunyi and decide to not visit this conference site,
why, may we ask, have you come to Zunyi? (*On Zijun Lu. Open daily 8:30am-5pm. Y5.*)

MONUMENT TO THE MARTYRS OF THE RED ARMY (hóng jūn lièshì língyuán;
红军烈士陵园). The monument is a real masterpiece of Soviet-style revolutionary
art, complete with valiant but nondescript faces topped with a golden hammer and
sickle. The structure dates back to the days when Sino-Soviet relations were
friendly, and is an interesting variation on the martyrs' monuments present in so
many Chinese towns. Such a monument is particularly poignant here on the route
of the Long March, which took the lives of a full three-quarters of its 80,000 participants. (*Just off Fenghuang Lu. From Zunyi Park, proceed up the road and turn left at the end;
the entrance is on the right. Free.*)

ZUNYI PARK (zūnyì gōngyuán; 遵义公园). A pleasant, lighthearted diversion
from the martyrs and Maoism of Zunyi's other sights, this park is filled with lots of
open space and flanked in the rear by a host of amusement park rides, including a
rollercoaster (Y5), a small roller skating zone (for children only), and a small zoo.
(*On Shilong Lu, just off Zijun Lu. Take bus #3 and ask the bus driver to let you off at the end of
Shilong Lu; from there, the park is up the road on the right. Open daily 7am-10pm. Y0.5.*)

MILITARY FORTRESS (jūnshī chéngbǎo; 军事城堡). This fort was built in the Ming dynasty by a rebellious general who also delighted in many Romanesque gladiatorial performances. As for the general himself? He burned to death when the fortress was attacked by the emperor. Today, the area offers the makings of a grueling two- to three-hour hike. Although the enemy's long gone, climbers can still celebrate the thrill of victory when taking in the magnificent view from the top. *(Zunyi CITS arranges shuttles for 5 or more people (Y70-80). Free.)*

OTHER SIGHTS. The small but dense **Xiangshan Temple Complex** (xiāngshān sì; 湘山寺), off Zhonghua Nan Lu, sits on a hill that affords a comprehensive view of the city, factories, TV towers, and all. Continue from the traffic circle at the base of the street and turn left up a small winding alley; the temple is a few minutes up ahead. *(Open daily 7am-7pm. Y0.5.)* The smaller **Baiyun Temple** (báiyún sì; 白云寺), off Zhonghua Nan Lu in the direction of the train station, is near a slightly more interesting covered market. *(Free.)*

CHISHUI 赤水 ☎ 0852

The little-visited but beautiful town of Chishui lies on the Guizhou-Sichuan border, about 300km northwest of Zunyi, in the middle of a subtropical forest that keeps the area isolated and untrampled. Chishui's landscape, cityscape, and cuisine have a distinct Sichuanese flavor, and the surrounding scenery is utterly stunning and virtually tourist-free. **Shizhangdong Falls** (shízhàngdòng pùbù; 十丈洞瀑布), 40km south of Chishui, are not as high or as touristed as the Huangguoshu Falls near Anshun. The **Four Caves and Gorges** (sì dòng gōu; 四洞沟) has four waterfalls and a famous "sea of bamboos and ferns."

Buses run between Chishui and Zunyi (10hr., 2 per day, Y50). There are few budget accommodations officially open to foreigners, although it may be possible to stay at one of the cheaper guesthouses. The **Chemical Factory** (chìtiānhuà; 赤天化) has Y180 doubles in the older part of the hotel, and luxurious Y250 doubles in the newer part. For information on trekking possibilities, contact the **Chishui Tourism Bureau** (chìshuǐ lǚyóu jú; 赤水旅游局; ☎ 282 1329).

HOME SWEET HOME Supported by wooden stilts that keep flood waters at bay in rainy Banna, Dai houses consist of two levels. The lower one acts as a barn where farm animals and equipment are kept, and the upper level contains the kitchen, enormous living room, and closed-off bedroom. A pole representing good luck stands in the living room which guests may stroke, and another pole is in the bedroom which no one except family members are allowed to touch. This pole, and the bedroom itself, is the family's sacred space, where the spirits of ancestors are said to inhabit. If a man steps inside a family's bedroom, he has to marry one of the daughters or else the family spirits will be taken away and the family's luck destroyed. The bedroom is divided up into three sleeping areas by curtains of different color. Only cloth can be used as divisions because the spirits must be able to wander freely around the room. Old people sleep in a black and blue colored partition, unmarried members in a white partition, and couples in a red partition.

SICHUAN 四川

Blessed with vigorous rivers, a mild climate, and endless rows of terraced green-ery, Sichuan is justifiably known as China's "Heaven on Earth." The major bread-basket of the southwest, the province is home to a whopping 110 million people. Most live in the fertile and flat Sichuan basin centered around the provincial capi-tal of Chengdu. The bustling city was the capital of Sichuan's own Kingdom of Shu in the 3rd century AD, spawning the hell-fire spicy food and the local dialect that are both unique to the region. Once the area's largest city, Chengdu's rival Chong-qing (and the entire eastern quarter of the province) was penciled in as a munici-pality in 1997, instantly becoming the largest "city" in the world, with a population of over 30 million. In contrast, the western hinterlands of Sichuan, once a separate province called Xikang, are sparsely populated with Tibetans, Qiang, and Yi minor-ities as well as wildlife such as the giant panda. The area's thundering rapids, snowy peaks, and yaks signal the cultural, if not geographic, border with Tibet.

Sichuan has historically thrived in isolation from the rest of China. However, even isolation cannot last forever. The region's magnificent scenery has made Sichuan a popular destination for Chinese tourists. As the major state-sanctioned springboard to Tibet, Sichuan attracts its share of adventure-seeking Western tourists, too. Indeed, Sichuan's remarkable mix of culture, nature, and adventure means that it is quickly losing its status as one of China's best-kept secrets.

HIGHLIGHTS OF SICHUAN

A BUDDHIST PILGRIMAGE to the incense-shrouded temples of **Emeishan** (p. 631), the Big Buddha of **Leshan** (p. 628), and the colorful **Dazu Grottoes** (p. 644).

PANDA-MONIUM at **Chengdu's Giant Panda Research Center** (p. 623) or the **Wolong Nature Reserve** (p. 626).

BACK TO NATURE with the primeval forests and pristine pools of **Jiuzhaigou** (p. 634) and **Huanglong** (p. 637).

WATERWORKS in the form of the 2200-year-old irrigation project at **Dujiangyan** (p. 625) or the famed **Three Gorges** (p. 646).

CHENGDU 成都 ☎028

Beautiful tree-lined streets, soaring skyscrapers, and glitzy department stores con-ceal Chengdu's 2300-year history well. Where there were once only lush green fields, there is now a major metropolis of 9.8 million residents, many of whom are riding high atop the waves of economic reforms implemented by Sichuan native Deng Xiaoping. Construction in the city continues at a frenzied pace as mobile phones and DVD stores rub shoulders with traditional tea houses.

Visitors today can still find traces of a long history scattered throughout Chengdu. The Qin dynasty (221-206 BC) established the city's remarkably success-ful irrigation system, Dujiangyan, which diverts the Min River and supports one of the densest agricultural populations in the world. During the Eastern Han dynasty (AD 25-220), Chengdu garnered fame for its silk brocade, traded as far west as Rome. After the fall of the Han, loyalist Liu Bei and his brilliant advisor Zhuge Liang sought to revitalize the dynasty by establishing the short-lived Shu Han King-dom (AD 221-263) and making Chengdu its capital—an endeavor immortalized by the novel *Romance of the Three Kingdoms*. During the Tang dynasty, the great poet Du Fu (AD 712-770) lived in a thatched cottage in the western part of Chengdu, where he penned over 240 poems. Numerous Daoist and Buddhist mon-asteries also dot the city's historic landscape. The ancient city wall and many other monuments were destroyed in the 1960s, replaced by tributes to commu-nism including a gigantic statue of Mao that gazes over the city center to this day.

More mellow than most overcrowded Chinese cities, Chengdu offers plenty of life, history, and culture to pique the interest of every type of traveler. spicy, taste-bud-tantalizing Sichuanese restaurants, tranquil tea houses, and famous historical sites. Chengdu's proximity to some gorgeous, mountain-in-the-clouds nature parks—most notably Emeishan, Leshan, and Jiuzhaigou—makes it an ideal point for starting or ending one's journey through Sichuan.

✦ ORIENTATION

Chengdu sits in a basin of fog held in by the surrounding mountains, and its residents are known for having beautiful skin due to the lack of direct sunlight. The city center moves outward in concentric circles toward quieter and slightly less clean areas—the urban layout resembling something of a spider web. The city of Chengdu lies within two large ring roads, each of which is further divided into numbered sections or *duan*. The first ring road, **Yihuan Lu** (一环路), encompasses the city center, where most of the government offices, business centers, sights, shopping centers, luxury hotels, and restaurants are located. The second ring road, **Erhuan Lu** (二环路) surrounds the outlying areas, including Sichuan Union University, the US Consulate, and the Provincial Hospital. **Renmin Lu** (人民路), divided into south, central, and north sections, serves as the city's main drag running north-south through the city center. Numerous other streets also cut through the two ring roads, forming a web-like configuration with the city's main arteries. Countless alleyways branch off from these streets, making navigation of city streets very difficult for foreigners. The best form of transportation in the city is to take the taxis, tricycles, or local buses.

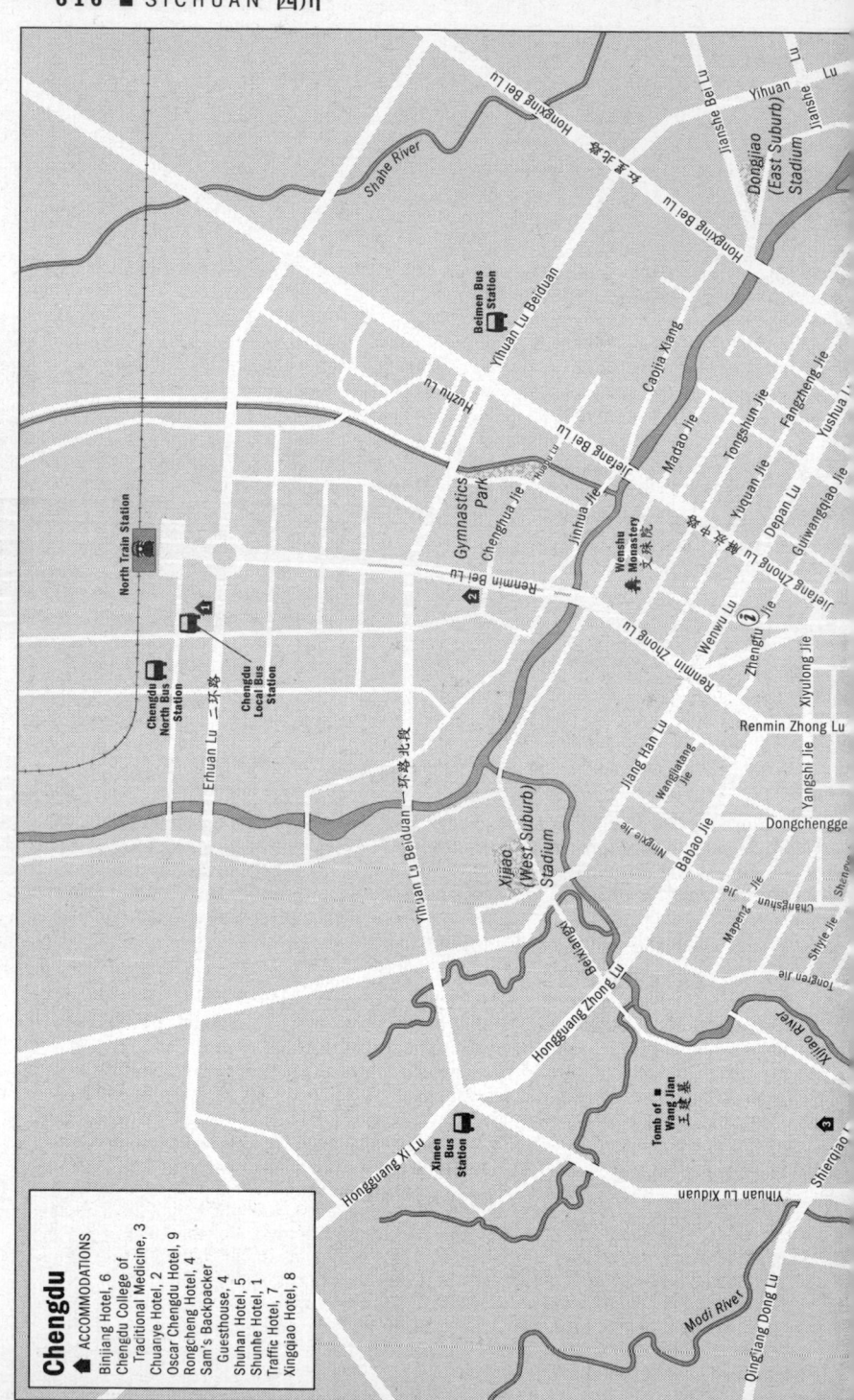

Chengdu

▲ ACCOMMODATIONS

Binjiang Hotel, 6
Chengdu College of
  Tracitional Medicine, 3
Chuarye Hotel, 2
Oscar Chengdu Hotel, 9
Rongcheng Hotel, 4
Sam's Backpacker
  Guesthouse, 4
Shuhan Hotel, 5
Shunhe Hotel, 1
Traffic Hotel, 7
Xingqiao Hotel, 8

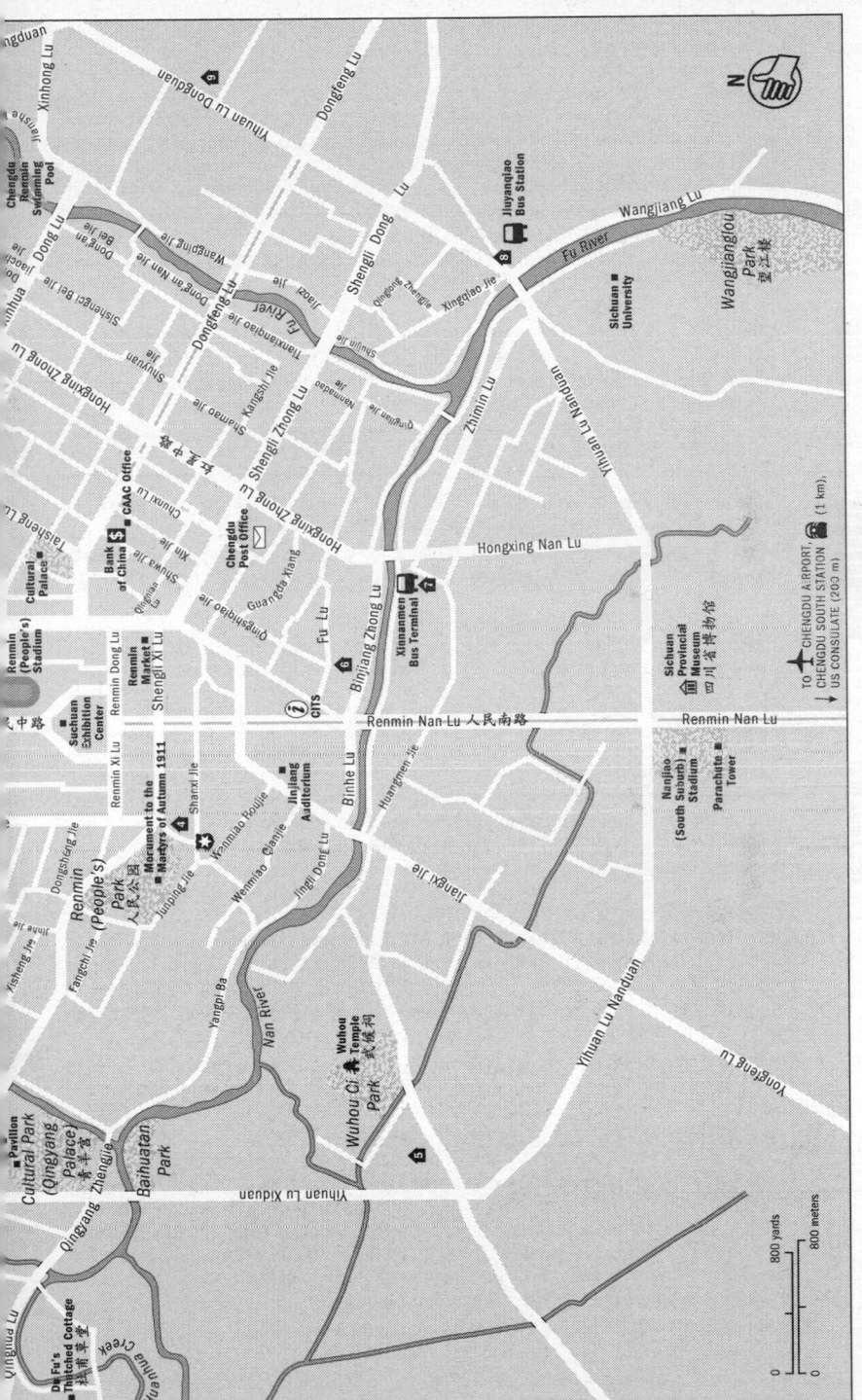

N

Yingduan

Xinhong Lu

Yinhua Lu Dongduan

Dongfeng Lu

Chengdu Renmin Swimming Pool

Xinhua Dong Lu

Dong'an Bei Jie

Dong'an Nan Jie

Sishengci Bei Jie

Dong'an Bei Jie

Wangping Jie

Dongfeng Lu

Tianxiangjiao Jie

Shengli Dong Lu

Shengli Dong Lu

Jiaxi Jie

Qingdong Zheng'e

Jiuyanqiao Bus Station

Fu River

Wangjiang Lu

Wangjiangou Park 望江楼

Hongxing Zhong Lu

Taisheng Lu

Sishengci Bei Jie

Shengli Zhong Lu

Sishengci Jie

Kangshi Jie

Shamao Jie

Snyuan Jie

Xinjie Jie

Namanba Jie

Shujin Jie

Xingqiao Jie

Sichuan University

Cultural Palace

Bank of China $

CAAC Office

Chunxi Lu

Xin Jie

Chengdu Post Office

Shengli Zhong Lu

Hongxing Zhong Lu

Zhimin Lu

Qinglian Jie

Yihuan Lu Nanduan

Guangda Xiang

Qingshibao Jie

Fu Lu

Hongxing Nan Lu

Renmin (People's) Stadium

Renmin Market

Renmin Dong Lu

Shengli Xi Lu

Binjiang Zhong Lu

Xinnanmen Bus Terminal

Sichuan Provincial Museum 四川省博物馆

TO CHENGDU AIRPORT, ✈ (1 km), CHENGDU SOUTH STATION 🚉, US CONSULATE (203 m)

Sichuan Exhibition Center

Renmin Xi Lu

(i)

CITS

Renmin Nan Lu 人民南路

Renmin Nan Lu

Dongsheng Jie

Monument to the Martyrs of Autumn 1911

Shanxi Jie

Binhe Lu

Huangmen Jie

Nanjiao (South Suburb) Stadium

Parachute Tower

Yisheng Jie

Fangzi Jie

Renmin (People's) Park 人民公园

Jinjiang Auditorium

Wenmiao Houjie

Wenmiao Qianie

Jingli Dong Lu

Jiangxi Jie

Yihuan Lu Nanduan

Yongfeng Lu

Junjing Jie

Yangpi Ba

Nan River

Wuhou Ci Temple 武侯祠

Wuhou Ci Park

Pavilion

Cultural Park (Qingyang Palace) 青羊宫

Baihuatan Park

Qingyang Zhengjie

Yihuan Lu Xiduan

Qinghua Lu

Du Fu's Thatched Cottage 杜甫草堂

Huanhua Creek

800 yards

800 meters

0

0

▛ TRANSPORTATION

Airplanes: Shuangliu Airport (shuāngliú jīchǎng; 双流机场; ☎570 0114), 16km southwest of the central business districts, mainly served by China Southwest Airlines, Dragon Air, and Sichuan Airlines. Public buses leave for the city from 20m outside the arrival gate (approx. every 30min., Y8). The first and last departures of the bus depend on the earliest and latest arrivals at the airport (approx. 4:30am-9pm). A taxi to city center costs Y70-80 and takes 40min. To: **Beijing** (multiple flights per day, Y1150); **Guangzhou** (multiple flights per day, Y1040); **Guiyang** (M, F, and Su; Y500); **Kunming** (multiple flights per day, Y560); **Lanzhou** (multiple flights per day, Y750); **Lhasa** (3-5 per day, Y1200); **Shanghai** (multiple flights per day, Y1290); **Xian** (multiple flights per day, Y500); and **Xining** (Tu and F, Y790).

Trains: Chengdu North Train Station (chéngběi chēzhàn; 成北车站; ☎337 7523; inquiries 333 2633; schedule and reservations 666 4758), at the northernmost end of Renmin Bei Lu, between sections 2 and 3 of Erhuan Lu. To: **Beijing** (33-56hr., 3-4 per day, Y113-642); **Chongqing** (11hr., 5 per day, Y42-127); **Emeishan** (2-3hr., 6 per day, Y12); **Guangzhou** (48-56hr., 2-4 per day, Y206-754); **Guiyang** (19hr., 1 per day, Y72-226); **Kunming** (20-24hr., 3 per day, Y94-389); **Lanzhou** (27hr., 1 per day, Y72-254); **Nanjing** (37hr., 3-4 per week, Y107-327); **Panzhihua** (14-15hr., 3 per day, Y59-248); **Shanghai** (40-44hr., 2 per day, Y126-737); **Taiyuan** (30hr., 1 per day, Y88-304); **Ürümqi** (49hr., 1 per day, Y150-519); and **Xian** (19-40½hr., 2 per day, Y55-193).

Buses: Chengdu has bus stations in every direction of town, including **Baihua Central, Jiuyanqiao, Beimen,** and **Wuguiqiao** stations. Nearly all offer buses to nearby attractions like Dujiangyan.

Chengdu North Bus Station (chéngběi kèyùn zhōngxīn; 城北客运中心; ☎317 5758, info 317 5992, booking 317 3612), Chengdu's main bus terminal, is next to the train station. Exit North Train Station and stay on the right side of the square. Make a right on the first street after you exit the square and go straight, following signs until the street ends and you enter a large gate at the opposite side. Buses #2, 16, 25, 28, 44, 64, and 65 stop nearby. Open daily 6:30am-6pm. To: **Chongqing** (4hr., every 30min., Y70-80); **Dujiangyan** (1hr., every 20min., Y7); **Emeishan** (2hr., every 30min., Y15-25); **Kanding** (at least 12hr., 1 per day, Y102-110); **Leshan** (2hr., every 15min., Y19-26.5); and **Wudu** (15-16hr., 1 per day, Y80-112) via **Jiuzhaigou** and **Songpan.**

West Gate Bus Station (xīmén qìchē zhàn; 西门汽车站), in the northwest just beyond Yihuan Lu, on Menkou Lu by the Aba Hotel. Open daily 8am-6pm. To **Jiuzhaigou** (2 per day, Y78) and **Xiaojin** (10-11hr., 1 per day at 6am, Y72) via **Wolong.**

New South Gate Bus Station (xīnnánmén qìchē zhan; 新南门汽车站), on Daxue Lu off Xinan Lu, next to the Traffic Hotel on the south bank of the river. Buses for **Jiuzhaigou** (Y105) leave at 8am and arrive at 5pm. Open daily 8am-6pm.

Local Transportation: The **Chengdu North Bus Station** also has a local station (☎317 6210). Exit the North Train Station and stay on the right side of the square. Take your first right; the local bus station, 100m away, will be on your left. **Buses #55** and **64** go to the city center, while bus **#16** runs from the North Train Station through the city center to the South Train Station. Fare Y1, A/C Y2.

Taxis: Most taxis charge a base fee of Y5 during the day and Y6 at night, with Y1 for each additional 1.3km. **Tricycles** are a cheaper alternative; negotiate prices in advance.

▟ PRACTICAL INFORMATION

Tourist Office: China Chengdu Tourism Bureau (chéngdūshì lǚyóu jú; 成都市旅游局), 80 Zhengfu Jie, 7th Fl. (24hr. ☎662 9858; complaints 662 2062; fax 662 0420), in the far north of the city. The office's main purpose is quality control, and it helps to settle disputes between tourists and hotels or travel agencies. They also offer maps in Chinese, English, French, German, Japanese, and Korean. Open M-F 8am-noon and 2:30-6pm; in winter 8am-noon and 2-5:30pm.

Travel Agencies: CITS, 65 Renmin Nan Lu, Er Duan (☎665 8731). Open M-F 8:30am-8:30pm, Sa and Su 9am-6pm. **CYTS** (zhōngguó qīngnián lǚxíngshè; 成都中国青年旅行社), 6 Renmin Nan Lu, San Duan (☎558 3854), on the 7th floor of the Baiyun Hotel. Open M-F 9am-6pm. There are also four travel agencies in the Traffic Hotel specializing in tours to Tibet, Emeishan, Leshan, and Jiuzhaigou. Open daily 8am-10pm. **Mr. Lee,** 16 Yihuan Nan Lu (☎(1390) 803 5353, voicemail 555 4250, pager 95812), best contacted by phone. The humorous Mr. Lee arranges private vans and tours to both popular and less touristed sights around Chengdu and Sichuan.

Consulates: US (měiguó lǐngshìguǎn; 美国领事馆), 4 Lingshiguan Lu (☎558 3992; emergency 137 800 1422), off Renmin Nan Lu, between the 1st and 2nd ring roads. Accessible via bus #16. Open M-F 8:30am-6pm.

Bank of China: 35 Renmin Zhong Lu, Er Duan (☎613 2194). ATM for cash advances. Open M-F 8:30-11:45am and 2:30-5:30pm; in winter 8:30-11:45am and 2-5pm.

Bookstore: Foreign Language Bookstore (wàiwén shūdiàn; 外文书店), 5 Zhongfu Lu (☎662 7582), offers a small range of foreign language books, mostly in English. Books on Chinese medicine, literature, folklore, English-Chinese dictionaries, and a few English classics available. Open daily 9am-7:30pm.

PSB: 144 Wenwu Lu (☎640 7114).

Hospitals: Sichuan People's Hospital (sìchuānshěng rénmín yīyuàn; 四川省人民医院), 32 Yiyuan Xi Lu, Er Duan (☎776 9982). **No. 1 Hospital Attached to Huaxi Medical College** (huáxī yīkē dàxué fùshǔ dìyī yīyuàn; 华西医科大学附属第一医院), 37 Guoxue Xiang (☎555 1255). **Hospital Attached to Chengdu Chinese Medical College,** 17 Shierqiao Lu (☎776 9902).

Pharmacy: Tongrentang Pharmacy (tóngréntáng yàodiàn; 同仁堂药店), 1 Zhongfu Lu (☎674 2926), 3min. from the Holiday Inn Crowne Plaza. Sells mostly Chinese medicine, with some Western medicine and supplies. Chinese doctor upstairs. Open daily 8:30am-8:30pm.

Internet Access: Eachnet (yìqù; 易趣), 13 Binjiang Zhong Lu. Across the river from the Traffic Hotel. 9 computers, printing and scanning services. Y6 per hr. Open daily 9am-midnight, or when last customer leaves. **Tianfu Internet Bar** (tiānfǔ zhíxiàn wǎngbā; 天府执线网吧), Chengdu Telecom Mansion, 155 Taisheng Nan Lu, 2nd Fl. (☎678 3302). 28 computers. Y10 per hr. Open daily 9:30am-11pm. The **Traffic Hotel** has 5 computer terminals (Y10 per hr.) Open daily 10am-midnight.

Post and Telecommunications: Chengdu Post Office, 25 Shuwa Jie (☎674 2685). EMS and Poste Restante. Open daily 9:30am-6:30pm. **Postal Code:** 610000.

English Speakers' Corner: On the corner of Renmin Nan Lu and Binjiang Zhong Lu, east of the intersection along the river. Locals will eagerly question English-speaking visitors about politics, current events, and culture—as well as offer travel advice.

◤ ACCOMMODATIONS

Like most other Chinese cities, Chengdu suffers from a lack of inexpensive accommodations open to foreigners. As the political atmosphere loosens up, some cheaper places of varying quality are bending the rules, but this may depend upon your language ability and powers of persuasion.

Traffic Hotel (jiāotōng fàndiàn; 交通饭店), 6 Lingjiang Zhong Lu (☎545 1017; ☎/fax 548 2777), within the first ring road, near Renmin Nan Lu. From the North Train Station, take bus #55 or 28 to the New South Gate Bus Station; the hotel is next door. Long considered the flagship of Chengdu's budget hotels, the Traffic attracts foreign travelers by the packful. Clean rooms with A/C and TV. Knowledgeable English-speaking staff. Travel agencies, Internet access (Y10 per hr.) and bike rental (Y15 per day) available. 3-bed dorms Y30. Credit cards accepted.

Sam's Backpacker Guesthouse, 130 Shanxi Jie (☎609 9022; fax 447 6823; email santour@yahoo.com). Attached to Rongcheng Hotel, near People's Park, Sam's popularity has been growing quickly among travelers, for both its price and its comprehensive tour services. Helpful service and centrally located. Travel service, cafe, and currency exchange. 6-bed dorms Y20; 3-bed dorms Y25.

Shunhe Hotel (shùnhé jiǔdiàn; 顺和酒店), Erhuan Lu, Bei San Duan (☎317 2886; fax 317 5509). A 2-star establishment on the west side of the North Train Station. Pristine rooms with private baths and Western toilets. A/C, TV, IDD phones, and refrigerators. Although the staff does not speak English, try to ask for a room facing the street to compensate for the dim lighting. Popular hotpot and barbecue eatery and a Sichuanese restaurant inside, with complimentary breakfast. Doubles Y180.

Chuanye Hotel (chuānyè zhāodàisuǒ; 川冶招待所), 12 Renmin Bei Lu, Yi Duan (☎332 1238), across the street from the Tibet Hotel. From the North Train Station, walk about 1km toward the Wenshu Monastery. Chuanye is not supposed to accept foreigners, but travelers report that speaking some Chinese will greatly increase your chances, and looking Asian will even more so. Clean, communal bathrooms. The tiled rooms are particularly bright and spacious, with fan and TV. Breakfast included. 4-bed dorms Y20; singles Y40; doubles Y70, with bath and A/C Y80.

Chengdu College of Traditional Medicine (chéngdū zhōngyīyào dàxué; 成都中医药大学), 33 Shierqiao Lu (☎773 0506), just north of Cultural Park. You may want to call in advance to nab a bed. These rooms are particularly spacious and have private bathrooms and Western-style toilets. Unfortunately, the spaciousness makes up for the lack of cleanliness. Triples Y20-35.

Rongcheng Hotel (róngchéng fàndiàn; 蓉城饭店), 130 Shanxi Jie (☎663 2687; fax 613 5532), just off Renmin Nan Lu, slightly south of the city center. Well-lit, clean rooms, including A/C, TV, IDD phones and private bathrooms with Western-style toilets. Although Rongcheng offers a nice living environment in a central location, its rooms are a little overpriced and the service is somewhat unfriendly. Doubles Y220.

Shuhan Hotel (shǔhàn jiǔdiàn; 蜀汉酒店), 258 Wuhou Ci Dajie (☎555 6988), near Wuhou Ci park within the first ring road, and close to the historical sights in the city's western half. Spartan rooms are comfy, with IDD phone and bath. Doubles Y160.

Binjiang Hotel (bīnjiāng fàndiàn; 滨江饭店), 16 Binjiang Lu, Yi Duan (☎665 6451; fax 666 8092). From the North Train Station, take bus #16 to the Jinjiang Hotel and walk 3min. to the left. Although slightly cheaper and more spacious than the Shuhan Hotel, the rooms are dimly lit and have a peculiar aroma. A/C, private baths with Western-style toilets, and complimentary breakfast. Doubles Y140-190. MC, Visa accepted.

Xingqiao Hotel (xīngqiáo lǚguǎn; 星桥旅馆), 70 Banxien Lu (☎451 2838). From the northern side of the Fu River and Jiuyenqiao Bus Station, walk left along the river and walk 50m under the overpass. On your left, red doors signal the entrance to this "hotel," which seems more like an army hideout. Not officially supposed to accept foreigners, but some foreigners may be able to get a room. The rickety stairs lead to hole-ridden cement floors and hard wooden beds. Guests may want to hold their breath when passing the communal bathrooms. 4- to 5-bed dorms Y5; with mosquito netting Y6.

Oscar Chengdu Hotel (chéngdū fàndiàn; 成都饭店), 1 Shudu Lu, East Section (☎444 2389; fax 444 1603). One of the cheaper top-end hotels in the city, the Oscar offers services typical of a four-star hotel: travel agency, indoor swimming pool, restaurants, bars, and entertainment. Reservations recommended. Doubles Y600 and up.

FOOD

At sundown, venture over to **Chunxi Lu** near the city center to see a massive night market quickly constructed on Chengdu's sidestreets. Sidewalk vendors often sell *shao kao* (烧烤), barbecued sticks of meat, tofu, vegetables, and other food that are glazed in extra spicy seasonings (Y1-2).

Even more famous are the *xiaochi* (小吃; literally "small eats"; Y2-5), which can easily be obtained in the area around **People's Park,** as well as in the night street markets. *Xiaochi* offers a wide variety of options from noodles to dumplings, and standard cuts of rabbit and pork to cow intestine. Rejoice ye fainthearted ones—not all small eats are spicy.

Sichuan (and Chengdu) are also famous for its hotpot, *huoguo* (火锅), in which a basin of boiling, seasoned water is built right into the center of your table. Although Chongqing is perhaps better known for *huoguo*, there are plenty of great

NAME, PLEASE? To many, "Sichuanese food" refers to "really spicy Chinese food," but there are actually thousands of specific dishes originating in this province. One specific spice is *mala wei* (麻辣味), a flavoring that first excites, then deadens taste buds (true to its name, which means "flavor which brings searing pain"). One explanation for *mala wei*'s popularity is an old wives' tale that claims that *hua jiao* (the seed from which it is made) combats health problems such as arthritis. This seasoning is most commonly experienced in Sichuan's famous *mapo doufu* (麻婆豆腐), a dish cooked with pieces of soft tofu, minced pork, and lots of red-hot spice.

Many local Sichuanese dishes have peculiar names. For example, the spicy tofu dish *chen mapo doufu* is literally translated as "pockmarked Mother Chen's tofu." How did the dish get its name? Locals say a man during the Qing dynasty opened a restaurant that specialized in delicious, spicy bean curd. The locals loved the dish and knew it was cooked by the man's wife, who had pockmarks on her face.

The name of the popular dish *gongbao ji ding* (Kungpao chicken) also has a colorful origin. In the 19th century, a high-ranking, virtuous government official named Ding Baozhong executed a subversive eunuch in the empress's palace and became very famous throughout China. For some odd reason, everyone knew that Ding's favorite dish consisted of small pieces of chicken with peanut sauce and spices. Because his official title was *gongbao*, Ding's favorite dish was named *gongbao ji ding*, or "Gongbao's pieces of little chicken."

places in Chengdu. Streetside restaurants will generally cook you a whole meal for Y20 per person, or sell individual sticks of food for Y2-4. There is also a strip of more expensive, upscale places in the Sichuan Opera district along **Qintai Lu,** on the eastern edge of **Cultural Park**.

Other famous eats and eateries include **Dan Dan Noodles** (dān dān miàn; 担担面; ☎ 674 4134), on the first section of Renmin Zhong Lu. **Lai Tang Yuan** (lài tāngyuán; 赖汤圆; ☎ 351 6011), on Zongfu Jie, right next to the Holiday Inn Crowne Plaza Hotel and Parkson Shopping Center, specializes in glutinous balls (usually sweet, with ground black sesame, Y2 for 6). **Laohao Zhangyazi Duck Restaurant** (lǎoháo zhāngyāzi; 老号张鸭子), down the street from Lai Tang Yuan, is also a wonderful place, where a plate of the famous duck costs Y18.

🍴 **Paul's Oasis,** 1-28 Bingjiang Zhong Lu (☎ 667 3074), across from the Traffic Hotel. With graffiti-covered walls, plush couches, and Western music from breakbeat to flamenco, the Oasis is a watering hole in a desert of spices. The owner is an affable former professor of Chinese philosophy, and he cooks up Chinese and Western dishes—including a mean pizza. Imported beer available. A great place to meet other travelers (Paul is keen on introducing them to each other). Open daily 9am until the last customer leaves.

Shu Feng Garden Restaurant (shǔfēng yuán cāntīng; 蜀风园餐厅), 79 Huangmen Jie (☎ 558 7653), in the southwest section of the city, near Renmin Lu. The dining rooms feature Chinese paintings, ceiling lanterns, and beautiful wood carvings. A doting staff dressed in traditional red silk dresses serves up scrumptious food. Some famous Sichuanese dishes to try: roast duck (zhāngchá yāpià; 樟茶鸭片; Y30); bear paw tofu (xióngzhǎng dòufǔ; 熊掌豆腐, Y15); and sizzling pork (tiěbǎn huìguō ròu; 铁板烩锅肉, Y25). Open daily 11am-2am.

Sucai Restaurant (sùcài cānguǎn; 素菜餐馆), in the Wenshu Monastery. This vegetarian restaurant comes highly recommended, even for carnivores. Situated in Chengdu's largest Buddhist monastery, Sucai provides plenty of traditional atmosphere and excellent, cheap vegetarian food skillfully disguised as Sichuanese meat dishes. Open daily 11:30am-2:30pm and 5:30-6:30pm.

Yi Guo Eatery (yìguó dàpáidàng; 义国大排档), 7-13 Xinhong Nan Lu (☎ 433 1030), in the eastern part of the city, accessible by buses #8, 33, 71, or 61. Big portions of great-tasting food include the ribs and melon soup (Y20) and chili beef (Y28). Open daily 11am-1pm and 2-11pm.

High Fly Cafe (gāofēi kāfēi; 高飞咖啡), Renmin Nan Lu, San Duan (☎550 1572), a 5min. walk from the Nan River away from the city center, on the right side of the street. Both locals and foreigners warm up to the candlelight and good music. Western and Chinese food. After dinner, stuff down a brownie à la mode (Y10). High Fly throws Saturday night parties that run until morning. Otherwise, open daily 8:30-1am.

Chen Mapo Doufu (chén mápó dòufǔ diàn; 陈麻婆豆腐店), 197 Xiyulong Jie (☎675 4512), right smack in the city center (north of the Chengdu Stadium, bus #16 stops right in front). Bright chandeliers and refreshing air-conditioning join delectable servings of *mapo doufu* (Y6). Open daily 10:30am-9pm.

Longchaoshou Dumpling Restaurant (lóngchāoshǒu; 龙抄手), 8 South Chunxi Lu (☎666 6947). A haven for dumpling addicts with myriad snacks served on the ground floor. Meals Y15-30. Open daily 11:30am-2pm and 5:30-8pm.

Huangcheng Laoma Restaurant (huángchéng lǎomā; 皇城老马), 20 Qintailou Lu (☎613 1752), a large stone relief marks the door. Be forewarned, however, that when purchasing *huoguo*, you must take care in what you order—the Chinese often fill their pots with things such as cow brains and duck intestines. Hotpot Y25-65. If organs aren't your thing, there are many other options available. Open daily 10am-11:30pm.

🎋 TEA GARDENS

Chengdu has exceptional food, and, in China, food always implies a pot of tea. Accordingly, it is no surprise that tea-drinking, accompanied by playing cards, *mahjong*, and gossiping, counts among the favorite pastimes of Chengdu's residents. Despite the abundance of teashops, few have seats to spare. Bamboo furniture provides gossip forums for elderly women and cardtables for men. The tea gardens found in virtually every park offer an escape from the city's endless cacophony of bicycle bells and car horns. Locals willingly shell out Y3-8 for the peace of mind that accompanies a cup of tea.

One of Chengdu's most attractive tea gardens is in secluded **Wangjianglou Park** (wàngjiānglóu; 望江楼; entrance fee Y2, tea Y4), near Sichuan Union University. A more buzzing and energetic tea garden sits in **People's Park** (rénmín gōngyuán; 人民公园), along Jinhe Lu. Here, a tea pavilion perches beside a lake shaded by willow trees where large crowds gather in the early afternoon and evening (entrance fee Y2, tea Y5). For a more secluded and introspective tea experience, check out the park surrounding the **Tomb of Wang Jian** (wángjiànmù; 王建墓; entrance fee Y3, tea Y4), in the northwest of the city. Enjoy your beverage in a pavilion that stretches over a lily pond.

👁 SIGHTS

Apart from spicy food and huggable pandas, Chengdu and its surrounding areas are renowned for their history and breathtaking scenery.

🎍 **DU FU'S THATCHED COTTAGE** (dùfǔ cǎotáng; 杜甫草堂). A few blocks west of Qingyang Temple is Chengdu's most famous cultural relic, Du Fu's thatched cottage. During the chaotic An Lushan Rebellion that divided the Tang and Late Tang dynasties, Du Fu (AD 712-770) escaped to Chengdu, where he stayed for four years. Du Fu (dubbed "Poet Saint"), while at his cottage, wrote about missing the court and the harshness of his life in exile. Although this majestic complex itself may not seem too harsh, it is because most of the buildings were constructed later during the Northern Song dynasty, including a large tea pavillion, the "Verse Hall" filled with poetry, and the "waterside Balustrade" where Du Fu supposedly wrote and fished. The legendary Tang poet produced about 240 poems, including the famous "verse for the destruction of my thatched-roof cabin by the autumn windstorm." Although the original cottage (perhaps after several more windstorms), has been replaced by a replica, the sheer beauty and mystique of the grounds still makes this site a very worthwhile visit. *(On Qinghua Lu. ☎731 9258. Open daily 7am-5pm. Y30, young children and disabled travelers free.)*

QINGYANG TEMPLE (qīngyáng gōng; 青羊宫). Qingyang Temple, also known as the Green Ram Monastery, is one of China's most famous Daoist temples, serving as an active center of Daoist worship for Chengdu and the surrounding region. Enter the giant "Hall of Hunyuan Originator," where a deified Laozi holds a large golden ring representing the state of chaos before creation. Beyond this, in the central courtyard, is the remarkable "Eight Diagrams Pavilion," built completely without nails. The pavilion is a great place for dragon-lovers, with 81 carvings of the mythical creature representing the 81 transmigrations of Laozi. The main building, the "Hall of Three Purities," contains statues of the supreme Daoist deities and the 12 golden immortals. *(On Qingyang Lu, just inside Yihuan Lu, near the West Gate.* ☎ *776 6584. Open daily 8am-8pm. Y1.)*

GIANT PANDA BREEDING RESEARCH CENTER (dàxióngmáo fánzhí zhōngxīn; 大熊猫繁殖中心). The recently opened breeding center contains 12 to 13 adorable giant and red pandas housed in a pseudo-natural environment. Besides lounging, sleeping, and napping, their favorite activities include climbing trees and eating. Come between 8:30am and 10:30am to see them while they are being fed and are most active. The **Giant Panda Museum** also features life-size dioramas and detailed information on the evolution, feeding, and mating behavior of pandas, not to mention an exhibit displaying one lucky panda's carefully preserved reproductive organs, as well as photos of "electrical stimulation" of male artificial insemination. On higher floors, the complex contains the perhaps better named "Chengdu Museum of Dead Butterflies" and "Museum of Poorly Taxidermed Vertebrates." Sam's Guesthouse runs tours for Y40, which includes admission and transportation. *(About 16km northeast from the city center. No buses go to the breeding center; taxis cost Y80-90.* ☎ *350 9613. Open daily 7am-6pm. Y10.)*

WUHOU TEMPLE (wǔhóu cí; 武候祠). Wuhou Temple is over 1500 years old and holy ground to thousands of Three Kingdom enthusiasts, but less interesting to visitors unfamiliar with the *Romance of the Three Kingdoms* (see **A True Romance Needs Three,** p. 37). It is the most famous commemorative sight of Zhuge Liang (AD 181-234), the outstanding Shu prime minister of the Three Kingdoms period. In the beginning of the Ming dynasty, it combined with the Han Zhao Lie Temple dedicated to the Shu emperor, Liu Bei. Surrounded by trees and a large red wall, the Wuhou Temple houses over 40 stone tablets, the most valuable of which is "The Tablet of Three Wonders," carved in the Tang dynasty (AD 618-907). The 41 clay statues are the temple's most captivating aspects, each 1.7m to 3m tall. Liu Bei's statue in Liu Bei Hall is coated with gold and flanked by his sworn brothers and highest-ranking generals, Zhang Fei and Guan Yu. Leading up to it are the Officials' and Officers' corridors, with 28 detailed statues backed by traditional paintings. The temple also houses Zhuge Liang's chapel and Liu Bei's tomb, which is surrounded by a 180m-long brick wall. *(231 Wuhou Ci Jie, in the southwestern part of the city across the Nanhe River from downtown. Accessible by buses #1, 10, 26, 53, 57, and 59.* ☎ *555 2397. Open daily 8am-6pm. Y30, young children and seniors 70+ free.)*

PEOPLE'S PARK (rénmín gōngyuán; 人民公园). Near the city center, People's Park is, just as its name suggests, heavily populated by Chengdu urbanites seeking a brief respite from the frenzy of city life. The park is highly varied, with sectioned-off gardens containing plums, flowers, crabapples, *bonsai,* and of course, a tea garden. A "Children's Paradise" houses rides and a swimming pool (Y7, children Y5). At the center of the complex is a large circular lake with small rentable boats floating about (Y15 per hr.). The park also boasts a 31m-tall monument to those who perished during the Xinhai Revolution (1911), when Chengdu residents fought imperial powers for the right to build the Chengdu-Chongqing railway on their own. *(At the junction of Junpin Jie and Banbian Chao Jie. Open daily 7am-5pm. Y2.)*

TOMB OF WANG JIAN (wáng jiàn mù; 王建墓). Revered for his bravery, wisdom, and kindness, Wang Jian (AD 847-918) climbed the ranks as a soldier from a poor family to become emperor of the Shu Kingdom. His mausoleum is reputed to be the largest of the royal tombs from the so-called Five Dynasties and Ten Kingdoms

SICHUAN

Period (AD 907-979). Originally built into a small hill, only the stone platform upon which Wangjian's coffin once rested still remains. It is decorated by exquisite stone reliefs, which include depictions of 23 different types of ancient Chinese musical instruments. As an attraction itself, the mausoleum is limited, but it is made infinitely more worthwhile by wandering through the well-kept gardens arranged circularly around the tomb. Narrow, bamboo-lined pathways lead to collections of *bonsai* trees and pavilions where you can enjoy a cup of tea. *(7 Fuqing Dong Jie, inside the first ring road and northwest of downtown. Accessible by bus #48. ☎ 774 4480. Open daily 8:30am-5:30pm. Park admission Y3, tomb admission Y15.)*

WENSHU MONASTERY (wénshū yuàn; 文殊院). Founded in the Sui dynasty (AD 589-618), Wenshu is a maze of gardens, shrines, and some 400 Buddhist statues gazing upon incense-filled courtyards. Some, like the fine iron figures of the 10 *bodhisattvas*, are recognized as great works of art. Wenshu also houses the 1000 Buddha Pagoda, The Hall of 500 Arhats, and various paintings and calligraphy. The monastery is an ideal place to have a cup of tea (Y2-3) if you enjoy observing socializing and card-playing locals. You can catch the monks chanting everyday at 5pm, or come earlier to dine at the fantastically cheap vegetarian restaurant (see p. 621). *(On Wenshu Yuan Jie, close to Renmin Zhong Lu, north of the city center. Accessible by buses #16, 55, and 64. ☎ 693 2375. Main gate open daily 8am-6pm, back gate 6am-9pm. Y1.)*

WANGJIANGLOU PARK (wàngjiānglóu; 望江楼). Wangjianglou Park, or "River-Viewing Park," is dedicated to the famous Tang poetess Xue Tao. The park itself is a peaceful, less crowded alternative to People's Park (see p. 623). The top of the park's elegant 28m-tall pagoda provides a wonderful view of the Fuhe River and the surrounding area, including Sichuan Union University. Along with a serene tea garden, the park also features relics of the poetess, Qing dynasty architecture, and rare species of bamboo. There are in fact over 150 types of bamboo within the park, and it is sometimes called the "Kingdom of Bamboo of Endless Charms." *(On Wangjiang Lu, near Sichuan Union University. Accessible by bus #35. Open daily 6am-9pm. Y2.)*

SICHUAN PROVINCIAL MUSEUM (sìchuān shěng bówùguǎn; 四川省博物馆). On display are some 160,000 artifacts from the Stone Age (17000-4000 BC) to the Qing dynasty (AD 1644-1911). Peruse the first floor in a clockwise fashion to see a timeline of civilization that arose in Sichuan, ranging from the reconstruction of a primitive hut to detailed stone statues of Ming dynasty soldiers. The second floor exhibit changes on a monthly or annual basis. *(3 Renmin Nan Lu, Si Duan. About 100m on your left from the intersection of Renmin Nan Lu and the second ring road walking away from the city center. ☎ 522 2907. Open daily 9am-5pm. Y10, students Y5, children free.)*

SICHUAN UNIVERSITY MUSEUM (sìchuān dàxué bówùguǎn; 四川大学博物馆). On the grounds of Sichuan University, this museum, founded in 1914, has an impressive collection of over 40,000 well-preserved artifacts. These include Eastern Han and Tang dynasty stone sculptures, the ancient costumes, housewares, and weapons of various ethnic minority groups, and a room of Tibetan artifacts. *(☎ 541 2451. Open daily 8:30am-4:30pm. Y10, children free.)*

SANXINGDUI MUSEUM (sānxīngduī bówùguǎn; 三星堆博物馆). The Sanxingdui Museum opened in late 1997 with a focus on the relics of the ancient state of Zhou (1050-226 BC), featuring over 1000 priceless pieces of pottery, jade, and bone from that period. The bronze relics here are rough-hewn; lovers of the intricate and delicate aspects of more recent Chinese antiques should look elsewhere. *(40km southeast of Chengdu in Guanghan. Buses run from the North Station Square Gao Shun Tang Station and West Gate Station. Trains from North Train Station to Guanghan every 30min. 7am-7pm. ☎ (0838) 550 0873. Open daily 9am-4:30pm. Y20.)*

🎵 🎭 ENTERTAINMENT AND NIGHTLIFE

Chengdu has entertainment options for everyone, from night markets to hopping discos and karaoke bars.

■ **Focus** (jiāodiǎn; 焦点), 100 Yandai Jie, Transport Bldg., 6th Fl. (☎ 666 0326). The city's hot spot for the young, rich, and beautiful, Focus sports a pulsating dance floor, a bandstand, an enormous circular bar, 6 bowling lanes (Y60-80 per hr.), darts, two pool tables (Y40 per hr.), and private karaoke rooms. There are nightly live performances, featuring local pop stars, dancers, and bizarre touring acts. Acts featuring more famous performers require a ticket (Y150). Known as Chengdu's best club, it is also the most upscale and expensive. Open daily 7pm until people leave.

Top One (kǎkǎdù; 卡卡嘟), 16 Yihuan Lu, South Section (☎ 555 8999), near Sichuan Province Swimming Pool. Top One's *feng shui* is top notch. A large bar encircles an elevated stage, where musical and dance acts perform until 11pm. Red lights and plush seating fill the room, which is bordered by private karaoke rooms. After the performances, much of the youthful crowd heads downstairs to a hypnotic dance room. Although the lightboards and spinning strobes are exciting, you may have trouble grooving to the bassed-up Chinese pop. Open daily 7pm-3am.

Kinglane Club (xīnlěi; 鑫磊), 8 Dongcheng Gen Lu (☎ 677 0408), just off Renmin Nan Lu, south of the city center. A local nightlife scene in full bloom, replete with teeny boppers and middle-aged men. Two floors of bars and table-seating gaze upon a dance floor filled with smoke and strobelights, where local singing and dancing acts perform. At about 12:30am, Kinglane starts spinning surprisingly good House music. But if dancing is not your thing, head upstairs for some *xiaochi*, or talk to one of Kinglane's 30 "companion girls" who sit behind the bar. Open daily 7:30pm-1:30am.

Garden Cinema (huāyuán yǐngchéng; 花园影城), 21 Renmin Nan Lu (☎ 554 4206), next to the Sichuan Province Swimming Pool. Year-old undubbed English movies run all day. Let the surprisingly comfortable fake leather sofas whisk you away from China for an hour or two. Tickets Y10-15. Open daily 11:20am-10:55pm.

⚑ DAYTRIPS FROM CHENGDU

DUJIANGYAN IRRIGATION SYSTEM 都江堰
56km west of the city. Take the bus from the West Gate Long-distance Bus Station, northwest of downtown Chengdu (1hr., every 10min. 7am-5pm, Y6.5-9). From Dujiangyan Transportation, take bus #1 to the system (every 10min. Y1). Open daily 8am-5pm. Y60.

The Dujiangyan Irrigation System is on the Min River in the northwest of Dujiangyan City. The river, a tributary of the Yangzi, flooded frequently thousands of years ago and did great harm to surrounding inhabitants. In 256 BC, Li Bing, the governor of the Shu prefecture of the Qin state, and his son, diverted the river into a manmade channel through Mount Yulei and constructed an ingenious irrigation system. This system divides the Min into an inner and outer river, and two spillways control flooding and collect silt. Since Dujiangyan's construction over 2000 years ago, the region has been converted to a "Land of Abundance," with a yearly bumper crop and over $5,300km^2$ of gravity irrigation system.

Dujiangyan is divided into three parts: the **Fishmouth Pier** (yúzuǐ; 鱼嘴) splits the river in two; the **Feishayan Weir** (fēishàyàn; 飞沙堰) drains flood water and rids sediment deposits; and the **Mouth of the Precious Jar** (bǎopíng kǒu; 宝瓶口), or the trunk canal, cuts through Mount Yulei and diverts water to irrigate nearby farmlands. To get to the Fishmouth Pier, cross the beautiful **Anlan Bridge** (ānlán qiáo; 安澜桥), suspended by (at least outwardly) woven bamboo cables. Once called Fuqi Bridge (Husband and Wife Bridge) because it was built by a devoted couple, the chain railing of the re-named Anlan Bridge is held together by locks that symbolize the pair's never-ending devotion. Up the hill and overlooking the irrigation project are various temples and pavilions separated by forest and gardens, the most important of which is **Erwang Temple** (èrwáng sì; 二王寺; "Two Kings Temple"), built as a tribute to Li Bing and his son. You may also run into the **oldest tree in China,** measuring 3.6m across and dating back to the Yin Shang dynasty (1700-1100 BC). Get a bird's-eye view of the whole system and surrounding areas by continuing up the hill to the five-story high Qin Yen Lou, which is proud of the fact that

Mao, Deng, and Jiang Zemìn all gazed out from its upper platform. Cable cars (Y25 per stop) run from Yulei Hill Park to Erwang Temple and Lidui Park.

Several cheap **eateries** (Y5-15 a meal) serving basic Sichuanese food line the street close to the entrance and the riverfront area. Although pure scenery-seekers may find Dujiangyan disappointing, the sheer ingenuity and history surrounding the ancient waterworks complex compensate for its rather drab appearance.

QINGCHENG MOUNTAIN 青城山

About 70km from Chengdu. Daily buses depart from the West Gate Bus Station northwest of the city (1½hr., daily 7-10am, Y10-12). You can also take a bus from Dujiangyan (1hr., every 20-30min., Y3). Buses return only to Dujiangyan (1hr.; 4pm, 6pm, 7pm; Y3). Train ride round-trip Y12. Cable car one-way Y25. Ferry ride one-way Y3. Or hike up the mountain (3½hr.). Y41, children less than 1.3m tall half-price.

Immersed in a sea of green trees and veiled in layers of chiffon mist, Qingcheng (Green City) Mountain is so named for good reason. A less rigorous climb than the one at Emeishan, a hike up (or a combination boat and cable car ride for the lazy) Qingcheng nonetheless offers much of the same captivating beauty. Apart from providing spectacular views of an ocean of greenish mist, the south face of the mountain, known as Qingcheng Front Mountain, is also home to numerous Daoist temples. The best preserved of these monuments, **Jianfu Temple** (jiànfú gōng; 建福宫), lies at the foot of the mountain. Jianfu has been around since the Tang dynasty, when it was known as Zhangren Temple. According to myth, a male fairy once lived on Zhangren Mountain, practicing Daoism in seclusion. For good luck, a king visited the fairy there before heading into battle. When the king later won the battle, he built Zhangren Temple in the fairy's honor. Today, the temple continues to house ancient relics in the Rugian and Weixin Pavilions.

Halfway up Qingcheng lies **Tianshi Cave** (tiānshī dòng; 天师洞), a mazelike temple dedicated to the Daoist master Zhang Ling. Built up on the mountainside, it eventually dips into the cave where Zhang once lived. Tianshi also houses a giant gingko tree planted by Zhang Ling in the Han dynasty and a colossal boulder that supposedly split when a sky demon hurled a lightning bolt at a visiting master.

The **Shangqing Temple** (shàngqīnggōng; 上清宫), a multi-layered pavilion, dominates the mountain's first peak. A wood carving of the Daoist Scriptures on morality is kept here, and three Daoist deities are consecrated: the High Lord Lilaojun, and Daoism's founders Chui Yang and Sin Feng. From the rear of the temple, visitors can walk farther up the mountain to enter the six-story **Laojun Ge Pavilion** (Y3). This massive structure is the highest point on Qingcheng, and contains a huge bronze statue of Laozi on his ox. But best of all, Laojun offers a stunning 360° bird's-eye-view of the greenery and mist below.

Jianfu Temple, Tianfu Temple, and Shangqing Temple, near the exit of the second cable car, all offer **food** and **accommodation** (Y20-30). Qingcheng Front Mountain can be done as a long daytrip out of Chengdu, or can perhaps be shortened by taking the cable car one way. Another option is to stay one night on the mountain, perhaps at Shangqing Temple, in order to catch the sunrise.

About 30km from Qingcheng Front Mountain is **Qingcheng Rear Mountain** (qīngchéng hòu shān; 青城后山), the north face of Qingcheng. Minibuses run frequently from Qingcheng Front Mountain to the Rear Mountain (30min., Y10). While the south face of Qingcheng is the more famous Daoist haven, the north face is better known for its picturesque natural scenery, caverns, waterfalls, gardens, and ancient graves. Tranquil and unspoiled, Qingcheng Rear Mountain offers a more secluded and less touristed alternative to the Front Mountain.

WOLONG NATURE RESERVE 卧龙自然保护区

100km northwest of Chengdu, the Wolong Nature Reserve is accessible from West Gate Bus Station by a bus bound for Xiaojin (3hr., 1 per day at 6am, Y30). The only returning buses are to Dlujiangyan (2hr., 8am and noon, Y10). ☎ (0837) 624 6615. Admission to the Giant Panda Research Center Y8.

PANDA-MONIUM Now listed as an endangered species, the charismatic giant panda once ranged over huge tracts of land in China and Myanmar in dense, high-altitude bamboo or coniferous forests. Today, fewer than 1000 wild pandas remain in small, isolated patches of Sichuan, Gansu, and Shaanxi provinces. The Wolong Nature Reserve in Sichuan (see p. 626) is one of 11 natural areas protected by the Chinese government to preserve pristine, bamboo-bejungled panda habitat. Of late, panda conservation has captured the attention of the entire world. The adorable creatures are the emblem of the World Wildlife Fund, and over 100 pandas have been taken from the wild and placed in Chinese and foreign zoos.

Illegal poaching continues despite stiff laws, but China's pandas are threatened most by habitat destruction due to the burgeoning Sichuanese population. Because they eat tremendous amounts of only one species of bamboo, pandas need an exceptionally large area of continuous habitat to survive. When the arrow-shoot bamboo in one area goes through its normal cycle of self-destruction every dozen years or so, pandas have to be able to migrate to other areas. So in isolated patches, pandas end up starving.

Because pandas are clownish, theatrical, and adorable animals that easily win over audiences, they are highly sought after by zoos. The Chinese government has given or lent pandas to foreign zoos in the past as a gesture of friendship and goodwill. In 1936, fashion designer Ruth Harkness brought the first giant panda to be exhibited overseas to the United States. The panda, Su-Lin, arrived as an infant at the Brookfield Zoo near Chicago, IL, and was one of the zoo's biggest attractions until his death in 1938. Mao Zedong gave President Nixon a pair in 1972; Xing-Xing (Hsing-Hsing) and Ling-Ling were installed in the National Zoo in Washington, D.C. Ling-Ling died at the ripe old age of 23 in December 1992, and Xing Xing died seven years later.

The Wolong Nature Reserve was established by the Chinese government in the late 1970s to protect the highly endangered and highly adorable giant panda. The panda has thus induced the protection of some of the most stunning and dramatic wilderness in Sichuan, and you may find your face pressed against the glass during the entire last hour of the bus ride to the reserve.

The pandas are best seen in the **Giant Panda Research Center** (dà xíongmāo guǎn; 大熊猫馆), halfway up the mountain, where they can be observed from behind bars (unfortunately, your chances of catching a glimpse of a panda in the wild are extremely limited). It is at times difficult to believe that these furry and innocent-looking creatures can actually inflict serious injury upon bystanders, but the bars protect onlookers from their powerful claws and 200kg bodies. The best time to visit the center is from 11am-3pm, when the pandas are active and more likely to take an interest in the curious creatures peering into their private homes. Visitors can also pose for photos with the reserve's baby pandas (Y200). 25m farther up the mountain, the **Red Panda Center** (xiǎo xíongmāo guǎn; 小熊猫馆) is home to the less rare and more raccoon-like red pandas.

Up in the mountains, pandas, golden monkeys, takins, and pheasants can, with a little luck, be observed in their natural habitat. If no animals are seen, visitors can find solace in nature's wondrous beauty. Unlike other areas in Sichuan, Wolong lacks major tourist facilities and thus offers the only real pristine hiking around Chengdu. In the **Valley of the Heroes** (3hr. climb), the path begins in the town of Wolong 5km up the road from the Research Center and runs through a beautiful gorge. The scenery of the 4487m Balangshan Pass is amazing; pristine alpine scenery provides a perfect backdrop for grazing yaks and fields of wildflowers.

Wolong is a pretty long haul from Chengdu, and transportation is limited, so if you plan on hiking, also plan on spending the night. There is a small **hotel** outside the Giant Panda Research Center on the way to the red panda center. Doubles run for Y200, but bargain for discounts. There is also lodging available in the town of Wolong (Y30 per bed). If your only intent is to see a panda, you may opt to stay in Chengdu and visit the Giant Panda Breeding Research Base instead (see p. 623).

LESHAN 乐山   ☎0833

The six-million-strong city of Leshan is augmented by hordes of summer tourists who descend upon the city to visit the celebrated Big Buddha, tallest in the world. Once known as an education center that produced several members of the Chinese literati (Su Dongpo's poet family included), Leshan has caught the nasty building bug currently infecting southwest China: massive construction efforts have turned parts of the town into bustling commercial centers, complete with neon signs, skyscrapers, and glistening advertisements. But Leshan still retains its natural beauty: it sits on the point of juncture of three major rivers and emanates a local feel as sunsets over the fast waters draw out crowds of tea-sipping locals and line-dancing old ladies. Tourism accounts for much of Leshan's income; the best time of year to visit Leshan is in the late spring or early autumn, to avoid both the summer heat and the camera-toting tourists the season brings with it.

▐ TRANSPORTATION

Buses: Leshan Long-distance Bus Station (lèshān chángtú qìchē zhàn; 乐山长途汽车站), 165 Jiading Zhong Lu (☎213 1080). Buses run roughly 7am-5pm. To: **Chengdu** (2-4hr., every 30min., Y15-35); **Chongqing** (7hr., every hr., Y80); **Dujiangyan** (3-5hr., 2 per day, Y23-28); **Emeishan** (1hr., every 10min., Y40); **Kanding** (at least 15hr., every other day 8:20am, Y66); and **Yibin** (6hr., 5-6 per day, Y50).

Boats: Near Yutang Jie and Binjiang Lu. Ticket booth open daily 8:30-11:30am and 3-6pm. A boat heads for **Yibin** (1 per day, Y80), where passengers can catch boats to **Chongqing**. However, the boat only runs when the seasonal river waters are favorable. Check with a local travel agent prior to going to Leshan.

Local Transportation: Buses go between Leshan's 2 ferry piers along Binjiang Lu, near the Taoyuan Hotel. **Speedboats** give 30min. tours of the Buddha and the island for Y30 (☎211 7217; open daily 7am-7pm). The cheapest and most common way to get to the Buddha is to take the **ferry** (Y1) directly across the river to the left side of Lingyun Hill. A ferry that fills up somewhat less frequently goes to the front of Wuyou Hill (Y2). After heavy rains, the ferries cease operation. Minimum 10 passengers.

Taxis: Base fare Y3, each additional km Y1.

Tricycles: Y4-5 for any destination in the city.

✈ ℹ ORIENTATION AND PRACTICAL INFORMATION

About 166km southwest of Chengdu, Leshan occupies the flat northwestern shores of the T-shaped intersection formed by the emerald ripples of the Min River and the muddy currents of the Dadu. All of Leshan's attractions are carved on or built atop the rocky embankment on the far shore facing the city. The **Leshan Bridge** (乐山大桥) farther upstream and the **Minjiang Bridge** (岷江大桥), closer to the docks, connect the Big Buddha bank with the city bank of the river. On the city side, **Jiangbin Jie** (江滨街) runs right along the waterfront while **Jiading Lu** (嘉定路) also runs parallel to the Min but farther inland. Farther inland still, **Renmin Lu** (人民路) crosses **Daqiao Xi Jie** (大桥西街), the road across the Minjiang Bridge.

Tourist Office: Leshan Tourism Bureau (lèshānshì lǚyóu jú; 乐山市旅游局; ☎213 6296), on Binhe Lu, in the city government's office. Open M-F 8am-noon and 3-6:30pm. The **Foreign Affairs Office** (wàiguórén bànshì chù; 外国人办事处), 17 Shanxi Lu (☎213 0971), has some English speakers and is a better office to visit with complaints or questions. Open M-F 8-11:30am and 3-6pm.

Bank of China: 36 Renmin Nan Lu, Huangjia Shan (☎212 5121). The only bank providing currency exchange services. Credit card advances. Open daily 8am-6pm.

PSB: 5 Nan'an Lu (☎249 9048), in the far west. Open daily 8-11:30am and 3-6pm.

Hospitals: Leshan City People's Hospital (lèshān shì rénmín yīyuàn; 乐山市人民医院), 76 Baita Jie (☎211 9328), up the street from the Jiashou Hotel.

Leshan City Red Cross Hospital (lèshān shì hóngshízì yīyuàn; 乐山市红十字医院), 45 Xincun Jie (☎213 9082), appears slightly cleaner and newer than the People's Hospital. Both open 24 hr.

Pharmacy: Leshan City Medical Company (lèshān shì yīyào gōngsī; 乐山市医药公司), 3 Tuqiao Jie (☎213 2064). Open daily 8:30am-8:30pm.

Post and Telecommunications: ▧**Post and Telecommunications Office** (yóudiàn guǎngchǎng; 邮电广场; ☎211 8384), on Yutang Jie. EMS, IDD service, and Internet access (Y3 per hr.) available. Post office open daily 8am-8pm. Telecommunications office (2nd Fl.) open daily 8am-10pm. **Postal Code:** 614000.

ACCOMMODATIONS

Unfortunately, accommodations in Leshan do not cater to the average budget traveler. With most tourists arriving in high-rolling tour groups, individual travelers are often left stranded.

Taoyuan Hotel (táoyuán bīnguǎn; 桃源宾馆), 12 Binjiang Jie, lower section (☎213 1810; fax 213 2102), near the ferry pier and facing the river. Situated across the river from the Big Buddha. The cement-floored rooms are dirty and have hard beds, but they also come equipped with a TV and ceiling fan. Communal showers with 24hr. hot water have green moss on the walls that add color to your showering experience. A late-night pharmacy and restaurants next door. Doubles Y50; triples Y60.

Dongfeng Hotel (dōngfēng bīnguǎn; 东风宾馆), 176 Jiading Nan Lu (☎213 4728). Enter under the "Tiangong" sign. The winds of change have blown: the Dongfeng features large, carpeted rooms with tiger-skin bedsheets, A/C, sparkling private baths, and use of a sleek, black-paneled elevator. Doubles Y198.

Jifenglou Hotel (jìfēnglóu bīnguǎn; 集凤楼宾馆; ☎230 2807), next to Lingyun Temple. Opened in 1999, this charming hotel sports new hardwood floors, clean bathrooms, A/C, TV, IDD, and 24hr. hot water. Doubles Y120.

Jiuri Feng Hotel (jiurì fēng bīnguǎn; 就日峰宾馆; ☎230 2891), follow the path from Lingyun Temple for about 400m, past a private house on the left; the path branches a few times, so ask for directions. A self-defined "quasi-three-star hotel," Jiuri Feng offers bright rooms, firm beds, and balconies offering stunning views of the mountain slopes. A/C, business center, gardens, and a swimming pool that opens in July. Doubles Y218.

FOOD

Leshan is renowned for its *xiba doufu* (西坝豆腐), said to be especially delicious because of the waters used to prepare it. The muddy Min River hardly inspires a great appetite, but the tofu is indeed excellent. Both sides of the Taoyuan Hotel are lined with tofu restaurants serving many variations of *xiba doufu*. If you're looking for an upscale environment, try **Xiba Doufu Restaurant** (xībà doùfǔ dàjiǔlǒu; 西坝豆腐大酒楼), 121 Binjiang Lu (☎210 0848) in the same area.

Plain (if it can be called that) and cheap Sichuanese food can be found on the strip along the river from the pier to the Jiazhou Hotel (if coming out of Taoyuan, turn right), which is lined with small restaurants and tea houses where you can eat outside (dishes costing only Y5-10 each). A foreigner hangout with an English menu is the small and dusty **The Yang's Restaurant,** 49 Baita Jie, just across from the Leshan City People's Hospital. The food is relatively inexpensive, and the English-speaking Mr. Yang aids travelers well, arranging popular tours to the countryside. For a real (albeit expensive) escape, check out the zany and well-furnished **Newcastle Pub** (jīngdiǎn shíguāng; 经典时光), 5 Baita Jie, attached to the Jiazhou Hotel and a little closer to the river than Mr. Yang's. They offer imported coffees (Y20-50), milkshakes, limited foods and snacks (Y5-12), and a few imported beers.

👁 SIGHTS

BIG BUDDHA (dà fó; 大佛)

Across the river from the city. The best way to get there is by taking the ferry (Y1); make a right off the dock and walk 200m to the entrance of Lingyun Temple. Tour boats (Y30) from the Leshan pier (see Practical Information, p. 628) provide a river view of the Big Buddha but only pause briefly. Lingyun Temple and Big Buddha Y40, children under 1.2m tall free.

Begun in AD 713, 90 years of construction finally completed what is still today the world's largest (and least imaginatively named) Buddha. The Big Buddha was conceived by the monk Haitong to control the menacing waters of the Min, Dadu, and Qingyi rivers that once wreaked havoc on the people of Leshan. The slowing down of the river brought a peace to the people of Leshan that was surpassed only by the peace attained through the Buddha's wisdom.

The Big Buddha has a serene look and an artistic touch no photograph can betray. Unfortunately, old age has taken its toll on even the Enlightened One, and curious patches of body hair have sprouted up in the form of green vegetation. At the top, visitors can stick a finger into the Buddha's ear or pat his nose for good luck. On the way down the flight of steps from his head to his manicured toes, a white scar can be detected on the Buddha's chest, where a thief dug a book of Buddhist scriptures and a jade statue of Avalokiteshvara out of the Buddha's chest. The entire descent takes about 10 minutes.

OTHER SIGHTS

LINGYUN TEMPLE (língyún sì; 凌云寺). Also known as Dafo Temple (Big Buddha Temple), Lingyun Temple was built in the 7th century and has magnificent gold-plated statues of Sakyamuni, the 5 *bodhisattvas*, and 18 *arhats*. The main courtyard is lined with corridors containing the history of the Big Buddha and other large buddhas. Behind the main chapel is **Zangyanfazheng Hall,** which pays tribute to the monk Haitong (now missing his eyes) and two others who contributed to the taming of rivers: Li Bing, the builder of Dujiangyan, and Zhao Yu, a hero who is said to have slain a ferocious flood-causing river dragon in the Sui dynasty. Legend has it that Haitong dug out his eyes to convey his sincerity and good faith, as well as to blind himself to the corruption of the age. The small chapel next door, dedicated to a statue of Sakyamuni, is carved out of just one piece of wood. *(On Lingyun Hill. Enter from the Big Buddha entrance.)*

WUYOU TEMPLE (wūyóu sì; 乌尤寺). Wuyou Hill and Lingyun Hill were attached until Li Bing, the Dujiangyan engineer, sliced a waterway between the two hills 2000 years ago to rid the island of its flooding problems. Said to resemble the head of a sleeping Buddha, Wuyou Hill has a temple perched atop it from which magnificent views of the surrounding rivers and hills peek through the bamboo growth in all directions. At the entrance to Wuyou Temple, four giant gods boldly stand guard. Inside the main chapel stand gold-plated statues of the Buddha of Boundless Life, Sakyamuni, Puxian Bodhisattva of Wisdom, and Wenshu Bodhisattva of Behavior, as well as a statue of the Goddess of Mercy in a small side chapel. The rear of the main chapel holds the temple's best-regarded statues, Song dynasty iron casts of the three Saints of the West: Amitabhu, Guanyin, and Dashizhi. While in the Wuyou Temple complex, you may want to check out Arhat Hall, with contemporary, life-like sculptures of each of the 500 *arhats*. *(Accessible by bridge from Lingyun Hill, or by ferry from the main pier (Y2). Open daily 8am-6pm.)*

MAHAO CAVE TOMBS (máhào yá mù; 麻浩崖墓). Cave tombs were popular in Sichuan during the Former and Later Han dynasties, during which time people believed heavily in ghosts, superstitions, and the afterlife. These well-preserved tombs still contain original stone coffins and funerary objects; the caves themselves are a little bland (especially since access is restricted). *(At the foot of Lingyun Hill, left of the Haoshang Bridge. Open daily 8am-6pm. Y2, children under 1.3m tall free if accompanied by an adult.)*

DONGFANG FODU MUSEUM (dōngfāng fódū; 东方佛都). The museum is constructed in an Indian architectural style, complete with red earth and curved domes. Dongfang Fodu boasts one of the largest collections of replicated Buddha statues around, ranging from the huge, 173m-long reclining Buddha on the hill (constructed in just two years) to the modern copies of statues taken from China by foreign powers. With authentic buddhas all over the island, you may find that this site is not worth the price or time. *(To the right of Haoshang Bridge. Take the passenger scooters (Y5). If walking, go past the minibuses and down the dirt path; veer left when it becomes a paved road, and continue walking for about 1km. Open daily 8am-7pm. Y25.)*

EMEISHAN 峨眉山 ☎0833

One of the four famous Buddhist mountains in China, Emeishan lies 20km west of Leshan. The two mountain peaks are said to resemble the graceful curves of a pair of well-defined eyebrows, hence the name Emeishan (Lofty Eyebrows Mountain). In the past, worshipers impatient to become Buddhist deities believed one could swap a life of self-sacrifice and abstinence for a leap off Sheshen Cliff near the Golden Summit onto a rocky platform resembling Buddha's outstretched palm.

Today, devout Buddhists armed with sticks and bamboo slippers conquer the steep hills (fending off ferociously greedy monkeys all the way), and hordes of chattering tourists and tough old nannies march to the various temples around the peaks, aiming ultimately for the Golden Summit Temple, where Myriad Buddhas Peak towers 3099m above sea level.

The number of temples that dot Emeishan's peaks may be impressive, but the views steal the show. Looking down on a sea of clouds or a sparkling sunrise, very lucky visitors may witness the phenomenon known as **Buddha's Light** (fóguāng; 佛光), said to occur only 14 times a year on unpredictable days. On these rare occasions, your shadow is cast from the peak into the mist before you, while a colorfully glowing halo encircles your head, as if you have attained Enlightenment. You will more likely be enveloped in Emeishan's frequent thick fog and drizzle, but the trailside scenery of jungle forest and ancient, gnarled trees will still make you feel like a mystical wanderer.

▐ TRANSPORTATION

Trains: Emeishan Train Station (éméishān huǒchē zhàn; 峨眉山火车站; ☎547 0699), on Mingshan Lu, east section, Shengli Town. To: **Chengdu** (2½hr., 6 per day, Y12-16); **Chongqing** (6hr., 1 per day, Y52); **Kunming** (19hr., 3 per day, Y109); **Panzhihua** (14hr., 6 per day, Y41-71); and **Xian** (21hr., 2 per day, Y113).

Buses: The **Long-distance Bus Station** (éméishān kèyùn zhàn; 峨眉山客运站; ☎553 3084) is on Mingshan Lu. To: **Chengdu** (2hr.; regular bus every 30 min. 5am-6pm, Y19; A/C bus every 40min. 6am-6pm, Y31); **Chongqing** (5-6hr., 8am, Y90); **Dujiangyan** (3hr., 8:50am and 4pm, Y36); **Leshan** (30-40min., every 10min. 6am-6:15pm, Y4); **Yibin** (5hr., 7:20am, Y36); and **Zigong** (3hr., 3 per day, Y21). The **Baoguo Monastery Lianyun Bus Co.** (bàoguó sì liányún qìchē gōngsī; 报国寺联云汽车公司; ☎552 2299), near Baoguo Monastery, has buses to **Chengdu** (several per day, Y30) and **Emeishan** (200 per day; up Y20, down Y15). The travel agencies in **Emeishan Grand Hotel** (éméishān dàjiǔdiàn; 峨眉山大酒店) and **Hongzhushan Hotel** (hóngzhūshān bīnguǎn; 红珠山宾馆), near Baoguo Monastery, arranges buses to Dazu, Dujiangyan, Jiuzhaigou, Leshan, Qingcheng Mountain, and even Yunnan's Xishuangbanna.

Local Transportation: Buses run throughout the city 7am-6pm. Fare Y0.5. In the Baoguo Monastery Scenic District, buses run from the monastery parking lot to the summit, dropping passengers near Qingyin Pavilion and Wannian Temple (7am-6pm; one-way Y20, round-trip Y35). 5-seater **vans** (Y2) run from the fountain in Mingshan Lu, Zhong Duan, to Baoguo Monastery 6:30am-7:30pm.

Taxis: Unmetered taxis within the city Y10. To the foot of Emeishan (past the toll booth) and the Baoguo Monastery Y20, from the monastery parking lot to near the top of the mountain Y15. Bargain.

Tricycles: Y3-4. Trips to the foot of the mountain Y45 and up.

✦ ❷ ORIENTATION AND PRACTICAL INFORMATION

Situated 131km south of Chengdu and 30km west of Leshan, Emeishan (not to be confused with the city of Meishan) is actually 6.6km from the park entrance gate. **Baoguo Monastery,** the first major sight and a cluster of lodgings at the base of the mountain, is another 5km beyond the park gates. Most of the city streets are named after landmarks on the mountain. **Foguang Lu** (佛光路) forms a ring road around the city. **Wannian Lu** (万年路) and **Mingshan Lu** (明山路) run parallel to the Bowen River and are bisected by **Jinding** (Golden Summit; 金顶路) **Lu.** There is little reason to stay in the city, as the Baoguo area contains places to stay and eat.

Travel Agency: Emeishan International Travel Service (éméishān lǚxíng shè; 峨眉山旅行社; ☎552 7555, ext. 5766; fax 522 4244), at the intersection of Jinding Nan Lu and Mingshan Zhong Lu. A travel agency and CAAC ticket office. Open daily 7am-noon and 1-10pm. For other travel-related inquiries, try the **Foreign Affairs Office** (wàishì bànshì chù; 外事办事处; ☎552 2831).

Bank of China: 73 Bailong Nan Lu (☎552 3737). The only bank in town providing foreign currency exchange services. English spoken. Open daily 8am-6pm.

PSB: 73 Wenmiao Jie (☎552 2741). Open daily 8am-noon and 3-6pm.

Hospital: Emeishan City Hospital (éméishān shì yīyuàn; 峨眉山市医院), 81 Santaishan Jie (☎552 2408), off Jinding Nan Lu.

Pharmacy: Emeishan City Kangjia Pharmacy (éméishān shì kāngjiá yàofáng; 峨眉山市康佳药房; ☎552 0290), on Yangliu Jie. Open daily 8am-8pm.

Internet Access: Emeishan Hotel (éméishān fàndiàn; 峨眉山饭店; ☎562 6888), in the Baoguo Monastery Scenic Area, next to the Post and Telecommunications Hotel. One fast computer (Y8 per hr.). Open daily 8am-11pm.

Post and Telecommunications: Post and Telecommunications Office (☎553 7217), on Foguang Nan Lu. EMS and IDD available. Open daily 8am-8pm. Another branch on Baoguo Bei Lu across from the Emei Hotel. **Postal Code:** 614200.

▌ ACCOMMODATIONS

Like neighboring Leshan, the city of Emeishan lacks budget accommodations for individual travelers, due mostly to the influx of Chinese tour groups that embark on widely popular three-day tours of Leshan and Emeishan. The monasteries dotting the mountain are cheap (Y15); however, they are often overcrowded, dirty, or chilly. There are also hotels on the mountain and at the base. All listings below are in the **Baoguo Monastery Scenic Area.** Due to the dramatic fluctuations in the number of tourists, off-days are prime bargaining opportunities.

Post and Telecommunications Hotel (yóudiàn bīnguǎn; 邮电宾馆; ☎559 0777; fax 559 0019), on the right along the main road leading to Baoguo Monastery. Pleasant buildings with tree-lined outdoor hallways and sunny rooms. IDD service. Hot water 4pm-midnight. 2-bed dorms Y30; 3-bed dorms Y20.

Sanxin Hotel (sānxīn dàjiǔdiàn; 三鑫大酒店), just across from the well-marked Emeishan Hotel. Dorms are bright and squeaky-clean, with tiled floors and common bathrooms. 2- and 3-bed dorms Y30; doubles with bath Y180-240. MC, Visa accepted.

Qinggong Hotel (qīnggōng bīnguǎn; 轻工宾馆; ☎559 0921), on the small road opposite Baoguo Monastery's parking lot, right before the entrance to the Hongzhushan Hotel. Beautiful surroundings and glowing red lanterns. Slightly less beautiful rooms with electric fans, large mosquito-netted windows, firm mattresses, and 24hr. hot water. IDD service. Doubles with A/C and bath Y160; triples Y80.

Jinye Hotel (jīnyè bīnguǎn; 金叶宾馆; ☎552 3666), up the hill on the left, at the end of the straight section of the main road. Going up the hill, take the left branch of the road. Clean and comfy, the Jinye offers everything you need—A/C, TV, balconies, and clean bathrooms with Western toilet, not to mention incredibly friendly service. A mainstay for roving Chinese tour groups. Doubles Y220.

☼ FOOD

A number of restaurants line the main road to Baoguo Monastery, near the Post and Telecommunications Hotel. The ▥ **Teddy Bear Cafe** (wánjù xióng cānguǎn; 玩具熊餐馆), in the Baoguo Monastery Scenic Area, is noticeable for its teddy bear sign on the second floor. Cuddly, inviting, and popular among foreigners, this cafe serves delicious Sichuanese and Western dishes. Menus are available in various languages. Don't miss the eggplant with garlic and ginger (Y10) and the pancakes (Y10) with chocolate and banana. (☎ 559 0135. Open daily 7am-last customer leaves.) Farther up the road from the Teddy Bear Cafe, **Dengyue Restaurant** (dēngyuè jiǔlóu; 登月酒楼) serves the standard Sichuanese food, with the bonus of an English menu. The fried egg noodles (Y8) and crispy fish (Y25) are a good bet. (☎ 559 0085. Open daily 6:30am-midnight.)

⚠ HIKING EMEISHAN

Buses leave from the Baoguo Monastery Lianyun Bus Station 6am-5pm (off-season 6am-4pm), and go between 3 stops: the parking lot (Y10); the cable-car station leading to Wannian Temple (Y15); and Thundering Cave Terrace (Y30), 7.5 km from the peak. Take the bus and **cable car** *(Y40) to Wannian Temple, hike 2 days to the peak, and then hike down the other path (1-2 days) to the parking lot. A time and knee-saving option is to take the bus all the way up, catch a cable car from Jieyin Hall (a 20min. walk from the bus drop-off) to the Golden Summit (Y40), spend the night there, and hike down the next day.*

The Emei mountains, 7km southeast of Emeishan city, cover some 300 km^2. In addition to the three dozen historical sites connected by 100km of trails, the 60 km^2 park area is also a nature reserve home to red pandas, takins (sumen antelope), bearded frogs, hundreds of kinds of butterflies, and over 3000 species of plants, including 60 varieties of Indian azalea flowers.

The main trail up the mountain diverges at **Qingyinge**. The left branch leads up a scenic gorge. Although this is a difficult route, including the **"99 turns path"** and greedy monkey roadblocks, it contains the most natural beauty of the two. The right path covers more historical sites including Wannian Temple. Both trails eventually converge and lead to the Golden Summit.

Due to the 2500m elevation difference, mountain weather can be unpredictable and much cooler (7 10 °C lower) than city temperatures. Locals say that the best weather for visiting the peak is right after a rainstorm, when fast-fleeing clouds are accompanied by rainbows and perchance the rare Buddha's Light. Climbs on clear days offer less dramatic views of verdant valleys, and cloudy weather visits are the least rewarding as the mountain is cloaked with dense mist.

BAOGUO MONASTERY (bàoguó sì; 报国寺). Built in 1615, Baoguo is the largest monastery on Emeishan, sitting 550m above sea level at the foot of the mountain. It was originally known as the Huizong (Assembled Religions) Hall, because it united the three popular beliefs in China at the time: Buddhism (represented by Guangchengzi), Daoism (by Chukuang), and Confucianism (by Puxian, later known as Samantabhadra Bodhisattva). During the early part of the Qing dynasty, the hall was renovated and became known as Baoguo Monastery. *Baoguo* ("dedication to one's country"), is considered one of the four acts of benevolence. The temple's interior is filled with plant life, home to many small gardens and *bonsai*.

Baoguo's main historic relic is the **Shengji bell**. Reputedly the second-largest bell in China (after Beijing's Great Bell), the 25-ton bronze bell was cast in 1564 and has some 61,600 words from Buddhist scripture inscribed upon it. At the start of the 20th century, the bell was taken from the monastery to make ammunition. By the time the monks got it back, the bell had a small crack. During the Great Leap Forward (1957-58), the bell was damaged again and now it can no longer be used. Behind Daxiong Hall sits a 2m porcelain Buddha that also dates back to the Ming. The Buddha is particularly remarkable for the thousand-petal lotus that it rests upon, representing attainment of *nirvana*. (**Accommodations** *available in Baoguo Monastery. 4-bed dorms Y20; 3-bed dorms Y30; 2-bed dorms Y40. Open daily 6:30am-9pm. Y8.)*

FUHU MONASTERY (fúhǔ sì; 伏虎寺). Named for a tiger that used to harass and intimidate the monastery's inhabitants, Fuhu (Crouching Tiger) Monastery, is "crouched" farther up the mountain and into the woods than Baoguo is. Although the monastery is ancient, it spent many years as an empty building until the 1980s, when a small group of nuns took up residence. There are few statues of note, but the luxuriant surrounding forests and mountains are beautiful and home to the rare Withered Leaf Butterfly. The ancient and rare plant, *shaluo*, once fulfilled the appetites of herbivorous dinosaurs 200 million years ago and still grows today. (*Accommodations consist of basic 4-bed dorms (Y14). Open daily 6:30am-8pm. Y6.*)

QINGYIN PAVILION (qīngyīn gé; 清音阁). Farther up the mountain weary hikers can catch their breath at the Qingyin Pavilion, situated between the Black and White Dragon streams, flanked by symmetric bridges and surrounded by deep green growth. The crisp sound of water cascading down sleek ebony stone gives Qingyin (literally Clear Sound Pavilion) its name.

WANNIAN TEMPLE (wànnián sì; 万年寺). Higher up the mountain at 1020m sits Wannian Temple, dating back to the Jin dynasty (AD 280-316). The oldest building on the mountain is the ancient brick chapel that escaped unscathed from the fires that consumed the rest of the temple in 1945. It was once known as Baishui Puxian Monastery, after the famous *bodhisattva* Puxian (Samantabhadra), who is the main deity worshiped at Emeishan. In AD 980, the Tang Emperor Taizong commissioned the most important statue in the temple—a bronze 7.4m, 62-ton statue of Puxian Bodhisattva riding atop his white elephant. During the Ming dynasty, Emperor Wanli had the temple renovated and renamed it Wannian Temple (Ten Thousand Year Temple). The statue of Puxian is housed in **Wuliang Hall,** where he is surrounded by 1000 small copper statues of Buddha seated around the dome.

Wannian Temple is also famous for its melodious **musical frogs.** Their vocal cords are usually only active in the early mornings, so it is unlikely that late-comers will be able to catch the frogs in concert. (*Temple **accommodations** Y15 per bed. Vegetarian restaurant open during temple hours (Y5-10). Temple open daily 11am-7pm. Y10.*)

ELEPHANT-BATHING TEMPLE (xǐ xiàng sì; 洗象寺). At 2100m, and seated upon a small precipice with tremendous drops on both sides, Xixiang Temple used to be known as Lotus Flower Temple, because a large piece of yellow rock resembling a lotus flower was once found there. Some years later, a medicine man on the mountain is said to have seen Puxian Bodhisattva bathing his white elephant in the small hexagonal pond in front of the temple. It seems doubtful that this miniscule pool could accommodate the girth of Puxian's pachyderm, but we won't argue. (*Temple **accommodations** Y15 per bed. Open daily 7am-8pm. Y1.*)

GOLDEN SUMMIT HUAZANG TEMPLE (jīndǐng huázàng sì; 金顶华藏寺). First constructed during the Eastern Han, the Golden Summit Huazang Temple stands 3077m above sea level. The temple itself is a simple structure and not terribly interesting, but it provides a platform from which to admire the opaque and mystical scenery, from the distant cloud-clad mountains to the deep gullies below. All it takes to witness a dazzling sunrise over a sea of clouds, and perhaps even Buddha's Light, is a little luck, the determination to wake up at 5:30am, and the patience to wait around in the cold wind until daybreak. (*Temple **accommodations** Y20-30 per bed. Small restaurant on site. Cable cars from Jeyin Hill to Golden Summit Y40, Y30 down. Open daily 6am-7pm. Y10.*)

JIUZHAIGOU 九寨沟 ☎ 0837

Against a backdrop of thundering waterfalls, snow-capped mountains, and virgin forest, 108 iridescent turquoise lakes fan out across panoramic valleys like a strutting peacock unfurling its plumage. Named after the nine native Tibetan villages in the gully, Jiuzhaigou's dazzling scenery reinvigorates jaded senses and leaves onlookers speechless. This northern Sichuanese national park doubles as a giant panda reserve and has been recognized as a UNESCO World Heritage Site. But fame has its price: the park is already filled with Chinese tourists who hop buses from sight to sight.

ORIENTATION AND PRACTICAL INFORMATION

Over 450km north of Chengdu, Jiuzhaigou is tucked into the Minshan Range in Nanping County, a part of the Aba and Qiang Autonomous Prefecture near the Gansu border. It spreads across 60,000 hectares and has a gorgeous 80km long scenic area, largely concentrated in a Y-shaped valley that splits near the mighty Nuorilang Falls. The left branch leads on to Zechawa Village and Long Lake, while the right spills into Mirror Lake, Pearl Shoal Waterfall, and the Primeval Forest. In winter, Jiuzhaigou gets enough snowfall to render it inaccessible; even in summer, heavy rainfall can make the roads to the reserve treacherous.

Buses and Tours: The **Jiuzhaigou Long-distance bus station** (jiǔzhàigōu qìchē zhàn; 九寨沟汽车站; ☎773 2030), has several buses to **Songpan**. A bus (10hr., 7am, Y130) from Ximen Bus Station in Chengdu drops passengers at the entrance to the nature reserve. Alternatively, an 8am bus from Ximen Bus Station provides a 5- to 6-day tour of Jiuzhaigou for Y200-288 (includes admission but not accommodations). Chengdu hotel travel agencies also offer packaged trips to Jiuzhaigou. Inside Jiuzhaigou, buses constantly go up and down the main road. The bus pass (Y90) gives you unlimited rides, and is included in the park admission price.

PSB: On the small street leading to the entrance to the nature reserve, opposite the parking lot (☎773 4033; complaints 12315). Open daily 8:30am-5:30pm; someone is on duty 24hr.

Hospital: Jiuzhaigou County Hospital (jiǔzhàigōu xiàn yīyuàn; 九寨沟县医院; ☎773 2156 or 2146), 43km past the turnoff point to the Jiuzhaigou entrance, down the road to Nanping County and on the right. Ambulance service. Open 24hr. Also, located 4km up the road in the other direction is the **Jiuzhaigou County Clinic** (jiǔzhàigōu xiàn yīyuàn zhàngzhá fēnyuàn; 九寨沟县医院障扎分院; ☎773 4007). Open 24hr.

Post and Telecommunications: On the right (coming from Chengdu) in a 3-story building, 5-6km from the entrance to Jiuzhaigou. IDD service. Open daily 10am-5pm.

ACCOMMODATIONS

Many of the newer hotels sprouting up along the road to Jiuzhaigou are resorts catering to high-rolling tour groups. Fortunately, within Jiuzhaigou itself, there are cheaper accommodations, pretty much all of which have the same prices: doubles Y22, "luxury" doubles with shower Y30 (hot water is generally available for a few hours in the evening). Included in your admission ticket is one night's free stay in any of the standard rooms. All three **cultural villages** (Heyezhai, Shuzhengzhai, and Zechawazhai) offer such accommodations.

INSIDE JIUZHAIGOU

Shuzheng Hotel (shūzhèng bīnguǎn; 树正宾馆), in Shuzheng Village. Check in at the "Front Office" sign; the rooms are up the hill. Standard doubles and triples (Y22) are dimly lit and have dingy concrete floors. Questionably clean communal outdoor toilets, and no shower facilities. Quite the opposite, though, are the hotel's Y40 doubles and triples, which are clean and carpeted, and in a traditional Tibetan-style building.

Silver Fall Hotel (yíngpù bīnguǎn; 银瀑宾馆; ☎773 8083), in Shuzheng Village, before the road forks at Nuorilang Falls. Carpeted rooms are bright and clean, with TV and private bathrooms. Doubles Y60.

Zechawa Village Hotel (zèchāwá zhài bīnguǎn; 则查洼寨宾馆), in Zechawa Village, up the hill from Nuorilang bus stop. Doubles Y22; with carpeted floors, TV, and bath Y30.

OUTSIDE JIUZHAIGOU

Jiuzhaigou Cabins (jiǔzhàigōu mùwū; 九寨沟木屋; ☎773 4127), 25m from the entrance to the nature reserve. When facing the gate, the cabins are on up a small path on the left. This newly opened, all-wooden hotel practically sparkles. Some rooms overlook the rushing river, and all have bright, fluorescent-free lighting. Heaters, TVs, and baths. Singles Y100; doubles Y300.

Jiuzhaigou Grand Hotel (guìbìnlóu fàndiàn; 贵宾楼饭店; ☎ 773 4163; fax 773 4163), in the entrance parking lot area, behind the bank and police station. Rooms are dirty and crowded, and have common bathrooms with no showers. 3- to 4-bed dorms Y40.

🍴 FOOD

The best dishes to try are the wild vegetable dishes of Jiuzhaigou, such as the **sliced pork with edible tree fungus** (mùěr ròupiàn, 木耳肉片, Y30) and the **walnut flower dish** (hétáohuā, 核桃花, Y30). The **yak** (máo níu, 牦牛, Y60) is also worth trying if you have money to spare. Budget travelers, be forewarned: the food prices are greatly inflated within Jiuzhaigou; vendors ask Y5-8 for dried noodles and Y5 for just a bottle of water. If you're on a budget, carry your own snacks and drinks into the park. There are several good and inexpensive restaurants inside the nature reserve. In the Heye Village, there is the **Lotus Leaf Restaurant** (héyè cāntīng; 荷叶餐厅), in the Zechawa Village, there is the **Nuorilang Restaurant** (nuòrìlǎng cāntīng; 诺日郎餐厅), and in Shuzheng Village, there is **Shuzheng Restaurant** (shūzhèng cāntīng; 树正餐厅). These three are where most tour groups gather for meals; all serve similar Sichuanese food at comparable prices.

👁 SIGHTS

JIUZHAIGOU NATURE RESERVE (jiǔzhàigōu, 九寨沟)
Open daily 7am-9pm. Y185, students Y140; a Y20 price increase is anticipated sometime within the next year.

Juizhaigou's beauty is as legendary as its origins. According to a local tale, the warrior god Dage presented a beautiful magic mirror, painstakingly crafted from clouds and wind, to his beloved goddess Wunosemo. One day, a meddling devil, envious of the couple's love and happiness, caused Wunosemo to drop her treasured mirror. It fell to earth, where it shattered over Jiuzhaigou and formed glittering lakes. This story seems less far-fetched to those who have beheld the unearthly beauty of this idyllic area. Reflections of the richly colored foliage (deep green in summer, fiery red and golden yellow in autumn) glisten in the 118 turquoise, crystalline lakes. Some, such as **Five Flower Lake** (wǔ huā hǎi; 五花海) and **Panda Lake** (xióng māo hǎi; 熊猫海), both along the right branch of the road after it splits at the Nuorilang bus stop, extend to mythic depths. Other pools create long series of waterfalls that rush between trees and crash over the rocky cliffs of **Shuzheng Falls** (shùzhèng pùbù; 树正瀑布) and **Pearl Shoal Falls** (zhēnzhū tān pùbù; 珍珠滩瀑布). All told, Jiuzhaigou contains 17 waterfalls; the grandest cascade, **Nuorilang Falls** (nuòrílǎng pùbù; 诺日郎瀑布), is 30m tall and 320m wide, the widest in the world.

LONG LAKE (cháng hǎi; 长海) **AND ZARU TEMPLE.** One of the most beautiful sights in the reserve is Long Lake, at the end of a 30-minute, 18 km bus climb along the left branch from the Nuorilang bus stop. At an elevation of 3150m, this tranquil lake is one of the least crowded areas of the park. Crystal clear and strikingly deep (130m, 40m visible depth), the azure blue waters attract migratory wild swans. Near the entrance stands a small Tibetan monastery, Zaru Temple, happy to accept visitors and their donations. At the center of the main assembly hall is a prominent statue of Sakyamuni, and over a thousand smaller Sakyamunis line its side walls. An elderly monk (one of five who reside in Zaru) will sound the gong and chant while the devout pray to the main statue. He then presents visitors with Tibetan ceremonial scarves *(hadas)* as good luck charms. *(Open daily 8am-7pm.)*

HIKING. Escape the clicking of cameras and the roar of tour buses by hiking the several trails in Juizhaigou. In Shuzheng, reach an unmarked trail by crossing the small footbridge on Tiger Lake and then either heading right toward Nuorilang Falls or left toward Sleeping Dragon Lake. Farther up the road, an official trail circumnavigates **Pearl Shoal Falls** (30min.), and a boardwalk connects **Five-flower Lake** with **Panda Lake** (25min.), passing an epic series of waterfalls along the way.

WHAT GOES AROUND COMES AROUND The

beauty of Jiuzhaigou has inspired many creation myths about the origins of some of the more scenic vistas in the area. One such story is the story of **Pearl Shoal Falls**. Once upon a time, a Tibetan man fell in love with a fairy and gave her a sparkling pearl necklace as a symbol of his affection. In return, the fairy gave him an axe—more a practical gift than a romantic one—that was used to help the local people dig a canal to relieve the area's flooding waters. When a god heard that the fairy's gift to the man had bestowed such power on the people, he became furious and ordered his underlings to seize the lovestruck fairy. In the ensuing struggle, the fairy's pearl necklace was broken and her pearls fell to the earth, forming sparkling waterfalls and cascades. From that point on, the locals called the falls "Pearl Shoal."

CULTURAL EVENTS. Each of the three villages hosts an evening cultural event, usually nightly, but depending on tour groups' demand. In Heye Village from 8 to 10pm, there is a kitschy, Tibetan-style **Bonfire Party** (Y60), complete with Tibetan dancing, a Tibetan-style tug-of-war, a mock Tibetan wedding ceremony (in which a fortunate winner from the audience plays the part of bridegroom), and a whole lamb delectably crackling over the flames. In Shuzheng, from 8:30 to 10:30pm, there is a show that focuses specifically on different forms of Tibetan dancing (Y50). If you really want to get down and dirty, you can witness a Yak-Slaughtering Ceremony (Y30-50) in Zechawa Village from 8 to 10pm, and then feast on the freshly flayed flesh of everyone's favorite furry friend.

⚑ DAYTRIP FROM JIUZHAIGOU: HUANGLONG

*In Songpan County, 397km north of Chengdu. **Buses** (2hr.) from the county seat of Songpan drop passengers at the mouth of the valley, which is also the source of the Lujiang River. From here, visitors take the trail into the wilderness, as the entire reserve is open only to foot traffic. Horse treks from Songpan (see p. 638) involve a 1 day ride to Huanglong, 1 day hiking in the park, and 1 day return. The round-trip **hike** from the entrance to Huanglong Temple is 7.5km and takes 3-4hr. Bring ample drink and food, as there are no vendors along the trail. **Open** daily 8am-7pm. **Admission** Y75, students Y35.*

Guarded by 10 majestic 5000m peaks surrounding another jagged Minshan Valley, the Huanglong Scenic Reserve is just as enchanting, if not more so, than its more famous counterpart and fellow UNESCO World Heritage Site 128km to the east. Locals named the valley Huanglong (huánglóng; 黄龙) or Yellow Dragon, because it reminded them of a dragon leaping down from the mountains. Like Jiuzhaigou, Huanglong's dense old-growth forest and alpine slopes shelter endangered wildlife like giant pandas, snow leopards, golden silk monkeys, crown deer, and bent-horned antelope. Unlike Jiuzhaigou's wide, crashing waterfalls, however, Huanglong's terraced pools of iridescent blue, supported by kilometer after kilometer of intricate calcium formations, create an endless mosaic of broken mirrors that reflect the sky and snow-capped mountains.With no roads running through it, Huanglong attracts far fewer tourists, making it infinitely more tranquil and intimate than Jiuzhaigou.

The gently climbing trek takes hikers past aquamarine pools and babbling brooks that flow just below **Lintai Falls** and **Body-Washing Falls,** providing picturesque photo-ops and the soothing sounds of crashing water. The long stretch of cascading golden steps, known as **Golden Sand On Earth,** is the result of several centuries' accumulation of calcium sediments. Near the top, a few temples dot the mountainscape, the largest of which is **Huanglong Temple.** Although the temple itself is unremarkable, the beautiful cave, to the left of the monastery, is worth exploring (bring a flashlight). Behind Huanglong Temple, the brilliant **Five Colored Lake** features a gradient of colors; the lake's stunning beauty is ample reward for the two-hour hike to the upper end of the trail. Behind the lake, a footpath leads to the hills and boulder fields beyond, offering the more energetic hiker a heart-stopping view of Huanglong. The path back down to the entrance takes slightly less time, bypassing the pool and weaving instead through a forest of towering trees.

SONGPAN 松潘   ☎0837

Songpan is set in lush green mountains with thousands of terraces piled up to the peaks. A quick hike takes you to small monasteries and huts from where you can gaze into the quiet valley below. Songpan's ancient gates grandly mark the entrance to the city center. Most visitors to Songpan are either en route to Jiuzhaigou or Huanglong, or embarking on a horse trek in the neighboring mountains. The town itself consists of aging wooden buildings and cobblestoned streets, with a few shiny hotels spawned by the recent influx of money and tourists.

Lodgings during peak season (July-Oct.) are often packed. **Songzhou Hotel** (sōngzhōu bīnguǎn; 松洲宾馆), near the north gate on the town's main drag, has cement-floors and hot water from 7 to 10:30pm. (☎723 2371. 2-bed dorms Y15.) Farther down the road, with rooms of the same quality and price, friendly service, and a great view, is the **Songpan (Fandian) Hotel** (sōngpān fàndiàn; 松潘饭店). Classier rooms are available at the **Songpan (Binguan) Hotel** (sōngpān bīnguǎn; 松潘宾馆) on Shuncheng Lu, about a 10-minute walk from Shunjiang Horse Treks. (☎723 2662. Doubles with bath Y280.)

Many claim that the **horse treks** out of Songpan are the highlight of their travels in Sichuan. The price (Y60, including meals, tents, bedding, cold weather gear, and lovable guides) is absolutely unbeatable. The two competing companies, **Happy Trails Horse Treks** (kuàilè de xiǎolù qímǎ lǚyóu; 快乐的小路奇马旅游; ☎723 1064) and **Shun Jiang Horse Treks** (shùnjiāng lǚyóu mǎduì; 顺江旅游马队; ☎723 1201), are right next to each other and offer the same tours with the same high quality. Treks to Erdao Hai Hot Springs take two days, with Zhaya Waterfall an extra three days (Y30 entrance fee to both parks); the trek to Ice Mountain takes four days (with a camp at 4000m). The popular tour to Huanglong and back is three days. You can also take a two-hour bus ride to Huanglong from the **Songpan Bus Station** (sōngpān qìchē zhàn; 松潘汽车站; ☎728 2543).

ZÖIGÊ 若尔盖

Pronounced *ruòěrgài* in Mandarin, Zöigê serves mostly as a night's stopover for north or south-bound bus riders. This dusty little town is somewhat inhospitable: the uniform, cement buildings block the views of the beautiful surrounding hills and grasslands, and bands of sarcastic teenage boys roam the streets. Buses leave Zöigê every morning to Songpan, Langmusi, and Hezuo. Zöigê's accommodations are minimal and often lack showers. The **Grain Bureau Guesthouse** (liángjú bīnguǎn; 粮局宾馆) accepts foreigners and has Y15 dorm beds in spacious triples. The **Ruoliang Hotel** (rūoliáng bīnguǎn; 若粮宾馆; ☎298 360) has cleaner doubles for Y25. There is a public shower (Y3) just down the street.

LANGMUSI 郎木寺   ☎0941

Langmusi is a hidden treasure on the traveler's itinerary between Chengdu and Xiahe. You'd think you were on the Tibetan Plateau if it weren't for the giant mountains and rock structures that surround this tiny town: the streets are filled with robed Tibetan monks and women clad in the ornate costumes of Tibetan herders. It's also one of the last places a tourist can witness a traditional **sky-burial**, which occurs nearly every morning. Be respectful and keep a good di-si-tan-si.

The town's main attraction is its giant monastery, **Langmusi Temple** (làngmùsì; 郎木寺), which is divided into two complexes on two hills that straddle the village. For great views of Langmusi and surrounding villages, hike up through the main temple with the aid of some very friendly monks, and continue up over the ridge to see the stunning distant mountain ranges. From there, go down toward the sky-burial grounds (surrounded by prayer flags) and a small cave.

Buses go daily to **Hezuo**, where you can change for Xiahe, and to **Zöigê**, where you can change for Songpan. The cheapest lodgings are available at the **Langmusi Guesthouse** (làngmùsì duōděisuǒ; 郎木寺垛得所), which has spacious four-bed dorms (Y10), but distant toilets and no showers. The **Langmusi Hotel** (làngmùsì fàndiàn; 郎木寺饭店; ☎667 1086) next door has similar rooms (Y15), with showers. Both places have remarkably friendly staff. Langmusi offers some tasty food and some restaurants with English menus. In **Lesha's Little Restaurant** (dīxuéwén fànguǎn; 丁学文饭馆; ☎667 1179), you can try to beat the 27-minute record for finishing their frisbee-sized yak burger (Y12). If you still have room for dessert, order a slice of the delicious apple, peach, or apricot pies (Y8). **Hotel Restaurant** (bīnguǎn cāntīng; 宾馆餐厅; ☎667 1164) has a somewhat larger selection of Western food and Chinese favorites, especially Sichuanese dishes. The **Langmusi Restaurant** (làngmùsì fànguǎn; 郎木寺饭馆) is cheaper and has smaller portions.

CHONGQING 重庆   ☎023

Over the years, Chongqing (meaning "Double Blessed") has come to be seen by some as a serviceable and lackluster interior city. Nothing could be farther from the truth. Everything in Chongqing is hot, from the sweltering sub-tropical summer heat to the spicy food. The visual and aural landscape of this attractive Yangzi-side city is quirky and unique: steep hills make biking unfeasible, and honking car horns has been declared illegal. At the same time, air raid tunnels and Guomindang prison camps hint at a turbulent, troubled, and intriguing past.

The city only became an integral part of the Chinese empire during the Ming dynasty. Chongqing was opened up first to British trade in 1890 and then to Japanese trade in 1895. The Japanese left in 1937, once the Sino-Japanese War broke out (see p. 16), and Chongqing became the capital of the Republic of China after the Guomindang evacuated Nanjing. In the final days of the civil war between the CCP and the GMD, Chongqing became the site of intense fighting. The city was part of Sichuan province until 1997, when it was granted the special status of independent municipality, a title shared with Beijing, Tianjin, and Shanghai. Chongqing municipality is now about the size of Austria, home to 30 million people.

These days, this booming industrial city, seething with heat, humidity, and dust, and trapped in the sultry Yangzi Valley, is best known as the beginning point of Three Gorges cruises down the Yangzi. But its burgeoning nightlife, historical sights, and unmistakable atmosphere make it worthwhile on its own.

▐▀ TRANSPORTATION

Airplanes: Jiangbei Airport (jiāngběi jīchǎng; 江北机场; ☎6715 2337), 35km north of the city center. **Shuttle buses** (40-50min., every 30min. 6am-6pm, Y15) leave from the **CAAC office,** 161 Zhongshan San Lu (☎6360 0444), in the Shangqingsi district. Chongqing is mainly served by **China Southwest Airlines** (xīnán hángkōng gōngsī; 西南航空公司), which has a convenient branch (☎6382 5926) between the Liberation Monument and Huixianlou Hotel in the same building as the China Industrial Bank. Open daily 8am-6pm. **Sichuan Airlines** (sìchuān hángkōng gōngsī; 四川航空公司), 17 Minquan Lu (☎6381 3022 or 6301 6241), just below the Liberation Monument on the left. Open daily 8:30am-8pm. To: **Beijing** (2 per day, Y1250); **Guangzhou** (1 per day, Y940); **Kunming** (1 per day, Y570); **Shanghai** (M, W, and F-Sa, Y1190); and **Xian** (1 per day, Y460).

Trains: Caiyuanba Train Station (càiyuánbà huǒchē zhàn; 菜园坝火车站; ☎6386 2607), near Binjiang Lu, Yuzhong district. Ticket office open daily 8:30-11:30am, 2:30-5:30pm, and 6:30-11:30pm. The station area is full of rip-off artists. Do not take a taxi from the group just opposite the exit; they don't use meters. The official taxi stand is on the right, on the main road leading away from the station. To: **Beijing** (32-35hr., 1:16 and 6:13pm, Y181-658); **Chengdu** (4hr.; midnight, 6:41am, and 9:06pm; Y88-130); **Guangzhou** (50hr., 4 per day, Y105-339) via **Nanning; Guiyang** (10hr., 8:47pm, Y34-120); **Kunming** (24hr., 9:41am and 3:49pm, Y81-304); and **Shanghai** (45hr., 5:14pm, Y271-756).

Buses: Chongqing Long-distance Bus Station (chóngqìng chángtú qìchē zhàn; 重庆长途汽车站), 38 Caiyuan Lu (☎6387 3196), left of the train station. Open daily 5:30am-midnight. To: **Chengdu** (4hr., every 20min. 6:30am-10pm, Y107-199); **Dazu** (2hr., every 40min. 6:30am-7pm, Y29); and **Emeishan** (7hr., 8:45am, Y94).

Boats: See the **Three Gorges,** p. 646.

Local Transportation: Buses are cheap and efficient but can be confusing. Fare Y0.5. Bus **#102** connects Chaotianmen Dock with the Caiyuanba Train Station, running along Jiabang Lu; **#103** runs past the Great Hall of the People from near the Liberation Monument; and **#401** links Chaotianmen Dock with the Liberation Monument. Bus stops are far apart; ask drivers to let you off closer to your destination. **Minibuses** run the same routes (Y2) and are more flexible about stopping anywhere.

Taxi: Base fare Y5, each additional km Y1.2.

✴ 🔀 ORIENTATION AND PRACTICAL INFORMATION

At the confluence of the **Yangzi** and **Jialing** rivers, Chongqing municipality is divided into five central districts, of which **Yuzhong** (渝中) is the dominant one. **Jiangbei** (江北) to the north and **Shapingba** (沙坪坝) to the west are also important. Steep and narrow winding streets make Chongqing difficult to navigate. The most conveniently located accommodations, shops, and transport facilities are all in Yuzhong, bounded to the southwest by the train station and to the northeast by the Chaotianmen Docks. Yuzhong's central orientation point is the **Liberation Monument**.

Travel Agencies: CITS, at 120 Zhaozhi Lanyan Lu (☎6885 2216; fax 6385 0196). Another branch on the 6th floor of the Huixianlou Hotel (☎6370 9934). Both branches open daily 8:30am-5:30pm. **China Youth Travel Service** (zhōngguó qīngnián lǚxíngshè; 中国青年旅行社), 125 Renmin Lu (☎6386 0814), in Yuzhong district. Open M-F 9am-5:30pm. **Chongqing International Travel Ticket Agency** (chóngqìngshì guójì lǚyóu hángkōng shòupiàochù; 重庆市国际旅游航空售票处), 173 Renmin Lu (☎6385 8283). Open M-F 8:30am-5:30pm. The **Huixianlou Hotel** (☎6382 5148) also books tickets at no extra cost.

Consulates: Canada: Metropolitan Tower, Ste. 1705, Wuyi Lu (☎6373 8007; email cdncon@cta.cq.cn). **UK:** Metropolitan Tower, Ste. 2868, Wuyi Lu (☎6381 0321). Both open M-F 9am-5pm.

Bank of China: On 1804 Minzhu Lu (☎6370 1294), near the Liberation Monument. Exchanges traveler's checks. Open daily 8:30am-9pm.

Market: Carrefour (jiālèfú; 家乐福; ☎6372 9010), on Minhua Jie. *Oui, oui,* it's a real live French supermarket. Open daily 9am-10pm.

PSB: 1 Linjiang Lu (☎6384 4403). Open 24hr.

Hospital: Both are in the Yuzhong district. **Chongqing Emergency Center** (chóngqìngshì jíjiu yīliáo zhōngxīn; 重庆市急救医疗中心), 1 Jiankang Lu (☎6387 4000). Emergency room open 24hr. **Chongqing No. 1 People's Hospital** (chóngqìngshì dìyī rénmín yīyuàn; 重庆市第一人民医院), 40 Doamen Kou (☎6384 4283). Open 24hr.

Internet Access: Yuzhong district is home to several Internet bars. From the Huixianlou Hotel, turn right at the Liberation Monument and then left when the street splits. Stay right until the street ends; turn right and go to the 3rd floor next to the Xinhua Bookstore. Y3 per hr. Open 24hr.

Post Office: Each district has a main **post office.** The most convenient one is located in Yuzhong at 3 Mingnan Lu, just down from the Liberation Monument on the left. IDD service available downstairs until 8pm. Open daily 8:30am-9:30pm. Chongqing is not a good place for Poste Restante. **Postal Code:** 630011.

🔝 ACCOMMODATIONS

Chongqing accommodations are all about skyscrapers with skyscraping prices (try US$150 per night); foreigners looking for budget hotels will have to look far and wide. Fortunately, the cheapest district, Yuzhong, is also the most convenient.

Huixianlou Hotel (huìxiānlóu fàndiàn; 会仙楼饭店), 186 Minzhu Lu (☎6384 5101; fax 6384 7495), Yuzhong district. The best deal in town, in the heart of the fun district. This place is plush; even dorms have carpets, A/C, and TV. Books river cruises, plane tickets, and tours. 6-bed dorms Y50; singles Y180-280; doubles Y140-280.

SICHUAN

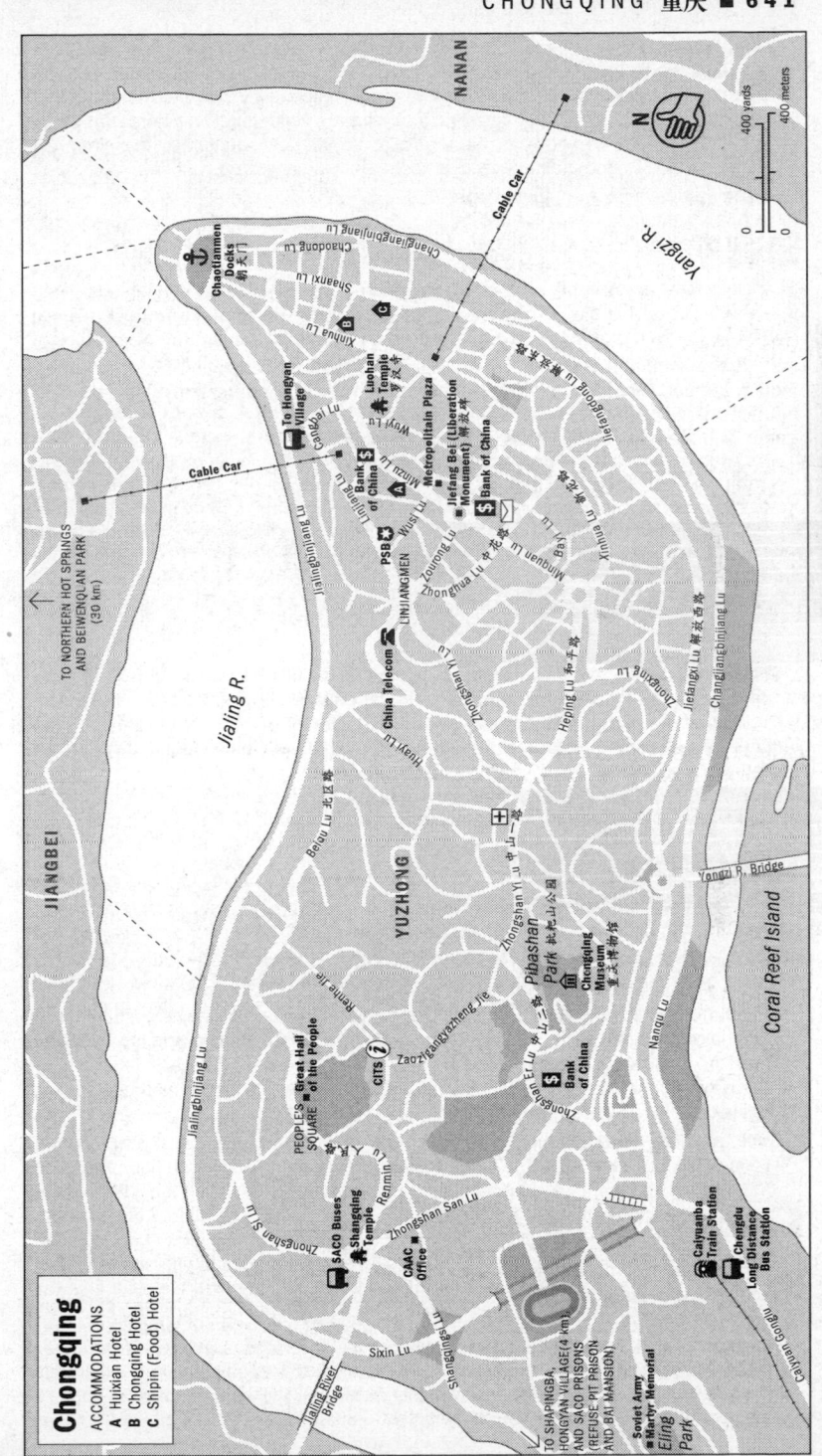

Chongqing

ACCOMMODATIONS
A Huixian Hotel
B Chongqing Hotel
C Shipin (Food) Hotel

NANAN

Yangzi R.

N

400 yards
400 meters

Cable Car

Changjiangbinjiang Lu

Chaodong Lu

Shaanxi Lu

Xinhua Lu

Chaotianmen
Docks 朝天门

C

B

Luohan
Temple
罗汉寺

Metropolitain Plaza

Wuyi Lu

Jiefang Bei (Liberation
Monument) 解放碑

To Hongyan
Village

Cangbai Lu

Bank
of China

$

Mizu Lu

A

Bank of China $

Minquan Lu

Bayi Lu

Xinhua Lu

Jiefangbei Lu

Lingjiang Lu

Lingjiangmen Lu

Wusi Lu

PSB

Zoutong Lu

LINJIANGMEN

Zhonghua Lu

Heping Lu 和平路

Jiefanglu Lu 解放东路

Changjiangbinjiang Lu

Zhongxing Lu

China Telecom

Huayi Lu

Beipu Lu 北区路

Cable Car

Jialing R.

JIANGBEI

TO NORTHERN HOT SPRINGS
AND BEIWENQUAN PARK
(30 km)

YUZHONG

Zhongshan Yi Lu 中山一路

Pipashan
Park 枇杷山公园

Chongqing
Museum
重庆博物馆

Nanqu Lu

Yangzi R. Bridge

Coral Reef Island

Renmin Jie

Great Hall
of the People

PEOPLE'S
SQUARE

CITS

Zaozigangzizheng Jie

Bank of China $

Zhongshan San Lu

Jialingbinjiang Lu

Zhongshan Er Lu 中山二路

SACO Buses

Shangqing
Temple

CAAC
Office

YHA

Zhongshan San Lu

Renmin Lu

Zhongshan Si Lu

Caiyuanba
Train Station

Chengdu
Long Distance
Bus Station

Caiyuan Gonglu

Sixin Lu

Shangqingsi Lu

Jialing River Bridge

TO SHAPINGBA,
HONGYAN VILLAGE (4 km)
AND SACO PRISONS
(REFUSE PIT PRISON
AND BAI MANSION)

Soviet Army
Martyr Memorial

Eling
Park

Shipin Hotel (shípĭn bīnguǎn; 食品宾馆), 72 Shanxi Lu (☎6384 7300; fax 6384 5844), Yuzhong district. Another clean, convenient cheapie. All rooms have A/C, TV, and attached bath. Singles Y140; doubles Y150-180; triples Y180.

Fanzhuang Hotel (fànzhuāng bīnguǎn; 范庄宾馆), 256 Renmin Zhong Lu (☎6385 2083; fax 6385 3267), Yuzhong district, opposite the stand for airport buses. Rooms have A/C, TV, heater, phone, and bath. Singles Y100-150; doubles Y130-160; triples Y165; quads Y220; sextuples Y330.

FOOD

Those who love inhumanly chillie-laden morsels will find that Chongqing has some wonderful food. The local specialty is **Sichuanese hotpot** (sìchuān huǒguō; 四川火锅), which is said to have originated in Chongqing. Unlike the clear Mongolian variety, Chongqing hotpot broth is an ultra-spicy psychedelic red concoction, which used to be laced with opium for added flavor. The omnipresent hotpot joints are easily recognizable, with rows of tables with holes in their middles.

The hotpot craze began in the area of **Xiaomishi** (xiǎomíshì; 小米市), but the family-run joints there have been replaced by hundreds of sidewalk eateries and flashier high end restaurants. Only a few of the original places remain, like **Fatso's Hotpot** (pàngzĭmā huǒguō; 胖子妈火锅). Beef, mushrooms, kidney slices, and liver slices are hot add-ins (Y10-20 per plate). From the Marriott Tower, walk downhill and turn left down the first alley. (Open daily 10am-midnight.) There are more stalls near the Huixianlou Hotel; from the hotel, walk toward the Liberation Monument, take the first right, and then turn into an alley to the left. A small night market on Canbai Lu also features hotpot; walk up Minzhu Lu away from the Monument, and turn right at the end.

Vienna Restaurant (wéiyěnà dàjiǔdiān; 维也纳大酒店), in Cangbai (沧白) district serves heavenly hotpots. From the Carrefour (see **Markets,** p. 640), waltz down the right fork of the road and Vienna is on the left. The lunch (Y36) and dinner (Y38) buffets garner praise. (Open daily 11am-10pm.) **Taipei Stone Hotpot City** (táiběi shítóu huǒguō chéng; 台北石头火锅成), 23 Zhongshan San Lu (☎6386 9081), serves over 200 dishes--even sushi, quail eggs, and fish heads—in its Y48 buffet. From the top of the Crown Escalator, turn right; the restaurant is on the right.

NIGHTLIFE

In the world of Chongqing nightlife, any pub or club that's been around for a year must be on the downswing. Word of mouth (not hard to find among the city's hip young English speakers) should always be your first guide to this booming scene. In Yuzhong district, the most happening area is around the Liberation Monument.

Ling Dian Pub (língdiǎn jiǔbā; 零点酒吧). From Huixianlou, walk straight past the Liberation Monument for 5min. On the left corner will be a large, modern complex. Take the elevator to the 4th Fl. This place is the expat choice because it actually attempts to move away from Chinese pop around 2am. After midnight, tables are hard to come by. Heineken Y25. Open daily 8pm-5am.

Reunion Club (huíguī jiǔláng; 回归酒廊; ☎6376 2882), in the Yutian Bldg., 8th Fl. From Huixianlou, turn left at the Liberation Monument; the building is a block ahead on the right. This is the only other option for the "in" crowd. The Reunion's large dance floor and exuberant crowd keep the place moving to Chinese pop until closing time. Corona Y25. Open daily 7pm-2:30am.

SIGHTS

Surging urbanity aside, the darker side of Chongqing's economic situation is still very much in evidence. Chongqing's attractive architecture and steep winding streets lend it a unique feel. Chongqing does not have much in the way of natural scenery or ancient relics, but it does offer a glimpse of the grim and not-so-ancient past of the 1947-49 Civil War.

LOOK MA, NO HANDS! Long years of battle between the Ming and the invading Manchurians of the Qing left Chongqing's population severely depleted. During the reign of Qing Emperor Kangxi, large numbers of people were brought into Chongqing from Hunan and Hubei provinces to repopulate the city. Because many of them were brought in against their will, the emperor's soldiers handcuffed the forced migrants to one another for the long walk to Chongqing. The only time they could have their hands released was when they needed to use the toilet. Hence the birth of the phrase "free my hands" (jiěshǒu; 解手), which is used even today in Chongqing when excusing oneself to go to the bathroom.

LIBERATION MONUMENT (jiěfàng bēi; 解放碑). This is the most prominent meeting point in Yuzhong district, built to commemorate the Communist liberation of Chongqing from Guomindang control. Now a pedestrian area surrounded by flashing neon lights, fast food joints, and signs saying "Times Square," this area looks more and more like it's celebrating Chongqing's "liberation" from the era of high Maoism and socialist austerity. The Monument area is a great place to watch a parade of fashion-conscious children strutting by with new clothes from the huge **Metropolitan Plaza** (dàdūhuì guǎngchǎng; 大都会广场), the city's largest mall.

PEOPLE'S SQUARE (rénmín guǎngchǎng; 人民广场). The massive People's Square is dominated by the **Great Hall of the People** (rénmín dàlǐtáng; 人民大礼堂), designed by the famous Chinese architect Zhang Jiade and completed in 1954. Modeled after the Temple of Heaven in Beijing (see p. 122), it contrasts sharply with the relative paucity of classical architecture in Chongqing. The rotunda under the central dome seats 4000 during music, opera, and dance performances. In 1981, "the people" to whom the hall is dedicated sacrificed the south and north wings and turned them into the expensive and palatial Chongqing People's Hotel. Every night (7:30-9:30pm) the People's Square becomes a massive dance hall; hundreds of people coordinate dance steps to music blasted over giant loudspeakers. *(Great Hall at 135 Renmin Lu, accessible by bus #103. Open daily 8am-6pm. Y3.)*

SITE OF SINO-AMERICAN SPECIAL TECHNICAL COOPERATION ORGANIZATION (zhōngměi hézùo suǒjí zhōngyíng jiùzhǐ; 中美合作所集钟营旧址). The site is a cluster of former concentration camps. The larger camp, known as **Refuse Pit Prison** (zhāzí dòng; 渣滓洞), once held some 200 Communist Party members for questioning and, later, elimination. The interrogation room, with its faintly bloodstained rope and torture apparatus, has been kept just the way it was, as have some of the prison rooms. On November 27, 1949, after the Communist Party proclaimed the People's Republic of China, the Guomindang commander in charge of Chongqing ordered the massacre of the prisoners. Only a handful of people managed to escape. *(On Gele Mountain, 50min. from the city center. Take bus #215 to Sapingba and change to #210, which runs past the entrance. ☎ 6531 3028 or 6351 0908. Performances enacting interrogation scenes (Y40) are held nightly at 7pm; the more gruesome techniques are left out. Open daily 8:30am-5:30pm. Y15.)*

3 kilometers down the hill is the **Bai Mansion** (báigōngguǎn; 白公馆), which shares the same sordid past, albeit on a smaller scale. Perhaps the best-remembered prisoner is Child Carrot Head, so named because malnutrition caused his head to seem considerably larger than his body. The child entered the prison when he was only months old and was killed at the age of nine. The interrogation room is in a small cave at the back of the mansion. Cool, damp air and manipulative red lights enhance the eeriness of the chamber, which still contains various 50-year-old tools. Another 3-4km away, down the hill back toward the road, is the **Martyrs' Tomb** (lièshì mù; 烈士墓), where a large stone carving commemorates the members of the Communist Party who died at Gele Mountain. A museum here displays photographs, clothes (most bearing marks of suffering), and writings of the deceased, as well as a larger collection of tools used during interrogation sessions.

RED CLIFF VILLAGE (hóngyán cūn; 红岩村). This modest complex was built by members of the Communist Party to serve as their headquarters during the shaky Communist-Nationalist alliance. In the building nearest to the entrance is a small museum that holds revolutionary photographs and essays. Slightly farther on are the southern headquarters and living quarters of the Communist Party and the 8th Route Army. Mao's greatly respected right-hand man, Zhou Enlai, lived here for several years during the war with Japan. Despite Chongqing's scorching summers, the only electric fan around is the one in the room used by Mao, who stayed here for 43 days during his talks with Chiang Kai-shek. The people at Hongyan Village endured hardships that have been held up as an example of resilient revolutionary spirit. *(Take bus #104 from Cangbei Lu (35-45min.); Hongyan village is at the terminus, on the other side of the road. ☎ 6330 1887. No English captions. Open daily 8:30am-5:30pm. Y6.)*

CHAOTIANMEN DOCKS (cháotiānmén; 朝天门). The docks are the gateway to the Yangzi, the starting and ending point for all river cruises. It's worth going to the docks just to take a look at the wide river; with all the pollution and steamers belching smoke, it will simultaneously impress and depress. **Chaotianmen Square** (cháotiānmén guǎngchǎng; 朝天门广场) is a good viewing platform.

NORTHERN HOT SPRINGS (běi wēnquán; 北温泉). These three pools can reputedly cure skin ailments. Those who fear that the water's healing powers may be diluted by the crowds can rent private bath and shower facilities. The grounds of Beiwenquan Park invite aimless wanderings or a trip to the fish aquarium or deep mountain cave, where stalactites, stalagmites, and bats prove amiable company. *(A bus (2hr., Y6) runs daily from the Chongqing Hotel on Xinhuan Lu to Bei Pei; from there, bus #516 (Y1) takes you to the springs. ☎ 6822 2324. Open daily 6am-8pm. Y8.)*

SOUTH HOT SPRINGS (nán wēnquán; 南温泉). This small park offers boat rides, swimming, and a mountain cable car (Y30) in addition to the crowded hot springs. A weekend favorite with locals. *(Take the bus from in front of Jiao Chang Kou (40-50min., Y8) to its terminus at the park entrance. ☎ 6283 8008. Open daily 6am-8pm. Y8.)*

OTHER SIGHTS. **Luohan Temple** (luóhànsì; 罗汉寺) is an unusual temple complex, worth visiting even for those already jaded by too many sacred carvings. Built over 1000 years ago, the temple has been renovated a great deal since. Small statues carved into the wall lead to a large red and yellow painted temple area to the left. To the right are 500 carved and painted terracotta figures, each different, guarded by a large gold Buddha. *(On Minzhu Lu. Open daily 7am-5:30pm. Y2.)*

Pibashan Park (pībāshān gōngyuán; 批杷山公园) stretches between Zhongshan Er Lu and Pibashan Zhenjie, with north and south exits. The central pavilion, provides fantastic views of Chongqing, particularly at night. *(Open daily 7am-10pm. Y5.)* On the path from the road on the south side of the park is the lackluster **Chongqing Museum** (chóngqìng bówùguǎn; 重庆博物馆), housing relics from Chongqing's past. The photo exhibition of modern Chongqing on the first floor is best. All captions are in Chinese. *(Open daily 8:30am-5pm. Y5.)*

NEAR CHONGQING: DAZU 大足

Dazu is one of those one-trick towns, but it's definitely a good trick. Nearby cave art includes more than 60,000 splendid statues dating from the Tang and Song dynasties, the most accessible of which are at Beishan in Dazu and Baoding just outside. Dazu is currently bidding for UNESCO recognition as a World Heritage Site, an honor that it certainly deserves. The town itself, hospitable but not too interesting, is a good base from which to grope your way through the grottoes. In a pinch, Dazu can be done as a daytrip from Chongqing, but staying overnight allows for more comfort.

⚡🛈 ORIENTATION AND PRACTICAL INFORMATION

Dazu is based around the **Lanxi River** (lánxī hé; 濑溪河), 70km east of Chongqing. The bus station is at the southern end of town, and the city center is just north of the river. **Bei Jie** (北街) runs from north to south perpendicular to **Tangxiang Jie** (棠杏街), where the bank and most shops are set. From **Dazu Bus Station** (dàzú qìchē zhàn; 大足汽车站), on Nanhuan Xi Lu, buses go to: Baoding (30min., every 30min. 8am-4pm, Y2); Chengdu (4hr., every 30min. 6:30-9:30am and 2pm, Y51); and Chongqing (2hr., every 30min. 6:30am-5:30pm, Y27). Unmetered **taxis** will take you anywhere in the city for Y3. Going to Baoding will be around Y30-35. Minibuses run between Baoding and Beishan (Y4). The **Bank of China,** 67 Tangxiang Jie, a 5min. walk from Bei Jie, exchanges traveler's checks and currency. (☎4372 4034. Open daily 8am-8pm.) **China Telecom,** 1 block south of the bank, is across a small park. (Open daily 8am-6pm.) The **post office,** on Bei Jie, is in front of the Tancheng Hotel. (Open daily 8am-6pm.)

🏠🍴 ACCOMMODATIONS AND FOOD

Accommodations in Dazu costs more than the offerings merit. As far as food goes, you can get your hands around some hotpot at the food stalls down by the river. **Bei Lu** has a cluster of small point-and-choose restaurants. Beds at the **Dazu County Guesthouse** (dàzú xiàn jīguān zhāodàisuǒ; 大足县机关招待所), 10 Lao Bei Jie, get a little rough in the cheaper rooms. Turn left out of the bus station, cross the bridge, go up Bei Jie, and turn left at the 3rd traffic circle; the hotel is on the left through a small courtyard. (☎4372 2867. Singles Y50, with bath Y150; doubles Y70, with bath Y150; quads Y240.) The **Tangcheng Hotel** (tángchéng jiǔdiàn; 棠城酒家), 75 Bei Jie, is more grit than glitz. Turn left out of the bus station, cross the bridge, and walk up the main road almost to the end. Rooms (all with attached baths) have peeling wallpaper and windows that look out into the hallway. (☎4373 3936. Singles Y20-40, with A/C Y60; doubles and triples Y50/Y70.)

👁 SIGHTS

Dunhuang it's not, but Dazu's Buddhist cave art is quite remarkable.

BEISHAN (běishān; 北山). There are nearly 1000 statues at Beishan, in caves numbered 1 to 290. The first statues here were carved in AD 892 by Wei Junying, a military commander. His work was continued by others over the next 250 years, and reached its present state in 1162. The statues include both literal portraits of Buddhist narratives and abstract portraits of Buddhist philosophies. Look out for Guanyin (#122), the Cave of the Prayer Wheel (#136), and the Peacock King on his lotus throne (#155). Many of the caves have a central figure surrounded by hundreds of smaller statues, each wearing a different expression. This is an enjoyable place to wander through, though less spectacular than Baoding; if you will be going to both, go here first. The **White Pagoda Temple** (duǒbǎotǎ; 多宝塔) is atop the hill to the right. To get here, follow Bei Jie away from the river to the end, go around the traffic circle, and continue in the same direction along Beishan Lu; the entrance is a 20-minute walk away. *(White minibuses run between Beishan and Baoding (Y4) and leave whenever they are full. Motorbikes can also give you a ride. Open daily 8am-6pm. Signs all in English. Y40, students Y20; a double ticket for Beishan and Baoding Y85.)*

BAODING (bǎodǐng; 宝顶). The art at Baoding is really something else. The carvings were produced under the supervision of Zhao Zhifang, a very dedicated monk, in AD 1174-1252. The nearly 10,000 carvings constitute one of Tantric Buddhism's most deeply venerated sites. According to the blurb on the Chinese sign, "the carvings tell people the truth of life, arouse their sentiments, captivate them with Buddhism and blessings and happiness, or warn them against afterlife misfortunes and sufferings." The statues are eerily well preserved, with much of the original paintwork intact and still vibrant. The various niches are built in a circle; the most impressive is the Ritual Site of Liu Benzun (a lay Buddhist of the late Tang

SICHUAN

dynasty) and a huge set of carvings covering a rock face, depicting a series of different narratives (cave 21). Outside this area is a small pavilion, the **Tower of Ten Thousand Years** (wànnián lóu; 万年楼). Farther along, beckoning those with grotto-fried brains, is the Shou Temple, reaching up into the hill above (Y4). *(Take the bus or a taxi (Y20) from Dazu. Open daily 8am-6:30pm. Y50, students Y25.)*

THREE GORGES 三峡

Above colored cloudscape the White Emperor at dawn,
Ten thousand *li* to Jiangling is but a single day's jaunt.
While the cry of apes from atop twin banks cannot be halted,
The light raft has sped past mountains ten grand.
—Tang poet Li Bai

From the White Emperor City (near Chongqing) to Jiangling (near Yichang), the mighty Yangzi rolls through 192km of death-defying rapids and odd-shaped peaks known as the Three Gorges (Sanxia). The Three Gorges are studded with historical sites and have been immortalized in poetry and literature, captivating the imagination of everyone from Li Bai to Bill Gates. In a decade's time, this ancient landmark will disappear off the face of the earth. Contemporary China's obsession with development at all costs and traditional China's infatuation of undertaking outlandishly ambitious projects have fused into the project of constructing a hydroelectric mega-dam due to be completed in 2009 (see p. 648). When finished, the Three Gorges Dam will be one of two manmade structures visible from the moon (the other, of course, is the Great Wall).

The cruise down the Three Gorges allows tourists to experience mass tourist culture up close. Many tourists come away feeling distinctly disappointed by the experience. Certain segments of the trip are impressive, but most portions feel like an ordinary (albeit long) boat ride. Contrived, manmade attractions and the souvenir feeding frenzy that awaits at each stop may temper the sense of wonder that the trip is meant to inspire.

Most tourists make the downstream journey from Chongqing and disembark at either Yichang (see p. 400) or Wuhan (see p. 394) in Hubei province; some cruises go as far as Jiujiang in Jiangxi. The **Official Port Ticket Office** (chóngqìng gǎng shòupiào chù; 重庆港售票处; ☎ 6384 2861) is perhaps the best place to get a ticket. Most reputable companies have a booth here and all share the same fixed prices. Business is monitored by CQG ("Chongqing Port") officials, who can be distinguished by blue shirts, black pants/skirts, and small red pins. Questions or concerns can be addressed at the CQG desks in the back and far side of the terminal.

As always, be on the lookout for con artists. If it seems too good to be true, it probably is. One way to avoid unpleasant scams is to travel individually, bypassing tour groups and commission fees, and purchase admission tickets upon arrival at the attraction. The cruise tickets are computer-issued and about the same size as the computer-issued train tickets. Be sure the price and class printed on the ticket corresponds to the full list price. Some tourists fall victim to English-speaking con artists who promise all-inclusive private or small-group tours led by English-speaking guides only to be herded on to the big boats once the money is handed over. While higher-end cruises with genuinely small tours do exist, they cost considerably more (Y1600-3000) and often fall below expectations.

There are several different classes of **berths:** 1st class (2 beds, A/C, TV, and bath), 2nd class (2-4 beds, A/C, TV, and bath on some boats), 3rd class (6-8 beds, A/C, TV, and washbasin on some boats), 4th class (8-12 beds), and 5th class (any space you can find on the deck). Facilities and room configurations vary somewhat by boat. Posted prices are as follows: to **Yichang** (1st class Y929, 2nd class Y466, 3rd class Y220, 4th class Y150, 5th class Y106) and **Wuhan** (1st class Y1369, 2nd class Y686, 3rd class Y322, 4th class Y231, 5th class Y153). Most departures are 5-8pm; the dock number and boat name are printed on the ticket. Some companies also run non-tour boats to **Shanghai** (6 days; 1st class Y1887, 2nd class Y1031, 3rd class Y480, 4th class Y339, 5th class Y229).

FENGDU 丰都

If there is any truth behind Fengdu's nickname, "City of Ghosts" (guǐ chéng; 鬼城), then the grand Yangzi must be the River Styx. The surrounding riverbank heights are fabled to be the abode of demonic spirits, and this tourist town feeds off the legend with an eerie, Halloween-esque atmosphere. Once they open the floodgates to create the enormous Three Gorges Reservoir, however, the entire city of Fengdu will really be an underwater ghost town, leaving only "Mt. Olympus" (Ming Mountain) unscathed. Most evening-departing cruises allow passengers three hours in this town, usually beginning at around 6 or 7am on the first full day. From the docks, follow the crowd of visor-wearing tourists and hawkers straight ahead; if arriving at Dock No. 4, head left along **Dongmen Lu** (东门路) and **Beimen Lu** (北门路) before turning right on **Zhongshan Lu** (中山路).

MING MOUNTAIN (míng shān; 名山). Said to be the hilltop capital of a ghost kingdom, Ming Mountain now sees enough activity to wake the dead—and empty your wallet. The mountain's ghost-ornamented temples and the garish **God Palace** (guǐguó shéngōng; 鬼国神宫) are supplemented by palm readers (Y60), picture takers (Y10), tea houses (Y20), and trinket sellers (Y10-100). The suspension bridge leading to the mountain is where a soul's destination in the afterlife, be it nirvana or the abyss of hell, is said to be determined. On festival days, the demons go marching in, as the temple complex overflows with goblins, ogres, and horse-headed monsters. *(Open daily 6am-6pm. Y55. Chairlift Y15.)*

SHIBAOZHAI (shíbǎozhài; 石宝寨). Three and a half hours downstream from Fengdu, the "Stone Treasure Block" of Shibaozhai (proclaiming itself the "Pearl on the Yangzi"), is an impressive 12-storied, red-walled, green-eaved pagoda built against a vertical cliff. Most tour boats stop here for only one hour to allow passengers to scramble up the ramp, through the vendor-crammed streets, and up the "Stairs to the Clouds" of the 56m Ming-era tower dedicated to the Jade Emperor, the omnipotent heavenly ruler of folk religion. Legend has it that the "hillside block" is the elaborately colored jade chop left behind by the goddess Nü Wa when she mended the broken sky. *(Open daily 8:30am-4pm. Y15.)*

FENGJIE 丰节

Guarding the entrance to Qutang Gorge at the river's confluence with Plum Creek is Fengjie, a small town laden with history. Two thousand-year-old coffins, discovered in the exposed valley wall, confirm that Fengjie was the capital of the Kui Kingdom of the Ba people, ancestors of today's Tujia minority. Kuizhou, the Tang-era name of Fengjie, was a hot spot for itinerant Tang poets like Li Bai, Du Fu, and Lu You, who all braved the gorges. But Fengjie's greatest claim to fame is White Emperor City and the Three Kingdoms episodes that happened there.

White Emperor City (bái dì chéng; 白帝城) was built during the Han dynasty by Gongsun Shu, then ruler of Sichuan. One day some white gas escaping from a well appeared to him as a white imperial dragon, which he took as a propitious sign for him to assume the title of White Emperor. Oddly enough, none of the statues in the temple are dedicated to him and it is not for Gong that the city is renowned. About 450 years ago, *Romance of the Three Kingdoms* buffs tossed out Gong's altar and replaced it with one for their hero, Liu Bei. According to the novel, in AD 221 Liu, King of Shu, launched a 750,000-man invasion against a former ally, the Kingdom of Wu, to avenge King Sun Quan's decapitation of Liu's blood brother, Guan Yu. Against the better judgment of his advisor Zhuge Liang, Liu stationed his enormous army in the forests of Yichang, which Wu's troops promptly set ablaze. Liu Bei escaped thanks to his brilliant advisor Zhuge, who thought of the **Eight Diagram Formation** (bā guà zhèn; 八卦阵), a labyrinth created out of mist-enshrouded boulders around Fengjie that trapped pursuing Wu troops. Scenes in White Emperor City temples depict the mortally wounded Liu offering his kingdom to Zhuge Liang and the loyal marquis refusing and handing the lineage down to Liu's young son, Liu Chan. The site also houses various steles and calligraphy amid the bamboo gardens. *(Open daily with no set admission hours. Y40, chairlift Y15.)*

SICHUAN

Many boats drop anchor in Fengjie for the night before entering the Three Gorges the next morning. If you have more time, explore the Fengjie environs, which are loaded with unusual geological formations. The 500m wide, 600m deep crater-like funnel called the **Heavenly Pit** (xiāotiān zhài; 小天寨) leads to a myriad caverns fed by underground rivers, the **Black Wind Cave** (hēifēngdòng; 黑风洞), the **Maze River** (mígōng hé; 迷宫河), and the **Mysterious Big Crevice** (dàdìfèng; 大地缝), all south of Fengjie.

LITTLE THREE GORGES

The more intimate Little Three Gorges (xiǎo sānxiá; 小三峡) is a good contrast to the austere majesty and historic gravity of its counterpart. The most expensive portion of the trip, it is also the most rewarding. Unless the water levels are too high or the weather too frightful, most cruises park for six-hour-long small tours in the town of Wushan, which meets the Daning River right before Wu Gorge. More time allows for visits to river caves and the archaeological site where a two-million-year-old ape man was unearthed, or even hunting. Up the Daning and its Madu River tributary are the Longmen, Bawu, and Dicui gorges, which are known collectively as the Little Three Gorges. The charming Daning river turns into a splendid stream as it spindles through lush, uninhabited limestone gorges. While monkeys call and egrets coo in the dense forests high above, boatsmen propel wooden *sampan* by thrusting bamboo poles into the clear creek bed full of smooth, iridescent pebbles. Unfortunately, it will all be lost to the flood of 2009. *(Tickets bought directly from the boat steward can be fully refunded without difficulty if conditions preclude the tour; tour group members may be stuck with a partial refund or substitutes of other sights. Y100.)*

QUTANG GORGE

Just east of Fengjie, Qutang Gorge (qūtáng xiá; 瞿塘峡), full of hidden shoals, is the first and narrowest of the Three Gorges, measuring 50m at its narrowest point. The most spectacular stretch of the gorge is the 8km segment flanked by knife-cut vertical cliffs on both sides. The north bank, called the **Red Armor Cliff,** is named after a battalion outfitted with red armor from the Spring and Autumn Period. The south bank, called the **White Salt Cliffs,** still has remnants of an ancient plankway, a treacherous road built by placing wooden planks into grooves in the cliff. During the Spring and Autumn Period, soldiers were stationed on the peak. Vividly named formations such as Phoenix Drinking Spring, Upside-down Monk, and Rhinoceros Gazing at the Moon gaze over the river.

WU GORGE

Wu Gorge (wū xiá; 巫峡), the "gorge of witches," is generally considered to be the most enchanting and bewitching of the Three Gorges. The 2000m high canyon walls block out the sun's rays, and the dappled sunlight and misty showers give the area a surreal feel. The western section of the 40km-long gorge is called Gold-Helmet Silver-Armor Gorge, and the eastern section, the Iron Coffin Gorge. Wushan, towering over the river, has 12 peaks, six on either side, which are thought to be ossified offsprings of Wangmu Niang Niang, wife of the Jade Emperor and Empress of the Heavens.

XILING GORGE

The longest and last of the Three Gorges, the 120km-long Xiling Gorge (xīlíng xiá; 西陵峡) is no lazy homestretch. Once infamous as a ship graveyard, most of this catastrophe canyon's hidden shoals have been blasted clear. But landslides continue to smash villages, and navigating down the treacherous 42km section that includes the Art-of-War, Cow-Liver-Horse-Lung (supposedly named after the cliff-side imagery), and Yellow Cow and Yellow Cat Gorges used to be a heart-stopping affair. Past the **Nanjin Gate** is the placid Gezhou Dam Lake.

FRANKLY MY DEAR, I DO GIVE A DAM At

Sandouping, before the Nanjin Gate and some 40km from Yichang is the **Three Gorges Project** (sānxiá gōngchéng; 三峡工程), the world's largest dam construction site, an overwhelming (and depressing) sight. The sheer scale of the project dwarfs bulldozers, drills, and other mechanical monstrosities, making them look like mere sandbox Tonka toys manned by some 60,000 action figures. When completed in 2009, this 200m high, 2000m wide Great Wall across the Yangzi and its 28 superturbines will harness more energy than 18 nuclear power plants. The price tag? Only US$17 billion, according to official figures.

When the final stage of this super-project kicks in less than a decade from now, the Three Gorges as we know it will vanish forever, along with the homes of nearly 2 million people and some 8000 unexcavated archeological sites. Proponents envision railway links, rapid regional development, and better living standards for residents around the pristine lake and flood control downriver. Furthermore, the creation of this deep-water reservoir along the Yangzi will allow ocean-going freighters to penetrate as far upstream as Chongqing, more than 2000km inland from the East China Sea. Naysayers warn of dams clogged by soil erosion, reservoirs foaming with water pollution, inadequate compensation for dislocated residents, mountains of debt forcing corporations into bankruptcy, endangered species facing extinction, tectonic pressures causing rock slides and earthquakes, and even increased susceptibility to foreign nuclear missiles.

After decades of debates and countless rounds of expert testimony, the Three Gorges Dam, often described as the pet project of former Premier and Department of Hydropower Secretary Li Peng, is pushing full steam ahead. Although the pragmatic wing of the Politburo led by Zhu Rongji remains cool to the dam, most analysts believe that too much money has already been spent for the project to stop.

Tours of the site include transportation, a guide, and visits to a couple of lookout points providing views of the cranes, boats, workers, and the river itself. Markings on cliffs indicate flood levels; 135m above the current river is the predicted water level in 2003, and 175m above is where the final flood should level off upon project completion. Tours leave from Gezhou Hotel (gézhōu bà bīnguǎn) daily at 9am and 2pm (Y45).

SICHUAN

THE NORTHWEST

Vast, sparsely populated, and blanketed by dune-swept deserts, plateaus, mountains, and inland salt seas, China's Northwest is often dismissed as an inhospitable backwater frontier. Ningxia, Gansu, Qinghai, and Xinjiang have historically lagged behind the coast in development. But a long history of contact with "outsiders" along the famed Silk Roads left a lasting legacy; imperial tombs, Buddhist grottoes, city ruins, and desert mummies offer a glimpse of past wonders. Now the region, and Xinjiang in particular, serves as a gateway to Central Asia and Pakistan. A trip in the Northwest today often appears hauntingly surreal: against the flat monotone brown of the Taklimakan Desert, the eerie fluorescent orange of the masked highway sweepers, the piles of sparkling green glass raked to the side of the road, even the mottled reds and blues of passing vehicles seem brighter and more vivid than usual. The area is home to amazing geographic diversity: within an hour or two, the landscape can change from desert to rock mountains to alpine forest to snow-capped mountain peaks. A colorful collage of faces, hats, and costumes surfaces in the area's Uighur bazaars, Tibetan monasteries, Mongol yurts, and Hui mosques, showcasing the region's cultural diversity. The Northwest is also a fantastic place to delve into the great and unexplored outdoors, be it by sheepskin-rafting down the Yellow River, departing on a camel expedition through the vast desert, or hiking through awesome (and unexplored) alpine valleys.

HIGHLIGHTS OF THE NORTHWEST

FOLLOWING THE SILK ROAD along its fabled route, with stops in **Xian** (p. 214), **Zhongwei** (p. 659), **Jiayuguan** (p. 677), **Turpan** (p. 698), and **Kuqa** (p. 704). For more information, see the Silk Road itinerary, p. 6.

CAVING IN to the charms of Dunhuang's **Mogao** (p. 686), Guyuan's **Xumishan** (p. 662), and Tianshui's **Maijishan** (p. 675) **Grottoes.**

TIBETAN TREASURES in **Xiahe** (p. 669) and **Matisi** (p. 682), near Zhangye.

ALL-NATURAL GOODNESS at Tianshan's "Heavenly Pool" (**Tianchi,** p. 694) and in the remote Yili River Valley near **Yining** (p. 695).

SHOPPING UNTIL YOUR DONKEY DROPS at Kashgar's Sunday Bazaar (p. 711).

NINGXIA 宁夏

Wedged between Shaanxi and Gansu and capped by the Great Wall, the tiny Ningxia Hui Autonomous Region is roughly the size of the Republic of Ireland. Once the heart of the great Western Xia empire, Ningxia has been something of an orphan state in recent times, swallowed by Gansu in 1914 and declared a nationalist province in 1928. After the Long March, Red armies found the impoverished local Hui farmers and herders ideal for guerrilla recruitment, and incorporated Ningxia into the Shaanxi-Gansu-Ningxia Soviet Area. Military rule continued after 1949, and only in 1958 did the autonomous region come into existence.

Although much of the region is covered with arid hills and desert dunes, Ningxia relies on an extensive Yellow River irrigation system (first constructed during the Qin-Han period) to sustain agriculture. From meager natural resources, local peasants scratch out fields of corn, wheat, millet, and sorghum visible for miles along country roads. Ningxia herdsmen boast their very own stock of high-cashmere-wool-yielding, fast-growing, and tender-tasting Zhongwei sheep.

A hodgepodge of civilizations has emerged along the banks of the great river—living testament to the province's strategic position along the Silk Routes. While the majority of the more than five million people who inhabit the region are Han

NORTHWEST

Chinese, a full third are Hui, with pockets of Tibetan, Mongolian, and Manchu scattered throughout. Descendents of Muslim traders from the Middle East, the Hui, or "Chinese Mohammedans," have left a firm imprint upon the architectural and religious landscape and to this day carry on their merchant tradition all over the country. For travelers to northwestern China, Ningxia is a transitional region where Han influence melts into the Islamic culture farther west.

YINCHUAN 银川   ☎0951

One of ancient China's more dynamic outposts of civilization, Yinchuan has seen its fair share of conquerors swoop down from the surrounding grasslands to invade the city. With the life-giving waters of the Yellow River to the east, the protective ranges of the Helan Mountains to the west, and the natural beauty of the city itself, it is no wonder that Han, Tangut, and Mongol all have vied for dominance over this cultural center.

The city's recent surge in investment and infrastructure has made it one of the fastest growing places in China—although it still has a lot of catching up to do. These days, Yinchuan is a city of lights—multicolored bulbs wrap around every lamppost. Certain avenues are blocked off from traffic and open to strolling pedestrians; even the street barriers glow with an ethereal neon pulse. Yinchuan's beautiful city parks come replete with fishing ponds, alabaster bridges, traditional pagodas, and the locals decked out in their finest: from the grizzled old brownskinned man in a white cap playing "Go" on the corner to young girls dressed up in Japanese-style neon kiddie outfits. Old men chat alongside fishermen, while lovers seek privacy in the recessed corners of the parks. Genuinely friendly hawkers, plentiful accommodations, and an interesting balance of Hui and Han cultures combine to make Yinchuan a pleasant two- or three-day sojourn.

▛ TRANSPORTATION

Airplanes: Yinchuan's new **Minhang Yinchuan Airport** (mínháng yínchuān jīchǎng; 民航银川机场; ☎691 2218) is 25km east of the Old Town. Frequent minibuses make the 30min. trip to the Old Town center (Y40). Shuttle buses (Y15) also run to the **CAAC ticket office** (☎691 3688), near the South Gate. Walk south on Yuhuangge Nan Jie for 10min.; it's on the left. Open M-F 8am-6pm; in winter 8:30am-5:30pm. To: **Beijing** (1-3 per day, Y870); **Chengdu** (M, W, and F-Sa; Y810); **Dunhuang** (Su-M, W, and F; Y710); **Guangzhou** (Tu, F, and Su, Y1510); **Shanghai** (1 per day, Y1080); and **Xian** (1-4 per day, Y430).

Trains: The **Yinchuan Train Station** (yínchuān huǒchē zhàn; 银川火车站; ☎504 6271) is in the eastern quarter of the New Town, inconvenient since all the sights, night spots, and parks are in the Old Town. The train schedules posted and sold in the station are deceptively incomplete—ask before assuming there is no convenient train to your next destination. To: **Beijing** (22hr., 2 per day, Y165-301); **Lanzhou** (8hr., 2 per day, Y46-70); **Pingliang** (9hr., 1 per day, Y34-64); **Shanghai** (48hr., 1 per day, Y126-261); **Xian** (17hr., Y55-122); **Xining** (14hr., Y160); and **Zhongwei** (3½hr., 2 per day, Y13).

Buses: The **Yinchuan Long-distance Bus Station** (yínchuān chángtú qìchē zhàn; 银川长途汽车站; ☎603 1571) is in the southeastern corner of the Old Town, on the east side of South Gate Square. To: **Beijing** (24hr., 1 sleeper per day, Y180); **Lanzhou** (11hr.; 4 non-sleepers per day, Y38; 1 sleeper per day, Y55-60); **Taiyuan** (17hr., 1 sleeper per day, Y114); **Xian** (16hr., 4 sleepers per day, Y104); and **Zhongwei** (4hr., every 25min. 7:55am-5:30pm, Y13).

Local Transportation: Buses **#1, 2, 4, 17,** and **18** make the 15min. commute between the New Town and the Old Town (Y1). Bus **#1** leaves from the train station in the New Town and heads east on Yinxin Bei Lu, passing the Old Drum Tower and Yuhuang Pavilion on Jiefang Xi Jie. Bus **#2** departs from across from the train station and heads east on Yinxin Nan Lu past the Western Pagoda before terminating at the Old Town's South Gate, next to the long-distance bus station. Buses generally depart every 30min.

The Northwest

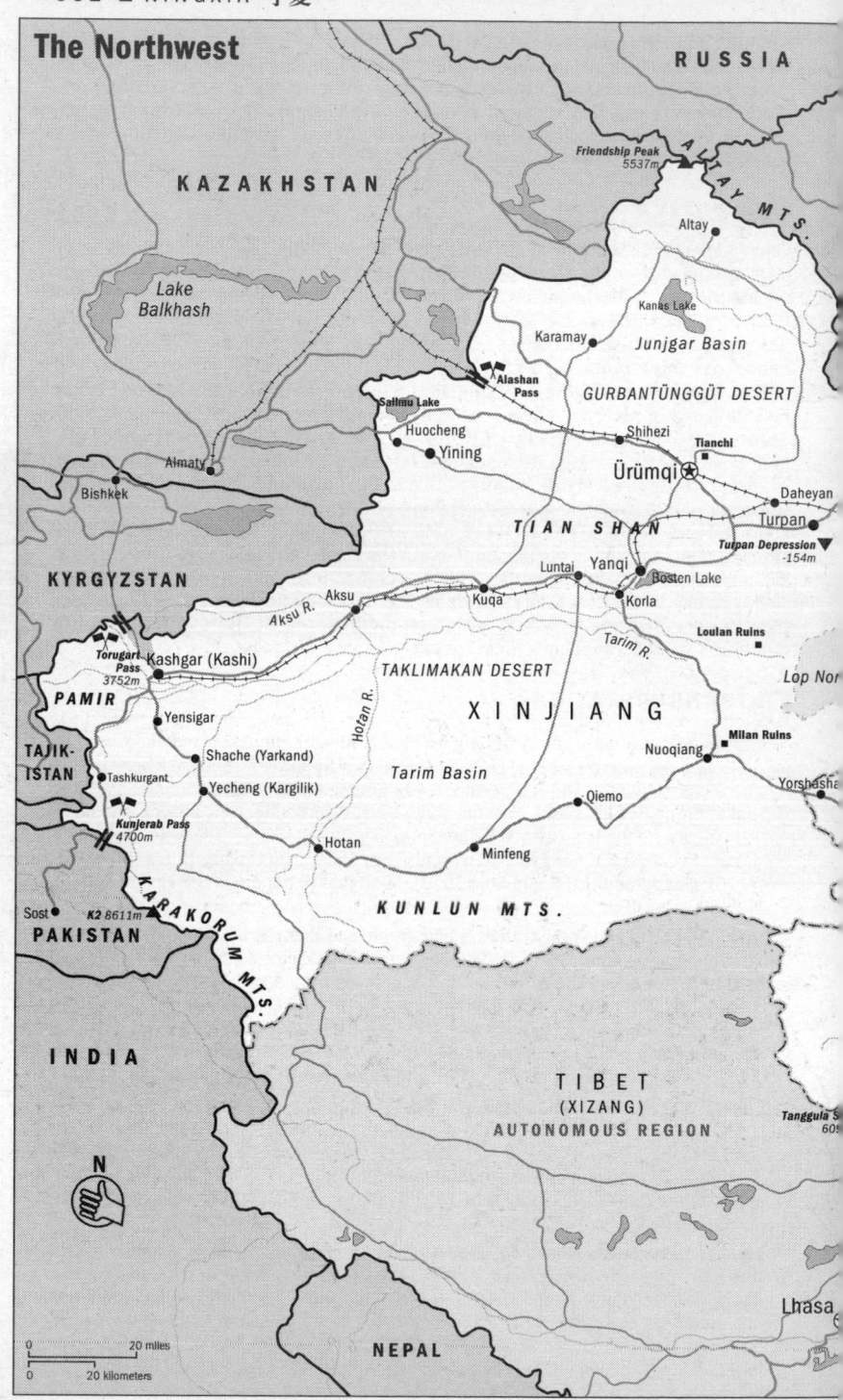

RUSSIA

KAZAKHSTAN

Friendship Peak
5537m

Altay

Lake
Balkhash

Kanas Lake

Karamay

Junjgar Basin

GURBANTÜNGGÜT DESERT

Alashan
Pass

Sailmu Lake

Huocheng

Shihezi

Tianchi

Yining

Ürümqi ⊛

Almaty

Daheyan

Bishkek

Turpan

TIAN SHAN

Turpan Depression ▼
-154m

KYRGYZSTAN

Luntai

Yanqi

Aksu R.

Aksu

Bosten Lake

Kuqa

Korla

Loulan Ruins ■

Torugart
Pass
3752m

Kashgar (Kashi)

Tarim R.

Lop Nor

PAMIR

Yensigar

TAKLIMAKAN DESERT

XINJIANG

Hotan R.

TAJIK-
ISTAN

Tashkurgant

Shache (Yarkand)

Milan Ruins ■

Nuoqiang

Yecheng (Kargilik)

Tarim Basin

Qiemo

Yorshasha

Kunjerab Pass
4700m

Hotan

Minfeng

Sost

K2 8611m

KUNLUN MTS.

PAKISTAN

KARAKORUM MTS.

INDIA

TIBET
(XIZANG)
AUTONOMOUS REGION

Tanggula S
60

N

Lhasa

0   20 miles
0   20 kilometers

NEPAL

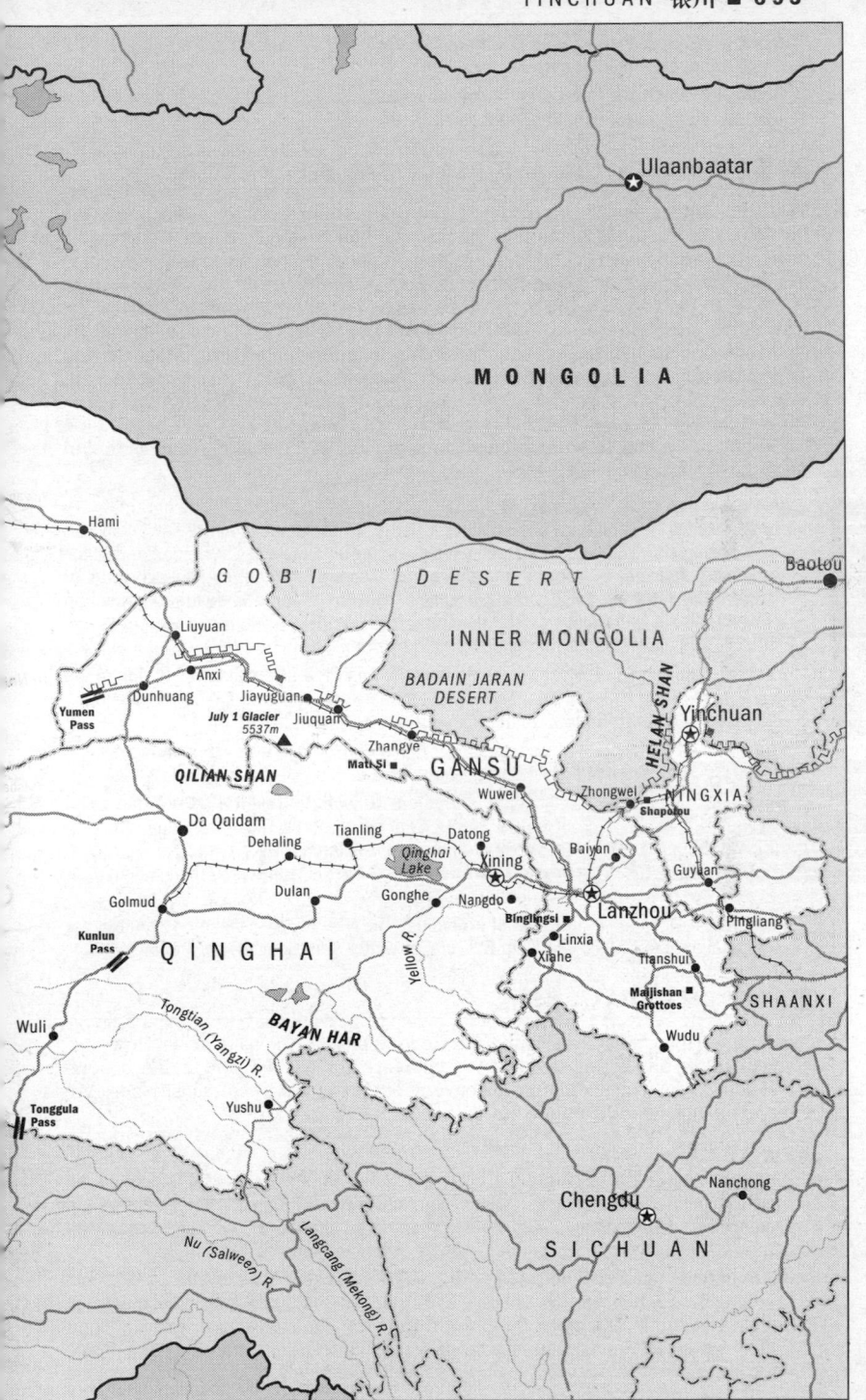

Taxis: Most trips, such as from downtown Old Town to the train station, cost about Y15. Trips are rarely metered; bargain beforehand.

Bikes: The **Yinchuan Hotel** (see **Accommodations,** p. 655) has the best deal on bike rentals. Y3 for 4hr., each additional hr. Y0.5.

ORIENTATION AND PRACTICAL INFORMATION

Yinchuan is divided into two distinct communities approximately 11km apart: the **Old Town** (lǎo chéng; 老城) in the east and the **New Town** (xīn chéng; 新城) in the west. The two towns are connected by three main roads. **Yinxin Nan Lu** (银新南路) is sandwiched between **Yinxin Bei Lu** (银新北路) to the north and **Changcheng Lu** (长城路) to the south. While the vast majority of accommodations options in the New Town are centered around **Tiedong Bei Lu** (铁东北路) and **Xincheng Xi Jie** (新城西街), hotels and sights are more liberally interspersed throughout the Old Town. The Old Town's bustling main road, **Jiefang Xi Jie** (解放西街), is an excellent starting point in the search for housing and culinary and visual delights. Jiefang Xi Jie and **Jiefang Dong Jie** (解放东街) intersect with **Minzu Jie** (民族街) to form the backbone of the Old Town. The **Drum Tower** (gǔ lóu; 鼓楼) is at the intersection of **Gulou Jie** (鼓楼街) and Jiefang Jie.

Travel Agency: CTS, 116 Jiefang Xi Jie, Ste. 301 (☎504 8006, 504 5555, or 504 3720; email nxcits@126.com), on the southwest corner of the intersection of Fenghuang Jie and Jiefang Xi Jie, marked by a small red sign squeezed between 2 store fronts. English-speaking staff member. Maps and brochures available. Organizes package tours of **Sand Lake** (shā hú; 沙湖), the Xia tombs, and other famous destinations within Ningxia. Also a good resource for planning group excursions along the Silk Road and into Qinghai. Open M-F 8:30am-noon and 2:30-6pm.

Bank of China: On Jiefang Xi Jie, a 10min. walk west of the Yinchuan Hotel, on the left hand side of the street. Exchanges traveler's checks at counters #7 and 8. Open M-F 9am-noon and 2:30-6pm; in winter 9am-noon and 2-5:30pm.

PSB: On the northern end of Yuhuangge Bei Jie (☎691 5080). **Visa extensions** available M-F 2:30-6pm. Open M-F 8am-6pm.

Hospitals: Yinchuan's best hospital is **Medical University Hospital** (yī xuéyuàn fùshǔ yīyuàn; 医学院附属医院; ☎409 1488), 2km south of the Old Town. Within the city, the **Yinchuan People's Hospital** (yínchuān shì dìyī rénmín yīyuàn; 银川市第一人民医院; ☎602 5831) and the **Autonomous Region Hospital** (zìzhì qū yīyuàn; 自治区医院; ☎206 3134) are other options.

Post Office: Yinchuan's central **post office** is in the New Town, to the left as you exit the train station. EMS. Open M-F 8am-6:30pm; in winter 8am-6pm. **Postal Code:** 750001.

ACCOMMODATIONS

In the New Town, most hotels are near Tiedong Lu and Xinchang Xi Jie. However, since all of the interesting sights in Yinchuan are in the Old Town, finding accommodations there is generally more convenient. In the Old Town, most places are located on or around Jiefang Xi Jie.

NEW TOWN

Taoyuan Hotel (táoyuán bīnguǎn; 桃园宾馆), 2 Tiedong Bei Jie (☎306 6485), on the left, just before Xincheng Xi Jie. The Taoyuan has newly painted walls and carpeting and large, bright baths. Iron-studded leather doors and headboards give added character. No A/C. Deposit Y100. Y25 per bed, with TV, bath, and breakfast Y50.

Alashan Hotel (ālāshàn fàndiàn; 阿拉善饭店), 51 Xincheng Xi Jie (☎306 6086). From Tiedong Bei Lu, turn right on Xincheng Xi Jie; the hotel is on the right corner. Alashan caters more to businessmen than budget travelers. The surreal new "ethnic village" offers a chance to experience "traditional" Mongolian living in a modern setting. Inside a massive greenhouse, guests swelter in paneled yurts with a tiny living room, bath and

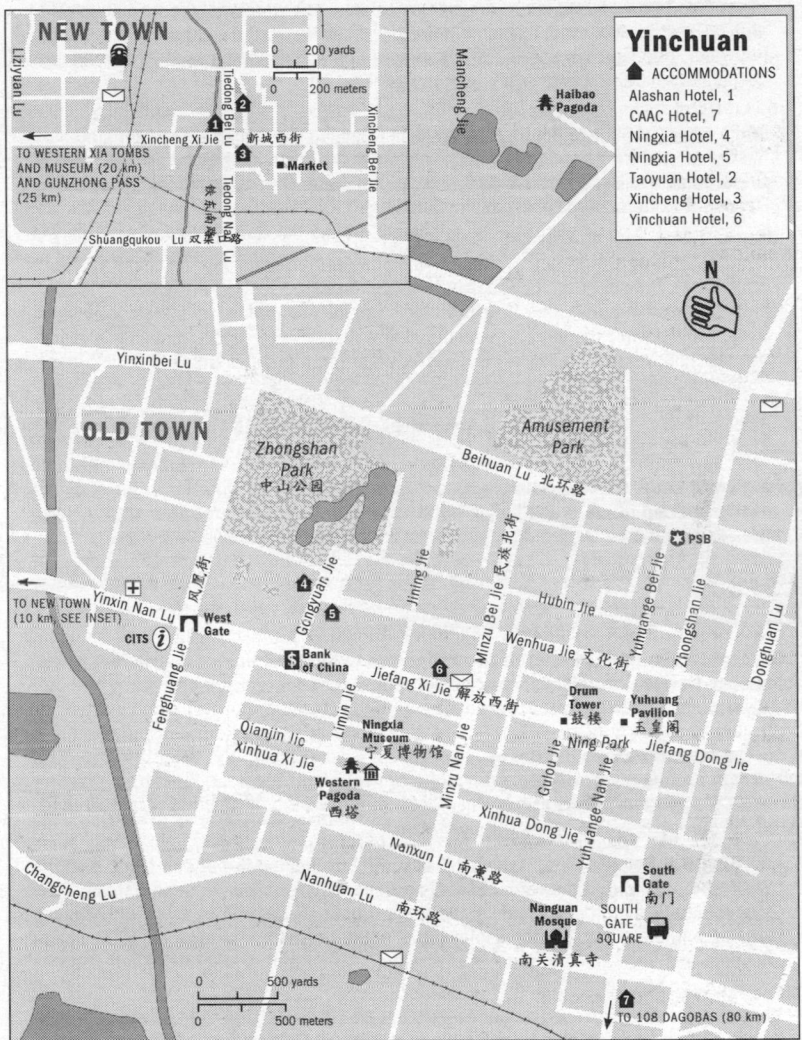

NEW TOWN

Liziyuan Lu

TO WESTERN XIA TOMBS AND MUSEUM (20 km) AND GUNZHONG PASS (25 km)

Tiedong Bei Lu

Xincheng Xi Jie 新城西街

Tiedong Nan Lu

■ Market

Shuangqukou Lu 双渠口路

Xincheng Bei Jie

Manchengi Jie

Haibao Pagoda

Yinchuan
ACCOMMODATIONS
Alashan Hotel, 1
CAAC Hotel, 7
Ningxia Hotel, 4
Ningxia Hotel, 5
Taoyuan Hotel, 2
Xincheng Hotel, 3
Yinchuan Hotel, 6

N

OLD TOWN

Yinxinbei Lu

Zhongshan Park 中山公园

Amusement Park

Beihuan Lu 北环路

PSB

TO NEW TOWN (10 km, SEE INSET)

Yinxin Nan Lu

凤凰街

West Gate

CITS

Gongyuan Jie

Jining Jie

Minzu Bei Jie 民族北街

Hubin Jie

Yuhuange Bei Jie

Zhongshan Jie

Donghuan Lu

Bank of China

Jiefang Xi Jie 解放西街

Wenhua Jie 文化街

Qianjin Jie

Fenghuang Jie

Limin Jie

Minzu Nan Jie

Ningxia Museum 宁夏博物馆

Drum Tower 鼓楼

Yuhuang Pavilion 玉皇阁

Ning Park

Jiefang Dong Jie

Xinhua Xi Jie

Western Pagoda 西塔

Gulou Jie

Yuhuange Nan Jie

Xinhua Dong Jie

Changcheng Lu

Nanxun Lu 南薫路

Nanhuan Lu 南环路

South Gate 南门

SOUTH GATE SQUARE

Nanguan Mosque 南关清真寺

TO 108 DAGOBAS (80 km)

NORTHWEST

shower, and double bed, all for Y108. Alashan also offers standard rooms with wooden floors, clean towels, 24hr. hot water, and TV. 10% student discount. Singles and triples with A/C and breakfast Y168; doubles Y100.

Xincheng Hotel (xīnchéng fàndiàn; 新城饭店; ☎306 6010), on the corner of Tiedong Lu and Xincheng Xi Jie, opposite the Alashan. A 10min. taxi ride from the station. Aging, but with tough-to-beat prices. Hot water 7am-11pm. Deposit is twice room cost. Doubles Y43-60, with bath Y76 (ask for the double with living room); triples Y66.

OLD TOWN

Yinchuan Hotel (yínchuān fàndiàn; 银川饭店), 17 Jiefang Xi Jie (☎602 3053), on the left just after Jiangning Jie, if coming from the New Town train station. Although the Yinchuan has poorly lit and less than sanitary communal bathrooms, the rooms are clean and the staff speaks some English. On-site travel service (Y20 ticket commission). 24hr. hot water. Deposit Y10. Lockout 1-5am; knock and someone should let you in. Singles Y80; doubles Y50-98, with A/C Y108; triples Y75-120.

CAAC Hotel (mínháng dàshà; 民航大厦; ☎691 3688), right of the CAAC ticket office, at the corner of Shengli Bei Jie and Nanhuan Dong Lu. Immaculate Western bathrooms, freshly painted walls, and thick wood trimming make this hotel a good escape from the world outside. All rooms have A/C and TV. Hot water 6am-1am. Breakfast included. Deposit is twice room cost. Doubles Y168.

Ningxia Hotel (níngxià bīnguǎn; 宁夏宾馆; ☎504 5131, ext. 3611). From Jiefang Xi Jie, turn right on Gongyuan Jie, then right again onto Wenhua Jie; the Ningxia Hotel is 5min. down the street on the left. Not to be confused with the luxury hotel of the same name across the street, this Ningxia Hotel is one of Yinchuan's cheapest accommodations. You get what you pay for: peeling yellow walls, concrete floors, rusting bathrooms, but still relatively clean rooms. Deposit is twice room cost. Doubles Y50, with larger bath and living room Y70.

Ningxia Hotel (níngxià bīnguǎn; 宁夏宾馆; 3 Gongyuan Jie (☎504 5131, ext. 2901), opposite its cheaper counterpart. Medium-sized rooms come equipped with refrigerators, new carpets, sparkling bathrooms, wood closets, and TVs. The building wraps around a beautiful park dotted with ponds, bridges, and mini-gazebos. Philosophize over a hot cup of joe in the coffee bar as you plan your next expedition into the city. Breakfast included. Deposit Y250. 10% student discount. Doubles Y178-398.

🍴 FOOD

While not renowned for its culinary specialties, Yinchuan has many good, clean, and cheap **restaurants** scattered around town. Establishments along **Jiefang Xi Jie, Yuhuangge Bei Jie,** and **Xinhua Dong Jie** serve up local specialties like grabbed lamb meat and lamb kebabs (yángròu chuān; 羊肉串); Yuhuangge Bei Jie in particular has a large selection of restaurants and side-street fruit markets. Simple fried rice with egg and tomatoes for flavor and protein is also a popular standby. Plentiful ice cream stands are a wonderful relief from the summer heat. Be sure to try the *meiguo da jiaoban* (American Big Foot), a delicious jab at most tourists' oversized clod-hoppers. The toe is the best part.

Lao Bing Hot Pot (lǎo bīng huǒguō; 老兵火锅), on Jiefang Xi Jie, one block past the West Gate fountain at the corner of Xi Qiao Xiang. When walking west on Jiefang Xi Jie, the restaurant is on the right side of the street. True to its name, Lao Bing ("old soldier") houses warheads and guns in display cases in the back. Choose from over 20 kinds of noodles and vegetables to dunk in a yin-yang shaped hotpot with two different brews (Y10 all you can eat). Open daily 11am-9:30pm.

Xinglongshui Restaurant (xìnglóngshuǐ fànguǎn; 兴隆水饭馆), 112 Limin Jie, just south of Jiefang Xi Jie. This 5-table restaurant is a great option for breakfast or lunch. A big bowl of steaming *jiaozi* with local vegetables costs Y6. Open daily 10am-8pm.

Nationalities Restaurant (mínzú cāntīng; 民族餐厅), on Jiefang Xi Jie, just 2 doors from the Yinchuan Hotel. This Muslim restaurant offers a range of Yinchuan specialty dishes. Try one of the many lamb dishes made with locally grown peppers (Y15 for 2 people, including a frothy mug of Ningxia beer). Breakfast dishes include dumplings, porridge, and soybean milk. Open daily 6:30am-10pm.

🎵 ENTERTAINMENT

Night markets abound (open approx. 7pm-midnight) in Yinchuan. There is a large market at the very end of Gulou Nan Jie; walk south away from the Drum Tower and enter under the rainbow-colored arches. In **Ning Park** (níng yuán; 宁园), just south of the Yuhuang Pavilion, locals fish, play cards, or sip tea under the leafy boughs of the low-hanging trees and the gazebos. Just south of Zhongshan Park, and most easily reached by walking west on Wenhua Xi Lu, is the lively and festive **Guangming Square** (guāngmíng guǎngchǎng; 光明广场), centered around a lit fountain. People of all ages congregate on the steps of the stadium and opposite the People's Congress Building, enjoying the cool and breezy Yinchuan evenings. Unfortunately, the fountain is shut off around 10:30pm and everyone heads home.

■ SIGHTS

OLD TOWN

YUHUANG PAVILION (yùhuáng gé; 玉皇阁). Built over 450 years ago in much the same architectural style as the South Gate, the Yuhuang Pavilion is a great starting point for exploring the city. Breezy and cool, the second floor contains a painting and calligraphy gallery highlighting local artists. Climb to the third floor to see various metal and earthenware artifacts documenting Ningxia's history, as well as a beautiful long scroll with both Arabic and Chinese *kaisu* style script. A historical survey of the area, beginning with the mysterious Xia dynasty, is displayed in Mandarin. *(One block east of the Drum Tower. Open daily 8:30-11am and 2-5pm. Y2.)*

NANGUAN MOSQUE (nánguān qīngzhēn sì; 南关清真寺). Easily visited on the way to or from the 108 Dagobas (see p. 658), this magnificent mosque is a welcome architectural respite from typical Chinese temples. Erected in the late Ming dynasty, the mosque was rebuilt in 1981 after its destruction during the Cultural Revolution. The main dome is over 25m tall, surrounded by four turquoise domes (representing the four sects of Islam). The sound of running and splashing water greets visitors in the main courtyard, and pheasants, peacocks, and parakeets chatter in the aviary that wraps around the garden. A small museum on the right displays pictures of Mecca during Ramadan and of Muslim leaders who have paid homage at this mosque. *(A 15min. walk south of the Yuhuang Pavilion on Yuhuangge Nan Jie, at Nanhuan Dong Lu. Be considerate when peering in the main prayer chamber; it is an active place of worship. Open daily 8:30am-8pm. Y8.)*

SOUTH GATE (nán mén; 南门). The short climb up to the South Gate is rewarded by a cool breeze, hot tea, and a great view of Yinchuan's South Square. Built from 1004 to 1007 during the Song dynasty, Yinchuan's city wall was nearly destroyed in a 1739 earthquake. The wall was again damaged during the chaos of the 1911 Revolution and rebuilt in 1917. The surrounding walls were torn down in 1953 and only the South Gate remains, although that, too, is under construction. The tunnel running through the center of the structure has also changed with the times, now sporting a mini-market with hawkers and trinkets in every corner. Stairs are on the north side, and the woman who runs the shop on top can recite the entire history of the gate—in Mandarin only. *(Y2 during daylight hours.)*

HAIBAO PAGODA TEMPLE (hǎibǎo tǎ sì; 海宝塔寺). Built in the early 5th century and reinforced in the late 18th century, this nine-story pagoda is part of an active temple complex just beyond the north edge of the Old Town. On the climb to the top, contemplate the extensive graffiti scrawled in Chinese along the walls. Once up there, view the city fading into farmland through windows that face the four compass points. *(By bicycle, ride north on Jinning Bei Jie; the street becomes a dirt road after Beihuan Xi Lu. The pagoda is clearly visible along the entire length of this street, about a 20min. ride. Open daily sunrise-sunset. Y5.)*

NINGXIA MUSEUM (níngxià bówùguǎn; 宁夏博物馆). This regional museum has an extensive collection of Northern Zhou and Western Xia objects. Dusty and poorly maintained, the museum is still worth a quick look. In the center of the courtyard is the **Western Pagoda,** which offers a commanding view of the city after an exhausting 12-story climb. *(Entrance to the courtyard on Jinning Nan Jie. Walk west along Xinhua Xi Jie and take a left onto Jinning Nan Jie; the entrance is on the right. Open Tu-Su 9am-5pm; in winter 9am-noon and 2-5pm. Museum admission Y2; pagoda Y5.)*

NORTHWEST

NEAR YINCHUAN

Yinchuan's best sights are beyond the city limits and most easily accessible by taxi. The Western Xia Tombs and Museum and Gunzhong Pass can be visited together in a day of sightseeing; take a *miandi* taxi from the Old Town (Y150 round-trip) or take bus #2 from the depot on Xinhua Jie, about four blocks west of Gulou Jie, to the last stop, Huagongchang (化工场). From here the taxi fare to the Xia tombs and Gunzhong Pass should be no more than Y100 round-trip.

WESTERN XIA TOMBS (xī xià wánglíng; 西夏王陵). Undoubtedly the primary reason to visit Yinchuan, the Western Xia Tombs pay silent and surreal tribute to an empire rumored to have killed Genghis Khan with poison-tipped arrows only to be obliterated in 1227 by vengeful Mongol hordes. Initially a tributary state of the Chinese Song dynasty, the Tangut tribes (a Qiang-Tibetan people) revolted in 1038 and established a kingdom consisting of Han, Tibetans, Uighurs, and even Nestorian Christians from Central Asia. The Western Xia triumph over the Seljuk Turks halted Islam's advance into China; their armies may actually have been the fabled armies of Prester John that supposedly assisted the Crusader cause. The tombs of the Western Xia kings are scattered across the rocky plains: the nine large earth mounds are said to house the remains of the nine emperors, while the 200 smaller structures spanning the horizon may have been erected for various nobles. When visiting the tombs, don't confine yourself to the museum and the one fenced-off, easily accessible tomb. Wander out among the scrub desert scenery, and discover the less visited tombs on the horizon—they are well worth the walk. *(20km west of the New Town, about 30min. Open daily sunrise-sunset. Y20, students Y10.)*

WESTERN XIA MUSEUM (xī xià bówùguǎn; 西夏博物馆). A short distance from the largest tombs lies this worthwhile exhibition of Western Xia culture. The first floor displays well-preserved relics of the Western Xia, ranging from 800-year-old leather shoes to imperial seals. On the second floor, massive horse, ox, and dog figures in bronze, gold, and stone maintain their ancient vigilance, encased in modern glass displays. There is also a beautiful collection of Buddhist icon paintings, some flaking off in cloudlike patterns, as well as *sutra* scrolls written in Chinese and Arabic. The museum is a good warm-up, but the real treat are the tombs themselves and the barren Helan Mountains rising in the distance. *(Open daily sunrise-sunset. Admission included in tombs ticket.)*

GUNZHONG PASS (gǔnzhōng kǒu; 滚钟口). Consisting of several paved trails that wind along the bleeding-red foothills of the Helan Shan mountain range, this hiking reserve offers spectacular views of the Yellow River Plain. The greener rock faces near the pass recede into stark clay and sand farther south toward the Western Xia Tombs. There are also possibilities for longer day or multiple-day hikes into the craggy peaks looming high above, some rising over 5000 ft. *(Lodging is available year-round at the small hostel just above the front gate to the left for Y10 per bed or Y30 for a double room. Ask at the front gate for information. Open daily sunrise-sunset. Y5.)*

108 DAGOBAS (qíngtóngxiá yībǎilíngbā tǎ; 青铜峡一百零八塔). Eighty kilometers south of Yinchuan, the 108 Dagobas are a testament to good intentions gone awry. Despite the impressive scenery and attractive garden, the dagobas (Buddhist commemorative shrines) themselves are unfortunate victims of modern repair. Whereas the pictures of the old dagobas do make one wonder, the current renditions, replete with gaudy coloring and now-rusting tin roofs, strip all mystery from the silent figures. Arranged in a pyramidal schema, the dagobas' original function is still unknown. *(The fastest way to reach the dagobas is to take a taxi (Y60-100) to the dam, 3.5km from the site. Then walk left along the east bank of the river until you reach the ferry. The ferry or a smaller boat should cost around Y10. Bus #153 is rumored to leave South Gate in the Old Town at 10am and 2pm in the direction of the dagobas, but its existence is still in dispute. Open daily sunrise-sunset. Y5.)*

ZHONGWEI 中卫   ☎0953

A mere 160km southwest of Yinchuan, Zhongwei has the low-key atmosphere of a beach town—minus the beach. Instead, visitors can surf sand dunes, raft the Yellow River aboard traditional sheepskin rafts, explore the Tengger Desert atop occasionally cranky camels, and learn about the science of desert reclamation. All within an easy 40-minute minibus or train ride from town, such activities are a welcome relief from the monotony of small rural villages in central Ningxia. Life in Zhongwei is enjoyed at a markedly slower pace than in most Chinese cities, evidenced by the multitude of card games littering the sidewalks, gossip beneath the tree-lined avenues, and idle markets that fill the town every Thursday. The relaxed attitude has seemingly affected the pickpockets as well—they lack the speed and subtlety of their east coast counterparts, but beware nonetheless.

◪▧ ORIENTATION AND PRACTICAL INFORMATION

Navigation in Zhongwei is made simple by a grid-like layout. From the **Drum Tower** (gǔ lóu; 鼓楼) in the city center, **Bei Dajie** (北大街), **Nan Dajie** (南大街), **Dong Dajie** (东大街), and **Xi Dajie** (西大街) mark the northern, southern, eastern, and western neighborhoods of town, respectively. The train station is at the northern end of Bei Dajie, and the bus station is at the eastern end of Dong Dajie. Xi Dajie is lined with China Telecom, the PSB, a good hotel, Internet access, and the hospital. Taxis and bike rentals are unnecessary, as Zhongwei's small size puts all restaurants, shops, and points of interest within a 20-minute walk.

Trains: Zhongwei Train Station (zhōngwèi huǒchē zhàn; 中卫火车站), on Bei Dajie, a 15min. walk north of the Drum Tower. Taking the train from Zhongwei is often more convenient than the bus. To: **Beijing** (28hr., 10:05pm, Y179); **Guyuan** (4½hr., 5 per day 12:10am-5:58pm, Y14-17); **Lanzhou** (6hr., 4 per day 1-7:52am, Y18-47); **Ürümqi** (20hr., 9 and 11am, Y105-122); and **Yinchuan** (2½-3hr., 7 per day, Y11-25).

Buses: Zhongwei Long-distance Bus Station (zhōngwèi chángtú qìchē zhàn; 中卫长途汽车站; ☎701 2775), on Dong Dajie, a 15min. walk east of the Drum Tower. Schedules and routing often depend on traveler demand, and many trips involve a stop and change of bus. To **Yinchuan** (4hr., approx. every 30min., Y14). Buses may also run to **Guyuan** and **Lanzhou**.

Travel Agency: Ningxia Shapotou Travel Service (níngxià shāpōtóu lǚxíngshè; 宁夏沙坡头旅行社), 2 Bei Dajie (☎701 2961), in the Yixing Hotel. Group tours to Shapotou, as well as Yellow River rafting tours (Y120 for 1hr.) and day- to week-long Tengger Desert camping expeditions (Y250-380). English-speaking guides and staff.

Bank of China: 1 Dong Dajie, next to the Drum Tower. Exchanges traveler's checks. Open M-F 8am-6:30pm; in winter 8am-6pm; year-round Su 9:30am-4:30pm.

PSB: Opposite the post office (☎701 2914, ext. 8000 or 8030). Open daily 8am-noon and 2:30-6:30pm.

Hospital: The **hospital** (☎701 1632) is on Xi Dajie, just past the Shangye Hostel.

Pharmacy: North Street Chemist's Shop (běi jiē yào diàn; 北街药店), just south of the train station, on the east side. Western medicines available. Open daily 8am-9:30pm.

Phones: China Telecom, on the corner of Xi Dajie and Zhongshan Jie, just before the PSB. IDD available. Open daily 8am-7pm.

Internet Access: Computer World (diànnǎo dàshìjiè; 电脑大世界; ☎703 0086), on the left side of Xi Dajie when you walk west from the Drum Tower, around the corner from China Telecom. Y8 per hr.

Post Office: The new **post office** is in a large glass-faced building on Xi Dajie, a 15min. walk west of the Drum Tower on the left side of the road. EMS available. Open daily 8am-7pm. **Postal Code:** 751700.

COFFEE, TEA, "AN MO" Some hotels in China's western provinces have recently added another service, one that before was only offered by the occasional three- or four-star establishment: the all-encompassing "massage." While in no way discouraged by most male guests, and indeed good business sense for many hotels, many of the eager solicitors are frankly a bit overzealous. Some tenants may appreciate phone calls saying *"yao bu yao xiaojie?"* (Do you want a girl?) or *"yao bu yao an mo?"* (Do you want a massage?), but calls made every 30 minutes from 10pm to 5am push the limits of any man's patience. Simply unplug the phone (responding with jokes, anger, disgust, silence, and threats have all proved fruitless) or have a woman answer; the "masseuses" are deterred by a female voice.

Reintensified efforts have yielded a new, more subtle approach. Given only a thin bedspread by hotel maids, guests may welcome a late night phone call offering more bedding. Upon opening the door, however, guests may find hotel "personnel" quite insistent upon offering more than just an extra blanket or two.

ACCOMMODATIONS AND FOOD

A few good dining options in Zhongwei are several excellent noodle shops lining Bei Dajie, stalls in the night market on Shangye Nan Jie, and the sparkling restaurant in the Yixing Hotel. Be sure to try *haoyou niurou* (beef with onions, mushrooms, and brown sauce; 耗油牛肉; Y10), *rishi wudongmian* (a pasta-like local dish; 日式乌冬面; Y5), and *haozi mian* (spicy noodle soup; 蒿子面; Y3). Lamb dishes are also popular. In the summer, apricots and other fresh fruit abound.

Railway Hotel (zhōngtiě bīnguǎn; 中铁宾馆; ☎703 1948). Take a quick left out of the train station; look for the hotel's green-colored glass facade. All rooms are newly renovated and spotlessly tiled, with 20in. TVs. Breakfast included. Singles with bath and living room Y120; doubles with bath Y80; triples with bath Y84; quads Y60.

Zhongwei Hotel (zhōngwèi bīnguǎn; 中卫宾馆), 33 Xi Dajie. Part of the Zhongwei government complex, this hotel's clean, bright, quiet rooms overlook a small flower garden. Breakfast included. Double rooms with bath, telephone, and fan Y84-128; triples Y90; luxury rooms Y190-388.

Yixing Hotel (yìxìng dàjiǔdiàn; 逸兴大酒店; ☎701 7666), in a large, modern building next to the Drum Tower. An excellent restaurant on the 2nd floor, a travel service, and a business center are just the beginning. Rooms (most with bath and fan) are spacious and clean. Deposit Y500. Singles Y80-150; doubles Y60-120, with A/C Y280 and up; triples Y75-140; quads Y80.

Zhongwei Hotel (zhōngwèi fàndiàn; 中卫饭店; ☎701 2219), at the intersection of Bei Dajie and Changcheng Dong Jie. With questionably clean sheets and a distinctly odorous dorm atmosphere, prices here are optimistic. The common bath is a bit of a trough, and before 8pm, showers are out back. At least the rooms have mosquito screens. Singles Y35; doubles Y50, with bath Y70; triples Y52/Y96; quads Y52.

SIGHTS

While the must-see Gao Temple is an easy five-minute walk north of the Drum Tower, the equally fascinating Shapotou sand dunes lie 22km west of the city. Nonetheless, both can comfortably be seen in a daytrip, giving travelers time for a lazy, enjoyable dinner.

SHAPOTOU (shāpōtóu; 沙坡头). Sandwiched between the stark and arid Tengger Desert and the loess-filled Yellow River, Shapotou is Zhongwei's prime getaway destination. Worth the trip for its natural beauty alone, Shapotou offers unique experiences in a truly fantastic setting. A haven for outdoor enthusiasts, Shapotou boasts camel rides into the desert (short trip Y20; 2-day camel excursion to the Inner Mongolian border, including 5hr. non-stop camel journeys and yurt accom-

TEMPLE KNOW-HOW Although many tourists quickly pass by Buddhist temples, pausing only to take a brief look at the statue inside the altar before heading on their way, participating in the simple ritual of bowing and lighting incense allows a deeper experience. Taking part in this ritual in no way implies your conversion to Buddhism or the belief in the deity that stands before you; the act of humbling oneself by bowing and kindling feelings of spirituality implies respect for yourself and for the world. As you approach the altar, take three sticks of incense (xiāng; 香) or accept three from the attendant monk, and light them in the candle in the altar. Rather than blowing on the sticks, wave them gently to extinguish the flame. Then move behind the cushions to the front, grasp the incense sticks with two hands, and raise them to the level of your forehead. Pause for a moment, then lower the sticks to about chin level, pausing again before moving them in toward your chest. Bow and then place the sticks upright into the box of ashes on the front of the temple altar.

modations Y150-200), rafting in inflated sheepskin rafts down the Yellow River (Y30), and six-hour motorboat cruises to a giant waterwheel (Y180). Perhaps the most exciting adventure is the toboggan ride (Y15) down the face of a 100m sand dune at the entrance.

For those seeking to escape the packs of red-hatted tourist groups that normally overrun the small resort's riverbanks, ride the chairlift back up to the top of the sand cliff and walk along a small hiking path that meanders through flowering shrubs and patterned dunes as it skirts the high bank of the Yellow River below. From here, one can see the latticework of planted straw that attempts to reclaim land from the encroaching desert dunes. To learn more, visit the free **Desert Research Center,** across the train tracks from the Shapotou resort entrance, where shrubs and trees are made ready for transplanting to sensitive areas along the desert's edge. *(From Zhongwei, the 3pm Lanzhou-bound train stops at Shapotou station. Alternatively, take a taxi (35min., round-trip Y100) from Zhongwei; bargain hard. Upon arrival, go to the resort ticket booth and plan activities with director Dong Jianzhong (☎ 769 8053); the Shapotou staff is flexible and accommodating. No tours are necessary. Except for the dune ride, all activities are down at the riverbank. Y15.)*

GAO TEMPLE (gāo miào; 高庙). Built between AD 1403 and 1424, the Gao Temple is an intriguing architectural and spiritual conglomeration, housing Confucian, Buddhist, and even Christian religious figures. The temple complex covers an impressive 4100m^2 of tall, spiraling towers and over 200 rooms. Elegant open-air walkways seamlessly connect multiple pavilions, allowing visitors to seemingly float from level to level. Each feature is painstakingly unique: intricate latticework, carved faces on the end of each roofing tile, flowers engraved upon boughs, and magnificent paintings and calligraphy on every partition make the entire structure an object of appreciation in itself.

Swallows make their nests in the soaring eaves, darting through even the narrowest of the temple's passages. Take time to wander through the string of small prayer rooms, each containing a Buddhist deity and wall murals illustrating legends and facets of the Buddhist path. For an extra Y5, go underground and receive an eye-opening lesson on the numerous forms of punishment waiting for you in the netherworld. Black lights, neon paint, styrofoam, and eerie 80s music are the backdrop to "Zhongwei's High Temple of Hell." The 18 jails display unlucky souls in various stages of decapitation, disembowelment, and some acts that words simply fail to convey adequately. *(On Bei Dajie, across from the Zhongwei Hotel. Open daily sunrise-sunset. Y5.)*

GUYUAN 固原 ☎ 0954

A drab, dusty small town in southern Ningxia, Guyuan nevertheless serves as a convenient staging post for a trip to the impressive Xumishan Grottoes, 55km to the northwest. While the Guyuan Museum contains a surprising array of artifacts, the town itself is of little interest.

✚🛈 ORIENTATION AND PRACTICAL INFORMATION

Guyuan's 24hr. **train station** is 3km east of the town center, an eight-minute ride (Y3) on the ever-plentiful *bengbeng che* (motorized three-wheeled cabs). Trains go to: Lanzhou (10hr., 10:20pm, Y29); Xian (9hr.; 3:30am, 2:05, and 9:40pm; Y34); and Yinchuan (6hr., 1:15 and 6:20am, Y27). On the western end of **Wenhua Jie** (文化街) near downtown, the **bus station** is about a five-minute walk west of the town's major north-south axis, **Zhongshan Jie** (中山街). Buses go to: Lanzhou (8hr., 1 per day, Y27); Xian (10hr., 9:30am and 6:30pm, Y35-66); and Yinchuan (4½-7hr., 8:50am and 6:30pm, Y27-40). The **Bank of China** is on Zhongshan Jie just before the Zhongyin Hotel. (Open daily 8am-noon and 2-5:30pm.) The **hospital** is directly across the street from the Dianli Hotel. **Internet access** (Y5 per hr.) is available in the post office branch next to the main building. Guyuan's newly renovated **post office** is on Zhongshan Nan Jie, at Wenhua Jie. (Open daily 8am-6pm.) The **postal code** is 756000.

▨🏠 ACCOMMODATIONS AND FOOD

Guyuan has only a few food and accommodations options, most clustered around the bus station and along Zhongshan Jie. Hotel restaurants tend to more reliable than the small one-room street restaurants that are found throughout the town.

▨ **Dianli Hotel** (diànlì bīnguǎn; 电力宾馆), 219 Renmin Jie (☎203 2192). Turn right from the bus station onto Wenhua Jie, walk through the intersection, and take the first right; the hotel is on the right. While the glass doors, massive reception area, and army of doormen may scare budget backpackers away, the Dianli is actually the best value in town, with 24hr. hot water, scrubbed communal bathrooms, and new TVs. Deposit Y100-200. Lockout 2am, but knock and the night guard will let you in. 3-bed dorms Y20-25; singles with bath Y380; doubles Y70, with bath Y120.

Plum Garden Hotel (méi yuán fàndiàn; 梅园饭店), ☎203 9788), near the bus station. From the bus station, turn right and walk 50 ft.; the hotel is on the left. Though the hotel is conveniently located and offers bright rooms with TVs, clean sheets, and spotless concrete floors, the Meiyuan's stained and molding common bathroom troughs still leave something to be desired. Hot water 6:30-8am and 8:30-11:30pm. 4-bed dorms Y4; 3-bed dorms Y12; doubles with bath Y56-120.

Guyuan Hotel (gùyuán bīnguǎn; 固原宾馆), 94 Zhengfu Jie (☎203 2479). Walk left out of the bus station, make the first left, and continue to Zhengfu Jie. Make a right; the hotel is on the left side of the street. The common bathrooms are clean, although the smell won't attract anyone—except maybe the flies. Additional 6% Guyuan "education" fee goes toward improving local schools. Deposit Y100-200. Singles with bath Y180; doubles Y60, with bath Y120-180; triples Y75/120; quads with bath Y100.

Shangye Hostel (shāngyè zhāodàisuǒ; 商业招待所), right out of the bus station, across the first intersection. This hostel has clean sheets, white walls, and a nice view of the town's main thoroughfare. The bathrooms are rusting and stained, and the hallways have a few flies, but at this price, who's complaining? Doubles with bath Y14-28.

👁 SIGHTS

Guyuan's main claim to fame is the Xumishan Grottoes. For those with extra time, the Guyuan Museum and Guyuan Garden are worth a visit.

XUMISHAN GROTTOES (xūmíshān shíkū; 须弥山石窟). Beautiful bleeding red dust mountains, dry red waterfalls coursing over baked rock caves, and a slow march of dark green pines advancing up crumbling ridges herald the approach to the grottoes. Children from the small villages nearby follow visitors up and down the paths, often saying nothing and gazing into your eyes with a kind of blankness seen in holy men. Cuckoos call; the echo bounces off the narrow gulleys. All the while, weather-worn Buddhas and *bodhisattvas*, sometimes just shrouded figures of stone with an outstretched hand in mantra, seem to fade back into the rock from which they were carved.

Xumishan is a surreal collection of eight cliff art sites, 70 Buddhist statues, 130 Buddhist relief carvings, and 350 caverns. The rulers of the Northern Wei (AD 386-534) and Northern Zhou (AD 557-584) dynasties embraced Buddhism and began construction of Xumishan, Longmen (Luoyang), Mogao (Dunhuang), and Yungang (Datong) grottoes. The most commanding of the statues, a 22m high Tang-era Maitreya Buddha, maintains silent watch over the riverbed below. Locals attribute the Buddha's incredible condition to an ancient covering that has since eroded and been replaced with a subtle arch protecting it from the sun and rain. Caves 21, 25, 30, and 31, all containing buddhas of various forms, are of particular interest; caves 24 and 32 are notable for their prayer columns. *(Direct buses from Guyuan bus station to Xumishan leave irregularly. From around 7:30-11am, frequent minibuses (Y3.5) from Guyuan travel in the direction of Xumishan, stopping at a dirt road about 16km away. From here, local taxis go the rest of the way; Y20 round-trip, Y5 per hr. waiting time. Minibuses return to Guyuan until late evening. Walking around Xumishan can take a good 4-5hr., and the sun is relentless, so bring sunscreen and a wide-brimmed hat. Open daily sunrise-sunset. Y20, students Y10.)*

GUYUAN MUSEUM (gùyuán bówùguǎn; 固原博物馆). Housing a spectacular set of displays on the county's amazingly rich history, the museum holds artifacts ranging from the New Stone Period to the Qin dynasty, as well as an electronic map depicting the Silk Road routes. Bronze, clay, jade, and iron works mingle with ancient fishing weapons, musical instruments, and stone axes. The exhibits are a living record of the many minority cultures that have swept through Ningxia, with explanations of everything from the belligerent to the divine: battle techniques, staple crops, burial rites, and important religions. Also of interest is a statue of a Northern Zhou General, Li Xian, complete with a small troop of miniature guardian soldiers, not a few of which are inexplicably female. Although the tour guide may speak only a little English, the tour is still recommended; all posted signs and explanations are in Chinese. *(On the southern end of Zhengfu Jie. Open Tu-Sa 8am-noon and 2:30-6pm. Y20, students Y10.)*

GUYUAN GARDEN (gùyuán gōngyuán; 固原公园). This park is centered around a dusty ridge that overlooks the town below and the inviting vastness of the Helan Mountains in the distance. A once lush pond is now dried up, and the garden on the park map has withered away, leaving a walkway and pavilion hovering over bare stone-littered fields. Southern Ningxia at its essence, here there are no colors but the gray-green handful of trees digging shallow roots into the baked earth and the ubiquitous tan-brown of dust particles floating across the city. *(On Zhengfu Jie, a 3min. walk north of the Guyuan Museum. Y1.)*

GANSU 甘肃

Reaching westward like a greedy finger of land, cordoned between the Qilian and Zoulan mountain ranges to the south and the Gobi to the north, Gansu province is a crossroads of Han, Mongolian, Tibetan, and Turkic influences. Chinese domination of the region began in the 2nd century BC, when Han Emperor Wudi sent two million colonists to the northwest. Chinese hegemony alternated with interludes of Xiongnu (Hun), Tibetan, Uighur, and Mongol control. The lush foothills in the southwest corner of the province are home to a sizeable Tibetan contingent, centered around the enchanting town of Xiahe. West of the fertile Yellow River valley surrounding Lanzhou, the flat and featureless Hexi corridor is laced with a string of Silk Road outposts protected by the Great Wall. Oases like Dunhuang and Jiayuguan are a practice in paradox, with their leafy avenues, poplar-lined parks, and fresh springs, all hemmed in by relentless desert. Corridor highlights include the spectacular Buddhist art of the Mogao Grottoes and the awe-inspiring Ming Great Wall fort. Farther west, pebble flats give way to dunes, and the Han and Hui presence fades into Uighur and Yughur culture.

Though still lagging far behind the booming seaboard in standard of living, Gansu has begun to feel the winds of development. Highway construction and mining investment have left the ancient trade routes abuzz with oil tanker trucks. Ambitions soar higher than the passenger jets that shuttle between Lanzhou, Jiayuguan, and Dunhuang; the national space center in Jiuquan plans to put the first Chinese into space very soon. Truly, Gansu is blasting off into the 21st century.

LANZHOU 兰州 ☎0931

Although it sits smack in the geographical center of the country, Lanzhou was long considered a peripheral outpost of China. It flourished as a pit stop along the Silk Road and was elevated to the status of provincial capital in 1666, but Lanzhou didn't really shed its backwater reputation until the post-1949 Marxist-Maoist makeover transformed it into a center for petrochemical refining, bauxite smelting, and atomic energy, as well as an important stop on the Sino-Soviet Highway.

Massive skyscrapers, wide boulevards, numerous shopping centers, and fantastic restaurants now complement the stark natural scenery of the surrounding mountains and the Yellow River. Despite being the world's most heavily polluted city, Lanzhou pleasantly surprises many visitors. Its most popular attraction, the cave art at Bingling Temple, is actually a few hours away, but the bustling outdoor cafes, locally brewed beer, impressive provincial museum, and rapidly developing western district also merit exploration. The city also is a gateway to the Tibetan village of Xiahe. With an ever-expanding skyline, present-day Lanzhou seeks to reap the benefits of its fortuitous location: a mere outpost no longer, Lanzhou is one of the last bastions of modern conveniences en route to China's otherwise underdeveloped western frontier.

⌐ TRANSPORTATION

Travel insurance, compulsory for travel within Gansu, costs Y30 and is valid for 14 days. It can be purchased at any hotel, travel agency, or bus station; large hotels and travel agencies also often sell it for Y3 per day. Buy it before you leave—it is generally more expensive if purchased en route.

Airplanes: Lanzhou Airport (lánzhōu jīchǎng; 兰州机场), 73km north of the city, is a major regional hub. Buses (Y25) shuttle between the airport and the **China Northwest Airlines ticket office** (xīběi hángkōng gōngsi shòupiào chù; 西北航空公司售票处), 512 Donggang Xi Lu (24hr. ☎882 1964; free ticket delivery ☎883 9064). Turn left at the Legend Hotel and walk 5min.; the office is on the right. Open daily 8am-9pm. To: **Beijing** (3 per day, Y1070); **Chengdu** (1-2 per day, Y750); **Dunhuang** (1-3 per day, Y820); **Guangzhou** (1 per day, Y1510); **Jiayuguan** (W and F-Sa, Y730); **Shanghai** (1 per day, Y1400); **Ürümqi** (Sa-M and W-Th, Y1040); and **Xian** (1-3 per day, Y430).

Trains: Lanzhou Train Station (lánzhōu huǒchē zhàn; 兰州火车站; ☎882 2142), at the southern end of Tianshui Lu, at Pingliang Lu, in Lanzhou's eastern district. Tickets sold 2-5 days in advance. Buying tickets (especially hard sleepers) for trains not originating in Lanzhou is extremely difficult, particularly in summer. To: **Beijing** (25-35hr., 9:45am and 4:30pm, Y390); **Guangzhou** (35hr., 3:55pm, Y493); **Shanghai** (31hr., 7:20am and 9:02pm, Y409); **Ürümqi** (32hr., 9:30pm, Y225); and **Xian** (13hr., 6:18pm, Y175).

Buses: East Station (lánzhōu dōng zhàn; 兰州东站; ☎841 8411), on Pingliang Lu, a 20min. walk north of the train station. To: **Dunhuang** (24hr., 2:30 and 6pm, Y84-167); **Jiayuguan** (17hr., 3:30pm, Y56); **Pingliang** (4½-8hr., every 30min. 6:30am-7:30pm, Y32-43.5); **Ürümqi** (38hr., 6pm, Y100-140); **Xian** (16hr., 6:30pm, Y180); and **Yinchuan** (12hr., 3 per day 7am-7pm, Y60.4). The **West Station** (lánzhōu xī zhàn; 兰州西站; ☎233 3285), on Xijin Dong Lu, has buses to: **Linxia** (3hr., every 30min. 6:30am-7pm, Y12); **Pingliang** (6hr., every 30min. 7am-7pm, Y19-32); **Xiahe** (6hr., 6:30 and 7:30am, Y19-27); **Xining** (5hr., every 30min. 9am-7pm, Y20); and **Yongjing** (2½hr., 2 per day, Y6). There is a much smaller bus station on Pingliang Lu across from the train station, but departures are sporadic and prices erratic.

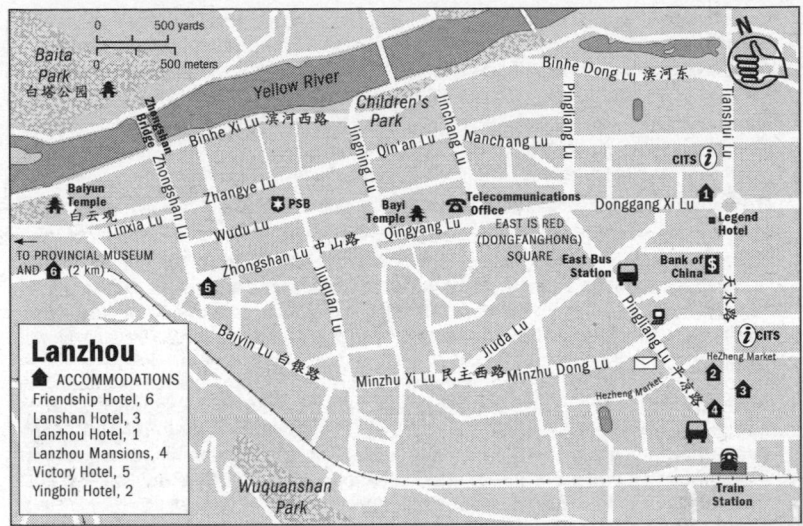

Lanzhou

🏠 **ACCOMMODATIONS**
Friendship Hotel, 6
Lanshan Hotel, 3
Lanzhou Hotel, 1
Lanzhou Mansions, 4
Victory Hotel, 5
Yingbin Hotel, 2

Local Transportation: The extensive public **bus** system makes the cross-town commute almost enjoyable. Fare Y0.4-1.1. Buses **#1, 7, 10,** and **31** travel north from the train station, while bus **#6** heads northwest. Bus #1 goes from the train station to the Lanzhou Hotel and the Legend Hotel, at the intersection of Donggang Xi Lu and Tianshui Lu, before proceeding westward along Zhongshan Lu. To head east of town, take bus #6 to the intersection of Pingliang Lu and Minzhu Dong Lu and change to bus **#33**. From the same junction, change to bus **#34** to get to Zhongshan Bridge.

✳️🔋 ORIENTATION AND PRACTICAL INFORMATION

On the southern shores of the Yellow River, Lanzhou is divided into two distinct districts. Visitors usually enter Lanzhou from the **eastern district.** This part of the city, radiating out from the train station in the south, offers dozens of street markets, cheap accommodations, and bustling restaurants and noodle shops. In contrast, the shimmering and glitzy **western district,** with brand new high-rises, upscale fashion stores, and dim sum joints, invokes a sense of Shanghai on the eve of a great boom. The riverfront **Binhe Lu** (滨河路) and the main thoroughfare of **Xijin Lu** (西津路) link the two ends of town.

Xijin Xi Lu forks into three main roads, each changing names several times as it crosses the eastern end of town: nearest the river, it becomes Linxia Lu (临夏路), Zhangye Lu (张掖路), and Nanchang Lu (南昌路); a little farther south, Zhongshan Lu (中山路), Qingyang Lu (庆阳路), and Donggang Lu (东岗路); farthest south and nearest the train tracks, Baiyin Lu (白银路) and Minzhu Lu (民主路). In the heart of the eastern district, **Tianshui Lu** (天水路) bisects Donggang Lu at the Xiguan Traffic Circle, terminating at the train station. **Pingliang Lu** (平凉路) cuts diagonally across the eastern end of town, from **East is Red Square** (dōngfāng hóng guǎngchǎng; 东方红广场) to the train station. The main Yellow River crossing is the **Zhongshan Bridge** (zhōngshān qiáo; 中山桥).

Travel Agencies: CITS, 10 Nongmin Xiang (☎841 6164 or 886 1333), directly behind the Lanzhou Hotel. Another location at 290 Tianshui Lu (☎862 5678), a 10min. walk north from the train station. Tours to Bingling Temple around Y300 (negotiable). Both branches open daily 9am-9pm. **Lanzhou Golden Eagle Aviation Ticket Center** (lánzhōu jīnyīng hángkōng piàowù zhōngxīn; 兰州金鹰票务中心), 143 Zhongshan Jie (☎847 6496 or 843 6064), next to the Victory Hotel. Take a left out of the hotel entrance; the sign is on the left. English-speaking staff member. Full-day tours to Bingling Temple Y640, 2-day tours to Xiahe Y640. Open daily 8:30am-6pm. **Gansu Western Tour Service** (gānsù xībù lǚxíngshè; 甘肃西部旅行社; ☎885 2929; 24hr. ☎908 9110), in the Lanzhou Hotel. Open daily 8am-noon and 2:30-6pm.

Bank of China: 589 Tianshui Lu, a 20min. walk from the train station. Exchanges traveler's checks at counters #40 and 50. Credit card advances (4% commission) on the 2nd floor (M-F only). Open M-F 8:30am-5:30pm, Sa-Su 9:30am-4pm.

Bookstore: Foreign Language Bookstore (wài wén shūdiàn; 外文书店), on Zhangye Lu, a 5min. walk east of the provincial government building. Open daily 8am-6:30pm.

PSB: 310 Wudu Lu (☎846 2851, ext. 8550). From Zhongshan Lu, turn left on Jiuquan Lu, and left again on Wudu Lu. Although there is a sign pointing you to the right, down a small street, the branch that deals with foreigners actually faces Wudu Lu. **Visa extensions** Y320 UK citizens, Y280 US citizens. Open M-F 8am-noon and 2:30-6pm.

Hospital: ☎233 5411.

Internet Access: Qidian Internet Bar (qǐdiǎn wǎngbā; 起点网吧), on the 3rd floor of the building opposite the post office, marked by a large blue sign. Y3 per hr. Open 24hr.

Post Office: At the corner of Minzhu Dong Lu and Pingliang Lu, a 15min. walk northwest of the train station (☎878 9692). Parcel pickup on the left. EMS and Poste Restante. Open daily 8am-7pm. **Postal Code:** 730000.

ACCOMMODATIONS

Most budget accommodations are in the city's eastern district along Tianshui Lu, within a 20-minute walk of the train station. A few cheap lodgings can also be found amid the pricey real estate in the western district.

EASTERN DISTRICT

Lanzhou Mansions (lánzhōu dàshà; 兰州大厦; ☎841 7210), opposite the train station. The undisputed favorite among backpackers, this hotel offers clean sheets, bathtubs, bed lamps, and TVs. Deposit Y100. 4-bed dorms Y27; 3-bed dorms Y31; 2-bed dorms Y48; singles with breakfast Y109; doubles Y82-152.

Yingbin Hotel (yíngbīn fàndiàn; 迎宾饭店; ☎888 6552), on Tianshui Lu, a 5min. walk from the train station, on the left. The Yingbin has renovated the majority of its rooms, most recently in the middle building. Remarkably clean baths, white linens (satin bedspreads in the back building), and a quiet setting create an inviting atmosphere. Hot water 8-11pm in front building, 24hr. everywhere else. Deposit Y100. Singles Y50, with bath Y158; doubles Y44-50/178; triples Y36-51; quads Y52.

Lanshan Hotel (lánshān bīnguǎn; 兰山宾馆; ☎861 7211), on Tianshui Lu, a 5min. walk from the train station, on the right. Staff is open to a bit of bargaining and always ready with a smile. Rooms are clean and well lit. There are concrete floors and green hostel paint in the rooms without attached baths. Breakfast included. Deposit Y20. Singles Y38, with bath Y66; doubles Y52/84; triples Y66; quads Y68.

Lanzhou Hotel (lánzhōu fàndiàn; 兰州饭店), 434 Donggang Xi Lu (☎841 6321, ext. 8777 or 8260), on the Xiguan Traffic Circle, a 25min. walk north on Tianshui Lu from the train station. Take bus #1 from the station. Primarily geared toward wealthy foreigners and high-rolling Chinese businessmen. New carpets and sparkling sheets grace most rooms. Traveler's check exchange (for guests only) and travel agency. Deposit varies. Singles Y230; doubles Y180-460; triples Y120. Credit cards accepted.

WESTERN DISTRICT

Friendship Hotel (lánzhōu yǒuyì bīnguǎn; 兰州友谊宾馆; ☎233 3051), on Xijin Xi Lu, opposite the Provincial Museum in the western district. Well-maintained common bathrooms and accommodating English-speaking staff make this an excellent option for anyone planning to explore the west end. Deposit double the room rate, Y100 minimum. Dorms Y38; doubles Y98, with bath Y222; triples Y114. Credit cards accepted.

Victory Hotel (shènglì bīnguǎn; 胜利宾馆; ☎846 5221, ext. 2500), on Zhongshan Lu. Accessible from the train station by bus #1. Scrubbed common showers and bathrooms and a few English-speaking staff members make the Victory an economy-class winner. The best rooms are on the 5th and 8th floors. Deposit double the room rate. 3-bed dorms Y30; doubles with bath Y160-260; triples Y90, with bath Y150.

⬛ FOOD

A trip to Lanzhou is not complete without a taste of its honeydew melon (called the "White Melon of Lanzhou" in Chinese) or a cup of the local **eight treasure tea** (bā bǎo chá; 八宝茶; Y1), a wonderful mix of herbs and dried fruit that will leave you thirsting for more. Numerous restaurants line **Tianshui Lu** between the train station and Xiguan Traffic Circle. **Nongmin Xiang** (农民巷), the strip of Muslim noodle shops and kebab stands near the Xiguan Traffic Circle and directly behind the Lanzhou Hotel, is an old backpacker favorite. Just south of Minzhu Dong Lu, running between Pingliang Lu and Tianshui Lu, is **Hezheng Market** (hézhèng shìchǎng; 和政市场), which is filled with vendors selling lamb kebabs (yángròu chuān; 羊肉串; Y3 for 10), egg pancakes (jīdàn bǐng; 鸡蛋饼; Y0.8), and delicious sweet porridge blends (hēimǐ zhōu or xiǎomí zhōu; 黑米粥 or 小米粥; Y0.5 per bowl). Dozens of hotpot restaurants cluster around the Pingliang Lu gate. **Zhongshan Jie,** near the Victory Hotel, has many excellent cafes and dim sum spots unmatched in quality and atmosphere; some stay open until 2:30am. **Donggang Xi Lu** is the place to go for outdoor cafes.

■ **Caesar-Rome International Food City** (káisálóng měishí chéng; 恺撒龙美食城; ☎848 0969), on Zhongshan Lu, immediately to the right of the Victory Hotel. Dim sum begins at 8:30pm and lasts until the wee hours of the morning. Two people can stuff their faces in the very fancy dining hall for about Y30 each. Open daily 7am-2:30am.

Yiqing Garden Lamb Restaurant (yīqīng yuán yánggāoròu diàn; 伊清园羊羔肉店), on Nongmin Xiang. From in front of the Lanzhou Hotel, turn left; the Yiqin is the first restaurant on the left upon entering the alley. Though it doesn't look like much from outside, this tiny Muslim restaurant dishes up delicious lamb dishes (Y8-12) and *yuxiang* beef (Y12). Open daily variable hours.

Yueyuehong Restaurant (yuèyuèhóng cānyín; 悦月红餐饮), 19 Tianshui Lu, 2min. from the Lanzhou Mansions, on the same side of the street. The food is nothing spectacular, but the English menu and stir-fry options (Y6-10) make ordering cheap and easy.

WHAT'S IN A NAME? Always Coca-Cola? Not always. Although

the swirly red-and-white trademark of the Coca-Cola Corporation is pretty much universal, the folks at Coke wanted to give the world's most popular drink a more "native" name when it hit the Middle Kingdom. At first, the closest phonetic match they could find was "Kedou Kela" (kēdǒu kēlà; 蝌蚪磕蜡), and the beverage elite from Hong Kong to Harbin almost found themselves downing cool sips of "bite the wax tadpole" or "female horse stuffed with wax" (depending on the dialect). Coke nixed the wildlife theme and, after an exhaustive search through 40,000 characters, hit upon the infinitely more successful "Kekou Kele" (kěkǒu kělè; 可口可乐), which roughly translates to "brings happiness in the mouth." Not to be outdone, Pepsi Co. made the choice of a new generation "Baisi Kele" (bǎishì kělè; 百事可乐) or "everything enjoyable." In an attempt to elbow in on the competition, the local yokel Wahaha Corporation came out with "Feichang Kele" (非常可乐) or "Future Cola," whose suspiciously curlicued, red-and-white packaging doesn't mask its decidedly non-cola taste (although the sweet, soda water-like drink is being vigorously promoted in Western cities like Yinchuan and Lanzhou). But the phonetic fun goes beyond cola wars. American automotive giant Chrysler first thought of bombarding Chinese car buyers with advertisements for their reliable "Kuaisele" brand (kuàisǐle; 快死了), but nixed the idea when they figured out the name meant "swiftly careening toward death." A final note: next time the summer sun starts getting to you, cool off with a bowl of Häagen-Dazs ice cream—better known in China as "Haigan Dao" (háigǎn dào; 孩感到)—and you'll be "happy to feel it arrive."

🧭 SIGHTS

The provincial museum and a smattering of city parks aside, the Bingling Temple Grottoes far outside the city are Lanzhou's featured tourist attraction. Those with a bit of extra time on their hands may want to visit the **White Cloud Temple** (bái yún guān; 白云观), a 10-minute walk west of Zhongshan Bridge along the river. The most important Daoist temple in Lanzhou, it is pleasant enough, although street noise envelops even the darkest recesses inside. *(Open daily sunrise-sunset. Free.)*

🏛 **GANSU PROVINCIAL MUSEUM** (gānsù shěng bówùguǎn; 甘肃省博物馆). This splendid museum is a fountain of information on the 3000-year history of Gansu civilization. One of the most interesting sights in Lanzhou, it is a must-see for all travelers, history junkies or not. The first floor galleries, previously home to a massive stegodon skeleton and a collection of minority nationality costumes, were undergoing extensive renovations in June 2000. The second floor gallery displays art and tools from the Neolithic period to the Tang and beyond, including bronze and jade ritual objects, Han wooden horses, and beautiful pottery artifacts from before 2000 BC. The world-renowned **Han Horse of Wuwei**, a marvelous bronze sculpture of a divine prancing horse with one hoof on a flying swallow's back, takes center stage in the second room. The flying horse is followed by an army of armed guards and bronze chariots. There is also a massive electronic map showing the various branches of the Silk Road, and a fascinating collection of scrolls printed on bamboo slats. Perhaps the most interesting exhibit is of a Tang dynasty camel driver's woolen expense log from Turpan, displayed in the final room of the front hall. *(On Xijin Xi Lu, directly across from the Friendship Hotel, in the western district. Open Tu-Sa 9am-noon and 2:30-5:30pm. Y25, students Y15.)*

WUQUAN SHAN PARK (wǔquán shān gōngyuán; 五泉山公园). Far less touristed than the White Pagoda Park across town, this park consists of a series of small temples, pavilions, and tea houses terraced into the steep, rocky hills south of the city. Dotted with flowering bushes in the summer and sheltered by towering grandfather cypress trees, the courtyards offer lounge chairs, an expansive view of Lanzhou's skyline, and a perfect spot to sip leisurely from a cup of *ba bao cha*. *(South of town, at the terminus of bus #8. Taxi from the main train station Y5. Also accessible via bus #141 from Lanzhou West Train Station. Open daily sunrise-sunset. Y3.)*

WHITE PAGODA PARK (bái tǎ gōngyuán; 白塔公园). After entering the right set of stairs, visitors are overwhelmed by a barrage of circus games, neon lights, food hawkers, and animated afternoon karaoke sessions. However, climbing the steep staircases to the now tanning pagoda rewards persistent visitors with a good view of Lanzhou. The covered terrace that surrounds the site is a convenient place to take a breather, and during the summer months, locals gather around tables, playing card games and nibbling on sunflower seeds. *(At the end of Zhongshan Lu, on the north bank of the Yellow River, near Zhongshan Bridge. Open daily 7:30am-7:30pm. Y3.)*

📷 DAYTRIP FROM LANZHOU: BINGLING TEMPLE GROTTOES

*Take a **bus** (7:30am, Y5-8) to Liujiaxia Dam (刘家峡), making sure that the driver knows you want to get off at Bingling Temple. The bus drops you at a ticket office along the main road; at that point, either pay the steep admission fee (which only gets you as far as the reservoir 5min. away) or take a taxi (Y10 per person) and bypass the gate entrance fee. Depending on the water level, you may be forced to take a speedboat (Y50 per person round-trip, less for larger groups) rather than the ferry. Regular **admission** Y20; admission to locked caves additional Y70-300 per cave (caves 140, 144, 169, and 182 are the most expensive). Depending on whether the speedboat or ferry is taken, the whole trip includes 4-5hr. on a bus, 2-6hr. on a boat, and a mere 1-1½hr. of cave viewing. Public buses from Lanzhou often stop many times along the way to the reservoir, leaving less time at the caves; consider taking an all-inclusive **tour** (about Y150, with speedboat Y230) through a travel agency to save transit time and maximize your cave-viewing time. Take a **bus** back to Lanzhou from the first ticket booth along the main road (last bus leaves 5-5:30pm) or share a miandi taxi to the far west end of town (Y10-20 per person) and then take bus #41 (1hr., Y1.1) into the center of town.*

HOT, HOT, HOT A Northwestern China specialty, hotpot is literally that: a hot, steaming pot of spicy broth kept boiling by a special burner built into the table. The broth is seasoned with fish heads, Chinese dates, star of anise, and more spices than you can count. Into this, people dunk thinly sliced meats, often beef or lamb, as well as any local vegetable or noodle imaginable. Cooked within seconds, these morsels are fished out and dunked again into a spicy peanut sauce before being eaten. Both a festive occasion and a culinary delight, hotpot brings together a sweaty, teary-eyed group of friends to linger for hours over the steaming pot, often while playing drinking games and laughing uproariously. Hotpot generally costs Y20-30 per person.

Hailed as one of the best-preserved collections of Buddhist cave art in China, the Bingling Temple Grottoes (bǐnglíng sì shíkū; 炳灵寺石窟) are nonetheless attracting fame in travelers' circles for being not quite worth all the hype. Although grotto art is definitely the highlight of the trip, the scenic Yellow River cruise and vibrant farmland along the banks tempt many travelers to use up a few rolls of film before even reaching the caves. The ride from Lanzhou is pleasurable if rough, offering glimpses of vast corn fields, improbably fertile soil along riverbeds, and distinctive red-clay banks carved by the incessant river current. The upriver cruise from the dam rewards passengers with streaming landscapes of open skies, multicolored peaks, and contoured banks. The river narrows upstream and the boats snake through a rocky gorge. Spectacular finger-like stone spires, rising 30 to 50m above the rushing waters, signal your arrival at the small dirt path leading to the caves.

Reality, in the form of a pastel billboard advertising exorbitant prices, rudely awakens travelers upon their arrival at the caves. The extra money to visit various locked caves buys the chance to climb bamboo ladders to trapdoors that lead four stories up into the cliffs, an experience unworthy of the steep price; these particular caves are rather dull compared to the caves included in the basic admission.

While Yungang and Longmen Grottoes were major imperial sites of worship in northern capitals (and Dunhuang was a pilgrimage site along the Silk Road), secluded Bingling Temple actually outdates its three more famous counterparts. Construction on the first of the 183 caves, 694 stone statues, and 82 clay figures began in AD 366 and continued for 1000 years. Many Northern Zhou statues were retouched in the Ming, giving them more depth and perspective, as well as the brighter colors visible today. Caves 69, 82, 134, 136, and the curiously black-and-white 28 (all visible when you pass to the left of the Maitreya) are well preserved, placed as they were deep into their respective niches. Murals and calligraphic *sutras* adorn the inner caverns. The strategic square holes in the wall supported ancient construction scaffolding, much like that used today to access the caves.

At the far end of the access bridge sits a 27m tall Tang-era Maitreya sitting Buddha. Legend has it that the upper body, carved out of the rock cliff, symbolizes the internal, psycho-physical realm, and the lower body, molded out of excavated stone and clay, symbolizes the external physical world. The Buddha is said to sit equally mindful of both realms.

XIAHE 夏河 ☎0941

Xiahe is undoubtedly one of the best kept secrets in China. One of the six most important religious centers of Tibetan Lamaism's Yellow Hat (Gelugpa) sect, the Labrang Monastery is awe-inspiring. Surrounded by expansive grasslands and the rearing Phoenix (Fengshan) and Dragon (Longshan) Mountains, Xiahe's cool alpine air contrasts with the incredible warmth of the Tibetan people and monks who call the town home. Especially for those who cannot make the increasingly popular (and increasingly expensive) pilgrimage to Tibet, Xiahe is a must-see.

NORTHWEST

▲★? ORIENTATION AND PRACTICAL INFORMATION

Xiahe lies along a single road starting at the bus station in the east and running 4-5km westward, changing from a fully Hui community to a Tibetan one, complete with mud-brick houses, prayer flags, and colorful door fronts. The post office and administrative buildings are in the east, while Labrang Monastery is out west.

Buses: Xiahe is accessible only by bus. **Xiahe Bus Station** (xiàhé chángtú qìchē zhàn; 夏河长途汽车站; ☎712 1462), is on the eastern edge of town. To: **Hezuo** (2hr., every 30min. 6:10am-5pm, Y6.5); **Lanzhou** (5-7hr., 4 per day, Y20-26); **Linxia** (3hr., every 25min., Y9); **Maqu** (6hr., 2 per day, Y22); and **Tongren** (5hr., 1 per day, Y12).

PSB: Take a right up the road out of the bus station; the office is a 3min. walk (☎712 1526). The officer is nearly fluent in English and will gladly help with visa extensions. Open M-F 8am-noon and 2:30-6pm.

Internet Access: Xiahe Internet Club, a 5min. walk away from the monastery toward the bus station. Y18 per hr. Open daily 10am-6:30pm.

Post Office: A 10min. walk on the right from the PSB (☎712 1944). EMS and IDD service available. Open daily 8am-6pm. **Postal Code:** 747100.

▌ ACCOMMODATIONS

Xiahe has several pleasant and inexpensive accommodations, most run by a friendly management that accepts foreigners.

Overseas Tibetan Hotel (huá qiáo fàndiàn; 华侨饭店; ☎712 2642), just before the monastery. The friendly, English-speaking owner is the son of a Tibetan refugee. A variety of clean rooms at great prices. Hotel taxi, Internet access (Y16 per hr.), bike rental (Y10 per day), IDD service, and a book exchange. 24hr. hot water. 4-bed dorms Y15; doubles Y50, with bath Y150.

Tara Guesthouse (zhuómǎ lǚshè; 卓玛旅社; ☎712 1274), right around the corner from the Overseas Tibetan, near the monastery. Schooled in the United States and a part-time resident of New York City, the owner has a knack for helping travelers. Rooms are slightly small, and the two-headed showers can sometimes be difficult to operate. Several comfortable, sun-filled common areas where you can seek advice from other travelers. All rooms have common bathrooms. Bike rental Y10 per day. Hot water 7am-noon and 6-10pm. 3- to 6-bed dorms Y15; doubles Y40-50.

Daxia Hotel (dàxià bīnguǎn; 大夏宾馆; ☎712 1546), a short walk up the road from the bus station, on the right. The Daxia has clean, tiled floors and spacious rooms with great views. Less frequented since the construction of the Tara and Overseas Tibetan Hotels; you're more likely to have a quiet stay in a large room all to yourself. Common bathrooms with hot water 8-11:30pm. 3-bed dorms Y21; doubles Y62; singles Y60.

White Conch Hotel (bái hǎiluó bīnguǎn; 白海螺宾馆; ☎712 2486). Guests can fall asleep to the soothing sounds of the Daxia River; rooms to the right of the staircase are closest to the water. White sheets, heavy blankets, clean carpets, and well-kept bathrooms. Hot water 7-10:30pm. 3-bed dorms Y31; doubles with bath Y180.

◖ FOOD

Han, Hui, and Tibetan cuisines are all widely available in their respective sections of town; a dozen or so restaurants display outdoor English menus. For genuine Tibetan food, steer clear of the various mutations of the "Yak Restaurant" in the east and cross the little bridge into the west. On the right side of the road, just before the monastery, the **Labrang Monastery Restaurant** (lābǔlèng sì fànguǎn; 拉卜楞寺饭馆) is a backpacker's dream, with a huge English menu. The breakfast foods are especially delicious; make sure you get a loaf of their piping hot Tibetan bread (Y2) to complement your morning meal. Just across the street, the **Snowlands Restaurant** (xuěchéng cāntīng; 雪城餐厅) is another little haven of Tibetan,

Han, and creative Western food. The restaurant is particularly clean and tidy, with some outdoor seating, and a great chicken sandwich (Y5). The Nepali chef at the **Everest Restaurant** (☎712 2642), attached to the Overseas Tibetan Hotel, cooks up some of the best chicken curry outside India.

▣ SIGHTS

Xiahe's city proper itself lacks any major sights, but people come mostly for the monastery. A trip out to the **Sangke Grasslands** (sāngkē cǎoyuán; 桑科草原) is well worth the 14km bike ride. Follow the road west out of town and you will come to this vast prairie, a great picnic spot by a picturesque lake. Sangke is a quick way to escape buildings and check out the home of local Tibetan herders. Some travelers, however, report that it is typical of the stuff you'll see the whole busride into Xiahe, so if you can afford it, rent a private vehicle to be driven farther out into the grasslands. *(Round-trip taxi Y25. 45min. bike ride each way. Y3.)*

LABRANG MONASTERY
Tours of the monastery leave from the ticket office to the right of the entrance daily at 10am and 2pm. Office open daily 8:15am-noon and 2-6pm. Y23.

Labrang Monastery (làbülèng sì; 拉卜楞寺) is spectacular inside and out. This magnificent monastery is surrounded by 2.5km of prayer wheels, numbering over 1200 in all and punctuated by several massive wheels housed in separate towers. It's possible to sit for hours watching pious pilgrims performing their clockwise circuit about the grounds.

Founded in 1709 by Eang Zongahe, a monk who thereafter was named the first Jiamuyang, or "living Buddha," the monastery has been the site of numerous acts of violence. As any monk will forcefully attest, the current version of the monastery is only a shell of its former self. Large-scale bloody disputes between Tibetan and local Hui power-holders in the 1920s and the ravages of the Cultural Revolution reduced the monastery's population by 75%. One thousand temples were destroyed, leaving only 27. Today, monks number only 1500 and nuns 100. The monastery's most important colleges are to the north of the road.

The main prayer hall greeting visitors at the entrance gate was rebuilt in 1990 following an electrical fire in 1985. Able to hold the entire monk contingent, the hall is illuminated by yak-butter lamps, draped with hangings called "umbrellas," and filled with statues of the past, present, and future buddhas (Akshobhya, Sakyamuni, and Maitreya).

The monks study at six institutes: the institutes of philosophy, astrology, medicine, law, lower and higher theology, and Eastern Buddhism. Labrang monks study for the majority of the day, with the remainder of their time devoted to prayer and rest. The "normal" schedule is as follows: general studies 4:30 to 7:30am, manual work 10am to 8pm, study 9 to 10pm, and prayer 10pm to 2am. All monks are equired to have reading knowledge of Hindi, Tibetan, and Sanskrit, as well as spoken comprehension of English.

To appreciate all that the monastery has to offer, be sure to take part in the tours. After the tour, you may wander about the entire complex on your own. Leaving through the exit, take the first left and follow the right wall to the entrance to a small garden. At certain times of the day, you may be able to view monks at recess, either exercising or practicing meditative gymnastics. Upon leaving the northern complex, travel up the road and follow the covered prayer wheels counterclockwise until you reach the **Gongtang Pagoda** (gòngtáng bǎotǎ; 贡唐宝塔), surrounded by an impressive array of prayer wheels. *(Open daily 9am-5pm. Y5.)*

PINGLIANG 平谅　　　　☎0933

A growing industrial town in Gansu just across the Ningxia border, Pingliang is most famous for the nearby Daoist mountain of Kongtong Shan. Sadly, Pingliang suffers greatly from the growing pains of modernization. Despite the surrounding

high ridges of terraced farmlands and green, rocky cliffs, the city is crisscrossed
by large, noisy transport trucks and often choked by careless waste disposal and
industrial smoke. Oppressive in the daytime, Pingliang fortunately comes alive at
night with many night markets and a festive town square.

✴ 🛈 ORIENTATION AND PRACTICAL INFORMATION

The town of Pingliang is oriented along a north-south-east-west grid pattern, with
the **Panxuan Lu** (盘旋路) **traffic circle** in the center. Running west of the circle is
National Highway 312 (sānyāoèr guódào; 312国道). **Jiefang Bei Lu** (解放北路) runs
north from the city center to the train station.

Trains: Pingliang Train Station (píngliàng huǒchē zhàn; 平凉火车站; ☎862 8878), on
Jiefang Bei Lu north of the city center. Accessible via bus #1 or by *bengbeng che*. Open
daily 9am-noon, 1:30-5:30pm, 7:10-9pm, and 10:30pm-8am. From Pingliang, trains
are often a more reliable means of travel than buses are. To: **Chengdu** (20½hr.,
1:15am, Y57); **Lanzhou** (11hr., 8:50pm, Y32); **Ürümqi** (4 and 6:16am, Y118-137);
Xian (8hr., midnight, Y27); and **Yinchuan** (9 hr., 4:55am and 11:15pm, Y34).

Buses: Pingliang Long-distance Bus Station (píngliàng chángtú qìchē zhàn; 平凉
长途汽车站), on National Highway 312, about 2.5km west of the town center. Open
daily 5:30am-10pm. To: **Lanzhou** (5-8hr.; every hr. 6am-5pm; Y31, express Y41); **Xian**
(8 hr., every hr. 6am-1:30pm, Y25); and **Yinchuan** (8hr., 7am and 6pm, Y32).

Local Transportation: Bus #1 services the train station, and **#2** runs from Panxuan Lu
traffic circle along Zhongshan Jie. Fare Y0.2. **Motorized three-wheeled cabs** (bēngbēng
chē; 蹦蹦车) to most destinations cost Y2.

Bank of China: On Zhongshan Jie, about 5min. from the post office. Exchanges traveler's
checks. Open M-F 9am-5pm.

Hospitals: District Hospital (dìqū yīyuàn; 地区医院), on Kongtong Dong Lu, a 10min.
walk east of Panxuan Lu traffic circle. There is a hospital across from the post office.

Post Office: Pingliang Post Office, on Zhongshan Jie, a 10min. walk from Xinmin Jie.
From Panxuan Lu traffic circle, walk south on Jiefang Nan Lu. Turn right onto Zhongshan
Jie; the building is on the left. Open daily 8am-7pm. **Postal Code:** 744000.

🏠 ACCOMMODATIONS AND FOOD

Cheap and relatively clean accommodations are available for about Y10 per bed in
the many hostels a short walk from both the train and bus stations. Much nicer
rooms are available for slightly higher prices in the town center. The downtown
area offers a lively atmosphere to walk off an evening meal.

Blue Star Hotel (lán xīng fàndiàn; 蓝星饭店; ☎863 0844), on Jiefang Nan Lu, about
5min. from Panxuan Lu traffic circle. Carpeted rooms with bright white walls, clean
sheets, and sanitary common bathrooms and showers make this feel like a high-end
hotel. Deposit Y100-200. Singles and doubles Y50; triples Y60-75; quads Y60.

Yuanheng Hotel (yuánhéng bīnguǎn; 元亨宾馆; ☎861 2322, ext. 8999), on the southeast side of Panxuan Lu traffic circle. Given spotless rooms with carpeting, TVs, wood
furniture, and decent common bathrooms, the sparkling glass-lined lobby is only a
bonus. Deposit Y150 and up. Doubles Y50, with bath Y136-268; triples with bath Y105.

Traffic Hotel (jiāotōng fàndiàn; 交通饭店; ☎821 6111), a 5min. walk to the left when
you leave the bus station. Dormitory-style lodging, complete with wet hallway floors,
noisy groups of people, and pungent common bathrooms. Rooms come with washed
sheets and new carpets. Doubles Y30-36.

👁 SIGHTS

KONGTONG MOUNTAIN (kōngtóng shān; 崆峒山). This, China's foremost Daoist
mountain, is undoubtedly the best reason to visit Pingliang. Kongtong's 42 Qin-
and Han-dynasty temples and pavilions were built right into the edge of high, for-

ested cliffs—once accessible only by chiseled steps and dangling chains. Formerly the realm of the eight famous immortals and the hermitage of ascetic priests, the area is now invaded by a newly opened road and a parking lot full of vendors. The spectacular view of the surrounding terraced farmland and the bright smiles of the mountain priests are more than enough to restore the sense of lofty spirit that was so central to the place. Visitors seeking to follow the traditional pilgrimage route can start at **Qianshan** (qiánshān; 前山) and ascend the 3km or so of steps, stopping at smaller temples along the way to burn incense. *(15km west of Pingliang. A taxi from Pingliang to Qianshan costs about Y20; taxis also stop at Houshan (hòushān; 后山). From there, it is a long wait for an all-terrain vehicle (Y20) to the top. Y30.)*

OTHER SIGHTS. Back in Pingliang, the **Bao Pagoda** (bǎo tǎ; 宝塔) is southeast of the Panxuan Lu traffic circle. Walk south on Jiefang Nan Lu and turn left on Zhongshan Lu, which becomes Baota Lu after several blocks; Bao Pagoda is on the left. The seven-story Ming structure houses bronze Buddha statues on each level. Near the bus station on National Highway 312, about 10 minutes from Panxuan Lu traffic circle, **Liu Lake Park** (liǔ hú gōngyuán; 柳湖公园), with meandering garden paths and frequent music performances, stays open until around midnight.

TIANSHUI 天水 ☎ 0938

During the past 10 years, this large industrial city has become an oasis of modern life for the many young people who come from small surrounding towns seeking industry and technology jobs and the pulse of a growing city. Although large-scale development seeks to create a uniform city of glass and steel, for now traditional tile-roofed, plaster wall architecture remains interspersed among even the most prosperous shopping streets. This sense of historical continuity is further defined by Tianshui's vital artists' community, which continues to practice ancient traditions of painting and sculpture in a modern context.

Tianshui is perhaps most famous for its nearby Maijishan Grottoes, housing amazingly well-preserved Buddhist sculptures in over 200 cliff caves that date back more than 1500 years. Tianshui also offers convenient access to several other scenic and religious sights of interest, most notably the Immortal's Cliff Area and the Stone Gate Mountains, both ideal hiking spots made even more enjoyable by the breezy and dry climate. Tianshui is an ideal two- or three-day layover point for those traveling the southern route of the Silk Road.

✸❓ ORIENTATION AND PRACTICAL INFORMATION

Tianshui is comprised of two main sections, separated by 15km of industrial development and small rural communities. The eastern section, **Beidao** (北道), consists of several large avenues radiating out from the train station in the north. **Yi Malu** (一马路) gallops from east to west directly in front of the train station. Running directly south of the train station, crossing Yi Malu and the parallel **Erma Lu** (二马路), is **Weihe Bianqiao Lu** (渭河便桥路). Public buses and minibuses make the 45-minute trip to the much more modern and lively **Qincheng** district (秦城), leaving every 10 minutes and dropping passengers off at a bus stop on **Dazhong Lu** (大众路), just southwest of the **central square** (zhōngxīn guǎngchǎng; 中心广场). **Minzhu Lu** (民主路) runs past the north side of the square, and **Jiefang Lu** (解放路) borders the south side, extending to the western end of the city. In most cases, walking is feasible for destinations within each district.

Trains: Tianshui Train Station (tiānshuǐ huǒchē zhàn; 天水火车站), in Beidao, faces a large square, the departure point for Qincheng- and Maijishan-bound minibuses. Ticket office open 24hr. Tickets can also be bought at the Industrial and Commercial Bank of China on Dazhong Lu, a 5min. walk south of the Qincheng central square. Open daily 9am-6pm. To: **Lanzhou** (7hr., 9 per day, Y26-52); **Ürümqi** (4:35, 11:43am, and 11pm; Y131-245); **Xian** (7hr., 10 per day, Y25-51); and **Xining**.

Buses: Tianshui Long-distance Bus Station (tiānshuǐ chángtú qìchē zhàn; 天水长途 汽车站) is in the northern part of Qincheng. From the central square, walk 3 blocks east on Minzhu Lu, and turn left on Hezuo Bei Lu. Walk for 5min. until you reach the first major intersection; turn left again. The station is visible on the right side of the street. To: **Lanzhou** (8hr.; 6, 7, 8am, and 5pm; Y29); **Linxia** (13hr., 6:30am, Y33); and **Pingliang** (8hr., 6am, Y22). Often a more sensible option for shorter trips, the **local bus station,** just past the Industrial and Commercial Bank on Dazhong Lu in Qincheng, has frequent morning buses to **Gangu** and **Wushan.** Buses to local and long-distance destinations are rarely crowded, and arriving 30min. in advance is sufficient time to buy a ticket and find the bus.

Local Transportation: Buses #1, 6, and **9** shuttle between Qincheng central square and the train station in Beidao, leaving every 10-15min. (Y2). Bus #6 is an express bus (approx. 30min.); the others take about 45min. **Private minibuses** also travel between these 2 points, but take a much longer time. These minibuses often look very similar to city buses; be certain that the bus number is clearly displayed in the front windshield. **Taxis** and *bengbeng che* to Jade Springs Park Y3-10.

Travel Agency: CITS (☎821 3621), on the northwest corner of Minzhu Lu and Hezuo Lu, in Qincheng. Walk east from the central square for 7-8min.; the office is on the left. Although the office staff is friendly to individual travelers, it specializes in group package tours—including high-priced tours of Maijishan (English-speaking guides available). English speaker on staff. Open daily 9am-6pm.

Bank of China: On Minzhu Lu, in Qincheng. From the city square, walk east for 10min.; the bank is on the left, in a clearly visible glass high-rise. Exchanges traveler's checks. Open daily 8am-6pm. Another location on Yi Malu, in **Beidao.** From the train station, walk 5min. east on Yi Malu; the bank is on the left side of the street.

Internet Access: Internet Bar (wǎngbā; 网吧), on Qingnian Bei Lu, Qincheng. From the central square, walk east on Minzhu Lu, taking the first left onto Qingnian Bei Lu; it's 5min. ahead on the left. Look for a pair of mirrored columns with the Chinese name written in red; the bar is on the 2nd floor. Y4 per hr. Open daily 9am-8pm.

Post and Telecommunications: At the corner of Dazhong Lu and Minzhu Lu, Qincheng, just north of the central square. Open daily 8am-8:30pm. **China Telecom** is next door. No IDD service. A **post office** on Yi Malu, a 5min. walk west of the train station, Beidao.

ACCOMMODATIONS AND FOOD

Most of Beidao's accommodations are within minutes of the train station; the area itself is of little interest, and dining options are limited. Qincheng offers centrally located and inexpensive lodging with easy access to major city sights and the bustling night markets near the central square.

Streetside stalls and restaurants abound; at **Wenmiao Market** (wénmiào shāngchǎng; 文庙商场), over 100 vendors sell local specialties. For breakfast, try the small, round yellow breads, eaten with a spiced hash and a bowl of porridge.

Railway Hostel (tiělù zhāodàisuǒ; 铁路招待所; ☎273 5154), Beidao, near the train station. From the station, take a right and follow Yi Malu for about 3min; the hostel is on the right. With a restaurant, a 24hr. service desk, spotless showers, and bright, white rooms, this is one of Tianshui's more upscale hostels. Mosquito netting and 24hr. hot water. Singles Y26, with living room and TV Y36; doubles Y36; triples Y42; quads Y40.

Huaxi Hotel (huáxī bīnguǎn; 华西宾馆; ☎821 5356), Qincheng. From the Qincheng bus stop, walk straight ahead, with the central square on your left. Cross Minzhu Lu at the first intersection; the hotel entrance is around the corner to the left. The communal balconies overlooking the bustling city square more than make up for the aging yellow wallpaper and pockmarked red rugs. Showers are clean, although occasionally flooded with ankle-deep water. 24hr. hot water. Solo travelers report having decent luck buying just one bed in the triples. Doubles Y58, with bath Y86-106; triples Y78; quads Y86.

Maiji Hotel (màijī dàjiǔdiàn; 麦积大酒店; ☎261 2207), Beidao, on the right side of the train station square, as you exit the station. The Maiji's large budget rooms with electric fans, TVs, and clean bathrooms and showers offer most of the benefits of living in a luxury hotel—although the sheets are less than snow-white. 24hr. hot water. 10% student discount. Doubles Y80; triples Y84; quads Y80; rooms with bath Y130-400.

Tianshui Hotel (tiānshuǐ fàndiàn; 天水饭店), 37 Minzhu Lu, Qincheng (☎821 4056). Walk east on Minzhu Lu away from the central square for about 5min.; the entrance is on the right side of the street. Although a fresh coat of hostel-green paint coats the walls, the common bathrooms smell and look neglected (and the rear rooms overlook a construction site). Hot water 7:30-10pm. Deposit Y100-200. Singles Y35; doubles Y36; triples Y45; quads Y64.

⬛ SIGHTS

In and around the Qincheng district are several worthwhile spots to visit, all of which can be seen in one day. The Nanguo Temple is also open at night, and makes for a relaxing after-dinner excursion. South of the Beidao lie the Maijishan Grottoes, and nearby, the Immortals' Cliffs and **Stone Gate Mountain hiking reserve.**

MAIJISHAN GROTTOES

Minibuses leave from Tianshui's Beidao Train Station (40-45min.; Y8, round-trip Y20-25). Tours in Mandarin Y20, in English Y70. For an additional Y100-600, visitors can tour some of the caves that are closed to the general public. For information on tours, check with the tourist office just left of the museum. Gate admission Y10; caves Y30, groups of 2 or more students with ID Y15 per person.

Named after their resemblance to the stacks of harvested wheat that punctuate the surrounding terraced hillsides, the sheer rock cliffs of Maijishan (màijīshān shíkū; 麦积山石窟) rise dramatically from the forest below; from a distance, the latticework of caves and exterior sculptures appear to be the natural texture of the rock. However, climbing the scaffolding to the caves hundreds of feet up reveals the intricacy with which the cliff face has been carved and painted.

The cliff's largest sculptures, over 16m tall, consist of several buddhas radiating waves of sculpted clouds and surrounded by attendant *bodhisattvas*, each with a unique character and expression. Each cave is dominated by a central figure whose expression and gestures permeate a particular realm of the Buddhist cosmos, as depicted in the surrounding sculpture and mural art. Reflecting the steady process of expansion that began in the late Qin (AD 384-417) and continued into the Qing dynasty 1600 years later, different sculptural styles and spatial arrangements dominate different parts of the mountain. The Western Wei and Northern Wei additions are particularly captivating, expressing a delicate and subtle refinement of facial features and a strong physical presence in the sculpted forms. Although Maijishan's caves are now locked, often leaving visitors peering through metal screens into the dim worlds inside, guided tours offer the privilege of stepping inside the locked areas. Well worth the additional *yuan*, these tours reiterate the incredible devotional energy that has defined the Buddhist tradition in China for over 2000 years. The **Maijishan Museum** (màijīshān bówùguǎn; 麦积山博物馆), near the parking lot of the main entrance, displays "the cream of Maijishan's sculptures," truly some of the most delicate and well-preserved objects from the site.

OTHER SIGHTS

IMMORTALS' CLIFFS (xiānrén yá; 仙人崖). Surrounded by forested ridges and terraced wheat fields, the Immortals' Cliffs area is best known for the Buddhist and Daoist temples built under the shelter of an enormous overhanging cliff. Tucked into this cave-like niche are over 50 prayer halls, housing some powerfully evocative sculptures and murals that date back over 1600 years. To get a good look at the recessed figures, you must approach an altar at the front of the prayer hall; it is appropriate to burn a stick of incense and donate some small change as a sign of respect. There are many small pavilions and shrines dotting the surrounding hills. Hiking to them can be the best part of the trip, as you wind through a network of small dirt trails crisscrossing the lush, fragrant farmland. Next to the main parking lot, there is a small lake at the base of a cliff where paddle boats can be rented. *(Although this area merits a full day of exploration, the best deal is to arrange with a mini-bus driver at Beidao Train Station to go to Maijishan and then here, spending a few hours at each spot; this should cost about Y40 round-trip for a group. A taxi for a full day costs Y130-150. Y15.)*

FUXI TEMPLE (fúxī miào; 伏羲庙). This beautiful Ming-dynasty temple is devoted to Fuxi, the chief of a southeastern Gansu Neolithic clan society, who is said to be the original ancestor of the Chinese people. Cypress trees over 1000 years old grow in the courtyard, and a pair of enormous phoenix and dragon reliefs—reputed to be carved from a single piece of wood—decorate the intricate temple facade. On the left as you enter is the **Tianshui Museum** (tiānshuǐ bówùguǎn; 天水博物馆), which houses an impressive collection of Neolithic pottery, excellent examples of local sculpture and ritual vessels, and even some prized sculptures taken from Maijishan. As you walk around the temple complex, take a peek into the rooms bordering the courtyard: many are studios for local painters and calligraphers. *(On Jiefang Lu. From the Qincheng central square, walk west for 15min.; the temple is on the right. Open daily sunrise-sunset. Y5.)*

ANTIQUE MARKET (gǔwán chéng; 古玩城). Underneath the Qincheng central square is a collection of fascinating art studios and antique shops, offering everything from Ming-dynasty furniture and model architecture to a unique style of contemporary sculpture that uses gnarled roots and branches. Run by well-spoken collectors and often by artists themselves, this is a must-see for tourists in the Qincheng area. *(On Jiefang Lu. The entrance is across the street from a small mosque. Open daily 8:30am-5:30pm. Free.)*

JADE SPRINGS DAOIST TEMPLE (yùquán guān gōngyuán; 玉泉观公园). First built during the Yuan dynasty, this temple in the dusty hills northwest of the Qincheng city center has only its 700-year-old cypress trees and a sweeping view of the city to distinguish it from the generic Chinese temple complex. It is a pleasant place to relax and sip tea on a long, hot afternoon, though. *(From Fuxi Temple, turn left on Jiefang Lu, take the first left on Shuangqiao Bei Lu, and turn right onto Renmin Xi Lu. Walk for 5min.; the temple will be visible up a small street to the left. Open daily sunrise-sunset. Y5.)*

NANGUO TEMPLE. In a mountain valley a bit south of downtown Qincheng, this large park wraps around a pond lit by colored lights at night. Two 2000-year-old cypress trees, each 3m thick, stand in front of the temple's main gate. In 759, the Tang dynasty poet Du Fu, who was at the time exiled to Qinzhou (present-day Tianshui), visited the temple and wrote a poem singing its praises. In the courtyard of the temple is another old cypress, verified to be over 1600 years old; this is the very tree that caught Du Fu's fancy. *(2km south of Qincheng. Taxi from the central square about Y10. Open daily 6am-midnight. Y5.)*

NEAR TIANSHUI: GANGU 甘谷

2hr. west of Tianshui. Trains leave frequently from Pingliang to Lanzhou (1-2hr., about Y10-17); train #387 leaves at noon. Buses to Gangu (2hr., every hr., Y6) run from the Qincheng local bus station in Tianshui, on Dazhong Lu. Return buses to Tianshui depart every hour until 6pm.

Gangu's wheat fields and communist style block housing stretch out beneath **Great Statue Mountain** (dà xiàng shān; 大象山), a temple complex hugging a high ridge and centered around a 23m tall statue of Sakyamuni Buddha that is carved into the cliff face. *(Open daily sunrise-sunset. Y10.)* Although exploring the temple takes no more than a few hours, accommodations are cheap and transportation options plentiful, making Gangu a relaxing overnight stop on the way to Lanzhou.

Virtually the only place to stay is the **Gangu (Fandian) Hotel** (gāngù fàndiàn; 甘谷饭店), accessible by taxi (Y5 from the bus station, Y2 from the train station). Well situated on the edge of the town center and a 40-minute walk from Great Statue Mountain, the Gangu offers a range of prices and a helpful staff. Dorm beds have newly painted walls, concrete floors, and one-inch thick mattresses; there are no common showers, but the bathrooms are sanitary and well kept. Other rooms have proper mattresses, TV, phone, and bath, although the rugs are pock-marked and stained. (Singles Y21; doubles Y13, with bath Y39 and up; triples Y11; quads Y8.) The best place to eat is the **Gangu (Dajiudian) Hotel** (gāngù dàjiǔdiàn; 甘谷大酒店), now converted into a multi-floor restaurant. Walk due south from the Gangu (Fandian) Hotel, with the mountains at your back; after about 50m, you'll see a blue glass high-rise on the left. Those who are missing home may enjoy the Chinese version of french fries (tǔdòu kuài; 土豆块; Y4-5). For breakfast, vendors all along the main street in town sell delicious sticky rice and dates (Y2).

JIAYUGUAN 嘉峪关 ☎0937

Despite the town's grim historical reputation as the final frontier of 14th-century Ming China—the place beyond which the pale of civilization ended—modern-day Jiayuguan is a pleasant enough place to spend a slow-paced day or two. Jiayuguan Fort, the end of the Great Wall, is an impressive display of the empire's vast reach and serves as an effective expression of the outer limits of Beijing's influence at the time. Effectively, Jiayuguan is a one-hit wonder: while there are a few other sights, they could be skipped at no great cost.

⌐ TRANSPORTATION

Airplanes: Jiayuguan Airport (jiāyùguān jīchǎng; 嘉峪关机场) is 11km northeast of town. CAAC shuttle buses depart 1½hr. before flights (20min., Y10; do not let them charge double). The **CAAC ticket office**, 1 Xinhua Nan Lu (☎622 6237), is about 50m before the central traffic circle and opposite the post office. Open M-Sa 8:30am-noon and 2:30-5:30pm. To **Lanzhou** (W, F, and Su 5pm; Y730).

Trains: Jiayuguan Train Station (jiāyùguān huǒchē zhàn; 嘉峪关火车站; ☎631 5074) is on Yingbin Xi Lu, several kilometers southwest of the town. Accessible by pedicab or minibus #1. Open 24hr. Purchase tickets 3-5 days in advance if possible. To: **Beijing** (45hr., 3:30pm, Y300); **Chengde** (38hr., 6:40am, Y108); **Shanghai** (22hr., 1 per day, Y300); and **Xian** (13hr., 6 per day 9:40am-5pm, Y86). All westbound trains (8 per day 12:02am-10:40pm) stop at: **Liuyuan** (6hr., Y22); **Turpan** (14hr., Y62); **Ürümqi** (19hr., Y81); and **Korla** (22hr., Y86).

Buses: A **Gansu PICC insurance ticket** (Y30) is required to purchase bus tickets in Gansu. The **PICC office** (zhōngguó rénmín bǎoxiǎn; 中国人民保险), 36 Xinhua Nan Lu (☎622 6362), about 100m to the right of the Bank of China, with a "PICC LIFE" sign. Buses are generally unreliable; even express buses may stop frequently to pick up passengers. Open M-F 8:30am-12:30pm and 2:30-6:30pm, Sa 10am-4pm. The **Jiayuguan Bus Station** (jiāyùguān qìchē zhàn; 嘉峪关汽车站; ☎622 5528) is at the corner of Jingtie Xi Lu and Shengli Nan Lu. To: **Dunhuang** (4½hr., 3 per day 9-11:40am; 7½hr., 2:30pm; Y8.8-38.4); **Lanzhou** (15hr.; 4 per day 2-5:40pm; hard seat Y80, sleeper Y180); **Wuwei** (10hr., 3 per day 7am-8pm, Y52); and **Zhangye** (6hr., every hr., Y27). **Xining** can be reached via Zhangye and Wuwei.

Local Transportation: There are 4 **minibus** routes. Minibuses **#1** and **2** run from the train station through the center of town, along Xinhua Lu; **#3** runs west along the Gansu Highway, departing from the Jiayuguan Hotel; **#4** runs from the southeast to the northwest of town.

Taxis: Base fare Y4-6. **Pedicabs** cost about Y3 within the city.

Bike rental: The place right outside the Great Wall Hotel rents bikes for Y3 per hr., deposit Y40. The **Xiongguan Hotel** rents rather run-down bikes. Y1 per hr., deposit Y10 or a student ID.

◀✳🛈 ORIENTATION AND PRACTICAL INFORMATION

The small city of Jiayuguan lies on a tilted grid sliced horizontally by the **Gansu Highway** (National Route 312; sānyāoèr guódào; 312国道) heading to the Jiayuguan Fort in the west. **Xinhua Lu** (新华路) runs from northwest to southeast, meeting **Xiongguan Lu** (雄馆路) at the main traffic circle. The road proceeds south to bisect

Jingtie Lu (镜铁路), **Jianshe Lu** (建设路), and **Yingbin Lu** (迎宾路) at another small traffic circle. The bus station is at the intersection of Route 312, Jingtie Xi Lu, and **Shengli Lu** (胜利路), and the train station is banished off to the southwest corner, at the west end of Yingbin Xi Lu. Almost all services are within a 10-minute walk of the hotels; none of the far-flung sights are accessible by public transportation.

Travel Agencies: Tours of Jiayuguan are offered through the 2 formal travel agencies in town, most large hotels, and any taxi driver; arrange a driver through your hotel for the best rates. **Xiongguan Travel Agency** (xióngguān lǚxíngshè; 雄关旅行社; ☎622 6258), in the Jiayuguan Hotel. Enter through the main doors and take the first left; the entrance is to the right. Efficient and helpful, with English-speaking guides. One-day tours (Jiayuguan Fort, First Beacon Tower, Overhanging Great Wall, and Wei Tombs) Y150 per person, Y200-300 for a 10-person bus; multiple-day excursions to Gansu cities such as Dunhuang; and a 70-day camel-back expedition to Kashgar (min. 10 people). Ticket commission Y30-50. Open M-Sa 8:30am-12:30pm, 2:30-6:30pm, and 8-10pm. **Gansu Jiayuguan International Travel Service (JIT)** (gānsù jiāyùguān guójì lǚxíngshè; 甘肃嘉峪关国际旅行社), 2 Shengli Bei Lu, 2nd Fl. (☎622 6471), a 5min. walk west of the Jiayuguan Hotel. Pass the courthouse on Xiongguan Xi Lu and take a right on Shengli Bei Lu; the agency is to the right of the CITS restaurant. Knowledgeable multilingual staff. Guides Y50, additional Y200 for a full day tour. Open 24hr.

Bank of China: On Xinhua Nan Lu, just south of the PICC building. The center counter exchanges traveler's checks. Open M-F 9:30am-5:30pm, Sa 10am-4pm. A branch office in the Great Wall Hotel also exchanges traveler's checks. Open daily 10am-4pm. The Great Wall Hotel often exchanges traveler's checks for non-guests.

PSB: On the corner of Qilian Xi Lu and Xinhua Nan Lu, in the south of town (☎631 1043). Issues visa extensions. Open M-F 8:30am-12:30pm and 2:30-6:30pm.

Internet Access: In the **China Telecom** building, to the left of the post office. Y10 per hr. The **Jiayuguan** (Y12 per hr.) and **Great Wall** (Y10 per hr.) **Hotels** also have Internet.

Post and Telecommunications: The **post office** (☎622 6255) is opposite the Jiayuguan Hotel, on the central traffic circle. EMS and Poste Restante can be unreliable. Open daily 8:30am-7pm. IDD service is available to the left of the post office counters. Open M-F 7am-9pm. **Postal Code:** 735100.

ACCOMMODATIONS

At the time of writing, only three relatively large, high-end hotels are open to foreigners; fortunately, most of these have a floor or two of budget rooms. Many establishments tack on a 6% "education fee" to rooms.

Xiongguan Hotel (xióngguān bīnguǎn; 雄关宾馆; ☎622 5115), at the intersection of Xinhua Nan Lu and the Gansu Highway, diagonally opposite the Traffic Hotel. Accommodating staff (some English spoken), an excellent Sichuanese restaurant in back, average rooms, and sparkling common bathrooms. Single travelers can pay by the bed. Hot water 7-10am, 1-3pm, and 8pm-1am. Deposit Y10. Service charge Y1 per day. Doubles with bath Y80-200; triples Y56; quads Y64.

Jiayuguan Hotel (jiāyùguān bīnguǎn; 嘉峪关宾馆; ☎622 6231), on the corner of Xiongguan Xi Lu and Xinhua Bei Lu, diagonally across from the post office. This is where most tour groups end up. The older west wing rooms have hot water 7-9:30am, noon-2pm, and 8pm-midnight; renovated east wing rooms have A/C, attached bath, and 24hr. hot water. Foreigners should have no problems paying by the bed. Deposit twice room rate. East wing: singles Y60; doubles Y120. West wing: 4-bed dorms Y48; 3-bed dorms Y54; doubles with bath Y380.

Jiugang Hotel (jiǔgāng bīnguǎn; 酒钢宾馆; front building ☎671 3662; back building ☎671 4425), around the corner from the Jiayuguan Hotel. The Jiugang's front building offers doubles and triples with sparkling tile floors, the occasional peeling wall, and hot water noon-2pm and 9pm-1am. The back building, through a gate to the left, has more upscale rooms with tubs, 24hr. hot water, and IDD service. Deposit twice room rate.

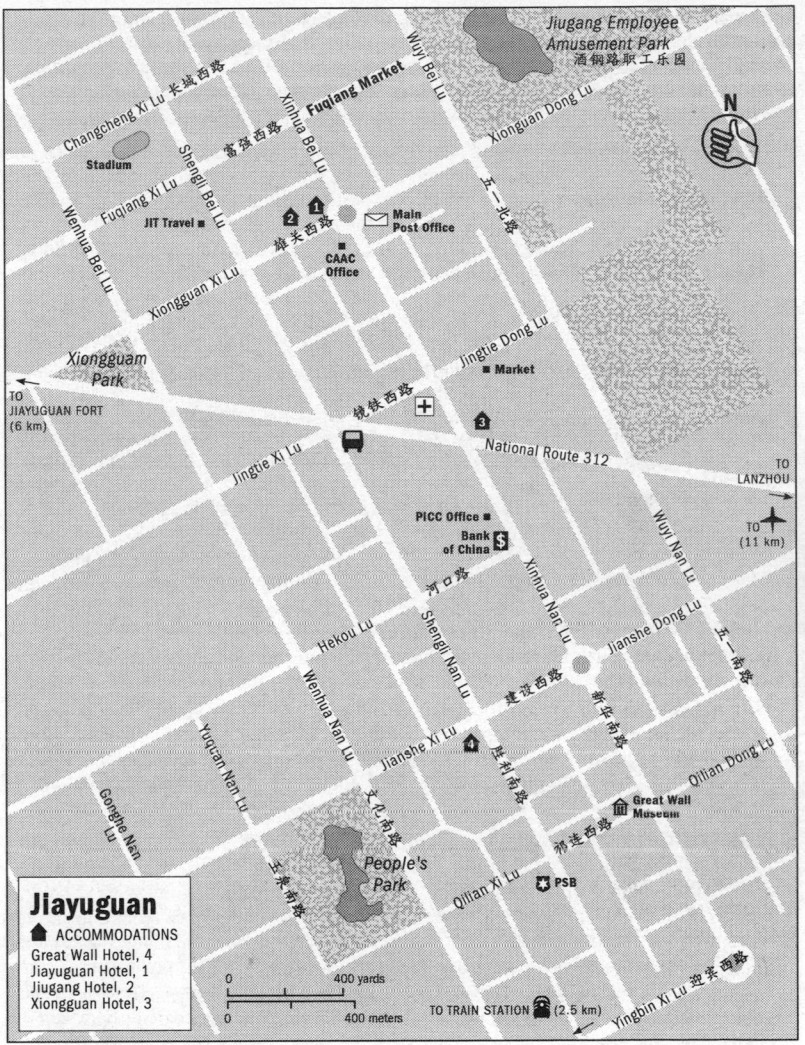

Front building: 3-bed dorms without shower Y15; 2-bed dorms with bath Y30; singles with bath Y60. Back building: singles and doubles with bath Y100-180.

Great Wall Hotel (chángchéng bīnguǎn; 长城宾馆), 6 Jianshe Xi Lu (☎ 622 5788). This luxury fortress is equipped with business center, sauna, massage parlor, and more; more useful for budget travelers are its bank and travel agency. Deposit 20% room rate. Student discount 10-20%. Make reservations a few days in advance. Doubles Y298-880; triples Y220.

FOOD

Jiayuguan food is nothing to write home about. For fine dining, try the restaurants at the **Jiayuguan** and **Xiongguan Hotels.** Most people eat at roast meat and noodle restaurants which serve both Han and Uighur foods. **Jingtie Market** (jìngtiě shìchǎng; 镜铁市场) and its larger counterpart, **Fuqiang Market** (fùqiáng shìchǎng; 富强市场), above the post office off Xinhua Bei Lu, offer excellent roast meat (Y8-10), a Jiayuguan specialty. Fill your belly with 10 different parts of a lamb, seasoned and skewered to perfection over an open grill. Sample everything from hot noodles to seasoned and roasted round breads (kǎobǐngzi; 考饼子; Y1), available from most roast meat vendors.

🧭 SIGHTS

After seeing the fort, those with time, money, and inclination can try **paragliding** (huáxiángjī; 滑翔机) off the dunes near the airport.

JIAYUGUAN FORT (jiāyùguān chénglóu; 嘉峪关城楼). One of the most photographed spots in northwest China, Jiayuguan Fort stands in the midst of the desert, against a backdrop of snow-capped peaks. The prime spot furnishes an absolutely awe-inspiring scene at sunset. Built in 1372, the fort is the final point of the 2000km Ming Great Wall. It consists of a 10m high outer wall that measures 733m in length. After entering through a small gate in the east, visitors are confronted with a set of inner walls guarded by 17m tall watch towers and an "entrapping rampart," between whose walls doomed raiders would be trapped and annihilated. Today, those who ram their way into the inner stronghold find a large open square. The booty? Camel rides and snack stands.

A massive tower to the west guards the main entrance and welcomes arriving traders and tourists with its title characters. The ramps on the north side of each gate once allowed teams of horses onto the wall, enabling mounted archers to speed about. It is said that the masons conscripted to build the fort were of such high caliber that they calculated in advance the number of bricks needed for the entire structure. Somehow, one brick was left unused. The odd-brick-out still rests on the ledge, taunting the math whiz who forgot to carry the 1. (*Although you can bike here in 30-45min. on the Gansu Highway (turn right at the posted sign and then left at the next posted sign), the 6km trip is best accomplished by pedicab or taxi (one-way Y15-20, round-trip Y30-35). The ticket office is to the right. Open daily 8:30am-8pm; in winter 8am-8pm. Y25; western tower Y5; western gate Y3. Interior entry tickets can be bargained down.*)

OVERHANGING GREAT WALL (xuánbì chángchéng; 悬壁长城). To fill up a day in the area, take a 30-minute bike ride or a taxi (round-trip Y15) to the Overhanging Great Wall, a 750m peripheral defense wall extending from Jiayuguan Fort along the cliffs of the Heishan (Black Mountains) gorge. Consisting of two main lookout towers, this section of the wall offers a panoramic view of surreal black wasteland and lifeless mountains extending hundreds of kilometers to the northwest. (*From the Jiayuguan Fort parking lot, exit left and make your first left onto a small paved road. You should see the wall to your left as you bike toward the entrance. Open daily 8:30am-8pm. Y8.*)

A WINNING HAND
A social phenomenon pervasive throughout Han Chinese culture in northwest and central China is a game called *Hua Quan*. An amazingly simple hand game, *Hua Quan* dominates the Han social scene, and its signature sounds penetrate every street corner, restaurant, and home throughout the region, especially once dusk begins to fall. While such matches are initially mistaken by most foreigners for violent arguments, the syncopated bursts of manic shrieking that issue forth from tables or from behind closed doors constitute no need for worry. The game is played one-on-one, with the two participants facing one another. Each player throws one hand into the center, holding out anywhere from zero to five fingers. Simultaneously, both participants must yell out a number from zero to 10. If the total number of fingers equals the number either player called out, that player wins the round. If there is no victor, the players go right into the next round. Simple, fun, and, above all, incredibly raucous.

FIRST BEACON TOWER (dì yī fēnghuǒ tái; 第一烽火台). The only portion of the original Jiayuguan Fort is the beacon tower that was used to relay warnings using windborne smoke signals. Fragments of the wall are scattered in the surrounding area, including the First Beacon Tower. The walk from the main complex to the tower entails crossing a main road and provides not-so-stunning views of Jiayuguan's industrial center. (*7km southwest of Jiayuguan Fort.*)

🢒 DAYTRIP FROM JIAYUGUAN: JULY 1 GLACIER

July 1 Glacier (qī yī bīngchuān; 七一冰川), 120 km south of Jiayuguan in the Qilian Mountains, offers fantastic 65m ice walls, caves, and nice views of the snowy mountains. July 1 Glacier is generally accessible from April to September. This trip is best made by at least four people. Asking prices for daytrips (approx. 3-4hr. of driving, 6hr. climbing or hiking) are Y600 for taxis with good clearance and power, Y800 for 10-person minibuses. Some drivers claim that *miandi* taxis are the best bet, but in fact the *miandis* cannot handle the roads. The best option is to talk to Jin Yufang (金玉芳), the manager at the Xiongguan Hotel. She will refer you to Wang Jun (王军), a driver experienced in making trips out to the glacier.

In July 2000, the road to the glacier was under construction and packed with dirt instead of gravel; it is not advisable to go if it is raining or if it has rained heavily in the past two days. A new road is scheduled for completion by 2001, which should improve travel greatly. The driver will drop you at a parking lot with a plaque indicating the location. Even in summer, take warm clothes and some food, as both hiking and road conditions can change quickly.

ZHANGYE 张掖 ☎0936

Zhangye was one of the most important Silk Road outposts along the Hexi Corridor, a narrow strip of fertile land running between the Qilian Mountains to the south and the Gobi and Budain Jaran Deserts to the north. However, the relics of Zhangye's rich history are for the most part swallowed up by monotonous block housing, commercial centers, and industrial smokestacks, which crowd a skyline once dominated by the Wood and Earth Pagodas to the south and the Drum Tower to the north. Though part of a layover day can be easily spent at a few sites within the city, most notably the giant reclining Buddha at Big Buddha Temple, Zhangye serves best as a transportation hub for the gorgeous temple town of **Matisi**, set in the foothills of the Tibetan Plateau.

✦ ORIENTATION AND PRACTICAL INFORMATION

From the South Bus Station, make a right on **Huancheng Nan Lu** (环城西路) and the first right onto **Xianfu Nan Jie** (县府南街) to reach the Big Buddha Temple, the Earth Pagoda, and the Zhangye Hotel.

Trains: Zhangye Train Station (zhāngyē huǒchē zhàn; 张掖火车站; ☎822 6749), is 8km northwest of the town center. *Miandi* taxis to the southwest part of town cost Y6 (with some haggling). Open 24hr. All trains running between **Lanzhou** and **Ürümqi** stop here; most also stop at **Jiayuguan** and **Wuwei**.

Buses: South Bus Station (nánguān qìchē zhàn; 南关汽车站; ☎821 3554 or 821 3449) is a 5min. walk from the Zhangye Hotel and within 10min. from most city sights. Open daily 6:30am-7:30pm. Although it supposedly only serves destinations to the west and south, buses also go to: **Dunhuang** (10hr.; 5pm; hard seat Y49, sleeper Y94); **Jiayuguan** (4hr., 4 per day 7:30-11:30am, Y17); **Lanzhou** (10hr.; every 30min. 7-8am; hard seat Y38.2, sleeper Y85); and **Matisi** (2hr.; every 30min.-1hr. 7am-5pm; Y6.3, foreigners Y12.6). **East Bus Station** (qìchē dōng zhàn; 汽车东站; ☎821 4073) is open daily 7am-8:30pm. To **Dunhuang** (10hr.; 7:20am and 5:30pm; hard seat Y46, sleeper Y92) and **Lanzhou** (11hr.; every 30min. 8am-8:30pm; hard seat Y38, sleeper Y80).

Travel Agency: CITS, 56 Xianfu Nan Jie (☎821 3505), in the lobby of the Zhangye Hotel.

Bank of China: On Dong Jie, a 5min. walk from the Drum Tower, on the left side of the street. Exchanges traveler's checks. Open M-F 8am-6pm. A more convenient option is a smaller branch on Xianfu Nan Jie, just north of the Zhangye Hotel. Exchanges currency only. Open daily 8am-6pm.

Post Office: A 3min. walk west of the Drum Tower, on the right side of the street. Open daily 8am-noon and 2:30-6pm. **Postal code:** 734000.

ACCOMMODATIONS

Zhangye has only two hotels that are officially open to foreigners.

Zhangye Hotel (zhāngyē bīnguǎn; 张掖宾馆), 56 Xianfu Nan Jie (☎821 2601, ext. 6289). Upon exiting the South Bus Station, make a right on Huancheng Nan Lu and then the first right onto Xianfu Nan Jie. The lobby of the economy building is 2min. ahead, on the right side of the street. Bright, clean dorm rooms with mopped linoleum floors and slightly yellow-tinged sheets overlook the garden in the rear. The rear building (hòu lóu; 后楼) has a CITS office and more luxurious rooms. Foreigners are charged double; with some effort, students should be able to get regular rates. 4-bed dorms Y14; 3-bed dorms Y18; singles with bath Y160; doubles with bath Y90-480.

Ganzhou Hotel (gānzhōu fàndiàn; 甘州饭店, ☎821 4749), on the northeast corner of the intersection of Nan Jie (南街) and Qingnian Xi Jie (青年西街), just south of the Drum Tower. The dim hallways with peeling paint seem to have received less attention than the rooms, which have spotless floors, impressively clean common baths, and somewhat questionable blue sheets. 24hr. hot water. 5-bed dorms Y10; 4-bed dorms Y12; 3-bed dorms Y13; 2-bed dorms Y15-18; singles Y38.

SIGHTS

BIG BUDDHA TEMPLE (dà fó sì; 大佛寺). Built in 1098 and restored during the Qing dynasty, this temple houses China's largest reclining Buddha, over 34m long. The temple also includes an array of guardian *lohans* surrounding the torpedo-like shape of the Holy One. Several small art galleries and a mediocre archeological survey of Zhangye's past are behind the temple. Although fenced off from the temple grounds and accessible only from Nan Jie, the **Earth Pavilion** (tǔ tǎ; 土塔) is worth a quick look; it embodies an interesting architectural confluence of Indo-Tibetan *stupa* forms and traditional flying-eave Chinese pagoda styles. *(On Minzhu Xi Jie, behind the Zhangye Hotel. Open daily 7:30am-6:30pm. Y11.)*

WOOD PAGODA (mù tǎ; 木塔). This 31m tall, nine-story pagoda was built in the 6th century and restored in 1925. Today it competes with a high-rise building just behind, although it is still a pleasant climb to the top. The small **Wanshou Temple** (wànshòu sì; 万寿寺) is also part of the complex. *(On Xianfu Nan Jie, just north of the Zhangye Hotel. Open daily 8am-6pm. Y5.)*

XILAI TEMPLE (xīlái sì; 西来寺). The tiny temple is perhaps more interesting for the throngs of old people who come to pray and socialize than for its interior. Several old monks will certainly offer to show you around the various nooks and crannies. *(Exiting the Wooden Pagoda complex, turn right on Minzhu Xi Jie, and then make the first left onto a small alley called Xilaisi Jie (there is no sign); the temple is on the right. Open daily sunrise-sunset. Free.)*

NEAR ZHANGYE: MATISI

Matisi (mǎtí sì; 马蹄寺), literally **Horse Hoof Temple**, has come to include both the main attraction in the area, the 33rd Heaven Grottoes, as well as several other smaller temples in the area. The temples are built into a vein of sheer cliffs that mark the foothills of the 2300m high Qilian Mountains. The surrounding landscape is breathtaking; several large waterfalls cascade from the ice-capped peaks above, winding down through cool pine forests and expanses of valley wildflowers. The hike along the high ridge above the 33rd Heaven Grottoes ends at the largest waterfall in the area. Many of the Tibetan villagers in the area rent horses and will gladly guide visitors to the most beautiful spots.

The **33rd Heaven Grottoes** (sānshísān tiān shíkū; 三十三天石窟) are strongly Tibetan in character. Richly detailed tapestries and sculptures emphasize the stages of the path to enlightenment, from peaceful smiling Buddhas holding lotus flowers to frightening guardians of the Southern Sea Realm. The name itself refers to the highest level of heavenly existence in the Tibetan Buddhist tradition (see **Tibetan Buddhism,** p. 729), which nonetheless falls short of enlightenment and Buddhahood. The five levels of caves are accessible by narrow, tunnel-like passages through the rock and overlook two white *stupas* to the west. Each contains an altar and several beautiful stone and bronze statues. Look for the horse hoof imprint in stone that gives the temple its name displayed in a glass case on the floor of the first temple.

Buses (2hr., every 45min.-1hr. 7am-5pm, Y6.3) go from Zhangye South Station to Matisi. The bus stops at the entrance gate (admission Y15) before continuing along the town's only road. Return buses to Zhangye are more erratic. Take a *miandi* taxi (Y3) to the nearby bus stop; you might have to wait up to an hour. The bus that departs at 4:30pm is fairly reliable, but arrive early to be sure. Miandi taxis back to Zhangye cost about Y100. The temple is open daily from 8am to 6pm. Admission is Y4 to the site, plus Y4 to climb the caves.

Small hostels of comparable price and quality line the main road just after the 33rd Heaven Temple complex. A good bet is the **Golden Horse Hostel** (jīn mǎ lǚshè; 金马旅社), just across from the two *stupas* up on the hill. Rooms have clean sheets and nice brick floors. (4-bed dorms Y15.) Several encampments at the top of the road provide accommodation and entertainment in Tibetan-style tents in the "ethnic village" at the foot of the mountains. This is a good way to experience a bit of Tibetan culture, though the area has a distinctly cheapened touristy feel. (Accommodation and food Y50-100 per person.)

DUNHUANG 敦煌 ☎0937

Long the natural junction of the southern and northern trade routes curving around the arid Tarim Basin, Dunhuang was one of ancient China's major trading posts. In the 2nd century BC, the ambitious Han Emperor Wudi incorporated the city into the Chinese empire. Hungry for more territory, he sent General Zhang Qian west to exploit tribal rivalries and forge allies for his next offensive. Zhang returned after eight years of tireless wandering through Central Asian and Indian kingdoms and reported that local leaders were reluctant to make war but eager to trade. Thus, caravans laden with precious Rome-bound silk ventured from the oasis of Dunhuang across the trans-Eurasian Silk Road. Dunhuang's location on this route made it a magnet for up-and-coming tribes. The Huns, Jie, Xianbei, Qiang, Tubo (Tibetan), Tangut, Mongols, and Uighurs all took turns wresting the outpost from Han control.

Lately, Dunhuang has been profiting from its past by promoting its fantastic desert scenery and the Mogao Grottoes' unrivaled Buddhist cave art to tourists. Dunhuang is a relaxing, beautiful area that easily merits a stay of three or four days. Excellent beer gardens, restaurants, and night markets abound, while the surrounding dunes and Crescent Lake are simply stunning.

⌐ TRANSPORTATION

Airplanes: Dunhuang Airport (dūnhuáng fēijīchǎng; 敦煌飞机场) is 13km east of the city. An unreliable shuttle service is offered by a private contractor; CAAC advises taking a taxi (20min., Y20-30) instead. **CAAC ticket office** (☎882 2389), on Yangguan Dong Lu, near Xinhua Bookstore. Open daily 8-11:30am and 3-6pm. Beware that many Dunhuang hotels pay commission to drivers to bring them potential guests. To: **Beijing** (Su-M and W-F, Y1500); **Lanzhou** (1 per day, Y820); **Ürümqi** (1-2 per day, Y570); and **Xian** (1 per day, Y1340).

Trains: Liuyuan Train Station (liŭyuán huŏchē zhàn; 柳园火车站; ☎(0937) 557 2995) is 2½hr. north of Dunhuang, along the Ürümqi-Lanzhou rail line. Frequent buses and minibuses to Liuyuan leave from the Dunhuang Bus Station. It is usually more difficult to get tickets on trains heading east. For longer trips, make arrangements 2-3 days in advance. Schedules change seasonally; check with John's Cafe, CITS, or Charley at Charley Johng's Cafe for up-to-date information. "Station fee" Y30 for hard sleepers, Y50 for soft sleepers. To: **Beijing** (40hr., 9:58am, Y544); **Lanzhou** (20hr., 3 per day, Y159); **Ürümqi** (13-15hr., 3 most available trains 6:08, 7:40, and 10:18pm, Y194) via **Turpan** (12hr.); and **Xian** (36hr., 3 per day 11:50am-7:24pm, Y229).

Buses: For long-distance travel beyond Liuyuan, most foreigners need the Y30 Gansu Insurance Ticket available at the **PICC office** (zhōngguó rénmín băoxiăn gōngsī; 中国人民保险公司), 12 Yangguan Zhong Lu (☎882 7469), near the Bank of China. Open M-F 8:30am-noon and 3-6:30pm. Most buses have a side compartment for storing bags; be prepared to have a wet pack if you leave yours on the roof, as short but furious rainstorms are frequent during the summer. There are 2 bus stations diagonally across from each another on Mingshan Lu. The **Dunhuang Bus Station** (dūnhuáng qìchē zhàn; 敦煌汽车站; ☎882 2174) is on the west side of the intersection. Open daily 6:30am-10:30pm. To: **Anxi** (7hr., 10 per day 7am-5:50pm, Y9.5); **Jiuquan** (5-6½hr.; 13 per day 7am-10:30pm, express buses at 8:30am and 2:30pm; Y31) via **Jiayuguan; Lanzhou** (22hr., 3 per day 8:30am-3pm, Y84); **Liuyuan** (2½hr., 8 per day, Y10); and **Wuwei** (10-12hr., 5 per day 8:30am-6pm, Y65) via **Zhangye. Dunhuang Long-distance Bus Station** (dūnhuáng chángtú qìchē zhàn; 敦煌长途汽车站; ☎882 3072, ext. 8115), is on the east side of the road. Open daily 6am-10pm. Buses go to Lanzhou, making frequent stops in all major towns along the way and taking much longer than buses from the other bus station.

Local Transportation: Taxis are not metered. Pedicabs, minibuses, and motorbikes abound, although walking or renting a bike is usually preferable. Most hotels offer **bike rental** for about Y1 per hr.

ORIENTATION AND PRACTICAL INFORMATION

All points of interest are within easy walking distance of each other; walking from the far northeast to the far southern part of Dunhuang takes under 20 minutes. The city is quartered by **Shazhou Lu** (沙州路) and **Yangguan Lu** (阳关路), which forms a traffic circle near the China Telecom building. Most tourist and commercial services are along Yangguan Lu, while budget accommodations and outdoor cafes line **Mingshan Lu** (鸣山路).

Travel Agencies: Dunhuang's 3 main sights (Mogao Grottoes, Crescent Moon Lake, and the Singing Sand Dunes) can all be toured without the aid of a travel agency. Ticket booking and travel information are offered at larger hotels, several tourist-oriented restaurants, and John's Information Cafe (see p. 686). **CITS,** 39 Mingshan Lu (☎882 3312), has English-, French-, German-, and Japanese-speaking staff. Commission Y30-50. Open daily 8am-noon and 2:30-6pm. Smilar "CITS" travel services in various hotels are in-house operations and not branches of the national agency.

Bank of China: On Yangguan Zhong Lu, a 5min. walk from Mingshan Lu. Exchanges traveler's checks and issues credit card advances. Open M-F 8am-noon and 3-6:30pm; in winter 8:30am-noon and 2:30-6pm. Currency exchange available in the Dunhuang, Taiyang, and International Hotels as well.

PSB: A short walk west from the intersection of Yangguan Lu and Mingshan Lu (☎882 2660). Issues **visa extensions** in the office to the right of the main gate. Open M-F 8am-noon and 3-6:30pm.

Internet Access: There is a small **Internet cafe** a few doors down from the post office. Y6 per hr. Open daily 8am-midnight, although they often siesta noon-3pm. **Charley Johng's Cafe, Shirley's Cafe,** and **John's Information Cafe,** all on Mingshan Zhong Lu, have access for Y20 per hr.

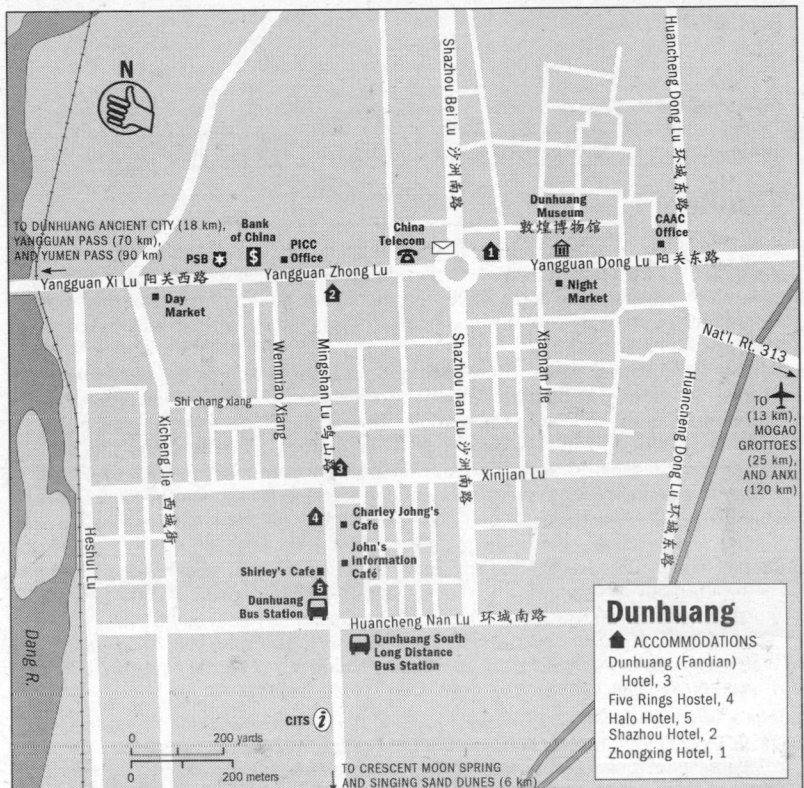

N

TO DUNHUANG ANCIENT CITY (18 km),
YANGGUAN PASS (70 km),
AND YUMEN PASS (90 km)

Bank
of China

PICC
Office

PSB 🏛 | $

Yangguan Xi Lu 阳关西路

Yangguan Zhong Lu

China
Telecom
☎ ✉

Dunhuang
Museum
敦煌博物馆
🏛

CAAC
Office

Yangguan Dong Lu 阳关东路

Shazhou Bei Lu 沙洲北路

Huancheng Dong Lu 环城东路

Nat'l. Rt. 313

TO
✈ (13 km),
MOGAO
GROTTOES
(25 km),
AND ANXI
(120 km)

Night
Market

■ Day
Market

Wenmiao Xiang

Mingshan Lu 鸣山路

Shi chang xiang

Shazhou nan Lu 沙洲南路

Xiaonan Jie

Xinjian Lu

Huancheng Dong Lu 环城东路

Xicheng Jie 西城街

Heshui Lu

Dang R.

Charley Johng's
■ Cafe

John's
■ Information
Café

Shirley's Cafe ■

Dunhuang
Bus Station 🚌

Huancheng Nan Lu 环城南路

🚌 Dunhuang South
Long Distance
Bus Station

CITS ⓘ

0   200 yards
0   200 meters

TO CRESCENT MOON SPRING
AND SINGING SAND DUNES (6 km)

Dunhuang

▲ ACCOMMODATIONS
Dunhuang (Fandian)
Hotel, 3
Five Rings Hostel, 4
Halo Hotel, 5
Shazhou Hotel, 2
Zhongxing Hotel, 1

NORTHWEST

Post and Telecommunications: Dunhuang's **post office** (☎882 1204) is on the corner
of Shazhou Bei Lu and Yangguan Zhong Lu, on the western side of the traffic circle. EMS
and Poste Restante available at the left counter. **China Telecom** is on the 2nd floor.
IDD service available. Both open daily 8am-7pm. **Postal Code:** 736200.

ACCOMMODATIONS

Most of Dunhuang's affordable hotels are along **Mingshan Lu.** Due to oversupply,
rates are often negotiable, and travelers usually do not pay the posted price.

Dunhuang (Fandian) Hotel (dūnhuáng fàndiàn; 敦煌饭店), 16 Mingshan Lu (☎882
7588), not to be confused with the expensive Dunhuang (Binguan) Hotel. Newly renovated, this hotel has decent service, clean and breezy rooms, and sparkling private
baths (but bare-bones communal bathrooms). 24hr. hot water. Deposit Y50. 10-bed
dorms Y10; doubles with bath and A/C Y100; triples Y60, with bath Y80; quads Y60.

Shazhou Hotel (shāzhōu fàndiàn; 沙洲饭店; ☎882 2380), on Mingshan Bei Lu. This
simple and straightforward hotel has free advice and bikes for guests. Well-maintained
rooms are bright and airy. 50% discount may be possible. Deposit Y100. Doubles with
bath Y60-80; triples Y90; quads Y100.

Five Rings Hostel (wǔ huán zhāodàisuǒ; 五环招待所; ☎882 2620), on Mingshan Lu,
across from the Feitian Hotel. Rooms are comfortable; like the Dunhuang, the communal bathrooms are this hostel's weakness. Deposit Y80-100. Doubles with bath Y100;
triples with bath Y120; quads Y60; quints Y50.

Halo Hotel (fóguāng dàjiŭdiàn; 佛光大酒店; ☎882 5040). Some English-speaking staff and great service give this hotel a good name. Deposit Y50. Bargain prices down at least Y15. Doubles Y160, with A/C Y320; triples Y90/150; quads Y160.

Zhongxing Hotel (zhōngxìng bīnguǎn; 中兴宾馆), 2 Yangguan Dong Lu (☎882 6488), opposite the post office, in the east end of town. Offers a spectrum of rooms, 24hr. hot water, and prompt service. Deposit Y300. Doubles Y60, with bath and A/C Y240-380.

🍴 FOOD

Chinese, Muslim, Western, and fusion restaurants are exploding in Dunhuang. Signs with the English word "cafe" are extremely popular, and the town is starting to resemble Yangshuo, the backpacker mecca outside Guilin. Here, fruit pancakes (Y3), chilled yogurt (Y2.5), freshly squeezed fruit juices, and attempts at chocolate soufflé are the norm.

Perhaps the liveliest place to try local and national cuisine is the **night market.** On the south side of Yangguan Dong Lu, in a rather grand open-air courtyard roughly opposite the museum, the market brims with stalls selling roasted chickens (dàpán jī; 大盘鸡; Y40-45), Chinese-style hamburgers, dumplings, hotpot, pastries, beer, and assorted teas. The market peaks around 7:30pm, lasting until 12:30am. For an interesting food experience, try **donkey meat yellow noodles** (lǘròu huángmiàn; 驴肉黄面; Y4).

■ **Charley Johng's Cafe** (☎883 3039), a 5min. walk from the post office, on the left side of the street. Owner Charley is affable and offers great Chinese and fusion food at great prices. Internet Y20 per hr., bike rental Y1 per hr. Charley can also reserve train and bus tickets for Y30-40 commission. What's more, he even lets you play your own music! Be sure to sign his log book. His sister runs **Shirley's Cafe** across the street (☎882 6387). Same prices, hours, and services. Open daily 7:30am-midnight.

John's Information Cafe (☎282 4816), left of the Feitian Hotel. A modern Silk Road refueling stop for travelers, with franchises in Kashgar, Ürümqi, and Turpan. A covered outdoor terrace greets guests, and the food is acceptable but a bit overpriced. Manager Jian Jun Wang can arrange bus tickets for no commission and air and train tickets for Y40-50 per ticket. IDD calls cost a one-time Y2 fee. Internet Y20 per hr., bike rental Y2 per hr. Open daily 7:30am-midnight.

👁 SIGHTS

There is little to see in Dunhuang itself. The dilapidated **Dunhuang Museum** (dūnhuáng bówùguǎn; 敦煌博物馆; ☎882 2981) is on Yangguang Dong Lu, with a 1950s-era fighter jet parked in the front courtyard. Lacking English explanations, staff, and housekeeping, this grim display of Han pottery, "New Stone Age" tools, and ancient Tibetan script should be only a last resort. *(Open daily 8am-6:30pm. Y10.)*

MOGAO GROTTOES (mògāo shíkū; 莫高石窟)

*25km southeast of Dunhuang. **Minibuses** cruise along Mingshan Lu daily 7:30-10:30am going to the grottoes for Y5 one-way; for the return trip, the same men wait around the parking lot area next to the hotel until 6pm or so. **Open** daily 8am-5pm; **guides** available 8:30-9:30am and 2-4:30pm. All of the **tours** only cover 10-15 caves, and the best preserved caves require a Y60-240 per person surcharge to enter. The most worthwhile are caves 45 and 57, both dripping with colors that remain amazingly bright after hundreds of years (Y60 per person per cave). Arrange at the front ticket office for access and a guide. Arrive at 8am and keep pressing the ticket office about getting a guide and tour; many tourists complain of having been told to wait, only to discover the English tour had already left. The quality of the guides varies widely, some knowing neither English nor the history of the grottoes. French-, German-, Russian-, and Japanese- speaking guides are also available. Chinese-speaking **tours** Y66. Because the morning tours end at noon and the guides have a siesta until 2pm, it is best not to wait around too long for a tour; otherwise, guides might limit the number of caves visited. **Tour-hopping** to spend more time at your favorite caves is also an option. **Photography** is pro-*

*hibited; cameras and bags must be stored to the right of the entrance for Y4. Light in the caves is poor at times; **flashlights** are available for rent for Y13, with a Y10 deposit. Weak and heavy, these ancient tubes are ineffective; bring your own with fresh batteries (available in town at many small vendors and at an electronics store on Mingshan Lu, near John's Information Cafe; Y1.5-6 per battery). **Admission** to grottoes Y88, students with any valid ID Y33.*

As the story goes, in AD 366, an Eastern Jin monk named Le Zun saw thousands of Buddhas—manifested as rays of light—glimmering from the cliff shafts of the Sanwei Mountain gully one night. He immediately threw himself to the desert ground in prayer and began digging into the cliff, determined to make a cave in honor of the buddhas. A few years later, another monk passed by and, after seeing the first monk hard at work, began a second cave. The project snowballed.

The clay of Mogao, unlike the cliff boulders of grottoes farther east, is ill-suited to large carvings, so artists created stucco figurines and frescoes. Over the next 11 dynasties, more than a thousand niches were created. Nearly 500 niches remain, containing an astounding 2150 statues and 43,000 murals. Most of the original reds, greens, ochres, and blues created out of metal oxides have ionized to a dark black, giving the murals an austere appearance. The motif is overwhelmingly Buddhist, but scenes illustrating Confucian virtues, historical events, landscapes, and daily life have also been discovered. In addition to endless numbers of buddhas, *arhats*, and *bodhisattvas*, Mogao is unique for its "flying *apsaras*," hovering angelic buddhas with fluttering drapery. This trademark has even made its way onto the tails of China Northwest Airlines' jets. During the Cultural Revolution, the caves escaped unharmed, thanks to the protection of Premier Zhou Enlai. In 1987, Mogao was named a UNESCO World Heritage Site.

SIXTEEN KINGDOMS (AD 304-439). Heavily weathered, the murals still show the heavy influence of Indian styles, with thick folds of skin on the Buddha and arbitrary shading. The open eye sockets and awkward flying postures of the flying *apsaras* give them a rather grotesque appearance. These statuettes, such as those of cave 275, show simple facial features reminiscent of Han terracotta figures.

NORTHERN WEI (386-534) AND WESTERN WEI (535-551). Immensely devout Buddhists, the Xianbei had a huge appetite for grottoes, patronizing not only Dunhuang but also Yungang and Longmen. The Mogao murals of this era (caves 432 and 259) feature elongated figures with flowing drapery and dashing *apsaras* with trailing ribbons. The battle scene of cave 120 reflects the mood of the period.

NORTHERN ZHOU (557-581) AND SUI (581-619). During the transition period between northern and southern dynasties and the end of 300 years of division, the once-slender statuettes begin to stiffen. Flying *apsaras* bear drapery festooned with abstract images and the occasional simple stylized representations of landscape imagery. Cave 15 shows a trinity scene with buddhas framed in pearls.

TANG (618-907). The Tang was the heyday of the Mogao Grottoes. Cave 51E exemplifies the cosmopolitan Tang empire with a genre painting of a congregation of Central Asian traders. Unlike earlier Indian depictions of nudity, the fully clothed Tang statues in caves 238 and 428 have unmistakably Chinese facial characteristics. Amitabha (Buddha of Eternal Paradise) and his Western Paradise were a favorite motif of the period. Painted using models from Beijing palace architectural styles, the radiating courtyards of attendant *bodhisattvas* reflect the hierarchy of the Buddhist cosmos. Larger buddhas are scattered over the surface of the wall, each with smaller and smaller layers of attendants and devotees. The mural in cave 139A shows the Amitabha seated on a lotus lantern under a pavilion, overlooking souls being reborn in the pool of reincarnation positioned in the foreground. The composition's symmetry is intentionally broken to highlight the dancing girl. Landscape frescoes, such as in cave 70, reflect the popular water and ink mountains and river themes of the time. The swirling halos behind most of the Tang-era Buddhas are surprisingly modern in their style and form.

LATER WORKS, REDISCOVERY, AND THE GREAT CALAMITY. After the Tibetan invasion of Dunhuang in 781, the quality and quantity of Mogao art suffered. Cave 55's haunting warrior from after the fall of the Tang has been compared by art historians to the degeneration in late Roman works. Later dynasties such as the Song and Ming steered China back toward Confucianism, and the Mogao Grottoes were eventually forgotten.

In 1900, Wang Yuan, a poor monk, discovered a vast collection of scriptures in cave 17. The 50,000-volume *Dunhuang Books*, written from AD 359 to 1136, contained Buddhist, Confucian, and Daoist documents, Bön poetry (see p. 728), travelogues, statistical records, and even musical scores. European and Japanese adventurers purchased or pillaged most of the collection, hence the "Great Calamity." When American Langdon Warner arrived in 1924, no volumes remained, so he used chemical adhesives and stripped off the murals from caves 323, 325, and 329. He returned with two of his students and began ripping into cave 285, but locals drove him out of the province.

Today, Dunhuang artwork in China and around the world (Warner donated his heist to Harvard University's Fogg Museum) has created a field in art history and religion known as Dunhuangology. The **Dunhuang Research Institute,** to the left of the caves, presents eight hand-painted, professional replica caves, brightly lit to give a much more detailed study of the art than the original caves. Photographs of the various explorers who traveled through the caves and an impressive collection of Tibetan Buddhist bronze art are displayed on the second floor. (☎886 9050. Open daily 8:20am-5:30pm. Free with Y66 or Y88 Mogao Grottoes ticket.)

OTHER SIGHTS

CRESCENT MOON SPRING AND SINGING SAND DUNES (yuèyā quán; 月牙泉; and mínshā shān; 鸣沙山). One of the most stunning vistas in northwest China, this shimmering crescent-shaped pool is surrounded by golden sand dunes. Legend has it that the pool, fed by an eternal spring, has been in the same location for 2000 years. Dunhuang's fantastic sand dunes, surging up from the oasis frontier, are visible from the center of town. The highest dunes rise from a series of windbrushed sand valleys that stretch for kilometers. Even the lesser peaks, best scaled on a wooden "ladder" (Y5-10) pressed into the slope, reward climbers with enchanting views of a vast, barren expanse interrupted only by the remarkable green of Dunhuang's fields and orchards. Although the sands are scalding before 5:30 or 6pm, the earlier you arrive, the farther you can place yourself from the hordes of tourists that flood the area around 6:30 or 7pm. You can also join them in "sand surfing" on a primitive sled (Y5), paragliding (Y20), or camel-riding (Y30-40). In the summer, the sun sets around 9 or 9:30pm, providing a prime photo-op; people often stay at the dunes until midnight or later. (An easy 30min. bike ride from Dunhuang. Ride south on Mingshan Lu, turn left at the Jinye Hotel, and follow the road for 6km to the gate. Due to the intense summer heat, departing Dunhuang about 5:30pm is best. The small dirt roads through the vast fruit orchards surrounding the front entrance gate lead to a 3 ft. barbed wire fence, down in many places. Y25.)

DUNHUANG ANCIENT CITY (dūnhuáng gǔchéng; 敦煌古城). A bit peculiar, even for China, is Dunhuang's "Ancient" City, actually a movie set built in 1987 to resemble a Song dynasty village. The price is hardly worth it. (18km southwest of Dunhuang. Minibuses cost Y70-90; tours also leave from CITS and John's Cafe. Y20.)

JADE GATE PASS AND SUN PASS (yùmén guān; 玉门关; and yángguān; 阳关). The ruins of Jade Gate Pass and Sun Pass would likely interest history buffs more for their historical import than their current state. Quickly deteriorating under the relentless heat and wind, these once-great gateways are nothing more than fading mounds in the desert. A trip consumes the better part of a day, costs Y300-600, and should probably by considered only by those who have time (and money) to burn. For better ruins, head west to Turpan. (80km west of Dunhuang. Organized tours generally also include a military storage facility (hé cān chéng; 河仓城) and the Han dynasty Great Wall relics (hàn cháng chéng; 汉长城). Jade Gate Pass Y30; Sun Pass Y10.)

XINJIANG 新疆

Covering a sixth of China's landmass with its deep basins (Tarim and Dzungar) and titanic mountain ranges (Altay, Tianshan, and Kunlun), the Xinjiang Uighur Autonomous Region stretches over an area 10 times the size of England. In this land of extremes, freezing peaks rise 8600m while depressions plunge well below sea level, and luscious melons ripen in oasis orchards while ancient ruins languish in parched deserts. The people who make the region their home are just as varied as Xinjiang's terrain, counting Uighurs, Kazakhs, Uzbeks, Mongols, Hui, and Han among their ranks. A world unto itself, Xinjiang has a little of everything, including unspoiled wilderness, well-preserved ruins, and a fascinating cultural landscape.

Easy to conquer but hard to manage, Xinjiang has seen plenty of invaders in its time, but few long-lasting governments. The region's earliest contacts with the Chinese came in the 2nd century BC, when Han armies pushed Xiongnu (Hun) tribes into the Tarim Basin. Han Emperor Wu's emissary Zhang Qian's journey into Central Asia helped open the Silk Routes (see also p. 683). After the Han folded and the Huns packed up and headed west, a loosely networked Turkish empire filled the power vacuum, stretching across Central Asia, Mongolia, and into Siberia. An alliance between Tang and Uighur forces drove out the Turks in 657, forming a Uighur kingdom under Tang suzerainty. But Tang influence receded in the wake of defeats by Muslim invaders, and the Uighurs fell to the Kyrgyzs in the 8th century. A string of invaders, including the Tibetans, Khitans, Karakhitans, and Mongols, followed, and it wasn't until 1759 that Qing armies reasserted Chinese control. In 1864, a Tajik general, Yakub Beg, took charge of a Muslim rebellion and formed the short-lived independent kingdom of Kashgaria. It was brought down by Hunanese commander Zuo Zongtang (of General Tso's Chicken fame) in 1876, only to face threats of annexation from soon-to-be-defunct Czarist Russia.

The first half of the 20th century saw Xinjiang running for shelter from a series of military coups, political backstabbings, makeshift coalitions, assassinations, and mysterious disappearances. Only the arrival of the PLA in 1949 imposed some stability on the region, but the Cultural Revolution brought back chaos, as thousands of mosques were destroyed. Heavy state-sponsored Han immigration in past decades has dramatically altered Xinjiang's ethnic composition and animosity between Han Chinese and Uighurs flares up from time to time, spurred by legal injustices, unequal opportunities, and mutual distrust. Ethnic riots rocked Kashgar in 1992 and 1997, while car bombs set by Uighur extremists shook Ürümqi and Beijing. A September 2000 bombing in Ürümqi, allegedly the act of Islamic fundamentalists, killed over 100 people. Although things have calmed down since, hope for autonomy from China lives on in the Uighur population.

NORTHWEST

IT'S ALL UIGHUR TO ME
The Uighur language is commonly spoken in China's Northwest, particularly in Xinjiang. There are no tones in Uighur; spew these words out to the best of your ability, and someone is sure to echo back the correct pronunciation. The "shi" sound is pronounced like "ship"; the "h" is reminiscent of coughing; and the "z" is similar to the "h" sound in its guttural pronunciation.

Hello, how are you?	yak-shimi-sis	to eat	tam-ak
Okay	yak-shi	invite to eat	tam-ak yang
Goodbye	hara-hosh	hami melon	how-hun
What are you doing?	azer ne-mar-ish-ka-li-sis	sweet	tat-let
How much does this cost?	nai-chi-po	tea	chai

In Xinjiang, time is generally told in Beijing time. However, informally, many people go according to Xinjiang time, two or three hours behind Beijing time. When you buy a bus or train ticket, verify which time is the right one. In Xinjiang more so than in many other parts of China, money can be an issue. Do not pay for tours before you return and are satisfied that the conditions have been met. If you charter a taxi or minibus, do not pay in advance. Many men in Xinjiang carry knives, so above all, handle disagreements as calmly as possible.

ÜRÜMQI 乌鲁木齐   ☎0991

Ürümqi is an expansive industriopolis of over 1.4 million inhabitants. Ironically, the capital of the Xinjiang Uighur Autonomous Region is very much a Han city, in both urban appearance and racial composition. Only small numbers of Uighur, Xibo, Hui, and Kazakh people continue to make a living here, creating a strange and fascinating mix. The flashing stripes of color in Uighur skirts, the bob of the *fez* in a thick crowd, and the rich tapestry of Uighur, Cyrillic, and Chinese scripts adorning virtually every street facade impart a sense of a 21st-century Silk Road, an exciting confluence of people and cultures on the move. Ürümqi really comes alive after sunset, disregarding the cues of Beijing time as it pulses deep into the night. While you're in the city, enjoy the rich food culture by strolling through night bazaars and smoky, vibrant back alleys where the scent of freshly baked bread and roasting meat wafts through galleries filled with fresh fruit, nuts, and sweet snack vendors.

Occupying a strategic access point through the Tianshan mountain range, Ürümqi has seen its share of power struggles. The 1955 discovery of oil in nearby Karamay kick-started the economy, and now Ürümqi oil executives are competing with those in Texas and Tokyo in the rush to cash in on the petroleum reserves around the Caspian Sea. Ürümqi offers travelers a magnificent museum, transportation links to China, Russia, and Central Asia, and a network of backpackers and travel agencies from which to glean advice about further travel in Xinjiang.

▢ TRANSPORTATION

Airplanes: Ürümqi Airport (wūlǔmùqí jīchǎng; 乌鲁木齐机场; ☎371 9511, ext. 113) is 20km from town. Shuttle buses (40min., Y8) leave the **Xinjiang Airlines ticket office** (xīnjiāng hángkōng shòupiào chù; 新疆航空售票处; ☎264 1826; 24hr. ☎265 2826), on the east side of Youhao Nan Lu, about 2hr. before departure. From the airport into town, the buses wait until full, up to an hour. Taxis cost about Y50. Xinjiang destinations include: **Aksu** (2pm, Y590); **Hotan** (Tu, Th, and Sa 1:30pm; Y1000); **Kashgar** (3 per day 9am-9:30pm, Y980); **Yining** (2-3 per day 8:40am-7pm, Y590). Other domestic flights to: **Beijing** (2-3 per day 8:30am-3pm, Y1930); **Dunhuang** (1 per day M-Sa, Y570); **Guangzhou** (1 per day Su-M and W-F, Y2270); **Lanzhou** (1 per day Tu-Th and Su, Y1040); **Shanghai** (W-Th and Sa-M 8:50am, Y2240); **Xian** (several morning flights per day, Y1330); and **Xining** (4 per week, Y900). Xinjiang Airlines international flights to: **Almaty** (M-F 6:05pm, Y1660); **Islamabad** (W 10:10am, Y2270); and **Moscow** (F 9:30am, Y2490). **Siberian Air,** 51 Xinhua Nan Lu (☎286 4327), in the Overseas Chinese Hotel compound, has flights to **Moscow** (Tu and Sa 3pm, US$200) via **Novosibirsk** (US$150). Open M, W-F, and Su 11am-7pm, Th 4-7pm.

Trains: Ürümqi Train Station (wūlǔmùqí huǒchē zhàn; 乌鲁木齐火车站; ☎344 5222), in the southwest part of town off the Ürümqi-Turpan highway. Take bus #2 or 10 or a taxi (Y6-9) from Xinhua Lu. Scalpers gobble up tickets to popular destinations; to avoid a Y30-40 commission, do as they do and buy tickets 2-4 days in advance. Within Xinjiang, daily trains head to **Kashgar** (30hr., Y199), via **Korla** (9hr., Y155), **Kuqa** (15hr., Y170), and **Aksu** (20hr., Y186). Express trains to Korla depart at 9:23pm. Also to: **Beijing** (59hr., 9:05pm, Y650); **Chengdu** (11:52am, Y340); **Lanzhou** (33hr., midnight, Y225); **Liuyuan** (13hr., variable departures, Y194); **Shanghai** (65hr., 11pm,

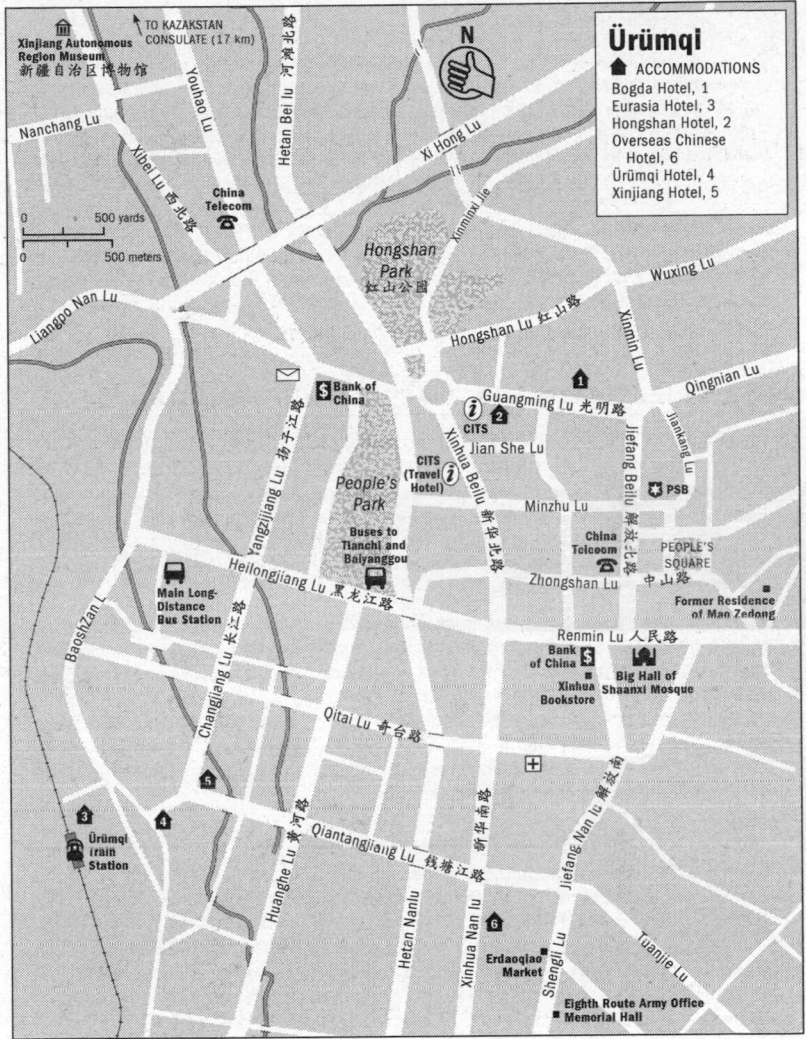

Y698); and **Xian** (3pm, Y400). Train #13 (30hr., M and Sa 11pm) goes to **Almaty, Kazakhstan,** via Alashankou.

Buses: Ürümqi has several long-distance bus stations. International buses depart from the Main Long-distance Bus Station.

Ürümqi Main Long-distance Bus Station (wūlǔmùqí chángtú qìchē zhàn; 乌鲁木齐长途汽车站), on Heilongjiang Lu, north of the train station and before Baoshan Lu. To: **Almaty, Kazakhstan** (16hr., 7 and 8pm, Y95-108); **Lanzhou** (40hr., 5pm, Y110); and **Yining** (16hr.; 11am, 1pm, and every hr. 3-9pm; Y90-100).

Southern Bus Station (nánjiāo qìchē zhàn; 南郊汽车站; ☎286 6635), on the south side of Xinhua Lu and Shengli Lu, serves destinations to the south and west and Turpan in the east. Accessible via bus #109 from across Changjiang Lu from the Xinjiang Hotel or by taxi (Y8). Open daily 8:30am-8:30pm. To: **Aksu** (every 30min. 1:30-8:30pm, Y95-108); **Kashgar** (30hr., every hr. 2-8pm, Y140-156); **Korla** (5 per day 11am-8pm; Y67-126, night bus Y46-71); **Kuqa** (every hr. 2-7pm, Y74-85); **Lanzhou** (1 per day, Y220); and **Turpan** (3hr., every 30min. 8:40am-8pm, Y20).

Kashgar Long-distance Bus Station (kāshí chángtú qìchē zhàn; 喀什长途汽车), 44 Qian-tangjiang Lu (☎581 1572), a 5min. walk east of the train station on the left and facing the Ürümqi Hotel, has buses to Kashgar at the same times and prices as the Southern Bus Station. Open daily 9am-9pm.

Buses arriving from **Hotan** stop at the Hotan District Office (hétiān zhù wūshì bànshì chù; 和田驻乌市办事处), on Hetan Bei Lu, north of Hongshan Park. Walk south on the left side of the road (the park's big hill is visible) until the sidewalk ends; make a left into an industrial goods alley. When you come to the next intersection, look right for the bus stop; take bus #109 (Y0.50) to the train station area and the Xinjiang Hotel.

Local Transportation: Buses lumber along Xinhua Lu: **#7** and **28** are the most frequent. Bus **#2** runs from the train station northwest to the Kazakh Consulate. Bus **#101** cuts through the Uighur area of Erdaoqiao, while **#1** runs south from the Hongshan Hotel to the Main Bus Station. Fare Y0.5-0.8.

Taxis: Base fare Y6. Trips around town generally under Y10.

■🛈 ORIENTATION AND PRACTICAL INFORMATION

Ürümqi lacks any discernible city center. **Xinhua Lu** (新华路) cuts from north to south through the sprawl, running past most budget hotels and tourist services. **Heilongjiang Lu** (黑龙江路) leads to the main bus station, and **Qiantangjiang Lu** (钱塘江路) leads to the train station farther south. **Guangming Lu** (光明路), dividing People's and Hongshan Parks, absorbs the north end of Xinhua Lu and leads to a number of tourist and financial services. The Uighur quarter of the city is in the southern neighborhood of **Erdaoqiao** (二道桥).

Travel Agencies: Well-established hotel agencies are often more reliable than the one-man business card-toting operations that seek you out on the street or in hotel lobbies. The **Hongshan Hotel** houses 2 agencies. **Tianshan Tianchi International Travel Service** (tiānshān tiānchí guójì lǚxíngshè; 天山天池国际旅行社; ☎281 6018, ext. 321), 3rd Fl., runs a popular 1-day trip to Tianchi (Y140). **Dabancheng Domestic Travel Agency** (dábǎnchéng guónèi lǚxíngshè; 达坂城国内旅行社; ☎231 6975), 1st Fl., also runs all-inclusive tours to Tianchi (Y150) and can arrange drivers to all parts of Xin-jiang for about Y600 per day. Both open 24hr.

Adventure Travel: Some agencies offer more rigorous mountain climbing and wilderness backpacking tours, as well as long guided camping excursions into the desert. One of the most reputable and hard-core guided trips is a 1- to 2-week ascent of 5000m Bogda Peak near Tianchi, led by the **Ürümqi Mountain Climbing Club**. Contact Wang Tienan (☎(130) 09681695; pager (127) 1031177), the head of the club, for details. Guided trips including tents, gear, cooks, and pack animals run US$40-50 per day. **Xinjiang International Sports Travel Service** (xīnjiāng guójì tǐyù lǚxíngshè; 新疆国际体育旅行社; ☎231 8481), next to Mark's Internet Cafe, specializes in guided trekking around Tianchi and the Altai region in northern Xinjiang.

Visas: Visas for travel to Kazakhstan are now handled in the **Kazakh Airlines office,** 31 Kunming Lu (☎381 6186), north of the Hotel World Plaza. 7-day processing. US$150 fee. Open M-Th 10:30am-2:30pm.

Bank of China: 1 Yangzijiang Lu, opposite the post office. Open M-F 10am-6pm, Sa-Su 11am-2:30pm. Exchanges traveler's checks (counter #23) and offers credit card advances (counter #9). Also at 343 Jiefang Nan Lu, at Renmin Lu, just west of Xinhua Bookstore. Open M-F 9:30am-1:30pm and 4-7pm, Sa-Su 11am-3pm.

Bookstore: Xinhua Bookstore (☎281 8136), has a good selection of English-Uighur phrasebooks and Xinjiang maps. Open daily 10am-8pm.

PSB: Foreigner Reception Office (wàiguórén jiēdàishì; 外国人接待室; ☎281 0452, ext. 3646), on the corner of Minzhu Lu and Jiankang Lu. **Visa extensions** (US citizens Y186) and lost and found. Open M-F 9:30am-1pm and 4-8pm.

Internet Access: Qisheng Network (qíshēng wǎngluò; 奇生网络), just inside the night market on Changjiang Lu. Walk north on Changjiang Lu and enter right into the bazaar;

the shop is the 2nd door on the left. Fast connections and telnet access. Y4 per hr. Open 24hr. **New Silk Road Internet Cafe,** Dejing Bldg., 4th Fl., on Zhongshan Lu. Fast connections as well as student and teacher discounts (Y5 per hr.). Y8 per hr. **Mark's Internet,** next to the Hongshan Hotel, has a few computers with slow connections. Y10 per hr. Open M-Sa 10am-1am. **China Telecom,** 105 Zhongshan Lu, a 4min. walk east of Xinhua Bei Lu. Y15 per hr. Open daily 9:30am-7:30pm.

Post Office: Main post office (☎585 7329), on Yangzijiang Lu, opposite the Bank of China, a 10min. walk west of the Hongshan Hotel. Descend the underground walkway in front of the bank, and re-emerge at the post office entrance. EMS and Poste Restante available in the room to the right. Open daily 9:30am-10:30pm. **Postal Code:** 830000.

▐▗▍ ACCOMMODATIONS AND FOOD

Budget accommodations are clustered around the train station to the southeast, less convenient for exploring the city, but nonetheless relatively safe and cheap.

Ürümqi has a distinct lack of must-chow-down-at restaurants. On the other hand, the thousands of little eateries along Xinhua Lu and in the Erdaoqiao Muslim district always satisfy. Night markets abound in the train station area; the best is on **Changjiang Lu,** about a five-minute walk from the Xinjiang Hotel. Most night markets start around 8:30pm Beijing time. Try the many kinds of lamb kebabs (yángròu chuān; 羊肉串), usually Y1 a piece. Cold Xinjiang beer is served up at nearly every stand (Y2.5-3 per bottle). A great meal with drinks costs around Y15.

📧 **Xinjiang Hotel** (xīnjiāng fàndiàn; 新疆饭店), 107 Changjiang Lu (☎585 2511, ext. 2000), facing the traffic circle at Qiantangjiang Lu and Changjiang Lu, a 10min. walk from the train station. Rooms have a view of the traffic circle, TV, phone, and clean sheets. Deposit Y20-200. 6-bed dorms Y17; 5-bed dorms Y22; 2-bed dorms Y35; doubles with bath Y170-688; quads Y80.

Eurasia Hotel (yà'ōu bīnguǎn; 亚欧宾馆), in the train station area. When you exit the station from the main doors, turn left. The Eurasia offers well-maintained rooms, and the reception desk can handle all your transportation needs. The cheaper dorms have bunk-beds with 1 in. thick mattresses. Showers in the nicer dorms 8-9pm only. Deposit Y50-100 per person. Key deposit Y20. 8-bed dorms Y12; 4-bed dorms with bath Y20; 3-bed dorms with bath Y80; doubles with bath Y198, with A/C Y228.

Hongshan Hotel (hóngshān bīnguǎn; 红山宾馆), 108 Xinhua Bei Lu (☎281 6018), across from Hongshan Park. Although foreigners cannot pay by the bed, the Hongshan is still a great place to meet other travelers. Rooms in the right wing off the lobby are generally in better condition. Deposit Y40 per person. Reservations recommended. Singles Y120, doubles Y90, with bath Y130; triples with bath Y195.

Bogda Hotel (bógédá bīnguǎn; 博格达宾馆), 10 Guangming Lu (☎282 3910, ext. 2119), a 10min. walk east of the Hongshan Hotel, in a pretentious "First Guesthouse of the Xinjiang Military Region" compound. This privatized ex-military hostel has bargain dorms (without showers) and pricey rooms. Off-season discounts available. 4- to 5-bed dorms Y20; doubles with bath Y288-388.

Overseas Chinese Hotel (huá qiáo bīnguǎn; 华侨宾馆), 51 Xinhua Nan Lu (☎286 0793), in the south of town, past Qiantangjiang Lu. In the Uighur part of town near the Kashgar and Turpan long-distance bus stations, this hotel houses the Siberian Airlines office and lots of Russian signs. Rooms are small, though bright and clean. Deposit Y100. 3-bed dorms Y60; singles Y100; doubles Y120-300. Traveler's checks accepted.

Ürümqi Hotel (wūlūmùqí bīnguǎn; 乌鲁木齐宾馆), 45 Qiantangjiang Lu (☎582 2888), across the traffic circle from the Xinjiang Hotel, a 5min. walk from the train station. Rooms have good views, immaculate sheets, and sparkling bathrooms. The glitter and marble attract guests like a flame attracts moths. Prices might zap you, though. Deposit twice room rate. Singles Y168-198; doubles Y238; triples Y180.

👁 SIGHTS

XINJIANG UIGHUR AUTONOMOUS REGION MUSEUM (xīnjiāng wéiwūěrzú zìzhì qū bówùguǎn; 新疆维吾尔族自治区博物馆). The brilliant Xinjiang Uighur Autonomous Region Museum is the lone star among Ürümqi's sights. Off the main lobby and behind a tourist shop is a hall devoted to the tools, dwellings, and dress of China's Uighur, Manchu, Xibo, Mongol, Hui, Uzbek, Tajik, Russian, and Tatar minorities. The rear part of this building displays massive felt- and fur-covered yurts surrounded by a hilarious array of stiff-looking stuffed sheep and goats intended to make the diorama more authentic.

The second and third halls, to the right of the lobby, boast to Xinjiang's archeological treasures, from a Western Han biscuit still in its wrappings to a Tang metal eye-protector. The fantastic mummies include an infant who died about 3800 years ago and "Loulan Beauty," the corpse of a 45-year-old woman of Indo-European ethnicity, reputed to be 4000 years old. The gift shop sells spectacular Uighur rugs. *(In the north part of town, recognizable by its green-tiled dome roof. A 25min. walk along Xibei Lu from the post office, or a 5min. ride on bus #7. Bus #2 runs from in front of the Xinjiang Hotel to just across from the museum. Free tours in Mandarin; most exhibits have English captions. Open M-F 9:30am-7:30pm, last admission 6pm; Sa-Su 10:30am-5pm. Y25, students Y12.)*

ERDAOQIAO MARKET (èrdàoqiáo shìchǎng; 二道桥市场). One of the best stops in town, this market sits in the heart of Ürümqi's Uighur quarter. On weekends, shop selling textiles and crafts spread out over an area almost one-fourth the size of Kashgar's famous Sunday bazaar (see p. 711). The main market is on Shengli Lu, stretching for several blocks south of where it turns into Jiefang Lu. A large gateway leads to a back alley full of rugs, silk, and food.

NEAR ÜRÜMQI: TIANCHI

Buses (2-2½hr., same-day round-trip Y15-20) leave for Tianchi daily from the south end of People's Park and from Hongshan Park, across from the Hongshan Hotel. Buy tickets at 8:15am; buses leave at 9am. Be sure to ask whether your ticket includes a highway toll fee, often tacked on at the last minute by the drivers. If you plan to spend the night at Tianchi, you will have to buy another Y15 ticket the next day. Buses back leave daily 4:30-5:30pm, stopping at the mid-mountain as well as at the bottom parking lot before heading back to Ürümqi. Public buses leave Tianchi every 30min. or so 8:30 10:30am, although you will need to change buses at Fukang (Y10) and Ermao (Y1.5-5); delays and complications are common. We recommend that you not take the small minibuses back to Ürümqi; take one of the large tourist buses (running in the afternoon only) instead. Bring warm clothes, especially for overnight stays. Although the yurts have stoves in them, it can get surprisingly chilly in the mountains, even in summer. Most Kazakhs here speak some English, but communication still requires gesturing.

Nestled high in the Tianshan mountains, 115km east of Ürümqi, the charming mountain lake of Tianchi lies 1950m above sea level, guarded by the stately 6000m Bogda peak. Tianchi rewards visitors with unforgettable experiences like alpine hiking, star-gazing, and camping in Kazakh yurts. According to myth, the Mother of the Western Skies would hold a feast at this lake whenever a local peach tree bore fruit. As this only happened about once every 3000 years, the banquets were understandably grand affairs. All the immortals would gather for such a long-awaited festival, converting the lake area into something of a Little Heaven; hence the name, "heavenly pool."

While immortals are hard to come by these days, Tianchi's natural beauty attracts hordes of worldly Chinese tourists. Breaking away from the paved lakeside paths and up into the surrounding hills will put plenty of distance between you and them. Several horse trails will take you to the high ridges that overlook the snow-capped mountains in the distance; small Kazakh encampments are scattered in pockets of grassland at amazingly high altitudes. Back at the lake, swimming is a great summer activity.

Overnight stays are highly recommended, as the lake regains its heavenly tranquility only after the majority of daytrippers exit around 5pm. Finding lodging in the many lakeside yurts is simple. Just ask, or more likely, you will be asked. Three meals and lodging costs about Y40; establish the price early on. **Rashit**, an endearing Kazakh guide, has been entertaining guests in his nine-yurt camp on the southwest bank of the lake for over 12 years. He speaks Mandarin and English, and is a great cook, too. While many backpackers go to Tianchi in search of solitude, they usually find their way to Rashit's by nightfall, attracted by the warm food and convivial atmosphere.

YINING 伊宁 ☎ 0999

Most travelers following the Silk Road through Xinjiang do not make the northern detour up to Yining, accessible only by a long bus ride or by a flight from Ürümqi or Korla. Although the city itself has little of interest, the road trip there passes through several wildlife preserves and the famous Sailimu Lake, offering magnificent views of snow-capped mountains, barren deserts, and alpine river valleys. As buses between Yining and Ürümqi are frequent, making a stop in an appealing camp area is quite feasible; buses often drop off and pick up roadside passengers. Most accessible is a stop at Sailimu Lake, 180km east of Yining, where you can easily find yurt accommodation. The ride from Korla to Yining (or vice versa) is also fantastic, with several alpine forests offering yurt accommodation (visible from the gravel highway). Stopping at these camps provides access to one of Xinjiang's most pristine wilderness areas; day hiking and camping options are limitless, though hailing a bus headed toward Yining may be difficult, making a Y400-500 taxi the only way back to the city.

✴ ORIENTATION AND PRACTICAL INFORMATION

Jiefang Lu (解放路) runs from the bus station in the northwest down to the post office near the southern limits of the city. **Sidalin Jie** (斯大林街) runs from east to west, crossing **Qingnian Square** (qīngnián guǎngchǎng; 青年广场) and then Jiefang Lu at the post office. Hotels are clustered near the bus station in the west, and around the Qingnian Square in the southeast.

Airplanes: The airport is a 15min. taxi ride north of the city (Y10; drivers try to charge Y20). **CAAC ticket office** (☎ 804 4328; 24hr. ☎ 803 2332), in the Yilite Hotel. Cancellations and delays are common; check in advance with the CAAC ticket office or the travel agency. To **Ürümqi** (1-2 per day, Y590).

Buses: Yining Long-distance Bus Station (yīníng chángtú qìchē zhàn; 伊宁长途汽车站; ☎ 802 3413), on the northwest end of Jiefang Lu, across the street and 100m down from the bus station. Open daily 8am-8pm. To: **Kashgar** (48hr.; Su-M, W, and F 3pm; Tu, Th, and Sa every hr. 11:30am-1:30pm, Y132); **Korla** (18-30hr., 12:30pm, Y63); and **Ürümqi** (17hr., every hr. 3:30-7:30pm, Y101-115).

Local Transportation: Bus #1 (Y0.5) runs along Jiefang Lu from the bus station to Qingnian Square in the east. Bus **#2** runs from the northwest end of Qingnian Square west along Sidalin Jie before heading south to the Yili River Park (Y1.2) along Yili He Lu.

Travel Agencies: Yili International Travel Agency (yílí guójì lǚxíngshè; 伊犁国际旅行社; ☎ 802 4939), on Xinhua Lu, in the southeast part of town. Accessible by pedicab (Y3) from the bus station or downtown. Open daily 9:30am-1:30pm and 4-8pm. **Yining International Travel Agency** (yīníng guójì lǚxíng shè; 伊宁国际旅行社; ☎ 8120298), on Ahetouti Jiang Lu, in Jianyin Mansion (jiànyín dàshà; 建银大厦), a 5min. walk south from Jiefang Lu. Both agencies offer 1- to 3-day package tours of Sailimu Lake, Nalati Grasslands, and other Yili Valley sites (about Y50 per day), although single travelers may have to wait to tag along with a larger tour group. Ticket commission Y20 at both.

Bank of China: On Jiefang Lu, just west of and across the street from the bus station. Exchanges traveler's checks at counters #2, 3, and 4. Open M-F 9:30am-1:30pm and 4-8pm; in winter 10am-2pm and 3:30-7:30pm; Sa-Su year-round 11am-5pm.

Post Office: On the corner of Sidalin Lu and Jiefang Lu. **Postal Code:** 835000.

NORTHWEST

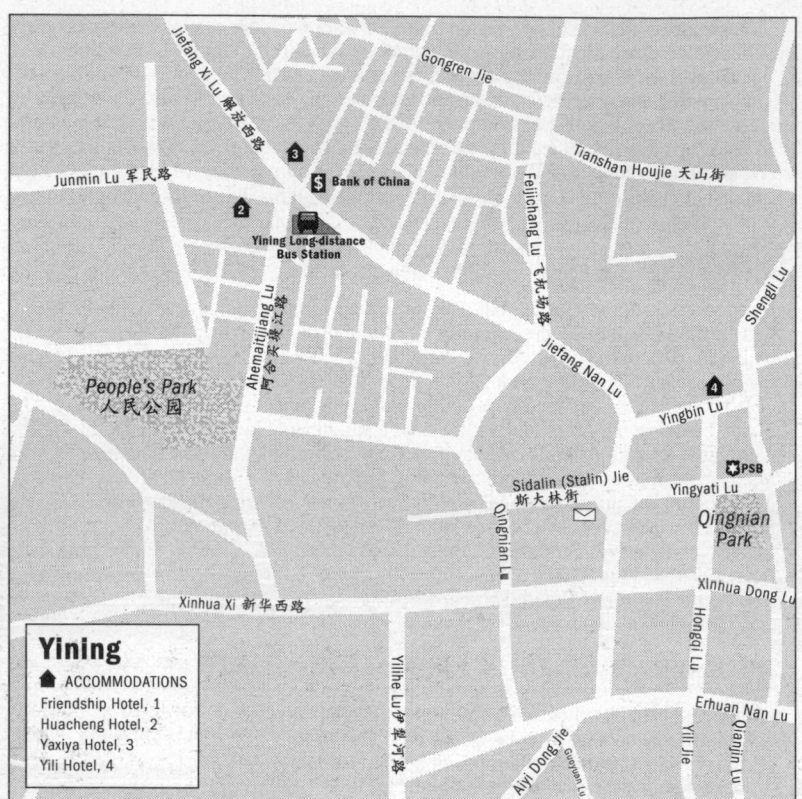

Yining

⌂ ACCOMMODATIONS
Friendship Hotel, 1
Huacheng Hotel, 2
Yaxiya Hotel, 3
Yili Hotel, 4

ACCOMMODATIONS

Yining has limited options for the budget traveler; dorm beds open to foreigners are rare. In addition, many hotels require single travelers to pay for an entire room, a policy that can be almost impossible to get around. However, mid-range singles are available in the gorgeous Yili Hotel and with some haggling in the conveniently located Yaxiya Hotel.

Yili Hotel (yīlí bīnguǎn; 伊犁宾馆) 22 Yingbin Lu (☎802 2794 or 802 3799), a 5min. walk north of Qingnian Square, at the end of Hongqi Lu. A beige gate leads to the forest-like grounds of the complex, housing three unassuming buildings and a few old Russian-style restaurants and conference centers with frequent music and dance performances in the evening. Rooms in the beautiful west wing have large breezy bathrooms and windows opening out onto the thick canopy of trees outside. The main building is more modern and sterile. 30% discounts possible. All rooms in both wings have private baths. West wing doubles Y50 per bed; triples Y30 per bed; luxury rooms Y160-228.

Yasiya Hotel (yàsīyà bīnguǎn; 亚绸亚宾馆; ☎803 1800, ext. 5100). From the bus station, turn left on Jiefang Lu and then turn right on the street directly across from the Bank of China; the Yasiya is on the left. Although policy is to rent rooms, not beds, a bit of haggling could do the trick; the lucky guest will pay Y40 to "fill" the room. Rooms have nice bedspreads, clean sheets, bed lamps, and functional private baths. Doubles Y90, with A/C Y120; triples Y90-108.

Huacheng Hotel (huāchéng bīnguǎn; 花城宾馆; ☎8125050, ext. 828). Veer east on Junmin Lu, a slight left off Jiefang Lu at the trisection just east of the bus station; the hotel is about 100m ahead on the left. The dorms are falling apart, with little of the wall not peeling away, an endless expanse of brick wall visible from the windows, and no showers. The cheaper doubles are not much better, but the more expensive ones are newly renovated and clean. 4-bed dorms Y11; 3-bed dorms Y13; doubles with bath Y40-50, new rooms Y80-164.

Friendship Hotel (yóuyì bīnguǎn; 友谊宾馆; ☎802 3901), down the street from the Yaxiya Hotel. Singles and doubles are newly painted, with a fresh smell and sparkling bathrooms. Triples are clean and cool, but have rusting bathrooms. High demand often makes these rooms hard to come by. Singles Y100; doubles Y120; triples Y90.

▣ SIGHTS

Part of a day can be spent in the city poking around **People's Park** (rénmín gōngyuán; 人民公园), on Ahetoutijiang Lu, about 10 minutes south of the Huacheng Hotel. The park itself is nothing much, but the tiny museum, housed in a beautiful 1948 Russian-style government building, is quite nice. Fading blue paint, large stars in the windows, creaky wooden floors, and long archway corridors recall its Russian influence. Ask, or be offered, a Chinese tour of the limited contents—pottery, some neat Tibetan-style Buddhist plates, and many photos. There is a photo gallery and historical timeline of the area in a separate complex. Neither place has English captions or tours, but you can glean plenty just by looking. *(Open daily sunrise-sunset. Park admission Y3; museum Y2.)*

Another nice spot is the **Yili River Park** (yīlí jiāng gōngyuán; 伊犁江公园), 6km south of the city, centered around the Yili River Bridge. From the Yili Hotel, take either bus #2 to the bridge (Y1.2) or a taxi (Y7). Buses run every 20 minutes or so in both directions. Although the scenery here is less than astounding, a walk along the far bank takes you through some picturesque farmland along grassy poplar-lined dirt paths. The near bank is full of tourist booths and hawkers selling speed boat rides and instant photos.

NEAR YINING: SAILIMU LAKE

*Just off the main Ürümqi-Yining highway, 135km north of Yining. If you are coming from the east, take a long-distance **bus** from Ürümqi; the road is in relatively good condition and buses are fairly reliable. Most buses will stop at the lakeside town, but ask anyway. Heading back to Yining, frequent buses run approx. 8am-5pm; be prepared to hail them down. To go from Yining to the lake, take a 11:40am bus to **Bole** (博乐) or a 1pm bus to **Jinghe** (精河); both stop at the lake (Y21 or Y27). Going directly to Ürümqi from Sailimu Lake is not advised, as sleeper buses are often full and ticket prices are inflated. The road from Sailimu Lake to Korla is not as good, and bus rides can turn into marathons.*

The beauty and isolation of Sailimu Lake (sàilǐmù hú; 赛里木湖) make this one of the best options for exploring nature in northern Xinjiang. This huge lake surrounded by snow-capped mountains is one of Yili's most awe-inspiring sites. While Tianchi's small size encourages hiking forays up into the surrounding alpine cliffs, Sailimu Lake has the relaxing feel of a small ocean, with pebble beaches bleeding out of the lowland pastures, and the quiet sound of the tides lapping at the shore. Although the stretch of highway running alongside the lake has become a nauseating tourist center (complete with food stands, trashy cinder block housing, and even a go-cart track), you have only to walk along a small dirt road clockwise around the lake from the bus stop to enjoy the lakeside wildflower meadows and camel-, goat-, and horse-grazing pastures. The lake's pristine grasslands and wildflower coves are home to a few hundred scattered Mongol and Kazakh family yurts; many offer a night's lodging with meals (Y30). Although more isolated yurts may take you in if you offer a simple gift (and payment), yurts with Chinese characters written on their sides are more accustomed to hosting guests. Bring warm clothes, as evenings are downright cold, even in the summer.

NORTHWEST

TURPAN 吐鲁番 ☎0995

Turpan is a stunning introduction to the inhospitable, rugged, and inspiring terrain of Xinjiang. Nicknamed "The Oven," the town is in the Turpan Depression, a baking $50,000km^2$ desert. The merciless sun shines for over 3000 hours a year, and summer temperatures hover around 40°C (100°F), hotter still in the nearby Flaming Mountains. Most of the cloud moisture evaporates before reaching the ground; the region receives a whopping 1-2cm of rain per year. But don't get too depressed; despite this inferno, Turpan and the neighboring town of Hami are famous for their grapes, multicolored melons, cantaloupes, apricots, and sun-dried raisins.

Turpan's slow-paced atmosphere is due partly to the laid-back hospitality of the Uighurs, who make up roughly 70% of the population, and also to the excruciating heat, which at midday immobilizes even the locals. Public transport is still dominated by donkey carts, which patrol the shaded, grape vine-covered thoroughfares. Tombs and ruins in the nearby valleys keep archeologists occupied for eons, but two days in the stifling heat is more than enough for most visitors.

▐ TRANSPORTATION

Trains: Turpan Train Station (tǔlǔfān zhàn; 吐鲁番站) is actually in the town of **Daheyan** (大河沿), 50km to the northwest. Minibuses leave every 30min. or when completely packed. The cheapest way to get there from Turpan is to take a public bus from the downtown station (1-2hr., every 30min. 7am-7pm, Y6). Taxi drivers may be willing to make the trip for the same price. CITS runs minibuses to the station if there are more than 3 people (Y50). To: **Kashgar** (27hr., 5:30pm, Y195); **Korla** (9hr., 2 per day, Y120); **Liuyuan** (11hr., several evening trains, hard seat Y160); and **Xian** (40-45hr., 5:03 and 8:58pm, Y305) via **Lanzhou** (32hr., Y242).

Bus: The **long-distance bus station** (☎852 2325) on Laocheng Lu resembles a white and green tiled mosque. Open daily 6:30am-8pm. Roads to Hami are not good; take the train instead. To **Kashgar** (24hr., 10am, Y130 sleeper) via **Korla** (6-7hr., Y38), and **Ürümqi** (2½hr., every 30min. 7:30am-7:30pm, Y24).

Local Transportation: Minibus #1 travels from east to west along Xincheng Lu, Laocheng Lu, and Munaer Lu; **#2** runs from north to south along Gaocheng Lu; **#5** runs north on Gaocheng Lu before heading east; **#6** runs south on Gaocheng Lu before heading east in front of the Turpan Hotel, out to Emin Minaret. Fare Y4. **Donkey-pulled wagons** and **taxis** also help to beat the heat. Fare about Y2-4 within the city.

✦❓ ORIENTATION AND PRACTICAL INFORMATION

This oasis town is just big enough to fit two major streets: **Gaochang Lu** (高昌路) runs north to south, intersected by **Xincheng Lu** (新城路), which becomes **Laocheng Lu** (老城路) and eventually **Munaer Lu** (木纳尔路) to the east. The long-distance bus station and many tourist offices are along Laocheng Lu, while the Turpan Museum is on Gaochang Lu. Hotels are spread rather evenly throughout the area. The center for nightlife and entertainment is the **Cultural Square** (wénhuà yóu guǎngchǎng; 文化游广场), sandwiched between Qingnian Lu and Gaochang Lu, just north of John's Information Cafe.

Travel Agency: CITS (☎852 1352 or 852 2491, ext. 2443), in the Oasis Hotel to the right of the gated entrance. A second branch in the Turpan Hotel is open only during the summer. Commission Y30-60. The employees at the main office are more efficient and speak English, although both offices provide tours of Turpan for Y40-50. The better (and cheaper) bet is to bargain for a tour of the surrounding sights (usually 8 in all) with the Uighur taxi drivers who hang out at John's Information Cafe. A full-day affair costing Y200-300 can be split among 4-5 people.

Bank of China: 18 Laocheng Lu (☎852 3067), across from the bus station. Exchanges traveler's checks; no credit card advances. Open M-F 9am-1pm and 5-7:30pm; in winter 9:30am-1:30pm and 3:30-7:30pm.

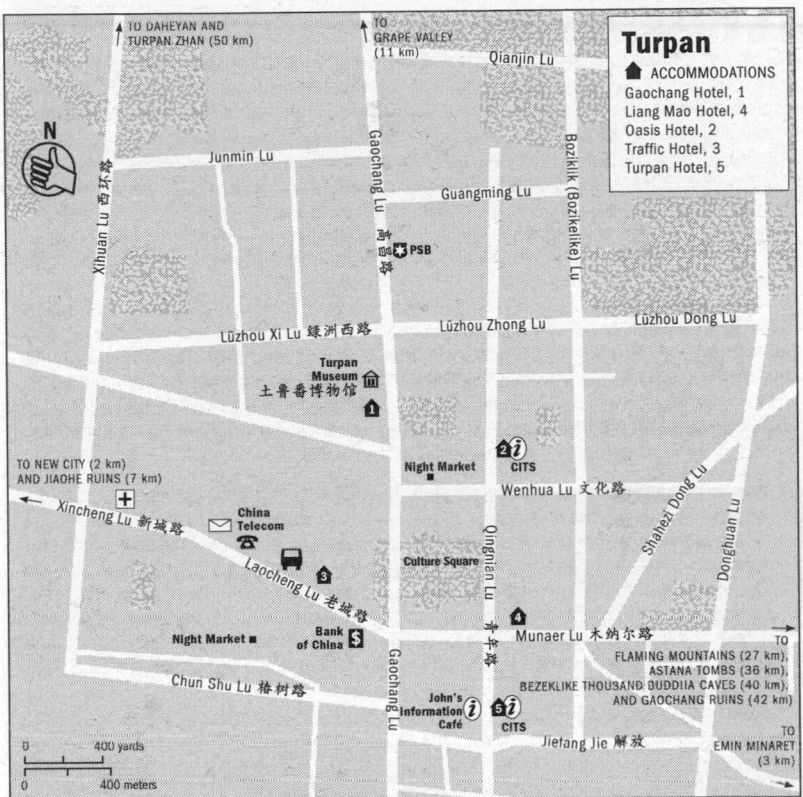

Turpan

🏠 ACCOMMODATIONS

Gaochang Hotel, 1
Liang Mao Hotel, 4
Oasis Hotel, 2
Traffic Hotel, 3
Turpan Hotel, 5

Bookstores: Xinhua Bookstore (☎852 6044), on the north side of Laocheng Lu, diago nally opposite the Bank of China. No English novels, but bilingual maps (Y2.5) and handy pocket English-Uighur translation books (Y6.5; no pronunciation key) are available. A small bookstore just up the street from the Turpan Hotel has a better selection of phrasebooks, including *Travelling in Xinjiang: A Uighur Conversation Guide for Tourists* (Y12) by Brewster and Abdullah, which has basic grammar and pronunciation tips.

PSB: 47 Gaochang Lu (☎95938 983 610), opposite the Victory Hotel, in the north part of town. The **Foreign Affairs Office** for visa extensions is on the 2nd floor of the building immediately to the right inside the compound gate. Open M-F 9am-noon and 5-8pm.

Telephones and Internet Access: China Telecom (☎852 3070), is to the right of the post office. IDD service. Internet access Y4 per hr. Open daily 9am-8pm. **John's Information Cafe** has IDD service and Internet access for Y30 per hr. For fast connections, head to the **168 Hotel** (168 dàjiǔdiàn; 168大酒店), on Gaochang Lu at Luzhou Lu, in the northern part of the city. Y10 per hr.

Post Office: China Post (☎852 2731), on Laocheng Lu west of the bus station. EMS and Poste Restante available. Open daily 9am-8pm. **Postal Code:** 838000.

🏠🍴 ACCOMMODATIONS AND FOOD

Almost all hotel rooms in Turpan, except for some of the cheap dorms, have air-conditioning. All are within walking distance of the central square and the night bazaar, although the Turpan Hotel is closest.

WEIGHT FOR ME Perhaps one of the more peculiar forms of entertainment cropping up in China these days is the omnipresent "weight and height machine." These 7 ft. gadgets, some in the form of friendly (if eccentric) robots, scream "Welcome!" and tell passersby to step on the platform. Participants, perhaps eager for greater physiological self-awareness, hop onto the scale and deposit their coins, causing an automatic bar to lower down and tap them on the cranium. Then, to add insult to injury, the tactless lump of metal broadcasts their measurements across the square for all to hear. Most intriguing is the fact that this activity seems quite popular among couples, as men usually pay to have their dates weighed and measured.

John's Information Cafe, on Gaochang Lu across from the Turpan Hotel, offers overpriced Western food (hamburgers Y20) in addition to Internet access and travel info. (Open daily until 1am.) The **Red Curtain Cafe,** a five-minute walk north from John's and a quick left at the intersection, offers cold beer, Chinese dishes, and genuine humor. A lively **night market** is south of the Bank of China; take a left after the bank on Laocheng Lu. The city square and surrounding night markets are perhaps the best options for a cheap meal and cold beer.

🚩 **Turpan (Binguan) Hotel** (tǔlǔfān bīnguǎn; 吐鲁番宾馆), 2 Qingnian Lu (☎852 2301; fax 852 3262), across from John's Cafe, on the east side of Qingnian Lu. Not to be confused with the Turpan (Fandian) Hotel on Gaochang Lu, which doubles its prices for foreigners, this *binguan* is the cheapest option in Turpan. A swimming pool of questionable cleanliness and massage/sauna center are in the nearby building. IDD calls can be made from the lobby. Hot water 7am-2am, public showers 3-9pm. Deposit Y50; no deposit on dorms. 10% student discount on standard rooms. Y17 dorms have no A/C but are remarkably cool in their subterranean location. Dorms with A/C Y30; doubles Y380; triples Y280-300. Credit cards accepted.

Traffic Hotel (jiāotōng bīnguǎn; 交通宾馆), 125 Laocheng Lu (☎853 1320), close to the bustle of downtown. The 2- to 4-bed dorms have somewhat unreliable A/C window units. Hot water 7-10am, 1-3pm, and midnight-1am. 6- to 10-bed dorms Y10; 4-bed dorms Y22; 3-bed dorms Y24; 2-bed dorms with bath Y40-60.

Gaochang Hotel (gāochǎng bīnguǎn; 高昌宾馆), 22 Gaochang Lu (☎842 3229), just south of the museum. A slick, renovated look and an accommodating staff make the Gaochang a good choice. 24hr. hot water. Deposit Y200. Bargaining possible. Dorms Y20; doubles Y140; triples Y90.

Oasis Hotel (lǜzhōu bīnguǎn; 绿洲宾馆), 41 Qingnian Lu (☎852 2491), a 10min. walk north on Qingnian Lu from the Turpan Hotel. With 24hr. hot water (not always the case in the dorms), beautiful terraced walkways, and flower gardens, the hotel is for those willing to cough up the cash. Dorms are ridiculously priced, with ancient A/C and concrete floors. Dorms Y50; doubles Y400.

Liangmao Hotel (liángmào bīnguǎn; 粮贸宾馆), 7 Laocheng Lu (☎852 4301). Walk 5min. north of the Turpan Hotel on Qingnian Lu to the first intersection and take a right; the white-tiled structure is on the left. Rooms are clean and bright. 24hr. hot water. Deposit Y30. Doubles Y168-180; triples Y150-180; quads Y160.

👁 SIGHTS

Turpan's sights can be visited in one busy day, a highly recommended plan, especially during the blistering summer months. Taxis average Y250-300 for the day, excluding admission. Although there is no need for guides to the sights in and around Turpan, they can help you make arrangements for further travel within Xinjiang. Most private Uighur guides speak fluent Japanese and excellent English. Drivers speak Uighur and Mandarin only. **Alim Arken** (☎853 2483) speaks fluent English and can be of great assistance. John's Information Cafe, across from the

Turpan Hotel, is the place to go to bargain for a local Turpan tour; guides and drivers congregate here at all times of the day. Although the cheapest deal for individual travelers is to tag along with four or five other people, you may have little say in how much time is spent at each place.

TURPAN CITY

EMIN MINARET (émǐn tǎ; 额敏塔). Also known as **Sugong Minaret** (sūgōng tǎ; 苏公塔), this active mosque has an impressive tower rising over 43m and built by Emin Hoja in 1778. The interior is simple, with white gates and domes that have light cascading in through small windows arranged in circular formation. The late afternoon light illuminates the unique brick formation used to construct the Minaret's top. A climb up the smaller structure to the right provides an excellent view of the surrounding vineyards. *(2km east of town center. Included in most tours. Open daily sunrise-sunset. Y20.)*

TURPAN MUSEUM (tǔlǔfān bówùguǎn; 吐鲁番博物馆). This recently renovated complex is well lit and well financed, but it lacks English captions. However, it is enough to browse through the stages of human evolution and to learn about the incredible variety of prehistoric animals and dinosaurs that roamed Xinjiang in times past. Colorful models, fossilized remains, and reconstructed skeletons offer a fascinating survey of Xinjiang's pre-desertification landscape. The second floor contains an eerie collection of 1500-year-old preserved and withered bodies, vacant-eyed in their glass cases. *(On Gaochang Lu, just north of the Gaochang Hotel. ☎852 3774. Open daily 9am-8pm. Y20.)*

NEAR TURPAN

JIAOHE RUINS (jiāohé gǔchéng; 交河古城). Founded atop a 30m cliff carved by two river ravines (the name means "intersecting rivers"), the once flourishing city of Jiaohe enjoyed a history spanning two millennia. Han records indicate that the city had 700 families, 6050 citizens, and 1856 soldiers by 109 BC. It served as the capital of the Kingdom of Jushi in AD 450 before it was eventually abandoned, probably due to a lack of water. Still there are the small rooms, temples, courtyards, and streets that were all sculpted out of sun-baked earth. In 1994, archeologists found the graves of more than 200 infants northwest of the site. The reason for their burial is still a mystery. *(7km west of town. Open daily sunrise-sunset. Y30.)*

ASTANA TOMBS (āsītǎnà gǔmù qún; 阿斯塔那古墓群). The tombs are a resounding disappointment for many visitors; overpriced and uninteresting, they can be seen in about 20 minutes. The large earth mounds house over 350 graves, only three of which are open to visitors. Each chamber is entered via a set of shallow stairs leading 5m underground. The first tomb displays wall paintings of Confucian model scholars and two "piggy bank" vessels that symbolize the Confucian ethic of investment without reward; the second is painted with birds said to fly south for the winter, symbolic of the buried official's unfulfilled wish to die in his hometown; and the third displays two well-preserved corpses, a female of supposed Indo-European origins, and a smaller man of Mongolian descent. *(Northwest of Gaochang. Open daily sunrise-sunset. Tours in Mandarin Y20.)*

GAOCHANG RUINS (gāochāng gùchéng; 高昌故城). The center of the Uighur empire in the 9th century, Gaochang has largely crumbled away and is a lesser cousin to the impressive Jiaohe Ruins. Founded in the Liang dynasty (397-439), Gaochang was conquered by Tang Emperor Taizong in 640. Later, the famous monk Xuan Zang taught Buddhism here for a month during his 18-year epic journey to obtain Indian scriptures. The only visible structure left is the city's massive outer wall. The many windows and doorways leak views through layers of earthen walls to the Flaming Mountains beyond. *(A good 40km east of Turpan. Those wary of the oppressive heat can take a donkey cart (Y7-10 round-trip) from the entrance to the main temple site. Open daily sunrise-sunset. Y20.)*

GRAPE VALLEY (pútáo gōu; 葡萄沟). Although your driver will undoubtedly try to take you here for a midday rest, the steep admission grants you a nice walk underneath miles of grape trellises, but not much else. *(Open daily sunrise-sunset. Y20.)* Food options are also limited, with only two or three vendors inside selling noodles and wine. A far better option is to go to the strip of restaurants just along the cliff edge bearing the huge characters 葡萄沟. Here you can sample the local noodle specialty, *laghman*, lamb kebabs, and fresh grapes for about Y15 per person. The rainbow of fresh and dried fruits is delicious and cheap; the wine, however, turns out to be no pot of gold. Cheaper wine ends up tasting remarkably like bad cough medicine; higher-quality wine costs Y30-40 per bottle. After lunch, most guides offer to take visitors swimming in the irrigation canals just up the hill, a popular leisure spot for local youngsters.

FLAMING MOUNTAINS (huǒyán shān; 火焰山). Aptly named the Flaming Mountains, these reddish slopes feature temperatures that top 55°C at midday! According to the novel *Journey to the West,* when Tang monk Xuan Zang came to this impasse, fires raged for hundreds of miles. His companion the Monkey King was able to extinguish the flames with a magical palm fan whisked from the throat of the ever-protective Iron Fan Princess. *(Free.)*

OTHER SIGHTS. One other stop on the average tour is the **Karez Irrigation System,** an exposed 10m section of the ancient Persian-style underground irrigation tunnels, also visible elsewhere in Turpan and offering essentially the same attractions as the Grape Valley. You (and hordes of tourists, as well as more trinket vendors than you can count) can also crowd into a tiny section of the original baked earthen wall canals. *(Open daily sunrise-sunset. Y15.)* The road to **Bezeklik Thousand Buddha Cave** (bózīkèlǐkè qiānfó dòng; 柏孜克里克千佛洞), 10km north of Gaochang Ruins, is under construction and requires a lengthy detour, so few tours include it. This once grand collection has been largely destroyed by profit-hungry local Muslims and prestige-hungry foreign archeologists-cum-art thieves such as Aurel Stein and Albert von Le Coq. *(Open daily sunrise-sunset. Y20.)*

KORLA 库尔勒 ☎0996

This predominantly Han Chinese city west of Ürümqi is Xinjiang's third largest economic center; the surrounding lower-class districts and farming villages are predominantly Uighur. Entering the city from the east is a surreal experience, as the highway, winding through barren desert canyons and red and black rock mountains, suddenly opens onto a hazy Lego-block city of industrial factories, office towers, and neon lights. Although in the daytime the bleak cityscape can be oppressive, at night, the streets teem with food bazaars, live music performances, and fashionable young women. Korla's claim to fame is the nearby Bosten Lake, the largest in Xinjiang, which, though pleasant, does not warrant a special visit. There are several interesting ancient ruins and spots to visit on the edge of the Taklimakan Desert, the best of which is undoubtedly the Ancient Poplar Forest, a spectacular grove of two- to 3000-year-old trees growing gnarled and weathered out of rippling white sand dunes.

▐ TRANSPORTATION

Airplanes: Flights from the **Korla Airport** (kùěrlè fēijīchǎng; 库尔勒飞机场) have currently stopped; when they resume, there will likely be flights to **Ürümqi.**

Trains: Korla Train Station (kùěrlè huǒchē zhàn; 库尔勒火车站), in the far southeast corner of the city. Accessible by bus #1 from People's Square or by taxi (Y10). Booking sleeper tickets to **Kashgar** is virtually impossible, as there is only 1 train per day (20hr., 3:20am, Y80 hard seat), and it originates in Ürümqi. To **Aksu** (express 8:15am, Y143; Kashgar night train hard seat Y63) and **Ürümqi** (11hr.; 9:25am, hard seat Y86; 6:15, 10:18, and 11:25pm, sleeper Y150).

Buses: The **bus station** (kèyùn zhōngxīn; 客运中心; ☎207 6390) is on Beishan Lu, in the north part of the city. Bus #2 connects it to People's Square. Although roads are often in terrible condition (especially heading west), buses are the most convenient option to Kuqa and Ürümqi. To: **Aksu** (12hr., 9am and noon, Y60; 7:30pm, Y80-91 sleeper); **Hotan** (26hr., 9am and 7:30pm, Y140); **Kashgar** (24hr., 4pm, Y160 sleeper; 7:30pm, Y109 seat); **Kuqa** (7hr.; 9:20am and 2pm, or take the Kashgar-bound night bus); **Ürümqi** (12hr.; 10am and noon, Y150 seat; 1 and 8pm, Y70 sleeper); and **Yining** (30hr., 8:30am, Y73).

Shuttle Taxis: Immediately to the right of the bus station, this stand offers regulated ticket sales and high speed Santana transport for about double the bus rates and half the time. The rates apply only if the car is full (4 passengers); otherwise, you must either wait or pay for the empty seats. To: **Aksu** (Y135-160); **Kuqa** (Y70-85); **Lotus Lake** or **Western Bosten Lake** (Y12); **Luntai** (Y40); and **Ürümqi** (Y115-140).

Local Transportation: Bus #2 runs north to the long-distance bus station and west to the Bosten Hotel. **Taxi** base fare is Y5. From People's Square to the train station Y10, most other points Y5.

✴ ORIENTATION AND PRACTICAL INFORMATION

The downtown is clustered around the central **People's Square** (rénmín guăngchăng; 人民广场). **Renmin Lu** (人民路) runs from east to west on the south side of the square. Most tourist services and accommodations are within a 20-minute walk of here. The bus station to the north is on **Beishan Lu** (北山路), which runs south into **Jiaotong Lu** (交通路). From the station, make a right and then the first left onto **Jianshe Lu** (建设路), which passes the square on the left before intersecting Renmin Lu. The train station is in the southeast part of town.

Travel Agencies: All 3 of Korla's foreigner-friendly hotels have travel agencies, and it's worthwhile to inquire about their rates to the Poplar Forest, especially if you have a larger group. **Jianggeer Travel Agency** (jiānggéěr lǚxíngshè; 江格尔旅行社; ☎202 2248, ext. 89008), just outside the Bayin Hotel's main gate, to the left. Arranges transportation to the Poplar Forest for Y600.

Bank of China: On Renmin Lu, a 10min. walk west of the People's Square, on the right side of the street (☎202 5086). Exchanges traveler's checks (counter #4); the door is to the right as you enter. Open daily 9:30am-1:30pm and 4:30-7:30pm.

Internet Access: On Renmin Lu, just before the Bank of China, is a small Internet cafe with a big red sign reading 创联网络 (chuànglián wǎngluò). Y3 per hr. for fast connections. Open daily past midnight.

Post Office: Korla's main **Post and Telecom Office** (☎202 3788), just off People's Square on Renmin Lu, with a large neon sign visible from the street. Open daily 9:30am-1:30pm and 4:30-7:30pm.

▐ ACCOMMODATIONS

Korla's first baby steps as a tourist center have not been in a budget-friendly direction (at least not for foreigners). According to regulations, only three luxury hotels can take foreigners, and of the three, only the Bayin Hotel offers dorm rooms.

Bayinguoleng Hotel (bāyīnguōlèng bīnguǎn; 巴音郭愣宾馆; ☎202 4441), also known as the Bazhou Hotel (bāzhōu bīnguǎn; 巴州宾馆), on Renmin Lu, a 15min. walk west of People's Square. The dorms share the main tower's luxury feel, with A/C, TV, wooden decor, and sparkling tile floors. 24hr. hot water. Dorms Y30; doubles Y270.

Loulan Hotel (lóulán bīnguǎn; 楼兰宾馆; ☎202 2999), on Renmin Lu, a 5min. walk east of People's Square. Very centrally located but ridiculously expensive. 20% discount for students or individual travelers. Doubles Y300; triples Y360.

Bosten Hotel (bósíténg bīnguǎn; 博斯腾宾馆; ☎202 2118), on Renmin Lu, quite far west of People's Square and the night bazaars. English speaker and on-site travel agency (☎203 3444). This luxury hotel has just 1 option for foreigners: Y200 doubles.

NORTHWEST

SIGHTS

Korla's claim to fame is the nearby Bosten Lake, but the best reason to come to Korla is to see the northern border of the **Taklimakan Desert** (tǎkèlāmǎgān shāmò; 塔克拉玛干沙漠), a fabulous ecosystem of flowering bushes, white sands, and ancient poplar trees growing in the widely variable watershed of the **Tarim River** (tǎlǐmù hé; 塔里木河), whose tiny streams and rivulets branch through the desert during brief rainy periods.

POPLAR FOREST PARK (húyáng sēnlín gōngyuán; 胡杨森林公园). About 120km south of **Luntai** (轮台), the highway that passes through the heart of the Taklimakan Desert en route to the southern rim town of Hotan enters a surreal landscape of two- to 3000-year-old poplar trees, their gnarled and weathered trunks emerging from seemingly barren white sands. Sending roots down to basins of water deep beneath the desert surface, these trees grow at an absurdly slow pace, giving the area a feel of eclipsed time and humbling power. The park itself, about a 15-minute drive from the roadside groves, is of little interest, as the trees there grown next to a large pond and are much younger and more natural-looking. However, you should probably tell the driver that you want to go to the park in order to simplify things; have him stop at the roadside groves along the way. Hiking the dunes can easily fill an entire afternoon. *(Take an early morning taxi shuttle (2hr., Y40 per person) from Korla to Luntai; you may have to wait for other people to fill the car's 4 seats. From Luntai, hire a taxi (Y100 round-trip, more if you want to do some hiking) to take you to the forest. Make sure the driver understands that you will be gone a long time; pay him once you return to Luntai. To return to Korla, take the bus (4-5hr., Y20) or a shuttle taxi. With careful planning and a light pack, you could take the train straight to Luntai from Ürümqi, skipping a potentially expensive night in Korla. After seeing the forest, take a taxi or bus back to Korla. Park Y8.)*

BOSTEN LAKE (bósíténg hú; 博斯腾湖). Although it is touted as Korla's premier tourist attraction, Bosten Lake, Xinjiang's largest, is a resounding disappointment. Only two spots on the lake are accessible by public transportation: the Golden Sands Resort and the Lotus Pond. The **Golden Sands** (jīn shātān; 金沙滩) is a tacky beach resort with plenty of inflatable air mattresses and plastic umbrellas to spare. If you are willing to shell out Y200-250 for an afternoon, you can hire a boat to explore the reed covered marshes and small fishing towns nearby, but even this is probably not worth it. If you really want to see the lake, a better option is to visit the much closer **Lotus Pond** (liánhuā chí; 莲花池), where you can spend a few hours strolling about the thickly growing lotuses and water lilies. If it has been raining a lot (as it does in the summer), you are unlikely to see anything but high rushes. *(Buses to Golden Sands (2hr., Y50 round-trip) leave daily at 9-10am from the south side of People's Square, across from the PICC Building, and depart from the lake at 6pm. Y20. Lotus Pond is best reached by shuttle taxi (Y12 per person in a 4-person car) from Korla Bus Station.)*

KUQA 库车 ☎ 0997

Present-day Kuqa is probably the most interesting stop you can make between Ürümqi and Kashgar. This area in the foothills of the Tianshan mountains was once an important nexus in the transmission of Buddhism east across the Northern Silk Road. Many grottoes and ancient ruins are scattered to the north of the city, a testament to the rich history of the area, as well as to the remarkable desert climate that preserves these traces of 1500-year-old civilization. Today, the compact New Town quickly fades into an entrancing network of small dirt roads that weave through the mud-brick architecture of traditional Uighur housing, revealing colorful archways, shady grape trellises, small mosques, and food markets. Taking a stroll through this area is a great way to immerse yourself in Uighur culture and traditional living without the glare of tour bus glass.

■ ❷ ORIENTATION AND PRACTICAL INFORMATION

Kuqa is divided into two sections. To the east is the predominantly Han Chinese **New Town** (xīn chéng; 新城), a relatively modern area containing foreigner-friendly hotels, tourist services, and the slightly peripheral bus and train stations. To the west is the Uighur section of the city known as the **Old Town** (lǎo chéng; 老城) which changes from the bustling market streets to the south into residential areas in the north, connected by small farm plots and poplar-lined dirt roads. **Tianshan Lu** (天山路) connects the southern edges of the two sections; upon entering the easternmost end of the new town, it passes the bus station and the Jiaotong and Kuqa Hotels, before intersecting with the two main new city avenues running from north to south: **Youyi Lu** (友谊路) and **Jiefang Lu** (解放路), about 1.5km to the west. Tianshan Lu branches north just past the western limits of the new city, entering the Uighur residential district. The southern fork becomes **Linji Lu** (林基路), which crosses a large bridge, the effective center of the Friday bazaar, and heads into the heart of the old town, passing the Kuqa Mosque on the right.

Airplanes: The airport was closed as of July 2000. Dates for reopening were uncertain.

Trains: Kuqa Train Station (kùchē huǒchē zhàn; 库车火车站), 7km southeast of the new town, accessible by a Y10 taxi ride or by taking bus #2 or 3 from in front of the post office. Arrive at the station early and expect delays. At the time of writing, regulations required that tickets for westbound trains be purchased only at the station; tickets for eastbound trains can be purchased at a ticket window adjacent to the Industrial and Commercial Bank, on Wenhua Lu between Jiefang Lu and Youyi Lu. Open daily 10am-1:30pm. To: **Aksu** (3-4hr., 3 per day 7:20am-3:30pm, Y20); **Kashgar** (13hr., 7:20am; 16hr., 3:30pm; Y48 hard seat only); and **Ürümqi** (express: 13hr.; 6:45pm; hard seat Y56, sleeper Y120; regular: 19hr., 1:04pm, sleeper Y120).

Buses: Kuqa Long-distance Bus Station (kùchē chángtú qìchē zhàn; 库车长途汽车站; ☎ 712 2379) is in the far southeast center of the new town. Take any bus running east on Tianshan Lu, or a Y6 taxi from most hotels. Open daily 8am-8:30pm. Buses to Hotan and Kashgar originate in Korla or Ürümqi; departure times from Kuqa are irregular, and seats or sleepers are not guaranteed. To: **Aksu** (7hr., every hr. 9:30am-2:30pm, Y23); **Hotan** (morning departures, Y90-180); **Kashgar** (20hr., 11am 2pm, Y75-110); **Korla** (8hr., every hr. 9:30am-2:30pm, Y25); **Ürümqi** (20hr., 2 and 4pm, sleeper Y80-90); and **Yining** (2 days, 9:30am, Y77).

Travel Agencies: Kuqa's only travel agency is on Tianshan Lu, in the main lobby of the Quici Hotel (☎/fax 712 2524). Although their rates for private tours of the Kuqa area are slightly more expensive than arrangements through hotel associate drivers, they are friendly and accommodating, and can help single travelers link up with others to share the expense. Be sure to specify which of Kuqa's sites you want to see, as there are too many to see in 1 day, and some of the popular sites are a waste of time. Standard 1-day tours of Kuqa Y300 per car. 1-day tours to Big Dragon Lake (dà lóng hú; 大龙湖) 140km to the north Y400 per car. Open daily 9:30am-1:30pm and 4-8pm.

Bank of China: On Jiefang Lu, just north of Tianshan Lu, on the left when you are coming from downtown. Exchanges currency and traveler's checks. Open daily 9:30am-1:30pm and 4-8pm; in winter 10am-1:30pm and 4-7pm.

Hospital: Kuqa County People's Hospital (kùchē xiàn rénmín yīyuàn; 库车县人民医院), 36 Jiefang Lu. Open 24hr.

Bookstore: Xinhua Bookstore, on the corner of Youyi Lu and Wenhua Lu, in the center of the New Town. Sells maps of Kuqa and surrounding tourist sights for Y3.

Post and Telecommunications: On the central downtown corner of Wenhua Lu and Youyi Lu. The **post office** is on the left, and **China Telecom** is a few doors down on the right. No EMS or IDD service. Both open daily 9:30am-8pm; in winter 10am-7:30pm.

ACCOMMODATIONS AND FOOD

When staying in Kuqa, decide how much you care about being in the center of town. While the centrally located Minmao, Qiuci, and Kuqa (Binguan) Hotels offer easy access to night **food markets** and the Uighur quarter of the old city, the Traffic Hotel and the Kuqa (Fandian) Hotel next to the bus station in the southeast part of the new city easily are the best values in town.

Kuqa (Fandian) Hotel (kùchē fàndiàn; 库车饭店; ☎713 1156), on Tianshan Lu. Take a left out of the bus station and walk 5min.; the hotel is on the right side of the street. The reception area is just off the parking lot to the rear. All rooms have A/C and bath, and some have been newly renovated. Front desk can book eastbound train tickets. 24hr. hot water. Singles and doubles Y80; triples Y100.

Kuqa Hotel (kùchē bīnguǎn; 库车宾馆; 76 Jiefang Lu (☎712 2901), on the far north end. Bright, clean rooms surround a pleasant garden courtyard. Dorm showers (8am-midnight; Y2) are in a separate building next door; all other rooms have A/C and attached bath. 4-bed dorms Y30; doubles with bath Y150; triples with bath Y200.

Minmao Hotel (mínmào bīnguǎn; 民贸宾馆), 16 Wenhua Lu (☎712 2999), at Jiefang Lu, in the heart of the new city. This small 2-floor hotel shares its tower with a lawyer's office. Although hallway carpets are badly stained, a nice surprise awaits inside: doubles are well lit and well decorated, with new carpets and tiled baths. Doubles Y100, with A/C Y120; triples with A/C Y165.

Traffic Hotel (jiāotōng bīnguǎn; 交通宾馆; ☎712 2682), facing the parking lot on the right side as you exit the bus station. The cheaper doubles (both with and without TV) have decent sheets, concrete floors, and a new coat of hostel-green paint. The higher-priced doubles are small and cramped, with cracking walls, rusty bathrooms, and a dismal view. Hot water 10pm-1am. Doubles Y30-40, with A/C Y60.

Quici Hotel (qiūcí bīnguǎn; 龟兹宾馆), 93 Tianshan Lu (☎712 2005), a good 3km west of the bus station. The closest hotel to the Uighur old town is also Kuqa's most expensive option. Most rooms have views of the lush arbors and flower gardens, and all have sparkling tile floors, new A/C, TV, and phone. The dorms have tiny multi-use bathroom compartments, while the doubles are more upscale and spacious. Kuqa's only travel service is just off the main lobby. 4-bed dorms Y60; doubles Y250; triples Y300.

SIGHTS

The mountains around Kuqa abound with Buddhist grottoes and remnants of Silk Road-era cities, although there is no public transportation available and roads are often in poor condition. The travel agency in the Qiuci Hotel is a good source of information; check with them to plan out your day in advance. If you have time and money enough to spend on chartering a taxi, some of the lesser-known areas can yield some amazing finds. Otherwise, the standard one-day tour (Y300) includes the Kizil Grottoes, the Kizilgaha Beacon Tower, the Subashi Temple Ruins, and the Kuqa Mosque. Perhaps the best part of the tour is the desolate length of highway leading to the Kizil Grottoes, which winds its way through the fragmenting red canyons of the Tianshan foothills. Known as **Tianshanmai** (tiānshānmài; 天山脉), literally, "the veins of the Tianshan mountains," this amazing area is a great place to stop and take some photos, although the rough terrain makes hiking extremely difficult. The best prices are found through independent taxi drivers, who often charge Y50-100 less than the Qiuci Hotel Travel Agency charges. A friendly and reliable Uighur- and Mandarin-speaking driver named **Hai Lin Shan** (海林山) hangs out in the lobby of the Kuqa (Binguan) Hotel's dorm building. He can be reached directly (☎(127) 201 3172), or ask the lobby desk.

KIZIL GROTTOES (kèzěěr qiān fó dòng; 克孜尔千佛洞). Considered the richest and best preserved Buddhist grotto site in the Kuqa area, this cliffside network of caves is actually in rather poor condition. Built in the beginning of the 3rd century AD, the caves have been vandalized several times by Islamic fundamentalists, who often gouged out the painted eyes of the Buddhas and scraped away their hand *mudras* (teaching gestures). The caves also suffered extensive looting by the German archeologist Albert Von Le Coq in the beginning of the 20th century, leaving few murals and zero sculptures intact for visitors to see. Many of the caves included in the 10-cave tour are sadly bare, with only a few holes in the walls and a story of what once was. Like at Dunhuang's Mogao Grottoes, the best preserved caves require a special ticket (Y100 and up), although many visitors feel that these are not worth the extra cash. The photos on the gate's tourist board are taken of the special caves 38 and 67, and do not indicate what you will be seeing in either section. *(At the main gate, you must buy a ticket for either the west caves, slightly closer, or the east caves, which are very similar in content. Y25; Y50 for both, including an English-, Japanese-, or Mandarin-speaking guide.)*

SUBASHI TEMPLE RUINS (sūbāshí gǔchéng; 苏巴什古城). This is the post-lunch destination for most tours, as there are no roads connecting the site to the nearby Beacon Tower. Set against the backdrop of the 2000m Tianshan Mountains, the amorphous mud brick shapes rising from the barren scrubland hint at the scope of the original construction while still remaining hauntingly similar to the textures of the surrounding landscape. This is quite a spectacular spot to see the sun set if you can convince the driver to head out in the late afternoon. *(50km north of the old city, accessible only by a small dirt road.)*

KIZILGAHA BEACON TOWER (kèzēěrgǎhā fēnghuǒ tái; 克孜尔烽火台). During the Han dynasty, this 13m high packed-earth watchtower used to light signal fires when an enemy approached. Similar beacon towers along the ancient Silk Road would transmit the signal over great distances of inhospitable desert. *(13km from Kuqa. Open daily sunrise-sunset. Y5.)* You will usually have to ask the driver to take you to the nearby **Kizilgaha Grottoes** (kèzēěrgǎhā qiān fó dòng; 克孜尔尕哈千佛洞).

KUQA OLD TOWN MOSQUE (kùchē dàsì; 库车大寺). In the old Uighur quarter, the Mosque's intricately masoned brick dome and minaret-flanked facade overlook a bustling neighborhood of grape-covered courtyards and trodding donkey carts full of fruit and breads. The interior is dim and breezy, with sunlight pouring in through large lattice windows. *(4km northwest of the new city. You may have to yell for the gatekeeper to let you in. Y5.)*

KASHGAR 喀什 ☎ 0998

Kashgar's relative inaccessibility has had a potent effect on its character, setting it a world apart even from the rest of Xinjiang, much less from the rest of China. Once a major post along the Silk Road, this predominantly Uighur city still retains vestiges of a trading-outpost ambience. Bustling markets are squeezed full of wizened-faced Uighurs, animated Central Asian traders, and veiled Muslim women. Mosques rise up above mud-thatched houses and donkey carts clip-clop down small alleys. The completion of the Ürümqi-Kashgar rail line in late 1999 has provided the definitive stamp of Han Chinese control over the area, breaching the expanse of Taklimakan Desert that has long isolated Kashgar from significant government intervention. Since then, Kashgar's Han population has been steadily rising, although like most of Xinjiang's cities, there continues to be a severe polarization of Uighur and Han parts of town.

Of course, Kashgar's position at the junction of the Taklamakan Silk Routes has not left it untouched by outside influence and invasion. The Chinese gained a toehold in the early 2nd century BC, but maintained only sporadic control until the 1800s. In the meantime, endless rounds of nomads conquered Kashgar, including the all-mighty Genghis Khan and Tamerlane, resulting in

NORTHWEST

the Uighurs' settlement and the influence of Islamic culture brought by the Umayyad Arabs. Europeans arrived in the late 1800s as a part of the tug-of-war between Russia and Britain. Muslim warlords with varying allegiances then ruled in the aftermath of the Qing dynasty, until the Communists began the current stint of rule in 1949. Kashgar more than ever is becoming an international city and an important nexus for travelers headed for the more unexplored regions of Pakistan and Central Asia.

▐ TRANSPORTATION

Airplanes: Kashgar Airport (kāshí jīchǎng; 喀什机场) is 18km north of the city. Taxis take 25min. and cost about Y20. The **CAAC ticket office** (huīhuáng jīpiào dàilǐ gōngsī; 辉煌机票代理公司; ☎283 6444), on Jiefang Nan Lu, is open daily 9:30am-9:30pm. **Xinjiang Airlines** (xīnjiāng hángkōng gōngsī; 新疆航空公司; ☎283 7998), on the right side of the People's Hotel lobby. Open daily 9:30am-8pm. All flights out of Kashgar go through Ürümqi; flights halve in number during winter. To **Ürümqi** (summer 1-2 per day, Y980).

Trains: The new **Kashgar Train Station** (kāshí huǒchē zhàn; 喀什火车站) is on Renmin Dong Lu, about 15km east of the city. Accessible by bus (Y0.5) from Renmin Dong Lu, or by taxi (Y10). From the station, look for an army of pink city buses, most of which will drop you in front of the Id Kah Mosque. Although tickets (especially sleepers) are in high demand, the **Industrial Commercial Bank of China** (gōngshāng yínháng; 工商银行), on the northeast corner of Renmin Lu and Jiefang Lu, has a ticket office with no commission that often can obtain tickets with 1-2 days notice. Open daily 10:30am-1:30pm and 3:30-6pm. A branch in the **People's Hotel** (☎252 0551) sells tickets (commission Y5), but seems to be less successful for booking at short notice. Open daily 9:30am-1:30pm and 4-8pm; in winter 10am-2pm and 3:30-7:30pm. Trains go to **Ürümqi** (28hr., 11:58pm, hard sleeper Y199) via **Kuqa** (13hr.; hard seat Y49, hard sleeper Y104) and **Korla** (16hr.; hard seat Y64, hard sleeper Y140).

Buses: International buses leave from the **International Bus Station** (kāshí guójì qìchē zhàn; 喀什国际汽车站), on Jiefang Lu, north of the Qini Lake Hotel across the Tuman River. The ticket office is next to the Tuman River Hotel on the left. Open daily 8:30am-9pm. Buses run to **Sost, Pakistan** on the Karakorum Highway, via **Tashkurgan** and the **Khunjerab Pass** (40hr., 1 per day, hard seat Y270). Buy your tickets at 11am; buses leave about noon. Buses run to **Bishkek, Kyrgyzstan** via the **Torugut Pass** (16hr., M, US$50); to take the public bus, you will need a transit permit (pīzhào; 批照) to make the border crossing. Only a travel agency can get you this permit, and most will require you to take their tour. It's worth asking, though, as most agencies itemize their tour packages, listing the permit price at around Y300-350 (for groups of 2-5). Make sure you have a valid entry visa to Kyrgyzstan, available only in Beijing (see p. 48) or Hong Kong. Anything more than a 3-day visa is reportedly hard to arrange, though this may not always be the case. The International Bus Station also has buses to **Korla** (25hr., 5 and 6pm, sleeper Y119) via **Kuqa** (20hr., sleeper Y76-86), and **Ürümqi** (40hr., 5 per day 1:30-9pm; sleeper Y149-170). The **Kashgar Long-distance Bus Station** (chángtú qìchē zhàn; 长途汽车站), on Tiannan Lu, off Renmin Dong Lu. Open daily 7:30am-8pm. To **Hotan** (10hr., every 2hr. 9:30am-9pm, Y50) and **Shache** (3hr., every hr. 9am-9pm, Y18).

Local Transportation: Kashgar is best appreciated by foot or by bike. Local **buses** are unreliable; **#9** goes from the Seman Lu area to the Mosque area and **#10** runs east toward the Abokh Hoja Tomb. The **Oasis Cafe, Qiniwake Hotel**, and **John's Information Cafe** all have **bike rentals** for Y2 per hr.

◢▓ ⑦ ORIENTATION AND PRACTICAL INFORMATION

The geographical and practical center of Kashgar is the intersection of **Jiefang Lu** (解放路) and **Renmin Lu** (人民路), while the religious and cultural center as well as the site of nightly food bazaars is the **Id Kah Mosque** and **Id Kah Square**, which lie on

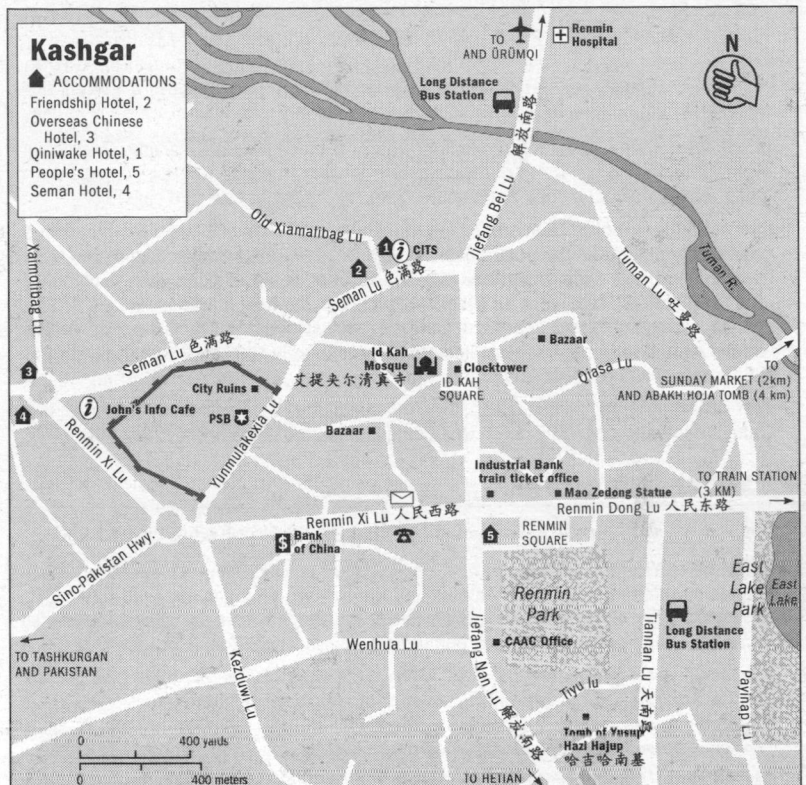

Kashgar

🏠 ACCOMMODATIONS
Friendship Hotel, 2
Overseas Chinese
  Hotel, 3
Qiniwake Hotel, 1
People's Hotel, 5
Seman Hotel, 4

TO ✈ AND ÜRÜMQI
⊞ Renmin Hospital
Long Distance Bus Station
Old Xiamalibag Lu
Jiefang Bei Lu 解放北路
Tuman Lu 吐曼路
Tuman R.
ℹ️ CITS
Seman Lu 色满路
Xaimolibag Lu
■ Bazaar
Seman Lu 色满路
Qiasa Lu
TO SUNDAY MARKET (2km) AND ABAKH HOJA TOMB (4 km)
City Ruins
Id Kah Mosque
艾提夫尔清真寺
ID KAH SQUARE
■ Clocktower
ℹ️ John's Info Cafe
PSB
Yunmulakexia Lu
Renmin Xi Lu
Bazaar ■
Industrial Bank train ticket office
■ Mao Zedong Statue
TO TRAIN STATION (3 KM)
Renmin Xi Lu 人民西路
Bank of China
Renmin Dong Lu 人民东路
RENMIN SQUARE
Sino-Pakistan Hwy.
Kezduwi Lu
Renmin Park
East Lake Park
East Lake
TO TASHKURGAN AND PAKISTAN
Wenhua Lu
Jiefang Nan Lu 解放南路
■ CAAC Office
Tiyu Lu
Tianman Lu 天南路
Long Distance Bus Station
Paynap Lu
0 400 yards
0 400 meters
TO HETIAN
Tomb of Yusup Hazi Hajup 哈吉哈南基

Jiefang Bei Lu north of Renmin Lu. Numerous small streets and alleys wind their way behind the mosque to the Qiniwake Hotel area. The long-distance bus station is on Jiefang Bei Lu, just across the **Tuman River** (tǔmàn jiāng; 吐曼江) in the far north of town. The Great Sunday Bazaar is west of the Tuman River on the south side of **Yizirete Lu** (艾孜热特路), while the foreigner-oriented part of town is in the far west near the Seman Hotel off **Seman Lu** (色满路).

Travel Agencies: Kashgar's travel agencies are useful for checking travel conditions and regulations to Pakistan and Kyrgyzstan.

John's Information Cafe (☎/fax 255 1186; mobile (139) 0998 1722; email Johncafe@hotmail.com), opposite the Seman Hotel. John speaks fluent English. Organizes trips around **Kashgar** (1 day, Y300 per car); **Lake Karakul** (1 day, Y800-1000 per car); and the **Taklimakan Desert** (daytrip). John also facilitates trips to **Bishkek** (4-5 people max., US$260 total); fax or email your name, passport number, nationality, and itinerary, and John will obtain the border patrol permit, jeep, and driver. For an extra fee, he arranges transport to Bishkek from the border.

CITS has a main branch to the left of the Qiniwake Hotel with unreliable hours; a smaller, more helpful branch to the right of the hotel entrance sticks to advertised hours (☎ 282 2103, ext. 4079; fax 282 9630; email Loxik@mail.xjcninfo.net). Tours include: **Lake Karakul trek** (4-5 days; Y800 per car, Y500 per day for trekking guide); **Kashgar** (Y250 per car, English-speaking guide Y200); **Taklimakan Desert** (1 day, Y800); and **Torugut Pass** (1-2 days; Y350 permit for 2-5 people, Y1000 transport, Y200 guide). Sleeper ticket commission Y50, 3 days in advance in summer. Open daily 9:30am-1:30pm and 3:30-8pm.

Bank of China: 239 Renmin Xi Lu (☎ 282 3562). Exchanges traveler's checks and issues credit card advances. Open daily 9:30am-1:30pm and 4-8pm, credit card advances M-F only. A branch office is in a hotel across from the International Hotel in the Qiniwake compound (☎283 3235). Open daily 9am-11pm.

PSB: On Yunmulakexia Lu (☎282 2064, ext. 3041), just south of Seman Lu, with an entrance at the far right. Issues visa extensions (UK Y160, US citizens Y125). Open M-F 9:30am-1:30pm and 4-8pm.

Telephones: China Telecom, across from the post office, has IDD service. Open daily 9am-2pm and 4-8pm. Street booths with English signs reading "IDD" or "long-distance calls" are plentiful and open until around 2am (Y2-2.5 for calling card calls).

Internet Access: China Telecom, on the immediate right of the China Telecom building, across the street from the post office. Y10 per hr. Open daily 8am-midnight. The business center of the **Qiniwake Hotel** also has Y10 per hr. access, but only 1 computer. The swankiest establishment for cyber satisfaction is the **New Era Shop** (☎282 9674), on the left side of Yunmulakexia Lu, just before the Qinibagh Hotel. Y10 per hr. **John's Information Cafe** is by far the most convenient option in the Seman area, although it has only 2 computers. Y15 per hr.

Post Office: 7 Renmin Xi Lu (☎282 7336), 3min. east of the bank. EMS and Poste Restante on the 2nd floor (M-F only). Open daily 10am-7pm. **Postal Code:** 844000.

■ ACCOMMODATIONS

Kashgar is a great place to kick back for a week; budget rooms are easy to find.

✦Qiniwake Hotel (qíníwǎkè bīnguǎn; 其尼瓦克宾馆), 93 Seman Lu (☎284 2299). There's no better deal in town. Rooms and dorms have fans and attached bath. IDD, Internet access, English-speaking staff, and 2 travel agencies right outside. Breakfast included. 4-bed dorms Y20; 3-bed dorms Y25; singles Y120; doubles Y160-260.

Friendship Hotel (yóuyì bīnguǎn; 友谊宾馆), 148 Seman Lu (☎823 5949), on the left side of Seman Lu just before the Qiniwake Hotel. This newly renovated facility eager to customers offers bright, immaculate rooms and dorms, all with private bath. In-room IDD calls possible. Deposit Y100. 4-bed dorms Y25; doubles Y160; triples Y120.

Seman Hotel (sèmǎn bīnguǎn; 色满宾馆), 170 Seman Lu (☎255 2129), has 2 branches under the same name. The foreigner-oriented, showier branch, across from John's Cafe, is easily recognizable by its colorful tiled minarets. Deposit Y100. Offers humid 3- to 4-bed dorms (Y15), nicer 2-bed dorms (Y30), surprisingly dilapidated 2-bed dorms with bath (Y60), and triples (Y180). The second branch, just to the right as you face John's Cafe, is a much better deal. Doubles with bath Y80.

People's Hotel (rénmín fàndiàn; 人民饭店), 1 Jiefang Nan Lu (☎282 4681), at Renmin Dong Lu. Standard rooms have simple balconies overlooking the busy street below, but common baths are not well kept. Hot water 7pm-3pm. Dorms Y25; singles with bath Y100; doubles Y68, with A/C and bath Y98-128.

Overseas Chinese Hotel (huá qiáo bīnguǎn; 华侨宾馆), 380 Seman Lu (☎255 3242), opposite the Seman Hotel. Views of the flower-festooned traffic circle cheer up aging showers and gloomy hallways. Hot water 8am-noon and 8pm-midnight. Rooms are often full. Deposit Y100. Singles with living room Y160; doubles Y100; triples Y90.

◉ FOOD

Kashgar's street food is not for the faint of heart; markets teem with ant-head stew, carcasses and intestines drape from massive hooks, and the pungent scent of barbecue smoke fills the air. The delicious Uighur *laghman* (Y3), noodles with tomatoes, onions, garlic, and an assortment of meats, is filling and readily available in streetside shops. Kebabs are everywhere, but beware the liver kebabs; the meat or vegetable-packed *kao bao* (Y0.5) are excellent. For breakfast or lunch, a big bowl of a rice, carrot, and squash mixture (zhuā fàn;

抓饭) costs Y2, or Y7 with hunks of lamb meat thrown on top. Other street delights include hot sweet milk (Y1), sweetbreads (Y0.5-1), deep-fried raisin, walnut, and sugar pastries (Y0.5), and bagel-like creations (Y0.2-0.5).

Relaxing ambience and Sino-Western fare combine to make the **Oasis Cafe,** just west of the Seman Hotel, one of the most enjoyable Western-style eateries around. Be sure to try their delicious in-house fruit jams. **John's Information Cafe** across the traffic circle serves its own rendition of Western dishes; let's just say that the information part is better than the cafe part. No visit to Kashgar is complete without a cup of tea at the **Chakhana Tea House,** on a corner south of Id Kah Mosque. Catapulted back in time, guests gain a rare glimpse into Kashgar's trading heyday amid greasy dishes, dark back rooms, and, of course, great tea.

🔊 SIGHTS

SUNDAY BAZAAR (kāshí xīngqī tiān shìchǎng; 喀什星期天市场). Nothing can truly prepare visitors for the grandeur and exoticism of Kashgar's Sunday Bazaar. With an impressive green-tiled dome and a multilingual sign proclaiming "Kashgar International Trade Market of Central and Western Asia," the bazaar is hard to miss. Every Sunday, the lot is transformed into a bubbling cauldron of human activity. A wild reminder of the days when Kashgar was a major crossroads on the Silk Road, the bazaar even today hosts a diverse ethnic mix of Uighurs, Tajiks, Kyrgyz, Uzbeks, Han, Russians, and, of course, foreigners. Livestock and all other creatures are contained within what looks like the holding pen for Noah's ark, while vegetables and food are sequestered in a separate section. The market tantalizes passersby with silks, knives, clothes, and more; bargain for 60 to 70% off the stated price. All sorts of tasty treats are also available in the alleys: just point and you shall receive. *(On Yizirete Lu to the northeast of town. Guard your cash and belongings carefully. The bazaar begins about 11am and ends around 6pm.)*

TOMB OF YUSUP HAZI HAJUP (hājíhānán mù; 哈吉哈吉南墓). Here lies the tomb of a much-beloved 11th-century Uighur poet who was also a prolific philosopher. Locals can't get enough of him, and they love the fact that visitors stop by. The tomb is a beautifully detailed structure with a main dome containing intricate lattices and high minarets. *(From Id Kah Square, follow Jiefang Bei Lu through the main intersection until it turns into Jiefang Nan Lu; take a left on the small Tiyu Lu (体育路) after about 1.8km, just after the stadium on the left.)*

TOMB OF ABOKH HOJA (ābākè huòjiā mù; 阿巴克霍加墓). Also known as the **Tomb of Xiangfei** (xiāngfēi mù; 香妃墓), this sight inspires a different emotion in most Uighurs than the tomb of Yusup Hazi Hajup. While the reason for such angst is at times unclear, many Uighurs seem to pin the blame on Abokh for increasing the tides of Han peoples to the west. Locals say the tomb was built by Abokh's son around 1635 to honor his dead father. Perhaps the most famous resident of this spot is a Uighur concubine of Emperor Qianlong named **Ikparhan** (Xiangfei in Mandarin). After her death, the heartbroken emperor had her carried by imperial caravan all the way back to her motherland. *(About 2km northeast of town on a road off Yizirete Lu, a 45min. bike ride along Yizirete Lu. A small, white English sign on the left will mark a turnoff; continue 700m ahead, through an alley on the right. Bike parking Y0.5. Open daily 8am-8pm. Main room Y15, students Y7.5; Niya Cultural Exhibit Y4; camera Y2, video camera Y200.)*

OTHER SIGHTS. Id Kah Mosque (àitígǎěr qīngzhēn sì; 艾提尕尔清真寺), on Jiefang Bei Lu north of Renmin Lu, was constructed in 1442. The religious epicenter of the Xinjiang Uighur community, it boasts a capacity crowd of 21,000 on festival days. Please respect local worshipers by covering your arms and legs and remaining silent. *(Free.)* The **Kashgar Museum** (kāshí bówùguǎn; 喀什博物馆) is not terribly thrilling, especially if you've already seen Ürümqi's museum—the Early Iron Age corpses may be of some interest, though. Returning to town along Yizirete Lu from

NORTHWEST

the Tomb of Abokh Hoja, take a left onto Taukuz Lu and continue for 1km; the museum is on the right before Renmin Dong Lu. *(Open daily 9:30am-1:30pm and 4-8pm. Y6, students Y3.)* The quickly deteriorating tomb of **Sayyid Ali Asla Khan** (sàiyītí yīlǐyī sīlāhàn mù; 赛衣提艾里斯拉罕墓) is farther south, along Yiliyisilahan Lu, a 10-minute walk south of Renmin Dong Lu. While there is little left of the mausoleum, walk around to left and a field of nearly 100 mud mounds lies undisturbed.

KARAKORUM HIGHWAY

The eastern segment of the Karakorum Highway (kālākūnlún; 喀拉昆仑) runs from Kashgar (see p. 707) to **Sost, Pakistan,** via Tashkurgan and the 4700m **Khunjerab Pass** (hónqílā nándápō; 红其拉南达坡). There are no overland connections from **Tashkurgan** (tǎshíkùěrgān; 塔什库尔干) to Shache, Hotan, or other southern Silk Road towns. The trip from Kashgar to Tashkurgan in theory takes eight hours.

This is far from a safe journey and is very dependent on weather conditions. During the summer months, the roads become treacherous. Mudslides (especially following summer rains) have caused fatal accidents. In late July and August, the snow from the mountains melts at its highest rate of the year, causing the river next to the highway to rise. The swift and torrential current eats away huge chunks of the road, leaving a very narrow passageway between the river and a sheer rock face/mud slope on the other side. Because communication is poor, it is almost impossible to know before leaving if the road has been washed out. If you get stuck, there is a good chance that you can walk farther along the road and then catch a bus or truck returning to Tashkurgan. From Kashgar to **Lake Karakul,** a 150km trip, costs Y43; to **Tashkurgan,** Y61; and to **Sost,** Y270.

Staying at lakeside yurts at the breathtaking Lake Karakul (kālā hú; 喀拉湖) is quite feasible. For onward travel (when the roads are good), look for a noon bus heading toward Kashgar and a 3pm bus heading toward Tashkurgan; be assertive in hailing them down. Luggage can cost an extra Y10-50, depending on the size. Check with John's Information Cafe and other travelers about road conditions, but be aware that conditions can change extremely rapidly.

BEYOND YECHENG

From **Yecheng** (叶城), the road splits: one way links Kashgar and Hotan via Shache, the other is an illegal overland route to Tibet. Late summer is not a good time to go, as melting snow runoff can wash away the dirt and gravel mountain roads, making the journey even more perilous. Expect to hitch a ride in a truck from Yechang. It can take weeks, rarely if ever under 10 days, to reach Lhasa. Temperatures are often below freezing, even during summer, and altitude sickness is a risk, as many of the mountain passes are over 5000m. The route is extremely dangerous; conditions are poor and can change rapidly. Some travelers report that if they reach the Tibetan border, they are often fined Y300 and allowed to continue into Tibet; as always, regulations, enforcement, and penalties are subject to change.

SHACHE 莎车

About halfway between Kashgar and Hotan, the small oasis town of Shache, also known as **Yarkand,** is a relaxing place to break the long desert crossing, although many people choose to bypass it entirely. Shache's one worthwhile tourist sight is the **Tomb of the Sultan of the Yarkand-Saxidia dynasty** (which controlled most of the southern Taklimakan during the 16th century), as well as a mausoleum for a famous Uighur musician and imperial concubine named Amannisahan. The tomb complex consists of a series of intricately decorated Islamic-style buildings, including a Qur'an reading room, a densely latticed dome housing the sultan's father, and an active mosque, off-limits to foreigners but still visible from the tombs. A reconstructed section of the old palace structure across the street is now used as housing for a few local families. To get to the tombs, walk along the main street heading east away from the bus station.

About a 10-minute walk past the Shache Hotel are two minarets rising behind a few low buildings on the left. Turn left onto a small market street; the main gate is on the right. (*Open daily 8am-10pm. A local Uighur guide speaks rudimentary English and decent Mandarin. Y10, students Y3.*)

The **Shache Long-distance Bus Station** (shāchē chángtú qìchē zhàn; 莎车长途汽车站) has buses to: Hetian (6hr., 11am, Y26); Kashgar (4hr., every hr. 8:30am-9:30pm, Y18); and Ürümqi (33hr., 3 per day, sleeper Y142-162) via Korla (24hr., sleeper Y99-117), but roads conditions are unpredictable. (☎851 5410. Open daily 8am-10pm.) Local branches of the **Bank of China** do not accept traveler's checks. **China Telecom** is on the main street; turn right out of the bus station, and take a right again. There is no calling card service, but IDD service is available. (Open daily 9:30am-midnight.)

Two pleasant, comfortable hotels within walking distance of the long-distance bus station accept foreigners. The **Traffic Hotel** (jiāotōng bīnguǎn; 交通宾馆), to the left as you exit the station, charges foreigners double and often refuses to rent by the bed. Chinese speakers and students may have better luck haggling for a cheaper room or for Chinese prices. Rooms are bright and nicely decorated, with fans; common baths have showers 8pm to midnight. (☎851 6402. Doubles with bath Y160; triples Y120; quads Y120.) The **Shache Hotel** (shāchē bīnguǎn; 莎车宾馆), about a 15-minute walk from the bus station, has an abandoned feel; on the bright side, few guests means that staff is often willing to greatly discount rates or to permit foreigners to purchase only a bed. The triples have almost the same conditions as doubles. (☎851 2365. Doubles Y200; triples Y60, bargain to Y40-50.) Shache is a good spot to kick back with a delicious meal and a cold beer, and night markets and small Uighur and Han Chinese restaurants abound. Be sure to be thorough in checking prices before you sit down to eat. A large **night market** runs along the street directly in front of the bus station, and another is a 10-minute walk from the Shache Hotel, just off the main street.

HOTAN 和田 ☎0903

One of the most isolated cities in all of China, Hotan is connected by road to Kashgar and, via the new Desert Highway, to Korla. Brought to life by the Karakash (Black Jade) and Yorungkash (White Jade) Rivers, this oasis town has long been a center of trade and religion along the Southern Silk Road. City ruins and Buddhist temples abound, although nowadays there is little to see but a few crumbling walls and the gorgeous desert scenery. More impressive reminders of Hotan's rich history are the ongoing traditions of silk production and carpet weaving. The mosaic of patterns and colors that adorn every market stall and drape from the backs of veiled Uighur women lend a sense of magic to this remote desert oasis, made more potent by the large amounts of white jade that lie hidden among the river stones just east of the city, renowned as China's finest.

ORIENTATION AND PRACTICAL INFORMATION

Beijing Lu (北京路) runs from **Wulumuqi Lu** (乌鲁木齐路) in the west to the **White Jade River** (bái yù hé; 白玉河), 5km east of town. Intersecting Beijing Lu in the town center is **Hetian Lu** (和田路) to the east, running south from the long distance bus station, and **Tanaiyi Lu** (塔乃依路) to the west.

Airplanes: Hotan Airport (hétiān fēijīchǎng; 和田飞机场), a Y15-20 taxi ride south of the city. **CAAC ticket office** (☎251 2178), on Wulumuqi Lu, a 5min. walk south of Beijing Lu. Open daily 9:30am-1pm and 4-7:30pm. To **Ürümqi** (Tu, Th, and Sa 10:35am, Y1070).

Bus: Hotan Long-distance Bus Station (hétiān chángtú qìchē zhàn; 和田长途汽车站; ☎203 2700, ext. 8874) lies along the highway in the north part of town. To go to the city center, exit right, walk 5 min. to the first intersection, and turn right to get to Beijing Lu, a 10min. walk. Open daily 8am-8:30pm. To: **Kashgar** (15hr.; 9 and 11:30am, Y37;

4:30pm, sleeper Y82; 8:30pm, soft seat Y56); **Qiemo** (2 days, 9am, Y56); **Shache** (7hr., 9am or any Kashgar bus, Y23); **Ürümqi** (25hr., 5 afternoon and evening buses, Y145-312) via **Korla** (19hr.) and the **Desert Highway** (the best desert scenery is seen from the 1pm bus); and **Yining** (at least 40hr., noon, Y161).

Local Transportation: All points of interest within the city are within a 15min. walk.

Travel Agencies: CITS (☎251 6090), on Wulumuqi Lu, about 20min. southwest of the town center. Ask for Aliv, who speaks English. Offers day tours (Y100 transportation plus Y100 guide fee), a convenient though costly option. A better bet is to haggle for a similar price to see 3 or 4 of the surrounding ruins and some desert scenery, and check out the factories and the White Jade River on your own. Open daily 9:30am-1:30pm and 4-8pm. A smaller branch in Rm. 228 of the Hotan City Hotel has unreliable hours.

Bank of China: On Beijing Lu, next to Xinhua Bookstore. Exchanges traveler's checks. Open M-F 9:30am-1:30pm and 4-8pm; in winter 10am-2pm and 3:30-7:30pm; Sa-Su year-round 11am-6pm.

Bookstore: Xinhua Bookstore, on Beijing Lu between Hetian Lu and Youyi Lu, sells city maps on the 2nd floor. Open daily 9:30am-9pm.

Post and Telecommunications: On Beijing Lu, across the street from Xinhua Bookstore. EMS, IDD service (no calling card calls), and Poste Restante. Open daily 9:30am-8:30pm. **Postal Code:** 848000.

▌ ACCOMMODATIONS

▨ **Hotan Guesthouse** (hétián yíngbīnguǎn; 和田迎宾馆; ☎202 2824), on Tanaiyi Lu. From the bus station walk right until you reach a tiny park, and then make a very sharp right. Walk 5min., making your first left on Tanaiyi Lu; the hotel is on the left. Set in a pleasant poplar tree courtyard. Dorms have fans, TVs, wood decor, and sparkling common baths. 24hr. hot water. 3-bed dorms Y20. 2-bed dorms with bath Y45.

Hotan City Hotel (hétián shì bīnguǎn; 和田市宾馆; ☎202 6101), at the corner of Beijing Xi Lu and Tanaiyi Lu. Buses #1 and 2 stop nearby, and there is a CITS office onsite. The cheaper, run-down rooms, complete with old concrete floors and peeling paint, are often full. Rooms with bath are bright, but bathrooms are sub-par. Hot water 9am-11pm. 4-bed dorms Y15; 3-bed dorms Y20, with bath Y40; 2-bed dorms with bath Y40.

Yiyuan Hotel (yíyuàn bīnguǎn; 怡苑宾馆; ☎202 5631), on Tanaiyi Lu, just south of the Hotan Guesthouse. The cheapest dorms are ridiculously tiny; other rooms are much more spacious and comfortable. 24hr. hot water. 3-bed dorms with A/C and bath Y45; 2-bed dorms Y30, with A/C and bath Y55.

◤ SIGHTS

Although Hotan boasts a great number of Silk Road-era ruins, these sites for the most part offer little for the casual observer; most relics have been carted off to local or Ürümqi museums, and the ancient city structures are no more than eroded mounds surrounded by vast stretches of sand dunes. If you are planning on crossing the Taklimakan via the Desert Highway to Korla and Ürümqi, these sites can be easily missed. Check with the Hotan CITS if you are interested in the ruins, as it is necessary to hire a vehicle (Y100-400, guide Y100 per day). CITS can also arrange a trip to the closest ruin, **Melikawat**, as part of the standard one-day Hotan tour. There are a number of grape vineyards and fruit orchards nearby, though visiting the silk, jade, and carpet factories is much more interesting; each offers an amazing perspective on the skill, coordination, and sheer volume of labor that goes into the production of Hotan's specialty items.

HOTAN CARPET FACTORY (hétián dìtǎn chǎng; 和田地毯厂). Check out the amazing process of carpet-weaving, often involving complex patterns of symmetry and the cutting and tying of hundreds of thousands of pieces of yarn or silk into a massive foundation grid. The history of Hotan's carpet industry is said to date back over 2000 years; more recently, in 1992, the factory wove a carpet for

Beijing's Great Hall of the People (see p. 117). *(From in front of the Hotan City Hotel, take east-bound bus #2 to the last stop. From here, either continue walking east or take bus #3, getting off as soon as you cross the White Jade River. Make a left on the 1st street across the bridge; the factory is 10min. ahead on the right. Open daily 9:30-5:30pm; avoid midday rest hours.)*

WHITE JADE RIVER (bái yù hé; 白玉河). Also known as the Yorungkash River, this is the area's primary source of white jade. Particularly in the late afternoon, you can see dozens of locals raking through piles of stones at the river's edge. Although real jade is scarce, the incredible beauty and variety of stones scattered about the banks is reason enough to visit the area. In the hot afternoon, you can pause in your search for a refreshing swim in the fast current. *(About 6km east of the city center. Take bus #2 from in front of the Hotan City Hotel to its last stop, then walk 10min. or take bus #3 east to the river.)*

HOTAN BAZAAR (hétiān dà bāzhá; 和田大巴札). The bazaar is best visited on Sundays when it has a similar feel to Kashgar's famous bazaar, but a visit during the week is also worthwhile, as there are hundreds of permanent silk, carpet, and clothing shops lining the market's covered alleyways. *(Walk north on Hetian Lu from the post office; turn right on Aiyitikaer Lu after the small park. Continue straight for 10min. along a wide dirt road; the market alleys branch off this main street.)*

SILK FACTORY (sīchóu chǎng; 丝绸厂). The most impressive part of the factory is a huge room where cocoons are boiled in long troughs and almost invisible strands of silk are wrapped around thousands of spinning reels. Long rows of Uighur women carry out this task with amazing dexterity. Visit the silk-weaving room, in which hundreds of electric looms crank out a ceaseless flow of silk sheets ready for dyeing. It may be difficult to wander around on your own, as security guards are often suspicious. If you arrive at the factory in the late morning or afternoon, head to the second floor of the office building opposite the main gate. Someone here should understand your intentions; it is often possible to arrange a tour. *(From the bus stop on Hetian Lu just south of Aiyitikaer Lu, take bus #1 (Y0.8) to the last stop; the factory, with a white tile gate and tan office building, is about 200m back toward town, on the right.)* About 1.5km south of the silk factory is **Hotan Winery** (hétiān zhìjiǔ chǎng; 和田制酒厂), which specializes in Hotan pomegranate and rice wines. Bottles can be purchased here at factory prices (Y20-120 per bottle). The security guard at the gate will call to arrange a guide.

HOTAN CITY MUSEUM (hétiān bówùguǎn; 和田博物馆). This small, one-room exhibit is nonetheless quite impressive, housing quite a few relics of the Buddhist-era Uighur culture excavated from the local Niya, Yotkan, and Aksepil city ruins. Pottery, sculpture, and even a preserved body make this museum a must-see while in Hotan. An excellent guide speaks Uighur and Mandarin. *(On Tanaiyi Lu, about 2min. from the Hotan City Hotel. Look for a small white building with blue windows. Open daily 9:30am-1:30pm and 4-8pm. Y7.)*

SOUTHERN SILK ROAD: BEYOND HOTAN

Beyond Hotan, the towns may appear progressively more dusty and drab. However, this journey offers the prospect of circumnavigating the entire Taklimakan Desert before leaving Xinjiang through the south, experiencing in the process some of the most untouched and isolated Uighur towns in all of Xinjiang. The route affords direct access to Golmud and Tibet and puts travelers close to Dunhuang. take the bus to **Qiemo** (且末), at least two days of rough travel along poor roads. The bus generally stops in **Minfeng** (民丰) along the way. From Qiemo, take the bus to **Ruoqiang** (若羌). In Ruoqiang, arrange a land cruiser with CITS. Some travelers have attempted to hitch rides east to the Qinghai border and on to **Golmud** (see p. 720), and have found the trip to take a minimum of one week to 10 days (if the road and weather conditions are favorable and breakdowns are few). During the rainy season, especially in August, many roads are washed out, and rivers may be too high to cross.

QINGHAI 青海

Besides its enormous salt lake and acclaimed herbal fungus, Qinghai has few claims to fame. More a political construct than a separate geographical entity, Qinghai province (*Amdo* in Tibetan), occupying the northern half of the Tibetan Plateau, has traditionally been a part of Eastern Tibet rather than China. The majority of the population is Han Chinese, though there are large numbers of Tibetans, Hui, Mongols, and Kazakhs. But most of the province is uninhabitable due to severe winds and freezing winter temperatures.

With a history as harsh as its lands, the region experienced a mass Han migration beginning in 1717, and Qinghai was made a province of the Republic of China in 1928, though it continued to be ruled by Hui warlords. Long March straggler Zhang Guotao split from Mao's main Red Army, hoping to slip into Russia with his 20,000 men. His ill-fated Qinghai expedition ended with two truckloads of weary survivors crawling back to Yanan. Later on, the better-equipped PLA easily drove out the local strongmen and solidified control over the region. Qinghai quickly became a prime spot for penal colonies, most of which were closed in the 1980s due to high operating costs.

To the traveler, Qaidam Basin in the northwest seemingly offers little more than desert and the occasional salt marsh, but the living portrait of vast herds tended by Amdowa Tibetan nomads, sketched onto the backdrop of Qinghai Lake, is unbeatable. The central-east Bayan Har mountain range is the source of the Yellow River, while the southern Tanggula Mountains give birth to both the Yangzi and the Mekong. The combination of high altitude (3600m), towering glaciers, and thundering gorges attract daredevil adventurers, nature documentary crews, and local tour groups, but transportation is difficult and conditions uncompromising.

One of the poorest in China, the province is turning to mining and manufacturing to pull itself out of decades of doldrums. Part of Qinghai's beauty is personally discovering whether or not its reappearance in the ebb and flow of Chinese life will not only be possible, but also, whether or not it will be a fruitful showing.

XINING 西宁 ☎0971

Guarding the overland route to Tibet at 2200m above sea level, Xining has always been desired for its strategic position on the edge of the Tibetan Plateau. From the Han dynasty through the Sui and later Tang, the region around modern Xining was controlled originally by Qiang tribesmen and then overrun by Tibetans. During the Song, the area earned its current name of Xining, or "Western Peace," and was granted the status of provincial capital in 1928. Xining has a diverse populace of Han, Hui, Tibetan, and even a handful of Chinese Christians. Although the city itself has no distinctive sights, it is nonetheless a pleasurable starting point from which to venture out to the Kumbum Monastery and Qinghai Lake.

✳❷ ORIENTATION AND PRACTICAL INFORMATION

The city center is centered around **Da Shizi** (Big Cross; 大十字) and **Xi Men** (West Gate; 西门), about a five-minute walk from one another. **Dongguan Dajie** (东关大街) runs through the eastern part of the city and across the river. It is home to the main Bank of China, the Great Mosque, and the train and long-distance bus stations.

> **Airplanes: Xining Airport** (xīníng jīchǎng; 西宁机场), is 30km to the east. Buses (30min., Y10) run from the **CAAC ticket office**, 34 Bayi Lu (☎817 4616), accessible by bus #28. Open daily 9am-12:30pm and 2:30-6pm. To: **Beijing** (1 per day, Y1160); **Chengdu** (Tu and F, Y790); **Guangzhou** (Tu and Sa, Y1300); **Lhasa** (Su-M and W-F, Y1290); **Shanghai** (Tu, Th, and Sa; Y1480); **Ürümqi** (Tu and Sa, Y900); and **Xian** (M-F and Su, Y520).

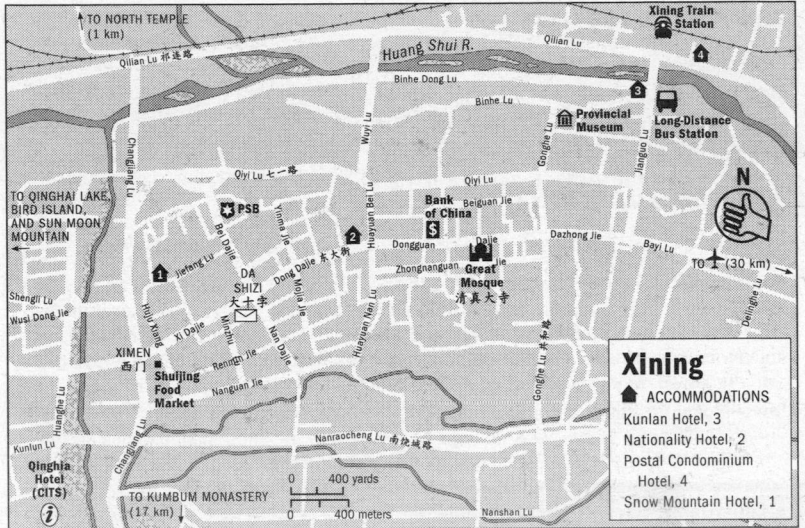

Xining

🏠 ACCOMMODATIONS

Kunlan Hotel, 3
Nationality Hotel, 2
Postal Condominium
Hotel, 4
Snow Mountain Hotel, 1

NORTHWEST

Trains: Xining Train Station (xīníng huǒchē zhàn; 西宁火车站; ☎(09851) 819 2262), on Qilian Lu across the river. Tickets are easy to procure. To: **Beijing** (32hr., 1 per day, Y230-658); **Golmud** (16hr., 2 per day, Y65-204); **Lanzhou** (3hr., 1 per day, Y29); and **Shanghai** (38hr., 1 per day, Y227-690).

Buses: Xining Long-distance Bus Station (xīníng qìchē zhàn; 西宁汽车站; ☎814 9611), on Jianguo Lu, across the river from the train station. Open daily 6am-6pm. To: **Dunhuang** (24hr., 1 per day, Y180); **Golmud** (18hr., 1 per day, Y75); **Heimahe** (6hr., 3 per day, Y20) via **Qinghai Lake**; **Lanzhou** (5hr., every 25min. 7am-5pm, Y20); **Lhasa** (50hr., 1 per day, Y340); **Linxia** (8hr., 4 per day, Y25-27); **Maduo** (15hr., 3 per day, Y44); and **Zhangye** (12hr., 1 per day, Y31).

Local Transportation: Buses cost Y0.5. Bus **#1** runs from the station area to the Great Mosque, Da Shizi, and Xi Men; **#2** goes east from the station area; **#11** goes to Chengjiang Lu, near the North Temple.

Travel Agencies: CTS (☎817 8629), in the lobby of the Postal Condominium Hotel. English-speaking staff. Offers trips to Qinghai Lake and Bird Island. Open 24hr. **Qinghai CTS** (qīnghǎi shěng zhōngguó lǚxíng shè; 青海省中国旅行社; ☎823 9240), on the 2nd floor of the Overseas Chinese Hotel, is somewhat pricier, but vice-manager Zhao Yueling speaks proficient English and can tailor trips to your needs. Open M-Sa 8:30am-6pm. **Nationality Travel Service** (mínzú lǚxíng shè; 民族旅行社; ☎822 4774 or 822 5951, ext. 2227), in the back of the Nationality Hotel, has decent deals on trips to Bird Island. Open daily 9am-6:30pm.

Bank of China: On Dongguan Jie, a 2min. walk east of Da Shizi (☎817 8888, ext. 8179 or 8205). Exchanges traveler's checks (1st Fl., counter #8) and issues credit card advances (2nd Fl., counter #8). Open M-F 8:30am-noon and 2:30-5:30pm, Sa-Su 10am-4:30pm. The branch in the Qinghai Hotel lobby also exchanges traveler's checks. Open M-F 8:30am-5:30pm, Sa-Su 9:30am-5pm.

Bookstore: Xinhua Bookstore (☎824 8475), at the Da Shizi intersection. Great maps of the city (Y4) and some English novels. Open daily 9:30am-9pm.

Hospital: Qinghai Medical College Hospital (qīnghǎi yī xuéyuàn fù yīyuàn; 青海医学院附医院; ☎611 1999). **Medical Emergency:** ☎817 7911, ext. 120.

PSB: 35 Bei Dajie (☎824 8190), a 5min. walk north of Da Shizi. Friendly and knowledgeable, with visa extensions available daily 8:30am-noon and 2:30-6pm. Open 24hr.

Internet Access: Yellow River Internet (huáng hé wángjǐng; 黄河网景), 59 Wusi Dajie (☎612 5070), in the far west of the city. Y4 per hr., Y3 for students and soldiers. Free tea while you browse. Open 24hr.

Post Office: On Da Shizi (☎824 7584), diagonally opposite the Xinhua Bookstore. EMS and Poste Restante (in a small glass cabinet) to the right; IDD service to the left and on the 2nd floor (open until 11pm). Open daily 8:30am-6pm. **Postal Code:** 810000.

ACCOMMODATIONS

Choosing a place near either Xi Men or Da Shizi is probably most convenient.

Postal Condominium Hotel (yóuzhèng gōngyù; 邮政公寓), 138 Huzhu Lu (☎814 9484, ext. 2751), near the train station. This is the best deal in Xining, even if you might have to walk up 6 flights of stairs to get to your room. The rooms are spartan but clean, with nice showers and bathrooms. Hot water 9-11pm. 4-bed dorms Y64; singles with bath Y46, with phone Y50; doubles Y48, with bath Y80.

Snow Mountain Hotel (xuěshān bīnguǎn; 雪山宾馆), 6 Bei Dajie (☎823 1010). Just north of Xi Men, a 10min. walk up Huju Jie, on the left. The Snow Mountain has accommodating staff, spotless attached bathrooms, and a prime location for the Shuijing food market. 24hr. hot water. Deposit Y200, key deposit Y20. Doubles Y138.

Kunlun Hotel (kūnlún bīnguǎn; 昆仑宾馆), 2 Jianguo Lu (☎813 3890, ext. 2065), directly across from the long-distance bus station. The 1st and 2nd floors are old military supply and hardware department outlets; the perfect place to pick up a cheap army parka. Aside from army accoutrements, the hotel has a friendly civilian staff. Hot water 9pm-midnight. Lockout midnight; knock and someone should let you in. Deposit Y20. Singles Y60-80; doubles Y70; triples Y75.

Nationality Hotel (mínzú bīnguǎn; 民族宾馆), 1 Huayuan Bei Jie (☎822 5951), at Dong Dajie, a 3min. walk east of Da Shizi. Mini-balconies with great views fill the spacious rooms with natural light. There are no public showers, so the bath-less Y30 per bed triples might leave you high and dry. Hot water 7-9am and 7:30pm-2am. Deposit Y20. Singles with bath Y100; doubles Y110-130; triples Y90, with bath Y165. Reservations recommended.

FOOD

Xining is a market town of magnificent ethnic variety. The **Traffic Market** along Huzhu Lu and east of the train station is the largest in Xining, followed by **Da Shizi Market,** on Nan Dajie. The best place to feast is at the giant night market on Yinma Jie, near Da Shizi. You can buy all types of food here, especially *xiaochi* ("small eats"; 小吃) of noodles and dumplings. Xining's most famous *xiaochi* are the savory beef noodles (niúròu miàn; 牛肉面) and the often garlicky chopped noodles (miàn piàn; 面片), both usually around Y4. The **Shuijing food market,** opposite Huju Xiang and east of Xi Men, sells mostly fruit and candy, but there are also some places that cook up Xining's famous *shaguo* (沙锅), a delicious hotpot of meat, vegetables, and *doufu* (Y5-9). Don't miss the vendors selling mouth-watering bowls of sugar-topped yogurt (suānnǎi; 酸奶; Y1). **Lanmuhan Bao,** just up the street from the PSB, serves some Western dishes, including deep-dish pizzas (Y8).

SIGHTS

KUMBUM MONASTERY (tǎěr sì; 塔尔寺). Kumbum Monastery and Labrang Monastery (see p. 671) are the two most important Tibetan Buddhist monasteries outside Tibet. Meaning "100,000 roaring images of the Buddha" in Tibetan, the Kumbum Monastery was founded in 1560 to pay respects to Qinghai native Tsong Khapa, founder of the Yellow Hat sect of Tibetan Buddhism (see p. 33). Currently home to 600 monks, Kumbum's monks study Sutra, the Tantra of Tibetan Medicine, and the Kalachalcra. Many of the embroideries, frescoes, and butter sculptures were destroyed in the Cultural Revolution, but enough artwork remains to overwhelm the average traveler.

There are tours available, but unfortunately none in English. The numbers written on the buildings themselves are completely different than the set of numbers used for the map legend on the admission ticket. Using the map legend numeration, you will see the **Eight Stupas** (#2), representing the life story of Sakyamuni, the Buddha of the Present, on your right just upon entering the complex. Farther up the road on the right is the giant **Hall of Meditation** (#20), which can hold all the monks at one time. Behind this is the beautiful **Golden Roof Pavillion** (#18) with a giant bodhi tree in the courtyard (Y3). At the end of the road and on the right is Kumbum's most unique attraction, the **Hall of Butter Sculpture** (#27). It is said that Master Tsong Khapa had a dream in which the grass turned to flowers, the thorns to bright lights, and the air to jewels. He thus ordered the monks to construct a series of reliefs out of yak butter and dedicate them to Buddha. *(27km southeast of Xining. Buses go from the leftside of the Xining Gymnasium, west of Xi Men, to the tiny village of Huangzhong (45min., every 30min. 7am-6pm, Y3). The monastery is a 3min. walk up the main road. There are few restaurants; bring snacks. Open daily 9am-6pm. Y21.)*

OTHER SIGHTS. The **Great Mosque** (qīngzhēn dà sì; 清真大寺) is on Dongguan Jie, a 10-15 minute walk east of Da Shizi. Built in 1380, it is now a spiritual center for Xining's Hui residents. Access is greatly restricted; non-Muslims can peek into the Great Prayer Hall through bars. The experience may be enlivened by stopping in during a prayer service. *(Prayer service daily 5:15am, 1:15, 5:30, 8:45, and 9:45pm—the largest on Fridays 1:15pm. Open daily 6am-9pm. Y5.)* The **North Temple** (běi shān sì; 北山寺) is an excellent one-hour hike to the northwest of Xining along Changjiang Lu, and offers fresh air and rolling hills. *(Open daily sunrise-sunset. Y6.)*

⚡ DAYTRIP FROM XINING: QINGHAI LAKE

*155km west of Xining. The trip is possible on public transportation, but is more reliable and hassle-free if arranged through a travel agency. Long-distance **buses** go daily from Xining to Heimahe (4hr.), roughly 1hr. from Bird Island, but there are no public buses going to the lake itself; travelers have been known to hike or thumb a ride the rest of the way. Return buses can be very crowded and you most likely will end up standing for 4hr. **Tours** should cost about Y80 (9-10hr. total, departing at 6:30am). **Admission** to Bird Island and Sun Mountain Y38.*

Qinghai (qīnghǎi hú; 青海湖) means "green sea" in Chinese. *Koko Nor* means "blue ocean" in Mongolian. *Tso Ngonpo* means "turquoise sea" in Tibetan. Whatever the name and whatever the hue, this enormous lake, China's largest, stretches 4583km² across the Tibetan Plateau at an elevation of 3250m. In addition to its seemingly unending horizon and abundant supply of fish, the lake is a summer nesting ground for hundreds of thousands of migratory birds. From April until July, flocks of gulls, terns, geese, swans, and cranes arrive on **Bird Island** (niǎo dǎo; 鸟岛), a peninsula on the south side of the lake, to mate before heading to the plains of India for the winter. From a tourist's vantage point, however, Bird Island appears to be more of a "bird rock," and even avid birdlovers may return disgruntled by the piles of tour buses, the long drive, and the overpriced admission.

Even though the road to Qinghai Lake offers expansive views of plateau, lake, and open stretches of sky, tour buses do tourism the Chinese way, namely, stopping at the less interesting spots (i.e. Bird Island), waiting in line to take a quick photo, and then jumping back into the van. Most tours do make a pleasant first stop at **Sun Moon Mountain** (rìyuèshān; 日月山), a beautiful mountain pass separating the grasslands from the plateau. There is typically a lunch stop, then, it's off to view birds. All in all, you've gotta love birds and not mind long drives for this trip to be worthwhile.

GOLMUD 格尔木 ☎ 0979

Golmud is Qinghai's second largest city. The arid, elevated plateau brings blaring hot days and cool nights, creating a rough habitation for the primarily Han residents who have come here to work in mining and oil plants. The lack of interesting sights makes it a one-day stop for travelers on their way to Lhasa through the only official overland route. While the train ride from Xining to Golmud is full of magnificent scenery ranging from lush terraces to salt flats to truly lunar landscapes, the bus ride from Golmud to Lhasa is a cramped and bumpy nightmare. Travelers are urged strongly to shell out the extra Y300 for a flight from Chengdu to Lhasa, or even the extra Y1000 to fly from Xining. As you crawl into your wormhole in the Lhasa-bound bus after the 25th bathroom break, you'll be wishing you were still enjoying Golmud's wide, tree-lined streets and pervasive "easy does it" attitude.

✷🛈 ORIENTATION AND PRACTICAL INFORMATION

Golmud is arranged in a small grid. The bus and train stations are in the south, from which **Jiangyuan Lu** (江源路) runs from the north through the city to the train and bus stations. One street west and parallel to Jiangyuan Lu is **Kunlun Lu** (昆仑路), which is home to hotels, the bank, and most restaurants.

Trains: Since road quality is poor around Golmud, trains are the preferable means of transport. **Qinghai Train Station** (qīnghǎi huǒchē zhàn; 青海火车站; ☎ 423 591, ext. 2222), on Jiangyuan Lu, in the south part of town. Open 24hr. To **Lanzhou** (1 per day, Y78-156) and **Xining** (19hr., 3 per day, Y46-122).

Buses: Qinghai Bus Station (qīnghǎi qìchē zhàn; 青海火汽车站; ☎ 423 688), just north of the train station. Open daily 7:30am-10pm. To: **Dunhuang** (11hr., 2 per day, Y50-84); **Lhasa** (at least 30hr., 1 per day, Y180); and **Xining** (20hr., 1 per day, Y40). **Tibet Bus Station** (xīzàng qìchē zhàn; 西藏火汽车站) in northwest Golmud has one bus to **Lhasa** (at least 30hr., 4:30pm, Y200).

Travel Agencies: CITS (☎ 412 764), on the 2nd floor of the Golmud Hotel, is the only travel agency in town. You *must* pay Y1660 for a bus and permit into Lhasa—no ifs, ands, or buts. This fee includes: Y1380 for bus, permit, and a 3-day "tour" of Lhasa that does not include admission fees, plus another Y280 as an advance payment on your means of departure from Lhasa. If you want to see your Y280 again, you must book through **Nag Qu International Travel Service** on the 2nd floor of Lhasa's Kirey Hotel, and you have only 4 options: Lhasa to Kathmandu by air; Lhasa to Chengdu by air; Lhasa to Zhangmu by bus; and Lhasa to Golmud by sleeper bus. Open daily 8:30am-12:30pm and 3-6:30pm.

Bank of China: 19 Taidamu Lu (☎ 413 727), at Kunlun Lu, 1 block south of the Golmud Hotel. Exchanges traveler's checks. No credit card advances. Open daily 8:30am-noon and 3-6pm.

PSB: In the eastern part of the city (☎ 412 375). Will not grant Tibet travel permits. Open daily 8:30am-noon and 3-6pm.

Post Office: On Jiangyuan Lu (☎ 413 094), a 5min. walk east from the Bank of China. EMS and IDD service. Open daily 8am-6pm. **Postal Code:** 816000.

▌◖◗ ACCOMMODATIONS AND FOOD

Only two hotels accept foreigners. The **Qinggang Hotel** (qīnggǎng bīnguǎn; 青港宾馆), 108 Kunlun Lu, is definitely worth the extra money. Rooms are carpeted and well furnished, with pristine private bathrooms and showers; a swimming pool, two free games in the bowling alley, and an on-site CITS are added perks. (☎ 421 808. Standard doubles Y128.) Across the street, the **Golmud Hotel** (gé'ěrmú bīnguǎn; 格尔木宾馆), 219 Kunlun Lu, has bleak but spacious rooms, with clean white sheets. There are no public showers. (☎ 412 061. 3-bed dorms Y22; singles Y28; doubles with bath Y77; triples Y66.)

Golmud has enough good cuisine to keep travelers satisfied; both the Han and Hui throw their regional fare into the mix. The **night market,** one intersection north of the Golmud Hotel and along the street to the right, has stalls with Muslim foods. The kebabs (Y1) are tender and delicious. There is also a fantastic restaurant across and just down the street from the Golmud Hotel. Although **Yinmiao Zhen Fast Food** (yínmiǎo zhèn; 银秒针快餐店) does not have an English menu, the Kungpao chicken (gōngbǎo jīdīng; 宫保鸡丁; Y10) will turn even cynics into worshipers of the spicy peanut. The sweet and sour pork (Y10) is also quite tasty. More popular with travelers, however, is the **Happy Peace Restaurant** (xīníng hépíng jiǔjiā gé fēndiàn; 西宁和平酒家格分店), which has an English menu consisting of mostly Han dishes and inexpensive beer.

NORTHWEST

༄༅· TIBET 西藏

Closed to foreign eyes until scarcely a decade ago, Tibet's remoteness and famed religiosity has long captured the imagination of Westerners enchanted with a mystical "Shangri-La" high in the Himalayas and untainted by the dull grime of civilization. When Tibet's doors were opened in the mid-1980s, Western visitors were startled to see Chinese soldiers marching beside ruined monasteries. Clearly, the Chinese invasion and communist transformation had left their mark on Tibet. But the amalgam of past, present, and future that is shaping the spirit of this intensely spiritual land is very different from anything else in China.

Tibet today is a place shaped by heartbreaking historical trauma, heart-stopping natural beauty, and a headstrong traditional culture. Surrounded by the world's loftiest mountains, Tibet is still the physical Roof of the World, but these days being so close to the heavens means being dangerously close to the world's third largest hole in the ozone layer. The cultural landscape of pre-1959 Tibet is gone forever. Travelers should not be fooled by the easing of religious restrictions and the sight of open Tibetan Buddhist festivities; the lack of political freedoms and the presence of mechanisms of repression are in many ways greater than they have ever been.

However, for most Tibetans, life remains rich despite the odds. Buddhism (see p. 728) dominates all aspects of life. Even the hawkers sweet-talking tourists in the capital city of Lhasa are likely, when work is over, to join the devout pilgrims walking the sacred circuit around the Jokhang Temple. With the influx of tourists and increasing international attention, no one knows what the future has in store for Tibet. Through the marvelous and confusing haze of the otherworldly and the earthy, one thing is certain: Tibet will never be what you imagined it to be.

HIGHLIGHTS OF TIBET

THE PALATIAL PALACES of the Dalai and Panchen Lamas at Lhasa's **Potala Palace** (p. 735) and Shigatse's **Tashilhunpo** (p. 749).

THE HOLY CIRCUIT around the **Jokhang Temple** (p. 736), and shopping around **Barkhor Market** (p. 736).

MONASTIC TRADITION at **Sera** (p. 738), **Sakya** (p. 749), and **Samye** (p. 740).

A LONG, STRANGE TRIP down the **Friendship Highway** (p. 742) to Nepal, which takes you past the base camp of **Mt. Everest** (p. 751).

TIBET ESSENTIALS

DOCUMENTS AND FORMALITIES

Traveling in Tibet is tightly restricted and monitored by the authorities. To enter Lhasa Prefecture, visitors also must obtain a Chinese visa and a Tibet Tourism Bureau (TTB) Permit (See **Travel Permits** below), issued only to travelers in tour groups. To travel elsewhere in Tibet, you must also be with a group and obtain an Alien Travel Permit.

VISAS. Travelers to the PRC need to obtain visas prior to arrival, and Tibet is no exception. The visa application form asks travelers to list their intended destinations in the PRC; as the itinerary given on the visa application is not binding, most travelers find it easier to omit Tibet in favor of less politically sensitive places like Beijing or Shanghai. Most embassies and consulates issue standard, single-entry, 30- to 60-day tourist visas. Multiple-entry visas are most easily obtained through a travel agency in Hong Kong. For more information on Chinese visas, see p. 50.

Tibet

TIBET

For those planning to enter Tibet via Kathmandu (p. 753), it is best to get a Chinese visa; once in the Nepalese capital, it is virtually impossible for individual travelers to get a Chinese visa. Instead, travelers are herded into tour groups and given group visas. Those wishing to stay in Tibet after their tour must apply for visa extensions at the Chinese affiliate of the Nepalese travel agency. The whole process is a bureaucratic nightmare and can be quite pricey (Y500-2500).

TRAVEL PERMITS. In addition to high altitude and nearly impassable terrain, individual travelers to Tibet are further burdened by an overwhelming amount of bureaucracy. The **Tibet Tourism Bureau (TTB) Permit** can only be obtained by going through a travel agency and joining a tour. The TTB grants access only to Lhasa and Lhasa Prefecture, including Namtso Lake. To travel anywhere else, you need to purchase an **Alien Travel Permit** (Y150 per person), which is only issued to guided groups. A travel agency can arrange for a guide (Y120-150 per day), a jeep with driver (Y2-3 per km), and documentation. The PSB offices in Lhasa and Tsetang reject individual travelers. Travelers might be able to acquire a permit (US$150) in Shigatse. However, policies and regulations change according to the whims of the local authorities. Ask around for the most current information.

The PSB conducts frequent sweeps for foreign travelers and trekkers. If caught without a permit, resist the temptation to flail about and yell obscenities. There have been documented cases of fines up to US$100 and even deportations; those who react calmly tend to receive less outrageous penalties.

GETTING TO TIBET

The three main gateways into Tibet are Chengdu (p. 614) in Sichuan province, Xining (p. 716) or Golmud (p. 720) in Qinghai province, and Kathmandu (p. 753) in Nepal. See also the **Transportation** and/or **Practical Information** sections of Lhasa (p. 730), Chengdu (p. 614), Xining (p. 716), and Zhangmu (p. 752) for further information on getting to and from Tibet.

FROM SICHUAN PROVINCE. Chengdu is the most popular gateway into Tibet from the Chinese interior. Almost all travelers to Tibet take the two-hour flight (3-5 per day, Y1200) to Lhasa's **Gonggar Airport.** Before buying an airline ticket, you will most likely need to obtain a Tibet Tourism Bureau Permit, sold only to those traveling in tour groups. Chengdu teems with travel agencies promoting three-, five-, and ten-day packaged deals. The usual routine for independent travelers involves purchasing a three-day tour (Y1950) that includes the TTB Permit, a one-way air ticket, transportation from Gonggar Airport to Lhasa, and several nights' accommodations. After three days in Lhasa, the tour group dissolves and travelers go their separate ways. Currently, overland routes on the Sichuan-Tibet highway are closed to foreigners.

FROM QINGHAI PROVINCE. Until the Xining-Lhasa air route (flight Y1290; TTB permit Y800) opened in the spring of 1999, most travelers took a train (Y123) from Xining to **Golmud** (p. 720), where they applied for the TTB Permit and embarked on a grueling 1115km bus journey (30-50hr., 1 per day, sleeper Y1380) on the Qinghai-Tibet highway. This route spends several hours above 5000m, high enough to make many people suffer from altitude sickness (see p. 725). Foreigners can purchase bus tickets from the 2nd floor of the **Golmud Hotel** (géěrmù bīnguǎn; 格尔木宾馆), 219 Kunlun Lu (☎(0979) 412 061, travel permit service ☎412 764), but considering the cost and difficulty of the overland trip, you might as well fly. A third option is the more expensive CITS and private tours (Y5000) that wind slowly (12-15 days) through the Qinghai plateau on their way to Lhasa.

FROM NEPAL. The flight from Kathmandu (Y2300) to Lhasa passes over the Himalayas, sometimes permitting a glimpse of Mt. Everest. Tickets can only be purchased with a TTB Permit and tour group credentials; three-day tours (more than US$400) can be arranged in Kathmandu, and include a one-way air ticket to

Lhasa, the TTB Permit, a few nights' accommodation, and transportation from Gonggar Airport. A new regulation strictly enforces the rule that Lhasa-bound tour groups must consist of at least 5 people.

Buses cross the China-Nepal border at Zhangmu. Individual travelers are not allowed to pass Zhangmu without a TTB Permit. Most people hire a land cruiser and guide (around US$200 per person) for the remainder of the trip to Lhasa. It is easier simply to join a budget tour in Kathmandu for the overland journey along the 920km long **Friendship Highway** (see p. 742); such tours generally stop in Zhangmu, Lhatse, and Lhasa (3 days, US$250-300 per person). Land cruisers also can be hired from Kathmandu for longer and more flexible trips.

The health risks of the overland route from Kathmandu into Tibet are considerable; the road passes through some very high altitudes before travelers have had sufficient time to acclimate. Anyone bent on adding Nepal to a Tibet itinerary should seriously consider arriving in Lhasa from Chengdu and departing for Kathmandu via the border at Zhangmu, not the other way around.

HEALTH

In addition to the normal ailments suffered by travelers to China, Tibet has several health risks of its own, particularly Acute Mountain Sickness and Giardiasis. Tibet's high altitude also means ultra-violet rays are more intense, increasing the risk of **sunburn,** even in cold weather. Tibetan winters are no joke; travelers should come prepared for **cold and snow.** Much of the tourist infrastructure shuts down. For more information on **sunburn** and **hypothermia,** see p. 62; for advice on general health concerns for the region, see p. 60.

ACUTE MOUNTAIN SICKNESS (AMS). Much of the Tibetan Plateau is at an altitude above 4000m, high enough to make many new arrivals in the region suffer the effects of the decreased air pressure and oxygen levels. Acute Mountain Sickness (AMS), also known as altitude sickness, typically appears about four hours after arrival, and it may take three or four days for the body to adjust. **Rate of ascent** affects the onset of AMS; ascending too quickly without allowing your body time to adjust can be very dangerous. The most prevalent symptoms of AMS are headache, insomnia, fatigue, shortness of breath, dizziness, and nausea. AMS is aggravated by dehydration, alcohol and other depressants, and overexertion.

Mild AMS (headache, vomiting, fatigue) is best alleviated by staying hydrated, avoiding sedatives (like alcohol), and taking it easy. Travelers should consider budgeting a few days in Lhasa simply to get used to the altitude. Mild symptoms of AMS can be treated by normal over-the-counter pain relievers; some physicians prescribe **Diamox** (acetazolamide), which stimulates respiration. Moderate AMS (persistent vomiting and severe headache) is sometimes treated by supplemental oxygen and steroids, and a descent of 300-700m is recommended.

Severe AMS is a life-threatening condition. **High Altitude Pulmonary Edema** (HAPE) often results in blueness or paleness of the lips and face and a cough or gurgling respiration as a result of fluid accumulation in the lungs. **High Altitude Cerebral Edema** (HACE) causes changes in consciousness; sufferers may stagger and be unable to walk straight. Severe fatigue and shortness of breath are other symptoms. Severe AMS can cause coma or even death. Travelers who suspect it should descend 600-1300m and seek medical assistance immediately.

GIARDIASIS. Commonly called **giardia,** giardiasis is caused by the protozoan parasite *Giardia lamblia.* This parasite is present in untreated water, particularly in cold and mountainous regions. Travelers should avoid unboiled tap water and raw food washed with unboiled tap water. Swimming in lakes and streams can also lead to infection, especially if you swallow the water. Symptoms of giardiasis include diarrhea, abdominal cramps, and nausea; they usually appear one to two weeks after infection and last for four to six weeks. Giardia is treatable by an anti-amoebic drug such as Flagyl (metronizade), usually available only by prescription.

TIBET

HISTORY

EARLY HISTORY

Legend says that the Tibetan people are descended from the unlikely union of a monkey and a female demon. Fossils and historical records say that Tibetans are descended from the Qiang, mentioned in Chinese records as early as 200 BC. However, it was probably not until the 7th century that the Tibetans developed as a discreet ethnicity. A collection of squabbling small princedoms occupied the region until the end of the 6th century, when Tibet's first *tsanpo* (king), **Namri Songtsen,** assembled an army of 100,000 and conquered a number of his neighbors on the Chinese border. His son, **Songtsen Gampo,** established diplomatic relations with the Tang court in exchange for a Chinese princess as his bride. This same renaissance man also extended the Tibetan empire to northern India, introduced the Tibetan script, and embraced **Buddhism.** Not long after his death, relations with China deteriorated.

In the 9th century, struggles over succession to the throne once again divided Tibet. Political authority languished but Buddhism flourished as missionaries flooded in from India. Monasteries, including the one at **Sakya** (p. 749), were founded in this period, and Tibetan priests **(lamas)** allied themselves with local nobility to create a viable political and religious power complex. When the **Mongols** stormed into the region in 1240, their leader declared himself the "patron" of the lama at Sakya, assuming effective political control while claiming to be subject to the lama's spiritual authority. During the Yuan dynasty, the Sakya lamas ruled Tibet as puppets of the Mongol emperor. When the emerging Ming dynasty overthrew Mongol rule in 1368, Tibet regained its independence. The development of Buddhism continued at a redoubled pace, and under the influence of India and Nepal, the seeds of present-day Tibetan Buddhist art were sown; monasteries, *stupas*, and frescoes appeared across the land.

COMING OF THE YELLOW HAT SECT

In the early 15th century, **Tsong Khapa,** disillusioned with the infighting and mysticism that characterized Tibetan Buddhism under the Sakya lamas, founded a new sect that emphasized scholastic philosophy and monastic discipline. Only after his death did his school, now known as the **Yellow Hat sect** or **Gelugpa sect,** really take off. During the mid-16th century, Mongol leaders recognized the Gelugpa lama (believed to be the living reincarnation of the *bodhisattva* Avalokiteshvara) as the ultimate spiritual head of Tibetan Buddhism, granting him the title of Dalai ("Ocean-wide") Lama. This declaration was violently opposed by the **Red Hat sect** (not to be confused with the red-hatted tour group hordes that are everywhere in China), but eventually the Dalai Lama was installed as the political ruler of Tibet. The Dalai moved the capital to **Lhasa,** which thereafter supplanted Sakya as the nation's foremost city. In the 17th century, the Dalai Lamas cemented the strongest government yet to govern a united Tibet. The construction of the **Potala Palace** (p. 735) was undertaken as a symbol of their authority. The Gelugpa sect and the divine authority of the Dalai Lama have dominated Tibetan Buddhism ever since.

CHINESE SUZERAINTY AND TIBETAN AUTONOMY

A series of disputes over who was to be the next Dalai Lama led the Dzungar Mongols from northern Xinjiang to invade. In 1717, the Qing, loathe to see any increase in Mongol power, invaded to kick out the Mongols. Welcomed by the Tibetans as a counterweight to the overbearing Mongols, the Chinese established a small garrison in Tibet. Under **Chinese "suzerainty,"** the Tibetans were left to govern internal affairs on their own, the Dalai Lama's government maintained peaceful relations with China, and Tibetan culture absorbed little Chinese influence.

As the strength of the Qing waned and British influence in India increased, sparks began to fly in the region. In the mid 1800s, Tibet, like much of China, was closed to western trade. Numerous attempts by the British to enter Tibet were repelled by the Tibetans. In 1903-4, the British military adventurer Younghusband led an "expedition" into Tibet, marching into Lhasa and slapping indemnities on the Tibetans. This forced the 13th Dalai Lama to flee to Mongolia. The British then backtracked and acknowledged Chinese sovereignty over Tibet. Emboldened by this declaration, the dying Qing dynasty brutally "pacified" Tibetan areas in Sichuan and Qinghai and sent the 13th Dalai Lama into exile in India. After the Chinese revolution of 1911, the indignant Tibetans (led by the newly returned Dalai Lama) declared complete independence and expelled all Chinese residents.

Over the next forty years, Tibet enjoyed complete sovereignty but failed to maintain internal harmony. The **Panchen Lama** (Tibet's second most important leader) was based in Shigatse (p. 746) and refused to pay taxes to the Dalai Lama, finally fleeing to China. The 13th Dalai Lama's attempts at reform and modernization were rejected by the conservative aristocracy, and Tibet remained a pious but impoverished theocracy. Tibet's neutrality during WWII did not help its drive for international recognition; when Chiang Kai-shek declared Tibet a province of Nationalist China, the victorious allied powers did not protest.

UNDER CHINESE RULE (1949-PRESENT)

EARLY YEARS (1949-1980). After the PLA beat a poorly equipped Tibetan army in 1950, the young **14th Dalai Lama**'s appeals to the United Nations were rebuffed. The Tibetan government was forced to sign a treaty whose terms were dictated by the Chinese: Tibet would maintain cultural and religious autonomy even as it fell under Chinese control.

While adopting a laissez-faire attitude toward the economy and domestic affairs of Tibet proper, the CCP collectivized Tibetan areas of western Sichuan and Qinghai. In the mid 1950s, after a failed rebellion, Tibetan rebel leaders retreated to Lhasa and carried on a guerrilla war in southern Tibet. The US Central Intelligence Agency (CIA), eager to strike a blow at the communists, covertly supplied the Tibetan rebels with arms and training. In 1959, a gathering of Sichuanese Tibetans near the Norbulingka in Lhasa began a **mass rebellion.** The Dalai Lama, accompanied by relatives, ministers, wealthier supporters, CIA-trained rebels, and much of the country's gold reserves, fled to exile in India. Shortly thereafter, the PLA swiftly quashed the uprising, although Tibetan fighters continued to foment unrest from bases in Nepal for another decade.

After the rebellion, the CCP declared **martial law** in Tibet. It liquidated the traditional ruling classes, replacing them with Beijing-appointed officials and communist Tibetan cadres. From 1959 on, Tibet was subject to the same economic reforms of collectivization and central planning as the rest of China, with disastrous effects (p. 18). During the Cultural Revolution, Chinese Red Guards and riotous Tibetan youths demolished legions of monasteries. Nuns and monks were forced to marry, and thousands were sent to prison camps. All told, well over a million Tibetans died in the turmoil.

RECENT EVENTS (1980-PRESENT). After the rise of Deng Xiaoping in 1979, liberal officials acknowledged past mistakes in Tibet and urged "ethnic sensitivity." Monasteries were rebuilt, economic activity was normalized, and the region was opened to tightly regulated tourism. Nominal religious practice was permitted so long as religious leaders stayed out of politics. Moves toward liberalization in the 1980s led Tibetans to clamor for greater political freedom, but demonstrations in Lhasa during the late 1980s were met with brutal police and army suppression. Three days before the Tiananmen Square protests in 1989 (p. 20), a large group of Tibetan protestors were killed in the streets, after which the Chinese government declared martial law. The display of Dalai Lama photographs was banned in 1994.

TIBET

Today, monasteries are tightly monitored, and monks are required to undergo political education and swear allegiance to the Chinese state. Although primary education is conducted mainly in Tibetan, almost all forms of higher education require students to speak Chinese. China's development projects from the Great Leap Forward to the new "Exploit the West" campaign have led the government to clear massive strips of Tibet's precious forests. This, combined with the poaching of many of Tibet's large animals and the greenhouse effect, threaten to turn the "Roof of the World" into an environmental tragedy that its inhabitants will have little to no part in writing.

As any visitor to Tibet will quickly realize, the Tibetan way of life has withstood many challenges. The **Tibetan Government in Exile,** based in Dharamsala, India, is a democratic, constitutional body that rules over the 131,000 Tibetans currently in exile. The Dalai Lama has succeeded in drawing world attention to his homeland, but when it comes to action, the new Chinese market apparently speaks louder than the Dalai Lama's pleas. Although in 1999 lobbyists for Tibet stopped a World Bank loan that would have funded increased Chinese immigration, China's forthcoming acceptance into the WTO will end international human rights inspections.

PEOPLE

ETHNIC COMPOSITION. About 4.6 million Tibetans live in China, most in the ethnically Tibetan areas of Qinghai, Gansu, Sichuan, and Yunnan. Since the 1950s, large numbers of Han and Hui Chinese, mainly merchants and government-sponsored cadres, have settled in these regions. Most Tibetans make their living through agriculture, nomadic herding, or small-scale commerce. Few cultures on earth invest as much in religion as the Tibetans do. In Tibet, politics, art, science, and literature all derive from and support spiritual faith. Prior to the Cultural Revolution, many Tibetans had based their livelihoods around Buddhist monasteries or nunneries. Chinese intervention and policies such as the 18 years minimum age for entry into the monastic life are also slowly turning Tibetans away from their traditional lifestyle.

LANGUAGE. Although part of the Sino-Tibetan language family, Tibetan is distinct from Chinese. The Tibetan script, introduced around AD 600, is derived from and similar to Indian writing systems, and is read from right to left like many of those scripts. Modern Tibetan is more closely related to Burmese than Chinese. Regional dialects vary widely; the Lhasa dialect is regarded as the standard.

FOOD. Tibetan **cuisine,** likewise, would never be mistaken for Chinese. The staple is barley flour (*tsampa*), which is mixed with water to form a porridge that is the foundation of most Tibetan diets. The yak, a big, pungent, and hairy creature well-suited to high altitudes, is another staple. Yak butter, yak meat, yak milk—any slaughtered yak is bound to be a very well-utilized yak. The yak and barley also haunt (and warm up) diners in the form of yak-butter tea and barley beer, known as *chang*. Wheat, mutton, and pork are also widely consumed; *thukpa* (noodle soups) and *momos* (fried dumplings) are popular.

RELIGION

BÖN

Before Buddhism, there was Bön. Elements of Bön are a good part of what make Tibetan Buddhism unique. As a largely practical faith, Bön is concerned with magic, soothsaying, and sacrifice. The Tibetan Buddhist concept of a divine king, a leader of both the political and the spiritual realms, originated with Bön, as did many of Tibetan Buddhism's minor deities and its tradition of religious oracles. Bön still has some staunch adherents, mostly nomads in the remote north and east of Tibet. When seven Bön aristocrats formally renounced secular life, pledging their loyalty to the *dharma*, they became Tibet's first monks, known as the "Seven Examined Men."

TIBETAN BUDDHISM

The Tibetan school of Buddhism integrates what it views as the three schools of Indian Buddhism: **Hinayana,** or individual practice; **Mahayana,** the ethical practice; and **Vajrayana,** or "diamond vehicle." A monk usually adopts one of the deities from India's **Tantric Sect** and studies and imagines the deity until he can exist as this buddha in meditation for hours on end. In the second phase, the monk manipulates his physical energies in order to exist eventually in the foundation of all being, "clear light." The key to Tibetan Buddhism is to channel the energy of emotion into the quest for sacred consciousness.

Before the Chinese occupation, an estimated 25% of Tibetans were monks or nuns. **Monastic life** would generally involve years of grueling, intensive study and meditation. Tibetan monasteries are headed by teachers called **lamas,** addressed by the title *rimpoche* (precious one), who are distinct from ordinary monks and nuns. Each living lama is said to be the reincarnation of an earlier lama, usually identified through astrology and consultations with oracle monks; child candidates for lamahood are typically asked to prove their legitimacy by identifying the former lama's possessions. The **Dalai Lama** and his traditional second-in-command, the **Panchen Lama,** are the most elevated representatives of these individuals.

While monks and nuns engage in theological argument and meditation, common people worship a number of *bodhisattvas*, deities, and demons. Among the most revered of these is **Avalokiteshvara,** represented as both the monkey demon (p. 726) and as the *bodhisattva* of compassion (like the Chinese Guanyin). **Circumambulating** (taking walks along designated sacred paths), the burning of yak-butter lamps (to represent the triumph of enlightenment over ignorance), the offering of bowls of water (to represent one's pure essence), and the **turning of prayer wheels** play an important role in popular practice.

Religious art in Tibetan temples reveals the complexity of Buddhist myth and symbolism. The range of depictions reflect the all-encompassing, multifaceted nature of enlightenment. Many buddhas are involved in a sexual embrace, meant to symbolize the unification of the male and female into a singular consciousness. Elsewhere, smiling, tranquil *bodhisattvas* appear alongside wrathful demons. The circular **mandalas** that turn up everywhere are abstract portraits of deities within the worlds they inhabit; the two-dimensional circle is meant to represent a three-dimensional sphere, at the center of which the deity is encased. An especially powerful symbol is the **wheel of life,** representing an infinite circular expanse along which an individual can travel through countless incarnations.

FESTIVALS AND HOLIDAYS

Most Tibetan festivals are local affairs, unique to a village or region and buoyed by strong community spirit. National festivals are mostly Buddhist holidays, but a few are the lingering remains of Tibet's distant pagan past. All dates follow the Tibetan calendar, which differs from both the Chinese and Western calendars.

Tibetan New Year (in February or March) is a huge affair. Offerings ranging from liquor to lamb's heads are prepared in the pre-dawn hours, and families venture out to temples and shrines at daybreak. Three days after the New Year, the 15-day **Prayer Festival** begins, marked by special prayers, mock theological debates, and the performance of miracles. This festival honors the philosophical victory of Buddha over those who critiqued his religious claims. The **Buddha's birth, enlightenment, and death** are all celebrated on the 15th day of the fourth month.

On the 25th day of the tenth month, Tibetans commemorate the **death of Tsong Khapa,** founder of the Yellow Hat Buddhist sect, by lighting yak-butter lamps in the windowsills of residences. On the 29th day of the last month of the year, bunches of burning straws are carried into every room of Tibetan homes to **cast out evil spirits.** These are eventually thrown outside to burn themselves out.

ဩན LHASA 拉萨   ☎ 0891

The name *Lhasa* blends the mystical and the mundane. During the building of the Jokhang Temple on Lake Wothang some 1300 years ago, goats *(ra)* were used to transport sand *(sa)* to fill the lake, and the city that grew around the construction site came to be known as *Rasa*. It was only after the various temples were built and holy statues installed in them that the name changed to *Lhasa* (Abode of the Gods). At first glance, Lhasa can seem poverty-stricken, with its pervasive street muck and pungent smells. Its name conjures up images of mysticism and monks. But anyone expecting a mystical Shangri-la from Lhasa had better wake up and smell the yak-butter tea. Immersion reveals a very festive mini-metropolis. The stalls of Barkhor Market sell all sorts of marvelous merchandise, from eye-catching *tangkas* to shiny prayer wheels. Lhasa's vitality even manages to stretch past the spirited Tibetan quarters in the east to infuse life and vigor into the Chinese areas in the west.

✳ ORIENTATION

At 3700m above sea level, Lhasa sits on the lowland northern bank of the **Lhasa** or **Kyichu River.** Lhasa's jurisdiction extends over some 29,052km^2 of terrain, but the populated area covers a much less intimidating 554km^2. Lhasa's intriguing city center spans only 20km^2, and visitors tend to get around just fine with a map and their own two feet. Bounded to the north by **Beijing Lu** (北京路) and to the south by **Jinzhu (Chingdol) Lu** (金珠路), Lhasa proper is divided into two main sections, with the dividing line loosely marked by the **Potala Palace.** The western half of the city is predominantly Chinese and holds little of interest for the average traveler, except perhaps for the **Norbulingka** and a slew of karaoke bars and Sichuanese restaurants. The predominantly Tibetan eastern half of town surrounds the **Jokhang Temple** and **Barkhor Market** area, the true heart of the city. Most tourists head to this lively and colorful quarter, complete with travel agencies, Western-style restaurants, and cheap accommodations.

▤ TRANSPORTATION

Airplanes: Lhasa Gonggar Airport (lāsà gònggā jīchǎng; 拉萨贡嘎机场; ☎ 618 2221), is 95km to the southwest, the greatest distance between any city and its municipal airport in the world. An **airport bus** runs from Gonggar Airport to Lhasa (1½hr., departure times dependent on daily arrival times, Y30). Buses also run from the Lhasa CAAC Ticket Office to Gonggar (1½hr., every other day, Y30). **Land cruisers** (1½hr., Y400-500) also ferry passengers between the airport and city center. Check the boards at the Yak, Banak Shol, Pentoc, and Kirey Hotels, where notices from passengers looking to share a taxi or land cruiser to the airport are often posted. **China Southwest Airlines,** a subsidiary of CAAC, has direct flights to and from Tibet. In Lhasa, tickets can be booked up to 15 days in advance at the **CAAC Ticket Office,** 1 Niangre Lu (☎ 683 3446; fax 683 8609). Open daily 9am-8:30pm. To: **Beijing** (W and Su, Y2940); **Chengdu** (2-3 per day, Y1000); **Chongqing** (Sa, Y1300); **Kathmandu** (Tu, Th, and Sa; Y2290); **Xian** (Su-M, W, and F; Y1320); and **Xining** (Su-M, W, and F; Y1290).

Buses: Lhasa Long-distance Bus Station (☎ 682 4469), on the corner of Jinzhu (Chingdol) and Minzhu Lu, is in the southwestern section of Lhasa. To: **Chengdu** (4 days, 3 per day, Y230); **Shigatse** (5hr., 1 per day, Y38); and **Tsetang** (4hr., 3 per day, Y26-30) via the **Samye Monastery ferry crossing.** Privately owned minibuses go to **Shigatse** (5-6hr., Y38) and the **Samye ferry crossing** (3hr., Y10). Boarding begins at 7am in front of Kirey Hotel and buses leave when full.

Local Transportation: Minibuses (Y2) are privately owned and run 7 routes: **#1** goes from the Leather Factory to the Tibetan Hospital; **#2** from the Tibetan Hospital to the Petroleum Storehouse; **#3** from the cement factory to Qingnian Lu; **#4** from the Electronic Machinery Factory to Ramoche Temple; **#5** from Ramoche Temple to Sera Monastery; **#6** from Najin Lu to Ramoche Temple; **#7** from No. 1 Middle School to the

N

TIBET

Lhasa

▲ ACCOMMODATIONS

Banak Shol Hotel, 8
Eight Auspicious (Tashi
Tagel) Hotel, 3
Kirey Hotel, 6
Lhasa Gang-gyen Hotel, 7

Lhasa Yak Hotel, 1
Mandala Hotel, 5
Pentoc Guesthouse, 2
Snowland Hotel, 4
Sunlight Hotel, 9

→ TO DREPUNG AND
NECHUNG MONASTERIES (8 km)

Duode Lu

Lingkuo Dong Lu

Telecommunications Office 📞

PSB ➕

Beijing Dong Lu

PSB ➕

Main Mosque

Lingkuo Dong Lu

Lingyu Bei Lu

Lingyu Nan Lu

Sera Lu

PSB ➕

Lingkuo Bei Lu 林廓北路

Ramoche Lu

Ramoche Temple 小昭寺

Dosenggge Lu

Bank of China 💲

6 7

8

Ani Tsangkung Nunnery

Jokhand Temple 大昭寺 ▲

5

FIT Travel ▲ 1

2 3

Zangyuan Lu

Dong Lu

Barkhor Market 八角街

Barkhor Lu

Lingkuo Nan Lu

Lingkuo (Chingdol) Dong Lu 金珠东路

People's Hospital ➕

Niangre Lu

CAC Office ✈

Lhasa City Post and Telecommunications 📞

Kharnga Dong Lu

Yuthok Lu

Jinzhu (Chingdol) Dong Lu 北京东路

Beijing Dong Lu 北京东路

TO SERA MONASTERY (3 km) ↑

Liberation Park

Lukhang Temple ▲

Lingkuo Xi Lu

Potala Palace 布达拉宫

Beijing Zhong Lu

0   400 yards
0   400 meters

Bank of China 💲

Golden Yaks Statue ■

Chakpori Hill ▲

Kundeling Lu

Lobhunke (Norbulingka) Lu

Library

Jinzhu (Chingdol) Zhong Lu 金珠中路

Beijing Zhong Lu 北京中路

Lhasa (Kyichu) R.

Minzu Lu

Nepal ▲

Norbulingka 罗布林卡

Beijing Xi Lu

Tibet Hotel (CITS) ■

Baiding Storehouse. **Tricycles** comfortably transport 2 passengers. From the end of Beijing Dong Lu to Potala Palace (3-4km) Y3-4. Tricycles are prohibited from passing the square in front of the Potala Palace before 7:30pm.

Taxis: Taxis cost Y10 anywhere in the city (north of the Kyichu River, excluding Sera and Drepung monasteries). Bargain for destinations beyond city limits.

Bike Rental: The **Snowland** (p. 733) and **Yak** (p. 733) Hotels rent bikes for Y3 per hr.

🛈 PRACTICAL INFORMATION

Tourist Offices: Lhasa Tourism Bureau (lāsàshì lǚyóu jú; 拉萨市旅游局), 33 Jiangshu Lu (☎632 3632, English ☎632 4097, fax 633 1175), does not deal with visas or entry permits, but arbitrates between tourists and travel agencies or hotels when necessary. Open daily 9:30am-12:30pm and 3:30-6pm.

Travel Agencies: CITS, 208 Beijing Xi Lu (☎683 6626; fax 683 6315), next to the Lhasa Hotel. Open daily 9:30am-1pm and 3:30-6:30pm. **Shigatse Travel** (rìkāzé guójì lǚxíngshè; 日喀则国际旅行社; ☎633 0489), a subsidiary branch in the Yak Hotel, can reliably arrange visas, permits, guides, and jeeps. Open daily 9am-1pm and 3-7:30pm. Both branches of CITS may charge much more than other travel agencies. For short trips in particular, travelers can usually count on the agencies in the Barkhor Market area, many of which are based in local hotels. Price varies more than quality; shop around. Anyone renting a land cruiser should look at the vehicle beforehand. **F.I.T. Travel Agency** (☎634 4397), next to Tashi Restaurant on Zangiyuan Dong Lu. Open daily 9am-9pm. They also have a branch (☎634 9239) in the Snowland Hotel. Open daily 9am-7:30pm. These 2 offices are the most common agents for tourists' trips to Namtso, Samye, and spots along the Friendship Highway.

Adventure Travel: Tibet International Sports Travel (☎633 4082), in the Himalaya Hotel (xǐmǎlāyǎ fàndiàn; 喜马拉雅饭店) on 6 Lingkuo Dong Lu, is considerably more expensive and caters to those interested in hard-core, action-packed vacations.

Bank of China: 28 Lingkuo Xi Lu. Exchanges currency and traveler's checks and issues credit card advances. 188 Najin Lu, 1km from Barkhor Market. Both branches open M-F 9am-1pm and 3:30-6:30pm, Sa-Su 10am-3pm. Authorized hotels also exchange foreign currency for a fee.

Consulate: Nepal, 13 Luobulinka (Norbulingka) Lu (☎682 2881; fax 683 6890), close to the Lhasa Hotel and on the #3 bus route. 60-day Nepalese visas Y230; overnight processing. Instant processing at the border crossing to Kathmandu (same price, only US currency). The consulate closes at 6pm; arrive in the morning for visa applications.

Bookstore: Xinhua Bookstore, 45 Renmin Lu, with branches in Barkhor Market and next to the Tibet Hotel. Mainly Chinese and Tibetan books; some English maps of Lhasa and Tibet. Open M-F 9:30am-8pm, Sa-Su 6:30am-7pm.

Libraries: Lhasa City Library (xīzàngshì túshūguǎn; 西藏市图书馆; ☎683 2954), on Luobulinka (Norbulingka) Lu. Limited selection of foreign reference books on the 2nd floor, including 2000 English books and 1000 books in Japanese, Spanish, French, and German. Open M-F 9am-12:30pm and 3:30-6pm, Sa-Su 10am-5pm.

PSB: 8 Lingkuo Bei Lu (☎632 5312; 24hr. ☎632 4422). Branches at 1 Barkhor Xi Lu (☎632 3393) and 157 Beijing Zhong Lu (☎682 3809). Will no longer issue travel permits or visa extensions; do this before entering Tibet (see p. 50 for more info on travel permits and visas).

Hospital: People's Hospital of the Tibet Autonomous Region (xīzàng zìzhìqū rénmín yīyuàn; 西藏自治区人民医院), 18 Lingkuo Bei Lu (☎633 2462; emergency ☎632 2200). Specializes in treating altitude sickness. A 70% cost increase for foreign expats, teachers, and students; 50% increase for diplomats and PRC-related experts; and 40% increase for residents of Hong Kong, Macau, Taiwan, and overseas Chinese. Many doctors speak English. Open daily 9am-12:30pm and 3:30-6pm. 24hr. emergency.

Pharmacy: Shengjie Pharmacy (shèngjié yàodiàn; 圣洁药店), 2 Beijing Zhong Lu, Diguang Ju Hostel. Open daily 8am-midnight. Bang on the door if there is an emergency; the proprietors live right behind the drug counter.

Internet Access: Boiling Point Cafe (fèi diǎn; 沸点), on Zangiyuan Dong Lu, just down the street from Tashi restaurant. The biggest and most popular place in town. Y20 per hr. Open daily 9am-11pm. The **Kirey Hotel** and **Makye Ame Restaurant** both have Internet access for Y20 per hr.

Post Office: Lhasa City Post Office, on Beijing Zhong Lu. Sells postcards and stationery. International letters Y6.4; postcards Y4.2. EMS and Poste Restante available. Open daily 9am-8pm; in winter and spring 9:30am-7pm.

Telephones: Lhasa City Telecommunications Office, 64 Beijing Zhong Lu. A few doors down the street from the post office walking away from the Potala. 13 phone booths with IDD service (no calling card calls). On weekends international calls are majorly discounted. Open daily 8am-midnight. The main **Lhasa City Telecommunications Office** is on 59 Lingkuo Dong Lu. IDD service. Open daily 9am-12:30pm and 3:30-6:30pm.

▐ ACCOMMODATIONS

Travelers to Tibet tend to be more interested in Tibet itself than in the comfort of its budget hotel rooms. Lhasa's simple, no-frills accommodations usually provide weary backpackers with little more than a place to sleep. Most of the establishments that accept foreigners line **Beijing Dong Lu** and **Zangyi Yuan Dong Lu,** one of two main roads (the other being Yuthok Lu) leading to Barkhor Market. Unless otherwise stated, all establishments have travel agencies, provide IDD service at the reception desk, have 24hr. hot water, and offer luggage storage.

▨ **Eight Auspicious Hotel,** also known as the **Tashi Tagel Hotel** (zāxī dájíe bīnguǎn; 扎西达杰宾馆), 8 Zangyi Dong Lu (☎632 5804 or 632 3271). Rooms and hallways are clean, bright, and airy. Communal showers and toilets are cleaner than those at most other local hotels. Your stay includes lovable service and often a spectacular view of the Potala Palace. The popular **Tashi 1** restaurant is a 2min. walk away. 3 bed dorms Y20; doubles Y50, with bath Y250.

▨ **Pentoc Guesthouse** (pānduō lǚguǎn; 攀多旅馆), 5 Zangyi Dong Lu (☎632 6686), a few doors down from Tashi 1 Restaurant. Next to a billiards room, this 57-bed guesthouse is popular with the younger set. The sunny, carpeted rooms have Tibetan-style furniture and wall designs. Immaculate communal bathrooms. English movies nightly. 2 bed dorms Y35; singles Y50; doubles Y80.

Lhasa Yak Hotel (lāsà yā bīnguǎn; 拉萨亚宾馆), 100 Beijing Dong Lu (☎632 3496). Look for the yak head above the red doors lining the street. The clean, tiled rooms are some of the best Lhasa has to offer in this price range. Friendly staff and in-house **Shigatse Travel Agency.** Bike rental Y3 per hr. Internet access Y20 per hr. 6- to 10-bed dorms Y25; doubles with bath Y100-260.

Kirey Hotel (jín bīnguǎn; 吉日宾馆), 105 Beijing Dong Lu (☎632 3462). Tibetan-style rooms, a large courtyard, and a view of the mountains attract throngs of backpackers and tour groups to the Kirey. **Mad Yak Restaurant** and **Tashi 2 Restaurant** on Kirey's grounds. Gates close at midnight. Communal showers have hot water 8:30-9:30pm. 3- to 4-bed dorms Y25; doubles Y50-60, with bath Y130.

Banak Shol Hotel (bāxuě bīnguǎn; 八雪宾馆), 43 Beijing Dong Lu (☎632 3829), a 20min. walk up Beijing Dong Lu from Zangyi Dong Lu. Banak Shol is Lhasa's oldest guesthouse (opened in 1985) and is still one of the most popular, especially with young people. Communal toilets on every floor, showers on 1st Fl. Free safety deposit boxes. 4- to 5-bed dorms Y25; 2-bed dorms Y70; singles Y35; doubles with bath Y160.

Mandala Hotel (mǎnzhài jiǔdiàn; 满斋酒店), 31 Bakuo Nan Jie (☎632 4783 or 633 8940), on the right side of Barkhor Market when you face the Jokhang Temple. Opened in August of 1998, Mandala is a first-rate addition to Lhasa's backpacker venues. The bright, shiny, wood-paneled rooms have A/C, heaters, and TV. Restaurant (dishes Y12-25) open 24hr. The nearby **Makye Ame Restaurant** (see **Food,** p. 734) lures many a guest astray. Doubles with bath Y100-180.

Snowland Hotel (xuěyù bīnguǎn; 雪域宾馆), 4 Zangyi Dong Lu (☎632 3687), a 7min. walk down Zangyuan Dong Lu leading to Barkhor Market, on the left. Well equipped

and conveniently located, with a large courtyard and social balconies. The old-fashioned rooms are cozy, bordering on cramped. Bike rental Y2 per hr. **F.I.T. Travel Service**
on 2nd floor. **Snowland Hotel Restaurant** open daily 7am-11pm. 5- to 10-bed dorms
Y24; doubles Y60-80, with bath Y260.

Lhasa Gang-Gyen Hotel (lāsà gāngjiān fàndiàn; 拉萨刚坚饭店), 83 Beijing Dong Lu
(☎633 7666 or 633 3004), about a 20min. walk east of Barkhor Market. Restaurant
open 24hr. 4-bed dorms Y40; doubles Y180.

Sunlight Hotel (rìguāng bīnguǎn; 日光宾馆), 27 Linju Lu (☎632 2227), a 15min. walk
southwest of Barkhor Market, far enough away from Beijing Lu to escape the noise pollution that afflicts most of Lhasa's other hotels. Rooms in this 2-star hotel are reasonably clean. **Lhasa Travel Agency** on premises. Doubles Y280.

◪ FOOD

The "Land of Yaks" extends straight onto your dinner plate, and after catching a
whiff of your entree, it may just stay there. Adventurous travelers can sample a
wide assortment of yak dishes and products in Lhasa, including yak *momos*
(dumplings), stewed yak, stir-fried yak, barbecued yak, and, of course, the wildly
popular Tibetan equivalent to coffee, yak-butter tea. Used in a great number of
dishes, *tsampa* (barley flour) is a staple of the local diet, and *tsampa* beer is a
must on festive occasions. Beware—it is strong stuff.

Due to the mass influx of foreigners into Lhasa in recent years, dozens of Western-style restaurants have sprung up in and around Lhasa's Barkhor Market.
Although the food is tasty, prices are fairly high, and it is easy to get in the habit of
dropping Y20-30 per meal while lingering in Lhasa.

The Chinese section of Lhasa along Beijing Xi Lu and near the Norbulingka is
home to several good Sichuanese restaurants. If Lhasa's western half is too expensive or too out of the way, there are venues for Chinese food in the eastern section
of town, particularly around the Banak Shol Hotel. Lhasa is also home to over 1500
Muslims and several Muslim restaurants, most of which are located along Lingkuo
Lu. Walk or bike down Beijing Dong Lu, past the Kirey and Banak Shol Hotels, and
turn left (north) at the intersection of Lingkuo Lu with Beijing Dong Lu.

▨ **Makye Ame Restaurant,** on the 2nd floor of the yellow building in the southeast corner
of the Barkhor Market, behind the Jokhang Temple. Although portions are dainty and
prices are high, the Bohemian atmosphere and massive menu of taste-bud-titillating
international foods draw budget travelers back time and time again. There's no better
place in the city to kick back, chug a few beers, and gaze down at the foot traffic circling
the Barkhor below than Makye's rooftop patio. Mini-library and Internet cafe (Y20 per
hr.). Dishes Y20-38. Open daily 9am-11pm.

▨ **Snowland Restaurant** (xuěyù cāntīng; 雪域餐厅), next to the Snowland Hotel. Fillled
with Westerners, the overworked and slightly grumpy staff serves delicious Western,
Tibetan, and Chinese dishes (Y20-40) in a surprisingly posh and peaceful dining area.
Open daily 8am-10:30pm.

▨ **The Third Eye,** 74 Zangyi Dong Lu, opposite Snowland Restaurant. An Indian atmosphere
and outstanding Indian food. Friendly and not as tourist-infested as other venues on the
same street. TV lounge in back. Open daily 6:30am-11:30pm.

Tashi 1, on the corner of Zangyi Dong Lu and Beijing Dong Lu. Wildly popular with backpackers. Foreign travelers often congregate to chow down on Western and Tibetan food
and compare travel plans. Open daily 7:30am-11pm; in winter 8:30am-11pm. **Tashi 2,**
in the Kirey Hotel, is less popular but just as good and more intimate than its counterpart. Open daily 7am-11pm; closed Nov.-Feb.

Lightfull Restaurant, on Bejing Dong Lu, a few doors from the Yak Hotel . The preparation takes a while, but the food is worth the wait. Typical array of Tibetan, Western, and
Chinese dishes (Y15-25) served in a cozy little Tibetan atmosphere. The authentic
omelettes (Y10-12) are particularly de-lightfull. Open daily 9am-10pm.

YAKKITY YAK In Tibet, it is impossible to escape from the omnipresent yak, also known as the long-haired cow. The yaks' black backs dot the landscape throughout the countryside. Yak oil lamps light most monasteries, and worshipers bring yak butter packets and yak oil candles to sprinkle or dip into the big oil lamps of Tibetan temples. Tibetans claim the yak can only breed at 3000m above sea level or higher, and that its meat and milk provide better nutrition than that of the normal cow. Perhaps its high alimentary value accounts for the animal's strong odor, a scent that all travelers to Tibet encounter sooner or later. The smell pervades restaurants offering savory yak "beef" dishes, yak *momos* (dumplings), and yak-butter tea. Yak-scented air wafts through Tibet's temples. Anyone hoping to escape the yak by skipping Tibet's temples and avoiding Tibetan cuisine should think again. The grounds and walls of Potala Palace itself are made from a mixture of ground stone, cement, and yak oil.

Mad Yak Restaurant, in the Kirey Hotel. Cheap Tibetan food and nifty, Tibetan-carpeted seats. Dishes Y8-25. Every night 7-8:30pm, there is a Tibetan dance show and a 25-course Tibetan buffet (Y50). Caters largely to tour groups. Open hours variable.

Mingchun Garden (míngchūn yuán; 明春园), about 200m from the Tibet Hotel. Great Sichuanese restaurant with an out-of-Tibet feel and large, spicy dishes (Y30-40). Open daily 9am-9pm.

ENTERTAINMENT

Most tourists are so worn out after hours of hiking and temple visiting that the most popular evening activity tends to be sitting around a table and chatting or playing cards over a few beers. For those desperate to dance, Lhasa has a few options. The largest discos in town are **J.J.** (jié jié; 结杰; ☎682 3131), just across from the Potala, followed by **Summit Disco**, 51 Jinzhu Dong Lu (☎632 7191). Both cater mostly to Han Chinese, with pop acts and contests; if you are offended by the occasional drag show 100m in front of the Potala, avoid the former. **Zhizun** (zhìjūn; 至尊), facing the CAAC ticket office on Niangre Lu, is a Tibetan club with traditional music and dancing. There are also numerous places to go for song, dance, and comedy performances by local troupes. An excellent troupe performs nightly at the **Gediga** on Lingkuo Lu. (☎633 2571. Open nightly 8:30pm-midnight.)

SIGHTS

Most of Lhasa's sights come in the form of monasteries. The remote **Tsurphu Monastery** (楚布寺), where the Karma (Black Cap) sect originated, has been closed indefinitely by the Chinese government. Pilgrims used to travel over horrendous roads to pay respects to the Karmapa (Living Buddha), the most highly regarded religious figure currently residing in Tibet.

POTALA PALACE
At the western end of Beijing Dong Lu, just before it becomes Beijing Zhong Lu. New arrivals to Tibet should not visit the palace until after the initial effects of altitude sickness have passed. Open M, W, and F 9am-12:30pm and 3:30-5:30pm, Tu and Th 9am-12:30pm and 4-5:30pm, Sa-Su 10am-noon and 3:30-5pm. The best time to go is in the morning. Admission M-F Y40, Sa-Su Y50, children under 1.2m free; an additional fee for pictures. Relics Museum and the Roof of Gold Y10.

The silhouette of the Potala Palace (bùdálā gōng; 布达拉宫) against the Tibetan sky has long been a symbol of Lhasa. While the Dalai Lama's court no longer inhabits the Potala's 1000 rooms, the palace retains a somber and awe-inspiring grandeur. During the Cultural Revolution, Premier Zhou Enlai used his personal unit of the PLA to protect the Potala from rioting Red Guards, sparing the palace the destruction visited upon so many of Tibet's other religious sites.

TIBET

King Songsten Gampo, the same ruler who built the Jokhang, chose the Potala's Red Hill as the site for his palace in the 7th century. Long after his death, political and military officials continued to mingle with scholarly priests in the court. Today, his likeness (the one with two heads) stands in **Dharmraja's Cave.** When the Great 5th Dalai Lama, Lobsang Gyatso, united Tibet in the 17th century, he formally recognized the Dalai Lama's dual role as the religious and political leader of the nation by rebuilding and dividing the palace into the White Palace (for overseeing political matters) and the Red Palace (for dealing with religious issues).

RED PALACE. The remains of the Dalai Lamas are in the western part of the palace, held in jewel-encrusted gold **stupas.** The 12.6m tall *stupa* of Lobsang Gyatso, the 5th Dalai Lama, is gilded with 3721kg of gold foil, 10,000 pearls, and precious stones. Since then, the only Dalai Lama not entombed in the Potala Palace is the 6th Dalai Lama, who was driven into exile by Mongolian conquerors. This section of the palace also houses the Dharmraja's Cave and some marvelous Buddha and *bodhisattva* statues. The treasures also include an exquisite 200,000 pearl **mandala,** the "Wheel of Time," made of coral, turquoise, and gold thread (see p. 729). A mural in the **Western Audience Hall** depicts the historic meeting between the 5th Dalai Lama and Emperor Shunzhi, founder of the Qing dynasty. Supposedly, they sat on chairs of the same height to symbolize the equality of their countries.

WHITE PALACE. All the Dalai Lamas were crowned in the **Great Eastern Assembly Hall.** The White Palace was the abode of the 13th and 14th Dalai Lamas; the 14th Dalai Lama's chambers, including his study, meeting rooms, and meditation chambers, are open to visitors. The balcony from which the Dalai Lama made infrequent contact with the Tibetan people overlooks the palace square.

ﾠ JOKHANG TEMPLE
Open daily 8am-midnight. Y25 for non-Tibetans.

The old saying, "the Jokhang is Lhasa, Lhasa is the Jokhang," rings true. Many visitors are drawn to the Jokhang (dàzhāo sì; 大昭寺) because of its Nepali, Indian, Buddhist, and Tang dynasty architectural elements. Most, however, are ultimately captivated by the mystical spirit of this active place of worship. Oil candles illuminate mural-lined corridors depicting tales from the temple's past, and the hum of devotees outside echoes off the walls.

A rich mosaic of myth surrounds the 7th-century temple. Legend holds that King Gampo's Nepali bride believed that the Tibetan Plateau was a demon that could be subdued only by building Buddhist temples on its key body parts. The king's Chinese wife, Princess Wencheng, used divinination and astrological calculation to select the temple site. Builders eventually laid Jokhang's foundations on Lake Wothang, thought to be the heart of the demon. The **Golden Buddha,** an image of Sakyamuni as a 12-year-old boy, was brought by Princess Wencheng and now resides at the back of the Jokhang's great prayer hall. Believers claim that the statue was consecrated by Sakyamuni himself while he lived in India. Other notable figures in the temple include the 1000-arm statue of **Avalokiteshvara** (Guanyin) and various statues of the **Maitreya Buddha.**

Nearly every night at 7:30pm, monks congregate in the main assembly hall to **chant.** Filtered with bells, drumming, and horn blowing, this, along with the view from the rooftop, is the true highlight of the Jokhang. Head up top after the chanting to catch the sunset, or come anytime for a stunning panorama of the city, as well as the classic shot of the Potala in the background, flanked by the glistening, golden spires of the Jokhang.

ﾠ BARKHOR MARKET
The Jokhang's Barkhor Market (bājiǎoshì chǎng; 八角市场) environs, also known as **Chongsaikang Market,** have managed to flourish without becoming excessively commercialized. The scent of burning incense mingles happily with the odor of yak, and monks interrupt their daily circumambulatory routine around the Jokhang to bargain for prayer beads. The market is a good place to shop for Tibetan trinkets;

Barkhor's myriad stalls display everything from *hadas* (ceremonial scarves) and prayer wheels to lamb skulls and photographs of religious figures. The entire Barkhor circuit proceeds in a clockwise direction, encircling the Jokhang and branching off into various side streets. Be sure to inspect the goods carefully, but don't touch if you're not going to buy. Hard bargaining can usually bring the price down 40 to 50% from the original quote; be respectful in your haggling. The market usually begins in the wee hours of the morning and shuts down at about 7:30pm.

RAMOCHE TEMPLE
On Ramoche Lu, about 500m north of Jokhang Temple, off Beijing Dong Lu. Open W-M 8am-5pm. Y20.

While not the grandest of Lhasa's temples, Ramoche is greatly loved: 115 monks join countless pilgrims in circumambulating the 4000m^2 complex, which also houses the Upper Tantric College. Ramoche Temple was built in the 7th century, when Princess Wencheng of the Tang court married King Songsten Gampo of Tibet. On her journey to Tibet, the princess brought with her the precious gold statue of the Sakyamuni Buddha (now in the Jokhang Temple) as part of her dowry. However, Princess Wencheng's carriage wheels got stuck in the mud, and her attendants could not budge the statue from its position at Lhasa's north gate. Four pillars were placed around the statue and a brocade draped over it to protect it from harm. Princess Wencheng decided that the gods intended the statue to remain where the muds had left it, so King Songsten Gampo built Ramoche Temple around it. Whether she was making a political statement or was simply homesick, the Princess decreed that all the gates and doors of the temple face east toward Chang'an (now Xian).

During the reign of King Mangsong Mangtsen, not long after the Ramoche Temple was built, Sino-Tibetan relations soured. Fearful that the Chinese would capture the Sakyamuni statue, the king ordered its transfer to the Jokhang, where it lay hidden under piles of sand. After relations improved and another Chinese princess traveled to Tibet with a dowry, Princess Wencheng's Sakyamuni statue was brought out from hiding and displayed in the Ramoche. The statue of a child Sakyamuni brought by King Songsten Gampo's Nepali wife was also moved from the Jokhang to the shrine in the Dukhang, the center room of Ramoche's Assembly Hall; statues of Sakyamuni's spiritual sons surround their eight-year-old father.

DRALHALUPUK TEMPLE AND CHAKPORI HILL
Across from the left foot of the Potala on the other side of Beijing Dong Lu, a road runs along the side of Chakpori Hill; the entrance is near the large chorten at the site of the old West Gate to the city. Follow the road until you see stairs leading up to 2 temples on the right, about halfway up the hill. Open daily 9:30am-7pm. Y15.

Dralhalupuk Temple served as a cave temple and private retreat for King Songsten Gampo. Although many of the 1000-year-old rock carvings were damaged during the Cultural Revolution, extensive renovation has restored some of them to their original splendor. Over 60 *bodhisattva* carvings decorate the cliffside temple. A second temple, a few meters above Dralhalupuk, served as a meditation cave for King Songsten Gampo's Nepali queen, Bhrikuti. A path to the top of Chakpori Hill (15min.) starts from just outside the entrance to the two temples. The southwest face of Chakpori Hill features a colorful collection of 9000 buddhas, the oldest dating back to the reign of King Gampo. To get there, walk about six minutes down Norbulingka Lu from Potala Square. When you see the Xin Xin Eatery (鑫鑫小吃), turn left down the dirt path and continue for six minutes, past a military station.

८८भ्रश्चित NORBULINGKA
On Norbulingka Nan Lu, a 10min. walk south of the Lhasa Hotel. Take bus #2 (Y2). Open M-Sa 9:30am-noon and 3:30-6pm, Su 10am-12:30pm and 4-5:30pm. Y25.

A refreshing contrast to the barren Tibetan landscape, the Norbulingka's (luōbùlínkǎ; 罗布林卡) beautifully manicured grounds consist of three main palaces totaling 370 rooms as well as a now-dry pool. This "Jeweled Garden" served as the summer residence for several Dalai Lamas. The **Daktonmiju Palace** was built in 1956 by the 14th Dalai Lama; however, the Dalai lived here for only two summers before fleeing to India in 1959. Visitors are greeted by two gigantic paintings of a lion and tiger. On the second floor, an elaborate mural traces Tibetan history from a heaven-sent monkey who mated with a demon (see p. 727) to the 14th Dalai Lama sitting with Chairman Mao. His Holiness's private living quarters, a radio sent as a housewarming gift by the Prime Minister of India, and a richly decorated throne made of solid gold are all on display. **Gesang Palace,** the oldest of the three palaces, served as the main summer residence of the 7th to the 12th Dalai Lamas. Various *tangkas* (painted scrolls) and Eight Medicine Buddhas adorn the walls of the main assembly hall. The two-story **Jianse Palace,** the summer home of the 13th Dalai Lama, is closed to the public periodically.

འབྲས་སྤུངས་ DREPUNG MONASTERY

10km from Lhasa. Buses #3 and 4 (8am-4pm, Y2) run from Lhasa to Drepung, stopping at the minibus station at Yatuo Lu and Niangre Lu, a 5min. walk southwest of the Barkhor Market area. Open daily 9am-4pm. Y30, children under 13 free.

Nicknamed "rice pile" because of its white, heap-like appearance, Drepung (zhébèng sì; 哲蚌寺) is the largest monastery in Tibet, covering over 20,000m² and housing 600 monks. The gargantuan monastery was built in 1416 by Jamygang Choje, fourth disciple of Tsong Khapa (see p. 729), after a dream in which he envisioned the site. Until the 5th Dalai Lama moved the court to the Potala Palace, Drepung's Garden Palace served as the seat of the Dalai Lamas.

Drepung's first structure, at the back of the great assembly hall, was a chapel dedicated to **Manjushri,** one of the great *bodhisattvas* of wisdom. It is said that the discovery of a slab of rock bearing Manjushri's likeness determined the exact site of Drepung; the revered rock now serves as one of the chapel's three walls. In the main kitchen next door, monks use huge electric mixers to mix yak-butter tea in army-sized cauldrons. Set in gold on the roof is a pair of deer (representing Sakyamuni's disciples) holding a wheel (representing Sakyamuni and his success). Tibetans have adopted the Indian concept that the wheel guarantees success if brought onto the battlefield, even if soldiers do not fight.

TIBET

Although its first chapel was dedicated to Manjushri, **Maitreya,** Buddha of the Future, is the main god of Drepung. A large statue of Maitreya, one of Drepung's three holy relics, sits above a great assembly hall that can hold 6000 people. When Drepung was undergoing expansion in 1416, the magistrate of Niu made a large donation under the condition that the statue be placed in the temple, facing east. Apparently, the magistrate's daughter, who died while reaching for some precious stones in a lake, had been reincarnated as a worm because of her greed. This worm lived in an eastern cave until the statue of Maitreya was consecrated. At that moment, the earth shook and the entrance to the cave broke open, releasing the daughter in human form and sending her to heaven. The mere sight of this statue can relieve suffering; a monk will aid you by serving you holy water and tapping your head against the statue's base. The other sacred relics are a conch shell that Tsong Khapa uncovered while digging Drepung's foundations and the *stupas* of the 1st, 2nd, and 3rd Dalai Lamas. The chapel across Maitreya's statue holds one of Tsong Khapa's teeth in a glass case.

Drepung also contains four Buddhist *tratsang* (colleges). Students meet daily 2:30 to 4:30pm (except Sundays, when they attend general assemblies); lucky visitors can catch them debating.

སེ་ར་ SERA MONASTERY

*At the foot of **Phurpa Chokri Mountain,** 3km northeast of Lhasa. **Bus #5** (Y2) from near the Barkhor Market stops in front. Alternatively, rent a bike or take a long walk; follow Beijing Dong Lu past the Kirey and Yak Hotels, and turn right on Niangre Lu, past the gold statue of a man on a horse and about 200m before the Potala Palace. Follow Niangre Lu for 2-3km; a small road before the General Military Hospital leads to the monastery. **Open** daily 9am-4pm. **Admission** Y30.*

When the Ming court invited Tsong Khapa to China to teach Buddhist doctrine, the disciple Jamchen Choje was sent in his master's place. The Ming emperor, pleased with Jamchen's teachings, proclaimed him "Buddha of Benevolence." When Sakya Yeshe, another of Tsong Khapa's leading disciples, founded Sera Monastery (sèlā sì; 色拉寺) in 1419, he intended the main Buddha of the monastery to be the Benevolence Buddha, in Jamchen's honor. A strange occurrence caused the main Buddha to be the Horse-Headed Buddha, Tamdrin (see **Sera Je Tratsang,** below).

Sera Monastery has three *tratsang* (colleges): the Me and Je debate colleges and the Ngagpa tantric college, where most of Sera's 550 monks live and study. As in all Tibetan Buddhist temples, visitors walk in a clockwise procession. Pilgrims to Sera Monastery should thus start with Sera Me, continue to Ngagpa, and end with Sera Je.

SERA ME TRATSANG. Sera Me's chapels and assembly hall house several statues of Sakyamuni, a large statue of the Longevity Buddha, and a revered statue of Tsong Khapa (see **The Coming of the Yellow Hat Sect,** p. 726).

NGAGPA TRATSANG. Ngagpa Tratsang, built by Sakya Yeshe in 1419, is the oldest existing building in Sera Monastery. Although the wall paintings in the main assembly hall are in poor condition, the statues are not. In the center and flanked by famous lamas of Sera Monastery, Sakya Yeshe sports a black cap presented to him by a Ming emperor. The huge chamber also contains statues of the Longevity Buddha, the 5th Dalai Lama, Tsong Khapa, and a chapel full of Sakyamuni statues. Large prayer meetings are held in this huge chamber every month on the 8th, 10th, 15th, 18th, 25th, and 30th days of the Tibetan lunar calendar.

SERA JE TRATSANG. The founder of the Sera Je Tratsang used to walk about the temple daily, and each day his robe would get caught in the thorny branch of a thistle tree. One day, while unfastening his robe from its clutch, he saw a horse's head on the offending branch. Believing it to be an omen, he covered the horse head with his robe and constructed a statue of it, proclaiming the **Horse-Headed Buddha** to be Sera's main protector. The central chapel of the Sera complex now houses the statue in a copper shrine. Many pilgrims kneel to place their heads in a hollow at the base of the shrine, thus receiving a blessing of longevity from the Horse-Headed Buddha. Sera's largest building, **Tsokchen** assembly hall, also houses Tsong Khapa's chapel, which holds statues of him, his important disciples, Manjushri, a *bodhisattva*, and Maitreya. Behind the Assembly Hall is the **Debate Courtyard,** the point of greatest interest for many tourists. Here monks sit and some stand, arguing loudly over interpretations of the Buddha's teaching. Movement of the left hand represents the relief of suffering, and the right, the destruction of evils. Participants slap the two together furiously to build confidence while making a point, and consistently successful debaters are raised in rank as monk. Debates take place Monday to Saturday 3 to 5pm.

NORTH OF LHASA

་བོ་སྣམ་མཚོ NAMTSO LAKE

*200km northwest of Lhasa. No additional Alien Travel Permit needed. There is no public transportation to the lake. Most tourists hire a **land cruiser** (Y1500-2500 per car for 2-3 days). Check the boards at the Lhasa Yak, Banak Shol, Pentoc, and Kirey Hotels (see **Accommodations,** p. 733). The other option is to take the bus (Y20) from the Lhasa Bus Station or from the Kirey Hotel headed for Naqu, get off at Damshung, and trek the remaining 40km. Some travelers choose to hitchhike this portion of the journey. This final stretch, known as the **Lhachen La Pass,** cuts across the Nyanchen Thanglha Range, which towers over Namtso. **Admission** to grasslands Y35, plus Y5 to enter monastery and guesthouse area.*

At 4627m above sea level, Namtso (nàmù cuò; 纳木错) is the highest lake in the world. Namtso's name, "Sky Lake," only hints at the appearance of this piece of brilliant blue heaven fallen to earth. After a bumpy and hellish six hour ride,

SKY BURIAL The traditional Tibetan "sky burial" involves burning the hair of the deceased and feeding the rest of the body to birds of prey. When a commoner dies, the corpse is bound up in white twine for the three- to five-day mourning period. The body is then transported by special porters to a flat platform in the mountains, where eagles and vultures devour the remains. Everything has to go if the person is to go to heaven; when the bones are left, they are crushed, dipped in the brain, and offered again to the raptors. If anything remains unconsumed at the end, monks are invited to meditate and chant *sutras* in order to atone for the misdeeds of the dead. Anyone who has committed grievous sins in their lifetime cannot receive a sky burial, nor can those who died of an infectious disease. The latter have their limbs torn off and cast into lakes instead. The bodies of living Buddhas, noblemen, and others destined for reincarnation are either cremated or, as in the case of religious holy men, preserved and placed in bejeweled *stupas* (such as those in the Red Palace of Potala Palace, p. 736) for all to view and worship.

Namtso's turquoise waters and immense scope (70km long and 30km wide) are a stunning and welcome sight. One of Tibet's holiest lakes, Namtso has long attracted devout pilgrims, who often cast *hadas* (ceremonial scarves) or other precious objects into the lake while meditating, in the hopes of being granted a vision in return. The enormous valley surrounding the lake is moist and fertile; bright wildflowers, grazing yaks, and colonies of pikas, burrow-dwelling plateau rodents, all thrive. Many visitors head straight to the bird sanctuary and caves at the **Tashi Dorje Monastery**, at the foot of the two large hills on the southeastern bank of the lake, which is actually nothing more than two massive boulders and an old, cave-dwelling lama.

Pilgrims and hikers often take 14 to 18 days to navigate this enormous salt-water lake, China's second largest. However, the beautiful terrain is flat and unvarying, so one full day at the lake is more than sufficient for most travelers. The best hikes involve climbing up the two large hills above Tashi Dorje Monastery. The smaller hill takes approximately 45 minutes to ascend, while the larger one takes 1½ hours. The climb provides a sweeping panoramic view of the lake and the snow-covered **Nyanchen Thanglha Mountains.** Spending the night by Namtso is highly recommended. Bring your own tent, or find **accommodation** in the Tashi Dorje Monastery (3- to 4-bed dorms Y25-30). Two small **restaurants** next to the guesthouses, both labeled "canteen," serve overpriced Chinese and Tibetan food (Y18-25); it might be a good idea to bring your own food.

SOUTH OF LHASA

ἆ᠊ᠨᠶᠡᠷ **SAMYE MONASTERY**

Buses between Lhasa and Tsetang pass the pier for boats to Samye Monastery (3hr., 3 per day, Y25-30). *Travel permits* are required; there is a checkpoint at the ferry crossing. *Motorboats* (45min., Y10) at the pier take tourists and pilgrims across the river. Upon reaching the island, passengers typically ride on the back of a *truck* or rent a *jeep* (30min., Y10) to Samye. Samye can also be approached on foot from Ganden Monastery. The two monasteries are separated by a mountain pass; the trek usually takes 4-5 days. There is no official checkpoint at Samye, so permits technically should not be needed if trekking from Ganden, but the PSB has been known to raid hotels and check for permits at Samye Monastery. Monastery **open** daily 8am-6pm. **Admission** Y25.

Surrounded by rolling dunes and sand-colored shrubs camouflaged against a sienna desert backdrop, Samye's golden roof sparkling in the sun is a magical sight. Built in the 8th century by King Trisong Detsen of the Yarlung dynasty, Samye Monastery (sāngmù yēsì; 桑木耶寺) is thought to be Tibet's first monastery and the home of Tibetan Buddhism. In his attempt to introduce Buddhism to Tibet,

ज़ैरꞏ TSETANG 泽当 ■ **741**

King Trisong Detsen invited two Indian masters, Shantarakshita and Padmasambhava, to his land. On their way from India to the Yarlung Valley, they passed by the Samye area and decided that the site was an auspicious location. Although the Jokhang and Ramoche Temples in Lhasa both have older foundations, neither went as far as Samye to strip Tibetans of their indigenous Bön religion and to establish Buddhism as a state religion as Samye did.

The monastery was constructed according to the design of a *mandala*, which represents the cosmological order of Buddhism. The main temple signifies **Mount Sumeru**, the center of the universe, surrounded by four small temples called *lings*, representing the four continents. Each *ling* is straddled by two smaller ones, representing the eight sub-continents. There is also a moon chapel, where a giant statue of Sakyamuni stares into the heavens, and a now-destroyed sun chapel.

The first floor has an indigenous Tibetan flavor. An entire chapel on the first floor is devoted to **Avalokiteshvara** and the main assembly hall on the first floor also houses statues of certain Tibetan kings and various founders of the different sects of Tibetan Buddhism. The second floor mainly houses the monks' dormitories and the living quarters of the Dalai Lama. The third floor is dominated by a giant, three-dimensional *mandala* model. Find the ladder around the back to climb to the still unfinished top floor.

The **Monastery Guesthouse** provides basic facilities for Y10-30 per bed; bargain. There are several restaurants outside the monastery's eastern gate, the best being **Friends Snowland Restaurant**. A shop next to the guesthouse sells basic supplies.

ज़ैरꞏ TSETANG 泽当 ☎0893

Although Tsetang, 185km southeast of Lhasa, is Tibet's third largest city, most visitors just pass through on their way from Lhasa to the ancient sites of Chongye and Yumbulagang in the Yarlung Valley. The uninspiring town, full of Han influence, has little to offer beyond a couple of hotels charging exorbitant prices.

⚡▐▚ PRACTICAL INFORMATION AND ACCOMMODATIONS

Travel permits (Y150 per person) are required for Tsetang. Individual travelers rarely are given permits; it is best to travel in a group with a guide. Lhasa travel agencies will arrange for land cruiser rentals and all necessary permits to take groups of travelers to Tsetang, Samye, and Yumbulagang (Y2500-3000 for 3 days).

Naidong Lu (乃东路), Tsetang's main road, leads out of Tsetang towards Tranduk Monastery and Yumbulagang Palace. The **Shannan Prefecture PSB** (☎782 0359) is open 24hr. a day. The **People's Hospital of Tsetang Town**, 4 Gesang Lu, has no English-speaking staff. (☎782 0289. Open daily 9am-12:30pm and 3:30-6:30pm.) The **Post and Telecommunications Office,** 12 Naidong Lu, opposite the Shannan Prefecture Government building, has IDD service. (Open daily 9am-7:30pm.) The **postal code** is 856000.

The **Regional Guesthouse**, on Naidong Lu, has musty rooms, with hot water from 9am to midnight. (☎782 1927. Y280 per person.) The **Tsetang Hotel,** also on Naidong Lu, provides somewhat luxurious but ludicrously priced rooms. (☎782 1899. Doubles Y550.) There are several cheap restaurants scattered around town.

🄳 DAYTRIPS FROM TSETANG

ཡུམབུ་བླ་སྒང་ YUMBULAGANG PALACE
15km south of Tsetang, past Tranduk Monastery, on the left as you come from Tsetang. A separate Alien Travel Permit is not needed for Yumbulagang. Yumbulagang can be reached on foot or by taxi (Y80) from Tsetang. Open daily 9am-5pm. Y15.

Yumbulagang (yāngbùlākāng; 雍布拉康) is awe-inspiring, even from a distance. The thin but imposing structure juts out of the mountain like a sword stuck in stone. The photogenic palace, which subscribes to the teachings of the Yellow Hat sect, was built more than 2000 years ago by the first ruler of the Yarlung dynasty, King Nyatre Tsanpo. Perhaps inspired by the shape of the mountain, Yumbulagang means "palace on the hind of a female deer." The palace itself has three floors. The first holds statues of Sakyamuni, the main object of worship here, and of a lineage of Yarlung monarchs: Nyatre Tsanpo, Lha-tho-tho-ri, Songsten Gampo, Trisong Detsen, and Triral Pachen. More bronze statues wait on the second floor, including one of Tsong Khapa. Murals of Nyatre Tsanpo and Yumbulagang itself grace the walls, along with a scene from the reclamation of the first wasteland in the Yarlung Valley. From the roof, Yumbulagang offers a picturesque panorama of the Yarlungzanbo (Brahmaputra) River Valley, with burnt umber mountains and mud houses in one direction and verdant fields in the other. For a good view of Yumbulagang, go around the back, climb over a low stone wall, and walk up the slope.

སྒྲ་བྲུག་ TRANDRUK MONASTERY

5km southwest of Tsetang, on the way to Yumbulagang. A separate Alien Travel Permit is not needed for Tranduk. Easily accessible on foot or by taxi (Y50). Open daily 7am-7pm. Admission for foreigners Y25.

One of Tibet's oldest monasteries, Trandruk (chāngzhū sì; 昌珠寺) was built in the 8th century by King Songsten Gampo. The king was persuaded by his Nepalese wife to build Tranduk and other temples to control the topographical beast known as the Tibetan Plateau; he and his Chinese wife used it as their winter palace.

The main assembly hall enshrines the king and his entourage, along with Tsong Khapa. Five Dhanyani Buddhas are found at the back of the hall in a locked room. A far more interesting and unique relic is the beautiful pearl *tangka* (Tibetan religious painting) on the second floor, colored in shades of silver, turquoise, and coral. To the right of the room holding the *tangka* is a chapel dedicated to the Indian goddess White Brahma.

FRIENDSHIP HIGHWAY

The week-long journey from Lhasa to Nepal over the 920km Friendship Highway strings together some of the region's most impressive attractions: the turquoise Yamdroktso Lake, gleaming glaciers near Gyantse, the Panchen Lama's capital of Shigatse, the rustic monastery at Sakya, the world's highest temple at Rongphu, Everest Base Camp, the Himalayan town of Tingri, and the subtropical border post of Zhangmu. Most areas of the highway are very well traveled, and road conditions are decent. Travel permits are required to make stops at any of the sights listed above. Some travelers have hitchhiked the entire distance on the Friendship Highway without permits although this is illegal. The typical cost for hiring a land cruiser ranges from Y6000-8000 per vehicle for a six- to eight-day trip, not including the Y350 entrance fee to Everest Base Camp.

ཡར་འབྲོག་མཚོ་ YAMDROKTSO LAKE

*100km southwest of Lhasa. The **Khambala Pass** (4900m) must be scaled to reach Yamdroktso on foot. No public buses pass through the area; Yamdroktso is usually visited by land cruiser en route to Gyantse and Shigatse from Lhasa. Some travelers have succeeded in taking public transportation to Gyantse and then hitchhiking to Yamdroktso. An **Alien Travel Permit** is required.*

Yamdroktso is one of Tibet's largest and holiest lakes, covering an area of more than 600km². The name Yamdroktso (Scorpion Lake; yángzhuō yāng hú; 羊卓雍湖) derives from the unique curves and curls of the lake's outline. Surrounded by distant snow-capped mountains, the colorful salt waters of the lake become bright sapphire at some times and an exquisite aquamarine at others. Its depths are home to plenty of fish, and its islands shelter wild ducks and green vegetation. Although a hydroelectric power plant has diminished the vibrancy of the lake's waters in recent years, Yamdroktso remains beautiful.

TIBET

SPORTS UTILITY VEHICLES. Those gas-guzzling, road-hogging beasts that annoy the living daylights out of so many drivers on well-paved Western roads are a lifesaver for travelers in rural Tibet. Due to rugged terrain and frequent mud slides, most attractions are inaccessible by public transportation; only 4-wheel-drive jeeps can conquer washed-out highways, tackle Himalayan inclines, and ford glacier streams. Since the lion's share of money visitors spend in Tibet will be spent on transportation, it's worth it to be an informed consumer.
1. Hire only imported vehicles—the newer the model the better. Check out the car (and the driver) the night before your trip, especially for longer journeys. If the jeep breaks down frequently along the way, demand that the driver change jeeps in the next town; companies usually keep vehicles in several towns.
2. Some travelers choose to pick up stragglers along the way. They claim that standard practice is for the stragglers to pay them, and they recommend giving a share to the driver. *Let's Go* does not recommend picking up hitchhikers.
3. Plan your itinerary to allow plenty of travel time during daylight hours under reasonable speeds. **Accidents are frequent** and are usually the result of daredevil drivers or impatient passengers. In the summer of 1998, a jeep carrying Swiss tourists plunged into a shallow ravine near Tingri, killing the driver; the severely injured survivors, one paralyzed, were airlifted to Hong Kong.

West of the lake and out of its view lies the small town of **Nagartse** (pop. 1400). A few cheap hotels line the main street. Near the town exit is the reasonably clean **Grain Guest House** (rìguāngliáng lüdiàn; 日光粮旅店), marked by a red, yellow, and green sign that reads "Guest House." (Dorms Y10-15.) None of the hotels in town have bath or shower facilities; there is a **public shower** (Y5) across from the Grain Guesthouse. There are also several decent Chinese restaurants along the street. The **Sichuan Village Restaurant** (shǔcūn táng cāntīng; 蜀村堂餐厅), right under the Grain Guesthouse's sign, serves some tasty dishes for Y15-30. (Open daily 8am-11:30pm.) The **post office** at the end of the street has IDD service. (Open daily 9:30am-1pm and 3:30-5:30pm.)

RALUNG MONASTERY

About 60km from Gyantse. Ralung Monastery is on the way from Yamdroktso to Gyantse; a red sign on the left indicates the direction. Travel down the track for about 10km; Ralung appears soon after some ruins. Beware the ferocious sheep dogs; wait for the monks to tie them up before entering. Open 24hr.; ask the monks to let you in. Y25.

The once-famous Ralung Monastery used to house a grand *stupa*, but much of the complex was destroyed during the tumultuous years of the Cultural Revolution. Since little of the monastery still stands, and most of what does has only been restored in recent years, Ralung is less touristed than many other monasteries in Tibet. Nevertheless, Ralung's thriving monastic life and idyllic natural setting make it an interesting stop.

According to myth, Sakyamuni predicted in his *sutra* that Tsangpa Gyare, a manifestation of Avalokiteshvara, would appear at a place called Sa Padmasambhava; a great Indian master invited by King Trisong Detsen to spread Buddhism in Tibet, confirmed this prophecy. It was later concluded by a great *tertön* (treasure finder) that the site on which Ralung stands was indeed the fabled Sa. At one time, Ralung was the main seat of the Drugpa Kagyu school of Tibetan Buddhism; the only reminder of this monastic complex is a vivid mural in the assembly hall. The most important relic in the monastery today is the 400-year-old footprint of the monastery chief's young child, captured on a piece of rock in the assembly hall.

卬ୟୟ· GYANTSE 江孜 ☎ 0892

Gyaltse means "top of the imperial palace" in Tibetan, and it is probably from this word that Gyantse derived its name. Tibet's fourth largest city is little more than a

TIBET

bustling town, with streets full of honking trucks and donkey carts and men shooting pool or playing bingo at roadside stands. Gyantse's carefree atmosphere belies
its strategic location and history of military conflicts. The imposing Dzong Fort
and the red, cliff-top walls are lasting monuments of the "Great Game," when British and Russian imperialists competed to fill the power vacuum left in Tibet by the
decline of the Qing during the late 19th century. With the magnificent Palkhor
Choiden Pagoda and its well-preserved architecture, Gyantse now attracts foreigners of a different type. The surrounding farmlands, the most fertile in Tibet, come
alive during the traditional Gyantse **horse-racing festivals** (June 8-14).

■ ? ORIENTATION AND PRACTICAL INFORMATION

The only crossroads in Gyantse serve as the heart of this compact city. Travelers
arriving from Yamdroktso enter the city from the east on **Weiguo Lu** (卫国路),
which becomes **Baiju (Palchoi) Lu** (白居路) after the intersection. Baiju (Palchoi)
Lu, as the name indicates, leads to Palchoi Monastery. Visitors departing for Shigatse exit Gyantse on **Yingxiong Nan Lu** (英雄南路), known as **Yingxiong Bei Lu**
(英雄北路) on the other side of the crossroads. Yingxiong Bei Lu passes the
entrance to Dzong Fort. The intersection gets its own street name, **Jiangzi (Gyantse)
Zhong Lu** (江孜中路).

As there is no long-distance bus station in Gyantse, **taxis** and **minibuses** depart
for Shigatse from the crossroads (taxis Y200, minibuses Y25).

Travel Permits: An **Alien Travel Permit** is required for Gyantse and all of its sights.
Obtain a permit at the Shigatse PSB (see p. 748; Y150) or through a travel agency.

Bike Rental: Gyantse Hotel, on Yingxiong Nan Lu, rents bikes to hotel guests (Y5 per hr.).

PSB: Gyantse County (24hr. ☎817 2032), on Weiguo Lu behind the Gyantse cinema.
Gyantse town (☎817 2084), on Baiju (Palchoi) Lu. Open daily 9am-1pm and 4-7pm.

Hospital: People's Hospital of Gyantse County (☎817 2003), on Yingxiong Bei Lu, near
No. 1 Middle School. Ambulance service. Open daily 9:30am-12:30pm and 3:30-
6:30pm.

Pharmacy: Tongji Drugstore, on Weiguo Lu, opposite Gyantse County Hotel. Open daily
8am-10pm.

Post and Telecommunications: On 17 Weiguo Lu. IDD service available. Open daily
9am-12:30pm and 4-7pm. **Postal Code:** 857400.

▌ ACCOMMODATIONS

Gyantse has several decent budget accommodation options. **Public showers** (Y5)
are available on Yingxiong Lu, across from the Canda Hotel.

Wutse Hotel (wūzī fàndiàn; 乌孜饭店; ☎817 2880), on Yingxiong Lu, next to the Canda
Hotel. The sterile dorms have tile floors and TV, and doubles have absolutely beautiful
private showers. 24hr. hot water. 4-bed dorms Y40; doubles Y300.

Gyantse Foodstuff Storage Hotel (jiāngzī guójiā liángshì chǔbèi zhāodàisuǒ; 江孜国家
粮食储备招待所), 11 Jiangzi (Gyantse) Zhong Lu (☎817 2873). Look for the red and
blue "Hotel" sign. Foodstuff has definitely got the stuff for budget travelers. Clean, carpeted rooms and not so clean public toilets. 3-bed dorms Y30; 2-bed dorms Y35.

Hotel of Gyantse Town Furniture Factory (tiánmù jiājù chǎng zhāodài; 田牧家具场招
待; ☎817 2254), on Baiju (Palchoi) Lu. The more basic rooms, decorated in Tibetan
style and tainted only by the dirty cement floors, are across the courtyard. The deck
area has a great view of the Dzong. Rooms Y30-40 per person.

Canda Hotel (càndá bīnguǎn; 灿达宾馆; ☎817 2573), on Yingxiong Lu. Look for the
tinted blue windows. Worn rooms are still comfy. Tiny singles Y50 (the proprietor may let
you shower in an open double); doubles with bath Y160.

FOOD

Wutse Restaurant (wūzī cāntīng; 乌孜餐厅; ☎817 2880), in the Wutse Hotel. Wutse Restaurant has Gyantse's cheapest menu and a cozy Tibetan feel. A wide selection of Western, Chinese, Tibetan, Nepali, and Indian foods. The deep dish cheese pizza (Y20) is a rare treat. Open M-F 6:30am-8pm, Sa-Su 6:30am until the last customer leaves.

Zhuangyuan Restaurant (zhuāngyuán fàntīng; 庄园饭厅; ☎817 2526), on Yingxiong Nan Lu, across from Wutse. English menus in this Sichuanese restaurant include pictures of hungry foreigners munching away. Sweet and sour pork (Y25), french fries (Y15), and pancakes (Y8-12) are popular choices. Open daily 7am-11pm.

Tashi Restaurant (☎817 2793), on Baiju (Palchoi) Lu, near the crossroads and the entrance to Dzong Square. For some reason, most foreigners choose to eat here, perhaps because of the Western music and atmosphere so many tourists crave. Dishes Y15-45; pastas Y25-30. Open daily 8am until the last customer leaves.

SIGHTS

PALCHOI MONASTERY
Open daily 9am-1:30pm and 3-10pm. Y30. Y10 to take photographs inside.

Founded in 1418 by Rapdan Gunsang and the first Panchen Lama, Keldrup Je, the Palchoi Monastery is where the Gelug, Sakya, and Boton sects of Tibetan Buddhism are said to peacefully coexist. The throne in the main assembly hall was once occupied by the Dalai Lama; now a photograph of the 10th Panchen Lama occupies the seat. In the center chapel, the large statue of Buddha, embodying the Buddhas of Past, Present, and Future, is surrounded by ministers and messengers responsible for bringing his knowledge to mankind.

Although the murals of Buddha upstairs appear identical at first, they are not— some carry bowls, representing compassion, while others are empty-handed, symbolizing the Buddha of Knowledge. In the upstairs chapel to the left is an intricate *mandala* with a multitude of figures capped by an orb. The solitary figure clothed in blue is **Vajrapani,** *bodhisattva* of energy and power.

Palkhor Choiden Pagoda (qiānfó tǎ; 千佛塔) surpasses the monastery in both age and fame. The pagoda is one of the world's most famous *stupas,* built almost 800 years ago. It is 32m high and has 108 doors, 77 chapels, and at least 100,000 images of Buddhist deities. A large statue of Sakyamuni awaits those who conquer the *stupa's* five stories. On the floors below, small chapels encase statues of Buddha incarnations, *bodhisattvas,* and important teachers.

DZONG FORT
After reaching the large red doors that lead to Dzong Square at the city's main intersection, walk down Baiju Lu for 3min.; turn left and follow the road up to the fort (20-30min.). Enter via a small dirt alleyway off Baiju Lu. Open daily 8am-8pm. Y20.

Some believe that touching the top of this mountain brings good luck and certainly an incredible view; others are content to admire the stately fort from below. Flanked by its crumbling auburn walls, this imposing and handsome citadel overlooks Gyantse. Here, Tibetan defenders fought to the bitter end in a losing cause against the onslaught of the British Younghusband "Expedition."

Built in AD 967 by the grandson of Tibet's last *Tsanpo,* the Dzong (quán shān kàngyīng yízhǐ; 泉山抗英遗址) was expanded and used by various regimes, dynasties, and religious sects (Sakya, Padru, Gadan, and Podrang in particular) to defend Gyantse from separatist regimes. Gyantse occupies a crossroads linking Lhasa with Shigatse and Yadong; the fortress guarding this crucial juncture was long considered impregnable until Younghusband and his troops marched in (see **Expedition or Execution?,** p. 746). The bloody aftermath is commemorated in the **"Anti-British Museum,"** an exhibition that describes the British invasion and displays matchlocks used by soldiers. A monastery is farther up the mountain.

TIBET

EXPEDITION OR EXECUTION?

EXPEDITION OR EXECUTION? In early 1903, a British adventurer named Younghusband led a Sepoy army from India to "check out" suspected Russian activity in Lhasa. After mowing down 1400 bewildered Tibetan troops with hilltop machine guns south of Gyantse in April, Younghusband marched into the city, predicting little resistance. A wave of reinforcements from Lhasa nearly captured Younghusband, but British firepower and deceit eventually prevailed.

Younghusband lured the Tibetan leadership into a "peaceful meeting;" his troops then opened fire, killing the two main Tibetan generals, the heads of Tibet's three largest monasteries, the Panchen Lama's chief representative, and 500 Tibetan soldiers. A hero was created, however, as the Panchen Lama's bodyguard managed to kill 10 Englishmen with his knife before eventually passing—his body filled with bullets. The Tibetan defenders withdrew to Palchoi Monastery and then to Dzong Fort. As the battle dragged on into July, Tibetans resorted to drinking out of mud pools and hurling boulders after they ran out of ammunition. The fort finally fell to a barrage of artillery fire, and the survivors retreated through hidden tunnels. According to British accounts, some 300 Tibetans lay dead while the British suffered only four dead and 30 wounded. A smug Younghusband marched into Lhasa, the first foreigner ever to do so.

PALA MANOR HOUSE

About 3km from Gyantse's city center. Walk down Yingxiong Nan Lu and turn right after the big "A" structure. A sign indicating the direction of the house is on the left, past the cement factory; the entrance is about 1km down a dirt road. Open daily 8am-8pm. Y20.

Pala Manor House (pà lā zhuāng yuán; 帕拉庄园 in Tibetan, Pachou Lakang) once belonged to a wealthy aristocrat of the Pala family. During Tibet's feudal period in the late 17th century, the Pala family supplied the Tibetan government with several officials of the highest rank. Perhaps as a result of their services, the family eventually came to own 37 manors and 3000 serfs. The original Pala Manor House was in Gyanka village, about 1km from Gyantse, but was destroyed during the British invasion of Tibet. Pala Manor House as it now stands was rebuilt in 1937. When the PLA crushed the rebellion of 1959, the heir to the Pala family fortunes, Tashi Wangjiu, fled to India and then to Switzerland, where he died in 1984. Reputedly the best-preserved manor house in all of Tibet, Pala Manor House escaped the ravages of the Cultural Revolution by acting as the PLA's regional headquarters.

A visit to this three-story house can be the perfect antidote to an overdose on monasteries. The third floor once served as the nobleman's private living quarters, and now contains the sunlight room, once used by the nobleman as a winter solarium and now containing a wide collection of Tibetan rugs, as well as the private prayer hall. During important religious days and festivals, lamas were invited here to pray and meditate. A porcelain statue of the Goddess of Mercy on display here supposedly dates back to the Tang dynasty. The second floor holds the manor's eclectic assortment of historical and religious items, including a photo of Tashi Wangjiu taken in 1956, turn-of-the-century *tangkas*, old Tibetan stamps (of which only 13 remain in the world), the master's alcohol collection, and even a bowl made from a human skull and used to hold wine for the gods.

A short walk across the street leads to the servants' houses, where over 3000 serfs lived on an average of 2.5m^2 per person. Chinese commentary lines the walls of the shacks, outlining each servant's success story following liberation in 1959.

གཞིས་ཀ་རྩེ SHIGATSE 日喀则 ☎0892

Tibet's second largest city, Shigatse is most famous for being the seat of the Panchen Lama, who is traditionally regarded by Tibetans (discounting those in Lhasa) to be on equal footing with the Dalai Lama. A visit to Shigatse requires a stop at Tashilhunpo Monastery, where all of the Panchen Lamas since the 4th have lived (including the controversial 11th, chosen by the Chinese government to

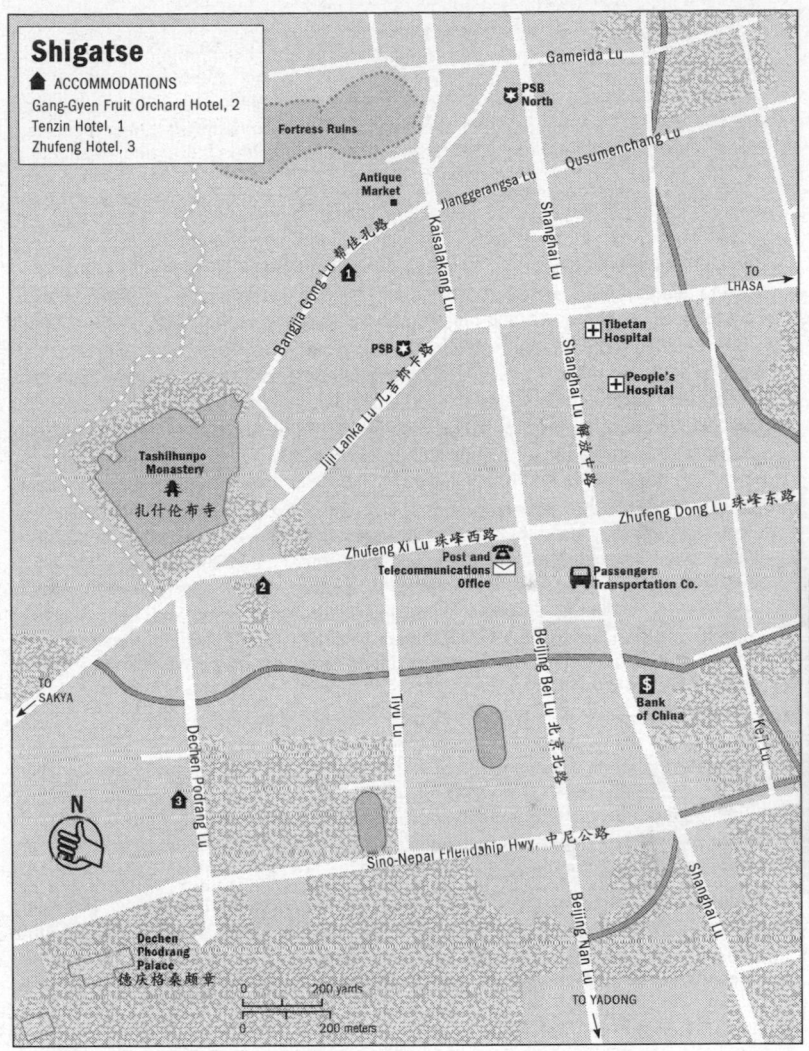

Shigatse

♦ ACCOMMODATIONS
Gang-Gyen Fruit Orchard Hotel, 2
Tenzin Hotel, 1
Zhufeng Hotel, 3

Gameida Lu

PSB
North

Fortress Ruins

Qusumenchang Lu

Antique
Market

Jianggerangsa Lu

Shanghai Lu

Bangjia Gong Lu 邦佳孔路

Kaisalakang Lu

TO
LHASA

Tibetan
Hospital

PSB

People's
Hospital

Shanghai Lu 解放中路

Jiji Lanka Lu 几吉拉卡中路

Tashilhunpo
Monastery

扎什伦布寺

Zhufeng Dong Lu 珠峰东路

Zhufeng Xi Lu 珠峰西路

Post and
Telecommunications
Office

Passengers
Transportation Co.

TO
SAKYA

Dechen Podrang Lu

Tiyu Lu

Beijing Bei Lu 北京北路

Bank
of China

Kei Lu

N

Sino-Nepal Friendship Hwy. 中尼公路

Shanghai Lu

Dechen
Phodrang
Palace
德庆格桑颇章

Beijing Nan Lu

0   200 yards

0   200 meters

TO YADONG

TIBET

replace the imprisoned six-year-old). Shigatse has most of the resources of a
larger city, set in traditional Tibetan architecture. Take a shaded stroll, shop in the
flea markets opposite Tenzin Hotel and at the Gang-gyen Carpet Factory near
Tashilhunpo, or lounge in one of the omnipresent red-light tea houses. Cheap,
comfortable accommodations make the city a good stop on the way from Lhasa to
Sakya and on to the border with Nepal.

🛈 PRACTICAL INFORMATION

An **Alien Travel Permit** is not necessary for Shigatse. The Shigatse PSB is a good
place to obtain permits for the Friendship Highway, Sakya, Everest Base Camp,
Gyantse, Nangartse, Yadong, and elsewhere in Shigatse Prefecture.

Buses: Passengers Transportation Co., 14 Jiefang Zhong Lu (☎882 2903), is the terminus for buses arriving in Shigatse. Open daily 9:30am-9pm. There are 2 roads from Lhasa to Shigatse: the more scenic old dirt road passes through Yamdrokso and Gyantse, while the new route is a paved highway winding along Yarlungzanbo River. Bus traffic runs only along the new one, which is 2-3hr. faster. All buses to Gyantse originate in Shigatse. Travel time depends on road conditions. To: **Gyantse** (2hr., 5 per day, Y25); **Lhasa** (6hr., 2 per day, Y38); **Sakya** (4hr, alternate days, Y27); and **Yadong** (5-6 hr.; Tu, Th, and Sa; Y34; travel permit required).

Local Transportation: There are no buses, but **tricycle** rides are always an option, and **motorcycles** have a fixed rate of Y3. **Taxis** are easy to come by, even after dark (Y10).

Bike Rental: Tenzin Hotel has 2 bikes to rent to hotel guests for Y3 per hr.

Travel Agencies: CITS (☎882 2516), in the Fruit Hotel, is the only travel agency in town. Shigatse CITS will grant some individual travel permits and arranges guideless jeep trips.Open M-F 9am-12:30pm and 4-7pm.

Bank of China: 7 Jiefang Zhong Lu. Exchanges traveler's checks. Open M-F 9am-1pm and 4-7pm, Sa-Su 10am-4pm.

Markets: There are 2 major flea markets in the northwest part of the city. The **Antique Market,** on Bangjia Gong Lu opposite the Tenzin Hotel, sells mostly bead necklaces and other handicrafts. The market across the road sells mainly clothing and essentials.

Department Store: Shigatse Commercial City (☎882 3674), at the corner of Beijing Lu and Gongjiu Lin Lu. Used mainly by locals. Karaoke facilities, a tea garden, and restaurants on the 3rd and 4th floors. Open daily 9am-7pm.

PSB: 4 Jiji Langka Lu (24hr. ☎882 2241). The **Foreign Affairs Office** (☎882 2240) is the place to obtain travel permits. On weekends, foreigners can contact Mr. Laba Ciren (☎882 3268) at his home. Other local branches on Renbu Lu, behind the Sanzuzi Hotel on Gangjielin Lu, on Xingong Lu, and on Yanhe Lu near the river. All PSB offices open daily 9am-1pm and 4-7pm.

Hospitals: People's Hospital of Shigatse Prefecture (xiàn rénmín yīyuàn; 县人民医院), 5 Shanghai Zhong Lu (outpatient ☎882 5900; emergency ☎882 2650). Ambulance service. Open daily 9am-12:30pm and 4-6:30pm. **Zang (Tibetan) Hospital** (zàng yīyuàn; 藏医院), 3 Shanghai Zhong Lu (☎882 2654). Tibetan and Western medicine. Open M-Sa 9am-12:30pm and 4-6:30pm. Emergency ward open until 9pm.

Pharmacy: Shigatse New and Special Medicines, 8 Shanghai Zhong Lu (24hr. ☎882 3101). Open daily 9am-9pm.

Post and Telecommunications: Main Post and Telecommunications Office, 12 Beijing Bei Lu. **Internet access** Y5.8 per hr. Post office open daily 9am-1pm and 4-8pm; **China Telecom** open 9am-midnight. IDD service also available at Shigatse Commercial City (see **Department Store,** above). Open daily 9am-8pm. **Postal Code:** 857000.

⌐ ACCOMMODATIONS

Although not as backpacker-friendly as Lhasa, Shigatse offers a handful of excellent budget hotels.

▩ **Tenzin Hotel,** 8 Banjia Ling Lu (☎882 2018). The destination of choice for the backpacker contingent. Clean and convenient, the hotel has a nice patio area and rooms with Tibetan decor. Hot water 8:30am-10:30pm. Large dorms Y25; 3-bed dorms Y34; 2-bed dorms Y60; singles Y50; doubles with bath Y180.

Gang-gyen Fruit Orchard Hotel (☎882 2282), across from the Tashilhunpo Monastery; look for the "Fruit Hotel" sign. Very basic accommodations. Solar-heated hot water depends on the weather. Dorms Y15, with carpets and TV Y25; doubles Y80.

Zhufeng Hotel (zhūfēng bīnguǎn; 珠峰宾馆), 14 Dechen Podrang Lu (☎882 1929). Follow signs for the "Zhufeng Friendship Hotel" opposite Tashilhunpo Monastery. Rooms have carpet and TV. 4-bed dorms Y30; doubles with bath Y120.

TIBET

🍴 FOOD

As can be expected of a city its size, Shigatse offers a wide variety of scrumptious food, although most Westerners tend to stick to the eateries near the Tenzin Hotel.

Tashi 1 Restaurant (☎882 2018), a few doors downhill from the Fruit Hotel. Tashi 1 technically has no relation to the popular Tashi 1 in Lhasa (see p. 734), but it has much the same feel. The joint serves tasty Tibetan, Chinese, and Western food (Y7-15) and is almost exclusively populated by Westerners. Open daily 6am-11:30pm.

Tenzin Restaurant (☎882 2018), in the Tenzin Hotel. A slightly more expensive version of Tashi 1 (dishes Y10-40). Mainly Chinese food, mainly Western clients. Open when people arrive until they leave.

Deler Tibetan Restaurant (☎882 3328), 2min. from the Tashilhunpo Monastery, up the hill from the Fruit Orchard Hotel. Look for the yak head on the sign. The pleasant atmosphere and authentic, cushioned seats make Deler a prime location to sip warm milk tea (Y1) as you wait for the Tashilhunpo to open. Hard-core Tibetan food (Y10-30), including yak lung (Y25), sheep head (Y20), and deep fried chicken (Y25). Open daily 8am-11pm.

👁 SIGHTS

གཀཔ་གར TASHILHUNPO MONASTERY
Open M-Sa 9am-12:30pm and 4-6pm. Y30.

Tashilhunpo Monastery (zhāshílúnbù sì; 扎什伦布寺) is to the Panchen Lama what the Potala is to the Dalai Lama. **Gedun Dup,** the first Dalai Lama, was responsible for building Tashilhunpo in 1447. The monastery shelters a large, impressive statue of the Maitreya Buddha, the 10th Panchen Lama's splendid funerary *stupa*, and packs of yelping dogs. Tour the monastery along the traditional circumambulatory route (walking clockwise; see p. 729 for more info on circumambulating).

Built by the 9th Panchen Lama in 1914, the chapel that houses the **Maitreya Buddha** is adorned by rich murals. The statue itself stands 26m, with a crown studded with jewels. Colorful *mandala* murals and depictions of numerous Buddhas cover the walls above the **10th Panchen Lama's Stupa,** made out of 547kg of gold, 75kg of silver, and precious stones. On the walls are 1000 gold-flake paintings of Buddhas and protector gods, including three large paintings of the Buddhas of the Past, Present, and Future. The **4th Panchen Lama's Funerary Stupa,** built in 1662, is not as spectacular as the 10th Panchen Lama's Stupa.

A long corridor leads to the *stupas* of the 5th through the 9th Panchen Lamas. Their individual *stupas* were destroyed during the Cultural Revolution, but their bodies escaped unharmed. Because of monetary constraints, the 10th Panchen Lama decided to house them together. Beautiful murals of important Yellow Hat sect members line the walls. On the floor below, on the same side as the entrance, is a kitchen with big vats of brewing yak-butter tea. The assembly hall next door houses a statue of Sakyamuni; a room on the floor above provides a good view. The body of Gedun Dup supposedly rests in a room next door.

ཆྲ SAKYA 萨迦   ☎08024

The town of Sakya, 150km west of Shigatse, shows few signs of Chinese influence, save the PSB checkpoint and military base at the edge of town. Sakya means "pale earth," and the city's distinctive pale gray buildings with vertical white and red stripes certainly render the name appropriate. Besides its multicolored structures, Sakya's distinguishing feature is the gigantic, fortress-like monastery that dominates the town center. Not many travelers spend the night, but the feel of this quiet monastery town merits what time you can afford.

FOUR'S A CROWD As you visit monasteries across Tibet, you will notice frequent depictions of an elephant with a monkey, a hare, and a bird piled upon each others' backs. This description is not born of an incredibly simplistic view of the animal food chain, but rather of an ancient Tibetan fable known as the "The Union of the Four Brethren." Once upon a time, on a hot sunny day, these four creatures decided to seek shelter under the same tree. The elephant exclaimed: "The tree is only big enough to shade me!" "No, no, there is only room for me," said the monkey. The rabbit also made the same claim. It is only when the tiny little bird squeaked, "I planted the seed for that tree," that they realized they were all being a bit selfish, so the four animals piled onto each others' backs and spent the afternoon together in the shade. The moral of the story is known as "friendship." Perhaps you can remind people of it next time you duke it out with child-trampling Chinese tourists to catch the bus to the next monastery.

█▐ ORIENTATION & PRACTICAL INFORMATION. An **Alien Travel Permit** is required; travelers must stop at the PSB checkpoint at the town entrance. The enormous **Sakya Monastery** effectively serves as the town center, and a handful of hotels, shops, and eateries are clustered east of the monastery walls. From Shigatse, **buses** (Y27) depart for Sakya every other day. From Sakya, Shigatse-bound buses depart every other day from the Sakya County Guesthouse. There is a **post office** across the street from the County Guesthouse. (Open daily 9:30am-12:30pm and 4-7pm.) The **postal code** is 857800.

▐▐ ACCOMMODATIONS AND FOOD. Accommodations options in Sakya are extremely limited. The most passable establishment is the **Sakya Hotel,** just outside the monastery's northeast corner. Enter through the gates just to the right of the **Sichuan Flavor Restaurant.** Dorm beds (Y10) have communal toilets.

The **Sichuan Flavor Restaurant** is a good place to chow down. Food is "imported," but on the whole prices are still quite reasonable. (Pancakes Y5-6, french fries Y20, noodle soup Y12. Open daily 8am-10pm.) Across the street is **Sakya Restaurant,** a little Tibetan joint serving decent food for under Y20. (Open daily 8am-11pm.)

Most travelers to Sakya actually end up spending the night in nearby **Lhatse** (30km west of the Sakya turn-off), where creature comforts are more plentiful. The **Lhatse Hotel** has musty, crowded dorm rooms and fancier Tibetan-style rooms with carpets and TV. Be sure to ask for a room facing the inner courtyard, or face the wrath of karaoke for the duration of the night. (☎(08032) 2208. Showers Y5. Dorms Y20-40; doubles Y90.) The **Tashi 2** restaurant, next to the Lhatse Hotel, serves tasty but overpriced Chinese dishes (Y18-30). A row of Sichuanese restaurants lines the other side of the street.

◎ SIGHTS. Sakya Monastery (sàjiā sì; 萨迦寺) is the only worthwhile sight in Sakya. The impressive, castle-like complex, completed in 1268, is home to the Red Hat (Sakyapa) sect of Tibetan Buddhism (see p. 726). Climbing the monastery walls and walking along the top ridge affords incredible views of the monastery and the surrounding valley. Be careful; there are no side railings. A ground floor entrance is via the east wall, which leads to the central courtyard.

To the left is the **Purkhang Chapel,** which houses the 700-year-old figure of Sakyamuni, 7000 glass-encased *bodhisattvas,* and other relics. The central figure is Manjushri, the Bodhisattva of Wisdom; Sakyamuni is a few paces to the left. The temple across from the chapel contains the *stupas* of 11 Sakya abbots, a dusty *mandala,* and hundreds of ancient scripts. Directly opposite the main entrance is the cavernous **assembly hall,** where the familiar figure of Sakyamuni is flanked by a symmetrical arrangement of statues. The remains of the founder of Sakya Monastery, Kon Konchog Gyelpo, are preserved inside the enormous central Buddha. The remarkable assortment of figures on display include Manjushri, Maitreya, and Kunga Nyingpo (the center figure of the trio to the right of Sakyamuni), a famous abbot of Sakya. The pillars themselves are single tree trunks, brought from India. Bring a flashlight to observe the mesmerizing murals on the walls. *(Open daily 8am-5pm; closed for a 1hr. lunch break. Y30; Y20 fee for photos taken inside the monastery.)*

ᇊᠪᠭᠤᠭᠠᠰᠤ MT. EVEREST

The approach to Mt. Everest (zhǔmúlángmǎfēng; 珠穆朗马峰) via **Pangla Pass** is one of the most beautiful and stunning routes in the world. After hours zig-zagging across the moonscaped plateau, the majestic Himalayas unfold in full force, with four of the six highest peaks in the world—Cho Oyu (8201m), Malaku (8463m), Lhotse (8516m), and Qomolangma (Everest, 8848.13m)—looming before the awe-struck traveler. The most magnificent view of the "Third Pole of the World," how-ever, is from Rongphu Monastery. On the rare clear day, lucky visitors can clamber up to base camp and watch the sun's rays slowly illuminate the mountain.

From Lhatse, the Friendship Highway continues for three hours, past **Shegar** (New Tingri) to the 65km **Everest access road.** After the turn-off, the bumpy and windy access road winds up for one-and-a-half hours, passing Pangla Pass, 5220m above sea level, before descending to the village of **Tashi Dzom.** Most visitors stop here for lunch or stay the night. After crossing a large valley and several tiny vil-lages, the road ends up at **Rongphu Monastery. Base camp** is a few kilometers up the Rongphu glacier bed. The Everest access road trip takes about five hours.

⚡ PRACTICAL INFORMATION

An **Alien Travel Permit** is required for Rongphu Monastery and Everest Base Camp. Permits can be obtained at Shigatse PSB (Y150) or at any travel agency. There is a Y65 **admission** fee per person to enter the Everest region, as well as a hefty Y405 vehicle fee (some travel agencies include this fee in land cruiser packages). These fees are collected at the village of **Chay,** about 3km after the turn-off from the Friendship Highway.

In Tashi Dzom, there are basic accommodations at the **Qomolangma Palber Hotel.** The rooms are slightly better—and much warmer—than those at Rongphu Monas-tery. For Y15-30, a guest gets a bed, access to outdoor pit toilets, and a lantern. A cozy **restaurant** serving mediocre Chinese food (Y5 10) is open daily 8am to 11pm.

👁 SIGHTS

The unbeatable views from the Rongphu Monastery and the Everest Base Camp are the only reason to come all this way—enjoy.

RONGPHU MONASTERY (róngbù sì; 绒布寺). Two hours farther up the Everest access road from Tashi Dzom is Rongphu Monastery, the small and run-down home of 21 nuns and nine monks. At 4980m, the monastery offers basic **accommo-dations** in cold rooms (dorms Y25), but at least you can brag that you've slept in the highest temple in the world. There are no electricity or door locks, but an incredi-ble view. Camping on the grounds costs Y10-15. There is a small restaurant that serves simple but tasty fried rice and noodles (Y10-20).

EVEREST BASE CAMP (zhūfēng dàbĕn yíng; 珠峰大本营). For centuries, the sight of Everest's peak has taken many a breath away. From 5000m above sea level, the grandeur of the mighty peak may not be apparent at first glance, but the shimmering beauty of the pyramidal north face quickly dissipates any initial disap-pointment. The best time for viewing is early morning, when the chances of a cloudless sky are highest and the sun's first rays glint off the perpetually snow-clad peak. During the monsoon summer months, clouds from Nepal can enshroud the Himalayas for up to a week; only the lucky may catch a glimpse of the peak.

For the intrepid, a hike from Rongphu Monastery to Everest Base Camp takes about two hours. For the faint-hearted, a 20-minute ride in a land cruiser will do the trick. Although there isn't that much to do at Base Camp, the "Mt. Qomolangma Base Camp" marker provides an unbeatable photo-op. One word of caution: do not attempt to hike to Base Camp if you have just arrived in Tibet via Kathmandu. Acute Mountain Sickness (see p. 725) can strike without warning and debilitate even the fittest trekker. Spend a few days getting acclimated before setting out on any long hikes.

১নৰ TINGRI 定日

The small village of Tingri is little more than a few houses along the Friendship Highway. Foreigners need an **Alien Travel Permit** (although only an individual one), to get there. Tingri is where most travelers spend either their last night (if heading to Kathmandu) or first night (if coming from Kathmandu) in Tibet. There is little to do in the town except admire the wonderful view of the Himalayan Range in the gorgeous natural backdrop to the town.

The **Everest Snow Leopard House**, on the Friendship Highway a few hundred meters before the center of town, is the cheapest place in town. There are communal toilets but no showers; plenty of hot boiled water is available for rinsing. (2- to 4-bed dorms Y15.) In the center of town, the **Amdo Hotel** has a nice shower available, as well as outdoor pit toilets with nice views of the surrounding valley. (Showers Y10, for non-guests Y15. 3- to 4-bed dorms Y30.)

There are a bunch of eateries lining the Friendship Highway, each re-hashing the same pricey menu. On the Nepal-bound side of town, the **Amdo Restaurant** is about as cheap and good as it gets (Tibetan dishes Y10-20). If you're looking for more variety, be patient; you'll probably be in Kathmandu soon.

ঝ্যম্ ZHANGMU 樟木 ☎08704

After charging across the arid Tibetan Plateau, the vivid green scenery of Zhangmu is a refreshing change. The lush green cliffs sloping above the border town of Zhangmu are a dead giveaway that Nepal is near, and many travelers feel it to be the most spectacular scenery they have seen in either Tibet or Nepal. Beautiful waterfalls splash down thousands of feet, sometimes drenching passing cars in the process. The entire town lies along the Friendship Highway as it curves and descends. The population, consisting of a curious mix of Tibetan, Nepalese, and Chinese, is growing at a rapid rate, in large part due to brisk border trade.

An **Alien Travel Permit** is technically required for Zhangmu, as there is a PSB checkpoint at the entrance to town. There is a **post office** near the top of town, as well as a **Bank of China** opposite the Zhangmu Hotel. Money changers also work the streets in front of the bank, offering better rates than in Kathmandu.

The lap of luxury in town is the **Zhangmu Hotel,** a two-star behemoth with a top-floor lobby and a restaurant that serves excellent buffets. (☎2221. Breakfast buffet Y60, lunch and dinner Y90. 4-bed dorms Y50.) The **Gang-gyen Hotel** has bright and airy dorms with communal toilets and nice views of the valley below. (☎2188. 24hr. hot water. 5-bed dorms Y50.) The **Zhangmu Friendship Guesthouse** is of similar quality to the Gang-gyen Hotel. (☎2261. Dorms Y20.) The Chinese-Tibetan restaurant next door to the Gang-gyen Hotel, **Gang-gyen Restaurant,** is popular with the backpacking crowd. (Open daily 8am-10:30pm.)

BORDER CROSSING INTO NEPAL: ZHANGMU

The customs checkpoint for China is at Zhangmu. From Zhangmu, most travelers pay for a ride on a truck (US$5-7) or walk the remaining 8km to **Kodari** (about 2hr.) and the Friendship Bridge, where the customs checkpoint for Nepal is located. Nepali **visas** are available at the border (1st entry to Nepal US$30, subsequent entries US$50), but it's more convenient to get one at the Nepalese consulate in Lhasa (see p. 732). From Kodari, two buses depart in the morning for Kathmandu, leaving from the Friendship Bridge when full. A taxi to Kathmandu costs Y1600-2400 per person. Barring landslides and other delays, the trip from Kodari to Kathmandu takes about five hours.

KATHMANDU काठमाण्डौ   ☎ 01

A half century after Nepal opened its borders to the world, Kathmandu has become a hippie haven, a mecca for trekkers, and a thriving cosmopolitan cultural center. As Nepal's largest city, Kathmandu has a gravity that pulls together tourists, *sadhus*, Tibetan refugees, and work-seeking Nepalis. There are so many temples in Kathmandu that the word "templescape" has been coined to describe the city's skyline. If you are arriving here at the end of a jaunt down Tibet's Friendship Highway, the city may seem brashly frenetic, but hidden along its crowded streets are many of the creature comforts you've likely been missing since you left Lhasa.

▐ TRANSPORTATION

Airplanes: Flights depart from **Tribhuvan International Airport,** 5km east of the center of town. The cheapest way there is by **bus: bus #1** runs from **Ratna Park** (frequent, 30min., Rs4) to a stop down the hill from the airport. Ratna Park is 20min. from Thamel; head to the end of Durbar Marg and walk south. Alternatively, **pre-paid taxis** cost Rs200 from Thamel and Rs250 from Freak Street.

Visas: Issued upon arrival at the airport to anybody with a passport, photograph, and hard currency or at the border crossing from Tibet (see p. 752).

Buses: Most buses arrive and depart from **New Bus Park,** Ring Rd., in Balaju. Almost all city buses make a stop at the New Bus Park. **Bus #23** from Ratna Park takes one of the most direct routes; it also stops along Kantipath, north of Rani Pokhari (every 5min., 5am-8pm, 30min., Rs3-6). You can also take a taxi (Rs58 from Thamel, Rs65 from New Rd.). The departure bays are not labeled in English, but the staff of the 24hr. "Police Room" will direct you to the right counter; most of the ticket vendors speak English.

Local Transportation: Despite their appearance, Kathmandu buses do work; many are even painted with route numbers these days. **Always confirm that the bus is going to your destination.** The valley bus station is known as **Ratna Park** (named for the park across the street); Nepalis also call it *purano* (old) bus park. Bus #7 (to Bhaktapur) leaves from **Bagh Bazaar,** one block north of Ratna Park. Buses generally leave as soon as they're full. Haggard, Chinese-built electric trolleybuses creak between Kathmandu and Bhaktapur (frequent, 45min., Rs6). The first stop is on **Tripureswar Marg,** just south of the National Stadium.

Taxis: Shiny new red, green, or yellow **taxis** are all metered, as are the older ones (identifiable by their black license plates). Rates typically start at Rs7-9. Fares within the city should be less than Rs150. After 9pm, rates go up by over 50%, and drivers may be reluctant to take you where you want to go. Taxis queue on Tridevi Marg near the entrance to Thamel. **Auto-rickshaws** are cheaper than taxis, if you can persuade the driver to use his meter. Aggressive **cycle-rickshaw** drivers bargain hard, charging almost as much as auto-rickshaws. **Tempos** (larger, sturdier versions of auto-rickshaws) use the same route numbers as buses but leave from different places. They can be flagged down anywhere along their routes; to request a stop, bang on the metal ceiling.

Bike Rental: Bicycles can be rented from shops in Thamel, especially around Thamel Chowk and Chhetrapati. Mountain bikes (Rs150 per day) are better for trips outside the city; heavier, bell-equipped one-speeders (Rs60 per day) are fine for the city.

▐ PRACTICAL INFORMATION

Kathmandu is best toured on foot. Many of Kathmandu's interesting and historic buildings are in the bustling **Durbar (Palace) Square,** which is the heart of the old city. A good way to explore the sights is to start from Basantapur Square (the large open plaza by Freak Street) and head west and then north in a clockwise arc.

Tourist Office: The Nepal Tourism Board's main office, the **Tourist Service Center,** Bhrikuti Mandap (☎256909), is south of Ratna Bus Park, just east of Durbar Marg. Open Su-F 9am-5pm. They also have an office at the **airport** (☎470537). Open daily

9am-5pm. The **Thamel Tourism Development Committee** (☎429750) has an office north on Thahity, near the small Bhagwati temple. Open Su-F 9am-4pm.

Embassy: China, Baluwatar (☎411740, visa services ☎419053). Visas Rs2200; bring your passport and 1 photo. Allow 4 days for processing. Visas to **Tibet** available only to organized groups of 5 or more and only obtainable through a travel agency. Open M-F 10am-5pm. Visa dept. open M, W, and F 9:30-11:30am.

Currency Exchange: As of September 2000, US$1 was equal to 72.85 **Nepalese rupees** (Rs) and Y1 was equal to Rs 8.79. **Nepal Bank Ltd.** (☎221185), New Rd., has the lowest commission around for traveler's checks (0.5%). Open daily 8am-1pm and 1:30-6pm. **ANZ Grindlays** (☎421787), on Tridevi Marg, gives cash advances on MC and Visa and sells AmEx traveler's checks. Commission on traveler's checks Rs200 or 1.5%. Open Sept.-May Su-F 9:30am-7:30pm; June-Aug. M-F 9:30am-4:45pm. The several official **exchange counters** around Thamel generally charge 2% commission. **Western Union** is in Annapurna Travel and Tours, on the east side of Durbar Marg (☎223530; fax 222966). Money can be wired here within a minute. Open daily 9:30am-7:30pm.

American Express: Yeti Travels, Hotel Mayalu, Jamal, P.O. Box 76 (☎226172; fax 226152). Open Su-Th 10am-1pm and 2-5pm, F 10am-1pm and 2-4:45pm.

Emergency: Red Cross Ambulance (☎228094). **CIWEC** (☎228531 or 241732) has 24hr. emergency service.

Police: The **Tourist Police** handles petty thefts and rip-offs and can be reached at any of the city's tourist offices: Bhrikuti Mandap (☎256909), Tribhuvan Airport (☎470537), and Thamel (☎429750). Contact the city police for more serious issues (☎100).

Hospital/Medical Services: Kathmandu has numerous reliable **clinics** geared toward Westerners. In case of illness, visit one of these first. **CIWEC Clinic** (☎228531 or 241732), is off Durbar Marg, behind the Yak and Yeti sign, to the right. US$45 per consultation, US$65 after hours or on weekends. Open M-F 9am-noon and 1-3:30pm. On call 24hr. MC, Visa accepted. **Nepal International Clinic** (☎434642; fax 434713), opposite the Royal Palace, 3min. east of the main gates, down a lane to the right. Consultation US$34. Open Su-F 9am-1pm and 2-5pm. On-call 24hr. for emergencies. AmEx, MC, and Visa accepted.

Pharmacy: Om Pharmacy (☎244658), on New Rd., opposite RNAC. Open daily 8am-9pm. Several other pharmacies are opposite Bir Hospital.

Internet Access: Internet cafes are everywhere around Thamel and Durbar Square. The Easy Link **Cybercafe** (☎416239), in Thamel, has fast connections, A/C, the lowest rates, and a standing offer of 10 free minutes after your first visit. There's even a **Moneygram** service for quick money transfers. Rs40 per hr. Walk north on Thahity-Thamel and take a left at the small Bhagwati temple.

▐ ACCOMMODATIONS

The prices listed are for high-season and do not include the 10% government tax. Rates are usually negotiable, depending on the season and the length of your stay. **Beware of touts:** don't let anyone lead you to their friend's hotel; a hefty commission will appear on your bill. **Freak Street** is Kathmandu's original tourist district. Ever since it hit its peak back in the 70s, Freak Street has been cheaper, less hectic, and less populated than Thamel. The places below, unless otherwise noted, have hot water, Western-style seat toilets, laundry service, luggage storage, and a noon check-out, but no towels or toilet paper.

▨ **Kathmandu Guesthouse** (☎413632 or 418733; fax 417133; email ktmguest@ecomail.com.np). All directions in Thamel are given in relation to this place, so you'd better figure out where Kathmandu's original "budget hotel" is. Old wing rooms have best access to the guesthouse's communication center, swank lobby with satellite TV, ticket booking, bike rental, and barber shop. 10% discount for stays of over a week. Reserve ahead Sept.-Nov. and Feb.-Apr. Old wing: singles US$6-10; doubles US$8-12. New wing: singles US$17-50; doubles US$20-60. Credit cards accepted.

■ **Hotel Potala** (☎419159; fax 416680), opposite K.C.'s, at the center of Thamel. Well-managed by a friendly Tibetan family, Potala has clean, comfortable rooms with common baths, and its low prices make it one of the best values in Thamel. Rooms (some with fans) have shared balconies. Singles Rs125; doubles Rs175-250.

■ **Hotel Sugat** (☎246454; fax 221824; email maryman@mos.com.np), along the southern edge of Basantapur Square (facing the royal palace). The rooftop garden has fantastic views. Large, carpeted rooms overlook Durbar Square; some have tubs and balconies. Fans, toilet paper, towels. Singles Rs110-300; doubles Rs300-400.

Hotel The Earth, Chhetrapati-Thamel (☎260312; fax 260763). South of Kathmandu Guesthouse, on the west side of the street. A range of large, clean, and generously furnished rooms at economy prices. One of the few places in Thamel with dorm beds. 50% discount for students and volunteers; 20% discount for stays over 1 week. Dorm beds Rs100; singles Rs150-400; doubles Rs250-550.

Prince Guesthouse (☎414456; fax 220143), Satghumti-Thamel, north of Kathmandu Guesthouse—turn left at the intersection. The Artist Formerly Known As would die for the pink 'n' purple decor and wall-to-wall carpeting. Brand-new, spotless rooms with fans, phones, and attached baths complete with seat toilets and shower curtains. Rooftop garden and restaurant. Singles US$7; doubles US$10.

Hotel Garuda (☎416340 or 414766; fax 413614), around the curve north of the Kathmandu Guesthouse. 5-star service and low prices have made Garuda popular with Himalayan expeditions for years. Rooftop "garden" is actually a garden, unlike other places in Thamel. Attached baths with towels and toilet paper. 25% off-season discount. Singles US$9-29; doubles US$13-36. AmEx, MC, Visa accepted.

Holy Lodge (☎437763; fax 413441), Satghumti, opposite the Prince Guesthouse. Spotless rooms with fans off a quiet courtyard. Singles US$4-9; doubles US$6-12.

Journeyman Hotel (☎253438; fax 253999), Ganabahal, Pipalbot, along the paved road leading southwest from Bhimsen Tower; continue west past the pipal tree and it's on your right. Large rooms with fans are old but well maintained. Friendly, accommodating management. Dorm beds Rs100; singles Rs170-250; doubles Rs200-500.

◘ FOOD

Nepal's undisputed national dish is *dahl bhat tarkari* (rice, lentils, and vegetable curry) available on nearly every menu as the "Nepali Set Meal."

■ **Typical Nepali Restaurant,** Chhetrapati-Thamel, south of Kathmandu Guesthouse, down an alley on the left. The singing, dancing manager, who identifies himself as J.J. (for "John Joker") persistently refills clay bowls of *raksi* (rice wine) while live Nepali music plays in the background. Complimentary bananas and popcorn accompany the all-you-can eat regional plates (Rs80-140), including *dahl bhat tarkari, roti, momos,* and *achaar.* Open daily 6:30am-10pm.

■ **New Tibetan Restaurant,** a short distance down Thahiti-Thamel, up the second set of stairs to your left. With a friendly staff and a cozy atmosphere, the New Tibetan serves delicious Nepali, Chinese, Tibetan, and continental food at down-to-earth prices. Nepali set meal Rs60; vegetarian chow mein Rs35. Try the uncommonly good yogurt with mixed fruit and honey (Rs35) for dessert. Open 7am-10pm.

Pumpernickel Bakery, opposite K.C.'s. A Thamel institution. At breakfast time, the line to order freshly baked croissants, cakes, and cinnamon rolls (Rs20-35) spills onto the street. The pleasant garden patio and wicker furniture in the back make it a nice place to linger and watch the tourists. Open daily 7am-9pm.

Angan Sweet Namkeens and Vegetarian Fast Food, at the intersection of New Rd. and Dharma Path. Serves ice cream (Rs36-50), Indian sweets, *dhosas* (Rs40-65), and other vegetarian treats (Rs20-65) on the go. Pay in front and shoulder your way into the back room to find a table. Free mineral water. Open daily 9:30am-8:30pm.

Oasis Restaurant, Freak St., with its outdoor dining area, is the only place where you can eat sheltered by big leafy plants and rainbow umbrellas. Mexican dishes Rs90-110; pizza Rs95; burgers Rs85-95. Open daily 8am-9:30pm.

TIBET

APPENDIX

GLOSSARY

apsara: Buddhist angel

arhat: one who has attained spiritual enlightenment

avos: the smallest denomination of Mecanese currency; 1/100th of a pataca

bei: north; 北

binguan: hotel; 宾馆

bodhisattva: a devout Buddhist who has attained enlightenment but stays on earth to help others

CAAC: Civil Aviation Administration of China; 中国民航

CCP: Chinese Communist Party; 中国共产党

CITS: China International Travel Service; 中国国际旅行社

CTS: China Travel Service; 中国旅行社

CYTS: China Youth Travel Service; 中国青年旅行社

dadao: boulevard; 大道

dagoba: a bell-shaped Buddhist commemorative shine

dajie: avenue; 大街

dasha: mansions; 大厦

DDD phones: Domestic Direct Dial phones; telephones from which domestic long-distance numbers can be dialed directly

dim sum: Cantonese bite-sized dumplings and buns usually eaten for breakfast or lunch

dong: east; 东

fandian: hotel or restaurant; 饭店

fen: the smallest denomination of Chinese currency; 1/100th of a *yuan*; 分

feng: peak; 峰

feng shui: literally "wind and water"; a system of geomancy used to determine auspicious locations or positions for buildings or other structures; 风水

GMD: Guomindang; the Nationalist People's Party led by Chiang Kai-shek that lost to the Communists in 1949 and fled to Taiwan; also called KMT (Kuomintang); 国民党

Guanyin: Buddhist goddess of mercy

gulou: drum tower; 鼓楼

gwailo: Cantonese "slang" for foreigner

hai: sea; 海

Han Chinese: China's ethnic majority; comprises 91% of the population

he: river; 河

Hong Kong dollars: unit of currency of Hong Kong

hu: lake; 湖

hutong: an alleyway

IDD phones: International Direct Dial phones; telephones from which international long-distance numbers can be dialed directly

jiang: river; 江

jie: street; 街

jiudian: a hotel or restaurant; may be more upscale than a fandian or binguan; 酒店

jiao: 10 *fen;* also called "mao"; 角

jiaozi: dumplings

Hui: ethnic Chinese Muslims

karst: eroded limestone formation

lama: spiritual leader in Tibetan Buddhism

laowai: Mandarin slang term for "foreigner"

loess: fine, yellowish silt

lu: road; 路

mahjong: popular Chinese game played with tiles that resembles gin

men: gate or door; 门

miandi: yellow mini-van taxis, the cheapest taxis around; the literal name "loaf of bread car" refers to the shape

nan: south; 南

pataca: unit of currency of Macau

PLA: People's Liberation Army; the CCP's military

PSB: Public Security Bureau (China's police force); 公安局
pagoda: an elongated, multi-story tower which tapers at the top
pinyin: a system of romanization which transliterates Chinese sounds in the Roman alphabet
PRC: People's Republic of China; 中华人民共和国
qiao: bridge; 桥
renminbi: the official name for Chinese currency; literally, "people's money"; 人民币
sampan: small, motorized boat used in Hong Kong harbors
SEZ: Special Economic Zone
shan: mountain; 山
si: temple; 寺
shui: water; 水
sinicization: the process of assimilation into Han Chinese society or culture; a sinicized ethnic minority is one that is hard to distinguish from the Chinese
stele: an upright stone tablet with carvings or inscriptions
stupa: Buddhist monument which often houses sacred relics
sutra: sacred Buddhist text
ta: pagoda; 塔
tai chi: slow speed martial art generally practiced as a form of early morning exercise
taipan: a 19th-century term for a powerful foreign businessman in Hong Kong
tian: heaven or sky; 天
tratsang: a Tibetan college
Uighur: Turkic-speaking Muslim minority group living primarily in Xinjiang; also spelled Uygur
xi: west; 西
yuan: unit of Chinese currency; 元
yurt: circular tent used by Central Asian nomads
zhan: station; 站
zhaodaisuo: guesthouse; 招待所
zhong: middle; 中
Zhongguo: China, literally "Middle Kingdom"; 中国

PINYIN PRONUNCIATION GUIDE

The most difficult aspect of the Chinese language for foreigners is the **tone system.** Do not let the challenge posed by tones prevent you from trying out a few Chinese phrases; even with no grasp of them, you should be able to make yourself understood. Most Chinese are very receptive to your attempting to speak Chinese; even a simple thank you may elicit much praise. Mandarin uses four tones, designated 1st tone, 2nd tone, 3rd tone, and 4th tone. The differences between them are based on the pitch at which one pronounces a syllable. The **1st tone** is indicated by a flat marker over the vowel (ā, ē, etc.) and is pronounced as a steady, unchanging, high-pitched sound. The **2nd tone** (á, é, etc.) is a rising tone; the voice goes from a lower to a higher pitch. The **3rd tone** (ǎ, ě, etc.) is probably the most difficult; the voice falls dramatically in pitch, and then rises again. The **4th tone** (à, è, etc.) is a short burst of a high pitch, producing an emphatic sound. Vowels without markers are tone-free: just spit them out. Beijingers add another twist to the language, in the form of an "R" tacked on to near every word ending. Thus, "men" would become "mer," and so on.

Most letters used in the pinyin system are pronounced just as they are in English. The exceptions are the following:

a	as in father	u	"oo" as in boot
ai	"i" as in eye	ü	"u" as in cute or mute
ao	"ow" as in allow	ui	"way" as in away
ang	"on" as in dawn	uo	"wo" as in war
e	"uh" as in duh	un	"wen" as in Wendy
ei	"ay" as in way or say	c	"ts" as in cats
i	"ee" as in feet after most consonants "rih" sound after "ch," "sh," "zh," and "r" silent after "c," "s," and "z"	ch	as in churn
ia	"ya" as in yahoo	q	"ch" as in cheat; an airy sound produced by pushing short burst of air while the tongue is pressed against the palate

ie	"ye" as in **ye**s	r	as in **r**ain
iu	"eo" as in L**eo**	sh	as in **sh**op
ong	"oan" as in l**oan**	x	"sh" as in **sh**eet; produced by releasing a stream of air while the tongue is pressed against the palate
ou	"o" as in **o**cean	z	"ds" as in rea**ds**
o	"wo" as in m**o**re	zh	soft "g" as in **G**eorge; pronounced like "j" but with the tongue rolled back

PHRASEBOOK

NUMBERS	PINYIN	CHINESE	NUMBERS	PINYIN	CHINESE
0	líng	零	20	èrshí	二十
½	yíbàn	一半	21	èrshíyī	二十一
1	yī or yāo	一	22	èrshíèr	二十二
2	èr or liǎng	二 or 两	100	yìbǎi	一百
3	sān	三	200	liǎngbǎi	两百
4	sì	四	1000	yìqiān	一千
5	wǔ	五	2000	liǎngqiān	两千
6	liù	六	10,000	yíwàn	一万
7	qī	七	20,000	liǎngwàn	两万
8	bā	八	100,000	shíwàn	十万
9	jiǔ	九	200,000	èrshíwàn	二十万
10	shí	十	1,000,000	yìbǎiwàn	一百万
11	shíyī	十一	100,000,000	yíyì	一亿
12	shíèr	十二	1 billion	shíyì	十亿

THE BASICS	PINYIN	CHINESE
Hello	nǐhǎo	你好
Good bye	zài jiàn	再见
How are you?	nǐ hǎo ma?	你好吗?
Please	qǐng	请
Thank you	xièxiè	谢谢
You're welcome	búkèqi or búxiè	不客气 or 不谢
Help!	jiùmìng!	救命!
I'm sorry	duìbùqǐ	对不起
It doesn't matter (either is okay)	dōu kěyǐ or méi guānxì	都可以 or 没关系
It doesn't matter (it's not a big deal)	wú suǒwèi	无所谓
Forget about it	suàn le ba	算了吧
What's your name?	nǐ jiào shénme míngzi?	你叫什么名子?
My name is...	wǒ jiào...	我叫...
I	wǒ	我
you	nǐ (standard) or nín (formal)	你, 您
he, she, it	tā	他, 她, 它
plural: we, you, they	add mén to singular: wǒmén, nǐmén, tàmén	我们, 你们, 他们
to be	shì (invariable)	是
Yes	shì	是
No	búshì	不是
to have	yǒu (invariable)	有
to not have	méiyǒu	没有

THE BASICS	PINYIN	CHINESE
Do you have...?	yǒu méiyǒu...?	有没有...?
okay	kéyǐ or xíng	可以 or 行
not okay	bùxíng or bùkéyǐ	不可以 or 不行
to want, would like	yào	要
to not want	búyào	不要
I want ...	wǒ yào...	我要...
I don't speak Chinese	wǒ bú huì shuō zhōngwén	我不会说中文
Do you speak English?	nǐ huì shuō yīngwén ma?	您会说中文吗?
I can't hear you	wǒ tīng bú jiàn	我听不见
Speak more slowly	màn yī diǎr	慢一点儿
Repeat that	chóngfù yíbiàn or zài shuō yī cì	重复一便 or 再说一次
I don't understand	wǒ bù míngbái/wǒ bù dǒng	我不明白/我不懂
I need help	wǒ xūyào bāngzhù	我需要帮助
You are cheating me	nǐ piàn wǒ	你骗我
What time do you open?	nǐ jǐdiǎn kāi mén/nǐ jǐdiǎn shàng bān?	你几点开门/你几点上班?
What time do you close?	nǐ jǐdiǎn guān mén/nǐ jǐdiǎn xià bān?	你几点关门/你几点下班?
restroom	cèsuǒ	厕所
man	nán	男
woman	nǚ	女
toilet paper	wèishēng zhǐ	卫生纸
Western toilet	mǎtǒng	马桶
squat toilet	dūnkēng	蹲坑
big	dà	大
small	xiǎo	小

DIRECTIONS	PINYIN	CHINESE
Where is...?	...zài nǎr	...在哪儿?
How do I get to ...?	qù...zěnme zǒu?	去...怎么走?
I want to go to...	wǒ yào qù...	我要去...
How far is...from here?	...yǒu duō yuǎn?	有多远?
How long does it take to get to...?	qù...děi huā duōcháng shíjiān?	去...得花多长时间?
north	běi	北
south	nán	南
east	dōng	东
west	xī	西
left	zuǒ	左
right	yòu	右
front, forward /in the front	qián/qiánmiàn	前/前面
back, rear/behind	hòu/hòumiàn	后/后面
center, middle	zhōng	中
upper, above, ascend	shàng	上
lower, below, descend	xià	下
between...and...	zài...hé...zhījiān	在...和...之间
to enter/entrance	jìn/jìnkǒu	进/进口
to exit/exit	chū/chūkǒu	出/出口
far, distant	yuǎn	远
close, near/nearby	jìn/fùjìn	近/付近
next to...	zài...pángbiān	在...旁边

APPENDIX

TRANSPORTATION	PINYIN	CHINESE
passenger	kèyùn	客运
insurance	bǎoxiǎn	保险
People's Insurance Company of China (PICC)	zhōngguó rénmín bǎoxiǎn gōngsī	中国人民保险公司
I want to take [a plane, train, bus] to...	wǒ yào zuò [fēijī, huǒchē, qìchē] qù...	我要座[飞机,火车,汽车]去...
ticket office	shòupiào chù	售票处
ticket	piào	票
I want to reserve a ticket	wǒ xiǎng dìng piào	我想订票
I want to buy a ticket to...	wǒ xiǎng mǎi qù...de piào	我想买去...的票
one-way ticket	dānchéng piào	单程票
round-trip ticket	wǎngfǎn piào	往反票
Can I cancel my ticket?	kěyǐ tuì piào ma?	可以退票吗?
Can I change my ticket?	kěyǐ huànpiào ma?	可以还票吗?
There are no seats (sleepers)	méi yǒu zuòwèi (wòpù)	没有座位(卧铺)
commission	shǒuxù fèi	手续费
schedule	shíkèbiǎo	时刻表
What time does it leave?	jǐ diǎn chūfā?	几点出发?
What time does it arrive?	jǐ diǎn dào?	几点到?
How long does it take?	yàohuā duōshǎo shíjiān?	要花多少时间?
Check (verify) ticket	chá piào	查票
waiting room	hòuchē shì	候车室
luggage storage	jìcùn chù	寄存处
airplane	fēijī	飞机
airport	fēijīchǎng	飞机场
CAAC ticket office	zhōngguó mínháng shòupiào chù	中国民航售票处
train	huǒchē	火车
train station	huǒchē zhàn	火车站
hard/soft seat	yìng zuò/ruǎn zuò	硬座/软座
hard/soft sleeper	yìng wò/ruǎn wò	硬卧/软卧
upper/middle/lower bunk	shàng pù/zhōng pù/xià pù	上铺/中铺/下铺
platform	zhàntái	站台
Can I upgrade my ticket?	kěyǐ bǔpiào ma?	可以补票吗?
long-distance bus	chángtú qìchē	长途汽车
bus station	qìchē zhàn	汽车站
sleeper bus	wòpù chē	卧铺车
boat	chuán	船
docks	mǎtóu	码头
1st, 2nd,...class cabin	yī, èr,...děng cāng	一,二,...等舱
city bus	gōnggòng qìchē	公共汽车
minibus	zhōngbā	中巴
To get off, say: I get off	xià	下
subway	dìtiě	地铁
taxi	chūzū chē	出租车
breadbox (miandi) taxi	miàndì	面的
To request a cab, say: get a cab	dǎ ge dì	打个的
Turn on the meter	dǎ biǎo	打表
bicycle	zìxíngchē	自行车
I want to rent a bicycle	wǒ xiǎng zū zìxíngchē	我想租自行车

MONEY	PINYIN	CHINESE
money	qián	钱
Chinese currency	rénmínbì	人民币
one (two, three) yuan	yī (èr, sān) kuài	一(二,三)块
1/10th of one yuan	máo	毛
1/100th of one yuan	fēn	分
cash	xiànjīn	现金
US dollars	měi yuán	美元
traveler's checks	lǚxíng zhīpiào	旅行支票
credit card	xìnyòng kǎ	信用卡
Can I use a credit card?	kěyǐ yòng xìnyòng kǎ ma?	可以用信用卡吗?
bank	yínháng	银行
Bank of China	zhōngguó yínháng	中国银行
change money	huàn qián	换钱
Can I exchange money (traveler's checks) here?	zhèr kěyǐ huàn qián (lǚxíng zhīpiào) ma?	这儿可以换钱(旅行支票)吗?
ATM	zìdòng qǔ kuǎn/zìdòng yínháng	自动取款/自动银行
price	jiàqián/jiàgé	价钱/价格
pay/pay for	fù qián	付钱
spend money	huā qián	花钱
give change	zhǎo qián	找钱
bargain	tǎojià huànjià	讨价还价
How much does it cost?	duōshǎo qián?	多少钱?
inexpensive	piányi	便宜
most inexpensive	zuì piányi	最便宜
expensive	guì	贵
too expensive	tài guìle	太贵了
This is fake	zhè shì jiǎ de	这是假的
Can I have a discount/do you give discounts?	kěyǐ piányi yìdiǎn ma/nǐ dǎ bù dǎ zhé?	可以便宜一点吗/你打不打折?
Write a receipt	kāi piào	开票
I want a receipt	wǒ yào fāpiào	我要发票
HEALTH & EMERGENCY	PINYIN	CHINESE
sick/disease	bìng	病
Western medicine	xī yī	西医
Chinese medicine	zhōng yī	中医
I am sick	wǒ bìng le	我病了
I don't feel well	wǒ bù shūfu	我不舒服
I am injured	wǒ shòushāngle	我受伤了
hurt/pain	téng	疼
My head hurts	wǒ tóu téng	我头疼
My stomach hurts	wǒ dùzi téng	我肚子疼
I'm allergic to...	wǒ duì...guòmín	我对...过敏
I feel nauseous	wǒ ěxīn	我恶心
I've caught a cold	wǒ gǎnmào le	我感冒了
I have a fever	wǒ fāshāo le	我发烧了
AIDS	àizībìng	爱滋病
altitude sickness	gāoshān fǎnyìng	高山反应
diarrhea	lā dùzi	拉肚子
hepatitis	gānyán	肝炎
malaria	nüèji	疟疾
rabies	kuángquǎnbìng	狂犬病

HEALTH & EMERGENCY	PINYIN	CHINESE
tetanus	pòshāngfēng	破伤风
hospital	yīyuàn	医院
Where is the hospital?	yīyuàn zài nǎr?	医院在那儿?
doctor	dàifu	大夫
Please use sterilized equipment	qǐng yòng yīcìyòng yīqì	请用一次用医器
I do not want a blood transfusion	wǒ bù yào shū xuè	我不要输血
shot/injection	zhùshè	注射
Please use my own syringe	qǐng yòng wǒ zìjǐ de zhùshèqì	请用我自己的注射器
pharmacy	yàodiàn/yàofáng	药店/药房
medicine	yàopiàn	药片
antibiotic	kàngshēngsù/kàngjùnsù	抗生素/抗菌素
aspirin/painkiller	āsīpǐlín	阿斯匹林
condom	bìyùntào	避孕套
contraceptive	bìyùnyào	避孕药
rehydration salts	fùshuǐ yán	复水盐
Fire!	huǒzāi!	火灾!
police	jǐngchá	警察
Thief (pickpocket)!	xiǎotōu!	小偷!
My money/passport has been stolen.	yǒurén tōu le wǒde qián/hùzhào	有人偷了我的钱/护照
I've lost my money/passport.	wǒ bǎ wǒ de qián/hùzhào diū le	我把我的钱/护照丢了
danger/dangerous	wéixiǎn	危险
Go away!	zǒukāi!	走开!

ACCOMMODATIONS	PINYIN	CHINESE
hotel	bīnguǎn/fàndiàn/jiǔdiàn/lǚguǎn	宾馆/饭店/酒店/旅馆
hostel	zhāodàisuǒ/lǚshè	招待所/旅社
yurt	ménggǔ bāo	蒙古包
room	fángjiān	房间
dormitory	duōrén fáng/jiān	多人房/间
single room	dānrén fáng/jiān	单人房/间
double room	shuāngrén fáng/jiān	双人房/间
triple room	sānrén fáng/jiān	三人房/间
economy room	jīngjì fáng/jiān	经济房/间
standard room	biāozhǔn fáng	标准房/间
luxury room	háohúa tàofáng	豪华套房/间
bed	chuángwèi	床位
You must fill the room	nǐ xūyào bāofáng	你需要包房
check-out	tuìfáng	退房
key	yàoshi	钥匙
deposit	yājīn	押金
attendant	fúwùyuán	服务员
settle account	shùfáng	数房
Can I look at the room?	wǒ kěyǐ kànkan fángjiān ma?	我可以看看房间吗?
Is it okay for men and women to stay together?	néng nánnǚ tóngjū ma?	能男女同居吗?
We are a married couple	wǒmen jiéhūnle	我们结婚了
(24hr.) hot water	(èrshísì ge xiǎoshí) rè shuǐ	24个小时热水
When is hot water available?	shénme shíhòu yǒu rè shuǐ?	什么时候有热水?

ACCOMMODATIONS	PINYIN	CHINESE
air-conditioning	kòngtiáo	空调
free breakfast	miǎnfèi zǎocān	免费早餐
Please wash these clothes	qǐng bǎ zhè xiē yīfu xǐ hǎo	请把这些衣服洗好

COMMUNICATIONS	PINYIN	CHINESE
post office	yóujú	邮局
letter	xìn	信
envelope	xìnfēng	信封
postcard	míngxìnpiàn	明信片
stamp	yóupiào	邮票
package	bāoguǒ	包裹
Express Mail International Service (EMS)	guójì tèkuài zhuāndì	国际特快专递
air mail	hángkōng xìn	航空
surface mail	píngyóu	平邮
registered mail	guà hàoxìn	挂号信
Poste Restante	cúnjú hòulǐng	存局候领
telephone office	diànxùn dàlóu	电讯大楼
China Telecom	zhōngguó diànxìn	中国电信
telephone	diànhuà	电话
phone card	diànhuà kǎ	电话卡
long-distance call	chángtú diànhuà	长途电话
international call	guójì chángtú diànhuà	国际长途电话
collect call	duìfāng fùqián diànhuà	对方付钱电话
I want to make a long-distance phone call	wǒ yào dǎ chángtú diànhuà	我要打长途电话
What is the number for...?	...de diànhuà hàomǎ shì duōshǎo?	...的电话号码是多少?
First dial "0"	xiān bō líng	先拨零
I want to [send/receive] a fax	wǒ yào [fā/shōu] chuánzhēn	我要 [发/收] 传真
internet bar	wǎngbā	网吧
computer	diànnǎo	电脑
I want to get on the Internet	wǒ yào shàng wǎng	我要上网
I want to send an email	wǒ yào fā diànzi yóujiàn	我要发电子邮件
How much is it per hour?	yī ge xiǎoshí duōshǎo qián?	一个小时多少钱?

PASSPORT & VISA	PINYIN	CHINESE
passport	hùzhào	护照
visa	qiānzhèng	签证
I need to extend my visa	wǒ xūyào yáncháng wǒ de qiānzhèng	我需要延长我的签证
PSB Division of Exit and Entry	gōng ān jú chūrù jìng guǎnlǐ chù	公安局出入境管理处
PSB Foreign Affairs Branch	gōng ān jú wàishì kē	公安局外事科
embassy	dàshǐguǎn	大使馆
consulate	língshìguǎn	领事馆

LEISURE	PINYIN	CHINESE
film	diànyǐng	电影
I want to watch a film	wǒ xiǎng kàn diànyǐng	我想看电影
movie theater	diànyǐng yuàn	电影院
music	yīnyuè	音乐

LEISURE	PINYIN	CHINESE
music concert	yīnyuè huì	音乐会
opera	xìjù	戏剧
sports	tǐyù	体育
stadium	tǐyùchǎng	体育场
to play (a sport)	dǎ	打
soccer	zúqiú	足球
table tennis	pīngpāng qiú	乒乓球
basketball	lánqiú	篮球
ice skating	liūbīng	溜冰
swimming (pool)	yóuyǒng (chí)	游泳 (池)
martial arts	wǔshù	武术
tai chi	tàijí quán	太极拳
mahjong	májiàng	麻将
I am here strictly to travel	wǒ shì zhuānmén lái lǚyóu de	我是专门来旅游的
How old are you?	nǐ duō dà/nǐ duō dà niánlíng?	你多大/你多大年龄?
I am 20 (30, ...) years old	wǒ [èrshí, sānshí, ...] suì	我 [20, 30, ...] 岁
What do you do (what is your occupation)?	nǐ zuò shénme?	你作什么?
I am a student/I go to school	wǒ shì xuéshēng/wǒ shàng xué	我是学生/我上学
I am a teacher/I teach school	wǒ shì lǎoshī/wǒ jiàoshū	我是老师/我教书
I work	wǒ shàngbān	我上班
I am retired	wǒ tuìxiú le	我退休了
I (don't) have any children	wǒ (méi) yǒu háizi	我 (没) 有孩子
bar	jiǔbā	酒吧
nightclub	jùlèbù	俱乐部
cover	ménpiào	门票
entertainment center	yúlè chǎng	娱乐场
massage	àn mó	按摩
sauna	sāngná	桑拿
karaoke	kǎlā OK	卡拉 OK
I am drunk	wǒ hē zuì le	我喝醉了
I want to be your friend	wǒ xiǎng jiāo hǎo péngyǒu	我想交好朋友
boyfriend/girlfriend	nán péngyǒu/nǚ péngyǒu	男朋友/女朋友
Do you want a massage?	nǐ yào bù yào xiǎojiě?	你要不要小姐?
You are very pretty/handsome	nǐ hěn piàoliang/hǎokàn	你很漂亮/好看
You are truly remarkable	nǐ zhēn liǎo bù qǐ	你真了不起
I love you	wǒ ài nǐ	我爱你
to make love	zuò ài [colloquial: qí mǎ]	做爱 [骑马]
I am not that casual	wǒ bù nàme suíbiàn	我不那么随便

TIME	PINYIN	CHINESE	TIME	PINYIN	CHINESE
minutes	fēnzhōng	分钟	week	xīngqī/lǐbài	星期/礼拜
hour	xiǎoshí	小时	Monday	xīngqī yī	星期一
...o'clock	...diǎn	...点	Tuesday	xīngqī èr	星期二
What time is now?	xiànzài jǐ diǎn?	现在几点?	Wednesday	xīngqī sān	星期三
morning	zǎochén	早晨	Thursday	xīngqī sì	星期四
noon	zhōngwǔ	中午	Friday	xīngqī wǔ	星期五
afternoon	xiàwǔ	下午	Saturday	xīngqī liù	星期六
evening	bāngwǎn	傍晚	Sunday	xīngqī rì/tiān	星期日/天
night	yèwǎn	夜晚	month (moon)	yuè	月
midnight	bànyè	半夜	Months are referred to numerically starting with Jan.:		

TIME	PINYIN	CHINESE
daytime	báitiān	白天
nighttime	wǎnshàng	晚上
now	xiànzài	现在
day	tiān or rì	天 or 日
today	jīn tiān	今天
day before yesterday	qián tiān	前天
yesterday	zuó tiān	昨天
tomorrow	míngtiān	明天
day after tomorrow	hòutiān	后天

FOOD	PINYIN	CHINESE
to eat	chīfàn	吃饭
supermarket	chāoshì	超市
restaurant	cānguǎn	餐馆
street stall	dài pái dáng	大排挡
to go	dàizǒu	带走
delivery	sòng	送
waitstaff/waitress	fúwùyuán/xiǎojiě	服务员/小姐
how many people are in your party?	nǐ jǐ wèi?	你几位?
menu	càidān	菜单
check/bill	zhàngdān	账单
chopsticks	kuàizi	筷子
napkin	cānjīnzhǐ	餐巾纸
fork	chāzi	叉子
knife	dāozi	刀子
spoon	sháozi	勺子
bowl	wǎn	碗
plate	pánzi	盘子
Is the food ready yet?	fàn zuò hǎo le ma?	饭做好了吗?
I am full	wǒ chī bǎo le	我吃饱了
delicious	hǎochī	好吃
This has no flavor	zhè méi yǒu wèidào	这没有味道
hot (temp.)	tàng	烫
cold	liáng	凉
Not too much...	shǎo yòng...	少用...
hot (spicy)	là	辣
garlic	dàsuàn	大蒜
MSG	wèijīng	味精
oil	yóu	油
pepper	jiāo	椒

TIME	PINYIN	CHINESE
January	yīyuè	一月
February	èryuè	二月
March	sānyuè	三月
December	shíèr yuè	十二月
year	nián	年
last year	qù nián	去年
1978	yī jiǔ qī bā nián	一九七八年
past	yǐqián	以前
future	jiānglái, wèilái	将来, 未来

FOOD	PINYIN	CHINESE
I am vegetarian	wǒ chī sù	我吃素
I don't eat meat	wǒ bù chī ròu	我不吃肉
I am on a diet	wǒ jiǎnféi	我减肥
set meal	tào cān	套餐
buffet	zìzhù cān	自助餐
dim sum	diǎnxīn	点心
snacks	xiǎochī	小吃
Muslim	qīngzhēn	清真
fast food	kuài cān	快餐
box lunch	hé cān	盒餐
KFC	kěndéjī	肯德鸡
McDonald's	màidānglào	麦当劳
hamburger	hànbǎobāo	汉堡包
rice	mǐfàn	米饭
fried rice	chǎofàn	炒饭
noodles	miàn	面
Northwest noodles	xīběi lāmiàn	西北拉面
mixed noodles	bàn miàn	拌面
kebab	ròuchuàn	肉串
bean curd/tofu	dòufǔ	豆腐
soup	tāng	汤
noodle soup	shāguǒ	沙锅
beef noodle soup	niúròu miàn	牛肉面
hotpot	shuàn yángròu	涮羊肉
hotpot (Sichuan)	huǒguō	火锅
curry	gālí	咖喱
wontons	húndùn	馄饨
dumplings	jiǎozi	饺子
steamed dumplings	bāozi	包子

FOOD	PINYIN	CHINESE
salt (salty)	yán (xián)	盐(咸)
soy sauce	jiàng yóu	酱油
sugar (sweet)	táng (tián)	塘(甜)
vinegar	cù	醋
vegetables	shūcài	蔬菜
Chinese cabbage	báicài	白菜
corn	yùmí	玉米
cucumber	huángguā	黄瓜
fish-flavored eggplant	yúxiāng qiézi	鱼香茄子
green vegetables	qīngcài	青菜
mushrooms	xiānggŭ/mógŭ	香菇/蘑菇
peas	wāndòu	豌豆
fried tomato and egg	xīhóngshí chăo jīdàn	西红柿炒鸡蛋
fruit	shuĭguŏ	水果
apple	píngguŏ	苹果
banana	xiāngjiāo	香蕉
dragon eyes	lóngyăn	龙眼
grape	pútáo	葡萄
lychee	lìzhī	荔枝
mango	mángguŏ	芒果
peach	táozi	桃子
pineapple	bōluó	菠萝
watermelon	xīguā	西瓜
almond jello	xìngrén dòufu	杏仁豆腐
ice cream	bīngqílín	冰淇淋
shake	năixī	奶昔
sweet soy milk	dòujiāng	豆浆
yogurt	suānnăi	酸奶
moon cake	yuè bĭng	月饼
New Year's cake	nián gāo	年糕
sweet bean paste rolls	dòushāgāo/bāo	豆沙糕/包
soft drinks	qìshuĭ	汽水
Future Cola	fēicháng kĕlè	非常可乐
Coke	kĕkŏu kĕlè	可口可乐
Pepsi	băishì kĕlè	百事可乐
Sprite	xuĕbì	雪壁

PLACES	PINYIN	CHINESE
sea	hăi	海

FOOD	PINYIN	CHINESE
Shanghai-style dumplings	xiăolóng bāo	小龙包
egg	jīdàn	鸡蛋
steamed buns	mántóu	馒头
bread	miànbāo	面包
fried bread sticks	yóutiáo	油条
porridge	zhōu/xīfàn	粥/稀饭
beef	niúròu	牛肉
chicken	jī	鸡
Kungpao chicken	gōngbăo jīdīng	宫保鸡丁
dog	gŏu	狗
Beijing duck	kăoyā	烤鸭
fish	yú	鱼
frog	qīngwā	青蛙
lamb	yángròu	羊肉
pork	zhūròu	猪肉
seafood	hăixiān	海鲜
shrimp	xiā	虾
snake	shé	蛇
to drink	hē	喝
beverage	yínliào	饮料
water	shuĭ	水
bottle	píng	瓶
cup	bēi	杯
mineral water	kuàng quán shuĭ	矿泉水
hot water	bái kāi shuĭ	白开水
tea house	chá guăn/chá fáng	茶馆/茶房
cafe	kāfeiguăn	咖啡馆
tea	chá	茶
eight-treasure tea	bā băo chá	八宝茶
milk pearl tea	zhēnzhū nāi chá	珍珠奶茶
coffee	kāfēi	咖啡
beer	píjiŭ	啤酒
Tsingtao beer	qīngdăo píjiŭ	青岛啤酒
red wine	hóng pútáo jiŭ	红葡萄酒
white wine	bái pútáo jiŭ	白葡萄酒
Long Island iced tea	cháng dăo bīng chá	长岛冰茶

PLACES	PINYIN	CHINESE
What country are you from?	nĭ shì năguó rén? or nĭ shì năĭ de?	你是哪国人? or 你是哪里的?

PLACES	PINYIN	CHINESE
river	jiāng or hé	江 or 河
lake	hú	湖
pond	chí	池
stream	xī	溪
waterfall	pùbù	瀑布
marsh	zhǎozé	沼泽
island	dǎo	岛
peninsula	bàndǎo	半岛
beach	hǎitān (shātān)	海滩 (沙滩)
forest	sēnlín	森林
grasslands	cǎoyuán	草原
desert	shāmò	沙漠
plateau	gāoyuán	高原
mountain	shān	山
glacier	bīngchuān	冰川
cave	dòng	洞
grotto	shíkū	石窟
hot springs	wēnquán	温泉
countryside	nóngcūn	农村
downtown	shì zhōngxīn	市中心
city	chéngshì	城市
county	xiàn	县
square	guǎngchǎng	广场
temple	sì	寺
park	gōngyuán	公园
museum	bówùguǎn	博物馆
road	lù	路
street	jiē	街
boulevard or avenue	dàjiē or dàdao	大街 or 大道
intersection	shízilùkǒu	十字路口
highway	gōnglù	公路

WEATHER	PINYIN	CHINESE
weather	tiānqì	天气
How's the weather?	tiānqì zěnme yàng?	明天天气怎么样?
weather forecast	tiānqì yùbào	天气预报
°C	shèshì wēndù	摄氏温度
clear	tiānqíng	天晴
sun	tàiyáng	太阳
cloudy	duōyún	多云
windy	guāfēng	刮风
hot and humid	mēnrè	闷热
extremely hot	rè sǐ le	热死了

PLACES	PINYIN	CHINESE
I am a native of (country).	wǒ shì...rén.	我是...人
Chinese	zhōngguó rén	中国人
foreigner	wàiguó rén	外国人
Where are you going?	nǐ qù nǎ ge guójiā?	你去哪个国家?
border crossing	jièxiàn	界线
Australia	aōdàlìyǎ	澳大利亚
Canada	jiānádà	加拿大
France	fǎguó	法国
India	yìndù	印度
Indonesia	yìnní	印尼
Ireland	āiěrlán	爱尔兰
Japan	rìběn	日本
Kazakhstan	hāsàkèsítǎn	哈萨克斯坦
Kyrgyzstan	jíěrjísítǎn	吉尔吉斯坦
Laos	lǎowō	老挝
Mongolia	ménggǔ	蒙古
Myanmar	miǎndiàn	缅甸
Nepal	níbóěr	尼泊尔
New Zealand	xīn xīlán	新西兰
North Korea	běi cháoxiān	北朝鲜
Pakistan	bājīsítǎn	巴基斯坦
Russia	éluósí	俄罗斯
South Africa	nánfēi	南非
South Korea	hánguó	韩国
Taiwan	táiwān	台湾
Thailand	tàiguó	泰国
UK	yīngguó	英国
US	měiguó	美国
Vietnam	yuènán	越南
expressway	gāosù gōnglù	高速公路
bridge	qiáo	桥

WEATHER	PINYIN	CHINESE
Is it going to rain?	huì xiàyǔ ma?	会下雨吗?
rain	xiàyǔ	下雨
thunderstorms	léizhènyǔ	雷阵雨
hail	bīngbáo	冰雹
typhoon	táifēng	台风
flood	shuǐzāi	水灾
raincoat	yǔyī	雨衣
umbrella	yǔsǎn	雨伞
snow	xiàxuě	下雪
extremely cold	lěng sǐ le	冷死了

APPENDIX

USEFUL CONVERSIONS

DISTANCE CONVERSIONS

Meters	1	15	50	100	200	500	1000
Feet	3.281	50	164	328	656	1640	3280

TEMPERATURE CONVERSIONS

°Celsius	-40	-20	-18	0	15	25	35
°Fahrenheit	-40	-4	0	32	59	77	95

MEASUREMENT CONVERSIONS

1 inch (in.) = 25.4 millimeters (mm)	1 millimeter (mm) = 0.039 in.
1 foot (ft.) = 0.30 m	1 meter (m) = 3.28 ft.
1 yard (yd.) = 0.914m	1 meter (m) = 1.09 yd.
1 mile = 1.61km	1 kilometer (km) = 0.62 mi.
1 ounce (oz.) = 28.35g	1 gram (g) = 0.035 oz.
1 pound (lb.) = 0.454kg	1 kilogram (kg) = 2.202 lb.
1 fluid ounce (fl. oz.) = 29.57ml	1 milliliter (ml) = 0.034 fl. oz.
1 gallon (gal.) = 3.785L	1 liter (L) = 0.264 gal.
1 acre (ac.) = 0.405ha	1 hectare (ha) = 2.47 ac.
1 square mile (sq. mi.) = 2.59km^2	1 square kilometer (km^2) = 0.386 sq. mi.

CLIMATE

To convert from °C to °F, multiply by 1.8 and add 32. For a rough approximation, double the Celsius and add 25. To convert from °F to °C, subtract 32 and multiply by 0.55 (approx. 5/9). For a rough approximation, subtract 25 and cut it in half.

AVG. TEMP. (LO/HI)	JANUARY		APRIL		JULY		OCTOBER	
	°C	°F	°C	°F	°C	°F	°C	°F
Beijing	-10/1	14/34	7/21	45/70	21/31	70/88	6/20	43/68
Chongqing	5/9	41/49	16/23	60/73	24/34	76/93	16/22	61/71
Harbin	-24/-5	-5/14	0/13	32/54	18/26	65/83	0/12	32/53
Hong Kong	13/18	56/64	19/24	67/75	26/31	78/87	23/27	73/81
Lhasa	-10/7	14/44	1/16	33/60	9/23	49/74	1/17	34/62
Shanghai	1/8	33/46	10/19	50/66	23/32	74/90	14/23	57/74
Ürümqi	-22/-11	-7/13	2/16	36/60	14/28	58/82	-1/10	31/50

AVG. RAIN (MM)	JAN	FEB	MAR	APR	MAY	JUN	JULY	AUG	SEP	OCT	NOV	DEC
Beijing	4	5	8	17	35	78	196	244	58	16	11	3
Chongqing	15	20	38	99	142	180	142	122	150	112	48	20
Harbin	5	5	15	20	35	90	150	110	40	25	10	5
Hong Kong	33	46	74	137	292	394	381	367	257	114	43	31
Lhasa	0	13	8	5	25	64	122	89	66	13	3	0
Shanghai	48	58	84	94	94	180	147	142	130	71	51	36
Ürümqi	15	8	13	38	28	38	18	25	15	43	41	10

Station at which ticket was bought. Some stations are booking centers for rail tickets to and from any station in China.

Train number.

Seat number.

Carriage number.

Arrival station. Details same as for departure station.

Time of departure.

Departure station. If in a city with several stations, look for telltale 东, 南, 西, 北, to determine which station. If it doesn't say, then it is the main (or only) station.

Date of departure.

Price.

This specifies the type of train and seat you have. Hard seat will only have the characters 硬座. Hard sleeper will have the character 硬卧 at the end. Train types include: regular (普快), direct (直快), express (特快) and international (国际).

F0081544
北京南
1999年07月03日
全價7.00元
限乘當日當次車
在2日內到有效

十渡　京A售
795次
06:30開
硬座普快 04車 43號

CTOKYLEC F081544　6465581222543668374133698844452446684523335 7994314

INDEX

MAP INDEX

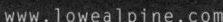

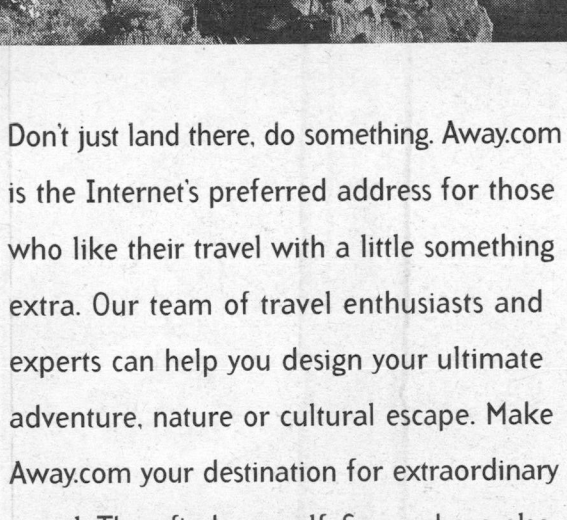

Find Yourself. Somewhere Else.

Don't just land there, do something. Away.com is the Internet's preferred address for those who like their travel with a little something extra. Our team of travel enthusiasts and experts can help you design your ultimate adventure, nature or cultural escape. Make Away.com your destination for extraordinary travel. Then find yourself. Somewhere else.

away.com
1.877.769.2929